Marketing Management

Marketing

Management

analysis, planning, and control

FOURTH EDITION

PHILIP KOTLER

NORTHWESTERN UNIVERSITY

PRENTICE-HALL, INC., ENGLEWOOD CLIFFS, NEW JERSEY 07632

Library of Congress Cataloging in Publication Data

KOTLER, PHILIP.
   Marketing management.

   Includes bibliographical references and indexes.
   1. Marketing management.
HF5415.13.K64   1980   658.8   79-21989
ISBN 0-13-557975-9

MARKETING MANAGEMENT   analysis, planning, and control   FOURTH EDITION
Philip Kotler

© 1980 by Prentice-Hall, Inc., Englewood Cliffs, New Jersey 07632

Printed in the United States of America

10   9   8   7   6   5   4   3   2

Editorial/Production Supervision by Maureen Wilson
Interior and Cover Design by Janet Schmid
Cover Photograph by © Reginald Wickham
Page Layout by Jenny Markus
Interior Illustrations by Herbert Daehnke
Acquisitions Editor: John Connolly
Manufacturing Buyer: John Hall

Prentice-Hall International, Inc., *London*

Prentice-Hall of Australia Pty. Limited, *Sydney*

Prentice-Hall of Canada, Ltd., *Toronto*

Prentice-Hall of India Private Limited, *New Delhi*

Prentice-Hall of Japan, Inc., *Tokyo*

Prentice-Hall of Southeast Asia Pte. Ltd., *Singapore*

Whitehall Books Limited, *Wellington, New Zealand*

TO NANCY

CONTENTS

Preface

No one knows what the 1980s will have in store for companies, consumers, and society at large. The 1970s was truly a turbulent and trying decade marked by (1) high and persistent worldwide inflation, (2) material and energy shortages, (3) economic stagnation, (4) consumerism, (5) environmentalism, (6) increased government regulation, (7) changing consumer life styles, and (8) undermarketed public sector needs. Some of these developments will continue into the 1980s and indeed intensify. New and unsuspected shocks will emerge. The challenge facing marketers in the 1980s will be to find constructive ways to reconcile company profitability, customer satisfaction, and social responsibility.

Properly viewed, these problesm are also opportunities. Marketing is the link between a society's needs and its industrial responses. It is the function through which organizations adjust their offerings to the ever-changing needs and wants of the marketplace. It is through external sensors that organizations adapt and grow.

This fourth edition has been written with three objectives:

1. To bring marketing management into closer alignment with the rapidly growing practice of corporate strategic planning;
2. To enlarge the discussion of several marketing topics of increased importance, particularly the strategic-planning process, competitive-marketing strategies for manufacturers and retailers, sales promotion and publicity decisions, new forces in the environment, buyer behavior theory, the marketing audit, exchange theory, organizational-buying behavior, marketing of services, product-line strategies, contents of marketing plans, marketing organization developments, and distribution-channel developments;
3. To update the text material so that it is as relevant as possible to the marketing problems of the 1980s.

The book remains true to its original principles. These principles are:

1. *A managerial orientation.* This book focuses on the major decisions facing marketing executives and top management in their attempt to harmonize the objectives and resources of the organization with the opportunities found in the marketplace.

2. *An analytical approach.* This book does not provide pat answers so much as ways of thinking about and analyzing recurrent marketing problems. Descriptive material is held to a minimum in order to permit the greatest latitude in developing the analytical content of marketing.

3. *A reliance on basic disciplines.* This book draws heavily on the basic disciplines of economics, behavioral science, and mathematics. *Economics* provides the fundamental tools and concepts for seeking optimal results in the use of scarce resources. *Behavioral science* provides fundamental concepts and findings for the interpretation of consumer and organizational buying behavior. *Mathematics* provides the means of developing explicit statements about the relationships among variables in a problem.

4. *A universal approach.* This book develops marketing thinking for the broadest of contexts. Marketing is treated as relevant to industrial as well as consumer markets, service industries as well as goods industries, small companies as well as large ones, nonprofit organizations as well as profit companies, and buyers as well as sellers.

Marketing remains one of the most difficult areas of analysis and decision making for the company. Marketing problems do not exhibit the neat quantitative properties of many of the problems in production, accounting, or finance. Psychological variables play a large role; marketing expenditures affect demand and costs simultaneously; marketing plans shape and interact with other corporate plans. Marketing decisions must be made in the face of insufficient information about processes that are dynamic, nonlinear, lagged, stochastic, interactive, and downright difficult. However, this is not taken as a case for intuitive decision making; rather it suggests the need for improved theoretical frameworks and sharper tools for analysis.

The book is organized into six parts. *Part I* develops the conceptual and strategic underpinnings of marketing. *Part II* presents concepts and tools for analyzing any market and marketing environment to discern opportunities. *Part III* presents principles for selecting target markets and planning effective marketing programs over the product's life cycle. *Part IV* deals with assembling the specific elements of the marketing mix based on their unique contributions. *Part V* develops the administrative side of marketing: organization, information handling, and control. *Part VI* broadens the discussion of marketing to cover international, nonbusiness, and contemporary issues.

ACKNOWLEDGMENTS

This fourth edition bears the imprint of many persons. My colleagues in the marketing department at Northwestern University made an important contribution through their zest in blending marketing theory with managerial practice: Bobby J. Calder, Richard M. Clewett, John Hauser, Sidney J. Levy, Louis W. Stern, Brian Sternthal, Alice Tybout, and Andris A. Zoltners. Two doctoral students in marketing, John Martin and Amy Seidel Marks, provided valuable assistance in numerous tasks connected with updating this edition. Donald P. Jacobs, dean of the Graduate School of Management, provided constant encouragement. Our secretaries, Marion Davis, Sabra Van Cleef, and Phyllis Van Hooser, provided invaluable help in manuscript preparation for the fourth edition.

I am indebted to colleagues at other universities who reviewed this edition and provided insightful suggestions: C. L. Abercrombie, Ralph Gaedeke, O. C. Ferrell, David J. Luck, Patrick E. Murphy, Edward Bonfield, and James C. Petersen.

My overriding debt is to my wife, Nancy, who provided me the time, support, and inspiration needed to regenerate this book. It is truly our book.

PHILIP KOTLER
Northwestern University
Evanston, Illinois

UNDERSTANDING MARKETING MANAGEMENT

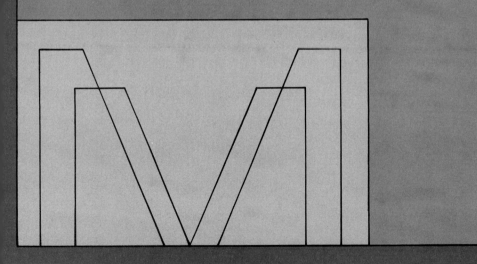

The Role of Marketing in Today's Organizations

Marketing is so basic that it cannot be considered a separate function. . . . It is the whole business seen from the point of view of its final result, that is, from the customer's point of view.
PETER DRUCKER

As human history speeds toward the year 2000, with its awe-inspiring problems and opportunities, the subject of marketing is attracting increasing attention from companies, institutions, and nations. Marketing has evolved from its early origins in distribution and selling into a comprehensive philosophy for relating any organization dynamically to its markets. Marketing is a cornerstone of policy and practice in such giant concerns as General Electric, Procter & Gamble, Sears, and IBM. Large and small business firms everywhere are beginning to appreciate the difference between selling and marketing and are organizing to do the latter. Nonprofit organizations such as museums, universities, churches, and government agencies are seeing marketing as a new way of looking at their relations with their publics. Developing nations are examining marketing principles to see how their domestic distribution system can be improved and how they can compete more effectively in world markets. Socialist nations are beginning to study how they could use marketing research, advertising, and pricing to increase their effectiveness in planning and distributing their goods.

The intensifying interest in marketing is paradoxical because while marketing is one of man's newest action disciplines, it is also one of the world's oldest professions. From the time of *simple barter* through the stage of a *money economy* to today's modern *complex marketing system, exchanges* have been taking place. But marketing—the study of exchange processes and relationships—

made its formal appearance only in the early part of the twentieth century out of questions and issues neglected by its mother science, economics.

In this short time, marketing has achieved the image of society's savior in the minds of many, and society's corrupter in the minds of others. Marketing's good deeds have been described in various ways:

> Aggressive marketing policies and practices have been largely responsible for the high material standard of living in America. Today through mass low-cost marketing we enjoy products which were once considered luxuries and which are still so classified in many foreign countries.[1]

> Advertising nourishes the consuming power of men. It creates wants for a better standard of living. It sets up before a man the goal of a better home, better clothing, better food for himself and his family. It spurs individual exertion and greater production. It brings together in fertile union those things which otherwise would not have met.[2]

Others take a dimmer view of marketing's contribution to society:

> For the past 6,000 years the field of marketing has been thought of as made up of fast-buck artists, con-men, wheeler-dealers, and shoddy-goods distributors. Too many of us have been "taken" by the tout or con-man; and all of us at times have been prodded into buying all sorts of "things" we really did not need, and which we found later on we did not even want.[3]

> What does a man need—really need? A few pounds of food each day, heat and shelter, six feet to lie down in—and some form of working activity that will yield a sense of accomplishment. That's all—in a material sense. And we know it. But we are brainwashed by our economic system until we end up in a tomb beneath a pyramid of time payments, mortgages, preposterous gadgetry, playthings that divert our attention from the sheer idiocy of the charade.[4]

It is clear that various social commentators have vastly different views on the meaning and social worth of marketing. The position taken in this book is that marketing makes a vital contribution to the advancement and satisfaction of human needs and wants. It is the means by which organizations identify unfulfilled human needs, convert them into business opportunities, and create satisfaction for others and profit for themselves. The capacity of organizations to survive and prosper depends on their ability to continuously create value for target markets in an environment of ever-changing human needs and wants.

THE AGE OF ORGANIZATIONS

To understand marketing, we must first understand organizations. Our society abounds in organizations, which stand ready to serve every need, whether large or small, good or bad, elevated or prosaic. With little effort, citizens of Chicago

---

[1] William J. Stanton, *Fundamentals of Marketing* (New York: McGraw-Hill Book Company, 1964), pp. 4–5.

[2] Sir Winston Churchill.

[3] Richard N. Farmer, "Would You Want Your Daughter to Marry a Marketing Man?" *Journal of Marketing*, January 1967, p. 1.

[4] Sterling Hayden, *Wanderer* (New York: Alfred A. Knopf, 1963).

can walk down Clark Street and instantly satisfy their appetite for chicken, hamburger, or pizza, courtesy of Kentucky Fried Chicken, McDonald's, or Pizza Hut. If they want new clothes, they can drive to the Old Orchard Shopping Center and rummage through racks of suits and dresses at Marshall Field's, Baskin's, or Montgomery Ward's. Their desire for recreation or entertainment can be satisfied instantaneously through the courtesy of the Touhy Tennis Club or the Biograph Theater. If the weather is too cold, they can board a 747 at O'Hare Airport and reach the balmy shores of Miami three hours later, courtesy of Delta Airlines. All said, an incredibly large number of organizations stand ready to serve human needs by holding them as business opportunities. The twentieth century is the Age of Organizations.

Organizations are so omnipresent that it is hard to believe that life ever existed without them. Yet throughout most of human history, people had to satisfy their needs through their own exertions. There was not the fast-food outlet, the health club, or the local movie theater to serve their needs.

Today's organizations come in all shapes and sizes. They may be publicly or privately owned. They may be run for profit, service, or some other goal(s). They may be organized as single proprietorships, partnerships, corporations, or conglomerates. They may range from a small private law practice to an IBM with 270,000 employees scattered throughout the world. They may have a single product line, such as paper, or sell as many as 150,000 different items, as in the case of Sears. They may operate in one locality, in a region, or nationally or internationally.

Organizations begin as ideas in the head of one or more entrepreneurs. The motivation for starting an organization could be to perform a great deed, make a great fortune, or meet an important need. The organizers must raise funds, attract personnel, establish a production or service facility, and find a market for its output. Many organizations do not survive these hurdles.

An organization can survive only if it is able to acquire the resources necessary to its sustenance. Such survival can be achieved in one of three ways. The first is through possessing legitimate or illegitimate *power*, which it uses to command resources. Thus public agencies obtain their resources through the imposition of taxes; the Mafia obtains its resources through other means. The second way is through *solicitation*, which comes about by convincing one or more persons or groups to contribute financial support freely. Opera companies and private universities survive through generous gifts that cover the large annual deficits between their normal income and cost. The third mode of survival is *exchange*, whereby an organization creates and offers goods and services that are able to attract and satisfy purchasers. This is the marketing solution to survival. The organization identifies a set of buyers and needs in the marketplace, develops a set of products and services to satisfy these needs, communicates the benefits of these products, makes them available and accessible, prices them in a reasonable manner, and convinces buyers to exchange their resources for these products.

The marketing solution calls for more than the ability of the organization to produce the needed goods and services. The organization must know how to produce better offers to the target market than its competitors. Buyers normally can buy from several sources. Their needs, preferences, and interests keep changing. The organization must keep abreast of these changes and constantly revise and improve its offer to the market. Playboy, Inc., one of the most successful publishing companies in history, has watched sales of its major magazine fall from a peak of 6.9 million copies in 1972 to 4.5 million. Kentucky Fried Chicken, one of the most successful fast-food franchisers in history, has experienced a declining market share for the past several years. Zenith, one of the most successful American manufacturers of television sets, has watched its market share erode in recent years in the face of increasing competition from Japanese television manufacturers.

The truth is that most organizations are not geared to maintain their marketing leadership in times of rapidly changing consumer wants and aggressive competition. They achieved their market positions in times when people spent more freely and when competitors were less sophisticated. They could survive by making and selling the same products year after year. These organizations can be said to lack a *marketing culture*. Only a handful of major companies—IBM, Procter & Gamble, Gillette, Eastman Kodak, Avon, McDonald's, Xerox, General Electric, and Caterpillar—are *master marketers*. The rest of them practice average marketing and are in a position of high marketing vulnerability as their markets shift and their competitors start to work harder or smarter.

The marketing function is not fully developed in most companies today for a number of reasons:

1. *Recent origins of marketing.* Marketing is a relatively new business discipline that is too often confused with one of its subfunctions, such as sales or advertising.
2. *Hostility toward marketing.* Marketing is normally resisted by vested interests in the company and must fight an uphill battle to establish its role, scope, and authority.
3. *Law of slow learning.* Marketing passes through several stages of misconception as it grows in the company.
4. *Law of fast forgetting.* Marketing principles tend to be forgotten with success, and executives have to be reminded of them periodically.

These propositions are examined in the following paragraphs.

RECENT ORIGINS OF MARKETING

How old is marketing? This question always brings about interesting speculations. Some people date marketing as beginning with earliest man and call it the world's oldest profession. Some even say marketing predates man. Consider the following case for subspecies marketing:

> I do not think it would be stretching the point too far to say that the reproductive cycle of plants is a natural exchange for profit system. After all, a flower, with its colour and perfume, is an advertisement for nectar. The exchange deal is quite straightforward—the bee has the nectar in return for pollen it has picked up elsewhere and for taking that flower's pollen onto the next one. At the next stage of the cycle the colour and perfume of the fruit is an advertisement for food. The bird eats the fruit and distributes the seeds in return.[5]

Others advance the argument that marketing began when mankind first engaged in exchange, that is, when two parties with surpluses resorted to barter as an alternative to employing force, stealing, or begging to obtain goods. Barter

---

[5] F.H. Elsby, in private correspondence.

evolved into the fine art of selling which received high expression in very early civilizations.

Peter Drucker thinks marketing first arose in the seventeenth century—and in Japan, not in the West.

> Marketing was invented in Japan around 1650 by the first member of the Mitsui family to settle in Tokyo as a merchant and to open what might be called the first department store. He anticipated by a full 250 years basic Sears, Roebuck policies: to be the buyer for his customers; to design the right products for them, and to develop sources for their production; the principle of your money back and no questions asked; and the idea of offering a large assortment of products to his customers rather than focusing on a craft, a product category, or a process.[6]

Drucker then suggests that marketing did not appear in the West until the middle nineteenth century at the International Harvester Company.

> The first man in the West to see marketing clearly as the unique and central function of the business enterprise, and the creation of a customer as the specific job of management, was Cyrus H. McCormick (1809–1884). The history books mention only that he invented a mechanical harvester. But he also invented the basic tools of modern marketing: market research and market analysis, the concept of market standing, pricing policies, the service salesman, parts and service supply to the customer, and installment credit.[7]

Yet another fifty years had to pass before marketing became very visible on the academic or business scene in America. The term *marketing* first appeared in college course titles in the early 1900s. In 1905, W. E. Kreusi taught a course at the University of Pennsylvania entitled "The Marketing of Products."[8] In 1910, Ralph Starr Butler offered a course entitled "Marketing Methods" at the University of Wisconsin. Butler explained how he conceived marketing:

> In considering the whole field of selling I developed the idea that personal salesmanship and advertising had to do simply with the final expression of the selling idea. My experience with the Procter & Gamble Company had convinced me that a manufacturer seeking to market a product had *to consider and solve a large number of problems* before he ever gave expression to the selling idea by sending a salesman on the road or inserting an advertisement in a publication. [italics added][9]

Marketing departments within business firms had their roots in the development of marketing research in the early twentieth century. The Curtis Publishing Company in 1911 installed the first marketing research department (called commercial research at the time) under the direction of Charles C. Parlin. Marketing research departments were subsequently established at U.S.

---

[6] Peter F. Drucker, *Management: Tasks, Responsibilities, Practices* (New York: Harper & Row, 1973), p. 62.

[7] Ibid.

[8] Robert Bartels, *The History of Marketing Thought,* 2nd ed. (Columbus, Ohio: Grid, 1976), p. 24.

[9] Ibid.

Rubber (1916) and Swift and Company (1917).[10] These departments were viewed as adjuncts to the sales department. Their task was to develop information that would make it easier for sales departments to sell. Over time, marketing research departments accepted additional responsibilities, such as sales analysis and marketing administration. Some time later, companies began to combine marketing research, advertising, customer services, and other miscellaneous marketing functions into marketing departments.

Marketing entered into the consciousness of different industries at different times. A few companies, such as General Electric, General Motors, Sears, and Procter & Gamble, saw its potentialities early. Marketing spread most rapidly in consumer packaged goods companies, consumer durable companies, and industrial equipment companies—in that order. Industrial commodity companies—steel, chemical, paper—came later to marketing consciousness, and still have a long way to go. In the last decade, consumer service firms—especially airlines and banks—have opened themselves to marketing. Airlines began to study travelers' attitudes toward different features of their service—schedule frequency, baggage handling, in-flight service, friendliness, seat comfort. Soon afterwards they shed the notion they were in the air carrier business and began to operate on the idea that they were in the total travel business. Bankers initially showed great resistance to marketing but in the end embraced it enthusiastically. Marketing has begun to attract interest in the insurance industry and the stock brokerage industry, although marketing is still poorly understood in these industries.

Marketing's most recent entry has been in the nonprofit sector of the economy. Such diverse organizations as colleges, hospitals, police departments, museums, and symphonies are currently taking a look at marketing. Marketing has attracted different degrees of interest and understanding in these various industries. American colleges and universities, troubled with declining enrollments, are eager to try out marketing ideas in their admissions operation. An increasing number of hospitals are beginning to look seriously into marketing as their bed counts go down. As a sign of the times, the Evanston Hospital of Evanston, Illinois, recently appointed the world's first vice president of marketing for a hospital.

What leads companies to suddenly discover marketing? An interest in marketing can be triggered by any of five circumstances:

1. *Sales decline.* This is the most common cause. For example, newspaper publishers are experiencing falling circulation as more people turn to television news. Some publishers are beginning to realize that they know very little about why people read newspapers and what they want out of newspapers. These publishers are commissioning consumer research and, on the basis of the findings, attempting to redesign newspapers to be contemporary, relevant, and interesting to readers.

2. *Slow growth.* Companies often reach the limits of their growth in their given industries and start to cast about for new markets. They recognize that they need marketing know-how if they are to successfully identify, evaluate, and select new opportunities. Dow Chemical, wanting new sources of profits, decided to enter consumer markets and invested heavily in acquiring marketing expertise to carry out the job.

3. *Changing buying patterns.* Many companies are experiencing increasingly turbulent markets marked by rapidly changing customer wants. These companies

[10] Ibid., pp. 124–25.

must adopt a marketing orientation in order to keep producing value for the buyers.

4. *Increasing competition.* A complacent company may suddenly be attacked by a master marketer and forced to learn marketing to meet the challenge. Consider the following:

> In the late 1950s when P&G moved into paper products, Scott Paper didn't pay much attention. From a standing start P&G has built a $1.3-billion business in toilet and facial tissues and diapers. Along the way it reduced Scott . . . to an also-ran, earning last year a paltry 4.3% on its total assets, versus P&G's 10.3%.[11]

5. *Increasing sales expenditures.* A company's expenditures for advertising, sales promotion, marketing research, and customer service, may increase without rhyme or reason. When management sees that happening, it often decides to improve its organization and control of these marketing functions.

HOSTILITY TOWARD MARKETING

For all these reasons, companies sooner or later are forced to improve their marketing capacity. Yet marketing is rarely greeted with open arms. Many financial and manufacturing executives see marketing as glorified "hucksterism" and as a threat to their power and status. Some marketers contribute to this by their aggressiveness and overclaiming of the results that stem from marketing.

The nature of marketing's threatening quality is illustrated in Figure 1-1. Initially, the sales/marketing function is seen as one of several *equally* important business functions in a check-and-balance relationship (Fig. 1-1A). A dearth of demand then leads marketers to argue that their function is somewhat more important than the others (Fig. 1-1B). A few marketing enthusiasts go further and say marketing is the major function of the enterprise, for without customers, there would be no company. They put marketing at the center with other business functions serving as support functions (Fig. 1-1C). This view incenses the other managers, who do not want to think of themselves as working for marketing. Enlightened marketers clarify the issue by putting the customer rather than marketing at the center of the company (Fig. 1-1D). They argue for a *customer orientation* in which all functions work together to sense, serve, and satisfy the customer. Finally, some marketers say that marketing still needs to command a central position in the firm if customers' needs are to be correctly interpreted and efficiently satisfied (Fig. 1-1E).

The marketer's argument for the concept of the corporation shown in Fig. 1–1E is summarized as follows:

1. The assets of the firm have little value without the existence of customers.
2. The key task of the firm is therefore to create and hold customers.
3. Customers are attracted through promises and held through satisfaction.
4. Marketing's task is to define an appropriate promise to the customer and to insure the delivery of satisfaction.
5. The actual satisfaction delivered to the customer is affected by the performance of the other departments.
6. Marketing needs influence or control over these other departments if customers are to be satisfied.

[11] Paul Gibson, "Procter & Gamble: It's Got a Little List," *Forbes*, March 20, 1978, p. 34.

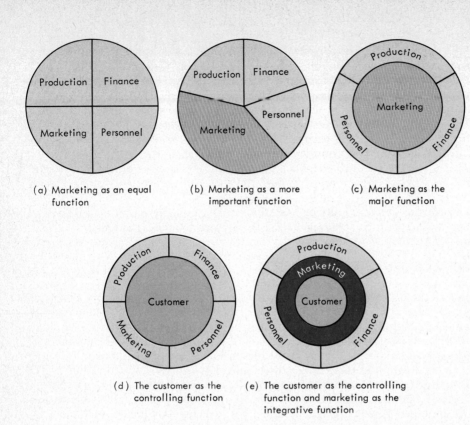

(a) Marketing as an equal function

(b) Marketing as a more important function

(c) Marketing as the major function

(d) The customer as the controlling function

(e) The customer as the controlling function and marketing as the integrative function

FIGURE 1-1
Evolving Views
of Marketing's Role
in the Company

Consider the following situation. The Plumrose Company is a Danish manufacturer of high-quality packaged sliced meats—bacon, ham, balogna, and salami. The company's products sell in U.S. supermarkets at a premium price to match their premium quality. The vice president of marketing sees the Plumrose name as making a promise to the customer that the products are of consistently high quality. Yet from time to time, the manufacturing people fail to exercise adequate quality control; for example, some fatty bacon will be packaged instead of being discarded. Some consumers will find that they have paid a premium price for poor-quality bacon. The company's implicit promise to the customer has been broken. The resulting dissatisfaction can lead to customer loss. Marketing wants the power to insure that this does not happen by asking for some influence or control over manufacturing.

Customer satisfaction can be hurt in other ways. Poor production scheduling might result in late deliveries to the trade and out-of-stock conditions facing the customer. Poor research in the research and development (R&D) department may lead to new products that fail to satisfy real customer needs. Inadequte funds allocated to marketing may prevent the development of improved packaging. The interests of different departments often come into conflict.[12] Marketing's continuous effort to keep every department's attention riveted on producing customer satisfaction interferes with the felt autonomy of

[12] For a discussion of conflicts between marketing and other departments, see chap. 22, pp. 592–96.

these departments. It is no wonder that the other departments react with some hostility to marketing for trying to take center stage in the firm.

Not only is marketing an issue in industries where it is well established but it is a hot issue in industries that are on the brink of marketing. In the law, accounting, and medical professions, a few practitioners have advocated liberalizing the professions' canons of ethics to permit more explicit marketing of professional services. For example, lawyers have already won the right to advertise, and that is causing considerable consternation among many lawyers who regard marketing as unprofessional and unbecoming. Marketing is a growing issue in college and hospital circles, as these institutions struggle to find enough clients for their services. Those colleges and hospitals that have established marketing positions face the animosity of professors and doctors who consider marketing of their service to be degrading. In the newspaper industry, the hostility of old-liners is shown by one newspaper editor who wrote a diatribe entitled "Beware the 'Market' Thinkers."[13] This editor warned newspapers not to let marketers in because they do not understand the function of newspapers, which is to print news. Marketing is not the solution, he feels, to the national decline in newspaper readership. Marketers would corrupt all that is good about today's newspapers.

LAW OF SLOW LEARNING

In spite of resistance in many quarters, most companies eventually allow some marketing to enter their hallowed doors. Marketing is not allowed to enter full blown, ready to work its magic. Marketing is allowed to enter in highly constrained forms so as not to provoke too much opposition. The company adds a single advertising manager or a marketing research manager who can hardly cause any trouble. It does not hire a vice president of marketing to bring in a full marketing orientation. It takes years for a company to arrive at a mature understanding of marketing. Even with determination and a clear understanding of marketing, it may take the firm five to ten years to build a well-functioning marketing organization.

In the typical company, marketing enlightenment grows slowly and tends to pass through five distinct stages. The stages are described below in the context of the banking industry.

Before the mid-1950s, banks had no understanding or regard for marketing. Banks were supplying needed services. They did not have to make a case for checking accounts, savings, loans, or safe-deposit boxes. The bank building was created in the image of a Greek temple calculated to impress the public with the bank's importance and solidity. The interior was austere, and the tellers rarely smiled. One lending officer arranged his office so that a prospective borrower would sit across from his massive desk on a lower chair than his own. The office window was located behind the officer's back and the sun would pour in on the hapless customer as he or she tried to explain why he or she needed a loan. This was the bank's posture before the age of marketing.

---

[13] William H. Hornby, "Beware the 'Market' Thinkers," *The Quill*, 1976, pp. 14 ff. However, see William A. Mindak, "Do Newspaper Publishers Suffer from 'Marketing Myopia'?" *Journalism Quarterly*, summer 1965, pp. 433–42.

Marketing Is Advertising, Sales Promotion, and Publicity

Marketing came into banks in the late 1950s, not in the form of the "marketing concept" but in the form of the "advertising and promotion concept." Banks and other financial institutions were experiencing increased competition for savings. A few financial institutions decided to adopt the marketing tools of the soap companies. They established budgets for advertising and sales promotion and managed to attract many new customers. Their competitors were forced into adopting the same measures and scurried out to hire advertising agencies and promotion experts.

Marketing Is Smiling and a Friendly Atmosphere

The banks that first introduced modern advertising and promotion soon found their advantage cancelled by the rush of imitators. They also learned another lesson: Attracting people to a bank is easy; converting them to loyal customers is hard. These banks began to formulate a larger concept of marketing, that of trying to please the customer. Bankers had to learn to smile. The tellers had to be retrained. The bars had to be taken off the tellers' windows. The interior of the banks had to be redesigned to produce a warm, friendly atmosphere. Even the outside Greek-temple architecture had to be changed.

The first banks to implement this change began to outperform their competitors in attracting and holding new customers. However, their competitors quickly figured out what was happening and rushed into programs of institutionalizing thoroughgoing friendliness. Soon all banks became so friendly that it was impossible for a customer to find an unfriendly bank. Friendliness became so widespread that it lost its potency as a determinant factor in bank choice.

Marketing Is Innovation

Banks had to search for a new basis for differential advantage. Bankers who read Professor Levitt's article "Marketing Myopia"[14] began to realize that marketing transcends advertising and friendliness, although those are important ingredients. Banks are not narrowly in the savings business: They are in the business of meeting the varied and changing financial needs of customers. These banks began to think in terms of continuous innovation of new and valued customer services, such as credit cards, Christmas savings plans, and automatic bank loans. Bank of America, for example, today offers over 350 financial products to customers.

A successful innovation provides the innovative bank with a competitive lead. However, financial services are easily copied and advantages are short-lived. But, if the same bank invests in continuous innovation, it should stay ahead of the other banks in its area.

Marketing Is Positioning

What happens when all banks advertise, smile, and innovate? Clearly they begin to look alike. They are forced to find a new basis for distinction. They begin to realize that no bank can be the best bank for all customers. No bank can offer all products. A bank must choose. It must examine its opportunities and "take a position" in the market.

Positioning goes beyond image making. The image-making bank seeks to cultivate an image in the customer's mind as a large, friendly, or efficient bank. It often develops a symbol, such as a lion (Harris Bank in Chicago) or kangaroo (Continental Bank in Chicago) to dramatize its personality in a distinctive way. Yet the customer may see the competing banks as basically alike, except for the chosen symbols. Positioning is an attempt to distinguish the bank from its competitors along real dimensions in order to be the preferred bank to certain segments of the market. Positioning aims to help customers know the real differences between competing banks so that they can match themselves to the bank that can be of most value to them.

[14] Theodore Levitt, "Marketing Myopia," *Harvard Business Review*, September–October 1965, pp. 26–44, 173–81.

There is a still higher concept of bank marketing that represents the ultimate essence of modern marketing. The issue is whether the bank has installed effective systems for market analysis, planning, and control. One large bank, which had achieved sophistication in advertising, friendliness, innovation, and positioning, nevertheless lacked good systems of marketing planning and control. Each new fiscal year, commercial loan officers submitted their volume goal, usually a figure 10 percent higher than the previous year's goal. They also requested a budget increase of 10 percent. No rationale or plans accompanied these submissions. Top management was satisfied with its officers who achieved their goals. One loan officer, judged to be a good performer, retired and was replaced by a younger man, who proceeded to increase the loan volume 50 percent the following year! The bank painfully learned that it had failed to measure the potentials of its various markets, to require marketing plans, to set quotas, and to develop appropriate reward systems.

Thus, financial institutions demonstrate a law of slow learning with regard to grasping the revolutionary character of marketing. This pattern is repeated as marketing enters each new industry. The interesting question is whether organizations must go through these stages to learn their marketing or whether they can come to it more quickly. The truth is that each stage is so revolutionary in its potential not only for business growth but also for internal disruption that perhaps institutions are wise in coming to terms with marketing one step at a time. As each stage is installed and proves itself, it makes company management more receptive to further advances in marketing thought and practice.

LAW OF FAST FORGETTING

Even after marketing is installed in an organization and matures through the various stages, management must fight a strong tendency to forget basic marketing principles. Management tends to forget marketing principles in the wake of success. For example, a number of major American companies entered European markets in the 1950s and 1960s expecting to achieve high success with their sophisticated products and marketing capabilities. A number of them failed, and a major reason is they forgot the marketing maxim: Know your market and know how to satisfy it. American companies came into these markets with their current products and advertising programs instead of building them up on the basis of what the market needed. General Mills went into the British market with its Betty Crocker cake mixes only to have to withdraw a short time later. Angel cake and devil's food cake sounded too exotic for British housewives. And many housewives felt that such professional-looking cakes as those pictured on the Betty Crocker packages must be hard to make. American marketers failed to appreciate the major cultural variations between and even within European countries and the need to start where the consumers are, not where their products are. Sorenson noted:

> In the United States, the marketing concept appears to be well into the mature phase of its own life cycle. It is increasingly being questioned, criticized, and—in some instances—ignored or discarded. By contrast, the marketing concept in Europe is alive and vigorous and just entering the rapid growth stage of its life cycle.[15]

[15] Ralph Z. Sorenson II, "U.S. Marketers Can Learn from European Innovators," *Harvard Business Review*, September–October 1972, p. 97.

There is a tendency in successful firms toward marketing regression—going back to an earlier stage of marketing thinking, for instance, seeing marketing primarily as sales and promotion. A good illustration is the case of a management consulting firm that was founded with the objective of achieving sustained long-term growth.[16] The firm's management developed a long-range plan based on the application of the following marketing principles:

1. Marketing was recognized as a company-wide activity with clearly defined areas of responsibility. Staff men and supervisors were expected to work on expanding services to existing clients; officers were expected to develop new clients and to close sales leads opened by the staff.
2. There was a carefully planned and vigorous program for building referral sources. Each officer belonged to several clubs and associations. Bank contacts were pursued systematically as a source of leads. Officers were encouraged to fill speaking engagements or to write articles.
3. Frequent meetings were held to coordinate and plan new business development activities. Training sessions were conducted to improve new business development skills.
4. A public relations consultant was retained to obtain favorable newspaper and trade paper publicity. Seminars were held from time to time on important management techniques.
5. Every effort was made to motivate new business development activity. Staff men were paid bonuses for successful leads. Ability to generate new business was made a significant element in promotion to supervisor and the major element in promotion to officer. Officers' compensation was based almost entirely on the volume and rate of growth of the client assignments under their supervision.

Within ten years, this program produced outstanding results. Fee billings had risen to over $4 million a year from offices located in six major cities. However, this represented a high point from which the firm began a decline, at first slowly and then precipitously. As the fortunes of the company declined, the organization fell into disarray. All the branch offices were closed. Several officers resigned to establish their own consulting firms.

The reversal of the company's fortunes was not the result of new factors or conditions in the marketplace. Rather the company paid a deferred penalty for long-term overemphasis on selling to the detriment of marketing. Having committed itself to a rapid growth goal, it neglected other things, specifically:

1. The original objective was for a sustained rate of growth of over 15 percent a year. This rate was achieved, but the effort involved did not leave sufficient time for the acquisition, training, and development of the professional staff. The firm was developing business at a rate somewhat faster than it was developing the capacity to handle it.
2. This problem was exacerbated by the effects of the emphasis placed on new-business development and the methods that were adopted to motivate it. Staff men perceived that high awards were given for business development but not necessarily for professional excellence. A number of staff men of great professional promise, but with little interest in selling, left the firm to join competitors. The multiplier effect of these resignations increased the difficulty of coordinating staff development with growth.

[16] This description is taken from a letter from a well-known management consultant, who prefers anonymity.

3. In view of the fact that officers were selected primarily for their ability to develop new business, they occasionally lacked the technical background to supervise properly the assignments handled by their own staff, who were more likely to have been selected on the basis of proven professional skills. The difference in compensation between officers and staff consultants was substantial, giving rise to poor morale, increasing the problem of turnover, and making it impossible to give proper supervision to complex and important assignments.

4. The high financial rewards for new-business development led to savage competition and infighting between company officers and contributed to an unhealthy atmosphere throughout the firm.

Thus a firm can overemphasize the job of selling to the detriment of really serving the customers' interests. An intense passion for volume and growth can ultimately hurt quality and long-run profitability. Companies have to constantly remind themselves that the name of the business game is not short-term sales but long-run profitability. And long-run profitability is attained not through hard selling but through sound customer-oriented marketing, which produces value and long-run buyer satisfaction.

THE HIGHER PURPOSE OF MARKETING

This brings us to the final question in this chapter. What is the higher purpose of marketing? What should an enlightened marketer try to accomplish?

This question is raised because managers sometimes lose sight of their ultimate goals and settle for short-term gains of dubious benefit to themselves and others. When they lose a sense of higher purpose, their work becomes unsatisfying and their attitude cynical.

Different goals have been proposed to guide the marketing practitioner. The most common view is that the marketer's goal is to maximize the market's *consumption* of whatever the company is producing. In this view, the marketer is a technician who engineers sales gains. Marketing success means selling more and more gum, cars, and ice cream bars as if the consumer were a huge consumption machine that must constantly be stuffed with goods and services. Even if consumers don't want this much consumption, it is good for the economy and creates jobs. Yet Adam Smith observed that hunger is limited by the size of the human stomach. More generally, people will eventually run out of time to consume all that they could buy. They may rebel against overeating and overdressing, and start thinking "enough is enough" or even "less is more." Frederick Pohl wrote a science-fiction short story, "The Midas Touch," in which factories are completely automated and the goods roll out continuously and people consume as much as they can in order not to be buried under the goods. In the story, ordinary people are given high consumption quotas, while the elite are excused from having to consume so much. Furthermore, the elite are given the few jobs that are still left to do, so that they don't have to face the bleakness of no work.

A sounder goal for the marketer is to aim to maximize *consumer satisfaction*. The marketer's task is to track changing consumer wants and influence the company to adjust its mix of goods and services to those that are needed. The marketer makes sure that the company continues to produce value for the target customer markets.

Even consumer satisfaction, however, is not a complete goal for the marketer. The act of creating "goods" to satisfy human desires also creates some "bads" in the process. Every car that is produced satisfies a transportation need and at the same time contributes to the level of pollution in society. The economist Kenneth Arrow noted that high gross national product also means high gross national pollution. The sensitive marketer has to take responsibility for the totality of outputs created by the business. First, the marketer is a member of the public and therefore victimizing himself to some extent. Second, the society has spawned consumerists, environmentalists, and other public-action groups, who make life difficult for those firms that are indifferent to the "bads" they create in the process of pursuing profits.

Ultimately, the enlightened marketer is really trying to contribute to the *quality of life.* The quality of life is a function of the quantity and need-satisfying quality of goods and services, the quality of the physical environment, and the quality of the cultural environment. Too often the firm rests its case on its ability to produce great quantities of goods and services and does not pay enough attention to its impact on the other components of life quality.

Profits will still be a major test of business success in serving society. However, as Drucker observes, profits are really a by-product of doing business well and not the moral aim of business. Business, like other institutions of society, prospers only by maintaining legitimacy in the eyes of consumers, employees, and the general public. Legitimacy is grounded in the institution's commitment to serve higher moral aims.

SUMMARY

Marketing—the management of exchange processes and relationships—is the cornerstone discipline of some of the most successful companies in America and a discipline of growing interest to companies and nonprofit organizations throughout the world. All organizations face the problem of how to increase value for target markets that are undergoing continuously changing needs and wants. Organizations must thoughtfully define their products, services, prices, communications, and distribution in a way that meets real buyer needs in a competitively viable way. That is the task of marketing.

Although selling is a very old subject, marketing is a relatively new subject. It represents a higher-order integration of many separate functions—selling, advertising, marketing research, new-product development, customer service, physical distribution—that impinge on customer needs and satisfaction. Many organizations at first resist marketing because it threatens vested interests within the organization and their own concepts of how to manage the organization effectively. Marketing gradually gets established, however, first as a promotion function, later as a customer service function, still later as an innovation function, then as a market positioning function, and ultimately as an analysis, planning, and control function. Few companies understand and install marketing in its full form when first considering it. Even after marketing is effectively implemented in an organization, there is a tendency for many managers to forget its main principles in the wake of success.

Marketing's task in the organization is not only to help it recognize business opportunities and serve the various publics but also to harness the organization's energy to enhance the quality of life in society.

1. There are several different approaches to the study of marketing. A *managerial* approach is one of them. What are some other possible approaches?

2. "Marketing is not simply the job of a group of people in the company who are responsible for selling the company's products. Every member of the firm should know how to function as a marketer." What does it mean for a company recruiter, for example, to function like a marketer?

3. A company president recently told the author: "I cannot see how marketing can be taught. The only way to learn marketing is to go out and try to sell something." How would you answer this?

4. The five stages through which many organizations pass as they develop their use of marketing were discussed in the context of the banking industry. Discuss them in the context of four-year private liberal arts colleges that are facing declining enrollment.

5. Do you think that the adoption of marketing by companies in developing nations will follow the same patterns as in the U.S.? Why?

6. What would a perfume company be doing differently in the way of marketing if its objective were to maximize sales? profits? consumer satisfaction? consumers' life styles? quality of life? In other words, how does the company's objective make a difference to its marketing practice?

7. What should the aim of marketing be in an affluent society? One prominent marketing educator said: "Herein lies a challenge for marketing: to justify and stimulate our age of consumption . . . to enjoy (the affluent life) without pangs of guilt." Would you defend this as an appropriate philosophy for the times?

8. "With the supermarkets as our temple and the singing commercial our litany, are we likely to fire the world with an irresistible vision of America's exalted purposes and inspiring way of life?" This statement by Adlai Stevenson suggests that business is too dominant and enshrined in American life. Do you agree?

Tasks and Philosophies of Marketing Management

2

The purpose of this chapter is to describe how a marketer views social phenomena. A marketer thinks in a particular way, as does a psychologist, a sociologist, an economist, and a political scientist. The marketer is trained to think about a certain set of issues, concepts, and relationships. Obviously if a marketer and the other social scientists were all shown a supermarket, each would be interested in different aspects of it and interpret a supermarket's role in different ways.

We will look at the structure of marketing thought first in terms of *marketing,* then in terms of *marketing management,* and finally in terms of *marketing philosophies.*

MARKETING

Various definitions of marketing have appeared through time:

It has been described by one person or another as a business activity; as a group of related business activities; as a trade phenomenon; as a frame of mind; as a coordinative, integrative function in policy making; as a sense of business purpose; as an economic process; as a structure of institutions; as the process of exchanging or transferring ownership of products; as a process of concentration, equalization,

18

and dispersion; as the creation of time, place, and possession utilities, as a process of demand and supply adjustment; and as many other things.[1]

All of these definitions provide useful but partial perspectives on the nature of marketing. We would like to propose a definition of marketing that is rooted in human behavior:

> *Marketing* is human activity directed at satisfying needs and wants through exchange processes.

Human Needs and Wants

The starting point for the discipline of marketing lies in *human needs and wants.* Mankind needs food, air, water, clothing, and shelter to survive. Beyond this, people have a strong desire for recreation, education, and other services. They have strong preferences for particular versions of basic goods and services.

There is no doubt that people's needs and wants today are staggering. In one year, in the United States alone, Americans purchased 67 billion eggs, 250 million chickens, 5.5 million hair dryers, 133 billion domestic air travel passenger miles, and over 20 million lectures by college English professors. These consumer goods and services led to a derived demand for more fundamental products, such as 150 million tons of steel and 3.7 billion pounds of cotton. These are a few of the wants and needs that get expressed in a $1.3 trillion economy.

A useful distinction can be drawn between *needs, wants,* and *intentions,* although these words are used interchangeably in common speech. *A need is a state of felt deprivation of some generic satisfaction arising out of the human condition.* People require food, clothing, shelter, safety, belonging, esteem, and a few other things for survival. People actually need very little. These needs are not *created* by their society or by marketers; they exist in the very texture of human biology and the human condition.

Wants are desires for specific satisfiers of these ultimate needs. A person needs food and wants a steak, needs clothing and wants a Pierre Cardin suit, needs esteem and buys a Cadillac. While people's needs are few, their wants are many. Human wants are continually shaped and reshaped by social forces and institutions such as churches, schools, corporations, and families.

Intentions are decisions to acquire specific satisfiers under the given terms and conditions. Many persons want a Cadillac; only a few intend to buy one at today's prices.

These distinctions shed light on the frequent charge by marketing critics that "marketers create needs" or "marketers get people to buy things they don't need." Marketers do not create needs; needs preexist marketers. Marketers, along with other influentials in the society, influence wants. They suggest to consumers that a particular car would efficiently satisfy the person's need for esteem. Marketers do not create the need for esteem but try to point out how a particular good would satisfy that need. Marketers also try to influence persons' *intentions* to buy by making the product attractive, affordable, and easily available.

Products

The existence of human needs and wants gives rise to the concept of *products.* Our definition of product is very broad:

[1] Marketing staff of Ohio State University, "A Statement of Marketing Philosophy," *Journal of Marketing,* January 1965, p. 43.

A *product* is something that is viewed as capable of satisfying a need or
want.

A product can be an *object, service, activity, person, place, organization,* or
idea. Suppose a person feels depressed. What might the person do to get out of
his or her depression? What products might meet the need to feel better? The
person can turn on a television set (object); go to a movie (service); take up
jogging (activity); see a therapist (person); travel to Hawaii (place); join a Lonely
Hearts Club (organization); or adopt a different philosophy about life (idea). All
of these things can be viewed as products available to the "feeling depressed." If
the term *product* seems unnatural at times, we may substitute the term *resource*
or *offer* or *satisfier* to describe that which may satisfy a need.

In the case of physical objects, it is important to distinguish between them
and the services they represent. People do not buy physical objects for their own
sake. A tube of lipstick is bought to supply a service: helping the person look
better. A drill bit is bought to supply a service: making a needed hole. Every
physical object is a means of packaging a service. The marketer's job is to sell
the service packages built into physical products. The seller who becomes
enamored of the physical features has a case of "marketing myopia." Fixated on
the features, he loses sight of the function. He forgets that a physical object is a
tool to solve a problem. People do not remain loyal to horses and carriages when
the modern automobile meets their needs better.

Exchange

The fact that people have needs and wants and the fact that there are products
capable of satisfying them are necessary but not sufficient to define marketing.
Marketing exists when people decide to satisfy needs and wants in a certain way
that we shall call *exchange.* Exchange is one of four ways in which a person can
obtain a product capable of satisfying a particular need.

The first option is *self-production.* A hungry person can relieve hunger
through personal efforts at hunting, fishing, or fruit gathering. The person does
not have to interact with anyone else. In this case there is no market and no marketing.

The second option is *coercion.* The hungry person can forcibly wrest food
from another. No benefit is offered to the other party except the chance not to
be harmed.

The third option is *supplication.* The hungry person can approach someone and beg for food. The supplicant has nothing tangible to offer except gratitude.

The fourth option is *exchange.* The hungry person can approach someone
who has food and offer some resource in exchange, such as money, another good,
or some service.

Marketing centers on that last approach to the acquisition of products to
satisfy human needs and wants. Exchange assumes four conditions:

1. There are two parties.
2. Each party has something that could be of value to the other.
3. Each party is capable of communication and delivery.
4. Each party is free to accept or reject the offer.

If these conditions exist, there is a potential for exchange. Whether exchange
actually takes place depends upon whether the two parties can find *terms of*

exchange that will leave them both better off (or at least not worse off) than before the exchange. This is the sense in which exchange is described as a value-creating process; that is, exchange normally leaves both parties with a sense of having gained something of value.

Market The concept of exchange leads naturally into the concept of a market:

> A *market* is the set of all actual and potential buyers of a product.

An example will illustrate this concept. Suppose an artist spends three weeks creating a beautiful sculpture. He has in mind a particular price. The question he faces is whether there is anyone who will exchange this amount of money for the sculpture. If there is at least one such person, we can say there is a market. The *size of the market* will vary with the price. The artist may ask for so high a price that there is no market for his sculpture. As he brings the price down, normally the market size increases because more people can afford the sculpture. The size of the market depends upon the number of persons who have (1) an interest in the object, (2) the necessary resources, and (3) a willingness to offer the resources to obtain it. These three things make up the *level of demand*.

Wherever there is a potential for trade, there is a market. The term "market" is often used in conjunction with some qualifying term that describes a *human need* or *product type* or *demographic group* or *geographical location*. An example of a *need market* is the relaxation market, which exists because people are willing to exchange money for lessons on yoga, transcendental meditation, and disco dancing. An example of a *product market* is the shoe market, so defined because people are willing to exchange money for objects called shoes. An example of a *demographic market* is the youth market, so defined because young people possess purchasing power that they are willing to use for such products as education, bikinis, motorcycles, and stereophonic equipment. An example of a *geographic market* is the French market, so defined because French citizens are a locus of potential transactions for a wide variety of goods and services.

The concept of a market also covers exchanges of resources not necessarily involving money. The political candidate offers promises of good government to a *voter market* in exchange for their votes. The lobbyist offers services to a *legislative market* in exchange for votes for the lobbyist's cause. A university cultivates the *mass-media market* when it wines and dines editors in exchange for more publicity. A museum cultivates the *donor market* when it offers special privileges to contributors in exchange for their financial support.

Marketing The concept of markets finally brings us full circle to the concept of marketing. *Marketing* means working with *markets,* which in turn means attempting to actualize *potential exchanges* for the purpose of *satisfying human needs and wants.* Thus we return to our definition of *marketing* as *human activity directed at satisfying needs and wants through exchange processes.*

MARKETING MANAGEMENT

Coping with exchange processes calls for a considerable amount of work and skill. Persons become fairly adept at buying to meet their household needs. Occasionally, they also undertake selling—selling their car, selling personal services.

21

Organizations are more professional in handling exchange processes. They must attract resources from one set of markets, convert them into useful products, and trade them in another set of markets. *Nations* also plan and manage exchange relations with others. They search for beneficial trade relations and exchanges with other nations. In this book we will take the perspective primarily of *organizational marketing* rather than that of personal or national marketing.

Our position is that *marketing management* takes place when at least one party to a potential exchange gives thought to objectives and means of achieving desired responses from other parties. Our formal definition of marketing management is:

> *Marketing management* **is the analysis, planning, implementation, and control of programs designed to create, build, and maintain mutually beneficial exchanges and relationships with target markets for the purpose of achieving organizational objectives. It relies on a disciplined analysis of the needs, wants, perceptions, and preferences of target and intermediary markets as the basis for effective product design, pricing, communication, and distribution.**

Marketing management can occur in an organization in connection with any of its markets. Consider an automobile manufacturer. The vice president of personnel deals in the *labor market;* the vice president of purchasing, the *raw materials market;* and the vice president of finance, the *money market.* They have to set objectives and develop strategies for producing satisfactory results in these markets. Traditionally, however, these executives have not been called marketers or trained in marketing. Instead, marketing management is historically identified with tasks and personnel dealing with the *customer market.* We shall follow this convention, although what we shall say about marketing concepts and principles applies to all markets.

Marketing work in the customer market is carried out by sales managers, sales representatives, advertising and promotion managers, marketing researchers, customer service managers, product managers, market managers, and the marketing vice president. Each of these job positions goes along with well-defined missions and responsibilities. Many of these job positions center around the management of particular marketing *resources,* such as advertising, sales force, or marketing research. On the other hand, product managers, market managers, and the marketing vice president manage *programs.* Their job is to analyze, plan, and implement programs that will produce a desired level of transactions with specified target markets.

Marketing-Management Tasks

The popular image of the marketing manager is someone whose task is primarily to stimulate demand for the company's products. However, this is too limited a view of the range of marketing tasks carried out by marketing managers. *Marketing management has the task of regulating the level, timing, and character of demand in a way that will help the organization achieve its objectives.* Simply put, marketing management is demand management.

The organization forms an idea of a *desired level of transactions* with a market. At any time, the *actual demand level* may be below, equal to, or above the *desired demand level.* This leads to the eight distinguishable demand states listed in Table 2–1. The marketing task and the formal name of each task is shown next to each demand state.[2]

TABLE 2–1 The Basic Marketing Tasks		
DEMAND STATE	MARKETING TASK	FORMAL NAME
I. Negative demand	Reverse demand	Conversional marketing
II. No demand	Create demand	Stimulational marketing
III. Latent demand	Develop demand	Developmental marketing
IV. Faltering demand	Revitalize demand	Remarketing
V. Irregular demand	Synchronize demand	Synchromarketing
VI. Full demand	Maintain demand	Maintenance marketing
VII. Overfull demand	Reduce demand	Demarketing
VIII. Unwholesome demand	Destroy demand	Countermarketing

Conversional marketing   Conversional marketing grows out of the state of negative demand. *Negative demand is a state in which all or most of the important segments of the potential market dislike the product or service and in fact might conceivably pay a price to avoid it.*

Negative demand, far from being a rare condition, applies to many products and services. Vegetarians feel negative demand for meats of all kinds. Numerous Americans feel negative demand for kidneys and sweetbreads. People have a negative demand for vaccinations, dental work, vasectomies, and gall bladder operations. Many travelers have a negative demand for air travel; others have a negative demand for rail travel. Places such as the North Pole and the desert wastelands are in negative demand by tourists. Atheism, ex-convicts, military service, and even work are in negative demand by certain groups.

The challenge of negative demand to marketing management, especially in the face of a positive supply, is to develop a plan that will cause demand to rise from negative to positive and eventually equal the positive supply level. We call this marketing task *conversional marketing.* Conversional marketing is one of the two most difficult tasks a marketer might face (the other is countermarketing). The marketer must discover whether the market resists the product because of beliefs, values, emotions, or costs and take appropriate measures. When the product is considered good for consumers (e.g., auto safety belts), the conversional marketer is a hero; when the product is considered bad (e.g., junk food), the conversional marketer is a villain.

Stimulational marketing   There is a whole range of products and services for which there is no demand. Instead of having negative or positive feelings toward the offer, people are indifferent or uninterested. *No demand is a state in which* *all or important segments of a potential market are uninterested in or indifferent to a particular offer.*

Three different categories of offers are characterized by no demand. First, there are those familiar objects that are perceived as having no value. Examples would be urban junk, such as Coke bottles, old barbed wire, and political buttons right after an election. Second, there are those familiar objects that are recognized to have value but not in the particular market. Examples would include boats in areas not near any water, snowmobiles in areas where it never snows, and burglar alarms in areas where there is no crime. Third, there are those unfamiliar objects that are innovated and face a situation of no demand because the relevant market has no knowledge of the object. Examples would include trinkets of all kinds that people might buy if exposed to them but would not normally think about.

The task of transforming no demand into positive demand is called *stimulational marketing*. Stimulational marketing is a tough task because the marketer faces a market that does not have a felt want for the offer. He can proceed in three ways. The first is to try to connect the product or service with some existing need in the marketplace. Thus antique dealers can attempt to stimulate interest in old barbed wire on the part of those who have a general need to collect things. The second is to alter the environment so that the offer becomes valued in that environment. Thus sellers of motorboats can attempt to stimulate interest in boats in a lakeless community by building an artificial lake. The third is to distribute information or the object itself in more places in the hope that its pervasive presence leads to desire and purchase.

Developmental marketing Developmental marketing is associated with a state known as latent demand. *A state of latent demand exists when a substantial number of people share a strong need for something that does not exist in the form of an actual product or service.* The latent demand represents an opportunity for the marketing innovator to develop the product or service that people have been wanting.

Examples of products and services in latent demand abound. Many cigarette smokers would like a good-tasting cigarette that does not contain nicotine and tars damaging to health. Such a product breakthrough would be an instant success, just as the first filter-tip cigarette won a sizable share of the market. Many people would like a car that promised substantially more safety and substantially less pollution than existing cars. There is a strong latent demand for fast city roads, efficient trains, uncrowded national parks, unpolluted major cities, safe streets, and good television programs.

The process of effectively transforming latent demand into actual demand is that of *developmental marketing*. The marketer must invest in marketing research and product development to bring about an offer that promises to satisfy the latent demand.

Remarketing All kinds of objects, services, activities, places, organizations, and ideas eventually experience *faltering demand. Faltering demand is a state in which the demand for a product or service is less than it used to be and where further decline is expected in the absence of remedial efforts to revise the target market, offer, and/or marketing effort.*

For example, railway travel has been a service in steady decline for a number of years, and it is badly in need of imaginative remarketing. Many churches have seen their membership thin out in the face of competition from secular recreations and activities. The downtown areas of many large cities are in need of remarketing. Many popular entertainers and political candidates lose their following and badly need remarketing.

The challenge of faltering demand is revitalization, and the marketing task involved is *remarketing*. Remarketing is based on the premise that it is possible in many cases to start a new life cycle for a declining product or service. *Remarketing is the search for new propositions for relating the offer to its potential markets.*

Synchromarketing   An organization might be satisfied with the average level of demand but quite dissatisfied with its temporal pattern. Some seasons are marked by demand surging far beyond the supply capacity of the organization, and other seasons are marked by a wasteful underutilization of the organization's supply capacity. *Irregular demand is a state in which the current timing pattern of demand is marked by seasonal or volatile fluctuations that depart from the timing pattern of supply.*

Many examples of irregular demand can be cited. In mass transit much of the equipment is idle during the off-hours and in insufficient supply during the peak hours. Hotels in Miami Beach are insufficiently booked during the summer and overbooked in the winter. Hospital operating facilities are overbooked at the beginning of the week and underutilized toward the end of the week to meet physician preferences.

The marketing task of trying to resolve irregular demand is called *synchromarketing* because the effort is to bring the movements of demand and supply into better synchronization. Many marketing steps can be taken to alter the pattern of demand. For example, a museum that is undervisited on weekdays and overvisited on weekends could (a) shift its special events to weekdays instead of weekends, (b) advertise only its weekday programs, (c) charge a higher admission price during the weekends. In some cases a pattern of demand can be readily reshaped through simple changes in incentives or promotion; in other cases the reshaping may require years of patient effort to alter habits and desires.

Maintenance marketing   The most desirable situation that a marketer faces is that of *full demand. Full demand is a state in which the current level and timing of demand is equal to the desired level and timing of demand.* Various products and services achieve this state from time to time. However, it is not a time for resting on one's laurels and doing perfunctory marketing. Market demand is subject to two erosive forces. One force is changing needs and tastes in the marketplace. The demand for barber services, as well as the demand for mass magazines and college educations, has undergone an unexpected decline because of changing market preferences. The other force is active competition. When a product is doing well, competitors quickly move in and attempt to attract away some of the demand.

The task of the marketer facing full demand is *maintenance marketing*. Maintenance marketing calls for maintaining efficiency in the carrying out of day-to-day marketing activities and eternal vigilance in spotting new forces that threaten to erode demand. The maintenance marketer is primarily concerned with tactical issues such as keeping the price right, keeping the sales force and dealers motivated, and keeping tight control over costs.

Demarketing   Sometimes the demand for a product or service begins to outpace the supply substantially. That is known as *overfull demand, a state in which demand exceeds the level at which the marketer feels able or motivated to supply it.*

The problem may be due to *temporary shortages,* as when producers suddenly find themselves facing an unexpected surge in demand or unexpected interruptions of supply. Or the problem may be due to *chronic overpopularity.* For example, the state of Oregon felt that too many people were moving to Oregon and spoiling its natural environment; and the city of San Francisco felt that too many motorists were using the Golden Gate bridge and weakening its structure.

The task of reducing overfull demand is called *demarketing. Demarketing deals with attempts to discourage customers in general or a certain class of customers in particular on either a temporary or a permanent basis.* Demarketing calls for marketing in reverse. Instead of encouraging customers, it calls for the art of discouraging them. Prices may be raised and product quality, service, promotion, and convenience may be reduced. Demarketers must have thick skins because they are not going to be popular with certain groups.[3]

Countermarketing   There are many products or services for which the demand may be judged unwholesome from the viewpoint of the consumer's welfare, the public's welfare, or the supplier's welfare. *Unwholesome demand is a state in which any demand is felt to be excessive because of undesirable qualities associated with the offer.* Classic examples of unselling efforts have revolved around the so-called vice products: alcohol, cigarettes, and hard drugs.

The task of trying to destroy the demand for something is called *countermarketing,* or *unselling.* Whereas demarketing tries to reduce the demand without impugning the product itself, countermarketing is an attempt to designate the product as intrinsically unwholesome. The offer may be the organization's own product, which it wishes to phase out, a competitor's product, or a third party's product, which is regarded as socially undesirable. Efforts by organized groups to countermarket undesirable social ideas or practices, or to promote desirable social ideas or practices, are called *social marketing.*[4]

MARKETING-MANAGEMENT PHILOSOPHIES

We have described marketing management as the conscious effort to achieve desired exchange outcomes with target markets. Now the question arises, What is the philosophy that guides these marketing efforts? What is the relative weight given to serving the interests of the *organization,* the *customers,* and *society?*

[3] See Philip Kotler and Sidney J. Levy, "Demarketing, Yes, Demarketing," *Harvard Business Review,* November–December 1971, pp. 74–80.

[4] See Philip Kotler and Gerald Zaltman, "Social Marketing: An Approach to Planned Social Change," *Journal of Marketing,* July 1971, pp. 3–12.

Very often these conflict. It is desirable that marketing activities be carried out under a clear concept of responsive and responsible marketing.

There are five alternative concepts under which business and other organizations can conduct their marketing activity.

The Production Concept

The production concept is one of the oldest concepts guiding sellers:

> The *production concept* is a management orientation that assumes that consumers will favor those products which are available and affordable, and that therefore the major task of management is to pursue improved production and distribution efficiency.

The implicit premises of the production concept are:

1. Consumers are primarily interested in product availability and low price.
2. Consumers know the prices of the competing brands.
3. Consumers do not see or attach much importance to nonprice differences within the product class.
4. The organization's task is to keep improving production and distribution efficiency and lowering costs as the key to attracting and holding customers.

The production concept is an appropriate philosophy of management in two types of situations. The first is where the demand for a product exceeds supply. Here consumers are ready to buy any versions of the product they can find. Thus companies in developing nations that are able to sell all they produce put their energy into improving production. The second situation is where the product's cost is high and has to be brought down to expand the market. Texas Instruments provides a contemporary example of the production concept:[5]

> Texas Instruments, the Dallas-based electronics firm, is the leading American exponent of the "get-out-production, cut-the-price" philosophy that Henry Ford pioneered in the early 1900s in connection with developing the market for automobiles. Ford put all of his talent into perfecting the mass production of automobiles to bring down their costs so that Americans could afford them. Texas Instruments puts all of its efforts in building production volume and improving technology in order to bring down costs. It uses its lower costs to cut prices and expand the market size. It goes after and usually achieves the dominant position in its markets. It has become number one in pocket calculators and is about to do the same with digital watches, having recently introduced a $10 model, and is hoping to bring down the price in the early 1980s to somewhere around $5. To Texas Instruments, marketing means one thing: bringing down the price to buyers. This orientation is also found in many Japanese companies and makes Texas Instruments well prepared to compete with them in world markets.[5]

Service and nonprofit organizations also follow the production concept when they focus their main energy on achieving work efficiency. Many medical and dental practices are organized on assembly line principles, as are some gov-

[5] "Texas Instruments Shows U.S. Business How to Survive in the 1980s," *Business Week*, September 18, 1978, pp. 66ff.

ernment agencies, such as unemployment offices and license bureaus. While this type of management results in the handling of many cases per hour, it is open to the charge of impersonality and consumer insensitivity.

The Product Concept

The product concept is another venerable concept guiding sellers.

> The *product concept* is a management orientation that assumes that consumers will favor those products that offer the most quality for the price, and therefore the organization should devote its energy to improving product quality.

The implicit premises of the product concept are:

1. Consumers buy products rather than solutions to needs.
2. Consumers are primarily interested in product quality.
3. Consumers know the quality and feature differences of the competing brands.
4. Consumers choose among competing brands on the basis of obtaining the most quality for their money.
5. The organization's task is to keep improving product quality as the key to attracting and holding customers.

The best-known example of the product concept is the manufacturer who built a better mousetrap.[6] He followed Emerson's advice: "If a man . . . makes a better mousetrap . . . the world will beat a path to his door." But to his surprise, he found few customers panting at his door. People do not automatically learn about new and improved products, believe that they are really superior, or show a willingness to pay a higher price. The inventor of a better mousetrap will get nowhere unless he or she takes positive steps to design, package, and price the new product attractively, place it into convenient distribution channels, bring it to the attention of persons concerned with rodent problems, and convince them that it has superior qualities. He should even have considered whether people want mousetraps in the first place as opposed to other solutions that could have been developed to meet this problem.

Companies can be found in all fields that tend to operate on a product concept. Railroad management was so sure that it had a superior form of transportation that it underserved the customers and overlooked the emerging challenge of the airlines, buses, trucks, and automobiles. In another vein, a manufacturer of office files complained that his files should be selling better because they are the best in the world. "They can be dropped from a four-story building and not be damaged." "Yes," agreed his sales manager, "but our customers aren't planning to use this feature." Too often product-oriented manufacturers fall in love with their products and think of marketing as simply proving to customers they are the best of their kind. An example is provided by the Elgin National Watch Company:[7]

---

[6] See "So We Made a Better Mousetrap," *The President's Forum,* Fall 1962, pp. 26–27.

[7] The full case is described in Ralph Westfall and Harper W. Boyd, Jr., *Cases in Marketing Management* (Homewood, Ill.: Richard D. Irwin, 1961), pp. 16–24.

> Since its founding in 1864, the Elgin National Watch Company had enjoyed a reputation as one of America's finest watchmakers. Elgin placed its major emphasis on maintaining a superior product and merchandising it through a large network of leading jewelry and department stores. Its sales rose continuously until 1958, and thereafter its sales and market share began to slip. What happened to undermine Elgin's dominant position?
>
> Essentially, Elgin's management was so enamored with fine, traditionally styled watches that it didn't notice the major changes taking place in the consumer watch market. With regard to *customers,* many of them were losing interest in the idea that a watch needed superior timekeeping accuracy, had to carry a prestigious name, and last a lifetime. They expected a watch to tell time, look attractive, and not cost too much. Consumers had growing desires for convenience (self-winding watches), durability (waterproof and shockproof watches), and economy (pin-lever watches). With regard to *channels,* an increasing number of watches were being sold through mass-distribution outlets and discount stores. This suggested that many Americans wanted to avoid the higher markups of the local jeweler, and also that buying watches had impulse characteristics that could be exploited by increased store exposure, with resulting increased sales. With regard to *competitors,* many had added lower-priced watches to their line and had begun to sell them through mass-distribution channels. Elgin's problem was that it had riveted its attention to a set of products instead of interpreting and serving a changing set of wants.

Nonprofit organizations frequently exhibit a product orientation. Opera companies assume that the public will want the standard fare of Mozart, Verdi, and Puccini year after year. Colleges assume that high school graduates will continue to want their product. Churches, police departments, and the post office feel that they are offering the public the right product and that the public should be grateful. This concentration on the purity and immutability of the product eventually gets these organizations into deep trouble, as many are finding out. These organizations too often are looking in a mirror when they should be looking out of the window.

The Selling Concept

The selling concept (also called the sales concept) is another hallowed way in which producers have sought to guide their exchange activity.

> The *selling concept* is a management orientation that assumes that consumers will either not buy or not buy enough of the organization's products unless the organization makes a substantial effort to stimulate their interest in its products.

The implicit premises of the selling concept are:

1. Consumers have a normal tendency to resist buying most things that are not essential.
2. Consumers can be induced to buy more through various sales-stimulating devices.
3. The organization's task is to organize a strong sales-oriented department as the key to attracting and holding customers.

Companies practicing the selling concept typically assume their goods are "sold, not bought." For example, insurance agents hold that people do not feel a strong need for insurance and do not beat a path to their door; therefore it is necessary to aggressively search out potential customers and hard-sell them on the benefits of insurance. The same philosophy pervades the thinking of encyclopedia and bible companies, land developers, and home repair contractors. Auto dealers often are prime practitioners of the selling concept:

> From the moment the customer walks into the showroom, the auto salesman will engage in "psyching him out," exaggerating, baiting, and occasionally lying. The new model is described as an excellent car. If the customer likes the floor model, he may be told that there is another customer about to buy it and that he should decide as soon as possible. If the customer balks at the price (which is artificially high to begin with), the salesman offers to talk to the manager to get a special concession. The customer waits ten minutes and the salesman returns with "the boss doesn't like it but I got him to agree." The aim is to "work up the customer" to buy then and there.[8]

Obviously, there are great risks in practicing the selling concept, especially in its hard-driving form where customer satisfaction is considered secondary to getting the sale. This practice will spoil the market for this seller in that eventually there will be no customers who trust him. For the selling concept to work for an extended period of time, the following circumstances are required:

1. Many of the customers come in knowing that the dealers are hard sellers and feel they can handle the situation.
2. Customers who are dissatisfied soon forget their dissatisfaction.
3. Dissatisfied customers do not talk very much to other customers.
4. Dissatisfied customers probably will not complain to consumer organizations.
5. There are a great number of potential customers out there; the company does not have to depend upon repeat business.

Although we have used business organizations to illustrate the selling concept, it is frequently practiced by nonprofit organizations as well. A perfect example is the political party seeking votes for its candidate. Having chosen a candidate on whatever grounds, it must vigorously sell this candidate to the voters as a fantastic person for the job.[9] The candidate and his or her supporters stomp through voting precincts from early morning to late evening shaking hands, kissing babies, meeting power brokers, making breezy speeches. Countless dollars are spent on radio and television advertising, posters, and mailings. Any flaws in the candidate are shielded from the public because the aim is to get the sale, not worry about postpurchase satisfaction. After the election, the new official continues to take a sales-oriented view toward the citizens. There is little research into what the public wants and a lot of selling to get the public to accept policies that the politician or party wants.

[8] See Irwin J. Rein, *Rudy's Red Wagon: Communication Strategies in Contemporary Society* (Glenview, Ill.: Scott, Foresman & Company, 1972).

[9] See Joseph McGinness, *The Selling of the President* (New York: Trident Press, 1969).

The Marketing Concept

The marketing concept is a more recent idea in the history of exchange relations.[10]

> The *marketing concept* is a management orientation that holds that the key task of the organization is to determine the needs and wants of target markets and to adapt the organization to delivering the desired satisfactions more effectively and efficiently than its competitors.

In short, the marketing concept says "find wants and fill them" rather than "create products and sell them." This orientation is reflected in various contemporary ads: "Have it your way" (Burger King); "You're the boss" (United Airlines); and "No dissatisfied customers" (Ford).

The underlying premises of the marketing concept are:

1. Consumers can be grouped into different market segments depending on their needs and wants.
2. The consumers in any market segment will favor the offer of that organization which comes closest to satisfying their particular needs and wants.
3. The organization's task is to research and choose target markets and develop effective offers and marketing programs as the key to attracting and holding customers.

The selling concept and the marketing concept are frequently confused by the public and many business people. Levitt draws the following contrast between these two orientations:

> Selling focuses on the needs of the seller; marketing on the needs of the buyer. Selling is preoccupied with the seller's need to convert his product into cash; marketing with the idea of satisfying the needs of the customer by means of the product and the whole cluster of things associated with creating, delivering and finally consuming it.[11]

The marketing concept replaces and reverses the logic of the selling concept. The two concepts are contrasted in Figure 2–1. The selling concept starts with the firm's existing products and considers the task as one of using selling and promotion to stimulate a profitable volume of sales. The marketing concept starts with the firm's target customers and their needs and wants; it plans a coordinated set of products and programs to serve their needs and wants; and it derives profits through creating customer satisfaction. In essence, the *marketing concept* is a *customer needs and wants orientation* backed by *integrated market-*

---

[10] See John B. McKitterick, "What Is the Marketing Management Concept?" *The Frontiers of Marketing Thought and Action* (Chicago: American Marketing Association, 1957), pp. 71–82; and Fred J. Borch, "The Marketing Philosophy as a Way of Business Life," *The Marketing Concept: Its Meaning to Management*, Marketing Series, no. 99 (New York: American Management Association, 1957), pp. 3–5. Also see the statement by a former president of Pillsbury: Robert J. Keith, "The Marketing Revolution," *Journal of Marketing*, January 1960, pp. 35–38.

[11] Theodore Levitt, "Marketing Myopia," *Harvard Business Review*, July–August 1960, pp. 45–56.

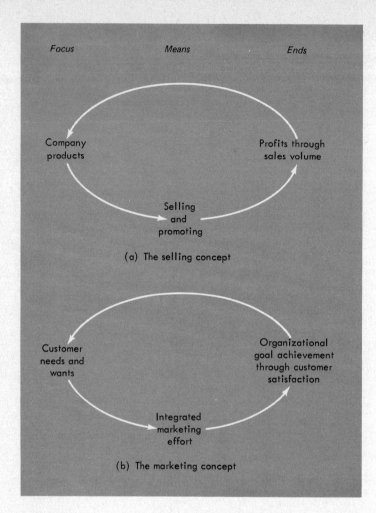

Focus   Means   Ends

Company products

Profits through sales volume

Selling and promoting

(a) The selling concept

Customer needs and wants

Organizational goal achievement through customer satisfaction

Integrated marketing effort

(b) The marketing concept

FIGURE 2–1
The Selling and Marketing Concepts Contrasted

ing effort aimed at generating *customer satisfaction* as the key to satisfying *organizational goals*. Drucker makes the contrast even more extreme:

> Indeed, selling and marketing are antithetical rather than synonymous or even complementary. There will always, one can assume, be need for some selling. *But the aim of marketing is to make selling superfluous.* The aim of marketing is to know and understand the customer so well that the product or service fits him and sells itself. Ideally, marketing should result in a customer who is ready to buy. All that should be needed then is to make the product or service available, i.e., logistics rather than salesmanship, and statistical distribution rather than promotion. [Italics added.] [12]

The marketing concept is the company's commitment to the time-honored concept in economic theory known as *consumer sovereignty*. The determination

[12] Peter F. Drucker, *Management: Tasks, Responsibilities, Practices* (New York: Harper & Row, 1973), pp. 64–65.

of what is to be produced should not be in the hands of the companies or in the hands of government but in the hands of consumers. The companies produce what the consumers want, and in this way maximize consumer welfare and earn their profits.

Among the prime practitioners of the marketing concept is McDonald's Corporation, the fast-food hamburger retailer.[13]

> In its short, twenty-year existence, McDonald's has served Americans and citizens of several other countries over 27 billion hamburgers! Today it commands a 20 percent share of the fast-food market, far ahead of its closest rivals, Kentucky Fried Chicken (8.4 percent) and Burger King (5.3 percent). Credit for this leading position belongs to a thoroughgoing marketing orientation. McDonald's knows how to serve people well and adapt to changing needs and wants.
>
> Before McDonald's, Americans could get hamburgers in restaurants or diners, but not without problems. In many places, the hamburgers were poor in quality, service was slow, decor was poor, help was uneven, conditions were unclean, and the atmosphere noisy. McDonald's was formulated as an alternative, where the customer could walk into a spotlessly clean outlet, be greeted by a friendly and efficient order-taker, receive a good-tasting hamburger less than a minute after placing the order, with the chance to eat it there or take it out. There were no jukeboxes or telephones to create a teenage hangout, and in fact, McDonald's became a family affair, particularly appealing to the children.
>
> As times changed, so did McDonald's. The sit-down sections were expanded in size, the decor improved, a very successful breakfast menu featuring Egg McMuffin was added, and new outlets were opened in high-traffic parts of the city. McDonald's was clearly being managed to evolve with changing customer needs and profitable opportunities.
>
> In addition, McDonald's management knows how to efficiently design and operate a complex service operation. It chooses its locations carefully, selects highly qualified franchise operators, gives them complete management training and assistance, supports them with a high-quality national advertising and sales promotion program, monitors product and service quality through continuous customer surveys, and puts great energy into improving the technology of hamburger production to simplify operations, bring down costs, and speed up service.

A marketing orientation is also relevant to nonprofit organizations. Most nonprofit organizations start out as product oriented. When they begin to suffer declines in support or membership, they resort to selling tactics. Thus many colleges facing declining enrollments are now investing heavily in advertising and recruitment activities. But these selling steps turn out to be only stopgap measures. These organizations begin to realize the need to define their target markets more carefully; research their needs, wants, and values; modernize their products and programs; and communicate more effectively. Such organizations turn from selling to marketing.

The Societal Marketing Concept

In recent years people have begun to raise a number of questions about the marketing concept. One of the major questions is whether the marketing concept is really being practiced by American business firms, or only given lip service. The marketing concept has such a nice-sounding rhetoric when used by businessmen

---

[13] See "The Burger That Conquered the Country," *Time*, September 17, 1973, p. 84.

in their speeches. They may even mean what they say. But there is a great deal to do between the utterance and the deed. Establishing the marketing concept in an organization is an extremely difficult task, and it takes considerable planning, persuasion, education, and reorganization.[14] Consequently, a great number of companies really do not practice the marketing concept even when they espouse it. Drucker considers *consumerism* to be evidence of this:

> That after twenty years of marketing rhetoric consumerism could become a powerful popular movement proves that not much marketing has been practiced. Consumerism is the "shame of marketing." [15]

There is a second, more disturbing doubt raised about the marketing concept, one that questions its validity. Some marketers have raised the question of whether the marketing concept is an appropriate organizational goal in an age of environmental deterioration, resource shortages, explosive population growth, worldwide inflation, and neglected social services.[16] The question is whether the firm that does an excellent job of sensing, serving, and satisfying individual consumer wants is necessarily acting in the best long-run interests of consumers and society. The marketing concept sidesteps the conflict between consumer wants, consumer interests, and long-run societal welfare.

As a concrete instance, consider once again McDonald's. It is doing an excellent job of meeting the wants of the American people for quick, inexpensive, tasty food in attractive surroundings. But is it really serving their long-run interests? Two recent criticisms that have been leveled against it by consumer and environmental groups are that:

1. McDonald's serves tasty but not necessarily nutritious food. The hamburgers have a lot of fat in them. McDonald's promotes fries and pies, two products that are dear to American taste but are high in starch and fat.
2. McDonald's uses up a great amount of paper in providing its food. The hamburgers are first wrapped in tissue paper and then placed in paper boxes, presumably to keep them warm. This results in substantial paper wastage and cost to the consumer.

Thus in the effort of a company to serve consumers' wants, questions can be raised about the uncovered social costs. The same thing occurs in many other instances:

1. The American auto industry has traditionally catered to the American demand for large automobiles, but meeting this desire results in high fuel consumption, heavy pollution, more fatal accidents to those in small cars, and higher auto purchase and repair costs.
2. The soft-drink industry has catered to the American demand for convenience by

---

[14] See Edward McKay, *The Marketing Mystique* (New York: American Management Association, 1972), pp. 22–30.

[15] Drucker, *Management*, p. 64.

[16] Laurence P. Feldman, "Societal Adaptation: A New Challenge for Marketing," *Journal of Marketing*, July 1971, pp. 54–60; and Martin L. Bell and C. William Emery, "The Faltering Marketing Concept," *Journal of Marketing*, October 1971, pp. 37–42.

increasing the share of one-way disposable bottles. The one-way bottle presents a great waste of resources in that approximately seventeen containers are necessary where one two-way bottle makes seventeen trips before it can no longer be used; many one-way bottles are not biodegradable; and these bottles often are a littering element.

3. The detergent industry has catered to the American passion for whiter clothes by offering a product that at the same time pollutes rivers and streams, killing fish and injuring the recreational possibilities.

These situations have led in recent years to the call for a new concept to revise or replace the marketing concept. Among the proposals are "the human concept," "the intelligent consumption concept," and "the ecological imperative concept,"[17] all of which get at different aspects of the same problem. We would like to propose "the societal marketing concept" as an answer to the dilemmas in the simple marketing concept. Our definition of societal marketing concept is:

> The *societal marketing concept* is a management orientation that holds that the key task of the organization is to determine the needs and wants of target markets and to adapt the organization to delivering the desired satisfactions more effectively and efficiently than its competitors in a way that preserves or enhances the consumers' and society's well being.

The underlying premises of the societal marketing concept are:

1. Consumers' wants do not always coincide with their long-run interests or society's long-run interests.
2. Consumers will increasingly favor organizations which show a concern with meeting their wants, long-run interests, and society's long-run interests.
3. The organization's task is to serve target markets in a way that produces not only want satisfaction but long-run individual and social benefit as the key to attracting and holding customers.

The societal marketing concept differs from the simple marketing concept by adding two considerations. First, it calls upon the marketer to concentrate on the buyers' needs and interests as well as on their wants. People have needs for which they have no defined solutions. Thus, consumers would like to find tasty food that is low in calories. Industrial buyers would like to find better machinery that will lower their production costs. The societal marketer will sense these needs and seek solutions. The solutions may amount to new products that the consumer never dreamed of. In this sense, the societal marketer is more attuned to the buyers' unexpressed needs than overexpressed wants. Consider the following case.[18]

---

[17] Leslie M. Dawson, "The Human Concept: New Philosophy for Business," *Business Horizons,* December 1969, pp. 29–38; James T. Rothe and Lissa Benson, "Intelligent Consumption: An Attractive Alternative to the Marketing Concept," *MSU Business Topics,* Winter 1974, pp. 29–34; and George Fisk, "Criteria for a Theory of Responsible Consumption," *Journal of Marketing,* April 1973, pp. 24–31.

[18] See Theodore Levitt, *The Marketing Mode: Pathways to Corporate Growth* (New York: McGraw-Hill Book Company, 1969), pp. 7–8.

American Airlines, in the effort to expand its air freight business, undertook a search for companies that would logically derive the most benefit from incorporating air freight into their physical distribution system. One such prospect was Raytheon. Raytheon executives had not expressed a want for air freight services. They told American Airlines, however, that they were always ready to save money and that if American could prove that they could save money through air freight, Raytheon would reorganize its physical distribution system and use air freight. American Airlines proceeded to work out the details of warehouse location, production scheduling, inventory control, and data transmission. They advanced a proposal for reorganizing Raytheon's physical distribution system that was so persuasive it was accepted by Raytheon. Thus, American Airlines started with Raytheon's need to save money and created a solution that the customer ended up wanting.

The other consideration added in the societal marketing concept is the emphasis on "long-run consumer and societal well being." It calls for a shift of the organization's perspective to include more marketing participants and longer-lasting effects. Societal marketing calls for including four considerations in marketing decision making: *consumer needs and wants, consumer interests, company interests,* and *society's interests.*

The major question facing companies is how societal marketing will affect their profitability. Companies cannot be expected to absorb losses or lower profits in the pursuit of societal marketing. Yet there have been cases where companies have actually increased their profits through practicing the societal marketing concept (see Chapter 27, p. 694). To the extent that societal marketing appears profitable, companies can be expected to give it serious consideration.

SUMMARY

Marketing has its origins in the fact that man is a creature of needs and wants. Needs and wants create a state of discomfort in persons, which is resolved through acquiring products to satisfy these needs and wants. These products are obtainable in several ways: self-production, coercion, supplication, and exchange. Most human society works on the principle of exchange, which means that people become specialists in the production of particular products and trade them for the other things they need. A market is an arena for potential exchanges—there are need markets, product markets, demographic markets, and geographic markets. Marketing encompasses all those activities that represent working through markets, that is, trying to actualize potential exchanges.

Marketing management is the conscious effort to achieve desired exchange outcomes with target markets. The marketer's basic skill lies in regulating the level, timing, and character of demand for a product, service, organization, place, person, or idea. The marketer faces up to eight different types of demand situations. If demand is negative, it must be reversed (conversional marketing); if nonexistent, it must be created (stimulational marketing); if latent, it must be developed (developmental marketing); if faltering, it must be revitalized (remarketing); if irregular, it must be synchronized (synchromarketing); if full, it must be maintained (maintenance marketing); if overfull, it must be reduced (demarketing); and if unwholesome, it must be destroyed (countermarketing).

Five alternative philosophies can guide organizations in carrying out their exchange activity. The production concept assumes that consumers will readily respond to products that are available and affordable and therefore that management's major task is to improve production efficiency and bring down prices. The product concept assumes that consumers will respond favorably to good products that are reasonably priced, and therefore little marketing effort is required. The selling concept assumes that consumers will normally not buy enough of the company's products unless they are reached with a substantial selling and promotion effort. The marketing concept holds that the main task of the company is to determine what a chosen set of customers' needs, wants, and preferences are and to adapt the company to delivering the desired satisfactions. The societal marketing concept holds that the main task of the company is to generate customer satisfaction and long-run consumer and societal well being as the key to satisfying organizational goals and responsibilities.

QUESTIONS AND PROBLEMS

1. Exchange is one of several ways of acquiring things. Propose some hypotheses explaining how trade or exchange may have begun.

2. The term *market* has many different usages. What does market mean to a stockbroker, produce merchant, sales manager, economist, and marketer?

3. Is there a contradiction between marketing something to people that is negatively demanded and practicing the marketing concept?

4. In the face of a long-term energy shortage, many public utilities have sought to reduce their customers' use of electricity. Propose a demarketing plan that will bring down the level of demand and help utilities avoid "brownouts."

5. Is the purpose of the marketing concept to maximize the customers' satisfaction or to maximize the company's long-run profitability?

6. Do you think the railroad passenger business is doomed? Why or why not? Could the passenger business be remarketed and made profitable through adoption of the marketing concept? Give illustrations.

7. Airlines seem to practice the marketing concept. They show a concern for passenger satisfaction, as exemplified by an attentive crew, complimentary flight meals, and other amenities. Would you agree that they deserve a high rating for their marketing orientation?

8. Do you think the marketing concept should provide the major orientation for every company? Could you cite companies which do not particularly need this orientation? Which companies need it most?

9. McDonald's faces two alternatives with respect to adopting the societal marketing concept. It can argue that its present practices are sound and in the public's interest. Or it can make some adjustments that will bring it closer to the societal marketing concept. Develop each possibility.

10. "Marketing is the science of actualizing the buying potentials of a market for a specific product." Does this definition reflect a product, selling, or marketing concept?

11. Coca-Cola has been accused of not practicing the societal marketing concept. Identify some aspects of the product that might be criticized.

The Marketing System

No substantial part of the universe is so simple that it can be grasped and controlled without abstraction. Abstraction consists in replacing the part of the universe under consideration by a model of similar but simple structure. Models . . . are thus a central necessity of scientific procedure.
ARTURO ROSENBLUETH and NORBERT WIENER

3

A marketer is someone skilled in knowing how to analyze and improve the ability of an organization to survive and grow in a complex and changing environment of markets and publics. This means that marketers must have a set of concepts and tools that enables them to grasp the complexity of the organization's environment and opportunities.

The two major tools are marketing system analysis and marketing process analysis. *Marketing system analysis* deals with identifying the major institutional components in an organization's environment that interact to produce results in the marketplace. *Marketing process analysis* consists of a set of logical steps to plan the organization's optimal adaptation to the marketplace of opportunities. These two forms of analysis handle the *structural* and *functional* aspects, respectively, of marketing phenomena. Marketing systems analysis is treated in this chapter, and marketing process analysis is treated in Chapter 4.

Marketing systems analysis consists of three levels of analysis of increasing scope and complexity. The first, *exchange system analysis*, deals with analyzing simple two-or-more person exchanges in a form that depicts what the individual parties are seeking through exchange. The second, *organizational marketing analysis*, deals with analyzing the major institutions and publics in the environment of the organization that affect its performance in the marketplace. The third, *macroenvironment analysis*, deals with analyzing the totality of interacting institutions in society, including the economic system, legal system, political system, and cultural system. This chapter will deal with exchange system analysis and organizational marketing analysis, and Chapter 5 will take up macroenvironment analysis.

EXCHANGE SYSTEM ANALYSIS

The core idea underlying marketing is that of exchange. The potential for exchange exists when two or more parties each possess something-of-value, which they might conceivably trade. The something-of-value could be *goods, services, money,* or *goodwill*. If the potential exchange is actualized, we say that a transaction takes place. A transaction signifies an agreement between two or more parties on the use, ownership, or transfer of resources. A transaction is the basic unit of exchange. Trillions of transactions take place each year.

In the simplest exchange situation, there are two parties. If one party is more actively seeking an exchange than the other, we call the first party a *marketer* and the second party a *prospect*. *A marketer is someone seeking a resource from someone else and willing to offer something-of-value in exchange.* The marketer is seeking a response from the other party in the form of a sale of what the marketer wants to sell or in the form of a purchase of what the marketer wants to buy. The marketer, in other words, can be a seller or a buyer.[1] In the event that both parties are actively seeking an exchange, we say that both of them are marketers and call the situation one of bilateral marketing.

A simple exchange system can be mapped by showing the two actors and the typical exchange media that flow between them. Figure 3–1 shows five familiar exchange situations. The most familiar is the commercial transaction—a seller offers a good or service to a buyer in exchange for money. The second is the employment transaction—an employer offers wages and fringe benefits to an employee in exchange for the employee's productive services (made up of time, energy, and skill). The third is the civic transaction—a police force, for example, offers protective services to citizens in exchange for their taxes and cooperation. The fourth is a religious transaction—a church offers religious services to members in exchange for their contributions of money and time. Finally, the fifth is a charity transaction—a charity organization offers gratitude and a feeling of well being to donors in return for contributions of money and time.

Figure 3–1 shows only the basic resources being exchanged by the two parties. A marketer interested in actualizing a potential transaction will make a more careful analysis of what the other party wants and what the marketer might offer in return. Suppose the Caterpillar Company, a leading manufacturer of earth-moving equipment, is interested in increasing its sales to target prospects, mainly construction companies. It researches the benefits that a typical construction company may be seeking in buying earth-moving equipment.

[1] This point is elaborated upon in Philip Kotler and Sidney J. Levy, "Buying Is Marketing, Too," *Journal of Marketing*, January 1973, pp. 54–59.

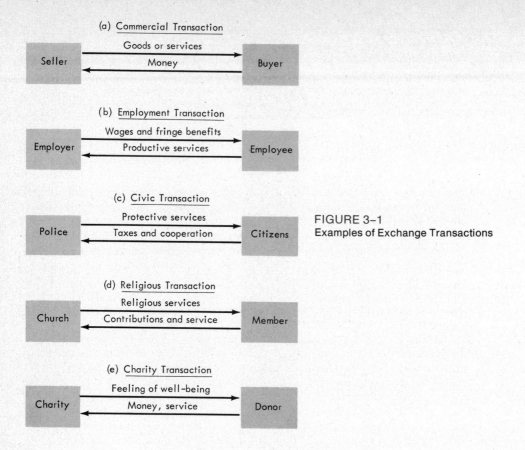

(a) Commercial Transaction

Seller → Goods or services → Buyer
Seller ← Money ← Buyer

(b) Employment Transaction

Employer → Wages and fringe benefits → Employee
Employer ← Productive services ← Employee

(c) Civic Transaction

Police → Protective services → Citizens
Police ← Taxes and cooperation ← Citizens

(d) Religious Transaction

Church → Religious services → Member
Church ← Contributions and service ← Member

(e) Charity Transaction

Charity → Feeling of well–being → Donor
Charity ← Money, service ← Donor

FIGURE 3–1
Examples of Exchange Transactions

Those benefits are listed at the top of the exchange map in Figure 3–2. The prospect wants high-quality equipment, a fair price, on-time delivery, good financing, and good service. This is the *want list* (or *wish list*) of the buyer. The wants are not all equally important and may vary from buyer to buyer. One of Caterpillar's tasks is to find out the importance of these different wants of the buyer.[2] At the same time, Caterpillar as the marketer has a want list, as shown below the Caterpillar arrow in Figure 3–2. Caterpillar wants a good price for the equipment, on-time payment, and good word of mouth. If there is a sufficient match or overlap in the want lists, there is a basis for a transaction. Caterpillar's task is, then, to formulate an *offer* (also called a *benefit bundle* or *value package*) designed to motivate the construction company to buy the Caterpillar equipment. The construction company might in turn make a counteroffer. The process of trying to find mutually agreeable terms is called *negotiation*. Negotiation either ends in mutually acceptable terms of exchange or a decision not to transact.

Although we have been dealing with two-party exchange systems, we can extend the analysis to three-or-more-party exchange systems. Suppose a YMCA camp is trying to attract more campers for the coming summer season. The deci-

---

[2] See chap. 6, pp. 157–64 for further elaboration.

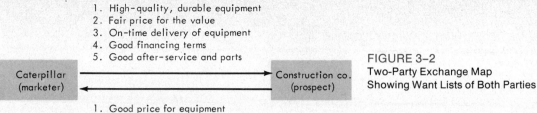

1. High-quality, durable equipment
2. Fair price for the value
3. On-time delivery of equipment
4. Good financing terms
5. Good after-service and parts

Caterpillar (marketer) → Construction co. (prospect)

1. Good price for equipment
2. On-time payment
3. Good word of mouth

FIGURE 3-2
Two-Party Exchange Map
Showing Want Lists of Both Parties

sion to go to a summer camp is jointly made by the child and parents. If either objects, the child is not likely to go. Therefore a YMCA camp director must develop a good understanding of what children and parents each want from summer camp. The analysis is shown in Figure 3-3. The parents want the camp to be a safe place and to provide fun and an opportunity to meet nice children. The parents want the child to learn good values, show good behavior, and be happy. The child wants the camp to be fun and have good counselors and good food. The child wants the parents' love and pampering. Against these want lists, the YMCA wants a fee, satisfaction, and good word of mouth from the parents and good behavior, satisfaction, and social learning from the child. The camp director's challenge is to formulate a camp experience that will jointly satisfy the wishes of the two markets and of the camp. Since other camps are also competing for the same family's patronage, the YMCA camp director must develop a distinctive value package that meets the needs of its target prospects better than competitors.

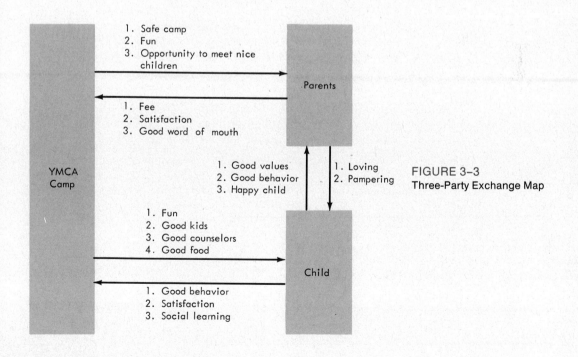

1. Safe camp
2. Fun
3. Opportunity to meet nice children

Parents

1. Fee
2. Satisfaction
3. Good word of mouth

1. Good values
2. Good behavior
3. Happy child

1. Loving
2. Pampering

YMCA Camp

1. Fun
2. Good kids
3. Good counselors
4. Good food

Child

1. Good behavior
2. Satisfaction
3. Social learning

FIGURE 3-3
Three-Party Exchange Map

41

Exchange analysis, as we have formulated it, is based on the assumption that, basically, people behave to maximize their self-interest. Marketers have found that the postulate of self-seeking behavior is the most useful one for understanding the actual behavior of parties in a market transaction. That people are motivated by self-interest is a long-standing philosophical postulate going back to Jeremy Benham, Adam Smith, and even earlier to Greek philosophers such as the hedonists. Acting out of self-interest does not necessarily mean acting selfishly. Acting selfishly implies the pursuit of self-gratification at the expense of others. Acting out of self-interest can include a concern for the interests of others (called enlightened self-interest), since the welfare of others can have an impact on one's self-interest. The self-interest postulate asks us to look at each potential exchange situation and identify what each party might be seeking.

To take an extreme case, consider a donor who gives some money to a charity. On the surface, this looks like a one-way transfer of value rather than a transaction. It is reasonable to assume, however, that the donor expects something in return. The donor expects the gift to be used productively and might also expect a show of gratitude. If the charity organization appears irresponsible or ungrateful, the donor is not likely to give next year. Even an anonymous donor of a large gift gets something back for giving. The reward may be purely the private pleasure of being able to give a large gift without requiring acknowledgment. Thus even extreme altruism can be interpreted in terms of what the giver is getting or expecting. Interpreting human behavior from the perspective of self-interest provides the marketer with guidelines for developing effective value packages.

ORGANIZATIONAL MARKETING ANALYSIS

The exchanges that take place between two or more parties occur in a larger framework known as the organizational marketing system.

> An *organizational marketing system* is an organization and the set of significant interacting institutions and forces in the organization's environment that affect its ability to serve its markets.

The simplest marketing system consists of a single organization serving a single market with no intermediaries, suppliers, or other parties involved. This system is shown in Figure 3–4. The organization and its market are connected by four

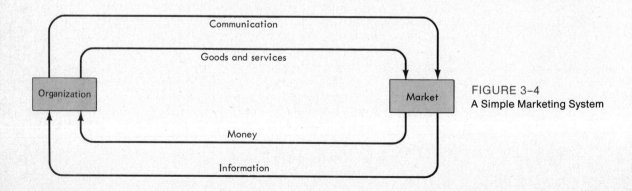

FIGURE 3–4
A Simple Marketing System

flows. The organization dispatches (1) goods and services and (2) communications to the market; in return it receives (3) money and (4) information. The inner loop shows an exchange of money for goods; the outer loop shows an exchange of information.

In reality, organizational marketing systems have many more components. We can distinguish five levels of successively larger environments in which the organization operates. These environments are shown in Figure 3–5 and described in the following sections, starting with the organization itself.

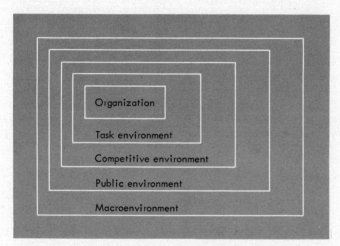

FIGURE 3–5
The Components of an Organizational
Marketing System

ORGANIZATION ENVIRONMENT

The first thing to notice is that the organization itself contains a number of components that will affect its ability to perform in the marketplace. An organization—whether a company, college, or church—can be viewed as a resource conversion machine that takes inputs from the outside world, converts them into useful products and services, and makes them available to others as outputs. To accomplish this, the organization must carry on a number of functions, such as research and development, engineering, purchasing, manufacturing, financing, and marketing.

Let us focus on marketing, which is typically organized as a department. Assume that the organization sells many products to many end users in many geographical areas. This means that the marketing part of the organization must attend to *marketing functions* (e.g., field sales, advertising, marketing research, and customer service), *organization products*, *customer end-users*, and *geographical markets*. The design of an effective marketing department is itself a major challenge.[3] In addition, we must recognize that the other departments of the organization constitute an environment for the marketing department. If the marketing department wants to open a new geographical market, it must present a case to top management and the financial vice president, in particular, for support. If the marketing department wants useful new products, it must influence the work of the research and development department.

[3] See chap. 22.

An organization, however, is not just an economic machine. It has a culture, that is, the major participants share a set of attitudes toward what they want to accomplish and what they think is important. The organizational culture may be favorable or inimical to the marketing department. These are the facts of life, and they constitute an organizational environment that affects the marketing performance of the company.

TASK ENVIRONMENT

The organization operates in a task environment that consists of those basic institutions that cooperate to create marketing value for a marketplace. The task environment consists of the company and the three major institutions shown in Figure 3–6, namely, *suppliers, marketing intermediaries,* and the *market*. The four constitute a *total marketing channel* for meeting a particular set of customer needs. The channel begins with heterogeneous raw materials found in nature, which are converted by successive processes into an assortment of final products that bring form, place, time, and possession utility to final buyers.

FIGURE 3–6
The Task-Marketing System of an Organization

Suppliers The organization, in order to produce value for the marketplace, must acquire a number of inputs needed in the production process from outside suppliers. For example, the Talon Company, the largest American producer of zippers, must obtain textiles, aluminum strip, brass strip, steel, dye, and other supplies in order to produce zippers. More generally, the main classes of inputs needed by sellers are labor, equipment, materials, fuel and energy, money, and information.

The company's task is to determine the optimal input mix for the given output mix that it wants to produce. The optimal input mix is influenced by the prices and availabilities of the various input goods. The company may decide to produce some of its own needed inputs and buy the rest from outside suppliers. The company's purchasing executive is responsible for buying the needed inputs at the best possible prices. This executive will check suppliers for the quality of their goods, prices, delivery reliability, warranties, credit terms, and miscellaneous services. For the more important inputs, the executive will negotiate contracts with multiple sources of supply to assure a sufficient supply and to be able to compare and watchdog prices.

The marketing department has a direct interest in the efficiency of the company's purchase of inputs. Before developing plans to increase sales, the marketing executive will check with the purchasing executive to make sure that the necessary materials can be obtained at the planned prices for producing the planned output, with the financial officer to make sure that the company has the necessary working capital, and with the personnel officer to make sure that the company has adequate manpower to produce the planned output.

The real "marketing" mettle of a purchasing department is tested during periods of shortages of needed inputs. During 1974, companies could not get enough plastic, fuel, paper, aluminum, copper, textiles, or glass. The purchasing manager had to scramble for additional suppliers, offer higher prices, and accept fewer services. The company's president had to make a personal appeal to the supplier for special consideration. Essentially, purchasing found that it had to "market" the company to suppliers.

The marketing executive is a direct purchaser of certain services to support the marketing effort, such as advertising, marketing research, sales training, and marketing consulting. In going outside, the marketing executive evaluates different advertising agencies, marketing research firms, sales-training consultants, and marketing consultants. The executive has to decide which services to purchase outside and which to produce inside by adding specialists to the staff.

Marketing Intermediaries

Marketing intermediaries are institutions that facilitate the distribution of the company's outputs to the final markets. For example, the Talon Company uses manufacturers' reps, wholesalers, jobbers, and retailers to sell its zippers to final markets. More generally, there are three main types of marketing intermediaries and many variants of each.[4] *Merchant middlemen* are business units—such as wholesalers and retailers—that buy, take title to, and resell merchandise (often called resellers). *Agent middlemen* are business units—such as brokers and sales reps—that negotiate purchases or sales but do not take title to merchandise. *Facilitators* are business units—such as transportation companies, warehouses, and banks—that assist in the performance of distribution but neither take title to goods nor negotiate purchases or sales.

The company that is seeking distribution for its output must either use established marketing intermediaries or set up its own. A company normally chooses established intermediaries because they have the experience and economies of scale for efficiently reaching the target markets. The company has to consider the cost of using these intermediaries against their sales performance, reliability, and cooperativeness. When the company finds existing intermediaries to be inadequate or unavailable, it may be forced to establish its own routes to the market. *Direct marketing* is the best example, in which the company seeks to reach the final market with its own sales force or by direct mail or telephone solicitation.

Marketing intermediaries perform one or more of several functions for the company. Among them are *research, promotion, contact, matching, negotiation, physical distribution, financing,* and *risk taking*.[5] The company that decides to sell through marketing intermediaries will look for those institutions that most efficiently perform the needed channel functions.

Markets

The final component of the company's task environment is the market itself. We have been referring to "the market" as a single entity although in fact the company usually sells to several markets. We can distinguish between *industrial markets* and *consumer markets*. Industrial markets buy for the sake of manufacture or resale, whereas consumer markets buy for the sake of consumption. For example, the Talon Company sells zippers to manufacturers, tailor shops, and consumers. Each of these markets in turn can be divided into submarkets called

[4] See chap. 16, p. 420.

[5] See chap. 16, p. 419.

market segments. Thus the manufacturers' market to which Talon sells zippers can be divided into manufacturers of clothing, of upholstery, of luggage, of automobiles, and of closet accessories. Similar breakdowns of the tailor market and the consumer market could be identified.

A company must decide whether it wants to sell to one, two, or all the market segments making up the larger market. Smaller companies tend to specialize in one or a few market segments and pick them carefully. A sound choice is a segment that the company has the resources to serve well and for which it can create a distinctive product.

Large companies serve several markets and market segments. They are wise if they formulate different marketing programs to meet the needs of the various served markets rather than trying to serve all the markets with the same marketing program. The latter is dangerous in that the company will lose share in those markets where competitors have tailored a superior marketing program. An example is the sale of ketchup to various markets. For example, the Heinz Company sells ketchup to such markets as food retailers, restaurants, industrial companies, colleges, hospitals, and prisons. Were it to sell one brand of ketchup to all these markets at the same price, it would have uneven success. The prison market wants to buy a cheap ketchup, not the expensive Heinz brand. To win a share of this market, Heinz has to formulate and offer a cheaper ketchup product for this market.

We might consider at this point how a map of a *total marketing channel* would look for an actual company, such as Heinz. Figure 3–7 presents a simplified version of how Heinz serves one of its final markets, namely, food retailers. Heinz acquires its raw materials from food producers and other inputs from other suppliers. These goods are warehoused by the suppliers and shipped to Heinz's plants as needed. The Heinz Company uses food brokers to contact wholesalers of several types: cooperatives, voluntaries, independents, and jobbers. Heinz ships its products to regional warehouses and from there, to wholesalers. The wholesalers in turn sell and ship Heinz products to such food retailers as discount supermarkets, convenience stores, independent supermarkets, and chain supermarkets. The retailers in turn sell the Heinz products to consumers.

The total marketing channel map is oversimplified to permit easy reading. The oversimplifications include the following:

1. The map shows only product flows and omits flows of title, payment, information, and promotion.[6]
2. The map omits the activities of other institutions in the task environment, such as auction markets, advertising agencies, and financial intermediaries.
3. Heinz sells and ships directly to large national chain supermarkets, but this bypass of brokers and wholesalers is not shown.

Nevertheless, Figure 3–7 gives the flavor of a company's marketing system at the level of the task environment.

[6] See chap. 16, pp. 414–16.

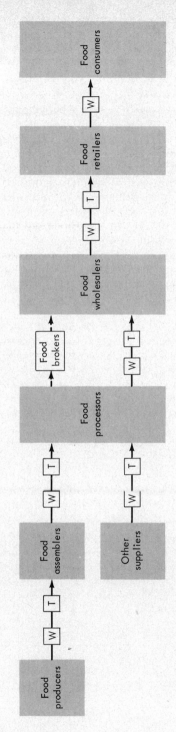

Legend: W: Warehouse
         T: Transportation carrier
         → : Flow of product

FIGURE 3–7
Heinz Task-Marketing System

47

COMPETITIVE ENVIRONMENT

An organization rarely stands alone in its effort to serve a given market. Its efforts to build an efficient task-marketing system to serve the market are matched by similar efforts on the part of others. The organization, in fact, operates within a rich environment of competitors. These competitors have to be identified, monitored, and outmaneuvered to gain and maintain the loyalty of the market.

The competitive environment consists not only of other companies but also of more basic things. The best way for a company to grasp its competition is to take the viewpoint of a buyer. What does a buyer think about in the process of arriving at the answer to a question that might result in the purchase of something? Suppose a consumer has been feeling tired and asks, "How can I get more physical exercise?" (See Figure 3–8.) Several possibilities come to mind, including bicycling, jogging, weight lifting, yoga, and using exercise machines. The possibilities make up the set of *generic competitors*. If bicycling turns out to arouse the most interest, the consumer next thinks about what type of bicycle to purchase. This leads to a set of *product-form competitors*, such as three-speed, five-speed, or ten-speed bikes. The consumer might decide on a ten-speed. The consumer might then consider which brand to buy and recall a set of *enterprise competitors*. Further things should be noted:

1. The consumer will normally be aware of less than the *total set* of existing brands, and what he or she is aware of is called the *awareness set*. Even fewer brands will be seriously considered (the *consideration set*). Only a few brands will remain in the final running (the *choice set*).
2. The consumer may restrict shopping to a few favorite retailers who can be called the *merchant competitors*.
3. This picture of bicycle competition was formed out of a consumer's interest in physical exercise. If the consumer had raised the question, "How can I find another means of getting to work?" or the question, "What can I do with my leisure time?" different sets of generic competitors would have emerged. Thus a bicycle competes with other sets of generic competitors, depending on the consumer's need.

The company's enterprise competitors are typically the competitors it watches most closely. The enterprise competitors will differ in the quality of

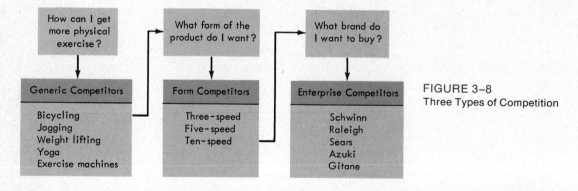

FIGURE 3–8
Three Types of Competition

their product, features, prices, service, and other factors. The company competes most closely with those enterprises occupying a similar position or niche in *product/market space.*[7] The company must therefore identify and monitor most closely those competitors who are seen to be closest to itself in the consumers' minds.

As an example, consider a gasoline marketer such as Shell, operating its stations in the Washington, D.C., market. A score of other gasoline marketers operate in this area, not all of equal competitive standing. Table 3–1 classifies these gasoline marketers according to their size and price policy in the marketplace. Shell is a major brander, in fact a market leader, and most of its competition is *intratype competition.* Its major marketing effort is spent in competing against the other market leaders, important majors, and minor majors. There is also some *intertype competition* between the major branders and price discounters. Furthermore, the price discounters are busy competing against each other. Thus, Shell competes differentially against a whole set of enterprise competitors. The market, given the range of choice, distributes itself among the enterprises according to their preference.

Our basic observation about the task and competitive environments can now be summarized. A company, in trying to successfully serve a set of customers, must keep four basic dimensions in mind, which can be called the four C's of market positioning. It must consider the nature of the *Customers, Channels, Competition,* and its own characteristics as a *Company.* Successful marketing is a matter of achieving an effective alignment of the company with customers, channels, and competitors.

TABLE 3–1
Classification of Gasoline Marketers in the Washington, D.C., Area.

I. *Major branders:* large, vertically integrated oil companies emphasizing many stations, strong advertising, strong service, nongasoline products (tires, batteries, and accessories), and minor repairs.
   A. *Market leaders:* relatively large numbers of stations, good market acceptance, large market share. Examples: Exxon, Amoco, and Shell.
   B. *Important majors:* thinner market representation, weaker market acceptance, average market share. Examples: Sun, Gulf, Texaco, and Mobil.
   C. *Minor majors:* relatively few stations, poor market acceptance, small market share. Examples: Chevron, Citgo, Arco, and Phillips.
II. *Price discounters:* small, nonvertically integrated oil companies emphasizing low price, little service, few other products, long hours.
   A. *Deep discounters:* lowest prices, least service. Example: Poor Boy.
   B. *Limited-service operators:* low price, limited service. Example: Scot.
   C. *Stamp and premium givers:* below normal prices plus giveaways. Example: Star.

SOURCE: Assembled from information in Fred C. Allvine and James M. Patterson, *Competition, Ltd: The Marketing of Gasoline* (Bloomington: Indiana University Press, 1972).

---

[7] See chap. 7, pp. 84–85.

Not only does an organization have to contend with competitors in seeking to satisfy a target market but it must also acknowledge a large set of publics that take an interest, whether welcome or not, in its methods of doing business. Because the actions of the organization affect the interest of other groups, these groups become significant publics to the organization. We shall define a public in the following way:

> A *public* is any group that has an actual or potential interest or impact on an organization's ability to achieve its objectives.

The main publics of an organization are shown in Figure 3–9.

A public can facilitate or impede the ability of an organization to accomplish its goals. For example, a regulatory government agency, such as the Federal Trade Commission, typically constrains the actions of companies with respect to pricing, advertising, product design, and selling methods. Yet this short-term inhibition may in the long run enhance a company's ability to serve its markets. The regulations prevent predatory tactics by competitors, help to build consumer trust, and lead to better products. The media, too, can turn out to be a benign, neutral, or negative force in the company's fortunes. Good press can increase sales and bad press can substantially hurt sales. In general, a company can view its publics in three ways. A *reciprocal public* is one that the company is interested in and that is interested in the company (e.g., stockholders). A *sought public* is one that the company is interested in but that does not take a strong interest in the company (e.g., the press in regard to good news coverage). An *unwelcome public* is one that the company shuns but that insists on taking an interest in the company (e.g., a citizen-action group).

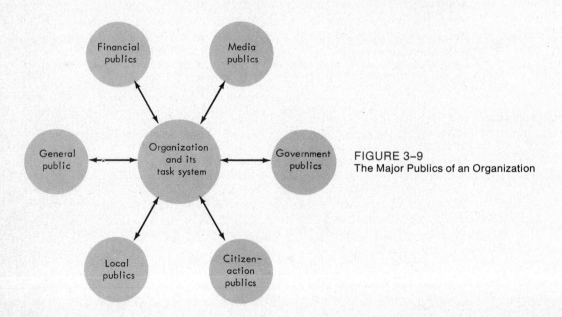

FIGURE 3–9
The Major Publics of an Organization

50

Since publics can substantially influence an organization's fortunes, the wise organization takes concrete steps to manage successful relations with its key publics, rather than sit back and wait. Most organizations establish public relations departments to plan constructive relations with various publics. These departments monitor the attitudes of the organization's publics and distribute information and communications to build goodwill. When negative publicity breaks out, these departments act as trouble shooters. In the best departments, there is an emphasis on counseling top management to adopt positive programs and to eliminate questionable practices so that negative publicity does not arise in the first place.

It would be a mistake for an organization to leave public relations entirely in the hands of the public relations department. All the employees of the organization are involved in public relations, from the chief officer who meets the general public to the financial vice president who addresses the financial community to the field sales representative who calls on customers.

We would propose that public relations should be conceived of as a broad marketing operation rather than a narrow communication operation.[8] A public is a group from which an organization wants some response, such as goodwill, favorable mentions, or donations of time or money. The organization must ask what that public is seeking that it could satisfy. It then plans a benefit package that is designed to build goodwill. We will take this point of view in describing the major publics surrounding an organization.

Financial Publics

Financial publics include all the groups who take an interest in, and might influence, the company's ability to obtain funds. Banks, investment houses, stock brokerage firms, and stockholders are the major financial publics. Management tries to cultivate the goodwill of these groups by issuing annual reports, answering financial questions, and satisfying the financial community that its house is in order.

Nonprofit organizations, such as universities, museums, and churches must mount a major marketing campaign every year to "sell" financial and donor markets on supporting them generously. This is often a greater marketing challenge than the problem of attracting and satisfying final customers with their services.

Media Publics

Media publics include mass and trade media companies that carry news, features, and editorial opinion: specifically, newspapers, magazines, and radio and television stations. Companies are acutely sensitive to the role played by the press in affecting their capacity to achieve their marketing objectives.

The company has two concerns. The first is how much coverage the press gives to the company's activities and products. Companies are hungry for news attention and free publicity, which substitute for paid advertising that the company would have to buy to build the same level of awareness in the marketplace.

The second issue is what the press says about the company's activities and

---

[8] The interrelations between marketing and public relations are examined in Philip Kotler and William Mindak, "Marketing and Public Relations: Partners or Rivals," *Journal of Marketing*, October 1978, pp. 13–20.

products. There is nothing more valuable to a company than favorable publicity, nor more damaging than unfavorable publicity. When the Mazda automobile (with the Wankel engine) was first introduced in the United States, it received extensive and favorable press coverage as a car with high performance and pollution control. This coverage boosted U.S. sales considerably. After the gasoline shortage erupted, the Environmental Protection Agency published the tested mileages of different automobiles and cited the Mazda as giving only about ten miles per gallon. This publicity caused a collapse of sales that completely upset Mazda's planned export level and marketing program.

Getting more and better coverage from the press calls for understanding what the press is really interested in and giving them what they want. The effective press relations manager knows most of the editors in the major media and systematically cultivates a mutually beneficial relation with them. The manager does not approach the press with threats or supplications but offers instead interesting news items, informational material, and quick access to top management. In return, the media reporters are more likely to give the company fair coverage.

Government Publics

Management is increasingly finding it necessary to take government developments into account when they formulate marketing plans and policies. In the past, companies were relatively free to set their marketing-mix variables—product features, packaging, price, advertising, sales promotion—at any level; they had to worry only about their consumers and competitors. In recent years, there has been a major and probably irreversible trend toward more government regulation and intervention in these marketing decisions. Manufacturers of drugs, toys, automobiles, appliances, and food items must carefully consider product safety and ecology in designing their products. Company pricing came under price controls for a while and might return at any time. Companies have to be careful about "truth in advertising" or face a suit by the Federal Trade Commission.

Companies have responded in three ways to growing government regulation. The first is to increase the company's *legal staff* to advise marketing managers as to what they can and cannot do. An understaffed legal department might seriously delay the company in making important decisions on advertising messages, price changes, and packaging moves. The second is to establish a *government relations department* or enlarge an existing department. Government relations managers must know the various agencies at the local, state, and federal levels as well as the key legislators. They must anticipate unfavorable developments, visit the right people, express the company's interests, and rally support. Lobbying is essentially company marketing in the arena of the legislative market. Lobbyists must know how to segment the legislative market; they must analyze legislators' needs and motives; they must know how a bill is passed, defeated, and influenced; and they must make personal calls and presentations. The third company response is to join with other companies in *trade associations* to lobby for the common interests of their industry.

Citizen-Action Publics

A company's marketing decisions are increasingly being affected by consumer organizations, environmental groups, minority organizations, neighborhood associations, and other vocal public-interest groups.

One morning not long ago a major Philadelphia bank found thirty senior citizens at its door demanding to talk to the bank's president. They called themselves the Gray Panthers and presented the bank's president with a list of ten nonnegotiable demands for citizens over sixty-five, including free checking, free safety-deposit boxes, and reduced interest rates. The bank president did his best to handle the situation diplomatically and in the end offered a few "senior citizen bank privileges." This kind of citizen action is becoming more frequent and is facing all organizations, from business firms to universities to churches.

Companies would be foolish to attack or ignore demands of public-interest groups. Progressive companies have made three responses. First, they are training their decision makers to introduce social criteria into their decision making, to strike a better balance between the needs of consumers, citizens, and stockholders. Second, they have established public-affairs departments to stay in touch with these groups to learn their interests and to express the companies' goals and activities to these groups. Third, these companies hold conferences with other companies to search for judicious ways to deal with these groups. Some companies have staked out a leadership role by identifying their interests with these groups and playing the role of leader and model company in furthering worthwhile social causes.

Local Publics

Every organization is physically located in one or more areas and comes into contact with local publics, such as neighborhood residents, community organizations, and local public officials. These groups will take an active or passive interest in the activities of the organization. The residents surrounding a hospital usually get concerned about ambulance sirens, parking congestion, and other things that go with running a hospital. Community groups are interested in the organization's employment policies, and the possibilities of its making donations to worthwhile local causes.

Organizations usually appoint a community relations officer whose job is to keep close to the community, attend meetings, answer questions, and make contributions to worthwhile causes. Smart organizations do not wait for local issues to erupt. They make investments in their community to help it run well and to build up a bank of company goodwill in case it is needed.

General Public

The company is ultimately concerned with the attitude of the general public toward its products and activities. The general public does not act in an organized way toward the company, as interest groups do. But the members of the general public carry around images of the company's standing as a corporate citizen and these images affect their patronage.

The company undertakes several activities to improve its public image. The company lends its officers to community fund drives and makes substantial contributions to charities. It sets up systems to respond to consumer grievances. It resorts to institutional advertising to describe what it is doing in the social field. In recent years the telephone company has run a campaign on "How to Save on Long-Distance Calls," the electrical utilities have run a campaign on "How to Conserve Electricity," and the Ford Motor Company has distributed tens of thousands of booklets on "How to Purchase a Car." These steps are designed to help the public become more intelligent buyers and users of the company's products.

MACROENVIRONMENT

The organization, its connected task institutions, competitors, and publics, all operate in a larger environment of macroforces and institutions that shape opportunities and pose threats to the successful functioning of the organization. These forces make up the "uncontrollables" to which organizations must adapt through judicious choice of the "controllable" factors, such as the markets they elect to serve and their marketing programs.

The major macroforces are six in number: demography, economics, natural resources, technology, law and politics, and culture. We mention these forces here to complete our modeling of the hierarchy of environments that affect a company's performance. They will be discussed in detail in Chapter 5 when we begin to look at marketing opportunities.

AN EXAMPLE OF A COMPANY MARKETING SYSTEM

The first task of a marketer in dealing with any marketing system is to depict the structure and components of that system. We shall illustrate by mapping the marketing system of a leading manufacturer of a popular soft-centered, chocolate-covered candy bar.[9] Instead of repeating the diagrams that have already been covered, we introduce some new mapping forms.

Figure 3–10 shows the major components and flows in the candy company marketing system. The diagram is divided into six elements.

1. The *environment* or, more precisely, those forces in the environment that affect candy demand and supply, such as population growth, per capita income, attitudes toward candy, and raw material availability and cost.
2. The *company and competitors' marketing strategies.*
3. The major *marketing decision variables* in this market—product characteristics, price, sales force, physical distribution and service, and advertising and sales promotion.
4. The major *marketing channels* that the company uses for this product.
5. The *buyer behavior model*, which shows customer response to the activities of the manufacturers and the distribution channels as well as to the environment.
6. The total *industry sales, company sales, and company costs.*

The various arrows show key flows in the marketing system. Flow 5, for example, would refer to a detailed diagram and description showing types of product characteristics decisions, the inputs that influence each of these decisions, and the sources of data for each of the inputs.

Let us select one element in Figure 3–10, the *company marketing strategy* box, and list on the right side of this box all the major marketing decisions made by the company (see Figure 3–11). There are two major types of decisions, trade decisions and consumer decisions. To influence the trade, the company uses the wholesale price, trade allowances, credit policy, and delivery policy. To influence consumers, the company uses product characteristics, packaging characteristics, retail price, consumer deals, and consumer advertising.

---

[9] This section is adapted from the author's "Corporate Models: Better Marketing Plans," *Harvard Business Review*, July–August 1970, pp. 135–49.

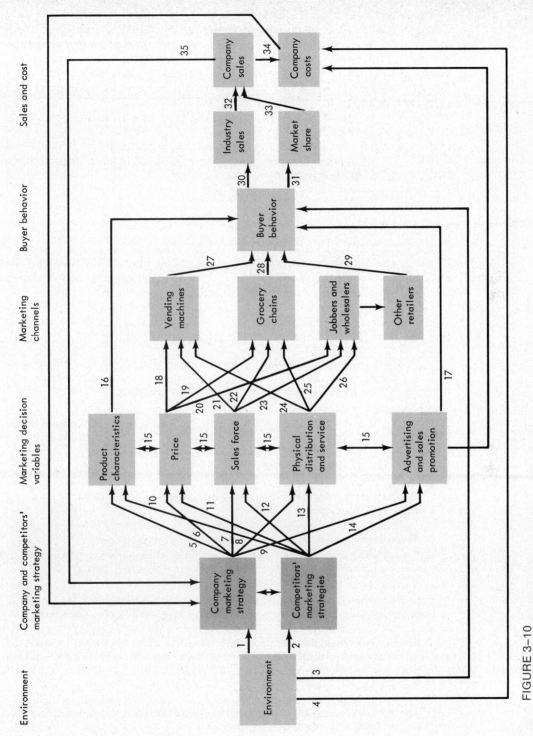

FIGURE 3–10
Comprehensive Marketing System Map: Candy Company

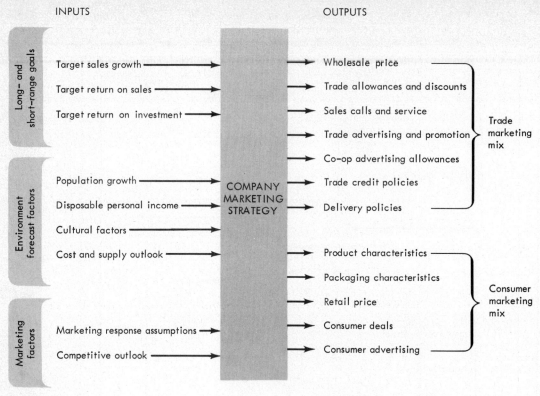

INPUTS | OUTPUTS

Long- and short-range goals

Target sales growth →
Target return on sales →
Target return on investment →

Environment forecast factors

Population growth →
Disposable personal income →
Cultural factors →
Cost and supply outlook →

Marketing factors

Marketing response assumptions →
Competitive outlook →

COMPANY MARKETING STRATEGY

→ Wholesale price
→ Trade allowances and discounts
→ Sales calls and service
→ Trade advertising and promotion
→ Co-op advertising allowances
→ Trade credit policies
→ Delivery policies

Trade marketing mix

→ Product characteristics
→ Packaging characteristics
→ Retail price
→ Consumer deals
→ Consumer advertising

Consumer marketing mix

FIGURE 3–11
Input-Output Map of Company Marketing Decisions: Candy Company

The next step is to list the various inputs and influences on these decisions, which fall into one of three groups:

1. The company's long- and short-range goals for sales growth, return on sales, and return on investment.
2. Forecastable factors in the environment, such as population growth, disposable personal income, cultural factors, and the cost and supply outlook.
3. Assumptions about the sales effectiveness of different marketing instruments as well as expectations concerning competition.

Any input can be elaborated further. For example, it is possible to isolate four cultural factors that will have a significant effect on future candy consumption:

Weight consciousness—if there is any relaxation of the pressures in American society toward the idea that "thin is beautiful," that will lead to a substantial increase in the sales of candy.

Cavity consciousness—as better dentifrices are developed, people will worry less about the negative effects of sugar on their teeth, and that will reduce their inhibitions against eating candy; on the other hand, some companies will see cavity-consciousness as an opportunity to develop a tasty, sugarless candy.

Nutrition consciousness—if recent interest in the ill effects of refined sugar on the human metabolism continues to grow, an increasing proportion of nutritionally conscious people will steer away from candy.

Cigarette consumption—if people reduce their cigarette consumption, we can expect candy, gum, and other oral gratifiers to replace cigarettes.

We can now trace how the various outputs feed into other parts of the system. Consider the output described as the trade marketing mix. This output becomes input into each of the distribution channels—for example, the grocery-chain model (see Figure 3–12). The trade marketing mix becomes the "handle" that the manufacturer uses to influence the retailer to provide favorable shelf facings and location, special displays and promotions, advertising, and in-stock maintenance.

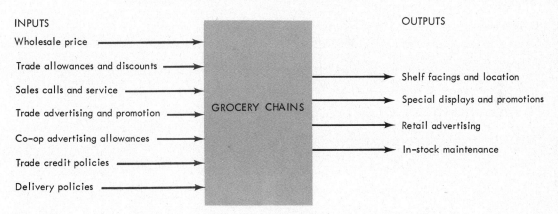

INPUTS

Wholesale price

Trade allowances and discounts

Sales calls and service

Trade advertising and promotion

Co-op advertising allowances

Trade credit policies

Delivery policies

GROCERY CHAINS

OUTPUTS

Shelf facings and location

Special displays and promotions

Retail advertising

In-stock maintenance

FIGURE 3–12
Input-Output Map of Grocery-Chain Decisions: Candy Company

The influence of the dealers' decisions on the final consumers is shown in Figure 3–13 along with influences coming from other parts of the marketing system. The various influences are classified into product and promotion factors (outputs coming from the company marketing decision model), distribution factors (outputs coming from the channels of distribution models), and environmental factors (outputs coming from the environmental model). These factors influence consumers' buying behavior to bring about a certain level of industry sales and brand-share sales of candy bars.

At some point it is necessary to estimate the quantitative relationships between various key elements. Figure 3–14 shows the estimated effect of chocolate weight percentage—a product characteristic—on candy bar sales. The company would like to keep this percentage down because chocolate is an expensive ingredient compared with the ingredients that make up the soft center. However, consumer tests reveal that as the chocolate content of the bar is reduced, the bar loses its appeal, and sales decline. The soft center begins to appear through the chocolate and leads consumers to feel that the bar is poorly made. Furthermore, their palates desire more chocolate to offset the soft center. When the layer of chocolate gets too thick (above 35 percent of the weight of the bar), consumer

INPUTS   OUTPUTS

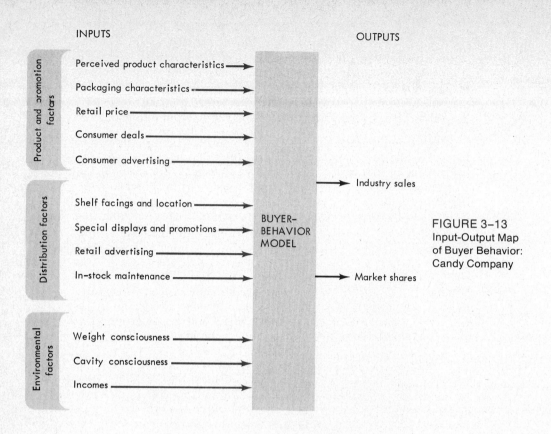

FIGURE 3–13
Input-Output Map
of Buyer Behavior:
Candy Company

preference for the bar also falls. The consumers begin to think of it not as a soft-centered bar but as a chocolate bar with "some stuff in it." They compare this bar with pure chocolate bars, and it suffers by comparison. To the best of management's knowledge, sales have the curvilinear relationship to percentage chocolate weight that is shown in Figure 3–14.

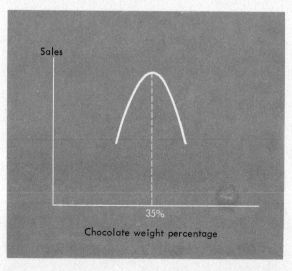

FIGURE 3–14
Functional Relationship Map:
Candy Company

Given this functional relationship, what is the optimum level of chocolate? If the company wishes to maximize sales, chocolate should constitute 35 percent of the candy bar's weight. However, since the company is primarily interested in maximizing profit, management needs the ingredient-cost functions, as well as the sales-response function, to determine the profit-maximizing amount of chocolate.

Other functional relationships should be studied—the relationship between the amount spent on advertising and the resulting sales, the number of sales representatives and the resulting sales, and so on. At some point, the various functional relationships must be put together into a model for analyzing the sales and profit consequences of a proposed marketing plan. A useful graphical-analytical device is shown in Figure 3–15.[10]

Quadrant 1 shows a relationship between population and the total sales of chocolate-covered, soft-centered candy bars. The functional relationship shows that sales tend to increase with population, but at a decreasing rate. The part of the curve describing candy consumption for stages where the American population was under 220 million persons is historically derived through least-squares regression analysis. The part of the curve showing sales for future sizes of the U.S. population is extrapolated and is influenced by anticipated cultural and economic trends. The curve indicates that a population of 220 million persons consumes approximately $105 million of soft-centered candy bars.

The second quadrant shows the relationship between total sales of soft-centered candy bars and company sales. When industry sales are $105 million, the company in question enjoys sales of $70 million—that is, a market share of approximately 67 percent. The part of the curve toward the lower level of industry sales is derived from historical information; the part toward the higher levels of sales is extrapolated on the assumption that there will be no dramatic changes in company and competitors' marketing efforts. Although the function is linear, it does not necessarily indicate that the company expects its market share to remain constant. This would be true only if the line started at the 0,0 origin of this quadrant (not shown). Actually the line indicates that the company expects its share of market to fall slightly as total sales increase. For example, when industry sales are $140 million, the expectation of company sales is $90 million, or an estimated market share of 61 percent as compared with 67 percent now.

The third quadrant shows the relationship between company sales and company profits. Again the company assumes that the relationship is basically linear. At the present time, profits are $7 million on company sales of approximately $70 million, or 10 percent. If company sales go up to $105 million, the company expects profits of approximately $10.2 million—that is, 9.7 percent.

This kind of graphical device, which assumes that all the underlying relationships have been combined and expressed in terms of three basic relationships, allows us to visualize the effect of a particular level of an environment factor and continued marketing program on company sales and profits. To this extent, it is a forecasting device. Its use extends beyond this, however, into marketing planning as well. Suppose, for example, that the company expects the

[10] This device was adapted to the candy company example and derives from a suggestion of Robert S. Weinberg, in "Multiple Factor Break-Even Analysis: The Applications of Operations-Research Techniques to a Basic Problem of Management Planning and Control," *Operations Research*, April 1956, pp. 152–86.

new antismoking campaign to have a big impact on candy bar sales, shifting the curve in the first quadrant higher (see Figure 3–15). Furthermore, suppose the company is considering intensifying its marketing effort to increase its market share even further. The anticipated effect of this on company market share can be seen by shifting the function in the second quadrant to the right, as shown in Figure 3–15. At the same time, the company's marketing costs increase and therefore shift the sales-profit curve to the right, as shown in the third quadrant of Figure 3–15. What is the net effect of this complicated set of shifts? The result is that, although sales have increased, profits have fallen. Apparently, the cost to the company of attaining a still higher market share exceeds the profits on the extra sales. The company would be wise not to intensify its marketing effort, at least according to the specific plan it is considering and its estimated effects.

FIGURE 3–15
Profit-Forecasting and Planning Map: Candy Company

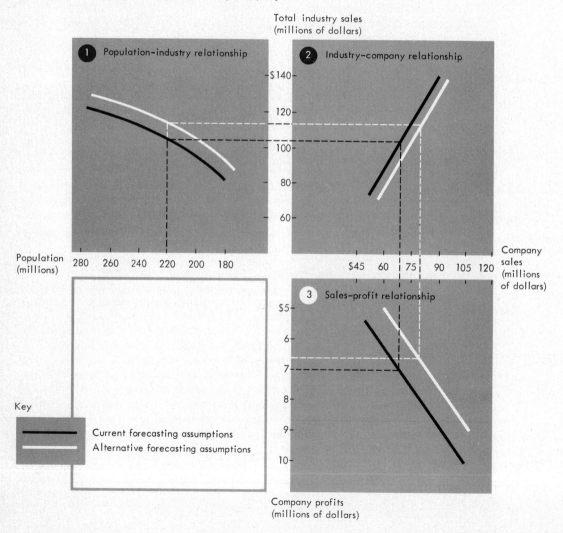

The four-quadrant model assists management in visualizing the impact of specific environmental assumptions and marketing plans on final sales and profits. It can be improved further by introducing more variables and representing their relationships in an overall mathematical model of the candy company's marketing system.

SUMMARY

A marketer is someone who is skilled in marketing system analysis and marketing process analysis. Marketing system analysis, the subject of this chapter, consists of three levels of analysis of increasing scope and complexity: exchange system analysis, organizational marketing analysis, and macroenvironment analysis.

An exchange system involves two or more parties each with something-of-value they might offer in trade. A transaction is the actualization of a potential exchange. The marketer who is seeking an exchange must understand the items making up the want list of the other party and formulate an offer that would be sufficient to motivate a transaction. Exchange maps, whether of two or more parties, assume each party to be pursuing its self-interest.

An organizational marketing system describes the organization and the set of significant interacting institutions and forces in the organization's environment that affect its ability to serve its markets. This system can be conceptualized on five levels. The first level involves the organization's internal environment and the factors and forces that facilitate or inhibit successful marketing action. The second level involves the task system, which consists of the basic institutions that cooperate to create marketing value for a marketplace: specifically the suppliers, organization, marketing intermediaries, and the final market. These four constitute a total marketing channel for meeting a particular set of customer needs. The third level involves the sets of competitors vying for the same market: generic competitors, product form competitors, and enterprise competitors. The fourth level consists of all the publics that have an actual or potential interest or impact on the organization's ability to achieve its objectives: financial publics, media publics, government publics, citizen-action publics, local publics, and the general public. The fifth level consists of the major macroenvironmental forces impinging on the organization: demography, economics, natural resources, technology, law and politics, and culture.

The various concepts of marketing systems analysis are illustrated for a major candy company that produces a candy bar for the mass market.

QUESTIONS AND PROBLEMS

1. Develop a comprehensive marketing system map of some company of your choice. Be sure to show the marketing mix elements and the channels of distribution.

2. Develop an input-output map for the advertising submodel in Figure 3–10.

3. Develop a functional relationship map which shows the relationship between (a) retail price and candy bar sales; (b) advertising and candy bar sales.

4. List as many specific marketing actions to stimulate sales as you can think of available to (a) supermarkets; (b) airlines.

5. Develop a diagram showing the major publics of a privately owned hospital.

6. Develop a three-party exchange map for a hospital's exchange system with the other two parties being the doctor and the patient.

7. "I hold strongly that marketing people should confine themselves to the marketing

field. I don't think most marketing oriented persons have the experience, aptitude, or approach for sound public relations." Do you agree?

8. The text distinguishes three types of competition: generic, product form, and enterprise. Illustrate the three types of competition for a firm in the photocopying machine industry.

9. Describe the marketing channel of a company of your choice.

The Strategic Management and Marketing Process

4

> There are three types of companies. Those who make things happen. Those who watch things happen. Those who wonder what happened.
>
> ANONYMOUS

The preceding chapter examined the structural components of organizational marketing systems but not their functioning. The task now is to show how organizations use the marketing process to convert unfulfilled market needs into profitable business opportunities.

A marketer's work starts long before the organization's products are produced and continues long after their sales are consummated. The professional marketer is involved in studying consumer needs and desires, developing product concepts aimed at satisfying unfulfilled needs, testing the validity of these product concepts, designing product features, developing packaging and a brand name, pricing the product to recover a reasonable return on investment, arranging for regional, national, and international distribution, creating effective marketing communications to let the public know about the product's availability, purchasing the most efficient media for the commercial messages, auditing sales, monitoring customer satisfaction, and revising marketing plans in the light of results. The marketer is a marketing researcher, inventor, psychologist, sociologist, economist, communicator, and lawyer all rolled into one.

There is a larger context for these specific activities, which we would like to consider in this chapter. Let us assume that we are dealing with a large *corporation* that has several *business divisions* and several *product lines* within each division. Marketing plays a role at each level, and we want to understand in what fashion. At the corporate level, marketing contributes perspectives and estimates to help top management decide on the corporation's mission, opportunities, growth strategy, and product portfolio. The policies set by corporate management then provide the context for strategy formulation in each of the business divisions by the divisional managers. Finally, the managers of each product and/or market within each division develop their marketing strategy within the context of the policies and constraints developed at the higher divisional and corporate levels.

We shall use the term *strategic management process* to describe the steps taken at the corporate and divisional levels to develop long-run master strategies for survival and growth. The term *strategic marketing process* will describe the steps taken at the product and/or market level to develop viable marketing positions and programs. The strategic marketing process takes place within the larger strategic management process of the corporation. We shall look first at the strategic management process and then the strategic marketing process.

STRATEGIC MANAGEMENT PROCESS

Many of today's major corporations got their start by coming out with the right products at the right time in a rapidly growing market. Many of their past decisions were made without the benefit of formal strategic thinking and planning. Wise, or lucky, management decisions carried these companies to where they stand today. However, management is recognizing that intuition alone is no longer enough for succeeding in today's environment. More and more companies are turning to formal planning systems to guide their course.

The early planning systems consisted of extrapolating current sales and environmental trends five or ten years out and basing plant and investment decisions on these numbers. Companies recognized the likely occurrence of cyclical and seasonal swings but basically assumed the dependability of the trends themselves. Within the last decade, however, the belief in a continuously growing economy gave way to the actuality of a highly discontinuous one. Companies experienced unexpected cost inflation, shortages of needed material, new technological breakthroughs, unwanted government regulations, high interest costs, aggressive international competition, and the end of the baby boom. As a result, management has come to believe that the only thing certain will be surprises and more surprises. The question becomes: How should a company carry on its planning in an "age of discontinuity" and "future shock"?

The answer of many companies is to switch from extrapolative planning to *strategic planning*. Strategic planning is based on the key concepts of *market evolution* and *strategic fit*. All markets undergo an evolutionary unfolding marked by changing customer needs, technologies, competitors, channels, and laws. The firm should be looking out of a "strategic window" watching these changes and assessing the requirements for continued success in each market.[1] There is only a limited period when the fit between the requirements of a particular market and the firm's competencies is at an optimum. At these times, the strategic window is

[1] See Derek F. Abell, "Strategic Windows," *Journal of Marketing*, July 1978, pp. 21–26.

open, and the firm should be investing in this market. In some subsequent period, the firm will find that the evolutionary path of this market is such that it can no longer be effective and efficient in serving this market. It should consider disinvesting and shifting its resources to areas of growing opportunity.

The increased pace of environmental change and rising cost of capital has shifted corporate power in recent years to strategic planners and financial vice presidents. They are calling the shots as to what businesses and products should be built, maintained, reduced, and terminated. Selective growth, rather than total product-line growth, is the key. Company marketers participate in the decision process by supplying estimates of market size and opportunity and presenting their views. Once business objectives are decided, marketing helps carry them out, even if they involve demarketing a product line or business. That is why strategic marketing must be seen today in the context of the strategic management process of the firm.

The strategic management process can be defined as *the managerial process of developing and maintaining a viable relationship between the organization and its environment through the development of corporate purpose, objectives and goals, growth strategies, and business portfolio plans for company-wide operations.* The major steps in this process are shown in Figure 4–1. The result is a strategic plan. We will look at how each component decision is made in terms of marketing inputs and implications.

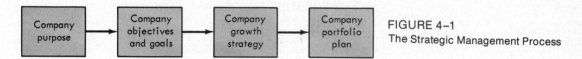

FIGURE 4–1
The Strategic Management Process

Company Purpose

An organization exists to accomplish something in the larger environment. Its specific purpose or mission is usually clear at the beginning.[2] Over time, however, one or more of the following things will happen. (1) The purpose becomes unclear as the organization grows and develops new products and markets. (2) The purpose remains clear but some managers lose their interest in the original purpose. (3) The purpose remains clear but loses its appropriateness to new conditions in the environment.

When management becomes aware that the organization is drifting, it is time to renew the search for purpose. The need is not simply to define a mission that helps management feel good or that serves public relations. A well-worked-out statement of purpose provides employees with a shared sense of opportunity, direction, significance, and achievement. An explicit purpose is an invisible hand, which guides widely scattered employees to work independently and yet collectively toward the realization of the organization's potentials.

In a large company that decides to take a fresh look at its purpose, the

---

[2] We shall use "purpose" and "mission" interchangeably. However, some authors distinguish the two. Steiner and Miner use "purpose" to describe the economic and ethical motivation of the business, e.g., "to strive for high product quality and corporate integrity." They use "mission" to describe the product and market domain of the firm, e.g., "to produce educational games for adults." See George A. Steiner and J. B. Miner, *Management Policy and Strategy: Text, Readings, and Cases* (Homewood, Ill.: Richard D. Irwin, 1977), p. 7.

people in top management bear the major responsibility. They may solicit ideas from stockholders, employees, customers, and distributors concerning the current and ideal character of the business. They will ask, "What is our business?" and "What should it be?"[3] These sound like simple questions but are among the most difficult ones the company will ever have to answer. A major company recently worked two years to forge a new and satisfactory statement of its purpose.

The purpose of the organization must take into account five key elements. The first is the *history* of the organization. Every organization has a history of aims, policies, and accomplishments. In reaching for a new purpose, the organization must honor the salient characteristics of its past history. It would not make sense for Harvard University, for example, to become a community college, even if such a move were a growth opportunity. The second consideration is the *current preferences* of the management and owners. Those who direct the company have their personal goals and predilections. If Sears's current management wants to serve higher-income consumers, this goal is going to influence the statement of corporate purpose. Third, *environmental considerations* influence the purpose of the organization. The environment defines the main opportunities and threats that must be realistically taken into account. The Girl Scouts of America would not get far in today's environment with the purpose "to prepare young girls for motherhood and wifely duties." Fourth, the organization's *resources* make certain missions possible and others not. Piedmont Airlines would be deluding itself if it adopted the mission to become the world's leading airline. Finally, the organization should base its choice of purpose on its *distinctive competences*. Although it may be able to accomplish many things, it should aim for that which it can do best. McDonald's could probably enter the solar energy business but that would not be making use of its main competence—providing low-cost food and fast service to large groups of customers.

More and more organizations are developing formal statements of corporate purpose that are shared with division heads, employees, and in many cases, customers and the public at large. Some of these statements, unfortunately, are very general and high minded and not very useful in corporate decision making. "We want to be the leading company of its kind producing the highest quality products with the widest distribution and service at the lowest possible prices." This sounds very good but fails to supply clear guidelines when tough business decisions need to be faced.

A number of characteristics should be embodied in a statement of purpose to make it maximally useful. The purpose should be stated in terms of accomplishing something *outside* of the organization. Statements such as "to make money" or "to become the market leader" fail to define a sufficient concept. Profits and leadership are the result of successful accomplishment of purpose rather than the purpose itself.

The statement of purpose should be *specific* as to the *business domain(s)* in which the organization will operate.[4] The business domain can be defined as a

[3] See Peter F. Drucker, *Management: Tasks, Responsibilities, Practices* (New York: Harper & Row, 1973), chap. 7.

[4] Exceptions are holding and investment companies, which operate over a wide range of business domains. They seek to make money wherever it can be made. A few companies, such as the 3M Company and Mobil, also seem ready to enter any business that shows promise of a substantial return.

product class, technological field, customer group, market need, or some combination. Companies have traditionally defined their business domain in product terms, such as "we are a computer manufacturer," or in technological terms, such as "we are a chemical processing company." An increasing number of companies have been moving in recent years to a customer-group definition of their business, such as "we help farmers increase their productivity," or a customer-need definition, such as "we are an entertainment company."

Some years ago, Levitt advanced the thesis that market definitions of a business are superior to product or technological definitions of a business.[5] His main argument is that products and technologies are transient, while basic market needs generally endure forever. A horse carriage company will go out of business as soon as the automobile is invented. But the same company, defined as a people-moving business, would switch from horse carriage manufacture to car manufacture. Levitt's widely read article, along with the economy's increasing uncertainty, encouraged many companies to shift their business domain definition from a product to a market focus. Several examples are given in Table 4–1.

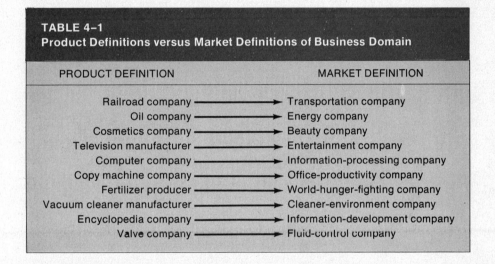

TABLE 4–1
Product Definitions versus Market Definitions of Business Domain

PRODUCT DEFINITION	MARKET DEFINITION
Railroad company	Transportation company
Oil company	Energy company
Cosmetics company	Beauty company
Television manufacturer	Entertainment company
Computer company	Information-processing company
Copy machine company	Office-productivity company
Fertilizer producer	World-hunger-fighting company
Vacuum cleaner manufacturer	Cleaner-environment company
Encyclopedia company	Information-development company
Valve company	Fluid-control company

Ansoff, however, has challenged some market-based definitions as being too broad to provide real direction:

> . . . the term "transportation business" fails to supply the common thread. First, the range of possible missions is very broad: intraurban, interurban, intracontinental, and intercontinental transportation; through the media of land, air, water, underwater; for moving passengers, and/or cargo. Second, the range of customers is wide: the individual, family, business firm, or government office. Third, the "product" varies: car, bus, train, ship, airplane, helicopter, taxi, truck. The number of practical combinations of the variables is large, and so is the number of common threads.[6]

---

[5] Theodore Levitt, "Marketing Myopia," *Harvard Business Review,* July–August 1960, pp. 45–56.

[6] H. Igor Ansoff, *Corporate Strategy* (New York: McGraw-Hill Book Company, 1965), p. 107.

In developing a market-based definition of a business, management should steer between being too narrow and too broad. A lead pencil manufacturer that believes it is in the business of making communication equipment is stating its mission too broadly. A useful approach is to move from the current product to successively higher levels of abstraction and then decide on the most realistic level of abstraction for the company to consider. Figure 4–2 shows two examples. A candy bar manufacturer can see itself operating in the broader candy market, the still broader snack market, or the still broader food market. A motorcycle manufacturer can see itself expanding to automobiles (motorized pleasure vehicles), trucks (motorized vehicles), or bikes (transportation vehicles). Each broadening step opens a vision of new opportunities but also may lead the company into unrealistic business ventures beyond its capabilities.[7]

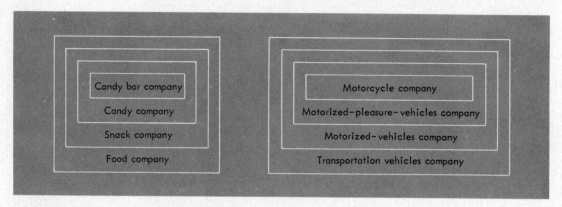

FIGURE 4–2
Successive Expansions of Business Domains

In its development of a definition of business domain, the company may want to specify up to four dimensions: customer need, customer group, product, and technology. Volkswagen, for example, may define its domain as "meeting the need for low-cost personal motorized transportation for low- to moderate-income consumers through providing small cars designed with the most fuel-efficient technology." The statement makes it clear that Volkswagen wants to serve the public's need for efficient cars and is not seeking to enter the large or expensive car market. On the other hand, this business domain would be too narrow for General Motors. However, it might not be too narrow for one of the business divisions of General Motors, and in fact, each division should carefully define its business domain.

Another useful characteristic of a corporate statement of purpose is that it

[7] The abstraction process is somewhat arbitrary. A yogurt producer can expand the domain as *yogurt → health food → health business* or as *yogurt → dessert → food business*. Much depends on what characteristic of a product is initially expanded.

is elevated and motivating in character. Employees would like to feel that their work is important and that they are making a contribution to people's lives. When the prosaic task of producing fertilizer is reshaped into the larger idea of improving agricultural productivity to feed the world's hungry, a new sense of purpose comes over the employees. When the task of selling vacuum cleaners is transformed into the larger idea of creating a cleaner and healthier environment, management is able to visualize a more exciting challenge.

Finally, a corporate statement of purpose should outline major policies that the company plans to honor in the pursuit of its mission. Policies describe the value system of the company: how employees are expected to deal with customers, suppliers, distributors, competition, and other actors and publics. Policies narrow the range of individual discretion, so that the company takes a consistent stand on important issues.

The company's mission, once settled upon, becomes the focus of its energy for the next ten or twenty years. Missions are not something to change every few years simply in response to environmental changes or new unrelated opportunities. On the other hand, sometimes a company has to reconsider its mission statement within a few years of its formulation because it no longer works or it does not define an optimal course for the company. The more rapid the pace of change in the environment, the more often companies will have to reexamine their basic statement of purpose.

Company Objectives and Goals

Management must translate the company's purpose into a set of specific objectives and goals that will support the realization of this purpose. The objectives indicate specific spheres of aim, activity, and accomplishment. The most common objectives of companies are *profitability, sales growth, market share improvement, risk diversification,* and *innovation.* These objectives may flow directly from the basic purpose or be considered as ancillary necessities for carrying out the basic purpose. To be useful, the organization's various objectives should be hierarchical, quantitative, realistic, and consistent.

Hierarchical A company always pursues a large number of objectives. When possible, these objectives should be stated in a hierarchical fashion from the most important to the least important.[8] An excellent example of hierarchical objectives is provided by Interstate Telephone Company (name disguised).[9] The company has not been earning the allowed rate of 7.5 percent in recent years, giving various "stakeholders" a real cause for concern.[10] One of management's major objectives is to increase its return on investment to 7.5 percent. Starting from this objective, a whole hierarchy of further objectives can be derived, as shown in Figure 4–3.

There are only two ways to increase the return on investment: increase the

---

[8] Charles H. Granger, "The Hierarchy of Objectives," *Harvard Business Review,* May–June 1964, pp. 63–74.

[9] Leon Winer, "Are You Really Planning Your Marketing?" *Journal of Marketing,* January 1965, pp. 1–8.

[10] "Stakeholders" are stockholders and all the other parties who have a "stake" in the firm, such as bankers and managers.

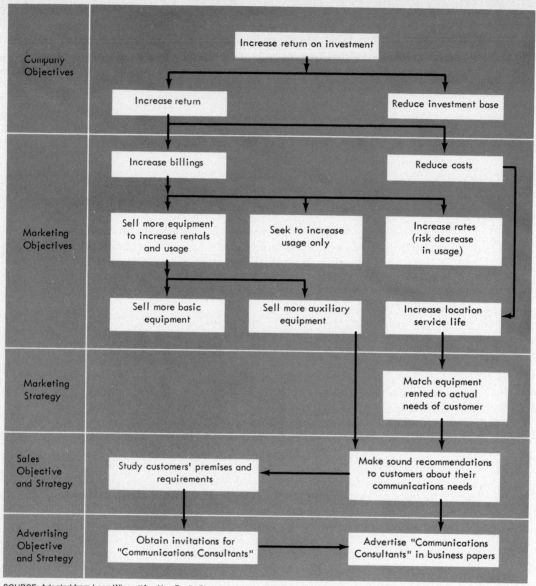

SOURCE: Adapted from Leon Winer, "Are You Really Planning Your Marketing?" *Journal of Marketing,* January 1965, pp. 1–8, here p. 3.

FIGURE 4–3
Hierarchy of Objectives for the Interstate Telephone Company

total return or reduce the investment base. The company is not about to do the latter. To increase its return, the company can strive to increase its billings or reduce its costs, or both. To increase its billings, the company can (1) sell more equipment to increase rentals and usage, (2) seek to increase usage of present equipment, and (3) increase its rates, providing this does not reduce customer usage and is allowed by the rate commission. As for reducing costs, this could be accomplished by increasing the service life of rented telephone equipment, which in turn suggests doing a better job of matching rented equipment to the actual needs of customers. To the extent that the company tries to increase its billings, subsidiary objectives must be set for sales force, advertising, and other elements of the marketing mix. For example, each sales district will be assigned a sales quota based on its potential. Each sales district quota in turn will be broken down and assigned to individual sales representatives. In this way a major objective of the company is ultimately translated into more specific objectives.

Quantitative To the extent possible, objectives should be stated in quantitative terms. The objective "increase the return on investment" is not as satisfactory as "increase the return on investment to 7.5 percent," or even better, "increase the return on investment to 7.5 percent by the end of the second year." Analysts use the term *goals* to describe an objective that has been made highly specific with respect to *magnitude* and *time*. Turning the objectives into concrete goals facilitates the whole process of management planning and control.

Realistic A company has to be careful in choosing target levels for its objectives. Not all levels will do. The levels should come out of an analysis of its opportunities and resources, not out of wishful thinking.

Consistent A company's objectives are sometimes inconsistent, as when management says that it wants "to maximize sales and profits," or "achieve the greatest sales at the least cost," or "design the best possible product in the shortest possible time." These objectives are in a trade-off relationship. It is not possible to maximize sales and profits simultaneously. One can increase sales by lowering price, improving product quality, and increasing marketing effort, although these steps, beyond a point, are likely to reduce profit. Robert Weinberg has identified eight basic strategic trade-offs facing any firm:[11]

1. Short-term profits versus long-term growth
2. Profit margin versus competitive position
3. Direct sales effort versus market development effort
4. Penetration of existing markets versus the development of new markets
5. Related versus nonrelated new opportunities as a source of long-term growth
6. Profit versus nonprofit goals (that is, social responsibilities)
7. Growth versus stability
8. "Riskless" environment versus high-risk environment

A company has to determine the relative emphasis to give to these conflicting objectives, or else they will fail to serve as useful guidelines.

Company Growth Strategy When an organization has clarified its purpose and objectives, it knows where it wants to go. The question is how best to get there. The company needs a "grand design" for achieving its objectives. That is called strategy. Strategy involves the choice of major directions for pursuing objectives and the allocation of support-

---

[11] Presented in a seminar, "Developing Management Strategies for Short-Term Profits and Long-Term Growth," sponsored by Advanced Management Research, Inc., Regency Hotel, New York City, September 29, 1969.

ing resources. Strategy is the company's concept of how to win the war. It should not be confused with tactics, which are derived activities designed to win battles.

Most companies have growth of sales and profits as one of their major objectives. They don't want to stand still. Lack of growth drains the company of new challenge, leads to the loss of its entrepreneurial managers, and exposes it to possible technological obsolescence. In wanting growth, companies need a growth strategy. They need to select from a whole set of possible investment directions those that are most likely to produce the desired growth. Consider the following case:

> Musicale Corporation (name disguised) is a leading phonograph records company, which along with other companies in the industry, faces some basic challenges. The costs and competition for top recording artists have been escalating. An alternative form of packaging music, tape cassettes, has been making rapid inroads. Channels of distribution have been shifting in favor of mass-merchandise outlets over small retailers. Larger promotion budgets are becoming necessary for launching new releases.
>
> Musicale has not sat idly by in the face of these challenges. It acquired a magnetic-tape-producing company and proceeded to market its music in cassette form with some success. Because its tape-manufacturing capacity exceeded its music-business needs, it formed a division to market magnetic tape to computer manufacturers and users. The company also tried its hand at manufacturing a complete line of phonographs under its own name; it later withdrew because their marketing required more resources than the company chose to invest. Still later Musicale entered the electronics business but withdrew in a few years.
>
> Although Musicale has been willing to venture away from the recording business, it has not done this with any great success. It did not show much patience with its new ventures because of their initial unprofitability. Its various ventures, while all loosely related to its major business, represented a set of ad hoc responses to fortuitous opportunities rather than the working out of a well-designed master plan for company growth. Musicale, sorely aware of its aimless growth history, is seeking a more systematic strategy for growth.

Alternative growth strategies can be generated for a company by mapping its marketing system and then moving to three levels of analysis. The first level identifies those opportunities available to the company in its current sphere of operations; we call them *intensive growth opportunities*. The second level identifies those opportunities available through integration with other parts of this marketing system; we call them *integrative growth opportunities*. The third level identifies those opportunities present completely outside the present marketing system; we call them *diversification growth opportunities*. Table 4–2 lists the specific possibilities latent in each of these broad opportunity classes.

Intensive growth   Intensive growth makes sense for a company if it has not fully exploited the opportunities latent in its current products and markets. Ansoff has proposed a useful classification of intensive-growth opportunities based on a *product/market expansion matrix*.[12] The matrix is shown in Figure 4–4 and the three major types of intensive growth opportunities are described as follows:

---

[12] H. Igor Ansoff, "Strategies for Diversification," *Harvard Business Review*, September–October 1957, pp. 113–24. The same matrix can be expanded into nine cells by adding modified products and modified markets. See S.C. Johnson and Conrad Jones, "How to Organize for New Products," *Harvard Business Review*, May–June 1957, pp. 49–62.

TABLE 4–2
Major Classes of Growth Opportunities

I. INTENSIVE GROWTH	II. INTEGRATIVE GROWTH	III. DIVERSIFICATION GROWTH
A. Market penetration	A. Backward integration	A. Concentric diversification
B. Market development	B. Forward integration	B. Horizontal diversification
C. Product development	C. Horizontal integration	C. Conglomerate diversification

	Existing products	New products
Existing markets	1. Market penetration	3. Product development
New markets	2. Market development	4. Diversification

FIGURE 4–4
Product/Market
Expansion Matrix

1. *Market penetration.* *Market penetration consists of the company's seeking increased sales for its current products in its current markets through more aggressive marketing effort.* There are three possibilities:
   a. The company can try to stimulate current customers to increase their *current rate of purchase.* This is a function of the *purchase frequency* times the *purchase amount.* Musicale can try to encourage customers to buy records more frequently and to buy more on each occasion. New releases, price promotion, advertising, publicity, and wider distribution aid in this effort. More basically, Musicale can think of opportunities to increase the *current rate of consumption,* which underlies the current rate of purchase. The consumption rate is a function of the *number of use occasions* times the *amount used per occasion.* If consumers start listening to their records on more occasions (say, early morning as well as evening) and listen to more records each time, they will buy more records.
   b. The company can increase its efforts to attract competitors' customers. To increase their market share, Musicale can develop bigger stars, record better performances, design more attractive record jackets, offer more attractive prices, use stronger advertising, and gain wider distribution.
   c. The company can increase its efforts to attract nonusers located in its current market areas. Such steps might be taken as exposing nonusers to more music, reducing the price of phonographs, and developing more publicity about music listening as a hobby.
2. *Market development.* *Market development consists of the company's seeking increased sales by taking its current products into new markets.* There are two possibilities:
   a. The company can open additional geographical markets through regional, national, or international expansion. The company is currently underrepresented in certain U.S. cities and is doing only an average job of participating in the growing international market.

73

b. The company can try to attract new market segments through developing product versions that appeal to these segments, entering other channels of distribution, or advertising in other media. The company, for example, is not well represented in the preteen segment of the market.

3. *Product development.* Product development consists of the company's seeking increased sales by developing new or improved products for its current markets. There are three possibilities:

a. The company can develop new product features or content through attempting to adapt, modify, magnify, minify, substitute, rearrange, reverse, or combine existing features.[13]

b. The company can create different-quality versions of the product.

c. The company can develop additional models and sizes. For example, Musicale might research and develop a new type of record that carries more sound track or better quality. It might produce all-plastic sheet records, such as those that are increasingly being inserted in magazines. It might produce new program content, such as a do-it-yourself series or a basic education series.

Integrative growth Integrative growth makes sense for a company if the basic industry has a strong growth future and/or the company can increase its profitability, efficiency, or control by moving backward, forward, or horizontally within the industry. Figure 4–5 shows the task-marketing system for Musicale. Three integrative-growth possibilities are discussed below.

1. *Backward integration. Backward integration consists of a company's seeking ownership or increased control of its supply systems.* Musicale relies heavily on plastic-material producers and recording equipment manufacturers. Musicale might see an advantage in backward integration if any of these suppliers is enjoying high growth or profits, or if there is some uncertainty over the availability or cost of future supplies.

2. *Forward integration. Forward integration consists of a company's seeking ownership or increased control of its distribution systems.* Musicale might see an advantage in forward integration if any of these marketing intermediaries is enjoying high growth or profits, or if Musicale is not getting satisfactory service. It might also start a direct-mail-order record club to reduce its dependence on middlemen.

3. *Horizontal integration. Horizontal integration consists of a company's seeking ownership or increased control of some of its competitors.* Musicale has seen several new companies enjoy phenomenal growth in a short time, based on a sharp ability to spot new recording talent. These companies could be attractive targets for takeover and could provide Musicale with new management talent and some new stars. Musicale would have to be sure that the acquisitions would not be challenged by the government as "tending substantially to lessen competition."

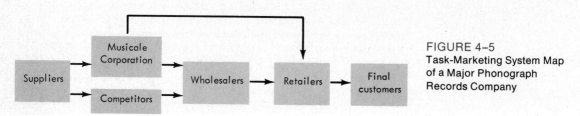

FIGURE 4–5
Task-Marketing System Map
of a Major Phonograph
Records Company

[13] See Alex F. Osborn, *Applied Imagination,* 3rd ed. (New York: Charles Scribner's Sons, 1963), pp. 286–87.

Diversification growth   Diversification growth makes sense for a company if the task-marketing system does not show much additional opportunity for growth or profit or if the opportunities outside of the present task-marketing system are superior. Diversification does not mean that the company will take up any opportunity that comes along. The company would attempt to identify fields that make use of its distinctive competences or help it overcome a particular problem. There are three broad types of diversification moves:

1. *Concentric diversification. Concentric diversification consists of the company's seeking to add new products that have technological and/or marketing synergies with the existing product line; these products normally will appeal to new classes of customers.* Musicale, for example, would search for other products that make use of its ability to work with plastics, sound recording, or artistically talented performers. One intriguing idea is for Musicale to go into other businesses with the talent under contract (such as name franchising) and manage other classes of talent (business executives, writers, and professors).

2. *Horizontal diversification. Horizontal diversification consists of the company's seeking to add new products that could appeal to its current customers though technologically unrelated to its current product line.* The products might appeal to the company's ultimate customers or its intermediate customers. For example, Musicale might publish a teenage magazine or make teenage clothing because of its great understanding of teenage tastes and life styles. Or it might manufacture other products that are carried by record retailers, such as phonographs or tape recorders. However, we saw that these horizontal diversification moves did not work out well for Musicale, primarily because the company did not have the competences to meet the success requirements in these businesses.

3. *Conglomerate diversification. Conglomerate diversification consists of the company's seeking to add new products for new classes of customers either because such a move promises to offset some deficiency or because it represents a great environmental opportunity; whichever the case, the new products have no relationship to the company's current technology, products, or markets.* Most companies experience seasonal or cyclical fluctuations, which are costly in terms of manpower, inventory carrying costs, or cash-flow management. Musicale has high sales in certain seasons, such as Christmas and Easter, and low sales during business recessions. These factors might lead it to look for business opportunities that have a different seasonal or cyclical pattern. Or companies like Musicale may be attracted to environmental opportunities, such as pollution control or health sciences, simply because they are very attractive. It might feel that it could acquire whatever competences were necessary to be successful in the new business. This optimism often proves, however, to be very naive.

Thus we see that a company can systematically identify growth opportunities through application of a marketing systems framework, looking first at current product-market opportunities, then at opportunities in other parts of the task-marketing system, and finally at relevant opportunities outside of the task system.

Company Portfolio Plan

Another major task of top management is the shaping of a business portfolio plan. At any point in time, a company consists of a portfolio of businesses (divisions, product lines, products, brands). This is true for nonprofit organizations as well as industrial companies. For example, a university consists of a number of schools, departments, and courses; and the YMCA consists of hotels, schools, summer camps, and recreational facilities. In the past, most organizations encouraged all their business units to grow by giving all of them a larger budget each year. All were held to increased sales and profit goals. The exceptions were seriously declining or troubled products. In recent years, organizations have moved to more selectivity because cash is scarce and opportunities differ greatly. Organizations now view themselves as managing a portfolio of businesses, and top management's job is to decide which businesses to build, maintain, phase down, and phase out. Thus a major company objective is to keep refreshing the company's portfolio of businesses by flushing out poor ones and adding promising new ones.

To carry out this objective, management first has to identify the *strategic business units* (SBUs) making up the company. An SBU has, ideally, the following characteristics:

1. It is a single business or collection of related businesses.
2. It has a distinct mission.
3. It has its own competitors.
4. It has a responsible manager.
5. It consists of one or more program units and functional units.
6. It can benefit from strategic planning.
7. It can be planned independently of the other businesses.

An SBU can, depending on the circumstances, be one or more company divisions, a product line within a division, or sometimes a single product.

The next step calls for management to classify all of the SBUs in a way that would reveal their resource-allocation merit. The two best-known classification schemes are those of the Boston Consulting Group and General Electric.

Boston Consulting Group approach   In this approach, pioneered by the Boston Consulting Group, the company classifies all of its SBUs in the *business portfolio matrix* (also called growth-share matrix) shown in Figure 4–6.[14] There are several things to notice.

1. The vertical axis, *market growth rate,* shows the annualized rate at which the various markets are growing in which each business unit is located. Market growth is arbitrarily divided into high and low growth by a 10 percent growth line.
2. The horizontal axis, *relative market share,* shows the market share for each SBU relative to the share of the industry's largest competitor. Thus a relative market share of .4 means that the company's SBU stands at 40 percent of the leader's share; and a relative market share of 2.0 means that the company's SBU is the leader and has twice the share of the next strongest company in the market. Relative market share gives more information about competitive standing than absolute market share; an absolute market share of 15 percent may or may not mean market leadership until we know the leader's share. The more that its SBUs have a relative market share greater than 1.5, the more the company is a leader in its various markets. The relative market share is drawn in log scale.

[14] For additional reading, see Charles W. Hofer and Dan Schendel, *Strategy Formulation: Analytical Concepts* (St. Paul, Minn.: West Publishing Company, 1978); George S. Day, "Diagnosing the Product Portfolio," *Journal of Marketing,* April 1977, pp. 29–38; and "Olin's Shift to Strategic Planning," *Business Week,* March 27, 1978, pp. 102–5.

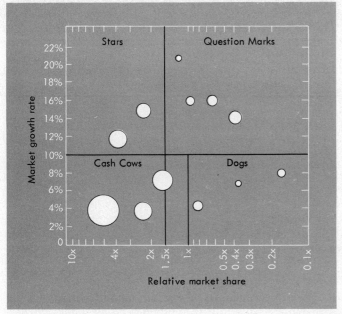

FIGURE 4–6
The BCG Business Portfolio Matrix

SOURCE: B. Hedley, ''Strategy and the 'Business Portfolio','' *Long-Range Planning,* February 1977, p. 12.

3. The circles depict the growth-share standings of the company's various SBUs. The areas of the circles are proportional to the SBUs' dollar sales.

4. Each quadrant represents a distinct type of cash-flow situation, leading to the following classification of SBUs:
   - **Stars.** Stars are high-growth, high-share SBUs. They are often cash-using SBUs because cash is necessary to finance their rapid growth. Eventually their growth will slow down, and they will turn into cash cows and become major cash generators supporting other SBUs.
   - **Cash cows.** Cash cows are low-growth, high-share SBUs. They throw off a lot of cash that the company uses to meet its bills and support other SBUs that are cash using.
   - **Question marks.** Question marks (also called problem children or wildcats) are low-share SBUs in high-growth markets. They require a lot of cash to maintain their share, let alone increase their share. Management has to think hard about whether to spend more to build these question marks into leaders; if not, the question marks will have to be phased down or out.
   - **Dogs.** Dogs (also called cash traps) are low-growth, low-share SBUs. They may generate enough cash to maintain themselves but do not promise to be a large source of cash.

5. The higher an SBU's market share, the higher its cash-generating ability. That is because higher market shares appear to be accompanied by higher levels of profitability. On the other hand, the higher the market-growth rate, the higher the SBU's cash-using requirements in order for it to grow and maintain its share.

6. The distribution of the SBUs in the four quadrants of the business portfolio matrix suggests the company's current state of health and desirable future strategic directions. The company in Figure 4–6 is fortunate in having some large cash cows

to finance its question marks, stars, and dogs. The company should seriously consider some decisive actions concerning its dogs and question marks. The picture would be worse if the company discovered that it had no stars, or had too many dogs, or had only a few weak cash cows.

7. As time passes, SBUs will change their positions in the business portfolio matrix. Many SBUs start out as question marks, move into the star category if they succeed, later become cash cows as market growth falls, and finally turn into dogs toward the end of their life cycle. Companies must be willing to let go of their weakening cash cows and not treat them as sacred cows.

8. Management's job is to project a future matrix showing where each SBU is likely to be assuming no change in its strategy. By comparing the current and future matrices, management can identify the major strategic issues facing the firm. The task of strategic planning is then to determine what role should be assigned to each SBU in the interest of efficient resource allocation. Four basic strategies can be pursued.

- **Build.** A strategy aiming at an improved market position with the willingness to forego short-term earnings to achieve this goal. This strategy is particularly appropriate for question marks, whose share has to grow if they are to become stars.

- **Hold.** A strategy designed to preserve the market position of an SBU. This strategy is particularly appropriate for strong cash cows if they are to continue to yield a large, positive cash flow.

- **Harvest.** A strategy that aims at getting short-term increase in cash flow regardless of the long-term effect. This strategy is particularly appropriate for a weak cash cow whose future is dim and from which more cash flow is needed. It can also be used with question marks and dogs.

- **Divest.** A strategy that aims at selling or liquidating the business because resources can be used better elsewhere. This stragegy is particularly appropriate for dogs and for question marks that the company decides it cannot finance for growth.

General Electric approach   The appropriate objective to assign to an SBU cannot be determined solely on the basis of its position in the growth-share matrix. If additional factors are introduced, the growth-share matrix can be seen as a special case of a more fundamental portfolio classification system, one that General Electric (GE) has pioneered, called a *nine-cell strategic business screen* (see Figure 4–7). Several things should be noticed.

1. The vertical axis represents the *industry's attractiveness*, which is based on rating such factors as *market growth rate* (used earlier in the growth-share analysis), *market size, profit margin, competitive intensity, cyclicality, seasonality,* and *scale economies.* Each of these factors is given a certain weight, a procedure that results in classifying a particular industry as high, medium, or low in overall industry attractiveness.[15]

2. The horizontal axis represents the SBU's *business strength* or ability to compete in that industry. Each industry has certain success requirements, which must be matched by the SBU having the required competences. Business strength is a

[15] An example of the weighting of factors is described in a future evolution of the business screen developed by the Shell Company which they call the directional policy matrix. See S. J. Q. Robinson, R. E. Hichens, and D. P. Wade, "The Directional Policy Matrix—Tool for Strategic Planning," *Long-Range Planning,* June 1978, pp. 8–15; and D. E. Hussey, "Portfolio Analysis: Practical Experience with the Directional Policy Matrix," *Long-Range Planning,* August 1978, pp. 2–8.

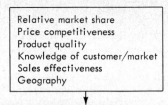

```
┌─────────────────────────────────┐
│ Relative market share           │
│ Price competitiveness           │
│ Product quality                 │
│ Knowledge of customer/market    │
│ Sales effectiveness             │
│ Geography                       │
└─────────────────────────────────┘
              ↓
        Business strength
   Strong    Average    Weak
```

Industry attractiveness — High / Medium / Low

A B C
F
D E G

┌─────────────────────────┐
│ Market size   │
│ Market growth   │
│ rate   │
│ Profit margin   │
│ Competitive   │
│ intensity   │
│ Cyclicality   │
│ Seasonality   │
│ Scale economies   │
└─────────────────────────┘

FIGURE 4–7
General Electric's Nine-Cell
Business Screen

SOURCE: Modified from Charles W. Hofer and Dan Schendel, *Strategy Formulation: Analytical Concepts* (St. Paul, Minn.: West Publishing Co., 1978), p. 32.

weighted rating of such factors as the SBU's *relative market share* (used earlier in the growth-share analysis), *price competitiveness, product quality, knowledge of customer/market, sales effectiveness,* and *geography.*

3. The screen is divided into three zones, which are known as green, yellow, and red. The green zone consists of the three cells at the upper left (vertical lines) indicating those industries that are favorable in industry attractiveness and SBU business strength, suggesting that the company has the green light to "invest and grow." The yellow zone consists of the diagonal cells stretching from the lower left to upper right, indicating industries that are medium in overall attractiveness. The company usually decides to maintain the SBU's share rather than have it grow or reduce its share. The red zone consists of the three cells in the lower right (horizontal) indicating those industries that are low in overall attractiveness, and here the company gives serious consideration to harvesting or divesting.

4. The circles represent individual SBUs. The areas of the circles are proportional to the size of the industries in which the various businesses compete, while the pie slices within the circles represent each SBU's market share. Thus G represents an SBU with a very small market share in a fair-size industry that is not very attractive and in which the company has little business strength.

5. The management should also plot a business screen showing projected positions of the SBUs if there is no change in strategies. By comparing the current and projected business screens, management can identify the major strategic issues and

79

opportunities it faces. For example, this type of analysis led GE to sort its current mix of SBUs into five investment groups:[16]

a. *High-growth products deserving the highest investment support*—engineering plastics, medical systems, transportation
b. *Steady reinvestment products deserving high and steady investment*—major appliances, steam and gas turbines, lamps
c. *Support products deserving steady investment support*—meters, specialty transformers
d. *Selective pruning or rejuvenation products deserving reduced investment*
e. *Venture products deserving heavy R&D investment*—"10-ton aircraft engine," microwave ovens, man-made diamonds

Many companies first classify their business using the Boston Consulting Group approach and then go into greater detail with the General Electric approach. Decisions are made on each SBU as to whether it will be built, held, harvested, or divested. Managers of SBUs in the latter three groups are given the opportunity to take issue with the judgment by supplying market data showing an SBU's greater potential. However, once the decision is made, the manager has to carry it out. For marketers, this means that their task is not always to build sales volume. If a business is slated for harvesting, then the marketer has to develop an optimal harvesting marketing plan, which might call for reducing plant and equipment expenditure, reducing R&D investment, reducing product quality and services, reducing advertising and sales-force expenditures, and raising price.[17]

The other implication of portfolio planning is that company marketers bear the main burden for coming up with new ideas for products and businesses to replace those that are being eliminated from the company's portfolio. Finding sound new ideas and developing them successfully calls for a well-worked-out theory of the strategic marketing process, to which we now turn.

STRATEGIC MARKETING PROCESS

Here we will examine the *strategic marketing process*, which defines the larger context for carrying out the day-to-day marketing activities of the firm. The strategic marketing process is *a managerial process of analyzing market opportunities and choosing marketing positions, programs, and controls that create and support viable businesses that serve the company's purpose and objectives*. The specific steps in the strategic marketing process are shown in Figure 4–8 and discussed in the following paragraphs.

Market Opportunity Analysis

The strategic marketing process begins with the effort to develop an attractive set of opportunities for the firm. Although new opportunities can be generated anywhere in the company, the marketing department bears this as a major responsibility. Some firms are chronically short of good ideas; here the marketer's task is to generate new ones. Other firms feel they have too many opportunities; here the marketer's task is to assist in selecting among them. In general, market-

---

[16] "GE Growth Plans Outline by Jones," *Bridgeport Telegram*, November 8, 1974.

[17] For the art of harvesting, see Philip Kotler, "Harvesting Strategies for Weak Products," *Business Horizons*, August 1978, pp. 15–22.

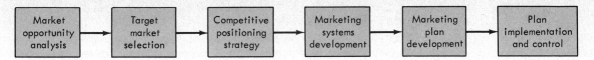

FIGURE 4–8
The Strategic Marketing Process

ers make a major contribution in generating, evaluating, and selecting attractive opportunities.

It is important to distinguish between *environmental opportunities* and *company opportunities.* There are countless environmental opportunities available in any economy as long as there are unsatisfied needs. Currently there are great opportunities to develop new sources of energy, new food products, improved agricultural methods, improved forms of transportation, new forms of leisure, and improved teaching technology. There are opportunities in refuse disposal, low-cost legal services, containerization, prefab housing, water purification, day-care centers, and biomedical instruments. But none of these necessarily represents opportunities for any specific company. Day-care centers are probably not an opportunity for U.S. Steel, nor are biomedical instruments an opportunity for Kentucky Fried Chicken.

The company should be concerned with relevant marketing opportunities. These are suggested by the purpose, objectives, growth strategies, and portfolio decisions of the company. We define a *company marketing opportunity* as follows:

> A *company marketing opportunity* is an attractive arena of relevant marketing action in which a particular company is likely to enjoy a differential advantage.

An opportunity is attractive if it is consistent with the company's purpose and likely to advance the company's objectives. The question is whether the company can bring more to this environmental opportunity than its potential competitors can. We make the following assumptions:

1. Every environmental opportunity has specific *success requirements.*
2. Each company has *distinctive competences,* that is, things that it can do especially well.
3. A company is likely to enjoy a *differential advantage* in an area of environmental opportunity if its distinctive competences match the success requirements of the environmental opportunity better than its potential competition.

Suppose General Motors, General Electric, and Sears all become interested at the same time in developing and marketing an electric car. Which firm would enjoy the greatest differential advantage? First we consider the success requirements. The success requirements would include (1) having good relations with suppliers of metal, rubber, plastic, glass, and other materials needed to produce an automobile, (2) having skill at mass production and mass assembly of complicated pieces of equipment, (3) having a strong distribution capacity to store, show, and deliver automobiles to the public, and (4) having the confidence of buyers that the company is able to produce and service a good auto product. Now General Motors has distinctive competences in all four of these areas. General Electric has distinctive competences in (1) supply and (2) production but not in (3) distribution or (4) automobile reputation. It does have great know-how in electrical technology. Sears's major distinctive competence is its extensive retailing system, but it would have to acquire the other competences. All said, General Motors would enjoy a major differential advantage in the production and marketing of electric cars.

The set of marketing opportunities available to a company at a particular time can be called the *company opportunity set.* The marketer's main technical contribution is to evaluate the *sales potential* of each opportunity. Who would buy the product? How much would they pay? What would be the optimal features? How many would buy? Where are they located? Who will the competition be? What distribution channels would be needed? These and other questions would be researched to estimate the sales potential. Financial and manufacturing executives would add their estimates of costs for a final evaluation of each opportunity.

Target Market Selection

Each market opportunity that looks good would have to be analyzed more closely from the point of view of how to enter that market. Each market is filled with many more customer groups and customer needs than one company can possibly serve, or serve in a superior fashion. The task calls for *market segmentation,* that is, breaking the total market into logical market segments (also called submarkets) that differ in their requirements, buying habits, or other critical characteristics. Once a useful segmentation approach is developed, the company can consider what part of the market it wants to serve.

A useful approach to segmentation is to develop a *product/market grid.* Possible products (or customer needs) can be shown in the rows and market segments (or customer groups) in the columns. Consider the following situation. A large equipment manufacturer has reviewed a set of opportunities and finds the idea of entering the boating industry to be attractive in terms of sales potential and company fit. The marketing vice president undertakes to examine in depth the product/market structure of the boating industry. The result is shown in Figure 4–9. The product/market consists of three distinguishable types of boats (shown in the rows) and three distinguishable customer markets (shown in the columns). The marketing vice president now proceeds to estimate, for each of the nine segments, the degree of market attractiveness and the company's degree of business strength, using the factors cited earlier on page 78. Suppose the segment that looks best is the "small lake speedboat" segment that is shaded in Figure 4–9.

Even this market segment may be larger than the company can serve, in which case *subsegmentation* is warranted. Figure 4–10 shows a subsegmentation of the "small lake speedboat" segment by geographical areas and family incomes. Suppose the company reviews each subsegment and decides that its best opportunity lies in designing and selling speedboats to families with incomes from $20,000 to $35,000 who live near small lakes in the Midwest. The company has now arrived at a clear idea of its *target market.*

This target market may constitute the total ambition of the company or may be viewed as a launching pad for later invasions of the larger market. In

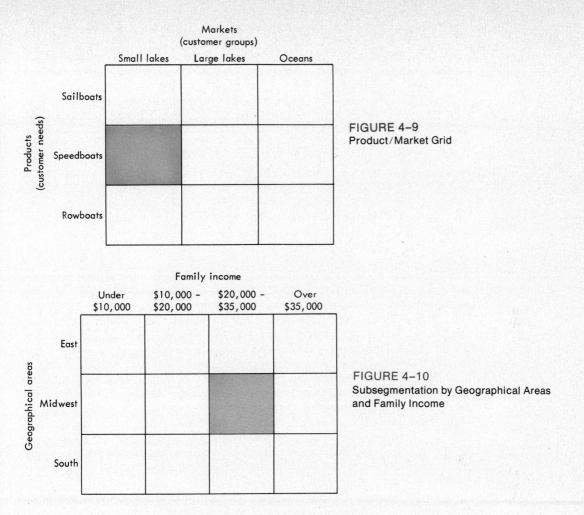

FIGURE 4–9
Product/Market Grid

FIGURE 4–10
Subsegmentation by Geographical Areas
and Family Income

fact, companies have been observed to entertain one of five *market-coverage strategies,* shown in Figure 4–11. In the first, called *product/market concentration,* a company niches itself in one part of the market. Usually smaller companies choose this pattern of market coverage. In the second, *product specialization,* a company decides to produce a full line of speedboats for all customer groups. In the third, *market specialization,* a company decides to make a full line of boats that serve the sundry needs of boaters on small lakes. In the fourth, *selective specialization,* a company enters multiple niches that have no relation to each other except that each provides an individually attractive opportunity. This pattern is usually the end result of an opportunistic acquisition program. The last strategy, *full coverage,* is typically undertaken by larger companies that seek market leadership. In general, a company might initially enter the most attractive market segment and spread out systematically as opportunities arise.

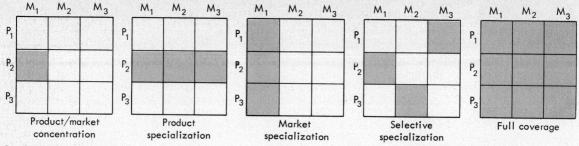

P = Product   M = Market

SOURCE: Adapted from Derek F. Abell, *Defining the Business: The Starting Point of Strategic Planning* (Englewood Cliffs, N.J.: Prentice-Hall, Inc., forthcoming, 1980), Chapter 8, pp. 13–17.

FIGURE 4–11
Five Patterns of Market Coverage

Competitive Positioning

The third step in the strategic marketing process is called *competitive positioning* and requires the firm to develop *a general idea of what kind of offer to make to the target market in relation to competitors' offers.*[18] Recall that the boat company decided to produce speedboats for medium-income people living near small lakes. The company should now make an effort to learn what competitors are offering to customers in this market and what customers really want. On the basis of the findings, the company is ready to choose a competitive positioning.

Suppose the company learns that boat buyers look at boat size and boat complexity as two product attributes of interest. The company can ask prospective customers and dealers where they perceive competitors' boats to be located along these dimensions, and the results can be plotted in the *product space map* shown in Figure 4–12. Competitor A is seen as producing large/complex boats, B, medium-size/medium-complex boats, C, medium-size/simple boats, and D, small/simple boats.[19] The areas of the circles are proportional to the competitors' sales.

Given these competitor positions, what position should the new manufacturer seek? The company has two basic choices. One is to take a position next to one of the existing competitors and fight for the customers who want that type of boat. The company might choose to do this if it feels that (1) it can build a better boat of this type, (2) the market buying this kind of boat is large enough for two competitors, (3) it has more resources than the existing competitor, and/or (4) this position is the most consistent with the company's reputation and competence.

The other choice is to develop a boat that is not currently offered to this

---

[18] Other terms that will be used interchangeably with competitive positioning are *market positioning* and *product positioning*. Market positioning suggests defining where the company and competitors stand in relation to market needs or attributes within the target market. Product positioning suggests defining where existing products of the company and/or competitors stand in terms of product attributes.

[19] These maps must be interpreted with care. Not all customers share the same perceptions. The map shows the average perception. Attention should also be paid to the scatter of perceptions. See chap. 13, pp. 322–23.

market, such as a small complex boat (see empty northwest quadrant of Figure 4–12). The company would gain instant leadership in this part of the market since competitors are not offering this type of boat. But before making this decision, the company has to be sure that (1) it is technically feasible to build a small complex speedboat, (2) it is economically feasible to build a small complex speedboat at the planned price level, and (3) there are a sufficient number of buyers who would prefer a small complex speedboat to any other kind. If the answers are all positive, the firm has discovered a "hole" in the market and should quickly move to fill it.

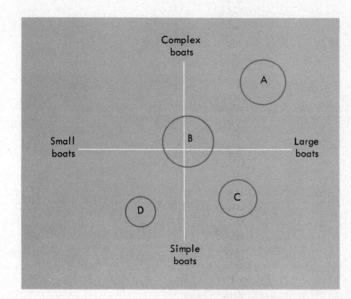

FIGURE 4–12
A Product Space Map Showing
Perceived Offers of Four Competitors

Suppose, however, the company decides there is more profit potential and less risk in building a large complex boat to compete with competitor A. In this case, the company would study A's boat and other aspects of A's offer, seeking a way to differentiate its offer in the eyes of potential buyers. Instead of competitive positioning through product-feature differentiation, it might seek competitive positioning through price/quality differentiation. In this case, the company faces the nine options shown in Figure 4–13. If competitor A, for example, is producing an average-quality boat and charging an average price, the new company could consider introducing a high-quality boat selling at a higher price (called a premium strategy). Or it can give careful consideration to one of the other strategies in Figure 4–13.

Two further factors affect the decision on target market and competitive position. The first is how the firm will acquire the resources to enter the boating industry. The company can proceed through acquisition, internal development, or collaboration with other companies.

Acquisition of an existing product or company is the easiest and quickest way to enter a new market. Acquisition obviates the costly and time-consuming process of attempting to build up internally the knowledge, resources, and repu-

tation necessary to become an effective participant in that part of the market.
The following conditions would favor acquisition:

1. The acquiring company has very little knowledge of the industry.
2. There is a strong advantage in entering the new market as soon as possible.
3. The company would face several barriers to entry through internal development,
   such as patents, substantial economies of scale, closed or difficult-to-enter channels of distribution, costly advertising requirements, or lack of raw materials or
   other supplies.

Product quality	Price High	Price Medium	Price Low
High	1. Premium strategy	2. Penetration strategy	3. Superbargain strategy
Medium	4. Overpricing strategy	5. Average-quality strategy	6. Bargain strategy
Low	7. Hit-and-run strategy	8. Shoddy-goods strategy	9. Cheap-goods strategy

FIGURE 4–13
Nine Competitive
Positioning Strategies
on Price/Quality

Some companies prefer to achieve most of their growth through *internal
development.* They may feel that true leadership is achieved by innovation.
They may feel that acquiring a company will raise the brows of antitrust people.
They may feel that acquirable companies are not very good or are asking for too
much. Or there may be no companies to acquire.

Entry into a new market or market segment may also be accomplished by
collaboration with others to jointly exploit the new opportunity. A major advantage is that the risk is shared, and therefore reduced, for each of the participating companies. Another advantage may be that each company brings specific
skills or resources, the lack of which makes it impossible for either company to
venture by itself. In the best joint-venturing combinations, there is not only com-
plementarity but synergy.

In addition to mode of entry, there is the question of timing. Just because a
company has spotted a good opportunity does not mean it should immediately

move in. It may lose by moving in too soon or too late. Is the nation headed for recession or prosperity? Is the major competitor back-ordered or hungry for business? These and other questions must be considered in determining the best moment to strike.

Marketing Systems Development

Once the company has chosen a target market and defined its competitive position, it is ready to undertake *marketing systems development. Marketing systems development is the task of developing a marketing organization, information system, planning system, and control system that promises to accomplish the company's objectives in the target market.*

Returning to our illustration, the company must establish a new SBU to take responsibility for the boating venture. The first step should be a marketing department, consisting of a divisional vice president of marketing, a sales force, and one or more staff members handling marketing research, promotion, customer service, and marketing planning. The size of the marketing organization will be small initially but will grow over time.

The SBU will need an information system to process inquiries and orders, gather marketing intelligence, forecast market and sales potential, survey buyers and dealers, and analyze sales and profits results. The information will have to be current, accurate, relevant, and comprehensive if the company is going to outperform competitors in meeting customer needs. The SBU will need a planning system that will lead to the annual development of goals, strategies, and tactics and their review and approval by higher levels of management. The overall sales goals will have to be broken down into quotas for sales territories and individual salespersons. The marketing budget will have to be allocated to various marketing-mix elements and territories.

Finally, the SBU will need to establish a system of controls to monitor performance, detect problems, improve efficiency, and take corrective actions when needed. The controls will have to address major questions, such as whether the business unit is going after the right market with the right marketing mix, as well as smaller questions, such as whether the sales force is using its time optimally and whether the advertising money is being spent efficiently.

Marketing Plan Development

The key to the SBUs success will lie in the quality of the long-range and annual marketing plans developed for the target market. A marketing plan is a written document that spells out the goals, strategies, and tactics that will be used to gain and maintain the competitive position and results that the company is seeking. The major elements of a marketing plan are as follows:

Situation analysis   A marketing plan begins with a summary of recent performance followed by a presentation of trends and issues connected with the macro-environment, competitors, customers, suppliers, distributors, and other parties. Major problems and opportunities are laid out, and strategic alternatives are posed and evaluated.

Marketing objectives and goals   This section states the major marketing objectives for the coming period and translates them into goals that are achievable and measurable. The overall sales goal is allocated to the sales units of the company, such as sales regions, sales districts, and finally individual salespersons. In

87

this form the goals are called sales quotas and are based on the past performance and estimated potential facing each of these units.

Marketing strategy, action program, and budget. To achieve the marketing objectives and goals, the SBU must develop a sound marketing strategy and action program. Rough strategic ideas were presumably established earlier in the competitive positioning decision. In the marketing-planning stage, the actual marketing strategy must be worked out in detail. We will define a marketing strategy as follows:

> **Marketing strategy** is a set of objectives, policies, and rules that guides over time the firm's marketing effort—its level, mix, and allocation—partly independently and partly in response to changing environmental and competitive conditions.

Here we will look more closely at the three elements of marketing strategy: marketing expenditure level, marketing mix, and marketing allocation.

MARKETING EXPENDITURE LEVEL   Management has to make a decision on what scale of marketing effort will be needed to achieve its goals. Companies typically establish their marketing budget at some conventional percentage of the sales goal. For example, a perfume company might set its marketing budget at about 35 percent of sales and a fertilizer company at 15 percent of sales. Companies entering a new market are especially interested in learning what the marketing *budget-to-sales ratio* is in the typical company. A particular company may spend more than the normal ratio in the hope of achieving a higher market share. Ultimately, the company should analyze the marketing work that has to be done to attain a given sales volume or market share and then price this work; the result is the required marketing budget.

MARKETING MIX   The company has to decide how to allocate the total marketing budget for a product to the various marketing-mix elements. Marketing mix is one of the key concepts in modern marketing theory.

> **Marketing mix** is the set of controllable variables and their levels that the firm uses to influence the target market.

Any variable under the control of the firm that can influence the level of customer response is a marketing-mix variable. Commodity firms usually assume that their marketing mix is narrow, consisting primarily of price and service. Other firms see dozens of controllable elements that might affect customer response. Various attempts have been made to develop a list of basic marketing variables. McCarthy popularized a four-factor classification called the four *P*s: *product, place, promotion,* and *price.*[20] A list of the particular marketing variables under each *P* is provided in Table 4–3.

[20] E. Jerome McCarthy, *Basic Marketing: A Managerial Approach,* 6th ed. (Homewood, Ill.: Richard D. Irwin, 1978), p. 39 (1st ed., 1960). Two alternative classifications are worth noting. Frey proposed that all marketing-decision variables could be divided into two factors: (1) *the offering* (product, packaging, brand, price, and service), and (2) *methods and tools* (distribution channels, personal selling, advertising, sales promotion, and publicity). See Albert W. Frey, *Advertising,* 3rd ed. (New York: Ronald Press, 1961), p. 30. Lazer and Kelley proposed a three-factor classification: (1) *goods and service mix,* (2) *distribution mix,* and (3) *communications mix.* See William Lazer and Eugene J. Kelley, *Managerial Marketing: Perspectives and Viewpoints,* rev. ed. (Homewood, Ill.: Richard D. Irwin, 1962), p. 413.

TABLE 4–3 Elaboration of the "Four *Ps*"			
PRODUCT	PLACE	PROMOTION	PRICE
Quality	Channels	Advertising	List price
Features	Coverage	Personal selling	Discounts
Options	Locations	Sales promotion	Allowances
Style	Inventory	Publicity	Payment period
Brand name	Transport		Credit terms
Packaging			
Sizes			
Services			
Warranties			
Returns			

The company's marketing mix at time t for a particular product can be conveniently represented by the vector:

$$(P, A, D, E)_t$$

where:

P = price
A = promotion (advertising)
D = place (distribution)
E = product (product-effectiveness rating, with 1.00 = average)

If the firm decides to produce a boat priced at $3,000, supporting it with advertising expenditures of $20,000 per month and distribution expenditures of $30,000 per month, and the product's quality is rated at 1.20, the company's marketing mix at time t is:

$$(\$3,000, \$20,000, \$30,000, 1.20)_t$$

One can readily see that a marketing mix is selected from a great number of possibilities. If the product's price is constrained to lie between $3,000 and $4,000 (to the nearest $100), its advertising and its distribution expenditures are constrained to lie between $10,000 and $50,000 (to the nearest $10,000) each, and its product quality can take on one of two values, then 550 (11 x 5 x 5 x 2) marketing-mix combinations are possible.

It should also be recognized that marketing-decision variables are not all adjustable in the short run. The firm can typically change its price, increase the size of its sales force, and raise its advertising expenditures in the short run. It can only develop new products and modify its marketing channels in the long run. Thus, the firm typically makes fewer period-to-period marketing-mix changes in the short run than the number of marketing-mix variables suggest.

Marketing staff members will have different opinions on how incremental marketing funds should be used. The sales manager would like to hire another salesperson; the advertising manager would like to buy another ad; the product manager would like to improve product quality or packaging; and the marketing research manager would like to carry out a deeper study of the market. In principle, the decision should be based on estimates of the net marginal revenue produced by alternative marketing investments. In practice, much debate will occur over the estimates of the net marginal revenues.

MARKETING ALLOCATION   In addition to determining the level and mix of marketing effort, management must determine how to allocate marketing resources among its products, customer segments, and sales areas. Typically, the company allocates a higher proportion of its marketing resources to those entities that are larger and/or have more unrealized market potential. In other words, it is looking for the highest return when allocating marketing funds to different uses.

We can represent a distinct allocation in the following way: Suppose management sets a price of $3,000, a monthly advertising budget of $5,000, a monthly distribution budget of $10,000, and a product quality of 1.00 for product i selling to customer type j in area k at time t. This is represented by the vector:

$$(\$3,000, \$5,000, \$10,000, 1.00)_{i,j,k,t}$$

Plan Implementation and Control

A plan is nothing "unless it *degenerates into work.*"[21] The goals and tasks must be assigned to specific persons to accomplish within specific time periods. Those responsible must accept them and be motivated to achieve them. Implementation requires good and continuous communication up and down the management ladder as well as across.

Control requires that each manager knows what to watch. The district sales manager examines the sales volumes and expenses of each sales representative against individual quotas and budgets. The manager gets on the phone and asks questions of the sales representatives who are lagging behind. The approach is constructive rather than critical, trying to pinpoint the trouble and determine how it can be corrected. In the meantime the regional sales manager scans the actual sales of this district sales manager and the other district sales managers, getting on the phone when noting deviations from quotas. The president of the company watches total sales and calls in the sales vice president when the sales are off.

This aspect of control is called *annual-plan control.* Management also exercises *profitability control* by examining the profitability of its various products, markets, territories, and marketing channels. It exercises *efficiency control* by looking for ways to improve the impact of its marketing expenditures. Finally, there is the major issue of *strategic control,* that is, the question of whether the company's products, resources, and objectives are properly matched to the right markets. In times of rapid change, a company's marketing strategy rapidly becomes obsolete. A marketing auditor might be called in to evaluate the question of strategic control.

[21] Drucker, *op. cit.,* p. 128.

SUMMARY

Management is the entrepreneurial agent that interprets market needs and translates them into meaningful products and services. To do so, management goes through a strategic management process and a strategic marketing process. The strategic management process consists of the steps taken at the corporate and divisional levels to develop long-run strategies for survival and growth. This process provides the context for the strategic marketing process, which consists of the steps taken at the product and market level to develop viable marketing positions and programs.

The strategic management process consists of defining the company's purpose, objectives, growth strategies, and portfolio plans. A clear statement of company purpose provides employees with a shared sense of opportunity, direction, significance, and achievement. It should define the company's business domain, preferably in market-oriented terms.

Strategic management then calls for developing a set of objectives, such as growth in sales and market share, profitability, and innovation to support the company purpose. These objectives should be hierarchical, quantitative, realistic, and consistent.

To achieve growth, the company must identify market opportunities where it would enjoy a differential advantage over competitors. The company can generate relevant opportunities by considering intensive growth opportunities within its present product-market scope (such as market penetration, market development, and product development), then considering integrative growth opportunities within its task-marketing system (such as backward, forward, and horizontal integration), and finally considering diversification growth opportunities outside of its task-marketing system (such as concentric, horizontal, and conglomerate diversification).

Finally, strategic management must define, for each strategic business unit (SBU) in the company's portfolio, whether that SBU will be built, maintained, harvested, or terminated.

Within this context, the strategic marketing process can be enacted. The first task consists of generating, evaluating, and recommending market opportunities. For any sound opportunity, the next step is to examine the product/market structure and identify the best target market. The third step is to decide on the best competitive position for the company within that target market, as well as the best mode of entry and timing. The fourth step calls for designing a marketing organization, information system, planning system, and control system to operate within that market. The fifth step calls for developing long-range and annual marketing plans that specify sales goals, marketing expenditures, marketing mix, and marketing allocation. The final step calls for implementing and controlling the marketing plan so that the marketing objectives are achieved. In addition to annual-plan control, management must carry out profitability, efficiency, and strategic control.

QUESTIONS AND PROBLEMS

1. Develop a market-oriented definition of the business domain of computer equipment manufacturers.

2. An automotive parts manufacturer produces three products: mufflers, filters, and silencers. The company is seeking new growth opportunities. Develop a product-market matrix showing some potential expansion opportunities for this manufacturer.

3. What is the major distinctive competence of (a) Sears; (b) Polaroid Company; (c) Procter & Gamble; (d) Ford Foundation?

4. Develop some propositions of the form "if . . . then" indicating whether a company should pursue an intensive, integrative, or diversification strategy.

5. Develop expansions of the business domains for each of the following types of organizations: (a) ballpoint pen company; (b) wristwatch manufacturer; (c) local swimming pool.

6. What kind of diversification growth strategy is illustrated by: (a) General Foods' acquisition of Burger Chef, a fast-food service chain; (b) Philip Morris' acquisition of Miller Brewing Company; (c) Mobil Oil's acquisition of Montgomery Ward?

7. The Kraftco Corporation states that it is seeking to provide a *quality* product that will *maximize customer satisfaction,* provide an *adequate return,* and increase the company's total *market share.* Is this a helpful statement of objectives that will help resolve major marketing issues facing the company?

8. A local high school has operated a night school program with only marginal success for several years. Due to a recent tax referendum, the school board has decided it must either significantly increase night school enrollments or cancel the entire program. Suggest a statement of purpose for the night school program and a hierarchy of objectives based upon the intention to increase enrollments.

9. Develop a list of specific growth strategies (in each of the opportunity categories under intensive, integrative, and diversification growth) for a medium-sized stapler manufacturing company.

10. An industrial equipment company consists of five strategic business units (SBUs), as shown below. Using the Boston Consulting Group portfolio analysis, determine whether the company is in a healthy condition. What future strategies should it consider?

SBU	DOLLAR SALES (IN MILLIONS)	NUMBER OF COMPETITORS	DOLLAR SALES OF THE TOP 3 (IN MILLIONS)	MARKET GROWTH RATE
A	.5	8	.7, .7, .5	15%
B	1.6	22	1.6, 1.6, 1.0	18%
C	1.8	14	1.8, 1.2, 1.0	7%
D	3.2	5	3.2, .8, .7	4%
E	.5	10	2.5, 1.8, 1.7	4%

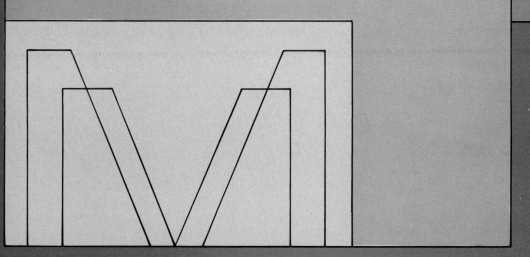

Analyzing Marketing Opportunities

2

THE MARKETING ENVIRONMENT

> *We are all continually faced with a series of great opportunities brilliantly disguised as insoluble problems.*
> JOHN W. GARDNER

5

Marketing planning begins with the analysis of marketing opportunities. The job of spotting and evaluating marketing opportunities breaks down into a logical sequence of questions:

1. What are the main environmental trends, opportunities, and threats facing the industry and the firm? *(Environmental analysis)*
2. What are the major operating characteristics of each basic type of market? *(Market analysis)*
3. How do buyers buy in this market? *(Buyer behavior analysis)*
4. What are the major segments making up this market? *(Market segmentation analysis)*
5. What is the current and future size of this market? *(Demand measurement and forecasting)*

This chapter takes up environmental analysis, and the following four chapters will deal with the remaining topics.

Modern marketing theory holds that the key to an organization's success is the ability to make timely and appropriate adaptations to a complex and ever-changing environment. *The marketing environment is the totality of forces and institutions that are external and potentially relevant to the firm.* We saw in

Chapter 3 that the marketing environment surrounding a firm consists of four levels: (1) the *task environment*, consisting of the institutions that help the organization carry out its major task, such as suppliers, distributors, and final buyers; (2) the *competitive environment*, consisting of the institutions that compete with the organization for customers and scarce resources; (3) the *public environment*, consisting of institutions that watch or regulate the activities of the organization, and (4) the *macroenvironment*, consisting of the major societal forces that shape the character of business opportunities and threats. This chapter will examine the major trends in the macroenvironment that affect marketing, leaving the more immediate environments of the organization to be analyzed elsewhere. The major components of the macroenvironment are demography, economics, natural resources, technology, politics, and culture.

ORGANIZATION / ENVIRONMENT ADAPTATION

A major fact about the macroenvironment is that it does not stand still. The decade of the 1970s, for example, was marked in different periods by shortages, runaway inflation, and high unemployment. It was also marked by various movements, such as consumerism, environmentalism, and women's liberation.

No firm can afford to ignore the changing times. An organization's performance in the marketplace is a matter of the degree of alignment between the *organization's environmental opportunities, objectives, marketing strategy, organizational structure,* and *management systems*. In the ideal case,

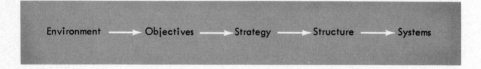

This says that the organization first studies the environment in which it is operating and specifically the opportunities and threats in this environment. It then develops a set of objectives describing what it wants to achieve in this environment. Then it formulates a corporate strategy that promises to achieve the corporate objectives. It then builds an organizational structure that is capable of carrying out the corporate strategy. Finally, it designs various systems of analysis, planning, and control to support the effective implementation of the strategy by the organization.

In practice, various things happen to prevent this ideal from being realized. The main problem is that these various components alter at different rates, resulting in a lack of optimal alignment. A typical situation is:

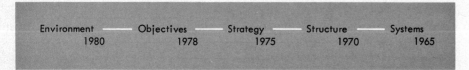

This says that the company is operating in a 1980 environment but with objectives that were set in 1978 for the environment at that time. Its strategy lags even more, having been the strategy that was successful in 1975. Its organizational structure is not even geared to supporting its strategy, having been designed almost ten years earlier in a quite different environment. Finally, its systems were developed many years ago and have not been adjusted to the new conditions.

Too often, in fact, organizations are run in a reverse (and perverse) way of thinking:

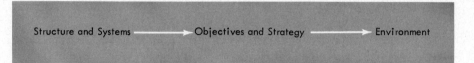

Structure and Systems ⟶ Objectives and Strategy ⟶ Environment

The organization believes that its structure and systems are sound because they worked during the firm's most successful years. Using these, it chooses objectives and strategies that are manageable under the present systems and structure. Then it scans the environment to find the opportunities that are best suited to its objectives and strategy.

> An example would be a hospital that primarily serves tuberculosis patients. Its organization, staffing, and systems are maximally adapted to providing health care to this type of patient. As a result, it sets its objectives in terms of attracting a certain number of tubercular patients and its strategy as one of appealing to patients who are self-paying and want quality care. Then it searches the environment broadly for this type of patient. The irony is, however, there are fewer such patients around thanks to various miracle drugs.

This is an example of bureaucratic thinking at its worst. The organization has set up a very *efficient* machine, but not an effective machine. Peter Drucker made the observation long ago that it is more important to do the *right thing* than to do *things right*.

The main problem is that the environment is the fastest changing element in the picture. Progressive companies are not even satisfied to bring the various elements into alignment in the current year. Instead, a company like IBM or Xerox will attempt to forecast what their business environment will be like in (say) 1985. Given this 1985 environmental forecast, they will set objectives that describe where they want to be in 1985. They will then formulate a strategy that will deliver these objectives by 1985. They will begin to alter the organization and its systems so that these will support the new strategy, rather than act as a drag on its fulfillment. This forward-looking thinking is summarized below:

Environment ⟶ Objectives ⟶ Strategy ⟶ Structure ⟶ Systems
1985   1985   1985   1985   1985

Environmental Change

A successful organization is one that has found a useful niche within the larger environment where it produces and receives value. The part of the environment it occupies is called its *habitat*. The various institutions and forces that support the organization in its habitat constitute its *ecosystem*.

> The auto industry is central to a vast *business ecosystem* consisting of rubber, glass, and steel plants, petroleum refineries, gasoline stations, superhighways, the economy of Detroit, and the incomes of millions of people.

As long as the institutions and forces in the ecosystem remain in balance, the ecosystem will persist from year to year without major change.

We can distinguish between the degrees of stability of an environment. The first is a *stable environment*, in which the major forces of economics, technology, law, and culture remain stable from year to year. The second is a *slowly evolving environment*, in which smooth and fairly predictable changes take place. The individual firm survives in this type of environment to the extent that it foresees change *and* takes intelligent steps to adapt. The third is a *turbulent environment*, in which major and unpredictable changes occur often.[1]

> Sudden changes in fuel availability, auto technology, or safety legislation can threaten auto manufacturers and the character of the auto ecosystem itself. Suppose a company develops an efficient electric automobile. The petroleum industry and the familiar gas station would be threatened with near extinction. Used car dealers would panic. Industries selling major consumer durables such as boats, small planes, and kitchen appliances would see their sales slow down. Such a major innovation, through its "creative destruction" of the present ecosystem, would pose a tremendous threat to many and a tremendous opportunity to others.

There is increasing evidence that more and more firms are finding themselves operating in turbulent environments. In his *Future Shock*, Toffler documents how key technological, economic, and social forces show an "accelerative thrust." One study shows that the average span between introduction and peak production of appliances introduced in the United States before 1920 was thirty-four years; for a group of appliances that appeared between 1939 and 1959, the span was only eight years. Many products that have appeared since 1959 have had even shorter spans.[2] Other forces, such as consumer life styles and government legislation, also show an accelerative thrust.

The firm operating in a turbulent environment has three tasks: (1) systematically scanning its environment, (2) identifying environmental threats and opportunities, and (3) making intelligent adaptations to the changing environment.

Environmental Scanning

The more energy a firm devotes to broad environmental scanning, the greater its capacity to survive. Environmental scanning calls for identifying the major environmental areas of interest to management, assigning responsibility for each area, and developing efficient systems for collecting and disseminating the information.

---

[1] For a useful discussion of types of environment and their implications, see F. E. Emery and E. L. Trist, "The Causal Texture of Organizational Environments," *Human Relations*, February 1965, pp. 21–32.

[2] See Alvin Toffler, *Future Shock* (New York: Bantam Books, 1970), p. 28.

> An automobile company will have a high interest in monitoring congressional thinking, among other things. It will hire one or more intelligence officers, locate them in a Washington office, and give them a budget for initiating and maintaining contacts with knowledgeable people. These officers will assemble information and relay the highlights to the company decision makers for whom they are relevant.

Opportunity and Threat Analysis

Within the large amount of information flowing into the firm, management must be able to spot the *environmental forces* that have the greatest import for future marketing strategy. They can be classified as either threats or opportunities facing the firm. We define an *environmental threat* as follows:

> An *environmental threat* is a challenge posed by an unfavorable trend or specific disturbance in the environment that would lead, in the absence of purposeful marketing action, to the stagnation or demise of a company, product, or brand.

A major threat is one that (1) would cause substantial damage to profits if it became a reality and (2) has a moderate to high probability of occurring. No company is free of such threats, and every manager should be able to identify several such threats.

> An automobile executive would readily identify the following threats: (1) successful development of an efficient electric car by a competitor, (2) growing preference for foreign-made cars by American consumers, (3) growing preference for mass transportation or for bicycles and motorcycles, and (4) a sudden and lasting fuel shortage.

A business facing several major threats is highly vulnerable. Its management should prepare contingency plans and give serious thought to diversification moves.

We define a *company marketing opportunity* as follows:

> A *company marketing opportunity* is an attractive arena of relevant marketing action in which a particular company is likely to enjoy a differential advantage.

A major company marketing opportunity is one that (1) has a high dollar potential for the firm and (2) a moderate-to-high probability that the firm would have success with it.

> Among the major marketing opportunities facing an auto company are: (1) developing an extremely fuel efficient small car, (2) developing a successful electric car, or (3) developing a successful mass-transportation vehicle.

To the extent that there are strong opportunities facing that business, we simply say that the business faces high opportunity.

An important exercise for the management of any company is to periodically identify the major threats and opportunities facing the company and each of its business units (divisions, product lines, and products). This is best done when management is preparing its annual or long-range marketing plans. Each threat and opportunity is assigned a number and then evaluated according to its probable level of impact and occurrence. The threats and opportunities can then be plotted in the threat and opportunity matrices shown in Figure 5–1.

The threat matrix shows seven identifiable threats. Management should give the greatest attention to threats 1 and 2 because they would have a high impact on the company and have a high probability of occurrence. Threat 3 can also substantially hurt the company but it has a low probability of occurrence; and threat 4 would not hurt much but is highly likely to occur. Management can safely ignore minor threats 5, 6, and 7.

Probability of occurrence   Probability of success

	High	Low				High	Low
High	1 2	3		High		8	9
Low	4	6 5 7		Low		10 11	12 13

Level of impact (threat)   Level of impact (opportunity)

(a) Threat matrix   (b) Opportunity matrix

FIGURE 5–1

Threat and Opportunity Matrices

The opportunity matrix shows six identifiable opportunities. The best is opportunity 8 which would have a high positive impact if the company is successful at developing this opportunity, and the company is highly likely to be successful. Opportunity 9 is an attractive opportunity but the company may not have the resources or competence to succeed in this opportunity. Opportunities 10 and 11 are minor in their impact although easy to carry off successfully. Opportunities 12 and 13 can be ignored.

Considering the two matrices together, this business unit faces two major threats and one major opportunity. This makes it a somewhat speculative business: it is high on opportunity and high on risk. In fact, four outcomes are possible with this analysis. They are shown in the opportunity-threat matrix in Figure 5–2. An *ideal business* is one which is high in major opportunities and low or devoid of major threats. A *speculative business* is high in both major op-

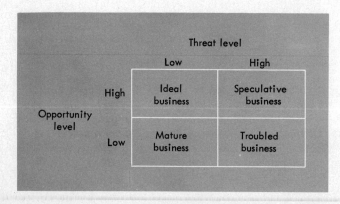

Threat level

	Low	High
High	Ideal business	Speculative business
Low	Mature business	Troubled business

Opportunity level

FIGURE 5–2

Opportunity-Threat Matrix

portunities and threats. A *mature business* is low in major opportunities and threats. Finally, a *troubled business* is low in opportunities and high in threats.

Organizational Response
Each business unit can seek to better its situation by moving toward its major opportunities and away from its major threats. With respect to opportunities, the firm must carefully appraise their quality. There is a whole profession of "futurologists" who conjure up wonderful products and services the public needs. Levitt has cautioned business men to judge opportunities carefully:

> There can be a need, but no market; or a market, but no customer; or a customer, but no salesman. For instance, there is a great need for massive pollution control, but not really a market at present. And there is a market for new technology in education, but no customer really large enough to buy the products. Market forecasters who fail to understand these concepts have made spectacular miscalculations about the apparent opportunities in these and other fields, such as housing and leisure products.[3]

Even in pursuing a marketing opportunity, the firm can control its level of risk taking. The firm might make a *token investment* in marketing research and R&D just to keep up, without getting sidetracked from its main business. Or it might make a *moderate investment* in the hope of becoming one of the leaders. Or it might make a *substantial investment* in the hope of becoming the leader, although this may involve great risk to its present business.

In facing a major threat, the firm has three modes of adaptation available:

1. *Opposition.* The firm can try to fight, restrain, or reverse the unfavorable development. Opposition may be used to "buy" the time needed to make more fundamental adjustments.
2. *Modification.* The firm can try to improve its environmental fit through changing its customer mix or marketing mix.
3. *Relocation.* The firm can decide to shift to another market in which it can produce more value.

The key implication for company marketing strategy in a turbulent environment is that the company must invest more to keep abreast of significant social changes and be prepared to adapt faster than before. It must not stick to the tried-and-true after this has become dysfunctional. It must not become a bundle of obsolete responses. It must be prepared to adapt creatively to the changing environment.

ENVIRONMENTAL FORECASTING

We saw that the key to organizational survival and growth is the firm's ability to adapt its strategies and organization to a rapidly changing environment. This puts a big burden on the firm of correctly anticipating the character of the future environment. The price can be enormous when a mistake is made. For example, Montgomery Ward lost its leadership in the chain-store retailing field after the Second World War because its chairman, Sewell Avery, bet on a stag-

[3] Theodore Levitt, "The New Markets—Think Before You Leap," *Harvard Business Review*, May–June 1969, pp. 53–67, especially pp. 53–54.

nant economy, while its major competitor, Sears, bet on an expanding economy. Major investments in products, markets, and marketing channels ride on the management's strategic judgments about the future environment. That is why a growing number of companies are getting into formal *environmental forecasting.*

Strategic planning has to begin with an environmental forecast that identifies the most important and likely developments for several years to come. Since any long-run forecast is tentative, the environmental forecast has to be revised at least once each year to bring in new factors.

No one disputes that environmental forecasting is still more art than science. While there has been some progress in the methodologies for forecasting economic and technological developments, there has been little progress in the reliable forecasting of political and cultural developments. These latter factors interact so much with the former factors that forecasts can be much in error. Some people even question the whole exercise of long-range forecasting. Our position, however, is that long-range forecasting contributes greatly to the identification of opportunities and the assessment of risks.

How do firms develop their forecasts? Large firms usually operate planning departments that are responsible for developing long-run forecasts of key environmental factors affecting their markets. General Electric, for example, has a large staff of forecasters, who conduct numerous studies of domestic and worldwide forces that are affecting its operations in various parts of the world. It makes its forecasts available to various divisions and also sells certain forecasts to other firms. Few firms, of course, can afford to do their own forecasting at this level of intensity and must find other ways to obtain sound forecasts.

These firms can buy forecasts from several types of suppliers. *Marketing research firms* can be hired to develop a forecast for a particular market through interviewing customers, distributors, and other knowledgeable parties. *Specialized forecasting firms* will produce long-range forecasts of particular macroenvironmental components, such as the economy, the population, natural resources, or technology. Finally, there are *futurist research firms* that produce total future scenarios that are rich in speculation and creative ideas. Among the latter are the Hudson Institute, the Futures Group, and the Institute for the Future.

A variety of methodologies are used in producing long-range forecasts, the following being the key ones.[4]

1. *Expert opinion.* Here knowledgeable people are selected and asked to assign importance and probability rating to various possible future developments. The most refined version, the Delphi method, puts experts through several rounds of event assessment, where they keep refining their assumptions and judgments.
2. *Trend extrapolation.* Here researchers fit best-fitting curves (linear, quadratic, or S-shaped growth curves) through past time series to serve as a basis for extrapolation. This method can be very unreliable in that new developments can completely alter the expected direction of movement.
3. *Trend correlation.* Here researchers correlate various time series in the hope of identifying leading and lagging relationships that can be used for forecasting.
4. *Dynamic modeling.* Here researchers build sets of equations that attempt to de-

[4] James R. Bright and Milton E. F. Schoeman, *A Guide to Practical Technological Forecasting* (Englewood Cliffs, N. J.: Prentice-Hall, 1973).

scribe the underlying system. The coefficients in the equations are fitted through statistical means. Econometric models of more than three hundred equations, for example, are used to forecast changes in the U.S. economy.

5. *Cross-impact analysis.* Here researchers identify a set of key trends (those high in importance and/or probability). The question is then put: "If event A occurs, what will be the impact on all other trends?" The results are then used to build sets of "domino chains," with one event triggering others.

6. *Multiple scenarios.* Here researchers build pictures of alternative futures, each internally consistent and with a certain probability of happening. The major purpose of the scenarios is to stimulate contingency planning.

7. *Demand/hazard forecasting.* Here researchers identify major events that would affect the firm greatly. Each event is rated for its *convergence* with several major trends taking place in society. It is also rated for its *appeal* to each major public in the society. The higher the event's convergence and appeal, the higher its probability of occurring. The highest scoring events are then researched further.

Having considered the nature of environmental threats and opportunities, we will now examine the major components of the marketing environment: demography, economy, natural resources, technology, politics, and culture. These environmental forces exercise a greater impact on the company than the company exercises on them. They constitute the "uncontrollables" to which companies adapt through setting the "controllable" factors, namely the firm's selection of target markets and marketing mixes. We want to examine the main trends in each component and the implications of these trends for marketing strategy.

DEMOGRAPHIC ENVIRONMENT

The first environmental fact of interest to marketers is *population* because people make up markets. Marketers are keenly interested in the size of the world's population—geographical distribution; density; mobility trends; age distribution; birth, marriage, and death rates; and racial, ethnic, and religious structure. We shall review here the major demographic trends and indicate the implications for marketing planning.

Worldwide Explosive Population Growth

Perhaps the major fact about the world population is its "explosive" growth:

In 1650 the population numbered about 0.5 billion, and it was growing at a rate of approximately 0.3 percent per year. That corresponds to a doubling time of nearly 250 years. In 1970 the population totaled 3.6 billion and the rate of growth was 2.1 percent per year. The doubling time at this growth rate is 33 years. Thus, not only has the population been growing exponentially, but the rate of growth has also been growing.[5]

The world population explosion has been a major concern of many governments and groups throughout the world. Two factors underlie this concern. The

[5] Donella H. Meadows, Dennis L. Meadows, Jorgen Randers, and William W. Behrens III, *The Limits to Growth* (New York: New American Library, 1972), p. 41.

first is the possible finiteness of the earth's resources to support this much human life, particularly at levels of living that represent the aspiration of most people. The famous eighteenth-century economist, Thomas Malthus, was concerned in his time about the population explosion. He saw the population growing at a geometric rate, while the world's food supply grew at an arithmetic rate. To him, this spelled unavoidable disaster for mankind. If mankind could not regulate its own rate of growth, then natural and other forces such as famine, disease, and war would intervene to keep population down to the available food supply. The Malthusian specter has been resurrected many times since—most recently in the tour de force called *The Limits to Growth*.[6] This book presents an impressive array of evidence that unchecked population growth and consumption must eventually result in insufficient food supply, depletion of key minerals, overcrowdedness, pollution, and an overall deterioration in the quality of life. One of its strong recommendations is the worldwide *social marketing* of birth control and family planning.[7]

The second cause for concern is that the rate of population growth is not equal everywhere but is highest in the countries and communities that can least afford it. In many developing nations the death rate has been falling as a result of modern medical advances, while the birthrate has remained fairly stable. For these countries to feed, clothe, and educate the children and also provide a rising standard of living for the population is out of the question. Furthermore, the poor families have the most children, and this reinforces the cycle of poverty.

The rate of increase of the world's population has great importance for business. A growing population means growing human needs. It means growing markets, if there is sufficient purchasing power. On the other hand, if the growing population presses too hard against the available food supply and resources, costs will shoot up and possibly profit margins will be depressed.

Slowdown in U.S. Birthrate

In contrast to many countries experiencing a rapid increase in population, the U.S. is undergoing a population slowdown. The U.S. population stood at 216.8 million on July 1, 1977.[8] The birthrate dipped below the "replacement rate" of 2.0 children per family to a record low of 1.8 in 1977. The preschool population declined 11.2 percent between 1970 and 1977. Among the factors contributing to smaller families are (1) desire to improve personal living standards, (2) increasing desire of women to work and enjoy more life outside of the home, (3) improved technology and knowledge of birth control, and (4) increasing concern about the future of civilization on this planet.

The declining birthrate is a threat to some industries, a boon to others. It has produced anxiety attacks in the board rooms of companies involved in children's toys, clothes, furniture, and food. The Gerber Company for years advertised, "Babies are our business—our *only* business," but quietly dropped this slogan a few years ago. It has responded to the shrinking market by trying to introduce baby food in other countries of the world where the birthrate is still

---

[6] Ibid.

[7] See Eduardo L. Roberto, "Social Marketing Strategies for Diffusing the Adoption of Family Planning," *Social Science Quarterly*, June 1972, pp. 33–51.

[8] Most of the statistical data in this chapter, unless otherwise indicated, are found in the *Statistical Abstract of the United States* (Washington, D.C.: Government Printing Office, 1977).

high.[9] Johnson & Johnson has responded by trying to interest grownups in using their baby powder and baby hair shampoo. Abbott Laboratories has added a geriatric food line to complement its line of infant formulas.

Other industries have benefited from the declining birthrate. With fewer children, young couples have more time and income to spend on travel, eating out, and adult recreation, thus contributing to a boom in these industries.

Aging of U.S. Population

Recent generations have benefited from a substantial decline in the death rate thanks to the miracles of modern medicine and greater education in preventative health care. Average life expectancy is now 72.5 years and may reach 74 years by the year 2000. This, coupled with the declining birthrate, has meant an aging of the U.S. population. The median age at the time of the country's founding was 16; now it is about 30; and it should reach 35 by the year 2000.[10]

Different age groups, of course, will grow at different rates. The age group 14 to 24 will shrink about 4 percent in absolute numbers during the coming decade, resulting in a possible weakening in influence of America's youth culture. The decline forebodes sagging sales for motorcycles, baseball and football equipment, denim clothing, records, *Playboy*-type magazines, and other goods for the youth market. It means enrollment declines in American colleges, which are already experiencing overcapacity and having to think about attracting new groups to the campus, such as homemakers and retired people.

Meanwhile the age group 25 to 44 will have the largest spurt in growth, something on the order of 35 percent by 1990. Marketers who sell to this group—furniture makers, vacation planners, tennis and ski equipment manufacturers—have to watch trends in this group's social patterns carefully, particularly such phenomena as falling marriage and rising divorce rates, deferred childbearing, and the two-wage-earning household.

The age group 45 to 64 will shrink slightly until the second half of the 1980s, when it will enter a period of rapid growth. This is the "empty-nester" group, whose children leave home and who find themselves with increased time and income on their hands. This group is a major market for eating out, travel, expensive clothes, and golf and other recreations.

The over-65 group will show the second largest rate of growth in the years ahead, increasing by at least 23 million Americans and perhaps as many as 32 million by the year 2000. This expected increase foretells a burgeoning demand for retirement homes and communities, campers, quieter forms of recreation (fishing, golf), single-portion food packaging, and medical goods and services (medicine, eyeglasses, canes, hearing aids, and convalescent homes). This group also means more conservative politics, demands for new rights by senior citizens to protect their standard of living, and a slowing down in the adoption of new cultural ideas.

The Changing American Family

The American ideal of the two-children, two-car suburban family—which provided great marketing opportunity in the post-World War II period—has been losing some of its luster. There will be fewer families forming (and surviving), and they will show a different orientation. Here are the major forces at work:

[9] See "Gerber: 'Selling More to the Same Mothers Is Our Objective Now'," *Business Week*, October 16, 1978.

[10] See "The Graying of America," *Newsweek*, February 28, 1977, pp. 50–65.

1. *Later marriage.* While 96 percent of all Americans will marry, the average age of first marriage has been rising over the years and now stands at 23.8 years for males and 21.3 years for females. This will slow down the sales of engagement and wedding rings, bridal outfits, and life insurance.

2. *Fewer children.* Couples with no children under 18 now make up 47 percent of all families. The newly married are also delaying childbearing longer. Of those families that have children, the mean number is 1.8, down from 3.5 in 1955.

3. *Higher divorce rate.* America has the world's highest divorce rate, with about 38 percent of marriages ending in divorce. This has created over a million single-parent families and the need for additional housing units. About 79 percent remarry, leading to the phenomenon of the "blended" family. Currently about 72.2 percent of adult males are married and 66.2 percent of adult females.

4. *More working wives.* Today more than 40 percent of all married women with school-age children hold some kind of job. There is less stigma attached to working (in fact, often a stigma is attached to being "just a housewife"), a greater number of job opportunities, and new freedom resulting from birth-control acceptance. These working women constitute a market for better clothing, day nursery services, home cleaning services, and more frozen dinners. The growing number of working women means less viewing of television soap operas and reading of the traditional women's magazines. In families where both husband and wife work, the woman's salary represents 40 percent of the household income and influences the purchase of higher-quality goods and services. Marketers of such things as tires, automobiles, insurance, and travel service have found it necessary to change their advertising messages and media selections so as to reach the increasingly significant working women's market.[11]

The Rise of Nonfamily Households

An important development is the rapid rise in the number of *nonfamily households.* They take several forms, each constituting a different market segment with special needs:

1. *Single-adult households.* Many young adults leave home earlier and move into their own apartments. In addition, many divorced and widowed people live alone. Altogether, more than 15.5 million people live alone. They account for 21 percent of all the households. The SSWD group (single, separated, widowed, divorced) need smaller apartments; inexpensive and smaller appliances, furniture, and furnishings; and food that is packaged in smaller sizes. Their car preferences are different in that they buy half of all Mustangs and other small specialty cars, and only 8 percent of the large cars.[12] Singles are a market for various services that supply opportunities for singles to meet each other, such as singles bars, tours, and cruises.

2. *Two-person cohabitant households.* There may be as many as 3 to 6 million unmarried people living together today, primarily heterosexual couples but homosexual couples as well. Since their arrangements are more temporary, they are a market for inexpensive or rental furniture and furnishings.

3. *Group households.* Fewer in number, group households can nevertheless be found, consisting of three or more persons of the same or opposite sex sharing ex-

---

[11] See Ellen Graham, "Advertisers Take Aim at a Neglected Market: The Working Woman," *Wall Street Journal,* July 5, 1977, p. 1.

[12] See June Kronholz, "A Living-Alone Trend Affects Housing, Cars, and Other Industries," *Wall Street Journal,* November 16, 1977, p. 1.

penses by living together. This pattern is frequently found among college students and also among certain secular and religious groups who live in communes.

Marketers have to pay attention to the special needs and buying habits of these nonfamily households, which are growing more rapidly in number than family households.

Geographical Shifts in Population

Americans are a mobile people, with approximately one out of five, or 42 million Americans, moving each year. Among the major mobility trends are:

1. *Movement of people to the Sunbelt states.* Over the next ten years, the West's population will grow 17 percent and the South's population will grow 14 percent. Major cities in the North, on the other hand, have been losing population between 1970–1975 (New York, 4.7 percent; Pittsburgh, 4.1 percent; Jersey City, 5.8 percent; and Newark, 3.2 percent). These regional population shifts are of special interest to marketers because of marked differences in regional spending patterns and consumer behavior. Consumers in the West, for example, spend relatively less on food and relatively more on automobiles than their counterparts in the Northeast. The exodus to the Sunbelt will lessen the demand for warm clothing and home heating equipment and increase the demand for air conditioning.

2. *Movement from rural to urban areas.* This movement has been going on for over a century. In 1880 approximately 70 percent of the nation's population lived in rural areas; now approximately 70 percent live in urban areas. Cities are characterized by a faster pace of living, more commuting, typically higher incomes, and a greater variety of goods and services than the small towns and rural areas that dot America. The largest cities, such as New York, Chicago, and San Francisco, account for most of the sales of expensive furs, perfumes, luggage, and works of art, and they still boast most of what there is of opera, ballet, and other forms of "high culture." Recently, there has been a slight shift of population back to rural areas on the part of some people who have grown tired of the big city.

3. *Movement from the city to the suburbs.* Many persons have moved far away from their places of work, owing largely to the development of automobiles, major highways, and rapid rail and bus transit. Cities have become surrounded by suburbs, and these suburbs in turn by "exurbs." The U.S. Census Bureau has created a separate population classification for sprawling urban concentrations, called Standard Metropolitan Statistical Areas (SMSA).[13] Over 63 percent of the nation's entire population (and 95 percent of the nation's urban population) are estimated to live in the 212 recognized Standard Metropolitan Statistical Areas, and it is the SMSAs rather than the cities proper that constitute the primary market focus of firms.

   Firms normally distinguish between the city and the suburban segments of the metropolitan areas. About 60 percent of the total metropolitan population now live in suburbs. Suburban areas are frequently marked by a style of living different from that in the cities. Suburbs tend to be characterized by casual, outdoor living, greater neighbor interaction, higher incomes, and younger families. Suburban dwellers are the source of much of the demand for station wagons, home workshop equipment, garden furniture, lawn and gardening tools and supplies, and outdoor cooking equipment. Retailers have recognized the importance of

---

[13] An SMSA consists of the counties of an integrated economic area with a large volume of daily travel and communication between a central city of at least fifty thousand inhabitants and the outlying parts of the area.

convenience and have brought their goods out to the suburbs through the development of branch department stores and suburban shopping centers.

At the same time, marketers should recognize a recent counter movement back to the central city, especially in cities where urban renewal has been successful. Young adults as well as older families whose children have grown up are attracted by the superior cultural and recreational opportunities and less interested in suburban commuting and gardening. This means strong opportunities for new high-rise apartment construction and new retail outlets within the central city.

A Better-Educated Populace
The number of Americans who have attended or graduated from college will reach 44 million by 1985, or 19 percent of the population. This will present both opportunities and challenges to marketers. A greater white-collar and educated work force will mean increased affluence and demand for quality products, books, upscale magazines, and travel. It will also mean a decline in television viewing because educated consumers tend to watch less than the population at large.

The demographic trends stated above are highly reliable for the short and intermediate run. There is little excuse for a company to be suddenly surprised by a demographic development. The alert firm will have plenty of advance notice and can start searching for new-product lines and more attractive markets when it reads the writing on the wall.

ECONOMIC ENVIRONMENT

Markets require not only people but purchasing power. Total purchasing power is a function of current income, prices, savings, and credit availability. The main economic trends that have implications for marketers are described below.

Slowdown in Real-Income Growth
American per capita income stood in 1976 at $6,393 and median household income stood at $12,686. Although per capita income keeps rising in money terms, there has been little or no growth in real terms for the last several years, in contrast to the 1950s and 1960s when real incomes grew substantially and ushered in a period of great affluence and optimism. Real per capita income growth has been hurt by (1) an inflation rate exceeding the money-income growth rate, (2) the hovering of unemployment between 6 and 8 percent, and (3) the increase in the tax burden, which has reduced the disposable-income level. Although mitigated somewhat by the rise in two-income families, most Americans have turned to more cautious buying both in regard to product categories and brands chosen. A survey by *Better Homes and Gardens* indicated that 72 percent of the respondents were buying more store brands to save money.[14] Many companies have introduced economy versions of their products and have turned to price appeals in their advertising messages. As for durable goods purchases, some consumers have postponed their purchase, while others have decided to buy out of fear that

---

[14] Reported in *Grey Matter*, "Private Brands Seek Growth in Faltering Economy," June 1974, p. 1.

prices will be 10 percent higher next year. Many consumers feel that the elements of the good life—a large home, two cars, foreign travel, and private higher education—are now beyond their reach.

Marketers have to pay attention to income differences as well as to average income trends. Income distribution in the U.S. is still pronouncedly skewed. At the top are *wealthy consumers* whose expenditure patterns have not been affected by current events and who are a major market for luxury goods (Rolls Royces starting at $49,000) and services (around-the-world cruises starting at $10,000). There is a comfortable *upper middle class,* who must exercise some expenditure restraint but are able to afford expensive clothes, minor antiques, and a small boat or second home. The *working class* must stick closer to the basics of food, clothing, and shelter, husband their resources, and try hard to save. Finally, there is the *underclass* (persons on welfare and retirees), who have to carefully count their pennies when making purchases of even the most basic kind.

Income levels and growth rates also vary regionally. They are affected by the level of local economic activity and employment, the rate of in- and out-migration, and union wage scales. Marketers have to take geographical income differences into account in planning their marketing effort.

Continued Inflationary Pressure

Although the double-digit inflation of the early seventies has been brought under control, inflation continues to push up the prices of homes, furniture, medical care, and food at rates that many consumers find disheartening. The inflationary pressure is fed by (1) hikes in the price of oil and other natural resources due to real scarcity or cartel price fixing, (2) the lack of competition in certain sectors of the economy, (3) the demands of labor unions for wage increases that exceed productivity gains, (4) the unfavorable balance of foreign trade, which shrinks the value of the dollar and pushes up the prices of foreign goods, (5) rising interest rates that push up costs in an effort to reduce demand, (6) the high expenditures on public services and on nonproductive capital investment, and (7) a psychology of inflationary expectation, which in turn feeds the inflation. Inflation leads consumers to search for opportunities to save money, including buying cheaper brands in larger, economy sizes, buying from less-expensive retail outlets, performing more of their own services, and bartering services with others.

Changing Savings and Debt Pattern

Consumer expenditures are influenced not only by income but also by consumer savings and debt patterns. Eighty-four percent of American spending units hold some liquid assets, the median amount being $800. Americans hold their savings in the form of bank savings accounts, bonds and stocks, real estate, insurance, and other assets. In many cases, the inflation rate has reduced the purchasing power of these savings, but still they constitute a gigantic reservoir of purchasing power to supplement income and are a major source of financing major durable purchases.

Consumers can also expand their purchases through borrowing. In fact, consumer credit has been a major contributor to the rapid growth of the American economy, enabling people to buy more than their incomes and savings permitted, thus creating more jobs and still more income and more demand. In 1978, outstanding consumer credit (including home mortgages) stood at $1 trillion, or $4,600 for every man, woman, and child in America. The cost of credit, however, is also high (with interest rates around 10 percent), and consumers are paying around 21¢ of every dollar they earn to pay off existing debts. This retards the further growth of housing and other durable-goods markets that are heavily dependent on credit.

Changing
Consumer-
Expenditure
Patterns

As people's incomes change, marketers can expect pronounced shifts in the relative demand for different categories of goods and services. The particular types of shifts were stated as early as 1857 by the German statistician Ernst Engel, who compared the budgets of individual working-class families. Engel observed that while rising family income tended to be accompanied by increased spending in all categories, *the percentage spent on food tended to decline, the percentage spent on housing and household operations tended to remain constant, and the percentage spent on other categories (clothing, transportation, recreation, health, and education) and savings tended to increase.* These "laws" have been generally validated in subsequent budget studies. At the same time, a company involved in a particular product category will want to look more closely at how expenditures on this product category varies with income. In the case of food, for example, a higher income, while it may not lead to buying more food, may lead to buying higher-quality food, thus causing food expenditures to remain constant for a while. But in general, as incomes rise, people will spend a higher proportion of their incomes on major durables, luxury goods, and services.

NATURAL ENVIRONMENT

The 1960s produced a growing public concern over whether the natural environment was being irreparably damaged by the industrial activities of modern nations. Kenneth Boulding pointed out that the planet earth was like a spaceship in danger of running out of fuel if it failed to recycle its materials. The Meadows, in *The Limits to Growth,* raised concern about the adequacy of future natural resources to sustain economic growth. Rachel Carson, in *The Silent Spring,* pointed out the environmental damage to water, earth, and air caused by industrial activity of certain kinds. These cries led to the formation of various watchdog groups, such as the Sierra Club and Friends of the Earth, as well as concerned legislators who have proposed various measures to regulate the impact of industrial activity on the natural environment.

Marketers should be aware of the challenges and opportunities created by four particular trends in the natural environment.

Impending
Shortages of
Certain Raw
Materials

The earth's materials fall into three groups: the infinite, the finite renewable, and the finite nonrenewable. *Infinite resources,* such as water and air, pose no immediate problem, although some groups argue that there is too high a level of pollution. Environmental groups lobbied for the banning of aerosol cans because of their potential damage to the ozone layer of air; and they have fought against the pollution of lakes and streams, Lake Erie, for one, by unregulated industrial wastes.

Finite renewable resources, such as forests and food, pose no immediate problem, but perhaps there is one in the long run. Companies in the forestry business are now required to reforest timberlands in order to protect the soil and to insure a sufficient level of wood supply to meet future demand. Food supply can be a major problem in that the amount of arable land is relatively fixed and urban areas are constantly expanding to absorb farmland.

Finite nonrenewable resources, such as oil, coal, and various minerals, do pose a serious problem.

> . . . it would appear at present that the quantities of platinum, gold, zinc, and lead are not sufficient to meet demands . . . silver, tin, and uranium may be in short supply even at higher prices by the turn of the century. By the year 2050, several more minerals may be exhausted if the current rate of consumption continues.[15]

The marketing implications are many. Firms that rely on these minerals face substantial cost increases, even if the materials remain available. They may not find it easy to pass on these cost increases. There is a need to search for substitute minerals. Firms engaged in research and development and exploration have an incredible opportunity to develop valuable new sources and materials.

Increased Cost of Energy

One finite nonrenewable resource, oil, has created the most serious problem for future economic growth. Much of contemporary economic and political history has been shaped by oil politics. The major industrial economies of the world are heavily dependent on oil resources and until substitute forms of energy can be developed on a practical basis, oil will continue to dominate the world political and economic picture. The shortage of oil and its price manipulation have created a frantic search for alternative forms of energy. Coal is once again popular, and companies are searching for practical schemes to harness solar, nuclear, wind, and other forms of energy. In the solar energy field alone, hundreds of firms are putting out first-generation products to harness solar energy for heating homes and other uses.[16] Other firms are searching for ways to make a practical electric automobile, with a prize going to the winners amounting to billions.

Increased Levels of Pollution

Some portion of modern industrial activity will inevitably damage the quality of the natural environment. One has only to think of the disposal of chemical and nuclear wastes, the dangerous mercury levels in the ocean, the quantity of chemical pollutants in the soil and food supply, and the littering of the environment with nonbiodegradable bottles, plastics, and other packaging materials. The public concern constitutes a marketing opportunity in two ways. First, it creates a large market for pollution-control solutions such as scrubbers and recycling centers. Second, it creates a major marketing opportunity for finding alternative ways to produce and package goods that do not cause environmental damage. Many marketers have become interested in using social marketing to find new solutions and influence consumers and business firms to be more ecology minded.[17]

---

[15] *First Annual Report of the Council on Environmental Quality* (Washington, D.C.: Government Printing Office, 1970), p. 158.

[16] See "The Coming Boom in Solar Energy," *Business Week,* October 9, 1978, pp. 88–104.

[17] See Karl E. Henion II, *Ecological Marketing* (Columbus, Ohio: Grid, 1976).

Increasing Government Intervention in Natural Resource Management

The growing concern with the deteriorating quality of the natural environment has led government to take an active role in regulating and enforcing conservation and pollution-control behavior. The responsibility is dispersed and is in the hands of many federal, state, and local agencies, each attempting to monitor environmentally damaging actions. Ironically, the effort to protect the environment often runs counter to the attempt to increase employment and economic growth, as for example, when business is forced to buy expensive pollution-cleanup equipment instead of investing in capital producing goods. From time to time, conservation politics takes a back seat to economic-growth politics. Marketing management must be alert to regulatory developments and the opportunities that open up with the effort to protect the natural environment.

TECHNOLOGICAL ENVIRONMENT

The most dramatic force shaping human destiny is technology. Technology has released such wonders as penicillin, open-heart surgery, and the birth-control pill. It has released such horrors as the hydrogen bomb, nerve gas, and the submachine gun. It has released such mixed blessings as the automobile, television sets, and white bread. Depending upon whether one is more enthralled with the wonders or the horrors determines one's attitude toward technology.

Every new technology may potentially spawn a major industry. One only has to think of transistors, xerography, computers, and antibiotics. These industries not only create but destroy. Transistors hurt the vacuum-tube industry and xerography hurt the carbon-paper business. The auto hurt the railroads and television hurt the movies. Schumpeter saw technology as a force for "creative destruction." Every enterprise must watch what is new in the environment, for this might eventually destroy it. If it has the imagination, the new might save it. It is discouraging that most phonograph companies did not enter the radio field, wagon manufacturers did not enter the automobile business, and steam locomotive companies did not enter the diesel locomotive business.

The growth rate of the economy is intimately tied to how many *major* new technologies will be discovered in the coming years. Unfortunately, technological discoveries do not arise evenly through time—the railroad industry created a lot of investment, and then there was a dearth until the auto industry emerged; later radio created a lot of investment, and then there was a dearth until television appeared. In the absence of major innovations that open up great markets and opportunities, an economy can stagnate. Some scientists do not foresee further promising innovations of the magnitude of the invention of the automobile or television. Others see an unlimited number of important innovations on the horizon.

In the meantime there are sure to be small innovations filling the gaps. Freeze-dried coffee probably made no one happier and antiperspirant deodorants probably made no one wiser, but they meet certain daily needs in an improved manner.

New technology creates some major long-run consequences that are not always foreseeable at the time. The contraceptive pill, for example, led to smaller families, more working wives, and larger discretionary incomes resulting in higher expenditures on vacation travel, among other things. Little did the airlines foresee that the pill would increase their traffic. The pill also led to a larger average size in brassieres, something the women's lingerie industry has missed entirely.

Here are some of the main trends in technology that the marketer should watch.

Accelerating Pace of Technological Change

Most of the technological products we take for granted today were not present even one hundred years ago. Abraham Lincoln did not know of automobiles, airplanes, phonographs, radio, or the electric light. Woodrow Wilson did not know of television, aerosol cans, home freezers, automatic dishwashers, room air conditioners, antibiotics, or electronic computers. Franklin Delano Roosevelt did not know of xerography, synthetic detergents, tape recorders, birth-control pills, or earth satellites. And John Kennedy did not know of freeze-dried coffee, fuel injection engines, or laser technology. As much as 20 percent of our products and brands were not around a decade earlier.

Toffler sees an *accelerative thrust* in the invention, exploitation, and diffusion of new technologies.[18] More ideas are being worked on; the time lag between idea and successful implementation is falling rapidly; and the time between introduction and peak production is shortening considerably. He sees technology as feeding on itself. As someone observed, 90 percent of all scientists who ever lived are now alive.

Unlimited Innovational Opportunities

There seems to be no dearth of ideas for needed new products and services, only an inability to bring them into a technical or commercially successful form. Among the most important things researchers are working on are cancer cures, chemical control of mental illness, aging postponers, electric cars, desalinization of sea water, home computer systems, butler robots, and nonfattening foods. Researchers are also working on a host of other innovations, including small flying cars, lightweight single-person rocket belts, commercial space shuttles, space colonies, and human cloning.[19]

An astute student of the technological scene, James R. Bright, stated that the strongest technological developments are occurring in transportation, energy, life-extension research, new materials, instrumentation, mechanization of physical activities, and mechanization of intellectual activities. His detailed description of the specific types and means of advance, as well as the results, constitutes an excellent guide to new opportunities.[20]

High R&D Budgets

One of the fastest-growing budgets in this generation has been the nation's research and development budget. In 1928, R&D expenditures totaled less than $100 million. By 1953, the figure had grown fifty times larger, to $5 billion, and

[18] Toffler, *Future Shock*, pp. 25–30.

[19] For a long list of possible innovations, see Dennis Gabor, *Innovations: Scientific, Technological, and Social* (London: Oxford University Press, 1970).

[20] James R. Bright, "Opportunity and Threat in Technological Change," *Harvard Business Review*, November–December 1963, pp. 76–86.

113

by 1976, R&D stood at over $37 billion, or almost 2.3 percent of gross national product (GNP).

The federal government is the largest supplier of R&D funds, and industry is the largest user. Almost 90 percent of the funds go to applied R&D. The remainder is spent on basic research, almost half of which takes place in colleges and universities.

The five industries spending the most on R&D (in billions of dollars) are aircraft and missiles ($5.7), electrical equipment and communication ($5.5), chemicals and allied products ($2.6), machinery ($2.6) and motor vehicles and other transportation ($2.3). These five industries account for 54 percent of total R&D expenditures and boast such research-minded firms as Du Pont, General Electric, Minnesota Mining & Manufacturing, Pfizer, Searle, and Texas Instruments. The least R&D spending is found in such industries as lumber, wood products, furniture, textiles, apparel, and paper and allied products. Industries at the top range spend between 5 and 10 percent of their sales dollars for R&D expenditures, and those in the lowest range spend less than 1 percent of their sales dollar.

Most of today's research is carried out by scientific teams working in research laboratories rather than by lone independent inventors of the breed of Thomas Edison, Samuel Morse, or Alexander Graham Bell. Managing scientific personnel poses major challenges. They are professionals who resent too much cost control. They are more interested in solving scientific problems than in coming up with marketable products. Yet companies are making some progress in impressing a stronger marketing orientation on their scientific personnel.[21]

Concentration on Minor Improvements Rather than on Major Discoveries

Tight money in recent years has led many companies to concentrate more on pursuing minor product improvements than gambling on major innovations. In the past, such companies as Du Pont, Bell Laboratories, and Pfizer would invest heavily to make major breakthroughs and were successful in many cases. Even these companies seem to be pursuing more modest goals today. Most companies are content to put their money into such things as improving antiperspirant deodorants, restyling automobiles, and developing new soft-drink flavors. Some part of every R&D budget is spent simply to match or copy competitors' products rather than in striving to surpass them.

Increased Regulation of Technological Change

Technological change is encountering more regulation and opposition than ever before. As products get more complex, the public needs assurance of their safety. Government agencies have responded by expanding their powers to investigate and ban new products that might be directly harmful or have questionable side effects. Thus the federal Food and Drug Administration has issued elaborate regulations governing the scientific testing of new drugs, resulting in (1) much higher research costs, (2) lengthening of the time span between idea and introduction from five to about nine years, and (3) the driving of much drug research to other parts of the world where regulations are less stringent. Safety

---

[21] See chap. 22, p. 594.

and health regulations have substantially increased in other areas, such as food, automobiles, clothing, electrical appliances, and construction. Marketers must know these regulations and take them seriously when proposing, developing, and launching new products. Many companies have had the experience of spending millions to develop a new product only to have a government agency pronounce it unsafe and force its withdrawal from the market.

Technological change is also meeting opposition from those who see large-scale technology as destroying many of the values they cherish.[22] They see technology as threatening to destroy nature, privacy, simplicity, and even humankind. They have adopted Schumacher's philosophy in *Small Is Beautiful*,[23] and have replaced cars with bicycles, synthetic food with organic food, and fancy clothes with denim clothes. They have opposed the construction of new nuclear plants, high-rise buildings, and recreational facilities where they believe these threaten to destroy existing ecological balances. They have clamored for official groups to perform *technological assessment* on new technologies before permitting those technologies to be commercialized in this society.

Marketers must understand the technological environment and the nuances of technology. They must be able to envision how technology can be connected up with human needs. They must work closely with R&D people to encourage more market-oriented research. They must be alert to possible negative aspects of any innovation that might harm the users and bring about distrust and opposition.

POLITICAL ENVIRONMENT

Developments in the political environment are increasingly affecting decisions on the marketing of goods and services. The political system is a broad term covering the forms and institutions by which a nation is governed. It consists of an interacting set of *laws, government agencies,* and *pressure groups* that influence and constrain the conduct of various organizations and individuals in the society.

Here we will examine the main political trends and their implications for marketing management.

Increasing Amount of Legislation Regulating Business

In the United States and several other countries, the basic political model is that of *liberal democracy.* Consumers and business firms are free to pursue their self-interest except where this pursuit is clearly harmful to others or to the larger society. Government is to play a minor role, limiting itself to those activities that cannot be carried on by other groups, namely (1) war and defense, (2) public works (roads, public monuments), (3) public services (fire, police, schools, justice), and (4) regulation to maintain competition and protect public health. Over the years, the government sector has steadily increased its power, until it is now

---

[22] Theodore Roszak, *The Making of a Counter Culture: Reflections on the Technocratic Society and Its Youthful Opposition* (Garden City, N.Y.: Anchor Books, Doubleday & Company, 1969).

[23] E.F. Schumacher, *Small Is Beautiful* (New York: Harper & Row, 1973).

the major employer in the United States, accounting for 19 percent of the non-agricultural labor force and spending approximately 21 percent of the gross national product. Its growth has been abetted by the demands of pressure groups to receive favors or protection, rather than by a belief that government ought to be the major employer in the economy. While many nations have gone over to a socialist model of society with government owning and operating major industries, U.S. citizens prefer to view government as a regulator, not an initiator of economic activity.

Legislation affecting business has increased steadily over the years, partly in reaction to the growing complexity of technology and business practices. The legislation seeks to accomplish any of three purposes. *The first is to protect companies from each other.* Business executives all praise competition in the abstract but try to neutralize it when it touches them. If threatened, they show their teeth:[24]

> ReaLemon Foods, a subsidiary of Borden, held approximately 90 percent of the reconstituted lemon juice market until 1970. Fearing antitrust action, ReaLemon began to allow companies on the West Coast and in the Chicago area to make inroads. By 1972, however, a Chicago competitor, Golden Crown Citrus Corporation, had captured a share that ReaLemon considered too large. ReaLemon went on the offensive and in 1974, the Federal Trade Commission filed a complaint charging ReaLemon with predatory pricing and sales tactics.

So laws are passed to define and prevent unfair competition. These laws are enforced by the Federal Trade Commission and the Antitrust Division of the attorney general's office. Sometimes, unfortunately, the laws end up protecting the inefficient rather than promoting the efficient. Some students of business regulation go so far as to charge that "judges and the Federal Trade Commission have remade the law into a body of rules of which a large portion impair competition and the ability of the economy to operate efficiently."[25] But, by and large, regulations are needed to keep executives fearful about overstepping the line in trying to neutralize or harm competitors. It is hard to imagine that the economy would be more efficient if competition were not supervised by some regulatory agencies.

The second purpose of government regulation is to protect consumers from business firms. A few firms are ready to adulterate their products, mislead through their advertising, deceive through their packaging, and bait through their prices. Unfair consumer practices must be defined and agencies established to protect consumers. Many business executives see purple with each new consumer law, and yet a few have said that "consumerism may be the best thing that has happened . . . in the past 20 years."[26]

---

[24] Dennis D. Fisher, "ReaLemon Sales Tactics Hit," *Chicago Sun-Times*, July 4, 1974.

[25] See Yale Brozen, "Antitrust Out of Hand," *The Conference Board Record*, March 1974, pp. 14–19.

[26] Leo Greenland, "Advertisers Must Stop Conning Consumers," *Harvard Business Review*, July–August 1974, p. 18.

The third purpose of government regulation is to protect the larger interests of society against unbridled business behavior. Gross national product might be rising, and yet the quality of life might be deteriorating. Most firms are not charged with the social costs of their production or products. Their prices are artificially low and their sales artificially high until agencies such as the Environmental Protection Agency shift the social costs back to these firms and their customers. As the environment continues to deteriorate, new laws and their enforcement will continue or increase. Business executives have to watch these developments in planning their products and marketing systems.

The marketing executive cannot plan intelligently without a good working knowledge of the major laws and regulations that exist to protect competition, consumers, and the larger interests of society. The laws are numerous; only the key ones can be listed here. Table 5–1 lists the main federal laws that concern marketing executives. They should know these federal laws and particularly the evolving courts' interpretations.[27] And they should know the state and local laws that affect their local marketing activity.

In addition to these laws, new bills to regulate business are proposed in Congress each year, but very few of them are passed or passed in the intended form. Lobbying activity tends to compromise bills until they are only a shadow of the original proposal. For example, many consumerists hold that the Fair Packaging and Labeling Act (1966) failed to do the job of improving consumer information and protection in the area of packaging.[28] What is sorely lacking in the whole area of business legislation is a mechanism for formally evaluating the full effects of the law's enforcement upon companies and consumers, so that learning could take place on how to formulate more effective legislation, which fulfills its purpose.[29]

Several countries have gone further than the United States in the passage of strong consumerist legislation. Norway has banned several forms of sales promotion, such as trading stamps, contests, and premiums, as being inappropriate or "unfair" instruments for the sellers to use in promoting their products. The Philippines requires food processors selling national brands to also market low-price brands so that low-income consumers will find economy brands on the market. In India food companies need special approval to launch brands that duplicate what already exists on the market, such as another cola drink or brand of rice. These and other legislative developments have not surfaced prominently in the United States, but they suggest how far regulations might be pushed to constrain marketing practice.

[27] See chap. 27, pp. 701–5 for a further discussion of legal constraints on marketing decisions. For recent cases, see G. David Hughes, "Antitrust Caveat for the Marketing Planner," *Harvard Business Review*, March–April 1978, pp. 40 ff.; and Ray O. Werner, "The 'New' Supreme Court and the Marketing Environment 1975–1977," *Journal of Marketing*, April 1978, pp. 56–62.

[28] See Laurence P. Feldman, *Consumer Protection: Problems and Prospects* (St. Paul, Minn.: West Publishing Co., 1976), pp. 278–79.

[29] See Louis W. Stern, Robert Dewar, Allan R. Drebin, Lynn W. Phillips, and Brian Sternthal, *The Evaluation of Consumer Protection Laws: The Case of the Fair Credit Reporting Act* (Cambridge, Mass.: Marketing Science Institute, 1977).

TABLE 5–1
Milestone U.S. Legislation Affecting Marketing

Sherman Antitrust Act (1890)

Prohibited (a) "monopolies or attempts to monopolize" and (b) "contracts, combinations, or conspiracies in restraint of trade" in interstate and foreign commerce.

Federal Food and Drug Act (1906)

Forbade the manufacture, sale, or transport of adulterated or fraudulently labeled foods and drugs in interstate commerce. Supplanted by the Food, Drug, and Cosmetic Act, 1938; amended by Food Additives Amendment in 1958 and the Kefauver-Harris Amendment in 1962. The 1962 amendments dealt with pretesting of drugs for safety and effectiveness and labeling of drugs by generic names.

Meat Inspection Act (1906)

Provided for the enforcement of sanitary regulations in meat-packing establishments, and for federal inspection of all companies selling meats in interstate commerce.

Federal Trade Commission Act (1914)

Established the commission, a body of specialists with broad powers to investigate and to issue cease and desist orders to enforce Section 5, which declared that "unfair methods of competition in commerce are unlawful." (Amended by Wheeler-Lea Act, 1938, which added the phrase "and unfair or deceptive acts or practices.")

Clayton Act (1914)

Supplemented the Sherman Act by prohibiting certain specific practices (certain types of price discrimination, tying clauses and exclusive dealing, intercorporate stockholdings, and interlocking directorates) "where the effect . . . may be to substantially lessen competition or tend to create a monopoly in any line of commerce." Provided that corporate officials who violate the law could be held individually responsible; exempted labor and agricultural organizations from its provisions.

Robinson-Patman Act (1936)

Amended the Clayton Act. Added the phrase "to injure, destroy, or prevent competition." Defined price discrimination as unlawful (subject to certain defenses) and provided the FTC with the right to establish limits on quantity discounts, to forbid brokerage allowances except to independent brokers, and to prohibit promotional allowances or the furnishing of services or facilities except where made available to all "on proportionately equal terms."

Miller-Tydings Act (1937)

Amended the Sherman Act to exempt interstate fair-trade (price fixing) agreements from antitrust prosecution. (The McGuire Act, 1952, reinstated the legality of the nonsigner clause.)

Antimerger Act (1950)

Amended Section 7 of the Clayton Act by broadening the power to prevent intercorporate acquisitions where the acquisition may have a substantially adverse effect on competition.

Automobile Information Disclosure Act (1958)

Prohibited car dealers from inflating the factory price of new cars.

National Traffic and Safety Act (1966)

Provided for the creation of compulsory safety standards for automobiles and tires.

Fair Packaging and Labeling Act (1966)

Provided for the regulation of the packaging and labeling of consumer goods. Required manufacturers to state what package contains, who made it, and how much it contains. Permitted industries' voluntary adoption of uniform packaging standards.

Child Protection Act (1966)

Banned sale of hazardous toys and articles. Amended in 1969 to include articles that pose electrical, mechanical, or thermal hazards.

Federal Cigarette Labeling and Advertising Act (1967)

Required that cigarette packages contain the statement, "Warning: The Surgeon General Has Determined That Cigarette Smoking Is Dangerous to Your Health."

Consumer Credit Protection Act (1968)

Required lenders to state the true costs of a credit transaction, outlawed the use of actual or threatened violence in collecting loans, and restricted the amount of garnishments. Established a National Commission on Consumer Finance.

National Environmental Policy Act (1969)

Established a national policy on the environment and provided for the establishment of the Council on Environmental Quality. The Environmental Protection Agency was established by "Reorganization Plan No. 3 of 1970."

Consumer Product Safety Act (1972)

Established the Consumer Product Safety Commission and authorized it to set safety standards for consumer products as well as to exact penalties for failure to uphold the standards.

Magnuson-Moss Warranty/FTC Improvement Act (1975)

Authorized the FTC to determine rules concerning consumer warranties and provided for consumer access to means of redress, such as the "class action" suit. Also expanded FTC regulatory powers over unfair or deceptive acts or practices.

Other Laws

Many other federal laws affect business competition and regulate practices found in specific industries. A multitude of state and local laws also regulate competition and specific practices within each state and legally designated locality.

The real issue raised by business legislation is where the point is reached when the costs of regulation exceed the benefits of regulation. The laws are not always administered fairly by those responsible for enforcing them. They may hurt many legitimate business firms and discourage new investment and market entry. They may increase consumer costs much more than consumer protection. Whereas each new law may have a legitimate rationale, their totality may have the effect of sapping initiative and slowing down economic growth.

More Vigorous Government-Agency Enforcement

Government agencies, like other human organizations, seek to grow in power and influence. Their mandate is to carry out the law. They have to find cases and win them to demonstrate the agency's usefulness and need for larger budgets. Their self-interest drives them to take an adversarial position toward business. In addition, some of the persons attracted to regulatory agencies start out with an antibusiness attitude.

The adversarial and costly nature of business regulation is well illustrated in the long-drawn-out suit by the Federal Trade Commission (FTC) against the four leading ready-to-eat breakfast cereal companies, Kellogg, General Mills, General Foods, and Quaker Oats.[30] In 1972, the Federal Trade Commission charged these firms with practicing a *shared monopoly*. This is a new, untested legal concept, which if upheld in the courts, would allow the FTC to attack other oligopolistic industries, such as automobiles, steel, and oil. The charge was that the Big Four of this industry (1) do not compete on a price basis, (2) enjoy monopoly level profits, and (3) make it tough for other firms to enter this industry because of their large advertising budgets and their grip on shelf space through their brand proliferation. While the Big Four were not charged with any explicit price conspiracy, it was suggested that they had tacitly agreed to compete not on price but on promotion. Since the case began in 1972, the FTC staff working on the case has turned over several times, and both sides have spent millions of dollars prosecuting and defending the case, with very little progress. Recently, a court ordered the FTC to release Quaker Oats from the suit on the grounds that its market share (10 percent) was too small to be charged with shared monopoly—a move that came after Quaker Oats had spent millions of dollars defending itself. Cases like this tend to go on even after the original issues vanish, simply because the sides will fight to the end. Business firms complain that they are the ultimate victims because government agencies (1) do not have to show a profit and (2) are less accountable to others for their actions.

Growth of Public-Interest Groups

The third major political development is the rapid growth in recent years of public-interest groups dedicated to lobbying for increased consumer protection and business regulation. The most successful of these groups is Ralph Nader's *Public Citizen*, which acts as watchdog for consumers' interests. Nader, more than any other single individual, lifted consumerism into a major social force,[31] first with his successful attack on auto safety (culminating in the passage of the National Traffic and Motor Vehicle Safety Act of 1962), and then through fur-

[30] See "Too Many Cereals for the FTC," *Business Week*, March 20, 1978, pp. 166, 171.

[31] Many other factors contributed to the emergence of consumerism as a major force. See Philip Kotler, "What Consumerism Means to Marketers," *Harvard Business Review*, May–June 1972, pp. 48–57.

ther investigations into meat processing (resulting in the Wholesome Meat Act of 1967), truth-in-lending, auto repairs, insurance and X-ray equipment. In addition to Nader's, there are hundreds of other consumer-interest groups—private and governmental—operating on the national, state, and local levels. There are also various other groups that affect marketing decision making—groups seeking to protect the environment (Sierra Club, Environmental Defense) or to advance the rights of women, blacks, senior citizens, and so on. The eight major public-interest groups have attracted collectively more members and funds than the two national political parties! They represent a new and dynamic form of political representation.[32]

What are the main consumer issues that consumer-interest groups are pressing before legislators and the public? They are:

1. *More and better consumer information.* Consumer advocates want companies to supply consumers with more and better information about the things consumers buy. Among the proposals: (a) Food packagers should be required to put more information on their packaging, such as a fuller description of the ingredients and even the nutritional levels. (b) Appliance manufacturers should write their warranties in clearer English so that buyers are not surprised later to learn that certain things are not covered. (c) Banks should be required to state their interest rates in standard terms so that consumers can compare interest rates at different institutions. (d) Advertisers should be prevented from creating advertisements that mislead or deceive consumers about a product's qualities.

2. *More and better consumer protection.* Consumer advocates feel that government agencies should be given larger budgets for testing products for their safety and health levels and for prosecuting offenders. They feel that automobiles are not safe enough, our food contains too many chemical additives, and many drugs have damaging side effects that outweigh their benefits.

3. *More and better consumer education.* Consumer advocates feel that American consumers do not receive enough education on how to judge values in goods and services and how to interpret marketing communications. For example, Swedish children receive consumer-education training throughout their public schooling, in contrast to the U.S. where one course may be offered on a required or elective basis. Furthermore, Swedish media (broadcast and print) carry much more news about consumer affairs, including a weekly show where the host demonstrates some poorly made products and takes calls from consumers who complain about specific products.

Consumerism is a powerful force that marketing must reckon with. Rather than seeing it as a threat to the marketer's "freedom to act," it should be viewed as an opportunity to do a better job of sensing, serving, and satisfying consumer needs. Peter Drucker called consumerism "the shame of marketing," implying that if marketers were serving consumers as well as they should be, consumerism wouldn't exist.[33] Companies should strive to incorporate consumerist considerations in the design and marketing of their products, as a further step in the implementation of the marketing concept.

[32] See Milton Kotler, "New Life for American Politics," *The Nation*, October 30, 1976, pp. 429–31.

[33] Peter F. Drucker, "The Shame of Marketing," *Marketing/Communications*, August 1969, pp. 60–64.

Another key component of the macroenvironment is the cultural system. People grow up in a particular society that shapes their basic beliefs, values, and norms. They absorb, almost unconsciously, a world view that defines their relationship to themselves, others, institutions, society at large, nature, and the cosmos. The following things are important to understand about culture as it affects marketing decision making.

Core Cultural Values Have High Persistence

People in a given society hold many beliefs and values, not all of which are equally important. Those that are most central to people can be called their core beliefs and values.

The set of core beliefs and values in a society has a high degree of persistence. For example, most Americans believe in work, getting married, giving to charity, and being honest. These beliefs shape and color more specific attitudes and behaviors found in everyday life. Core beliefs and values are passed on from parents to children and are reinforced by the major institutions of society—schools, churches, businesses, and government.

People also hold secondary beliefs and values that are more open to change in the wake of new social forces. Believing in the institution of marriage is a core belief; believing that people ought to get married early is a secondary belief. When students of culture debate about whether cultural change is slow or fast in this society, they often fail to distinguish between core and secondary beliefs and values.

Marketers who would like to change core beliefs and values would be wise not to try. Suppose a women's clothing designer wanted to sell women on the idea of going topless. That designer would be attacking a core value held by both men and women. The same designer, however, might have success in selling women on wearing shorter skirts or lower necklines because these styles do less violence to their core beliefs.

Each Culture Consists of Subcultures

A society is made up of people who share the same core beliefs and values. Yet there are always certain groups of deviants, such as criminals or anarchists. Furthermore, there can be much variation in the secondary beliefs and values that people hold, giving rise to *subcultures*. For example, immigrants, the super-rich, and the intelligentsia, because they have had different life experiences and face different issues, will exhibit somewhat different systems of beliefs and values. Those will be reflected in different patterns of consumer wants and behavior.

One also finds intergenerational differences in culture stemming from differences in life experiences. In a modern American family, the grandparents are conservative in their tastes and careful in their expenditures; the parents work and play hard and purchase many things on credit; their eighteen-year-old son might show little interest in either work or consumption. Recently a ten-year-old boy was told by his mother to behave more like his fourteen-year-old brother, to which he retorted: "Mom, he's from a different generation."

A clear expression of different secondary patterns of belief and behavior is seen in *life-style groups*. A life-style group is one whose members share similar *attitudes, interests, and opinions*. The persons making up a life-style group are similar in what they like, want, and do. One study distinguished eight male life-style groups and reported on the percentages in the population: (1) *quiet family men* (8 percent); (2) *traditionalists* (16 percent); (3) *discontented men* (13 percent); (4) *ethical highbrows* (14 percent); (5) *pleasure-oriented men* (9 percent); (6) *achievers* (11 percent); (7) *he-men* (19 percent); and (8) *sophisticated men* (10 percent).[34] Another study distinguished five female life-style groups and reported their percentages in the sample: (1) *homemakers* (35 percent); (2) *matriarchs* (10 percent); (3) *variety women* (17 percent): (4) *Cinderellas* (13 percent); and (5) *glamour women* (23 percent).[35] The researchers found that the various life-style groups had somewhat different product, brand, and media preferences. Thus life style becomes a useful segmentation variable for certain types of markets.

Secondary Cultural Values Undergo Shifts Through Time

Although core cultural values are fairly persistent, there are always small shifts taking place through time that are worth monitoring. In the early 1960s, a small group of young people, particularly in New York and San Francisco, were developing a "hippie" life style. They drew widespread media coverage, and this led other young people to adopt this life style or some of its component attitudes toward life, work, and relationships. Elsewhere, certain cultural heroes emerged, such as the late Elvis Presley and the Beatles, whose music and styles had a major impact on young people's hairstyles, clothing, and sexual norms. Others were affected by new magazines such as *Playboy*, or films such as *Easy Rider* and *The Graduate*. The changing ideas of the young began to spill over to their parents, leading to changes in some of their attitudes and behavior.

The measurement and forecasting of cultural change is still highly speculative. Some major corporations, marketing research firms, and futures research firms put out reports from time to time that summarize cultural trends. One of the best known of these is the Monitor series put out by the marketing research firm of Yankelovich. Monitor tracks 41 different cultural values, such as "anti-bigness," "mysticism," "living for today," "away from possessions," and "sensuousness," describing the percentage who share the attitude as well as the percentage who are antitrend. For example, the percentage of people who place a strong value on physical fitness and well being has been going up steadily over the years (35 percent currently), with the main support group being people under thirty, especially young women, the upscale consumers, and people living in the West. About 16 percent of the population, however, is antitrend.

A distinction should be drawn between the *dominant value system* and *trends in the value system*. Most people in this society see themselves as "happy, home loving, clean, and square" (the dominant value system), and there is a slight trend toward less conventional behavior (e.g., open marriage, cohabitation).[36] But the less conventional behavior is never practiced by more than a small percentage of the population, despite the distorted coverage of the news media. Thus major producers will want to cater to dominant value groups, and minor producers might see less conventional groups as a market-niche opportunity.

Here we will attempt to summarize the major values and value shifts that

---

[34] Quoted in William D. Wells, "Psychographics: A Critical Review," *Journal of Marketing Research*, May 1975, pp. 196–213, found on p. 201.

[35] Daniel W. Greeno, Montrose S. Sommers, and Jerome B. Kernan, "Personality and Implicit Behavior Patterns," *Journal of Marketing Research*, February 1973, pp. 63–69, found on p. 65.

[36] William D. Wells, "It's a Wyeth, Not a Warhol, World," *Harvard Business Review*, January–February 1970, pp. 26–32.

characterize people's relationships to themselves, others, institutions, society, nature, and the cosmos.

People's relationship to themselves   People vary in how much emphasis they put on gratifying their own needs versus serving others. The doctrine of primarily serving one's own needs is called self-fulfillment. More people are concerned with self-fulfullment today, seeking to do the things they want to do rather than follow convention or please other people. They are attaching more importance to *instant gratification* in the *here-and-now* rather than delayed gratification in the future. They want to enjoy all that life offers rather than make sacrifices for parents, family, or even friends. Some are *pleasure seekers,* wanting to have fun, change, and escape from the humdrum. Others are pursuing *self-realization,* by joining therapeutic or religious groups. A Yankelovich study has shown that self-fulfillment has become a guiding principle in a growing number of families. The study reported that 43 percent of the parents in a large sample are "new breed" rather than "traditionalist" and stress "freedom over authority, self-fulfillment over material success, and duty to self over duty to others—including their own children." [37]

The marketing implications of this trend toward self-fulfillment are many. People seek self-expression through the product, brand, and service choices they make. They are more willing to buy their "dream cars," take "dream vacations," and "dress more elegantly." People will spend more time in the wilderness, in health activities (jogging, tennis, yoga), in introspection, in arts and crafts. The lesiure industry (camping, boating, arts and crafts, sports) has a good growth outlook as a result of this search for self-fulfillment.

People's relationship to others   People choose to live their lives with different degrees of sociability, from the hermit who completely avoids others to the gregarious person who feels happy and alive only in the company of others. One trend seems to be a desire for more *open and easy relationships* with others. Relationships in the past, whether with parents, teachers, employers, or friends, were more structured and formal. Today people are seeking more spontaneous and natural interactions with others. They want to be able to say things on their mind without causing offense ("tell it like it is") and to listen more empathically. They are against the charade of phoniness that drove Holden Caulfield mad in J. D. Salinger's *Catcher in the Rye.*

For marketers, this means several things. People may prefer such products as furniture to be more casual and less formal and pretentious. They may want packaging to provide more complete and honest information. They may want advertising messages to be straighter. They may want salespersons to be more honest and open in their dealings.

People's relationship to institutions   People vary in how they feel about the major institutions in their lives, such as corporations, government agencies, trade unions, universities, and hospitals. Most people accept these institutions, although there are always groups that are highly critical of particular institutions, whether business, government, labor, or others. By and large, people are ready to work in the major institutions and rely on them to carry out society's work.

---

[37] "Family: New Breed v. the Old," *Time,* May 2, 1977, p. 76.

There is at present a trend toward a *decline in institutional loyalty*. People are inclined to give a little less to these institutions and trust them a little less. The work ethic has been gradually eroding. Instead of the old ethic of "living to work," an increasing number of people are "working to live." They put in their time in order to make the money to enjoy "what really counts." Pride in doing the job well and in giving all one has to the institution seems to be waning.

The marketing implications of this decline in institutional loyalty are several. Companies will be challenged to find new ways to build the loyalty of their work force. Many see the answer in programs of *job enrichment*, to make the work more interesting; *job enlargement*, which will give employees more responsibility; and *incentive pay*, which will give a larger reward to the more-productive employees. Companies will also be challenged to find new ways to build consumer confidence in themselves and their products. They will have to review their advertising communications to make sure that their messages don't raise the question, Can you trust this company? They will have to review their various interactions with the public to make sure that they are coming across as good guys. More companies are turning to *social audits*[38] and to enlightened *public relations*[39] to maintain a positive relationship with their publics.

People's relationship to society People vary in their attitudes toward the society in which they live, from patriots who defend it, to reformers who want to change it, to discontents who want to leave it. There is a trend toward declining patriotism and stronger criticism and cynicism as to where the country is going. Recently, the concept of *life ways* has been used for classifying people's relationships to the society in which they live. People fall into one of six *life-way* groups:

1. *Makers.* Makers are those who make the system go. They are the leaders and the up-and-comers. They are much involved in worldly affairs, generally prosperous and ambitious. They are found in the professions and include the managers and proprietors of business.
2. *Preservers.* Preservers are people who are at ease with the familiar and proud of tradition. They are a powerful force in promoting stability, solidity, and examination before embracing the new and different.
3. *Takers.* Takers take what they can from the system. They live in the interstices of the work world, finding their pleasures outside the realm of making things go. They are attracted to bureaucracies and tenured posts.
4. *Changers.* Changers tend to be answer-havers; they commonly wish to change things to conform with their views. They are the critics, protestors, radicals, libbers, advocates, and complainers—and a significant segment of the doers. Their focus is chiefly outward.
5. *Seekers.* Seekers are the ones who search for a better grasp, a deeper understanding, a richer experience, a universal view. The pathways of their seeking and the rewards sought tend to be internal. They are often the originators and promulgators of new ideas.

[38] See Raymond A. Bauer and Dan H. Fenn, Jr., "What Is a Corporate Social Audit?" *Harvard Business Review,* January–February, 1973, pp. 37–48.

[39] Leonard L. Berry and James S. Hensel, "Public Relations: Opportunities in the New Society," *Arizona Business,* August–September 1973, pp. 14–21.

6. *Escapers.* Escapers have a drive to escape, to get away from it all. Escape takes many forms from dropping out to addiction to mental illness to mysticism.[40]

These types are found in all societies, and over time the relative size of the groups changes. Mitchell sees American society drifting toward a greater ratio of takers to makers, which does not augur well for future economic growth. He also sees an increasing ratio of escapers to changers, which means that society will grow more conservative and self-indulgent.

Marketers can view life-way groups as market segments with specific symbolic and material needs. Makers are high achievers who collect success symbols, such as elegant homes, expensive automobiles, and fine clothes, whereas changers live more austerely, drive smaller cars and wear simpler clothes. Escapers go in for motorcycles, chic clothes, surfing, and disco. In general, the consumption patterns of individuals will reflect to some extent their orientation toward society at large.

People's relationship to nature   People vary in their relation to nature, some feeling subjugated by it, others feeling in harmony with it, and still others seeking mastery over it. One of the major long-term trends in Western society has been humankind's growing mastery over nature through technology. People can turn on a heater when cold and an air conditioner when warm; they can buy food when hungry and get stomach relief when they overeat. Along with this has been an attitude that nature is bountiful and that it is all right to wrest nature's riches. More recently, there has been a growing awareness of nature's fragility and a desire to preserve its magnificence. People are becoming aware that nature can be destroyed or spoiled by human activities. People are showing a growing interest in achieving a harmonious relationship with nature rather than exploiting it.

Consumers are showing increasing participation in such activities as camping, hiking, boating, and fishing. Business is responding by producing a large assortment of hiking boots, tenting equipment, and other gear for nature enthusiasts. Various retail stores have emerged specializing in back-to-nature equipment. Tour operators are packaging more tours to wilderness areas in Alaska and northern Finland. Food producers have found growing markets for "natural" products such as 100 percent "natural" cereal, ice cream with no artificial flavor or color, and health foods, while construction material companies have found growing markets for wood, stone, and other natural materials. Marketing communicators are using beautiful natural backgrounds in advertising many of their products. Industrial companies have found growing markets for products related to conservation and pollution control.

People's relationship to the cosmos   People vary in their belief system about the origin of the universe and their place in it. Americans by and large are monotheistic, although their religious convictions and practices have been waning through the years. Church attendance has been falling steadily, with the exception of certain evangelical movements (e.g., Crusade for Christ) reaching out to bring people back into organized religion. Some of the religious impulse has not been lost but translated into a growing interest in Eastern religions, mys-

---

[40] Arnold Mitchell, private communication.

ticism, and the occult with more Americans than ever studying yoga, zen, and transcendental meditation. What has been changing is the grip of conventional religion and morality on the lives of people.

The marketing implications are several. As people lose their religious orientation, they increase their efforts to enjoy their one life on earth as fully as possible. Their interest grows in earthly possessions and experience. Secularization and materialism go hand in hand. "Enjoy yourself" becomes the dominant theme, and people gravitate to those goods and services that offer them fun and pleasure in this life. In the meantime, religious institutions face a continuing decline in membership and support and turn to marketers for help in reworking their appeals to compete against the secular attractions of modern society.

In summary, cultural values are showing the following long-run trends:

Other-centeredness	⟶ Self-fulfillment
Postponed gratification	⟶ Immediate gratification
Hard work	⟶ The easy life
Formal relationships	⟶ Informal, open relationships
Religious orientation	⟶ Secular orientation

Marketers should recognize that each trend is subject to exceptions. A long perspective on cultural change shows that much cultural change follows a model of long-term pendulum swings rather than one-way movements. Every force seems to breed a counterforce, and in many cases, the counterforce eventually becomes dominant.

SUMMARY   Those who plan and manage products operate within a complex and rapidly changing marketing environment, which the firm must continuously monitor and adapt to if it is to survive and prosper. The marketing environment has several layers: the task environment, the competitive environment, the public environment, and the macroenvironment. In this chapter we are concerned with the macroenvironment. The firm and its macroenvironment make up an ecosystem; disturbances in this ecosystem may spell profound threats or new opportunities for the firm. The alert firm will set up formal systems for identifying, appraising, and responding to the various opportunities and threats in its environment.

The marketing macroenvironment of the firm can be factored into six components: the demographic, economic, natural, technological, political, and cultural environments. The demographic environment is characterized by a worldwide explosive population growth, a slowdown in the U.S. birthrate, and aging of the U.S. population, a changing American family, the rise of nonfamily households, geographical shifts in population, and a better-educated populace. The economic environment shows a slowdown in real-income growth, continued inflationary pressure, changing savings and debt patterns, and changing consumption-expenditure patterns. The natural environment is marked by impending shortages of certain raw materials, increased cost of energy, increased levels of pollution, and increasing government intervention in natural resource management. The technological environment exhibits an accelerating pace of technological change, unlimited innovational opportunities, high R&D budgets, concentration on minor improvements rather than major discoveries, and increased regulation of technological change. The political environment shows an increasing amount of legislation regulating business, more vigorous government-agency enforcement, and the growth of public-interest groups. Finally, the cultural environment shows long-run trends toward self-fulfillment, immediate gratification, the easy life, informal and open relationships, and a more secular orientation.

QUESTIONS AND PROBLEMS

1. Many companies have defined the food industry as a major area of opportunity. Cite some trends and opportunities that characterize the food industry's future.

2. Describe the threats facing: (a) home diaper delivery services; and (b) night clubs.

3. Name two major threats and two major opportunities facing each of the following industries: (a) automobiles; (b) beer; (c) steel.

4. Indicate some of the ecological consequences of television on dating, automobile demand, eating habits, and housing.

5. Would you support or not support each of the following new legislative proposals (give your reasoning): (a) a bill to require companies in concentrated industries to go through federal hearings before each price boost; (b) a bill to allow auto makers to prevent dealers from selling outside their territories; (c) a bill to require manufacturers to grant wholesalers a bigger discount than they give to large retail chains; (d) a bill to protect independent retailers from price competition by a manufacturer who does retailing of his own?

6. Do you agree that the cultural trends cited in this chapter are taking place? Does it follow that firms should move with majority values?

7. A medium-sized candy bar company has experienced a serious decline in its market share in recent years, primarily because of the growing appeal of granola bars and other health food snacks. List different responses the company can make to this change in its environment.

8. What demographic trends are sure to affect Walt Disney Productions and how can it respond to these trends?

9. How can a company keep track of the technological trends that may affect it?

CONSUMER MARKETS AND BUYING BEHAVIOR

6

There is an old saying in Spain: To be a bullfighter, you must first learn to be a bull.
ANONYMOUS

The preceding chapter described the role of major *macroenvironmental forces* in creating broad opportunities as well as threats for the company. We are now ready to move to an understanding of *markets*, which are the starting point for all marketing planning and action. In this chapter, we will examine the nature of *consumer markets*. In the next chapter, we will examine *organizational markets*—specifically producer, reseller, and government markets.

We will first consider the general concept of a market, before turning to the consumer market.

THE CONCEPT OF A MARKET

What is a "market"? The term *market* has acquired many usages over the years.

1. One of the earliest usages is that a market is a *physical place* where buyers and sellers gather to exchange goods and services. Medieval towns had market squares where sellers brought their goods and buyers shopped for goods. Most American cities at one time had well-known sections called markets where owners of goods set up carts and buyers came from all over the city to look for bargains. Today, transactions occur all over the city in what are called shopping areas rather than markets.

2. To an economist, a market describes all the buyers and sellers involved in actual or potential transactions over some good or service. Thus the soft-drink market consists of major sellers, such as Coca-Cola, Pepsi-Cola, and Seven-Up, and all the consumers who buy soft drinks. The economist is interested in describing and evaluating the *structure, conduct,* and *performance* of the market. Market structure describes the number and size distribution of buyers and sellers, the degree of product differentiation, and entry barriers. Market conduct describes how firms set their policies on product development, pricing, selling, and advertising. Market performance describes the level of efficiency and innovation of a firm's operation and the major results achieved in sales and profits.

3. To a marketer, a market is *the set of all individuals and organizations who are actual or potential buyers of a product or service.* Thus the marketer limits market to mean the buyer side of the economist's definition of a market; the seller side is called the industry or competition. The marketer wants to know several things about the market, such as its size, purchasing power, needs, and preferences.

We will adopt the last definition of a market. The definition hinges on the definition of a buyer. A *buyer is anyone who might conceivably buy a given product.* This means someone (a person or organization) who (1) might have a latent interest in the product and (2) the means to acquire it. A buyer is someone who is potentially "willing and able to buy." Let us apply this to the market for microwave ovens. The market consists of both households and firms (such as restaurants). Focusing on households, we recognize that not all households will be in the market. Some consumers have no interest: their kitchens are too small; they feel these machines are too complex; they fear that they are dangerous. And among interested consumers, many are unwilling to pay $400 or more for one of these appliances.

This means that the size of a market at a given time is a function of existing parameters such as consumer beliefs and product prices. A seller can expand the size of a market by recognizing its dependence on these parameters. A manufacturer of microwave ovens can wage an educational campaign to convince consumers that microwave ovens are safe. Or the manufacturer might lower its prices below $400, which will expand the number of consumers who can afford it.

Whether there is a market for something is highlighted in the story of an American shoe company that sent a salesman to a large South Seas island to see if there was a market for shoes. He came back disappointed and said, "The people don't wear shoes; there is no market." The chief executive, however, decided to double check and he sent his ace salesman to the island. The day after arriving, the salesman wired back, "The people don't wear shoes; there is a tremendous market." The first salesman thought that a market consists of the current users of a product; the second salesman thought a market consists of everyone with two feet whose interest in shoes might be developed. The true market lies somewhere between these two extremes.

The job of a marketer is to know the market. To understand a specific market, one needs first a working knowledge of the operating characteristics of four generic types of markets: *consumer market, producer market, reseller market,* and *government market.* These markets are essentially distinguished on the basis of *the buyers' role and motives* rather than the characteristics of the purchased product. Consumers are individuals and households buying for personal use; producers are individuals and organizations buying for the purpose of producing; resellers are individuals and organizations buying for the purpose of reselling; and governments are governmental units buying for the purpose of carrying out governmental functions.

Because markets are complex, we need a common framework for grasping a market's operating characteristics. The marketer can develop a good understanding of any market by asking the following questions, which can be called the six Os of a market:[1]

1. Who is in the market?—*Occupants*
2. What does the market buy?—*Objects*
3. When does the market buy?—*Occasions*
4. Who is involved in the buying?—*Organization*
5. Why does the market buy?—*Objectives*
6. How does the market buy?—*Operations*

Just as in the alphabet the letter *O* precedes the letter *P*, the six Os of a market should be grasped before one contemplates the four Ps of the marketing mix (see Figure 6–1). For example, the fact that price and service are the most important marketing variables in selling steel, while advertising and sales promotion are the most important variables in selling soap, derives from the substantial differences in these markets regarding the six Os.

We will now examine the consumer market in terms of the six Os.

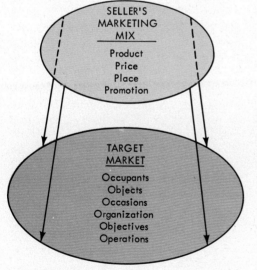

FIGURE 6–1
Marketing Strategy: Fine Tuning
the Marketing Mix to the Target Market

[1] Two other possible questions are, Where is the market? (outposts) and Where does the market buy? (outlets). The first will be treated in the next section (Who Is in the Consumer Market?), and the second will be treated in chap. 16.

WHO IS IN THE CONSUMER MARKET?

The consumer market consists of *all the individuals and households who buy or acquire goods and services for personal consumption*. We will use the American consumer market as an illustration of how a consumer market can be described. In 1976, the American consumer market consisted of 216.5 million persons who annually consume about $1.1 trillion worth of products and service—the equivalent of $5,080 worth for every man, woman, and child. Each year this market grows by another 1.5 million persons and another $100 billion, representing one of the most lucrative consumer markets in the world.[2]

Consumers vary tremendously in their ages, incomes, educational levels, mobility patterns, and tastes. Marketers have found it worthwhile to distinguish different groups and develop products and services tailored to their particular needs. If a market segment is large enough, some companies may set up special marketing programs to serve this market. Consider, for example, the black market:

> Comprising an important group in the United States are the 25 million blacks with a spending power of $60 billion. Blacks are especially good consumers—out of proportion to their numbers—of such products as soft drinks, clothing, and canned luncheon meats, making special marketing effort desirable on the part of manufacturers of those products. Furthermore, the rise in black "class consciousness" suggests the desirability of applying more differentiated marketing effort in terms of selling appeals, ad copy, ad media, and packaging.

Profitable marketing requires observing not only who the consumers are but also where they live. The 216 million Americans are scattered unevenly over an area of 3.6 million square miles. The major trends, as described in Chapter 5, are (1) movement of people to the Sunbelt states, (2) movement from rural to urban areas, and (3) movement from the city to the suburbs. Each of these has important implications for the formulation and location of marketing effort.

WHAT DO CONSUMERS BUY?

Available to the 216.5 million American consumers is a variety of products and services that until recently no one ever dreamed was possible. Today's consumer confronts an average of 6,800 grocery products in the modern supermarket. Each week that passes sees manufacturers trying to place 150 to 250 new products on the grocery shelves. The modern department store and mail-order catalog offer products in the tens of thousands.

Our interest is in finding some basis for classifying the vast number of consumer products. Two different classification schemes will be considered.

Durable Goods, Nondurable Goods, and Services

Three categories of goods can be distinguished on the basis of their rate of consumption and tangibility:[3]

[2] Major statistics on the consumer and other markets are taken from the *Statistical Abstract of the United States, 1977.*

[3] The definitions are taken from *Marketing Definitions: A Glossary of Marketing Terms,* compiled by the Committee on Definitions of the American Marketing Association, Ralph S. Alexander, chairman (Chicago: American Marketing Association, 1960).

Nondurable goods *Tangible goods which normally are consumed in one or a few uses* (examples: meat, soap). Since these goods are consumed fast and purchased frequently, they are likely to be made available in many locations, command a small margin, and develop strong brand loyalty.

Durable goods *Tangible goods which normally survive many uses* (examples: refrigerators, clothing). Durable products are likely to need more personal selling and service, command a higher margin, and require more seller guarantees.

Services *Activities, benefits, or satisfactions which are offered for sale* (examples: haircuts, repairs). Consumer services have the characteristics of being intangible, perishable, variable, and personal. As a result, they are likely to require more quality control, supplier credibility, and continuous availability.

Convenience Goods, Shopping Goods, and Specialty Goods

Goods can also be classified into three groups on the basis of consumer shopping habits:[4]

Convenience goods *Those consumers' goods which the customer usually purchases frequently, immediately, and with the minimum of effort in comparison and buying* (examples: tobacco products, soap, newspapers). Convenience goods can be further subdivided into *impulse goods* (for which the consumer puts forth no search effort) and *staple goods*.

Shopping goods *Those consumers' goods which the customer, in the process of selection and purchase, characteristically compares on such bases as suitability, quality, price, and style* (examples: furniture, dress goods, used automobiles, and major appliances). The consumer is likely to shop in a number of retail outlets to learn about the available goods and find the right item.

Specialty goods *Those consumers' goods with unique characteristics and/or brand identification for which a significant group of buyers are habitually willing to make a special purchasing effort* (examples: specific brands and types of fancy goods, hi-fi components, photographic equipment, and men's suits). Specialty goods do not involve shopping effort (since the consumer knows what he or she wants) but only shopping time to reach the outlets that carry these goods.[5]

WHEN DO CONSUMERS BUY?

The occasions for consumer buying can be analyzed along several dimensions. Whether consumers purchase a product frequently depends upon the rate of their consumption of the product. For example, households with young children

[4] *Marketing Definitions.*

[5] For further readings on the classification of goods, see Richard H. Holton, "The Distinction Between Convenience Goods, Shopping Goods, and Specialty Goods," *Journal of Marketing,* July 1958, pp. 53–56; Louis P. Bucklin, "Retail Strategy and the Classification of Consumer Goods," *Journal of Marketing,* January 1963, pp. 50–55; Leo V. Aspinwall, "The Characteristics of Goods Theory," in *Managerial Marketing: Perspectives and Viewpoints,* rev. ed., ed. William Lazer and Eugene J. Kelley (Homewood, Ill.: Richard D. Irwin, 1962), pp. 633–43; and Gordon E. Miracle, "Product Characteristics and Marketing Strategy," *Journal of Marketing,* January 1965, pp. 18–24.

consume milk at a much faster rate than childless households. Marketing strategy for such items is often based on segmenting the market into buyers with different consumption rates, that is, heavy, medium, and light users.

The purchase rate is also influenced by seasonal factors. Religious and secular holidays that entail entertaining and/or gift giving are eagerly anticipated by many industries as the time in which the highest percentage of the year's sales will be made. Seasonal fluctuations in the weather conditions affect the demand for swimsuits, snowmobiles, resort vacations, and air conditioners. Strong seasonal fluctuations in consumer purchasing can make cash flow and inventory management very difficult for businesses, and many try to counteract their effects by offering off-season discounts or sales.

Consumers also vary as to the time during the day or week they are most likely to make their purchases. The recent influx of women into the labor force with the consequent increase in men's participation in shopping has meant that an increased amount of shopping is done before or after work hours or on weekends. Stores of all kinds have extended their regular hours. Public transportation companies, restaurants, and museums have tried to minimize the effects of daily and weekly fluctuations in demand by offering discounts to users in off-peak hours.

Finally, economic conditions affect consumer purchase timing, particularly for durable or shopping and specialty goods. When the economic outlook is poor, consumers tend to postpone major purchases, although some will "buy now before it's too late."

WHO PARTICIPATES IN THE CONSUMER BUYING DECISION?

A key task facing a company is to determine who is the *customer* or *decision-making unit* for its product or service. For some products and services, the answer is relatively simple. For example, men are normally the decision-making unit for pipe tobacco, and women are the decision-making unit for pantyhose. On the other hand, the decision-making unit for a family automobile or vacation is likely to consist of husband, wife, and older children. In these cases the marketer must identify the roles and respective influence of the various family members in order to design the right product features and appeals.

There are five different roles that persons can play in a buying decision:

1. *Initiator.* The initiator is the person who first suggests or thinks of the idea of buying the particular product.
2. *Influencer.* An influencer is a person who explicitly or implicitly carries some influence on the final decision.
3. *Decider.* The decider is a person who ultimately determines any part or the whole of the buying decision: whether to buy, what to buy, how to buy, when to buy, or where to buy.
4. *Buyer.* The buyer is the person who makes the actual purchase.
5. *User.* The user is the person(s) who consumes or uses the product or service.

For example, in the decision to buy a new automobile, the suggestion might have come from the oldest child. Each member of the family may exert some influence on the decision or some component part, and even neighbors may have some influence. The husband and wife may make the final decision and act as the purchasing unit. The wife may be the prime user of the car.

The marketer's task is to study the roles played by different participants in each stage of the buying decision and the criteria that each typically applies in his or her role. For example, we noted that husbands and wives jointly participate in the family's decision to buy a new automobile. It would be helpful to know the roles played by husbands and wives in the different decision areas.

> Davis found that the decision of "when to buy an automobile" was influenced primarily by the husband in 68 percent of the cases, primarily by the wife in 3 percent of the cases, and equally in 29 percent of the cases.[6] On the other hand, the decision of "what color automobile to buy" was influenced primarily by the husband in 25 percent of the cases, by the wife in 25 percent of the cases, and equally in 50 percent of the cases.

An auto company would take these factors into account in designing a family car and promoting it.

Marketers have researched various family characteristics that might provide a clue to the relative influence of different family members in the purchase process. One characteristic is the *locus of family authority*. Herbst has observed four types of families: (1) *autonomic,* where an equal number of separate decisions is made by each partner; (2) *husband-dominance,* the husband dominates; (3) *wife-dominance,* the wife dominates; and (4) *syncratic,* where most decisions are made jointly.[7] All types of families may be found at any time, although the relative proportions may be changing over time. With rising education and income, families are moving away from a husband-dominance model toward a syncratic model, and this has important implications for marketers in their prospect targeting.

WHAT ARE CONSUMERS SEEKING?

The consumer market buys products and services to satisfy a variety of needs—physiological, social, psychological, and spiritual. Economists say that consumers are *utility maximizers,* that is, they will use their limited resources to acquire a bundle of goods that will put them on the highest utility curve.

In considering a particular good, the consumer will see it as a bundle of attributes. Thus a toothpaste offers a combination of dental protection, taste, and breath-freshening. Each brand of toothpaste will combine these attributes in different proportions. Furthermore, the individual consumer will place different values on these various attributes reflecting what he or she is seeking. Thus each brand offers the customer a certain total utility at a certain price. The consumer will choose the brand that maximizes the *value-to-cost* ratio.

[6] Harry L. Davis, "Dimensions of Marital Roles in Consumer Decision-Making," *Journal of Marketing Research,* May 1970, pp. 168–77.

[7] P. G. Herbst, "Conceptual Framework for Studying the Family," in *Social Structure and Personality in a City,* ed. O. A. Oeser and S. B. Hammond (London: Routledge & Kegan Paul Ltd., 1954), chap. 10.

This economic interpretation of consumer motivation is formally correct but lacks the rich explanations and insights of behavioral analysis. We will present a behavioral interpretation of motivation later in this chapter.

HOW DO CONSUMERS BUY?

We now come to a key task facing marketers, that of trying to understand how consumers buy. For example, camera manufacturers would like to know how consumers end up deciding to buy cameras in the first place and particular brands of cameras in the second place. Colleges would like to know how high school students decide to attend college in the first place and how they end up in particular colleges in the second place. What are the buyers' decision-making processes that lead to particular buying decisions?

The task of understanding consumer buying behavior is enormously complex, and whole books have been written on the topic.[8] Here we will attempt to present the main concepts and findings. We will present them in the course of answering four questions:

1. What are the major factors influencing the consumers' buying decisions? *(Buying influences)*
2. What is the role played by the type of buying situation? *(Buying situation)*
3. What subdecisions are involved in the buying decision? *(Buying decision)*
4. What is the buying process through which the buyer passes? *(Buying process)*

Major Factors Influencing Consumer Buying Behavior

If we were to analyze any specific consumer purchase, say a purchase of a Nikon camera by a Betty Smith, we would be able to identify a multitude of factors that played some role in influencing Betty Smith to end up buying that particular camera. These factors could be sorted into four major groups, those associated with the *buyer,* with the *product,* with the *seller,* or with the *situation* (see Figure 6–2). The various factors associated with each major component are described on p. 137.

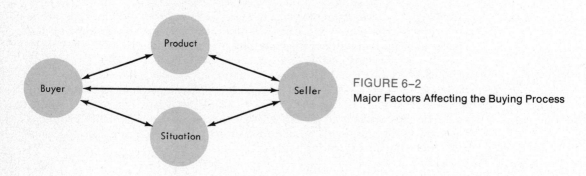

FIGURE 6–2
Major Factors Affecting the Buying Process

---

[8] See John A. Howard and Jagdish N. Sheth, *The Theory of Buyer Behavior* (New York: John Wiley & Sons, 1969); Francesco M. Nicosia, *Consumer Decision Processes* (Englewood Cliffs, N. J.: Prentice-Hall, 1966); and James F. Engel, Roger D. Blackwell, and David T. Kollat, *Consumer Behavior*, 3rd ed. (New York: Holt, Rinehart and Winston, 1978).

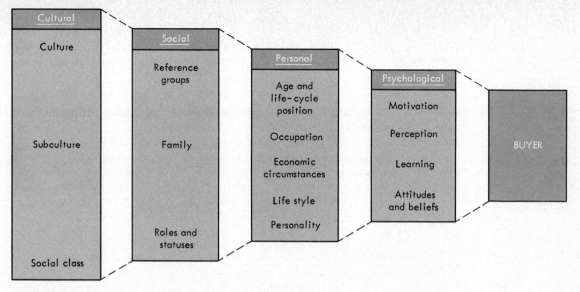

FIGURE 6–3
Buyer Characteristics Influencing Consumer Buying Behavior

1. **Buyer characteristics.** We would first need to know several things about Betty Smith to understand how she came to buy a Nikon camera. We would want to understand *cultural, social, personal,* and *psychological* factors that operate in her life (see Figure 6–3). Cultural factors include the *culture* from which she comes, her *subculture* identifications, and her *social* class. Social factors include the influence of other people in her life, particularly her *reference groups, family,* and *roles and statuses.* Personal characteristics include her *age and life-cycle position, occupation, economic circumstances, life style,* and *personality.* Finally, psychological characteristics include her *motivation, perceptions, attitudes and beliefs,* and *learning.* We will shortly examine these buyer characteristics in more detail.

2. **Product characteristics.** Various characteristics of the product will influence the buying decision. Betty Smith will pay attention to the Nikon's features, styling, quality, price, and backup services in making her decision. The marketer has control over these product attributes and can design them in a way to maximize the product's appeal to the target market.

3. **Seller characteristics.** Characteristics of the seller will influence the buying outcome. In this case, Betty Smith will form an opinion about the manufacturer, Nikon, and the retail outlet, say the ABC Camera Company. Betty will have a certain image of Nikon's reliability and service as a manufacturer. Betty will also form an impression of the retailer's knowledgeability, friendliness, and service. Thus the manufacturer and the retailer will want to consider the seller characteristics that affect Betty's decision as to whether she buys the camera.

4. **Situational characteristics.** Various situational factors also influence the buying decision. One such factor is the *time pressure* felt by Betty Smith to make a decision: under great time pressure, she might make the decision with less information, relying more on the salesperson than she would if she had more time to investigate. Other factors include the time of the year, weather, chance meetings with friends who have opinions about cameras, and the current economic outlook.

All four components of the buying situation—buyer, product, seller, and situation—interact to produce the buying outcome. We shall have much to say about the product, the seller, and the situation throughout the book. Here we will concentrate on the buyer's characteristics. We want to understand more deeply how the buyer's cultural, social, personal, and psychological characteristics influence the buying outcome.

Cultural characteristics The broadest influence on the buyer is the buyer's cultural characteristics, particularly the buyer's culture, subcultures, and social-class identifications. We shall look at the role played by each of these.

CULTURE Culture is the most fundamental determinant of a person's wants and behavior. Whereas the behavior of lower creatures is largely governed by instinct, human behavior is largely learned. The new baby as it grows up in a society will learn a basic set of values, perceptions, preferences, and behaviors, through a process of socialization involving the family and other key institutions.

Betty Smith's knowledge and interest in cameras are a function of being raised in a modern society where camera technolgy as well as a whole set of consumer learnings and values have developed. Betty is able to consider a camera because she knows what cameras are, because she knows how to read instructions on how to operate cameras, and because her society has accepted the idea that women use cameras. In another culture, say a remote backward tribe in central Australia, a camera would mean nothing to the tribespeople. It would simply be a curiosity. International marketers know that cultures are at different stages of development and interest with respect to buying cameras and other objects, and they have to consider this in choosing target markets and preparing marketing programs.

SUBCULTURES Each culture contains smaller groups or subcultures, and each of these provides more specific identification and socialization for its members. Four types of subcultures can be distinguished. *Nationality groups* such as the Irish, Polish, Italians, and Puerto Ricans are found within large communities and exhibit distinct ethnic tastes and proclivities. *Religious groups* such as the Catholics, Mormons, Presbyterians, and Jews represent subcultures with specific cultural preferences and taboos. *Racial groups* such as the blacks and Orientals have distinct cultural styles and attitudes. *Geographical areas* such as the Deep South, California, and New England are distinct subcultures with characteristic life styles.

Betty Smith's interest in various goods obviously will be influenced by her nationality, religion, race, and geographical background. Most likely her food preferences will be similarly influenced and also her clothing choices, recreations, and career aspirations. Her subculture identifications may or may not have played a prominent role on her wanting to buy a camera and choosing a Nikon. We can imagine that various subcultures attach different meanings to picture taking, and her interest could have been influenced by the meaning photography has in her subculture.

SOCIAL CLASS Virtually all human societies exhibit social stratification. Stratification may take the form of a caste system where the members of different castes are reared for certain roles and cannot change their caste membership. More frequently, stratification takes the form of social classes (see Table 6–1). *Social classes are relatively homogeneous and enduring divisions in a*

TABLE 6–1
Characteristics of Six Major American Social Classes

1. *Upper uppers* (less than 1 percent). Upper uppers are the social elite who live on inherited wealth and have a well-known family background. They give large sums to charity, run the debutante balls, maintain more than one home, and send their children to the finest schools. They are a market for expensive jewelry, antiques, homes, and vacations. While small as a group, they serve as a reference group for others to the extent that their consumption decisions trickle down and are imitated by the other social classes.

2. *Lower uppers* (about 2 percent). Lower uppers are persons who have earned high income or wealth through exceptional ability in the professions or business. They usually come from the middle class. They tend to be active in social and civic affairs and seek to buy the symbols of status for themselves and their children, such as expensive homes, schools, yachts, swimming pools, and automobiles. They include the *nouveaux riches,* whose pattern of conspicuous consumption is designed to impress those below them. The ambition of lower uppers is to be accepted in the upper-upper stratum, which is more likely to be achieved by their children than themselves.

3. *Upper middles* (12 percent). Upper middles are concerned with "career." They have attained positions as lawyers, physicians, scientists, and college professors. They believe in education and want their children to develop professional or administrative skills so that they do not drop into a lower stratum. This class likes to deal in ideas and "high culture." They are the quality market for good homes, clothes, furniture, and appliances. They seek to run a gracious home entertaining friends and clients.

4. *Lower middles* (30 percent). Lower middles are concerned with "respectability." They exhibit conscientious work habits and adhere to culturally defined norms and standards, including going to church and obeying the law. The home is important, and lower middles like to keep it neat and "pretty." They buy conventional home furnishings and do a lot of their own work around the home. The lower-middle-class wife spends a lot of time shopping for the family looking for buys. Although "white collars" make up a large part of this group, so do "gray collars" (mailmen, firemen) and "aristocrat blue collars" (plumbers, factory foremen).

5. *Upper lowers* (35 percent). Upper lowers lead a day-to-day existence of unchanging activities. They live in small houses and apartments in dull areas of the city. The men work at manual jobs and have only a moderate education. The working-class wife spends most of her time in the house cooking, cleaning, and caring for her children. She sees being the mother of her children as her main vocation, and she has little time for organizations and social activity.

6. *Lower lowers* (20 percent). Lower lowers are at the bottom of society and considered by the other classes as slum dwellers or "riffraff." Some lower lowers try to rise above their class but often fall back and ultimately stop trying. They tend to be poorly educated. They often reject middle-class standards of morality and behavior. They buy more impulsively. They often do not evaluate quality, and they pay too much for products and buy on credit. They are a large market for food, television sets, and used automobiles.

SOURCE: From *Consumer Behavior,* 3rd ed. by James F. Engel, Roger D. Blackwell, and David T. Kollat. Copyright © 1978 by The Dryden Press. Reprinted and adapted by permission of Holt, Rinehart and Winston.

society that are hierarchically ordered and whose members share similar values, interests, and behavior.

Social classes have several characteristics: (1) persons within a given social class tend to behave more alike; (2) persons are ranked as occupying inferior or superior positions according to their social class; (3) social class is not indicated by any single variable but is measured as a weighted function of one's occupation, income, wealth, education, value orientation, and so on; and (4) social class is continuous rather than discrete, with individuals able to move into a higher social class or drop into a lower one.

Social classes show distinct product-form and brand preferences in such areas as clothing, home furnishings, leisure activity, and automobiles. For example, Betty Smith's interest in an expensive and complex camera is more likely if she comes from an upper-middle-class background than from a lower-lower-class background. We can imagine that she attended an elite women's college in the East where she majored in writing and film making, and this experience led her to want to become a professional photographer. Even the retail stores that Betty patronizes for cameras and other goods may be heavily influenced by her social-class background.

Social characteristics The next group of factors affecting the buying outcome relates to people in the buyer's life and the impact they have on his or her buying behavior. We call these social factors, and they include reference groups, family, and the roles and statuses of the buyer.

REFERENCE GROUPS Reference groups are all those groups that influence a person's attitudes, opinions, and values. Some are *primary groups* (also called face-to-face groups), such as family, close friends, neighbors, and fellow workers, and others are *secondary groups*, such as fraternal organizations and professional associations. People are also influenced by groups they are not members of, called *aspirational groups*. Sports heroes and movie stars are typical members of these groups.

A person is significantly influenced by his or her reference groups in at least three ways. These reference groups expose the person to possible new behaviors and life styles. They also influence the person's attitudes and self-concept because the person normally desires to "fit in." And they create pressures for conformity that may affect the person's actual product and brand choices.

A company would like to know whether a consumer's decisions to purchase its product and brand are importantly influenced by reference groups, and if so, which reference groups. In the case of some products, such as soap and canned peaches, the buyer normally makes choices without any reference-group influence. Betty Smith's friends are not a factor in her decision to buy soap or in her brand choice. To the extent that product or brand choice is not subject to reference-group influence, the seller's marketing communications should stress the product's attributes, price, and quality, or other differential advantages.

There are other products where reference-group influence tends to be a strong factor in product and/or brand choice.[9] Reference-group influence tends to be strong when the product is visible and conspicuous to other people whom the buyer respects. Betty Smith's decision to buy a camera and her brand choice may be strongly influenced by some of her reference groups. Members of a pho-

[9] Bourne found that reference-group influence is strong for both product and brand choice in the case of cars and cigarettes; strong in product choice but weak in brand choice for air conditioners, instant coffee, and TV; strong in brand choice but weak in product choice for clothing, furniture, and toilet soap; and weak in both in soap, canned peaches, and radios. Francis S. Bourne, *Group Influence in Marketing and Public Relations*, Foundation for Research on Human Behavior (Ann Arbor, Mich.: The Foundation, 1956).

tography club that she belongs to may have a strong influence on her decision to buy a better camera and on the brand she chooses. At the same time, another reference group, such as her girl friends, probably had no influence on either decision. The more cohesive the reference group, the more effective its communication process, and the higher the person esteems it, the more influential it will be in shaping the person's product and brand choices.

If the company senses a high influence coming from certain reference groups, its task is to figure out how to reach the group's opinion leaders. At one time, sellers thought that *opinion leaders* were primarily community social leaders whom the mass market imitated because of "snob appeal." Today, it is recognized that opinion leaders are found in all strata of society and that a particular person may be an opinion leader in certain product areas and an opinion follower in other areas. The marketer then tries to reach the opinion leaders by identifying certain personal characteristics associated with opinion leadership, determining the newspapers and magazines read by opinion leaders, and developing messages that are likely to be picked up by opinion leaders.

FAMILY   Of all the face-to-face groups, a person's family undoubtedly plays the largest and most enduring role in influencing his or her attitudes, opinions, and values. From the family the person acquires a mental set not only toward religion, politics, and economics but also toward personal ambition, self-worth, and love. Even if the buyer no longer interacts very much with his or her family, the family's influence on the unconscious behavior of the buyer can be strong.

In the case of Betty Smith buying a camera, her family may or may not be an influence. They may state their opinions; they may support her career goal; they may loan or refuse to loan her money. They can make a difference in her behavior. With respect to the other products that she buys, the potential role of family members as coinfluencers should always be considered by the marketer.

ROLES AND STATUSES   A person participates in many groups throughout life—family, other reference groups, organizations, and institutions. The person will have a certain position in each group that can be defined in terms of *role* and *status*. For example, with her parents Betty Smith plays the role of *daughter;* in her family she plays the role of *wife;* in her part-time job she plays the role of *artist*. A role consists of a set of activities that the person is supposed to perform according to the definition and expectations of the individual and the persons around him or her.

Each role has a status attached to it, which reflects the general esteem accorded to that role in society or in the eyes of the immediate group. The role of Supreme Court Justice has extremely high status in this society; the role of artist has a lower status. Betty's interest in becoming an independent professional photographer is partly for self-fulfillment and partly to raise her status in society.

A person's roles and statuses influence not only general behavior but also buying behavior. Betty Smith's role within her own family as wife means that she will probably take responsibility for certain purchases for the family. Although the role of wives is changing, women still make the majority of buying decisions in connection with such household items as laundry supplies, food, paper products, and health-care products. Betty Smith's role as photographer means that she will be buying camera, film, developing paper, chemicals, an enlarger, and so on. If she aspires to be a high-status photographer, this aspiration will influence the type of equipment she will want to own and operate.

Personal characteristics   A buyer's decisions are also influenced by personal outward characteristics, notably the buyer's age and life cycle, occupation, economic circumstances, life style, and personality. We shall examine these personal characteristics below.

AGE AND LIFE CYCLE   There is no question that the goods and services that people buy change over their lifetime. While people eat throughout their lives, the type of food changes from baby food in the early years to most foods in the growing and mature years to a more restricted list in the later years because of special diets and food taboos. People's taste in clothes, furniture, and recreation is also age-related.

The concept of *family life cycle* has been developed to help identify possible changing wants, attitudes, and values as people grow older. Seven stages of the family life cycle have been distinguished:

1. *The bachelor stage:* Young, single people
2. *Newly married couples:* Young, no children
3. *The full nest I:* Young married couples with youngest child under six
4. *The full nest II:* Young married couples with youngest child six or over
5. *The full nest III:* Older married couples with dependent children
6. *The empty nest:* Older married couples with no children living with them
7. *The solitary survivors:* Older single people

Each life-cycle group has certain distinguishable needs and interests. The full nest I group is very much in the market for washers and dryers, TVs, baby food, and toys, whereas the full nest III group is in the market for nonessential appliances, boats, dental services, and magazines. The patterns of buying task specialization, authority, and relative influence vary for different life-cycle groups.

Some recent work has attempted to identify *psychological life stages*. Adults will experience certain *passages* or *transitions*.[10] Thus Betty Smith may move from being a satisfied housewife to a stage in which she is an unsatisfied one searching for new ways to fulfill herself. This may have contributed to her current strong interest in photography. Clearly, marketers ought to pay more attention to the changing needs of adults for goods and services that might be associated with adult passages.

OCCUPATION   A person's occupation will lead to certain needs and wants for goods and services. A blue-collar worker will buy workclothes, workshoes, lunch boxes, and bowling recreation. His or her company president will buy expensive cashmere jackets or ultra-suede dresses, air travel, country club membership, and a large sailboat. Betty Smith's interest in being a photographer will lead her to buy a whole range of photographic equipment and supplies as long as she remains in this occupation. In general, marketers can study whether certain occupational groups will have an above-average interest in their products and services. Or they can even choose to specialize in producing the particular products and services needed by a particular occupational group.

ECONOMIC CIRCUMSTANCES   People's economic circumstances will greatly affect the goods and services they consider and buy. Their circumstances consist

[10] Gail Sheehy, *Passages: Predictable Crises in Adult Life* (New York: E. P. Dutton & Co., 1974); and Daniel J. Levinson, *Seasons of a Man's Life* (New York: Alfred Knopf, 1978).

of their *income* (its level, stability, and time pattern), *savings and assets* (including the percentage that is liquid), *borrowing power,* and *attitude toward spending versus saving.* Thus Betty Smith can consider buying an expensive Nikon only if she has enough income, savings, or borrowing power and places more importance on spending now than on saving. Marketers of various income-sensitive goods and services pay continuous attention to trends in personal income, savings, and interest rates. If economic indicators indicate a worsening economic climate, they can take positive steps to redesign, reposition, and reprice their product, reduce their production and inventories, and do other things to protect their financial solvency.

LIFE STYLE   Another personal characteristic affecting buying behavior is the style of life that people choose to lead. People coming from the same subculture, social class, and even occupational group can choose to lead quite different life styles. Betty Smith, for example, can choose to be a solid homemaker, a career woman, or a "glamour woman." As it turns out, she plays several roles, and her way of reconciling them becomes her life style. Her wish to be a professional photographer has further life-style implications—she might be away from home more, stay out late at night, and enter somewhat marginal situations to take pictures.

Marketers believe that a person's product and brand choices are a key indicator of his or her life style. The following person is very real to us as a result of knowing his consumer preferences:

> He's a bachelor . . . lives in one of those modern high-rise apartments and the rooms are brightly colored. He has modern, expensive furniture, but not Danish modern. He buys his clothes at Brooks Brothers. He owns a good hi-fi. He skis. He has a sailboat. He eats Limburger and any other prestige cheese with his beer. He likes and cooks a lot of steak and would have filet mignon for company. His liquor cabinet has Jack Daniels bourbon, Beefeater gin, and a good Scotch.[11]

The implications of the life-style concept are well stated by Levy:

> Marketing is a process of providing customers with parts of a potential mosaic from which they, as artists of their own life styles, can pick and choose to develop the composition that for the time seems the best. The marketer who thinks about his products in this way will seek to understand their potential settings and relationships to other parts of consumer life styles, and thereby to increase the number of ways they fit meaningfully into the pattern.[12]

PERSONALITY   Another characteristic influencing the person's buying behavior is personality. Personality describes the organization of the individual's distinguishing character traits, attitudes, and habits. Each person has a distinct personality marked by such traits as their degree of extroversion versus introversion; impulsiveness versus deliberateness; creativity versus conventionality; and activeness versus passiveness. Suppose Betty Smith is extroverted,

---

[11] Sidney J. Levy, "Symbolism and Life Style," in *Toward Scientific Marketing*, ed. Stephen A. Greyser (Chicago: American Marketing Association, 1964), pp. 140–50.

[12] Harper W. Boyd, Jr., and Sidney J. Levy, *Promotion: A Behavioral View* (Englewood Cliffs, N. J.: Prentice-Hall, 1967), p. 38.

impulsive, creative, and active. This explains to some extent her interest in photography. It also implies that she will be active in searching for a camera, talking to people, asking them questions, and buying when it feels right.

Marketers of various products search for potential personality traits that their target market might show. For example, a beer company might discover that heavy beer drinkers are more outgoing, aggressive, and dogmatic. It might decide to develop a brand image for its beer that will appeal to that type of person. The likely step is to feature a real person in the ad who has these traits, so that heavy beer drinkers can identify and feel that this is their brand. While personality variables have not shown up that strongly in all product areas, some companies have been able to use personality segmentation to advantage.[13]

Many marketers use a related idea, that of a person's *self-concept*. Self-concept describes the way we see ourselves and think others see us. The theory holds that people generally choose products and brands that match their self-concept. Therefore the marketer tries to develop a brand concept that matches the target market's self-concept. This has worked with mixed success, however. Some of the problem stems from the fact that people have at least two types of self-concepts: their *actual self-concept* (the way a person really sees herself), and their *ideal self-concept* (the way a person would like to see herself). Thus it is not clear whether people like a product that is made for how they actually see themselves or for how they would like to see themselves.

Psychological characteristics   A person's buying choices are also influenced by four major psychological processes—motivation, perception, learning, and beliefs and attitudes. We shall explore the role of these psychological processes in the following paragraphs.

MOTIVATION   We saw that Betty Smith became interested in buying a camera. Why? What is she really seeking? What needs is she trying to satisfy?

A person will recognize himself or herself as having all kinds of needs at any point in time. Some needs are *biogenic,* so called because they arise from physiological states of tension such as might be caused by the need for food, drink, sex, and bodily comfort. Other needs are *psychogenic,* so called because they arise from psychological states of tension, such as the need for recognition, response, or variety of experience. Most of these needs, whether latent or recognized, do not necessarily move or motivate the person to act at a given point in time. A need must be aroused to a sufficient level of intensity for it to serve as a motive. A *motive* (or drive) is a stimulated need that is sufficiently pressing to direct the person toward the goal of satisfying the need. When the need is satisfied, the person's tension is discharged, and the person returns to a state of equilibrium.

Psychologists have offered various theories of human motivation. Two of the most popular are Maslow's and Freud's.

MASLOW'S THEORY OF MOTIVATION   Maslow's theory of motivation is based on the following premises:[14]

1. A person will have many needs.

---

[13] See chap. 8, pp. 201–2.

[14] Abraham H. Maslow, *Motivation and Personality* (New York: Harper & Row, 1954).

2. These needs will vary in importance (or potency level) and therefore can be ranked in a hierarchy.

3. The person will seek to satisfy the most important need first.

4. When the person succeeds in satisfying an important need, it will cease being a motivator for the time being.

5. The person will then turn his or her attention to the next important need.

According to Maslow, the needs, in order of their importance, are *physiological needs, safety needs, social needs, esteem needs,* and *self-actualization needs.* They are defined in Table 6–2.

What light does Maslow's theory throw on Betty Smith's interest in buying a camera? We can surmise that Betty has well satisfied her physiological, safety, and social needs, and therefore they are not motivators of her interest in cameras. We can consider the possibility that her camera interest grows out of a strong need she has for more esteem from others, a need that would come to a person who has been a homemaker for a long time. It may well be, however, that Betty is not even motivated by a need for self-esteem in that she feels quite secure about herself and her roles. Then we would surmise that her camera interest is aroused by a higher level of need, that of self-actualization. She wants to actualize her potential as a creative person and express herself through photography.

**TABLE 6–2
Maslow's Hierarchy of Needs**

PHYSICAL

1. *Physiological*—the fundamentals of survival, including hunger and thirst.
2. *Safety*—concern over physical survival, ordinary prudence, which might be overlooked in striving to satisfy hunger or thirst.

SOCIAL

3. *Belongingness and love*—striving to be accepted by intimate members of one's family and to be an important person to them. This striving could also include others to whom the person feels close.
4. *Esteem and status*—striving to achieve a high standing relative to others, including desire for mastery, reputation, and prestige.

SELF

5. *Self-actualization*—a desire to develop a personal system of values leading to self-realization.

FREUD'S THEORY OF MOTIVATION Freud asserts that people are not likely to be conscious of the real motives guiding their behavior because these motives have been shaped in early childhood and are often repressed from their own consciousness. Only through special methods of probing can their motives really be discovered and understood.

According to Freud, a child enters the world with instinctual drives and tries to gratify them through blatant means such as grabbing or crying. Very quickly and painfully the child becomes aware that instant need gratification is not possible. Repeated frustration leads the child to perfect more subtle means for gratification.

The child's psyche grows more complex as the child grows older. A part, the id, remains the reservoir of strong drives and urges. Another part, the ego, becomes the child's conscious center for planning to obtain satisfactions. A third part, the superego, causes the instinctive drives to be channeled into socially approved outlets to avoid the pain of guilt or shame.

The guilt or shame a person feels about some urges, especially sexual urges, leads to their repression. Through such defense mechanisms as rationalization and sublimation, these urges are denied or transmuted into socially acceptable behavior. Yet these urges are never eliminated or under perfect control; they emerge in dreams, in slips of the tongue, in neurotic and obsessional behavior, or ultimately in mental breakdowns when the ego can no longer maintain the delicate balance between the impulsive power of the id and the oppressive power of the superego.

A person's behavior, therefore, is never simple. His or her motivational wellsprings are not obvious to a casual observer or deeply understood by the person. If Betty is about to purchase an expensive camera, she may describe her motive to wanting a hobby or career. At a deeper level, she may be purchasing the camera to impress others with her talent. At a still deeper level, she may be buying the camera to feel young and independent again.

An important marketing implication of Freudian motivation theory is that buyers are motivated by *psychological* as well as *functional* product concerns. When Betty looks at cameras, she will not only process the functional information about the camera's performance but also react emotionally and intellectually to various other cues. The camera's shape, size, weight, material, color, and case are all capable of triggering deep emotions. A rugged-looking camera can arouse Betty's feelings about being independent, feelings that she either can handle or will want to avoid. Thus the manufacturer, in designing the product, should be aware of the role of visual and tactile elements in triggering deeper emotions that can stimulate or inhibit purchase.

The leading exponent of Freudian motivation theory in marketing is Ernest Dichter who for over two decades has been interpreting buying situations and product choices in terms of underlying unconscious motives. Dichter calls his approach *motivational research.* It consists of in-depth interviews with a few dozen target buyers designed to uncover deeper motives that the product has triggered in them. Various "projective techniques" are used to throw the ego off guard—techniques such as word association, sentence completion, picture interpretation, and role playing.

Motivation researchers have produced some interesting and occasionally bizarre hypotheses about what may be in the buyer's mind regarding certain purchases. They have suggested that:

Some businessmen don't fly because of a fear of posthumous guilt—if they crashed, their wives would think them stupid for not taking trains.

Men want their cigars to be odoriferous in order to prove their masculinity.

Women prefer vegetable shortening to animal fats because the latter arouse a sense of guilt over killing animals.

Men who wear suspenders are reacting to an unresolved castration complex.

A woman is very serious when baking a cake because she is going through the symbolic act of giving birth. She is averse to cake mixes that involve no labor because the easy life evokes a sense of guilt.

PERCEPTION   A motivated person is ready to act. How the motivated person decides to act is influenced by his or her perception of the situation. Two people in the same motivated state and objective situation may act quite differently because they perceive the situation differently. Betty Smith might see a fast-talking camera salesperson as pushy, insincere, and aggressive. Another camera buyer might see the same salesperson as intelligent, helpful, and articulate.

Why do people have different perceptions of the same situation? We start with the notion that all of us apprehend a stimulus object through *sensations,* that is, flows of information through one or more of our five senses: sight, hearing, smell, touch, and taste. However, each of us attends, organizes, and interprets this sensory information in an individual way. In fact, perception can be defined as "the process by which an individual selects, organizes, and interprets information inputs to create a meaningful picture of the world."[15] Perception depends not only on (1) the character of the physical stimuli but also on (2) the relation of the stimuli to the surrounding field (the gestalt idea) and on (3) conditions within the individual.

The following three mechanisms explain why people can have quite different perceptions of the same stimulus object or situation: selective exposure, selective distortion, and selective retention.

SELECTIVE EXPOSURE   People are exposed to a tremendous number of stimuli every moment of their lives. Consider the stimuli that come from various forms of advertising—people may be exposed to over 1,500 ads a day. It is impossible for a person to attend to all of the stimuli. Most of the stimuli will be screened out. The real challenge is to explain which stimuli people will notice. People will be selectively exposed to certain stimuli.

1. People are more likely to notice stimuli that bear on a current felt need of theirs. Betty Smith will notice all kinds of ads about cameras because she is motivated to buy one but will probably not notice ads about stereophonic equipment.

2. People are more likely to notice stimuli that they anticipate. Betty Smith is more likely to notice cameras in the camera store than a line of radios also carried by the store because she did not expect to see radios in the store.

3. People are more likely to notice stimuli whose change level is large in relation to the normal size of the stimuli. Betty Smith is more likely to notice an ad offering $100 off the list price of a Nikon than one offering $5 off the list price of a Nikon.[16]

[15] Bernard Berelson and Gary A. Steiner, *Human Behavior: An Inventory of Scientific Findings* (New York: Harcourt Brace Jovanovich, 1964), p. 88.

[16] This relationship is known as Weber's Law and is one of the main laws in psychophysics. See Steuart Henderson Britt, *Psychological Principles of Marketing and Consumer Behavior* (Lexington, Mass.: Lexington Books, 1978), p. 133.

Selective exposure means that marketers have to work especially hard to gain the attention of consumers in the marketplace. Their messages will be lost on most people who are not in the market for the product. Even people who are in the market may not notice a message unless it stands out from the surrounding sea of stimuli. Ads that are larger in size, or use four-color where most ads are black and white, or are novel and provide contrast are more likely to be noticed.

SELECTIVE DISTORTION Even stimuli that consumers note do not necessarily come across in the intended way. Each person has an organized mind set and attempts to fit incoming stimuli into preexisting modes of thinking. Selective distortion is the name given to the tendency of people to twist information into personal meanings. Thus Betty Smith may hear the salesperson mention some good and bad points about a competing camera brand. Since she already has a strong leaning toward Nikon, she is likely to distort the points she hears in order to conclude that Nikon is the better camera. People tend to interpret information in a way that will be consonant rather than dissonant with their preconceptions.

SELECTIVE RETENTION People will forget much that they learn. They will tend to retain information that supports their attitudes and beliefs. Because of selective retention, Betty is likely to remember good points mentioned about the Nikon and forget good points mentioned about competing cameras. She remembers Nikon's good points because she "rehearses" them more whenever she thinks about her decision to buy a camera.

These three perceptual factors—selective exposure, distortion, and retention—mean that marketers have to work hard to break through very strong perceptual filters. This explains why marketers have to buy so much message repetition, and why they place such an emphasis on message simplicity and clarity.

LEARNING When people act, they experience direct and indirect effects which influence their future behavior. Learning is the name given to changes in an individual's behavior arising from experience. Most behavior is learned. The exception is behavior based on instinctive responses, growth, or temporary physiological states of the organism such as hunger or fatigue.

Learning theorists hold that a person's learning is produced through the interplay of drives, stimuli, cues, responses, and reinforcement.

We have seen that Betty Smith has a drive toward self-actualization. A *drive* is defined as a strong internal stimulus impelling action. Her drive becomes a *motive* when it is directed toward a particular drive-reducing *stimulus object,* in this case a camera. Betty's response to the idea of buying a camera is conditioned by the surrounding configuration of cues. *Cues* are minor stimuli that determine when, where, and how the person responds. Her husband's opinion on buying a camera, the economic outlook, and the season of the year are all cues that may affect her *response* to the impulse to buy a camera.

Suppose Betty buys the camera. If the experience is *rewarding,* the probability is that she will use the camera more and more. Her response to cameras will be reinforced.

Later on, Betty may also want to buy a tape recorder and may experience cues similar to those she encountered when she bought a camera. If she responds in the same way to these cues and buys the tape recorder, and is satisfied, this reinforces her response to similar stimuli and drives in the future. We say that she *generalizes* her response to similar stimuli.

A countertendency to generalization is *discrimination.* When Betty has the opportunity to use two similar cameras on a trial basis and finds one more rewarding, her ability to discriminate between fairly similar cue configurations in the future improves. Discrimination means she has learned to recognize differences in sets of stimuli and can adjust her responses accordingly.

The practical import of learning theory for marketers is that they can build up demand for a product by associating it with strong drives, providing motivating cue configurations and providing positive reinforcement. A new company can enter the market by appealing to the same drives that competitors do and providing similar cue configurations because buyers are more likely to transfer loyalty to similar brands than to dissimilar brands (generalization). Or it may aim its brand to appeal to a different set of strong drives and offer cue inducements to switch.

BELIEFS AND ATTITUDES   Through the learning process, people acquire their beliefs and attitudes. These in turn influence their behavior.

A *belief* is a *descriptive thought that a person holds about something.* Betty Smith may believe that a Nikon takes great pictures, stands up well under rugged usage, and costs $550. These beliefs may be based on real knowledge, opinion, or faith. They may or may not carry any emotional charge. For example, Betty Smith's belief that a Nikon is black in color may or may not matter to her decision.

Manufacturers, of course, are very much interested in the beliefs that people carry in their heads about their products and services. These beliefs make up product and brand images, and people's behavior will be partly a function of their beliefs. If some of the beliefs are wrong and inhibit purchase, the manufacturer will want to launch a campaign to correct these wrong beliefs.

An *attitude* describes a person's *enduring favorable or unfavorable cognitive evaluations, emotional feelings, and action tendencies toward some object or idea.*[17] People carry attitudes toward almost everything: religion, politics, clothes, music, food, and so on. Attitudes put them into a frame of mind of liking or disliking things, moving toward or moving away from them. Thus Betty Smith may hold such attitudes as "buy the best," "the Japanese make the best products in the world," and "creativity and self-expression are among the most important things in life." The Nikon camera is therefore salient to Betty because it fits well into her preexisting attitudes. A company would benefit greatly from researching the various attitudes people have that might bear on their product.

Attitudes function in people's lives to enable them to have a fairly consistent behavior toward similar classes of objects. They do not have to interpret and react to everything in a fresh way. Attitudes economize in energy and thought. For this very reason, attitudes are very hard to change. A person's various attitudes have settled into some consistency and to change one may require painful adjustments in many other attitudes.

Thus a company is well advised to try to fit its products into existing attitudes rather than to try to change people's attitudes. There are exceptions, of course, where the greater cost of trying to change attitudes might pay off.

---

[17] See David Krech, Richard S. Crutchfield, and Egerton L. Ballachey, *Individual in Society* (New York: McGraw-Hill Book Company, 1962), chap. 2.

Honda entered the U.S. motorcycle market facing a major decision. It could either sell its motorcycles to a small market of people already interested in motorcycles or try to increase the number of people who would be interested in motorcycles. The latter would be more expensive because many people carried negative attitudes toward motorcycles and motorcycle riders. They associated motorcyclists with negative elements such as knives, black leather jackets, and crime. Honda took the second course and launched a major campaign based on the theme "You meet the nicest people on a Honda." Their campaign worked, and many people adopted a new attitude toward motorcycling.

We are now in a position to appreciate the incredible complexity involved in the act of someone's buying something. The person's choice is the result of the complex interplay of cultural, social, personal, and psychological factors. Many of these factors are beyond the influence of the marketer. However, they are useful in identifying those buyers who might be more interested in the product than others. Other factors are subject to marketer influence and clue the marketer on how to develop the product, and decide on price, place, and promotion elements for optimum impact on the marketplace.

Major Types of Buying Situations

The complexity of buyer behavior will of course vary with the type of purchase. There are great differences between buying toothpaste, a tennis racquet, an expensive camera, and a new car. Howard has suggested that consumer buying can be viewed as problem-solving activity and has distingushed three classes of buying situations.[18]

Routinized response behavior The simplest type of buying behavior occurs in the purchase of low-cost, frequently purchased items. The buyers are well acquainted with the product class, are aware of the major brands and their attributes, and have a fairly well-defined preference order among the brands. They do not always buy the same brand because the choice can be influenced by stockouts, special terms, and a wish for variety. But, in general, buyers' operations are routinized, and they are not likely to give much thought, search, or time to the purchase. The goods in this class are often called *low-involvement goods*.

The marketer's task in this situation is twofold. With respect to current customers, the brand should provide positive reinforcement. Its quality, stock level, and value must be maintained. With respect to noncustomers, the marketer must break normal buying routines by cues that call attention to the brand and its value in relation to the buyers' preferred brands. These cues include new features or benefits, point-of-purchase displays, price specials, and premiums.

Limited problem solving Buying is more complex when buyers confront an unfamiliar brand in a familiar product class. It requires information before making a purchase choice. For example, persons thinking about buying a new tennis racket may hear about an unfamiliar oversized brand called the Prince. They may ask questions and look at ads to learn more about the new brand concept before choosing. This is described as limited problem solving because buyers are

[18] Howard and Sheth, *Theory of Buyer Behavior*, pp. 27–28.

fully aware of the product class and the qualities they want but are not familiar with all the brands and their features.

The marketer recognizes that consumers are trying to reduce risk through information gathering. The marketer must design a communication program that will increase the buyer's brand comprehension and confidence.

Extensive problem solving   Buying reaches its greatest complexity when buyers face an unfamiliar product class and do not know the criteria to use. For example, a man may decide to buy a citizen band transceiver for the first time. He has heard brand names such as Cobra, Panasonic, and Midland but lacks clear brand concepts. He does not even know what product-class attributes to consider in choosing a good citizen band transceiver. He is in a state of extensive problem solving.

The marketer of products in this class must understand the information-gathering and evaluation activities of prospective buyers. The marketer's task is to facilitate the buyer's learning of the attributes of the product class, their relative importance, and the high standing of the brand on the more important attributes.

Major Subdecisions Involved in the Buying Decision   Whatever the type of buying situation, the buying decision is really a collection of decisions. Figure 6–4 illustrates nine decisions that a consumer may make on the way to concluding a particular transaction. Consider again Betty Smith. The process started with Betty feeling a need for some new activity. She tries to clarify the nature of her need and decides that she needs some new form of self-expression *(need-class decision)*. She considers various alternatives and decides

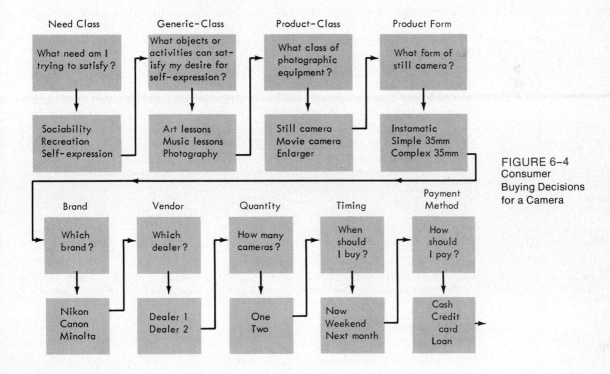

FIGURE 6–4
Consumer
Buying Decisions
for a Camera

that photography would satisfy her need *(generic-class decision).* In considering the different classes of photographic equipment, she concludes a camera would be the answer *(product-class decision).* She decides that a complex 35 mm camera would be best *(product-form decision).* Among the brands she recalls, Nikon gives her the most confidence *(brand decision).* She thinks that she will go to dealer 2, who is said to run the best camera shop for professional photographers *(vendor decision).* She also thought of suggesting that her girlfriend buy a camera and take up photography but dropped the idea *(quantity decision).* She thinks that she will buy the camera on the weekend *(timing decision).* And finally, she will pay for it using her credit card *(payment-method decision).*

Several things should be noted. The model suggests that the buyer behaves in a conscious and rational way in making buying decisions. This exaggerates the degree of deliberateness in the buying behavior of many consumers, who often go and buy a camera without much prior thought. In the case of everyday products such as soap and cigarettes, the decision detail would be even more compressed. On the other hand, the model allows the marketer to imagine the full decision structure on the chance that it will provide useful insight into the consumer's problem-solving behavior that can suggest effective marketing strategies.

In the second place, the number and nature of the decisions will vary for different buying situations. Suppose Betty Smith also decides to apply to graduate school and to major in film making. In this case, the college represents both the brand and vendor. The quantity decision has to be reinterpreted to mean whether she would go full- or part-time to school. Betty also chose a particular department in which to major, and this decision has to be interpreted as a product form.

Third, the consumer probably will not make all the decisions in the order shown. Betty may first notice a friend enjoying a new camera (product-class decision), then consider alternatives to photography (generic-class decision), then consider how she would pay for a camera (payment-method decision) and who would accept her credit card (vendor decision). While Figure 6–4 shows a logical movement from major to minor decisions, consumers may not make them in this order.

The top row of boxes in Figure 6–4 takes the form of questions and the lower row of boxes takes the form of sets of alternative solutions or, more technically, *evoked sets.*[19] *An evoked set is the set of alternatives that the buyer would actually consider at that stage of the decision process.* Marketers have a strong interest in the size and content of the evoked set at each decision point. The Nikon company would not have sold a camera to Betty Smith if she had not moved through the *decision chain:*

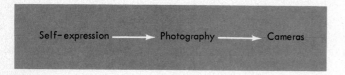

[19] Howard and Sheth, *Theory of Buyer Behavior,* p. 26.

Thus in selling cameras, the Nikon Company could gain from promoting the value of self-expression and the role of cameras in photographic self-expression. If Betty had followed a different chain, neither Nikon nor any other camera manufacturer would have had a sale.

Given that Betty got interested in a camera, Nikon needed to be one of the brands included in her brand-evoked set. If Betty had not heard of Nikon, Nikon would not have made the sale. The purpose of Nikon's advertising budget is to make sure that Nikon appears in almost every expensive-camera buyer's brand-evoked set. The purpose of Nikon's retail strategy is to make sure Nikon is widely carried and favorably promoted by dealers even if Nikon was not initially in the brand-evoked set of the buyer. Ideally, Nikon would like to be the only brand in the buyer's evoked set. The fact is, however, that a buyer will usually consider two or more brands of a shopping good. Nikon would find it useful to know how many brands of cameras the average buyer considers and the particular brands. They define Nikon's competition.

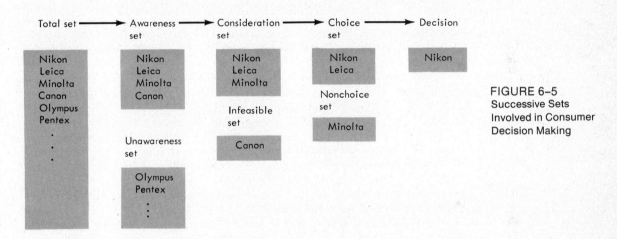

FIGURE 6–5
Successive Sets
Involved in Consumer
Decision Making

The notion of an evoked set can be refined further by recognizing that the buyer moves through a succession of sets on the way to a purchase decision.[20] Let us continue to stay at the level of the brand-evoked set. The various sets are shown in Figure 6–5. The *total set* represents all the brands of cameras that are available to this consumer (i.e., sold in the local area), whether or not the buyer knows about them. The total set can be divided into the consumer's *awareness set* (those brands that she recalls), and the *unawareness set*. Of the brands that Betty recalls, only some of them meet her buying criteria, and they constitute her *consideration* (or evoked) *set;* the others are relegated to an *infeasible set*. As she gets information or gives thought to these brands, a few of the brands remain strong choices and constitute her *choice set*, the others being relegated to a *nonchoice set*. She carefully evaluates the brands in the choice set and then makes her final decision, in this case choosing a Nikon camera.

[20] See Chem L. Narayana and Rom J. Markin, "Consumer Behavior and Product Performance: An Alternative Conceptualization," *Journal of Marketing*, October 1975, pp. 1–6.

The company's task is to work hard to get its brand included in the buyer's awareness set and to remain in the successive consideration and choice sets. The marketer must research the other brands that are likely to be included and the criteria used by the buyer as she moves to successively smaller sets in making her decision.

Major Stages in the Buying Process

The final step in attempting to understand how consumers buy is to map the actual stages they pass through to reach their buying decision. Each stage suggests certain things that marketers can do to facilitate or influence the consumer's decision making.

To map these stages, a sample of consumers can be asked to describe when they first felt a desire for the product, how they gathered information, what problems they tried to resolve, how they made their final choice, and how they felt afterwards.

Consumers, of course, vary in the way they buy any given object. In buying an automobile, for example, some consumers will spend a great deal of time seeking information and making comparisons; others will go straight to a dealer showroom, look at the cars, point to one, negotiate a price, and sign a contract. Thus consumers can be segmented in terms of *buying styles,* for instance, deliberate buyers versus impulsive buyers, and different marketing strategies directed at each segment.

How can marketers identify the typical stages in the buying process for any given product? They can introspect about their own behavior, although this is of limited usefulness *(introspective method).* They can interview a small sample of recent purchasers, asking them to recall the events leading to the purchase of the product *(retrospective method).* They can find some consumers who are contemplating buying the product and ask them to think out loud about how they would go through the buying process *(prospective method).* Or they can ask a group of consumers to describe the ideal way for people to go about buying the product *(prescriptive method).* Each method results in a *consumer-generated report* of the steps in the buying process.

An example of a consumer report of a car-buying decision is shown in Table 6–3. The buyer is a married male who first got the idea when he saw a neighbor's new car. He then developed reasons for possibly purchasing one. A few days later he saw an ad for a Ford. Two weeks later he stopped in a Ford showroom just to browse. He liked the car and the salesman, found that he could afford financing it, and purchased it. He picked it up a few days later and drove away. The car did not satisfy him completely, but an ad for a competitive brand made him feel that he had still bought the best make. He was annoyed a few days later when his salesman did not seem very cooperative in answering some questions.

The marketer should collect a number of consumer reports and attempt to identify one or more typical buying processes for that product. Some analysts have employed graph theory to summarize an individual or group's decision process in buying a product.[21] Figure 6–6 shows a graph version of several of the elements that appeared in the consumer-generated report in Table 6–3. The

[21] See James R. Bettman, "The Structure of Consumer Choice Processes," *Journal of Marketing Research*, November 1971, pp. 465–71.

TABLE 6–3
Consumer-Generated Report of a Purchase Decision

3/17	My neighbor just bought a new car. He says he likes it. It would be nice to buy a new car. My present car is getting ready to fall apart. New cars are safer.
3/19	There's an ad for a new Ford. It looks nice.
4/2	I don't have any plans this evening. I'll go over to the Ford showroom. The cars are nice, especially that deluxe model with air conditioning. Here comes a salesman. He's very helpful. I'm pleased that he is not trying to pressure me. I don't think I can afford the car. How much would it cost a month to finance? I can afford it. My wife has been nagging me for a new car. I'll buy it.
4/5	The car is ready. I wish I had driven it before buying. It seems a little stiff. It is hard to get in and out.
4/6	There's the new Chevy advertised. It doesn't look as good as my car.
4/8	My other neighbor wants to buy a car. I told him the good and bad points about the Ford.
4/11	I phoned the auto salesman for some information. He wasn't helpful. He told me to call the service department.

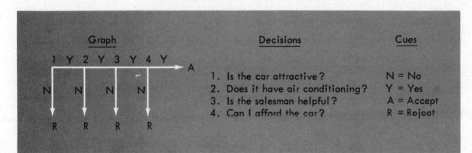

FIGURE 6–6
Graph of
Decision Process
with Four Cues

consumer experienced four cues, each having the capacity to lead him to accept or reject the car. The fact that he bought the car was the result of all four cues being positive.

Based on examining many consumer reports of the buying process, "Stage" models of the buying process have been conceptualized by consumer-behavior specialists. We will use the model shown in Figure 6–7, which shows the consumer as passing through five stages: *need arousal, information search, evaluation behavior, purchase decision,* and *postpurchase feelings.* This model emphasizes that the buying process starts long before the actual purchase and has consequences long after the purchase. It encourages the marketer to focus on the buying process rather than the purchase decision.

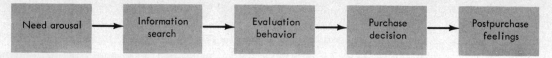

FIGURE 6–7
Five-Stage Model of the Buying Process

Need arousal The buying process starts with need arousal. A need can be activated through internal or external stimuli. In the first case, one of the person's normal needs—hunger, thirst, sex—rises to a threshold level and becomes a drive. The person has learned how to cope with this drive from previous experience and is motivated toward a class of objects that he or she knows will satisfy this drive.

Or a need can be aroused by an external stimulus, or *triggering cue*. A woman passes a bakery and the sight of freshly baked bread stimulates her appetite; she admires a neighbor's new car; or she watches a television commercial for a Jamaican vacation.

The marketing significance of the need arousal stage is twofold. First, the marketer must understand the drives that might actually or potentially connect to the product class and brand. An auto marketer recognizes that cars satisfy a need for mobility; cars also can satisfy the need for status, power, excitement. To the extent that a car can satisfy several drives simultaneously, it becomes a more intensely wanted object.

Second, the concept of need arousal helps the marketer recognize that need levels for the product fluctuate over time and are triggered by different cues. The marketer can arrange cues to conform better to the natural rhythms and timing of need arousal.

Information search If an aroused need is intense and a well-defined gratification object is near at hand, the person is likely to gratify the need right then. The hungry person who sees a candy bar will probably buy it and consume it immediately. In more cases, however, an aroused need is not gratified immediately. The need enters the memory's register as an item for future gratification.

Depending on the intensity of the stored need, the need produces one of two states in the individual. The first state is called *heightened attention*. The individual becomes alert to information bearing on the need and its gratification. Betty Smith may not search actively for information on cameras but is simply more receptive. She pays more attention to camera ads, cameras she sees being used, and remarks made about cameras by friends.

Under conditions of more intense need, the individual enters a state of active *information search*. The amount of information sought depends upon whether the person is facing limited problem solving or extensive problem solving. In the latter case, the person needs more information about the key attributes of the product class, about the qualities of the various brands, and about the outlets at which they are available.

Of key interest to the marketer are the various information sources that the consumer will turn to and the relative influence they will have on choice behavior. *Consumer-information sources* fall into four groups:

1. **Personal sources** (family, friends, neighbors, acquaintances)
2. **Commercial sources** (advertising, salesmen, dealers, packaging, displays)
3. **Public sources** (mass media, consumer rating organizations)
4. **Experiential sources** (handling, examining, using the product)

The relative influence of these information sources varies with the product category and the consumer's personal characteristics. Generally speaking, the consumer receives the most information exposure about a product from commercial sources, that is, marketer-dominated sources. On the other hand, the most effective exposures tend to come from personal sources. Each type of source may perform a somewhat different function in influencing the buying decision. Commercial information normally performs an *informing* function, and personal sources perform a *legitimizing* or an *evaluation* function. For example, physicians normally learn of new drugs from commercial sources but turn to other doctors for evaluation information.

The marketer will find it worthwhile to study the consumers' information sources whenever (1) a substantial percentage of the target market engages in overt search and (2) the target market shows some stable patterns of using the respective information sources. Identifying the information sources and their respective roles and importance calls for interviewing consumers and asking them how they happened to hear about the product, what sources of information they turned to, and what influence each source of information had. The marketer can use the findings to plan commercial communications and stimulate favorable word of mouth.

Evaluation behavior The incoming information helps the consumer clarify and evaluate the alternatives. The marketer needs to know how the consumer processes the incoming information to arrive at product judgments. Unfortunately, there is not a simple and single evaluation process used by all consumers, or even by one consumer in all buying situations. There are alternative processes, and recent research has been directed to studying them. Most current models of the consumer evaluation process are *cognitively oriented*—that is, they see the consumer as forming product judgments largely on a conscious and rational basis.

Certain basic concepts help in understanding consumer evaluation processes. The first concept is that of *product attributes*. The consumer sees products as multiattribute objects. A particular product is perceived in terms of where it stands on a set of attributes that are relevant to that product class. The attributes of normal interest to buyers in some familiar product classes are:

Beer: Smooth taste, alcohol content, bitterness, calorie content, price

Aspirin: Speed of relief, reliability, side effects, price

Tires: Tread life, safety, ride quality, price

Air travel: Departure time, speed, aircraft, preflight service, inflight service, price

Cameras: Picture sharpness, speed, closeup distance, size, ruggedness, price

While the above attributes are of normal interest, individual consumers will vary as to which they consider relevant. The market for a product can often be segmented according to the attributes that have primary interest to different buyers.

Second, the consumer is likely to attach different *importance weights* to the relevant attributes. A distinction can be drawn between *attribute importance* and *attribute salience.*[22] Salient attributes are those that come to the consumer's mind when asked about the attributes that will be considered. The marketer must not conclude that these are necessarily the most important attributes. Some of them may be salient because the consumer has just been exposed to a commercial message mentioning them or has had a problem involving them; hence these attributes are "top of the mind." Furthermore, in the class of nonsalient attributes may be some that the consumer has forgotten but whose importance would be recognized when they are mentioned. We shall be more concerned with attribute importance than attribute salience.

Third, the consumer is likely to develop a set of *brand beliefs*—beliefs about where each brand stands on each attribute. The set of beliefs held about a particular brand is known as the *brand image.* The consumer's beliefs or perceptions may be at variance with the true attributes due to the consumer's particular experience and the effect of selective perception, selective distortion, and selective retention.

Fourth, the consumer is assumed to have a *utility function* for each attribute.[23] The utility function describes how the consumer expects product satisfaction to vary with alternative levels of each attribute. For example, Mr. Smith may expect his satisfaction from a car to increase linearly with gas economy; to peak with an intermediate-size car as opposed to a subcompact or a very large car; to be higher for a red car than a green car. If we combine the attribute levels where the utilities are highest, they make up Mr. Smith's ideal car. This should not be confused with his fantasy car, but rather, it is the car he would most like to obtain if it were available and affordable.

Fifth, the consumer arrives at an attitude (judgment, preference) toward the brand alternatives through some *evaluation procedure.* Starting with an evoked set, the consumer compares products using some procedure and emerges with an order of preferences.

Consumers have been found to apply various evaluation procedures to make a choice among multiattribute objects.[24] Alternative evaluation procedures will be described using the following illustration.

---

[22] James H. Myers and Mark I. Alpert, "Semantic Confusion in Attitude Research: Salience vs. Importance vs. Determinance," in *Advances in Consumer Research*, vol. IV, proceedings of the Seventh Annual Conference of the Association of Consumer Research, October 1976, pp. 106–10.

[23] Some progress has been made in attempting to measure individual and market utility functions. One method, *conjoint analysis,* requires consumers to rank alternative product descriptions in order of their preferences. The data are then analyzed to reconstruct the implicit utility functions for the separate attributes. See Paul E. Green and Yoram Wind, "New Ways to Measure Consumers' Judgments," *Harvard Business Review,* July–August 1975, pp. 107–17. Another method, *tradeoff analysis,* presents consumers with matrices showing two attributes at a time, with different levels of each attribute, and asks them to enter numbers in each cell showing the most preferred to the least preferred combinations of attribute levels. See Richard M. Johnson, "Trade-Off Analysis of Consumer Values," *Journal of Marketing Research,* May 1974, pp. 121–27. For a comparison of these to direct utility assessment methods, see John R. Hauser and Glen L. Urban, "Assessment of Attribute Importance and Consumer Utility Functions," *Journal of Consumer Research,* March 1979.

[24] See Paul E. Green and Yoram Wind, *Multiattribute Decisions in Marketing: A Measurement Approach* (Hinsdale, Ill.: Dryden Press, 1973), chap. 2.

TABLE 6–4
A Buyer's Brand Beliefs about Alternative Brands

	CAR	PRICE	GAS MILEAGE (MILES/GAL)	CAR LENGTH (INCHES)	STYLE*	HANDLING*
			PRODUCT-CLASS ATTRIBUTES			
Evoked set	1	$6,000	10	220	10	10
	2	5,000	16	190	9	10
	3	4,000	14	210	5	6
	4	3,500	20	180	4	9

*A score of 10 represents the highest rating.

Mr. Smith wants to buy a new car and has seen ads and visited some dealer showrooms. His current information about the buying situation is summarized in Table 6–4. He is interested in the four brands shown in the rows (i.e., the evoked set) and the five product-class attributes shown in the columns. The cell numbers describe his brand beliefs. He perceives the first three attributes in terms of real numbers (although his perceptions may not be accurate). The last two attributes reflect his subjective ratings on a scale of 1 to 10.

Which car will Mr. Smith buy? Much depends upon his utility function for the various attributes. We will assume that Smith prefers a low price to a higher price, more gas mileage to less gas mileage, a car length of 180 inches, more style to less style, and better handling to poorer handling. The utility function can be further specified as to its actual shape, but we will assume linearity. Mr. Smith's choice is still not determinant. In fact, at least seven alternative models can explain how consumers form a preference ordering of objects.

DOMINANCE MODEL   Suppose one car was priced lowest, gave the highest mileage, and had the ideal length and the highest-rated style and handling. This car would be the buyer's choice. No car in the evoked set has this clear superiority. Dominance can be used, however, to remove a car that is inferior in all respects to some other car in the set. We can imagine a brand that the consumer dropped from consideration because it was exactly like brand 4 in the first four attributes and its handling was inferior. Dominance is used by consumers to reduce the number of brand alternatives in the evoked set.

CONJUNCTIVE MODEL   Mr. Smith can try to sort the cars into two classes, acceptable and unacceptable, and drop those in the latter class from consideration. He could establish minimum attribute levels that acceptable cars must possess. He might consider only cars costing less than $5,500, giving gas mileage of more than fifteen miles per gallon, not longer than 195 inches, and with a rated style of at least 4 and a handling of at least 6. These cutoffs eliminate brands 1 and 3 from further consideration. Conjunctive evaluation in the extreme could eliminate all brands. A consumer might not purchase any car because no brand meets his minimal requirements. Note that conjunctive evaluation does not pay attention to how high an attribute level is as long as it exceeds the minimum. A high level of one attribute does not compensate for a below-minimum level of another attribute. Conjunctive evaluation is non-compensatory.

DISJUNCTIVE MODEL   Mr. Smith might decide to consider only cars that exceed specified levels on one or a few attributes, regardless of their standing on the other attributes. Mr. Smith might decide that he will consider only cars that have superior styling (≥ 9) *or* handling (≥ 9). According to the evoked set in Table 6–4, Mr. Smith is left with cars 1, 2, and 4 as choices. The model is non-compensatory in that high scores on other variables have no bearing on keeping them in the acceptable set.

LEXICOGRAPHIC MODEL   Another noncompensatory process occurs if Mr. Smith arranges the attributes in order of importance and compares the brands on the first important attribute. If one brand is superior on the most important attribute, it becomes his choice. If two or more brands are tied on this attribute, Mr. Smith considers the second most important attribute; he continues this until one brand remains. Suppose Mr. Smith "prioritizes" the attributes in the following order: handling, style, gas mileage, car length, and cost. He looks at handling and finds cars 1 and 2 to be superior and equal to each other. He eliminates cars 3 and 4 from further consideration. Then he considers style and finds car 1 to be superior to car 2. At this point he has determined that car 1 is the preferred automobile.

EXPECTANCY-VALUE MODEL   Another evaluation model says that Mr. Smith forms an attitude toward each brand that is based on the importance weights he assigns to the brand attributes times his brand beliefs. This "expectancy-value" model takes the following form:[25]

$$A_{jk} = \sum_{i=1}^{n} W_{ik} B_{ijk} \qquad (6\text{–}1)$$

where:

A_{jk} = consumer k's attitude score for brand j

W_{ik} = the importance weight assigned by consumer k to attribute i

B_{ijk} = consumer k's belief as to the amount of attribute i offered by brand j

n = the number of attributes important in the selection of a given brand

To illustrate, suppose Mr. Smith feels that only two attributes, style and handling, are important to him in the selection of a car (the other three attributes have a zero weight). Furthermore, he feels that style is three times as important as handling. We would predict his attitude toward the four cars shown in Table 6–4 to be: $A_1 = 40[=3(10) + 1(10)]$; $A_2 = 37[= 3(9) + 1(10)]$; $A_3 = 21[=3(5) + 1(6)]$; and $A_4 = 21[=3(4) + 1(9)]$. Note that although cars 3 and 4 differ greatly in their style and handling, they emerge with the same level of overall attractiveness ($= 21$) because of compensatory attributes.

IDEAL-PRODUCT MODEL   One of the most interesting models is the ideal-product model (also called ideal-point model), which holds that consumers have

[25] The model also goes under other names (linear compensatory model, multiattribute attitude model). For an excellent review of this model, see William L. Wilkie and Edgar A. Pessemier, "Issues in Marketing's Use of Multi-Attribute Attitude Models," *Journal of Marketing Research*, November 1973, pp. 428–41.

or can form an image of the ideal product they want. An ideal product embodies the ideal combination of attributes for that consumer. The closer that existing products come to the consumer's ideal product, the more attractive they will be.

A consumer's concept of the ideal product is influenced by the *consumer's goal* and *self-concept,* among other things. If the consumer's goal in buying a car is cheap transportation, then the consumer will look for a car with such characteristics as low price, low operating costs, few options, and high durability. This goal may be further supported by the consumer's self-concept such as being a practical, plain person. A major premise is that consumers choose goods that express or enhance their self-concept. Every product includes symbolic content that communicates something to others about the consumer. The consumer will select products whose symbolic content is congruent with his or her self-concept.

To use the ideal-product model, the marketer would interview a sample of buyers and ask them to describe the characteristics of their ideal product in that product class. The marketer will obtain three classes of response. Some consumers will have clear pictures of their ideal product. Other consumers will mention two or more ideal products that would satisfy them equally. The remaining consumers will have trouble defining an ideal product and would find a wide range of product versions or brands equally acceptable.

Suppose Mr. Smith, who is buying a car, reports that his ideal car would be 180 inches in length and would average 15 miles per gallon. (He knows that more fuel economy would give him less power, and so he is satisfied with 15 miles per gallon.) Suppose these are the only two attributes of interest. Formula (6–1) can be modified to read:

$$D_{jk} = \sum_{i=1}^{n} W_{ik}|B_{ijk} - I_{ik}| \qquad (6\text{–}2)$$

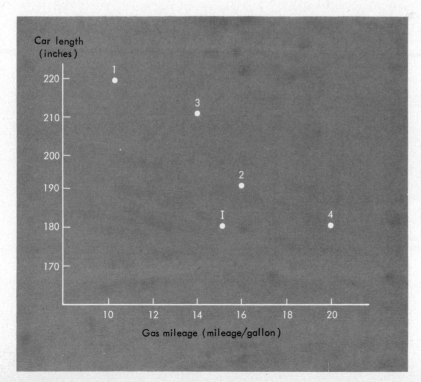

FIGURE 6–8

Brand Space Map Showing the Consumer's Perceptions of Four Brands and Ideal Brand *(I)* where D_{jk} is consumer k's *dissatisfaction* score with brand j, and I_{ik} is consumer k's *ideal level* of attribute i. Other terms remain the same. The lower the D, the more favorable consumer k's attitude toward brand j. For example, if there were a brand whose attributes were all at the ideal levels, the term $|B_{ijk} - I_{jk}|$ would disappear, and the dissatisfaction would be zero.

The ideal-product model is illustrated in Figure 6–8, which shows the consumer's perceptions of four brands as well as his ideal brand *(I)*. Cars closer to Mr. Smith's ideal product will be preferred more. Car 2 comes out best.

DETERMINANT-ATTRIBUTE MODEL   Several of the previous models employed the notion of *attribute importance* as being influential in brand choice. But in many buying situations, some attributes that consumers state are highly important to them do not seem to function strongly in their brand choice. For example, many consumers rate auto safety as highly important in buying a car. Yet they normally do not shop around and investigate the safety level of differ-

FIGURE 6–9
Determinant-Attribute Model

	Dealer	Dealer Attributes				Dealer preference (I)[d]	Dealer preference (D)[e]
		Good service	Convenience	Honesty	Friendliness		
Evoked set	1	20	20	50	30	27	301.0
	2	40	20	20	30	29	295.2
	3	20	20	10	10	17	142.6
	4	10	20	10	20	14	103.6
	5	10	20	10	10	13	93.6
Importance (I)[a]		.40	.30	.20	.10		
Variability (V)[b]		12.25	00.00	17.32	10.00		
Determinance (D)[c]		4.90	0.00	3.46	1.00		

[a] The attribute importance weights are assigned by the consumer and must add up to 1.
[b] The variability is measured by the standard deviation of the numbers in each column.
[c] The determinance is found by multiplying each importance weight by the corresponding standard deviation. A determinance score of 0 indicates a nondeterminant attribute; and the greater the determinance score, the more determinant the attribute.
[d] Dealer preference according to the importance weights is found by multiplying each dealer's attribute scores by the corresponding importance weights.
[e] Dealer preference according to the determinance scores is found by multiplying each dealer's attribute scores by the corresponding determinance scores.

ent cars. Although safety is important, the consumers largely believe that most cars are "safe enough." Cars that appear unsafe are not considered, and the safety levels of the remaining cars are not important. The irony is that competitors normally match each other on the important attributes, and therefore the less important attributes tend to be more determinant.[26]

To illustrate determinance, suppose that Mr. Smith wants to decide on the dealer from whom to purchase the car. Figure 6–9 shows five dealers in his evoked set and four attributes. He rates good service as most important (= .40), convenience next (= .30), then honesty (= .20), and finally friendliness (= .10). Figure 6–9 also shows his beliefs about where each dealer stands on each of these attributes. Note that the beliefs in each column are represented by scores that add up to 100.

Which dealer will Mr. Smith prefer? If we use the importance weights, we will predict that he will prefer dealer 2 (see the column scores in the next-to-last column). However, notice that the attributes differ in their variability among the dealers. For example, all five dealers are equally convenient. The model calls for measuring the variability of each attribute (using the standard deviation). The determinance of an attribute is then the product of its importance times its variability. Figure 6–9 shows, for example, that convenience is a nondeterminant attribute and has no influence over the outcome. The final step is to multiply the determinance scores by the dealer-attribute levels. The results are shown in the last column, and we can predict that this consumer will end up choosing dealer 1, not dealer 2.

MARKETING IMPLICATIONS   The preceding models indicate that buyers can form their product preferences in several different ways. A particular buyer, on a particular buying occasion, facing a particular product class, might be a conjunctive buyer, an expectancy-value buyer, or some other type of buyer. The same buyer may behave as a conjunctive buyer for large-ticket purchases and a disjunctive buyer for small-ticket items. Or the same buyer, in buying a large-ticket item, may behave first like a conjunctive buyer to eliminate many alternatives and then make a final choice as an expectancy-value buyer. When we realize that a market is made up of many buyers, it seems almost hopeless to assess the nature of buying behavior in that market.

Yet marketers can gain useful insights by interviewing a sample of buyers to find out how they form their evaluations in that product class. The marketer might find that the majority of consumers in that market use one particular evaluation procedure. In such a case, the marketer can consider the most effective ways to make his brand salient to consumers who are using that evaluation procedure.

For example, suppose the marketer discovers that most of the buyers form their preferences by comparing actual brands to their ideal products. Furthermore, suppose that there is a large market segment that has the same ideal product as Mr. Smith (see Figure 6–8). Suppose the marketer sells brand 4, which is less appealing to this market segment than brand 2. What can the marketer of brand 4 do to improve sales to this market segment?

---

[26] See James H. Myers and Mark I. Alpert, "Determinant Buying Attitudes: Meaning and Measurement," *Journal of Marketing*, October 1968, pp. 13–20.

The ideal-product model suggests at least seven alternative strategies. They are:[27]

1. ***Developing a new brand.*** The marketer could introduce a second brand that is closer to this segment's ideal brand.

2. ***Modifying the existing brand.*** The marketer could alter the attributes of the existing brand to bring it closer to this segment's ideal brand. This is called *real brand repositioning*.

3. ***Altering beliefs about the company's brand.*** The marketer could try to alter consumers' perceptions of where the company's brand actually stands on key attributes. The marketer may find that the market thinks its car is too long and may undertake a communication campaign to shift the market's perceptions of the company's brand closer to the ideal product. This is called *psychological brand repositioning*.

4. ***Altering beliefs about the competitors' brands.*** The marketer could try to alter consumers' perceptions of where a leading competitor's brand stands on different attributes. Thus the marketer may, through comparison advertising, represent car 2 as being much longer than its own car 4. This is called *competitive depositioning*.

5. ***Altering the attribute-importance weights.*** The marketer could try to persuade consumers to attach more importance to those attributes that the company brand happens to excel in. Thus the manufacturer of car 4 may promote the importance of gas mileage to consumers who may not have attached enough importance to it.

6. ***Calling attention to neglected attributes.*** The marketer could try to convince consumers to pay attention to an attribute that they are normally unaware of or indifferent to.

7. ***Shifting the ideal product.*** The marketer could try to persuade consumers to change their ideal levels for one or more attributes.

Purchase decision The evaluation stage leads the consumer to form a ranked set of preferences among the alternative objects in his or her evoked set. Normally, a consumer will buy the object he or she likes most. But there are a number of additional links between his or her evaluation behavior and the purchase decision. They are shown in Figure 6–10.

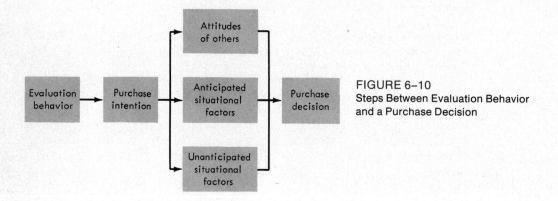

FIGURE 6–10
Steps Between Evaluation Behavior
and a Purchase Decision

---

[27] For further discussion, see Harper W. Boyd, Jr., Michael L. Ray, and Edward C. Strong, "An Attitudinal Framework for Advertising Strategy," *Journal of Marketing*, April 1972, pp. 27–33.

The consumer's evaluations will lead to an intention to purchase one of the objects. At that point, three additional factors intervene.[28]

The first is the *attitude of others*. Suppose a man prefers a Cadillac but his wife thinks a Cadillac is pretentious. His overall favorable attitude toward the Cadillac is consequently reduced. The extent to which the attitude of others will reduce a favorable attitude depends upon two things: (1) the intensity of the other person's negative attitude, and (2) the consumer's motivation to comply with the other person's wishes.[29] The more intense the other person's negativism, and the closer the other person is to the consumer, the more the consumer will revise downward his purchase intention.

Purchase intention is also influenced by *anticipated situational factors*. The consumer forms a purchase intention on the basis of such factors as expected family income, the expected total cost of the product, and the expected benefits of the product.

When the consumer is about to act, *unanticipated situational factors* may intervene to prevent her or him from carrying out the purchase intention. The buyer may not be able to negotiate desirable terms. He or she may not like the looks or manner of the salesperson or the way business is carried on in the showroom. There may be a sudden loss of nerve and worry about his or her income situation. Marketers believe that unanticipated factors in the *critical contact situation* can have a great influence on the final decision.

Thus preferences and even purchase intentions are not completely reliable predictors of actual buying behavior. They give direction to purchase behavior but fail to include a number of additional factors that may intervene.

The decision of an individual to modify, postpone, or avoid a purchase decision is heavily influenced by *perceived risk*. Marketers have devoted a lot of effort to understand buying behavior as *risk taking*.[30] Consumers cannot be certain about the performance and psychosocial consequences of their purchase decision. This uncertainty produces anxiety. The amount of perceived risk varies with the amount of money at stake, the amount of attribute uncertainty, and the amount of consumer self-confidence. A consumer develops certain routines for reducing risk, such as decision avoidance, information gathering from friends, and preference for national brand names and warranties. The marketer must understand the factors that provoke a feeling of risk in the consumer and attempt to provide information and support that will help reduce this risk.

Postpurchase feelings After buying and trying the product, the consumer will experience some level of satisfaction or dissatisfaction. If asked, she or he may report being very satisfied, somewhat satisfied, somewhat dissatisfied, or very dissatisfied. What determines the level of postpurchase satisfaction? The major theory holds that a consumer's satisfaction is a function of her or his *expectations (E)*

---

[28] See Jagdish N. Sheth, "An Investigation of Relationships among Evaluative Beliefs, Affect, Behavioral Intention, and Behavior," in *Consumer Behavior: Theory and Application*, ed. John V. Farley, John A. Howard, and L. Winston Ring (Boston: Allyn & Bacon, 1974), pp. 89–114.

[29] See Martin Fishbein, "Attitude and Prediction of Behavior," in *Readings in Attitude Theory and Measurement*, ed. Martin Fishbein (New York: John Wiley & Sons, 1967), pp. 477–92.

[30] See Raymond A. Bauer, "Consumer Behavior as Risk Taking" in *Risk Taking and Information Handling in Consumer Behavior*, ed. Donald F. Cox (Boston: Division of Research, Harvard Business School, 1967); and James W. Taylor, "The Role of Risk in Consumer Behavior," *Journal of Marketing*, April 1974, pp. 54–60.

and the product's *perceived performance (P)*, that is, $S = f(E, P)$.[31] If the product matches up to expectations, the consumer is satisfied; if it exceeds them, she or he is highly satisfied; if it falls short, the consumer is dissatisfied.

Consumers form their expectations on the basis of messages and claims sent out by the seller and other communication sources. If the seller makes exaggerated claims for the product, the consumer experiences *disconfirmed expectations*, which lead to dissatisfaction. The amount of dissatisfaction depends on the size of the difference between expectations and performance. Different psychological theories have been advanced suggesting that consumers may either magnify or diminish the importance of the differences between expectations and performance.[32] *Contrast theory* says that the amount of dissatisfaction will be larger than the performance gap. *Cognitive dissonance theory* says that the amount of dissatisfaction will be less because the consumer will try to reduce the dissonance by imputing higher performance.

The smart seller will make claims for a product that are congruent with its quality so that the buyer experiences satisfaction. Some sellers even understate performance levels so that consumers will experience higher-than-expected satisfaction with the product.

Thus we see that brand experience has an important effect on subsequent brand preference. If the purchased brand fails to deliver the expected satisfaction to the buyer, the buyer will revise downward his or her attitude toward the brand and may even eliminate it from his or her evoked set. On the other hand, a satisfying experience will tend to strengthen the buyer's brand preference.

The reinforcement effect of past brand choices on subsequent brand preferences has been described in a brand learning model developed by Kuehn.[33] This model postulates the existence of a pair of "learning operators" that explicitly alter current brand purchase probabilities on the basis of the last brand choice. The basic device is illustrated in Figure 6–11. The horizontal axis represents the probability of choosing brand j in period t, and the vertical axis represents the probability of choosing brand j in period $t + 1$. The figure contains a positively sloped 45-degree line as a norm. The figure also contains two positively sloped lines called the purchase and rejection operators. These operators show how the probability of purchasing brand j is modified from period t to period $t + 1$, depending on whether or not brand j was just purchased.

For example, suppose the probability of a person's purchasing brand j this period is .60. Suppose it is actually what he or she buys. The probability that the person will buy brand j again, assuming that he or she is satisfied, is found by running a dotted line up from the horizontal axis at .60 to the purchase-operator line (because brand j was purchased) and going across the vertical axis and reading the new probability. In this illustration, the new probability is .78. If the buyer had not purchased j, the dotted line from .60 would have been run up only to the rejection operator and read on the vertical axis. The probability of that person's buying j next time would have fallen from .60 to .31.

[31] See John E. Swan and Linda Jones Combs, "Product Performance and Consumer Satisfaction: A New Concept," *Journal of Marketing Research*, April 1976, pp. 25–33.

[32] See Rolph E. Anderson, "Consumer Dissatisfaction: The Effect of Disconfirmed Expectancy on Perceived Product Performance," *Journal of Marketing Research*, February 1973, pp. 38–44.

[33] Alfred A. Kuehn, "Consumer Brand Choice—A Learning Process?" in *Quantitative Techniques in Marketing Analysis*, eds. R. E. Frank, A. A. Kuehn, and W. F. Massy (Homewood, Ill.: Richard D. Irwin, 1962), pp. 390–403.

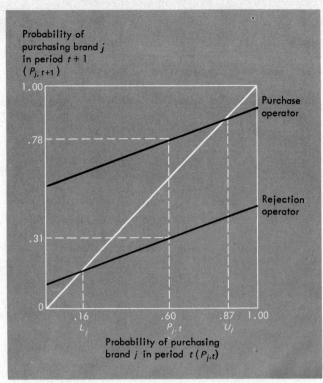

Probability of purchasing brand j in period $t + 1$ ($P_{j, t+1}$)

FIGURE 6–11
The Cumulative Learning Model

Purchase operator

Rejection operator

Probability of purchasing brand j in period t ($P_{j,t}$)

SOURCE: Kuehn, p. 391

If the consumer continues buying brand j, the probability of buying brand j approaches .87 in the limit. This upper limit, given by the intersection of the purchase-operator and the 45-degree line, represents a phenomenon known as *incomplete habit formation*. No matter how much brand j is bought, some probability still remains that the consumer may buy another brand. On the other hand, if the consumer does not buy brand j for a long time, the probability of his buying this brand falls continuously but never to zero. This is the phenomenon of *incomplete habit extinction*. There is always some positive probability that a consumer may buy a previously neglected brand.

The model has been fitted for some consumer staples (such as beer, coffee, frozen orange juice) and has found some limited empirical support. For example, Kuehn found that the probability of rebuying Snow Crop frozen orange juice was .33 with one past (last) purchase of this brand and .806 with four past purchases of this brand.

Brand purchase probabilities are less likely to be strengthened when consumers buy an expensive product. In the case of a car, the consumer finds attractive and unattractive qualities in each brand. Presumably the brand with the most attractive qualities is selected, but this does not resolve doubts about the unattractive qualities of the chosen brand or the attractive qualities of the rejected brands. The purchaser may subsequently hear information that reflects badly on the brand, for instance, that the brand will be discontinued or that the brand could have been purchased for less. Negative feelings can also arise through finding the brand's performance disappointing.

Postpurchase cognitive dissonance is common among purchasers of homes, automobiles, and major appliances. Cognitive dissonance means there is a lack of harmony in the buyer's various cognitions about purchased product and the foregone alternatives. According to Festinger, "The magnitude of postdecision dissonance is an increasing function of the general importance of the decision and of the relative attractiveness of the unchosen alternatives."[34] The dissonant consumer will seek to reduce the dissonance because of a drive in the human organism "to establish internal harmony, consistency, or congruity among his opinion, knowledge, and values."[35] Consumers will resort to one of two courses of action. They may try to reduce the dissonance by *removing* the product, returning it for a credit where that is possible, or selling it to someone else. Or they may try to reduce the dissonance by *confirming* the product, seeking information that might confirm its high value.

Marketers try to help buyers feel good about their purchase choice. A disappointed buyer may not only stop buying but also bad-mouth the product to others. The main step is to direct supportive communications to recent buyers. Auto manufacturers build assurances into the information brochures that accompany the product. They also run ads featuring recent purchasers showing satisfaction with their choice.

SUMMARY

Markets have to be understood before marketing can be planned. A market is the set of all individuals and organizations who are actual or potential buyers of a product or service. To understand a market, we ask six questions: Who is in the market? (occupants); What do they buy? (objects); When do they buy? (occasions); Who does the buying? (organization); Why do they buy? (objectives); and How do they buy? (operations). Answering these six Os of a market is a prerequisite to making decisions on the four Ps of marketing strategy.

We can distinguish between consumer markets and organizational markets (producers, resellers, government). This chapter examined the six Os of consumer markets.

The consumer market is the ultimate market for which economic activities are organized. It consists of the whole population, and it is important for the marketer to research age distribution, family formation, incomes, educational levels, mobility patterns, and tastes. The consumer market buys objects that can be classified according to their tangibility (durables, nondurables, and services) and according to how the consumers go about buying them (convenience, shopping, and specialty goods). The timing of consumer purchases is influenced by family size, seasonal factors, and economic conditions. The purchase decision is influenced by various parties playing various roles (initiator, influencer, decider, buyer, and user). In the family, which is the major purchasing organization for consumers, there is some buying task specialization, with the wife normally buying most of the household's goods, and other members buying or influencing the purchase of other things.

The objectives of consumers are to satisfy a variety of needs—phys-

[34] Leon Festinger, *A Theory of Cognitive Dissonance* (Stanford, Calif.: Stanford University Press, 1957), p. 262.

[35] Ibid., p. 260.

iological, safety, belongingness, status, and self-actualization. The consumer is not always fully conscious of the needs that are driving his or her behavior.

The buying situation itself can vary from one of routinized response behavior to limited problem solving to extensive problem solving. Buying is not a single act but a multicomponent decision on the need class, generic class, product class, product form, brand, vendor, quantity, timing, and method of payment. With each decision component, the buyer starts with an initial evoked set that gets narrowed down. The buyer goes through a process consisting of need arousal, information search, evaluation behavior, purchase decision, and postpurchase feelings. At each decision stage, characteristics of the buyer, product, seller, and selling situation interact to influence the buying outcome.

QUESTIONS AND PROBLEMS

1. Purchasing furniture is an uneasy experience for most families, one involving high perceived risk. Recommend a marketing approach that will help meet the buyer's concerns.

2. Recall some recent important purchase you made and construct a consumer buying protocol of what took place.

3. A grooming aid company has just developed a cologne product available in towelettes, that is, flat miniature packages with presoaked cloth that are handy to carry around and open when needed. Develop a map showing the structure of purchase decisions facing a buyer and the decision route he must follow to end up purchasing the new product and becoming a loyal customer.

4. Jim Beam, a brand of whisky, is advertised "Coffee, Tea, or Beam." What is the advertiser trying to accomplish?

5. A friend of yours is planning to buy a new car. He has a preference for foreign makes and his choice has narrowed down to Volkswagen, Opel, and Volvo. He is looking for three things in a car: economy, quality, and roominess, and he values them at .5, .3, and .2, respectively. He would rate Volkswagen as standing at .8, .8, and .2 on the three attributes; Opel, .3, .5, and .9; and Volvo, .5, .8, and .7. Predict the cars he is most likely to buy and least likely to buy if he evaluates cars according to the expectancy model.

6. "A person will tend to buy the brand in the product class whose image is most congruent with his self-image." Is a person's self-image a highly reliable prediction of his brand choice?

7. Develop a map showing the structure of purchase decisions as they may be made by potential buyers of paint. Indicate how a paint company such as DuPont can determine points at which advertising might favorably affect DuPont's share of the market.

8. Name some attitudes that you or others have expressed about prunes. Suggest some strategies and appeals that might overcome negative attitudes toward prunes.

9. A homebuilder is planning to design homes for "empty-nesters." Can this life-cycle group be further segmented? What kind of home design features fit the needs of empty nesters?

10. Describe the consumer market for briefcases, using the framework developed in this chapter.

ORGANIZATIONAL MARKETS AND BUYING BEHAVIOR

Companies don't make purchases; they establish relationships.
CHARLES S. GOODMAN

7

The needs and wants of consumers lead to the phenomenon of consumer markets described in the preceding chapter. In turn, those who supply consumer markets with goods and services are themselves in need of goods and services to run their business. These organizations—producers, resellers, and governments—therefore make up vast organizational markets that buy a multitude of things such as equipment, raw material, labor, and other services. Various organizations emerge to sell goods and services to these organizational buyers. A great many organizations sell exclusively to other organizations and never come in contact with consumer buyers.

Selling to organizations introduces several considerations not found in consumer marketing:

1. Organizations do not buy for personal consumption or utility but to obtain goods and services that will be used in further production, reselling, or servicing.
2. More persons normally get involved in organizational buying, especially for major items, than in consumer buying. The decision makers usually have different organizational responsibilities and apply different criteria to the purchase decision.
3. The organization imposes policies, constraints, and requirements that must be heeded by its buyers.
4. The buying instruments, such as requests for quotations, proposals, and purchase contracts, add another dimension not found in consumer buying.

Companies that sell such industrial products as steel, computers, and nuclear power plants need to understand organizational buying behavior. Webster and Wind define organizational buying as "the decision-making process by which formal organizations establish the need for purchased products and services, and identify, evaluate, and choose among alternative brands and suppliers."[1] No two companies buy in the same way. Yet the seller hopes to spot enough uniformities in organizational buying behavior to contribute to improved marketing-mix planning.

In this chapter, we shall examine each of three generic organizational markets—producers, resellers, and government units—in terms of the six Os framework developed in the preceding chapter: occupants, objects, occasions, organization, objectives, and operations.

THE PRODUCER MARKET

Who Is in the Producer Market?

The producer market (also called the industrial or business market) consists of all individuals and organizations who acquire goods and services that enter into the production of other products or services that are sold, rented, or supplied to others. The major types of industries making up the producer market are (1) agriculture, forestry, and fisheries; (2) mining; (3) manufacturing; (4) construction; (5) transportation; (6) communication; (7) public utilities; (8) banking, finance, and insurance; and (9) services. There are over 14 million different industrial units and each is a market for specific types of goods and services. They employ over 87 million workers, generate an annual national income of over $1 trillion, and constitute a buying market for the goods of most firms.

More dollars are involved in sales to industrial buyers than to consumers! To bring a simple pair of shoes into existence, hide dealers (mainly meat packers) must sell the hides to tanners, who sell the leather to shoe manufacturers, who sell the shoes to wholesalers, who in turn sell the shoes to retailers. Each party in the chain of production and distribution pays more than the previous party. The transactions based on one pair of finished shoes selling for $30 may have been $4 (hide dealer to tanner), $5 (tanner to shoe manufacturer), $20 (shoe manufacturer to wholesaler), and $24 (wholesaler to retailer), making a total of $53, whereas the transaction to the consumer involved but $30. More industrial marketing goes on than consumer marketing, although many people have the opposite impression.

Within the producer market, customers tend to be larger and fewer than in consumer markets. But even here, great variations are found. First, the number of industrial firms making up the market varies from one (monopsony), to few (oligopsony), to many. A French carburetor manufacturer has no choice but to sell to state-owned Renault; whereas an American carburetor manufacturer can sell to General Motors, Ford, Chrysler, and American Motors. Second, the size distribution of firms varies. We can distinguish between producer markets made up of only large firms, or a few large and many small firms, or only small firms. The seller's strategic problem is whether to sell to all firms or to concentrate on a few large firms or to concentrate on the many small firms.

---

[1] Frederick E. Webster, Jr. and Yoram Wind, *Organizational Buying Behavior* (Englewood Cliffs, N.J.: Prentice-Hall, 1972), p. 2.

Compared to ultimate consumers, producers tend to be concentrated geographically. The seven states of New York, California, Pennsylvania, Illinois, Ohio, New Jersey, and Michigan contain within their borders over half of the nation's manufacturing firms. Particular manufacturing industries, such as petroleum, rubber, and steel, show even greater geographic concentration. Most agricultural output comes from a relatively small number of states, and specific commodities, such as tobacco and citrus fruit, are grown in even fewer states. All of this geographical concentration of producers helps to reduce the costs of selling to them. Industrial marketers will want to watch any pronounced tendencies toward or away from further geographic concentration.

What Do Producers Buy?

The producer market buys a vast variety of products and services. An industrial-goods classification scheme would help us understand the varying marketing practices in the producer market. It is not particularly appropriate to base goods classification on the *shopping habits of the producers,* as we did in consumer-goods classification, because producers do not shop in the same sense. More often suppliers seek them out. Industrial goods are more usefully classified in terms of *how they enter the production process and their relative costliness.* These considerations determine who in the industrial firm buys (organization) and how they buy (operations). Using these principles, industrial goods fall into the three broad classes shown in Table 7–1.

TABLE 7–1
Goods Classification in the Industrial Market

I. *Goods entering the product completely—materials and parts*
  A. Raw materials
    1. Farm products (examples: wheat, cotton, livestock, fruits and vegetables)
    2. Natural products (examples: fish, lumber, crude petroleum, iron ore)
  B. Manufactured materials and parts
    1. Component materials (examples: steel, cement, wire, textiles)
    2. Component parts (examples: small motors, tires, castings)
II. *Goods entering the product partly—capital items*
  A. Installations
    1. Buildings and land rights (examples: factories, offices)
    2. Fixed equipment (examples: generators, drill presses, computers, elevators)
  B. Accessory equipment
    1. Portable or light factory equipment and tools (examples: hand tools, lift trucks)
    2. Office equipment (examples: typewriters, desks)
III. *Goods not entering the product—supplies and services*
  A. Supplies
    1. Operating supplies (examples: lubricants, coal, typing paper, pencils)
    2. Maintenance and repair items (examples: paint, nails, brooms)
  B. Business services
    1. Maintenance and repair services (examples: window cleaning, typewriter repair)
    2. Business advisory services (examples: legal, management consulting, advertising)

Each type of industrial good, as a result of its physical characteristics and use pattern in production, has acquired particular patterns of marketing effort and mix. Here are two examples:

Steel. Steel serves as an important component material in a large part of the industrial market, especially in durable-goods manufacture and construction. There are different grades and alloys of steel, but within any category most steel is identical. Therefore steel is basically a commodity, and the major product variables that count are (1) consistency of quality and (2) extent of the steelmaker's product line. The buyer's main concern is price, and a seller who offers his product for even a fraction of a cent less has the best chance of getting the order. The price reduction can come off the basic price or indirectly through volume discounts, freight absorption allowances, or more generous credit terms. Therefore these instruments figure importantly in steel marketing.

Because most sellers offer similar terms, competition also takes place on a nonprice front. An important variable is the seller's delivery reliability, because the buyer's production operation is geared to the continual delivery of steel or its emergency ordering. The steel seller who is located nearest to the buyer, or who reliably meets promised delivery dates, has a comparative advantage. Company salesmen cannot make much of a difference if their company's price or delivery reliability is not right, but can make a contribution by making contacts and being in the right place at the right time. Advertising plays only a small role, usually taking the form of either corporate-image advertising or new-product advertising to promote a new steel alloy. In this kind of business it is hard for a company to discover a marketing angle that helps it substantially increase its market share without competitors' being able to retaliate effectively with the same or an offsetting tactic.

Electric forklift trucks. The marketing mix for forklift trucks differs from that for steel because the trucks can be engineered in many variations to perform different tasks. The buyer seeks a truck that meets certain desiderata of size, lifting capacity, operating cost, features, and price. The seller's product-design capability is an important factor in getting business. A higher price can be charged for trucks with better performance or extra features. Some buyers are willing to pay more for such factors as the seller's reputation, extra styling, or comfort.

Another important marketing variable is the seller's backup for the purchase—particularly delivery times, parts availability, and service. Some of these things are in the hands of channel middlemen through whom the manufacturer sells. Advertising in trade journals plays a useful role in creating buyer awareness and interest in the company's product line. The promotional budget also goes into specification sheets, catalogs, training films, trade shows, and sales-force contests.

When Do Producers Buy?

A number of factors affect the frequency with which industrial goods and services are purchased. First, the characteristics of the product, such as its perishability, costliness, and bulk, affect how often it will be ordered or received. Thus a steel company will take almost continuous or daily delivery of iron ore as needed in its operations; it might order office supplies only monthly or quarterly; and it might purchase new furnaces once every few years.

Second, the inventory policies of the buyer will influence purchase frequency. Buyers can affect cost savings by ordering high volumes of regularly needed materials infrequently; they get volume discounts and engage in less paperwork. On the other hand, the company ties up more of its resources in inventory, thus incurring opportunity costs and risking some product obsolescence or spoilage. The industrial marketer has to take the industrial buyer's inventory policies into account in shaping offers and timing the sales calls.

Third, industrial purchase frequency is affected by the economic outlook. When the economic outlook is poor, companies will postpone purchases. They will carry minimum inventory levels and postpone larger capital investments. They have neither the funds nor the incentive to invest until they see improved economic conditions on the horizon. Industrial marketers find it harder to market their goods and services if they do not offer special terms, such as discounts and return privileges, to reluctant buyers. The buyers simply do not want to tie up their money. Their demand for goods and services is not *primary* but *derived* from the demand level for other goods into which their goods enter.

Who Participates in the Producer Buying Decision?

Who does the buying of the hundreds of billions of dollars of products and services needed by the industrial market? Buying organizations vary tremendously, from small firms with one or a few people in the purchasing function to huge corporations with large purchasing departments headed by a vice president of purchasing. In some cases the buyers make the entire decision as to product specifications and supplier, in other cases they are responsible for supplier choice only, and in still other cases they make neither decision but simply place the order. They typically make the decisions regarding smaller items and carry out the wishes of others regarding major capital items.

The challenge to the industrial marketer is to make a careful assessment of each customer's buying organization, roles, and influences and then determine the optimal marketing approach to that organization. Every industrial seller in approaching a prospective buying organization must try to answer three questions:

1. Who are the decision participants?
2. What is each member's relative influence in the decision?
3. What are each member's evaluation criteria and how does he or she rate each prospective supplier on those criteria?

Webster and Wind call the decision-making unit of a buying organization the *buying center,* defined as "all those individuals and groups who participate in the purchasing decision-making process, who share some common goals and the risks arising from the decisions."[2]

The buying center includes all members of the organization who play any of five roles in the purchase decision process:[3]

1. *Users.* Users are the members of the organization who will use the product or service. In many cases, the users initiate the buying project and play an important role in defining the purchase specifications.
2. *Influencers.* Influencers are those members of the organization who directly or indirectly influence the buying decision. They often help define specifications and also provide information for evaluating alternatives. Technical personnel are particularly important as influencers.
3. *Buyers.* Buyers are organizational members with formal authority for selecting the supplier and arranging the terms of purchase. Buyers may help shape product

[2] Ibid., p. 6.

[3] Ibid., pp. 78–80.

specifications, but they play their major role in selecting vendors and negotiating within the purchase constraints. In more complex purchases, high-level officers of the company might participate in the negotiations.

4. *Deciders.* Deciders are organizational members who have either formal or informal power to select the final suppliers. In the routine buying of standard items, the buyers are often the deciders. In more complex buying, the officers of the company are often the deciders.

5. *Gatekeepers.* Gatekeepers are members of the organization who control the flow of information to others. For example, purchasing agents often have authority to prevent salespersons from seeing users or deciders. Other gatekeepers include technical personnel and even switchboard operators. The main impact of gatekeepers comes from their ability to control the inflow of information on buying alternatives.

Within any organization, the buying center will vary in size and composition for different classes of products. More *decision participants* will be involved in buying a computer, for example, than in buying paper clips. The challenge to the industrial marketer is to figure out the major decision participants for any given type of purchase.

The well-known *How Industry Buys/1970*[4] study identified eight management groups that might get involved in the purchasing process: (1) overall corporate policy and planning, (2) operations and administration, (3) design and development engineering, (4) production engineering, (5) research, (6) finance, (7) sales, and (8) purchasing.

After identifying the decision participants, the industrial marketer has to figure out the participation level and influence of each participant in each stage of the buying process. The *How Industry Buys/1970* survey, for example, provides this kind of information. Consider the role, for example, of purchasing departments in the buying of industrial equipment. Purchasing departments rarely initiate the project; in about 10 percent of the companies, they participate in determining the kind of equipment, and in 46 percent of the cases, they participate in selecting the supplier.[5] An industrial salesperson, therefore, does not have to seek out the purchasing agent at the beginning of an effort to interest a company in a major piece of equipment. The salesperson should instead seek out production engineers because they are responsible for initiating purchase projects in 42 percent of the cases.

The salesperson must also recognize that each decision participant is likely to bring a different set of evaluation criteria to apply to the purchase decision. Consider the following:

The production manager of the buying organization may view a new component under consideration in terms of its effects on assembly cost and reliability of supply. Quality control may be concerned with the uncertainties introduced by the proposed change itself. Purchasing personnel are concerned with relative costs and the risks associated with shifting to a supplier whose performance is unknown. The sales manager is concerned with the effect of modification on the attractiveness and suitability of the changed end product for his customers and thus the effect of the specification change on sales. Customer service is concerned with expected breakdown rates, possible misuse by customer personnel, the costs of

---

[4] Published by *Scientific American*, 1970.

[5] Ibid., p. 7.

adding new items to the repair parts inventories and of additional training of maintenance, repair, and service personnel. Thus each possible buying influence employs his own criteria in evaluating the worth of the salesman's offer.[6]

The practical implication is that the industrial marketer must learn the relevant criteria of each decision participant in order to communicate effectively about the product's merits.

Since a buying center may include several persons (it is estimated that buying centers vary from three to twelve persons), the industrial marketer may not have the time or resources to reach them all or may not have access to all of them. Smaller companies try to figure out who the key buying influences are and concentrate their limited advertising and personal selling resources on them. Larger companies go for *multilevel in-depth selling* to reach as many decision participants as possible. Then salespeople "live" with the customer when it is a major account with recurrent sales.

Industrial marketers must periodically review their assumptions on the roles and influence of different decision participants. For example, for years Kodak's strategy for selling X-ray film to hospitals was to sell through lab technicians. The company did not notice that the decision was being made increasingly by professional administrators. As its sales declined, it finally grasped the change in buying practices and hurriedly changed its marketing strategy.

What Are Producers Seeking?

Industrial buyers are not buying goods and services for personal consumption or utility. They buy things for any of the following motives: (1) to make money, (2) to reduce operating costs, (3) to satisfy a social or legal obligation. A steel company will add another furnace if it sees a chance to make more money. It will computerize its accounting system if this will reduce the costs of doing business. It will add pollution-control equipment to satisfy legal requirements.

The main tradeoff faced by industrial buyers is between cost and quality. Some industrial buyers are partial to the best goods they can get, and others will buy the lowest-cost goods providing that these meet minimum standards. Often the producer can segment the market by identifying groups with different quality/cost preferences. An example is the transistor market:

> The market for transistors consists of three submarkets: military, industrial, and commercial. The buyer behavior differences among these three markets can be analyzed clearly.
>
> The military buyer attaches utmost importance to the producer's quality standards and the adequacy of his plant facilities. Only after these two considerations have been realized does price become a factor.
>
> Quality is also of great importance to industrial customers such as computer manufacturers, for their products are used by industrial manufacturers like themselves. Loyalties can be established in this segment through high quality and good service. Price itself is not a critical matter unless it becomes completely out of line.
>
> Commercial buyers, such as pocket-radio manufacturers, are in the most competitive user market and consequently buy their components completely on price and delivery. No loyalty to suppliers exists, and quality requirements are usually minimal.
>
> Because of these differences, marketing strategies have to be varied. In order

[6] See Charles S. Goodman, *Management of the Personal Selling Function* (New York: Holt, Rinehart and Winston, 1971), p. 204.

to sell transistors in the military market, firms must make a considerable investment in R&D, use salesmen who know military buying procedures, and specialize in limited-line products. In order to sell in the industrial market, firms must make a modest investment in R&D, use sales people who have technical knowledge concerning the product, and offer a broad line. In order to sell to the commercial market, firms need little or no R&D effort, use high-pressure sales people who are relatively nontechnical, and offer the most common lines that can be mass-produced.

Some buyers have a lot of latitude in selecting a quality/cost level of goods to buy. Consider the *institutional market:*

The institutional market consists of institutions that make purchases in order to provide goods and services to those they care for and are responsible for. Schools, hospitals, nursing homes, and prisons are prime examples of institutional buyers. They are generally characterized by low budgets and captive clienteles. A hospital purchasing agent has to decide on the quality of food to buy for the patients. The buying objective is not profit since the food is provided free to the patients. The basic objective is not cost minimization either, because patients served poor food in a hospital will complain to others and hurt the hospital's reputation. The hospital purchasing agent has to find institutional-food vendors whose quality meets a certain minimum standard and yet whose prices are low. Many food vendors set up a separate division to sell to institutional buyers because of their special buying needs and characteristics.

Over the years, company purchasing executives have been improving their purchasing skills and tools. The competency of buyers is a function of their degree of knowledge, analytical capacity, and negotiating ability. Buyers need to be fully informed about competing vendors, products, and terms. They have to be good at applying formal cost-evaluation models. When buying a computer, they have to know how much value to place on different attributes, such as calculation speed and information capacity. When evaluating the replacement of a generator, they have to know how to use payout-period and rate-of-return analysis. When considering different ways in which some function can be performed, they have to know value analysis.

Value analysis, which General Electric developed in 1948, is *an approach to cost reduction in which components are carefully studied to determine if they can be redesigned or standardized or made by cheaper methods of production.* The purchasing agent who is a value analyst will carefully examine the high-cost components in a given product—usually 20 percent of the parts will comprise about 80 percent of the costs. The examination proceeds through five steps:

1. Analyze a part's function to determine whether a standardized shelf item could be used.
2. See whether a nonstandardized part could be slightly redesigned into a standardized part. If so, competitive bidding could be solicited, and this generally leads to lower prices.
3. See whether two or more parts could be combined into one.
4. See whether cheaper substitute materials could be used. If so, there may be savings not only in the materials but also in the costs of molds and dies.
5. Contact suppliers and discuss whether certain parts could be made for less by improvements in tooling, by grouping similar work, or by increasing quantities.

Finally, the industrial buyer must have the knack of getting the vendors to compete for the business and have the negotiating skill to win the most favorable terms. . . . A good example of a cagey buyer is [the] vice president in charge of purchasing for Rheingold's big New York brewery. . . . Using the leverage of hundreds of millions of cans a year, like many other buyers, he takes punitive action when one company slips in quality or fails to deliver. "At one point American started talking about a price rise," he recalls, "Continental kept its mouth shut. . . . American never did put the price rise into effect, buy anyway, I punished them for talking about it." For a three-month period he cut the percentage of cans he bought from American.[7]

Most descriptions of industrial buyers portray them as rational, hard-nosed persons seeking to secure the best terms for their company. Other studies emphasize personal motives and influences in the industrial buyer's world. A study of buyers in ten large companies concluded:

> Corporate decision makers remain human after they enter the office. They respond to "image"; they buy from companies to which they feel "close"; they favor suppliers who show them respect and personal considerations, and who do extra things for them; they "over-react" to real or imagined slights, tending to reject companies which fail to respond to such items as reader service cards bound into magazines, or which delay in submitting requested bids. . . . Advertising and promotional materials are key factors in establishing a "good image." Good image qualities are said to include being "well known," being considered "big" or a "leader in the field," and having a reputation for providing good service.[8]

In truth, industrial buyers respond to both rational and subjective factors. Where there is substantial similarity in what suppliers offer in the way of products, price, and service, industrial buyers have little basis for rational choice. Since they can meet organizational goals with any one of a number of suppliers, buyers can bring in personal factors. On the other hand, where competing products differ substantially, industrial buyers are more accountable for their choice and pay more attention to objective factors. Short-run personal gain becomes less motivating than the long-run gain that comes from serving their organization well.

How Do Producers Buy?

How do industrial buyers carry out their buying operations? We want to consider the following four questions: (1) What factors influence the industrial buyer's decisions? (2) What are the major types of buying situations in industrial buying? (3) What are the major decisions made by industrial buyers? and (4) What are the major stages in the industrial buying process?

Factors influencing industrial buying decisions   Many theories have been advanced to explain how industrial buyers make their purchase decisions. Webster and Wind classify them into task- and nontask-oriented models.[9]

Task models view the organization as behaving in the manner of a rational

---

[7] Walter Guzzardi, Jr., "The Fight for 9/10 of a Cent," *Fortune*, April 1961, p. 152.

[8] The study was conducted by Motivational Programmers, Inc., a marketing research firm, and was reported in "Who Makes the Purchasing Decision?" *Marketing Insights*, October 31, 1966, pp. 16–18.

[9] "Who Makes the Purchasing Decision?" pp. 13–20.

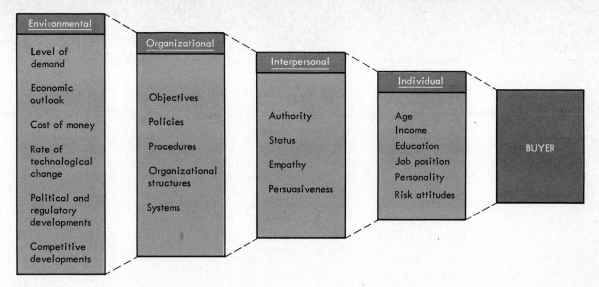

FIGURE 7–1
Major Factors Influencing Industrial Buying Behavior

buyer pursuing economic objectives in an efficient way. The organization is seen as making its decision in favor of the supplier with the minimum price, or the lowest total cost, or who buys things from the company in return (i.e., reciprocity), or who is the most ready to accommodate. Task models imply that industrial marketers should offer strong economic values to the buyer.

Nontask models emphasize the role of personal motives in the buying process, such as buyers who respond to personal favors (self-aggrandizement), or to attention (ego enhancement), or to personal-risk containment (risk avoiders). These nontask models suggest that industrial marketers should concentrate on the human and social factors in the buying situation and that they could overcome offer deficiencies by being more manipulative of emotional and interpersonal factors.

Webster and Wind see these factors as partial determinants in the total picture and prefer to classify all influences into four main groups: environmental, organizational, interpersonal, and individual[10] (see Figure 7–1).

Environmental factors are factors outside of the organization, such as are found in the macroenvironment, the public environment, and the marketing channel environment. Buying decisions are influenced by the level of primary demand, economic outlook, the cost of money, the rate of technological change, political and regulatory developments, and competitive developments. These environmental influences are normally beyond the control of both buyer and seller and have to be taken as given in the situation.

Organizational factors are another set of influences on the buying process. Each company spells out objectives, policies, procedures, structures, and systems to guide the buying process. Buying decisions are affected by the company's systems of reward, authority, status, and communication.

[10] Ibid.

Interpersonal factors constitute another important set of forces in the buying process. The buying center involves the interaction of several persons of different status, authority, empathy, and persuasiveness in the company. It is very hard for the seller to know in advance how interpersonal factors work in a particular company.

Individual factors constitute still another important set of determinants. The issue here is how the individual decision participants form their perceptions of and preferences for product characteristics and supplier offers. Furthermore, there is the issue of the role of such factors as the person's age, income, education, professional identification, personality, and attitudes toward risk in influencing his or her buying behavior.

Some of the most interesting work is going on in the area of trying to determine the relative importance of different attributes of the seller and the offer in creating preference among individual buyers. Cardozo and Cagley explored the role of four attributes in influencing the selection of suppliers and bids.[11] They found that a company that (1) is "in," (2) has a well-known name, (3) provides more information about its offer, and (4) stresses low-price appeals as a bidder will be unusually effective with professional buyers in large organizations. If the company lacks one or more of these attributes, it should direct its selling efforts to other participants in the buying center or to smaller organizations.

Lehmann and O'Shaughnessy undertook to research the relative importance of seventeen attributes in influencing purchase decisions: reputation, financing, flexibility, past experience, technical service, confidence in salesmen, convenience in ordering, reliability data on product, price, technical specifications, ease of use, preference of user, training offered, training required, delivery reliability, maintenance, and sales service.[12] They found that the relative importance of each attribute varied with the type of buying situation. For *routine-order products,* they found that delivery reliability and price were highly important, along with reputation of suppliers and experience with them. For *procedural-problem products,* such as a dry copying machine, the three most important attributes were technical service offered, flexibility of supplier, and product reliability. Finally, for *political-problem products,* those that stir rivalries in the organization, the most important attributes were price, reputation, product reliability, service reliability, and supplier flexibility.

Major types of buying situations   Organizational buying behavior varies with the type of buying situation. Some buying situations are highly routinized and programmed, and others are new tasks. Robinson et al. distinguish among three types of buying situations, which they call *buyclasses.*[13]

THE STRAIGHT REBUY   The straight rebuy describes the simplest buying situation—the company reorders something without any modifications. It is usually handled on a routine basis by the purchasing department. The company

[11] Richard N. Cardozo and James W. Cagley, "Experimental Study of Industrial Buyer Behavior," *Journal of Marketing Research,* August 1971, pp. 329–34.

[12] See Donald R. Lehmann and John O'Shaughnessy, "Difference in Attribute Importance for Different Industrial Products," *Journal of Marketing,* April 1974, pp. 36–42.

[13] Patrick J. Robinson, Charles W. Faris, and Yoram Wind, *Industrial Buying and Creative Marketing* (Boston: Allyn and Bacon, 1967).

chooses from suppliers already on its "list," giving much weight to its past buying experience with the various suppliers. The "in" suppliers make an effort to keep up product and service quality. They often propose automatic reordering systems so that the purchasing agent will save time on reordering from them. The "out" suppliers attempt to offer something new or create some dissatisfaction so that the buyer will reconsider the buying assumptions. Out suppliers will attempt to get their foot in the door with a small order and then try to enlarge their purchase share over time.

THE MODIFIED REBUY   The modified rebuy describes a situation in which the buyer is seeking to modify product specifications, prices, other terms, or suppliers in connection with something the company purchases. Somehow, the company thinks it can do better. The modified rebuy usually expands the number of decision participants. The in suppliers get nervous and have to put their best foot forward to protect the account. The out suppliers see it as an opportunity to make a better offer to gain some new business.

NEW TASK   A company faces a new task when it is considering buying a product or service for the first time. The greater the cost and/or risk, the larger the number of decision participants, and the greater their information seeking. The new-task situation is the marketer's greatest opportunity and challenge. The marketer must plan to reach as many key buying influences as possible and provide information and assistance in helping them resolve their problem, hoping, of course, that it will be in favor of his product. Because of the complicated selling involved in the new task, many companies use a specialized sales force, called a *missionary sales force,* to carry out this task.

New-task buying passes through several stages, each with its own requirements and challenges to the marketer. Ozanne and Churchill have applied an innovation diffusion perspective to the new task, identifying the stages as *awareness, interest, evaluation, trial,* and *adoption.*[14] They found that information sources varied in effectiveness at each stage. Mass media were most important during the initial awareness stage, whereas salespersons had their greatest impact at the interest stage. Technical sources were the most important during the evaluation stage. These findings provide clues to the new-task marketer as to efficient communications to use at different stages of the buying process.

Major types of buying decisions   The number of decisions involved in a particular buying project varies with the type of buying situation, the fewest being in the case of a straight rebuy and the most numerous in the new-task situation. In the new-task situation, the buying center will have to determine: (1) product specifications, (2) price limits, (3) delivery terms and times, (4) service terms, (5) payment terms, (6) order quantities, (7) acceptable suppliers, and (8) the selected supplier. Different decision participants will influence each decision, and the order in which the decisions will be made will vary.

The marketer's task is to anticipate the full range of decisions facing the buyer and offer an attractive and convenient total solution if possible. Suppose, for example, that a company wants to build a fertilizer plant. At one extreme, the company can make all the separate decisions and hire its own architects, en-

[14] Urban B. Ozanne and Gilbert A. Churchill, Jr., "Adoption Research: Information Sources in the Industrial Purchase Decision," *Proceedings,* Fall Conference (Chicago: American Marketing Association, 1968).

gineers, contractors, legal staff, and so on. At the other extreme, the company can hire one company that will put together the whole package. The second is called a *turnkey operation* because all the buyer has to do is turn the key when the plant is ready to start operating. The underlying idea is that the marketer should try to sell a system, not just a single component, because buyers find this more convenient and attractive. *Systems selling* is a key industrial-marketing strategy for winning and holding accounts.[15]

Major steps in industrial buying   The industrial marketer needs to grasp how the organizational buying process is carried out. The buying process consists of eight stages called *buyphases*.[16] They are (1) need recognition, (2) need definition, (3) need description, (4) seller identification, (5) proposal solicitation, (6) proposal evaluation and selection, (7) ordering procedure, and (8) performance review. The eight buyphases are listed in the rows of Figure 7–2 along with the three types of buyclasses. The model is called the *buygrid* framework.

All of the buyphases operate in new-task buying, whereas some are compressed or absent in the more straight rebuy situations. Each phase successively narrows the number of alternatives, indicating that sellers have to get into the act as early as possible.

BUYPHASES	BUYCLASSES		
	NEW TASK	MODIFIED REBUY	STRAIGHT REBUY
1. Anticipation or recognition of a problem (need) and a general solution			
2. Determination of characteristics and quantity of needed item			
3. Description of characteristics and quantity of needed item			
4. Search for and qualification of potential sources			
5. Acquisition and analysis of proposals			
6. Evaluation of proposals and selection of supplier(s)			
7. Selection of an order routine			
8. Performance feedback and evaluation			

FIGURE 7–2
The Buygrid Analytic Framework for Industrial Buying Situations

SOURCE: Redrawn from Patrick J. Robinson, Charles W. Faris, and Yoram Wind, *Industrial Buying and Creative Marketing* (Boston: Allyn & Bacon, 1967), p. 14.

[15] See chap. 14, footnote 1, p. 353.

[16] Robinson et al., *Industrial Buying.*

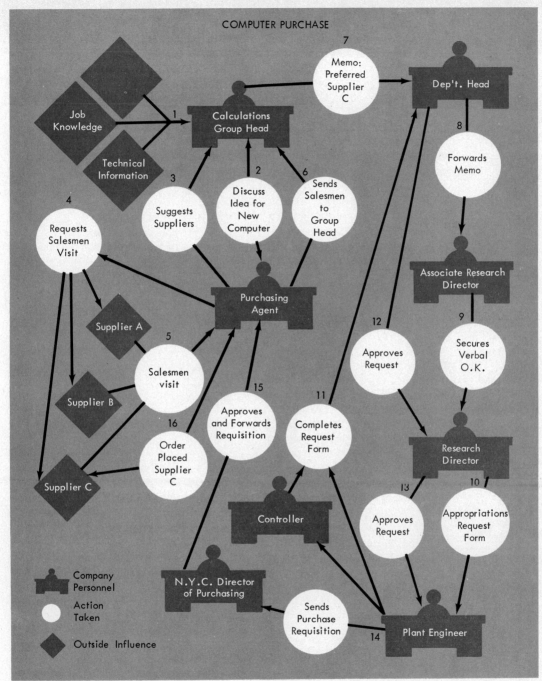

COMPUTER PURCHASE

Job Knowledge

Technical Information

1 → Calculations Group Head

7 Memo: Preferred Supplier C

Dep't. Head

8 Forwards Memo

3 Suggests Suppliers

2 Discuss Idea for New Computer

6 Sends Salesmen to Group Head

Associate Research Director

9 Secures Verbal O.K.

4 Requests Salesmen Visit

Purchasing Agent

Supplier A

5 Salesmen visit

Supplier B

15 Approves and Forwards Requisition

11 Completes Request Form

12 Approves Request

Research Director

16 Order Placed Supplier C

Supplier C

Controller

13 Approves Request

10 Appropriations Request Form

N.Y.C. Director of Purchasing

14 Sends Purchase Requisition

Plant Engineer

Company Personnel

Action Taken

Outside Influence

SOURCE: "Who Makes the Purchasing Decision?" *Marketing Insights.* October 31, 1966, p. 18.

FIGURE 7–3
Map of Company Events in the Purchase of a Computer

The actual sequence of buying steps should be studied by the marketer. Each buying situation involves a flow of work. This *buyflow* should be mapped when possible as a guide to developing effective marketing strategies. Mapping the buyflow is especially worthwhile with large prospective customers or when several customers can be identified who have similar buying operations. An example of a buyflow map for a computer purchase is shown in Figure 7–3. The map shows that eight different company employees (represented by desk symbols) were involved in this buying decision process at one time or another. Three suppliers also were involved, as well as other outside influences (shown in diamond-shaped figures). Finally, fifteen different events (shown as circles) fed up to the placing of the order ultimately with supplier C.

THE RESELLER MARKET

Who Is in the Reseller Market?

The reseller market consists of *all individuals and organizations who acquire goods for the purpose of reselling or renting them to others at a profit.* Instead of producing form utility, the reseller market produces time, place, and possession utility. The reseller market includes over 276,000 wholesaling firms employing 4,216,000 persons, and 1,665,000 retailing firms employing 11,961,000 persons; both sectors account for over 16 percent of the national income. Resellers are more dispersed geographically than producers but more concentrated than consumers.

What Do Resellers Buy?

Resellers purchase (1) goods for resale and (2) goods and services for conducting their operations. The latter are bought by resellers in their role as "producers," so we shall confine the discussion here to the goods they purchase for resale.

Resellers handle a vast variety of products for resale, indeed everything produced except the few classes of goods that producers choose to sell direct to final customers. The excluded class includes heavy or complex machinery, customized products, and products sold on a direct-mail or a door-to-door basis. With these exceptions, most products are sold to the final buyer through one or more selling intermediaries.

Each reseller faces the problem of determining its unique *assortment*—the combination of products and services that it will offer to the marketplace. The wholesaler or retailer can choose one of four assortment strategies:

1. *Exclusive assortment:* representing the line of only one manufacturer
2. *Deep assortment:* representing a given homogeneous product family in depth, drawing on many producers' outputs
3. *Broad assortment:* representing a wide range of product lines that still fall within the natural coverage of the reseller's type of business
4. *Scrambled assortment:* representing many unrelated product families

Thus a camera store can decide to sell only Kodak cameras (exclusive assortment), many brands of cameras (deep assortment), cameras, tape recorders, radios, and stereophonic equipment (broad assortment), or the last plus stoves and refrigerators (scrambled assortment). The assortment the reseller ultimately chooses will influence its customer mix, marketing mix, and supplier mix.

When Do Resellers Buy?	Resellers order goods according to their current stock level and anticipated demand level. Their ordering practice is influenced by two opposite forces. By placing large orders infrequently, they keep down their order-placement costs and may obtain good discounts. By placing small orders frequently, they keep down their inventory carrying costs. Resellers analyze the relative costs and make decisions on ordering points for replacing stock. Producers have to be aware of the inventory systems used by resellers in developing their marketing strategies.

Who Participates in the Reseller Buying Process?

Who does the deciding and buying for wholesale and retail organizations? In the smaller firms, the merchandise selection and buying functions may be carried out by persons who also carry out several other functions in the firm. In the larger firms, buying is a specialist function and often a full-time job. It is carried on in different ways by department stores, supermarkets, drug wholesalers, and so on, and differences can even be found within each type of distributive enterprise.

Much of the flavor of reseller buying practices can be sensed by examining the particular case of supermarket chains and the respective roles played by corporate-headquarter buyers, storewide buying committees, and the individual store managers. In the corporate headquarters of a supermarket chain specialist buyers will be found (sometimes called merchandise managers) for different product lines carried by the supermarket. These buyers have the responsibility for developing brand assortments and listening to presentations by salespersons offering new brands. In some chains these buyers have great latitude with respect to accepting or rejecting new items. In many chains, however, their latitude is limited to screening "obvious rejects" (and sometimes "obvious accepts"); otherwise they must bring the new-item proposals to the chain's buying committee at one of the weekly meetings.

There is some evidence that buying committees serve a "checking" function rather than an actual decision-making function. Borden found that the buyer's recommendation is highly important and influential in the committee decision.[17] The buyer decides what to communicate to the committee, thus exerting considerable influence on the decision. Buying committees exert some important indirect effects on product evaluations and decisions. By serving as a buffer between buyers and salespersons, committees provide buyers with an excuse for rejecting a seller's proposition.

Even if an item is accepted by a chain-store buying committee, it will not necessarily appear in a large number of the chain's outlets. According to one supermarket-chain executive: "No matter what the sales representatives sell or buyers buy, the person who has the greatest influence on the final sale of the new item is the store manager." In the nation's chain and independent supermarkets, two-thirds of the new items accepted at the warehouse are ordered on the individual store manager's own decision, and only one-third represent forced distribution.[18]

[17] Neil H. Borden, Jr., *Acceptance of New Food Products by Supermarkets* (Boston: Division of Research, Graduate School of Business Administration, Harvard University, 1968).

[18] Robert W. Mueller and Franklin H. Graf, "New Items in the Food Industry, Their Problems and Opportunities," a special report to the Annual Convention of the Supermarket Institute, Cleveland, Ohio, May 20, 1968, p. 2.

This picture of the reseller organization's buying procedure for new items points to the formidable problem faced by the producers of new items. Industry offers the nation's supermarkets between 150 and 250 new items each week, of which store space does not permit more than 10 percent to be accepted.

Several studies have attempted to rank the major criteria used by buyers, buying committees, and store managers. A. C. Nielsen Company carried out a study in which store managers were asked to rank on a three-point scale the importance of different elements in influencing their decision to accept a new item.[19] The final ranking showed:

Evidence of consumer acceptance	2.5
Advertising/promotion	2.2
Introductory terms and allowances	2.0
Why item was developed	1.9
Merchandising recommendations	1.8

The first three items are reported to be the most important criteria in other studies also.[20] They suggest that sellers stand the best chance when they can report strong evidence of consumer acceptance, present a well-designed and extensive introductory advertising and sales promotion plan, and provide incentives to the retailer.

These respective roles of chain buyers, chain buying committees, and store managers characterize, with some variation, the buying organizations of other distributive enterprises. Large department stores or chains rely on buyers for merchandise lines, and usually they have a lot of authority and latitude. They may report to buying committees. The buyers are aided by assistant buyers, who carry out a preliminary search as well as clerical tasks involved in ordering. The buyers may perform other functions such as demand forecasting, stock control, and merchandising. Individual store managers or their staff usually have some freedom with respect to which goods to order as well as which to display prominently.

What Are Resellers Seeking?

Resellers, like producers, are in business to make a profit. They must be adept at buying goods "cheap" and selling them "dear." This means they must know the various sources of supply, be able to negotiate, and be able to set services, prices, and promotional expenditures at levels that will generate a high level of revenue in relation to the costs of doing business. Buyers must master principles of demand forecasting, merchandise selection, stock control, space allocation, and display, not to mention the careful management of money and personnel resources. They must learn to measure return on a profit-per-cubic-foot basis

---

[19] Ibid., p. 5.

[20] "Merchandising New Items at Retail: The Payoff at Point of Purchase," *Progressive Grocer*, June 1968; also Borden, *New Food Products*, p. 203. Also see David B. Montgomery, *New Product Distribution: An Analysis of Supermarket Buyer Decisions* (Cambridge, Mass.: Marketing Science Institute, March 1973). Montgomery found the two most important variables to be company reputation and the perceived newness of the product.

rather than on a product-by-product basis.[21] In many retail lines the profit margin on sales is so low (for example, 1 to 2 percent in supermarkets) that a sudden decline in demand will drive profits into the red. Those who complain about middlemen profits overlook the enormous work and risk that must be borne by middlemen in their effort to create assortments that meet the wants and needs of final buyers.

Resellers tend to develop different buying styles to carry out their work. Dickinson has distinguished the following buyer types:

1. *Loyal buyer.* This type remains loyal to a resource, or group of resources, year after year, for reasons other than that he obtains the best deal.

2. *Opportunistic buyer.* This type selects mainly from a preselected list of those vendors who will further his long-term interests. Within his preselected list, he will pursue the best arrangement possible.

3. *Best-deal buyer.* This type looks for and selects the best deal available to him in the market at a given point in time.

4. *Creative buyer.* This type tries not to accept the marketing mixes offered by any of the vendors. He attempts to sell his offers to the market. This may or may not involve a change in the physical product.

5. *Advertising buyer.* This type attempts primarily to obtain advertising moneys; advertising moneys must be a part of every deal and are the prime target of each negotiation.

6. *The chiseler.* This type of buyer constantly negotiates extra concessions in price at the time of the offering. He tends to accept the vendor offer carrying the greatest discount from the price he feels that other accounts might pay.

7. *Nuts-and-bolts buyer.* This buyer selects merchandise that is the best constructed, assuming that the merchandise policies of the vendor are acceptable within a very broad range. He is more interested in the thread count than in the number that will sell.[22]

How Do Resellers Buy?

Resellers are influenced by the same set of factors—environmental, organizational, interpersonal, and individual—that were shown in Figure 7–1 as influencing producers.

The specific buying operations vary with the type of buying situation. Three situations can be distinguished.

The *new-item situation* describes the case where the reseller has been offered a new item. The new-item situation differs from the new-task situation faced by producers in that the former is a "yes-no" opportunity presented to the buyer while the latter means that the buyer is confronted with a new problem arising in the manufacturing process and must initiate research and evaluation of solutions and vendors.

The *best-vendor situation* faces the reseller who knows what is needed but must determine the best supplier. It occurs (1) when the reseller can carry only a subset of the available brands offered because of space constraints or (2) when

---

[21] See Robert D. Buzzell, *Product Profitability Measurement and Merchandising Decisions* (Boston: Harvard University Press, 1965).

[22] Roger A. Dickinson, *Buyer Decision Making* (Berkeley, Calif.: Institute of Business and Economic Research, 1967), pp. 14–17.

the reseller wants to sponsor a private brand and is seeking a willing and qualified producer. Resellers such as Sears and the A&P sell a substantial number of items under their own names; therefore much of their buying operation consists of vendor selection.

The *better-terms situation* arises when the reseller wants to obtain a better set of terms from current suppliers. The buyer is not eager to change the supplier but does want more advantageous treatment. Legally sellers are prevented, under the Robinson-Patman Act, from giving different terms to different resellers in the same reseller class unless these reflect corresponding cost differences, distress sales, or a few other special conditions. Nevertheless, individual resellers and classes of resellers (discounters, mass merchandisers) do press their suppliers for preferential treatment, and this treatment can take many forms, such as more supplier services, easier credit terms, and higher volume discounts.

Buying procedures in all three situations can be expected to grow more sophisticated over time, as better-trained persons are hired for these jobs, receive more extensive data with which to work, and learn how to use more analytical methods. Major changes in purchasing operations are being made possible by advances in computers and telecommunications. Computers are finding increased application in keeping current inventory figures, computing economic order quantities, preparing purchasing orders, developing requests for vendor quotations or expediting of orders, and generating printouts of dollars spent on vendors and products. Through telecommunications, the buyer can feed prepunched cards describing items and quantities needed into a transmitter that is linked to the supplier's receiving equipment. The supplier's equipment prepares cards or tapes, which become the input for mechanized preparation of shipping tickets, invoices, and other documents. Many resellers are going over to stockless purchasing of certain items, which means that the supplier inventories the items and supplies them to the buyer on short notice.

THE GOVERNMENT MARKET

Who Is in the Government Market?

The government market consists of federal, state, and local *governmental units that purchase or rent goods for carrying out the main functions of government.* In 1976, governmental units purchased $366 billion of products and services, or 21 percent of the gross national product, making it the nation's largest customer. The federal government accounts for approximately 60 percent of the total spent by government at all levels.

Although substantial government purchasing takes place in Washington, D.C., in state capitals, and in other major cities, it takes place in every county and village as well. The federal government operates an elaborate set of geographically dispersed buying information offices. Local products and services may be bought by local government offices, army posts, and so on. As one example, the naval complex at Hampton Roads, Virginia, paid local Virginia firms $500,000 in one year just for ice cream.

What Do Government Units Buy?

What else does government buy, besides ice cream? Practically everything. Governmental agencies buy bombers, sculpture, chalkboards, furniture, toiletries, clothing, materials-handling equipment, fire engines, mobile equipment, and fuel. In 1975, all government spent approximately $95 billion for education, $87 billion for defense, $39 billion for public welfare, $35 billion for health and hospitals, $23 billion for highways, $16 billion for natural resources, and smaller sums for postal service, space research, and housing and urban renewal. The mix of expenditures varied considerably with the particular type of governmental unit, with defense looming large in the federal budget (34 percent) and education looming large in the state and local budgets (38 percent). No matter how one feels about government marketing, it represents a tremendous market for any producer or reseller.

When Do Government Units Buy?

The factors determining when government buying occurs are the same as those for the previous markets. This is because there is a wide variety of government buyers who function essentially as industrial, reseller, or consumer buyers, even though the duration of the purchase process may be much longer.

Who Participates in the Government Buying Process?

Who in the government does the buying of the $366 billion of goods and services? Government buying organizations are found on the federal, state, and local levels. The federal level is the largest, and its buying units can be subclassified into the civilian and military sectors. The *federal civilian buying* establishment consists of seven categories: departments (e.g., Commerce), administration (e.g., General Services Administration), agencies (e.g., Federal Aviation Agency), boards (e.g., Railroad Retirement Board), commissions (e.g., Federal Communications Commission), the executive office (e.g., Bureau of the Budget), and miscellaneous (e.g., Tennessee Valley Authority). "No single federal agency contracts for all the government's requirements and no single buyer in any agency purchases all that agency's needs for any single item of supplies, equipment, or services."[23] Many agencies control a substantial percentage of their own buying, particularly of industrial products and specialized equipment. At the same time, the General Services Administration plays a main role in attempting to centralize the procurement of the items most commonly used by the civilian section (office furniture and equipment, vehicles, fuels, and so on) and to promote standardized buying procedures for the other agencies. It acts in the capacity of a wholesaler on its own account and as a reseller and an agent middleman for other government agencies.

Federal military buying is carried out by the Defense Department largely through the Defense Supply Agency and the three military departments of the Army, Navy, and Air Force. The Defense Supply Agency was set up in 1961 to procure and distribute supplies used in common by all military services in an effort to reduce costly duplication (thus it is the equivalent of the General Services Administration in the military sector). It operates six supply centers, which specialize in construction, electronics, fuel, personnel support, industrial, and general supplies. The trend has been toward "single managers" for major product classifications. Each individual service branch procures equipment and supplies in line with its own mission; for example, the Army Department operates special branches for acquiring its own material, vehicles, medical supplies and services, and weaponry.

State and local buying agencies include school districts, highway departments, hospitals, housing agencies, and many others.

[23] Stanley E. Cohen, "Looking in the U.S. Government Market," *Industrial Marketing*, September 1964, pp. 129–38.

Government buying is premised on a different fundamental objective than is found in the other sectors of the economy. Government does not pursue a personal consumption or a profit-making standard; rather it buys a level and mix of products and services that it or the voters establish as necessary or desirable for the maintenance of the society.

Government purchasing of specific goods and services largely follows the objective of *minimizing taxpayer cost*. Government buyers are supposed to buy from the lowest-cost bidders providing that their goods meet the stated specifications. Increasingly, however, the buyers will relax low-cost purchasing rules in the pursuit of other objectives, such as favoring depressed business firms or areas, small business firms, and business firms that do not practice racial, sex, or age discrimination.

Government buying practices appear complex to the uninitiated supplier because of the many agencies and procedures that characterize the government market. Yet most of the system can be mastered in a short time, and the government is generally helpful in diffusing information about its buying needs and procedures. In fact, government is often as anxious to attract new suppliers as the suppliers are to find customers. For example, the Small Business Administration publishes a useful booklet, *U.S. Government Purchasing, Specifications and Sales Directory*, listing thousands of items most frequently purchased by government and cross-referenced by the agencies most frequently using them. The Government Printing Office publishes *Commerce Business Daily*, which lists current proposed defense procurements estimated to exceed $10,000 and civilian agency procurements expected to exceed $5,000, as well as information about recent contract awards that can provide leads to subcontracting markets. The General Services Administration operates Business Service Centers in several major cities, whose staffs are set up to provide a complete education on the way GSA and other agencies buy and the steps that the supplier should follow. Various trade magazines and associations provide information on how to reach schools, hospitals, highway departments, and other government agencies.

Government buying procedures can be classified into two major types: the *open bid* and the *negotiated contract*. In both cases the emphasis is on competitive procurement. Open-bid buying means that the government procuring office invites bids from qualified suppliers for carefully described items, generally awarding a contract to the lowest bidder. Specifically, the interested supplier fills out an application requesting to be placed on the bidders' list. The supplier receives mailings of "invitations for bids," which carefully specify the item and quantity needed. The specifications include a description of the materials, dimensions, quality, reliability, and packing and crating requirements, as well as the terms of the contract that will be awarded to the successful bidder. The supplier firm must carefully consider whether it can meet the specifications and if it likes the terms. For commodities and standard items, such as fuel or school supplies, the specifications are not a hurdle. However, specifications may constitute a hurdle for nonstandard items, although the government unit is barred from issuing such narrow specifications that only one existing seller can meet them. Furthermore, the government procurement office is usually—but not always—required to award the contract to the lowest bidder on a winner-take-all basis. In some cases allowance can be made for the supplier's superior product or reputation for completing contracts. A more recent development is to ask for bids, particularly on equipment, to cover life-cycle maintenance as well as initial price. The award will go to the firm submitting the lowest life-cycle bid. This practice was started by the Defense Department in recognition of the fact that it might spend up to ten times the original purchase price to own and operate the equipment.

In negotiated-contract buying, the agency works with one or a few companies and directly negotiates a contract with one of them covering the project and terms. This occurs primarily in connection with complex projects, often involving major research and development cost and risk and/or where there is little effective competition. Contracts can have countless variations, such as *cost-plus pricing, fixed-pricing,* and *fixed price-and-incentive* (the supplier earns more if costs are reduced). Contract performance is open to review and renegotiation if the supplier's profits appear excessive.

Government contracts won by large companies give rise to substantial subcontracting opportunities, as much as 50 percent, for small companies. Thus government purchasing activity in turn creates derived demand in the producer market. Subcontracting firms going after this business, however, must be willing to place performance bonds with the prime contractor, thereby assuming some of the risk.

By and large, companies that have served the government have not manifested much of a marketing orientation—for a number of reasons. Total government spending is determined by elected officials rather than by marketing effort to develop this market. The government's procurement policies have emphasized price, leading the suppliers to invest all their effort in a technological orientation to bring their costs down. Where the product's characteristics are carefully specified, product differentiation is not a marketing factor. Nor are advertising and personal selling of much consequence in winning bids on an open-bid basis.

More companies are now establishing marketing departments to guide government-directed marketing. There is greater effort to coordinate bids and prepare them more scientifically, to propose projects to meet government needs rather than just to respond to government initiatives, to gather competitive intelligence, and to prepare better communication programs to describe the company's competence.

SUMMARY

The organizational market consists of all organizations that buy goods for purposes of further production or resale or distribution to others. Organizations are a market for raw and manufactured materials and parts, installations and accessory equipment, and supplies and services.

Producer organizations buy goods and services for the purpose of increasing sales, cutting costs, or meeting social and legal requirements. Compared to households, they show more skill in buying, are larger and more concentrated geographically, and are more influenced by the level of economic activity. In producer buying, more people are likely to participate; and they operate under a more specific set of policies and procedures. Their buying decisions are influenced by environmental, organizational, interpersonal, and individual factors. The decision-making unit of a buying organization, the buying center, consists of individuals who play any of five roles: users, influencers, buyers, deciders, and gatekeepers. Their involvement and behavior depend on the buying situation, whether a straight rebuy, modified rebuy, or new task. The number and type of buying decisions also vary with the type of buying situation, being the most complex in the new-task situation. The buying process itself consists of up to eight stages, called buyphases.

The reseller market consists of individuals and organizations who acquire and resell goods produced by others. Producers must apply modern marketing concepts and techniques in approaching resellers, because their buying organizations, needs, styles, and operations vary considerably.

The government market is a vast one that annually purchases $366 billion of products and services—for the pursuit of defense, education, public welfare, and other public needs. Government buying practices are highly specialized and specified, with open bidding and/or negotiated contracts characterizing most of the buying.

QUESTIONS AND PROBLEMS

1. Describe some of the major characteristics of commercial services firms (finance, insurance, and real estate) as a market for goods and services.

2. There are several important institutional markets: hospitals, educational institutions, welfare organizations, and the like. Discuss the characteristic buying needs and buying organization for, say, educational institutions.

3. Are industrial buyers more "rational" than household buyers?

4. The location of buying authority in a company will vary with the level of the *product's complexity* and with the level of the *commercial investment*. Given two levels (low, high) for each variable, predict who will make the buying decision in each of the four possible cases.

5. What types of assortment strategies are used by the following types of firms: (a) bicycle shop, (b) sports shop, (c) pawn shop, (d) Salvation Army Store, and (e) discount store.

6. Cessna Aircraft Company is interested in expanding its sales of small aircraft to business firms. Its marketing research analyst decides to study the buying process using the paradigm: (a) need arousal; (b) information search; (c) evaluation behavior; (d) purchase decision; and (e) postpurchase feelings. List factors under each that affect the potential industrial buyer of a private aircraft.

7. A home decorating service is confronted with the following paint mixing machines having the indicated attributes:

EVOKED SET	PRICE	NUMBER OF SPEEDS	SIZE (IN OUNCES)	NOISE LEVEL*
1	$30	10	32	3
2	$22	7	30	4
3	$25	5	48	5
4	$22	5	30	4

* A score of 5 represents the least noise.

Which machine(s) would this company prefer if its decision making could be explained by: (a) a dominance model; (b) a conjunctive model which used cut-off points of less than $28, at least 5 speeds and 32 ounces, and a quietness level equal to or greater than 4; (c) a disjunctive model based upon criteria of at least 8 speeds or at least 48 ounces; and (d) a lexicographic model with an importance ordering of least cost, size, speeds, and noise. (See chapter 7 for discussion of these models).

Market Segmentation
and Targeting

Never follow the crowd.
BERNARD M. BARUCH

8

An organization that decides to operate in some market—whether consumer, industrial, reseller, or government—recognizes that it normally cannot serve all the customers in that market. The customers are too numerous, widely scattered, or heterogeneous in their buying requirements or buying practices to be effectively and superiorly served by one organization. Some competitors will be in a better position to effectively serve particular customer segments of that market. The firm, instead of competing everywhere, sometimes against superior odds, should identify those parts of the market that are the most attractive and that it could serve the most effectively. This calls for two steps. The first is *market segmentation,* the act of subdividing a market into distinct and meaningful subsets of customers who might merit separate marketing programming and effort. The second is *target marketing,* the act of evaluating, selecting, and concentrating on those market segments that the company can serve most effectively. This chapter will deal with the major concepts and tools for market segmentation and targeting.

MARKET SEGMENTATION

Market segmentation represents an important recent advance in marketing thinking and strategy. In earlier years many business firms saw the key to profits to be in the development of a single brand that was mass produced, mass distributed, and mass communicated. This would lead to the lowest costs and prices and create the largest potential market. The firm would not recognize variations and would try to get everyone in the market to want what it produced.

As competition intensified, prices dropped and sellers' earnings declined. Sellers did not have much control over price because of the similarity of their products. At this stage, some sellers began to recognize the potential value of *product differentiation*—that is, the introduction of differential features, quality, style, or image in their brands as a basis for commanding a premium. This led to a proliferation of sizes, models, options, and other characteristics. It is important to recognize, however, that the product variations were not based on an analysis of natural market segments.

Market segmentation, the most recent idea for guiding marketing strategy, starts not with distinguishing product possibilities, but rather with distinguishing customer groups and needs. *Market segmentation is the subdividing of a market into distinct subsets of customers, where any subset may conceivably be selected as a target market to be reached with a distinct marketing mix.* The power of this concept is that in an age of intense competition for the mass market, individual sellers may prosper through developing offers for specific market segments whose needs are imperfectly satisfied by the mass-market offerings.

Nature of Market Segmentation

Markets consist of customers, and customers are likely to differ in one or more respects. They may differ in size, resources, geographical location, product requirements, buying attitudes, or buying practices. Any of these variables can make a difference in customer attractiveness or in company capability to effectively serve that customer. Any of these variables can be used to segment a market. Any market with two or more buyers is capable of being segmented.

Figure 8–1A shows a market consisting of six buyers before it is segmented. The maximum number of segments that a market can contain is the total number of buyers making up that market. Each buyer is potentially a separate market because of unique needs and desires. Ideally, a seller might study each buyer in order to tailor the best marketing program to that buyer's needs. Where there are only a few major customers, this is done to some extent. For example, the

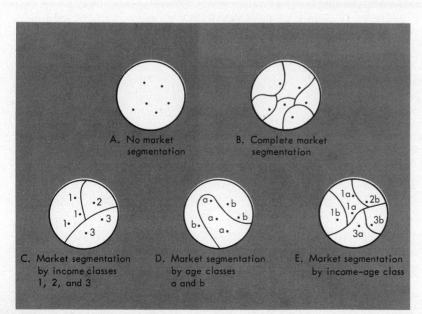

A. No market
   segmentation

B. Complete market
   segmentation

C. Market segmentation
   by income classes
   1, 2, and 3

D. Market segmentation
   by age classes
   a and b

E. Market segmentation
   by income-age class

FIGURE 8–1
Different Approaches
to Market Segmentation

major airframe producers such as Boeing and Douglas face only a few buyers and treat them as separate markets. This ultimate degree of market segmentation is illustrated in Figure 8–1B.

Most sellers will not find it worthwhile to customize their product to satisfy each buyer's specific wants. Instead, the seller identifies broad classes of buyers who differ in their product requirements and/or marketing susceptibilities. For example, the seller may discover that income groups differ in their product requirements and marketing susceptibilities. In Figure 8–1C a number (1, 2, or 3) is used to identify each buyer's income class. Lines are drawn around buyers in the same income class. Segmentation by income class results in three segments, the most numerous one being income class 1 in the illustration.

On the other hand, the seller may find pronounced differences in buyer behavior between younger and older buyers. In Figure 8–1D the same individuals are shown, but a letter (a or b) is used to indicate the buyer's age class. Segmentation of the market by age class results in two segments, both equally numerous.

It may turn out that income and age both count heavily in differentiating the buyer's behavior toward the product. The seller may find it desirable to partition the market according to those joint characteristics. In terms of the illustration, the market can be broken into the following six segments: 1a, 1b, 2a, 2b, 3a, and 3b. Figure 8–1E shows that segment 1a contains two buyers, segment 2a contains no buyers (a null segment), and each of the other segments contains one buyer. In general, as the market is segmented on the basis of a larger set of joint characteristics, the seller achieves finer precision but at the price of multiplying the number of segments and thinning out the populations in the segments. If the seller segmented the market using all conceivable characteristics, the market would again look like Figure 8–1B, where each buyer would be a separate segment.

Patterns of Market Segmentation

In the preceding illustration, the market was segmented by income and age, resulting in different *demographic segments.* Suppose that, instead, buyers are asked how much they want of each of two product attributes (say *sweetness* and *creaminess* in the case of an ice cream). This results in identifying different *preference segments* in the market. Three different patterns can emerge.

1. *Homogeneous preferences.* Figure 8–2 reveals a market where all the consumers have roughly the same preference. The market shows no *natural segments,* at least as far as the two attributes are concerned. We would predict that existing brands would be similar and located in the center of the preferences.

2. *Diffused preferences.* At the other extreme, consumer preferences may be scattered fairly evenly throughout the space with no concentration (Figure 8–2B). Consumers simply differ a great deal in what they want from the product. If one brand exists in the market, it is likely to be positioned in the center because it would appeal to the most people. A brand in the center minimizes the sum of total consumer dissatisfaction. A competitor coming into the market could locate next to the first brand and engage in an all-out battle for market share. This is the typical situation in a political market where the two candidates both go middle-of-the-road to gain the greatest following. The other choice is for the competitor to locate in some corner to gain the loyalty of a customer group that is not satisfied with the center brand. If there are several brands in the market, they are likely to eventually position themselves fairly evenly throughout the space and show real differences to match consumer preference differences.

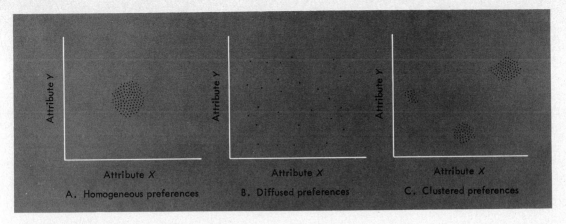

FIGURE 8–2
Basic Market-Preference Patterns

3. **Clustered preferences.** An intermediate possibility is the appearance of distinct preference clusters (Figure 8–2C). They may be called *natural market segments.* The first firm to enter this market has three options. (1) It might position itself in the center hoping to appeal to all the groups (undifferentiated marketing). (2) It might position itself in the largest market segment (concentrated marketing). (3) It might develop several brands, each positioned in a different segment (differentiated marketing). Clearly, if it developed only one brand, competition would come in and introduce brands in the other segments.

Market Segmentation Procedure

We have seen that market segments can be arrived at by applying a succession of variables to subdivide the market. As an illustration: An airline is interested in attracting nonflyers (segmentation variable: *user status*). Nonflyers consist of those who fear flying, those who are indifferent, and those who are positive toward flying (segmentation variable: *attitude*). Among those who feel positive are people with higher incomes and who have the ability to afford flying (segmentation variable: *income*). The airline may decide to target those higher-income persons who are positive about flying but simply have not been sufficiently motivated to travel by air.

How does the seller know which variables to apply in succession to the market? The answer is by interviewing a sample of consumers and attempting to discover the *hierarchy of variables* that these consumers use on their way to a purchase decision. Consider the purchase of an automobile. Figure 8–3A shows a few of the variables that buyers might consider in choosing a car. Years ago, many car buyers were primarily brand loyal and would first decide the brand they wanted and then on the car form. Thus buyer 1 in Figure 8–3A decided on a Chevrolet and then a station wagon. When most of the buyers buy this way, we call it a *brand-form market.* On the other hand, buyer 2 decided that he wanted a high-performance car, then an intermediate-size car, then a two-door, and finally a Cadillac. If most car buyers buy this way, we call it a *need-size-form-brand market.* In this kind of market, most of the brands do not compete against each other. The competitive brands are only those that satisfy the need-size-form prerequisites. The Hendry Corporation of New York has built a suc-

197

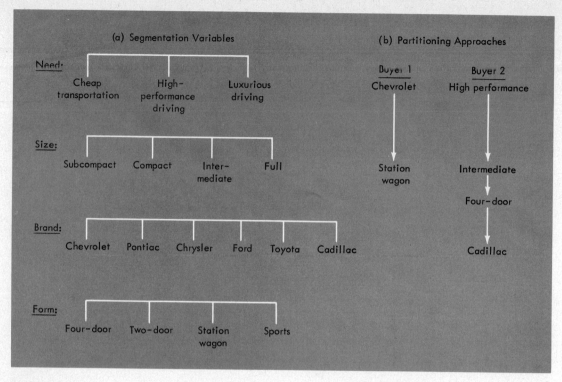

FIGURE 8–3
Market Partitioning

cessful brand-forecasting system based on examining how buyers buy and the character of the primary partitioning variables. They call this system *market partitioning theory* and have helped a number of companies understand their market segments and major competitors.[1]

Bases for Segmenting Consumer Markets

As we have seen, market segmentation involves the creative search for the most useful segmentation variables. The most market-oriented variables are *customers' product requirements* and *customers' responses to marketing stimuli*. These variables (called *bases of segmentation*) are often associated with other variables such as buyer demographics and media habits (called *market descriptors*). Some segmenters, in fact, go right to these later variables first because good data exist and the segments are more definable.

In this section, we will review the major geographic, demographic, psychographic, and behavioristic variables used in segmenting consumer markets. They are shown in Table 8–1. Then we will briefly review the major segmentation variables used in industrial market segmentation.

[1] See Manohar U. Kalwani and Donald G. Morrison, "A Parsimonious Description of the Hendry System," *Management Science*, January 1977, pp. 467–77.

TABLE 8–1
Major Segmentation Variables for Consumer Markets

VARIABLES	TYPICAL BREAKDOWNS
Geographic	
Region	Pacific, Mountain, West North Central, West South Central, East North Central, East South Central, South Atlantic, Middle Atlantic, New England
County size	A, B, C, D
City or SMSA size	Under 5,000, 5,000–19,999, 20,000–49,999, 50,000–99,999, 100,000–249,999, 250,000–499,999, 500,000–999,999, 1,000,000–3,999,999, 4,000,000 or over
Density	Urban, suburban, rural
Climate	Northern, southern
Demographic	
Age	Under 6, 6–11, 12–19, 20–34, 35–49, 50–64, 65 +
Sex	Male, female
Family size	1–2, 3–4, 5 +
Family life cycle	Young, single; young, married, no children; young, married, youngest child under six; young, married, youngest child six or over; older, married, with children; older, married, no children under 18; older, single; other
Income	Under $3,000, $3,000–$5,000, $5,000–$7,000, $7,000–$10,000, $10,000–$15,000, $15,000–$25,000, $25,000 and over
Occupation	Professional and technical; managers, officials and proprietors; clerical, sales; craftsmen, foremen; operatives; farmers; retired; students; housewives; unemployed
Education	Grade school or less; some high school; graduated high school; some college; graduated college
Religion	Catholic, Protestant, Jewish, other
Race	White, black, oriental
Nationality	American, British, French, German, Scandinavian, Italian, Latin American, Middle Eastern, Japanese
Social class	Lower-lower, upper-lower, lower-middle, upper-middle, lower-upper, upper-upper
Psychographic	
Life style	Straights, swingers, longhairs
Personality	Compulsive, gregarious, authoritarian, ambitious
Behavioristic	
Purchase occasion	Regular occasion, special occasion
Benefits sought	Economy, convenience, prestige
User status	Nonuser, exuser, potential user, first-time user, regular user
Usage rate	Light user, medium user, heavy user
Loyalty status	None, medium, strong, absolute
Readiness stage	Unaware, aware, informed, interested, desirous, intending to buy
Marketing-factor sensitivity	Quality, price, service, advertising, sales promotion

Geographic segmentation   In geographic segmentation, the market is divided into different locations—nations, states, counties, cities, or neighborhoods. The organization recognizes that market potentials and costs vary with market location. It determines those geographical markets that it could serve best. Thus the Coors Brewery until recently primarily served Denver and the surrounding area because its plant and supplies were concentrated there.

Demographic segmentation   In demographic segmentation, the market is subdivided into different parts on the basis of demographic variables—age, sex, family size, income, occupation, education, family life cycle, religion, nationality. Demographic variables have long been the most popular bases for distinguishing significant groupings in the market place. One reason is that consumer wants or usage rates are often highly associated with demographic variables; another is that demographic variables are easier to measure than most other types of variables.

For example, a furniture company may be interested in segmenting its market. Suppose that the company's marketing research reveals three important demographic variables: age of head of household, size of family, and level of income. Figure 8–4 shows a joint segmentation of the market according to these variables. Each variable is subdivided into the number of levels deemed useful for analysis; the result is 36(4 x 3 x 3) distinct segments. Every family belongs to one of these 36 segments. Having conceptualized the market in this way, management can proceed to determine the profit potential of each segment. This involves estimating for each segment the number of families, the average purchase rate, and the extent of competition. These pieces of information can be combined to estimate the value of each segment.

A company must be careful in its use of demographics because their influence on consumer buying potential does not always operate in the expected direction. For example, the Ford Motor Company used buyers' age in developing its target market for its Mustang automobile; the car was designed to appeal to young people who wanted an inexpensive sporty automobile. Ford found, to its surprise, that the car was being purchased by all age groups. It then realized that its target market was not the chronologically young but those who were psychologically young.

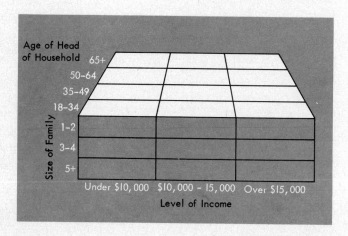

FIGURE 8–4
Segmentation of the Furniture Market
by Three Demographic Variables

Income is another demographic variable that can be deceptive. One would think that working-class families would buy Chevrolets and managerial-class families would buy Cadillacs. Yet many Chevrolets are bought by middle-income people (often as a second car), and some Cadillacs are bought by working-class families (such as high-paid plumbers and carpenters). Members of the working class were among the first purchasers of expensive color television sets; it was cheaper for them to buy these sets than go out to movies and restaurants. Coleman suggested that a distinction should be drawn between the "underprivileged" segments and the "overprivileged" segments of each social class.[2] The cheapest, most economic cars are not bought by the really poor, but rather by "those who think of themselves as poor relative to their status aspirations and to their needs for a certain level of clothing, furniture, and housing, which they could not afford if they bought a more expensive car." On the other hand, medium-priced and expensive cars tend to be purchased by the over-privileged segments of each social class.

Psychographic segmentation   In psychographic segmentation, buyers are divided into different groups on the basis of life style or personality differences. People within the same demographic group can exhibit very different psychographic profiles.

LIFE STYLE   Life style refers to the distinctive mode of orientation an individual or a group has toward consumption, work, and play. Such terms as hippies, swingers, straights, and jet-setters are all descriptive of different life styles. Marketers are increasingly being drawn to life style segmentation.[3] They are targeting versions of their products to life style groups and studying new-product opportunities arising out of life style analysis. Volkswagen, for example, is introducing life-styled automobiles: there will be a car for "the good citizen" emphasizing economy, safety, and ecology; and a car for the "car freak" emphasizing handling, maneuverability, and sportiness. Manufacturers of women's clothing have followed Du Pont's advice to design different clothes for the "plain woman," the "fashionable woman," and the "manly woman." Cigarette companies develop brands for the "defiant smoker," the "casual smoker," and the "careful smoker." Companies making cosmetics, alcoholic beverages, and furniture are seeing increasing opportunities in life style segmentation. At the same time, some companies have not found this variable to always work; for example, Nestlé introduced a special brand of decaffeinated coffee for "late nighters" and it failed.

PERSONALITY   Marketers have used personality variables to segment the market. They try to endow their products with *brand personalities* (brand image, brand concept) designed to appeal to corresponding *consumer personalities* (self-images, self-concepts). In the late fifties, Fords and Chevrolets were promoted as having different personalities. Ford buyers were thought to be "independent, impulsive, masculine, alert to change, and self-confident, while Chevrolet owners are conservative, thrifty, prestige-conscious, less masculine, and seeking to

[2] Richard P. Coleman, "The Significance of Social Stratification in Selling," in *Marketing: A Maturing Discipline,* ed. Martin L. Bell (Chicago: American Marketing Association, 1961), pp. 171–84.

[3] See Mark Hanan, *Life-Styled Marketing* (New York: American Management Association, 1972).

avoid extremes."[4] Evans investigated whether this was true by subjecting Ford and Chevrolet owners to the Edwards Personal Preference test, which measured needs for achievement, dominance, change, aggression, and so on. Except for a slightly higher score on dominance, Ford owners did not score significantly differently from Chevrolet owners, and Evans concluded that "the distributions of scores for all needs overlap to such an extent that [personality] discrimination is virtually impossible." Work subsequent to Evans on a wide variety of products and brands has occasionally turned up personality differences but more often has not. Westfall found some evidence of personality differences between the owners of convertibles and nonconvertibles, the former appearing to be more active, impulsive, and sociable.[5] Gottlieb found compulsive people to be heavier users of aspirin.[6] Tucker and Painter found some statistically significant but weak personality correlations for nine products in their study.[7]

Behavioristic segmentation   In behavioristic segmentation, buyers are divided into different groups on the basis of their knowledge, attitude, use, or response to the actual product or its attributes. Many marketers believe that behavioristic variables are the key starting point in identifying market segments.

PURCHASE OCCASION   Buyers may be distinguished on the basis of the occasion that gives rise to their purchasing the product. For example, the flying public includes people traveling on business, vacation, or family affairs. Those who are making long distance telephone calls may be conducting business or making personal calls.

BENEFITS SOUGHT   Buyers are drawn to products through different buying motives. In the case of toothpaste, various customers seek decay prevention, bright teeth, good taste, or low price. An attempt is made to determine the demographic or psychographic characteristics associated with each benefit segment. Haley has characterized those seeking decay prevention as worriers, bright teeth as sociables, good taste as sensories, and low price as independents.[8]

Further characteristics of each group may be found, such as that consumers concerned with decay prevention have larger families and those interested in bright teeth are often tobacco users or single people. Media habits may even vary with each group. The company can choose the benefit it wants to emphasize, create a product that delivers it, and direct a message to the group seeking that benefit.

Choosing a benefit group to market to has some difficulties. First, it is usually difficult to estimate the size of different benefit groups in the total population. It depends on the ease with which persons can cite one benefit as domi-

[4] Quoted in Franklin B. Evans, "Psychological and Objective Factors in the Prediction of Brand Choice; Ford versus Chevrolet," *Journal of Business*, October 1959, pp. 340–69.

[5] Ralph Westfall, "Psychological Factors in Predicting Product Choice," *Journal of Marketing*, April 1962, pp. 34–40.

[6] Maurice J. Gottlieb, "Segmentation by Personality Types," in *Advancing Marketing Efficiency*, ed. Lynn H. Stockman (Chicago: American Marketing Association, 1959), p. 154.

[7] W. T. Tucker and John J. Painter, "Personality and Product Use," *Journal of Applied Psychology*, October 1961, pp. 325–29.

[8] Russell J. Haley, "Benefit Segmentation: A Decision-Oriented Research Tool," *Journal of Marketing*, July 1968, pp. 30–35.

nating their interest in the product. Yankelovich found that people could do this with watches: as of 1962, "approximately 23 percent of the buyers bought [watches] for lowest price, another 46 percent bought for durability and general product quality, and 31 percent bought watches as symbols of some important occasion."[9] Second, the cited benefit might cover up something deeper; favoring the lowest-price watch may be a form of "sensibility snobbery." Finally, some buyers are interested in a particular benefit bundle rather than in a single benefit; this means the marketers may have to segment by benefit-bundle groups.[10]

USER STATUS   Many markets can be segmented into nonusers, exusers, potential users, first-time users, and regular users of a product. High-market-share companies such as Kodak (in the film market) are particularly interested in going after potential users, whereas a small film competitor will concentrate on trying to attract regular users to its brand. Potential users and regular users require different kinds of communication and marketing efforts. In the social marketing area, agencies such as antidrug agencies pay close attention to user status. They direct most of their effort at young people who might be potential users and try to immunize them against an interest in hard drugs. They sponsor rehabilitation programs to help regular users who want to quit their habit. They utilize exusers to lend credibility to various programs.

USAGE RATE   Many markets can be segmented into light-, medium-, and heavy-user groups of the product (called volume segmentation). Heavy users may constitute only a small percentage of the numerical size of the market but a major percentage of the unit volume consumed. For example, 50 percent of the beer drinkers account for 88 percent of beer consumption.[11] Naturally, beer companies will want to go after the "heavy half" of the market because every heavy drinker drinking their brand is worth several light drinkers. Unfortunately, when all the companies go after the same heavy drinkers, their campaigns look alike and cancel each other.

The hope is that the heavy users of a product have certain common demographics, personal characteristics, and media habits. One research company found that the "frequent beer drinker" earns less than $10,000 a year, is married (with two and a half children), and has simple manly tastes. He likes TV and he likes to watch sports.[12] Profiles like this are obviously helpful to the marketer in developing pricing, message, and media strategies.

In the area of social marketing campaigns, agencies often face a heavy-user dilemma. The heavy users are often the most resistant to the selling proposition. A family-planning agency, for example, would normally target its marketing effort to those families who would have the most children; but these families are also the most resistant to birth-control messages. The National Safety Council should target its marketing effort primarily to the unsafe drivers; but these drivers are also the most resistant to safe-driving appeals. The agencies

[9] See Daniel Yankelovich, "New Criteria for Market Segmentation," *Harvard Business Review*, March–April 1964, pp. 83–90, here p. 85.

[10] See Paul E. Green, Yoram Wind, and Arun K. Jain, "Benefit Bundle Analysis," *Journal of Advertising Research*, April 1972, pp. 31–36.

[11] See Dik Warren Twedt, "How Important to Marketing Strategy Is the 'Heavy User'?" *Journal of Marketing*, January 1964, pp. 71–72.

[12] See Norton Garfinkle, "A Marketing Approach to Media Selection," *Journal of Advertising Research*, December 1963, pp. 7–14.

must consider whether to use their limited budget to go after a few heavy users who are highly resistant or many light users who are less resistant.

LOYALTY STATUS   Loyalty status describes the amount of loyalty that users have to a particular object. The amount of loyalty can range from zero to absolute. We find buyers who are absolutely loyal to a brand (such as Budweiser beer), to an organization (such as the Republican party), to a place (such as New England), and so on.

Companies try to identify the characteristics of their hard-core loyals so that they can target their market effort to similar people in the population. Frank found some brand-loyal customers in the consumer-staples category but concluded that they "were not identifiable by socioeconomic or personality characteristics, did not have different average demand levels from nonloyal customers, and did not differ in sensitivity to promotion."[13] In this case, brand loyalty did not appear to be a useful basis for market segmentation.

Furthermore, the concept of brand loyalty has some ambiguities. What may appear to be brand loyalty may be explainable in other ways. Suppose a shopper purchased brand B on the last seven shopping occasions. The purchase pattern BBBBBBB would seem to reflect intrinsic preference for the product but may really reflect *habit, indifference, a lower price,* or the *nonavailability of substitutes.* The pattern BBBBAAA for another shopper would seem to indicate a switch in loyalty but may only reflect the fact that the store dropped brand B, or that she switched stores, or that she switched to brand A because of a price promotion. Marked brand continuity in brand-purchase sequences is not necessarily evidence that individual brand loyalty exists or is strong.

STAGES OF READINESS   At any point of time, there is a distribution of people in various stages of readiness toward buying the product. Some members of the potential market are unaware of the product; some are aware; some are informed; some are interested; some are desirous; and some intend to buy. The particular distribution of people over stages of readiness makes a big difference in designing the marketing program. Suppose a health agency wants to attract women to take an annual Pap test to detect cervical cancer. At the beginning, most of the potential market is unaware of the concept. The marketing effort should go into high-reach advertising and publicity using a simple message. If successful, more of the market will be aware of the Pap test and the advertising should be changed to dramatizing the benefits of taking an annual examination and the risks of not taking it, so as to move more people into a stage of desire. Facilities should also be readied for handling the large number of women who may be motivated to take the examination. In general, the marketing program must be adjusted to the changing distribution of readiness.

MARKETING FACTORS   Markets can often be segmented into groups responsive to different marketing factors such as price and price deals, product quality, and service. This information can help the company in allocating its marketing resources.[14] The marketing variables are usually proxies for particular benefits sought by buyers. A company that specializes in a certain marketing factor will

[13] Ronald E. Frank, "Is Brand Loyalty a Useful Basis for Market Segmentation?" *Journal of Advertising Research*, June 1967, pp. 27–33, here pp. 27–28.

[14] This approach is investigated in Henry J. Claycamp and William F. Massy, "A Theory of Market Segmentation," *Journal of Marketing Research*, November 1968, pp. 388–94. Also see Ronald Frank, William Massy, and Yoram Wind, *Market Segmentation* (Englewood Cliffs, N.J.: Prentice-Hall, 1972), part IV.

build up hard-core loyals seeking that factor or benefit. Thus Avon, which sells cosmetics on a door-to-door basis, appeals to women who like personal attention and service.

Bases for
Segmenting
Industrial Markets
Industrial markets can also be effectively segmented, although Wind and Cardozo observed that "industrial marketers typically fail to employ market segmentation as a foundation for planning and control of marketing programs."[15] In their study they proposed a two-stage approach to industrial market segmentation. The first stage calls for identifying *macrosegments* through the use of such characteristics as (1) end-use market, (2) product application, (3) customer size, (4) usage rate, (5) geographical location, and (6) organization structure. The second stage calls for dividing each selected macrosegment into *microsegments* through the use of such characteristics as (1) position in authority, (2) personal characteristics, (3) perceived product importance, (4) attitudes toward vendor, (5) buying decision criteria, and (6) stage in buying process.

As an example of industrial market segmentation, consider the following:

An aluminum company wants to select some market segments on which to focus its offers and market effort.[16] The first stage is macrosegmentation—determining which end-use market the company can best serve: automobiles, residential, or beverage containers. This can be called a horizontal product/market choice. Suppose the company decides that it can best serve the residential-housing market. The second step is to determine the best vertical level at which to enter the residential-housing market: semifinished material, building components, or end products. Suppose the company decides to enter the building-components market. The third step is to determine the best customer size to serve. Suppose the company decides to focus on large customers.

The second stage of analysis calls for forming microsegments within this macrosegment. For example, the company might discover that large customers fall into three groups—according to whether they buy on price, service, or quality. If the aluminum company has a high service profile, the company will probably decide to concentrate on the service-motivated microsegment of the market.

Requirements for
Effective
Segmentation
Clearly, there are many ways to segment a given market. Not all resulting segments are meaningful from a marketing point of view. The market for table salt, for example, could be subdivided into blond and brunet customers. But hair color is not relevant to the purchase of salt. Buyers of table salt are fairly homogeneous with respect to the relevant buying variables. In fact, if all salt buyers wanted to buy the same amount of salt each month, believed all salt was the same, and wanted to pay the same price, this market would be minimally segmentable from a marketing point of view.

To be useful, market segments must exhibit the following characteristics:

The first is *measurability*, the degree to which the size and purchasing power of the resulting segments can be measured. Certain segmentation variables are hard to measure. An illustration would be the size of the segments of

[15] Yoram Wind and Richard Cardozo, "Industrial Market Segmentation," *Industrial Marketing Management*, vol. 3, 1974, pp. 153–66.

[16] See E. Raymond Corey, "Key Options in Market Selection and Product Planning," *Harvard Business Review*, September–October 1975, pp. 119–28.

automobile buyers who are primarily motivated by automobile styling or by performance.

The second is *accessibility,* the degree to which the resulting segments can be effectively reached and served. It would be helpful if advertising could be directed mainly to the segment of opinion leaders, but their media habits are not always distinct from those of opinion followers.

The third is *substantiality,* the degree to which the resulting segments are large and/or profitable enough to be worth considering for separate marketing attention. A segment should be the smallest unit for which it is practical to tailor a separate marketing program. Segmental marketing is expensive, as we shall see shortly. It would not pay, for example, for an automobile manufacturer to develop special cars for midgets.

Benefits of Segmentation

The main conclusion from this discussion is that markets are made up of segments that are not all equally attractive to any one company. Given limited resources, a company should try to identify those market segments that it can best serve in terms of segment preferences, patterns of competition, and company strengths. The company can shape its marketing mix to be maximally effective in the chosen target market segments. Market segmentation offers companies at least three benefits.

First, *sellers are in a better position to spot and compare market opportunities.* They can examine the needs of each segment in the light of the current competitive offerings and determine the extent of current satisfaction. Segments with relatively low levels of satisfaction from current offerings may represent excellent market opportunities.

Second, *sellers can make finer adjustments of their product and marketing appeals.* Instead of one marketing program aimed to draw in all potential buyers (the "shotgun" approach), sellers can create separate marketing programs aimed to meet the needs of different buyers (the "rifle" approach).

Third, *sellers can develop marketing programs and budgets based on a clearer idea of the response characteristics of specific market segments.* They can allocate funds to the different segments in line with their likely levels of purchase response.

TARGET MARKETING

Market segmentation reveals the extent of market heterogeneity and the opportunities facing the firm from target marketing. This still leaves the firm a choice among three broad strategies for responding to the revealed market structure.

1. The firm might decide to go after the largest part of the market with one offer and marketing mix, trying to attract as many customers as possible. We call this *undifferentiated marketing.*

2. The firm might decide to go after a narrow market segment and develop the ideal offer and marketing mix. We call this *concentrated marketing.*

3. The firm might decide to go after several market segments, developing an effective offer and marketing mix for each. We call this *differentiated marketing.*

Here we will describe the rationale and merits of each of these strategies.

Undifferentiated Marketing

In undifferentiated marketing, the firm chooses not to recognize the different market segments making up the market. It treats the market as an aggregate, focusing on what is common in the needs of people rather than on what is different. It tries to design a product and a marketing program that appeal to the broadest number of buyers. It relies on mass channels, mass advertising media, and universal themes. It aims to endow the product with a superior image in people's minds, whether or not this image is based on any real difference.[17] An excellent example of undifferentiated marketing is the Coca-Cola Company's earlier production of only one drink in one bottle size in one taste to suit all.

Undifferentiated marketing is primarily defended on the grounds of cost economies. It is thought to be "the marketing counterpart to standardization and mass production in manufacturing."[18] The fact that the product line is kept narrow minimizes production, inventory, and transportation costs. The undifferentiated advertising program enables the firm to enjoy media discounts through large usage. The absence of segmental marketing research and planning lowers the costs of marketing research and product management. On the whole, undifferentiated marketing results in keeping down several costs of doing business.

Nevertheless, an increasing number of marketers have expressed strong doubts about the optimality of this strategy. Gardner and Levy, for example, admit that "some brands have very skillfully built up reputations of being suitable for a wide variety of people" but add:

> In most areas audience groupings will differ, if only because there are deviants who refuse to consume the same way other people do. . . . It is not easy for a brand to appeal to stable lower middle-class people and at the same time to be interesting to sophisticated, intellectual upper middle-class buyers. . . . It is rarely possible for a product or brand to be all things to all people.[19]

The firm practicing undifferentiated marketing typically develops a product and marketing program aimed at the largest segment of the market. When several firms in the industry do this, the result is hypercompetition for the largest segment(s) and undersatisfaction of the smaller ones. Thus the American auto industry for a long time produced only large automobiles, while foreign firms capitalized on the smaller segments. The "majority fallacy," as the American firms' policy has been called by Kuehn and Day, describes the fact that the larger segments may be less profitable because they attract disproportionately heavy competition.[20] The recognition of this fallacy has led many firms to reevaluate the opportunities latent in the smaller segments of the market.

Differentiated Marketing

Under differentiated marketing, a firm decides to operate in two or more segments of the market but designs separate product and/or marketing programs

[17] This strategy has also gone under other names, such as "product differentiation" or "market aggregation." See Wendell R. Smith, "Product Differentiation and Market Segmentation as Alternative Marketing Strategies," *Journal of Marketing*, July 1956, pp. 3–8; and Alan A. Roberts, "Applying the Strategy of Market Segmentation," *Business Horizons*, fall 1961, pp. 65–72.

[18] Smith, "Product Differentiation," p. 4.

[19] Burleigh Gardner and Sidney Levy, "The Product and the Brand," *Harvard Business Review*, March–April 1955, p. 37.

[20] Alfred A. Kuehn and Ralph L. Day, "Strategy of Product Quality," *Harvard Business Review*, November–December 1962, pp. 101–2.

for each. Thus General Motors tries to produce a car for every "purse, purpose, and personality." By offering product and marketing variations, it hopes to attain higher sales and a deeper position within each market segment. It hopes that a deep position in several segments will strengthen the customers' overall identification of the company with the product field. Furthermore, it hopes for greater loyalty and repeat purchasing, because the firm's offerings have been bent to the customer's desire rather than the other way around.

In recent years an increasing number of firms have moved toward a strategy of differentiated marketing. This is reflected in trends toward multiple product offerings and multiple trade channels and media. Coca-Cola now produces different drinks for different tastes; and International Harvester produces light, medium, and heavy trucks for different market segments.

The net effect of differentiated marketing is to create more total sales than undifferentiated marketing does. "It is ordinarily demonstrable that total sales may be increased with a more diversified product line sold through more diversified channels."[21] However, it also tends to be true that differentiated marketing increases the costs of doing business. The following costs are likely to be higher:

Product modification costs. Modifying a product to meet different market segment requirements usually involves some R&D, engineering, and/or special tooling costs.

Production costs. Generally speaking, it is more expensive to produce m units each of n differentiated products than mn units of one product. This is especially true the longer the production setup time for each product and the smaller the sales volume of each product. On the other hand, if each model is sold in sufficiently large volume, the higher costs of setup time may be quite small per unit.

Administrative costs. Under differentiated marketing, the company has to develop separate marketing plans for the separate segments of the market. This requires extra marketing research, forecasting, sales analysis, promotion, planning, and channel management.

Inventory costs. It is generally more costly to manage inventories of differentiated products than an inventory of only one product. The extra costs arise because more records must be kept and more auditing must be done. Furthermore, each product must be carried at a level that reflects basic demand plus a safety factor to cover unexpected variations in demand. The sum of the safety stocks for several products will exceed the safety stock required for one product. Thus carrying differentiated products leads to increased inventory costs.

Promotion costs. Differentiated marketing involves trying to reach different segments of the market through advertising media most appropriate to each case. This leads to lower usage rates of individual media and the consequent forfeiture of quantity discounts. Furthermore, since each segment may require separate creative advertising planning, promotion costs are increased.

Since differentiated marketing leads to higher sales and higher costs, nothing can be said a priori regarding the optimality of this strategy. Some firms are finding, in fact, that they have overdifferentiated their market offers. They would like to manage fewer brands, with each appealing to a broader customer

[21] Roberts, "Marketing Segmentation," p. 66.

group—reverse line extension or broadening the base. They seek a larger volume for each brand. Johnson and Johnson, for example, managed to attract adults to use its baby shampoo. Blue Nun was launched as a white wine equally good for meat and fish courses.

Concentrated Marketing

Both differentiated marketing and undifferentiated marketing imply that the firm goes after the whole market. Many firms see a third possibility, however, one that is especially appealing when the company's resources are limited. Instead of going after a small share of a large market, the firm goes after a large share of one or a few submarkets. Put another way, instead of spreading itself thin in many parts of the market, it concentrates its forces to gain a good market position in a few areas.

Many examples of concentrated marketing can be cited. Volkswagen has concentrated on the small-car market; Bobbie Brooks, on women's junior sportswear; Gerber, on the baby market; Richard D. Irwin, on the economics and business texts market. Through concentrated marketing the firm achieves a strong market position in the particular segments it serves, owing to its greater knowledge of the segments' needs and the special reputation it acquires. Furthermore, it enjoys many operating economies because of specialization in production, distribution, and promotion. If the segment of the market is well chosen, the firm can earn high rates of return on its investment.

At the same time, concentrated marketing involves higher than normal risks. The particular market segment can suddenly turn sour; for example, when young women suddenly stopped buying sportswear and turned to knit dresses one year, it caused Bobbie Brooks's earnings to go deeply into the red. Or a competitor may decide to enter the same segment. For these reasons, many companies prefer to diversify in several market segments.

Selecting a Target Marketing Strategy

Particular characteristics of the seller, the product, or the market serve to constrain and narrow the actual choice of a target marketing strategy.[22]

The first factor is *company resources*. Where the firm's resources are too limited to permit complete coverage of the market, its only realistic choice is concentrated marketing.

The second factor is *product homogeneity*. Undifferentiated marketing is more suited for homogeneous products such as grapefruit or steel. Products that are subject to great variation, such as cameras and automobiles, are more naturally suited to differentiation or concentration.

The third factor is *product stage in the life cycle*. When a firm introduces a new product into the marketplace it usually finds it practical to introduce one or, at the most, a few product versions. The firm's interest is to develop primary demand, and undifferentiated marketing seems the suitable strategy; or it might concentrate on a particular segment. In the mature stage of the product life cycle, firms tend to pursue a strategy of differentiated marketing.

The fourth factor is *market homogeneity*. If buyers have the same tastes, buy the same amounts per period, and react in the same way to marketing stimuli, a strategy of undifferentiated marketing is appropriate.

[22] R. William Kotrba, "The Strategy Selection Chart," *Journal of Marketing*, July 1966, pp. 22–25.

The fifth factor is *competitive marketing strategies*. When competitors are practicing active segmentation, it is hard for a firm to compete through undifferentiated marketing. Conversely, when competitors are practicing undifferentiated marketing, a firm can gain by practicing active segmentation if some of the other factors favor it.

Evaluating the Worth of Different Target Markets

The problem facing all firms that segment their market is how to estimate the value of operating in each of the segments. The firm that pursues differentiated marketing must know this in order to allocate its marketing effort over the various segments. The firm that pursues concentrated marketing must know this in order to decide which segments offer the best opportunities.

A useful analytical approach is illustrated in Figure 8–5.[23] The market is one for the mechanical line of a steel-fabricating company. Stage 1 shows a segmentation of this market, using as two variables the customer-prospect mix and the product-service mix. The customer-prospect mix consists of contractors in the electrical, general, and plumbing line, respectively. The product-service mix consists of three products sold to these contractors: pipe hangers, concrete inserts, and electrical supports. Nine cells result from this joint segmentation of the market. Each cell represents a distinct submarket, or product-market segment. A dollar figure is placed in each cell, representing the company's sales in that submarket.

Relative company sales in the nine submarkets provide no indication of their relative profit potential as segments. The latter depends upon market demand, company costs, and competitive trends in each submarket. Stages 2 and 3 show how a particular product submarket, the general-contractor market for concrete inserts, can be analyzed in depth.

Stage 2 appraises present and future sales in the selected submarket. The vertical axis accommodates estimates of industry sales, company sales, and company market share. The horizontal axis is used to project future sales in these categories and market share. The company sold in this submarket last year $200,000 worth of goods, or one-fourth of total estimated industry sales. Looking ahead, the company expects industry sales in this submarket to rise by 6 percent and its own sales to rise by 15 percent.

Stage 3 probes deeper into the marketing thinking behind the sales forecasts of Stage 2. The horizontal axis shows the promotional mix that the company is using or plans to use to stimulate the sales of concrete inserts to general contractors. The vertical axis shows the distribution mix that the company is using or plans to use to move concrete inserts into the hands of general contractors. The actual promotion-distribution mix could be detailed by placing budget figures (funds and men) in the relevant cells. The company will use all three types of distribution and rely mainly on personal selling and field service for stimulating sales to general contractors.

By carrying out this analysis, the seller is led to think systematically about each segment as a distinct opportunity. The analysis of the profit potential of each segment will help the seller decide on the appropriate target markets to serve.

[23] See William J. Crissy and Frank H. Mossman, "Matrix Models for Marketing Planning: An Update and Expansion," *MSU Business Topics*, autumn 1977, pp. 17–26.

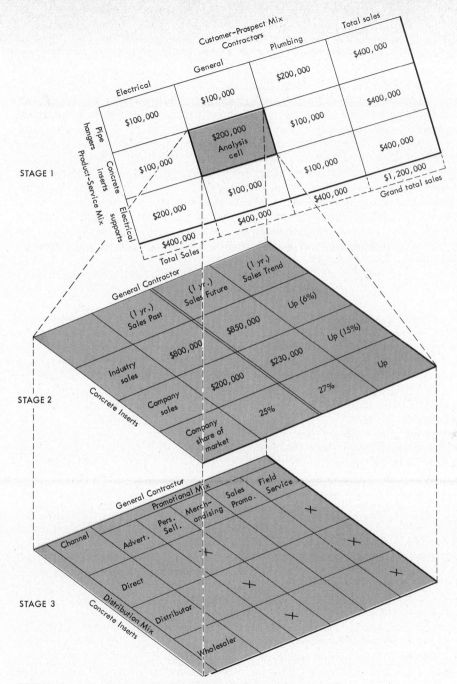

STAGE 1

STAGE 2

STAGE 3

SOURCE: From an unpublished paper by Rhett W. Butler, Northwestern University, 1964.

FIGURE 8–5
Analyzing the Worth of Different Market Segments for Steel-Fabricated Products

211

SUMMARY

Market segmentation is the subdividing of a market into distinct subsets of customers, where any subset may conceivably be selected as a market target to be reached with a distinct marketing mix. The opportunities present in a market increase when the marketer recognizes that it is made up of customer groups with varying preferences, not all of whom are likely to be receiving complete satisfaction from the current offerings of sellers.

Markets can be segmented on geographic, demographic, psychographic, and behavioristic variables. To be ultimately useful, the segments should be measureable, accessible, and substantial.

Firms have adopted different targeting strategies toward market segments, either ignoring the differences (undifferentiated marketing), developing a variety of products and marketing programs to meet different needs (differentiated marketing), or going after only a few segments (concentrated marketing). No particular strategy is superior in all circumstances. Much depends on company resources, product homogeneity, product stage in the life cycle, market homogeneity, and competitive marketing strategies. The firm must analyze the worth of the different market segments as a prelude to selecting its target markets.

QUESTIONS AND PROBLEMS

1. Market segments can be developed by cross-classifying different variables deemed to be important in the market. What are the problems that arise in trying to cross-classify more than a few variables?

2. Suggest a useful way to segment the markets for each of the following products: (a) household detergents; (b) animal feeds; (c) household coffee; (d) automobile tires.

3. A camera manufacturer is interested in developing a benefit segmentation of the camera market. Could you suggest some major benefit segments?

4. One critic has suggested that most segmentation is unnecessary. Buyers want variety and they switch around. The firm should produce various products, and it will catch those people who switch. Do you agree?

5. The Quaker Oats Company produces a dry breakfast cereal called Life. Life's brand manager is interested in ranking different market target groups for the cereal. The groups are to be formed by using age of housewife, family size, and size of city. Propose a list of market target groups ranging from extremely important to extremely unimportant.

6. A shaving cream manufacturer is planning to introduce a new aftershave lotion. Research indicates that light blue is the favored color by a strong margin. Does it follow that light blue should be adopted?

7. There are certain product markets where brand loyalty is weak and cannot be used as a segmentation variable. What are the characteristics of produce markets where brand loyalty is weak?

8. It is claimed that some markets are oversegmented, that is, the market segments are too small to be served profitably. Some companies are beginning to think of "desegmentation," that is, putting out fewer products, each designed to satisfy a larger group. How would you view this development?

9. A firm that manufactures wristwatches recognizes that it is basically in the time measurement business. It would like to segment the time measurement market in order to find new opportunities for expansion. Develop a segmentation of this market.

MARKET MEASUREMENT AND FORECASTING

9

> *Forecasting is hard, particularly of the future.*
> ANONYMOUS
>
> *Forecasting is like trying to drive a car blindfolded and following directions given by a person who is looking out of the back window.*
> ANONYMOUS

Marketing planning requires the conversion of the various qualitative understandings of a market into quantitative estimates of specific demand by product, territory, and type of customer. Furthermore, estimates must be made of the future course of market demand. These tasks are called *demand measurement* and *demand forecasting*, respectively. Demand estimates are essential in carrying out three important management functions—the *analysis* of market opportunities, the *planning* of marketing effort, and the *control* of marketing performance.

MAJOR CONCEPTS IN DEMAND MEASUREMENT

Demand measurement describes the activity of developing quantitative estimates of demand. Figure 9–1 shows *ninety* different types of demand measurement! Demand can be measured for six different *product levels* (product item, product form, product line, company sales, industry sales, national sales), five different *space levels* (customer, territory, region, U.S.A., world), and three different *time levels* (short-range, medium-range, and long-range).

Each type of demand measurement serves a specific purpose. Thus a company might make a short-range forecast of the total demand for a particular

213

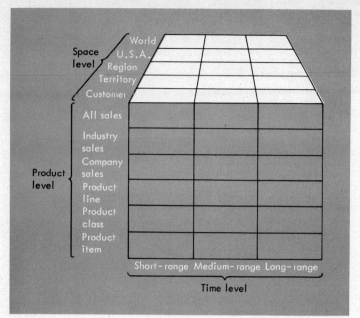

FIGURE 9–1
Ninety Types of Demand Measurement (6 x 5 x 3)

product item to provide a basis for ordering raw materials, planning production, and scheduling short-run financing. Or it might make a long-range forecast of regional demand for its major product line to provide a basis for considering market expansion.

The field of demand measurement is filled with a confusing number of terms. Company executives talk of forecasts, predictions, potentials, estimates, projections, goals, targets, quotas, and budgets. Many of these terms are redundant. The major concepts in demand measurement are *market demand* and *company demand.* Within each, we distinguish between a *demand function,* a *potential,* and a *forecast.*

Market Demand   In evaluating marketing opportunities, the first step is to estimate total market demand. It is not a simple concept, however, as the following definition makes clear:

> *Market demand* for a *product* is the *total volume* that would be *bought* by a defined *customer group* in a defined *geographical area* in a defined *time period* in a defined *marketing environment* under a defined *marketing program.*

There are eight elements in this definition.

PRODUCT   Market demand measurement requires a careful definition of the scope of the product class. A company that manufactures tin cans has to define whether its market is all metal-can users or all container users. It depends on how the company views its opportunities for penetrating adjacent markets.

TOTAL VOLUME   Market demand can be measured in terms of physical volume, dollar volume, or relative volume. The U.S. market demand for automobiles may be described as 10 million cars or $60 billion. The market demand for

214

automobiles in Greater Chicago can be expressed as 3 percent of the nation's total demand.

BOUGHT In measuring market demand, it is important to define whether "bought" means the volume ordered, shipped, paid for, received, or consumed. For example, a forecast of new housing for the next year usually means the number of units that will be ordered, not completed (called housing starts).

CUSTOMER GROUP Market demand may be measured for the whole market or for any segment(s). Thus a steel producer may estimate the volume to be bought separately by the construction industry and by the transportation industry.

GEOGRAPHICAL AREA Market demand should be measured with reference to well-defined geographical boundaries. A forecast of next year's passenger automobile sales will vary depending upon whether the boundaries are limited to the United States or include Canada and/or Mexico.

TIME PERIOD Market demand should be measured with reference to a stated period of time. One can talk about the market demand for the next calendar year, for the coming five years, or for the year 2000 A.D. The longer the forecasting interval, the more tenuous the forecast. Every forecast is based on a set of assumptions about environmental and marketing conditions, and the chance that some of these assumptions will not be fulfilled increases with the length of the forecast period.

MARKETING ENVIRONMENT Market demand is affected by a host of uncontrollable factors. Every forecast of demand should explicitly list the assumptions made about the demographic, economic, technological, political, and cultural environment. Demographic and economic forecasting are well developed, technological forecasting is coming into its own, but political and cultural forecasting are still in their infancy.[1] Much interest in the whole subject of predicting future environments is being stimulated by futurists such as Kahn and Weiner.[2] At the same time, Levitt has cautioned: "The easiest kind of expert to be is the specialist who predicts the future. It takes only two things: imagination and a good command of the active verb."[3]

MARKETING PROGRAM Market demand is also affected by controllable factors, particularly marketing programs developed by the sellers. Demand in most markets will show some elasticity with respect to industry price, promotion, product improvements, and distribution effort. Thus a market demand forecast requires assumptions about future industry prices, product features, and marketing expenditures. We shall use the term *marketing effort* to describe the sum of the company's demand-stimulating activities. Marketing effort has four dimensions that make a difference in its impact: (1) *marketing expenditure level*, the total expenditures spent on marketing, (2) *marketing mix*, the amounts and types of marketing tools the company is using at a particular time, (3) *marketing allocation*, the company's division of its marketing effort over different customer groups and sales territories, and (4) *marketing effectiveness*, the efficiency with which the company employs its marketing funds.

[1] For a discussion of environmental forecasting methods, see chap. 5, pp. 101–3.

[2] Herman Kahn and Anthony J. Weiner, *The Year 2000* (New York: Macmillan Company, 1967).

[3] Theodore Levitt, "The New Markets—Think before You Leap," *Harvard Business Review*, May–June 1969, pp. 53–68, here p. 53.

The most important thing to realize about market demand is that it is not a single number, but a function. For this reason it is also called the *market demand function* or *market response function*. The functional nature of market demand is shown in Figure 9–2A. Market demand is shown on the vertical axis, industry marketing effort on the horizontal axis. The market demand function is shown as

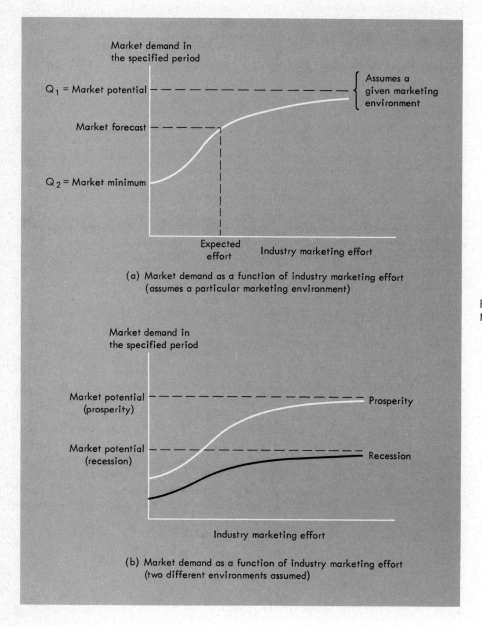

(a) Market demand as a function of industry marketing effort (assumes a particular marketing environment)

FIGURE 9–2
Market Demand

(b) Market demand as a function of industry marketing effort (two different environments assumed)

a curve that rises with higher levels of industry marketing effort. The curve is defined for a given marketing environment.

The shape of the curve has to be determined for each market. The curve in the illustration has the familiar S shape, suggesting that market demand shows first increasing, then diminishing, sales response to increased industry marketing effort. Some base sales, the *market minimum,* would take place without any demand-stimulating marketing expenditures by the industry. Positive marketing expenditures will yield increasing, then decreasing, returns. Still higher marketing expenditures would not stimulate much further demand, thus suggesting an upper limit to market demand, called the *market potential.*

The distance between the market minimum and the market potential shows the overall *marketing sensitivity of demand* in that industry. We can think of two extreme types of markets, the *expansible* and the *nonexpansible.* The expansible market, epitomized by markets for new products, is quite affected in its total size by the level of marketing expenditures. In terms of Figure 9–2A the distance between Q_1 and Q_2 is relatively large. The nonexpansible market, epitomized by cigarettes or steel, is not much affected by the level of marketing expenditures; the distance between Q_1 and Q_2 is relatively small. The firm selling in a nonexpansible market can take the market's size (the level of *primary demand*) for granted and concentrate its marketing resources on getting a desired market share (the level of *selective demand*).

It is important to emphasize that the *market demand function* is *not* a picture of market demand *over time.* Rather, the curve shows alternative current forecasts of market demand associated with alternative possible levels of industry marketing effort in the current period.

Market Forecast

Only one of the many possible levels of industry marketing effort will actually occur. The market demand corresponding to the expected effort is called the *market forecast.* The market forecast shows the expected level of market demand for the expected level of industry marketing effort and the given environment.

Market Potential

The market forecast shows the expected market demand, not the highest possible market demand. For the latter, we have to visualize the level of market demand for a very "high" level of industry marketing effort, where further increases in marketing effort would have little effect in stimulating further demand. *Market potential is the limit approached by market demand as industry marketing effort goes to infinity, for a given environment.*

The phrase "for a given environment" is crucial in the concept of market potential. Consider the market potential for automobiles in a period of recession versus a period of prosperity. The market potential is higher during prosperity. In other words, market demand is income-elastic. The dependence of market potential on the environment is illustrated in Figure 9–2B. Thus the analyst distinguishes between the position of the market demand function and movement along it. The sellers cannot do anything about the position of the market demand function; this is the result of a given marketing environment. The sellers influence their particular location on the function, however, in deciding how much to spend on marketing.

We are now ready to define company demand. *Company demand is the company's share of market demand.* In symbols:

$$Q_i = s_i Q \qquad (9\text{--}1)$$

where:

Q_i = company i's demand
s_i = company i's market share
Q = total market demand

Company demand, like market demand, is a function—called the *company demand function* or *sales response function*—and is subject to all the determinants of market demand *plus whatever influences company market share.*

But what influences company market share? The most popular theory is that the *market shares* of various competitors will be proportional to their *marketing-effort shares.* This normal expectation can be called *the fundamental theorem of market-share determination* and is expressed:

$$s_i = \frac{M_i}{\Sigma M_i} \qquad (9\text{--}2)$$

where:

M_i = company i's marketing effort.

For example, consider the simple case where two identical firms are selling the same product but spending different amounts on marketing: $60,000 and $40,000 respectively. Using equation (9–2), company one's market share is predicted to be 60 percent:

$$s_1 = \frac{\$60,000}{\$60,000 + \$40,000} = .60$$

If company one is not enjoying a .60 market share, additional factors must be brought in. Suppose the companies also differ in the *effectiveness* with which they spend marketing dollars. Then equation (9–2) can be revised to read:

$$s_i = \frac{\alpha_i M_i}{\Sigma \alpha_i M_i} \qquad (9\text{--}3)$$

where:

α_i = marketing effectiveness of a dollar spent by company i (with α = 1.00 for average effectiveness)
$\alpha_i M_i$ = company i's effective marketing effort

Suppose that company one spends its marketing funds less effectively than company two, with $\alpha_1 = .90$ and $\alpha_2 = 1.20$. Then company one's market share would be forecast to be 53 percent:

$$s_1 = \frac{.90(\$60,000)}{.90(\$60,000) + 1.20(\$40,000)} \cong .53$$

Equation (9–3) assumes a strict proportionality between market share and effective effort share. Yet if there are grounds for expecting diminishing returns as one firm's effective effort increases relative to the industry's effective effort, equation (9–3) should be modified to reflect this. One way to reflect diminishing returns is through the use of a marketing-effort elasticity exponent that is less than unity:

$$s_i = \frac{(\alpha_i M_i)^{em_i}}{\Sigma(\alpha_i M_i)^{em_i}}, \qquad \text{where } 0 < em_i < 1 \tag{9–4}$$

where:

em_i = elasticity of market share with respect to company i's effective marketing effort.

Assume that the marketing-effort elasticity is .8 for all companies. As a result, company one's market share would be

$$s_1 = \frac{[(.90)(\$60,000)]^{.8}}{[(.90)(\$60,000)]^{.8} + [(1.20)(\$40,000)]^{.8}} \cong .50$$

Thus company one's estimated market share is revised to take into account diminishing returns. Although company one is spending 60 percent of the marketing funds in the industry, its market share is only 50 percent, because of both a lower spending efficiency than its competition *and* diminishing returns.

A further improvement in the formulation of market-share determination can be introduced by breaking up each company's marketing effort into its major components and separately expressing the effectiveness and elasticity of each type of marketing effort. The equation becomes:

$$s_{it} = \frac{R_{it}^{eRi} P_{it}^{-ePi} (a_{it} A_{it})^{eAi} (d_{it} D_{it})^{eDi}}{\Sigma[R_{it}^{eRi} P_{it}^{-ePi} (a_{it} A_{it})^{eAi} (d_{it} D_{it})^{eDi}]} \tag{9–5}$$

where:

s_{it} = company i's estimated market share at time t
R_{it} = quality rating of company i's product in year t
P_{it} = price of company i's product in year t
A_{it} = advertising and promotion costs of company i in year t
D_{it} = distribution and sales-force costs of company i in year t
a_{it} = advertising-effectiveness index for company i at time t
d_{it} = distribution-effectiveness index for company i at time t

$\left.\begin{matrix} eRi, ePi \\ eAi, eDi \end{matrix}\right\}$ = elasticities of quality, price, advertising, and distribution, respectively, of company i.

Thus equation (9–5) is a flexible way to take account of four major influences on a company's market share: *marketing expenditures, marketing mix, marketing effectiveness,* and *marketing elasticity.* Although this would seem to be a great deal, the expression could be further refined (we shall not do so here) to take into account (1) *marketing allocation to territories,* (2) *carry-over effects of past marketing expenditures,* and (3) *synergistic effects of marketing decision variables.*[4]

Company Forecast

Company demand describes estimated company sales at alternative levels of company marketing effort. It remains for management to choose one of the levels.[5] The chosen level of marketing effort implies a particular level of sales, which may be called the company sales forecast:

> The *company sales forecast* is the expected level of company sales based on a chosen marketing plan and assumed marketing environment.

The company sales forecast is represented graphically in the same way as the market forecast was in Figure 9–2A; substitute company sales for the vertical axis and company marketing effort for the horizontal axis.

Too often the sequential relationship between the company forecast and the company marketing plan is confused. One frequently hears that the company should plan its marketing effort on the basis of its sales forecast. The forecast-to-plan sequence is valid if "forecast" means an estimate of national economic activity or if company demand is minimally expansible. The sequence is not valid, however, where market demand is expansible, nor where "forecast" means an estimate of company sales. The company sales forecast does not establish a basis for deciding on the amount and composition of marketing effort; quite the contrary, it is the *result* of an assumed blueprint for marketing action. The sales forecast must be viewed as a dependent variable that is affected, among other things, by the planned marketing activity of the firm.

Two other concepts are worth mentioning in relation to the company forecast.

> A *sales quota* is the sales goal set for a product line, company division, or sales representative. It is primarily a managerial device for defining and stimulating sales effort.

The sales quota set by management is arrived at through a joint consideration of the company forecast and the psychology of stimulating its achievement. The latter consideration generally leads to setting sales quotas that total to a slightly higher figure than the estimated sales forecast.

The other concept is a *sales budget.*

> A *sales budget* is a conservative estimate of the expected volume of sales and is used primarily for making current purchasing, production, and cash-flow decisions.

[4] For further development, see the author's *Marketing Decision Making: A Model-Building Approach* (New York: Holt, Rinehart and Winston, 1971). Also see David E. Bell, Ralph L. Keeney, and John D. C. Little, "A Market Share Theorem," *Journal of Marketing Research,* May 1975, pp. 136–41.

[5] The theory of choosing the best level of marketing effort is described in chap. 10, pp. 251–70.

The sales budget is arrived at through a joint consideration of the sales forecast and of the need to avoid excessive investment in case the forecast is not realized. The latter consideration generally leads to setting a sales budget slightly lower than the company forecast.

Company Potential

Company sales potential is *the limit approached by company demand as company marketing effort increases relative to competitors.* The absolute limit of company demand is, of course, the market potential. The two would be equal if the company achieved 100 percent of the market—that is, if the company became a monopolist. In most cases, company sales potential is less than market potential, even when company marketing expenditures increase considerably over those of competitors. The reason is that each competitor has a hard core of loyal buyers who are not very responsive to other companies' efforts to woo them away.

METHODS OF ESTIMATING CURRENT DEMAND

We are now ready to consider practical methods of estimating current demand. There are two types of current demand estimates in which a seller might be interested: *total market potential* and *territorial potential*. Total market potential is of interest whenever a seller is facing a decision to introduce a new product or drop an existing one. The seller wants to know whether the market is large enough to justify the company's participation.

Total Market Potential

Total market potential is the maximum amount of sales (in units or dollars) that might be available to all the firms in an industry during a given period under a given level of industry marketing effort and given environmental conditions. A common way to estimate it is as follows:

$$Q = n \times q \times p \qquad (9\text{--}6)$$

where:

Q = total market potential
n = number of buyers in the specific product/market under the given assumptions
q = quantity purchased by an average buyer
p = price of an average unit

Thus if there could be 121,000,000 buyers of books each year, and the average book buyer buys 3 books a year, and the average price is $4, then the total market potential for books is approximately $1,452,000,000 (= 121,000,000 × 3 × $4).

The most difficult component to estimate in (9–6) is n, the number of buyers in the specific product/market. One can always start with the total population in the nation, say 216,000,000 people. This can be called the *suspect pool.* The next step is to introduce criteria to eliminate groups that obviously would not buy the product. Let us assume that illiterate people, children under twelve, and persons with poor eyesight do not buy books, and they constitute 20 percent of the population. Then only 80 percent of the population, or 172,800,000 people, would be in the *prospect pool*. We might do further research and conclude that persons of low income and low education do not read books, and they are over 30 percent of the prospect pool. Eliminating them, we arrive at a *hot prospect pool* of approximately 121,000,000 for book buying. We would now use this as the number of potential buyers in formula (9–6) for calculating total market potential.

A variation on formula (9–6) is known as the *chain ratio method*. It is based on the notion that it may be easier to estimate the separate components of a magnitude than the magnitude directly.[6] Suppose a brewery is interested in estimating the market potential for a new dietetic beer. An estimate can be made by the following calculation:[7]

$$
\left.\begin{array}{l} \text{Demand} \\ \text{for the} \\ \text{new} \\ \text{dietetic} \\ \text{beer} \end{array}\right\} = \left\{\begin{array}{l} \text{Population} \times \text{ personal discretionary income per capita } \times \\ \text{average percentage of discretionary income spent on food } \times \text{average percentage of amount spent on food that is spent on beverages } \times \text{ average percentage of amount spent on beverages that is spent on alcoholic beverages } \times \text{ average percentage of amount spent on alcoholic beverages that is spent on beer } \times \text{ expected percentage of amount spent on beer that will be spent on dietetic beer.} \end{array}\right.
$$

Once the total market potential is estimated, it should be compared with the current market size. *Current market size* is the actual volume (in units or dollars) that is currently being purchased. Current market size is always smaller than the total market potential. It is important to estimate what percentage current market size is of the total market potential. In Figure 9–3, A and B show current market size as a high percentage of total market potential, which means that most of the people who could buy the product are buying it. C and D, however, show current market size at one-half of total market potential, a situation often typical of new-product markets.

The remaining factor is the company's current market share. A and C in Figure 9–3 show the company with a small market share, while B and D show the company with a large market share. The company has a choice in each case whether to go after its competitors' customers or after the untapped market potential. In case D, the company already has a large market share and its best growth opportunity is to go after the untapped market potential. In case C, however, the company could go after either its competitors' customers or the untapped market potential.

Here we must introduce another concept, that of the served market. *A company's served market are all those buyers for whom the company's product is available, accessible, and attractive*. If the company in C distributes its product in only one part of the country and if its price would not appeal to many of its competitors' customers, then the company could not penetrate its competition very much. It has a low share of the current market but a high share of its served

[6] J. Scott Armstrong, William B. Denniston, Jr., and Matt M. Gordon, "The Use of the Decomposition Principle in Making Judgments," *Organizational Behavior and Human Performance*, vol. 14, 1975, pp. 257–63.

[7] See Russell L. Ackoff, *A Concept of Corporate Planning* (New York: Wiley-Interscience, 1970), pp. 36–37.

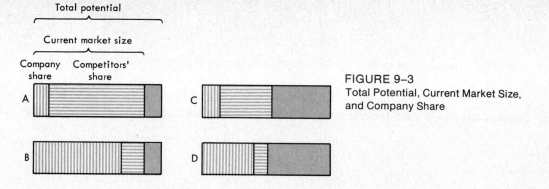

Total potential

Current market size

Company share / Competitors' share

A

B

C

D

FIGURE 9–3
Total Potential, Current Market Size,
and Company Share

market. Its best course is to go after the untapped potential in its served market rather than after its competitors' customers.

Territorial Potentials

All companies are concerned with (1) selecting the markets to sell in, (2) allocating their marketing budget optimally among these markets, and (3) evaluating their performance in the different markets. The basis for these decisions lies in competent estimation of the market potential of different territories. Two major methods are available. The first, or *market-buildup method,* is used primarily by industrial-goods firms. The second, or *index-of-buying-power method,* is used mainly by consumer-goods firms.

Market-buildup method   The market-buildup method calls for identifying all the potential buyers for the product in each market and adding up the estimated potential purchases of each. The market-buildup method is straightforward if one has available a list of all potential buyers *and* a good estimate of what each will buy. Unfortunately one, if not both, is usually lacking.

Consider the market-measurement problem faced by a machine tool company. Suppose it wants to estimate territorial market potentials for one of its machines, a medium-size wood lathe. Let us focus on one of the markets, the Greater Boston area.

The first step is to identify all potential buyers of lathes in the Boston area. Household buyers can be excluded because the lathe is too large for home-workshop purchase. The lathe is of no purchase interest to many other types of buyers, such as hospitals, retailers, and farmers. The market for this lathe is found primarily in manufacturing establishments. Even here, the lathe is of interest only to manufacturing establishments that have to shape or ream wood as part of their operation.

The company could go through a directory of all manufacturing establishments in the Greater Boston area and list those that might do woodworking. Then it might estimate the number of lathes each might purchase, based on some ratio of the number of lathes per thousand employees or the number of lathes per $1 million of sales. This would be an arduous task, especially considering that the task would have to be repeated for every other market.

A more efficient method of estimating territorial market potentials makes use of the Standard Industrial Classification System (S.I.C.). The system was developed by the federal government in connection with taking its Census of

Manufacturers. The classification is based on the *product produced* or *operation performed*. The S.I.C. System classifies all manufacturing into twenty major industry groups, each having a two-digit code. Thus, #25 is Furniture and Fixtures and #35 is Machinery, except electrical. Each major industry group is further subdivided into about 150 industry groups designated by a three-digit code (#251 is household furniture and #252 is office furniture). Each industry is further subdivided into approximately 450 product categories designated by a four-digit code (#2521 is wood office furniture and #2522 is metal office furniture).

For each four-digit S.I.C. number, the Census of Manufacturers provides the number of establishments subclassified by location, number of employees, annual sales, and net worth.

To use the S.I.C. System, the lathe manufacturer first must determine the four-digit S.I.C. codes that represent products whose manufacture is likely to require lathe machines. For example, lathes will be used by manufacturers in S.I.C. #2511 (wood household furniture), #2521 (wood office furniture), and so on. To get a full picture of all four-digit S.I.C. industries that might use lathes, the company can use three methods. (1) It can look at past sales and determine the S.I.C. codes of the past customers. (2) It can go through the S.I.C. manual and check off all the four-digit industries that in its judgment would have an interest in lathes. (3) It can mail questionnaires to a wide range of companies to inquire about their interest in wood lathes.

Once the company identifies the S.I.C. groups relevant to its product, its next step is to determine an appropriate base for estimating the likely number of lathes that will be used in each industry. Suppose customer industry sales are the most appropriate base. For example, in S.I.C. #2511, ten lathes may be used for every $1 million worth of sales; in S.I.C. #2521, five lathes for every $1 million sales. Once the company is able to establish the rate of lathe ownership relative to the customer industry's sales (or number of employees, net worth, or whatever), it can turn to the Census of Manufacturers' data and compute the market potential.

Table 9–1 shows a hypothetical computation for the Boston area involving two S.I.C. codes. In #2511 (wood household furniture) there are six estab-

TABLE 9–1
Market-Buildup Method Using S.I.C. Codes
(Hypothetical Lathe Manufacturer—Boston Area)

S.I.C.	1 ANNUAL SALES (IN MILLIONS $)	2 NUMBER OF ESTABLISHMENTS	3 POTENTIAL NUMBER OF LATHE SALES PER $1 MILLION CUSTOMER SALES	4 MARKET POTENTIAL $(1 \times 2 \times 3)$
2511	$1	6	10	60
	5	2	10	100
2521	1	3	5	15
	5	1	5	25
				200

lishments with annual sales of $1 million and two establishments with annual sales of $5 million. Furthermore, it is estimated that ten lathes can be sold in this S.I.C. code per every $1 million customer sales. Since there are six establishments with annual sales of $1 million, they account for $6 million of sales, which is a potential of 60 lathes (6 × 10). The other figures in the table are similarly computed. When the estimated sales for each S.I.C. code are added up, it appears that there is a market potential for 200 lathes in the Greater Boston area.

In a similar way, the company can estimate the market potential for other territories in the country. Suppose the market potentials for all the markets sum up to 2,000 lathes. In this case the company concludes that the Boston market contains 10 percent of the total market potential. Without further qualification, this might warrant the company's allocating 10 percent of its marketing effort (sales force, advertising, and so on) to the Boston market. In practice, the lathe manufacturer should determine additional things about each market, such as the extent of market saturation, the number of competitors, the market growth rate, and the average age of the equipment in use, before actually deciding on the amount of resources to allocate to each market.

If the company decides to sell lathes in Boston, it needs a system for identifying the best prospect companies. In the old days, sales reps called on companies door to door; this was called bird-dogging or smokestacking. This method is far too costly today. The answer is to get a list of all the companies in Boston, qualify them by some criteria, and then use direct mail or phone calls to identify the better prospects. The lathe manufacturer can use *Dun's Market Identifiers*, which lists twenty-seven key facts for over 3,250,000 establishments in the U.S. and Canada in manufacturing, wholesaling, retailing, transportation, communications, public utilities, agriculture, mining, and services.[8] The files can be screened for S.I.C. lines of business, company size (annual sales volume, number of employees, and net worth), and location by states, counties, cities, or ZIP code. The lathe manufacturer would buy a printout (and mailing labels) of all those companies in the Boston area that were in the high prospect S.I.C. lines of business and over a certain size.

Index-of-buying-power method   Consumer companies also face the problem of estimating territorial market potentials. Because their final customers are typically so numerous, they cannot list every potential customer and estimate its buying requirements. Nor is there such a thing as a Standard Household Classification that classifies households by types and provides the number of households of each type in each location. Therefore, the company that sells to households has to resort to a different solution.

The method most commonly used is a straightforward *index method*. Suppose the company is a drug manufacturer. It might assume that the market potential for drugs is directly related to a single factor, such as population. For example, if the state of Virginia has 2.28 percent of the U.S. population, the company might readily assume that Virginia would be a market for 2.28 percent of total drugs sold.

A single factor, however, is rarely a complete indicator of sales opportunity. Obviously, regional drug sales are also influenced by such factors as per

---

[8] *Dun's Market Identifiers (DMI)*, Dun & Bradstreet, New York, 1978.

capita income and the number of physicians per, say, ten thousand people. This leads to the desirability of developing a multiple-factor index, each factor being assigned a specific weight in the index.

One of the best-known, general-purpose, multiple-factor indices of area demand is the "Annual Survey of Buying Power" published by *Sales and Marketing Management*.[9] The index is designed to reflect the relative buying power in the different regions, states, and metropolitan areas of the nation. *Sales and Marketing Management*'s index of the relative buying power of an area is given by

$$B_i = .5y_i + .3r_i + .2p_i \qquad (9\text{--}7)$$

where:

B_i = percentage of total national buying power found in area i
y_i = percentage of national disposable personal income originating in area i
r_i = percentage of national retail sales in area i
p_i = percentage of national population located in area i

For example, suppose Virginia has 2.00 percent of the U.S. disposable personal income, 1.96 percent of U.S. retail sales, and 2.28 percent of U.S. population. The buying-power index for Virginia would be:

$$.5(2.00) + .3(1.96) + .2(2.28) = 2.04$$

That is, 2.04 percent of the nation's drug sales might be expected to take place in Virginia. *Sales and Marketing Management* holds that these weights reflect market potential for many consumer goods that are neither low-priced staples nor high-valued luxury goods. The weights, however, vary in their appropriateness for different products. A company can use multiple regression to find the weights that work best for estimating market potential for its products.

It should be understood that area market-potential estimates reflect relative industry opportunities rather than relative company opportunities. The company would adjust the market-potential estimates by factors left out of the index. It would want to consider such additional factors as its brand share, number and type of competitors, sales-force strength, physical-distribution system, local promotional costs, and local market idiosyncrasies.

Many companies will compute some specific additional indices for the various areas as a guide to allocating marketing resources. Suppose the company is reviewing the eight cities listed in Table 9–2. The first three columns show the percentage of total U.S. population, category sales, and brand A sales, respectively, in these eight cities. Column 4 shows the *category development index*, which is the ratio of consumption intensity to population intensity. Seattle, for example, has a category development index of 221 because it accounts for 2.71

[9] For a helpful exposition on using this survey and three other surveys published by *Sales and Marketing Management*, see "Putting the Four to Work," *Sales Management*, October 28, 1974, pp. 13 ff.

TABLE 9–2
Indices of Category Development, Brand Development, and Market Opportunity

TERRITORY	PERCENT OF TOTAL U.S. POPULATION (1)	PERCENT OF TOTAL SALES OF PRODUCT CATEGORY (2)	PERCENT OF TOTAL SALES OF BRAND A (3)	CATEGORY DEVELOP-MENT INDEX (4) = (2 ÷ 1)	BRAND DEVELOP-MENT INDEX (5) = (3 ÷ 1)	MARKET OPPORTUNITY INDEX (6) = (4 ÷ 5)
Seattle	1.23	2.71	3.09	221	252	.88
Portland	1.02	2.17	2.48	212	242	.88
Los Angeles	5.54	10.41	6.74	188	122	1.54
Boston	2.18	3.85	3.49	177	160	1.11
San Francisco	3.66	6.41	7.22	175	198	.88
Toledo	.79	.81	.97	102	123	.83
Albuquerque	.79	.81	1.13	102	143	.71
Baltimore	2.67	3.00	3.12	113	117	.97

percent of the nation's consumption of this category while it has only 1.23 percent of the nation's population. Column 5 shows the *brand development index*, which is the ratio of brand consumption intensity to population intensity. For Seattle, the brand development index is 252 because Seattle consumes 3.09 percent of this brand and has only 1.23 percent of the nation's population. Column 6 shows the *market opportunity index*, which is the ratio of category development to brand development. This ratio is .88 for Seattle, indicating that the company's brand is more developed in Seattle than in other cities. Seattle is therefore an area of low (incremental) opportunity in that the company brand is highly developed in Seattle. In Los Angeles, on the other hand, the market opportunity index stands at 1.54, indicating a high opportunity in that the company's brand is relatively underdeveloped. Companies do not necessarily put all of their money in the high market opportunity areas. Procter & Gamble, for example, uses an allocation of resouces such that 50 percent of the advertising budget for Tide is devoted to those geographic areas where the brand is weak (i.e., high-opportunity areas) and 50 percent to areas where the brand is strong.

After the company has decided on the amount of effort it wants to put into each territory, it can refine its allocations down to smaller units such as *census tracts* or *ZIP-code centers*. Census tracts are small areas about the size of city neighborhoods, and ZIP-code centers (which were designed by the U.S. Post Office Department) are larger areas, often the size of small towns. Information on population size, median family income, and other characteristics is available for each type of unit. Marketers have found these data extremely useful in identifying high potential retail areas within large cities or buying mailing lists for direct mail.[10]

[10] See Bob Stone, *Successful Direct Marketing Methods* (Chicago: Crain Books, 1975), pp. 57–63.

We are now ready to examine the problem of forecasting the future demand for a product. Very few products or services lend themselves to easy forecasting. The few cases generally involve a product whose absolute level or trend is fairly constant and where competitive relations are nonexistent (public utilities) or stable (pure oligopolies). In the vast majority of markets, market demand and especially company demand are not stable from one year to the next, and good forecasting becomes a key factor in company success. Poor forecasting can lead to overly large inventories, costly price markdowns, or lost sales because the product is out of stock. The more unstable the demand, the more critical is forecast accuracy, and the more elaborate is forecasting procedure.

Forecasting methods range from the crude to the highly sophisticated. Many technical aspects fall in the province of experts. Yet there are compelling reasons why marketing managers should be familiar with the major alternative forecasting methods. This familiarity is necessary in order to understand the limitations of the current methods as well as whether better methods are available. Furthermore, forecasting is influenced by marketing planning, requiring a continuous dialogue between marketing managers and company forecasters. This dialogue is aided considerably when marketing managers understand the basic forecasting techniques.

Six major methods of forecasting demand are discussed below.[11] The proliferation of forecasting methods should not be surprising, given the diversity of products, the variations in the availability, reliability, and types of information, and the variety of forecast objectives. Although six methods are discussed, there are actually only three information bases for building a forecast. The investigator can build the forecast on the basis of *what people say, what people do,* or *what people have done.*

The first basis—*what people say*—involves systematic determination of the opinions of buyers or of those close to them, such as salesmen or outside experts. It encompasses three methods: (1) surveys of buyer intentions, (2) composites of sales-force opinions, and (3) expert opinion. Building a forecast on *what people do* involves another method: (4) putting the product to a market test to provide indications of future buyer response. The final basis—*what people have done*—involves analyzing, with mathematical and statistical tools, records of past buying behavior, using either (5) time-series analysis or (6) statistical demand analysis.

Surveys of Buyer Intentions

Forecasting is essentially the art of anticipating what buyers are likely to do under a given set of conditions. This immediately suggests that a most useful source of information would be the buyers themselves. Ideally, a list of all potential buyers would be drawn up; each buyer would be approached, preferably on a face-to-face basis, and asked how much the company would buy of the stated product in the defined future time period under stated conditions. The buyers would also be asked to state what proportion of the total requirements would be

---

[11] For other classifications and discussions of forecasting methods, see *Forecasting Sales,* National Industrial Conference Board, Business Policy Study No. 106, 1963; Harry Deane Wolfe, *Business Forecasting Methods* (New York: Holt, Rinehart and Winston, 1966); and John C. Chambers, Satinder K. Mullick, and Donald D. Smith, "How to Choose the Right Forecasting Technique," *Harvard Business Review,* July–August 1971, pp. 45–74.

bought from the particular firm, or at least what factors would influence supplier choice. With this information, the firm would have an ideal basis for forecasting its sales.

Unfortunately, this method has a number of limitations in practice. Let us accept for the moment that the buyers could be identified and could and would convey valid information about their intentions. Would the value of this information be worth the cost of gathering it? In the case of consumer convenience goods, such as soda beverages, it would be prohibitively expensive to pay a personal call on every buyer. This objection is answered in part by taking a probability sample of consumers. The cost can also be reduced by substituting telephone or mail interviewing for personal interviewing.

Would the buyers freely report their intentions? In many situations buyers would not confide their buying intentions. A Defense Department official would not reveal how many atomic weapons will be purchased.

The value of this method would depend ultimately on the extent to which the buyers had clearly formulated intentions and then carried them out. The two areas where buyer-intention surveys have proved to be of some value are major consumer durable goods and industrial goods.

In regard to *major consumer durables,* such as automobiles, new housing, furniture, and appliances, several sampling services regularly produce reports on consumer buying intentions.[12] They ask some form of the question whether the consumer intends to buy within a stated period each of several different durables. In the past the question was usually worded:

> Do you intend to buy an automobile within the next six months?
> Yes _____ No _____ Don't know _____

While the proportion of automobile buyers tended to be higher for those reporting a purchase intention than for those who had not, the forecasting performance was far from satisfactory. It was believed that two problems were associated with the simple intention to-buy (0, 1) scale: (1) some consumers who said they didn't intend to buy had a finite, though small, probability of buying, and (2) the "don't know" category had too many responses. Juster suggested the use of a *purchase-probability scale,* such as

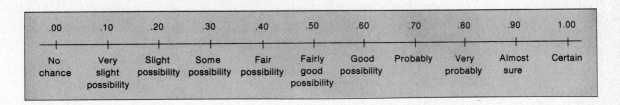

[12] The consumer pollsters include the Survey Research Center at the University of Michigan, Sindlinger & Company of Norwood, Pa., The Conference Board, Inc., and the Commercial Credit Corporation. For a discussion, see "How Good Are Consumer Pollsters?" *Business Week,* November 9, 1969, pp. 108–10.

Juster showed, on the basis of a random sampling of 800 households, that the purchase-probability approach accounted for approximately twice the actual purchase variance for automobiles as the intention-to-buy approach.[13] In addition to this improvement of the basic question, the various surveys also inquire into the consumer's present and future personal finances, and expectations about the economy. The various bits of information are combined into a *consumer sentiment measure* (Survey Research Center) or a *consumer confidence measure* (Sindlinger). Consumer durable-goods producers subscribe to these indices in the hope of learning in advance of major shifts in consumer buying intentions so that they can adjust their production and marketing plans accordingly. These surveys of consumer buying intentions have proved useful, though not completely accurate, for short-range consumer-durable sales forecasting.

In the realm of *industrial buying*, intention surveys regarding plant, equipment, and materials have been carried out by various agencies. The two best-known capital-expenditures surveys are the one conducted by the U.S. Department of Commerce in collaboration with the Securities and Exchange Commission and the one conducted annually in the late fall by McGraw-Hill through its publication *Business Week*. Most of the estimates have been within a 10 percent error band of the actual outcomes. This is a good record, considering that the business investment component of national income is highly variable.

Various industrial firms find it useful to carry on their own survey of customer buying intentions:[14]

> National Lead's marketing research personnel periodically visit a carefully selected sample of 100 companies and interview the manufacturer's technical research director, sales manager, and purchasing director, in that order. The technical research director is asked about the rate of incorporation of titanium in the manufacturer's various products; the sales manager is questioned about the sales outlook for the company's products that incorporate titanium; and the purchasing director is queried about the total amount of titanium his company plans to purchase in relation to past purchases. On the basis of these interviews and supplementary information, National's marketing research department estimates the market demand for titanium and prepares a "most favorable" forecast and a "least favorable" forecast. There are also indirect benefits. National Lead's analysts learn of new developments and modes of thinking that would not be apparent through published information. Their visits also promote National's image as a company that is concerned about buyers' needs. Another advantage of this method is that it yields subestimates for various industries and territories in the process of building an aggregate estimate.[14]

In summary, the appropriateness of the buyer-intentions survey method increases to the extent that (1) the buyers are few, (2) the cost of effectively reaching them is small, (3) they have clear intentions, (4) they follow out their original intentions, and (5) they are willing to disclose their intentions. As a result, it is of value for industrial products, for consumer durables, for product purchases where advanced planning is required, and for new products where past data do not exist.

[13] F. Thomas Juster, *Consumer Buying Intentions and Purchase Probability, An Experiment in Survey Design*, National Bureau of Economic Research, Occasional Paper No. 99 (New York: Columbia University Press, 1966).

[14] Adapted from *Forecasting Sales*, pp. 31–32.

Composite cf Sales-Force Opinion

Where it is impractical to make direct buyer inquiries, the company may decide to ask its sales representatives for estimates. An example is the Pennwalt Corporation:

> In August, the field sales personnel are provided with tabulating cards to prepare their sales forecasts for the coming year. Individual cards are prepared for each product sold to each major customer, showing the quantity shipped to the customer in the previous six months. Each card also provides space in which the field salesmen post their forecasts for the coming year. Additional tab cards are also supplied for those customers who were not sold in the current six-month period but who were customers in the prior year; and finally, blank cards are provided for submitting forecasts of sales to new customers. Salesmen fill in their forecasts (on the basis of current prices) using their own informed judgment; in some divisions, they are also in a position to substantiate their forecasts by obtaining purchase estimates from their customers.[15]

Few companies use their sales force's estimates without some adjustments. In the first place, sales representatives are biased observers. They may be congenitally pessimistic or optimistic, or they may go to one extreme or another because of a recent sales setback or success. Furthermore, they are often unaware of larger economic developments and of marketing plans of their company that will influence future sales in their territory. They may understate demand so that the company will set a low sales quota.[16] They may not have the time or concern to prepare careful estimates.

In the light of these contaminating factors, why are sales-force estimates used at all? There is the possibility that the over-and-under errors may cancel out, leaving a good aggregate forecast. Or a consistent bias in the forecast of individual sales representatives may be recognized and an adjustment made in each before aggregating the individual sales forecasts.

The company may supply certain aids or incentives to the sales force to encourage better estimating. The sales representatives may receive a record of their past forecasts compared with their actual sales, and also a set of company assumptions on the business outlook. Some companies will summarize individual forecasting records and distribute them to the sales force. A tendency for sales representatives to produce ultraconservative estimates to keep down their sales quota can be countered by basing territorial advertising and promotional expenditures on each sales representative's estimate.

Assuming these biasing tendencies can be countered, a number of benefits can be gained by involving the sales force in forecasting. Being closest to the customers, sales representatives may have more knowledge or better insight into developing trends than any other single group. This is especially likely where the product is fairly technical and subject to a changing technology. Second, because of their participation in the forecasting process, the sales representatives may have greater confidence in the derived sales quotas, and this confidence may increase their incentive to achieve those quotas. Finally, a grass-roots forecasting procedure results in estimates broken down by product, territory, customer, and sales representative.

---

[15] Ibid., p. 25.

[16] However, see Jacob Gonik, "Tie Salesmen's Bonuses to Their Forecasts," *Harvard Business Review*, May–June 1978, pp. 116–23.

In summary, the appropriateness of the composite-of-sales-force opinion method increases to the extent that the sales representatives (1) are likely to be the most knowledgeable source of information, (2) are cooperative, (3) are unbiased or can be corrected in their biases, and (4) will derive some benefits from participating in the procedure.

Expert Opinion   Another method of forecasting involves tapping the opinion of well-informed persons other than buyers or company sales representatives, such as distributors or outside experts.

The automobile companies gather estimates of sales directly from their dealers. These estimates are subject to the same strengths and weaknesses as sales-force estimates: the dealers may not give the necessary attention to careful estimating; their perspective concerning future business conditions may be too narrow; and they may supply biased estimates to gain some immediate advantage.

Firms also resort to outside experts for estimates of future demand. A firm may use or buy general economic forecasts or special industry forecasts prepared outside of the firm. Or a firm may invite a group of experts to estimate the probability of a development, such as a new technology or a change in business conditions.

There are at least three ways to gather the judgments of a group of experts. They may meet as a committee and come up with a group estimate (group discussion method). They may supply their separate estimates to a project leader who merges them into a single estimate (pooled individual estimates method). They may supply individual estimates and assumptions that are reviewed by the project leader, revised, and followed by a second round of individual estimation, a third round, and so forth, until the assumptions and estimates converge (Delphi method). The third method is becoming increasingly popular for developing market and technological forecasts.[17]

An interesting variant of the expert-opinion method has been used by Lockheed Aircraft Corporation.[18] A group of Lockheed executives pose as different major customers. In a hardheaded way, they evaluate Lockheed's offer in relation to competitors' offers. A decision on what and where to buy is made for each customer. The purchases from Lockheed are totaled and reconciled with an independent statistical forecast to become Lockheed's sales forecast.

The use of expert opinion has the following advantages: (1) forecasts can be made relatively quickly and inexpensively, (2) different points of view are brought out and balanced in the process, and (3) there may be no alternative if basic data are sparse or lacking. The main disadvantages are: (1) opinions are generally less satisfactory than hard facts, (2) responsibility is dispersed, and good and bad estimates are given equal weight, and (3) the method usually is more reliable for aggregate forecasting than for developing reliable breakdowns by territory, customer group, or product.

---

[17] See Norman Dalkey and Olaf Helmer, "An Experimental Application of the Delphi Method to the Use of Experts," *Management Science*, April 1963, pp. 458–67. Also see Roger J. Best, "An Experiment in Delphi Estimation in Marketing Decision Making," *Journal of Marketing Research*, November 1974, pp. 447–52.

[18] See, for example, Gerald A. Busch, "Prudent Manager Forecasting," *Harvard Business Review*, May–June 1961, pp. 57–64.

| Market-Test Method | The usefulness of opinions, whether those of buyers, sales representatives, or other experts, depends upon the cost, availability, and reliability of this type of information. In cases where buyers do not plan their purchases carefully or are very erratic in carrying out their intentions or where experts are not very good guessers, a more direct market test of likely behavior is desirable. A direct market test is especially desirable in forecasting the sales of a new product or the likely sales of an established product in a new channel of distribution or territory. Where a short-run forecast of likely buyer response is desired, a small-scale market test is usually an ideal answer.[19] |

| Time-Series Analysis | As an alternative to costly surveys or market tests, some firms prepare their forecasts on the basis of a statistical-mathematical analysis of past data. The underlying logic is that past data are an expression of enduring causal relations that can be uncovered through quantitative analysis. They can be used to predict future sales. Thus forecasting becomes an exercise in adroit backcasting. |

A time series of past sales of a product can be analyzed into four major temporal components.

The first component, *trend* (*T*), is the result of basic developments in population, capital formation, and technology. It is found by fitting a straight or gradually curved line through the time-series data. If the trend turns out to be statistically significant, then it becomes central in the preparation of a long-range forecast.

The second component, *cycle* (*C*), is seen in the wavelike movement of sales. Properly speaking, a cycle exists when the time series shows an undulation of a fairly constant amplitude and periodicity. Few if any business series exhibit pure cyclical behavior in this sense. Some, such as housing construction, hog sales, and pig-iron sales, exhibit approximate cyclical behavior. Many sales series are affected by swings in the level of general economic activity, which tends to be somewhat periodic. Isolation of the cyclical component can be useful in intermediate-range forecasting.[20]

The third component, *season* (*S*), refers to a consistent pattern of sales movements within the year. Although "season" suggests a distinct quarterly pattern induced by changes in the weather, it is used more broadly to describe any recurrent hourly, weekly, monthly, or quarterly sales pattern. The seasonal component may be related to weather factors, holidays, and/or trade customs. The seasonal pattern provides the investigator with a norm for forecasting short-range sales.

The fourth component, *erratic events* (*E*), includes strikes, blizzards, fads, riots, fires, war scares, price wars, and other disturbances. These erratic components have the effect of obscuring the more systematic components, and the problem becomes one of starting with the original "noisy" time series and separating the underlying systematic forces from the erratic.

Classical time-series analysis involves procedures for decomposing the original sales series (*Y*) into the components, *T*, *C*, *S*, and *E*. According to one model, these components interact linearly—that is, $Y = T + C + S + E$; ac-

---

[19] Market testing is discussed in chap. 13, pp. 334–40.

[20] The most careful methodology for isolating and studying cyclical movements is that developed by the National Bureau of Economic Research. Arthur F. Burns and Wesley C. Mitchell, *Measuring Business Cycles* (New York: National Bureau of Economic Research, 1946).

cording to another model, they interact multiplicatively—that is, $Y = T \times C \times S \times E$. The multiplicative model makes the more realistic assumption that the seasonal and cyclical effects are proportional to the trend level of sales. T is stated in absolute values, and C, S, and E are stated as percentages.

This is not the place to describe the methodology for decomposing a time series. The procedures are outlined in elementary business statistics textbooks.[21] The main caution is to avoid mechanical extrapolation. The forecast is not simply a matter of putting together systematic components but rather a creative and further act in itself. The systematic forces underlying past sales may not remain unchanged. Any one of the three components can take on a different form starting tomorrow; the past trend can be altered by the appearance of a competitive product; the cyclical pattern can be altered by new countercyclical government policies; the seasonal pattern can be altered by new counterseasonal company policies. A mechanical extrapolation ignores marketing plans, the effect of which has to be built into the final forecast. The impact of possible erratic forces can be conveyed by preparing an optimistic, pessimistic, and most likely forecast. The size of the forecast error band conveys to management a sense of how much confidence it can repose in the most likely forecast.

For a company with hundreds of items in its product line that wants to produce efficient and economical short-run forecasts, a newer time-series technique called *exponential smoothing* is available. In its simplest form, exponential smoothing requires only three pieces of information: this period's actual sales, Q_t; this period's smoothed sales, $\overline{Q}_t$; and a smoothing parameter, a. The sales forecast for next period's sales is given by

$$\overline{Q}_{t+1} = aQ_t + (1 - a)\overline{Q}_t \qquad (9\text{--}8)$$

where:

$\overline{Q}_{t+1}$ = sales forecast for next period
a = the smoothing constant, where $0 \le a \le 1$
Q_t = current sales
$\overline{Q}_t$ = smoothed sales

Suppose the smoothing constant is .4, current sales are $50,000, and smoothed sales are $40,000. Then the sales forecast is

$$\overline{Q}_{t+1} = .4(\$50,000) + .6(\$40,000) = \$44,000$$

In other words, the sales forecast is always between (or at an extreme of) current sales and smoothed sales. The relative influence of current and smoothed sales depends on the smoothing constant, here .4. Thus the sales forecast "tracks" actual sales.

For each of its products, the company determines an initial level of smoothed sales and a smoothing constant. The initial level of smoothed sales can

[21] See Ya-Lun Chou, *Statistical Analysis with Business and Economic Applications*, 2nd ed. (New York: Holt, Rinehart and Winston, 1975), chap. 2. For computer programs, see Julius Shiskin, *Electronic Computers and Business Indicators* (New York: National Bureau of Economic Research, 1957). For an application, see Robert L. McLaughlin, "The Breakthrough in Sales Forecasting," *Journal of Marketing*, April 1963, pp. 46–54.

be simply average sales for the last few periods. The smoothing constant, on the other hand, is derived by trial-and-error testing of different smoothing constants between zero and one to find the one that produces the best fit of past sales. The method can be refined to reflect seasonal and trend factors by adding two more constants.[22]

Statistical Demand Analysis

Time-series analysis treats past and future sales as a function of time, rather than of any real demand factors. Its main use is in markets where the underlying demand factors remain stable over time. Where this is not the case, it is much more desirable to try to discover the direct relationship between sales and real demand factors.

Numerous real factors, of course, affect the sales of any product. Statistical demand analysis is an attempt not to derive a complete set of factors but rather to discover the most important factors in the hope that they will explain a significant amount of the variations in sales. The factors most commonly analyzed are prices, income, population, and promotion.

The procedure consists of expressing sales (Y) as a dependent variable and trying to explain sales variation as a result of variation in a number of independent demand variables $X_1, X_2, \ldots, X_n$; that is,

$$Y = f(X_1, X_2, \ldots, X_n) \qquad (9\text{-}9)$$

For example, Palda found that the following demand equation gave a fairly good fit to the historical sales of Lydia Pinkham's Vegetable Compound between the years 1908 and 1960:

$$Y = -3649 + .665X_1 + 1180 \log X_2 + 774X_3 + 32X_4 - 2.83X_5 \quad (9\text{-}10)$$

where:

Y = yearly sales in thousands of dollars
X_1 = yearly sales (lagged one year) in thousands of dollars
X_2 = yearly advertising expenditures in thousands of dollars
X_3 = a dummy variable, taking on the value 1 between 1908 and 1925 and 0 from 1926 on
X_4 = year (1908 = 0, 1909 = 1, and so on)
X_5 = disposable personal income in billions of current dollars[23]

The five independent variables on the right helped account for 94 percent of the yearly variation in the sale of Lydia Pinkham's Vegetable Compound between 1908 and 1960. To use it as a sales-forecasting equation for 1961, it would be necessary to insert figures for the five independent variables. Sales in 1960 should be put in X_1, the log of the company's planned advertising expenditures for 1961 should be put in X_2, 0 should be put in X_3, the numbered year corre-

[22] See Robert G. Brown, *Smoothing Forecasting, and Prediction of Discrete Time Series* (Englewood Cliffs, N.J.: Prentice-Hall, 1963). For another interesting method, the *Box-Jenkins method*, see Box-Jenkins, *Time Series Analyses, Forecasting and Control* (San Francisco: Holden-Day, 1970).

[23] Kristian S. Palda, *The Measurement of Cumulative Advertising Effects* (Englewood Cliffs, N.J.: Prentice-Hall, 1964), pp. 67–68.

sponding to 1961 should be put in X_4, and estimated 1961 disposable personal income should be put in X_5. The result of multiplying these numbers by the respective coefficients and summing them gives a sales forecast (Y) for 1961.

Basically, demand equations are derived by trying to fit the "best" equation to historical or cross-sectional data. The coefficients of the equation are estimated according to the *least squares* criterion. According to this criterion, the best equation is one that *minimizes the sum of the squared deviations of the actual from the predicted observations*. The equation can be derived through the use of standard formulas. The closer the fit, the more useful the equation, all other things being equal.

With the advent of high-speed computers, statistical demand analysis is becoming an increasingly popular approach to forecasting. The user, however, should be wary of five problems that might diminish the validity or usefulness of any statistical demand equation: (1) too few observations, (2) too much correlation among the independent variables, (3) violation of normal distribution assumptions, (4) two-way causation, and (5) emergence of new factors not accounted for.[24]

SUMMARY

No firm can conduct its business successfully without trying to measure the actual size of markets, present and future. Quantitative measurements are essential for the analysis of market opportunity, the planning of marketing programs, and the control of marketing effort. The firm may make many measures of demand, varying in the level of product aggregation, the time dimension, and the space dimension. In all its studies, however, the company should be clear about its demand measurement concepts, particularly the distinction between market demand and company demand, and the corollary concepts of forecasts and potentials.

Current demand may be estimated for the market as a whole or for various territories. In the latter case, the market-buildup method is commonly used for industrial goods and the index of buying power is commonly used for consumer goods.

For estimating future demand, the company may use one or any combination of at least six different forecasting methods: surveys of buyer intentions, sales-force estimates, expert opinions, market tests, time-series analysis, or statistical demand analysis. These methods vary in their appropriateness with the purpose of the forecast, the type of product, and the availability and reliability of data.[25]

QUESTIONS AND PROBLEMS

1. Two forecasters working for the same automobile manufacturer arrived at substantially different estimates of next year's demand. Does this variance imply that forecasting is largely guesswork?

2. A manufacturer of printing equipment makes estimates of sales by first asking the district sales managers for district forecasts. Describe how these initial forecasts may be refined at higher company levels to arrive at a final companywide forecast.

[24] For further discussion, see the author's *Marketing Decision Making: A Model-Building Approach* (New York: Holt, Rinehart and Winston, 1971), pp. 596–602.

[25] For further reading on contemporary methods of demand analysis, see G. David Hughes, *Demand Analysis for Marketing Decisions* (Homewood, Ill.: Richard D. Irwin, 1973).

3. A beverage company wants to use multiple regression to determine what factors explain state-to-state variations in the consumption of soft drinks. (a) What independent variables should be tested? (b) If the fitted regression equation "explains" most of the state-to-state variation in sales, does it follow that it is a good device for indicating relative market potential by state?

4. A manufacturer of women's hair products (home permanents, hair rinses, shampoos, etc.) wanted to determine the relative market potential for its products in each county of the United States. What three or four factors are most likely to belong in a weighted index of potential?

5. A marketing researcher sought a multiple regression equation to explain past sales in an industry. Good industry data on the dependent and independent variables only went back five years. He fitted the following equation:

$$Y = 5{,}241 + 31X_1 + 12X_2 + 50X_3$$

where:

Y = yearly sales in thousands of dollars
X_1 = U.S. disposable personal income in billions of dollars
X_2 = U.S. population in millions of households
X_3 = time, in years (1960 = 0)

He was pleased to find that this equation accounted for 98 percent of the yearly variations in industry sales. List any reservations you would have about using this equation in forecasting future industry sales.

6. A chemical company wants to estimate the demand for sulphur next year. One of the many uses of sulphur is the manufacture of sulphuric acid, one of whose end uses is its application in polishing new cars. Automaker C is a customer of this manufacturer. Suggest the ratios that have to be linked to go from automaker C's new car production to its impact on the company's sulphur sales.

7. Suppose a company's past sales are: 10, 12, 15, 12, 11, 13, 18, 20. The company forecaster uses an exponential smoothing equation with $a = .4$ and initial $\bar{Q}_t = 10$. Estimate the exponentially smoothed sales that would have been predicted for the third period on.

8. An automotive manufacturer is attempting to develop a sales forecast for next year. The company forecaster has estimated demand for six different environment-strategy combinations:

SALES FORECASTS		
HIGH MARKETING BUDGET	MEDIUM MARKETING BUDGET	LOW MARKETING BUDGET
Recession 15	12	10
Normal 20	16	14

He believes that there is a .20 probability of recession and an .80 probability of normal times. He also believes the probabilities of a high, medium, and low company marketing budget are .30, .50, and .20, respectively. How might he arrive at a single point forecast? What assumptions are being made?

9. A motorboat company based in Washington state is considering opening up additional retail outlets in several counties on the Columbia River and Puget Sound. Using

market opportunity indexes, recommend in which counties the outlets should be located.

COUNTY	POPULATION	SALES OF MOTORBOATS (IN DOLLARS)	SALES OF COMPANY'S BOATS (IN DOLLARS)
Clark	161,300	2,800,000	186,200
Klickitat	13,400	140,000	38,000
Cowlitz	72,000	455,000	72,000
Snohomish	261,700	2,835,000	361,000
Pacific	16,200	1,750,000	836,000
Skagit	56,200	2,310,000	155,800
Total in State	3,583,400	3,500,000,000	3,800,000

Planning Marketing Strategy

3

Marketing Planning

10

Plans are nothing; planning is everything.
DWIGHT D. EISENHOWER

We are now ready to examine how an organization can efficiently develop plans and strategies for serving its markets. No organization will thrive simply through reacting to each new development as it occurs. Taking ad hoc initiatives will only result in inconsistent actions and uncontrolled expenditures, leaving the organization vulnerable to more-forward-planning competitors. Each organization must take a planned approach to the marketplace.

The four chapters in Part III will deal with the larger issues in planning, to be followed by several chapters in Part IV dealing with the individual elements of the marketing mix. This chapter examines the nature and role of marketing planning as a key element in effective marketing. Chapter 11 analyzes specific marketing strategies that are used by market leaders, aggressors, followers, and nichers. Chapter 12 discusses the tailoring of marketing strategies to the different stages of the life cycle through which a product passes. Finally, Chapter 13 deals with the company's need to find and successfully launch new products and services to replace those approaching the end of their product life cycle.

Many questions arise in connection with marketing planning. What are the stages through which business- and marketing-planning systems evolve? What is the nature and content of a marketing plan? What is the theory of effective marketing planning? We shall address each of these questions in this chapter.

EVOLUTION OF BUSINESS PLANNING

Business planning is a relatively new development in the corporate world. Businesses appear to pass through four stages on their way to sophisticated planning. Various companies today can be found in each of these stages.

Unplanned Stage

When businesses first get started, their managers are so busy hunting for funds, customers, equipment, and materials that they have no time for planning. Management is totally engrossed in the day-to-day operations required for survival. There is no planning staff and little time to plan.

Budgeting-system Stage

Eventually management recognizes the need to develop and install a budgeting system to facilitate orderly financing of company growth. An estimate is made by management of total sales for the coming year and the expected costs and cash flows associated with this sales level. Each departmental manager prepares a budget for carrying out the department's work for the coming year. These budgets are essentially financial and do not require the thought that goes into real business planning. Budgets are not to be confused with plans.

Annual-planning Stage

Management eventually turns to planning, usually annual planning. To carry this out, management adopts one of three basic approaches. The first is *top-down planning*, so called because top management sets *goals* and *plans* for all the lower levels of management. This model is taken from military organizations where the generals prepare the plans and the troops carry them out. In commercial organizations it goes along with a Theory X view of employees—that they dislike work and responsibility and prefer to be directed.[1]

The second system is *bottom-up planning*, so called because the various units of the organization prepare their own goals and plans, based on the best they think they can do, and send them to upper management for approval. This style is based on Theory Y thinking about human nature—that employees like work and responsibility and are more creative and committed if they participate in the planning and running of the enterprise.

Most companies use a third system known as *goals-down–plans-up planning*. Here top management takes a broad look at the company's opportunities and requirements and sets corporate goals for the year. The various units of the company are responsible for developing plans designed to help the company reach these goals. These plans, when approved by top management, become the official annual plan. A typical example is afforded by the Celanese Company:

> The annual planning process starts in late August, with top management receiving marketing research reports and sending out a guidance letter stating overall volume and profit goals. During September and October, product planning managers develop overall marketing plans in consultation with the field sales manager and the marketing vice president. In the middle of October, the marketing vice president reviews and approves the plans and submits them to the president for final approval. In the meantime, the field sales manager works with his regional sales managers and salesmen to develop field sales plans. Finally, in the fourth week in October, the controller prepares an operating budget; it goes, in early

[1] Douglas McGregor, *The Human Side of Enterprise* (New York: McGraw-Hill Book Company, 1960).

242

November, to top management for final approval. Thus, three months after the planning process started, a completed plan and budget are ready to be put into operation.[2]

Annual-planning systems may take several years before they work successfully. Initially, several of the executives will resist having to draft plans for their operations. Their resistance is based on: (1) not wanting to commit themselves in advance to goals and strategies in a rapidly changing environment; (2) resenting the time-consuming nature of preparing plans when they can be doing "more important" things; and (3) thinking of planning as something to satisfy higher levels of management rather than seeing it as a personal tool for improving business performance. Therefore top management must give thought to an effective strategy for introducing a planning culture into the organization. Management needs a plan for planning and a plan for selling employees on the benefits of planning.

The prime requisite is that the president be sold on planning. The president will then see to it that the senior officers carry out their planning responsibilities. The officers should be encouraged to discuss the pros and cons of formal planning. The following arguments can be presented in favor of planning:

Encourages systematic thinking ahead by management.

Leads to a better coordination of company efforts.

Leads to the development of performance standards for control.

Causes the company to sharpen its guiding objectives and policies.

Results in better preparedness for sudden developments.

Brings about a more vivid sense in the participating executives of their interacting responsibilities.[3]

To facilitate the acceptance of planning, a planning officer should be hired. The planning officer meets with various executives to get their ideas about a planning system, designs a planning methodology, and tests it further with various executives until it seems ready to launch. After the design and calendar for planning is approved, this officer assists the executives in gathering information and writing their plans. The initial plans should be short and practical. Over the years, desirable elaborations will be added in phase with the executives' readiness to engage in more-sophisticated planning.

Strategic-planning Stage

In this stage, the planning system of the company takes on several elaborations in an effort to improve its overall effectiveness.

The major change is the addition of *long-range planning*. Management realizes that annual plans make sense only in the context of a long-range plan. In fact, the long-range plan should come first, and the annual plan should be a detailed version of the first year of the long-range plan. For example, managers at American Hospital Supply Company prepare a strategic five-year plan early in the year and an annual operating plan later in the year. The five-year plan is re-

---

[2] *The Development of Marketing Objectives and Plans: A Symposium* (New York: Conference Board, 1963), p. 38.

[3] See Melville C. Branch, *The Corporate Planning Process* (New York: American Management Association, 1962), pp. 48–49.

worked each year (called *rolling planning*) because the environment changes rapidly and requires an annual review of the long-run planning assumptions. The choice of five years for a planning horizon is somewhat arbitrary. Brand managers at the Henkel Company of Germany annually prepare a three-year plan. Executives at Xerox prepare intermediate and long-range plans as well as annual plans. A Xerox executive described Xerox as being on a continuous planning basis, by which he meant that some plan is being written or revised every day of the year.

A further development is that the various plans begin to take on a more *strategic character*. When a company first turns to planning, the planning documents are very simple: they are long on statistics and specific tactical actions and short on strategy. One often looks in vain for a clear statement of strategy. In more-advanced planning systems, the plan formats are constructed so as to require a section on strategy.

As the company gains experience with planning, an effort is made to *standardize the plan formats* so that higher management can make more valid comparisons among similar units. It is important that the plans written for different comparable units, such as divisions, product lines, products, or brands, follow the same or a similar format to permit intelligent comparison by higher management.

As the planning culture takes hold in the company, further improvements are introduced. Managers receive more training in the use of *financial analysis* and are required to justify their recommendations not in sales volume terms but in terms of contribution margin, cash flow, and rate of return on manageable assets. *Computer programs* are developed to help product managers examine the impact of alternative marketing plans and environmental assumptions on sales and profit. The managers are eventually asked to develop *contingency plans* in addition to main plans, showing how they would respond to unexpected but critical developments. These and other developments mark the emergence of a true strategic-planning culture in the firm.

THE NATURE OF A MARKETING PLAN

As a company's planning system evolves, there is increasing talk of "marketing planning and marketing plans." Unfortunately, no common usage attaches to these terms. Companies that are highly market oriented sometimes use the term "marketing plan" synonymously with the overall business plan; perhaps a better title would be "market-oriented business plan." In other companies, "marketing plan" is used to describe the section within the larger business plan that deals specifically with marketing issues and strategies, in contrast to the financial and manufacturing sections of the same plan. In still other companies, it is used to describe a special marketing document for attaining some marketing goal, such as a successful new-product launch or an orderly development of a new market.

Because of these varying usages, the term "marketing plan" may not be as useful as a more specific designation of the particular type of plan being discussed. There are at least eight different plans that require marketing input:

1. *Corporate plan.* The corporate plan describes the overall business plan for the corporation. It might be an annual, intermediate, or long-range plan. The corpo-

rate plan deals with company missions, growth strategies, portfolio decisions, investment decisions, and current objectives and goals. It does not contain details on the activities of individual business units.

2. *Divisional plan.* The divisional plan is similar to the corporate plan and describes the division's plan for growth and profitability. It describes marketing, financial, manufacturing, and personnel strategies and may use a short, intermediate, or long-run planning horizon. In some cases, the divisional plan is the sum of all the separate plans prepared within the division.

3. *Product-line plan.* A product-line plan describes objectives, goals, strategies, and tactics for a specific product line. Each product-line manager prepares this plan.

4. *Product plan.* A product plan describes objectives, goals, strategies and tactics for a particular product or product category. Each product manager prepares this plan.

5. *Brand plan.* A brand plan describes objectives, goals, strategies, and tactics for a specific brand within the product category. Each brand manager prepares a brand plan.

6. *Market plan.* A market plan is a plan for developing and serving a particular market. If the organization has market managers as well as product managers, the market managers would prepare these plans.

7. *Product/market plan.* A product/market plan is a plan for marketing a particular product or product line of the company in a particular industrial or geographical market. An example would be a plan by a bank to market its lending services to the real estate industry.

8. *Functional plan.* A functional plan is a plan for one of the major functions, such as marketing, manufacturing, manpower, finance, or research and development. It also describes plans for subfunctions within a major function, such as, in the case of marketing, an advertising plan, a sales promotion plan, a sales-force plan, and a marketing research plan.

As noted earlier, most of these plans have a marketing component. In fact, the marketing component not only is essential but usually takes priority in the plan's development. Planning often starts with the question, How great a sales volume can we hope to obtain at a profit? This step is answered by marketing analysis and the development of a marketing plan. After this plan is approved, the nonmarketing executives start working on their manufacturing, financial, and personnel plans to support the marketing plan. Thus the marketing plan is a foundation for the planning of the other activities of the company.

THE COMPONENTS OF A MARKETING PLAN

How does a marketing plan look? A review of the planning formats used by various companies quickly reveals great variations in the topics included and in the sequence of topics addressed by the planner. Each company develops a format that reflects the planning capability of its executives, their tolerance for short or long plans, and the special topics that must be emphasized in that industry.

In spite of the variation, however, certain basic topics should find their way into every plan. We shall focus on product or brand plans in our discussion. A product or brand plan should contain the following sections: *executive summary, situation analysis, objectives and goals, strategy statement, action programs, budgets,* and *controls.*

Executive Summary   The plan should open with a one- or two-page summary of the main facts and recommendations contained within the plan. Here is an abbreviated example:

> The 1981 Marketing Plan seeks to generate significant increases in corporate sales and profits, in comparison to the previous year's achievements. The sales target is set at $80,000,000, which represents a planned 20 percent sales gain in comparison to last year. This increase is deemed to be attainable because of the improved economic, competitive, and distribution picture. The operating margin is forecast at $8,000,000, which represents a 25 percent increase in comparison with last year. To achieve these goals, the sales promotion budget will amount to $1,600,000, which amounts to 2 percent of projected sales. The advertising budget will amount to $2,400,000, which represents 3 percent of projected sales. . . . [More detail follows.]

The purpose of the executive summary is to permit higher management to grasp quickly the major thrust of each plan and then read further in search of the information that is most critical in evaluating the plan. To facilitate this, a table of contents should follow the executive summary.

Situation Analysis   The first major section of the plan is the *situation analysis* (also called "current situation" or "where we stand"). In this section, the manager describes the major features of the situation facing his or her operation that must be addressed by the subsequent objectives, strategies, and actions. The situation-analysis section itself can be usefully divided into four sections—background, normal forecast, opportunities and threats, and strengths and weaknesses—to encourage a systematic situation appraisal by the manager.

Background   This section usually starts with a summary of key sales and profit data for the last several years. An example of five years of past data is shown in Table 10–1.[4]
   Row 1 shows that the market volume is growing at 200,000 units a year. Row 2 shows that the company's brand rose from a 6 percent share to a fairly stable 10 percent share. Row 3 shows that the product's price of $2 has been increasing recently. Row 4 shows that variable cost per unit originally declined but has been increasing recently. Row 5 shows that the gross contribution margin per unit—the difference between price (row 3) and unit variable cost (row 4)—first increased and then decreased in the most recent year. Rows 6 and 7 show sales volume in both units and dollars, and row 8 shows the total gross contribution margin. Row 9 shows a stable and then rising level of overhead. Row 10 shows net contribution margin, that is, gross contribution margin less overhead. Rows 11 and 12 show advertising and distribution expenses, respectively. Finally, row 13 shows net operating profit after marketing expenses. The picture is one of growing sales, with profits, however, growing at a slower rate. These data should be followed by a description of noteworthy facts and trends about the market, distributors, and competitors. The market description should include the definition of the served market, major market segments, market size and trends, and buyer behavior. The distribution section should describe the major features and trends occurring in distribution. In the case of competitors, their

---

[4] For another example, see the case, "Concorn Kitchens," in Harper W. Boyd, Jr., and Robert T. Davis, *Marketing Management Casebook* (Homewood, Ill.: Richard D. Irwin, 1971), pp. 125–36.

246

TABLE 10-1
Historical Product Data

VARIABLE	COLUMNS	1975	1976	1977	1978	1979
1. Market—total units		1,000,000	1,200,000	1,400,000	1,600,000	1,800,000
2. Share		.06	.08	.10	.10	.10
3. Price per unit $		2.00	2.00	2.00	2.20	2.40
4. Variable cost per unit $		1.20	1.10	1.10	1.30	1.55
5. Gross contribution margin per unit $	(3 − 4)	.80	.90	.90	.90	.85
6. Sales volume in units	(1 × 2)	60,000	96,000	140,000	160,000	180,000
7. Sales $	(3 × 6)	120,000	192,000	280,000	352,000	432,000
8. Gross contribution margin $	(5 × 6)	48,000	86,400	126,000	144,000	153,000
9. Overhead $		20,000	20,000	20,000	30,000	30,000
10. Net contribution margin $	(8 − 9)	28,000	66,400	106,000	114,000	123,000
11. Advertising $		8,000	12,000	15,000	18,000	20,000
12. Distribution $		4,000	8,000	15,000	15,000	20,000
13. Net operating profit $	(10 − 11 − 12)	16,000	46,400	76,000	81,000	83,000

market shares, strategies, and strengths and weaknesses should be described. Some of the factors explaining the most recent sales and profit results should be presented.

Normal forecast The background should be followed by a forecast of market size and company sales under "normal conditions," that is, assuming no major changes in the *marketing environment* or *marketing strategies*. This forecast could be obtained in a number of ways. The simplest method is straightforward extrapolation of past growth rates of market size and company sales. For example, the market volume in Table 10-1 for the coming year can be forecast at 2,000,000 units, on the assumption that the 200,000 annual increase continues. Market share can be assumed to stay at 10 percent. Prices can be expected to rise by, say, twenty cents. Another method is to forecast the economy and other major variables affecting sales and then use a regression equation to forecast sales. Still another method is to gather sales-force estimates of what they expect to sell next year. Most companies use more than one method and take some average of the estimates.

The forecast would have to be revised if quite different environmental conditions are expected or strategies are planned. If the forecast does not satisfy higher management, the product or brand manager would have to consider new strategies, hoping to find one that promises a higher level of sales and profits.

Opportunities and threats The normal forecast section should be followed by a section in which the manager identifies the main opportunities and threats facing the business unit. Usually the manager is aware of a number of these but should be challenged to put them into words. Higher management can review

247

this list and raise questions about factors that are listed or missing. At year end, higher management can review the earlier list of opportunities and threats and see how many of them materialized and what actions were taken.

Table 10–2(A) shows the opportunities and threats listed by a product-line manager in charge of a company's line of television sets. The opportunities and threats describe *outside* factors facing the business unit. They are written so as to suggest some possible actions that might be warranted. The manager may be asked to list the opportunities and threats in order of importance, as an indicator of which deserve the most attention and planning.

TABLE 10–2(A)
Major Opportunities and Threats in the Television Business

Opportunities
1. There is a growing market for life-size home television. We should give thought to entering this market and attempting to establish leadership.
2. Our dealer coverage in the South is thin, although consumer preference for our brand is high.
3. The federal government is getting ready to slap a quota on foreign television sets.

Threats
1. Many consumers are shifting to lower-price brands. We may have to lower prices on our existing line or introduce some new lower-cost models.
2. The cost of cabinet wood is expected to jump 15 percent in the coming year. We may have to find new, substitute exterior materials.
3. The federal government may pass a more stringent product-safety law. This would necessitate some product redesign.

TABLE 10–2(B)
Strengths and Weaknesses of the Television Company

Strengths
1. Ninety-five percent of consumers know our brand. This awareness level is the highest in the industry.
2. Forty percent of consumers believe our brand to be the most reliable one in the industry. No one brand comes close to this.
3. Our dealers are the best trained in the industry in terms of knowledge and salesmanship.

Weaknesses
1. Our brand is considered high in price relative to other brands, and it loses the price-conscious buyer. Pricing strategy should be reevaluated.
2. The quality of the picture is no longer the best in the industry. We need to invest more in research and development.
3. Our advertising campaign is not particularly creative or exciting. We may want to consider switching advertising agencies.

Strengths and weaknesses   In this section of the plan the manager lists the main internal strengths and weaknesses of the business unit (see Table 10–2(B)). The list of strengths has implications for strategy formulation, while the list of weaknesses has implications for investments to correct weaknesses. Higher management can raise important questions about the business units based on the manager's list of strengths and weaknesses.

Objectives and Goals

The situation analysis points out where the business stands and where it might go. The next task now is to develop a statement about where the business should go. Management has to set specific objectives and goals that will be accepted by higher management.

Higher management typically defines overall goals for the coming period for the corporation as a whole. The top management of an electronics firm may state that they want the company to achieve (1) a 15 percent growth in sales volume, (2) a pretax profit of 20 percent on sales, and (3) a pretax profit of 25 percent on investment. Within this context, each business-unit manager develops goals that will support the corporate goals. Those business units that are in a good market situation will be expected to adopt even more ambitious goals than the corporate goals. Those in difficult markets will adopt more modest goals. Top management wants to "stretch" each business unit to its maximum potential level.

Assume that the managers of the television product line in this company see the key need to be that of increasing the profitability of the line. Suppose the line's current return on investment (ROI) is 10 percent, and higher management wants the television line to yield 15 percent. That can be accomplished by (1) increasing the sales revenue, (2) decreasing the cost (or not increasing it by as much as the higher sales revenue), and (3) decreasing the investment (or not increasing it by as much as the increase in profit). Any or all of these can be adopted as objectives for the coming period.

The objectives the manager decides to emphasize can be turned into goals, that is, given magnitudes and target dates. The manager might propose the following goals for attaining a 15 percent ROI in the television line: (1) attain a 12 percent increase in sales revenue for the coming year, (2) increase the expense budget by 8 percent for the coming year, and (3) hold the investment level constant for the coming year.

Strategy Statement

In this section of the plan, the manager formulates an overall strategy that will achieve the stated goals. To overcome the tendency toward tunnel vision, the manager should be requested to list some alternative marketing strategies. Unfortunately, many managers tend to avoid thinking deeply about alternative strategies. According to a study reported by Ames:

> In one company when each planner was asked by top management to outline alternative strategies . . . the request drew a complete blank. The planners were so locked into their accustomed way of thinking about their markets that they could not conceive of a different approach that made any commercial sense at all.[5]

---

[5] B. Charles Ames, "Marketing Planning for Industrial Products," *Harvard Business Review*, September–October 1968, p. 103.

A marketing strategy is not a collection of specific actions but rather a statement that indicates where major efforts should be directed in order to attain the goals. The strategy is made up of elements that can be generated by a further analysis of each objective.

For example, the objective "increase the sales revenue" can be broken down into three subobjectives. Sales revenue can be increased by (1) increasing the average price on all units, (2) increasing the overall sales volume, and (3) managing to sell more of the higher-price units. Each of these points can be examined further. For example, the overall sales volume can be increased by (1) increasing market growth and (2) increasing market share. In turn, increased market growth can come about by convincing people (1) to own more television sets per household and/or (2) to replace their old sets more frequently. By going down the path of each objective and its constituents, the manager will be able to identify in a systematic manner the major strategy opportunities facing the product line. Presumably the manager will choose the strategy that promises to produce the best results. The manager should state the basic strategy as clearly and succinctly as possible. For example:

> Our basic strategy for producing higher profit will be to lengthen the product line by adding some lower-price units at the lower end and some expensive units at the high end. The average price of the existing brands will be raised moderately. A new advertising campaign will be developed to further build the perceived superiority of our brand in the consumers' minds, with much emphasis on the higher-price units. New dealerships will be opened in our weaker areas. Dealers will receive a new high-impact training program.

In developing the strategy, the manager will want to discuss it with others whose cooperation will make the difference between failure and success. He or she will see the purchasing and manufacturing people to make sure that they are able to buy enough material and produce enough goods to meet the planned sales volume levels, the sales manager to make sure of obtaining the planned sales-force support, and important dealers to make sure that they will cooperate.

Action Program

The strategy statement represents the broad outline of how the manager hopes to accomplish the stated goals. The broad outline must be filled in with specific actions (also called tactics). A useful approach is to take each strategy element and make it someone's responsibility. For example, improving the advertising campaign might be assigned to Jane Jones, advertising manager. Jones should then proceed to list the various actions required to carry out the strategy, such as inviting proposals for competing advertising agencies, selecting the best agency, approving the final copy, and approving the media plan. Each activity is assigned to someone in the advertising department along with a completion date. This format would be repeated for each strategy element.

The overall action plan may take the form of a matrix, with the twelve months (or fifty-two weeks) of the year serving as columns and various marketing activities serving as rows. Dates can be entered when various activities or expenditures will be started, reviewed, and completed. This action plan is subject to change during the year as new problems and opportunities arise, but it serves as a general implementation framework for tactics.

Budgets   The goals, strategies, and planned actions allow the manager to formulate a supporting budget statement for the operation. The budget statement is essentially a projected profit-and-loss statement.[6] On the revenue side, it shows the forecasted number of units that would be sold and the average net realized price. On the expense side, it shows the costs of production, physical distribution, and marketing, broken into finer categories. The difference, or projected profit, is shown. In some companies, managers prepare alternative budgets for high and low levels of realized sales. Management reviews the budget and either approves or asks for modifications. Once approved, the budget is the basis for material procurement, production scheduling, manpower planning, and marketing operations.

Controls   The last section of the plan deals with the controls that will be applied to monitor the plan's progress. Normally the budget is spelled out for each month or quarter. This means that higher management can review the results each period and spot those businesses that are not attaining their goals. Managers of lagging businesses are asked to cite the new factors in the picture and the actions they are taking to improve plan fulfillment. Higher management usually resists lowering the sales and profit goals and instead recommends shifts or reductions of certain expenditures.

Some control sections require the manager to identify major contingencies and to state what steps would be taken in the event of each contingency. A contingency plan is not a complete plan but rather an outline of some steps that the manager would consider. The purpose of a contingency plan is to encourage the manager to face up to the most important challenges that might occur and to give prior thought to response strategies.

THE THEORY OF EFFECTIVE MARKETING RESOURCE ALLOCATION

We are now ready to examine more closely the task of developing an optimal marketing plan. Effective marketing planning calls for finding the relationships between different levels, types, and allocations of marketing resources and the corresponding impact on sales and profits. An effective marketing manager will utilize these relationships in preparing marketing plans. Assume that John Smith is a product manager at a large company and is preparing his annual plan. He has data on the product's recent history, the economic outlook, competitors' strategies, plant capacity, forecasted raw material costs, and other important variables. He has given some preliminary thought to the situation analysis, objectives and goals, and marketing strategy, and is at the point of trying to develop specific budget numbers. *With what budget item(s) should he start?* Should he start by estimating sales? Costs? Profits? At least three approaches are used by product managers in practice.

Profit and Sales   Before describing these approaches, we will introduce two tools—a *profit equa-*
Equations   *tion* and a *sales equation*. These equations can be used for the double purpose of sales planning and profit planning.

---

[6] For an example, see chap. 24, p. 640.

251

The profit equation The profit equation is developed in the following way. Profits (Z) by definition are equal to the product's revenue (R) less its costs (C):

$$Z = R - C \tag{10-1}$$

Revenue is equal to the product's net price (P') times its unit sales (Q):

$$R = P'Q \tag{10-2}$$

But the product's net price (P') is equal to its list price (P) less any allowance per unit (k) representing freight allowances, commissions, and discounts:

$$P' = P - k \tag{10-3}$$

The product's costs can be conveniently classified into unit variable non-marketing costs (c), fixed costs (F), and marketing costs (M):

$$C = cQ + F + M \tag{10-4}$$

Substituting equations (10–2), (10–3), and (10–4) into (10–1) and simplifying,

$$Z = [(P - k) - c]Q - F - M \tag{10-5}$$

where:

Z = total profits
P = list price
k = allowance per unit (such as freight allowances, commissions, discounts)
c = production and distribution variable cost (such as labor costs, delivery costs)
Q = number of units sold
F = fixed costs (such as salaries, rent, electricity)
M = discretionary marketing costs

The expression $[(P - k) - c]$ is the *gross contribution margin per unit*—the amount the company realizes on the average unit after deducting allowances and the variable costs of producing and distributing the average unit. The expression $[(P - k) - c]Q$ is the *gross contribution margin*—the net revenue available to cover the fixed costs, profits, and discretionary marketing expenditures.

The sales equation In order to use the profit equation for planning purposes, the product manager will need to develop an understanding of the determinants of sales volume (Q). The relation of sales volume to its determinants is specified in a sales equation (also called the *sales volume equation,* or *sales response function*):

$$Q = f(X_1, X_2 \ldots, X_n, Y_1, Y_2, \ldots, Y_m) \tag{10-6}$$

where:

$(X_1, X_2, \ldots, X_n)$ = sales variables under the control of the firm
$(Y_1, Y_2, \ldots, Y_m)$ = sales variables not under the control of the firm

Let us look at the Y variables first. They include such things as the cost-of-living index, the population size of the target market, and the market's average purchasing power. As these variables change, so does the buying rate of the target market. The manager has no influence over the Y variables but needs to estimate them and base the forecast partly on them. We shall assume that the manager has estimated the Y variables and their effect on sales volume, which is conveyed by:

$$Q = f(X_1, X_2, \ldots, X_n/Y_1, Y_2, \ldots, Y_m) \qquad (10\text{-}7)$$

which says that sales volume is a function of the X variables, for given levels of the Y variables.

The X variables are the variables that the manager can use to influence the sales level. The X variables include the list price (P), allowances (k), variable cost (C) (to the extent that high variable costs reflect improved product quality, delivery time, and customer service), and marketing expenditures (M). Thus sales, as a function of the manager's controllable variables, is described by:

$$Q = f(P, k, c, M) \qquad (10\text{-}8)$$

We can make one additional refinement. The marketing budget, M, can be spent in several ways, such as advertising (A), sales promotion (S), sales force (D), and marketing research (R).

The sales equation (or *marketing-mix equation*) (10-8) can be related as follows:

$$Q = f(P, k, c, A, S, D, R) \qquad (10\text{-}9)$$

where the elements in the parentheses represent the marketing mix elements.

Approaches to Developing Marketing Plans

We now are ready to contrast three approaches—sales volume planning, target profit planning, and profit-optimization planning—used by product managers to develop their plans.

Sales volume planning In this system, the product manager is told the target sales volume for the coming year. Higher management sets the sales goal on the basis of the economic outlook, the competitive picture, and the desire to run the plant at or near capacity. Sales volume planning is typically found in capital-intensive industries such as steel, autos, and chemicals where the task is to keep the equipment operating as much as possible and find ways to sell all of the output. The product manager may not even have much to say about the price that will be charged. In a few cases, the product manager will not even propose the marketing budget necessary to do the job, in that top management will develop a budget based on a conventional percentage of marketing expenditures to planned sales. The manager's main discretion comes in dividing the marketing budget among various elements of the marketing mix, such as advertising, sales promotion, and marketing research. He or she also determines or proposes how to allocate these expenditures among the different geographical and end-use markets for the product.

This system is also found in some consumer-packaged-goods companies. At Procter & Gamble, the brand manager is often given the sales volume goal, the product price, and the marketing budget, and his job is to produce and develop a plan (largely a promotion plan) for spending the budget in a way that will attain the planned sales. He usually does not even know the true profit being earned by the company on his own brand.

Target profit planning   In many companies, the product manager is responsible for proposing a marketing plan that promises to deliver a stated target level of profits. In some cases, the target profit level is set by higher management and it is the product manager's job to build a plan to achieve this level of profits. In other cases, the product manager proposes a target profit level that he or she believes will satisfy higher management, given the corporation's overall profit goal and the expected capacity of the product to contribute to profits.

Table 10–3 provides a realistic, though hypothetical, illustration of how a product manager at the Heinz Company makes up a marketing budget for the coming year. Heinz product managers are profit oriented rather than sales volume oriented in their marketing planning.

Let us assume that the product is ketchup. We will limit this illustration to the household market. The product manager first estimates the total market for ketchup for the coming year. An estimate can be formed by applying the recent growth rate of the market (6 percent) to this year's market size (23,600,000 cases). This forecasts a market size of 25,000,000 cases for next year. The product manager then forecasts Heinz's sales based on assuming the continuation of

---

**TABLE 10–3
A Target Profit-Oriented Product Plan**

1. *Forecast of total market* This year's total market (23,600,000 cases) × recent growth rate (6%)	25,000,000 cases
2. *Forecast of market share*	.28
3. *Forecast of sales volume* (2 × 3)	7,000,000 cases
4. *Price per case to distributor*	$4.45 per case
5. *Estimate of sales revenue* (3 × 4)	$31,150,000
6. *Estimate of variable costs* Tomatoes and spices ($.50) + bottles and caps ($1.00) + labor ($1.10) + physical distribution ($.15)	$2.75 per case
7. *Estimate of contribution margin to cover fixed costs, profits, and marketing* ([4–6] 3)	$11,900,000
8. *Estimate of fixed costs* Fixed charge $1.00 per case × 7 million cases	$7,000,000
9. *Estimate of contribution margin to cover profits and marketing* (7–8)	$4,900,000
10. *Estimate of target profit per case*	$1,900,000
11. *Amount available for marketing* (9–10)	$3,000,000
12. *Split of the marketing budget* Advertising Sales promotion Marketing research	 $2,000,000 $ 900,000 $ 100,000

its past market share of 28 percent. Thus Heinz's sales *(Q)* are forecasted to be 7,000,000 cases.

Next, the product manager sets a distributor price of $4.45 per case *(P)* for next year based on such factors as this year's price, expected rises in cost, and expected competitors' prices. For simplicity, assume that there are no allowances *(k = 0)*. Then the planned sales revenue *(PQ)* will be $31,150,000.

The product manager then estimates next year's variable costs at $2.75 per case. This means that the contribution margin to cover fixed costs, profit, and marketing is $11,900,000. Suppose the company charges this brand with a fixed cost *(F)* of $1.00 a case, or $7,000,000. This leaves a contribution margin to cover profits and marketing of $4,900,000.

At this step, the product manager brings in the target profit goal. Suppose a profit level of $1,900,000 will satisfy higher management. It is usually some increase, say 5 to 10 percent, over this year's profit. He then subtracts the target profit from what remains of the contribution margin to learn that $3,000,000 is available for marketing. To summarize:

$$[(P - k) - c]Q - F - Z = M \qquad (10\text{--}10)$$

$$[(\$4.45 - 0) - \$2.75]\,7,000,000 - \$7,000,000 - \$1,900,000 = \$3,000,000$$

Thus, the marketing budget is not determined on independent grounds but rather as a residual amount coming out of a budget-planning process. The marketing budget is established, in effect, as the amount the company can "afford." This method is nothing other than an elaboration of the first of Joel Dean's four methods of setting the advertising budgeting, which he dubbed the affordable method.[7]

The product manager accepts this as the necessary or desirable marketing budget if it appears reasonable in relation to last year's marketing budget and the new sales target. If it appears inadequate to produce the desired level of sales, he may do one of a number of things. He may reduce the profit goal. He may try to negotiate for lower fixed charges to his operations. He may consider raising next year's price by more than the initial planned increase. Or he may press manufacturing to find a way to reduce or keep down the unit costs of producing his product.

The last step involves the product manager in splitting the marketing budget into its mix elements, such as advertising, sales promotion, and marketing research. (We will assume that the sales force will remain fixed in size and is part of fixed cost.) The split is normally based on the previous year's split and on how competitors are using their marketing budgets. Table 10–3 shows two-thirds of the money going for advertising, almost a third for sales promotion, and the remainder for marketing research.

Against this method of developing the marketing budget, several criticisms can be leveled. In the first place, the manager estimated sales before he estimated the marketing budget, which is justified only on the inadmissible assumption that the level of marketing expenditures does not affect sales! This assumption is inadmissible. If it were true, marketing expenditures either should not be budgeted or should be kept very low. Second, this approach calls upon

---

[7] See chap. 19, p. 498.

the product manager to find a "satisficing" plan, not an optimizing one. That is, the manager seeks the price and budget that will achieve a satisfactory profit level rather than maximize profits. Third, the manager set next year's price largely on the basis of covering expected cost increases rather than by considering price jointly with other marketing-mix variables. Markup pricing is normally not a logically defensible pricing method. Finally, the allocation of the marketing budget to the marketing-mix elements seems highly arbitrary.

Profit-optimization planning   Profit optimization requires that the manager give explicit recognition to the relationship between sales volume and the various elements of the marketing budget as represented in the *sales equation*. We shall use the term *sales response function* to describe the relationship between sales volume and a particular element of the marketing mix. Specifically, *the sales response function forecasts the likely sales volume during a specified time period associated with different possible levels of a marketing-mix element, holding constant the other marketing-mix elements.* It should not be thought of as describing a relationship over time between the two variables. To the extent that managers have a good feel for the relevant sales response functions, they are in a position to formulate more effective marketing plans.

What are the possible shapes of sales response functions? Figure 10–1 shows some major possibilities. Part A shows the well-known relationship between price and sales volume, known as the Law of Demand. The relationship states that more sales will occur, other things being equal, at lower prices. The illustration shows a curvilinear relationship, although linear and other relationships are possible.

Figure 10–1B shows four possible shapes for the relationship between sales volume and the level of marketing expenditures. Marketing expenditure function *(A)* is the least plausible: it states that sales volume is not affected by the level of marketing expenditures. It would mean that the number of customers and their purchasing rates are not affected by sales calls, advertising, sales pro-

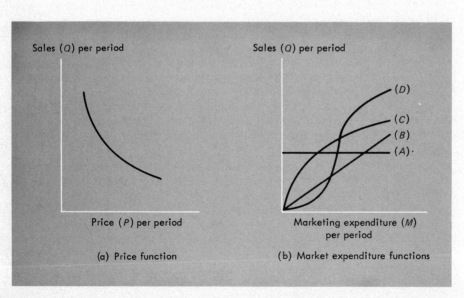

FIGURE 10–1
Sales Response
Functions

motion, or marketing research. Marketing expenditure function *(B)* states that sales volume grows linearly with the level of marketing expenditure. That is, $Q = a + bM$ where *a* is the intercept and *b* the slope, both to be estimated. In the illustration, the intercept is 0 but this is inaccurate if some sales would take place even in the absence of marketing expenditures.

Marketing expenditure function *(C)* is a concave function showing sales volume increasing throughout at a decreasing rate.[8] It is a plausible description of sales response to alternative-size sales forces. The rationale is as follows: If a field sales force consisted of one sales representative, that representative would call on the best prospects, and hence the marginal rate of sales response would be highest. A second sales rep would call on the next best prospects, and the marginal rate of sales response would be somewhat less. Successively hired sales reps would call on successively less responsive prospects, and this accounts for the continuously diminishing rate of sales increase.

Marketing expenditure function *(D)* is an S-shaped function showing sales volume initially increasing at an increasing rate and then increasing at a decreasing rate.[9] It is a plausible description of sales response to different levels of advertising expenditure.[10] The rationale is as follows: Small advertising budgets do not buy enough advertising to create more than minimal brand awareness. Larger budgets can produce high brand awareness, interest, and preference, all of which might lead to purchase response if the price and other things are right. Very large budgets, however, may not produce much additional response because the target market is already highly familiar with the brand.

The occurrence of eventually diminishing return to increases in marketing expenditures as shown in marketing expenditure functions *(C)* and *(D)* is plausible for a number of reasons. First of all, there tends to be an upper limit to the total potential demand for any particular product. The easier sales prospects are sold first; the more recalcitrant sales prospects remain. As the upper limit is approached, it becomes increasingly expensive to stimulate further sales. In the second place, as a company steps up its marketing effort, its competitors are likely to do the same, with the net result that each company experiences increasing sales resistance. In the third place, if sales were to increase at an increasing rate throughout, natural monopolies would result. A single firm would tend to take over in each industry because of the greater level of its marketing effort. Yet this is contrary to what we observe in industry.

How can a marketing manager estimate the sales response functions that apply to his business? Essentially, three methods are available. The first is the *statistical method,* where the manager gathers data on past sales and levels of marketing-mix variables and estimates the sales equation through standard statistical estimation procedures. Several researchers have done this with varying degrees of success, the success being related to the quantity and quality of avail-

---

[8] Mathematically, this concave function can be represented by a log function of the form $Q = a \log M$, a power function of the form $Q = aM^b$ (where $0 < b < 1$), or a modified exponential function of the form $Q = \bar{Q}(1 - e^{-aM})$. See Philip Kotler, *Marketing Decision Making: A Model Building Approach* (New York: Holt, Rinehart and Winston, 1971).

[9] Mathematically, this S-shaped function can be represented by a Gompertz function of the form $Q = \bar{Q}b^{cM}$ or a logistic function of the form $Q = \bar{Q}/1 + e^{-(a+bM)}$. See Kotler, *Marketing Decision Making.*

[10] However, see chap. 19, pp. 500–501.

able data and the seeming stability of the underlying relationships.[11] The second is the *experimental method,* which calls for deliberately varying the marketing expenditure and mix levels in matched samples of geographical or other units and noting the resulting sales volume.[12] The experimental method produces the most reliable results but is not used extensively enough because of its complex requirements, high cost, and inordinate level of management resistance. The third is the *judgmental method,* where experts are asked to estimate the needed magnitudes. This method requires a careful selection of the experts and a defined procedure for gathering and combining their estimates, such as the Delphi method.[13] The judgmental method is often the only feasible one, and under many circumstances it can be quite useful. We believe that getting informed estimates from experts is better than making no estimates at all.

In estimating sales response functions, some cautions have to be observed. The sales response function assumes that other variables remain constant over the range of the function. Thus the company's price and competitors' prices and marketing mix are assumed to remain unchanged, no matter what the company spends on marketing. Since this *ceteris paribus* condition is unrealistic, the sales response function would have to be modified to reflect competitors' probable responses. The sales response function also assumes a certain level of company efficiency in the expenditure of the marketing dollars. If the expenditure efficiency rises or falls, the sales response function would have to be modified accordingly. Also, the sales response function would have to be modified to reflect the delayed impacts of expenditures on sales beyond one year. These and other characteristics of sales response functions are spelled out in more detail elsewhere.[14]

Once the sales response functions are estimated, how are they used in profit optimization? Graphically, we must introduce some further curves to find the point of optimal marketing expenditure. The analysis is shown in Figure 10–2. The sales response function shown here is S-shaped, although the same analysis applies to any form. First the manager subtracts all nonmarketing costs from the *sales response function* to derive the *gross profit curve.* Next, marketing expenditures are drawn in such a way that a dollar on one axis is projected as a dollar on the other axis. This amounts to a 45-degree line when the axes are scaled in identical dollar intervals. The *marketing expenditures curve* is then subtracted from the *gross profit curve* to derive the *net profit curve.* The net profit curve shows positive net profits with marketing expenditures between M_L and M_U, which could be defined as the rational range of marketing expenditure. The net profit curve reaches a maximum at M. Therefore the marketing expenditure that would maximize net profit is $\$M$.

The graphical solution can alternatively be carried out in algebraic terms;

[11] For examples of fitted sales response functions, see Doyle L. Weiss, "Determinants of Market Share," *Journal of Marketing Research,* August 1968, pp. 290–95; Donald E. Sexton, Jr., "Estimating Marketing Policy Effects on Sales of a Frequently Purchased Product," *Journal of Marketing Research,* August 1970, pp. 338–47; and Jean-Jacques Lambin, "A Computer On-Line Marketing Mix Model," *Journal of Marketing Research,* May 1972, pp. 119–26.

[12] See Russell Ackoff and James R. Emshoff, "Advertising Research at Anheuser-Busch," *Sloan Management Review,* winter 1975, pp. 1–15.

[13] See the author's "A Guide to Gathering Expert Estimates," *Business Horizons,* October 1970, pp. 79–87.

[14] See the author's *Marketing Decision Making.*

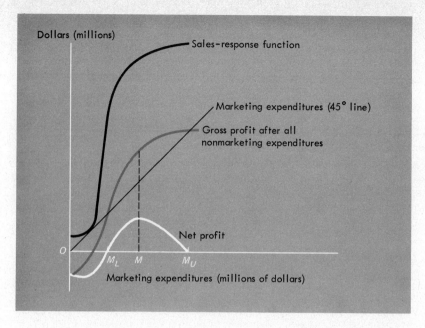

Dollars (millions)

Sales-response function

Marketing expenditures (45° line)

Gross profit after all
nonmarketing expenditures

Net profit

O M_L M M_U

Marketing expenditures (millions of dollars)

FIGURE 10–2
Relationship Between Sales
Volume, Marketing Expenditures,
and Profits

indeed it has to be if the sales volume is a function of more than one marketing-mix variable. Here we will present a numerical example of how this is done.

A numerical example Ms. Jones, a product manager, has been selling her product for some years using a low-price, low-promotion strategy. The current price is $16, and $10,000 is being spent on advertising and another $10,000 on sales promotion. Sales are around 12,000 units and profits around $14,000. Higher management considers this unimpressive. Ms. Jones is anxious to find a better strategy to increase profits.

Her first step is to generate a set of alternative marketing-mix strategies. She generates the eight strategies shown in the first three columns of Table 10–4

TABLE 10–4
Marketing Mixes and Estimated Sales

MARKETING MIX NO.	PRICE (P)	ADVERTISING (A)	PROMOTION (S)	SALES (Q)
1.	$16	$10,000	$10,000	12,400
2.	16	10,000	50,000	18,500
3.	16	50,000	10,000	15,100
4.	16	50,000	50,000	22,600
5.	24	10,000	10,000	5,500
6.	24	10,000	50,000	8,200
7.	24	50,000	10,000	6,700
8.	24	50,000	50,000	10,000

(the first strategy is the current one). They were formed by assuming a high and a low level of each of three marketing variables and elaborating all the combinations ($2^3 = 8$).

Her next step is to estimate the likely sales that would be attained with each alternative mix. She feels that the needed estimates are unlikely to be forthcoming through fitting past historical data or through conducting marketing-mix experiments. She decides to ask the sales manager for his estimates since he has shown an uncanny ability to be on target. Suppose he provides the sales estimates shown in the last column of Table 10–4.

The final step calls for determining which marketing mix maximizes profits, assuming the sales estimates are reliable. This calls for introducing a profit equation and inserting the different marketing mixes into this equation to see which maximizes profits.

Suppose fixed costs, F, are $38,000; unit variable costs, c, are $10; and the contemplated allowance off list price, k, is $0. Then profit equation (10–5) reads:

$$Z = (P - 10)Q - 38,000 - A - S \qquad (10\text{–}11)$$

Profits are shown to be a function of the chosen price and the advertising and sales promotion budgets.

At this point the manager can introduce each marketing mix and estimated sales level (from Table 10–3) into this equation. The resulting profits are #1($16,400), #2($13,000), #3(−$7,400), #4(−$2,400), #5($19,000), #6($16,800), #7(−4,200), and #8($2,000). Marketing mix #5, calling for a price of $24, advertising of $10,000, and promotion of $10,000, promises to yield the highest profits ($19,000).

There is one more step the product manager can take. Some marketing mix not shown might yield a still higher profit. To check on this possibility, the product manager can fit a sales equation to the data shown in Table 10–4. The sales estimates in the table can be viewed as a sample from a larger universe of expert judgments concerning the sales equation $Q = f (P,A,S)$. A plausible mathematical form for the sales equation is the multiple exponential:

$$Q = bP^pA^aS^s \qquad (10\text{–}12)$$

where:

b = a scale factor
p,a,s = price, advertising, and promotion elasticity, respectively

Using least-squares regression estimation (not shown), the manager finds the fitted sales equation to be:

$$Q = 100,000P^{-2}A^{1/8}S^{1/4} \qquad (10\text{–}13)$$

This fits the sales estimates in Table 10–4 extremely well. Price has an elasticity of −2, that is, a 1 percent reduction in price, other things being equal, tends to increase unit sales by 2 percent. Advertising has an elasticity of ⅛, and promotion has an elasticity of ¼. The coefficient 100,000 is a scale factor that translates the dollar magnitudes into sales volume in units.

The product manager now substitutes this sales equation into the Q term in profit equation (10–11). This yields, when simplified:

$$Z = 100{,}000\,A^{1/8}S^{1/4}[P^{-1} - 10P^{-2}] - 38{,}000 - A - S \qquad (10\text{–}14)$$

Profits are strictly a function of the chosen marketing mix. The manager can insert any marketing mix (including those not shown in Table 10–4) and derive an estimate of profits. To find the profit-maximizing marketing mix, she applies standard calculus.[15] The optimal marketing mix (P,A,S) is ($20, $12,947, $25,894). Twice as much is spent on promotion as on advertising because its elasticity is twice as great. The product manager would forecast a sales volume of 10,358 units and profits of $26,735. While other marketing mixes can produce higher sales, no other marketing mix can produce higher profits. Using this equation, the product manager has solved not only the optimum marketing mix but also the optimum marketing budget $(A + S = \$38{,}841)$.

Having examined the procedure for identifying the profit-optimizing marketing mix, let us return to the Heinz example in Table 10–3. We saw that the Heinz product manager arrived at a marketing plan involving a price of $4.45, an advertising budget of $2,000,000, a sales promotion budget of $900,000, and a marketing research budget of $100,000. Instead of stopping at this point, he should develop some alternative marketing-mix strategies and attempt to forecast the probable sales volume associated with each strategy. He could do a financial analysis to find out which strategy promises the highest profit level. Or he could fit a sales equation to the estimates to capture the implied elasticities. The sales equation could then be incorporated into the profit equation, and the latter could be maximized to find the best marketing mix and expenditure.

To facilitate profit-optimization planning, some companies have designed computer programs for use by marketing managers to identify and assess the impact of alternative marketing plans on profits and sales. The marketing manager goes to a computer terminal, types in a request for the particular program, and then proceeds to build and test a marketing expenditure plan. One well-known computer program consists of four subprograms.[16] First the marketing manager requests the computer to retrieve and display the major statistics on the product for the last several years. This material is called the *historical base* and is similar to Table 10–1. He then instructs the computer to produce a *straightforward projection* of the major statistics for the next several years, using extrapolation. He then modifies any projections based on his own knowledge, and the result is called the *profit-and-loss planning base*. This shows a normal "extrapolated" level of marketing expenditures, price, and sales, and the resulting profits. If the projected profits are satisfactory, the marketing manager can stop here. However, a fourth subprogram called a *marketing plan simulator* is available for trying out alternative marketing plans and estimating their sales and profits. The simulator incorporates an estimated sales equation. The marketing manager tests alternative marketing plans until he finds a highly satisfactory one.

[15] The derivation is shown in the appendix of the author's "Marketing Mix Decisions for New Products," *Journal of Marketing Research*, February 1964, pp. 43–49.

[16] See Boyd and Davis, *Marketing Management Casebook*, pp. 125–36.

Long-run profit projection Computer programs have also been designed to help marketing managers build and test long-run strategies for the development of a product or market. For example, the marketing manager may be asked to forecast, for a given product, the expected costs, prices, sales, profits, cash flow, and return on investment for the next several years as an indication of whether the particular product business should be built, maintained, harvested, or terminated. Table 10–5 shows the printout from one such computer program for a ready-to-eat cereal product.

The first line shows that this projection is for a seven-year planning horizon. Details then appear on the undepreciated value of plant and equipment devoted to this product, current opportunity cost, working capital, and expected terminal salvage value.

The rest of the printout shows the expected or planned year-to-year levels of important variables that ultimately affect the internal rate of return. Column 1 shows the retail price per unit, which is expected to rise from $.58 to $.70 in the course of seven years. Column 2 shows that the retail margin for this product (18 percent) is not expected to change. Column 3 shows the resulting wholesale prices. Since this company will sell direct to the retailers, there is no wholesale margin (column 4), and the factory price (column 5) is the same as the wholesale price.

Column 6 shows estimated variable manufacturing costs, and they too are expected to rise over the period, from a present level of $.19 to $.23 in 1982. The ratio of variable manufacturing costs to factory prices is shown in column 7, followed by the planned ratio of variable marketing costs to factory prices (column 8). Subtracting variable manufacturing and marketing costs per unit from the price, the result is the contribution to fixed costs and profits, which is shown in dollar and percentage form in columns 9 and 10 respectively.

The next step calls for estimating fixed manufacturing costs and fixed marketing costs over the next seven years, which are shown in columns 11 and 12. The symbol E + 06 is computer printout shorthand and means that the reader should move the decimal place, in the associated number, six places to the right. Thus $1.028E + 06 means $1,028,000. Columns 13 and 14 show the anticipated investments in plant, equipment, and building over the next seven years, and column 15 shows the estimated total depreciation expense.

We now arrive at the estimated sales and profits. Columns 16 and 17 show management's estimates of sales (in percentage and in unit terms, respectively) over the next seven years. The figures indicate that management expects company sales (in units) to rise at the rate of about 10 percent a year, on the basis of its planned levels of marketing expenditures. Column 18 presents management's estimates of industry sales for the next seven years.

The figures in column 19, market share, are derived by dividing estimated company sales (column 17) by estimated industry sales (column 18). We see that management expects market share to grow from 2.6 percent to 3.8 percent over a seven-year period. Column 20 expresses total marketing expenditures (columns 8 and 12) as a percent of sales, and this percentage is expected to fall. Examining this more closely, we see that management expects sales to rise faster than marketing expenditures; hence it is assuming an increase in marketing productivity.

Columns 21 and 22 are a derivation of the implied yearly profits after taxes in percentage and dollar terms. The computer program uses the following formula to calculate dollar profits after taxes:

TABLE 10–5
Sample Printout from Computer System

```
                    TIME HORIZON = 7                        YEARS

        REMAINING UNDEPR. P&E INVEST. AT BEGIN. YR. 1 = 900000    DOLLARS
        REMAINING NO. OF YEARS OF P&E DEPRECIATION    = 3         YEARS
        REMAINING UNDEP. BLDG. INVEST. AT BEGIN. YR. 1 = 210000   DOLLARS
        REMAINING NO. OF YEARS OF BLDG. DEPRECIATION  = 21        YEARS

        DEPRECIATION HORIZON FOR P&E INVESTMENTS      = 10        YEARS
        DEPRECIATION HORIZON FOR BLDG. INVESTMENTS    = 30        YEARS

        OPPORTUNITY COST (AT BEGINNING OF PERIOD)     = 2.E+06    DOLLARS
                             WORKING CAPITAL          = 13        PCNT SALES
        SALVAGE VALUE (AT END OF PERIOD)              = 10        X EARNINGS
```

	1	2	3	4
YEAR	RET.PRICE ($)	RET.MAR.(PCNT)	WHOLE.PRICE ($)	WHOLE.MAR.(PCNT)
1981	.577	18	.473	0
1982	.602	18	.494	0
1983	.621	18	.509	0
1984	.639	18	.524	0
1985	.659	18	.54	0
1986	.675	18	.554	0
1987	.698	18	.572	0

	5	6	7	8
	FACTORY	VARIABLE MAN.	VARIABLE MAN.	VARIABLE MKTG
YEAR	PRICE($)	COST($)	COST(PCNT)	COST(PCNT)
1981	.473	.191	40.4	5
1982	.494	.196	39.7	5
1983	.509	.202	39.7	5
1984	.524	.208	39.7	5
1985	.54	.214	39.6	5
1986	.554	.221	39.9	5
1987	.572	.227	39.7	5

	9	10	11	12
	CONTRIB. TO FIXED COSTS AND PROFIT		FIXED MAN.	FIXED MKTG.
YEAR	($)	(PCNT)	COST($)	COST($)
1981	.258	54.6	915000	4.25E+06
1982	.273	55.3	971000	4.9E+06
1983	.282	55.3	1.028E+06	5.5E+06
1984	.29	55.3	1.31E+06	5.75E+06
1985	.299	55.4	1.386E+06	6.25E+06
1986	.305	55.1	1.471E+06	6.85E+06
1987	.317	55.3	1.824E+06	7.6E+06

	13	14	15
YEAR	P&E INVEST.	BLDG. INVEST.	DEPREC. EXPENSE
1980	850000	0	
1981	0	0	395000
1982	0	0	395000
1983	850000	1.E+06	395000
1984	0	0	213333
1985	0	0	213333
1986	850000	1.E+06	213333
1987	0	0	331666

	16	17	18	19
	INDEX OF	COMPANY	INDUSTRY	MARKET
YEAR	COMPANY SALES	SLS(UNITS)	SLS(UNITS)	SHARE
1981	1	3.E+07	1.166E+09	2.6
1982	1.1	3.3E+07	1.182E+09	2.8
1983	1.2	3.6E+07	1.198E+09	3
1984	1.3	3.9E+07	1.215E+09	3.2
1985	1.4	4.2E+07	1.23E+09	3.4
1986	1.5	4.5E+07	1.247E+09	3.6
1987	1.6	4.8E+07	1.265E+09	3.8

	20	21	22	23
YEAR	MKTG. EXP. (PCNT SLS)	P.A.T.(PCNT SLS)	P.A.T.($)	CSH FLOW(A.T.)
1980				-2.85E+06
1981	34.9	7.7	1.097245E+06	-353001
1982	35.1	8.4	1.370807E+06	1.493337E+06
1983	35	8.8	1.610162E+06	-110272
1984	33.1	9.9	2.014062E+06	1.953967E+06
1985	32.5	10.4	2.361914E+06	2.281351E+06
1986	32.5	10.4	2.591395E+06	667228
1987	32.7	9.9	2.723974E+06	2.722089E+06

```
            CALCULATED INTERNAL RATE OF RETURN (AFTER TAXES) = 45      PCNT
```

SOURCE: Case material of the Harvard University Graduate School of Business Administration, prepared by Professors Derek Abell and Ralph Sultan, used by permission.

$$Z = (1 - t)(mQ - F - D) \qquad (10\text{--}15)$$

where:

Z = profits after taxes
t = tax rate
m = contribution margin to fixed costs and profit
Q = sales in units
F = fixed manufacturing and marketing costs
D = depreciation

For example, the profits after taxes for 1981 are

$$(1 - .4967)[(\$.258)(30{,}000{,}000) - \$5{,}165{,}000 - \$395{,}000] = \$1{,}097{,}245$$

Column 23 shows the results of the conversion of *profits after taxes* to *cash flow after taxes*. The formula for cash flow is

$$L = Z + D - W - I \qquad (10\text{--}16)$$

where:

L = cash flow after taxes
Z = profits after taxes
D = depreciation
W = working capital in dollars (that is, working capital as a percent of sales, times wholesale price, times sales in units)
I = new investment expenditure

For example, the cash flow after taxes for 1981 is

$$\$1{,}097{,}245 + \$395{,}000 - [.13(\$.473)(30{,}000{,}000)] - 0 = -\$353{,}001$$

The computer now calculates the internal rate of return implicit in the cash flow in column 23. This is found by taking the opportunity cost at the beginning of the period and searching for the interest rate that would discount the future cash flows so that the sum of the discounted cash flows is equal to the initial opportunity cost; this rate turns out to be 45 percent.

Thus computer programs enable the product manager to estimate the financial consequences implied by a particular strategy, environment, and set of costs. The manager can easily calculate the impact on profit of any alterations in the data or assumptions.

Optimal marketing mix The theory of profit optimization leads to finding the optimal marketing expenditure level. Now we want to examine the issue of finding the optimal marketing mix. Clearly, the elements of the mix are somewhat substitutable for each other. A company that is seeking increased sales can think of achieving them by raising the price, or increasing the sales force, advertising budget, or promotion budget. The issue is, What changes in an element, or what combination of elements, would produce the optimal response?

Let us assume that a product manager has identified advertising and promotion dollars as the two major elements of the marketing budget. In principle, there are an infinite number of combinations of spending on these two items. This is shown in Figure 10–3A. If there are no constraints on the levels of advertising and promotion, then every point in the A-S plane shown in Figure 10–3A is a possible marketing mix. An arbitrary line drawn from the origin, called a *constant-mix line*, shows the set of all marketing mixes where the two tools are in a fixed ratio but where the budget varies. Another arbitrary line, called a *constant-budget line*, shows a set of varying mixes that would be affordable with a fixed marketing budget.

Associated with every possible marketing mix is a resulting sales level. Three sales levels are shown in Figure 10–3A. The marketing mix (A_1S_1)—calling for a small budget and a rough equality between advertising and promotion—is expected to produce sales of Q_1. The marketing mix (A_2S_2) involves the same budget with more expenditure on advertising than on promotion; this is expected to produce slightly higher sales, Q_2. The mix (A_3S_3) calls for a larger budget but a relatively equal splitting between advertising and promotion, and with a sales estimate of Q_3. Given these and many other possible marketing mixes, the marketer's job is to find the sales equation that predicts the Qs.

For a given marketing budget, the money should be divided among the various marketing tools in a way that gives the same marginal profit on the marginal dollar spent on each tool. A geometrical version of the solution is shown in Figure 10–3B. Here we are looking down at the A-S plane shown in Figure 10–3A. A constant-budget line is shown, indicating all the alternative marketing mixes that could be achieved with this budget. The curved lines are called *iso-sales curves*. An iso-sales curve shows the different mixes of advertising and personal selling that would produce a given level of sales. It is a projection into the A-S plane of the set of points resulting from horizontal slicing of the sales function shown in Figure 10–3A at a given level of sales. Figure 10–3B shows iso-sales curves for three different sales levels: 75, 100, and 150 units. Given the budget line, it is not possible to attain sales of more than 100 units. The optimum marketing mix is shown at the point of tangency between the budget line and the last-touching iso-sales curve above it. Consequently, the marketing mix $(A°S°)$, which calls for somewhat more advertising than promotion, is the sales-maximizing (and in this case profit-maximizing) marketing mix.

This analysis could be generalized to more than two marketing tools. Dorfman and Steiner proved that the marketing mix of price, promotion, and product quality would be optimized when the following side conditions were met:[17]

| Price elasticity of demand | = | Marginal value product of promotion | = | Quality elasticity of demand times price markup over average cost of production |

Ferber and Verdoorn stated the rule more intuitively:

> In an optimum position the additional sales obtained by a small increase in unit costs are the same for all nonprice instruments and at the same time equal to additional sales accompanying a corresponding decrease in unit prices.[18]

[17] Robert Dorfman and Peter O. Steiner, "Optimal Advertising and Optimal Quality," *American Economic Review,* December 1954, pp. 826–36.

[18] Robert Ferber and P. J. Verdoorn, *Research Methods in Economics and Business* (New York: Macmillan Company, 1962), p. 535.

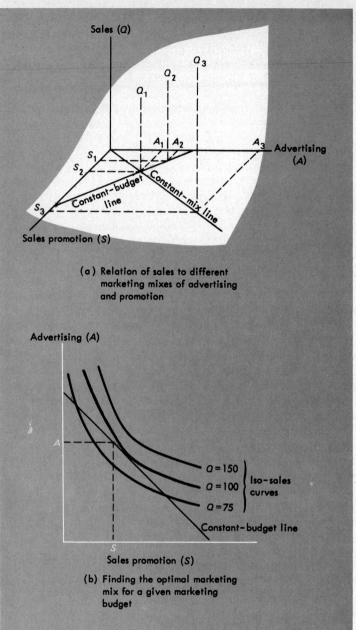

(a) Relation of sales to different marketing mixes of advertising and promotion

(b) Finding the optimal marketing mix for a given marketing budget

FIGURE 10–3
The Sales Function Associated with Two Marketing-Mix Elements

Optimal marketing allocation   A final issue facing the marketing planner is to optimally allocate a given marketing budget to the various *target markets* (TMs). The TMs could be different sales territories, customer groups, or other market segments. With a given marketing budget and mix, it may be possible to increase sales and profits by shifting funds among different markets.

Most marketing managers allocate their marketing budget to the various TMs on the basis of some percentage to actual or expected sales. Consider the following example:

> The marketing manager at the Guardian Oil Company (name disguised) estimates total gasoline sales volume (which combines regular and premium gasoline) and adds premium sales volume back to this figure to yield "profit gallons" (thus giving double weight to premium gasoline sales). The manager then takes the ratio of the advertising budget to the profit gallons to establish a figure for advertising dollars per profit gallon. This is called the prime multiplier. Each market receives an advertising budget equal to its previous year's profit gallons sold multiplied by the prime multiplier. Thus the advertising budget is allocated largely on the basis of last year's company sales in the territory.[19]

Unfortunately, size rules for allocating funds lead to inefficient allocations. They confuse "average" and "marginal" sales response. Figure 10–4A illustrates the difference between the two and makes it clear that there is no reason to assume they are correlated. The two dots in the figure show current marketing expenditures and company sales in two TMs. The company spends $3,000 on marketing in both TMs. Company sales are $40,000 in TM 1 and $20,000 in TM 2. The average sales response to a dollar of marketing effort is thus greater in TM 1 than in TM 2; it is $\frac{40}{3}$ as opposed to $\frac{20}{3}$, respectively. It might therefore seem desirable to shift funds out of TM 2 into TM 1 where the average response is greater. Yet the real issue is one of the marginal response. The marginal response is represented by the *slope* of the sales function through the points. A higher slope has been drawn for TM 2 than for TM 1. The respective slopes show that another $1,000 of marketing expenditure would produce a $10,000 sales increase in TM 2 and only a $2,000 sales increase in TM 1. Clearly, marginal response, not average response, should guide the allocation of marketing funds.

Marginal response is indicated along the sales response function for each territory. We will assume that a company is able to estimate TM sales response functions. Suppose the sales response functions for two TMs are those shown in Figure 10–4B. The company wishes to allocate a budget of B dollars between the two TM's to maximize profits. When costs are identical for the two TMs, then the allocation that will maximize profits is the one that will maximize sales. The funds are optimally allocated when (1) they exhaust the budget and (2) the marginal sales response is the same in both TMs. Geometrically, this means that the slopes of the tangents to the two sales response functions at the optimal allocations will be equal. Figure 10–4B shows that a budget of $6 million would be allocated in the amounts of approximately $4.6 million to TM 1 and $1.4 million to TM 2 to produce maximum sales of approximately $180 million. The marginal sales response would be the same in both TMs.

[19] Donald C. Marschner, "Theory versus Practice in Allocating Advertising Money," *Journal of Business,* July 1967, pp. 286–302.

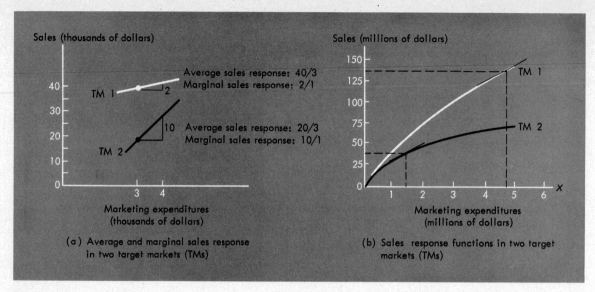

FIGURE 10-4
Sales Response Functions in Two Target Markets (TMs)

The principle of allocating funds to TMs to equalize the marginal response is used in the planning technique called *zero-based budgeting*.[20] The manager of each TM is asked to formulate a marketing plan and estimate the resulting sales for (say) three levels of marketing expenditure, such as 67 percent of the normal level, the normal level, and 133 percent of the normal level. An example is shown in Table 10-6, outlining what the Heinz marketing manager would do with each budget level and his estimate of sales. A sales response function can be fitted through these estimates for each TM. Then higher management reviews these functions and gives serious consideration to shifting funds from TMs with low marginal responses to TMs with higher marginal responses. Thus higher management at Heinz will consider whether it would be worthwhile withdrawing $1 million from the Heinz budget of $3 million (and losing 2 million case sales) or adding $1 million to gain another million in case sales. This depends on how productive the money would be in other parts of the business.

The result of measuring the shape of a sales response function can lead to substantial shifts in marketing strategy by a company. A major oil company had been locating its service stations in every major U.S. city.[21] In many markets, it operated only a small percentage of the total stations. Company management began to question whether this situation was wise. It decided to estimate how the company's city market share varied with its percentage share of marketing expenditures in each city (as measured by the share of outlets). A curve was fitted through observations of the share of outlets and share of markets in differ-

[20] See Paul J. Stonich, *Zero-Base Planning and Budgeting: Improved Cost Control and Resource Allocation* (Homewood, Ill.: Dow Jones-Irwin, 1977).

[21] See John J. Cardwell, "Marketing and Management Science—A Marriage on the Rocks?" *California Management Review*, summer 1968, pp. 3–12.

TABLE 10–6
Illustration of Zero-based Marketing Budgeting

BUDGET (M)	MARKETING PLAN	SALES FORECAST (Q)
$2,000,000	Try to maintain sales and market share in the short term by concentrating sales effort on largest chain stores, advertising only on TV, sponsoring two promotions a year, and carrying on only limited marketing research.	5,000,000 cases
$3,000,000	Implement a coordinated effort to expand market share by contacting 80 percent of all retailers, adding magazine advertising, adding point-of-purchase displays, and sponsoring three promotions during the year.	7,000,000 cases
$4,000,000	Seek to expand market size and share by adding two new product sizes, enlarging the sales force, increasing marketing research, and expanding the advertising budget.	8,000,000 cases

ent cities in its system. The resulting curve was S-shaped (see Figure 10–5). This meant that having a low percentage of stations in a city yielded an even lower percentage of market volume. The practical implication was clear: the company should either withdraw from its weak markets or build them up to, say, having

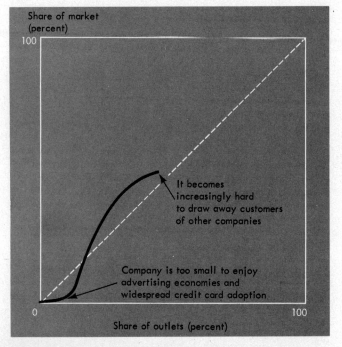

FIGURE 10–5
Share of Market as a Function of Share of Outlets

at least 15 percent of the competitive outlets. Instead of an allocation strategy of locating a few outlets in each of many cities, the oil company should set up a greater number of outlets in a more limited number of cities.

SUMMARY

Marketing planning is one of the key expressions of the modern marketing concept. Systems of formal company planning in general have been slow to evolve, with companies going first through an unplanned stage, then a budgeting-system stage, an annual-planning stage, and finally a strategic-planning stage. Even the term marketing plan has several usages. It turns out that marketing input is necessary in the formulation of various company plans, including the corporate plan, divisional plans, product-line plans, product plans, brand plans, market plans, product/market plans, and functional plans. The contents of marketing plans vary from company to company, but at a minimum should contain an executive summary, situation analysis, objectives and goals, strategy statement, action program, budgets, and controls.

In order to plan effectively, marketing managers must understand the key relationships between marketing expenditures of various types and their sales and profit consequences. These relationships are captured in a profit equation and a sales equation. Both equations can be used in any of three types of planning found in today's companies. Sales volume planning calls for developing a marketing plan to sell a target sales volume. Target profit planning calls for developing a marketing plan to achieve a target profit level. Finally, profit-optimization planning calls for finding the profit-maximizing plan. The latter involves methods of determining the optimal marketing expenditure level, marketing mix, and marketing allocation.

QUESTIONS AND PROBLEMS

1. What kinds of suboptimizing practices often take place in (a) setting sales targets; (b) setting departmental budgets?

2. A marketing decision maker evaluates two alternative marketing strategies and estimates their expected rates of return to be 8 percent and 12 percent, respectively. Which strategy should be chosen if this decision is to be made many times? Which strategy should be chosen if this decision is to be made only once?

3. Suppose the quantity sold (Q) of an item depends upon the price charged (P), the level of advertising expenditure (A), and the level of distribution expenditure (D). Develop a sales response equation (a) where the marginal effect of each marketing variable is uninfluenced by the level of the other marketing variables; (b) where the marginal effect of each marketing variable is influenced by the level of the other variables.

4. A firm is trying to decide how much quality to build into a new machine tool. Illustrate diagrammatically the logic of determining the optimal quality level.

5. How many different marketing mixes could be formulated given a dozen marketing activities that could each be performed at five different levels?

6. Suggest four improvements in the computer program shown in Table 10–5 for projecting sales and profits.

7. Suggest some equation forms that might be used to represent (a) a sales response function when sales increase at a decreasing rate with marketing expenditures; (b) a sales response function where sales increase at an increasing and then decreasing rate.

8. The product manager in charge of a well-established dry breakfast cereal has the following margin and expense statement:

Net Sales		100%
Manufacturing and shipping costs		
Fixed	12.9	
Variable	39.6	
Total		52.5
All other expenses (excluding advertising and merchandising expenses)		
Distribution and delivery expenses	5.4	
Administrative and general expenses	4.0	
Salesmen's expenses	3.5	
Market research	.5	
Total		13.4
Available for advertising and merchandising and profit		34.1

Name several ways the product manager can try to increase profit.

COMPETITIVE MARKETING STRATEGY

Success is a product of unremitting attention to purpose.
BENJAMIN DISRAELI

Top management today is putting increased pressure on marketing executives to think more strategically. And marketing executives are responding by spelling out their strategy in clearer terms in their plans. They are providing better rationales for favoring one strategy over another.

What do we mean by a marketing strategy? We will use the following definition:

> A *marketing strategy* is a consistent, appropriate, and feasible set of principles through which a particular company hopes to achieve its long-run customer and profit objectives in a particular competitive environment.

A company's marketing strategy will have to take several factors into account, including: (1) the company's competitive size and position in the market; (2) the company's resources, objectives, and policies; (3) the competitors' marketing strategies; (4) the target market's buying behavior; (5) the stage of the product life cycle; and (6) the character of the economy. Many of these factors are reviewed in other chapters of the book.

In this chapter, we will focus on the first factor, namely, the dependence of marketing strategy on the company's size and position in the market. Let us imagine a market that has the competitive structure shown in Figure 11–1.

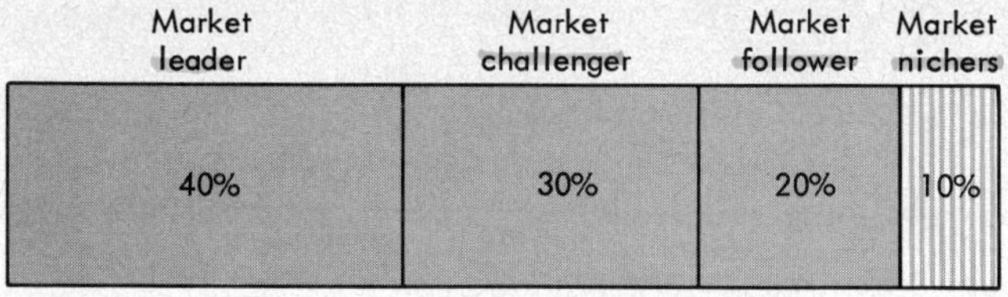

Market leader	Market challenger	Market follower	Market nichers
40%	30%	20%	10%

FIGURE 11–1
Hypothetical Market Structure

Forty percent of the market is in the hands of a *market leader,* the firm with the largest market share. Another 30 percent of the market is in the hands of a *market challenger,* a runner-up firm that is actively trying to expand its share using highly aggressive tactics. Another 20 percent is in the hands of a *market follower,* another runner-up firm that seeks to maintain its market share and not rock the boat. The remaining 10 percent is in the hands of several small firms called *market nichers,* which serve small market segments that they hope will not attract the interest of the larger firms.

We will examine and illustrate the various strategies that are used by market leaders, challengers, followers, and nichers.

MARKET-LEADER STRATEGIES

Almost every industry contains one firm that is acknowledged to be the market leader. This firm has the largest market share in the relevant product market. It usually leads the other firms in price changes, new-product introductions, distribution coverage, and promotional intensity. The leader may or may not be admired or respected, but other firms will acknowledge its dominance. The leader is an orientation point for competitors, a company to either challenge, imitate, or avoid. Some of the best-known market leaders are General Motors (autos), Kodak (photography), U.S. Steel (steel), IBM (computers), Xerox (copying), Procter & Gamble (consumer packaged goods), Caterpillar (earth-moving equipment), Coca-Cola (soft drinks), Sears (retailing), McDonald's (fast food), and Gillette (razor blades).

Unless a dominant firm enjoys a legal monopoly, its life is not altogether easy. It must maintain a constant vigilance. Other firms keep challenging its strengths or trying to take advantage of its weaknesses. The market leader can easily miss a turn in the road and plunge into second place. A product innovation may come along and make the leader's product obsolete (e.g., *Life* magazine was displaced by television). The leader might spend conservatively, expecting hard times, while a challenger spends liberally, expecting a buoyant economy (Montgomery Ward's loss of its retail dominance to Sears after World War II). The dominant firm might grow to look old-fashioned against new and peppier rivals (*Playboy* magazine falling to second place in newsstand circulation after *Penthouse*). The dominant firm may grow sloppy in its costs and find its profits slipping (Food Fair's decline, resulting from poor cost control).

A dominant firm's objective is to remain number one. This objective breaks down into three subobjectives. The first is to find ways to make the total market grow larger. The second is to protect the current market share through good offensive and defensive strategies. The third is to expand the current market share further.

273

Expanding the Total Market

The dominant firm usually stands to gain the most from any increases in market size. If Americans decide to buy ten million cars instead of eight million, General Motors stands to gain the most because they sell one out of every two cars in the U.S. To the extent that General Motors can convince Americans to own two or three cars per family or replace their cars more often, they will benefit. In fact, dominant firms can attempt to expand the total market in three ways.

New users   The first way is to attract *new users* to the product class. Every product class has the potential of attracting buyers who are currently unaware of the product or resisting it because of its price or failure to supply certain features or take certain forms. A manufacturer can search for new users among three groups. For example, a perfume manufacturer can try to convince women who do not use perfume to use perfume *(market-penetration strategy)*, or convince men to start using perfume *(new-market strategy)*, or sell perfume in other countries *(geographical-expansion strategy)*.

One of the modern success stories in developing a new class of users is that of Johnson & Johnson's baby shampoo, the leading brand of baby shampoo. The company became concerned with the future sales growth of this product when the birthrate started to slow down. Their marketers noticed that other members of the family occasionally used the baby shampoo and liked it for their own hair. Management decided to launch an advertising campaign to create adult preference for the baby shampoo. In a short time, Johnson & Johnson baby shampoo became the leading brand in the total shampoo market.

In another case, the Boeing Corporation faced a sharp decline in orders for B-747 jumbo jets when the airlines felt they had acquired enough aircraft to serve the existing level of demand. Boeing concluded that the key to more B-747 sales was to help the airlines attract more people to flying. They analyzed potential flying segments and concluded that the working class did not do much flying, although the cost was within their reach. Boeing encouraged the airlines and the travel industry to create charter travel packages that could be sold to unions, churches, and lodges to get their members to fly. This strategy had proven very successful in Europe and seemed like a natural way to expand the size of the American flying market.

New uses   Another way to expand a market is to discover and promote new uses for the product. For example, the average American eats a dry breakfast cereal three mornings a week. Manufacturers would gain if they could convince people to eat breakfast cereal on other occasions during the day. Some cereals are specifically promoted for their tastiness as snacks, to increase their use frequency.

Du Pont's nylon provides a classic story of new-use expansion. Every time nylon seemed to enter a mature stage of its life cycle, some important new use was discovered. Nylon was first used as a synthetic fiber for parachutes; then as a major material in women's stockings; later, a major material in women's blouses and men's shirts; still later, it entered automobile tires, seat upholstery, and carpeting.[1] Each new use started the product on a new life cycle. Credit goes to the

[1] See Theodore Levitt, "Exploit the Product Life Cycle," *Harvard Business Review*, November–December 1965, pp. 81–94. The original study is reported in Jordan P. Yale, "The Strategy of Nylon's Growth," *Modern Textiles Magazine*, February 1964, pp. 32, 49. By permission.

continuous research and development program conducted by Du Pont to discover new uses.

In even more cases, the credit goes to users rather than the company for discovering new uses. Vaseline petroleum jelly started out as a simple machine lubricant, and over the years users have reported all kinds of new uses for the product, including use as a skin ointment, a healing agent, and a hair dressing.

Arm & Hammer, a manufacturer of baking soda, had a product on its hands whose sales were on a plateau for 125 years. Baking soda had hundreds of uses but no single important use. The company discovered some consumers were using it as a refrigerator deodorant. It decided to mount a heavy advertising and publicity campaign focusing on this single use and succeeded in the first year of promotion in getting half of the homes in America to place an open box of baking soda in their refrigerator.

In these cases, the company's task is to do a good job of monitoring consumer usages through periodic inquiries and surveys. This is as true for industrial products as consumer products. Von Hippel, who has studied how ideas for new industrial products originate, claims that most of the ideas come from users rather than company research-and-development laboratories.[2] This makes *marketing research* an important contributor to company growth and profits.

More usage A third market-expansion strategy is to convince people to *use more of the product per use occasion.* If a cereal manufacturer can convince consumers of the benefits of eating a full bowl of cereal instead of half a bowl, total sales will increase. Procter & Gamble advises that its Head and Shoulders shampoo is more effective in reducing dandruff with two applications instead of one.

A very creative example of a company stimulating higher usage per occasion is the Michelin Tire Company (French). The company was seeking ways to encourage French car owners to drive their cars more miles per year—thus leading to more tire replacement. They conceived the idea of rating restaurants throughout France on a three-star system and publishing the results in a guidebook. Many of the best restaurants were reported in the south of France, leading many Parisians to consider making weekend excursions to the south of France.

Protecting Market Share

In addition to expanding the total market size, the dominant firm must be eternally vigilant in protecting its current market share. Challenger firms are constantly stalking the market leader looking for possible weaknesses. Fuji attacks Kodak; Avis attacks Hertz; Bic attacks Gillette; *Penthouse* attacks *Playboy.* The plight of a number-one firm, such as Procter & Gamble, is aptly described below.

> Colgate can pick and choose where it wants to hit the giant; the giant, by contrast, must defend itself everywhere. It's not unlike the situation in guerilla warfare, where the guerillas, with a lot less to defend, can concentrate their forces on one or two points and take a heavy toll. This is what Colgate has been doing: attacking first one P&G strong point, then another, hoping to keep P&G off balance.[3]

---

[2] See Eric von Hippel, *A Customer-Active Paradigm for Industrial Product Idea Generation,* unpublished working paper, Sloan School of Management, MIT, Cambridge, Mass., May 1977.

[3] "Colgate vs. P&G," *Forbes,* February 1, 1966, pp. 27–28.

Dominant firms cannot be expected to sit idly by as smaller firms nibble away at them. Some years ago, Chrysler's share of automobile sales started to rise from 12 percent to 18 percent, following the appointment at Chrysler of a new top management team, the restyling of their line of cars, and the intensive grooming of dealers. At this point, one rival marketing executive was overheard to say, "If they (Chrysler) go to 20 percent, it will be over our dead bodies. We've still got some leverage."[4] Thus the Big Two (General Motors and Ford) have an idea of a proper maximum share for the third largest firm in the industry, and they will initiate a counteroffensive when this share is approached.

What can the market leader do to discipline an upstart firm? From a military point of view, they can try "brinkmanship," "massive retaliation," "limited warfare," "graduated response," "diplomacy of violence," "threat systems," and so on. From a business point of view, they can practice one of four broad strategies:

1. *Innovation strategy.* A strategy of innovation is the most constructive from the point of view of the firm and the society. It means that the dominant firm refuses to be content with the way things are and leads the industry in new-product ideas, customer services, means of distribution, and cost-cutting discoveries. By continuously creating new customer values, the dominant firm takes the best course possible to discourage competitors. It is applying the military "principle of the offensive": the commander must exercise initiative, set the pace, and exploit enemy weaknesses. It makes use of the principle that the best defense is a good offense.

2. *Fortification strategy.* A strategy of fortification is also a positive approach to maintaining leadership. The dominant firm keeps its prices reasonable in relation to the perceived value of its offer and competitors' offers. It produces its brand in a variety of sizes and forms so as to cover the varying preferences of the market instead of letting competitors get a foothold. It creates additional brands to fortify its hold on shelf space and dealers' efforts.

3. *Confrontation strategy.* Often the dominant firm will face an extremely aggressive challenger whose actions demand a quick and direct response. The dominant firm can wage a *promotional war,* engaging in massive promotional expenditures that the aggressor cannot match. The promotional increases can take the form of more or better deals to the trade if that leads the trade to stock up and push the dominant firm's brand. The dominant firm may engage in a *price war,* being careful, however, to avoid the charge of *predatory pricing.*[5] A large pharmaceutical company uses the threat of a price war whenever another firm is considering entering its markets. The dominant firm leaks information to the press that it is contemplating a price reduction. The word reaches the potential competitor, who gets frightened and withdraws.

4. *Harassment strategy.* The dominant firm will sometimes resort to a *harassment strategy.* It might go to major suppliers and threaten to reduce its purchases if the latter supply the upstart firm. Or it might put pressure on distributors not to carry the competitor's product. Or their salesmen might bad-mouth the competitors. Or it might try to hire away the better executives of an aggressive firm. When a dominant firm is bent on taming or destroying a competitor, there is very little it is not capable of, except as it is constrained by its own policies and the threat of triple-damage suits by the aggrieved competitor.

[4] "If the Big Three's a Crowd, Blame Chrysler," *Newsweek,* May 20, 1968, p. 84.

[5] See Ralph Cassady, Jr., "The Price Skirmish—A Distinctive Pattern of Competitive Behavior," *California Management Review,* winter 1964, pp. 11–16.

The dominant firm can often restrain its competitors through legal devices. It might push legislation that would be more unfavorable to the competitors than to itself. A common example is that of the Sunday blue laws banning business on Sunday, which established merchants' support because these laws retard the growth of the discount house. These and other laws have been used at various times by dominant interests in the drug, hardware, and grocery business to prevent the growth of pesky new channels of distribution.[6]

A harassment strategy is apt to be used by dominant firms that have grown sluggish, inefficient, or overly content. Their expenses rise rapidly; their aspirations do not keep up with the available resources, and the firm gets soft. This condition becomes a strong attractor of competitors, and the dominant firm is thrown back to confrontation or harassment tactics to defend its position.

The principles of protecting market leadership are admirably illustrated by companies such as Procter & Gamble, Caterpillar, IBM, General Motors, and Hertz, all of whom have shown a remarkable ability to protect their market shares against repeated attacks by very able challengers. Their viability is not based on doing one thing well but rather on doing everything right. They don't leave themselves exposed in any respect. We shall examine the cases of Procter & Gamble and Caterpillar.

Procter & Gamble   P&G is considered to be the nation's most skillful marketer of consumer packaged goods. It enjoys market leadership in virtually every market in which it sells. It has the leading toothpaste (Crest), the leading disposable diaper (Pampers), the leading laundry detergent (Tide), and the leading anti-dandruff shampoo (Head and Shoulders). Its market leadership rests on several principles:

1. *Product innovation.* P&G is a practitioner of product innovation that relies heavily on benefit segmentation. It enters markets by introducing a new product with a new benefit rather than launching a me-too product backed by heavy advertising. For example, P&G spent ten years researching and developing the first effective anticavity toothpaste, Crest. It spent several years researching the first effective over-the-counter antidandruff shampoo, Head and Shoulders. The company thoroughly tests its new products with consumers, and only when real preference is indicated does it proceed with launching them in the national market.

2. *Quality strategy.* P&G designs its products with higher-than-average quality. Furthermore, the company makes a continuous effort to improve the product quality over the product's life. When they announce "new and improved," they mean it. This is in contrast to many companies that, after establishing the quality level, rarely improve it, and to some companies that deliberately reduce the quality in an effort to squeeze out more profit.

3. *Product flanking.* P&G makes a practice of producing each of its brands in several sizes and forms to satisfy varying preferences in the marketplace. This practice also gives its brands more total shelf space and prevents competitors from spotting uncovered needs in the market.

4. *Multibrand strategy.* P&G is the originator and master practitioner of the art of launching several brands in the same product category. For example, it produces ten brands of laundry detergent, each positioned somewhat differently in the consumers' mind. The trick is to design brands that compete against specific

[6] See Joseph C. Palamountain, Jr., *The Politics of Distribution* (Cambridge, Mass.: Harvard University Press, 1955).

competitors' brands rather than each other. Each brand manager runs the brand independently of the other brand managers but knows he or she is competing for resources and results. Having several brands on the shelf, the company "locks up" shelf space and gains more clout with distributors.

5. **Brand-extension strategy.** P&G will often exploit its good brand names by introducing new products under the same brand name. For example, the Ivory brand has been extended from a soap to also include liquid soap and a detergent. Launching a new product under a well-known brand name gives it more recognition and credibility with much less advertising outlay.

6. **Heavy advertising.** P&G is the nation's largest consumer-packaged-goods advertiser, spending over $460 million per year. It never stints on spending money to create strong consumer awareness and preference.

7. **Aggressive sales force.** P&G has a top-flight field sales force, which is very effective in gaining shelf space and retailer cooperation in point-of-purchase displays and promotions.

8. **Effective sales promotion.** P&G has a sales promotion department that stands ready to advise brand managers on the most effective promotions to achieve particular objectives. The department collects the results of different types of consumer and trade deals and develops an expert sense of their effectiveness under varying circumstances. At the same time, P&G prefers to minimize the use of sales promotion, preferring to rely on the long-term buildup of consumer preference through advertising.

9. **Competitive toughness.** P&G carries a big stick when it comes to constraining aggressors. P&G is willing to spend large sums of money to outpromote new competitive brands and prevent them from getting a foothold in the market.

10. **Manufacturing efficiency.** P&G's reputation as a great marketing company should not obscure its greatness as a manufacturing company. The company spends large sums of money developing and improving production operations to keep its costs among the lowest in the industry.

11. **Brand-management system.** Some fifty years ago P&G originated the brand-management system in which one executive is totally responsible for the development of each brand. The system has been copied by many competitors, but frequently without the success that P&G has achieved through perfecting its system over a number of years.

Thus we see that P&G's market leadership strategy is not based on doing one thing well but on a successful orchestration of all the factors that count in market leadership.

Caterpillar Since the 1940s, Caterpillar has enjoyed the dominant position in the construction equipment industry. Its tractors, crawlers, and loaders, painted in familiar yellow, are a common sight at any construction area and account for 50 percent of the world's sales of heavy construction equipment. Caterpillar has managed to retain leadership in spite of charging a premium price for its equipment and being challenged by a number of able competitors, including John Deere, Massey-Ferguson, International Harvester, and J.I. Case. Several principles combine to explain their success:

1. **Premium-product quality.** Caterpillar produces high-quality equipment known for its reliability. Reliability is a major consideration in the purchase of heavy industrial equipment. It is said that Caterpillar designs its equipment with a heavier gauge of steel than necessary, to convince buyers of its superior quality.

2. *Extensive-and-efficient-dealership system.* Caterpillar maintains the largest number of independent construction-equipment dealers in the industry. Its 260 dealers are located throughout the world and carry a complete line of Caterpillar equipment. Caterpillar dealers can focus all of their attention on Caterpillar equipment without needing to carry other lines. Competitors' dealers, on the other hand, normally lack a full line and have to carry complementary, non-competing lines. Caterpillar is in a position to enfranchise the finest dealers (a new dealership costs the franchisee $5,000,000) and spends the most money in training, servicing, and motivating them.

3. *Superior service.* Caterpillar has built a worldwide parts and service system that is second to none in the industry. Caterpillar can deliver replacement parts and service anywhere in the world within a few hours of equipment breakdown. This degree of service is very hard for competitors to match without a substantial investment. Any competitor duplicating the service level would only neutralize Caterpillar's advantage rather than gaining any net advantage.

4. *Superior parts management.* Thirty percent of Caterpillar's sales volume and over 50 percent of its profits come from the sale of replacement parts. Caterpillar has developed a superior parts-management system to keep margins high in this end of the business.

5. *Premium price.* Caterpillar is able to charge a price premium of 10 to 20 percent on comparable equipment because of the extra value perceived by buyers.

6. *Full-line strategy.* Caterpillar produces a full line of construction equipment to enable buyers to do one-stop buying.

7. *Good financing.* Caterpillar arranges generous financial terms to customers buying its equipment. This is important because of the large sums of money involved.

Expanding Market Share

Market leaders can also try to grow through further expansion of their market share. The well-publicized Profit Impact of Market Strategies (PIMS) studies indicate that *profitability* (measured by pretax ROI) rises with *market share.*[7] The empirical relationship is shown in Figure 11–2A.[8]

> According to a PIMS report, "The average ROI for businesses with under 10 percent market share was about 9 percent. . . . On the average, a difference of 10 percentage points in market share is accompanied by a difference of about 5 points in pretax ROI." The PIMS study shows that businesses with market shares above 40 percent earn an average ROI of 30 percent, or three times that of those with shares under 10 percent.

These findings have been taken by many major firms to mean that they should not only strive for market dominance but also try to push their market share higher. This is a sound pursuit for dominant marketers whose market share is less than (say) 50 percent. But for dominant marketers with a share of over 50 percent—such as General Motors, Eastman Kodak, IBM, Campbell's, Gillette, Coca-Cola, Kellogg, and Caterpillar—market share expansion may be both ex-

[7] Sidney Schoeffler, Robert D. Buzzell, and Donald F. Heany, "Impact of Strategic Planning on Profit Performance," *Harvard Business Review,* March–April 1974, pp. 137–45; and Robert D. Buzzell, Bradley T. Gale, and Ralph G. M. Sultan, "Market Share—A Key to Profitability," *Harvard Business Review,* January–February 1975, pp. 97–106.

[8] See Buzzell et al., "Market Share," pp. 97, 100. The results, however, should be interpreted cautiously because (1) the data came from a limited number of industries and (2) there was some variance around the main line of relationship.

pensive and risky. They might be better off spending their time building up market size rather than market share.

The first reason for self-restraint has to do with the possibility of provoking antitrust action. Jealous competitors and antitrust legislators are likely to cry "monopolization" if the dominant firm makes further inroads on market share. Each company has to assess the shape of the antitrust probability function it faces. The hypothetical function in Figure 11–2B indicates that the firm feels the antitrust risk rises after it achieves a 25 percent market share and becomes almost a certainty at a 75 percent market share. This rise in the risk would cut down the attractiveness of pushing market share gains too far.

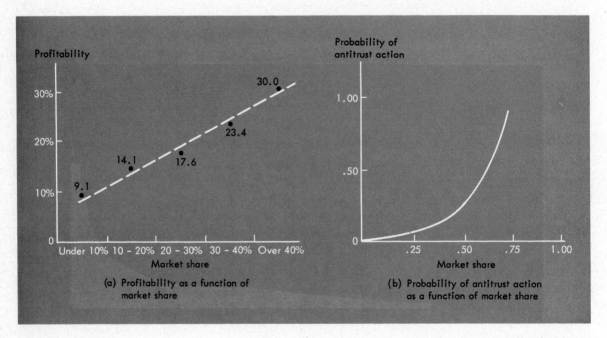

FIGURE 11–2
Market Share Functions

The second reason is economic. The cost of making further gains in market share after a large share has been achieved may rise fast and reduce the profit margin. A company that has (say) 60 percent of the market must recognize that the "holdout" customers and distributors may be holding out because of negative attitudes toward the company, loyalty to competitive suppliers, unique needs that cannot be met by the leader, or the desire to deal with smaller suppliers. Furthermore, the competitors are likely to fight harder to defend their diminishing market share. The cost of legal work, public relations, and lobbying rises with market share. After a certain point, profitability may stabilize or decline with further market share gain. This, combined with the risk of antitrust action, may caution the leader to stabilize rather than expand the existing market share. In fact, some dominant marketers may even consider reducing their share to reduce their risk, and there are techniques for doing this.[9]

MARKET-CHALLENGER STRATEGIES

The firms that occupy second, third, and fourth place in an industry can be called runner-up or trailing firms. They may be quite large in their own right although smaller than the leader. Examples include Colgate, Ford, Montgomery Ward, Avis, Westinghouse, Schlitz, and Pepsi-Cola. These runner-up firms can adopt one of two postures. They can decide to attack the leaders and others in a grab for further market share (market challengers). Or they can be content to play ball and not rock the boat (market followers). We shall examine the strategies of market challengers in this section.[10]

Market challengers can attempt to gain market share in three ways. The first is through a *direct-attack strategy* (also called head-on strategy) in which a challenger tries to best the market leader through sheer doggedness and fight. For years, Colgate launched direct attacks on Procter & Gamble but without much success.[11] The second way is through a *backdoor strategy* (also called end-run or blindside) in which the challenger runs *around* the dominant firm rather than *into* it. Timex gained its leadership in the low-price watch market by selling its watches through mass-merchandise outlets rather than through conventional jewelry stores that were "locked up" by the major watch manufacturers. The third way is through a *guppy strategy* of attacking smaller competitors rather than the market leader. Many major beer companies owe their growth not to taking share away from the leader or each other but to the gobbling up of smaller regional and local beer companies in the process of competition.

Basically the market challenger has to decide whether to aggress against the leader, other runner-ups, or smaller firms, based on discovered weaknesses. It then builds a strategy to take advantage of the weakness. Yet challengers are found from time to time going after competitors with nothing more than a strong determination to win. Recently the second-place razor blade manufacturer in Brazil decided to go after Gillette, the market leader. Management was asked if they were offering the consumer a better blade. "No," was the reply. "A lower price?" "No." "A better package?" "No." "A cleverer advertising campaign?" "No." "Better allowances to the trade?" "No." "Then how do you expect to take share away from Gillette?" they were asked. "Will power," was the reply. Needless to say, their offensive failed.[12]

[9] See Paul E. Bloom and Philip Kotler, "Strategies for High Market-Share Companies," *Harvard Business Review*, November–December 1975, pp. 63–72.

[10] For additional reading, see C. David Fogg, "Planning Gains in Market Share," *Journal of Marketing*, July 1974, pp. 30–38; and Bernard Catry and Michel Chevalier, "Market Share Strategy and the Product Life Cycle," *Journal of Marketing*, October 1974, pp. 29–34.

[11] "How to Be Happy Though No. Two," *Forbes*, July 15, 1976, pp. 36, 38.

[12] Also see William E. Fruham, Jr., "Pyrrhic Victories in Fights for Market Share," *Harvard Business Review*, September–October 1972, pp. 100–107.

In fact, several strategies are available to the market challenger who is seeking an advantage vis-à-vis competition. They are described here.

1. *Price-discount strategy.* A major attack strategy for challengers is to offer buyers a product of comparable quality to the leader's at a lower price. (See Figure 4–13, p. 86. Leader in cell 1, challenger in cell 2.) The Fuji Corporation used this strategy to attack Kodak's preeminence in the photographic-paper field. Its paper is of comparable quality and is priced 10 percent lower than Kodak's. Kodak chose not to lower its price, with the result that Fuji made strong gains in market share. Bristol-Meyers adopted a price-discount strategy in launching its new-type aspirin called Datril against Johnson & Johnson's leading brand, Tylenol.[13] It budgeted a heavy advertising campaign to announce its lower price and to convince consumers that all the new-type aspirins are identical. Tylenol, however, countered by lowering its price and Bristol-Meyers's brand never achieved the expected market share. Texas Instruments is perhaps the prime practitioner of price cutting. It will enter a market by offering a comparable-quality product that is progressively lowered in price to gain market share and lower costs. Texas Instruments is willing to forego profits in the first few years in order to gain unchallenged market leadership. They did this with transistors and hand calculators and now seem bent on doing it in the low-price watch market.[14]

For a price-discount strategy to work, three assumptions must be fulfilled. First, the challenger must be able to convince buyers that its product and service are of comparable quality to the leader's. Second, the buyers must be sensitive to the price difference and feel comfortable about turning their back on existing suppliers. Third, the market leader must stubbornly stick to its price in spite of the competitor's attack.

2. *Cheaper-goods strategy.* Another strategy to gain market position is to offer the market an average- or low-quality product at a much lower price. (See Figure 4–13, p. 86. Leader in cell 1, challenger in cell 5 or 9.) This works when there is a sufficient segment of price-conscious buyers. Firms that get established through this strategy, however, are vulnerable to attack by "cheaper-goods" firms whose prices are even lower. In defense, they try to upgrade their quality gradually to the level of the market leader or slightly less.

3. *Prestige-goods strategy.* A market challenger can attempt to get around the market leader by launching a higher-quality product and charging a higher price. (See Figure 4–13, p. 86. Leader in cell 1, challenger goes to northwest of cell 1.) Mercedes gained on Cadillac in the American market by offering the American public a car that was of even higher quality and higher priced. Some attackers, after gaining market acceptance for their premier products, later roll out lower-price products.

4. *Product-proliferation strategy.* The challenger can go after the leader by launching a large number of product variants. Hunt went after Heinz's leadership in the ketchup market by creating several new ketchup flavors and bottle sizes, in contrast to Heinz's reliance on one flavor of ketchup, sold in a limited number of bottle sizes. The success of this strategy depends upon the new product's managing to attract and hold customers and the failure of the leader to react fast enough with its own product variants.

5. *Product-innovation strategy.* The challenger may pursue the path of product innovation to attack the leader's position. Polaroid and Xerox are two examples of companies whose success is based on continuously introducing outstanding in-

---

[13] See "A Painful Headache for Bristol-Myers?" *Business Week*, October 6, 1975, pp. 78–80.

[14] See "The Great Digital Watch Shake-Out," *Business Week*, May 2, 1977, pp. 78–80.

novations in the camera and copying fields, respectively. Miller recently took over second place in the beer industry because of its successful development of a light beer and its introduction of "pony-sized" bottles for light-beer drinkers. In many ways, the public gains most from challenger strategies oriented toward product innovation.

6. *Improved-services strategy.* The challenger may attack the leader by finding ways to offer new services or better service. IBM achieved its success in the computer market by recognizing that customers were more interested in the quality of the software and the service than in the hardware. Avis's famous attack on Hertz, "We're only second. We try harder," was based on promising and delivering cleaner cars and faster service than Hertz.

7. *Distribution-innovation strategy.* A challenger should examine the possibility of expanding its market share by developing a new channel of distribution. Avon became one of the largest and most profitable cosmetics companies by perfecting the ancient method of door-to-door selling instead of battling other cosmetic firms in conventional store outlets. U.S. Time Company decided to sell its low-price Timex watches through mass merchandise channels, thus bypassing the jewelry stores.

8. *Manufacturing-cost-reduction strategy.* Some companies see the key to building market share as lying in achieving lower manufacturing costs than their competitors'. The lower manufacturing costs can be achieved by more efficient purchase of materials, lower labor costs, and more modern production equipment. A company can use its lower costs to price more aggressively to gain market share. This strategy has been the key to the successful Japanese invasion of various world markets. A company like Texas Instruments reverses the process by first lowering its prices aggressively, then winning market share, and then finding its costs falling through the "experience curve."[15] As it captures more volume, its costs continue to fall, thus providing a basis for further price cutting or profit taking.

9. *Intensive advertising promotion.* Some challengers seek to gain on the leader by increasing the quantity and/or quality of their advertising and promotion. When Hunt went after Heinz in the ketchup market, it built its annual spending level to $6.4 million as against Heinz's $3.4 million. Miller Beer has similarly been outspending Budweiser in its attempt to achieve first place in the U.S. beer market. Substantial promotional spending, however, is usually not a sensible strategy unless the challenger's product or advertising message exhibits some superiority over competition.

A challenger rarely succeeds in improving its market share by relying on only one strategy element. Its success depends on designing a total strategy that will improve its position over time. This is shown in the following examples.

Pepsi-Cola and Coca-Cola Before the Second World War, Coca-Cola dominated the American soft-drink industry. There was really no second-place firm worth mentioning. "Pepsi raised hardly a flicker of recognition in Coke's consciousness."[16] Pepsi-Cola was a newer drink that cost less to manufacture and whose taste was generally thought to be less satisfying than Coke's. Its major

---

[15] The experience curve describes the rate at which costs fall as a function of accumulated production experience. See "Selling Business a Theory of Economics," *Business Week*, September 8, 1973, pp. 86–88.

[16] Alvin Toffler, "The Competition that Refreshes," *Fortune*, May 1961. Also see "Pepsi Takes on the Champ," *Business Week*, June 12, 1978, pp. 88–97.

selling point was that it offered more drink for the same price. Pepsi exploited this difference by advertising, "Twice as much for a nickel, too." Its bottle was plain, and it carried a paper label that often got dirty in transit, thereby adding to the general impression that it was a second-class soft drink.

During the Second World War, Pepsi and Coke both enjoyed increased sales as they followed the flag around the world. After the war ended, Pepsi's sales started to fall relative to Coke's. A number of factors contributed to Pepsi's problems, including its poor image, poor taste, poor packaging, and poor quality control. Furthermore, Pepsi had to raise its prices to cover increased costs, and this made it less of a bargain than before. Morale was quite low at Pepsi toward the end of the 1940s.

At this point, Alfred N. Steele came to the presidency of Pepsi-Cola with a great reputation for merchandising. He and his staff recognized that the main hope lay in transforming Pepsi from a cheap imitation of Coke into a first-class soft drink. They recognized that this turnaround would take several years. They conceived of a *grand offensive* against Coke that would take place in two phases. In the first phase, which lasted from 1950 to 1955, the following steps were taken: First, the taste of Pepsi was improved. Second, the bottle and other corporate symbols were redesigned and unified. Third, the advertising campaign was redesigned to upgrade Pepsi's image. Fourth, Steele decided to concentrate on hitting the take-home market, which Coke had relatively neglected. Finally Steele singled out twenty-five cities for a special push for market share.

By 1955, all of Pepsi's major weaknesses had been overcome, sales had climbed substantially, and Steele was ready for the next phase. The second phase consisted of mounting a direct attack on Coke's "on-premise" market, particularly the vending-machine and cold-bottle segments, which were growing fast. Another decision was to introduce new size bottles that offered convenience to customers in the take-home and cold-bottle markets. Finally, Pepsi offered to finance any of its bottlers who were willing to buy and install Pepsi vending machines. These various steps, running from 1955 to 1960, again led to considerable sales growth for Pepsi. Within one decade, Pepsi's sales had grown fourfold.

Yamaha versus Honda In the early 1960s, Honda had established itself as the number one motorcycle brand in the United States. Its lightweight machines with their great eye appeal, the slogan, "You Meet the Nicest People on a Honda," and an aggressive sales organization and distribution network all combined to greatly expand the market for motorcycles. Yamaha, another Japanese manufacturer, decided to enter the market against Honda. Its first step was to study the leader's major weaknesses, which included several dealers who had grown rich and lazy, abrupt management changes, discouragement of franchise-seeking dealers, and a neglect of promoting the mechanical aspects of their motorcycles. Yamaha offered franchises to the best of the Honda-rejected franchisees and built an enthusiastic sales team to train and motivate their dealers. They improved their motorcycle to the point that they could claim and demonstrate its mechanical superiority. They spent liberally on advertising and sales promotion programs to build buyer awareness and dealer enthusiasm. When motorcycle safety became a big issue, they designed superior safety features and advertised extensively. The sum of these strategies propelled Yamaha into a clear second position in an industry of over fifty manufacturers.

MARKET-FOLLOWER STRATEGIES

Not all runner-up companies choose to challenge the market leader. The effort to draw away the leader's customers is never taken lightly by the leader. If the challenger's lure is lower prices, improved service, additional product variants, the leader can match these all in sufficient time to defuse the attack. The leader probably has more staying power in an all-out battle. A hard fight might leave both firms worse off, and this means the challenger has to think twice before attacking. Unless the challenger is able to launch a preemptive strike—through a substantial product innovation or distribution breakthrough—he often settles in favor of following rather than attacking the leader.

Patterns of "conscious parallelism" are quite common in homogeneous product industries of high-capital intensity, such as steel, fertilizers, and chemicals. The opportunities for product differentiation and image differentiation are low; service quality is often comparable; price sensitivity runs high. Price wars can erupt at any time. The mood in these industries is against short-run grabs for market share, because that strategy only provokes retaliation. Most firms decide against stealing each other's customers. Instead they present similar offers and values to buyers, usually by copying the leader. Market shares tend to remain highly stable.

This is not to say that market followers are without strategies. A market follower must be clear on how it is going to hold on to current customers and win a fair share of new ones. Each follower must work a set of target markets to which it can bring distinctive advantages—location, services, financing. It must be ready to enter new markets that are opening up. The company must keep its manufacturing costs low and its product quality and services high. Followership is not the same as passivity or being a carbon copy of the leader. The follower has to define its own path to growth, but decides to do this in a way that does not create intense competitive retaliation.

Market followers, although they have lower market shares than the leader, may be as profitable or even more profitable. A recent study reported that numerous companies with less than half the market share of the leader had a five-year average return on equity that surpassed the industry median.[17] Burroughs (computers), Crown Cork & Seal (metal containers), and Union Camp Corporation (paper) were among the successful market followers. The keys to their success were conscious market segmentation and concentration, effective research and development, profit emphasis rather than market share emphasis, and strong top management.

MARKET-NICHER STRATEGIES

Almost every industry includes a number of minor firms that operate in some part of the market and try to avoid clashing with the majors. These smaller firms attempt to find and occupy market niches that they can serve effectively through specialization and that the majors are likely to overlook or ignore.

---

[17] R. G. Hamermesh, M. J. Anderson, Jr., and J. E. Harris, "Strategies for Low Market Share Businesses," *Harvard Business Review*, May–June 1978, pp. 95–102.

These firms are variously called market nichers, market specialists, threshold firms, or foothold firms. Market niching is of interest not only to small companies but also to smaller divisions of larger companies that are not able to achieve major standing in that industry.

The salvation of these firms is to find one or more market niches that are safe and profitable. An ideal market niche would have the following characteristics:

1. The niche is of sufficient size and purchasing power to be profitable.
2. The niche has growth potential.
3. The niche has been bypassed or neglected by major competitors.
4. The firm has superior competencies to serve the niche effectively.
5. The firm can defend its position against an attacking major because of the goodwill it has built up.

The key idea in nichemanship is specialization. The firm has to identify a viable form of specialization along market, customer, product, or marketing-mix lines. At least ten specialist roles are open to a market nicher.

1. *End-use specialist.* This firm decides to specialize in serving one type of end-use customer. For example, a law firm can decide to specialize in the criminal, civil, or business law markets.
2. *Vertical-level specialist.* This firm specializes at some vertical level of the production-distribution cycle. For example, a copper firm may concentrate on the production of raw copper, copper components, or finished copper products.
3. *Customer-size specialist.* This firm concentrates on selling to either small-, medium-, or large-size customers. Many nichers specialize in serving small customers because they are neglected by the majors.
4. *Specific-customer specialist.* This firm limits its selling to one or a few major customers. Many firms sell their entire output to a single company such as Sears or General Motors.
5. *Geographic specialist.* This firm focuses on the needs of a certain locality, region, or area of the world.
6. *Product or product-line specialist.* This firm produces only one product line or product. Within the laboratory equipment industry are firms that produce only microscopes, or even more narrowly, only lenses for microscopes.
7. *Product-feature specialist.* This firm specializes in producing a certain type of product or product feature. Rent-a-Junk, for example, is a California car rental agency that rents only "beat-up" cars.
8. *Job-shop specialist.* This firm stands ready to make customized products as ordered by the customer.
9. *Quality/price specialist.* This firm chooses to operate at the low or high end of the market. For example, Hewlett-Packard specializes in the high-quality, high-price end of the hand-calculator market.
10. *Service specialist.* This firm offers or excels in one or more services not readily available from other firms. An example would be a bank that takes loan requests over the phone or dispatches an officer to deliver the money at the client's home or office.

Thus we see that small firms have many opportunities to serve customers in profitable ways. Many small firms discover good niches through blind luck, although good opportunities can be detected and developed in a more systematic manner.

SUMMARY

Marketing strategy forms the heart of a marketing plan. Yet many marketing plans are vague on strategy, taking up most of the space with very specific tactics. A marketing strategy is a consistent, appropriate, and feasible set of principles through which a particular company hopes to achieve its long-run customer and profit objectives in a particular competitive environment.

A marketing strategy has to take several factors into account, a prime one being the company's position in the particular market, specifically whether it is a market leader, challenger, follower, or nicher.

A market leader has three problems, those of expanding the total market, protecting its market share, and expanding its market share. The market leader is usually extremely interested in expanding market size through looking for new users, new uses, and more usage. The leader also protects itself through strategies of innovation, fortification, confrontation, and occasionally harassment. The most sophisticated leaders cover themselves by doing everything right, leaving no openings for competitive attack. As for expanding their market share, leaders whose shares are already large will put less emphasis on that because it would increase the risk of antitrust action.

A market challenger is a firm that is seeking to aggressively expand its market share by attacking the leader, other runner-up firms, or smaller firms in the industry. Among the most common challenger strategies are price discounts, cheaper goods, prestige goods, product proliferation, product innovation, improved services, distribution innovation, manufacturing cost reduction, and intensive advertising.

A market follower is a runner-up firm that chooses not to rock the boat, usually out of fear that it stands to lose more than it might gain in the process. The follower is not without a strategy, however, and seeks to use its particular competences to participate actively in the growth of the market. Some followers enjoy a higher rate of return on equity than the leaders in their industry.

A market nicher is a smaller firm that chooses to operate in some part of the market that is specialized and not likely to attract the larger firms. Market nichers often become specialists in some end-use, vertical level, customer size, specific customer, geographic area, product or product line, product feature, or service.

QUESTIONS AND PROBLEMS

1. Many people have noted a similarity between business strategy and military strategy. There are the gasoline "price wars," the "border clashes" and "skirmishes" of the major computer manufacturers, the "escalating arms budgets" of the soap companies, "guerilla warfare" by Purex against the soap giants, the "sabotaging" of and "spying" on test markets by competitors, and so on. Without denying the usefulness of military insights and principles, name some limitations of the analogy between business and military competition.

2. Comment on the following statements made about the appropriate marketing strategy of smaller firms: (a) "The smaller firm should concentrate on pulling away the larger firm's customers, while the larger firm should concentrate on stimulating new customers to enter the market." (b) "Larger firms should pioneer new products and the smaller ones stick to copying them."

3. What information about each major competitor should a company regularly gather?

4. It might appear that Caterpillar has no vulnerabilities. However, this is not true. Name some potential threats to Caterpillar.

5. What are some of the marketing principles that General Motors has used to maintain its four decades of leadership in the U.S. auto industry?

6. Briefly critique the following marketing strategy statement: "The company will develop the best product and the best service at the lowest price."

7. The major producer of dance shoes is interested in expanding the total market for its ballet shoes. These are flat-soled slippers which are different from the pointed shoes used for toe dancing. Suggest ways they can do so.

8. Identify the specialist roles assumed by the following firms: (a) Kenmore; (b) Coors Beer; (c) Rolls Royce; (d) Mom and Pop grocery with home delivery.

Product Life-Cycle Strategy

12

We are now ready to examine the role played by product life cycle and market evolution in the formulation of marketing strategy. A product's marketing strategy needs periodical revision during its passage through the life cycle. The first part of the chapter will examine the concept of product life cycle and consider appropriate strategies during the stages of introduction, growth, maturity, and decline. The second part will examine how markets as a whole evolve under the impetus of innovation and competition.

THE CONCEPT OF PRODUCT LIFE CYCLE

A product's sales position and profitability can be expected to change over time. The product life cycle is an attempt to recognize *distinct stages* in the *sales history* of the product. Corresponding to these stages are distinct opportunities and problems with respect to marketing strategy and profit potential. By identifying the stage that a product is in, or may be headed toward, companies can formulate better marketing plans.[1]

---

[1] For some excellent articles on product life cycle, see Robert D. Buzzell, "Competitive Behavior and Product Life Cycles," in *New Ideas for Successful Marketing*, ed. John S. Wright and

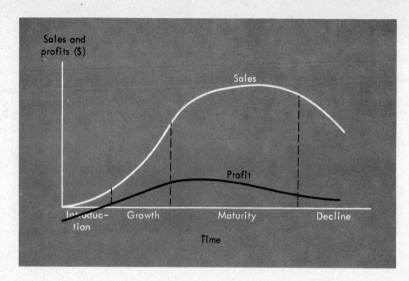

FIGURE 12–1
Sales and Profit Life Cycles

Most discussions of product life cycle (PLC) portray the sales history of a typical product as following the form of an S-shaped sales curve as illustrated in Figure 12–1. This curve is typically divided into four stages known as *introduction, growth, maturity,* and *decline*.[2] *Introduction* is a period of slow growth as the product is introduced in the market. The profit curve in Figure 12–1 shows profits as almost nonexistent in this stage because of the heavy expenses of product introduction. *Growth* is a period of rapid market acceptance and substantial profit improvement. *Maturity* is a period of a slowdown in sales growth because the product has achieved acceptance by most of the potential buyers. Profits peak in this period and start to decline because of increased marketing outlays (not shown) to sustain the product's position against competition. Finally, *decline* is the period when sales continue a strong downward drift and profits erode toward the zero point.

The designation of where each stage begins and ends is somewhat arbitrary. Usually the stages are based on where the rate of sales growth or decline tends to become pronounced. Polli and Cook proposed an operational measure based on a normal distribution of percentage changes in real sales from year to year.[3]

Not all products pass through the idealized S-shaped product life cycle

Jac L. Goldstucker (Chicago: American Marketing Association, 1966), pp. 46–68; William E. Cox, Jr., "Product Life Cycles as Marketing Models," *Journal of Business,* October 1967, pp. 375–84; Theodore Levitt, "Exploit the Product Life Cycle," *Harvard Business Review,* November–December 1965, pp. 81–94; Rolando Polli and Victor Cook, "Validity of the Product Life Cycle," *Journal of Business,* October 1969, pp. 385–400; and Thomas A. Staudt and Donald A. Taylor, *A Managerial Introduction to Marketing* (Englewood Cliffs, N.J.: Prentice-Hall, 1970), chap. 10.

[2] Some authors distinguish additional stages. *Maturity* describes a stage of sales growth slowdown and *saturation* a stage of flat sales after sales have peaked. A stage of *petrification* follows *decline* if sales again stabilize at some low but positive level. See George C. Michael, "Product Petrification: A New Stage in the Life Cycle Theory," *California Management Review,* fall 1971, pp. 88–91.

[3] Polli and Cook, "Product Life Cycle."

shown in Figure 12–1. Some products show a rapid growth from the very beginning, thus skipping the slow sales start implied by the introductory stage. Other products, instead of going through a rapid-growth stage, go directly from introduction to maturity. Some products move from maturity to a second period of rapid growth. Cox studied the product life cycles of 754 ethical-drug products and found six different product life-cycle patterns.[4] The most typical form was a "cycle-recycle" pattern (see Figure 12–2A). Cox explained the second "hump" in sales as being caused by a traditional promotional push in the decline stage. Some investigators have reported a "scalloped" life-cycle pattern (see Figure 12–2B), which represents a succession of life cycles for this product based on the discovery of new-product characteristics, new usages, or new markets. Often the more anomalous life-cycle patterns are really temporal sequences of the normal life-cycle pattern.

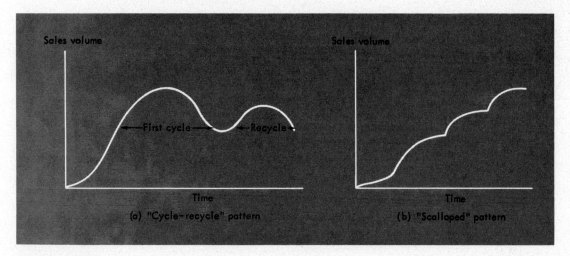

FIGURE 12–2
Some Anomalous Product Life-Cycle Patterns

Studies by Buzzell of grocery food products and Polli and Cook of various consumer nondurables showed the PLC concept to hold up well for many product categories. Those planning to use this concept must investigate the extent to which the PLC concept holds up for products in their industry. They will learn whether the normal sequence of stages is followed and the average duration of each stage. Cox found that a typical ethical drug that followed the normal PLC cycle spanned an introductory period of one month, a growth stage of six months, a maturity stage of fifteen months, and a decline stage that exceeded the sum of the previous three stages—mainly because of the reluctance of manufacturers to drop drugs from their catalogs. These lengths must be reviewed periodically. It appears that increasing competition is leading to a shortening of PLCs over time, which means that products make profits for shorter periods.

[4] Cox, "Product Life Cycles."

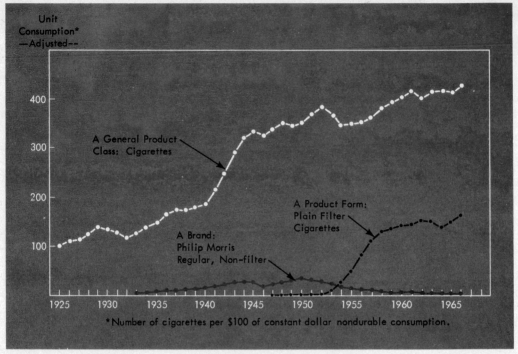

Unit
Consumption*
—Adjusted—

400 —

300 —

A General Product
Class: Cigarettes

200 —

A Product Form:
Plain Filter
Cigarettes

100 —

A Brand:
Philip Morris
Regular, Non-filter

1925   1930   1935   1940   1945   1950   1955   1960   1965

*Number of cigarettes per $100 of constant dollar nondurable consumption.

SOURCE: Rolando Polli and Victor Cook, "Validity of the Product Life Cycle," *Journal of Business,* October 1969, p. 389.

FIGURE 12–3
PLCs for a Product Class, Product Form, and Brand

The PLC concept should be defined with respect to whether the product is a product class (cigarettes), a product form (plain filter cigarettes), or a brand (Philip Morris regular nonfilter). (See Figure 12–3.) The PLC concept has a different degree of applicability in these three cases. Product classes have the longest life histories, longer than particular product forms, and certainly longer than most brands. The sales of many product classes can be expected to continue in the mature stage for an indefinite duration since they are highly related to population (cars, perfume, refrigerators, and steel). Product forms, on the other hand, tend to exhibit the standard PLC histories more faithfully than do product classes. Product forms such as the dial telephone and cream deodorants seem to pass through a regular history of introduction, rapid growth, maturity, and decline. As for brands, a brand's sales history can be erratic because changing competitive strategies and tactics can produce substantial ups and downs in sales and market shares, even to the extent of causing a mature brand to suddenly exhibit another period of rapid growth.

Fad and Fashion Life Cycles   There are two special categories of new-product life cycles that should be distinguished from the others: fads and fashions. *Fads* are practices or interests that come quickly into being, are adopted with great zeal, peak early, and decline very fast. Their acceptance cycle is short, and they tend to attract only a limited following. Fads often have a bizarre or capricious aspect, as when people start buying "pet rocks" or "streak" (run naked). Fads appeal to people who are searching for excitement or who want a way to distinguish themselves from others or have something to talk about to others. Fads do not survive because they normally do not satisfy a strong need, or at least do not satisfy it well. It is difficult to predict whether something will only be a fad, and if so, how long it will last—a few days, weeks, or months. The amount of media attention it receives, along with other factors, will influence its duration.

Fashions, in contrast, are interests that tend to grow slowly, remain popular for a while, and decline slowly. Fashion life cycles come closer to resembling the normal product life cycle. There are fashion styles in cars (long and low look), women's clothing (mini-skirt), and men's haircuts (long hair). Some fashions are classic and last a long time, such as a man's dark blue business suit and a woman's basic black dress.

The length of a fashion cycle is hard to predict in advance. Wasson believes that fashions come to an end because they represent an inherent purchase compromise such that the consumer starts looking for missing attributes after a while.[5] For example, as automobiles get shorter, they get less comfortable, and then a growing number of buyers start wanting longer cars. Furthermore, too many consumers adopt the fashion, thus turning others away. Reynolds suggests that the length of a particular fashion cycle depends on the extent to which the fashion meets a genuine need, is consistent with other trends in the society, as well as societal norms and values, and does not meet technological limits as it develops.[6] Robinson, however, sees fashions as living out inexorable cycles regardless of economic, functional, or technological changes in society.[7]

We have described the PLC concept without offering any underlying explanation in market terms. Support for it lies in the theory of the diffusion and adoption of innovations (see pp. 342–46). When a new product appears, steps must be taken by the company to stimulate awareness, interest, trial, and purchase. This takes time, and in the introductory stage only a few persons ("innovators") will buy it. If the product is satisfying, larger numbers of buyers ("early adopters") are drawn in. The entry of competitors into the market speeds up the adoption process by increasing the market's awareness and by exerting a downward pressure on prices. More buyers come in ("early majority") as the product is legitimized. Eventually the rate of growth decreases as the proportion of potential new buyers approaches zero. Sales become steady at the replacement purchase rate. Eventually they decline as new-product classes, forms, and brands appear and divert the interest of the buyers from the existing product. Thus the product life cycle is closely related to normal developments that can be expected in the diffusion and adoption of any new product.

The PLC concept is useful mainly as a framework for developing effective marketing strategies in different stages of the product life cycle. We now turn to the major stages and consider the appropriate marketing strategies.

[5] Chester R. Wasson, "How Predictable Are Fashion and Other Product Life Cycles?" *Journal of Marketing,* July 1968, pp. 36–43.

[6] William H. Reynolds, "Cars and Clothing: Understanding Fashion Trends," *Journal of Marketing,* July 1968, pp. 44–49.

[7] Dwight E. Robinson, "Style Changes: Cyclical, Inexorable, and Foreseeable," *Harvard Business Review,* November–December 1975, pp. 121–31.

The introduction stage starts when the new product is first made available for general purchase in the marketplace. Prior to introduction, the product has been under a long period of development, which might have included some test marketing in a few cities but not a full-scale launching. The actual introduction of the product in one or more markets takes time, and sales growth is apt to be slow. Such well-known products as instant coffee, frozen orange juice, and powdered coffee creamers lingered for many years before they entered a stage of rapid growth. Buzzell identified four causes for the slow growth of many processed-food products:

1. Delays in the expansion of production capacity
2. Technical problems (working out the bugs)
3. Delays in making the product available to customers, especially in obtaining adequate distribution through retail outlets
4. Customer reluctance to change established behavior patterns[8]

In the case of expensive new products, sales growth is retarded by additional factors such as:

5. Small number of buyers who are attuned to innovations
6. High cost of the product inhibits purchase

In the introductory stage, profits are negative or low because of the low sales and heavy distribution and promotion expenses. Much money is needed to attract distributors and "fill the pipelines." Promotional expenditures are at their highest ratio to sales "because of the need for a high level of promotional effort to (1) inform potential consumers of the new and unknown product, (2) induce trial of the product, and (3) secure distribution in retail outlets."[9]

There are only a few competitors and they produce basic versions of the product, since the market is not ready for product refinements. The firms direct their selling effort to those buyers who are the readiest to buy, usually higher-income groups. Prices tend to be on the high side because "(1) costs are high due to relatively low output rates, (2) technological problems in production may have not yet been fully mastered, and (3) high margins are required to support the heavy promotional expenditures which are necessary to achieve growth."[10]

In launching a new product, marketing management can set a high or a low level for each marketing variable such as price, promotion, distribution, and product quality. Working only with price and promotion, management can choose one of the four strategies shown in Figure 12–4.

A *rapid-skimming strategy* consists of launching the new product with a high price and a high promotion level. The firm charges a high price in order to recover as much gross profit per unit as possible. It spends a lot on promotion to convince the market of the product's merits even at the high-price level. The high promotion serves to accelerate the rate of market penetration. This

[8] Buzzell, "Competitive Behavior," p. 51.

[9] Ibid, p. 51.

[10] Ibid, p. 52.

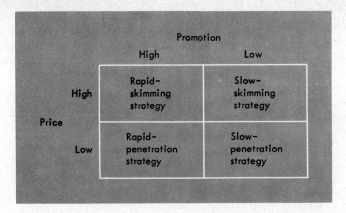

FIGURE 12–4
Four Introductory Marketing Strategies

strategy makes sense under the following assumptions: (1) a large part of the potential market is unaware of the product; (2) those who become aware of the product are eager to have it and are able to pay the asking price; (3) the firm faces potential competition and wants to build up brand preference.

A *slow-skimming strategy* consists of launching the new product with a high price and low promotion. The purpose of the high price is to recover as much gross profit per unit as possible; and the purpose of the low promotion is to keep marketing expenses down. This combination is expected to skim a lot of profit from the market. This strategy makes sense under the following assumptions: (1) the market is relatively limited in size; (2) most of the market is aware of the product; (3) those who want the product are prepared to pay a high price; and (4) there is little threat of potential competition.

A *rapid-penetration strategy* consists of launching the product with a low price and heavy promotion. This strategy promises to bring about the fastest rate of market penetration and the largest market share for the company. This strategy makes sense under the following assumptions: (1) the market is large in size; (2) the market is relatively unaware of the product; (3) most buyers are price sensitive; (4) there is strong potential competition; and (5) the company's unit manufacturing costs fall with the scale of production and accumulated manufacturing experience.

A *slow-penetration strategy* consists of launching the new product with a low price and low level of promotion. The low price will encourage the market's rapid acceptance of the product; at the same time, the company keeps its promotion costs down in order to realize more net profit. The company firmly believes that market demand is highly price-elastic but minimally promotion-elastic. This strategy makes sense if (1) the market is large; (2) the market is highly aware of the product; (3) the market is price sensitive; and (4) there is some potential competition.

GROWTH STAGE

If the new product satisfies the market, sales will start climbing substantially. The early innovators will continue their purchasing and a large number of conventional consumers will begin to follow their lead, especially if there is favorable word of mouth. New competitors will enter the market attracted by the opportunities for large-scale production and profit. They will introduce new features in the product and this will expand the market. The increase in the number of competitors leads to an increase in the number of distribution outlets, and factory sales jump just to fill the pipelines.

Prices tend to remain where they are or fall only slightly during this period, insofar as demand is managing to increase quite rapidly. Companies maintain their promotion expenditures at the same or at a slightly raised level to meet competition and continue educating the market. Sales rise much faster, causing a decline in the promotion-sales ratio.

Profit margins peak during this stage as promotion costs are spread over a larger volume, and unit manufacturing costs fall faster than price declines owing to the "experience-curve" effect. During this stage, the firm tries to sustain rapid market growth as long as possible. This is accomplished in several ways:

1. The firm undertakes to improve product quality and add new features and models.
2. It vigorously searches out new market segments to enter.
3. It keeps its eyes open to new distribution channels to gain additional product exposure.
4. It shifts some advertising copy from building product awareness to trying to bring about product acceptance and purchase.
5. It decides when the time is right to lower prices to attract the next layer of price-sensitive buyers into the market.

The firm that aggressively pursues any or all of these market-expanding strategies will increase its competitive position. But this comes at additional cost. The firm in the growth stage faces a tradeoff between high market share and high current profit. By spending a lot of money on product improvement, promotion, and distribution, it can capture a dominant position; but it forgoes maximum current profit in the hope, presumably, of making up for it in the next stage.

MATURITY STAGE

At some point a product's rate of sales growth will slow down, and the product will enter a stage of relative maturity. This stage normally lasts much longer than the previous stages, and it poses some of the most formidable challenges to marketing management. *Most products are in the maturity stage of the life cycle, and therefore most of marketing management deals with the mature product.*

The maturity stage can be divided into three phases. The first phase is called *growth maturity.* Here, the rate of sales growth starts to decline because of distribution saturation. There are no new distribution channels to fill, although some laggard buyers are continuing to enter the market. The second phase is *stable maturity,* when sales become level on a per capita basis because of market saturation. Most potential consumers have tried the product, and future sales are governed by the rate of population growth and replacement demand. The third phase is *decaying maturity.* The absolute level of sales now starts to decline as some of the customers move toward other products and substitutes.

The beginning of a slowdown in the rate of sales growth has the effect of producing overcapacity in the industry. This overcapacity leads to intensified competition. Competitors engage more frequently in markdowns and off-list pricing. There is a strong increase in promotional budgets, in the form of trade and consumer deals. Other firms increase their research and development budgets to find better versions of the product. These steps, to the extent that they do not stimulate adequate sales increases, mean some profit erosion. Some of the weaker competitors start dropping out. The industry eventually consists of a set of well-entrenched competitors whose basic orientation is toward gaining competitive advantage.

The product manager of a mature product should not be content to simply defend its current position. A good offense will provide the best defense of the product. Three basic strategies are available in this stage: market modification, product modification, and marketing-mix modification.

Market modification   The product manager first looks for opportunities to find new buyers for the product. There are several possibilities.

First the manager looks for *new markets and market segments* that have not yet tried the product. The key to the growth of air freight service, for example, is the constant search of the industry for new business markets to whom they can demonstrate the benefits of air freight over ground transportation.

Second, the manager looks at ways to stimulate *increased usage* among present customers. A common practice of food manufacturers, for example, is to list several recipes on their packages to broaden the consumers' uses of the product.

Third, the manager may want to consider *repositioning* the brand to achieve larger brand sales, although this will not affect total industry sales. For example, a manufacturer of a chocolate drink mix may find that its heavy users are mostly older people. This firm should give serious consideration to trying to reposition the drink in the youth market, which is experiencing faster growth.

Product modification   Managers also try to break out of a stagnant sales picture by initiating calculated changes in the product's characteristics that will attract new users and/or more usage from current users. The *product relaunch* can take several forms.

A strategy of *quality improvement* aims at increasing the functional performance of the product—such aspects as its durability, reliability, speed, and taste. A manufacturer can often make a real gain on competition by launching the "new and improved" automobile, television set, coffee, or cigarette. Grocery manufacturers often call this a "plus" launch and talk about a new additive or advertise the terms "stronger," "bigger," or "better." This strategy is effective to the extent that (1) the product is capable of quality improvement, (2) buyers believe the claims about improved quality, and (3) a sufficient number of buyers are highly responsive to improved quality.

A strategy of *feature improvement* aims at adding new features that expand the product's versatility, safety, or convenience. For example, the addition of power to hand lawn mowers increased the speed and ease of cutting grass. Manufacturers then worked on the problem of engineering better safety features. Some manufacturers have built in conversion features so that the lawn mower doubles as a snow plow. All of these feature improvements are distinguishable from quality improvements on the one hand and styling improvements on the other. Stewart outlines five advantages flowing from a strategy of feature improvement:

1. The development of new functional features is one of the most effective means of building a company image of progressiveness and leadership.
2. Functional features are an extremely flexible competitive tool because they can be adapted quickly, dropped quickly, and often can be made optional at very little expense.
3. Functional features allow the company to gain the intense preference of pre-selected market segments.
4. Functional features often bring the innovating company free publicity.
5. Functional features generate a great amount of sales-force and distributors' enthusiasm.[11]

The chief disadvantage is that feature improvements are highly imitable; unless there is a permanent gain from being first, the feature improvement may not pay.

A strategy of *style improvement* aims at increasing the aesthetic appeal of the product in contrast to its functional appeal. The periodic introduction of new car models amounts to style competition rather than quality or feature competition. In the case of packaged-food and household products, companies introduce color and texture variations and often put great emphasis on package restyling, treating the package as an extension of the product. The outstanding advantage of a style strategy is that each firm may achieve a unique market identity and secure some durable share of the market on the basis of that identification. Yet styling competition also brings a number of problems. First, it is difficult to predict whether people—and which people—will like a new style. Second, style changes usually mean discontinuing the old style, and the company risks losing some of the customers who liked the old style.

Marketing-mix modification As a final category of mature-product strategy, the product manager should consider the possibility of stimulating sales through altering one or more elements of the marketing mix. One tactic is to cut *prices* in order to attract new triers and competitors' customers. Another is to develop a more effective *advertising* campaign that attracts consumers' attention and interest. A more direct way to attract other brand users is through aggressive promotion—trade deals, cents-off, gifts, and contests. The company can also consider moving into higher-volume *market channels*, particularly discount channels, if they are in a growth stage. The company can also offer new or improved service to the buyer as a patronage-building step.

The main problem with relying exclusively on marketing-mix modification is that these steps are highly imitable by competition, especially price reductions, additional services, and mass-distribution penetration. This means that the firm may not gain as much as expected, and, in fact, all firms may pay a price in the form of profit erosion.

---

[11] John B. Stewart, "Functional Features in Product Strategy," *Harvard Business Review,* March–April 1959, pp. 65–78.

Most product forms and brands eventually enter a stage of sustained sales decline. The decline may be slow, as in the case of oatmeal; or rapid, as in the case of the Edsel automobile. Sales may plunge to zero and the product may be withdrawn from the market, or sales may petrify at a low level and continue for many years at that level.

Sales decline for a number of reasons. Technical advances may give birth to new product classes and forms that become effective substitutes. Changes in fashion or tastes lead to buyer migration. The lower costs of imported products hurt the domestic producers. All of these have the effect of intensifying overcapacity and price competition, leading to a serious erosion of profits.

As sales and profits decline, a number of firms withdraw from the market in order to invest their resources in more-profitable areas. Those remaining in the industry tend to reduce the number of product offerings. They withdraw from smaller market segments and marginal trade channels. The promotion budget is reduced. The price may also be reduced to halt the decline in demand.

Unfortunately, most companies have not developed a well-thought-out policy for handling their aging products. Sentiment plays a role:

> But putting products to death—or letting them die—is a drab business, and often engenders much of the sadness of a final parting with old and tried friends. The portable, six-sided pretzel was the first product The Company ever made. Our line will no longer be our line without it.[12]

Logic also plays a role. Sometimes it is expected, or hoped, that product sales will improve when the economy improves. Sometimes the fault is thought to lie in the marketing program, and so the company makes plans to revise it. Management may feel that the solution lies in product modification. When none of these explanations works, a weak product may be retained because of its alleged contribution to the sales of the company's other products. The ultimate argument may be that its sales volume at least covers out-of-pocket costs, and the company may temporarily have no better way of keeping its fixed resources employed.

Unless strong retention reasons exist, carrying a weak product is very costly to the firm. The cost of sustaining a weak product is not just the amount of uncovered overhead and profit. No financial accounting can adequately convey all the hidden costs:

> The weak product tends to consume a disproportionate amount of management's time.
>
> It often requires frequent price and inventory adjustments.
>
> It generally involves short production runs in spite of expensive setup times.
>
> It requires both advertising and sales-force attention that might better be diverted to making the "healthy" products more profitable.
>
> Its very unfitness can cause customer misgivings and cast a shadow on the company's image.

[12] R. S. Alexander, "The Death and Burial of 'Sick' Products," *Journal of Marketing*, April 1964, p. 1.

The biggest cost imposed by carrying weak products may well lie in the future. By not being eliminated at the proper time, these products delay the aggressive search for replacement products; they create a lopsided product mix, long on "yesterday's breadwinners" and short on "tomorrow's breadwinners"; they depress current profitability and weaken the company's foothold on the future.

A company faces a number of tasks and decisions to insure the effective handling of its aging products.

Identifying the weak products   The first task is to establish a system that will identify those products that are in a declining stage. Six steps are involved:

1. A product-review committee is appointed with the responsibility for developing a system for periodically reviewing weak products in the company's mix. This committee includes representatives from marketing, manufacturing, and the controller's office.

2. This committee meets and develops a set of objectives and procedures for reviewing weak products.

3. The controller's office supplies data for each product showing trends in market size, market share, prices, costs, and profits.

4. This information is run against a computer program that identifies the most dubious products. The criteria include the number of years of sales decline, market-share trends, gross profit margin, and return on investment.

5. Products put on the dubious list are then reported to those managers responsible for them. The managers fill out diagnostic and prognostic rating forms showing where they think sales and profits on dubious products will go with no change in the current marketing program and with their recommended changes in the current program.

6. The product-review committee examines the product-rating form for each dubious product and makes a recommendation (a) to leave it alone, (b) to modify its marketing strategy, or (c) to drop it.[13]

Determining marketing strategies   In the face of declining sales, some firms will abandon the market earlier than others. The firms that remain enjoy a temporary increase in sales as they pick up the customers of the withdrawing firms. Thus any particular firm faces the issue of whether it should be the one to stay in the market until the end. For example, Procter & Gamble decided to remain in the declining liquid-soap business until the end and made good profits as the others withdrew.

If it decides to stay in the market, the firm faces further strategic choices. The firm could adopt a *continuation strategy*, in which case it continues its past marketing strategy: same market segments, channels, pricing, and promotion. The product simply continues to decline until at last it is dropped from the line. Or the firm could follow a *concentration strategy*, in which case it concentrates its resources only in the strongest markets and channels while phasing out its efforts elsewhere. Finally, it could follow a *harvesting strategy*, in which case it sharply reduces its expenses to increase its current profits, knowing this will accelerate the rate of sales decline and ultimate demise of the product. In some sit-

[13] This system is spelled out in detail in the author's "Phasing Out Weak Products," *Harvard Business Review*, March–April 1965, pp. 107–18. Also see Paul W. Hamelman and Edward M. Mazze, "Improving Product Abandonment Decisions," *Journal of Marketing*, April 1972, pp. 20–26.

uations the hard-core loyalty may remain strong enough to allow marketing the product at a greatly reduced level of promotion and at the old or even a higher price, either of which will mean good profits. An interesting example is afforded by Ipana toothpaste:

> Ipana toothpaste was marketed by Bristol-Myers until 1968, when it was abandoned in favor of promoting new brands. In early 1969, two Minnesota businessmen picked up the Ipana name, concocted a new formula but packaged the product in tubes similar to those used by the former marketer. With no promotion, the petrified demand for Ipana turned out to be $250,000 in the first seven months of operation.[14]

The drop decision   When a product has been singled out for elimination, the firm faces some further decisions. First, it has the option of selling or transferring the product to someone else or dropping it completely. Second, it has to decide whether the product should be dropped quickly or slowly. Third, it has to decide what level of parts inventory and service to maintain to cover existing units.

The key characteristics of each of the four stages of the product life cycle are summarized in Table 12–1. In addition, the table summarizes the type of responses typically made by business organizations in each stage.[15]

[14] "Abandoned Trademark Turns a Tidy Profit for Two Minnesotans," *Wall Street Journal,* October 27, 1969, p. 1.

[15] A more elaborate version of normative marketing responses for each stage of the PLC cycle is found in Chester R. Wasson, *Dynamic Competitive Strategy and Product Life Cycles* (Austin, Texas: Austin Press, 1978).

TABLE 12–1
Product Life Cycle: Characteristics and Responses

	INTRODUCTION	GROWTH	MATURITY	DECLINE
Characteristics				
Sales	Low	Fast growth	Slow growth	Decline
Profits	Negligible	Peak levels	Declining	Low or zero
Cash flow	Negative	Moderate	High	Low
Customers	Innovative	Mass market	Mass market	Laggards
Competitors	Few	Growing	Many rivals	Declining number
Responses				
Strategic focus	Expand market	Market penetration	Defend share	Productivity
Mktg. expenditures	High	High (declining %)	Falling	Low
Mktg. emphasis	Product awareness	Brand preference	Brand loyalty	Selective
Distribution	Patchy	Intensive	Intensive	Selective
Price	High	Lower	Lowest	Rising
Product	Basic	Improved	Differentiated	Rationalized

SOURCE: Peter Doyle, "The Realities of the Product Life Cycle," *Quarterly Review of Marketing,* summer 1976, pp. 1–6.

To date, the PLC concept has been the major concept used by marketers to interpret product and market dynamics. Its usefulness varies in different decision-making situations. As a *planning* tool, the PLC concept appears useful in characterizing the main marketing realities of each stage and indicating the major alternative marketing strategies available to the firm in each stage. As a *control* tool, the PLC concept allows the company to roughly gauge how well a product is doing in relation to successful and comparable products that were launched in the past. As a *forecasting* tool, the PLC concept may be of less usefulness because sales histories exhibit various patterns in practice, and the stages last for varying durations.

At the same time, PLC theory has its share of criticism. Critics have said that the life-cycle patterns are too variable, that it is difficult to know what stage the product really is in, and the company marketing actions can influence the course of the product life cycle. Dhalla and Yuspeh have argued that management action based on the PLC is actually harmful in many cases:

> Suppose a brand is acceptable to consumers but has a few bad years because of other factors—for instance, poor advertising, delisting by a major chain, or entry of a "me-too" competitive product backed by massive sampling. Instead of thinking in terms of corrective measures, management begins to feel that its brand has entered a declining stage. It therefore withdraws funds from the promotion budget to finance R&D on new items. The next year the brand does even worse, panic increases. . . . Clearly, the PLC is a *dependent* variable which is determined by marketing actions; it is not an *independent* variable to which companies should adapt their marketing programs.[16]

To this can be added another criticism, that PLC focuses on what is happening to a particular product rather than on what is happening in the overall market. It produces a product-oriented picture rather than a market-oriented picture. It needs to be complemented by a theory that analyzes the evolution of the market itself and the opportunities that are continually emerging.

THE CONCEPT OF MARKET EVOLUTION

Firms need a way to understand not only market statics but also market dynamics. Market statics addresses the question: What are the nature, size, and operations of a particular market? Market dynamics addresses the question: How do markets evolve through time? Firms need a way to anticipate the evolutionary path of a market as it is marked by new needs, competitors, technology, channels, and other developments.

Stages in Market
Evolution

A market can be viewed as evolving through stages of market crystallization, expansion, fragmentation, reconsolidation, and termination. We shall describe and illustrate these stages below.

Market-crystallization stage Before a market materializes, it exists as a *latent market*. A *latent market* consists of people who share a similar need or want for

---

[16] Nariman K. Dhalla and Sonia Yuspeh, "Forget the Product Life Cycle Concept!" *Harvard Business Review*, January–February 1976, pp. 102–12, here p. 105.

something that does not yet exist. For example, people want a means of more rapid calculation than can be achieved by mental calculation or by using a paper and pencil. Until recently, this need was imperfectly satisfied through abacuses, slide rules, and large desk calculators.

Suppose John Smith, an entrepreneur, recognizes the latent interest of people in a more convenient and rapid means of calculation. Suppose he imagines a solution in the form of a small, hand-size electronic calculator. He works hard and succeeds in developing a workable prototype. Having solved the technical problem, this entrepreneur now must turn his attention to the marketing problem. He faces the problem of determining target markets, product attributes, price, distribution channels, and promotion for the initial version of this product. Here we will concentrate on only one of these problems, that of determining the product attributes. Suppose he has to decide on two product attributes: (1) *physical size* and (2) *number of arithmetic functions*. Being market oriented, the entrepreneur decides to interview a sample of potential buyers. They are asked to state their preference level for each attribute. Each person's preference, or ideal product, can be represented by a point (called ideal point) in a diagram showing the two attributes.

Suppose the resulting preferences are those shown in Figure 12–5A. Evidently target customers differ greatly in their design preferences. Some consumers want a simple four-function calculator (adding, subtracting, multiplying, and dividing) and others want more functions (calculating percentages, square roots, logs, and so forth). Some consumers want a small hand calculator and others want a large one. When buyer preferences are evenly scattered in a market, it is called a *diffused-preference market*.

The entrepreneur's problem is to design an optimal product for this market.[17] The entrepreneur faces three broad options.

1. He or she can locate the new product in one of the corners of the market *(a single-niche strategy)*;
2. He or she can simultaneously launch two or more products to capture two or more parts of the market *(a multiple-niche strategy)*;
3. He or she can locate the new product in the middle of the market *(a mass-market strategy)*.

For small firms, a single-niche market strategy makes the most sense. A small firm has insufficient resources for capturing and holding the mass market. Larger firms would enter and clobber the small firm. Its best bet is to specialize the new product in size, number of functions, or some other attributes and capture a corner of the market that won't attract competitors for a long time. If it has adequate resources, it might design and introduce products in two or more niches.

If the firm is large, it makes sense to go after the mass market by designing a product that is "medium" in size and number of functions. A product in the center will minimize the sum of the distances of existing preferences from the product. An electronic hand calculator designed for the mass market will create the minimum total dissatisfaction.

---

[17] This problem is trivial if consumers' preferences turn out to be concentrated; the product will be located where the market is. If there are distinct clusters of preference, the entrepreneur can design a product for the largest cluster or for the cluster that the company can serve best.

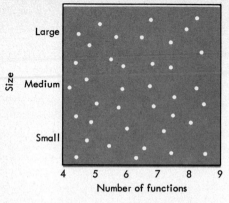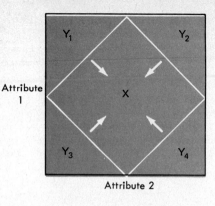

FIGURE 12–5
Market Space
Diagrams

(a) Market-crystallization stage—
consumer-preference distribution
for hand calculator

(b) Market-expansion stage —
illustration of a strangulation
strategy with four brands of
firm Y attacking firm X's
brand

We will assume that the pioneer firm is large and desires to design a product for the mass market. It is subsequently launched and sales start to climb. We can say that the stage of *market crystallization* has begun.

Market-expansion stage   An interesting question now arises. Where will a second firm enter the market, assuming that the first firm has established itself in the center? This begins the *market-expansion stage*. The second firm has three broad options:

1. It can locate its brand in one of the corners (*a single-niche strategy*).
2. It can locate its brand next to the first competitor (*a mass-market strategy*).
3. It can launch two or more products in different unoccupied corners of the market space (*a multiple-niche strategy*).

If the second firm is small, it will want to avoid head-on competition with the pioneer. It will launch a product in one of the market corners. Thus Hewlett-Packard chose to produce an advanced and premium-priced hand calculator instead of battling it out with Bowmar, the pioneer, for control of the mass market.

If the second firm is large, it might choose to launch its brand in the center against the pioneer firm. The two firms can easily end up sharing the mass market almost equally. In political markets, the two major candidates will each go after the mass market because a candidate needs 50-plus percent to win.

A large second firm can alternatively try to implement a multiniche strategy. Procter & Gamble will occasionally enter a market containing a large entrenched competitor, and instead of launching a me-too product or single-segment product, it introduces a succession of products aimed at different segments. Each entry creates its own loyal following and takes some business away from the major competitor. Soon the major competitor is surrounded, its revenue is weakened, and it is in no position to launch a counteroffensive of new brands in outlying segments. P&G, in a moment of final triumph, then launches a brand against the major segment. This is called a strangulation strategy and is illustrated in Figure 12–5B.

Market-fragmentation stage   Each successive firm that enters the market will go after some position, either locating next to a competitor or seeking to serve some new segment. A point is reached where the competitors now cover and serve all the major market segments. In fact, they go further and invade each other's segments, reducing everyone's profit levels in the process. The market splits into finer and finer fragments. This is called the *market-fragmentation stage.* There are a few uncovered segments whose needs are not met by existing products, but they are too small to be served economically. The market reaches maturity, with few new products emerging at this stage. This is illustrated in Figure 12–6A, with the letters representing different companies supplying various segments. Note that two segments are unserved.[18]

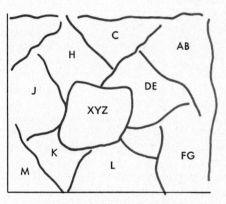

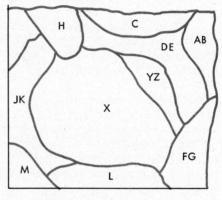

FIGURE 12–6
Market-Fragmentation
and Market-Reconsolidation
Stages

(a) Market-fragmentation stage   (b) Market-reconsolidation stage

Market-reconsolidation stage   This, however, is not the end of the evolution of a market. The stage of fragmentation is often followed by a *market-reconsolidation stage,* caused by the development of a new attribute that has cogent market appeal. This happened in the toothpaste market, for example, when P&G introduced its new fluoride toothpaste, Crest, which effectively retarded dental decay. Suddenly other toothpaste brands that claimed whitening power, cleaning power, sex appeal, taste, or mouthwash effectiveness were pushed into the corners because consumers predominantly wanted a toothpaste that gave anticavity protection. P&G's Crest won a lion's share of the market, as shown by the X territory in Figure 12–6B.

But even a reconsolidated market is not the terminal stage in the evolution of a market. Other companies will copy the successful brand, and the market will eventually become fragmented again. Markets seem to swing between mar-

---

[18] The product space is drawn with two attributes for simplicity. In point of fact, more attributes come into being as the market evolves. The product space grows from a two-dimensional to an *n*-dimensional space, which unfortunately cannot be drawn.

ket fragmentation and market reconsolidation. The fragmentation is brought about by competition and the reconsolidation is brought about by innovation.

Market-termination stage   Termination of this "see-saw" process occurs when a radically new innovation destroys the old market. If an entrepreneur discovers a spray that is more effective than toothpaste, the discovery will eventually destroy the toothpaste market. This is called the *market-termination stage*. Thus a product form ends when a new form emerges that meets consumer needs in a superior way.

Dynamics of Attribute Competition

We have seen how markets move through the stages of *market crystallization, market expansion, market fragmentation, market reconsolidation,* and eventually *market termination.* In the long run, markets have a tendency to deteriorate in their value to the sellers because of free entry and competition. The process is temporarily reversed through *innovation,* that is, the development of new customer benefits. The evolution of markets is very much the history of various firms identifying new benefits to offer to the buyers.

We can illustrate this process with the example of paper towels. Formerly, homemakers used only cotton and linen dish cloths and towels in their kitchens. A paper company, looking for new markets, developed paper towels to compete with the cloth. This development crystallized a new market. Other paper manufacturers entered and expanded the market. Eventually, the number of brands proliferated and created market fragmentation. Overcapacity in the industry led the various manufacturers to search for new features. One manufacturer, hearing consumers complain that the paper towels were not sufficiently absorbent, introduced "superabsorbent" paper towels and regained a large market share. This stage of market reconsolidation did not last long because competitors soon came out with their version of superabsorbent paper towels. Soon the market was fragmented again. Then another manufacturer heard consumers express a wish for a "superstrength" paper towel, and proceeded to introduce one. It was soon copied by other manufacturers. Later another manufacturer introduced a lint-free paper towel, which was subsequently copied. Thus paper towels evolved from a simple product to one with various absorbencies, strengths, and applications. Market evolution was driven by the forces of innovation and competition.

Competition in a market produces a succession of product attributes. If a new attribute draws demand, then several competitors soon offer it, and it loses its determinance. To the extent that most banks are now "friendly," friendliness is no longer a basis for consumer choice among banks. To the extent that most airlines serve in-flight meals, meals are no longer a basis for air-carrier choice. This suggests the strategic importance of a company's maintaining leadership in the innovation of new attributes. Each new attribute, if successful, creates a differential advantage for the firm, leading to temporarily higher-than-average market share and profits. The market leader must learn to routinize innovation.

The crucial question is, Can a firm look ahead and anticipate the sequence of attributes that are likely to be high in demand and technologically feasible over time? How can the firm search for new attributes? There are four possible approaches.

The first approach employs an *empirical process* to identify new attributes. The company surveys consumers to find out what attributes consumers would like added to the product and the relative demand intensity for each. The firm also considers the cost of developing each new attribute and likely competitive initiatives and reactions. It then seizes on those attributes promising to generate the highest profit contribution.

The second approach sees attribute search as primarily the outcome of an *intuitive process*. Entrepreneurs, in particular, prefer to use their intuition to identify new attributes. They go into product development without using marketing research to confirm their hunches. Natural selection determines the winners and the losers. If a manufacturer spots an attribute that the market turns out to want, that manufacturer is considered smart, although from another perspective, he or she was only lucky. This theory offers no guidance as to how to foresee new valued attributes.

A third approach says that new attributes unfold through a *dialectical process*. Any valued attribute gets pushed to an extreme through the competitive process. Thus blue jeans started out as an inexpensive article of clothing and over time have become fashionable and more expensive. This unidirectional elaboration, however, contains the seeds of its own destruction. Eventually some manufacturer will discover a new cheap material and consumers will flock to buy it. The message of dialectical theory is that the same innovators should not try to march ahead of their competitors but rather should head in the opposite direction toward market segments that are suffering from neglect.

A fourth approach holds that new attributes emerge through a *needs-hierarchy process*. On this theory, we would predict that the first automobiles would provide basic transportation and be designed for safety. At a later time, automobiles would start appealing to social acceptance and status needs. Still later, automobiles would be designed to help people "fulfill" themselves. The innovator's task is to assess when the market is ready to satisfy the next-higher level of need.

The actual unfolding of new attributes in a market is more complex than any simple theories would suggest. We should not underestimate the influence of technological and societal processes in influencing the emergence of new attributes. For example, the strong consumer interest in compact-size television sets remained unmet until miniaturization technology was sufficiently advanced. Technological forecasting is one important approach to trying to anticipate the timing of future technological developments that will permit new attribute offers to consumers. The societal factor also plays a major role in shaping attribute evolution. Developments such as inflation, shortages, environmentalism, consumerism, and new life styles create consumer disequilibrium and lead consumers to reevaluate actual and potential product attributes. For example, inflation increases the desire for a smaller car, and car safety increases the desire for a heavier car. The innovator must use marketing research to gauge the values that consumers put on different attributes in order to determine the company's best move vis-à-vis competition.

SUMMARY

Every new product that is launched enters a product life cycle marked by a changing set of problems and opportunities. The sales history of the typical product is commonly thought to follow an S-shaped curve made up of four stages. The *introduction* stage is marked by slow growth and minimal profits as the product is pushed into distribution. The company has to decide during this stage between the four strategies of rapid skimming, slow skimming, rapid penetration, or slow penetration. If successful, the product enters a *growth* stage marked by rapid sales growth and increasing profits. During this stage, the company attempts to improve the product, enter new market segments and distribution channels, and reduce its prices slightly. There follows a *maturity* stage in which sales growth slows down and profits stabilize. The company seeks innovative strategies to renew sales growth, including market, product, and marketing-mix modification. Finally, the product enters a stage of *decline* in which little can be done to halt the deterioration of sales and profits. The company's task during this period is to identify the truly declining products, develop for each one a strategy of continuation, concentration, or milking, and finally phase out the product in a way that minimizes the hardship to company profits, employees, and customers.

Product life-cycle theory must be complemented by a theory of market dynamics that provides guidelines as to the structure of the total market and the kinds of new attributes to which the market is ready to respond. The general theory of market evolution holds that new markets *crystallize* with the recognition of an unsatisfied need or a way to better satisfy existing needs. The innovator usually designs a product for the mass market. Competitors start entering the market with similar or different products leading to *market expansion*. The market undergoes increasing *fragmentation* until some firm recognizes a new determinant attribute that *reconsolidates* the market into fewer and larger parts. This stage does not last because firms are always seeking differential advantage and their actions continue to break large markets into smaller markets. There is often a cycling back and forth between market reconsolidation based on innovation and fragmentation based on competition. The market may ultimately terminate upon the discovery of a superior new product form.

Companies must know how to anticipate specific attributes that the market may want. Profits go to those who are early in introducing new and valued benefits. The search for new attributes can be based on empirical work, intuition, dialectical reasoning, or needs-hierarchy reasoning.

The main role of market evolution theory is to shift the attention of marketers from specific product and brand evolution to the evolution of the overall market. Each product tells only a limited story about the opportunities and evolution of the market. Successful marketing comes through creative interpretation of the market's evolutionary potential.

**QUESTIONS
AND
PROBLEMS**

1. Beer is a product that appears to be in the mature stage of its life cycle. Can you suggest some steps that can be taken by the industry to boost sales?

2. "In fact, it is this writer's contention that once one has stated that products are 'born' and that most 'die,' most of the usefulness of the life cycle model has been exhausted. It is simply not a very rich model." Do you agree?

3. Develop a long-range plan for marketing a new line of electric can openers, indicating for each stage in the product's life cycle (introductory, growth, maturity, and decline) the major objective and the likely policy on price, quality, advertising, personal selling, and channels.

4. For each appliance, indicate in which stage of the product life cycle it is found: (a) refrigerators; (b) room air conditioners; (c) wringer-type washing machines; (d) compactors.

5. As a product passes through the successive stages of its product life cycle, both its rate of sales growth and its rate-of-return on investment change. Using these two variables as axes, develop a diagram showing the typical trajectory of these variables over the product life cycle.

6. Discuss the changes in the promotion level and mix in the different stages of the product life cycle.

7. Select a fad and a fashion and plot their product life-cycle patterns on one graph. How do they differ from each other?

8. What is the difference between a product life-cycle analysis of the product class "paper towels" and the market evolution analysis of them found in the chapter?

New-Product-Development Strategy

Nothing in this world is so powerful as an idea whose time has come.
VICTOR HUGO

13

The message of the product life cycle is that companies cannot rely on their current products to produce the target rate of sales and profit growth. As some of the company's products enter the decline stage, the company will have to take concrete steps to replace them. The "planning gap" between desired and expected sales growth can be filled by the company in only two basic ways: *acquisition* or *innovation*.

The acquisition route can take one of three forms. First, the company can pursue a *corporate-acquisition* program involving the search for smaller companies that have attractive product lines. Acquisition-minded companies, such as Beatrice Food and Litton Industries, have developed great experience in spotting and negotiating with companies for takeover. Second, the company can pursue a *patent-acquisition* program in which it buys the rights to new products from their original inventors or patent holders. Third, the company can make an effort to become a *licensee* in the manufacture of various products that it wants to produce. In all three cases, the company does not contribute to the development of new products but simply acquires the rights to produce existing ones.

The innovation route can take one of two basic forms. The company can pursue *internal innovation* by setting up and operating its own research and development department. Or it can pursue *contract innovation*, which involves hiring independent researchers or new-product-development agencies to attempt to develop specified products for the firm.

Many companies will combine several of these strategies for growth. General Mills, for example, tries to base its growth on a fifty-fifty mix of acquisition and innovation. Its management feels that the economics favor acquisition at times and innovation at other times, and they want to be skilled at both.

This chapter will focus on innovation as growth strategy, because of the heavy role that marketing plays in finding, developing, and launching successful new products. "New products" for our purposes will mean *products, product modifications,* and *brands* that the firm brings into existence through research and development effort conducted either inside or outside the firm. We will also be concerned with whether the consumer sees them as "new," although this will not be our primary criterion.

THE NEW-PRODUCT-DEVELOPMENT DILEMMA

Under modern conditions of competition, it is becoming increasingly risky not to innovate. Consumers and industrial customers want and expect a stream of new and improved products. Competition will certainly do its best to meet these desires. A program of managed innovation seems to be a necessity.

At the same time, innovation can also be very risky. Ford lost an estimated $350,000,000 on its ill-fated Edsel; and Du Pont lost an estimated $100,000,000 on its Corfam (synthetic leather). Xerox's venture into computers was a disaster; and the French Concorde aircraft probably will never recover its investment. A survey of 125 companies indicated that the median percentage of major new products and services whose performance fell short of expectations was 20 percent for industrial product manufacturers, around 18 percent for service industries, and approximately 40 percent for consumer-product manufacturers.[1] The last rate is particularly discouraging and very costly to the consumer-product manufacturers who miss the mark.

Looking ahead, successful new-product development may be even harder to achieve as time goes on. There are several reasons for this.

1. *Shortage of important new-product ideas.* Some technologists think there is a shortage of fundamentally new technologies—on the order of the automobile, television, computers, xerography, and wonder drugs. Although there are many minor new products emerging, the nation needs major innovations to avoid economic stagnation.

2. *Fragmented markets.* Keen competition is leading to increasingly fragmented markets. Companies have to aim new products at smaller market segments rather than the mass market. This means lower sales and profits, although the companies may maintain their positions longer.

3. *Growing social and governmental constraints.* New products increasingly have to satisfy public criteria in addition to promising reasonable profits. They must be designed with consideration given to consumer safety and ecological compatibility. Government requirements have slowed down the rate of innovation in

---

[1] David S. Hopkins and Earl L. Bailey, "New Product Pressures," *The Conference Board Record,* June 1971, pp. 16–24.

the drug industry and have considerably complicated product design and advertising decisions in such industries as industrial equipment, chemicals, automobiles, and toys.

4. *Costliness of new-product-development process.* A company typically has to develop a great number of new-product ideas in order to finish with a few good ones. Booz, Allen & Hamilton studied this question for fifty-one companies and summarized its findings in the form of a decay curve of new-product ideas. (See Figure 13–1.) Of every fifty-eight ideas, about twelve pass the initial screening test, which shows them to be compatible with company objectives and resources. Of these, some seven remain after a thorough evaluation of their profit potential. About three survive the product-development stage, two survive the test-marketing stage, and only one is commercially successful. Thus, about fifty-eight new ideas must be generated to find one good one. This one successful idea must be priced at a profitable enough level to cover all the money lost by the company in researching fifty-seven other ideas that failed.

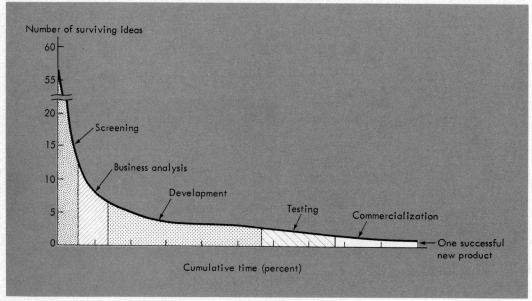

SOURCE: Redrawn from *Management of New Products,* 4th ed. (New York: Booz, Allen & Hamilton, 1968), p. 9.

FIGURE 13–1
Decay Curve of New-Product Ideas (Fifty-One Companies)

5. *Capital shortage.* The high cost of new-product development is no longer affordable by many companies because of the high cost of money. This is pushing many companies to favor product modification and imitation in preference to true innovation.

6. *Shorter life spans of successful products.* Even when a new product turns out to be a commercial success, rivals are so quick to follow suit that the new product is typically fated for only a short, happy life. The race to be first on the market sometimes assumes grotesque proportions. Alberto-Culver was so eager to beat a

new Procter & Gamble shampoo to the market that it developed a name and filmed a TV commercial before it had even developed its own product.

Thus management faces a dilemma; it should develop new products, yet the odds weigh heavily against their success. The answer must lie in conducting new-product development in a way that reduces the risk of failure. But what are the major causes of new-product failure? The most frequently cited causes are:

1. A high-level executive favors the idea and pushes it through in spite of the lack of supporting evidence.
2. Poor organizational systems for handling new-product ideas (poor criteria, poor procedures, poor coordination of departments).
3. Poor market-size measurement, forecasting, and market research.
4. Poor marketing planning, such as poor positioning, poor segmentation, under-budgeting, overpricing.
5. Lack of product distinctiveness or consumer benefit.
6. Poor product design.
7. Unexpectedly high product-development costs.
8. Unexpectedly intense competitive response.

The first two factors call for better organizational arrangements, and the last five factors call for improved techniques at each stage of the new-product-development process.

EFFECTIVE ORGANIZATIONAL ARRANGEMENTS

Top management must take the ultimate responsibility for the quality of the new-product-development work at the company. It cannot simply hire some new-product specialists and leave it to them to come up with useful new ideas. Effective new-product-development work must start with a clear definition by top management of its growth strategy, particularly in terms of the business domains and product categories in which it wants to do business. This will avoid lower management's working on ideas that top management won't ultimately buy. In one food company, the new-product manager spent thousands of dollars researching an exciting new snack idea only to hear the president say months later, "Drop it. We don't want to be in the snack business."

Top management should try to get quite specific about their criteria for new-product idea acceptance, especially in a large multidivisional company where all kinds of projects can bubble up as the favorites of specific managers. The Gould Corporation, for example, established the following acceptance criteria: (1) the product can be introduced within five years; (2) the product has a market potential of at least $50 million and a 15 percent growth rate; (3) the product will provide at least 30 percent return on sales and 40 percent on investment; and (4) the product will achieve technical or market leadership.

A major problem of top management is how much to budget for new-product development. Research and development is so uncertain in its outcomes that it is difficult to use normal investment criteria for budgeting. Some companies solve this problem by encouraging as many project proposals as possible

TABLE 13–1

Estimated Cost of Finding One Successful New Product (Starting with Sixty-four New Ideas)

STAGE	NUMBER OF IDEAS	PASS RATIO	COST PER PRODUCT IDEA	TOTAL COST
1. Idea screening	64	1:4	$ 1,000	$ 64,000
2. Concept test	16	1:2	20,000	320,000
3. Product development	8	1:2	200,000	1,600,000
4. Test marketing	4	1:2	500,000	2,000,000
5. National launch	2	1:2	5,000,000	10,000,000
			$5,721,000	$13,984,000

and financing as many as are promising. Other companies set their R&D budget by using a conventional percentage-to-sales figure, or by spending an amount comparable to competition. Still other companies develop a set of objectives with respect to how many successful new products they want, and work backwards to estimate the rough investment cost required.

Table 13–1 shows the worksheet for this last method. The manager of the new-products department reviewed the results of sixty-four recent new-product ideas processed in the company. Only one in four, or sixteen, ideas passed the idea-screening stage, and it cost the company an average of $1,000 per idea reviewed at this stage. Half of the surviving ideas, or eight, survived the concept-testing stage, at a cost of $20,000 each. Half of those, or four, survived the product-development stage, at a cost of $200,000 each. Half of those, or two, did well in the test market, at a cost of $500,000 each. When these two ideas were launched, at a cost of $5,000,000 each, only one was highly successful. Thus the one successful idea had cost the company $5,721,000 to develop. In the process, sixty-three other ideas fell by the wayside. Therefore the total cost for developing one successful new product was $13,984,000. Unless the company can find ways to improve the pass ratios and reduce the costs at each stage, it will have to budget nearly $14,000,000 for each successful new idea it hopes to find. If top management wants four successful new products over the next few years, it will have to budget $64,000,000 (= 4 × $14,000,000) for new-product development, and even more, to allow for inflation.

A key factor in effective new-product-development work is to establish workable organizational structures. Companies use five different organizational arrangements for handling the new-product development.[2]

1. **Product managers.** Many companies leave new-product development up to their product managers. In practice, this system has several faults. The product managers are usually too busy managing their product lines to give much thought to new products other than brand modification or extension; they also lack the specific skills and knowledge needed to successfully develop new products.

[2] See *Organization for New-Product Development* (New York: Conference Board, 1966); and David S. Hopkins, *Options in New-Product Organization* (New York: Conference Board, 1974).

2. *New-product managers.* General Foods and Johnson & Johnson have established positions of new-product managers who report to group product managers. This position adds professionalization to the new-product function; on the other hand, new-product managers tend to think in terms of product modifications and line extensions limited to their product market. The position often does not have sufficient authority or top-level support.

3. *New-product committees.* Most companies have a high-level management committee charged with reviewing new-product proposals. Consisting of representatives from marketing, manufacturing, finance, engineering, and other departments, its function is not development or coordination so much as the reviewing and approving of new-product plans.

4. *New-product departments.* Large companies often establish a new-product department headed by an executive who is given substantial authority and access to top management. This executive normally reports to the chief executive, or marketing vice president, or research and development vice president. The department's major responsibilities include generating and screening new ideas, directing and coordinating research and development work, and carrying out field testing and precommercialization work.

5. *New-product venture teams.* Dow, Westinghouse, Monsanto, and General Mills assign major new-product-development work to venture teams. A venture team is a group specifically brought together from various operating departments and charged with the responsibility of bringing a specific product to market or a specific new business into being.

We are now ready to look at the successive stages of the new-product-development process. Eight stages are involved: *idea generation, screening, concept development and testing, marketing strategy, business analysis, product development, market testing,* and *commercialization.*

IDEA GENERATION

The first stage in the new-product-development process is the generation of ideas. Firms vary in how they go about finding ideas. Some are very casual and simply keep their ears open to new possibilities. Others identify product categories in which to concentrate their search effort. The search effort is narrow gauged when they rely on one or a few sources for ideas; or broad gauged when they rely on many sources. Furthermore, ideas may be generated intuitively or through special techniques. Here we will examine the major sources and techniques for generating ideas.

Sources of New-Product Ideas
The major sources of new-product ideas are customers, scientists, competitors, company salesmen and dealers, and top management.

Customers   The marketing concept suggests that customers' needs and wants are the logical starting point in the search for new-product ideas. Hippel has shown that a great number of ideas for new industrial products are user generated, which means companies must design better systems for spotting these ideas.[3] Companies can identify customers' needs and wants in several ways: (1) direct customer surveys, (2) projective tests, (3) focused group discussions, (4)

---

[3] Eric A. von Hippel, "Users as Innovators," *Technology Review,* January 1978, pp. 3–11.

suggestion systems and letters received from customers, and (5) perceptual and preference mapping of the current product space to discern new opportunities. Many idea hunters claim to find more ideas by asking customers to describe their *problems* with current products rather than by asking them for new-product ideas directly.

Scientists   Many companies hope to find new-product ideas through their scientific research programs. Basic laboratory research has yielded television and transistors, new forms of packaging, and synthetic fibers for clothing. Du Pont and Bell Laboratories are particularly noted for basic research, whereas most companies' R&D labs carry out applied research and often make only minor modifications of existing products.

Competitors   Companies must carefully watch the new-product-development work being done by their competitors. They can catch certain gleanings by listening to distributors, suppliers, and sales representatives as to what seems to be in the works. The sales of new products launched by their competitors should be monitored. The company should assess why they are bought and by whom. Many companies will buy the competitors' products, take them apart, and build a better one. Their growth strategy is one of product imitation and improvement rather than product origination.

Company sales representatives and dealers   Company sales representatives and dealers are a particularly good source of new-product ideas. They have firsthand exposure to customers' unsatisfied needs and complaints. They are often the first to learn of competitive developments. An increasing number of companies are training and rewarding their sales representatives and dealers for producing new ideas.

Top management   Top management is another major source of new-product ideas. Some company leaders, such as Edwin H. Land of Polaroid, take personal responsibility for driving forward technological innovation in their companies. This isn't always constructive, as when a top executive pushes through pet ideas that are insufficiently researched or supported by the available data.

Miscellaneous sources   Other sources of new-product ideas include inventors, patent attorneys, university and commercial laboratories, industrial consultants, advertising agencies, marketing research firms, and industrial publications.

Idea-Generating Techniques

Really good ideas come out of a combination of inspiration, perspiration, and techniques. A large number of "creativity" techniques have been developed over the years to help individuals and groups generate better ideas.

Attribute listing   This technique involves listing the major attributes of an existing object and then imagining ways to modify each attribute in the search for a new combination that will improve the object. Consider a screwdriver.[4] Its attributes are the following: a round, steel shank, a wooden handle, manually oper-

---

[4] See John E. Arnold, "Useful Creative Techniques," in *Source Book for Creative Thinking,* ed. Sidney J. Parnes and Harold F. Harding (New York: Charles Scribner's Sons, 1962), p. 255.

ated, and torque provided by twisting action. Now a group can be asked to propose possible corrections in each attribute to improve product performance or appeal. The round shank could be changed to a hexagonal shank so that a wrench could be applied to increase the torque; electric power could replace manual power; the torque could be produced by pushing. Osborn suggested that useful ideas can be stimulated by putting the following questions to an object or its attributes: put to other uses? adapt? modify? magnify? minify? substitute? rearrange? reverse? combine?[5]

Forced relationships   This technique relies upon listing several objects and then considering each object in relation to every other object. Suppose an office-equipment manufacturer is looking for a novel piece of office equipment.[6] Several objects are listed—a desk, bookcase, filing cabinet, chair. If these pieces are paired, certain ideas occur, for instance, a desk with a built-in bookcase, or a desk with a built-in filing cabinet.

Morphological analysis   This method consists of singling out the most important dimensions of a problem and then examining all the relationships among them. Suppose the problem is described as that of "getting something from one place to another via a powered vehicle."[7] The important dimensions are the type of vehicle to use (cart, chair, sling, bed); the medium in which the vehicle operates (air, water, oil, hard surface, rollers, rails); the power source (pressed air, internal combustion engine, electric motor, steam, magnetic fields, moving cables, moving belt). The next step is to let the imagination loose on every combination. A cart-type vehicle powered by an internal-combustion engine and moving over hard surfaces is the automobile. The hope is that some other combinations will turn out to be quite novel and appealing.[8]

Problem analysis   The preceding creativity techniques have in common an effort to imagine new products without going to the consumer for any input. Problem analysis, on the other hand, starts with the consumer. Consumers are asked to name problems associated with the use of a particular product or product category. Thus Bell & Howell might ask consumers about problems they have with their movie projectors. Each problem can be the source of a new idea. For example: "It is time consuming to rewind the film" suggests automatic rewinding. "The scene is too small to see on the screen" suggests zoom lens. "Some of the film is boring" suggests a fast-forward mechanism. Not all of these ideas, however, are worth developing. The problems have to be rated by their *seriousness, incidence,* and *cost of remedying* in order to choose the ones to work on.

The technique can be reversed and consumers can be given a list of problems and asked to suggest which products come to mind as having each prob-

---

[5] See Alex F. Osborn, *Applied Imagination*, 3rd ed. (New York: Charles Scribner's Sons, 1963), pp. 286–87.

[6] Ibid., pp. 213–14.

[7] Arnold, "Useful Creative Techniques," pp. 256–57.

[8] See Edward M. Tauber, "HIT: Heuristic Ideation Technique—A Systematic Procedure for New Product Search," *Journal of Marketing*, January 1972, pp. 58–70; and Charles L. Alford and Joseph Barry Mason, "Generating New Product Ideas," *Journal of Advertising Research*, December 1975, pp. 27–32.

lem.[9] Thus the question: "The package of _____ doesn't fit well on the shelf" might lead consumers to name dog foods and dry breakfast cereals. A food marketer might think of entering these markets with a different shape package.

Brainstorming   Persons can also be stimulated to greater creativity through certain forms of organized group exercise. One well-known technique is *brainstorming*, whose principles were developed by Alex Osborn. A brainstorming session is held for the sole purpose of producing a lot of ideas. Generally the group size is limited to between six and ten. It is not a good idea to include too many experts in the group, because they tend to have a stereotyped way of looking at a problem. The problem should be made as specific as possible, and there should be no more than one problem. The sessions should last about an hour and may be held at almost any time of the day, although the morning is often the most effective time.

When the meeting takes place, the chairman starts with, "Remember now, we want as many ideas as possible—the wilder the better, and remember, no *evaluation.*" The ideas start to flow, one idea sparks another, and within the hour over a hundred or more new ideas may find their way into the tape recorder. For the conference to be maximally effective, Osborn believes the following four rules must be observed:

1. *Criticism is ruled out.* Adverse judgment of ideas must be withheld until later.
2. *Freewheeling is welcomed.* The wilder the idea, the better; it is easier to tame down than to think up.
3. *Quantity is wanted.* The greater the number of ideas, the more the likelihood of useful ideas.
4. *Combination and improvement are sought.* In addition to contributing ideas of their own, participants should suggest how ideas of others can be joined into still another idea.[10]

Freewheeling brainstorming sessions are highly productive of new-product ideas. Within forty minutes, one group of twelve men and women produced 136 ideas.

Synectics   William J. J. Gordon felt that the main weakness of the Osborn brainstorming session was that it produced solutions too quickly, before a sufficient number of perspectives had been developed. Gordon decided that instead of defining the problem specifically, he would define it so broadly that the group would have no inkling of the specific problem.

For instance, one of the problems was to design a vaporproof method of closing vaporproof suits worn by workers who handled high-powered fuels.[11] Gordon kept the specific problem a secret and sparked a discussion of the general notion of "closure," which led to images of different closure mechanisms, such as birds' nests, mouths, or thread. As a group exhausted the initial per-

[9] See Edward M. Tauber, "Discovering New Product Opportunities with Problem Inventory Analysis," *Journal of Marketing,* January 1975, pp. 67–70.

[10] Osborn, *Applied Imagination,* p. 156.

[11] John W. Lincoln, "Defining a Creativeness in People," in *Source Book for Creative Thinking,* Parnes and Harding, pp. 274–75.

spectives, Gordon would gradually interject facts that further defined the problem. Only when the group was close to a good solution would Gordon describe the exact nature of the problem. Then the group would start to refine the solution. These sessions would last a minimum of three hours, for Gordon believed that fatigue played an important role in unlocking ideas.

Gordon described five themes that guided these idea-conception conferences:

1. **Deferment.** Look first for viewpoints rather than solutions.
2. **Autonomy of object.** Let the problem take on a life of its own.
3. **Use of the commonplace.** Take advantage of the familiar as a springboard to the strange.
4. **Involvement/detachment.** Alternate between entering into the particulars of the problem and standing back from them, in order to see them as instances of a universal.
5. **Use of metaphor.** Let apparently irrelevant, accidental things suggest analogies which are sources of new viewponts.[12]

IDEA SCREENING

The purpose of idea generation is to create a number of good ideas. The main purpose of all the succeeding stages is to *reduce* the number of ideas. The first idea-pruning stage is screening.

In the screening stage, the company must seek to avoid two types of errors. A *DROP-error* occurs when the company dismisses an otherwise good idea because of a lack of vision of its potentialities. Some companies still shudder when they think of some of the ideas they dismissed:

> Xerox saw the novel promise of Chester Carlson's copying machine; IBM and Eastman Kodak did not see it at all. RCA was able to envision the innovative opportunity of radio; the Victor Talking Machine Company could not. Henry Ford recognized the promise of the automobile; yet only General Motors realized the need to segment the automobile market into price and performance categories, with a model for every classification, if the promise was to be fully achieved. Marshall Field understood the unique market development possibilities of installment buying; Endicott Johnson did not, calling it "the vilest system yet devised to create trouble." And so it has gone.[13]

If a company makes too many DROP-errors, its standards are obviously too conservative.

A *GO-error* occurs when the company lets a poor idea proceed to development and commercialization. We can distinguish at least three types of product failures that ensue. An *absolute product failure* loses money and its sales do not cover variable costs; a *partial product failure* loses money but its sales cover all the variable costs and some of the fixed costs; and a *relative product failure* yields a profit that is less than the company's normal rate of return.

[12] Ibid., p. 274.

[13] Mark Hanan, "Corporate Growth through Venture Management," *Harvard Business Review*, January–February 1969, p. 44.

The job of screening is to spot and drop poor ideas as early as possible. The rationale is that product-development costs rise substantially at each successive stage of the process. When products reach later stages, management often feels that so much has been invested in developing the product that it ought to be launched in the hope of recouping some of the investment. But this is letting good money chase bad money and the real solution is to not let poor product ideas get this far.

Product-Idea-Rating Devices

Most companies require their executives to write up each new-product idea on a standard form that can be reviewed by a new-product committee. At this stage, the ideas are rough, and the form simply requires a description of the product, the target market, competition, and some rough guesses as to market size, product price, development time and costs, manufacturing costs, and level of return.

Even if the idea looks good, the question arises whether the idea is appropriate for the particular company. Does it mesh well with the company's objectives, strategies, and resources? Table 13–2 shows a common type of rating form for this question. The first column lists factors required for successful launching of the product in the marketplace. In the next column, management allocates weights to these factors according to their importance. Thus management believes marketing competence will be very important (.20), and purchasing and supplies competence will be of minor importance (.05). The next task is to rate the company's degree of competence on each factor on a scale from .0 to 1.0. Here management feels that its marketing competence is very high (.9) and its location and facilities competence is low (.3). The final step is to multiply the

---

TABLE 13–2
Product-Idea-Rating Device

PRODUCT SUCCESS REQUIREMENTS	(A) RELATIVE WEIGHT	(B) COMPANY COMPETENCE LEVEL											RATING (A × B)
		.0	.1	.2	.3	.4	.5	.6	.7	.8	.9	1.0	
Company personality and goodwill	.20							✓					.120
Marketing	.20										✓		.180
Research and development	.20								✓				.140
Personnel	.15							✓					.090
Finance	.10										✓		.090
Production	.05									✓			.040
Location and facilities	.05				✓								.015
Purchasing and supplies	.05										✓		.045
Total	1.00												.720*

* Rating scale: .00–.40 poor; .41–.75 fair; .76–1.00 good. Present minimum acceptance rate: .70.

SOURCE: Adapted with modifications from Barry M. Richman, "A Rating Scale for Product Innovation," *Business Horizons,* summer 1962, pp. 37–44.

relative importance of the success requirements by the corresponding levels of company competence to obtain a single overall rating of the company's fitness to carry this product successfully into the market. Thus, if marketing is an important success requirement, and this company is very good at marketing, this will increase the overall rating of the product idea. In the example, the product idea scored .72, which, in the company's experience, places it at the high end of the "fair idea" level.

This basic rating device is capable of additional refinements.[14] Whether it is advisable to introduce them is largely a matter of how much more would be gained. The checklist serves as a means of promoting systematic evaluation and discussion of the product idea among management—it is not designed to make the decision for them.

CONCEPT DEVELOPMENT AND TESTING

Those ideas that survive screening must undergo further development into fully mature product concepts. It is important to distinguish between a product idea, a product concept, and a product image. A *product idea* is a possible product, described in objective functional terms, that the company can see itself offering to the market. A *product concept* is a particular subjective consumer meaning that the company tries to build into the product idea. A *product image* is the particular subjective picture consumers actually acquire of the product.

Concept Development

Assume that a large food processor gets the idea to produce a powder that consumers could add to milk to increase the nutritional level and improve the taste. This is a product idea. Consumers, however, do not buy product ideas; they buy product concepts.

A product idea can be turned into a large number of alternative product concepts. First, the question can be asked, Who is to use this product? The powder can be aimed at infants, children, teenagers, young or middle-aged adults, senior citizens, or some combination. Second, What primary benefit should be built into this product? Taste, nutrition, refreshment, energy? Third, What is the primary occasion for this drink? Breakfast, midmorning, lunch, midafternoon, dinner, late evening? By asking these questions, a company can form many alternative product concepts. One is an *instant breakfast drink* aimed at adults who want a quick way to get nutrition at breakfast without preparing a breakfast. Another is a *health supplement* aimed at senior citizens as a nighttime beverage; still another is a *tasty snack drink* designed for children for midday refreshment.

The company must narrow down the choice to one of these concepts. Here it introduces criteria that it wants to achieve with this new product: good rate of return, high sales volume, rounding out of product line, utilization of idle capacity. The criteria could be listed as rows of a matrix, and the alternative product concepts as columns. In each cell a number between 1 and 10 can be placed to indicate how high that product concept stands on that criterion. Certain concepts will profile very poorly on the set of criteria: the market is not large

---

[14] See John T. O'Meara, Jr., "Selecting Profitable Products," *Harvard Business Review*, January–February 1961, pp. 83–89; and John S. Harris, "New Product Profile Chart," *Chemical and Engineering News*, April 1969, pp. 110–18.

enough, the concept is too novel, and so forth. More data are then collected on the remaining concepts until one is finally chosen as the core product concept.

Product and Brand Positioning

Once the core product concept is chosen, it defines the character of the product space in which the new product has to be positioned. An *instant breakfast drink* means that this product will compete against bacon and eggs, breakfast cereals, coffee and pastry, and other breakfast alternatives. A *tasty snack drink* means that this product will compete against soft drinks, fruit juices, and other tasty thirst quenchers. Thus the product concept, and not the product idea, defines the product's competition.

Assume that the instant breakfast drink concept is selected. Figure 13–2A is a *product-positioning map* showing where an instant breakfast drink stands in relation to other breakfast products, using the two dimensions of cost and preparation time. An instant breakfast drink stands in a distinct part of the market, offering the buyer low cost and quick preparation. Its nearest competitor is cold cereal; its most distant competitor is bacon and eggs. This should be kept in mind and utilized in communicating the concept to the market.

If the company is entering an existing product market, then it also has to develop a *brand-positioning map*. Suppose companies A, B, and C have already introduced brands of instant breakfast drinks, which are positioned as shown in Figure 13–2B. The company must decide on how much to charge and how calorific to make its drink, assuming these are salient attributes used by buyers. One possibility is to position the new brand in the medium-price, medium-calorie part of the market; another is to position it in the low-price, low-calorie end of

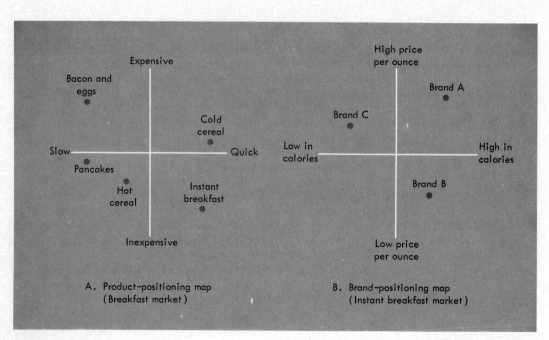

FIGURE 13–2
Product and Brand Positioning

the market. Both would give the new brand distinctiveness, as opposed to positioning the brand right next to another brand and fighting intensely for share-of-market. This decision requires researching the size of alternative preference segments of the market.

Concept Testing Through these steps, the company hopes to arrive at a set of viable product or brand concepts. Concept testing calls for taking these concepts to a group of target consumers and getting their reactions. The concepts may be presented symbolically or physically. At this stage, usually a word and/or picture description suffices, although the reliability of a concept test increases, the more concrete and physical the stimulus. The consumers will be shown a word description of a concept, such as:

> A powdered product that is added to milk to make an instant breakfast that gives the person all the breakfast nutrition he or she needs, along with good taste and high convenience. The product would be offered in three flavors, chocolate, vanilla, strawberry, and would come in individual packets, six to a box, at 79¢ a box.

The consumer will be asked to react to each concept and its specific attributes. The concept test should include the following questions:

1. *Is the concept clear and easy to understand?* (Often the concept test reveals that people are not really grasping the concept.)
2. *Do you see some distinct benefits of this product over competing offerings?* (The respondents must recognize distinct benefits of this product over its near substitutes.)
3. *Do you find the concept and claims believable?* (The respondents may have strong doubts about the product claims, which the manufacturer will have to overcome.)
4. *Do you like this product better than its major competitors?* (The respondents report whether they really prefer this product.)
5. *Would you buy this product?* (The company must find out if there is a sufficient percentage of respondents with an actual intention to buy this product.)
6. *Would you replace your current product with this new product?* (The company must find out if the consumer envisions not only trying this product but also substituting it permanently for the current product.)
7. *Would this product meet a real need of yours?* (If consumers do not feel a real need for the product, they may buy it only once for curiosity.) [15]
8. *What improvements can you suggest in various attributes of the product?* (This enables the company to bring about further improvements in form, features, pricing, quality, and so on.)
9. *How frequently would you buy this product?* (This indicates whether the consumer sees it as an everyday product or a specialty product.)
10. *Who would use the product?* (This question helps the marketer define the user target.)
11. *What do you think the price of this product should be?* (This question helps the marketer know the consumer's value perception of the product.)

[15] For a good discussion, see Edward M. Tauber, "Reduce New Product Failures: Measure Needs as Well as Purchase Intention," *Journal of Marketing*, July 1973, pp. 61–64.

The consumers' responses will enable the company to know which concept has the strongest appeal. For example, question 5 goes after the consumer's *intention to buy* and usually reads: "Would you *definitely, probably, probably not, definitely not* buy this product?" Suppose 40 percent of the consumers said "definitely" and another 30 percent said "probably." Most companies have developed norms from past experience to judge how well these intention-to-buy results predict actual buying. One food manufacturer rejects any product idea that does not draw a definite intention-to-buy score above 50 percent. Another food manufacturer takes the "definite" score plus half of the "probable" score and wants the sum to exceed 50 percent.

More advanced methods of concept development and testing are coming into general usage. In the method known as *conjoint analysis*,[16] the researcher develops a set of concepts that share the same attributes but differ in their attribute levels. For example, one concept is an instant breakfast drink that claims nutrition as a benefit, comes in one flavor, and is 79¢; another concept claims refreshment as a benefit, comes in three flavors, and is 69¢; and so on. Each consumer is asked to rank all the concepts from the most preferred to the least preferred. Then the researcher takes the consumers' rankings and applies a mathematical program that estimates the market's utility function for the levels of each attribute. The researcher might discover, for example, that the claim of nutrition adds a great deal to consumer utility but additional flavors add very little. With the aid of these estimated attribute-utility functions, the researcher can go ahead to develop the optimal characteristics for the new brand.

We have focused on a particular example in describing concept development and testing. But the methodology applies to any product, service, or idea, such as an electric car, a new banking service, a new type of museum, or a new health plan. Too many companies think their job is done when they get a product idea. They do not mature it into a full concept and subject it to adequate concept testing. Later the product encounters all kinds of problems in the marketplace that would have been avoided if the company had done a good job of concept development and testing.

MARKETING STRATEGY DEVELOPMENT

The new-product developer will have to develop a preliminary concept of the marketing strategy for introducing this product into the market. The marketing strategy will be rough at this stage and will be refined in subsequent stages.

The marketing strategy statement consists of three parts. The first part describes the size, structure, and behavior of the target market, the intended positioning of the new product in this market, and the sales, market share, and profit goals being sought in the first few years. Thus for the instant breakfast drink the statement might read:

> The target market is families with children who are receptive to a new, convenient, nutritious, and inexpensive form of breakfast. The company's brand will be positioned at the higher-price, higher-quality end of the market. The company

---

[16] See chapter 6, footnote 23, p. 158. One of the most impressive models for product-concept development and positioning is Glen L. Urban, "Perceptor: A Model for Product Positioning," *Management Science*, April 1975, pp. 858–71.

will aim initially to sell 500,000 cases or 10 percent of the market, with a loss in the first year not exceeding $1.3 million dollars. The second year will aim for 700,000 cases or 14 percent of the market, with a planned profit of $2.2 million dollars.

The second part of the marketing strategy statement will outline the product's intended price, distribution strategy, and marketing budget for the first year. For the instant breakfast cereal, the statement might read:

The product will be offered in a chocolate flavor in individual packets of six to a box at a retail price of 79¢ a box. There will be forty-eight boxes per case and the case's price to distributors will be $24. For the first two months, dealers will be offered one case free for every four cases bought, plus cooperative advertising allowances. Free samples will be distributed door to door. Coupons with 10¢ off will be advertised in newspapers. The total sales promotion budget will be $2,900,000. An advertising budget of $6,000,000 will be split between national and local 50:50. Two-thirds will go into television and one third into newspapers. Advertising copy will emphasize the benefit concept of nutrition and convenience. The advertising-execution concept will revolve around a weak little boy who drinks instant breakfast and grows strong. During the first year, $100,000 will be spent on marketing research to buy store audits and consumer panel information to monitor the market's reaction and buying rates.

The third part of the marketing-strategy statement describes the intended long-run sales and profit goals and marketing-mix strategy over time. For the breakfast drink the statement might read:

The company intends to ultimately capture 25 percent market share and realize an aftertax return on investment of 12 percent. To achieve this, product quality will start high and be further improved over time through technical research. Price will initially be set at a skimming level and lowered gradually to expand the market and meet competition. The total promotion budget will be boosted each year about 20 percent, with the initial advertising/sales promotion split of 63:37 evolving eventually to 50:50. Marketing research will be reduced to $60,000 per year after the first year.

BUSINESS ANALYSIS

Once management has developed a satisfactory product concept and a tentative marketing strategy, it is in a position to do a hardheaded analysis of the business attractiveness of the proposal. Management must review the future sales, costs, and profit estimates as to whether they satisfy the company's objectives. If they do, the product concept can be moved to the product-development stage. As new information comes in, some revision will probably have to take place in the product concept and marketing strategy, calling for revised estimates of sales, costs, and profits. Thus business analysis, which starts in this stage, will be revised at critical review periods during the product's development.

Estimating Sales   The key to whether a product should be developed is whether its sales will be high enough to return a satisfactory profit to the firm. One can obtain some helpful benchmarks by carefully examining the history of previous (analogous) products and surveying market opinion. At the very least, management finds it

helpful to have estimates of minimum and maximum sales to provide some indication of the risk involved.

Estimation methods differ depending upon whether they are designed to
estimate the sales of a one-time purchased product, an infrequently purchased
product, or a frequently purchased product. Figure 13 3A illustrates the product life-cycle sales that can be expected for one-time purchased products. Sales
rise at the beginning, peak, and later approach zero as the number of potential
buyers is exhausted. If new buyers keep entering the market, the curve will not
go down quite to zero.

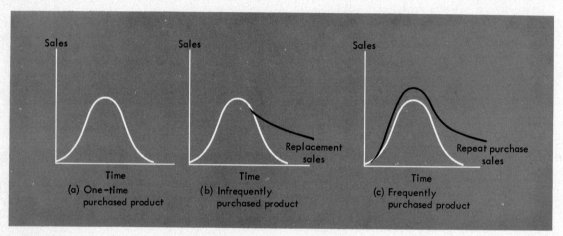

FIGURE 13–3

Product Life-Cycle Sales for Three Types of Products

Infrequently purchased products are exemplified by many durable goods,
such as automobiles, toasters, and industrial equipment. These goods exhibit replacement cycles, dictated either by their physical wearing out or their obsolescence associated with changing styles, features, and tastes. Sales forecasting for
this category of products consists of separately estimating sales and replacement
sales (see Figure 13–3B).

Frequently purchased products, such as consumer and industrial nondurables, have product life-cycle sales resembling Figure 13–3C. The number of
first-time buyers first increases and then decreases as there are fewer left (assuming a fixed population). Repeat-purchase sales occur soon, provided that the
product satisfies some fraction of people who become steady customers. The
sales curve eventually falls to a plateau level representing a level of steady repeat purchase volume; by this time the product is no longer in the class of new
products.

Estimating first-time sales   The first task, regardless of the type of product, is to
estimate first-time purchases of the new product in each period. Three examples
will be described.

MEDICAL EQUIPMENT   A medical-equipment manufacturer developed a
new instrument for rapidly analyzing blood specimens for various potential-

illness indicators. To estimate market potential, the company first defined the various market segments—they included hospitals, clinics, and unaffiliated laboratories. For each segment, management defined the minimum-size facility that would be a potential customer for the instrument. Then it turned to data indicating the number of such units in each segment. It reduced the number by the estimated purchase probability, which varied from segment to segment. It then cumulated the number of remaining potential customers over the segments and called this the *market potential. Market penetration* was then estimated, based on the amount of advertising and personal selling effort per period, the rate of favorable word of mouth, the price set on the machine, and the activity of competitors. These two estimates were then multiplied to form an estimate of sales.

ROOM AIR CONDITIONERS   A number of investigators have proposed that models of epidemics (sometimes called contagion models) provide a useful analogy to the new-product diffusion process. Bass has used an equation based on an epidemic model to forecast future sales of major appliances, including room air conditioners, electric refrigerators, home freezers, black-and-white television, and power lawn mowers.[17] He used sales data for only the first few years of product introduction to estimate sales for the subsequent years, until replacement demand became a big factor. For example, his sales projection for room air conditioners fit the pattern of actual sales with a coefficient of determination, R^2 = .92. The predicted time of peak was 8.6 years as against an actual time of peak of 7.0 years, and the predicted magnitude of peak was 1.9 million as against an actual peak of 1.8 million.

CONSUMER NONDURABLES   Fourt and Woodlock developed a useful first-time sales model that they tested against several new consumer nondurable products.[18] Their observation of new-product market penetration rates showed that (1) cumulative sales approached a limiting penetration level of less than 100 percent of all households, frequently far less, and (2) the successive increments of gain declined. Their equation is

$$q_t = r\bar{q}(1 - r)^{t-1} \qquad (13\text{–}1)$$

where:

q_t = percentage of total U.S. households expected to try the product in period t

r = rate of penetration of untapped potential

$\bar{q}$ = percentage of total U.S. households expected to eventually try the new product

t = time period

Assume that a new product is about to be introduced where it is estimated that 40 percent of all households will eventually try the new product ($\bar{q}$ = .4). Furthermore, it is estimated that in each period 30 percent of the remaining new-buyer potential is penetrated (r = .3). Therefore the percentage of U.S. households trying the product in each of the first four periods will be

[17] Frank M. Bass, "A New Product Growth Model for Consumer Durables," *Management Science,* January 1969, pp. 215–17.

[18] Louis A. Fourt and Joseph N. Woodlock, "Early Prediction of Market Success for New Grocery Products," *Journal of Marketing,* October 1960, pp. 31–38.

$$q_1 = r\bar{q}(1-r)^{1-1} = (.3)(.4)(.7^0) = .120$$

$$q_2 = r\bar{q}(1-r)^{2-1} = (.3)(.4)(.7^1) = .084$$

$$q_3 = r\bar{q}(1-r)^{3-1} = (.3)(.4)(.7^2) = .059$$

$$q_4 = r\bar{q}(1-r)^{4-1} = (.3)(.4)(.7^3) = .041$$

As time goes to infinity, the incremental trial percentage goes to zero. To estimate dollar sales from new triers in any period, the estimated trial rate for the period given by equation (13–1) is multiplied by the total number of U.S. households times the expected first-purchase expenditure per household on the product.

Estimating replacement sales   To estimate replacement sales, management has to research the *survival-age distribution* of its product. The lower end of the distribution will indicate when the first replacement sales are expected to take place. The actual timing of replacement will be influenced by such factors as the customer's economic outlook, cash flow, and product alternatives as well as the company's prices, financing terms, and sales effort. Since replacement sales are difficult to estimate before the product is in actual use, some manufacturers prefer to rest the case for launching the new product solely on the basis of first-time sales.

Estimating repeat sales   For a frequently purchased new product, the seller has to estimate repeat as well as first-time sales. This is because the unit value of frequently purchased products is low, and repeat purchases take place soon after the introduction. A high rate of repeat purchasing means buyer satisfaction with the product; sales are likely to remain high even after all first-time purchases take place. The seller should note the percentage of repeat purchases that take place in each *repeat purchase class:* those who buy once, twice, three times, and so on. Some products and brands are bought a few times and then dropped. It is important to estimate whether the repeat-purchase ratio is likely to rise or fall, and at what rate, with deeper repeat-purchase classes.[19]

Estimating Costs and Profits

After preparing the sales forecast, management can proceed to estimate the expected costs and profits of this venture. The costs are gathered through discussions with the R&D and manufacturing departments and include the planned marketing costs described in the marketing strategy statement. Table 13–3 illustrates a five-year projection of sales, costs, and profits for the instant breakfast drink product.

Row 1 shows the projected sales revenue over the five-year period. The company expects to sell $11,889,000 (approximately 500,000 cases at $24 per case) in the first year. Sales are expected to rise around 28 percent in each of the next two years, increase by 47 percent in the fourth year, and then slow down to 15 percent growth in the fifth year. Behind this increasing series is a specific set of assumptions about the rate of market growth, the company's market share, and the factory-realized price.

---

[19] See Robert Blattberg and John Golanty, "Tracker: An Early Test Market Forecasting and Diagnostic Model for New Product Planning," *Journal of Marketing Research,* May 1978, pp. 192–202.

TABLE 13–3
Projected Five-Year Cash Flow Statement (in Thousands of Dollars)

	YEAR 0	YEAR 1	YEAR 2	YEAR 3	YEAR 4	YEAR 5
1. Sales revenue	0	11,889	15,381	19,654	28,253	32,491
2. Cost of goods sold	0	3,981	5,150	6,581	9,461	10,880
3. Gross margin	0	7,908	10,231	13,073	18,792	21,611
4. Development costs	− 3,500	0	0	0	0	0
5. Marketing costs	0	8,000	6,460	8,255	11,866	13,646
6. Allocated overhead	0	1,189	1,538	1,965	2,825	3,249
7. Gross contribution	− 3,500	− 1,281	2,233	2,853	4,101	4,716
8. Supplementary contribution	0	0	0	0	0	0
9. Net contribution	− 3,500	− 1,281	2,233	2,853	4,101	4,716
10. Discounted contribution (15%)	− 3,500	− 1,113	1,691	1,877	2,343	2,346
11. Cumulative discounted cash flow	− 3,500	− 4,614	− 2,922	− 1,045	1,298	3,644

Row 2 shows the *cost of goods sold,* which hovers around 33 percent of sales revenue. This cost is found by estimating the average cost of labor, ingredients, and packaging per case.

Row 3 shows the expected *gross margin,* which is the difference between sales revenue and cost of goods sold.

Row 4 shows anticipated *development costs* of $3.5 million for researching and preparing to produce the new product. The development costs are made up of three components. The first is the *product-development costs* of researching, developing and testing the physical product. The second is the *marketing research costs* of fine-tuning the marketing program and assessing the market's likely response. It covers the estimated costs of package testing, in-home placement testing, name testing, and testmarketing. The third is *the manufacturing-development costs* of new equipment, new or renovated plant, and inventory investment.

Row 5 shows the estimated *marketing costs* over the five-year period to cover advertising, sales promotion, marketing research, and an amount allocated for sales-force coverage and marketing administration. In the first year, marketing costs stand at a high 67 percent of sales and by the fifth year are estimated to run at 42 percent of sales.

Row 6 shows the *allocated overhead* to this new product to cover its share of the cost of executive salaries, heat, light, and so on.

Row 7, the *gross contribution,* is found by subtracting the previous three costs from the gross margin. Years 0 and 1 involve losses and thereafter the gross contribution becomes positive and is expected to run as high as 15 percent of sales by the fifth year.

Row 8, *supplementary contribution,* is used to list any change in income from other products of the company that is due to the introduction of the new product. *Dragalong income* is the name given to any increase in the income on other company products resulting from adding a product to the line. *Cannibalized income* is the name given to any decrease in the income on other company products (such as replaced products) resulting from adding a product to the line.[20]

Row 9 shows the *net contribution*, which in this case is the same as the gross contribution since there was no supplementary contribution.

Row 10 shows the *discounted contribution*, that is, the present value of each of the future contributions discounted at 15 percent compounded per annum. For example, the company will not receive the contribution of $4,716,000 until the fifth year, which means that it is worth only $2,346,000 today if the company can normally earn 15 percent on its money.[21]

Finally, row 11 shows the *cumulative discounted cash flow*, which is the cumulation of the annual contributions in row 10. This cash flow is the key series on which management bases its decision on whether to go forward into product development or drop the project. Two things are of central interest. The first is the *maximum investment exposure*, which is the highest loss that the project can create. We see that the company will be in the hole for a maximum of $4,614,000 in year 1; this will be the company's loss if it terminates the project. The second is the *payback period*, which is the time when the company recovers all of its investment including the built-in return of 15 percent. The payback period here is approximately three and a half years. Management therefore will have to decide whether it can expose itself to a maximum investment loss of $4.6 million and wait three and a half years for payback.[22]

PRODUCT DEVELOPMENT

A product concept that scores high in a business analysis is now ready to be turned over to the R&D and/or engineering departments to be developed into a physical product. Up to now, it existed only as a word description, a drawing, or a very crude mock-up. This next step calls for a large jump in investment, which dwarfs the idea-evaluation costs incurred in the earlier stages. Much time and many dollars go into trying to develop a technically feasible product. This stage will provide an answer as to whether the product idea can be translated into a

[20] See Roger A. Kerin, Michael G. Harvey, and James T. Rothe, "Cannibalism and New Product Development," *Business Horizons*, October 1978, pp. 25–31.

[21] The *present value* (V) of a future sum (I) to be received t years from today and discounted at the interest rate (r) is given by $V = I_t/(1 + r)^t$. Thus $\$4,716/(1.15)^5 = \$2,346$.

[22] Companies use other financial measures to evaluate the merit of a new-product proposal. The simplest is *breakeven analysis*, where management figures out how many cases of the product the company would have to sell to break even with the given price and cost structure. If management is confident that the company can sell at least the breakeven number of cases, then it would probably move the project into product development. The most complex method is *risk analysis*. The basic approach is to obtain three estimates (optimistic, pessimistic, and most likely) for each uncertain variable affecting profitability under an assumed marketing environment and marketing strategy for the planning period. The computer simulates possible outcomes from which a rate-of-return probability distribution is drawn, showing the range of possible rates of returns and their probabilities. See David B. Hertz, "Risk Analysis in Capital Investment," *Harvard Business Review*, January–February 1964, pp. 96–106.

technically and commercially feasible product. If not, the company's accumulated investment will be lost except for any by-product information gained in the process.

Three steps involved in the product-development stage: prototype development and testing, branding, and packaging.

Prototype Development and Testing

The R&D department will undertake developing one or more physical versions of the defined product concept. It succeeds if it finds a prototype that satisfies the following criteria:

1. The prototype is seen by consumers as successfully embodying the key attributes of the product concept.
2. The prototype performs safely under normal use and conditions.
3. The prototype can be produced for the budgeted manufacturing costs.

The work of developing a successful product prototype can take days, weeks, months, or even years. Designing a new commercial aircraft, for example, will take several years of development work. Even developing a new taste formula can take time. For example, the Maxwell House Division of General Foods discovered, through consumer research, a strong preference for a brand of coffee that would strike the consumer as "bold, vigorous, deep tasting."[23] Its laboratory technicians spent over four months working with various coffee blends and flavors to formulate a corresponding taste. Even then it turned out to be very expensive to produce, and the company took steps to "cost reduce" the blend to meet the target manufacturing cost. This compromised the taste, however, and the new coffee brand failed to do well in the marketplace.

The lab scientists must know not only how to design the required functional characteristics but also how to convey the psychological aspects of the product concept through *physical cues*. This requires knowing how consumers react to different colors, sizes, weights, and other physical cues. In the case of a mouthwash, for example, a yellow color supports an "antiseptic" claim (Listerine), a red color "supports" a refreshing claim (Lavoris), and a green color supports a "cool" claim (Micrin). Or, to support the claim that a lawnmower is powerful, the lab people have to design a heavy frame and a noisy engine. Marketers often work with the lab people, who fill them in on how consumers make their judgments about product qualities they are seeking.

When the prototypes are ready, they must be put through a series of rigorous functional and consumer tests. The *functional tests* are conducted under laboratory and field conditions to make sure that the product performs safely and effectively. The new aircraft must be able to fly; the new snack food must be shelf-stable; the new drug must not create dangerous side effects. Functional product testing of new drugs now takes years of laboratory work with animal subjects and then human subjects before they obtain Federal Drug Administration approval. In the case of equipment testing, consider the experience of the Bissell Company with a combination electric vacuum and floor scrubber:

> . . . four were left with the research and development department for continued tests on such things as water lift, motor lift, effectiveness in cleaning, and dust

[23] See "Maxwell House Division (A)" (Boston: Intercollegiate Case Clearing House, ICH 13M83, 1970).

331

bag design. The other eight were sent to the company's advertising agency for test by a panel of fifty housewives. The research and development department found some serious problems in their further tests of the product. The life of the motor was not sufficiently long, the filter bag did not fit properly, and the scrubber foot was not correct. Similarly, the consumer tests brought in many consumer dissatisfactions that had not been anticipated: the unit was too heavy, the vacuum did not glide easily enough, and the scrubber left some residue on the floor after use.[24]

Consumer testing can take a variety of forms from bringing consumers into a lab to test and rate the product versions to giving them samples to use in their normal settings. *In-home product-placement tests* are common with products ranging from ice cream flavors to new appliances. When Du Pont developed its new synthetic carpeting, it installed free carpeting in several homes in exchange for the homeowners' willingness to report from time to time their likes and dislikes about the new carpeting in relation to conventional carpeting. Consumer-preference testing draws on a variety of techniques, such as paired comparisons, multiple choices, and ranking procedures, each with its own advantages and biases.[25]

Branding

The brand name should not be a casual afterthought but an integral reinforcer of the product concept. Among the desirable qualities for a brand name are:

1. *It should suggest something about the product's benefits.* Examples: Coldspot, Beautyrest, Craftsman, Accutron.
2. *It should suggest product qualities, such as action, color, or whatever.* Examples: Duz, Sunkist, Spic and Span, Firebird.
3. *It should be easy to pronounce, recognize, and remember.* Short names help. Examples: Tide, Crest.
4. *It should be distinctive.* Examples: Mustang, Kodak.

Some marketing research firms have developed elaborate name-research procedures including *association tests* (what images come to mind), *learning tests* (how easily is the name pronounced), *memory tests* (how well is the name remembered), and *preference tests* (which names are preferred).

The goal of many firms is to build a unique brand name that will eventually become identified with the generic product. Such brand names as Frigidaire, Kleenex, Levis, Jello, Scotch tape, and Fiberglas have succeeded in this way. However, their very success has threatened some of the companies with the loss of exclusive rights to the name. Cellophane and shredded wheat are now names in the common domain. Because of legal action, Du Pont has to describe its product as Du Pont Cellophane and Nabisco has to describe its product as Nabisco Shredded Wheat.

Packaging

Some years ago, packaging was a minor element in the marketing mix for a product. The traditional packaging concerns of manufacturers are product *protection* and *economy*. A third packaging objective, which comes closer to consid-

[24] Ralph Westfall and Harper W. Boyd, Jr., *Cases in Marketing Management* (Homewood, Ill.: Richard D. Irwin, 1961), p. 365.

[25] See Paul E. Green and Donald S. Tull, *Research for Marketing Decisions*, 4th ed. (Englewood Cliffs, N.J.: Prentice-Hall, 1978), chap. 6.

ering the consumer, is *convenience*. This means such things as size options and packages that are easy to open. A fourth packaging objective, *promotion*, has received increasing recognition from manufacturers. And a fifth objective, *ecology*, is becoming increasingly important as people become concerned with the disposal of packaging material and its effects on the environment.

Various factors account for the growing recognition of packaging as an independent and potent selling tool:

Self-service   An increasing number of products are sold on a self-service basis as a result of the growth of supermarkets and discount houses. The package must now perform many of the sales tasks. It must attract attention, describe the product's features, give the consumer confidence, and make a favorable overall impression.

Consumer affluence   The rise in consumer affluence has meant that consumers are willing to pay a little more for the convenience, appearance, dependability, and prestige of better packaging.

Company and brand image   Companies are recognizing the power of well-developed packaging to contribute to instant consumer recognition of the company or brand. There is hardly a film buyer who does not immediately recognize from a distance the familiar yellow packaging of Kodak film. Packaging is a tool not only in creating category identification but also in carrying out the brand's positioning concept in terms of quality, costs, and other factors.

Innovational opportunity   Innovative packaging can bring about large sales gains. The first companies to move into pop top cans and aerosol cans attracted many brand switchers. Hanes Corporation's L'eggs hosiery is one of the best recent examples of an innovative packaging approach—in this case, mass-marketed hosiery packaged in a unique egg-shaped container merchandised in free-standing display units. Hanes quickly gained a 10 percent share of the hosiery market with this product.

Developing the package for a new product requires a large number of decisions. The first task is to establish the *packaging concept*. The packaging concept is a definition of what the package should basically *be* or *do* for the particular product. Should the main function(s) of the package be to offer superior product protection, introduce a novel dispensing method, suggest certain qualities about the product or the company, or something else?

> General Foods developed a new dog-food product in the form of meatlike patties. Management decided that the unique and palatable appearance of these patties demanded the maximum visibility. Visibility was defined as the basic packaging concept, and management considered alternatives in this light. It finally narrowed down the choice to a tray with a film covering.[26]

A host of further decisions must be made on the component elements of package design—*size, shape, materials, color, text,* and *brand mark.* Decisions must be made on much text or little text, cellophane or other transparent film, a plastic or a laminate tray, and so on. Each packaging element must be harmo-

[26] See "General Foods—Post Division (B)," Case M-102, Harvard Business School, 1964.

nized with the other packaging elements; size suggests certain things about materials, materials suggest certain things about colors, and so forth. The packaging elements also must be guided by decisions on pricing, advertising, and other marketing elements.

After the packaging is designed, it must be put through a number of tests. *Engineering tests* are conducted to insure that the packaging stands up under normal conditions; *visual tests,* to insure that the script is legible and the colors harmonious; *dealer tests,* to insure that dealers find the packages attractive and easy to handle; and *consumer tests,* to insure favorable consumer response.

In spite of these precautions, a packaging design occasionally gets through with some basic flaw that is discovered belatedly:

> Sizzl-Spray, a pressurized can of barbecue sauce developed by Heublein, . . . had a potential packaging disaster that was discovered in the market tests. . . . "We thought we had a good can, but fortunately we first test marketed the product in stores in Texas and California. It appears as soon as the cans got warm they began to explode. Because we hadn't gotten into national distribution, our loss was only $150,000 instead of a couple of million." [27]

It should be clear why developing packaging for a new product may cost a few hundred thousand dollars and take from several months to a year. This may sound like excessive attention to pay to packaging, but for those who recognize the several functions it performs in consumer attraction and satisfaction, the attention is well warranted.

MARKET TESTING

After management is satisfied with the product's functional performance, the product moves into further market testing. Market testing is the stage where the product and marketing program are introduced into more authentic consumer settings to learn how well the product will do before making a final decision to launch it in the marketplace.

Not all companies choose the route of market testing. A company officer of Revlon, Inc., stated:

> In our field—primarily higher-priced cosmetics not geared for mass distribution—it would be unnecessary for us to market test. When we develop a new product, say an improved liquid makeup, we know it's going to sell because we're familiar with the field. And we've got 1,500 demonstrators in department stores to promote it. [28]

Most companies, however, know they can pick up valuable information about the users, trade, marketing program effectiveness, market potential, and other matters from market testing. The main issues are, how much market testing and what kind?

The amount of market testing is influenced by the amount of *investment*

---

[27] "Product Tryouts: Sales Tests in Selected Cities Help Trim Risks of National Marketings," *Wall Street Journal,* August 10, 1962, p. 1.

[28] Ibid.

cost and *risk* on the one hand, and the *time pressure* and *research cost* on the other. Products involving a substantial investment deserve to be market tested so as not to make a mistake; the cost of the market tests will be an insignificant percentage of the cost of the project itself. Products involving high risk—those that create new-product categories (first instant breakfast) or have novel features (first fluoride toothpaste)—warrant more market testing than those that represent simple modifications (another toothpaste brand). On the other hand, the amount of market testing may have to be severely limited if the company is under great pressure to introduce its brand, as might happen if the season is just starting or if competitors are about to rush their products into the market. The company may prefer the risk of a product failure to the risk of losing distribution or market penetration on a highly successful product. The cost of market testing will also make a difference in how much is done and what kind.

Market-testing methods differ somewhat in the testing of consumer versus industrial products, and they shall be discussed separately.

Consumer-Goods Market Testing

The purpose of consumer-goods market testing is to find out how consumers and the trade react to handling, using, and repurchasing the product, and how large the market is.

In testing consumers, the company is interested in forming estimates of the main components of sales, specifically *trial, first repeat, adoption,* and *frequency of purchase.* The company hopes to find all of these at high levels. In some cases, it will find many consumers trying the product but not rebuying it, showing a lack of product satisfaction. Or it might find high first-time repurchase but then a rapid wear-out effect. Or it might find high permanent adoption but low frequency of purchase (such as in the case of gourmet frozen food) because the buyers have decided to use the product only on special occasions.

In testing the trade, the company wants to learn how many and what types of dealers will handle the product, under what terms, and with what shelf-position commitments.

The major methods of consumer-goods market testing, going from the less to the more costly, are described in the following paragraphs.[29]

Sales-wave research   Sales-wave research is an extension of the ordinary home-use testing in which consumers who initially try the product at no cost are offered the opportunity to obtain more of the product, or any competitor's products, at slightly reduced prices. They may be reoffered the product as many as three to five times (sales waves), the company noting each time how many consumers selected that company's product again and what comments they reported about usage. Sales-wave research can also include exposing consumers to one or more advertising concepts in rough form to see what impact the advertising has on subsequent repeat-purchase behavior.

The main advantage of sales-wave research is that the company can estimate the repeat-purchase rate under conditions where consumers are spending their own money and have a choice among competitors' brands. Another advantage is that the company can gauge the impact of alternative advertising concepts on consumer repurchase behavior. Finally, sales-wave research can be

---

[29] See Edward M. Tauber, "Forecasting Sales Prior to Test Market," *Journal of Marketing,* January 1977, pp. 80–84.

conducted under relative competitive security, implemented in a short time, and carried out without needing to develop final packaging or advertising.

On the other hand, sales-wave research does not indicate the trial rates that would be achieved by a given-size promotion budget, since the consumers are preselected to try the product. Nor does it indicate anything about the brand's power to gain distribution and favorable shelf position from the trade.

A variation of sales waves is the *printed-shopping-list method.* This method uses a special consumer panel whose members continually buy products from a printed shopping list, which are then delivered to their homes. New products are inconspicuously added to the long shopping list from time to time and promoted earlier by a direct-mail piece to the home. The company can learn the trial and repeat-purchase rates without exposing the product to competitors in the open market. However, the company is not allowed to interview panel members for more information, and it has to worry about possible panel biases. The advertising exposure is limited to printed material, and therefore there is no test of the impact of a full advertising program.

Simulated store technique   The simulated store technique (also called "laboratory test markets," "purchase laboratories," or "accelerated test marketing") calls for finding thirty to forty shoppers (at a shopping center or elsewhere) and inviting them to a brief screening of some television commercials. Included are a number of well-known commercials and some new ones, and they cover a range of products. One of the commercials advertises the new product, but it is not singled out for attention. The consumers are given a small amount of money and invited into a store where they may use the money to buy any items or they may keep the money. The company notes how many consumers buy the new product and competing brands. This provides a measure of product trial and of the commercial's effectiveness against competing commercials. The consumers reconvene and are asked the reasons for their purchases or nonpurchases. Some weeks later they are reinterviewed by phone to determine product attitudes, usage, satisfaction, and repurchase intention and are also offered an opportunity to repurchase any products.

This method has several advantages, including the measuring of trial rates (and repeat rates if extended), advertising effectiveness, speedy results, and competitive security. The results are usually incorporated into mathematical models that are used to project ultimate sales levels. Marketing research firms that offer this service report surprisingly accurate prediction of sales levels of products that are subsequently launched in the market.[30]

Controlled test marketing   Several research firms have arranged controlled panels of stores that have agreed to carry new products for a certain fee. The company with the new product specifies the number, store types, and geographical locations it wants. The research firm takes responsibility for delivering the product to the participating stores, and for controlling shelf location, num-

---

[30] The best-known systems are Yankelovich's "Laboratory Test Market," Elrick and Lavidge's "Comp," and Management Decision Systems' "Assessor." For a description of "Assessor," see Alvin J. Silk and Glen L. Urban, "Pre-Test Marketing Evaluation of New Packaged Goods: A Model and Measurement Methodology," *Journal of Marketing Research*, May 1978, pp. 171–91.

ber of facings, displays and point-of-purchase promotions, and pricing, according to prespecified plans. Sales results can be audited both from shelf movement and from consumer diaries kept by a sample of consumers who stop at these stores. The company may also test small-scale advertising in local newspapers in conjunction with the test.

Controlled testing (also called "minimarket testing") allows the company to gauge the effectiveness of in-store factors and limited advertising on consumers' buying behavior toward a new product without the consumers' being contacted in advance or during the process. A sample of consumers could be interviewed later to gather their impressions of the product. The company does not have to use its sales force, give trade allowances, or take the time to buy into distribution. There are also disadvantages, in that this technique does not provide the company with experience in the problems of selling the new product to the trade. This technique also involves a greater exposure of the product to competition.

Test markets Test markets are the ultimate form of testing a new consumer product in a situation resembling the one that would be faced in a full-scale launching of the product. The company usually works with an outside research firm to locate a small number of representative test cities in which the company's sales force will try to sell the trade on carrying the product and giving it good shelf exposure. The company will put on a full advertising and promotion program in these markets similar to the one that would be used in national marketing. It is a chance to do a dress rehearsal of the total plan. Test marketing can cost the company several hundred thousand dollars, depending upon the number of cities tested, the duration of the test, and the amount of data the company plans to collect.

Test marketing is expected to yield several benefits. The primary motive is to *achieve a more reliable forecast of future sales*. If product sales fall below target levels, the company may have to drop or modify the product.

A second motive is to *pretest alternative marketing plans*. Some years ago Colgate-Palmolive used a different marketing mix in each of four cities to test market a new soap product.[31] The four approaches were: (1) an average amount of advertising coupled with free samples distributed door to door, (2) heavy advertising plus samples, (3) an average amount of advertising linked with mailed redeemable coupons, and (4) an average amount of advertising with no special introductory offer. Colgate found that the third alternative generated the best sales and profit level.

Through test marketing, the company may discover a product fault that escaped its attention in the product-development stage. It may pick up valuable clues to distribution-level problems. And the company may gain better insight into the behavior of different market segments.

Test marketing calls for several decisions.[32]

---

[31] *Wall Street Journal*, "Product Tryouts."

[32] For some good discussions, see N. D. Cadbury, "When, Where and How to Test Market," *Harvard Business Review*, May–June 1975, pp. 96–105; and Jay E. Klompmaker, G. David Hughes, and Russell I. Haley, "Test Marketing in New Product Development," *Harvard Business Review*, May–June 1976, pp. 128–38.

1. *How many test cities?* Most tests use between two and six cities, with an average of four. In general, a larger number of cities should be used, (1) the greater the maximum possible loss and/or the probability of loss from going national, (2) the greater the number of alternative marketing plans and/or the greater the uncertainty surrounding which is best, (3) the greater the number of regional differences, and (4) the greater the chance of calculated test-market interference by competitors.

2. *Which cities?* No single city is a perfect microcosm of the nation as a whole. Some cities, however, typify aggregate national or regional characteristics better than others and have become popular for test-marketing purposes, among them Syracuse, Dayton, Peoria, and Des Moines. Each company develops its own test-city selection criteria. One company looks for test cities that have diversified industry, good media coverage, cooperative chain stores, average competitive activity, and no evidence of being overtested. Additional test-city selection criteria may be introduced because of the special characteristics of the product. Patio Foods, in testing a new line of frozen Mexican dinners, selected cities according to the incidence of travel to Mexico, the existence of a Spanish-language press, and good retail sales of prepared chili and frozen Chinese food.

3. *Length of test?* Test markets have lasted anywhere from a few months to several years. The longer the product's *average repurchase period*, the longer the desired test period, to observe repeat-purchase rates. On the other hand, the period should be cut down if competitors are rushing to the market.

4. *What information?* Management must decide on the type of information to collect in relation to its value and cost. *Warehouse shipment data* will show gross inventory buying but not indicate weekly sales at retail. *Store audits* will show actual retail sales and competitors' market shares but will not indicate anything about the characteristics of the buyers buying the different brands. *Consumer panels* will indicate what people are buying what brands, and their loyalty and switching rates. *Buyer surveys* can be conducted to obtain information in depth about consumer attitudes, usage, and satisfaction. Among other things that can be studied during the test-market period are trade attitudes, retail distribution, and the effectiveness of advertising, promotion, and point-of-sale material.

5. *What action to take?* Table 13–4 shows four possible test-market findings bearing on trial and repeat-purchase rates. If the test markets show a high trial and high repurchase rate, this suggests the desirability of a GO-decision. If the test markets show a high trial and a low repurchase rate, then the customers are not satisfied with the product and it should be either redesigned or abandoned. If the test markets show a low trial and a high repurchase rate, then the product is essentially appealing but more people have to be influenced to try it earlier: this means increasing advertising and sales promotion. Finally, if the trial and repurchase rates are both low, then the product should be dropped.

TABLE 13–4
Alternative Actions Following Test-Market Results

TRIAL RATE	REPURCHASE RATE	ACTION
High	High	Commercialize the product
High	Low	Redesign product or drop it
Low	High	Increase advertising and sales promotion
Low	Low	Drop the product

In spite of the benefits of test marketing, some experts question its value. Achenbaum lists five concerns:

1. There is the problem of obtaining a set of markets that is reasonably representative of the country as a whole.
2. There is the problem of translating national media plans into local equivalents.
3. There is the problem of estimating what is going to happen next year based on what has happened in this year's competitive environment.
4. There is the problem of competitive knowledge of your test and of deciding whether any local counteractivities are representative of what competition will do nationally at a later date.
5. There is the problem of extraneous and uncontrollable factors such as economic conditions and weather.[33]

Achenbaum contends that test marketing's main value lies not in sales forecasting but in learning about unsuspected problems and opportunities connected with the new product. He points to the large number of products that failed after successful test-market results. Some large companies are beginning to skip the test-marketing stage altogether and are relying on the earlier market-testing methods.

Industrial-Goods Market Testing

New industrial goods typically undergo extensive *product testing* in the labs to measure performance, reliability, design, and operating costs. Following satisfactory results, many companies will proceed to commercialize the product by listing it in the catalog and turning it over to the sales force. Today, however, an increasing number of companies are turning to *market testing* as an intermediate step. Market testing can indicate: (1) how the product performs under actual operating conditions in the customer's hands; (2) who are the key buying influences; (3) how different buying influences react to alternative prices and sales approaches; (4) what is the market potential; and (5) what are the best market segments.

Test marketing is not typically used in the market testing of industrial products. It is too expensive to produce a small sample of Concordes or new computers, let alone actually put them up for sale in a select set of markets to see how they sell. Industrial buyers won't buy durable goods that are being test marketed only, since they want assurances of service and parts. Furthermore, marketing research firms have not generally built the test market systems in industrial markets that are found in consumer markets. Therefore, industrial-goods manufacturers generally have to use other methods to research the market's reactions to a new industrial product.

The most common method is a *product-use test*, similar to the in-home use test for consumer products.[34] The manufacturer selects a small group of potential customers who agree to use the new product for a limited period. The product may be used at the manufacturer's site but is more typically used at the customer's site. The manufacturer's technical people observe how the customer's

---

[33] Alvin A. Achenbaum, "The Purpose of Test Marketing," in *The Marketing Concept in Action,* ed. Robert M. Kaplan (Chicago: American Marketing Association, 1964), p. 582.

[34] The discussion of this and other methods draws heavily on Morgan B. MacDonald, Jr., *Appraising the Market for New Industrial Products* (New York: Conference Board, 1967), chap. 2.

workers use the product, which often exposes unanticipated problems of safety and servicing. This clues the manufacturer about customer training and servicing requirements. After the test, the customer is given an opportunity to express purchase intent and other reactions.

A second common market-test method is to introduce the new industrial product at *trade shows*. Trade shows draw a large number of buyers to view new exhibits in a few concentrated days. The manufacturer can see how much interest buyers show in the new product, how they react to various features and terms, and how many orders or purchase intentions they express. The disadvantage is that the trade show reveals the product to all competitors, and the manufacturer should be fairly ready to launch it at that point.

The new industrial product can also be tested in *distributor and dealer display rooms*, where it may stand next to the manufacturer's other products and possibly competitors' products. This method yields preference and pricing information in the normal selling atmosphere for the product. The disadvantages are that the customers may want to place orders that cannot be filled, and those customers who come in might not be representative of the total market.

Controlled or test marketing has been used by some manufacturers. They will produce a limited supply of the product, often through subcontractors, and give it to the sales force to sell in a limited set of geographical areas that will be given promotional support, printed catalogue sheets, and so on. In this way, management can gain experience about what might happen under full-scale marketing and be in a better position to make the final decision about launching.

COMMERCIALIZATION

At this point, management presumably has enough information to make a final decision about whether to launch the new product. If the company goes ahead with commercialization, it will face its largest costs to date. The company will have to build or rent a full-scale manufacturing facility. The size of the plant will be a critical decision variable. The company can build a smaller plant than called for by the sales forecast, to be on the safe side. This is what Quaker Oats did when it launched its 100% Natural brand of breakfast cereal. The demand so far exceeded their sales forecast that for about a year they could not supply enough product to the stores. Although they were gratified with the response, the low forecast cost them a considerable amount of lost profits.

Another major cost is marketing. To introduce a major new household detergent into the national market may require $10 to $20 million for advertising and promotion alone in the first year. In the introduction of new food products, marketing expenditures typically represent 57 percent of sales during the first year.

The decision to commercialize involves four component decisions.

When (Timing) The first decision concerns *timing* questions. If the new product replaces another product, the new product's introduction might be delayed until the old product's stock is drawn down through normal sales. If the demand is highly seasonal, the new product should not be introduced until the seasonal timing is right. If the new product could be improved further, the company may prefer to miss the selling season in order to come out with a better product.

Where (Geographical Strategy)	The next decision is whether the company should launch the new product in a *single locality,* a *region,* a *set of regions,* the *national market,* or the *international market.* Few companies have the confidence, capital, and capacity to put new products into full national distribution from the start. Instead, they will develop a *planned market rollout* over time. Small companies, in particular, will select an attractive city and put on a blitz campaign to win share. They will spread out to further cities as they gain footholds. Large companies will generally introduce their product into a whole region and then move on to the next region. A few companies with large national distribution networks, like the auto companies, will launch their new models in the national market unless there are production shortages.

In rollout marketing, the company has to rate the alternative markets for their attractiveness. The various candidate markets can be listed as rows, and rollout attractiveness criteria can be listed as columns. The major rating criteria are: *market potential, company's local reputation, cost of filling the pipeline, quality of research data in that area, influence of area on other areas,* and *competitive penetration.* In this way the company determines the prime markets and develops a geographical rollout plan.

The factor of competitive presence is very important. Suppose McDonald's wants to launch a new chain of fast-food pizza parlors. Suppose Shakey's, a formidable competitor, is strongly entrenched on the East Coast. Another pizza chain is entrenched on the West Coast but is considered weak. The Midwest is the battleground between two other chains. The South is open, but Shakey's is planning to move in. We can see that McDonald's faces quite a complex decision in choosing a rollout strategy.

To Whom (Target Market Prospects)	Within the rollout markets, the company must target its distribution and promotion to the best prospect groups. Presumably the company has already profiled the prime prospects on the basis of data gathered in the market testing or earlier stages. Prime prospects for a new consumer product would ideally have four characteristics:

1. They would be early adopters of the product.
2. They would be heavy users of the product.
3. They would give the product good word of mouth and influence others to buy it.
4. They could be reached at a low cost.[35]

Few profiled groups have all of these characteristics. The company can rate the various prospect groups by these characteristics and then target its initial efforts to them. The aim is to generate high sales as soon as possible to motivate the sales force and attract other new prospects.

How (Introductory Marketing Strategy)	The final step is to develop the marketing strategy for introducing the new product in the rollout markets. It calls for allocating the marketing budget among the marketing-mix elements and sequencing the various activities. Thus a new car might be launched by developing publicity several months before the product is available, then switching to advertising when the car is in the showrooms, and

[35] Philip Kotler and Gerald Zaltman, "Targeting Prospects for a New Product," *Journal of Advertising Research,* February 1976, pp. 7–20.

later developing promotional incentives to draw more people to the showrooms. To sequence and coordinate the multitude of activities involved in launching a new product, management increasingly is using network planning techniques, such as critical-path scheduling.[36]

THE CONSUMER-ADOPTION PROCESS

The *consumer-adoption process* begins where the *firm's innovation process* leaves off. It deals with the process by which potential customers come to learn about the new product, try it, and eventually adopt or reject it. It underlies the introduction and rapid growth stages of the product life cycle. The company must understand this process so that it can bring about early market awareness and trial usage. The *consumer-adoption process* should be distinguished from the *consumer-loyalty process*, which is the concern of the established producer.

The earliest approach used by new-product marketers for launching a new product was to distribute it widely and inform everyone who might be a potential purchaser. This *mass-market approach*, however, has two drawbacks: (1) it requires heavy marketing expenditures, and (2) it involves a substantial number of wasted exposures to nonpotential and low-potential buyers. These drawbacks have led to a second approach called *heavy-user target marketing*, that of directing the product to the group that tends to account for a substantial share of all purchasing. This makes sense, provided heavy users are identifiable and among the first to try the new product. But it was noticed that even within the heavy-user group, persons differed in how much interest they showed in new products and in how fast they could be drawn into trying them. Certain persons tended to be earlier adopters than others. The import of this finding is that the new-product marketer ought to direct marketing effort to those persons who are most likely to adopt the product early. *Early-adopter theory* grew around this view and held that:

1. Persons within a target market will differ in the amount of time that passes between their exposure to a new product and their trial of the new product.
2. Early adopters are likely to share some traits in common that differentiate them from late adopters.
3. There exist efficient media for reaching early-adopter types.
4. Early-adopter types are likely to be high on opinion leadership and therefore helpful in "advertising" the new product to other potential buyers.

We now turn to the theory of innovation diffusion and adoption, which provides clues to identifying the best early prospects.

Concepts in Innovation Diffusion and Adoption

The central concept is that of an *innovation*, which refers to any good, service, or idea that is *perceived* by someone as new. The idea may have had a long history, but it is still an innovation to the person who sees it as being new.

Innovations are assimilated into the social system over time. *Diffusion process* is the name given to "the spread of a new idea from its source of inven-

---

[36] See Yung Wong, "Critical Path Analysis for New Product Planning," *Journal of Marketing,* October 1964, pp. 53–59.

tion or creation to its ultimate users or adopters."[37] The *adoption process,* on the other hand, focuses on "the mental process through which an individual passes from first hearing about an innovation to final adoption." *Adoption* itself is a decision by an individual to use an innovation regularly.

The differences among individuals in their response to new ideas is called their *innovativeness.* Specifically, innovativeness is "the degree to which an individual is relatively earlier in adopting new ideas than the other members of his social system." On the basis of their innovativeness, individuals can be classified into different *adopter categories* (see p. 344).

Individuals also can be classified in terms of their influence on others with respect to innovations. *Opinion leaders* are "those individuals from whom others seek information or advice." Individuals or firms who actively seek to change other people's minds are called *change agents.*

Propositions about the Consumer-Adoption Process

We are now ready to examine the main generalizations drawn from hundreds of studies of how people accept new ideas.

Stages in the adoption process   The first proposition is that *the individual consumer goes through a series of stages of acceptance in the process of adopting a new product.* The stages are classified by Rogers as follows:

1. *Awareness:* the individual becomes cognizant of the innovation but lacks information about it.
2. *Interest:* the individual is stimulated to seek information about the innovation.
3. *Evaluation:* the individual considers whether it would make sense to try the innovation.
4. *Trial:* the individual tries the innovation on a small scale to improve his or her estimate of its utility.
5. *Adoption:* the individual decides to make full and regular use of the innovation.

The value of this model of the adoption process is that it requires the innovator to think carefully about new-product acceptance. The manufacturer of electric dishwashers may discover that many consumers are frozen in the interest stage; they cannot move to the trial stage, because of their uncertainty and the large investment. But these same consumers would be willing to use an electric dishwasher on a trial basis for a small fee. Recognizing this, the manufacturer may institute a trial-use plan with option to buy.

Individual differences in innovativeness   The second proposition is that *people differ markedly in their penchant for trying new products.* In each product area, there are apt to be "consumption pioneers" and early adopters. Some women are the first to adopt new clothing fashions or new appliances, such as the microwave oven, some doctors are the first to prescribe new medicines,[38] and some farmers are the first to adopt new farming methods.[39]

[37] The following discussion leans heavily on Everett M. Rogers, *Diffusion of Innovations* (New York: Free Press, 1962).

[38] See James Coleman, Elihu Katz, and Herbert Menzel, "The Diffusion of an Innovation among Physicians," *Sociometry,* December 1957, pp. 253–70.

[39] See J. Bohlen and G. Beal, *How Farm People Accept New Ideas,* Special Report No. 15 (Ames: Iowa State College Agricultural Extension Service, November 1955).

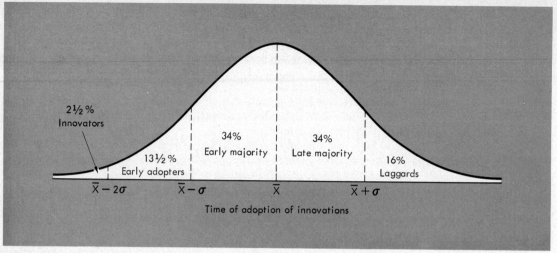

SOURCE: Redrawn from Everett M. Rogers, *Diffusion of Innovations* (New York: Free Press, 1962), p. 162.

FIGURE 13–4

Adopter Categorization on the Basis of Relative Time of Adoption of Innovations

Other individuals, however, tend to adopt innovations much later. This has led to a classification of people into the adopter categories shown in Figure 13–4. The adoption process is represented as following a normal (or near normal) distribution when plotted over time. After a slow start, an increasing number of people adopt the innovation, the number reaches a peak, and then it diminishes as fewer persons remain in the nonadopter category.

Convenient breaks in the distribution are used to establish adopter categories. Thus innovators are defined as the first 2½ percent of the individuals to adopt a new idea; the early adopters are the next 13½ percent who adopt the new idea, and so forth. Although this partitioning in terms of unit standard deviations is somewhat arbitrary, the model provides the needed standardization for comparing different studies of product adoption.

Rogers has characterized the five adopter groups in terms of ideational values. The dominant value of innovators is *venturesomeness;* they like to try new ideas, even at some risk, and are cosmopolite in orientation. The dominant value of early adopters is *respect;* they enjoy a position in the community as opinion leaders and adopt new ideas early but with discretion. The dominant value of the early majority is *deliberateness;* these people like to adopt new ideas before the average member of the social system, although they rarely are leaders. The dominant value of the late majority is *skepticism;* they do not adopt an innovation until the weight of majority opinion seems to legitimize its utility. Finally, the dominant value of the laggards is *tradition;* they are suspicious of any changes, mix with other tradition-bound people, and adopt the innovation only because it has now taken on a measure of tradition itself.

The marketing implication of the adopter classification is that an innovating firm should direct its communications to those people who are likely to

be early in adopting the innovation; messages reaching late adopters and laggards are wasted.

The identification of early adopters is not easy. So far no one has demonstrated the existence of a general personality factor called innovativeness. Individuals tend to be innovative in certain areas and laggard in others. We can
think of a businessman who dresses conservatively but who delights in trying unfamiliar cuisines. The firm's problem is to identify the characteristics of those
who are likely to be early adopters in its product area. The probability of being
an early adopter may turn out to be related to easily identified economic, educational, social, or personality characteristics. For example, studies show that
innovative farmers are likely to be better educated and more efficient than noninnovative farmers. Innovative housewives are more gregarious and usually of a
higher social status than noninnovative housewives. Certain communities, especially those with higher than average mobility, tend to be more ready to accept
new ideas. Drawing on several studies, Rogers offered the following hypotheses
about early adopters:

> The relatively earlier adopters in a social system tend to be younger in age, have
> higher social status, a more favorable financial position, more specialized oper-
> ations, and a different type of mental ability from later adopters. Earlier adopters
> utilize information sources that are more impersonal and cosmopolite than later
> adopters and that are in closer contact with the origin of new ideas. Earlier adop-
> ters utilize a greater number of different information sources than do later
> adopters. The social relationships of earlier adopters are more cosmopolite than
> for later adopters, and earlier adopters have more opinion leadership.[40]

Once the characteristics of early adopters are identified, a marketing communications program can be developed for the new product calculated to reach
and interest these people. The known media habits of these people can be used
to increase the effectiveness of the company's advertising. The company can also
supply samples to community leaders and utilize store demonstrations to attract
the early adopters.

Role of personal influence   The third proposition is that *personal influence
plays a very large role in the adoption of new products.* By *personal influence* is
meant the effect of product statements made by one person on another's attitude
or probability of purchase. Katz and Lazarsfeld reported:

> About half of the women in our sample reported that they had recently made
> some change from a product or brand to which they were accustomed to some-
> thing new. The fact that one third of these changes involved personal influences
> indicates that there is also considerable traffic in marketing advice. Women con-
> sult each other for opinions about new products, about the quality of different
> brands, about shopping economies and the like.[41]

Although personal influence is an important factor throughout the diffusion process, its significance is greater in some situations and for some individuals

[40] Rogers, *Diffusion of Innovations,* p. 192.

[41] Elihu Katz and Paul F. Lazarsfeld, *Personal Influence* (New York: Free Press, 1955), p. 234.

than for others. Personal influence seems to be more important in the evaluation stage of the adoption process than in the other stages. It seems to have more influence on the later adopters than the earlier adopters. And it appears to be more important in risky situations than in safe situations.

Influence of product characteristics on the rate of adoption   The fourth proposition is that *the character of the innovation itself affects the rate of adoption.* Five characteristics seem to have an especially important influence on the adoption rate. The first is the innovation's *relative advantage,* or the degree to which it appears superior to previous ideas. The greater the perceived relative advantage, whether in terms of higher profitability, reliability, or ease of operation, the more quickly the innovation will be adopted.

The second characteristic is the innovation's *compatibility,* or the degree to which it is consistent with the values and experiences of the individuals in the social system.

Third is the innovation's *complexity,* or the degree to which it is relatively difficult to understand or use. The more complex innovations are likely to take a longer time to diffuse, other things being equal.

Fourth is the innovation's *divisibility,* or the degree to which it may be tried on a limited basis. The evidence of many studies indicates that divisibility helps to increase the rate of adoption.

The fifth characteristic is the innovation's *communicability,* or the degree to which the results are observable or describable to others. Innovations that lend themselves to better demonstration or description of advantage will diffuse faster in the social system.

Other characteristics have also been found to influence the rate of adoption, such as initial cost, continuing cost, risk and uncertainty, scientific credibility, and social approval. The new-product marketer has to research the role of all these factors and give the key ones maximum attention in developing the new-product and marketing program.

Influence of organizational buyers' characteristics on the rate of adoption   The fifth proposition is that *organizations, like individuals, can be classified as to their likely rate of trying and adopting a new product.* Thus, the producer of a new teaching method would want to identify the schools that rank high in adoption probability. The producer of a new piece of medical equipment would want to identify hospitals that rank high in adoption probability. Some of the characteristics might be associated with the organization's environment (community progressiveness, community income), the organization itself (size, profits, pressure to change), and the administrators (education level, age, cosmopolitanism). Once a set of useful indicators are found, they can be used to identify the best target organizations.

SUMMARY

More and more organizations are recognizing the advantages, indeed the necessity, of developing new products and services. If anything, their current offerings are facing shortening life spans and must be replaced by newer products.

New-product development, however, is not a primrose path. The risks of innovation are as great as the rewards. A large percentage of new products fail in the marketplace, and a still larger number have to be dropped before commercialization. The key to successful innovation lies in developing better organizational arrangements for handling new-product ideas and developing sound research and decision procedures.

The new-product-development process consists of eight stages: idea generation, idea screening, concept development and testing, marketing strategy and development, business analysis, product development, test marketing, and commercialization. The purpose of each successive stage is to decide whether the idea should be further developed or dropped. The company seeks decision criteria for each stage that minimize the chances of poor ideas moving forward and good ideas being rejected. The last stage, commercialization, involves the introduction of the products that have passed the previous tests; it is benefited by marketing planning and strategy based on an understanding of the consumer-adoption process.

**QUESTIONS
AND
PROBLEMS**

1. The new-product development process starts with a search for good ideas. Suggest some concepts that can guide a company's search effort.

2. A candy store chain is seeking ideas for a new sales promotion campaign. Show how morphological analysis might be used to generate a large number of ideas for a campaign.

3. Complained a research executive: "Would fluorocarbon resins, nylon, or polyethylene have come out of a screening formula—or a check list, for that matter? The important things are intuition and judgment. Research is a creative art." Is this a valid argument against formal screening devices? Can you name any advantages of using formal screening devices?

4. (a) Expected profit and risk are two major dimensions for determining whether to introduce a new product nationally. Can you develop a diagram using these two dimensions to show how critical limits might be set up by a firm before a market test to guide its decision after the test? (b) Suppose a firm finds that the test-market results are borderline and concludes that the product would probably yield a below-average return. It has sunk a lot of money into the development of the product. Should it introduce the product nationally or drop it? (c) State the two opposing risks that a firm faces when it bases its new-product decision on test-market results. How can it reduce these risks? (d) In the test marketing of Colgate's new soap (described in the text), the third marketing mix yielded the highest sales. Does this mean that it should be preferred to the other mixes if the product is launched nationally?

5. In 1950, Charles Saunders introduced a store called the Keedozall. The customer would pass a series of closed displays and insert a key into slots for wanted merchandise. He would take a resulting punched tape to a check-out cashier who fed the tape to a register. The amount would be totaled and the assembled merchandise delivered at the check-out point. Do you think this innovation in retailing was successful? Why or why not?

6. General Foods developed a new dog food product, PC-33. Not a canned or dry dog food, this product had a meat formulation and the appearance of hamburgers and could be sold on the regular grocery shelves. It offered a new combination of convenience and nutritional values. Develop four alternative product concepts for this new dog food.

7. A school furniture company is eager to develop a new line of lightweight chairs for elementary school classrooms. Recommend a set of steps for researching, developing, and testing these chairs.

8. A company president asked his new product manager what a proposed new product

would earn if launched. "Profits of three million dollars in five years." Then he asked whether the product might fail. "Yes." "What would we lose if the product fails?" "One million dollars." "Forget it," said the president. Do you agree with the president's judgment?

9. The International Harvester Company is planning to introduce a new line of trucks with luxury cabin features. Propose a plan for encouraging the dealers to sell these trucks and to promote these trucks to their target customers.

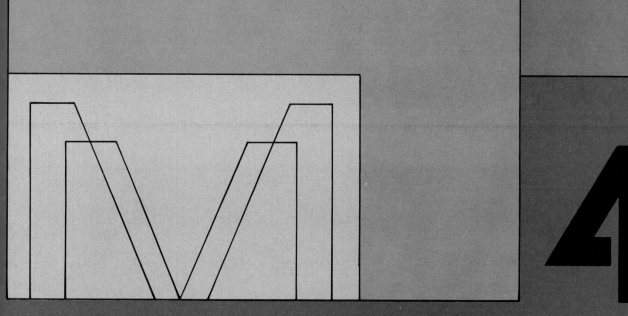

Assembling the Marketing Mix

4

PRODUCT DECISIONS

In the factory we make cosmetics, and in the drugstore we sell hope.
CHARLES REVSON

14

We are now ready to examine, in the chapters of Part 4, each of the major elements of the marketing mix. It is appropriate that we begin with product, the most important element of the marketing mix. In the first part of this chapter we will explore the concept of "product," and then we will examine the various decisions that management must make at the level of its overall product mix, product lines, brands, and services.

THE CONCEPT OF A PRODUCT

The word "product" has several meanings. We shall define it in the following way:

A *product* is anything that can be offered to a market for attention, acquisition, use, or consumption; it includes physical objects, services, personalities, places, organizations, and ideas.

Other names for a product would be the offering, offer, value package, or benefit bundle.

"Product" has three senses that are worth distinguishing.

At the most fundamental level we can talk about the *core product*. The core product answers the question, "What is the buyer really buying?" The product is simply the packaging of a problem-solving service. The woman purchasing lipstick is not buying a set of chemical and physical attributes for their own sake; she is buying hope. The woman buying a camera is not buying a mechanical box for its own sake; she is buying pleasure, nostalgia, a form of immortality. The marketer's job is to sell *core benefits*, not *product features*. Notice that the core benefit is the center of Figure 14–1.

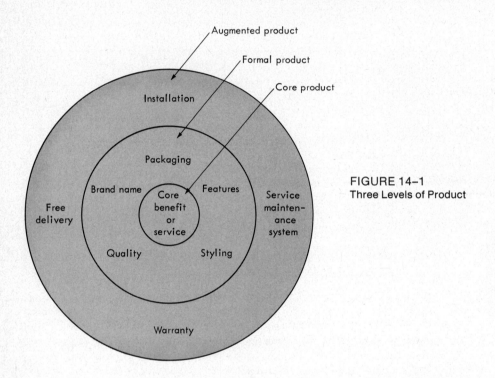

FIGURE 14–1
Three Levels of Product

The *formal product* is the larger "packaging" of the core product. It is what the target market recognizes as the tangible offer. Lipsticks, computers, educational seminars, political candidates, are all formal products. If the formal product is a physical object, it may be recognized by the market as having up to five characteristics: a *quality level, features, styling,* a *brand name,* and *packaging.* If it is a service, it may have some or all of these facets in an analogous manner. We can say that the U.S. Income Tax Advisory Service exhibits a certain quality level in that government tax advisers have a certain degree of competence. The service has certain features, such as being offered at no charge and usually requiring some waiting time. The service has a certain styling, such as being brief, cursory, and impersonal. The service has a certain formal name, that of "Federal Income Tax Advisory Service." Finally, the service is packaged within branch offices located in various cities.

Finally, the *augmented product* is the totality of benefits that the person receives or experiences in obtaining the formal product. The augmented product of IBM is not only the computer but a whole set of accompanying services, including instruction, canned software programs, programming services, maintenance and repairs, guarantees, and so on. IBM's outstanding position in the computer field is due in part to its early recognition that the customer wants all of these things when buying a computer. This recognition leads to the notion of *systems selling;* the company is selling a system, not just a computer.[1] It leads the sellers to look at the buyer's total *consumption system*—"the way a purchaser of a product performs the total task of whatever it is that he or she is trying to accomplish when using the product."[2] As a result, sellers are able to recognize many opportunities for augmenting their product offering as a competitive maneuver. According to Levitt, the *new competition* is not between what companies produce in their factories, but between *what they add to their factory output in the form of packaging, services, advertising, customer advice, financing, delivery arrangements, warehousing, and other things that people value.*[3] The firm that develops the right augmented product will thrive in this competition.

Product Hierarchy

Each product is related in a hierarchical fashion to a whole set of other products. We can postulate the existence of product hierarchies stretching from basic needs down to very particular items that might satisfy those needs. We can identify seven levels of the product hierarchy. Here they are defined and illustrated for life insurance.

1. *Need family.* The core need that actualizes the product family. Example: security.
2. *Product family.* All the product classes that can satisfy a core need with more or less effectiveness. Example: savings and income.
3. *Product class.* A group of products within the product family that are recognized as having a certain functional coherence. Example: financial instruments.
4. *Product line.* A group of products within a product class that are closely related, either because they function in a similar manner, are sold to the same customer groups, are marketed through the same types of outlets, or fall within given price ranges. Example: life insurance.
5. *Product type.* Those items within a product line that share one of several possible forms of the product. Example: term life.
6. *Brand.* The name associated with one or more items in the product line that is used to identify the source or character of the item(s). Example: Prudential.
7. *Item.* A distinct unit within a brand or product line that is distinguishable by size, price, appearance, or some other attribute. The item is sometimes called a *stockkeeping unit,* a product variant, or subvariant. Example: renewable.

[1] Systems selling really originated as systems buying, to describe government procurement practices in buying a major weapons or communication system. Instead of purchasing and putting all the components together, the government would solicit bids from prime contractors who would be willing to assemble the package or system. The winning prime contractor would then buy or bid for the subcomponents. Sellers have increasingly recognized that buyers like to purchase in this way and have responded with augmented-product offerings.

[2] See Harper W. Boyd, Jr., and Sidney J. Levy, "New Dimensions in Consumer Analysis," *Harvard Business Review,* November–December 1963, pp. 129–40.

[3] Theodore Levitt, *The Marketing Mode* (New York: McGraw-Hill Book Company, 1969), p. 2.

Another example: the need "hope" gives rise to a product family called toiletries and a product class within that family called cosmetics, of which one line is lipstick, which has different product forms, such as tube lipstick, which is offered as a brand called Revlon in a particular size, such as economy size.

Two other terms frequently arise. A *product system* is a group of diverse but related items that function in a compatible manner. For example, the Nikon Company offers a basic 35mm camera along with an extensive set of lenses, filters, and other options that collectively constitute a product system. A *product mix* (or *product assortment*) is the set of all products and items that a particular seller makes available to the buyers.

PRODUCT-MIX DECISIONS

Most companies, whether in manufacturing, wholesaling, or retailing, handle more than one product. The average supermarket handles 6,800 items, the American Optical Company manufactures over 30,000 items, and General Electric manufactures over 250,000 items.

The General Electric Company manages its incredible number of items by dividing its enterprise into several *sectors* headed by sector vice-presidents; each sector is divided into several *groups;* each group consists of several *divisions;* each division consists of several *product lines;* and each product line consists of several *products, brands, and items.* All of these products constitute the company's *product mix.*

Width, Depth, and Consistency of the Product Mix

The product mix of a company can be described as having a certain width, depth, and consistency. The *width* of the product mix refers to *how many different product lines are found within the company.* The Bissell Company at one time produced only one product line, carpet sweepers. General Electric, on the other hand, produces transformers, light bulbs, toasters, radios, jet engines, and scores of other product lines. The width of the product mix depends on the definitions established for product-line boundaries.

The *depth* of the product mix refers to the *average number of items* (or *length) offered by the company within each product line.* The Toni Company produces its Home Permanent Waves in nine versions to accommodate different hair types and styles and produces its Deep Magic Skin Creme in two versions to accommodate regular and dry skin. These and other product-line depths can be averaged to indicate the typical depth of the company's product mix.

The *consistency* of the product mix refers to *how closely related the various product lines are in end use, production requirements, distribution channels, or in some other way.* Contrast the product mixes of General Electric and Hunt Foods & Industries, Inc. In spite of the large number of General Electric's lines, there is an overall consistency in that most products involve electricity in one way or another. Hunt, on the other hand, produces tomato products, paint, matches, magazines, metal and glass containers, and steel.

All three dimensions of the product mix have a market rationale. Through increasing the width of the product mix, the company hopes to capitalize on its good reputation and skills in present markets. Through increasing the depth of its product mix, the company hopes to entice the patronage of buyers of widely differing tastes and needs. Through increasing the consistency of its product mix, the company hopes to acquire an unparalleled reputation in a particular area of endeavor.

The concepts of width, depth, and consistency are related to those of product item, lines, and mix. Figure 14–2 illustrates these relationships for a hypothetical company's product mix. The mix consists of twelve products, made up of four product lines with an average depth of three items to a line.

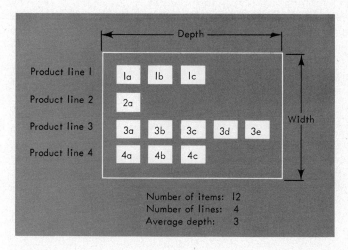

FIGURE 14–2
Conceptual Representation of a Product Mix

The illustration helps clarify the major issues in product policy. Product policy at the level of the product mix involves the issues of what lines to add, strengthen, or delete. Product policy at the level of the product line involves the issues of product-line stretching, filling, and pruning. Product policy at the level of the product item involves the issues of adding, modifying, or dropping individual items.

Evaluation of the Current Product Mix

The product mix of a company is the direct responsibility of top management. Top management must periodically review whether the current mix of product lines represent a good balance in terms of future sales growth, sales stability, and profitability. Markets are continuously changing in their needs and preferences; competitors keep entering and altering their marketing strategies; and the environment keeps changing. All of these changes favor certain of the company's product lines and hurt others. Some of the lines will just begin to show a profit, others will continue to produce good profits, and still others will be slipping badly.

This is illustrated in Figure 14–3. The company produces three product lines—A, B, and C. Projected earnings for the next six years are shown. A produces about 60 percent of the company's total profits, B about 30 percent, and C the remaining 10 percent. Typically, a small percentage of a firm's products account for a large percentage of its earnings. Looking ahead, the company expects A's earnings to decline, B's earnings to grow and then decline, and C's earnings to grow. By the sixth year, C will be contributing most of the profit, followed by B and A. The disturbing development is that the three product lines will not in total earn enough to sustain the company's desired profit-growth rate.

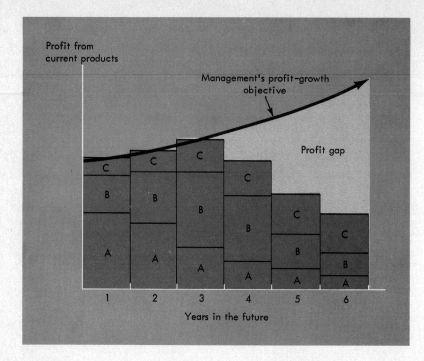

Profit from current products

Management's profit-growth objective

Profit gap

Years in the future

FIGURE 14–3

Projected Profit Growth from Current Products

The shaded area in the figure shows a profit gap that must be filled in one of two ways: (1) improving the performance of the current product lines; (2) adding new product lines.

Improving the Performance of the Current Product Lines

Top management must take a hard look at its current product lines to see whether resources can be reallocated among the lines to improve the mix's overall performance. In the past, companies tended to give all their product lines support that was proportionate to their sales or profit levels. Those lines that contributed the bulk of the sales and profits received more resources. However, companies lacked a definitive product-classification scheme to guide their resource allocation.

The answer came in the form of business portfolio analysis as developed by the Boston Consulting Group and General Electric and described earlier.[4] The various portfolio grids can be applied to strategic business units, product lines, as individual products in the line. Their application enables the company to decide which products to build, hold, harvest, and divest.

Adding New Product Lines

The other way to close a profit gap is to seek additional product lines to add to the current product mix. Here the company is guided by its corporate mission, natural growth opportunities, and kinds of strengths that give it a differential advantage in particular product markets. The company might also seek new lines whose sales behavior over time will balance the sales of its current lines. The company wants to avoid high sales variability because this means periodic excess capacity, employee layoffs, and so on.

[4] See chap. 4, pp. 75–80.

<table>
<tr><td>Product-Mix
Optimization</td><td>We are now ready to define product-mix optimization. The static product-mix optimization problem is defined as follows: Given n possible products, choose m of them (when $m < n$) such that profit is maximized subject to a given level of risk and other constraints.</td></tr>
</table>

This problem is found in a number of situations. Retailers and wholesalers typically have to ration scarce shelf space among a large competing set of products; candy manufacturers have to decide on the best mix of candies to produce and package; and companies facing equipment, labor, or material shortages have to decide which products to produce. The problem may be solvable through mathematical programming, the most important condition being the absence of strong demand and cost interactions among the various products being considered.

The dynamic product-mix optimization problem is the problem of timing deletions and additions to the product mix in response to changing opportunities and resources so that the product mix remains optimal through time. A logical approach would be to simulate possible sequences and timings of planned product deletions and additions over some future time period. The computer's contribution would be to present management with the profit, stability, and growth characteristics of the different possible transformations of the product mix through time.

PRODUCT-LINE DECISIONS

Each product line within a company or division is usually the responsibility of some particular executive. In General Electric's Consumer Appliance Division, for example, there are product-line managers for refrigerators, stoves, washing machines, dryers, and other appliances. In Northwestern University, there are separate academic deans for the medical school, law school, business school, music school, speech school, journalism school, and the college of liberal arts. Often there is arbitrariness in what a company or industry designates as product lines. Consider an office supply manufacturer whose products consist of staplers, staples, staple removers, electric pencil sharpeners, and sharpening blades. Are there five product lines? Or is there a line of staples and accessories and another line of electric pencil sharpeners and accessories? Or are there three lines: staples, electric pencil sharpeners, and accessories? If staplers are divided into home and office staplers, should they be treated as one or two product lines?

The real issue is, What is the best way to organize and manage these various products? If the accessories to the main products yield a high profit, the company will want to manage accessories as a separate product line. Ultimately, the question is, What is the best way to serve the customers and compete effectively in the marketplace?

<table>
<tr><td>Product-Line
Analysis</td><td>Product-line managers must master their lines in two important ways. First, they must know the sales and profits of the various items in the line. Second, they must know how the product line stacks up against the competitors' product lines in the same markets.</td></tr>
</table>

Product-line sales and profits The various items in a product line contribute differentially to total sales and profits. The product-line manager should prepare

357

an exhibit showing the percentage of total sales and profits contributed by each item in the line. An example of a product line with five products is shown in Figure 14–4.

According to the figure, the first item in the product line accounts for 50 percent of the product line's sales and 30 percent of its profits. The first two items account for 80 percent of the product line's sales and 60 percent of the product line's profits. If these two items were hit hard by a competitor, the product line's sales and profitability would decline drastically. A high concentration of sales in a few items means some vulnerability. These items must be carefully monitored and protected. At the other end, the last item only constitutes 5 percent of the product line's sales and profits. The product-line manager will want to consider whether this slow seller should be dropped from the line.

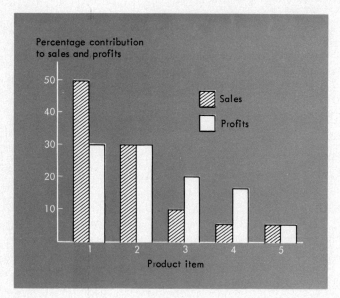

FIGURE 14–4

Product Item Contributions to a
Product Line's Total Sales and Profits

Product-line market profile The product-line manager must also review how the product line is positioned against competitors' product lines. Consider a paper company with a product line consisting of paper board.[5] Two of the major attributes of paper board are the paper weight and the finish quality. Paper weights are usually offered at standard levels of 90, 120, 150, and 180 weight. Finish quality is offered at three standard levels. Figure 14–5 is a product map showing the location of the various items in the product lines of company X and four competitors, A, B, C, and D. Competitor A offers two product items in the extra-high weight class with variable finish quality. Competitor B offers four items that vary in weight and finish quality. Competitor C offers three items such that the greater their weight, the greater their finish quality. Competitor D offers three items, all of which are lightweight but varying in finish quality. Fi-

[5] This illustration is found in Benson P. Shapiro, *Industrial Product Policy: Managing the Existing Product Line* (Cambridge, Mass.: Marketing Science Institute, September 1977), pp. 3–5, 98–101.

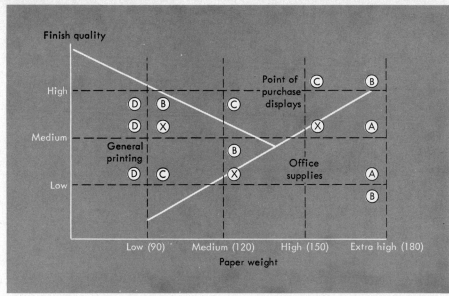

FIGURE 14–5
Product Map for a
Paper-Product Line

SOURCE: Benson P. Shapiro, *Industrial Product Policy: Managing the Existing Product Line* (Cambridge, Mass.: Marketing Science Institute, September 1977), p. 101.

nally, company X offers three items that range in weight and vary between low and medium finish quality.

This product mapping of the product line is highly useful for designing marketing strategy. It shows which competitors' items are competing against each of company X's items. For example, company X's low-weight/medium-quality paper competes against competitor D's paper. On the other hand, its high-weight/medium-quality paper has no direct competitor. The map reveals locations for possible new-product items. For example, no manufacturer offers a high-weight/low-quality paper. This product gap can be explained in one of four ways:

1. It is not technologically possible to produce this kind of paper.
2. It is not economically feasible to produce this kind of paper.
3. There is low or inadequate demand for paper of this kind.
4. This is a good opportunity, and the company is the first to discover it.

Another benefit of the product map is that it is possible to identify market segments and even particular customers according to their paper buying preferences. Figure 14–5 shows the types of paper, by weight and quality, preferred by the general printing industry, the point-of-purchase display industry, and the office-supply industry, respectively. The map shows that company X is well positioned to serve the needs of the general printing industry, but is on the borderline of serving the other two industries and will stay there unless it brings out more paper types that meet their needs.

Another chart that is helpful for marketing strategy is shown in Figure 14–6. The chart shows: (1) the number of items offered by the industry in each

359

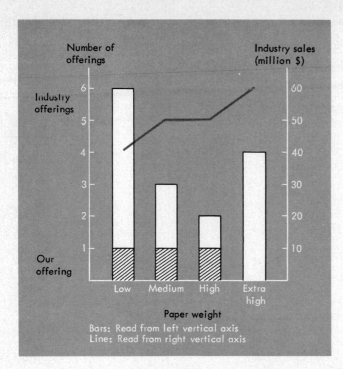

FIGURE 14–6

Number of Offerings and Sales in Each Paper-Weight Category

paper-weight class; (2) the number of items offered by the company in each paper-weight class; and (3) the industry sales of each paper-weight class. Thus, the industry offers six items in the low-paper-weight class (company X offers one of these), and the total sales are only $40 million. On the other hand, sales are $60 million in the extra-high-paper-weight class, and the company does not offer any items in this class. It looks like the company's market coverage is not broad enough and may in fact be mismatched to the real opportunities.

Product-Line Length

One of the major issues facing product-line managers is what the length (the number of items) of the product line should be. The line is too short if the manager could increase profits by adding items; the line is too long if the manager could increase profits by dropping items.

The question of the optimal length of the product line goes back to the company's objectives. Companies that want to be positioned as full-line companies and/or are seeking high market share and market growth will tend to have longer lines. They are less concerned that some items don't contribute an adequate amount of profit. Companies that are keen on high profitability, on the other hand, will carry shorter lines consisting of "cherry-picked" items.

Product lines show a strong tendency to lengthen over time, in an almost unplanned fashion. Several forces are at work:[6]

1. Excess manufacturing capacity puts pressure on the product-line manager to dream up new items.
2. New items are easy to design because they are variations on the existing items.

[6] See the discussion in Shapiro, *Industrial Product Policy*, pp. 9–10.

3. Sales personnel and distributors put pressure on the product-line manager for a more complete product line to satisfy their customers.

4. The product-line manager sees opportunities for additional product items in specific products and markets.

As a result, the product-line manager gradually adds items to the product line in the search for more volume and profits. But as items are added, the following costs go up: (1) designing and engineering costs, (2) inventory carrying costs, (3) manufacturing changeover costs, (4) order processing costs, (5) transportation costs, and (6) promotional costs to introduce the new items.

Eventually something happens to call a halt to the mushrooming growth of the product line. Manufacturing capacity may be in short supply and top management refuses to let the line grow any further. Or the controller raises questions about the line's profitability, and a study is instituted to improve margins. In the latter case, the study will show a large number of money-losing items, and they will be pruned from the line in one major effort to increase profitability. This pattern of gradual line growth followed by sudden line retrenchment will repeat itself many times, resulting in an undulating life-cycle pattern.

We are now ready to look at the major decisions product-line managers face in managing the product line. The decisions include stretching, filling, modernizing, featuring, pricing, and pruning the product line.

Line-Stretching Decision

Every company product line stretches over a certain range of the total range offered by the industry as a whole. For example, Lincoln automobiles are located in the high range of the automobile market, Granadas in the middle range, and Pintos in the low range. "Line stretching" is the act of lengthening the company's product line beyond its current range. It may be motivated by a desire to reach new customer groups, to adapt to changing customer desires, or to become a full-line company. Line stretching should be distinguished from line filling, the latter being concerned with adding items within the current range. Line-filling decisions are largely tactical, whereas line-stretching decisions are largely strategic. We shall examine three types of line-stretching decisions: a downward stretch, an upward stretch, and a two-way stretch.

Downward stretch Many companies establish themselves initially at the high end of a market and subsequently add products for the lower end. Here are two examples:

Caterpillar. For years, Caterpillar has been the dominant supplier of tractors above 100 horsepower (with five models), while John Deere has dominated the lower-horsepower end of the market (with three models). In the early 1970s, each company decided to invade the other's market segment. Caterpillar teamed up with a Japanese supplier to build a lighter tractor. Deere went for a high-end stretch by designing its first large tractor. Caterpillar's move toward the low end of the market was motivated by the wish to participate in a growing market segment that it was neglecting by not having lighter tractors.

IBM. IBM has historically operated in the large main-frame end of the computer market, leaving minicomputer manufacture to other firms, such as Digital Equipment or Data General. However, the slowdown in growth of the large-batch-oriented data processing units had led IBM to enter minicomputer manufacture as an avenue to further growth. IBM's interest in minicomputers is further stimulated by its growing interest in computer networks and distributed data processing systems.

Thus a company may decide to stretch toward the lower end of the market for any of the following reasons:

1. The company finds that slower growth is taking place at the high end and is forced to stretch its product line downward.
2. The company is attacked at the high end and decides to counterattack by invading the low end.
3. The company originally entered the high end in order to establish an image of quality and intended all the time to roll downward.
4. The company adds a low-end unit to fill a hole that otherwise would attract and give a start to a competitor.

In making a downward stretch, the company faces certain risks. The first is that it might provoke low-end companies to counterattack by moving into the higher end. The second is that the company's dealers may not be willing to handle or emphasize the lower-end products. For example, International Harvester truck dealers do not like to sell the lighter trucks because there is much less profit in them. The company may have to establish a second dealership system for its low-end trucks. Still another risk is that low-end items may dilute the company's quality image. If Cadillac added an inexpensive car bearing its name, this would detract from the prestigious Cadillac name. It would be better for Cadillac to design a second, less expensive line not bearing the Cadillac name.

Upward stretch   Companies that are positioned at the low end of the market may want to enter the higher end of the market for any of the following reasons:

1. The company may be attracted by the potential for faster growth rate or higher margins at the upper end of the market.
2. The company may evaluate the competitor(s) at the higher end as weak and easy to displace.
3. The company may want to reposition itself as a full-line manufacturer.

An upward-stretch decision is accompanied by several risks. Not only may the upper-end competitors be well entrenched but the move might tempt them to enter the lower end of the market. Prospective customers may not believe that the company has the wherewithal to produce quality products for the higher end of the market. Finally, the company's sales representatives and distributors may not have the talent or training to serve the higher end of the market, thus requiring intensive training or new sales reps and distributors.

Two-way stretch   Companies that are positioned strongly in the mid-range of a market may decide to go after market dominance by stretching their line in both directions. Texas Instruments' (TI) strategy in the electronic hand-calculator market provides an excellent illustration of a two-way stretch. Before TI entered this market, the market was dominated primarily by Bowmar at the low-price/low-quality end and Hewlett-Packard at the high-price/high-quality end (see Figure 14–7). TI introduced its first calculators in the medium-price, medium-quality end of the market. Gradually it added more machines at each end. It offered better calculators than Bowmar at the same price or lower, ultimately destroying it; and it designed high-quality calculators selling at a much lower price than Hewlett Packard calculators, taking away a good share of HP's sales at the higher end. This two-way stretch won TI the indisputable leadership position in the hand calculator market.

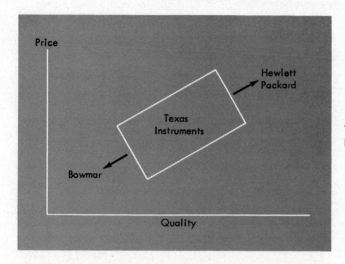

FIGURE 14–7
Two-Way Product-Line Stretch
Illustrated in the Hand-Calculator Market

Line-Filling Decision

A product line can also be lengthened by adding more items within the present range of the line. Looking back at Figure 14–5, we can spot several items that paper company X could add to its line. It can add items at standard levels that are not offered by anyone, such as a high-paper-weight/low-finish-quality paper. It can introduce items between the standard paper weights and/or finish quality levels. It can add items that competitors offer, pricing them the same as, a little higher, or a little lower than competitors' items.

The main motives for line filling are: (1) reaching for incremental profits; (2) trying to satisfy dealers who complain about lost sales because of missing items in the line; (3) trying to utilize excess capacity during slow times; (4) trying to be the leading full-line house; and (5) trying to keep the competitors from finding holes and getting in.

Line filling can be overdone, resulting in cannibalization and customer confusion. The company should strive to make each item differentiable in the consumer's mind. Each item should possess a *just noticeable difference.* According to Weber's Law, customers are more attuned to relative than to absolute differences.[7] They will perceive the difference between boards 2 and 3 feet long and between boards 20 and 30 feet long, but not between boards 29 and 30 feet long. The company should make sure that product item differences within its line are at least as large as just noticeable differences.

The company should check that the proposed item enjoys some market demand and is not being filled in simply to satisfy an internal gap. The famous Edsel automobile, on which Ford lost $350 million, was a case of line filling that met Ford's internal positioning needs but not the market's needs. Ford had no-

[7] See Steuart Henderson Britt, "How Weber's Law Can Be Applied to Marketing," *Business Horizons,* February 1975, pp. 21–29.

ticed that Ford car owners would trade up to General Motors' products like Oldsmobile or Buick rather than step up to a Mercury or Lincoln. Ford decided to create a stepping-stone car to fill its line. The Edsel was created, but it failed to meet a market need since a sufficient number of similar cars were available to the same buyers, and many buyers were beginning to switch to smaller cars.

Once the product-line manager decides to add another item to sell at a certain price, the task of designing it is turned over to the company engineers. The planned price will dictate how the item is designed, rather than the design dictating the price that will be charged.

Line-Modernization Decision

In some cases, the product line is adequate in length but has become old-fashioned looking over time. The line needs to be modernized. For example, a company's line of machine tools may have a 1920s look and lose out to better-styled competitors' lines.

When a company recognizes that its line needs modernization, the issue is whether to overhaul the line piecemeal or in one fell swoop. A piecemeal approach allows the company to test how customers and dealers feel about the new style before committing the whole line to that style. Furthermore, piecemeal modernization poses less of a drain on the company's cash flow. A major disadvantage of piecemeal modernization is that it allows competitors to see what the company is doing and gives them breathing time to redesign their own line.

Line-Featuring Decision

The product-line manager typically selects one or a few items for special featuring to draw attention to the line. Sometimes managers promote items at the low end of the line to serve as "traffic builders." Thus Sears will announce a special low-priced sewing machine to bring people into the sewing machine department. Recently Rolls Royce announced an economy model selling for only $49,000—in contrast to its high-end model selling for $108,000—to bring people into its showrooms. Once the customers arrive, some sales people will try to influence them to buy at the higher end of the line by disparaging the low-end model. (This is called bait-and-switch selling and could be held illegal.)

At other times, managers will feature a high-end item to give the product line "class." Stetson promotes a man's hat selling for $150, which few people buy but which acts as a flagship to enhance the whole line.

Sometimes a company finds one end of its line selling well and the other end poorly. The company may try to boost the demand for the slower sellers, especially if the slower sellers are produced in a separate factory that is idled by the lack of demand. This situation faced Honeywell when its medium-size computers were not selling as well as its large computers. But things are not this simple. It could be argued that the company should be promoting the product items that are selling well in a drive to achieve dominance in that segment of the market, rather than trying to stimulate demand where it is weak. Recently, the author of a successful textbook complained to his publisher that not enough money was being spent promoting his successful textbook, only to hear the editor say that promotion money should be used for the books that were not selling!

Line-Pricing Decision

A major task facing product-line managers is pricing the various items in their lines. Here we want to discuss two special situations. (Also see chap. 15, pp. 407–9 for additional discussion.)

The first has to do with a product line that consists of main products and satellite products. The satellite products take two forms. The first consists of *optional products* or *product features*. Here the buyer of the main product is free to buy none, one, or more optional products or features. The automobile customer can order such options as electric window controls, defoggers, and light dimmers. The restaurant customer can order or skip liquor in addition to the main course. The seller's task is to decide on prices for the optional items. If the prices are too high, customers will either forego purchase of the options or eventually switch to other sellers who price these options lower. Management can choose between pricing these options high in order to make them serve as an independent profit source or to price them low in order to act as a traffic builder. Many restaurants choose to price their liquor high and their food low. The food revenue covers the cost of the food and operating the restaurant, and the liquor produces the profit. This explains why customers may be looked at askance when they don't order something to drink from the bar. Other restaurants will price their liquor low and food high to draw in a crowd that likes to drink.

The other type of satellite product is a *captive product* (or *after-market product*). Examples are razor blades, camera film, and copier supplies. Manufacturers of the main products (razors, cameras, and copiers) often price them low in order to stimulate purchase and then make their profit through a high markup on the supplies. Thus Kodak prices its cameras low because it makes its money on the film. Those camera makers who do not sell film have to price their cameras higher than Kodak in order to make the same overall profit. As for the copier market, the early copier companies (such as Apeco and 3M) made their money selling specially coated paper that had to be used with their copiers. Part of Xerox's success lay in introducing a copying machine that did not require special paper, thus offering customers a way to save money on their copying costs.

The other interesting line-pricing situation arises in connection with *by-products*. In the production of processed meats, petroleum products, and other chemicals, there will often be by-products. If the by-products have no value, and in some cases a cost of disposal, this will have to be considered in pricing the main product. The manufacturer will normally have a strong incentive to develop value either through finding a market for the product in its raw state or processing it into a valued product, where the processing cost is less than its value. The manufacturer should be willing to accept any price for the by-product that covers more than its cost of processing and delivery, since this will conribute to profit or enable the seller to reduce the price of the main product to make it more competitive in the market.

Line-Pruning Decision

Product-line managers must periodically give consideration to pruning their product lines. There are two occasions for pruning. One occasion is when management notices that the product line includes deadwood that is acting as a drag on profits. The weak products can be identified through sales and cost analysis following the method outlined in Chapter 12, pages 299–301. Recently RCA cut down the number of its color television sets from 69 to 44 models, and a chemical company cut down its products from 217 to the 93 with the largest volume, contribution to profits, and long-term potential. Many companies that have implemented major prunings have often achieved stronger long-term profits.

The other occasion for product pruning is when the company is facing high demand and does not have the production capacity to produce all of the items in their desired quantities. Here the company should examine its profit margins and concentrate on the production of the higher-margin items, dropping temporarily or permanently some of the low-margin or losing items. Typically companies shorten their lines in periods of tight demand and lengthen their lines in periods of slow demand.

BRAND DECISIONS

Brand strategy is an intimate aspect of product strategy. A marketer has to decide which products to brand, how to brand them, and how to manage the brands.

First, some definitions are in order. A *brand* is "a name, term, sign, symbol, or design, or a combination of them which is intended to identify the goods or services of one seller or group of sellers and to differentiate them from those of competitors."[8] A *brand name* is "that part of a brand which can be vocalized—the utterable." Well-known brand names include Chevrolet, Coke, and Comet.

A *brand mark* is that part of a brand that can be recognized but is not utterable, such as a symbol, design, or distinctive coloring or lettering. Well-known brand marks include the Playboy bunny and the Metro-Goldwyn-Mayer lion. Finally, a *trademark* is "a brand or part of a brand that is given legal protection because it is capable of exclusive appropriation. . . ." Thus a trademark is essentially a legal term protecting the seller's exclusive rights to use the brand name and/or brand mark. *Branding* will be used as a general term describing the establishing of brand names, marks, or trade names for a product.

The Branding Decision

The first of several decisions in brand strategy is whether the company should even put a brand name on one or more of its products. The alternative to branding is simply to sell the product in bulk to middlemen or the final customers. Until recent times, most staple products—sugar, salt, bacon, cloth—went unbranded. Producers shipped their goods to middlemen who would sell them out of barrels, bins, or cases without any identification of the supplier. Finer goods were branded in some cases—Rubens paintings—and in other cases were unbranded—fine Chinese jade carvings.

A change began in the 1890s with the growth of national firms and national advertising media. The growth of brand names has been so dramatic that today, in the United States, hardly anything is sold unbranded. Salt is packaged in distinctive manufacturers' containers, oranges are stamped, common nuts and bolts are packaged in cellophane with a distributors' label, and various parts of an automobile—spark plugs, tires, filters—bear visible brand names different from that of the automobile itself.

In some industries today, there are occasional reappearances of unbranded, or "generic," goods, primarily as an effort by someone in the marketing system to offer consumers a low-cost alternative to branded goods. Thus, the Jewel Food Company has introduced a product line of plain-wrapped staples—soup, soap, toilet paper—with no brand name and carrying a low price. In many health food stores, several products are spooned from bins without supplier identification. In the pharmaceutical industry, many drugs are supplied in generic form.

[8] This and the following definitions are taken from *Marketing Definitions: A Glossary of Marketing Terms.*

366

Indeed, why should a producer rush into branding when it clearly involves a cost—packaging, stamping, legal protection—and a risk, if the product should prove unsatisfying to the user? It turns out that branding can perform a number of useful functions:

1. The producer may want a brand mark for identification purposes to simplify handling or tracing.
2. The producer may want a legal trademark and patent to protect unique product features from being imitated.
3. The producer may want to emphasize a certain quality level in the offer and make it easy for satisfied customers to find the product again.
4. The producer may see the brand name as an opportunity for endowing the product with an inherent drama that may create the basis for price differentiation.

Sometimes the pressure for branding comes not from the purchaser but from the distributor or ultimate buyer. Distributors may want brand names as a means of making the product easier to handle, identifying suppliers, holding production to certain quality standards, and increasing buyer preference. Ultimate buyers may want brand names to help them identify the products they want.[9] The brand name has informational value to buyers; without it, how could they shop in the modern supermarket with its 6,800 items?

Brand-Sponsor Decision

In branding, producers may use their own name(s) (*manufacturers' brands*), middlemen's names (*middleman brands*), or follow a mixed-brand policy, producing some output under their own name(s) and some output under middlemen's names.[10] For example, Kellogg's, International Harvester, and IBM produce virtually all of their output under their own brand names. A manufacturer such as Warwick Electronics produces virtually all of its output under various distributors' names. Whirlpool produces output both under its own name and under distributors' names.

Manufacturers' brands tend to dominate the American scene. Consider such well-known brands as Campbell's Soup and Heinz Ketchup. In recent times, however, large retailers and wholesalers have turned to developing their own brands. Middlemen are often able to make more profit because they do not bear the manufacturers' heavy promotional expenses. Their own brands give them more control over pricing and some measure of control over suppliers because they can threaten to change suppliers. Middlemen's brands have become an important factor in brand competition. Consider that over 90 percent of Sears products are under its own label, and that 25 percent of A&P's products are under its own label. More and more department stores, service stations, clothiers, drugstores, and appliance dealers are responding to these advantages by launching their own brands.

---

[9] Until recently, Soviet factories did not brand their products but used identification marks indicating the factory. Because of the variable quality, consumers began to buy the products produced at the better-known factories. Before long, state-sponsored advertising agencies emerged to tell consumers about the quality of the various factories.

[10] *Manufacturers' brands* also go under such names as national brands, regional brands, and advertising brands. *Middlemen's brands* also go under a variety of names: distributors' brands, private brands, store brands, dealer brands, house brands, and ghost brands. See Thomas F. Schutte, "The Semantics of Branding," *Journal of Marketing,* April 1969, pp. 5–11.

The competition between manufacturers' and middlemen's brands is called the "battle of the brands." In this confrontation, middlemen have many advantages. Retail shelf space is scarce, and many manufacturers, especially newer and smaller ones, cannot introduce products into distribution under their own name. Middlemen take special care to maintain the quality of their brands, building consumers' confidence. Many buyers know that the private label brand is often manufactured by one of the larger manufacturers anyway. Middlemen's brands are often priced lower than comparable manufacturers' brands, thus appealing to budget-conscious shoppers, especially in times of inflation. Middlemen give more prominent display to their own brands and make sure they are better stocked. For these and other reasons, the former dominance of the manufacturers' brands is weakening. Indeed, some marketing commentators predict that middlemen's brands will eventually knock out all but the strongest manufacturers' brands.

Manufacturers of national brands are in a very trying situation. Their instinct is to spend a lot of money on consumer-directed advertising and promotion to maintain strong brand preference. Their price has to be somewhat higher to cover this promotion. At the same time, the mass distributors put strong pressures on them to put more of their promotional money toward trade allowances and deals if they want adequate shelf space. Once manufacturers start giving in, they have less to spend on consumer promotion, and their brand leadership starts slipping. This is the national brand manufacturers' dilemma.[11]

Brand-Quality Decision

In developing a brand, the manufacturer has to establish the brand's quality level and other attributes that will support the brand's targeted position in the marketplace. Quality is one of the major positioning tools of the marketer. But what is quality and how is it measured? Quality stands for *the rated ability of the brand to perform its functions*. It is an overall measure reflecting the product's standings on durability, reliability, precision, ease of operation and repair, and other valued attributes. Some of these attributes can be measured objectively and combined, using a set of importance weights, into an index of quality. From a marketing point of view, however, quality is better measured in terms of the buyers' perceptions of quality. Buyers can be asked to rate a given set of brands on a quality scale.

Manufacturers do not all attempt to build the highest-quality products. Higher-quality products will cost consumers more. There will be markets for each quality level. Each manufacturer faces two decisions: (1) where to locate the brand's initial quality and (2) how to manage the brand's quality level through time.

Most brands can be established initially at one of four quality levels: low, average, above average, and superior.[12] The PIMS study attempted to determine the relationship between a brand's profitability (ROI) and its quality.[13] The in-

[11] See E. B. Weiss, "Private Label?" *Advertising Age*, September 30, 1974, pp. 27 ff. For an excellent example of decision theory, applied to a national bakery facing this dilemma, see Robert D. Buzzell and Charles C. Slater, "Decision Theory and Marketing Management," *Journal of Marketing*, July 1962, pp. 7–16.

[12] Or six levels could be used: shoddy quality, below-average quality, average quality, plus quality, double-plus quality, finest quality.

[13] See chap. 11, footnote, pp. for references.

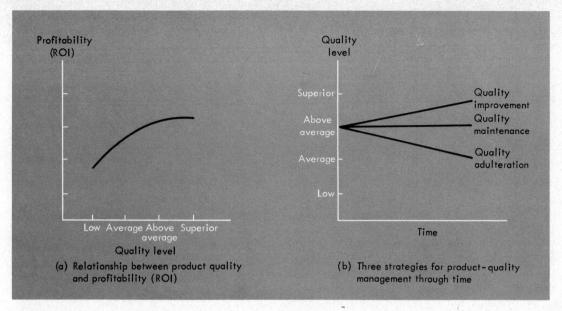

(a) Relationship between product quality and profitability (ROI)

(b) Three strategies for product-quality management through time

FIGURE 14–8
Brand-Quality Strategies and Profitability

vestigators found that profitability rose with brand quality but not in a linear fashion. The estimated relationship between quality level and profitability is shown in Figure 14–8A. This suggests that companies should aim to deliver above-average quality. Superior quality increases profitability only slightly, while inferior quality hurts profitability substantially. Furthermore, high marketing expenditures tend not to compensate for inferior product quality. "It doesn't pay to promote a poor product."

The other issue is how the company should manage brand quality through time. The three options are illustrated in Figure 14–8B: improve quality, maintain quality, or reduce quality. The first option, where the manufacturer invests in continuous research and development to make the product better, usually produces the highest return and market share. Procter & Gamble is a major practitioner of product-improvement strategy, which, combined with the high initial product quality, helps explain their leading position in many markets. The second option is to maintain product quality. Many companies leave their quality unaltered after its initial formulation unless glaring faults or opportunities occur. The third option is to reduce product quality through time. The company may experience a cost-price squeeze and decide to substitute cheaper materials. If they do this a number of times, the brand's deterioration will eventually be noticed.[14] A few companies will adulterate their products quite deliberately as a

[14] An interesting example is the Simmons Corporation, which substituted cheaper materials in its Beautyrest mattresses to fight rising costs. Consumers and retailers soon noticed the difference. Sales stagnated, market share fell, and profits plummeted. Now Simmons is engaged in a valiant effort to improve its product and image. See "Simmons: A Turnaround Proves Hard to Bring Off," *Business Week*, June 5, 1978, pp. 146–50.

way to increase profits, at least in the short run. The products that get the most adulteration are those in a late stage of their life cycle where they are being harvested or readied for withdrawal.

As a side note, many Japanese and German companies regard product quality as the major selling tool and pay great attention to statistical quality control. They want their products to come as close to zero defects as possible. In these cases, quality control is part of the marketing mix rather than regarded as only part of the production mix.

Family-Brand Decision

Manufacturers who choose to produce most of their output under their own name still face several choices. At least four brand-name strategies can be distinguished:

1. *Individual brand names.* This policy is followed by such companies as Procter & Gamble (Tide, Bold, Dash, Cheer, Gain, Oxydol, Duz) and Genesco, Inc. (Jarman, Mademoiselle, Johnson & Murphy, and Cover Girl).
2. *A blanket family name for all products.* This policy is followed by such companies as Heinz and General Electric.
3. *Separate family names for all products.* This policy is followed by Sears (Kenmore for appliances, Kerrybrook for women's clothing, and Homart for major home installations).
4. *Company trade name combined with individual product names.* This policy is followed by Kellogg's (Kellogg's Rice Krispies and Kellogg's Raisin Bran).

Competitors within the same industry may adopt quite different brand-name strategies. In the soap industry, for example, Procter & Gamble favors individual brand names. The name P&G will be used with new products during the first six weeks of television promotion and then be deemphasized. P&G wants each product to make it on its own. Colgate, on the other hand, makes much use of the phrase "the Colgate family" to help its individual products along.

What are the advantages of an individual-brand-names strategy? A major advantage is that the company does not tie its reputation to the product's acceptance. If the product fails, it is not a bad mark for the manufacturer. Or if the new product is of lower quality, the company does not dilute its reputation. The manufacturer of a line of expensive watches or of high-quality food products can introduce lower-quality lines without using its own name. On the positive side the individual-brand-names strategy permits the firm to search for the best name for each new product. Another advantage is that a new name permits the building of new excitement and conviction.

The opposite policy, that of using a blanket family name for all products, also has some advantages if the manufacturer is willing to maintain quality for all items in the line. The cost of introducing the product will be less because there is no need for "name" research, or for expensive advertising to create brand-name recognition and preference. Furthermore, sales will be strong if the manufacturer's name is good. Thus Campbell's is able to introduce new soups under its brand name with extreme simplicity and instant response. On the other hand, Phillips in Europe uses its name on all of its products, but since its products differ greatly in quality, most people expect only average quality in a Phillips product. That hurts the sales of its superior products; here is a case where individual branding might be better, or the company might decline to put its own name on its weaker products.

Where a company produces or sells quite different types of products, it may not be appropriate to use one blanket family name. Thus Swift and Company, in producing both hams and fertilizers, developed separate family names (Premium and Vigoro). When Mead Johnson developed a diet supplement for *gaining* weight, it created a new family name, Nutriment, to avoid confusion with its family brand for weight-*reducing* products, Metrecal. Companies will often invent different family brand names for different quality lines within the same product class. Thus A&P sells a primary, secondary, and tertiary set of brands—Ann Page, Sultana, Iona, respectively.

Finally, some manufacturers will want to associate their company name along with an individual brand for each product. In these cases, the company name legitimizes, and the individual name individualizes, the new product. Thus the Quaker Oats in *Quaker Oats Cap'n Crunch* allows the new product to benefit from the company's reputation in the breakfast cereal field, and Cap'n Crunch allows room to individualize and dramatize the product.

Brand-Extension Decision

A brand-extension strategy is any effort to use a successful brand name to launch product modifications or additional products. In the case of product modifications, it is commonplace in the detergent industry to talk about brand X, then the new, improved brand X, then the new brand X with additives. Brand extension also covers the introduction of new package sizes, flavors, and models. More interesting is the use of a successful brand name to launch new products. After Quaker Oats's success with Cap'n Crunch dry breakfast cereal, it used the brand name and cartoon character to launch a line of ice cream bars, T-shirts, and other products. Brand extension has also been used by Armour Dial soap to cover a variety of new products that could not easily find distribution without the strength of the Dial name.[15]

Another kind of brand extension occurs when durable-goods manufacturers add stripped-down models to the lower end of their line in order to advertise their brand as starting at a low price. Thus Sears may advertise room air conditioners as "starting at $120," and General Motors may advertise a new Chevrolet at $3,400. In both cases, these "fighter" or "promotional" models are used to draw in customers on a price basis who, upon seeing the better models, usually decide to trade up. This is a common strategy but must be used carefully. The "promotional" brand, although stripped, must be up to the brand's quality image. The seller must be sure to have the promotional product in stock when it is advertised. Consumers must not get the feeling they were taken, or else they may switch suppliers.

Multibrand Decision

A multibrand strategy is the development by a particular seller of two or more brands that compete with each other. Procter & Gamble pioneered this strategy. Following the phenomenal success of its Tide detergent brand introduced after World War II, it introduced another brand, Cheer, in 1950. Cheer took some sales away from Tide, but the combined sales volume was larger than if P&G had sold only Tide. P&G subsequently introduced other brands of detergents,

[15] See Theodore R. Gamble, "Brand Extension," in *Plotting Marketing Strategy*, ed. Lee Adler (New York: Simon and Schuster, 1967), pp. 170–71.

each launched with a claim of somewhat different performance. Other manufacturers in the soap field began to follow a multibrand strategy.

There are several reasons why manufacturers turn to multibrand strategy. First, there is the severe battle for shelf space in the nation's supermarkets. Each brand that the distributors accept gets some allocation of shelf space. By introducing several brands, a manufacturer ties up more of the available shelf space, leaving less for competitors.

Second, few consumers are so loyal to a brand that they won't occasionally try another. They respond to cents-off deals, gifts, and new-product entries that claim superior performance. The manufacturer who never introduces another brand entry will almost inevitably face a declining market share. The only way to capture the "brand switchers" is to be on the offering end of a new brand.

Third, creating new brands develops excitement and encourages efficiency within the manufacturer's organization. Companies such as General Motors and P&G see their individual managers competing to outperform each other.

Fourth, a multibrand strategy enables the company to take advantage of different market segments. Consumers respond to various benefits and appeals, and even marginal differences between brands can win a large following.

In deciding whether to introduce another brand, the manufacturer should consider such questions as

> Can a unique story be built for the new brand?
>
> Will the unique story be believable?
>
> How much will the new brand cannibalize the sales of the manufacturer's other brands versus the sales of competitors' brands?
>
> Will the cost of product development and promotion be covered by the sales of the new brand?

A major pitfall is introducing a number of multibrand entries, each of which obtains only a small share of the market and none of which is particularly profitable. In this case, the company has dissipated its resources over several partially successful brands instead of concentrating on a few brands and building each one up to highly profitable levels. Such companies should weed out the weaker brands and establish tighter screening procedures for choosing new brands to introduce. Ideally, a company's brands should cannibalize the competitors' brands and not each other.[16]

Brand-Repositioning Decision

However well a brand is initially positioned in a market, a number of circumstances may call for repositioning thinking:

1. A competitor may have placed its brand next to the company's brand, thus cutting into its market share in that segment.
2. Customer preferences may have shifted, leaving the company's brand less in the center of a preference cluster.
3. New customer preference clusters may have formed that represent attractive opportunities.

A classic repositioning success story is the campaign developed by Seven-Up. Seven-Up was one of many soft drinks on the market and was bought pri-

---

[16] For an excellent discussion of multibrand strategies, see Robert W. Young, "Multibrand Entries," in Adler, *Plotting Market Strategy*, pp. 143–64.

marily by older people who wanted a fairly bland, lemon-flavored drink. Some research indicated that while a majority of soft-drink consumers preferred a cola, they did not prefer it all the time, and furthermore, many consumers were noncola drinkers. Seven-Up decided to establish leadership in the noncola market and executed a brilliant campaign, calling itself the Uncola. The Uncola was featured as a youthful and refreshing drink in its own right, the one to reach for instead of a cola. Seven-Up thus created a new way for consumers to view the market, as consisting of primarily colas and uncolas, with Seven-Up leading the uncolas.

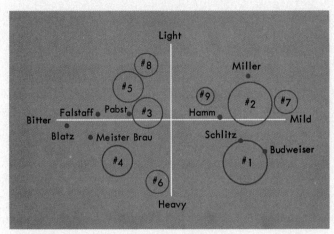

FIGURE 14–9
Distribution of Perceptions and Preferences in the Beer Market

SOURCE: Richard M. Johnson, "Market Segmentation: A Strategic Management Tool," *Journal of Marketing Research,* February 1971, p. 16.

The problem and method of analysis for considering repositioning alternatives for a brand can be illustrated in connection with Hamm's position in the beer market. Figure 14–9 shows the distribution of beer brand perceptions and taste preferences on two attributes: lightness and mildness. The dots represent the perceived positions of the various brands, and the circles represent preference clusters. The larger circles represent more-intense densities of preference. This information would reveal that Hamm no longer meets the preferences of any distinct segment.

To remedy this, Hamm's task is to identify the best preference cluster in which to reposition Hamm. Preference cluster #1 would not be a good choice because Schlitz and Budweiser are well entrenched. Preference cluster #2 seems like a good choice because of its size and the presence of only one competitor, Miller. Preference cluster #9 would be another possibility, although it is relatively small. Hamm can also think about a long-shot repositioning toward the supercluster #3, #5, and #8 or the supercluster #4 and #6.

Management must weigh two factors in making its choice. The first is the *cost* of shifting the brand to that segment. The cost includes changing the product's qualities, packaging, advertising, and so on. In general, the repositioning cost *rises* with the repositioning distance. The more radical the brand-image change that is contemplated, the greater the investment required to alter people's images. Hamm would need more money to reposition its brand in segment #8 than segment #2. It might be better for Hamm to create a new brand for segment #8 than to reposition its present brand.

The other factor is the *revenue* that would be earned by the brand in the new position. The revenue depends upon (1) the number of consumers in the preference segment, (2) their average purchase rate, (3) the number and strength of competitors already in that segment or intending to enter it, and (4) the price normally charged for brands selling to that segment.

CUSTOMER-SERVICE DECISIONS

A company's offer to the marketplace usually includes some service component. The service component can be a minor or major part of the total offer. In fact, the offer can range from a pure good on the one hand to a pure service on the other. Four categories of offer can be distinguished:

1. *A pure good.* Here the offer consists primarily of a tangible good such as soap, toothpaste, or salt. No explicit services accompany the product.

2. *A core good with associated services.* Here the offer consists of a core good along with one or more adjunct services that enhance its utility. For example, an automobile manufacturer sells an automobile that is accompanied by a warranty, service and maintenance instructions, and so on. Levitt observes: "The more technologically sophisticated the generic product (e.g., cars and computers), the more dependent are its sales on the quality and availability of its accompanying customer services (e.g., display rooms, delivery, repairs and maintenance, application aids, operator training, installation advice, warranty fulfillment). In this sense, General Motors is probably more service intensive than manufacturing intensive. Without its services, its sales would shrivel."[17]

3. *A core service with adjunct goods or services.* Here the offer consists of a core service along with some additional services and/or supporting goods. Examples include airline travel and car rental. Airline passengers essentially are buying transportation service. They arrive at their destinations without anything tangible to show for their expenditure. However, the trip included some tangibles such as food and drinks, a plane ticket stub, and an airline magazine. The service required a capital-intensive good called an airplane for its realization, but the primary item was a service.

4. *A pure service.* Here the offer consists of a core service and possibly some adjunct services. Examples include psychotherapy and massages. The client of a psychoanalyst receives a pure service with the only tangible elements in the service situation consisting of an office and a couch.

Thus the company's core product can be a good, or service and additional services might be included. We define a *service* as *activity that has value to a buyer.* A service is not a physical thing but rather an energy expenditure. It cannot be stored. A service that is not purchased at the moment it is available perishes. Thus while a car will stay in inventory until it is sold, an unoccupied seat on a particular flight is lost forever when the flight departs. Furthermore, a

---

[17] Theodore Levitt, "Production-Line Approach to Service," *Harvard Business Review,* September–October 1972, pp. 41–42.

service tends to be more variable in quality than a physical product, since it is often inseparable from the person offering it.

The services that accompany a core product or service can be extremely influential in the company's market share. As noted by Levitt:

> Whether the product is cold-rolled steel or hot-cross buns, whether accountancy or delicacies, competitive effectiveness increasingly demands that the successful seller offer his prospect and his customer more than the generic product itself. He must surround his generic product with a cluster of value satisfactions that differentiates his total offerings from his competitors! He must provide a total proposition, the content of which exceeds what comes out at the end of the assembly line.[18]

The marketer faces three decisions with respect to customer service: (1) what elements of customer service should be included in the customer-services mix? (2) what level of service should be offered? and (3) in what forms should the services be provided?

The Service-Elements Decision

The first task is to identify the main service elements in the industry and their relative importance to customers. Customers can be asked to name service elements that they consider important. Once a list is settled upon, customers can be asked to rank or rate the importance of these elements. For example, Canadian buyers of industrial equipment ranked thirteen service elements in the following order of importance: (1) delivery reliability, (2) prompt quotation, (3) technical advice, (4) discounts, (5) after-sales service, (6) sales representation, (7) ease of contact, (8) replacement guarantee, (9) wide range of manufacturer, (10) pattern design, (11) credit, (12) test facilities, and (13) machining facilities.[19] These importance rankings suggest that the company should at least match competition on delivery reliability, prompt quotation, and technical advice and other elements deemed most important by the customers.

But the issue of which service elements to emphasize is more subtle than this. It goes back to the discussion of the difference between the importance and determinance of an attribute (see chap. 6, pp. 162–63). A customer-service element can be highly important and yet not a determinant of customer preference if all of the suppliers are perceived to be equal on this attribute. Consider the following example.

The Monsanto Company was seeking a way to improve its customer-services mix. Purchasing agents were asked to rate Monsanto, Du Pont, and Union Carbide on several attributes. All three companies, it turned out, were seen by customers as offering high delivery reliability and having good sales representatives. These were not determinant attributes. All three companies, however, were viewed as rendering insufficient technical service. Monsanto then carried out a study to find out how important technical service is to chemical buyers. Their study showed that buyers attached a high importance to technical service. Monsanto then proceeded to hire and train additional technical people. Shortly thereafter, it launched a campaign describing itself as the leader in technical service. The discovery gave Monsanto an opportunity to develop a valued difference in the minds of buyers.

---

[18] Levitt, *The Marketing Mode*, p. 2.

[19] Peter G. Banting, "Customer Service in Industrial Marketing: A Comparative Study," *European Journal of Marketing* 10, no. 3 (1976): 140.

Customers not only expect important service elements to be included in the product offer but also want the services to be offered in the right amount and quality. If bank customers face lengthy waits in line or confront frowning bank tellers, they will be inclined to switch their business to other banks.

Normally, higher levels of customer service produce higher customer satisfaction and therefore higher repeat purchases. We can use the right-hand diagram of Figure 10–1 on page 256 to illustrate various relationships that might exist between sales and service level. A shows the benchmark case where a particular customer service, no matter how well it is provided, does not make a difference to the sales level. For example, a supermarket chain may offer additional labeling to help consumers understand nutrition, and this may not draw more sales. B shows a case where sales respond in a linear fashion to the level of service offered. For example, sales might rise linearly with the degree of ease of contact with the sales rep. C shows sales responding very rapidly to a service and increasing with higher levels of this service at a diminishing rate. Adding one sales person to a department in a store makes a big difference; adding a second person makes a smaller difference; adding a third person makes an even smaller difference. D shows a case where offering a small amount of a service has little impact on sales; the impact increases as more is offered; and later it falls off. An example would be a new automobile warranty. If the warranty covers thirty days, it is not very impressive; a year—it is more impressive; three years—it is still more impressive but may not produce that much more in sales.

Companies must maintain a constant check on their own and competitors' service levels in relation to customers' expectations. The company can monitor service deficiencies through a number of devices: comparison shopping, periodic customer surveys, suggestion boxes, and complaint-handling systems. The task is not to minimize complaining behavior but in fact to maximize it so that the company can really know how it is doing, and the disappointed customers can get satisfaction.

A useful device is to periodically survey a sample of customers to find out how they feel about each service element in terms of its importance and performance. An example is shown in Figure 14–10A. Fourteen different service attributes of an automobile dealer's service department were rated by customers on importance and performance. The importance of the service attribute was rated on a four-point scale of "extremely important," "important," "slightly important," and "not important." The dealer's performance was rated on a four-point scale of "excellent," "good," "fair," and "poor." For example, the first service attribute, "Job done right the first time," received a mean importance rating of 3.83 and a mean performance rating of 2.63, indicating that customers felt it was highly important, although not being performed that well by this service department. The ratings of the fourteen attributes are displayed in Figure 14–10B. The figure is divided into four quadrants. Quadrant A shows the important service attributes that are not being offered at the desired performance levels; they include attributes 1, 2, and 9. Dealers should concentrate their attention on improving their performance on these attributes. Quadrant B shows important service elements where the company is performing well; its job is to maintain the high performance. Quadrant C shows minor service elements that are delivered in a mediocre way but do not need any attention since they are not very important. Quadrant D shows a minor service element, "Send out maintenance notices," which is being performed in an excellent manner, a case of

ATTRIBUTE NUMBER	ATTRIBUTE DESCRIPTION	MEAN IMPORTANCE RATING[a]	MEAN PERFORMANCE RATING[b]
1	Job done right the first time	3.83	2.63
2	Fast action on complaints	3.63	2.73
3	Prompt warranty work	3.60	3.15
4	Able to do any job needed	3.56	3.00
5	Service available when needed	3.41	3.05
6	Courteous and friendly service	3.41	3.29
7	Car ready when promised	3.38	3.03
8	Perform only necessary work	3.37	3.11
9	Low prices on service	3.29	2.00
10	Clean up after service work	3.27	3.02
11	Convenient to home	2.52	2.25
12	Convenient to work	2.43	2.49
13	Courtesy buses and rental cars	2.37	2.35
14	Send out maintenance notices	2.05	3.33

[a] Ratings obtained from a four-point scale of "extremely important," "important," "slightly important," and "not important."

[b] Ratings obtained from a four-point scale of "excellent," "good," "fair," and "poor."

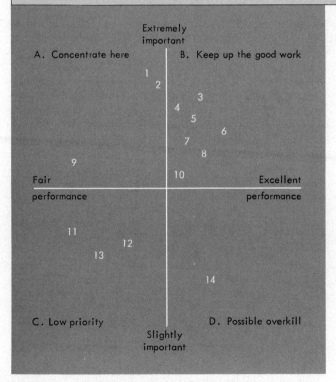

FIGURE 14–10
Importance and Performance Ratings
for Automobile Dealer's Service Department

SOURCE: John A. Martilla and John C. James, "Importance-Performance Analysis," *Journal of Marketing,* January 1977, pp. 77–79.

possible "overkill." This classification of service elements according to their importance and performance provides marketers with guidelines as to where they should concentrate their effort.

The Service-Form Decision

Marketers must also decide on the forms in which to offer various service elements. First, there is the question of how to price the service element. Consider, for example, what Zenith should do in connection with offering repair services on its television sets. Zenith has three pricing options:

1. Zenith could offer free television-repair service for a year with the sale of its set.
2. Zenith could offer the customer an option to buy a service contract.
3. Zenith could decide not to offer any repair service, leaving it to independent television-repair specialists.

Second, there is the question of how the repair service should be provided. Zenith has three choices:

1. Zenith can hire and train its own service repair people and locate them throughout the country.
2. Zenith can make arrangements with distributors and dealers to provide the repair services.
3. Zenith can leave it to independent companies to provide the necessary repair services.

For each such service element, various options exist on how it could be provided to customers. The company's decision depends very much on customers' preferences as well as competitors' strategies.

The Customer-Service Department

Given the importance of customer service as a competitive weapon, companies would do well to consider developing a strong customer-service department reporting to the vice president of marketing. Customer-service departments are found in many companies, although their scope and authority vary widely. Ideally, these departments should integrate and be responsible for a number of customer services, the most important of which are:[20]

1. *Complaints and adjustments.* The company should set up procedures for facilitating and handling complaints. By keeping statistics on the types of complaints, the customer-service department can recognize problems and press for changes in product design, quality control, high-pressure selling, and so on. It is much less expensive to preserve the goodwill of existing customers than to attract new customers or woo back lost customers.
2. *Credit service.* The company should offer customers a number of options in financing their purchase, including installment credit contracts, open book credit, loans, and leasing options. The costs of extending credit are usually more than made up by the gross profit on the additional sales and the reduced cost of marketing expenditures to overcome the customers' objection of not having enough money.
3. *Maintenance service.* The company should make provisions for supplying customers with a parts and service system that is effective, speedy, and reasonable in

---

[20] See Ralph S. Alexander and Thomas L. Berg, *Dynamic Management in Marketing* (Homewood, Ill.: Richard D. Irwin, 1965), pp. 419–28.

cost. While maintenance service is often run by the production department, marketing should monitor customers' satisfaction with this service.

4. **Technical service.** The company should provide customers who buy complex materials and equipment with technical services such as custom design work, installation, customer training, applications research, and process-improvement research.

5. **Information service.** The company should consider setting up an information unit that is responsible for answering customer inquiries and disseminating information on new products, features, processes, expected price changes, order backlog status, and new company policies. The information can be disseminated through company newsletters and selectively to specific customers.

All of the preceding services should be coordinated and used as tools in creating customer satisfaction and loyalty.

SUMMARY

Product is the most important element in the marketing mix. By a product, we mean anything that can be offered to a market for attention, acquisition, use, or consumption. Each product has three aspects. The core product is the essential service that the buyer is really buying. The formal product is made up of the features, styling, quality, brand name, and packaging that constitute the tangible product. The augmented product is the formal product plus the various services accompanying it, such as installation, service maintenance, and free delivery. Each product, furthermore, can be interpreted as fitting somewhere in a product hierarchy consisting of a need family, product family, product class, product line, product type, brand, and item.

Most companies handle more than one product, and their product mix can be described as having a certain width, depth, and consistency. The various lines making up the product mix have to be periodically evaluated for profitability and growth potential. The company's better lines should receive disproportionate support; weaker lines should be phased down or out; and new lines should be added in the effort to fill the profit gap.

Each product line should have a separate manager. The manager should study the sales and profit contributions of each item in the product line as well as how the items are positioned in the market against competitors' items. This provides information needed for making several product-line decisions. Line stretching involves the question of whether a particular line should be stretched downward, upward, or two ways. Line filling raises the question of whether additional items should be added within the present range of the line. Line modernization raises the question of whether the line needs a new look, and whether the new look should be installed piecemeal or all at once. Line featuring raises the question of which end of the line should be featured in promotions of the line. Line pricing raises the question of how optional features, by-products, and various satellite services should be priced. Line pruning raises the question of how to detect and remove weaker product items from the line.

Companies also develop a set of brand policies concerning whether to sell their products under their own name, distributors' names, or both, and whether to develop family or individual brands. Many manufacturers of consumer goods employ brand-extension and multibrand strategies.

Finally, companies have to develop a set of customer services that are wanted by customers and are effective against competitors. The company has to decide on the most important service elements to offer, the level at which each element should be offered, and the form in which each element should be provided. The service offer can be coordinated by a customer-service department that is responsible for complaints and adjustments, credit, maintenance, technical service, and information service.

1. Define the primary want-satisfying purpose(s) of the following goods: (a) cars; (b) bread; (c) oil; (d) pillows; (e) pens; (f) novels; (g) textbooks; (h) uniforms; (i) watches; (j) detergents.

2. Offer a definition of the basic business of each of the following large companies: (a) General Motors; (b) Bayer's (maker of aspirins); (c) Massachusetts Investors Trust (a mutual fund); (d) Sears; and (e) *Time* magazine.

3. Most firms prefer to develop a diversified product line to avoid overdependence on a single product. Yet there are certain advantages that accrue to the firm that produces and sells one product. Name them.

4. "As a firm increases the number of its products arithmetically, management's problems tend to increase geometrically." Do you agree?

5. Does the ranking of a company's products according to their relative profit contribution indicate the best way to allocate the marketing budget to these products? If yes, how should the budget be allocated to the products? If no, why?

6. Draw a graph showing how the length of a product line behaves over time.

7. Some supermarket chains have recently introduced a line of generic (unbranded) products, including soups, paper goods, dog food, and so on. Why are generics emerging now and how far are they likely to go?

8. Determine the category of the service component of each of the following items and list some of the elements in their service mixes: (a) museum tour; (b) food processor; (c) photocopies obtained from a coin-operated photocopy machine; (d) facial tissue.

PRICE DECISIONS

15

There ain't no brand loyalty that two-cents-off can't overcome.
ANONYMOUS

All profit organizations and many nonprofit organizations face the task of setting a price on their products or services. Price goes by many names: fares, fees, charges, tuitions, rents, assessments, and plain old price. Originally, price was considered one of the top two or three influences on buyer choice behavior. In the 1950s and 1960s, nonprice factors grew relatively more important and reached a point where over half of a sample of company managers "did not *select* pricing as *one of the five most important* policy areas in their firm's marketing success."[1] More recently, because of worldwide inflation, price has again attracted considerable attention and is now viewed by many marketers as the most important element in the marketing mix, following the product.[2]

Price is the only element in the marketing mix that creates sales revenue; the other elements are costs. In spite of the importance of setting the right price, most companies do not handle pricing well. The most common mistakes are the following: pricing is too cost oriented in that companies fail to take sufficient account of demand intensity and customer psychology, price is not revised often

[1] See Jon G. Udell, "How Important Is Pricing in Competitive Strategy?" *Journal of Marketing,* January 1964, pp. 44–48; also see Robert A. Robicheaux, "How Important Is Pricing in Competitive Strategy?" in *Proceedings: Southern Marketing Association,* ed. Henry W. Nash and Donald P. Robin, January 1976, pp. 55–57.

[2] See "Pricing Strategy in an Inflation Economy," *Business Week,* April 6, 1974, pp. 43–49.

enough to capitalize on changed conditions in the marketplace; price is too often set independently of the rest of the marketing mix rather than as an intrinsic element of market-positioning strategy; and price is not varied enough for different product items and market segments.

The pricing function is handled in a variety of ways in different companies. In small companies, pricing is often a decision of top management and may be out of the hands of the marketing or sales department. In large companies, price determination is typically in the hands of divisional and product-line managers. Even here, top management sets the general pricing objectives and policies and often has to approve the prices proposed by lower levels of management. In industries where pricing is a key factor (aerospace, railroads, oil companies), companies will often establish a separate pricing department to set prices or assist others in the determination of appropriate prices. This department reports in some cases to the marketing department and in other cases to top management. Others who exert an influence on pricing include sales managers, production planners and managers, finance specialists, and accountants.

Pricing is a problem in four general types of situations. It is a problem *when a firm must set a price for the first time.* This happens when the firm develops or acquires a new product, when it introduces its regular product into a new distribution channel or geographical area, or when it regularly enters bids on new contract work. Pricing is a problem *when circumstances lead a firm to consider initiating a price change.* The firm may wish to review whether its price is right in relation to its demand, costs, and competitors' prices. Repricing can be triggered by inflation, shortages, or excess inventories. Pricing is a problem *when competition initiates a price change.* The firm has to decide whether to change its own price, and if so, by how much. Finally, pricing is a problem *when the company produces several products that have interrelated demands and/or costs.* The problem is one of determining optimal price relationships for the products in the line.

SETTING PRICES

Pricing is a problem when a company develops a new product and must set its price for the first time. We can distinguish between pricing strategy and pricing tactics. *Pricing strategy* is the task of defining the price range and price movement through time that would support the sales and profit objectives and marketing positioning of the product in the target market. Thus if a television producer designs a new super-screen TV set that it wishes to position as the Cadillac of the industry, price and quality will have to be set high to support this positioning. *Pricing tactics* is the task of setting specific price levels and terms and altering them within the general parameters of the price strategy as conditions change.

The setting of price is rarely a simple matter. It is only simple in a *price-taking* market, that is, a market where each seller must charge the going price. As conditions approach perfect competition (i.e., homogeneous product, high information, and high mobility of resources), such as is found in several raw material markets, suppliers pretty much have to charge the same as their competitors. If they charge more (without offering any extra services), no one will buy; and there is no reason to charge less as long as buyers are paying the going price.

Most markets, however, do not meet the conditions of perfect competition and call for *price making*. Here the pricing decision can be very complex. The following example is presented to sensitize the reader to the complicated issues involved in price setting.[3]

Pricing a new mobile home   Modern Mobile Homes manufactures a single mobile home called the Knight, which is sold through its own franchised dealers at a retail price of $7,000. The dealers have been pressuring the company to add a second mobile home to the line at the higher end. In response, the company has designed the Queen and is about to set its dealer and retail price. Here are the major facts:

1. The company has enough extra plant capacity to produce up to 500 units a year. Any more than this would require investing in new plant capacity.

2. The fixed costs of producing the Queen are estimated at $120,000. The direct costs are estimated at $6,000 a unit.

3. There is one major competitor producing a high-quality mobile home, which is retailing for $7,800. The competitor charges its dealers $6,400, which is approximately an 18 percent dealer discount off the list price. The company estimates that the competitor's direct cost is $5,800, which means that the competitor makes $600 a unit. The competitor sells about 600 units a year.

4. The company would like to price the Queen to sell for at least $800 more than the Knight to establish its superior quality in the product line.

5. The company displayed the Queen at the latest retail trade show and over 60 percent of the visitors reported that the Queen seemed better designed than the competitor's model.

With this information, what dealer and retail price should Modern Mobile Homes establish for the Queen? If the company is cost-oriented, it could simply start with the fact that each unit costs $6,000 to manufacture and add a markup for the profit it wants per unit. If the company wants $600 profit, the dealers would pay $6,600 and in turn mark it up for the profit they want per unit. The fault with this approach is that it ignores the competitor's price and the relative perceived value of the Queen.

A market-oriented approach would attempt to start with what value potential buyers put on the Queen. For example, if market testing indicates that potential buyers think that the Queen is worth at least $200 more than the competitor's mobile home, then the company might consider a retail price of $8,000. It might decide to offer its dealers a 20 percent dealer discount to motivate them more highly than the competitor's dealers. Under that plan, dealers would pay $6,400, and the company would make $400 per unit. This pricing strategy, which is one of many possible ones, is displayed in Figure 15–1, along with the other information in this case.

What are the implications of pricing the Queen at $8,000? The first thing

---

[3] This example is adapted with several changes from David J. Schwartz, *Marketing Today: A Basic Approach*, 2nd ed. (New York: Harcourt Brace Jovanovich, 1977), pp. 542–44.

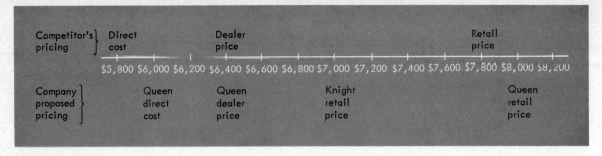

FIGURE 15-1
Illustration of a Pricing Problem

the company has to consider is how many units it would have to sell at $6,400 to break even. The *breakeven volume* is given by:

$$Q_B = \frac{F}{(P\text{-}c)} = \frac{\$120,000}{(\$6,400\text{-}\$6,000)} = 300 \text{ units} \tag{15-1}$$

where:

F = fixed cost
P = price
c = direct cost

The competitor is currently selling 600 units. If this is the total market potential, then Modern Mobile Homes will have to achieve a 50 percent market share to break even. And it would have to achieve this market share in spite of charging $200 more per unit. On the other hand, if the market potential might grow in response to strong market effort, then the company might feel more confident about being able to sell at least 300 units a year.

The company will also want to consider other pricing alternatives. The Queen might be priced slightly below $8,000 (say at $7,950) because buyers have a tendency to think of it as selling in the $7,000 rather than $8,000 price range. This is called *odd pricing* and assumes a certain buyer psychology. Or the Queen might be priced at the competitor's price of $7,800 so that the companies are left to fight for market share on the basis of nonprice competition. Or the company might price the Queen below the competitor's price to grab for a higher market share. However, this violates the wish to price the Queen at $800 more than the Knight; also, it could lead to a higher volume of orders than the company can fill, and this would require increased investment. On the other hand, the company might want to consider pricing the Queen higher than $8,000, to suggest a real Cadillac (called *prestige pricing*). For each possible price level, management would have to figure out the breakeven volume and its probability of attainment, the competitor's likely price and marketing-mix response, and the dealers' discount that makes sense.

Modern Mobile Homes's pricing problem is even more complicated. The company can produce the Queen with optional features (better plumbing, lighting, and so on) and will have to figure out a price structure for the different options. Price will also depend on the size of the planned marketing budget because that will make a difference in the company's ability to convince the market to pay a high price. The Queen could cannibalize some of the sales of the Knight, depending on how closely the Queen is priced to the Knight. Or conversely, the Queen could increase the sales of the Knight, since the dealers will be able to attract more traffic with the longer product line. The company will face opportunities to sell the Queen to large mobile-park developers and will have to decide whether these sales will be handled through their franchised dealers or through a national accounts sales department in the home office, and if so, at what price. The company may not have the freedom to charge less than dealer cost to mobile-park developers in order not to be charged with price discrimination under the Robinson-Patman Act. Finally, the example assumed only one competitor where normally several competitors would operate and complicate the pricing problem.

Thus actual pricing strategies require taking many factors into account. A company has to proceed by clarifying its *pricing objectives*, then considering the *policy constraints*, and then choosing a *pricing procedure*.

Pricing Objectives

A company must be clear on what it is trying to achieve in the way of overall business and marketing objectives before it can set the price on a product. Each possible price has a different implication for profits, sales revenue, and market share. This is shown in Figure 15–2 for a hypothetical product. If the company wants to maximize pretax profits, it should set a price of $97. If it wants to maximize sales revenue, it should set a price of $86. If it wants to maximize its market share, it should set an even lower price.

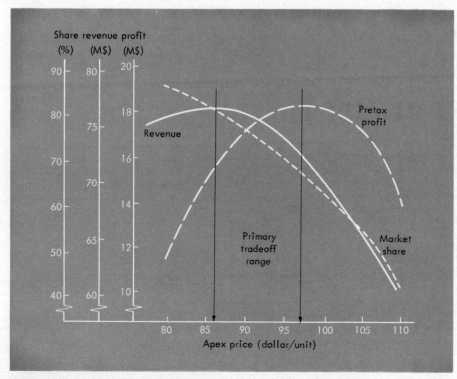

FIGURE 15–2
Relation Between Price, Revenue, Market Share, and Profits

SOURCE: Franz Edelman, *Decision Making in Marketing* (New York: Conference Board, 1971).

Here we will examine six frequently found pricing objectives.

Profit-maximization pricing   One of the most common pricing objectives is to maximize current profits. Economists have worked out a simple yet elegant model for pricing to maximize current profits. The model assumes that the firm has, or can acquire, knowledge of its demand and cost functions for the product in question. The demand function describes the estimated quantity (Q) that would be purchased per period at various prices (P) that might be charged. Suppose the firm is able to determine through statistical demand analysis that its *demand equation* is

$$Q = 1,000 - 4P \qquad (15\text{--}2)$$

This equation expresses the law of demand—less will be bought at higher prices.

The cost function describes the estimated total cost (C) for alternative quantities per period (Q) that might be produced. In the simplest case, the total cost function can be described by the linear equation $C = F + cQ$ where F is total fixed cost and c is unit variable cost. Suppose the company estimated the following *cost equation* for its product:

$$C = 6,000 + 50Q \qquad (15\text{--}3)$$

The company is almost in a position to determine the current profit maximizing price. It needs only two more equations, both definitional in nature. First, *total revenue (R)* is defined as equal to price times quantity sold—that is,

$$R = PQ \qquad (15\text{--}4)$$

Second, *total profits (Z)* are defined as the difference between total revenue and total cost—that is,

$$Z = R - C \qquad (15\text{--}5)$$

The company can now determine the relationship between profits (Z) and price (P) by starting with the profit equation (15–5) and going through the following derivation:

$$Z = R - C$$
$$Z = PQ - C$$
$$Z = PQ - (6,000 + 50Q)$$
$$Z = P(1,000 - 4P) - 6,000 - 50 (1,000 - 4P)$$
$$Z = 1,000P - 4P^2 - 6,000 - 50,000 + 200P$$
$$Z = -56,000 + 1,200P - 4P^2$$

Total profits turn out to be a quadratic (that is, second-degree) function of price. It is a hatlike figure (a parabola), and profits reach their highest point ($34,000) at a price of $150.[4]

---

[4] The optimal price of $150 can be found by drawing the parabola with some sample prices and locating the high point; or by using calculus.

The economist's model has value in showing the role played by the demand and cost function in setting price. But it also has several limitations in practice. (1) It assumes that the other marketing-mix variables are held constant, when in fact they would have to be adjusted for different price settings. (2) It assumes that competitors don't change their prices, when in fact they will react with different prices to different price settings of the company. (3) It ignores the reaction of other parties in the marketing system—government, suppliers, dealers, and so on—to various prices that might be charged. (4) It assumes that the demand and cost functions can be reliably estimated, when in fact great difficulties exist.[5]

Market-share pricing   A company could choose to set a price that maximizes its market-share penetration even though it foregoes current profits. An increasing number of companies believe that long-run profitability rises with market share.[6] Texas Instruments and other companies have set out to dominate their markets through *market-penetration pricing*. They will build excess plant capacity to produce a huge volume, set the price at or below competitors to win share, and keep bringing down their price as their costs fall. They will lose money for the first few years but make it up later when they dominate the market and have the lowest costs.

Any of several conditions might favor setting a low price:[7] (1) The market appears to be highly price sensitive, and therefore a low price will stimulate more rapid market growth. (2) The unit costs of production and distribution fall with accumulated production experience. (3) A low price would discourage actual and potential competition.

Market skimming   Firms may want to take advantage of the fact that some buyers stand ready to pay a much higher price than others because the product has high present value to them. They will initially price to yield a high profit margin per unit sold. This makes sense under the following conditions: (1) There are enough buyers whose demand is relatively inelastic. (2) The unit production and distribution costs of producing a smaller volume are not so much higher that they cancel the advantage of charging what some of the traffic will bear. (3) There is little danger that the high price will stimulate the emergence of rival firms. (4) The high price creates an impression of a superior product.

As time passes, the firm will lower its price to draw in the more price-elastic segments of the market. Du Pont is a prime practitioner of market-skimming pricing, particularly on patent-protected discoveries. They used it with cellophane and nylon, for instance. They will charge a high initial price and only lower it gradually over the years to bring in new price-sensitive segments. Polaroid is another practitioner. It will introduce an expensive version of a new camera and only gradually introduce lower-priced models in a bid for the mass market.

[5] Cost function estimation is described in Jack Johnston, *Statistical Cost Analysis* (New York: McGraw-Hill Book Company, 1960). Demand function estimation is described in Leonard J. Parsons and Randall L. Schultz, *Marketing Models and Econometric Research* (New York: North-Holland, 1976).

[6] See Chapter 11, pp. 279–80.

[7] See Joel Dean, *Managerial Economics* (Englewood Cliffs, N.J.: Prentice-Hall, 1951), pp. 420 ff.

Current-revenue pricing   A company may wish to set the price to maximize current sales revenue. This is a matter of finding the price/quantity combination that yields the largest sales revenue. The firm's interest in early cash recovery could arise because it is strapped for funds or regards the future as too uncertain to justify patient market development.

Target-profit pricing   Some companies describe their pricing objective as the achievement of a satisfactory rate of return. The implication is that although another price might produce an even larger return over the long run, the firm is satisfied with a return that is conventional for the given level of investment and risk. Target pricing (see pp. 390–91) is an example of this.

Promotional pricing   Firms will occasionally set a price designed to enhance the sales of the entire line rather than to yield a profit on the product by itself. An example is *loss-leader pricing*, in which a popular product is priced low to attract a large number of buyers who can be expected to buy the firm's other products. Another example is *prestige pricing*, in which a high price is set on a product item to enhance the quality image of the product line.

Pricing Policies and Constraints

A company's pricing policies answer such questions as the pricing image the company wants, its attitude toward price discounts, and its philosophy of meeting competitors' prices. Thus if Modern Mobile Homes wants an image as a high-quality manufacturer, its pricing policies would rule against introducing models at the low-price, low-quality end.

In setting prices, the decision maker has to consider the reaction of various parties affected by the pricing decision. The following parties are important.

Distributors   The firm must think through its pricing strategy for its distributors and dealers. Some companies set a price for distributors and allow them to set whatever final price they wish. This is done where it is thought that each distributor is in the best position to determine the price suited to local conditions and to set it high enough to provide sufficient selling incentive. The disadvantage is that the manufacturer relinquishes control over the final price. The other approach is for the manufacturer to determine the final price and how much of a distributor's margin is necessary to provide sufficient distributor incentive. The distributors must recognize that the important incentive variable is not the difference between the distributor's and final price (the margin) but rather the margin times the sales volume stimulated by the particular final price.

Competitors   The firm must consider how current competitors will react to its price. Competitors can do nothing, adjust their prices, and/or adjust other elements of their marketing mix. In addition, the price chosen is likely to influence the entry rate of new competitors.

Suppliers   The company's suppliers of materials, funds, and labor also must be considered. Many suppliers interpret the product's price as indicating the level of the firm's profits from the product. The reaction of labor unions will be that a high price, or price increase, constitutes grounds for higher wages. Farmers believe they deserve higher cattle prices if retail meat prices are high. The firm's bank often feels uneasy if product prices are on the low side.

Government Another price-interested party is the government. Under the Robinson-Patman Act, the seller cannot charge different prices to comparable customers unless the price differences are based strictly on cost differences. Under the Miller-Tydings Act, the seller may or may not be able to require retailers to sell their branded products at a uniform list price, depending upon the state laws. Public utilities must justify their rates before regulatory commissions. At various times, pricing in the steel, auto, meat, drug, and heavy-equipment industries has been subject to government pressure. The prices of agricultural goods and of imported goods are affected by agricultural and tariff legislation, respectively. And various state and local governmental units pass legislation and rulings affecting the prices that can be set by sellers.

Company executives Price is a concern of different parties within the company. The sales manager wants a low price so that the sales representatives can "talk price" to customers. The controller likes to see a price that will lead to an early payout. The price makes an important difference to the advertising manager as to copy and media tactics. The production planner is interested because the price will affect the rate of sales. These and other executives in the organization can be expected to have strong views on where to set the price.

Pricing Procedures

There is widespread agreement that actual price setting should be based on the three factors of *cost, demand,* and *competition.* Yet various pricing procedures used in practice will often pay undue attention to one of these factors. We shall examine cost-oriented, demand-oriented, and competition-oriented pricing procedures in this section.

Cost-oriented pricing A great number of firms set their prices largely or even wholly on the basis of their costs. Typically, all costs are included, including a usually arbitrary allocation of overhead made on the basis of expected operating levels.

MARKUP PRICING The most elementary examples of cost-oriented pricing are markup pricing and cost-plus pricing. In both cases price is determined by adding some fixed percentage to the unit cost. Markup pricing is most commonly found in the retail trades where the retailer adds predetermined but different markups to various goods. Cost-plus pricing is most often used to describe the pricing of jobs that are nonroutine and difficult to "cost" in advance, such as construction and military-weapon development.

Markups vary considerably among different goods. Some common markups on the retail price in department stores are 20 percent for tobacco goods, 28 percent for cameras, 34 percent for books, 41 percent for dresses, 46 percent for costume jewelry, and 50 percent for millinery.[8] In the retail grocery industry, items like coffee, canned milk, and sugar tend to have low average markups, while items like frozen foods, jellies, and some canned products have high average markups. In addition, quite a lot of dispersion is found around the averages. Within the category of frozen foods, for example, one study showed the markups on retail price to range from a low of 13 percent to a high of 53 percent.[9]

[8] *Departmental Merchandising and Operating Results of 1965* (New York: National Retail Merchants Association, 1965).

[9] See Lee E. Preston, *Profits, Competition, and Rules of Thumb in Retail Food Pricing* (Berkeley: University of California Institute of Business and Economic Research, 1963), p. 31.

Many hypotheses have been advanced to explain the variations in markups within selected product groups. Preston conducted a study to examine how much of the markup variance within common grocery-product groups could be explained by differences in unit costs, turnover, and manufacturers' versus private brands.[10] The principal finding was that over 40 percent of the variation remained unexplained in most product categories and was probably due to erratic decisions, random factors, and frequently better adaptations to the current market than could be provided by these factors.

Does the use of a rigid customary markup over cost make logical sense in the pricing of products? Generally, no. Any model that ignores current demand elasticity in setting prices is not likely to lead, except by chance, to the achievement of maximum profits, in either the short or long run. As demand elasticity changes, as it is likely to do seasonally, cyclically, or over the product life cycle, the optimal markup would also change.

Still, markup pricing remains popular for a number of reasons. First, there is generally less uncertainty about costs than about demand. By pinning the price to unit costs, sellers simplify their own pricing task considerably; they do not have to make frequent adjustments as demand conditions change. Second, where all firms in the industry use this pricing approach, their prices are likely to be similar if their costs and markups are similar. Price competition is therefore minimized, which would not be the case if firms paid attention to demand variations when they priced. Third, there is the feeling that cost-markup pricing is fairer to both buyers and sellers. Sellers do not take advantage of buyers when the latter's demand becomes acute; yet the sellers earn a fair return on their investment.

TARGET PRICING   A common cost-oriented pricing procedure is that of *target pricing*, in which the firm tries to determine the price that would give it a specified target rate of return on its total costs at an estimated standard volume. This pricing approach has been most closely associated with General Motors, which prices its automobiles so as to achieve a long-run average rate of return of 15 to 20 percent on its investment. It is also closely associated with the pricing policies of public utilities, which have a large investment and are constrained by regulatory commissions, in view of their monopoly position, to seek a fair rate of return on their costs.

The pricing procedures can be illustrated in terms of the breakeven chart in Figure 15–3. Management's first task is to estimate its total costs at various levels of output. The total-cost curve is shown rising at a constant rate until capacity is approached. Management's next task is to estimate the percentage of capacity at which it is likely to operate in the coming period. Suppose the company expects to operate at 80 percent of capacity. This means that it expects to sell 800,000 units if its capacity is 1 million units. The total cost of producing this volume, according to Figure 15–3, is $10 million. Management's third task is to specify a target rate of return. If the company aspires for a 20 percent profit over costs, then it would like absolute profits of $2 million. Therefore one point on its total-revenue curve will have to be $12 million at a volume of 80 percent of capacity. Another point on the total-revenue curve will be $0 at a volume of zero percent of capacity. The rest of the total-revenue curve can be drawn between these two points.

[10] Ibid., pp. 29–40.

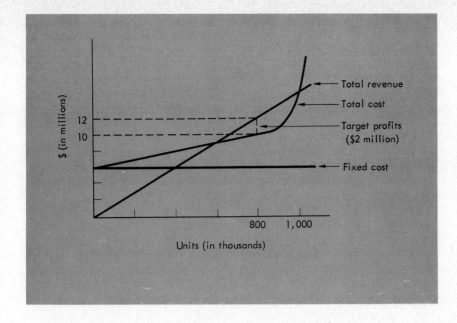

FIGURE 15–3
Breakeven Chart for
Determining Target Price

Where does price come in? The slope of the total-revenue curve is price. In this example, the slope is $15 a unit. Thus if the company charges $15 a unit and manages to sell 800,000 units, it will attain the target rate of return of 20 percent, or $2 million.

Target pricing, however, has a major conceptual flaw. The company used an estimate of sales volume to derive the price, but price is a factor that influences sales volume! A price of $15 may be too high or too low to move 800,000 units. What is missing is a demand function, showing how many units the firm could expect to sell at different prices. With an estimate of the demand curve and with the requirement to earn 20 percent on costs, the firm could solve for those prices and volumes that would be compatible with each other. In this way, the firm would avoid setting a price that failed to generate the estimated level of output.

Demand-oriented pricing Demand-oriented pricing calls for setting a price based on consumer perceptions and demand intensity rather than on cost.

PERCEIVED-VALUE PRICING An increasing number of companies are basing their price on the product's "perceived value." They see the buyers' perception of value, not the seller's level of cost, as the key to pricing. They attempt to measure the relative perceived value of their offer and utilize this in setting the price.[11]

Perceived-value pricing is in line with modern market-positioning thinking. A company develops a product for a particular target market with a particular market positioning in mind with respect to price, quality, and service. Thus, it makes an initial decision on offer value and price. Then the company

---

[11] See Daniel A. Nimer, "Pricing The Profitable Sale Has a Lot to Do With Perception," *Sales Management*, May 19, 1975, pp. 13–14.

estimates the volume it can sell at this price. This suggests the needed plant capacity, investment, and unit costs. Management then figures out whether the product would yield a satisfactory profit at the chosen price and cost. If the answer is yes, the company goes ahead with product development. Otherwise, the company drops the idea.

Among the major practitioners of perceived value pricing are Du Pont and Caterpillar. When Du Pont developed its new synthetic fiber for carpets, it demonstrated to carpet manufacturers that they could afford to pay Du Pont as much as $1.40 a pound for the new fiber and still make their current profit. Du Pont calls this the *value-in-use price*. Du Pont recognized, of course, that pricing the new material at $1.40 a pound would leave the market indifferent. So they set the price somewhat lower than $1.40, depending on the rate of market penetration they were seeking. Du Pont did not take into consideration its own unit-manufacturing cost in setting the price but only in judging whether there was enough profit to go ahead in the first place.

Caterpillar uses perceived value to set prices on its construction equipment. It might price a tractor at $24,000 although a competitor's similar tractor is priced at $20,000. And Caterpillar will get more sales than the competitor! When prospective customers ask a Caterpillar dealer why they should pay $4,000 more for the Caterpillar tractor, the dealer answers:

$20,000 is what the tractor's price would be if it were equivalent to the competitor's tractor
$ 3,000 is the price premium for superior durability
$ 2,000 is the price premium for superior reliability
$ 2,000 is the price premium for superior service
$ 1,000 is the price premium for the longer warranty on parts

$28,000 is the price to cover the value package
–$ 4,000 discount

$24,000 final price

The stunned customers learn that although they are asked to pay a $4,000 premium for the Caterpillar tractor, they are in fact getting a $4,000 discount! They end up choosing the Caterpillar tractor because they are convinced that the lifetime operating costs of the Caterpillar tractor will be smaller.

The key to perceived-value pricing is to make an accurate determination of the market's perception of the value of the total offer. Sellers with an inflated view of the value of their offer may be overpricing their product. In some cases, they underestimate the perceived value and are charging less than they could. Market research has to be carried out to establish the market's perceptions.

Suppose three companies, A, B, and C, produce rapid-relay switches, and a sample of industrial buyers are asked to examine and rate the respective companies' offers. Three alternative methods can be used.

Direct price-rating method. Here the buyers are asked to estimate a price for each switch that they think reflects the total value of buying the switch from each company. For example, they may assign $2.55, $2.00, and $1.52 respectively.

Direct perceived-value-rating method. Here the buyers are asked to allocate 100 points to the three companies to reflect the total value of buying the switch from each company. Suppose they assign 42, 33, 25 respectively. If the average market price of a relay switch is $2.00, we would conclude that the three firms could charge, respectively, $2.55, $2.00, and $1.52 and reflect the perceived value.

Diagnostic method. Here the buyers are asked to rate the three offers on a set of, say, four attributes. They are to allocate 100 points to the three companies with respect to each attribute. They are also asked to distribute 100 points to reflect the relative importance of the attributes. Suppose the results are those shown below:

IMPORTANCE		PRODUCTS		
WEIGHT	ATTRIBUTE	A	B	C
25	Product durability	40	40	20
30	Product reliability	33	33	33
30	Delivery reliability	50	25	25
15	Service quality	45	35	20
100	(Perceived value)	(41.65)	(32.65)	(24.9)

By multiplying the importance weights against each company's ratings, we find that company A's offer is perceived to be above average (at 42), company B's offer is perceived to be average (at 33), and company C's offer is perceived to be below average (at 25).

Company A, according to these findings, can set a high price for its switches because it offers more, and the buyers perceive this. If it wants to price proportionally to its perceived value, it can charge around $2.55 (= $2.00 for an average quality switch × $\frac{42}{33}$). If all three companies set their price proportional to perceived value, they all would enjoy some market share since they all offer the same value-to-price.

If a company prices at less than the perceived value of its offer, it would gain a higher-than-average market share because buyers will be getting more value for their money by dealing with this company. This is illustrated in Figure 15–4. The three offers, A, B, and C, initially lie on the same value/price line. Respective market shares will depend upon the relative density of ideal points (not shown) surrounding the three locations. Now suppose company A decides to lower its price to A'. This means its value/price is on a higher line (the dashed line), and it will pull market share away from both B and C, particularly B because it offers more value at the same price as B. B will be pressed to either lower its price or raise its perceived value. In the latter case, B would have to design better qualities and services and effectively inform the market. If the cost of doing this is less than the loss in revenue that would result from a lower price, B would probably invest in strengthening its perceived value.

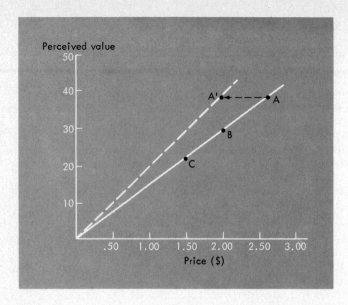

FIGURE 15–4
Perceived-Value Analysis

DEMAND-DIFFERENTIAL PRICING Another form of demand-oriented pricing is demand-differential pricing (also called *price discrimination*), in which a product or service is sold at two or more prices that do not reflect a proportional difference in marginal costs. Price discrimination takes various forms:

1. *Customer basis.* Here different customers pay different amounts for the same product or service. One car buyer pays the full list price and another car buyer bargains and pays a lower price.
2. *Product-form basis.* Here different versions of the product are priced differently but not proportionately to their respective marginal costs. An electric dishwasher with a $5 Formica top might be priced at $260 and the same dishwasher with a $10 wooden top might be priced at $280.
3. *Place basis.* Here different locations are priced differently, even though there is no difference in the marginal cost of offering the locations. A theatre varies its seat prices because of the different intensities of demand for the various locations.
4. *Time basis.* Here different prices are charged seasonally, by the day, and even by the hour. Public utilities typically vary their prices to commercial users by time of day and weekend versus weekday.

For price discrimination to work, certain conditions must exist.[12] First, the market must be segmentable, and the segments must show different intensities of demand. Second, there should be no chance that the members of the segment paying the lower price could turn around and resell the product to the segment paying the higher price. Third, there should be little chance that competitors will undersell the firm in the segment being charged the higher price. Fourth, the cost of segmenting and policing the market should not exceed the extra revenue derived from price discrimination. Fifth, the practice should not breed customer resentment and turning away.

[12] See George Stigler, *The Theory of Price*, rev. ed. (New York: Macmillan Company, 1952), pp. 215 ff.

394

Competition-oriented pricing   When a company sets its prices chiefly on the basis of what its competitors are charging, its pricing policy can be described as competition oriented. It is not necessary to charge the same price as competition, although this is a major example of this policy. The competition-oriented-pricing firm may seek to keep its prices lower or higher than competition by a certain percentage. The distinguishing characteristic is that it does *not* seek to maintain a rigid relation between its price and its own costs or demand. Its own costs or demand may change, but the firm maintains its price because competitors maintain their prices. Conversely, the same firm will change its prices when competitors change theirs, even if its own costs or demand have not altered.

GOING-RATE PRICING   The most popular type of competition-oriented pricing is that in which a firm tries to keep its price at the average level charged by the industry. Called *going-rate pricing*, it is popular for several reasons. Where costs are difficult to measure, it is felt that the going price represents the collective wisdom of the industry concerning the price that would yield a fair return. It is also felt that conforming to a going price would be least disruptive of industry harmony. The difficulty of knowing how buyers and competitors would react to price differentials is still another reason for this pricing.

Going-rate pricing primarily characterizes pricing practice in homogeneous product markets, although the market structure itself may vary from pure competition to pure oligopoly. The firm selling a homogeneous product in a *highly competitive market* has actually very little choice but to set the going price. In *pure oligopoly*, where a few large firms dominate the industry, the firm also tends to charge the same price as competition, although for different reasons. Since there are only a few firms, each firm is quite aware of the others' prices, and so are the buyers. The slightest price difference would attract business to the lower-price firm. The individual oligopolist's demand curve has a kink in it at the level of the present prices. The demand curve tends to be elastic above the kink because other firms are not likely to follow a raise in prices; the demand curve tends to be inelastic below the kink because other firms are likely to follow a price cut. An oligopolist can gain little by raising its price when demand is elastic or by lowering its price when demand is inelastic.

In markets characterized by *product differentiation*, the individual firm has more latitude in its price decision. Product and service differences desensitize the buyer to existing price differentials. Firms try to establish themselves in a pricing zone with respect to their competitors, assuming the role of a high-price, medium-price, or low-price firm. Their product and marketing programs are made compatible with this chosen pricing zone or vice versa. They respond to competitive changes in price to maintain their pricing zone.

SEALED-BID PRICING   Competitive-oriented pricing also dominates in those situations where firms compete for jobs on the basis of bids, such as original equipment manufacture and defense contract work. The bid is the firm's offer price, and it is a prime example of pricing based on expectations of how competitors will price rather than on a rigid relation based on the firm's own costs or demand. The objective of the firm in the bidding situation is to get the contract, and this means that it hopes to set its price lower than that set by any of the other bidding firms.

Yet the firm does not ordinarily set its price below a certain level. Even when it is anxious to get a contract in order to keep the plant busy, it cannot quote a price below marginal cost without worsening its position. On the other hand, as it raises its price above marginal cost, it increases its potential profit but reduces its chance of getting the contract.

The net effect of the two opposite pulls can be described in terms of the *expected profit* of the particular bid. Suppose a bid of $9,500 would yield a high chance of getting the contract, say .81, but only a low profit, say $100. The expected profit with this bid is therefore $81. If the firm bid $11,000, its profit would be $1,600, but its chance of getting the contract might be reduced, say to .01. The expected profit would be only $16. Table 15–1 shows these and some other bids and the corresponding expected profits.

TABLE 15–1
Effect of Different Bids on Expected Profit

COMPANY'S BID	COMPANY'S PROFIT	PROBABILITY OF GETTING AWARD WITH THIS BID (ASSUMED)	EXPECTED PROFIT
$ 9,500	$ 100	.81	$ 81
10,000	600	.36	216
10,500	1,100	.09	99
11,000	1,600	.01	16

One logical bidding criterion would be to state the bid that would maximize the expected profit. According to Table 15–1, the best bid would be $10,000, for which the expected profit is $216.

The use of the expected-profit criterion makes sense for the large firm that makes many bids and is not dependent on winning any particular contract. In playing the odds, it should achieve maximum profits in the long run. The firm that bids only occasionally and/or may need a particular contract badly will probably not find it advantageous to use the expected-profit criterion. The criterion, for example, does not distinguish between a $1,000 profit with a .10 probability and a $125 profit with an .80 probability. Yet the firm that wants to keep production going is likely to prefer the second contract to the first. In other words, the dollar value of expected profits may not reflect the utility value.[13]

INITIATING PRICE CHANGES

Pricing is a challenge not only when the firm sets a price for the first time but also when it is about to initiate a price cut or increase. We will examine these two moves and then consider how to estimate the likely reactions of various parties, particularly buyers and competitors, to these moves.

Initiating Price Cuts

Several circumstances may lead a firm to consider cutting its price even though such a move may threaten industrial harmony and provoke a price war. One circumstance is *excess capacity*. Here the firm needs additional business and pre-

---

[13] For further discussion, see C. West Churchman, Russell L. Ackoff, and E. Leonard Arnoff, *Introduction to Operations Research* (New York: John Wiley & Sons, 1957), pp. 559–73.

sumably has failed to generate it through increased sales effort, product improvement, and other normal means of sales expansion. In the mid-1970s, prices remained remarkably sticky in spite of widespread overcapacity, showing that firms preferred high margins on low sales to low margins on higher sales.[14] But in the late 1970s various companies, particularly small ones, began to break ranks with "follow the leader pricing" and turned to "flexible pricing" to gain as much business as they could.[15]

Another circumstance is *falling market share* in the face of vigorous price competition. Several American industries—such as automobiles, consumer electronics, cameras, watches, and steel—have been losing market share, particularly to Japanese competitors whose high-quality goods carry lower prices than American products. This has led Zenith, General Motors, and others to take more aggressive pricing action. GM, for example, has begun to price by geography and cut its subcompact car prices by 10 percent on the West Coast, where Japanese competition is stiffest.

Still another circumstance provoking price cutting is a *drive for dominance through lower costs*. Either the aggressive pricer starts with lower costs than its competitors or it initiates price cuts in the hope of gaining market share, which would lead to falling costs through larger volume.

Initiating Price Increases

Many companies have had to raise prices in recent years. They do this in spite of the fact that the price increases will be resented by customers, dealers, and even the company's own sales force. A successful price increase can increase profits considerably. For example, if the company's profit margin is 3 percent of sales, a 1 percent price increase will increase profits by 33 percent if sales volume is unaffected.

A major circumstance calling for upward price revision is the persistent worldwide *cost inflation* in recent years. Rising costs unmatched by productivity gains squeeze profit margins and lead companies to regular rounds of price hikes. Prices are often raised by more than the cost increases in anticipation of further inflation or government price controls. Companies hesitate to make price commitments in long-term contracts for fear that cost inflation will erode their profit margins. Companies have become adept at inflation pricing through such measures as:[16]

1. Adopting delayed quotation pricing
2. Writing escalator clauses into contracts
3. Unbundling goods and services and pricing them separately[17]
4. Reducing cash and quantity discounts and off-list pricing by sales force
5. Increasing minimum-acceptance order sizes
6. Putting more sales power behind higher marginal products and markets
7. Reducing product quality, features, or service

[14] See "Prices Rise in Spite of Spare Capacity," *Business Week*, March 21, 1977, pp. 120–26.

[15] See "Flexible Pricing," *Business Week*, December 12, 1977, pp. 78–88.

[16] See "Pricing Strategy in an Inflationary Economy," *Business Week*, December 12, 1977; and Norman H. Fuss, Jr., "How to Raise Prices—Judiciously—to Meet Today's Conditions," *Harvard Business Review*, May–June 1975, pp. 10 ff.

[17] The classic unbundling story is told of a customer buying an automobile in Mexico when inflation was at its worst. After the customer agreed to buy the car at the stated price, the salesperson asked if he also wanted to order tires and a steering wheel!

The other major circumstance leading to price increases is *overdemand*. When a company cannot supply all of its customers, it can raise its price, use allocation quotas, or both. Prices may be raised relatively invisibly through dropping discounts and adding higher-priced units to the line. Or prices may be pushed up boldly. U.S. Gypsum faced this problem when it fell into an oversold position on wallboard, fully recognizing that it would probably catch up with demand in six months and move to an undersold position. The issue was whether it should put through a sharp price increase then, followed by a sharp price decrease six months later, or a small price increase then and a small price decrease six months later. It decided on the former because it felt dealers were more concerned with availability than price and would make good money even at the higher price.

In passing price increases on to customers, the company should show a concern for their situation and not act as a ruthless price gouger. The price increases should be accompanied by a well-thought-out communication program in which the customers are told why the prices are being increased and how they might economize. The company's sales force should make regular calls on the customers and attempt to help them solve their problems.

Buyers' Reactions to Price Changes

Whether the price is to be moved up or down, the action is sure to affect buyers, competitors, distributors, and suppliers, and may interest government as well. The success of the move depends critically on how major parties, particularly buyers and competitors, respond.

The traditional analysis of buyers' reactions to price change utilizes the concept of *price elasticity of demand*.

Price elasticity of demand This term refers to the ratio of the percentage change in demand (quantity sold per period) caused by a percentage change in price. In symbols:

$$Eqp = \frac{(Q_1 - Q_0)/\tfrac{1}{2}(Q_0 + Q_1)}{(P_1 - P_0)/\tfrac{1}{2}(P_0 + P_1)} \tag{15-7}$$

where:

Eqp = elasticity of quantity sold with respect to a change in price
Q_0, Q_1 = quantity sold per period before and after price change
P_0, P_1 = old and new price

A price elasticity of -1 means that sales rise (fall) by the same percentage as price falls (rises). In this case, total revenue is unaffected. A price elasticity greater than -1 means that sales rise (fall) by more than price falls (rises) in percentage terms; in this case, total revenue rises. A price elasticity less than -1 means that sales rise (fall) by less than price falls (rises) in percentage terms; in this case, total revenue falls.

As an example, suppose a company lowers its price from \$10 to \$5 and, as a result, its sales rise from 100 units to 150 units. According to (15-7):

$$\frac{(150 - 100) / \tfrac{1}{2}(100 + 150)}{(\$5 - \$10) / \tfrac{1}{2}(\$10 + \$5)} = \frac{.40}{-.67} = -.60$$

Thus the demand elasticity is less than -1, or inelastic, and we know that total revenue will fall. Checking this, we note that the total revenue fell from $1,000 to $750.

Price elasticity of demand gives precision to the question of whether the firm's price is too high or too low. From the point of view of maximizing *revenue*, price is too high if demand is elastic and too low if demand is inelastic. Whether this is also true for maximizing *profits* depends on the behavior of costs.

In practice, price elasticity is extremely difficult to measure. There are definitional as well as statistical hurdles. Definitionally, price elasticity is not an absolute characteristic of the demand facing a seller but rather a conditional one. Price elasticity depends on the magnitude of the contemplated price change. It may be negligible with a small price change (one below the threshold level) and substantial with a large price change. Price elasticity also varies with the original price level. A 5 percent increase over current prices of $1 and $1.20, respectively, may exhibit a quite different elasticity. Finally, long-run price elasticity is apt to differ from short-run elasticity. Buyers may have to continue with their current supplier immediately after a price increase because choosing a new supplier takes time, but they may eventually switch suppliers. In this case, demand is more elastic in the long run than in the short run.[18] Or the reverse may happen: buyers drop a supplier in anger after being notified of a price increase but return later. The significance of this distinction between short-run and long-run elasticity is that sellers will not know for a while the total effect of their price change.

Major statistical estimation problems face the firm wishing to evaluate price elasticity. Different techniques have evolved, none completely appropriate or satisfactory in all circumstances. The problem can be brought into focus by considering the following case:

> One of the telephone companies in the Bell chain was considering a rate reduction on the extension (or second) phone, which it installed in a home for an extra monthly charge of 75 cents. The company had been using heavy promotion to sell families on second phones, but the advertising stimulation appeared to be showing diminishing returns. The company was wondering how many additional extension phones would be ordered if the charge was reduced to fifty cents.

A telephone company would not have any competitive reactions to worry about in contemplating a price change. The company could proceed to estimate the likely reactions of the ultimate customers, using one of four methods.

DIRECT ATTITUDE SURVEY   The company could interview a sample of potential users as to whether they would add another phone if the monthly service charge was lowered to fifty cents. The percentage who said yes could then be applied against the known total number of potential users to find the number of extra extensions this would mean.

STATISTICAL ANALYSIS   This could take the form of either a historical or a cross-sectional analysis of the relationship between price and quantity. A historical analysis consists in observing how extension usage was affected in the past by

---

[18] Stigler suggests that demand is generally more elastic in the long run because the short run is marked by the difficulty of rapid adjustment, the existence of market imperfections, and the presence of habit. Stigler, *Theory of Price*, pp. 45–47.

rate reductions. A cross-sectional analysis consists in observing how extension usage varies with the rates charged by different companies in the Bell System.

MARKET TEST The company could offer a representative sample of potential users the chance to have an extension phone for fifty cents a month if they acted on the offer within a specified time period. The percentage who took advantage could then be applied against the estimated number of potential users.

ANALYTIC INFERENCE The company could conjecture how many additional families would be likely to find a second phone worthwhile at the lower price. The issue of a second phone would be one of convenience versus cost. The company could segment the market into dwelling units of different sizes and different income levels. A family in a large home with a good income would tend to be more receptive to a second phone. The company could estimate how many families in this segment were without second phones and apply the probability that they would acquire the phone at the reduced rate. This could be done for all the segments, to build up an estimate.

Perceptual factors in buyers' response Perceptual factors constitute an important intervening variable in explaining market response to price changes. In the Bell case, this turned out to be particularly true. In a direct attitude survey, potential extension users were asked what they thought the extension service cost. Over 80 percent of the respondents named a price above seventy-five cents a month, in some cases as high as two dollars. The amount of price misinformation was profound, and this could be an important deterrent of purchase. The policy implication is quite interesting. It means that *bringing people closer to an understanding of the correct price would be tantamount to a price reduction.* If a housewife thought the monthly charge was one dollar and then learned that it was only seventy-five cents, this is tantamount to a price reduction *in her mind* of 25 percent. Rather than reducing the monthly rate to fifty cents, the company might gain more through an advertising campaign that clarified the current price.

Customers will not always put the most straightforward interpretation on a price change when it occurs.[19] A price reduction, which would normally attract more buyers, could mean other things to the buyers:[20]

The item is about to be superseded by a later model.
The item has some fault and is not selling well.
The firm is in financial trouble and may not stay in business to supply future parts.
The price will come down even further and it pays to wait.[21]
The quality has been reduced.

[19] For an excellent review, see Kent B. Monroe, "Buyers' Subjective Perceptions of Price," *Journal of Marketing Research*, February 1973, pp. 70–80.

[20] See Alfred R. Oxenfeldt, *Pricing for Marketing Executives* (San Francisco: Wadsworth Publishing Company, 1961), p. 28.

[21] Economists use the concept of *elasticity of expectations* to convey this possibility. The elasticity of expectations is the ratio of the future expected percentage change in price to the recent percentage change in price. A positive elasticity means that buyers expect a price reduction (increase) to be followed by another reduction (increase).

A price increase, which would normally deter sales, may carry a variety of different meanings to the buyers:

> The item is very "hot" and may be unobtainable unless it is bought soon.
> The item represents an unusually good value.[22]
> The seller is greedy and is charging what the traffic will bear.

Buyers' reactions to price changes will also vary with the buyers' perceptions of the product's cost in their total scheme of purchases. Buyers are most price sensitive to products that cost a lot and are bought frequently, whereas they hardly notice higher prices on small items that they buy infrequently. In addition, buyers are normally less concerned with the product's *price* than its *total costs*, where the costs include obtaining, operating, and servicing the product. A seller can charge a higher price than competition and still get the business if he or she is able to convince the customer that the total costs are low.

Competitors' Reactions to Price Changes

A firm contemplating a price change has to worry about competitors' as well as customers' reactions. Competitors' reactions are particularly important where the number of firms is small, the product offering is homogeneous, and the buyers are discriminating and informed.

How can the firm estimate the likely reaction of its competitors? Let us assume that the firm faces only one large competitor. The likely behavior of this competitor can be approached from two quite different starting points. One is to assume that the competitor has a set policy for reacting to price changes. The other is to assume that the competitor treats each price change as posing a fresh challenge. Each assumption has different research implications.

If the competitor has a set price-reaction policy, there are at least two ways to fathom it—through inside information and through statistical analysis. Inside information can be obtained in many ways, some quite acceptable and others verging on cloak-and-dagger methods. One of the more respectable methods is hiring an executive away from a competitor. In this way the firm acquires a rich source of information on the competitor's thought processes and patterns of reaction. It may even pay to set up a unit of former employees whose job is to think like the competitor. Information on the thinking of a competitor can also come through the financial community, suppliers, dealers, and the business community at large.

A set policy toward meeting price changes may be discerned through a statistical analysis of the firm's past price reactions. We can employ the concept "conjectural price variation" (V), defined as the ratio of the competitor's reactive price change to the company's previous price change. In symbols:[23]

$$V_{A,t} = \frac{P_{B,t} - P_{B,t-1}}{P_{A,t} - P_{A,t-1}} \tag{15–8}$$

[22] A cosmetics company introduced a new low-priced lipstick line, and it did not sell. The company raised its price substantially, and it began to sell extremely well. Price is taken by many buyers as an indicator of quality. See André Gabor and C. W. J. Granger, "Price as an Indicator of Quality," *Economica*, February 1966, pp. 43–70.

[23] See William Fellner, *Competition among the Few* (New York: Alfred A. Knopf, 1949); and Richard M. Cyert and James G. March, *A Behavioral Theory of the Firm* (Englewood Cliffs, N.J.: Prentice-Hall, 1963), chap. 5, esp. pp. 88–90.

where:

$$V_{A,t} = \text{the change in competitor B's price during period } t \text{ as a}$$
$$\text{proportion of company A's price change during period } t$$
$$P_{B,t} - P_{B,t-1} = \text{the change in competitor B's price during period } t$$
$$P_{A,t} - P_{A,t-1} = \text{the change in company A's price during period } t$$

The last-observed $V_{A,t}$ can be used by the company as an estimate of the probable reaction of the competitor. If $V_{A,t} = 0$, then the competitor did not react last time. If $V_{A,t} = 1$, then the competitor fully matched the company's price change. If $V_{A,t} = \frac{1}{2}$, then the competitor only matched half of the company's price change. However, it could be misleading to base the analysis only on the last price reaction. It would be better to average several of the past V terms, giving more weight to the more recent ones because they are reflections of more current policy. A possible estimate of future competitive price reaction ($V_{A,t+1}$) might be

$$V_{A,t+1} = .5V_{A,t} + .3V_{A,t-1} + .2V_{A,t-2} \tag{15-9}$$

where three past conjectural price-variation terms are combined in a weighted average.

The statistical method makes sense if the competitor shows a fairly consistent price reaction. Otherwise it would be better to assume that the competitor decides afresh on each occasion of a price increase what response to make. An analysis must be made of the competitor's self-interest. His current financial situation should be researched, along with recent sales and capacity, customer loyalty, and corporate objectives. If evidence points to a market-share objective, then the competitor is likely to match the price change. If evidence points to a profit-maximization objective, the competitor may react on some other policy front, such as increasing the advertising budget or improving the product quality. The task is to get into the mind of the competitor through inside and outside sources of information.

The problem is complicated because each price change by the company occurs under unique circumstances, and the competitor is capable of putting different interpretations on it. The competitor's reaction to a price reduction will depend on whether it is interpreted to mean:

The company is trying to steal the market.

The company is not doing well and is trying to improve its sales.

The company is hoping that the whole industry will reduce its prices in the interests of stimulating total demand.

When there is more than one competitor, the company must estimate each competitor's likely reaction. If all competitors behave alike, this amounts to analyzing only a typical competitor. If the competitors cannot be expected to react uniformly because of critical differences in size, market shares, or policies, then separate analyses are necessary. If it appears that a few competitors will match the price change, then there is good reason to expect the rest will also match it.

The following case illustrates how a major chemical company analyzed the probable reactions of various parties to a contemplated price reduction.[24]

> A large chemical company had been selling a plastic substance to industrial users for several years and enjoyed a 40 percent market share. The management became worried about whether its current price of one dollar per pound could be maintained for much longer. The main source of concern was the rapid buildup of capacity by its three competitors and the possible attraction of further competitors by the current price. Management saw the key to the problem of possible oversupply to lie in further market expansion. The key area for market expansion lay in an important segment of the market that was closely held by a substitute plastic product produced by six firms. This substitute product was not as good, but it was priced lower. Management saw a possible solution in displacing the substitute product in the recalcitrant segment through a price reduction. If it could penetrate this segment, there was a good chance it could also penetrate three other segments, which had resisted the displacement.

The first task was to develop a decision structure for the problem in which all components would be related. This meant defining the objectives, price alternatives, and key uncertainties. It was decided that the objective would be to maximize the present value of future profits over the next five years. Management decided to consider the four alternatives of maintaining the price at one dollar or reducing the price to ninety-three, eighty-five, and eighty cents, respectively. The following were considered among the key uncertainties that had to be evaluated:

How much penetration in the key segment would take place without a price reduction?

How would the six firms producing the substitute plastic react to each possible price reduction?

How much penetration in the key segment would take place for every possible price reaction of the suppliers of the substitute plastic?

How much would penetration into the key segment speed up penetration into the other segments?

If the key segment were not penetrated, what would be the probability that the company's competitors would initiate price reductions soon?

What would be the impact of a price reduction on the decision of existing competitors to expand their capacity and/or potential competitors to enter the industry?

The data-gathering phase consisted mainly in asking key sales personnel to place subjective probabilities on the various possible states of the key uncertainties. Meetings were held with the sales personnel to explain the concept of expressing judgments in the form of probabilities. The probabilities were filled out on a long questionnaire. For example, one question asked for the probability that the producers of the substitute product would retaliate if the company

[24] See Paul E. Green, "Bayesian Decision Theory in Pricing Strategy," *Journal of Marketing,* January 1963, pp. 5–14.

reduced its price to ninety-three cents per pound. On the average, the sales personnel felt that there was only a 5 percent probability of a full match, a 60 percent probability of a half match, and a 35 percent probability of no retaliation. They were also asked for probabilities if price were reduced to eighty-five and to eighty cents. The sales personnel indicated, as expected, that the probability of retaliation increased with an increase in price reduction.

The next step was to estimate the likely payoffs of different courses of action. A decision-tree analysis revealed that there were over four hundred possible outcomes. For this reason, the estimation of expected payoffs was programmed on a computer. The computer results indicated that in all cases a price reduction had a higher expected payoff than status quo pricing, and, in fact, a price reduction to eighty cents had the highest expected payoff. To check the sensitivity of these results to the original assumptions, the results were recomputed for alternative assumptions about the rate of market growth and the appropriate cost of capital. It was found that the ranking of the strategies was not affected by the change in the assumptions. The analysis clearly pointed to the desirability of a price reduction.

RESPONDING TO PRICE CHANGES

Let us reverse the previous question and ask how a firm should respond to a price change initiated by a competitor.

In some market situations the firm has no choice but to meet a competitor's price change. This is particularly true when the price is cut in a homogeneous product market. Unless the firm meets the price reduction, most buyers will shift their business to the lowest-price competitor.

When the price is raised by a firm in a homogeneous product market, the other firms may or may not meet it. They will comply if the price increase appears designed to benefit the industry as a whole. But if one firm does not see it that way and thinks that it or the industry would gain more by standing pat on prices, its noncompliance can make the leader and the others rescind any price increases.

In nonhomogeneous product markets, a firm has more latitude in reacting to a competitor's price change. The essential fact is that buyers choose the seller on the basis of a multiplicity of considerations: service, quality, reliability, and other factors. These factors desensitize many buyers to minor price differences. The reacting firm has a number of options: doing nothing and losing few or many customers, depending upon the level of customer loyalty; meeting the price change partly or fully; countering with modifications of other elements in its marketing mix.

The firm's analysis should take the form of estimating the expected payoffs of alternative possible reactions. It should consider the following questions:

Why did the competitor change the price? Is it to steal the market, to utilize excess capacity, to meet changing cost conditions, or to evoke a calculated industry-wide price change to take advantage of total demand?

Is the competitor intending to make the price change temporary or permanent?

What will happen to the company's market share and profits if it ignores the price change? Are the other companies going to ignore the price change?

What is the competitor's (and other firms') response likely to be to each possible reaction?

Market leaders, in particular, are frequent targets of aggressive price cutting by smaller firms trying to build market share. One only has to think of Fuji Film's attack on Kodak, Bic's attack on Gillette, and Datril's attack on Tylenol.[25] When the attacking firm brings a comparable quality to the market, its lower price will cut increasingly into the market leader's share. The leader at this point has several options.

1. *Price maintenance.* The leader might choose to maintain its price and profit margin. It may believe that (a) it would lose too much profit if it reduced its price on all the units it sells; (b) it would not lose much market share; and (c) it would be easy to regain market share when necessary. It may also feel that it could hold on to the good customers, giving up only the poorer ones to the competitor. The argument against price maintenance, however, is that the attacker gets more confident, the leader's sales force gets demoralized, and the leader ends up losing more share than expected. The leader then panics, lowers price in order to regain share, and finds it more difficult and costly to regain share than expected.

2. *Price maintenance with nonprice counterattack.* If the leader chooses to maintain price, it should take some steps to strengthen the value of its offer. It should improve its product, services, and communications so that customers see themselves as getting more value per dollar from the company than from its competitor. The firm will often find it cheaper to maintain its price and spend money to improve the value of its offer than to cut its price and operate at a lower margin.

3. *Price reduction.* The leader might prefer to lower its price to the competitor's price to hold its market share. It may choose this course of action because (a) its costs fall with volume; (b) it believes that the market is very price sensitive and it will lose a substantial market share; and (c) it believes that it would be hard to rebuild its market share once it is lost. This action will cut its profits in the short run. Some firms will be tempted to reduce their product quality, services, and marketing communications to maintain profits but this is shortsighted and can ultimately hurt their long-run market share. The company should try to maintain the value of its offer as it cuts prices.

4. *Price increase with product counterattack.* The leader, instead of maintaining or lowering its price, might raise it along with introducing some new brands to bracket the attacking brand. Heublein, Inc., used this strategy when its Smirnoff's vodka, which had 23 percent of the American vodka market, was attacked by another brand, Wolfschmidt, priced at one dollar less a bottle. Instead of Heublein's lowering the price of Smirnoff by one dollar, it raised the price by one dollar and put the increased revenue into its advertising. At the same time, Heublein introduced a new brand, Relska, to compete with Wolfschmidt and also introduced Popov, a low-priced vodka. This strategy effectively bracketed Wolfschmidt and gave Smirnoff an even more elite image.

The best response requires an analysis of the particular situation. The company under attack has to consider the product's stage in the life cycle, its importance in the company's portfolio, the intentions and resources of the competitor, the price sensitivity versus value sensitivity of the market, the behavior of costs with volume, and the company's alternative opportunities.

An extended analysis of company alternatives is not always feasible at the time of a price change. The competitor who initiated the price change may have spent considerable time in preparing for this decision, but the company may

---

[25] See "The Market Manhandles a Blue Chip," *Business Week*, June 20, 1977, p. 70 ff; "Razor Fighting," *Newsweek*, November 22, 1976, p. 103; and "A Painful Headache for Bristol-Myers?" *Business Week*, October 6, 1975, pp. 78–80.

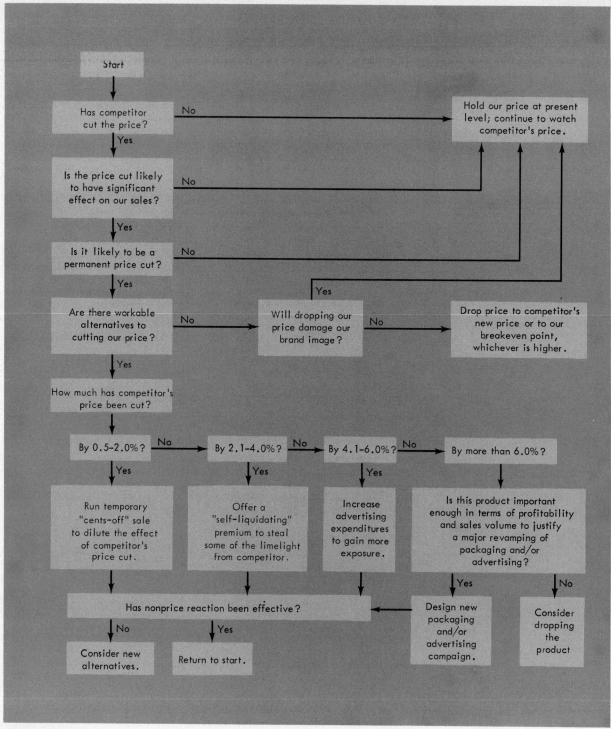

SOURCE: Redrawn, with permission, from an unpublished paper by Raymond J. Trapp, Northwestern University, 1964.

FIGURE 15–5

Decision Program for Meeting a Competitor's Price Cut

have to react decisively within hours or days. About the only way to place such decisions on a sure footing is to anticipate their possible occurrence and to prepare an advanced program to guide managers' responses. An example of such a program to meet a possible price cut is shown in Figure 15–5. Reaction programs for meeting price changes are likely to find their greatest application in industries where price changes occur with some frequency and where it is important to react quickly. Examples could be found in the meat-packing, lumber, and oil industries.[26]

PRICING THE PRODUCT LINE

The logic of setting or changing a price on an individual product has to be modified when the product is a member of a product line. In the latter case, the quest is for a set of mutual prices that maximizes the profits of the line. This quest is made difficult because various company products are interrelated in demand and/or cost and are subject to different degrees of competition.

Interrelated Demand

Two products are interrelated in demand when the price (or some other element of the marketing mix) of one affects the demand for the other. Economists use the concept of "cross-elasticity of demand" to express the interaction.[27] A positive cross-elasticity means that two goods are *substitutes,* a negative cross-elasticity means that two goods are *complements,* and a zero cross-elasticity means that two goods are *unrelated* in demand. If a television manufacturer lowered the price of its color television sets, this would decrease the demand for its black-and-white sets (substitutes), increase the demand for the components of its color sets (complements), and probably not affect the demand for its pocket radios. Before changing the price of any single item in its line, the seller should consider the various cross-elasticities to determine the overall impact of this move.

Interrelated Cost

Two products are interrelated in cost when a change in the production of one affects the cost of the other. By-products and joint products are related in this sense. If the production of ham is cut down, the production of pork will be also. As a result, the unit cost of the pork will rise because the overhead is spread over fewer units. More generally, any two products using the same production facilities are interrelated on the cost side even if they are not joint products. This is largely because accounting practice requires a full allocation of costs. The significance of all this is that if the company increases the price of A, for example, and causes its sales to fall, the cost of the other products, assuming they are not complementary goods, will be higher. Thus management must examine the cost interactions before it changes the price of a single product in the line.

[26] See, for example, William M. Morgenroth, "A Method for Understanding Price Determinants," *Journal of Marketing Research,* August 1964, pp. 17–26.

[27] Technically, the cross-elasticity of demand (E_c) is the percentage change in quantity sold of product B associated with a percentage change in price of product A.

Various products in a company line are exposed to different degrees of competition. The seller may have little latitude in pricing products in the line where existing or potential competition is keen and will have varying degrees of price discretion in the other cases. Therefore the prices of the products in the line should not simply be proportional to costs, for this would overlook profit opportunities that are associated with taking advantage of different degrees of competition.

In practice, costs have provided the usual starting point for determining the prices of interrelated products in the line. Even here there seems to be considerable disagreement over which costs should be used. The three most popular cost bases are full costs, incremental costs, and conversion costs. The price structures resulting from using these respective cost bases are illustrated for a hypothetical soap manufacturer in Table 15–2.

The soap manufacturer makes two types of specialty soap. The second soap requires more labor cost but less material cost per bar than the first soap. The second soap also requires more manufacturing overhead than the first. The specific costs per bar are shown in Table 15–2A.

The first pricing principle calls for pricing the soaps proportionately to their full costs. Since both soaps have the same full costs, they will bear the same price (here forty-two cents because of a 20 percent markup). The chief criticism against using the full cost is that the allocation of overhead unavoidably involves some arbitrariness. Therefore the resulting prices take on a partly arbitrary character. As a result, the company may be blind to profit opportunities that would exist if the prices of the two soaps were not geared so tightly to the recovery of a somewhat arbitrary overhead burden.

The second pricing principle calls for setting prices that are proportional

TABLE 15–2
Illustration of Alternative Product-line Pricing Principles

A. PRODUCT-LINE COST STRUCTURE

	SOAP 1	SOAP 2
1. Labor cost	.10	.15
2. Material cost	.20	.10
3. Overhead cost	.05	.10
Full cost (1 + 2 + 3)	.35	.35
Incremental cost (1 + 2)	.30	.25
Conversion cost (1 + 3)	.15	.25

B. ALTERNATIVE PRODUCT-LINE PRICES

	MARKUP	SOAP 1	SOAP 2
1. Full cost pricing	20%	.42	.42
2. Incremental cost pricing	40%	.42	.35
3. Conversion cost pricing	180%	.42	.70

to incremental costs. The underlying theory is that the company should charge customers proportionately to the extra costs it has to bear in supplying additional units of the two soaps. In the example, supplying an additional unit of soap 2 imposes less additional cost than supplying another unit of soap 1. The net effect of pricing on an incremental cost basis is to shift sales toward the soap that absorbs more company overhead.[28]

The third pricing principle calls for setting prices that are proportional to conversion costs. Conversion costs are defined as the labor and company overhead required to convert purchased materials into finished products. Conversion costs thus amount to the "value added" by the firm in the production process; it can be found by subtracting purchased material costs from the allocated full costs. The argument that has been advanced for using conversion costs is that the firm's profits should be based on the value its own operations add to each soap. The net effect of pricing on a conversion cost basis is to shift sales toward the soap that has more material cost. This pricing principle economizes on the use of scarce company resources, such as labor and machines.

Although costs can represent a starting point for developing the pricing structure, they hardly represent sufficient criteria. Incremental costs provide the lower limit to individual product pricing (except in special circumstances, such as loss leading). But a *uniform* markup over incremental or any other costs is fallacious in that it ignores the different demand intensities, cross-elasticities, competitive conditions, and life-cycle characteristics of each product.

SUMMARY

In spite of the increased role of nonprice factors in the modern marketing process, price remains an important element and especially challenging in certain situations.

In setting a price, the firm must pay attention to pricing objectives, policies, and procedures. The firm can draw guidance from the theoretical pricing model of the economists. The model suggests how the firm can find the short-run profit-maximizing price when estimates of demand and cost are available. The model, however, leaves out several factors that have to be considered in actual pricing situations, such as the presence of other objectives, multiple parties, marketing-mix interactions, and uncertainties surrounding the estimates of demand and cost. In practice, companies tend to orient their pricing toward cost (as in markup pricing and target pricing), or demand (as in perceived-value pricing and differential-demand pricing), or competition (as in going rate pricing and bidding).

When a firm considers changing its established price, it must carefully consider customers' and competitors' reactions. The probable reaction of customers is summarized in the concept of price elasticity of demand. There are several ways to estimate price elasticity and some problems in interpreting it, but it is a key factor in the determination of how much would be gained by the price change. Competitors' reactions also must be taken into account, and they depend very much on the nature of the market structure and the degree of product

---

[28] The principle of marking up incremental costs is analyzed and defended for retail pricing in Malcolm P. McNair and Eleanor G. May, "Pricing for Profit, A Revolutionary Approach to Retail Accounting," *Harvard Business Review*, May–June 1957, pp. 105–22.

homogeneity. Competitors' reactions may be studied on the assumption either that they flow from a set reaction policy or that they flow from a fresh appraisal of the challenge each time. The firm initiating the price change must also consider the probable reactions of suppliers, middlemen, and government.

The firm that faces a competitor's price change must try to understand the competitor's intent and the likely duration of the change. If swiftness of reaction is desirable, the firm should preplan its reactions to different possible pricing developments.

Pricing is complicated when it is realized that various products in a line typically have important demand and/or cost interrelationships. Then the objective is to develop a set of mutual prices that maximize the profits on the whole line. Most companies develop tentative prices for the products in the line by marking up full costs or incremental costs or conversion costs and then modifying these prices by individual demand and competitive factors.

QUESTIONS AND PROBLEMS

1. Does an "early cash recovery" pricing objective mean that the firm should set a high rather than a low price on its new product?

2. The statement was made that a firm might set a low price on a product to discourage competitors from coming in. Are there any situations (aside from anti-trust reasons) when a firm might deliberately want to attract competitors into a new market and set a high price for this reason?

3. Four different methods of estimating the price elasticity of demand for extension telephones were described in the text. What are the limitations of each method?

4. Xerox developed an office copying machine called the 914. The machine was more expensive than competitive machines but offered the user superior copy and lower variable costs: 1 cent per copy as opposed to between 4 and 9 cents for competing processes. The machine cost around $2,500 to produce, and management was considering pricing it at either $3,500 or $4,500. How could it estimate unit sales at the two alternative price levels?

5. Bell and Howell was the first company to develop an electric-eye camera by combining a regular $70 camera with a $10 electric-eye mechanism. What price do you think might be charged for the new camera?

6. A group of people were asked to choose between two raincoats, one bearing a brand label and a higher price and another bearing a store label and a lower price. The two coats happened to be identical, but the customers were not told this. If customers were completely knowledgeable, (a) what percentage would choose the higher-priced coat, and (b) what percentage do you think actually chose the higher-priced coat?

7. In principle, a reduction in price is tantamount to an increase in marketing effort. How can the price reduction be monetized into its equivalent in increased marketing effort?

8. The leading manufacturer of a food flavor intensifier has recently watched its market share fall from 100 percent to 85 percent. Its declining share is due to its insistence on maintaining a high price in the face of new competitors who have introduced the same product for substantially less. The company has fought the new competition by increasing its advertising expenditures and dealer promotions. Does this make as much sense as cutting its price?

9. Restate the following prose description of a pricing procedure in either (a) mathematical or (b) logical flow diagram form.

Given that my competitor is operating at or above his breakeven point with a price equal to mine, then: If I cut my price, my competitor will cut his to match mine providing the price cut is likely to be permanent and the competitor can break even at my new price. If I do not cut my price, my competitor will not cut his either. If I cut my price, and the price cut is not likely to be permanent, my competitor will watch price and volume but will do nothing now. If I cut my price, and if the price cut is likely to be permanent and my competitor cannot break even at my new price, he will cut his price down to his breakeven point.

10. How can a company increase its profits without raising a single price and managing to lower any of its costs?

11. Four companies, W, X, Y, and Z, produce electric can openers. Research asking consumers to allocate 100 points among the companies' products for each of four attributes produced the following results.

IMPORTANCE WEIGHT	ATTRIBUTE	COMPANY PRODUCTS			
		W	X	Y	Z
.35	Durability	30	15	40	15
.15	Attractiveness	20	20	30	30
.25	Noiselessness	30	15	35	20
.25	Safety	25	25	25	25

An average electric can opener sells for $20. What should company W do about the pricing of its product if company Y charges $22?

Marketing-Channels Decisions

The middleman is not a hired link in a chain forged by a manufacturer, but rather an independent market, the focus of a large group of customers for whom he buys. . . . As he grows and builds a following, he may find his prestige in his market is greater than that of the supplier whose goods he sells.

PHILLIP McVEY

16

In today's economy, most producers do not sell their goods directly to the final users. Between them and the final users stands a host of marketing intermediaries performing a variety of functions and bearing a variety of names. Some intermediaries—such as wholesalers and retailers—buy, take title to, and resell the merchandise; they are called *merchant middlemen*. Others—such as brokers, manufacturers' representatives, and sales agents—search for customers and may negotiate on behalf of the producer but do not take title to the goods; they are called *agent middlemen*. Still others—such as transportation companies, independent warehouses, banks, and advertising agencies—assist in the performance of distribution but neither take title to goods nor negotiate purchases or sales; they are called *facilitators*.

Two aspects of channel decisions place them among the most critical marketing decisions of management. The first is that *the channels chosen for the company's products intimately affect every other marketing decision*. The firm's pricing decisions depend upon whether it seeks a few franchised high-markup dealers or mass distribution; the firm's advertising decisions are influenced by the degree of cooperation from channel members; the firm's sales-force decisions depend upon whether it sells directly to retailers or uses manufacturers' representatives. This does not mean that channel decisions are always made prior to other decisions, but rather that they exercise a powerful influence on the rest of the mix.

The second reason for the significance of channel decisions is that *they involve the firm in relatively long-term commitments to other firms.* When an automobile manufacturer signs up independent franchised dealers to merchandise its automobiles, it cannot easily replace them with company-owned outlets if conditions change. When a drug manufacturer relies on independent retail druggists for the distribution of most of its products, it must heed them when they object to its entering its products into mass-distribution chain stores. Corey has observed:

> A distribution system . . . is a key *external* resource. Normally it takes years to build, and it is not easily changed. It ranks in importance with key *internal* resources such as manufacturing, research, engineering, and field sales personnel and facilities. It represents a significant corporate commitment to large numbers of independent companies whose business is distribution—*and* to the particular markets they serve. It represents, as well, a commitment to a set of policies and practices that constitute the basic fabric on which is woven an extensive set of long-term relationships.[1]

Thus there is a powerful tendency toward status quo in channel arrangements. Therefore, management must choose its channels carefully, with an eye on tomorrow's likely selling environment as well as today's.

THE NATURE OF MARKETING CHANNELS

Every producer seeks to link together the set of marketing intermediaries that best fulfill the firm's objectives. This set of marketing intermediaries is called the *marketing channel* (also trade channel, channel of distribution). We shall use Bucklin's definition of a marketing channel: "A *channel of distribution* shall be considered to comprise a set of institutions which performs all of the activities (functions) utilized to move a product and its title from production to consumption."[2]

Number of Channel Levels

Marketing channels can be characterized according to the number of channel levels. Each institution that performs some work to bring the product and its title to the point of consumption constitutes a *channel level*. Since both the producer and the ultimate consumer perform some work in bringing the product and its title to the point of consumption, they are included in every channel. We will use the number of *intermediary levels* to designate the *length* of a channel. Figure 16–1 illustrates several marketing channels of different lengths.

A zero-level channel, often called a *direct marketing channel,* consists of a manufacturer selling directly to a consumer. Many examples can be found. Avon's sales representatives sell cosmetics directly to homemakers on a door-to-door basis; IBM's sales representatives sell computer equipment directly to user firms; and Bell Apple Orchard invites the public to pick their own apples at a flat price per bushel.

A one-level channel contains one selling intermediary. In consumer mar-

---

[1] E. Raymond Corey, *Industrial Marketing: Cases and Concepts* (Englewood Cliffs, N.J.: Prentice-Hall, 1976), p. 263.

[2] Louis P. Bucklin, *A Theory of Distribution Channel Structure* (Berkeley: Institute of Business and Economic Research, University of California, 1966), p. 5.

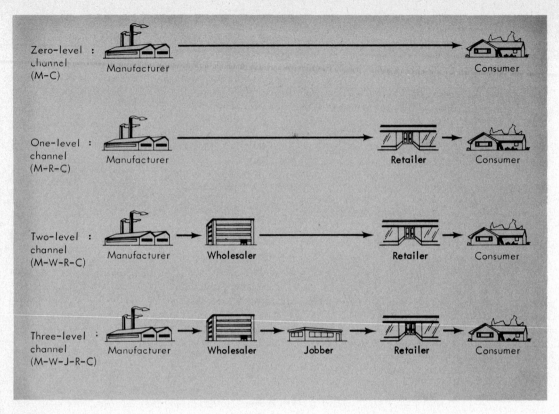

FIGURE 16–1
Examples of Different-Level Channels

kets this intermediary is typically a retailer (R); in industrial markets, it is often a sales agent or a broker.

A two-level channel contains two intermediaries. In consumer markets they are typically a wholesaler and a retailer; in industrial markets they may be a sales agent and a wholesaler.

A three-level channel contains three intermediaries. An example is found in the meat-packing industry, where a jobber usually intervenes between the wholesalers and the retailers. The jobber buys from wholesalers and sells to the smaller retailers, who generally are not serviced by the large wholesalers.

Higher-level marketing channels are also found, but with less frequency. From the producer's point of view the problem of control increases with the number of levels, even though the manufacturer typically deals only with the adjacent level.

Types of Channel Flows

The various institutions that make up a marketing channel are connected by several distinguishable types of flows. The most important are the physical flow, title flow, payment flow, information flow, and promotion flow. These are illustrated in Figure 16–2 for the marketing of forklift trucks.

The *physical flow* describes the actual movement of physical products from raw materials to final customers. In the case of a forklift-truck manufacturer, such as Allis-Chalmers or Clark Equipment, raw materials, subassemblies, parts, and engines flow from suppliers via transportation companies (transporters) to the manufacturer's warehouses and plants. The finished trucks are warehoused and later shipped to dealers in response to their orders. The dealers in turn sell and ship them to customers. Large orders may be supplied directly from the company warehouses or even from the plant itself. At each stage of movement, one or more modes of shipment may be used, including railroads, trucks, and air freight.

The *title flow* describes the actual passage of title (of ownership) from one marketing institution to another. In the case of forklift trucks, title to the raw materials and components passes from the suppliers to the manufacturer. The title to the finished trucks passes from the manufacturer to the dealers and then to the customers. If the dealers only hold the trucks on *consignment,* they would not be included in the diagram.

The *payment flow* shows customers paying their bills through banks and other financial institutions to the dealers, the dealers remitting payment to the manufacturer (less the commission), and the manufacturer making payments to the various suppliers. There will also be payments made to transporters and independent warehouses (not shown).

The *information flow* describes how information is exchanged among the

FIGURE 16–2

Five Different Marketing Flows in the Marketing Channel for Forklift Trucks

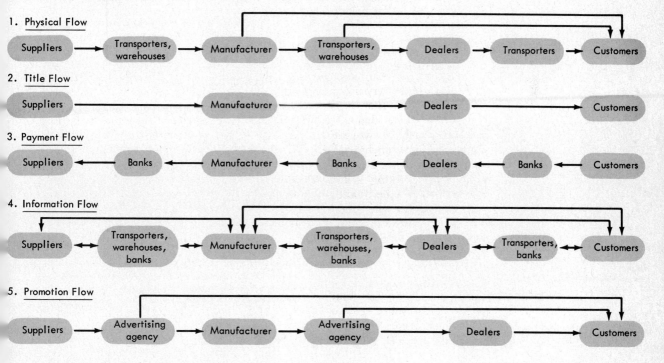

institutions in the marketing channel. A two-way information exchange takes place between each successive stage in the channel, and there are several information flows between nonadjacent institutions.

Finally, the *promotion flow* describes directed flows of influence (advertising, personal selling, sales promotion and publicity) from one party to other parties in the system. Suppliers promote their name and products to the manufacturer. They may also promote their name and products to final customers in the hope of influencing the manufacturer to prefer products embodying their parts or materials. A promotion flow is also directed by the manufacturer to dealers (trade promotion) and final customers (end-user promotion).

Were all of these flows superimposed on one diagram, they would emphasize the tremendous complexity of even simple marketing channels. This complexity goes even further, once we start distinguishing among different types of intermediaries, and customers.

Channels in the Service Sector

The concept of marketing channels is not limited to the distribution of physical goods. Producers of services and ideas also face the problem of making their output *available* and *accessible* to target populations.[3] "Educational-dissemination systems" and "health-delivery systems" are simply names for marketing channels to distribute services in the nonprofit sector. The problem is one of developing and locating a set of agencies and facilities to provide services to a spatially distributed population.

> Hospitals must be located in geographic space to serve the people with complete medical care, and we must build schools close to the children who have to learn. Fire stations must be located to give rapid access to potential conflagrations, and voting booths must be placed so that people can cast their ballots without expending unreasonable amounts of time, effort or money to reach the polling stations. Many of our states face the problem of locating branch campuses to serve a burgeoning and increasingly well educated population. In the cities we must create and locate playgrounds for the children. Many overpopulated countries must assign birth control clinics to reach the people with contraceptive and family planning information.[4]

Channels of distribution are also used in "person" marketing. A professional comedian seeking an audience before 1940 had available seven different channels: vaudeville houses, special events, nightclubs, radio, movies, carnivals, and theaters. In the 1950s television emerged as a strong channel and vaudeville disappeared. Politicians also must find cost-effective channels—mass media, rallies, coffee hours—for distributing their ideas to the voters.

Channels normally are thought to describe routes for the forward movement of products. Increasingly there is talk about the development of *backward channels:*

[3] *Availability* means that the goods and services could be obtained by consumers with a reasonable (not excessive) amount of effort. *Accessibility* means that the consumers feel comfortable in dealing with the channel outlets. For example, poor people might know that medical services are *available* from a particular hospital, but various social and psychological barriers might exist to make the hospital seem of low *accessibility.*

[4] Ronald Abler, John S. Adams, and Peter Gould, *Spatial Organization* (Englewood Cliffs, N.J.: Prentice-Hall, 1971), pp. 531–32.

The recycling of solid wastes is a major ecological goal. Although recycling is technologically feasible, reversing the flow of materials in the channel of distribution—marketing trash through a "backward" channel—presents a challenge. Existing backward channels are primitive, and financial incentives are inadequate. The consumer must be motivated to undergo a role change and become a producer—the initiating force in the reverse distribution process.[5]

The authors of this statement go on to identify several types of middlemen that can play a role in the backward channel, including (1) manufacturers' redemption centers; (2) "Clean-Up Days" community groups; (3) traditional middlemen such as soft-drink middlemen; (4) trash-collection specialists; (5) recycling centers; (6) modernized "rag and junk men"; (7) trash-recycling brokers; and (8) central-processing warehousing.

Why Are Middlemen Used?

Why is the producer generally willing to delegate some of the selling job to intermediaries? The delegation usually means the relinquishment of some control over how and to whom the products are sold. The producer appears to be placing the firm's destiny in the hands of intermediaries.

Since producers are free in principle to sell directly to final customers, there must be certain advantages or necessities for using middlemen. Some of the major factors are described below.

Many producers lack the financial resources to embark on a program of direct marketing. For example, General Motors's new automobiles are marketed by over 18,000 independent dealers; even as the world's largest manufacturing corporation, General Motors would be hard pressed to raise the cash to buy out its dealers.

Direct marketing would require many producers to become middlemen for the complementary products of other producers in order to achieve mass-distributional efficiency. For example, the Wm. Wrigley Jr. Company would not find it practical to establish small retail gum shops throughout the country or to sell gum door to door or by mail order. It would have to tie gum in with the sale of many other small products and would end up in the drugstore and foodstore business. It is much easier for Wrigley to work through the existing and extensive network of privately owned distribution institutions.

Those producers who have the required capital to develop their own channels often can earn a greater return by increasing their investment in other parts of their business. If a company is earning a 20 percent rate of return on its manufacturing operation and foresees only a 5 percent rate of return on investing in direct marketing, it would not make sense to put money toward vertically integrating its channels.

The use of middlemen boils down largely to their superior efficiency in making goods widely available and accessible to target markets. Marketing intermediaries, through their experience, their specialization, their contacts, and their scale, offer the firm more than it can usually achieve on its own.

Figure 16–3 shows just one source of the economies effected by the use of middlemen. Part A shows three producers using direct marketing to reach each of three customers. This system requires nine different contacts. Part B shows

[5] William G. Zikmund and William J. Stanton, "Recycling Solid Wastes: A Channels-of-Distribution Problem," *Journal of Marketing*, July 1971, p. 34.

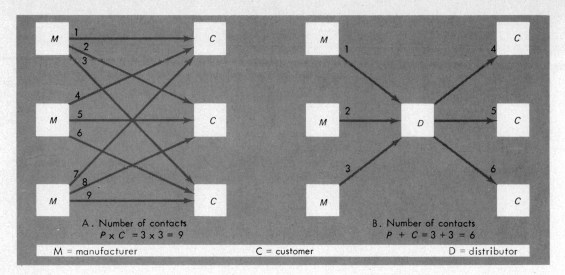

FIGURE 16–3
How a Distributor Effects an Economy of Effort

the three producers working through one distributor, who in turn contacts the three customers. This system requires only six contacts. Thus the use of middlemen reduces the amount of work that must be done.

From the point of view of the economic system, the basic role of marketing channels is to transform the heterogeneous supplies found in nature into meaningful goods assortments desired by humans:

> The materials which are useful to man occur in nature in heterogeneous mixtures which might be called conglomerations since these mixtures have only random relationship to human needs and activities. The collection of goods in the possession of a household or an individual also constitutes a heterogeneous supply, but it might be called an assortment since it is related to anticipated patterns of future behavior. The whole economic process may be described as a series of transformations from meaningless to meaningful heterogeneity.[6]

Alderson has summarized this in the statement that "the goal of marketing is the matching of segments of supply and demand."[7]

Marketing-Channel Functions   A marketing channel is essentially a method of organizing the work that has to be done to move goods from producers to consumers. The purpose of the work is to overcome various gaps that separate the goods and services from those who

[6] Wroe Alderson, "The Analytical Framework for Marketing," *Proceedings—Conference of Marketing Teachers from Far Western States* (Berkeley: University of California Press, 1958).

[7] Wroe Alderson, *Marketing Behavior and Executive Action: A Functionalist Approach to Marketing Theory* (Homewood, Ill.: Richard D. Irwin, 1957), p. 199.

would use them. The work of middlemen is designed to create *form, time, place,* and *possession utilities.* Several *functions* or tasks are involved in this work. The major marketing-channel functions are:[8]

1. *Research.* The gathering of information necessary for planning and facilitating exchange.
2. *Promotion.* The development and dissemination of persuasive communications about the offer.
3. *Contact.* The searching out and communicating with prospective buyers.
4. *Matching.* The shaping and fitting of the offer to the buyer's requirements. Includes such activities as manufacturing, grading, assembling, and packaging.[9]
5. *Negotiation.* The attempt to reach final agreement on price and other terms of the offer so that transfer of ownership or possession could be effected.
6. *Physical distribution.* The transporting and storing of the goods.
7. *Financing.* The acquisition and dispersal of funds to cover the costs of the channel work.
8. *Risk taking.* The assumption of risks in connection with carrying out the channel work.

The first five functions deal primarily with consummating transactions, while the last three act as facilitating functions.

It is not a question of whether these functions must be performed in order to bridge the gaps between producer and customer—they must be—but rather who is to perform them. All of the functions have three things in common: they use up scarce resources, often they can be performed better through specialization, and they are shiftable. To the extent that the manufacturer performs them, its costs go up and its prices have to be higher. When some of these tasks are delegated to middlemen, the producer's costs and prices are lower, but the middlemen must add a charge to cover the use of scarce resources. The issue of who should perform various channel tasks is largely one of relative efficiency and effectiveness. To the extent that specialist intermediaries achieve economies through their scale of operation and their knowhow, the producer can gain by transferring some of the channel functions to their charge.

A major point to keep in mind is that marketing functions are more basic than the institutions that at any given time appear to perform them. Changes in the number of channel levels and/or channel institutions largely reflect the discovery of more efficient ways to combine or separate the economic work that must be carried out if useful assortments of goods are to be provided to target customers.

---

[8] For other lists, see Edmund D. McGarry, "Some Functions of Marketing Reconsidered," in *Theory in Marketing,* eds. Reavis Cox and Wroe Alderson (Homewood, Ill.: Richard D. Irwin, 1950), pp. 269–73; and Bucklin, *Theory of Distribution Channel Structure,* pp. 10–15.

[9] Alderson adds the concept of *sorting* as part of the matching process. Sorting consists of four basic processes. *Sorting out* is separating a heterogeneous collection into homogeneous groupings. *Accumulation* is the building up of larger homogeneous collections out of smaller ones. *Allocation* is breaking down large homogeneous collections into smaller ones to meet the requirements of various markets. *Assorting* is the building up of a heterogeneous collection from various sources to meet the requirements of some market. See Alderson, *Marketing Behavior and Executive Action,* chap. 7.

TABLE 16–1
Definitions of Various Marketing Intermediaries

Agent. A business unit which negotiates purchases or sales or both but does not take title to the goods in which it deals. The agent usually performs fewer marketing functions than does the merchant. He commonly receives his remuneration in the form of a commission or fee. Examples are: broker, commission merchant, manufacturers agent, selling agent, and resident buyer.

Broker. An agent who does not have direct physical control of the goods in which he deals but represents either buyer or seller in negotiating purchases or sales for his principal. The broker's powers as to prices and terms of sale are usually limited by his principal.

Commission house (sometimes called *Commission merchant*). An agent who usually exercises physical control over and negotiates the sale of the goods he handles. The commission house usually enjoys broader powers as to prices, methods, and terms of sale than does the broker, although it must obey instructions issued by the principal. It generally arranges delivery, extends necessary credit, collects, deducts its fees, and remits the balance to the principal.

Dealer. A firm that buys and resells merchandise at either retail or wholesale.

Distributor. In its general usage this term is synonymous with "wholesaler."

Facilitating agencies in marketing. Those agencies which perform or assist in the performance of one or a number of the marketing functions, but which neither take title to goods nor negotiate purchases or sales. Common types are banks, railroads, storage warehouses, commodity exchanges, stock yards, insurance companies, graders and inspectors, advertising agencies, firms engaged in marketing research, cattle loan companies, furniture marts, and packers and shippers.

Jobber. This term is widely used as a synonym of "wholesaler" or "distributor." The term is sometimes used in certain trades and localities to designate special types of wholesalers.

Manufacturer's agent. An agent who generally operates on an extended contractual basis; often sells within an exclusive territory; handles noncompeting but related lines of goods; and possesses limited authority with regard to prices and terms of sale. He may be authorized to sell a definite portion of his principal's output.

Merchant. A business unit that buys, takes title to, and resells merchandise. The distinctive feature of this middleman lies in the fact that he takes title to the goods he handles. Wholesalers and retailers are the chief types of merchants.

Middleman. A business concern that specializes in performing operations or rendering services directly involved in the purchase and/or sale of goods in the process of their flow from producer to consumer. Middlemen are of two types, *merchants* and *agents.*

Retailer. A merchant, or occasionally an agent, whose main business is selling directly to the ultimate consumer.

Selling agent. An agent who operates on an extended contractual basis, sells all of a specified line of merchandise or the entire output of his principal, and usually has full authority with regard to prices, terms, and other conditions of sale. This functionary is often called a "sales agent."

Wholesaler. A business unit which buys and resells merchandise to retailers and other merchants and/or to industrial, institutional, and commercial users, but which does not sell in significant amounts to ultimate consumers. Those who render all the services normally expected in the wholesale trade are known as *service wholesalers;* those who render only a few of the wholesale services are known as *limited-function wholesalers.* The latter group is composed mainly of *cash-and-carry wholesalers,* who do not render the credit or delivery service; *drop-shipment wholesalers,* who sell for delivery by the producer direct to the buyer; *truck wholesalers,* who combine selling, delivery, and collection in one operation; and *mail-order wholesalers,* who perform the selling service entirely by mail.

SOURCE: *Marketing Definitions: A Glossary of Marketing Terms,* compiled by the Committee on Definitions of the American Marketing Association, Ralph S. Alexander, Chairman (Chicago: American Marketing Association, 1960).

We have been talking about various channel institutions, such as wholesalers, jobbers, and retailers, without defining them. The fact is that a large number of different channel institutions exist, each performing one or more functions in the channel. Table 16–1 provides a set of definitions of the more common channel institutions.

CHANNEL DYNAMICS

Channel institutions, like products, are subject to life cycles. A particular channel institution may emerge suddenly, enjoy rapid growth, reach a point of relative maturity, and eventually move into a period of slow decline. A major force behind the channel life cycle is changing economics, which makes new combinations of marketing functions suddenly more efficient than previous ones.

In retailing, totally new institutions have appeared in an industry that a hundred years ago consisted only of small general and specialty stores. *Department stores* first came on the American scene in the 1860s, about a decade after they started in Europe. Shortly thereafter *mail-order houses,* such as Montgomery Ward (1872) and Sears Roebuck (1886), were established. During the 1910s and 1920s, *chain-store organizations* emerged and entered a period of rapid growth. The principal retailing innovation in the 1930s was the *supermarket.* The late 1940s were marked by the appearance of *planned suburban shopping centers.* The major retailing development in the early 1950s was the *discount house.* The 1950s also produced a rapid expansion of *automatic merchandising,* that is, vending machines. The 1960s witnessed the rapid growth of *fast-food service outlets, superstores* and *hypermarkets,* and *convenience stores.* The 1970s marked the rapid development of *boutiques, discount grocery stores, home improvement centers, furniture warehouse showrooms,* and *catalog showrooms.* None of these retailing forms have passed out of existence, but they show changing capacities over time to deliver what the consumer wants.

The newer retailing forms appear to be reaching maturity much faster than earlier retailing forms, that is, institutional life cycles seem to be growing shorter. The time required to reach maturity was eighty years for department stores (1860–1940), forty-five years for variety stores (1910–1955), and thirty-five years for supermarkets (1930–1965), twenty years for discount department stores (1950–1970), and fifteen years for home improvement centers (1965–1980).[10]

Retailing innovations are emerging all the time in a dynamic economy. A soft-drink manufacturer opened a chain of soft-drink stores for the take-home market that sell private-brand colas, ginger ale, and so on, at substantial savings. American Bakeries started Hippopotamus Food Stores, featuring large institutional-sized packages at a 10 to 30 percent savings. One of the large New York banks recently instituted "house-call loans," for which they will qualify an applicant over the phone and then deliver the money in person. Adelphi University in New York developed a "commuter train classroom" in which executives who commute daily between Long Island and Manhattan can earn M.B.A.'s by sitting in on fifty-minute classes held in specially reserved cars on the commuter train. Marketers are continually seeking new ways to distribute their products and services.

[10] William R. Davidson, Albert D. Bates, and Stephen J. Bass, "The Retail Life Cycle," *Harvard Business Review,* November–December 1976, p. 94.

What explains the emergence of new retailing forms and decline of old retailing forms?[11] One major hypothesis is called the *wheel of retailing*.[12] According to this hypothesis, many new types of retailing institutions begin as low-status, low margin, low price operations. They become effective competitors of more conventional outlets, which have grown "fat" over the years. Their success gradually leads them to upgrade their facilities and proffer additional services. This increases their costs and forces price increases until they finally resemble the conventional outlets that they displaced. They, in turn, become vulnerable to still newer types of low-cost, low-margin operations. This hypothesis appears to explain the original success and later troubles of department stores, supermarkets, and, more recently, discount houses. On the other hand, it does not explain the growth of suburban shopping centers and automatic retailing, both of which started out as high-margin and high-cost operations.

When new institutions first appear, the typical pattern is one of institutional *conflict* followed later by *accommodation*. The established institutions band together and use all their power to thwart the new institution. They may threaten to break off business relations with those who supply the new institution. This happened when national-brand appliance manufacturers started dealing with discount houses, when milk producers allowed their brands to appear in vending machines, and when drug manufacturers started to sell their products through food outlets. The established retailers will also lobby for restrictive legislation against the new retailing outlets. They try to pass laws placing special taxes on these organizations, or restricting their hours of operation, or preventing them from selling certain goods.

But the newer firms, where they bring real advantages, generally survive this onslaught, and in the next phase the more progressive established firms begin to accommodate to the new ones. They reduce their margins, cut down some of their frills, form chains, expand their parking space, and in general reduce the competitive advantage of the newer firms. In time, the differences diminish.

Evolution of Wholesaling Institutions

Wholesalers are essentially middlemen who market products to retailers, other wholesalers, or industrial users. There are many types of wholesalers as indicated in the definition in Table 16–1. *Merchant wholesalers* buy title to the merchandise and resell it to others. *Agent wholesalers* buy and sell goods for others without taking title and receive fees or commissions. *Miscellaneous-type wholesalers* are usually found in specialized sectors of the economy such as the agricultural market (farm product assemblers) and the petroleum market (petroleum bulk plants and terminals).

Not all wholesalers are independent businesses, and in fact an increasing volume of products is going through producer-owned and retail-owned wholesalers. *Producer-owned wholesalers* include sales offices (which sell and promote

---

[11] Four theories of retail institutional change are described in Ronald E. Gist, *Retailing: Concepts and Decisions* (New York: John Wiley and Sons, 1968), chap. 4.

[12] Malcolm P. McNair, "Significant Trends and Developments in the Postwar Period," in *Competitive Distribution in a Free, High-Level Economy and Its Implications for the University,* ed. A. B. Smith (Pittsburgh: University of Pittsburgh Press, 1958), pp. 1–25. Also see the critical discussion by Stanley C. Hollander, "The Wheel of Retailing," *Journal of Marketing,* July 1960, pp. 37–42.

but do not stock product) and sales branches (which carry a limited inventory in addition to selling and promoting and customer services). *Retailer-owned wholesalers* have been set up by many large retailers to bypass independent wholesalers and include purchasing offices, warehouses, and wholesale cooperatives.

Changes in wholesaling have been less dramatic than changes in retailing, but no less important. At one time wholesalers dominated the marketing channels. Small manufacturers and small retailers could not operate without their services. But as manufacturers and retailers grew in size, the larger ones were able to find ways to avoid or reduce the charges of wholesaling middlemen. During the 1920s, many thought that the majority of wholesalers were doomed by the growth of chain operations. Wholesalers declined in relative importance from 1929 on, and did not regain their former relative position until as late as 1954. Absolute wholesale sales volume has continued to grow, but in relative terms wholesalers have just been holding their own. During the period 1950–1972, they suffered a major decline in their profitability, productivity, and liquidity.

The wholesalers who fell into deep trouble were those who failed to adapt to the dramatic changes taking place in retailing, materials-handling technology, and manufacturers' new marketing policies. Many wholesalers had enjoyed a protected position and had grown "fat and lazy." Their main activities were to break bulk-and-fill customer orders, rather than to carry on aggressive selling programs. They tended to render similar services and charges to all customers, even though some customers wanted more services and others wanted less. It is understandable why both manufacturers and retailers continually sought ways to circumvent the wholesaler.

The progressive wholesalers were those who were willing to change their ways to meet the challenges of chain organizations, discount houses, and rising labor costs. This meant (1) seeking to adapt their services to a clearer target group of customers and (2) seeking cost-reducing methods of transacting business. Wholesalers became much more selective in choosing their customers, preferring to drop those who appeared to be unprofitable according to an analysis of sales and service costs. They placed more emphasis on increasing order size and promoting the higher profit merchandise. They offered assistance to customers in locating, leasing, designing, opening, and modernizing stores and in doing a better job of selling, advertising, promoting, and displaying their wares. Progressive wholesalers selected and trained their salesmen better. Many wholesalers met the threat of chain organizations by organizing smaller retailers into voluntary chains. Many wholesalers went into private branding, supplying their customers with less expensive products. Others went into cash-and-carry or cost-plus wholesaling. Still others met the challenge by becoming specialty wholesalers and taking on functions that neither manufacturers nor customers were performing.

To meet the challenge of rising costs, alert wholesalers turned to advanced systems of material handling, billing, and shipping. Material-handling costs were brought down by time-and-motion studies of work procedures and ultimately by automating the warehouse so that orders could be processed through computers and items picked up by mechanical devices and conveyed on a belt to the shipping platform, where they were assembled. Billing, inventory control, and forecasting were improved through computerization and office automation. Finally, alert wholesalers were able to bring down their shipping costs by finding the right combinations of rail, truck, barge, and air freight.

Although the overwhelming majority of goods and services are still sold through marketing intermediaries, a growing number of producers have turned to direct marketing to either bypass or supplement their use of middlemen. Direct marketing (sometimes called in-home buying or nonstore retailing) in 1977 accounted for $75 billion or 12 percent of all consumer purchases. It takes four major forms:

1. *Mail-order selling.* Direct-mail expenditures reached $5 billion in 1975, or 15 percent of all advertising expenditures. Over sixty-five hundred companies sent out more than 2.26 billion catalogs targeted to appropriate households. Large general merchandise mail-order houses like Sears sent out general and specialized catalogs, and smaller operators sent out specialized ones. Catalog buying, while it normally does not save the buyer money, especially in the light of rising freight and postal charges, does offer a convenient way to shop and makes available certain goods that are absent or difficult to obtain in the buyer's home area. Direct mail also takes the form of mailed letters and foldouts promoting a particular item (books, insurance, magazine subscriptions) or making an appeal for funds for worthy causes (in 1975, nonprofit organizations raised $21.4 billion through the mail, or 80 percent of their total contributions).

2. *Mass-media selling.* Many direct marketers place direct-response ads in newspapers, magazines, radio, and television to sell phonograph records and tapes, small appliances, and myriad other items.

3. *Telephone selling.* The telephone is increasingly being used as a selling tool for selling everything from home repair services to newspaper subscriptions to zoo memberships. Some telephone marketers have developed computerized phoning systems where households are dialed automatically and computerized messages presented. Telephone selling has incurred the opposition of several groups who consider it an invasion of privacy and are proposing laws to ban or limit it.

4. *On-premise selling.* This old form of selling, which started centuries ago with itinerant peddlers, has burgeoned into a $6 billion industry, with over six hundred companies either selling *door to door* or arranging *home demonstration parties.* The industry still contains Fuller Brush and many encyclopedia- and bible-selling companies and their paid staffs of mainly male workers. But new personnel and selling concepts have emerged—for example, World Book enlists school teachers to sell encyclopedias to their neighbors; Avon trains attractive young women to sell cosmetics and act as beauty consultants to their neighbors; Tupperware has been a pioneer in home-demonstration cookware parties for small neighborhood groups.[13]

Why the boom in direct marketing? Direct marketing meets the needs of people who cannot easily find certain goods, are too busy to shop, or do not like to shop because of the crowds, parking difficulties, and poorly trained sales clerks. As the nation's educational level and affluence rise, people find their time growing scarcer, and also they feel more competent to select goods in private.

[13] See "How the 'New Sell' is Raking in Billions," *U.S. News and World Report,* May 8, 1978, pp. 74–75.

Add to this the improvements in communication technology and promotional techniques, and it becomes clear why direct marketing is soaring.[14]

Growth of Vertical Marketing Systems

While the retailing, wholesaling, and direct marketing sectors undergo their individual evolutions, a very significant development is occurring that cuts across all of these levels. This development is the emergence of *vertical marketing systems* (VMS).[15] To understand them, we should first define *conventional marketing channels*. Conventional channels are "highly fragmented networks in which loosely aligned manufacturers, wholesalers, and retailers have bargained with each other at arm's length, negotiated aggressively over terms of sale, and otherwise behaved autonomously."[16] By contrast, *vertical marketing systems* are "professionally managed and centrally programmed networks, pre-engineered to achieve operating economies and maximum market impact."[17] These systems offer effective competition to conventional marketing channels because they achieve impressive scale economies through their size, bargaining power, and elimination of duplicated services. In fact, they have emerged in the consumer-goods sector of American economy as the preferred mode of distribution, accounting for as much as 64 percent of the available market.

Corporate VMS Three types of vertical marketing systems can be distinguished. A *corporate vertical marketing system* has as its distinguishing characteristic the combining of successive stages of production and distribution under a single ownership. As examples:

> . . . Sherwin-Williams currently owns and operates over 2,000 retail outlets . . . Sears reportedly obtains 50 percent of its throughput from manufacturing facilities in which it has an equity interest. . . . Holiday Inns is evolving into a self-supply network that includes a carpet mill, a furniture manufacturing plant, and numerous captive redistribution facilities. In short, these and other organizations are massive, vertically integrated systems. To describe them as "retailers," "manufacturers," or "motel operators" oversimplifies their operating complexities and ignores the realities of the marketplace.[18]

Administered VMS An *administered vertical marketing system*, by contrast, achieves coordination of successive stages of production and distribution not through common ownership but through the size and power of one of the parties within the system. Thus, manufacturers of a dominant brand are able to secure strong trade cooperation and support from resellers. Such companies as General Electric, Procter & Gamble, Kraftco, and Campbell Soup are able to command

[14] Direct marketers must be skilled at prospect identification, communication planning, and promotion testing. For an excellent text, see Bob Stone, *Successful Direct Marketing Methods* (Chicago: Crain Books, 1975).

[15] The following discussion is indebted to Bert C. McCammon, Jr., "Perspectives for Distribution Programming," in *Vertical Marketing Systems*, ed. Louis P. Bucklin (Glenview, Ill.: Scott, Foresman & Company, 1970), pp. 32–51.

[16] Ibid., p. 43.

[17] Ibid.

[18] Ibid., p. 45.

unusual cooperation from their resellers and retailers in connection with displays, shelf space, promotions, and price policies.

Contractual VMS A *contractual vertical marketing system* consists of independent firms at different levels of production and distribution integrating their programs on a contractual basis to obtain more economies and/or sales impact than they could achieve alone. Contractual VMSs have expanded the most in recent years and constitute one of the most significant developments in the economy. There are three major types of contractual VMSs:

1. *Wholesaler-sponsored voluntary chains.* These originated in the effort of wholesalers to save the independent retailers they served against the competition of large chain organizations. The wholesaler develops a program in which independent retailers join together to standardize their practices and/or to achieve buying economies that enable them to stand as a group against the inroads of the chains.

2. *Retailer cooperatives.* These arose through the efforts of groups of retailers to defend themselves against the corporate chains. The retailers organize a new business entity to carry on wholesaling and possibly production. Members are expected to concentrate their purchases through the retailer co-op and plan their advertising jointly. Profits are passed back to members in the form of patronage refunds. Nonmember retailers may also be allowed to buy through the co-op but do not receive patronage refunds.

3. *Franchise organizations.* Here several successive stages in the production-distribution process are linked under an agreement with one entity of the system, which is considered the franchiser. Franchising has been the fastest growing and most interesting retailing development in recent years. Although the basic idea is an old one, some forms of franchising are quite recent. In fact, three forms of franchises can be distinguished.

The first is the *manufacturer-sponsored retailer franchise system*, exemplified in the automobile industry. A car manufacturer such as Ford licenses dealers to sell its cars, the dealers being independent business who agree to meet various conditions of sales and service.

The second is the *manufacturer-sponsored wholesaler franchise system*, which is found in the soft-drink industry. The soft-drink manufacturer licenses bottlers (wholesalers) in various markets who buy its concentrate and then carbonate, bottle, and sell it to retailers in local markets.

The third is the *service-firm-sponsored retailer franchise system*. Here a service firm organizes a whole system for bringing its service efficiently to consumers. Examples are found in the auto rental business (Hertz and Avis), fast-food service business (McDonald's, Burger King), and motel business (Howard Johnson, Ramada Inn). The motel franchiser, for example, uses its mass-purchasing power to obtain favorable terms from suppliers; in some cases it buys an equity interest or owns them entirely. The motels are standardized in their appearances, procedures, and services, allowing travelers to know what to expect in advance. The franchiser provides the franchisees with a large number of services, such as *national advertising and sales promotion, site selection, motel design, employee and management training, centralized reservation system, market surveys and management consulting*. In return, the franchisers buy certain equipment and supplies through the franchiser and pay franchising fees and a percentage of their revenue. No wonder individually owned motels and hotels are at a disadvantage in competing with these franchised systems. Franchising systems are rapidly replacing the "opportunistic and ad hoc linkages" that have historically prevailed in many lines of trade.[19]

Many independents, if they have not joined VMSs, have become specialty-store operators, serving special segments of the market that are not available or attractive to the mass merchandisers. Thus there is a polarization in retailing, with large vertical marketing organizations on the one hand and specialty independent stores on the other. This development creates a problem for independent manufacturers. They are strongly aligned with the traditional outlets, which they cannot easily give up. At the same time, they must eventually realign themselves with the high-growth vertical marketing systems. The manufacturers will probably have to accept less attractive terms from these large buying organizations. Vertical marketing systems can always decide to bypass large manufacturers and set up their own manufacturing. *The new competition in retailing is no longer between independent business units but rather between whole systems of centrally programmed networks (corporate, administrative, and contractual) competing against each other to achieve the best economies and customer· response.*

Growth of Horizontal Marketing Systems

Another significant development is the readiness of two or more companies to form alliances to jointly exploit an emerging marketing opportunity. Neither firm is able to amass the capital, know-how, production or marketing facilities to venture alone; or it prefers not to because of the high risk; or it envisions a substantial synergy in the proposed relationship. The companies may set up temporary or permanent arrangements to work with each other, or to create a third entity owned by the two parents. Such developments in horizontal marketing systems have been described by Adler as *symbiotic marketing*.[20] Here are two examples:

> In spite of Pillsbury Company's acceptance in grocery outlets, it lacked the resources to market its new line of refrigerated doughs for biscuits, cookies, and rolls because merchandising these products required special refrigerated display cases. But Kraft Foods Company was expert at selling its cheeses in this manner. Accordingly, the two firms set up an arrangement whereby Pillsbury makes and advertises its dough line while Kraft sells and distributes it.
>
> In the advertising field, *Million Market Newspapers, Inc.,* is the sales company held in common by five newspapers—*St. Louis Post-Dispatch, Washington Star, Boston Globe, Philadelphia Bulletin,* and *Milwaukee Journal-Sentinel.* By selling these five markets in one convenient package, a beneficial synergistic effect is created.

Growth of Multichannel Marketing Systems

Another important channel development is the movement of companies toward developing multichannel systems that reach the same or different markets, where some of these channel systems are in competition with each other. Here

[19] For background on franchising systems, see Dov Izraeli, *Franchising and the Total Distribution System* (London: Longman Group, 1972); and Charles L. Vaughn, *Franchising: Its Nature, Scope, Advantages, and Development* (Lexington, Mass.: Lexington Books, 1974).

[20] Lee Adler, "Symbiotic Marketing," *Harvard Business Review,* November-December 1966, pp. 59–71.

are examples of companies that have designed two or more channel systems for reaching the same customer level.

> The John Smythe Company, a Chicago based furniture retailer, sells a full line of furniture through its company-owned conventional furniture stores as well as through its Homemakers Division, which runs furniture warehouse show-rooms. Furniture shoppers can spot many similar items in both types of outlets, usually finding lower prices at the latter.
>
> A large liquor distiller in Kentucky bottles bourbon under 4,000 different labels for various distributors, chains, and supermarkets. Shoppers in a particular town buying different brands and paying different prices might unknowingly be getting the bourbon that came out of the same barrels of this Kentucky distiller.
>
> J.C. Penney operates department stores, mass-merchandising stores (called The Treasury), and specialty stores.

Tillman has labelled large retailing stores with diversified retailing channels "merchandising conglomerates" or "conglomerchants" and defined them as "a multiline merchandising empire under central ownership, usually combining several styles of retailing with behind-the-scenes integration of some distribution and management functions." [21]

A growing number of companies can also be found that operate multichannels that serve two different customer levels. This is called *dual distribution* and can be a source of many conflicts for the sponsoring company.[22] Some examples are:

> Shell Oil sells its gasoline through company dealerships and also to independent gasoline-marketing companies. Conflicts arise during gasoline shortages when the independent gasoline companies accuse Shell of favoring its own dealers with sure supplies and also of engaging in price squeezing.
>
> General Electric sells large home appliances through independent dealers (department stores, discount houses, catalog retailers) and also directly to large tract builders. The independent dealers would like General Electric to get out of the business of selling to tract developers because it competes with the retailers. General Electric defends its position by pointing out that builders and retailers are different classes of customers.

Alternative Roles of Individual Firms in a Channel

Our discussion of direct, vertical, horizontal, and multichannel marketing systems underscores the dynamic and changing nature of channels. Each firm in an industry has to define its relation to the dominant channel type and its pricing policies, advertising, and sales promotion practices. McCammon has distinguished five types of relationship of an individual firm to the dominant channel.[23]

[21] Rollie Tillman, "Rise of the Conglomerchant," *Harvard Business Review*, November–December 1971, pp. 44–51.

[22] See Robert E. Weigand, "Fit Products and Channels to Your Markets," *Harvard Business Review*, January–February 1977, pp. 95–105.

[23] Bert C. McCammon, Jr., "Alternative Explanations of Institutional Change and Channel Evolution," in *Toward Scientific Marketing*, ed. Stephen A. Greyser (Chicago: American Marketing Association, 1963), pp. 477–90.

The *insiders* are the members of the dominant channel who enjoy continuous access to preferred sources of supply and high respect in the industry. They have a vested interest in perpetuating the existing channel arrangements and are the main enforcers of the industry code. The *strivers* are those firms who are seeking to become insiders but have not yet arrived. They have discontinuous access to preferred sources of supply, which can disadvantage them in periods of short supply. They adhere to the industry code because of their desire to become insiders. The *complementors* neither are nor seek to be part of the dominant channel. They perform functions not normally performed by others in the channel, or serve smaller segments of the market, or handle smaller quantities of merchandise. They usually benefit from the present system and tend to respect the industry code. The *transients,* like the complementors, are outside of the dominant channel and do not seek membership. They go in and out of the market or move around as opportunities arise, but are really members of another channel. They have short-run expectations and little incentive to adhere to the industry code. Finally, the *outside innovators* are the real challengers and disrupters of the dominant channels. They come with an entirely new system for carrying out the marketing work of the channel; if successful, they cause major structural realignments. They are companies like McDonald's, Avon, and Holiday Inn, who doggedly develop a new system to challenge the old.

Another important role is that of *channel captain.* The channel captain is the dominant member of a particular channel, the one who organized it and leads it. For example, General Motors is the channel captain of a system consisting of a huge number of suppliers, dealers, and facilitators. The channel captain is not always a manufacturer, as the examples of McDonald's and Sears show. Some channels do not have an acknowledged captain in that the various firms do not even recognize that they are acting as part of a system.

Channel Cooperation, Conflict, and Competition

It should be clear that within and between marketing channels there are different degrees of cooperation, conflict, and competition.

Channel cooperation is usually the dominant theme among members of the same channel. The channel represents a coalition of dissimilar firms that have banded together for mutual advantage. Manufacturers, wholesalers, and retailers complement each other's needs and their partnership normally produces greater profits for each participant than could have been secured by trying to carry out individually all of the channel's work. The need for channel cooperation is a natural extension of the *marketing concept* in that firms are trying to effectively sense, serve, and satisfy the needs of the target market.

Channel conflict, nevertheless, also tends to occur within each channel system. *Horizontal channel conflict* refers to conflict between firms at the same level of the channel. Some Ford car dealers in Chicago may complain about other Ford dealers in the city being too aggressive in their pricing and advertising and stealing sales from them. Some Pizza Inn franchisees may complain about other Pizza Inn franchisees cheating on the ingredients, maintaining poor service, and hurting the overall Pizza Inn image. In cases of horizontal channel conflict, the responsibility lies with the *channel captain* to set clear and enforceable policies, to encourage information about intralevel channel conflict to flow upward to management, and to take quick and definitive action to reduce or control this type of conflict, which, if left unchecked, could hurt the channel's image and cohesiveness.

Vertical channel conflict is even more common and refers to conflicts of interest between different levels of the same channel. Consider the following examples:

> Auto manufacturers threaten to drop dealers who refuse to comply with the manufacturers' policies on service, pricing, or advertising.
>
> Toy wholesalers boycott those toy manufacturers who sell direct to large retail discounters.
>
> Drug retailers threaten to drop drug manufacturers who put their lines in supermarket outlets.

Some amount of vertical channel conflict is healthy, and the problem is not one of eliminating it but of managing it better. The solution lies in two possible directions. The first is the effort on the part of the channel captain to develop *superordinate goals* for the system, from which everyone would gain. Superordinate goals would include trying to minimize the total cost of moving the product through the system, improving information flows within the system, and cooperating to increase consumer acceptance of the product. The second is to develop *administrative mechanisms* that increase participation and trust and help to resolve conflicts, such as dealer and distributor councils and various conciliation, mediation, and arbitration mechanisms.[24]

Channel competition is another phenomenon of channel relations and describes the normal competition between firms and systems trying to serve the same target markets. *Horizontal channel competition* occurs between firms at the same channel level competing for sales in the same target market. Thus various appliance retailers, such as department stores, discount stores, and catalog houses, all compete for the consumer's appliance dollar. This competition is healthy and should result in consumers' enjoying a wider range of choice in the way of products, prices, and services. *Channel system competition* describes the competition between different whole systems serving a given target market. For example, are food consumers better served by conventional marketing channels, corporate chains, wholesale-sponsored voluntary chains, retailer cooperatives, or food-franchise systems? While each system will have some loyal followers, the share of the different systems in the total food business will shift over time in favor of those systems that are best able to meet consumer needs at the time.

CHANNEL-DESIGN DECISIONS

We shall now look at channel decision problems from the point of view of the producer. In the last section of this chapter, we will examine the channel-management decisions facing resellers.

In developing channels of distribution, producers have to struggle with what is ideal and what is available. In the typical case, a new firm starts as a local or regional operation selling to a limited market. Since it has limited capital, it usually utilizes existing middlemen. The number of middlemen in any local market is apt to be limited: a few manufacturers' sales agents, a small number of

---

[24] For an excellent summary of interorganizational conflict and power in marketing channels, see Louis W. Stern and Adel I. El-Ansary, *Marketing Channels* (Englewood Cliffs, N.J.: Prentice-Hall, 1977), chap. 7.

wholesalers, an established set of retailers, a few trucking companies, and a few warehouses. The best channels may be a foregone conclusion. The problem may be to convince one or a few of the available middlemen to handle the line.

If the new firm is successful, it may branch out to new markets. Again, the producer will tend to work through the existing intermediaries, although this may mean using different types of marketing channels in different areas. In the smaller markets, the firm may sell directly to the retailers; in the larger markets, it may work only through distributors. In rural areas, it may work with general-goods merchants; in urban areas, with limited-line merchants. In one part of the country it may grant exclusive franchises because the merchants are accustomed to work this way; in another, it may sell through any and all outlets willing to handle the merchandise. In this way, the producer's channel system evolves as an expedient adaptation to local opportunities and conditions.

Determining Channel Objectives and Constraints

The starting point for the effective planning of channels is a determination of which markets are to be reached by the company. In practice, the choice of markets and choice of channels may be interdependent. The company may discover that markets it would like to serve cannot be served profitably with the available channels.

> A producer of gypsum wallboard defined its target market as all contractors and dry-wall applicators. But this firm could not get lumber yards to handle its product, since existing lumber yards were tied to existing competitors. This led the firm to change its target market to large tract builders who wanted to deal directly with the producer rather than through lumber yard intermediaries. Thus the choice of market target was redetermined after the consideration of channels.

Each producer develops its channel objectives in the context of constraints stemming from the customers, products, intermediaries, competitors, company policies, and the environment.

Customer characteristics In designing their channels, producers are greatly influenced by customer characteristics. When the *number* of customers is large, producers tend to use long channels with many middlemen on each level. The importance of the number of buyers is modified somewhat by their degree of *geographical dispersion*. It is less expensive for a producer to sell directly to five hundred customers who are concentrated in a few geographical centers than to sell them if they are scattered over five hundred locations. Even number and geographical dispersion are further qualified by the *purchasing pattern* of these buyers. Where the ultimate customers purchase small quantities on a frequent basis, lengthier marketing channels are desirable. The high cost of filling small and frequent orders leads manufacturers of such products as hardware, tobacco, and drug sundries to rely chiefly on wholesalers. At the same time, these same manufacturers may also bypass their wholesalers and sell direct to certain larger customers (retail chains and cooperative associations) who can place larger and less frequent orders. The buyers' *susceptibilities to different selling methods* also influence the producer's channel design. For example, a growing number of furniture retailers prefer to make selections at trade shows, and that has increased the popularity of this channel.

Product characteristics Product characteristics also influence channel design. *Perishable* products require more direct marketing because of the dangers associated with delays and repeated handling. Products that are *bulky* in relation to their value, such as building materials or soft drinks, usually require channel arrangements that minimize the shipping distance and the number of handlings in the movement from producer to ultimate customers. *Unstandardized* products, such as custom-built machinery and specialized business forms, are usually sold directly by company salesmen because of the difficulty of finding middlemen with the requisite technical knowledge. Products requiring installation and/or maintenance *services* usually are sold and maintained directly by the company or by dealers given exclusive franchises. Products of *high unit value* are often sold through a company sales force rather than through middlemen.

Middleman characteristics Channel design must take into account the strengths and weaknesses of different types of intermediaries in handling various tasks. For example, manufacturers' representatives are able to contact customers at a relatively low cost per customer because the total cost is shared by several clients. But the selling effort per customer during the contact is often less intense than if the company's salesmen were doing the selling. In general, intermediaries differ in their aptitude for performing such functions as promotion, negotiation, storage, and contact, as well as in their requirements for credit, return privileges, training, and frequency of shipment.

Competitive characteristics Channel design is influenced by the channels that competitors use. The producers in some industries want their products to compete in or near the same outlets carrying the competitors' products. Thus food producers want their brands to be displayed next to competitive brands, and this means using the same middlemen. The marketing channels used by competitors sometimes define what the producer wants to avoid rather than imitate. Avon decided not to compete with other cosmetics manufacturers for scarce and inconspicuous positions in retail stores and established instead a profitable door-to-door selling operation.

Company characteristics Company characteristics play an important role in channel selection. The company's overall *size* determines the extent of its markets, the size of its larger accounts, and its ability to secure the cooperation of intermediaries it elects to use. Its *financial resources* determine which marketing functions it can handle and which ones to delegate to intermediaries. A financially weak company tends to employ commission methods of distribution and tries to use intermediaries who are able and willing to absorb some of the storage, transit, and customer-financing costs. The company's *product* mix influences its channel pattern. The wider the company's product mix, the greater the ability of the company to deal with its customers directly. The greater the average depth of the company's product mix, the more it is likely to favor exclusive or selective dealers. The more consistent the company's product mix, the greater the homogeneity of its marketing channels. The company's *past channel experience* and *current marketing policies* influence channel design. A policy of speedy delivery to ultimate customers affects the functions the producer wants intermediaries to perform, the number of final-stage outlets and stocking points, and the type of transportation system used. A policy of heavy advertising leads the producer to seek intermediaries willing to handle displays and join in cooperative advertising programs.

Environmental characteristics Channel design is further influenced by environmental factors. When *economic conditions* are depressed, producers want to move their goods to market in the most economical way. This means using shorter channels and dispensing with inessential services that add to the final price of the goods. *Legal regulations and restrictions* also affect channel design. The law has sought to prevent channel arrangements that "may tend to substantially lessen competition or tend to create a monopoly." The most sensitive areas have to do with agreements by manufacturers not to sell to certain types of outlets, attempts by a manufacturer to offer its line to dealers on condition they do not carry competitive lines, attempts by a manufacturer to force its full line on dealers, arbitrary action by a manufacturer in the withdrawal of or refusal to renew dealer franchises, and attempts to set up territorial restrictions that substantially lessen competition.

Identifying the Major Channel Alternatives

After specifying channel objectives and constraints, the firm should proceed to identify its major channel alternatives. A channel alternative specifies four elements:

The basic *types of business intermediaries* that will be involved in selling and facilitating the movement of the goods to the market

The *number of intermediaries* that will be used at each stage of distribution

The particular *marketing tasks* of the participating intermediaries

The *terms and mutual responsibilities* of the producer and intermediaries

Types of intermediaries The firm should first identify the alternative intermediaries available to carry on its channel work. Consider the following industrial example:[25]

A manufacturer of test equipment for public utilities developed an audio device for detecting poor mechanical connections in any machinery with moving parts. The company executives felt that this product would have a market in all industries where electric, combustion, or steam engines were either used or manufactured. This meant such industries as aviation, automobile, railroad, food canning, construction, and oil. The existing sales force was small, and the problem was how to reach these diverse industries in an effective way. The following channel alternatives came out of management discussions:

1. **Company sales force.** Expand the company's direct sales force. Assign sales representatives to territories and give them responsibility for contacting purchasing agents in the relevant industries. Or specialize the company sales force by end-use industries.

2. **Manufacturers' agencies.** Hire manufacturers' agencies operating in different regions or end-use industries to sell the new test equipment.

3. **Industrial distributors.** Find distributors in the different regions and/or end-use industries who will buy and carry the new line. Give them exclusive distribution, adequate margins, product training, and promotional support.

---

[25] Adapted from David E. Faville, *Selected Cases in Marketing Management* (Englewood Cliffs, N.J.: Prentice-Hall, 1961), pp. 98–101. For further reading on industrial distributors, see Frederick E. Webster, Jr., "The Role of the Industrial Distributor," *Journal of Marketing*, July 1976, pp. 10–16.

Here is another example:

A consumer electronics company decided to use its excess capacity to produce FM car radios. In considering channels of distribution, it came up with the following alternatives:

1. **OEM market.** The company could seek a contract with one or more automobile manufacturers to buy its radios for factory installation on original equipment. OEM stands for *original equipment manufacture.*

2. **Auto dealer market.** The company could sell its radios to various auto dealers for replacement sales when they service cars.

3. **Retail automotive parts dealers.** The company could sell its radios to the public through retail automotive parts dealers. They could reach these dealers through a direct sales force or through distributors.

4. **Mail-order market.** The company could arrange to have its radios advertised in mail-order catalogs.

Not only do conventional channel arrangements suggest themselves, but sometimes more innovative possibilities. This happened when the Conn Organ Company decided to merchandise organs through department and discount stores, thus drawing more attention to them than they ever enjoyed in the small music stores where they had always been merchandised. A daring new channel was exploited when a group decided to merchandise books through the mails in the now famous Book-of-the-Month Club. Other sellers, perceiving the success of the Book-of-the-Month Club, developed Record-of-the-Month clubs, Candy-of-the-Month clubs, and dozens of others.

Number of intermediaries The number of intermediaries to use at each stage is influenced by the degree of *market exposure* sought by the company. Three degrees of market exposure can be distinguished.

INTENSIVE DISTRIBUTION Producers of convenience goods and common raw materials generally seek *intensive distribution*—that is, the stocking of their product in as many outlets as possible. The dominant factor in the marketing of these goods is their place utility. The producers of cigarettes, for example, try to enlist every possible retail outlet and device to create maximum brand exposure and convenience. This policy has culminated in the use of over 1 million outlets, which is about as intensive as distribution can get.

EXCLUSIVE DISTRIBUTION Some producers deliberately limit the number of intermediaries handling their products. The extreme form of this is *exclusive distribution,* a policy of granting dealers exclusive rights to distribute the company's products in their respective territories; it often goes along with *exclusive dealing,* where the manufacturer requires the dealers not to carry competing lines. The latter is found at the retail level with respect to the distribution of new automobiles, some major appliances, and some brands of women's apparel. But why would a manufacturer want to limit its products' market exposure? Obviously, it must be gaining other advantages in limiting its distribution. Through granting exclusive distribution privileges, the manufacturer hopes to gain a more aggressive selling effort and be able to exercise more direct controls over intermediaries' policies on prices, promotion, credit, and various services. Exclusive distribution also tends to enhance the prestige or image of the product and allow higher markups.

SELECTIVE DISTRIBUTION   Between the two extreme policies of intensive distribution and exclusive distribution stand a whole range of intermediate arrangements that have been called *selective distribution*. Selective distribution involves the use of more than one but less than all of the intermediaries who are willing to carry a particular product. It is used both by established companies with good reputations and by new companies seeking to get distributors by promising them selective distribution. The company does not have to dissipate its efforts over a lot of outlets, many of which would be marginal. It can develop a good working understanding with the selected intermediaries and expect a better-than-average selling effort. In general, selective distribution enables the producer to gain adequate market coverage with more control and less cost than intensive distribution.

Specific marketing tasks of channel members   Every producer faces several tasks in moving goods to the target markets. Looking at a channel as a sequence of tasks rather than a linkage of business entities makes it immediately apparent that every producer faces a large number of alternatives, even when there is little choice regarding the basic types of intermediaries and the best degree of market exposure.

Assume that the following four tasks have to be performed:

T = *transit*, the work of transporting the goods toward the target markets
A = *advertising*, the work of informing and influencing buyers through advertising media
S = *storage*, the work of carrying an inventory out of which orders are filled
K = *contact*, the work of searching for and communicating with buyers.

Assume that there are three channel members—manufacturer (M), wholesaler (W), and retailer (R)—and each can perform one or more of these tasks. There are many possible patterns of task allocation to the various members of the channel. For example:

$$M(TA\text{--}) \rightarrow W(T\text{-}S\text{-}) \rightarrow R(\text{-}A\text{-}K)$$

In this channel, the manufacturer transports the goods and advertises them. (A dash means the absence of the corresponding task.) The wholesaler takes responsibility for transporting and storing the goods and therefore resembles a warehouse agent rather than a full-service wholesaler. The retailer is responsible for further advertising and contact work.

A different marketing channel is implied by the pattern

$$M(T\text{-}S\text{-}) \rightarrow W(\text{-}\text{-}\text{-}\text{-}) \rightarrow R(\text{-}A\text{-}K)$$

Here the manufacturer is reduced to a private-brand producer who stocks and ships on order, the wholesaler is eliminated, and the retailer assumes the complete selling function. This is the marketing channel developed by mail-order houses for many of their products.

There are a great number of other possible patterns of task allocation in a marketing channel.[26] Many can be ruled out because they would be uneconomic, unstable, or illegal. Management's task is to identify the feasible alternatives and select the one that promises the highest degree of effectiveness in serving customers relative to competition.

Terms and responsibilities of channel members   In conceiving the tasks to be performed by different channel members, the producer must also determine the mix of conditions and responsibilities that must be established among the channel members to get the tasks performed effectively and enthusiastically. The "trade-relations" mix is capable of many variations and introduces a still further dimension of alternatives.

The main elements in the trade-relations mix are the *price policies, conditions of sale, territorial rights,* and *the specific services to be performed by each party.*

Price policy is one of the major elements in the trade-relations mix. The producer usually establishes a list price and then allows discounts from it to various types of intermediate customers and possibly for various quantities purchased. In developing the schedule of discounts, the producer must proceed carefully because intermediate customers have strong feelings about the discounts they and others are entitled to.

Conditions of sale refers to the payment terms and to producer guarantees. Most producers grant discounts to their distributors for early payment. For example, "2 percent in 10 days, net 30" means that distributors can deduct 2 percent from the invoice price if they pay within ten days, or otherwise they must pay the full price within thirty days. The producer may also extend certain guarantees to distributors regarding defective merchandise or price declines. The offer of a guarantee against price declines may be necessary to induce distributors to buy in large quantities rather than on a hand-to-mouth basis.

Distributors' territorial rights are another element in the trade-relations mix. Distributors want to know where the producer intends to enfranchise other distributors. They also would like to receive full credit for all sales taking place in their territory, whether or not the sales were stimulated through their personal efforts.

Mutual services and responsibilities are a fourth element of the trade-relations mix. These are likely to be comprehensive and well defined in franchised and exclusive-agency channels where the relation between producer and distributor is close. For example, the Howard Johnson Company provides the restaurant leaseholders with the building, promotional support, a record-keeping system, training, and general administrative and technical assistance. In turn, the leaseholders are supposed to meet company standards regarding physical facilities, cooperate with new promotional programs, furnish requested information, and buy specified food products.

Evaluating the Major Channel Alternatives

By this time, the producer will have identified several major channel alternatives for reaching the market. The problem is to decide which of the alternatives would best satisfy the long-run objectives of the firm. Each alternative must be rated against *economic, control,* and *adaptive* criteria.

---

[26] The number of possible patterns of task allocation in a marketing channel is given by $(2^n)^m$, where n represents the number of tasks and m represents the number of channel members. In the example, there are $(2^4)^3 = 4,096$ possible task allocations.

Economic criteria   Of the three, economic criteria are the most important, since the firm is not pursuing channel control or adaptability as such but is pursuing profits. True, channel control and adaptability have implications for long-run profit, but the more outstanding a channel alternative is from an economic point of view, the less important are its potentialities for conflict and rigidity.

DIRECT SALES FORCE VERSUS MANUFACTURERS' SALES AGENCY   Economic analyses can be illustrated with the familiar problem facing many manufacturers: Should they hire their own sales force or use a manufacturers' sales agency?

> A company wishes to reach a large number of retailers in a certain region of the country. One alternative is to hire and train ten company sales representatives who would operate out of a sales office in the region. They would be paid a base salary with the opportunity for further earnings through a commission plan. The other alternative is to use a manufacturers' sales agency in the region that has developed extensive contacts with retailers. The agency has thirty sales representatives, who would receive commissions on the goods sold.

Each alternative will produce a different level of sales and costs. The better system is not the one producing the greater sales or the lesser cost but rather the one producing the higher profit.

The analysis should begin with an estimate of *sales* under each system, because some costs will be dependent upon the level of sales. Will more sales be produced through a company sales force or a manufacturers' agency? Most marketing managers believe that a company sales force will sell more. Company sales representatives concentrate entirely on the company's products; they are better trained to sell the company's products; they are more aggressive because their future depends on the company; they are more successful because customers prefer to deal directly with the company.

But these are abstract arguments. It is conceivable that the manufacturers' agency could produce as many or more sales than a company sales force. In the first place, the producer is considering hiring ten new company sales representatives versus using thirty agency sales representatives. The sheer difference in the size of the sales force could lead to more sales through the agency. Second, the agency's sales force may be just as aggressive as a direct sales force. This depends on how much pay incentive the line offers them in relation to the other lines they represent. Third, it is not unconditionally true that customers prefer to deal with company sales representatives over agents. Where the product and terms are standard, the customers may be quite indifferent. They may prefer dealing with the agent who represents a larger number of manufacturers to dealing with a salesperson representing a single company. Fourth, one of the chief assets of the agency is the extensive contacts built up over the years. A company sales force would have to cultivate contacts from scratch. The agency can often obtain more sales for the manufacturer, at least in the first few years.

Thus, estimates of the sales potential with a company sales force versus a manufacturer's agency require a detailed analysis of the concrete plans for each. Sales estimates can be developed by soliciting the opinions of experienced managers and experts in the field.

The next step calls for estimating the costs associated with selling different

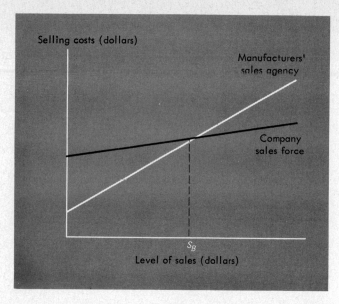

Selling costs (dollars)

Manufacturers'
sales agency

Company
sales force

S_B

Level of sales (dollars)

FIGURE 16–4
Breakeven Cost Chart for the Choice
Between a Company Sales Force
and a Manufacturers' Sales Agency

volumes under each system. They are shown in Figure 16–4. The fixed costs of engaging a manufacturers' agency are lower than those of conducting a sales office operation. On the other hand, costs rise faster with additional sales through a manufacturers' agency than through a company sales force. The reason is that sales agents get a larger fixed percentage of sales than company sales representatives, who are only on part commission.

Looking at the figure, we see one sales level (S_B) at which selling costs would be the same for the two channels. The sales agency would constitute a superior channel at any volume of sales below S_B, and the company sales branch would constitute a superior channel at any volume higher than S_B. This analysis accords with common observations of the circumstances under which the two channels have been used. Sales agents tend to be engaged by smaller firms, or by larger firms in their smaller territories, because in both cases the sales volume is too low to justify a fixed investment in a company sales force.

Control criteria The evaluation of the economics of sales agents versus a company sales force provides a rough guide to the probable economic superiority of one channel over the other. The evaluation must now be broadened by a consideration of the motivational, control, and conflict aspects of the two channel alternatives.

The use of sales agents can give rise to a number of control problems. The central fact is that the manufacturers' sales agency is an independent business interested in maximizing its own profits. The agent may not cooperate with the client's agent in an adjacent territory. The agent concentrates calls on the customers that are most important to the agency in terms of the total assortment of goods rather than on the customers who are most important to the client. The agent's sales force may not take the time to master the technical details concerning the client's product or to make use of the client's promotion materials carefully.

438

Adaptive criteria One other criterion should be considered—that of the producer's freedom to adapt to changing conditions. Each channel alternative involves some duration of commitment and loss of flexibility. A manufacturer who decides to use a sales agent may have to offer a five-year contract; during this period, other means of selling, such as direct mail, might become more efficient, but the manufacturer is not free to drop the sales agent. A channel alternative involving a long commitment must appear to be greatly superior on economic or control grounds in order to be considered.

CHANNEL-MANAGEMENT DECISIONS

After a company has determined its basic channel design, individual middlemen must be *selected, motivated,* and *evaluated.*

Selecting
Channel
Members

Producers differ in their ability to recruit qualified middlemen for the proposed channel operation. Some producers have no trouble finding specific business establishments to join the channel. Their proposal attracts more than enough middlemen either because of the high prestige of the firm or because the specific product or line appears to be a good moneymaker. For example, Ford was able to attract twelve hundred new dealers for its ill-fated Edsel. In some cases the promise of exclusive or selective distribution will influence a sufficient number of middlemen to join the channel. The main problem for the producer who can attract enough middlemen is one of selection. The producer must decide on what middlemen characteristics provide the best indication of their competence.

At the other extreme are producers who have to work hard to line up the desired number of qualified middlemen. U.S. Time Company found it very hard to line up jewelry stores to carry its inexpensive Timex watches and was forced to go to mass-merchandising outlets. When Polaroid started, it could not get photographic-equipment stores to carry its new cameras and was forced to go to mass-merchandising outlets. Often small producers of new food products find it very hard to get shelf space in food outlets. The producer should study how middlemen make their buying decisions—specifically, how much weight they give to gross margin, planned advertising and promotion, return guarantees, and so on. The producer must develop an offer that promises to make a lot of money for the middlemen.

Whether producers find it easy or difficult to recruit middlemen, they should determine what characteristics distinguish the better middlemen from the poorer ones. They will want to evaluate the middlemen's number of years in business, growth record, solvency, cooperativeness, and reputation. If the middlemen are sales agents, producers will also want to evaluate the number and character of other lines carried and the size and quality of the sales force. If the middleman is a department store being considered for exclusive distribution, the producer wants to evaluate the store's location, future growth potential, and type of clientele.

Motivating
Channel
Members

Middlemen must be motivated to do their best job. The factors and terms that led them to join the channel provided some of the motivation, but these must be supplemented by continuous supervision and encouragement from the producer. The producer must sell not only through the middlemen but to them. The question of motivation is a complex one, since there are grounds for both cooperation and conflict between producers and their distributors.

The job of stimulating channel members to top performance must start with the manufacturer's attempting to understand the needs and psychology of the particular middlemen. Middlemen are often criticized by manufacturers, according to McVey:

> for failure to stress a given brand, or for the poor quality of his salesmen's product knowledge, his disuse of suppliers' advertising materials, his neglect of certain customers (who may be good prospects for individual items but not for the assortment), and even for his unrefined systems of record keeping, in which brand designations may be lost.[27]

However, what are shortcomings from the manufacturer's point of view may be quite understandable from the middleman's point of view. McVey listed the following four propositions to help understand the middlemen:

> The middleman is not a hired link in a chain forged by a manufacturer, but rather an independent market. . . . After some experimentation, he settles upon a method of operation, performing those functions he deems inescapable in the light of his own objectives, forming policies for himself wherever he has freedom to do so. . . .
>
> [The middleman often acts] primarily as a purchasing agent for his customers, and only secondarily as a selling agent for his suppliers. . . . He is interested in selling any product which these customers desire to buy from him. . . .
>
> The middleman attempts to weld all of his offerings into a family of items which he can sell in combination, as a packaged assortment, to individual customers. His selling efforts are directed primarily at obtaining orders for the assortment, rather than for individual items. . . .
>
> Unless given incentive to do so, middlemen will not maintain separate sales records by brands sold. . . . Information that could be used in product development, pricing, packaging, or promotion-planning is buried in nonstandard records of middlemen, and sometimes purposely secreted from suppliers.[28]

These propositions serve as a provocative departure from otherwise stereotyped thinking about the performance of middlemen. The first step in motivating others is to see the situation from their viewpoint.

Producers vary in their level of sophistication with respect to handling distributor relations. We can distinguish between three approaches: *cooperation, partnership,* and *distribution programming.*[29]

Most producers see the problem of motivation as one of figuring out ways to gain *cooperation* from independent and sometimes difficult middlemen who "aren't loyal" or "are lazy." They will use the carrot-and-stick approach. They will dream up positive motivators, such as higher margins, special deals, premiums, cooperative advertising allowances, display allowances, and sales con-

---

[27] Phillip McVey, "Are Channels of Distribution What the Textbooks Say?" *Journal of Marketing,* January 1960, pp. 61–64.

[28] Ibid.

[29] See Bert Rosenbloom, *Marketing Channels: A Management View* (Hinsdale, Ill.: Dryden Press, 1978), pp. 192–203.

tests. If these don't work, they will apply negative sanctions, such as threatening to reduce the margins, slow down service, or terminate the relationship. The basic problem with this approach is that the producer has not really studied the needs, problems, strengths, and weaknesses of the distributors. Instead, the producer puts together a miscellaneous set of devices that are based on crude stimulus-response thinking. McCammon notes:

> Many programs (developed by the manufacturer) consist of hastily improvised trade deals, uninspired dealer contests, and unexamined discount structures. . . . This traditional attitude toward distributor programming is a luxury that no longer can be easily afforded.[30]

More-sophisticated companies try to forge a long-term *partnership* with their distributors. This calls for the manufacturer's developing a clear sense of what it wants from its distributors and what its distributors can expect from the manufacturer in terms of market coverage, product availability, market development, account solicitation, technical advice and services, and market information. It seeks agreement from the channel members on these policies and may even set up compensation based on adherence to these policies. In one case, the company, instead of paying a straight 25 percent sales commission, pays the following:

1. Five percent for carrying the proper level of inventory
2. Another 5 percent for meeting the sales quotas
3. Another 5 percent for servicing the customers effectively
4. Another 5 percent for proper reporting of final customer purchase levels
5. Another 5 percent for proper accounts receivables management

Distribution programming is still a further stage in the possible relation between manufacturers and their distributors. McCammon defines this as building a planned, professionally managed, vertical marketing system that incorporates the needs of both manufacturer and distributors.[31] The manufacturer sets up a special department within the marketing department called distributor relations planning, whose job is to identify the distributors' needs and build up the programmed merchandising and other programs to help each distributor operate as optimally as possible. This department and the distributors jointly plan the merchandising goals, inventory levels, space and visual merchandising plans, sales-training requirements, and advertising and promotion plans. The aim is to convert the distributors from the idea that they make their money primarily on the buying side (through an adversarial relation with the supplier) to the realization that they make their money on the selling side through being part of a sophisticated vertical marketing system.

Evaluating Channel Members

The producer must periodically evaluate middleman performance against certain standards. Where a middleman's performance is below standard, it is necessary to determine the underlying causes and to consider the possible remedies. The producer may have to tolerate the unsatisfactory performance if dropping

---

[30] Bert C. McCammon, Jr., "Perspectives for Distribution Programming," in *Vertical Marketing Systems,* ed. Louis P. Bucklin (Glenview, Ill.: Scott, Foresman & Co., 1970), p. 32.

[31] Ibid., p. 43.

or replacing the middleman would lead to even worse results. But if there are attractive alternatives to the use of this middleman, then the producer should require the middleman to reach a certain level of performance within a stated time or be dropped from the channel.

Much grief can be avoided if standards of performance and sanctions are agreed upon at the very beginning between the producer and the channel members. The areas posing the greatest need for explicit agreement concern sales intensity and coverage, average inventory levels, customer delivery time, treatment of damaged and lost goods, cooperation in company promotional and training programs, and middleman services owed to the customer.

The producer typically issues sales quotas to define current performance expectations. Automobile manufacturers and many appliance dealers set quotas not only for total units to be sold but often for types of units. In some cases these quotas are treated only as guides; in others, they represent serious standards. Some producers list the sales of various middlemen after each sales period and send the rankings out. This device is intended to motivate middlemen at the bottom of the list to do better for the sake of self-respect (and continuing the relationship) and middlemen at the top to maintain their performance out of pride.

A simple ranking of the middlemen by level of sales is not necessarily the best measure. Middlemen face varying environments over which they have different degrees of control; the importance of the producer's line in their assortments also varies. One useful measure is to compare each middleman's sales performance against its performance in the preceding period. The average percentage of improvement (or decline) for the group can be used as a norm. Another useful measure is to compare each middleman's performance against assigned quotas based on an analysis of the sales potential in the respective territories. After each sales period, middlemen are ranked according to the ratio of their actual sales to their sales potential. Diagnostic and motivational effort can then be focused on those middlemen who have underachieved.

CHANNEL-MODIFICATION DECISIONS

A producer must do more than design a good channel system and set it into motion. Every so often the system requires modification to meet new conditions in the marketplace.

This fact struck a large manufacturer of major household appliances who had been marketing exclusively through franchised dealers. A relative loss in market share made the producer take stock of several distributional developments that had taken place since the original channel was designed:

> An increasing share of major-brand appliances were being merchandised through discount houses.

> An increasing share of major appliances were being sold on a private-brand basis through large department stores.

> A new market was developing in the form of volume purchases by tract home builders who preferred to deal directly with the manufacturers.

> Door-to-door and direct-mail solicitation of orders was being undertaken by some dealers and competitors.

The only strong independent dealers were those in small towns, and rural families were increasingly making their purchases in large cities.

These and other developments in the ever-changing distribution scene led this manufacturer to undertake a major review of possible channel modifications.

Three different levels of channel change should be distinguished. The change could involve adding or dropping individual channel members; adding or dropping particular market channels; or developing a totally new way to sell goods in all markets.

The decision to add or drop particular middlemen usually requires a straightforward incremental analysis. The economic question is, What would the firm's profits look like with this middleman and without this middleman? The incremental analysis could be complex if the decision would have many repercussions on the rest of the system. An automobile manufacturer's decision to grant another dealer franchise in a city will require taking into account not only that dealer's probable sales but the possible losses or gains in the sales of the manufacturer's other dealers.[32]

Sometimes a producer contemplates dropping not an isolated middleman but all middlemen who fail to bring their unit sales above a certain level within a certain period. This happened when a large manufacturer of motor trucks selling through a network of franchised dealers noted that at least 5 percent of its dealers were selling fewer than three or four trucks a year. According to the controller's calculation, it cost more for the company to service these small dealers than the sale of three or four trucks was worth. If the issue were a matter of dropping a few of these weak dealers, then an incremental analysis would probably indicate that company profits would rise. But the decision to drop most of these dealers could have such large repercussions on the system as a whole that an incremental analysis would not suffice. Such a decision would raise the unit costs of producing trucks, since the overhead would have to be spread over fewer trucks; some employees and equipment would be idled; some business in the markets where the smaller dealers were cut out would go to competitors; and other company dealers might be made insecure by the decision. Nothing short of a detailed, total systems simulation would be adequate for comprehending all the effects.

A producer sometimes faces the question of whether its channel for reaching a particular geographical area or customer type is still optimal. A breakeven or rate-of-return analysis could be made of the present and alternative systems. The most difficult "channel-change" decision involves the revision of the overall system of distribution. For example, an automobile manufacturer may consider replacing independent dealers with company-owned dealers; a soft-drink manufacturer may consider replacing local franchised bottlers with centralized bottling and direct sales. These are decisions made at the highest level, decisions that not only change the channels but necessitate a revision of most of the marketing-mix elements and policies to which the firm is accustomed. Such decisions have so many ramifications that any quantitative modeling of the problem can only be a first approximation.

---

[32] See T. E. Hlavac, Jr., and John D. C. Little, "A Geographical Model of an Urban Automobile Market," in *Proceedings of the Fourth International Conference on Operational Research*, ed. David B. Hertz and Jacques Melese (New York: John Wiley & Sons, 1966), pp. 302–11.

In analyzing the desirability of changing a channel, the task is one of determining whether the channel is in equilibrium.[33] A channel is in equilibrium when there is no structural or functional change that would lead to increased profits. A structural change is one involving the addition or elimination of some middleman level in the channel. A functional change is one involving the reallocation of one or more channel tasks among the channel members. A channel is ripe for change when it is in disequilibrium—that is, when it provides an opportunity for gain through a structural or functional modification.

A simple example will convey the concept of channel disequilibrium. Assume there is a channel of the manufacturer-wholesaler-retailer type (M-W-R). (See Figure 16–5.) Each channel member makes a set of decisions on price, advertising, and distribution (P,A,D). for simplicity, assume that these decisions mainly affect the succeeding stage. Thus the producer makes decisions $(P,A,D)_1$, which influence the quantity (Q_1) ordered by the wholesaler. The producer calculates net profits (Z_1) by subtracting its costs from its revenue from the wholesaler. In the same fashion, each channel member makes an independent set of decisions that influence its revenue and cost and bring about a particular net profit.

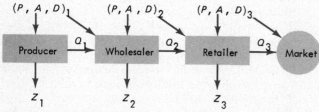

FIGURE 16–5

Conceptual Picture of the Profits in a Marketing Channel

SOURCE: Redrawn, with modifications, from Stanley Stasch, "A Method of Dynamically Analyzing the Stability of the Economic Structure of Channels of Distribution" (Ph.D. dissertation, School of Business, Northwestern University, 1964), p. 63.

Looking at the channel as a whole, a set of independent decisions is made $[(P,A,D)_1, (P,A,D)_2, (P,A,D)_3]$ that results in some total channel profit $(Z_1 + Z_2 + Z_3)$. The concept of channel disequilibrium can now be defined precisely. The channel is in disequilibrium if there exists an alternative set of decisions $[(P,A,D)_1, (P,A,D)_2, (P,A,D)_3]^*$ that would result in a different total channel profit $(Z_1 + Z_2 + Z_3)^*$ that is greater than $(Z_1 + Z_2 + Z_3)$. If this is the case, the channel presents an opportunity for increased profit. But the alternative decisions are not likely to be made as long as the channel members make their decisions independently. The greater the difference between $(Z_1 + Z_2 + Z_3)^*$ and $(Z_1 + Z_2 + Z_3)$, the greater will be the incentive of the channel members to pursue joint planning or for some channel member to absorb one or more of the others to achieve the extra profits from integrated decision making.

[33] This section leans heavily on Stanley Stasch's "A Method of Dynamically Analyzing the Stability of the Economic Structure of Channels of Distribution" (Ph.D. dissertation, School of Business, Northwestern University, 1964).

Let us turn from the channel decisions facing manufacturers to those facing middlemen, particularly wholesalers and retailers. We will look at the marketing decisions made by resellers in the areas of product, price, promotion, and place.[34]

Product Decisions of Resellers

Resellers have to make product decisions with respect to the assortment they will carry, the buying policies they will implement, and the services they will provide to customers.

A reseller's *product assortment* can be described in terms of decisions on width (narrow or wide) and depth (shallow or deep). Consider the restaurant business. A small lunch counter offers a food assortment that is narrow and shallow—a few sandwiches and some egg dishes. A delicatessen's assortment is narrow but deep—essentially smoked meat and smoked fish products with many varieties. A cafeteria usually offers a wide assortment of foods lacking much depth in any category. Finally, a major restaurant offers a wide assortment of foods with many variations of each. In the food store business, mom-and-pop stores, health food stores, convenience food stores, and supermarkets differ primarily in the width and depth dimensions of their respective assortments. In the area of industrial wholesaling, assortment profiles vary. For example, a rack jobber carries a narrow line of sundries that is shallow in depth. On the other hand, a full-line wholesaler carries a wide and deep assortment by definition. Typically, resellers begin as small-business people, with narrow and shallow lines. If successful, they expand by increasing either the width or the depth of their assortment. Those that are ultimately successful are able to carry assortments that are both wide and deep.

Resellers make their profit on the difference between what they pay for their merchandise and what they get for it. Because margins are usually small, they are under great pressure to buy carefully. Often they can make as much or more money through adept buying as adept pricing. So the *buying function* is usually a key resource that must be expertly staffed. The buying group develops product specifications, often invites competitive bidding, and buys from multiple sources.

Resellers also make decisions of the *mix of services* they will provide their customers. The old mom-and-pop grocery stores offered home delivery, credit, and conversation to their customers—services that today's modern supermarkets have completely eliminated. In industrial wholesaling, cash-and-carry operations offer minimal services whereas full-line wholesalers offer delivery, credit, sales aids and training, cooperative advertising, and return privileges to their customers.

Pricing Decisions of Resellers

Resellers typically base their prices on conventional markups over the costs of the original goods. For example, wholesalers average a gross margin of 20 percent. Gross margin is the difference between their selling price and their cost price of the goods sold. This gross margin has to cover their expenses, which may

[34] See Ben Enis, *Marketing Principles: The Management Process*, 2nd ed. (Pacific Palisades, Cal.: Goodyear Publishing Co., 1977), pp. 428–36.

run an average of 17 percent, leaving a profit margin of around 3 percent. The gross margins in retailing average 35 to 40 percent, but here too expenses consume most of the gross margin. There are wide variations around these margins for different types of wholesalers and retailers. For example, grocery wholesalers and retailers work with an average profit margin of less than 2 percent.

Resellers are continually looking for ways to improve their gross margin through smarter pricing. They will often put a low markup on a few items to act as *loss leaders* (or *traffic builders*) and put high markups on other items, hoping that buyers will buy them once the buyers are on the premises. They will also place the higher-markup items in prime exposure locations.

Promotion Decisions of Resellers

Resellers make regular use of the normal tools of promotion, such as advertising, personal selling, sales promotion, and publicity. In the case of wholesalers, they use both push and pull methods of promotion. Their sales force acts as a push force in calling on prospective and current customers, offering special prices and premiums, and asking for orders. Wholesalers use pull force by advertising their assortments and certain manufacturers' brands in media reaching retailers and ultimate consumers. The advertising is supplemented with such promotional tools as special discounts for off-season purchase and premiums.

Retailers use a number of promotion tools to reach final consumers. The major tool is advertising, and in many areas it takes the form of newspaper advertising to announce sales prices or special merchandise. The advertising is occasionally supplemented by hand-delivered circulars or direct-mail pieces. Sales promotion takes the form of in-store demonstrations, trading stamps, grand prizes, and visiting celebrities. Much effort goes into the designing of effective atmospheres for the retailing establishment that reinforce impulses to buy or consume the products.

Place Decisions of Resellers

Resellers compete in creating place utility for their customers. Wholesalers must develop well-located stocking points, carry sufficient inventories, and use reliable means of transportation to be able to fill customers' orders fast. In the case of retailers, their choice of locations will be a key competitive factor in their attraction of customers. For example, the major factor in the consumer's choice of a bank is its nearness to the customer. Department store chains, oil companies, and major fast-food franchisers must be particularly adept in making their location decisions, and the use of advanced methods of site selection and evaluation is critical.

SUMMARY

Marketing-channel decisions are among the most complex and challenging facing the firm. Each firm usually confronts a number of alternative ways to reach the market. They vary from direct selling, to using one, two, three, or more intermediaries. The firms making up the marketing channel are connected in different ways by physical, title, payment, information, and promotion flows. Marketing channels do not stay static but are characterized by continuous and sometimes dramatic change. Four of the most significant recent trends are direct, vertical, horizontal, and multichannel marketing systems.

Each channel system has a different potential for creating sales and producing costs. Once a particular marketing channel is chosen, the firm must usually adhere to it for a substantial period. The chosen channel will significantly affect and be affected by the rest of the marketing mix.

Good channel design should proceed with a clarification of channel objectives, alternatives, and likely payoffs. The objectives are conditioned by the particular characteristics of customers, products, middlemen, competitors, and environment. The alternatives are usually numerous because of the variety of types of intermediaries, the different possible intensities of market coverage, the various ways in which channel tasks can be allocated among channel members, and the many possible trade-relations mixes. Each feasible alternative way to reach the market has to be spelled out and evaluated according to economic, control, and adaptive criteria.

After the basic design of the channel is determined, the firm faces the task of effective channel management. It has to select particular firms to work with or find business firms willing to work with it. It has to supplement the motivations provided to channel members through the trade-relations mix by special incentives and supervision. It has to periodically evaluate the performance of individual channel members against their own past sales, other channel members' sales, and, possibly, sales quotas.

Because markets and the marketing environment are continually changing, the firm must be prepared to make channel revisions: individual members may be dropped or added, the channels in specific markets may be modified, and sometimes the whole channel system may have to be redesigned. Evaluating a proposed channel change may be approached through incremental analysis if only the particular unit or channel is affected; it may require a systems-level analysis if the change is likely to affect other units. The greater the disequilibrium in a channel, the more apparent it will be to observers that channel modification would lead to increased profits.

QUESTIONS AND PROBLEMS

1. If there are five producers and five customers in a market, how many contacts would have to be made (a) without a middleman? (b) with a middleman? What are the general formulas?

2. Explain how the characteristics of (a) peaches and (b) cement affect the channels for them.

3. Suggest some alternative channels for (a) a small firm which has developed a radically new harvesting machine; (b) a small plastic manufacturer who has developed a picnic pack for keeping bottles and food cold; and (c) a manufacturer of expensive watches.

4. Is the following channel pattern plausible? What kinds of institutions are implied?

$$M(---K) \rightarrow W(-AS-) \rightarrow R(TA--)$$

5. Produce a checklist of questions for rating prospective applicants for a distributorship.

6. "Discussions of merchandising practices in the oil industry have often proceeded from the premise that the existing distributive channel structure for gasoline is a millstone around the industry's neck." Can you think of innovations for improving the distribution of automobile fuel or for improving the profitability of service stations?

7. Can you think of a radically different way to organize the distribution of (a) automobiles; (b) beer?

8. "Middlemen are parasites." This allegation has been made by many over the centuries. Is this likely to be the case in a competitive economic system? Why or why not?

9. There is often conflict between manufacturers and retailers. What does each party really want from the other and why does this give rise to conflict?

Physical-Distribution Decisions

When is a refrigerator not a refrigerator? . . . when it is in Pittsburgh at the time it is desired in Houston.
J. L. HESKETT, N. A. GLASKOWSKY, R. M. IVIE

17

Throughout the years, the term *marketing* has connoted two different but related processes, the first dealing with the *search for and stimulation of buyers* and the second with the *physical distribution of goods.* With the increased competition for markets, marketing executives have devoted the bulk of their time to the search and stimulation function. Their attention has been given over to developing a mix of products, prices, promotion, and channels that would keep demand high and growing. They have viewed physical distribution, or the logistics of getting goods to the buyers, as a supportive and subsidiary activity.

More recently, several developments have awakened management's interest in the logistics problem and led them to wonder whether they were not overlooking many opportunities to increase customer service, outperform competition, and effect cost savings.

One of the alerting factors is the steady climb in the bill for such physical-distribution services as freight, warehousing, and inventory. Freight and warehousing bills are rising as a result of increased labor, energy, and equipment costs. The inventory bill is rising because buyers are tending to place smaller orders more frequently, and manufacturers are tending to expand the width and depth of their product lines. Many executives have been shocked to learn that the total costs of storing, handling, and moving their products are anywhere between 19 and 22 percent of their net sales![1] One study showed the cost breakdown as follows: inventory (44 percent), traffic service and customer freight (23 percent), warehousing and shipping (16 percent), interplant freight (9 percent), and sales order processing (8 percent).[2]

Authorities in increasing numbers argue that substantial savings can usually be effected in the physical-distribution area, which has been variously described as "the last frontier for cost economies"[3] and "the economy's dark continent."[4] There is much evidence that uncoordinated physical-distribution decisions result in profit suboptimization. Not enough use is being made of modern decision tools for blending economic levels of inventories, efficient modes of shipment, and sound plant, warehouse, and store locations.

Furthermore, physical distribution is a potent tool in the demand-stimulation process. Companies can attract additional customers by offering better service or by cutting prices through successfully reducing physical-distribution costs.

THE SCOPE OF PHYSICAL DISTRIBUTION

Physical distribution comprises the set of tasks involved in planning and implementing the physical flows of materials and final goods from points of origin to points of use or consumption to meet the needs of customers at a profit.

At least fourteen tasks are involved in physical distribution and they are shown in Figure 17–1. The system starts with sales forecasting, which allows the company to formulate plans with respect to production and inventory levels. The production plans suggest the materials that must be ordered by the purchasing department, and these arrive through inbound transportation, enter the receiving area, and are stored in raw material inventory. Raw materials are converted into finished goods. Finished goods inventory is the link between customers' orders and the company's manufacturing activity. Customers' orders draw down the finished goods inventory level, and manufacturing activity builds it up. Finished goods flow off the assembly line, and pass through packing, in-plant warehousing, shipping-room processing, outbound transportation, field warehousing, and customer delivery and servicing.

Under traditional thinking, physical distribution starts with goods at the plant and tries to find efficient ways to get them to customers. Under marketing thinking, physical-distribution planning should start with market considerations and work all the way back to raw material needs and sources. The company should start with its target customers, their locations, and their needs for product delivery and availability. It should know the service levels offered by competitors and plan to match or exceed these levels, or at least compensate for

[1] For further discussion of physical-distribution costs, see Ronald H. Ballou, *Basic Business Logistics* (Englewood Cliffs, N. J.: Prentice-Hall, 1978), pp. 17–19.

[2] Bernard J. LaLonde, "Integrated Distribution Management: The American Perspective," *Journal of Long-Range Planning*, December 1969, p. 64.

[3] Donald D. Parker, "Improved Efficiency and Reduced Cost in Marketing," *Journal of Marketing*, April 1962, pp. 15–21.

[4] Peter Drucker, "The Economy's Dark Continent," *Fortune*, April 1962, pp. 103 ff.

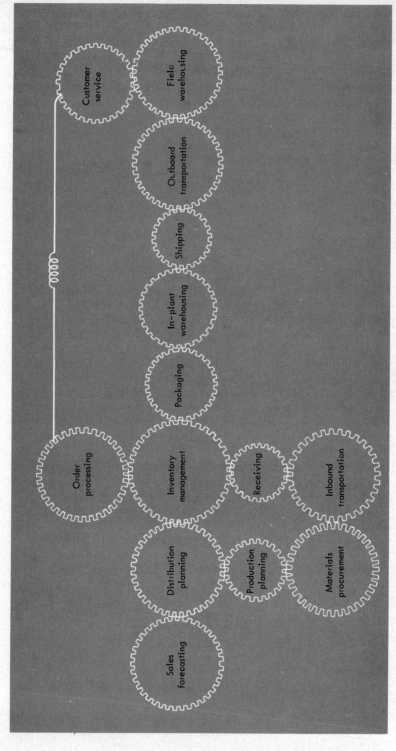

SOURCE: Redrawn, with modifications, from Wendell M. Stewart, "Physical Distribution: Key to Improved Volume and Profits," *Journal of Marketing,* January 1965, p. 66.

FIGURE 17–1
Major Activities Involved in Physical Distribution

them by other features of its offer. The company then makes an integrated set of decisions on warehouse and plant locations, inventory levels, and transportation modalities that are designed to supply the target levels of service to the target customers.

A growing number of practitioners prefer to call this way of thinking "market logistics" rather than "physical distribution." Too often, physical distribution is a planning of physical flows of the existing finished goods from the company out to the marketplace at the least cost. A market-logistics viewpoint reverses this thinking and often leads to an innovative approach to physical distribution. Consider the following case:

> In Germany, soft drinks are typically purchased from retailers in individual bottles. A soft-drink manufacturer, looking for an advantage, decided to design a six-pack. He tested who the idea with consumers who responded positively to the convenience aspect of carrying bottles in a six-pack. The retailers also responded positively because the bottles could be loaded faster on the shelves and could lead to the purchase of more bottles per occasion. The company designed the six-packs to fit on the shelf in a way that maximized utilization of the shelf space. Then it designed cases and pallets that would bring these six-packs to the store's receiving rooms efficiently. The plant operations were redesigned to produce the new bottles and six-packs. The purchasing department let out bids for the new needed materials. When implemented, this new way of packaging soft drinks was an instant hit with consumers, and the manufacturer's market share increased substantially. A market-logistics viewpoint led to a creative physical-distribution breakthrough.

THE PHYSICAL-DISTRIBUTION OBJECTIVE

Many companies state their physical-distribution objective as *getting the right goods to the right places at the right time for the least cost.* Unfortunately, this provides little actual guidance. No physical-distribution system can simultaneously maximize customer service and minimize distribution cost. Maximum customer service implies such policies as large inventories, premium transportation, and many warehouses, all of which raise distribution cost. Minimum distribution cost implies such policies as slow and cheap transportation, low stocks, and few warehouses.

The physical-distribution objective can be defined more carefully by introducing the notion of an *efficient system.* System efficiency is a matter of the ratio of a system's output to its input. By clarifying what the outputs and inputs are in a physical-distribution system, we can come closer to defining a clear objective for such a system.

Level of Service (Output)

A basic output of a physical-distribution system is the *level of customer service.* Customer service represents one of the key competitive benefits that a company can offer potential customers in order to attract their business. From the customer's view, customer service means several things:

1. The speed of filling and delivering normal orders
2. The supplier's willingness to meet emergency merchandise needs of the customer
3. The care with which merchandise is delivered, so that it arrives in good condition

4. The supplier's readiness to take back defective goods and resupply quickly
5. The availability of installation and repair services and parts from the supplier
6. The number of options on shipment loads and carriers
7. The supplier's willingness to carry inventory for the customer
8. The service charges, that is, whether the services are "free" or separately priced

The company's task is to research the relative importance and determinance of these various customer services to the target customers and what competitors are offering. The company then decides on a competitively viable mix of customer services.

Of all the services listed above, the first one, *delivery time,* is typically the most important to customers. Customers want the ordered merchandise or service delivered at the promised time. Late delivery of needed parts or service can idle expensive equipment, labor, and even whole factories. Actual delivery time is made up of two components, order cycle time and delivery reliability. *Order cycle time* is the normal time the company takes to fill an order after receiving it. It is what the company's sales representatives state as the expected time for delivery, such as "one-week delivery." *Delivery reliability* is the percentage of times the company actually fills the order within the stated order cycle time. Thus "60 percent reliability" means that the company meets the promised delivery date only 60 percent of the time.

The company can improve actual delivery time by cutting down the order cycle time, increasing delivery reliability, or both. Suppose a company has been operating on an order cycle time of seven days with a 60 percent reliability. In a bid for more customers, it is considering cutting delivery time down to five days with a 95 percent reliability. This will substantially increase its physical distribution costs. The trick is to measure whether this move will produce enough increased sales and profits to cover the added costs. To the extent that the management is able to estimate the relationship between levels of service and sales, it will have a means of determining the optimal level of customer service.

Several factors influence the optimal level of customer service. The *competitors' normal delivery time* is a major factor in that the company risks losing or failing to attract customers if it offers a lower standard; and to offer a higher standard would be costly and might even lead competitors to increase their service levels, thus raising everyone's costs. Another factor is the *degree of criticality of the needed parts or service;* delivery times have to be faster when expensive operations are dependent upon delivery. Still another factor is the *differential advantage or loyalty* enjoyed by the company; the higher this is, the less it has to offer in the way of a delivery-time advantage. Finally, the *cost of supplying higher levels of service* will influence the normal delivery time; a company is not going to improve the delivery time at a high cost unless this will substantially improve sales.

Once it decides on a delivery-time standard, the company can design the physical distribution system to meet that standard with a high degree of reliability. Pillsbury defines its delivery-time standard as "third-morning rail delivery anywhere in the U.S." Xerox defines its service-delivery standard as being able "to put a disabled machine anywhere in the continental United States back into operation within three hours after receiving the service request." To accomplish this, Xerox has a separate division consisting of 12,000 service personnel and parts managers.

Cost of Service (Input)

A company bears certain costs, of which freight, inventory, and warehousing are the main ones, in providing its present level of customer service. Often the total bill is not known because companies typically lack centralized management and accounting of their physical-distribution activities. These costs, however, must be measured as a prerequisite for distribution planning and control.

The present system can be said to be efficient if no reorganization of logistical inputs could reduce the costs *while maintaining the present service level.* Many companies think their physical-distribution system is efficient because each decision center—inventory, warehousing, and traffic—appears to do a good job of keeping down its own costs. However, this is an area where the sum of distribution costs is not necessarily minimized by a set of uncoordinated efforts to minimize the separate costs. As Parker points out:

> Pressures are applied by top management which encourage the separate functional units to control and reduce their costs of operation. Cost reduction becomes the primary way for these functional units to call attention to themselves. . . . As a result, when decisions are made about transportation, warehousing, packaging, inventory levels . . . they are based on an analysis of alternatives within that specific function, without regard for the possible effects upon other closely related functions. Functional costs are considered, but the all-important total cost of the related functions is ignored.[5]

Various physical-distribution costs interact, often in an inverse way:

> The traffic manager favors rail shipment over air shipment whenever possible. This reduces the company's freight bill. However, because the railroads are slower, this ties up company capital longer, delays customer payment, and may cause customers to buy from competitors offering more rapid service.
>
> The shipping department uses cheap containers to minimize shipping costs. This leads to a high damage rate of goods in transit and the loss of customer goodwill.
>
> The inventory manager favors holding low inventories to reduce total inventory cost. However, this results in many stockouts, backorders, accompanying paperwork, special production runs, and high-cost fast-freight shipments.

The import is that since physical-distribution activities are highly interrelated, decisions must be made on a total system basis.

The Objective

We are now ready to define the objective of physical-distribution design. A physical-distribution system consists of a set of decisions on the number, location, and size of warehouses; freight policies; and inventory policies. Each possible physical-distribution system implies a total distribution cost, as given by the expression:

$$D = T + FW + VW + S \qquad (17\text{--}1)$$

[5] Parker, "Improved Efficiency in Marketing," p. 17.

where:

D = total distribution cost of proposed system

T = total freight cost of proposed system

FW = total fixed warehouse cost of proposed system

VW = total variable warehouse costs (including inventory) of proposed system

S = total cost of lost sales due to average delivery delay under proposed system[6]

The choice of a physical-distribution system calls for examining the total distribution cost associated with different proposed systems and selecting the system that minimizes total distribution cost. Alternatively, if it is hard to measure S in (17–1), the company should aim to minimize the distribution cost $T + FW + VW$ of reaching a *given level of customer service*.

MAJOR ALTERNATIVES IN PHYSICAL-DISTRIBUTION STRATEGY

A firm faces a large number of alternatives in designing its physical-distribution system. The variety increases in number and complexity as we go from a firm with a single plant serving a single market to a firm with multiple plants and multiple markets. Many firms, in fact, follow a "logistic life cycle" going from a single plant in a single market to one of multiple plants in multiple markets, calling for various changes in physical-distribution arrangements along the way.

Single Plant, Single Market

The vast majority of the three hundred thousand manufacturers in the United States are single-plant firms doing business in single markets. The single markets served may be a small city, as in the case of small bakeries and printing firms, or a region, as in the case of local breweries and boat manufacturers.

Does the single-plant firm generally locate in the midst of its market? It often does, for the cost of serving a market increases with the distance. The distant firm has to absorb higher outbound freight costs and is normally at a competitive disadvantage.

Yet in some cases there are offsetting economies in locating a plant at some distance from the market. The higher market transportation cost may be offset by lower costs of land, labor, energy, or raw materials.

> A pickling plant serving the Chicago market was deliberately located in the midst of a cucumber-growing region two hundred miles from Chicago. This gave the company better control over crop selection. Labor costs were lower because pickling and packing were done only in certain months, when farmers had surplus time on their hands. Finally, the acreage for the plant cost only a fraction of what it would have cost near the city.

The merits of locating a plant near the market or near its sources depend

[6] Adapted from Alfred A. Kuehn and Michael J. Hamburger, "A Heuristic Program for Locating Warehouses," *Management Science*, July 1963, pp. 657–58.

mainly on relative transfer and processing costs. A substantial change in certain costs could upset the balance of advantages. The firm choosing between two alternative plant sites must carefully weigh not only present alternative costs but expected future alternative costs.

Single Plant,
Multiple Markets

The firm having a single plant and selling in a dispersed set of markets has a choice of several physical-distribution strategies. Consider a midwestern manufacturer who wishes to expand its operation into the East. The manufacturer can serve the eastern market in four ways: (1) *direct shipments* to customers on the East Coast, (2) *carload shipments to a warehouse* on the East Coast, (3) *fabricated-parts shipments to an assembly plant* on the East Coast, or (4) *establishment of a manufacturing plant* on the East Coast.

Direct shipments to customers   Any proposed system of physical distribution must be evaluated in terms of customer service and cost. The direct-shipment proposal would normally score poorly on both of these counts. Direct shipment implies slower delivery than shipments to the customer from an eastern-based warehouse. Direct shipment also implies higher cost, because the typical customer order is normally smaller than carload size. Carload rates (CL) are often 50 percent lower than less-than-carload rates (LCL).

But whether direct shipment does involve these disadvantages depends upon a number of things. It is conceivable that direct shipment from a distant plant could effect *faster* delivery than shipment from a nearby warehouse. A Kansas City manufacturer of colored, flavored ice cream cones learned that its customers in the East could receive shipments sooner by air freight direct from Kansas City than by truck shipments out of New York City. Furthermore, direct shipment of less-than-carload orders must be measured against the cost of maintaining warehoused inventories in the East. The decision on whether to use direct shipment depends on such factors as the nature of the product (its unit value, perishability, and seasonality), the required speed and cost of delivery, the size and/or weight of the typical customer order, and the geographical distance and direction.

The cost of direct shipment varies with selection of waterways, railroad, motor carriers, air freight, or some combination. Figure 17–2A shows how the cost of different modes of transportation may be compared. If the company receives eastern orders for shipments averaging less than ten pounds, it could minimize transportation cost by using air freight; between ten and thirty-five pounds, motor freight; over thirty-five pounds, rail freight.

This analysis is incomplete because each transportation alternative implies a different average delivery time. We can assume a higher cost of lost sales for longer delivery delays. Thus the slower modes of transportation cost less for freight but more in sales. These two diverging cost functions of delivery time are shown in Figure 17–2B. By adding the two cost curves vertically, we can find a total-cost curve. The total-cost curve tends to be U-shaped, and by projecting its minimum point down to the days-of-delivery axis, we can estimate the optimum delivery delay, D. This delay has the property that the marginal savings in freight from a slightly longer delay would just equal the marginal cost of lost patronage.

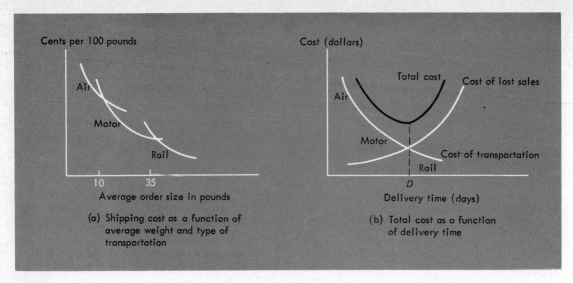

FIGURE 17–2
Costs as a Function of Shipping Mode and Average Weight

Bulk shipments to a warehouse near the market   The firm may find it less expensive to make bulk shipments to a regional warehouse in the East and to fill customer orders from that regional warehouse. The savings would arise mainly because of the substantial difference between carload and less-than-carload shipping rates. Suppose the midwestern manufacturer expects to sell 5,000 units annually in the East, and virtually all of the individual orders call for less-than-carload shipments. Assume that the shipping cost is $8 per unit on a carload basis, and $12 per unit on a less-than-carload basis. The cost of shipping the 5,000 units directly to customers at less-than-carload rates would be $60,000 (5,000 × $12). The cost of shipping carloads to a warehouse would be $40,000 (5,000 × $8). This represents a gross cost saving of $20,000.

From this, we have to subtract the cost of local delivery from the warehouse to the customer and the cost of warehousing. Suppose the typical local delivery charge is $1 a unit; then local delivery charges of $5,000 (5,000 × $1) must be subtracted from the gross savings, leaving savings of $15,000. Suppose the average unit stays in the warehouse one week before shipment and the warehouse charge per unit per week is $2, including handling, insurance, and all other charges. Then the annual warehousing bill would be $10,000 (5,000 × $2), leaving net savings of $5,000. Given these figures, the midwestern manufacturer could save $5,000 a year by making bulk shipments to a warehouse in the East as an alternative to direct shipments to customers.

To this possible freight savings should be added another advantage accruing from the use of a market-located stocking point. A regional warehouse typically makes it possible to make faster deliveries to customers and thereby increase customer patronage. In general, the optimizing rule for adding regional warehouses is simple enough. A regional warehouse should be added *if the freight savings and increased patronage resulting from faster delivery exceed the incremental costs of operating the warehouse.*

456

Large manufacturers must consider a whole system of regional ware-houses, or stocking points, to serve a national market. Maytag, a large manufac-turer of home laundry equipment, has over one hundred regional stocking points. Instead of sending small-volume orders of washing machines to over fif-teen thousand different dealers, the company sends carload shipments to its vari-ous stocking points. In this way it can promise speedier delivery and also save considerably on freight costs.

But an extensive regional warehouse system raises a number of new prob-lems: (1) What is the best number of stocking points?; (2) Where should they be located?; (3) What is the best inventory level to hold at each? Paper-and-pencil analysis is exceedingly inadequate to answer these questions. Companies are turning increasingly to computer models. Gerson and Maffei have described a computer simulation program for evaluating a system of up to forty warehouses, four thousand customers, and ten factories.[7] This program can be used to esti-mate quickly the cost of alternative arrangements in the existing number and lo-cations of factories and warehouses. Other models are available, which use mathematical programming or heuristic techniques to determine the optimal distribution system.[8]

Fabricated-parts shipments to an assembly plant near the market A third alter-native for the midwestern manufacturer is to establish an assembly plant near the market. Parts are shipped in carload quantities to the regional assembly plant at lower freight charges. The presence of a regional plant also stimulates the increased interest of local salesmen, dealers, and the community at large. Against this the company must consider the sunk investment cost in additional facilities.

Establishment of a regional manufacturing plant The midwestern manufac-turer's fourth alternative is to establish a regional plant in the East. The decision to build a regional manufacturing plant requires the most detailed factual infor-mation and analysis of the local scene. Many factors are involved, including the availability and costs of manpower, energy, land, transportation, and, not the least important, the legal and political environment.

One of the most important factors is the nature of mass-production econo-mies in the industry. In industries requiring a relatively heavy fixed investment, a plant has to be quite large in order to achieve cost economies. If unit costs of manufacture decrease continuously with the scale of plant, then one plant could logically supply the entire company volume at minimum *production* costs. How-ever, it would be fallacious to ignore distribution costs, because they tend to be higher at higher volumes. The two considerations are combined in Figure 17–3. Unit production costs decline steadily as increased volume is produced by a single plant, while unit distribution costs tend to rise as the volume requires di-rect shipment to more distant markets. When the two curves are summed verti-cally, total costs may in fact rise as a result of using only one plant location. The company should consider a second plant as an alternative to expanding the size of a single plant much past V. It is conceivable in this case that two plants, each involving higher unit production costs, may effect a large enough saving in dis-tribution costs to constitute the better arrangement.

[7] Martin L. Gerson and Richard B. Maffei, "Technical Characteristics of Distribution Simula-tors," *Management Science*, October 1963, pp. 62–69.

[8] See Kuehn and Hamburger, "Locating Warehouses."

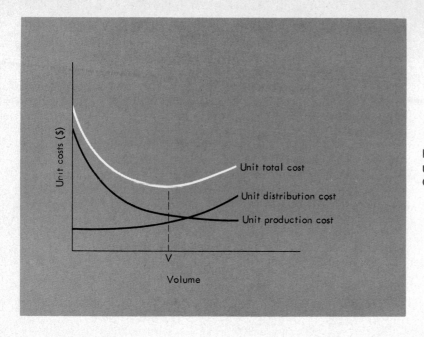

FIGURE 17–3
Unit Production and Distribution
Costs for a Single Plant

Multiple Plants, Multiple Markets   Many of the large companies that do not require extremely large plants to achieve production economies utilize a physical-distribution system consisting of many plants and many warehouses. These companies face two optimization tasks. The first is to set a factory-to-warehouse shipping pattern that minimizes total freight costs, given the present plant and warehouse locations. The second is to determine the number and location of facilities that will minimize total distribution costs. Here system simulation is a potent technique. A physical-distribution simulation at General Electric showed how a subsidiary with $50 million sales could save $2.9 million a year through system redesign.[9]

The physical-distribution system must be designed not so much for maximum economy for the present as for maximum flexibility for the future, even if present costs must be a little higher in order to gain this flexibility. The company's plans for entering new-product markets, for introducing new-product styles and models, and for changing the number of distributors all should count in designing the system. The system should be planned with an awareness of technological developments, particularly in the areas of communications, transportation, and automation. Such innovations as automated warehouses, piggy-back freight, electronic hookups between computers in different locations, containerization, and air freight are all factors to consider.

INVENTORY DECISIONS

While marketing management generally does not have control over inventory policy, it is inclined to seek a strong voice in the making of inventory policy. The marketer's chief concern lies in providing a high level of customer service. Inventory policy is thus a tool in the demand-creation and demand-satisfaction process. The marketer would like to promise customers that all their orders would

[9] "The Case for 90% Satisfaction," *Business Week*, January 14, 1961.

be filled immediately and would be shipped by the most rapid transportation. However, it is not realistic from a cost point of view for a company to carry the amount of stock that would virtually guarantee no stockouts. A major reason is that *inventory cost increases at an increasing rate as the customer-service level approaches 100 percent.* A typical cost relationship is illustrated in Figure 17–4A. To be able to fill 85 percent of the total received orders from existing stock, the company has to carry an inventory valued at $400,000. To raise the customer-service standard by five percentage points, to 90 percent, inventory investment must be increased by $100,000. To raise the customer-service standard another five percentage points, to 95 percent, inventory investment must now be increased by $200,000.

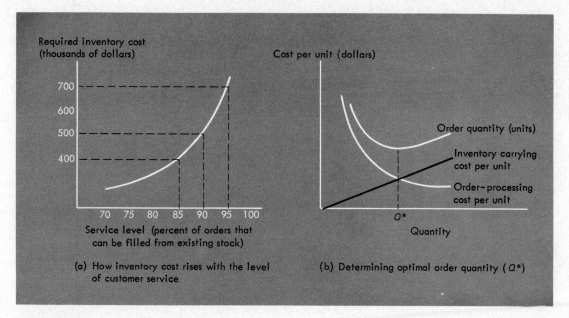

(a) How inventory cost rises with the level of customer service

(b) Determining optimal order quantity ($Q*$)

FIGURE 17–4
Important Inventory Relationships

This acceleration of inventory cost does not mean that increases in customer service are never warranted. Increases in service spell increases in patronage and sales. But how much do sales increase with service? The graph only tells us that an increase from 90 to 95 percent service requires another $200,000 of inventory investment. We need to know whether sales and profits would increase enough to justify the higher investment.

Types of Inventory Decisions

Inventories are carried because *producing* and *using* activities typically take place at different times, in different locations, and at different rates. In the case of agricultural food crops, rate of usage is usually even throughout the year, but harvesting occurs at discrete times. In the case of manufacturing output, factories achieve production economies by producing large runs of items infrequently. The savings in producing large runs generally exceed the cost of storing the goods over the period required for their complete sale.

Inventory decision making can be thought of as a two-step decision process: (1) when to order (order point), and (2) how much to order (order quantity).

When to order The basic characteristic of an inventory is that it is drawn down during the period. This calls for a determination of the level at which the remaining stock justifies the placement of a new order. This level is called the *order (or reorder) point*. An order point of 20 would mean that when the seller's supply of an item falls to 20 units, an order for more stock should be placed.

The determination of the order point depends upon the order lead time, the usage rate, and the service standard. The higher these are, the higher the order point. Furthermore, if the order lead time and customer usage rate are variable, the order point would have to be higher by an amount of *safety stock*. The final order point is set on the basis of balancing the risks of stockouts against the costs of overstock.

How much to order The decision the firm makes on how much to order directly influences how often it has to order. The larger the quantity ordered, the less often an order has to be placed.

Order-processing costs are somewhat different for the distributor and the manufacturer. The distributor's processing costs consist of whatever materials, machine accounting time, and labor are used up every time an order is placed, received, and inspected. Distributors have variously estimated their order-processing costs anywhere from a few dollars to one hundred dollars an order. The figure used makes quite a difference in the final determination of optimal order quantity.

Order-processing costs for a manufacturer consist of *setup costs* and *running costs* for the item. If setup costs are very low, the manufacturer can produce the item often and the cost per item is pretty constant and equal to the running costs. However, if setup costs are high, the manufacturer can reduce the average cost per unit by producing a long run and carrying more inventory.

Order-processing costs must be compared with *inventory carrying costs*. The larger the average stock carried, the higher the inventory carrying costs. These carrying costs include (1) storage charges, (2) cost of capital, (3) taxes and insurance, and (4) depreciation and obsolescence. Inventory carrying costs may run as high as 30 percent of the inventory value. That is a higher figure than the estimate used by many businessmen, but there is growing recognition that the cost is this high. This means that marketing managers who want their companies to carry larger inventories must be able to convince top management that the higher inventories will yield new sales with an incremental gross profit that would more than cover the incremental inventory carrying costs.

Many companies have higher inventory carrying costs than necessary because they try to offer their customers the same service standard on all their goods. It would be better for these companies to distinguish between their fast-moving, moderately moving, and slow-moving items and handle them differently. The fast-moving items would be highly stocked and carried in several locations, whereas the slow-moving items would be kept low in stock, carried in only one location, and possibly shipped by air freight when badly needed. Customers would expect to wait longer for nonstandard items, and the company will save a lot of money.[10]

[10] See James L. Heskett, "Logistics—Essential to Strategy," *Harvard Business Review,* November–December 1977, pp. 85–96.

The optimal order quantity can be determined by observing how order-processing costs and inventory carrying costs sum up at different possible order levels. In Figure 17–4B, the order-processing cost per unit is shown to fall with the number of units ordered, because the order costs are spread over more units. Inventory carrying charges per unit are shown to rise with the number of units ordered because each unit remains longer in inventory. The two cost curves are summed vertically into a total-cost curve. The lowest point on the total-cost curve is projected down on the horizontal axis to find the optimal order quantity Q°.[11]

LOCATION DECISIONS

Marketing managers have a keen interest in the location decisions made by the firm. Retail outlets must be carefully located near the greatest number of potential customers, because of the importance of shopper convenience in store patronage. Even warehouse locations should be located near the customer concentration points to ensure fast and cheap delivery to customers.

Types of Location Decisions Location decision making can be thought of as a two-step decision process: (1) selecting a general area, and (2) selecting a specific site.

We can illustrate the major issues in retail location by citing the experience of the Rayco Manufacturing Company.[12] Rayco was formed after World War II as a manufacturer of automobile seat covers. Its distribution network consisted of independently financed, franchised dealers who merchandised Rayco products exclusively. By 1955, it had over one hundred fifty dealers operating in sixty different cities. Its national retail structure continued to grow, and new lines were added: convertible tops, automobile replacement parts, and a line of home-furnishing fabrics. But auto seat covers remained its main product.

Selecting the area Rayco's Research Division has the responsibility of evaluating the profit potential of various areas of the country. The areas might be cities, standard metropolitan areas, or some other geographical unit. Suppose a set of n areas $(1, 2, 3, \ldots, i, \ldots, n)$ is to be evaluated. Let Z_i represent the expected profit potential of the ith area. Let X_i be a proposed company dollar investment in developing area i. The expected profit potential will vary with development expenses. That is, $Z_i = f(X_i)$. A larger outlet, a better dealer, or a larger promotion budget invested in a particular area would create higher profits, although the rate of profit increase can be expected to diminish beyond some level of investment.

[11] The optimal order quantity is given mathematically by the formula

$$Q^\circ = \sqrt{\frac{2DS}{IC}}$$

where D = annual demand, S = cost to place one order, and IC = annual carrying cost per unit. Known as the economic-order quantity formula, it assumes a constant ordering cost, a constant cost of carrying an additional unit in inventory, a known demand, and no quantity discounts. For the derivation of this and more complex formulas, see Martin K. Starr and David W. Miller, *Inventory Control: Theory and Practice* (Englewood Cliffs, N.J.: Prentice-Hall, 1962).

[12] The discussion that follows is adapted from "Rayco Manufacturing Company, Inc.: Pinpointing Store Locations by Electronic Computer," Case 3M38, Intercollegiate Case Clearing House. Harvard Graduate School of Business Administration, Boston, by permission of the author, Charles H. Dufton, Northeastern University, Boston.

Rayco's task is to estimate, for each candidate area, how profits would behave at different levels of investment. Once it derives a set of area profit functions, it can allocate its total "new locations" budget to these areas in such a way that the marginal profit is the same in all areas.

Although the area investment problem turns out to be simple to solve in principle, everything hinges on being able to estimate expected profits as a function of investment: $Z_i = f(X_i)$. Area profits are a complex function of area cost and area demand characteristics. The relevant cost characteristics of an area, such as land costs and advertising rates, are fairly easy to determine. It is the area's demand potential that is usually hard to determine.

Rayco initially identified about three hundred variables that could influence area sales. The Research Division examined the logical rationale for each variable and was able to reduce the set to seventy-four. Included were such variables as "average January temperature," "percent of the dwellings that were one-unit detached structures," and an "index for the physical appearance of a store." An equation was fitted to these seventy-four variables based on data from 150 existing outlets. Several of the variables failed to pass tests of statistical significance, and in the final equation, thirty-seven variables were retained, yielding an R^2 of .92. Rayco felt it could now estimate the "market potential" of any new area by inserting thirty-seven characteristics into the formula.

Selecting the site   After determining the areas of high potential, the firm must decide how many outlets to establish and where they should be specifically situated. If San Francisco appeared to be a high-potential market, Rayco could establish, for about the same investment, one large outlet in a central location or a few smaller outlets in separate parts of the city. If consumers behaved as though auto seat covers were specialty goods, they would be willing to travel longer distances, and this would favor one large, centrally located store. If consumers regarded Rayco's products as convenience goods, this would favor Rayco's establishing a few smaller outlets.

A store's trading area or reach is affected by a number of other factors besides the type of merchandise. One is the number of different items carried by the store. Baumol and Ide have developed an analysis in which they visualize each consumer as calculating his or her net gain from patronizing a store with N items at a distance D.[13] They assume that increases in N more than compensate for increases in D up to a point. Beyond this point, the cost of traveling to the store, and within the store, become dominant. The cost of traveling within a store, which is a function of N, would never reach discouraging proportions in the case of a Rayco outlet but could be a real factor in very large supermarkets and department stores, especially for the shopper who plans to purchase only a few items.

The *utility* expected by a consumer in location i of shopping at an outlet in location j is affected by many variables in addition to N and D. Included are such factors as store image, delivery, credit, service policies, promotion, parking facilities, and air conditioning. If consumer utility as a function of these variables could be measured, the choice of the best site and store size from a list of alternatives is solvable in principle.[14] Suppose there are three alternative proposed

[13] See William J. Baumol and Edward A. Ide, "Variety in Retailing," *Management Science,* October 1956, pp. 93–101.

[14] See David L. Huff, "Defining and Estimating a Trading Area," *Journal of Marketing,* July 1964, pp. 34–38.

sites—1, 2, and 3—offering utilities 40, 30, and 10, respectively, to a consumer in location i. The probability that this consumer would shop at site 1 is the ratio of the utility of site 1 to the total utility, in this case .50 ($= 40/80$). If there are 1,000 similar consumers clustered at location i, then half of them, or 500, can be expected to patronize proposed site 1. In a more advanced analysis, it would be desirable to distinguish major socioeconomic types of consumers at location i, because there are strong interactions of consumer type and store type.

In practice, firms vary considerably in how analytically they investigate the trade potential of proposed sites. Small firms rely on population census data and on simple traffic counts. Large firms carry out expensive surveys of consumer shopping habits and make extensive calculations of expected sales volume.

In undertaking a detailed *trade analysis* for a proposed site, the large firm first prepares area maps indicating density and the location of competitive intercepting facilities. An overlay on this map indicates major arteries to pinpoint traffic flows. Additional information is obtained by surveying the license plates in the parking lots of competitive facilities and through inquiries at noncompeting stores as to customer sources.

The real estate department then determines the availability and cost of potential sites within the general area. The trade potential of each site is then evaluated. A series of circles is drawn around each site at varying distances to indicate the primary trading area, the secondary trading area, and the fringe trading area. The secondary and fringe areas are further away from the new site and closer to competitive sites; they can be expected to contribute a progressively smaller amount of per capita sales.

The major chains utilize elaborate site-location checklists in their evaluation of sites. Nelson has published a very elaborate checklist containing over thirty factors, each of which has to be rated excellent, good, fair, or poor in evaluating a proposed site.[15] These factors relate to the site's trading area potential, accessibility, growth potential, competitive interception, and site economics. Some of the large chain organizations have gone beyond checklists into elaborate computer models for site location. One very large merchandising organization dropped its location consultant firm when it realized that the methods being used were at the checklist stage and undertook to build its own internal consultancy group for sophisticated location research.

ORGANIZATIONAL RESPONSIBILITY FOR PHYSICAL DISTRIBUTION

Divided Authority   By now it should be abundantly clear that decisions on warehousing, transportation, inventory levels, and location require the highest degree of coordination. Yet in the typical company, physical-distribution responsibilities tend to be divided in an ill-coordinated and often arbitrary way among several company departments. Furthermore, each department tends to adopt a narrow view of the company's physical-distribution objective. *Traffic managers* seek to minimize the freight bill. They prefer less-expensive modes of transportation and infrequent and large shipments. *Sales managers* seek to maximize the level of customer service. They prefer large inventories and premium transportation. *Inventory-control managers* seek to minimize inventory costs. They prefer small inventories because inventory carrying costs tend to be more tangible than

[15] Richard L. Nelson, *The Selection of Retail Locations* (New York: F. W. Dodge Corporation, 1958), pp. 349–50.

stockout costs. Various managers jealously guard their prerogatives. The result is system suboptimization.

Organizational Alternatives

Companies are increasingly recognizing the potential benefits of developing some coordinating mechanism and have generally chosen one of two forms. Many companies have set up a permanent committee, composed of personnel responsible for different physical-distribution activities, that meets periodically to work out policies for increasing the efficiency of the overall distribution system. A small number of companies have centralized their physical-distribution activities in the hands of a single authority.[16]

The example of the Burroughs Company is particularly illuminating.[17] Burroughs organized the Distribution Services Department to centralize control over its physical-distribution activities. Within two and one-half years following the reorganization, the company claimed savings of over $2 million annually (on $200 million of sales), plus a higher level of service to field branches and customers.

When a company establishes a separate department with responsibility for physical distribution, the major issue is whether the new department should have separate status or be placed within one of the major existing departments. For example, Heinz created a new department of coordinate stature with Marketing and Production which was headed by a vice-president of Distribution. Heinz hoped that this arrangement would guarantee respect for the department, develop a greater degree of professionalism and objectivity, and avoid partisan domination by Marketing or Production.

On the other hand, Burroughs placed its new Distribution Services Department within the Marketing Department. By this move, Burroughs was expressing the great importance it attached to good customer service relative to the costs of providing it. Wherever marketing is the crucial factor in competitive success, physical distribution is usually placed under the marketing department. This is especially true in such competitive industries as soap, food, and cosmetics, where marketing and physical distribution must be coordinated not only to minimize costs but also to harmonize distribution with frequent advertising campaigns and customer and dealer promotions.

But the location of the department, or even its creation, is a secondary concern. The important thing is the recognition by the company that if it does not coordinate the planning and operation of its physical-distribution activities, it is missing the opportunity for often sizable cost savings and service improvements. When this fundamental awareness takes place, each company can then make a determination of what would constitute the most appropriate coordinative mechanism.

SUMMARY

Just as the marketing concept is receiving increasing recognition by business firms, a growing number of firms are beginning to heed the physical-distribution concept. Physical distribution is an area of high potential cost savings, improved

---

[16] But in half the cases, the heads of distribution manage only transportation and warehousing and not the other physical distribution functions. See Robert S. Jeffries, Jr., "Distribution Management: Failures and Solutions," *Business Horizons*, April 1974, pp. 55–66. Also see Stephen B. Oresman and Charles D. Scudder, "A Remedy for Maldistribution," *Business Horizons*, June 1974, pp. 61–72.

[17] See L. O. Browne, "Total Distribution in an Age of Computers," *Distribution Age*, July 1964, pp. 33–40.

customer satisfaction, and competitive effectiveness. When traffic managers, inventory managers, and warehouse planners make decisions only with reference to their own framework, they affect each other's costs and demand-creation influences but do not take them into consideration. The physical-distribution concept calls for treating all these decisions within a unified total systems framework. Then the important task becomes that of designing physical-distribution arrangements that minimize the cost of providing a given level of customer service.

The firm can choose from a number of alternative physical-distribution strategies, ranging from direct shipment to field warehousing to local assembly plants to local manufacturing plants. It must develop inventory policies that reconcile the value of a high level of customer service with the need to economize on inventory carrying costs. It must find more accurate ways to evaluate alternative general areas and specific sites for marketing expansion. It must review the whole question of organizational responsibility for physical distribution, particularly how to coordinate the various decisions and where leadership should be located in the organization.

We have deliberately emphasized the planning rather than the operations aspects of physical distribution. Physical distribution is an area where good systems design counts for as much as or more than good operations management. Nevertheless, many of the potential economies come from improved management of the existing system.

QUESTIONS AND PROBLEMS

1. Does it follow that the company offering a high customer service level tends to bear high physical distribution costs in relation to sales?

2. A small midwestern boat company with good sales wants to expand into the eastern part of the country. What physical distribution strategy might it use to bring its boats to the East?

3. A national can manufacturer operates many local plants because cans are a low-cost, low-price product that has a relatively high transportation cost when shipped assembled, being mostly "air." Some of its plants appear uneconomic, and it is considering closing them. Much depends upon whether customers in the affected areas would accept a longer delivery time, switch business to a competitor's local plant, or manufacture their own cans. Develop a flow diagram showing how the company might analyze probable customer reactions to the elimination of a local plant.

4. What are the two inventory-production policy alternatives facing a seasonal producer?

5. Suppose a company's inventory carrying cost is 30 percent. A marketing manager wants the company to increase its inventory investment from $400,000 to $500,000, believing this would lead to increased sales of $120,000 because of greater customer loyalty and service. The gross profit on sales is 20 percent. Does it pay the company to increase its inventory investment?

6. The text mentioned that Rayco approached the problem of finding the characteristics of good locations through multiple regression. (a) Suggest some of the various ways in which the dependent variable, sales, might be defined. (b) How could the research department further reduce the number of independent variables in the market evaluation formula?

7. Suppose you are the marketing manager of a medium-sized manufacturing company. The president has just made the following statement: "The distribution activity is not a concern of the marketing department. The function of the marketing department is to sell the product ... let the rest of the company handle production and distribution." How would you reply to this statement?

MARKETING COMMUNICATIONS DECISIONS

People no longer buy shoes to keep their feet warm and dry. They buy them because of the way the shoes make them feel— masculine, feminine, rugged, different, sophisticated, young, glamorous, "in." Buying shoes has become an emotional experience. Our business now is selling excitement rather than shoes.
FRANCIS C. ROONEY

18

Modern marketing calls for more than developing a good product, pricing it attractively, and making it readily accessible to target customers. The company must design and disseminate information about the product's existence, features, and terms and how these will benefit the target market. Every company is inevitably cast into the role of a communicator and promoter.

Companies have responded by hiring sales forces to carry persuasive messages, advertising agencies to develop attention-getting ads, sales promotion specialists to develop sales campaigns; and public relations firms to enhance the company's image. They all continue to spend large and growing sums for promotion. For most companies the question is not whether to promote, but how much to spend and in what ways.

The company's communications responsibilities go beyond disseminating information to target customers. The company must communicate effectively with other parties in its *task environment,* particularly its dealers and suppliers. It must communicate with major *external publics,* such as its stockholders, the financial community, the media, and various government units. It must communicate effectively with its *internal publics,* particularly its directors, middle management, sales force, and wage workers.

This means that the company must know how to market itself to various groups in order to gain their confidence and goodwill. It must develop a clear corporate identity. This involves answering an extremely difficult question, What does it want to be? Whether or not the company answers this question, it *will be* something to its customers and other publics. Its products, employees, and actions will communicate something. And what is communicated should not be left to chance.

The company that can establish a reputation for trustworthiness, progressiveness, and social responsibility starts with an advantage over other firms in the minds of actual and potential customers and other publics. The corporate aura lends a halo effect to the individual corporate divisions, product lines, and brands. Many buyers, when it comes to explaining why they chose one company over another, in the end say they have more confidence in that company. Customer confidence is built through a combination of satisfying offers and effective communications. Neither alone will do the job. Companies are increasingly recognizing the value of creating an integrated communications program that reflects the company's identity in all of the things that it does.

This chapter will look at the major tools in the marketing communications mix and then at a model of the marketing communications process. Finally we will discuss planning the marketing communications program. The following three chapters will take up advertising, sales promotion and publicity, and sales force, and examine the major decisions involved in each.

THE MARKETING COMMUNICATIONS MIX

One can take a broad or a narrow view of the tools in the marketing communications mix. The broad view says that each of the four *P*s belongs in the marketing communications mix. The product's styling, the color and shape of the packaging, and the price all communicate something. Once the company decides on a target market position, all the marketing-mix tools should reinforce this position.

The narrow view says the marketing communications mix consists of the subset of marketing tools that are primarily "communicational" in nature. They are the tools normally classified under promotion, one of the four *P*s. They are called *promotools*, and include various forms of advertising, packaging, sales presentations and demonstrations, point-of-purchase displays, sales aids (catalogs, literature, films), incentive tools (contests, trading stamps, premiums, free samples, coupons), and publicity programs.

Each of these promotools has specific potentialities and complexities that could justify managerial specialization. Yet a company, even a very large one, typically does not have a specialist in each area but only in those areas where the importance and usage frequency of the tool warrant specialization. Historically, companies first made a separate function out of *personal selling*, later out of *advertising*, still later out of *sales promotion*, and ultimately out of *publicity*. These four major tools are defined as follows:

Advertising. Any paid form of nonpersonal presentation and promotion of ideas, goods, or services by an identified sponsor.

Personal selling. Oral presentation in a conversation with one or more prospective purchasers for the purpose of making sales.

Sales promotion. Short-term incentives to encourage purchase or sale of a product or service.

Publicity. Nonpersonal stimulation of demand for a product, service, or business unit by planting commercially significant news about it in a published medium or obtaining favorable presentation of it upon radio, television, or stage that is not paid for by the sponsor.[1]

Here we will discuss the special qualities of each promotional component.

Advertising

Advertising comes in many forms and has many uses. It involves such varied media as magazines and newspapers, radio and television, outdoor displays (such as posters, signs, skywriting), direct mail, novelties (matchboxes, blotters, calendars), cards (car, bus), catalogs, directories, and circulars. It can be carried out for such diverse purposes as long-term buildup of the company name (*institutional advertising*), long-term buildup of a particular brand (*brand advertising*), information dissemination about a sale, service, or event (*classified advertising*), announcement of a special sale (*sales advertising*), and so on.

Because of the many forms and uses of advertising, it is hard to advance all-embracing generalizations about its distinctive qualities as a component of the marketing communications mix. Yet the following qualities can be noted:

1. *Public presentation.* Advertising, unlike personal selling, is a highly public mode of communication. Its public nature confers a kind of legitimacy to the product and also suggests a standardized offering. Because many persons receive the same message, buyers know that their motives for purchasing the product will be publicly understood.

2. *Pervasiveness.* Advertising is a pervasive medium that permits the seller to repeat a message many times. It also allows the buyer to receive and compare the messages of various competitors. Large-scale advertising by a seller says something positive about the seller's size, popularity, and success.

3. *Amplified expressiveness.* Advertising provides opportunities for dramatizing the company and its products through the artful use of print, sound, and color. Sometimes the tool's very success at expressiveness may, however, dilute or distract from the message.

4. *Impersonality.* Advertising, in spite of being public, pervasive, and expressive, cannot be as compelling as a company sales representative. The audience does not feel obligated to pay attention or respond. Advertising is only able to carry on a monologue, not a dialogue, with the audience.[2]

Personal Selling

Personal selling also takes several forms, such as sales calls by a field representative (field selling), assistance by a salesclerk (retail selling), and a golf invitation from one company president to another (executive selling). It can be used for many purposes, such as creating product awareness, arousing interest, developing product preference, negotiating prices and other terms, closing a sale, and

---

[1] These definitions, with the exception of the one for sales promotion, came from *Marketing Definitions: A Glossary of Marketing Terms* (Chicago: American Marketing Association, 1960). The AMA definition of sales promotion covers, in addition to incentives, such marketing media as displays, shows and exhibitions, and demonstrations that can better be classified as forms of advertising, personal selling, or publicity. Some marketing scholars have also suggested adding packaging as a fifth element of the promotion mix, although others classify it as a product element.

[2] The distinctive qualities of advertising and personal selling, are adapted from Sidney J. Levy, *Promotional Behavior* (Glenview, Ill.: Scott, Foresman & Company, 1971), chap. 4.

providing posttransactional reinforcement. Personal selling has certain distinctive qualities:

1. *Personal confrontation.* Personal selling involves an alive, immediate, and interactive relationship between two or more persons. Each party is able to observe at close hand the characteristics and needs of the other and make immediate adjustments. Each party has the potentiality to help or hurt the other by showing interest or lack of it, and this can make the encounter stressful.

2. *Cultivation.* Personal selling permits all kinds of relationships to spring up, ranging from a matter-of-fact selling relationship to a deep personal friendship. In most cases, the sales representative must use art to woo the buyer. The sales representative at times will be tempted to put on pressure or to dissemble to get an order, but normally will keep the customer's long-run interests at heart.

3. *Response.* Personal selling, in contrast with advertising, makes the buyer feel under some obligation for having listened to the sales talk or using up the sales representative's time. The buyer has a greater need to attend and respond, even if the response is a polite "thank you."

Sales Promotion

Sales promotion is the catchall for various promotools that are not formally classifiable as advertising, personal selling, or publicity. These tools may be subclassified into items for *consumer promotion* (e.g., samples, coupons, money-refund offers, prices-off, premiums, contests, trading stamps, demonstrations), *trade promotion* (e.g., buying allowances, free goods, merchandise allowances, cooperative advertising, push money, dealer sales contests), and *sales-force promotion* (e.g., bonuses, contests, sales rallies).

Although sales promotion tools are a motley collection, they have two distinctive qualities:

1. *Insistent presence.* Many sales promotion tools have an attention-getting, sometimes urgent, quality that can break through habits of buyer inertia toward a particular product. They tell the buyers of a chance that they won't have again to get something special. This appeals to a broad spectrum of buyers, although particularly to the economy minded, with the disadvantage that this type of buyer tends to be less loyal to any particular brand in the long run.

2. *Product demeaning.* Some of these tools suggest that the seller is anxious for the sale. If they are used too frequently or carelessly, they may lead buyers to wonder whether the brand is desirable or reasonably priced.

Publicity

A company and its products can come to the attention of the public through being newsworthy. The seller pays nothing for the news coverage. The results of free publicity can sometimes be spectacular. Consider the case of the diet drink Metrecal:

> Almost overnight, Metrecal became part of the American tribal customs, fashions and language. The signs were everywhere. Drugstores served Metrecal across soda fountains. Newspapers printed Metrecal-inspired cartoons. Fashionable luncheon clubs served Metrecal cocktails. Steve Allen and a probate judge in Charleston, South Carolina, wrote songs about Metrecal. Don Wilson, the announcer, danced "The Metrecal Bounce" on television. Overweight football players in Chicago ate at "the Metrecal table."[3]

[3] Peter Wyden, *The Overweight Society* (New York: William Morrow & Co., 1965), p. 50.

Publicity has three distinctive qualities:

1. *High credibility.* News stories and features seem to most readers to be authentic, media-originated reports. They have a higher degree of credibility than if they came across as sponsored by a seller.
2. *Off guard.* Publicity can reach many potential buyers who otherwise avoid salesmen and advertisements. This is because the message is packaged in a way that gets to the buyers as news rather than as a sales-directed communication.
3. *Dramatization.* Publicity has, like advertising, a potential for dramatizing a company or product.

A MODEL OF THE COMMUNICATIONS PROCESS

We are now ready to examine how the process of communications works. Years ago, Lasswell suggested that communications involve five major questions: *who ... says what ... in what channel ... to whom ... with what effect.*[4] These can be rephrased into saying that communications consist of a *sender* transmitting a *message* through *media* to a *receiver* who *responds.* Communications specialists spend their time doing source analysis, message analysis, media analysis, audience analysis, and response analysis.

We will use a slightly expanded version of this model, the one shown in Figure 18–1. The model consists of eight major communications elements. Two of them (in rectangles) represent the major parties in a communication—sender and receiver. Two others (in diamonds) represent the major communications tools—message and media. The remaining four (in ovals) represent major communication functions—encoding, decoding, response, and feedback. Each of these is defined below.

Sender. The party sending the message to another party (also called the *source* or *communicator*).

Encoding. The process of putting thought into symbolic form.

Message. The set of symbols that the sender transmits.

Media. The paths through which the message moves from sender to receiver.

Decoding. The process by which the receiver assigns meaning to the symbols transmitted by the sender.

Receiver. The party receiving the message sent by another party (also called the *audience* or *destination*).

Response. The set of reactions that the receiver has after being exposed to the message.

Feedback. The part of the receiver's response that the receiver communicates back to the sender.

The model indicates the factors in effective communications. Senders must know what audiences they want to reach and what responses they want. They must be skillful in encoding messages that take into account how the target audience tends to decode messages. They must transmit the message over efficient media that reach the target audience. They must develop feedback channels so that they can monitor whether the audience got the intended message.

[4] Harold D. Lasswell, *Power and Personality* (New York: W. W. Norton & Company, 1948), pp. 37–51.

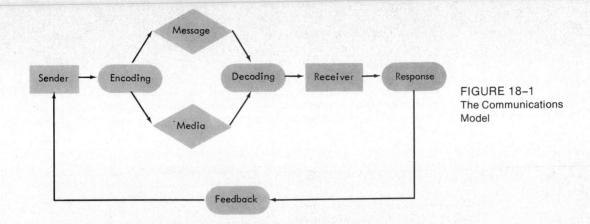

FIGURE 18–1
The Communications
Model

This might suggest that skillful communicators can exercise great powers of persuasion over their audiences, a view propounded in *The Hidden Persuaders*[5] and other books criticizing marketing communicators. However, the same model shows this is not the case. The audience is far from manipulable. The model shows an active rather than passive audience.[6] The audience, because of decoding, does not necessarily receive all of the message or receive it in the intended way.[7] Furthermore, the audience can show a wide variety of responses after decoding or interpreting the message. Finally, the audience may initiate or control the feedback to the sender, thus also playing the role of communicator. The audience, far from being passive, is an active party in the marketing dialogue.

The model permits the drawing together of many interesting findings about the communications process that have a bearing on effective marketing communications planning. We will discuss the elements not in the order of the *message flow* (from communicator to audience) but mainly in terms of the *planning flow* (from target audience backward to the communicator). The marketing communicator must make decisions on the following elements:

1. Who is the target audience? (Receiver)
2. What response should be sought? (Response and decoding)
3. What message should be developed? (Message and encoding)
4. What media should be used? (Media)
5. What source attributes should accompany the message? (Sender)
6. What feedback should be collected? (Feedback)

[5] Vance Packard, *The Hidden Persuaders* (New York: Pocket Books, 1957).

[6] See Joseph T. Klapper, *The Effects of Mass Communication* (New York: Free Press, 1960); Raymond A. Bauer, "The Limits of Persuasion," *Harvard Business Review*, September–October 1958, pp. 105–10; and Bauer, "The Initiative of the Audience," *Journal of Advertising Research*, June 1963, pp. 2–7.

[7] For example, an audience survey showed that many viewers of the popular "All in the Family" CBS program viewed Archie Bunker as a hero rather than as a narrow-minded and prejudiced American. See Neil Bidmar and Milton Rokeach, "Archie Bunker's Bigotry: A Study in Selective Perception and Exposure," *Journal of Communication*, winter 1974, pp. 36–47.

A marketing communicator must start with a clear target audience in mind. The audience may be potential buyers of the company's products or current users, deciders, or influencers. The audience may be individuals, groups, particular publics, or the general public. The target audience will critically determine *what* is to be said, *how* it is to be said, *when* it is to be said, *where* it is to be said, and *who* is to say it.

Given the target audience, the communicator has to research several audience characteristics, such as the audience's image of the company and its products, cognitive processing approach, needs and wants, product and brand preferences, and media habits. We will examine the first two characteristics here, the others being treated elsewhere in the book.

Audience image A major part of audience analysis is to assess the audience's current image of the company, its products, and its competitors. People's attitudes and actions toward an object are highly conditioned by their beliefs about the object. *Image* is the term used to describe the *set of beliefs that a person or group holds of an object.*

At any point in time, the current image of an object is likely to lag behind the reality of the object. For example, a particular company may continue to be seen as the market leader long after its quality has started to slip. Another company might have a second-class image long after it has transformed itself into a first-class institution. Images can be five to ten years obsolete in the same way that we are not seeing a real star in the sky but an image of that star as it was earlier, since light takes time to travel. *Image persistence* is the result of people continuing to see what they expect to see, rather than what is. This means that it is very hard for a company to improve its image in a short time, even given a willingness to spend a great deal of money.

Furthermore, a company cannot change its image simply through communications effort. The image is a function of "good deeds plus good words." The company must live out what it wants to be and must use communications to tell the story. Some companies attempt to create phony images through slick communications campaigns, but this rarely succeeds because there is too much discrepancy between the message and the reality.

The communicator's task is to research the current image as a basis for deciding on communications objectives. This requires contacting a sample of people in the target audience and using some instrument to measure their image of the object in question. There are many instruments for image measurement,[8] but we shall describe here the popular one known as the *semantic differential*.[9]

The semantic differential involves creating a set of attribute scales with each attribute defined by bipolar adjectives. Figure 18–2 shows a set of nine scales used to measure the image of three brewing companies. The scales each have seven intervals, although there could have been five, nine, or some other number. More scales could have been added, but many would be redundant, since only a certain number of basic image dimensions exist. In fact, the creators

---

[8] For a discussion of various image-measurement techniques, see the author's *Marketing for Nonprofit Organizations* (Englewood Cliffs, N.J.: Prentice-Hall, 1975), pp. 131–37.

[9] The semantic differential technique was originally developed in C. E. Osgood, C. J. Suci, and P. H. Tannenbaum, *The Measurement of Meaning* (Urbana: University of Illinois Press, 1957).

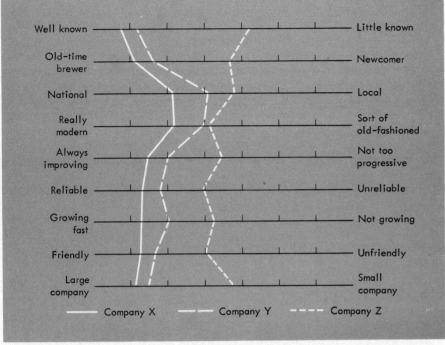

FIGURE 18–2
The Images of Three
Brewing Companies
as Measured by
a Semantic Differential

SOURCE: William A. Mindak, "Fitting the Semantic Differential to the Marketing Problem," *Journal of Marketing,* April 1961, pp. 28–33.

of the semantic differential suggest that images are measurable along three basic factors:

1. Evaluation (the good-bad qualities of the image)
2. Potency (strong-weak qualities)
3. Activity (active-passive qualities)

The various image attributes in Figure 18–2 all reflect either evaluation ("reliable, unreliable"), potency ("large company, small company"), or activity ("growing fast, not growing"). The image researcher simply has to make sure that enough scales have been developed to reflect these basic factors. Normally, the new instrument is tested on a small sample of people so that it can be refined before using it on a larger group.

Respondents are asked to place a mark on each scale according to their impression of the degree to which the object possesses that attribute. The image researcher then averages the responses on each scale and represents this average by a point. The points of the various scales are connected vertically, forming an image profile of the object. In Figure 18–2, company X has the best standing on each image attribute.[10] That is not always the case. More often, each company

[10] When administering the instrument, all of the favorable adjectives should not be on the same side, lest the respondents answer carelessly on the basis of a halo effect.

473

excels on certain attributes and lags on others. Even here, company X has some communication work to do in not being sufficiently "national" or "really modern." But even before concluding this, company X should ascertain where consumers see the ideal company (not shown) by asking them how "national" and how "modern" they would expect the ideal company to be.

To gain additional value from the data, the image profile should be recalculated for major groups in the market. For example, people in various parts of the country may hold different images of the same company. This would make a difference in establishing communications objectives for each group. Even within a given group, the image researcher should calculate the variance as well as the mean on each image attribute. We can imagine two extremes. The first is where there is high *image consistency,* in that most of the respondents see the object in approximately the same way. The way may or may not please the company, but nevertheless it is consistent. The other is where there is high *image diffusedness,* in that the respondents vary considerably in how they see the object. The company should not necessarily be disturbed by image diffusedness, and in fact, it may have deliberately cultivated some image ambiguity. This is essentially what politicians do who are running for office. They try to attain different images among diverse groups. Our main point is that the communicator will have to start with the existing images in the marketplace in determining the communication objectives.

Audience cognitive processing The communicator should also probe how the particular target audience processes incoming information. For example, people differ in cognitive complexity as a result of their native intelligence and education. A highly educated audience will be able to handle a larger and more complex set of symbols than will a group with a poor educational background. The communicator will want to know the tendencies of the target audience toward selective perception, distortion, and recall because this will affect the persuasive effectiveness of the message.

Of particular interest is the degree to which various audience groups are persuasible. Communicators have been looking for audience traits that correlate with persuasibility. For example, intelligence is widely thought to be negatively correlated with persuasibility, but the evidence is inconclusive. Women have been found to be more persuasible than men, but men who feel socially inadequate also show this trait.[11] Persons who accept external standards to guide their behavior and who have a weak self-concept appear to be more persuasible. Persons who are low in self-confidence are also thought to be more persuasible. However, research by Cox and Bauer and later by Bell showed a curvilinear relation between self-confidence and persuasibility, with those moderate in self-confidence being the most persuasible.[12] In general, the communicator should consider this research, look for audience traits that correlate with differential persuasibility, and use them to guide the message and media development.

[11] I. L. Janis and P. B. Field, "Sex Differences and Personality Factors Related to Personality," in *Personality and Persuasibility,* ed. C. Hovland and I. Janis (New Haven: Yale University Press, 1958), pp. 55–68.

[12] Donald F. Cox and Raymond A. Bauer, "Self-confidence and Persuasibility in Women," *Public Opinion Quarterly,* fall 1964, pp. 453–66; and Gerald D. Bell, February 1967, pp. 46–53. However, see the attempted refutation by Abe Shuchman and Michael Perry, "Self-confidence and Persuasibility in Marketing: A Reappraisal." *Journal of Marketing Research,* May 1969, pp. 146–54.

What Response Should Be Sought?

The next task of the marketing communicator is to define the target response it seeks. The ultimate response, of course, is purchase behavior. But purchase behavior does not occur *in vacuo*. In most cases, the consumer goes through a series of stages before deciding to purchase a product. It is critical that the marketing communicator know these buyer-readiness stages and assess where the target audience is at a particular time.

The marketer may be seeking a *cognitive, affective,* or *behavioral* response from the target audience. In other words, the purpose may be to put something into the consumer's mind, to change the consumer's attitude, or to get the consumer to undertake a specific action. Even here, there are different models of what each response consists of. Figure 18–3 shows four of the better-known *response hierarchy models.*

The AIDA model shows the buyer as passing through successive stages of awareness, interest, desire, and action. The "hierarchy-of-effects" model shows the buyer as passing through stages of awareness, knowledge, liking, preference, conviction, and purchase. The "innovation-adoption" model shows the buyer as passing through stages of awareness, interest, evaluation, trial, and adoption. The "communications" model shows the buyer as passing through stages of ex-

FIGURE 18–3
Response Hierarchy Models

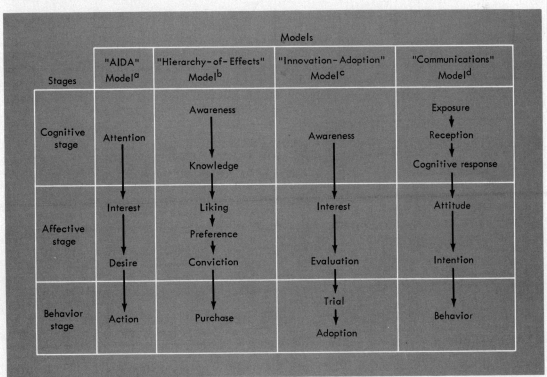

SOURCES: (a) E. K. Strong, *The Psychology of Selling* (New York: McGraw-Hill Book Company, 1925), p. 9; (b) Robert J. Lavidge and Gary A. Steiner, "A Model for Predictive Measurements of Advertising Effectiveness," *Journal of Marketing,* October 1961, p. 61; (c) Everett M. Rogers, *Diffusion of Innovations* (New York: Free Press, 1962), pp. 79–86; (d) Various sources.

posure, reception, cognitive response, attitude, intention, and behavior. Most of these differences are semantic.

The communicator normally assumes that buyers pass through these stages in succession on the way to purchase. However, there is some evidence that the stages can occur in different orders. Ray has distinguished three plausible response models.[13]

Learning response model   The learning response model is the hierarchy showing a person passing from *cognition to affect to behavior*. It is particularly applicable where the buyer feels *involved* and there are *clear differences among alternatives*. It applies to high-involvement goods such as automobiles, washing machines, and computers. It suggests that the marketer should plan a communication campaign to first build product awareness and knowledge, then interest and conviction, and finally motivation to purchase.

Dissonance-attribution response model   This model describes situations where buyers go through a *behavioral-affective-cognitive* sequence. They buy the product through the recommendation of a personal source, then their attitude changes through experience with the object, and then they learn about the product's attributes by paying attention to messages supporting that product. An example would be the purchase of insurance where a general agent recommends a particular policy and company, the customers buy it, then their attitude starts changing, and they watch for messages about this company. Their attitude changes after purchase to reduce dissonance, and their learning takes place as they attribute the purchase to their own volition. *Attribution (or self-perception) theory* says that when people are uncertain they develop their attitudes largely from making choices in actual situations rather than coming to these situations with strongly set attitudes.[14] This model applies primarily to situations where the audience is *involved,* but the alternatives are almost *indistinguishable.* For the marketer, it suggests that the main task is to induce trial or purchase through effective sales promotion incentives rather than relying on advertising to build up a favorable attitude. Attribution researchers have particularly investigated the effectiveness of the communication strategies of "foot-in-the-door" (making a small request as a prelude to a larger request) and "door-in-the-face" (making a large request that will probably be refused as a prelude to making a smaller request).[15] As for the role of mass media, according to this response model, its task is primarily to reduce dissonance *after* purchase and promote learning.

Low-involvement response model   Here the consumer is thought to pass from *cognition to behavior to attitude change*. Krugman proposed this sequence for products where there is *low involvement* or *minimal differences* between alter-

[13] Michael L. Ray, *Marketing Communication and the Hierarchy-of-Effects* (Cambridge, Mass.: Marketing Science Institute, November 1973).

[14] D. Bem, "Self-Perception Theory," in *Advances in Experimental Social Psychology*, ed. L. Berkowitz (New York: Academic Press, 1972).

[15] A. Cann, S. Sherman, and R. E. Elkes, "Effects of Initial Request Size and Timing of a Second Request on Compliance: The Foot in the Door and the Door in the Face," *Journal of Personality and Social Psychology*, 32, 1975, pp. 774–82.

natives (e.g., detergents, flour).[16] Low involvement means that there is a low "number of conscious 'bridging experiences,' connections, or personal references per minute that the viewer made between his own life and the stimulus." Television advertising for these products is a low-involvement learning experience where many messages penetrate the person's normal perceptual defenses (because of low involvement) and create gradual perceptual shifts, such as awareness, but not attitude change. In the purchase situation, the consumer recognizes the product and buys it, and a change in attitude occurs after use. According to this model, the function of marketing communications is to build product awareness and to support favorable attitudes after purchase.

We will now look more closely at the response variables that the communicator wants to influence. We will use the response variables listed in the "communications model" in Figure 18–3.

Exposure The first thing the communicator must do is to expose the message to the target audience. Exposure means that *the message physically appears in the target audience's immediate environment.* Thus a member of the target audience reads the newspaper or magazine, listens to the radio or television station or comes into contact with the person carrying the message.

To achieve exposure, the communicator must study the media habits of the target audience. Most media vehicles publish data, with varying degrees of accuracy, on the size and composition of their audiences. The communicator is guided by the media cost in relation to the size of the target audience delivered by a given vehicle. The most common measure of exposure efficiency is *cost-per-thousand exposures.* The communicator seeks to select media that minimize the cost-per-thousand exposures.

Reception Given an exposure, the next question is whether there is reception of the message. Did the message actually enter the receiver's consciousness? This breaks down into two issues: whether there is message *attention* and whether there is message *comprehension* by the receiver.

Any receiver who is exposed to a particular media vehicle has an *attention probability* somewhere between zero and one. Attention is a function of (1) the amount and strength of competing stimuli in the immediate environment, (2) the receiver's traits, (3) the receiver's media-using habits, and (4) the situational context. The receiver is bombarded by approximately fifteen hundred commercial messages every day. This gives rise to a condition known as *sensory overload.* The receiver copes with sensory overload by ignoring most of the messages in the environment. Receivers vary, of course, in the messages that they pay attention to, a phenomenon known as *selective attention.* A person in the market for a car will notice automobile advertising, whereas this advertising will be lost on other people. People also vary in their media-using habits. Thus some readers of *Newsweek* will read every ad of every issue (probability of attention = 1), other readers will read about half of the ads of every issue (probability of attention = ½), and still others will read about half of the ads in half of the issues (probability of attention = ¼). Finally, the situational context will influence attention, as when a person has an hour to read *Newsweek* versus only five minutes because of having to be somewhere.

[16] Herbert E. Krugman, "The Impact of Television Advertising: Learning without Involvement," *Public Opinion Quarterly,* fall 1965, pp. 349–56.

The challenge to the communicator is to design a message that wins attention in spite of the surrounding distractions. Schramm has suggested that the likelihood that a potential receiver will attend to a message is given by:[17]

$$\frac{\text{Likelihood}}{\text{of attention}} = \frac{(\text{Perceived reward strength}) - (\text{Perceived punishment strength})}{\text{Perceived expenditure of effort}}$$

This explains why ads with bold headlines promising something, such as "How to Make a Million," along with an arresting illustration and little copy have a high likelihood of grabbing attention. For very little effort, the reader has an opportunity to gain a great reward.

Communicators have developed several devices for attracting attention, including *novelty and contrast, arresting pictures or headlines, distinctive formats, message size and position,* and *color, shape, and movement.*[18]

Achieving attention is not enough. The communicator also wants the receiver to correctly *comprehend* the message. Comprehension is measured by asking people who have been exposed to a message to play it back or describe its intent. The more complex the message, the poorer the comprehension is likely to be. Some people will get the intended message, others will forget some important parts, and still others will completely misconstrue the major points. Loss of comprehension efficiency is due to audience tendencies toward *selective attention, recall,* and *distortion.* Receivers often add things to the message that are not there (*amplification*) and do not notice other things that *are* there (*leveling*). The communicator's task is to do the best job possible in achieving message simplicity, clarity, interest, and repetition to get the main points across.

Cognitive response   The communicator is really aiming to get the message accepted and assimilated into the receiver's long-term memory. Long-term memory is the repository for all information one has ever processed. In entering the receiver's long-term memory, the message has a chance of modifying the receiver's beliefs and attitudes. But first the message has to enter the receiver's short-term memory, which is conceived as a limited-capacity store that represents and processes incoming information. Whether the message actually passes from the receiver's short-term to long-term memory depends upon the amount and type of *message rehearsal* by the receiver. Rehearsal does not mean simple message repetition but rather the receiver's elaborating on the meaning of the information in a way that retrieves into short-term memory related thoughts in the receiver's long-term memory. If the receiver's initial attitude toward the object is positive and he or she rehearses support arguments, the message is likely to be accepted and have high recall. If the receiver's initial attitude is negative and the person rehearses counterarguments, the message is likely to be rejected but to stay in long-term memory. If there is no rehearsal of arguments but simply, "I've heard this before" or "I don't believe it," there is not likely to be high

---

[17] Wilbur Schramm and Donald F. Roberts, eds., *The Process and Effects of Mass Communication* (Urbana: University of Illinois Press, 1971), p. 32.

[18] For a summary of some findings on these attention-attracting devices, see James F. Engel, Roger D. Blackwell, and David T. Kollat, *Consumer Behavior,* 3rd ed. (Hinsdale, Ill.: Dryden Press, 1978), pp. 346–48.

recall or any attitude change. Generally speaking, much of what is called persuasion is self-persuasion.[19]

Attitude To the extent that the acceptance of a message alters the beliefs about the object or their relative weights, the receiver's attitude toward the object will be altered. This supposition is based on Fishbein's model showing attitudes as a function of beliefs (see expectancy value model, p. 160). An effective message will predispose the consumer to view the object more favorably. Since we have discussed attitude elsewhere, we will not elaborate on it here.

Intention People who have a positive attitude toward an object will not necessarily buy it. A person must form an intention to buy. The person has to feel like the kind of person who buys this object and must see others whom he respects as approving of the purchase. Fishbein calls these *personal normative beliefs* and *social normative beliefs* and says that they must support the person's attitude toward the object for a buying intention to be formed.

What can the communicator do to increase the person's intention to buy the object? The communicator can develop messages that weaken objections, such as that the product costs too much, or that it does not fit the buyer's personality, or that friends will look askance. Furthermore, the communicator can try to create a sense of urgency to buy the product now, such as implying that prices will go up or that the goods will go out of stock. Sales representatives use a number of devices to get a buyer to act, such as asking when the buyer will make a decision, or offering a discount or premium if the order is placed now.

Behavior We know that buyers do not always carry out their intentions. Their stated intentions are not the same as commitments; they are simply their own predictions as to what they might do. The main factors causing intentions not to be carried out are inertia or the occurrence of unpredictable events. The buyer might never quite make it to the auto showroom, dislike the salesperson, or lose a job. The communicator cannot do much to counteract extraneous events that undermine the buyer's purchase intention.

The communicator is interested not only in whether the consumer buys, but also in whether and how the consumer talks about the product to others. Part of the message strategy of the marketer is to provide information that will reduce postpurchase dissonance, refute inaccurate impressions, and provide a language for speaking favorably about the product.

What Message Should Be Developed?

Knowing the target audience and the desired response, the communicator can proceed to formulate an appropriate message. The communicator has to solve three problems: what to say (*message content*), how to say it logically (*message structure*), and how to say it symbolically (*message format*).

Message content The communicator has to figure out what to say to the target audience that will produce the desired response. This has been variously called the *appeal, theme, idea,* or *unique selling proposition.* It amounts to formulating

[19] A. Greenwald, "Cognitive Learning, Cognitive Response to Persuasion, and Attitude Change," in *Psychological Foundations of Attitudes,* ed. A. Greenwald, T. Brock, and T. Ostrom (New York: Academic Press, 1968).

some kind of benefit, motivator, identification, or reason why the audience should think or do something.

Ever since Aristotle, it has been traditional to distinguish between rational, emotional, and moral appeals. *Rational appeals* are appeals directed to the rational self-interest of the audience. They attempt to show that the product will yield the expected functional benefits. Examples would be messages demonstrating a product's quality, economy, value, or performance. It is widely believed that industrial buyers are most responsive to rational appeals. They are knowledgeable about the product class, trained to recognize value, and accountable to others for their choice. They have the time and incentive to compare different suppliers' offers and choose the best. Consumers, when they buy big-ticket items, are also thought to gather information and make careful comparisons of alternative offers. They will respond to quality, economy, performance, and other appeals.

Emotional appeals are appeals designed to stir up some negative or positive emotion that will motivate product interest or purchase. Communicators have worked with such negative emotional appeals as fear, guilt, and shame, especially in connection with getting people to start doing things they should (e.g., brushing their teeth, having an annual health checkup) or stop doing things they shouldn't (e.g., smoking, overdrinking of alcohol, drug abuse, overeating).

The use of fear appeals has been studied more than any other negative emotional appeal, not only in marketing communications but also in politics and child rearing. It used to be held that the message's effectiveness increased with the level of fear presented. The more fear building, the more tension, and the greater the drive to reduce the tension. Then the famous study of Janis and Feshbach, in which they tested the effectiveness of different fear levels in a dental-hygiene message directed to high school students, indicated that the strong fear appeal was less effective than a moderate one in producing adherence to a recommended dental hygiene program.[20] For a while, this finding became the standard, that neither extremely strong nor weak fear appeals were as effective as moderate ones. Ray and Wilke supported this position by hypothesizing two types of effects as fear increases:

> First, there are the facilitating effects that are most often overlooked in marketing. If fear can heighten drive, there is the possibility of greater attention and interest in the product and message than if no drive were aroused. . . . But fear also brings the important characteristic of inhibition into the picture. . . . If fear levels are too high, there is the possibility of defensive avoidance of the ad, denial of the threat, selective exposure or distortion of the ad's meaning, or a view of the recommendations as being inadequate to deal with so important a fear.[21]

Other researchers have found cases where high fear appeals appear maximally effective. This may mean that the buyers have different tolerances for fear, and the level of the fear message should be set separately for different segments. Further, if the fear message is to be maximally effective, the communication should

---

[20] Irving L. Janis and Seymour Feshbach, "Effects of Fear-Arousing Communications," *Journal of Abnormal and Social Psychology,* January 1953, pp. 78–92.

[21] Michael L. Ray and William L. Wilkie, "Fear: The Potential of an Appeal Neglected by Marketing," *Journal of Marketing,* January 1970, pp. 55–56.

promise to relieve in a believable and efficient way the fear it arouses; otherwise the buyers will ignore or minimize the threat.[22]

What about the effectiveness of positive emotional appeals, such as love, humor, pride, and joy? For example, a recent campaign to encourage young people to attach their auto seat belts showed a young man asking his woman friend to put on her belt as a way of saying, "I love you." Motivation researchers have found that persons may more often undertake to do something out of love for others than out of fear of harm to themselves. Marketers have also successfully used messages communicating joy (e.g., some soft-drink ads) associated with using the product. As for humor, the evidence has not established that a humorous message is necessarily more effective than a straight version of the same message.[23] On the positive side, humorous messages probably attract more attention and create more liking and belief in the source; but humor may also detract from comprehension. David Ogilvy, head of a major advertising agency, believes that humor is overused: "People are amused by clowns—they don't buy from them. . . . So many people in advertising are compulsive entertainers who seek applause rather than sales."

Moral appeals are appeals to the receiver's sense of what is right and proper to do. They are often used in messages exhorting people to support high-consensus social causes such as a cleaner environment, better race relations, equal rights for women, and aiding the disadvantaged. An example is the March of Dimes appeal: "God made you whole. Give to help those He didn't." They are less often used in connection with mundane products. This society is not highly responsive to moral appeals as such, although in many societies moral appeals are highly effective.

Message structure   The persuasive effect of a communication is affected not only by its content but also by the manner in which it is structured. Research carried on many years ago by Hovland and his associates at Yale shed much light on the major issues in message structure, namely, conclusion drawing, one- versus two-sided arguments, and order of presentation.

Conclusion drawing raises the question of whether the communicator should draw a definite conclusion for the audience or leave it to them. In a laboratory-type experiment, Hovland and Mandell found that more than twice as many persons changed in the direction advocated when the conclusion was stated than when they were left to form their own conclusions.[24] However, other studies produced conflicting results, and it appears that some situations are unfavorable to conclusion drawing:

1. If the communicator is seen as untrustworthy, the audience may resent the attempt to influence them.

---

[22] See Carl I. Hovland, Irving L. Janis, and Harold H. Kelley, *Communication and Persuasion* (New Haven: Yale University Press, 1953), pp. 87–88.

[23] See Brian Sternthal and C. Samuel Craig, "Humor in Advertising," *Journal of Marketing*, October 1973, pp. 12–18.

[24] Carl I. Hovland and Wallace Mandell, "An Experimental Comparison of Conclusion-Drawing by the Communication and by the Audience," *Journal of Abnormal and Social Psychology*, July 1952, pp. 581–88.

2. If the issue is simple, or the audience is intelligent, the audience may be annoyed at the attempt to explain the obvious.

3. If the issue is highly personal, the audience may resent the communicator's interference.

Sometimes drawing too explicit a conclusion, especially in the area of new products, can overly limit the product's acceptance. If the Mustang people had hammered away at the point that the car was for young people, this strong definition might have ruled out the many other age groups who were attracted to it. Some *stimulus ambiguity* can play a definite role in leading to a broader market definition and more spontaneous uses of new products. It permits more people to read their own meaning into the product. Conclusion drawing seems better suited for complex or specialized products where a single and clear use is intended.

One- or two-sided arguments raise the question of whether the communicator should only praise the product or also mention or anticipate some of its shortcomings. Intuitively, it would appear that the best effect is gained by a one-sided presentation: this is the predominant approach in sales presentations, political contests, and child rearing. Yet the answer is not so clear-cut. It depends on such things as the initial position of the audience, the audience's level of education, and the audience's exposure to subsequent communication.[25] (1) *One-sided messages tend to work best with audiences that are initially favorably predisposed to the communicator's position, whereas two-sided arguments tend to work best with audiences who are opposed.* A seller of a new brand whose other products are well accepted might think of favorably mentioning the existing products and then going on to praise his new product. (2) *Two-sided messages tend to be more effective with better-educated audiences.* A salesperson dealing with engineers might not pretend his or her product has it all over competing products but mention more factually where it excels and where it lags. (3) *Two-sided messages tend to be more effective with audiences who are likely to be exposed to counterpropaganda.* By mentioning a minor shortcoming in the product, a salesperson takes the edge off this mention when it comes from a competitor, much as a small discomforting inoculation now prevents a greater sickness later. But he or she must be careful to inoculate only enough negative vaccine to make the buyer resistant to counterpropaganda, not to his or her own product. The success of some products that emphasize minor limitations, such as Benson & Hedges, Volkswagen, and Avis, derives from a two-sided message strategy.

Order of presentation raises the question of whether a communicator should present his or her strongest arguments first or last. In the case of a one-sided message, presenting the strongest argument first has the advantage of establishing attention and interest. This may be especially important in newspapers and other media where the audience does not attend to all of the message. However, it means an anticlimactic presentation. If the audience is captive, as in a sales presentation or conference, then a climactic presentation may be more effective. Studies have yielded both findings, and we can say only that the strongest arguments do *not* belong in the middle of the message. In the case of a two-sided message, the issue is whether to present the positive argument

---

[25] See C. I. Hovland, A. A. Lumsdaine, and F. D. Sheffield, *Experiments on Mass Communication*, vol. III (Princeton, N.J.: Princeton University Press, 1948), chap. 8.

first (primacy effect) or last (recency effect). If the audience is initially opposed, it would appear that the communicator would be smarter to start with the other side's argument. This will tend to disarm the audience and allow him to conclude with his strongest argument. It does not appear that either the primacy or the recency effect dominates in all or most situations, and more research is needed into the underlying processes.

Message format   The remaining task in message development is to choose the most effective symbols to implement the message content and structure strategy. If the message is to be carried in a print ad, the communicator has to develop the format elements of headline, copy, illustration, and color. A good message strategy can be ruined by a poor message format. If the message is to be carried over radio, the communicator has to choose words, voice qualities (speech rate, rhythm, pitch, articulation) and vocalizations (pauses, sighs, yawns). The sound of an announcer promoting used automobiles has to be different from the sound of an announcer advertising a soft, comfortable bed mattress. If the message is to be carried over television or in person, then all of these elements plus body language (nonverbal clues) have to be planned. Thus politicians have to pay as much attention to their facial expressions, gestures, dress, posture, and hair style as to what they are saying. Finally, if the message is to be carried by a product and its packaging, the message designer will have to pay attention to texture, scent, noise, color, size, and shape. For example, it is well known that color plays an important communication role in food preference. When housewives sampled four cups of coffee next to brown, blue, red, and yellow containers (all the coffee was identical, although this was unknown to the housewives), 75 percent felt the coffee next to the brown container tasted too strong; nearly 85 percent judged the coffee next to the red can to be the richest; nearly everyone felt the coffee next to the blue can was mild and next to the yellow can was weak.

What Media Should Be Used?

Knowing the target audience, desired response, and message, the communicator can now turn to the selection of efficient media, that is, channels of communication or influence. Channels of communication are of two broad types, *personal* and *nonpersonal.*

Personal influence channels are means of direct contact with target individuals or groups. Three types can be distinguished. *Advocate channels* consist of company representatives in personal contact with the buyers, trying to influence them. *Expert channels* consist of independent persons (consultants, authorities) exercising an influence on the buyers through their expertise. *Social channels* consist of the buyers' associates, neighbors, friends, or family who may exercise an influence on the buyers. This last channel is also known as *word-of-mouth influence,* and it may be the strongest of the three personal channels, especially in the consumer-products area.

Nonpersonal influence channels are media that carry influence without involving direct contact. Three types of nonpersonal media can be distinguished. *Mass and selective media* consist of newspapers, magazines, radio, television, and billboards that people might buy or perceive. Mass media are aimed at large, often undifferentiated audiences; selective media are aimed at specialized audiences. *Atmospheres* are environments that are designed to create or reinforce the buyer's leanings toward purchase or consumption of the product. Thus dentists, lawyers, and boutique stores each design atmospheres that communicate confidence and other things that might be valued by the clients.[26] *Events* are occurrences that are designed to communicate particular messages to target audiences. Modern organizations, through their public relations department, arrange events that they hope will be newsworthy enough to be picked up and amplified by the news media.

We shall now look more closely at the major channels of influence.

Person-to-person communication   There has been much discussion of the relative effectiveness of personal versus nonpersonal influence in changing attitudes and behavior. Most observers believe that personal influence is generally the more potent of the two, especially in two cases:

1. *Where the product is expensive, risky, or purchased infrequently.* In such cases, buyers are likely to be high information seekers. They will probably go beyond mass-media information and seek out the product experiences and opinions of knowledgeable and trusted sources.
2. *Where the product has a significantly social, as opposed to private, character.* Such products as automobiles, clothing, and even beer and cigarettes have significant brand differentiation that implies something about the status or taste of the users. Here users are likely to choose brands acceptable to their groups.

This should normally incline marketers to favor personal influence channels over mass media. Unfortunately, marketers have limited control over personal influence channels. They cannot hire neighbors and friends to speak favorably about their products. Ironically what little control they have comes through the mass media! According to Klapper: "Personal influence may be more effective than persuasive mass communication, but at present mass communications seems the most effective means of stimulating personal influence."[27]

Thus the relationship and relative influence of personal influence and mass communication is more complicated than it at first appears. Many observers hold that mass communications affect personal attitudes and behavior through a *two-step flow-of-communication process.* "Ideas often flow from radio and print to opinion leaders and from these to the less active sections of the population."[28]

If true, this hypothesis has several significant implications. First it says that mass media's influence on mass opinion is not as direct, powerful, and automatic as supposed. It is mediated by *opinion leaders,* persons who are members of primary groups and whose opinions tend to be sought out in one or more areas. Opinion leaders are more exposed to mass media than the people they influence. They are the carriers of the messages to people who are less exposed to media, thus extending the influence of the mass media; or they may carry altered or no messages, thus acting as *gatekeepers.*

[26] See Philip Kotler, "Atmospherics as a Marketing Tool," *Journal of Retailing,* winter 1973–74, pp. 48–64.

[27] Joseph T. Klapper, *The Effects of Mass Communication* (New York: Free Press, 1960), p. 72.

[28] P. F. Lazarsfeld, B. Berelson, and H. Gaudet, *The People's Choice,* 2nd ed. (New York: Columbia University Press, 1948), p. 151.

Second, the hypothesis challenges the notion that persons are influenced in their consumption styles primarily from a "trickle-down" effect from the higher-status classes. Since people primarily interact with others in their own social class, they pick up their fashion and other ideas in this way—from people like themselves who are opinion leaders.

A third implication is that the mass communicator may accomplish message dissemination more efficiently by using a lower advertising budget and directing it specifically at opinion leaders, letting them carry the message to others. Thus a pharmaceutical firm may direct new-drug promotion to influential doctors. In many markets, however, opinion leaders and the people whom they influence are very much alike. It is hard to identify opinion leaders, aim communications specifically at them, and trust that they will say positive things about the product.

Although the two-step flow-of-communication hypothesis opened up some important new understandings about the flow of influence, it also has certain difficulties as a theory, and it could be misleading if used literally. The following qualifications must be made:

1. Opinion leadership is not a dichotomous trait. It is a matter of degree. All group members may have some opinion leadership in certain areas of consumption.
2. Opinion followers do not get their information only from opinion leaders. They too are in touch with mass media, although a little less so.
3. An effective mass-media strategy might be to aim messages at everyone and stimulate *opinion seeking;* this is a useful way to use opinion leaders.[29]

More recently, communications researchers have been moving toward a social structure view of interpersonal communication.[30] They see society as made up of *cliques,* that is, social subsystems whose members interact with each other relatively more frequently than with other members of the social system. The members of the cliques are highly similar, thus constituting an "interlocking network." Their similarity and close attraction facilitate effective communication but also act as barriers to new ideas entering the network. The challenge is to create more system openness whereby cliques exchange more information with each other and the larger environment. This is accomplished by persons who play roles as liaisons and bridges. A *liaison* is a person who interpersonally connects two or more cliques without belonging to either clique. A *bridge* is a person who is a member of one clique and who has a link to a person who is a member of another clique. Word-of-mouth communications flow most readily within cliques, and the problem is one of facilitating a communication flow between cliques.

Companies can take some steps to stimulate personal influence channels to work on their behalf, even if their actual control is somewhat limited. Among the things they can do are:

[29] For further discussion, see Elihu Katz, "The Two-Step Flow of Communication," *Public Opinion Quarterly,* spring 1957, pp. 61–78; and Everett M. Rogers, *Modernization among Peasants: The Impact of Communication* (New York: Holt, Rinehart and Winston, 1969), p. 222.

[30] See Everett M. Rogers, "New Product Adoption and Diffusion," *The Journal of Consumer Research,* March 1976, pp. 290–301.

1. Observe whether certain individuals or companies seem to stand out as influentials in their groups and devote extra effort to them, either through personal attention, direct mail, or advertising.

2. Create opinion leaders out of certain persons, by supplying them with the product on attractive terms, or selecting them as company representatives.

3. Work through community influentials such as disc jockeys, class presidents, and presidents of women's organizations.

4. Let the advertising feature interpersonal discussion of products or testimonials by influentials as part of the content.

5. Develop advertising that is high in conversational value.

6. Choose salesmen who are of the same general social status as their prospects.[31]

Mass communication   Mass-communication channels tend to have a less insistent presence than personal communication channels, which means that audience members can more easily avoid or tune them out. Even during high-saturation campaigns, many members of the audience will not be reached. Three psychological processes, commonly referred to as factors of *perceptual defense,* operate to cut down the reach and impact of mass media. *Selective attention* means that a person notes only a small fraction of all the media vehicles and only a small fraction of their content. *Selective distortion* means that the person perceives the content differently than intended—because it is filtered through personal needs and beliefs. *Selective retention* means that the person remembers certain things better than others—again because of the personal needs and beliefs.

Thus the communicator's ability to reach and persuade a target audience is highly constrained. The communicator's best course of action is to identify the major channels of influence that reach the target audience: groups they are in touch with, newspapers and magazines they read, people they respect. These are then rated according to the influence they have on members of the target audience and the costs of trying to activate them to carry the message. For each communication channel, a benefit-cost analysis is made. The communicator then develops a media mix that optimizes message distribution and impact for a given budget or minimizes the message cost of achieving a given level of message distribution and impact. We shall say more about media selection in chapter 19, pages 508–16.

What Source Attributes Should Accompany the Message?

Communicators influence their audience through their choice of message and media and through how they are perceived by the audience. The latter is called the *source effect.*

Source credibility   Marketers have known for years that messages delivered by highly credible sources will add to the persuasiveness of a message. Pharmaceutical companies will quote doctors' opinions to testify to their products' benefits because doctors have high credibility. Antidrug crusaders will use former drug addicts to warn high school students against drugs because exaddicts have higher credibility than teachers. Other marketers will hire well-known personalities, such as newscasters or athletes, to carry their messages.

But what factors underlie source credibility? The three factors most often

---

[31] These and other points are discussed in Thomas S. Robertson, *Innovative Behavior and Communication* (New York: Holt, Rinehart and Winston, 1971), chap. 9.

identified are expertise, trustworthiness, and likability.[32] *Expertise* is the degree to which the communicator is perceived to possess the necessary authority for what is being claimed. Doctors, scientists, and professors rank high on expertise where their advocacy pertains to their field of specialization. *Trustworthiness* is related to how objective and honest the source is perceived to be. Friends are perceived to be more trustworthy than strangers or salespeople. *Likability* is related to how attractive the source is to the audience. Qualities such as candor, humor, and naturalness tend to make a source more likable.

The most highly credible source, then, would be a person who scored high on all three dimensions. If such a message carrier could not be found, it would be helpful to know the relative influence of expertness, trustworthiness, and likability on message acceptance. This will of course vary for different products and situations.

Source incongruity   If a person has a positive attitude toward a source and a message—or a negative attitude toward both—a state of congruity is said to exist. But what happens if the person holds one attitude toward the source and the opposite toward the message? Suppose, for example, a homemaker hears a celebrity whom she likes praise a brand that she dislikes. Osgood and Tannenbaum posit that *attitude change will take place in the direction of increasing the amount of congruity between the two evaluations.*[33] In this example, the homemaker will end up respecting the celebrity somewhat less and respecting the brand somewhat more. If on further occasions she encounters the same celebrity praising other negatively valued brands, she will eventually develop a negative evaluation of the celebrity and maintain her negative attitudes toward the brands. The principle of congruity says that communicators can use their own good image to reduce some negative feelings toward a brand, but in the process may lose some of their trusted standing, especially if they do that often.

What Feedback Should Be Collected?   After the messages have been developed and distributed, the communicator must research the effects that these messages have on the target audience. This generally involves contacting a sample of members of the target audience and asking them whether they recognize or recall seeing or hearing the message, how many times, what points they recall, how they felt about the message, and their previous and current attitudes toward the product and company. Ultimately, the communicator would like to collect behavioral measures of audience response, such as how many people were moved to buy the product or to talk about it to others. Many companies settle for low-level measures of communications effectiveness, such as recall scores, when in fact the correlation of these measures with actual behavior may be very weak or even negative. If people counterargue with specific message content, they will recall counterarguments, associate them with message arguments, and exhibit good recall—but reject the message. Companies tend to spend comparatively little money researching what they are accomplishing with their communications, and yet careful monitoring of the results is at the heart of improving the impact of their communications.

[32] Herbert C. Kelman and Carl I. Hovland, " 'Reinstatement' of the Communicator in Delayed Measurement of Opinion Change," *Journal of Abnormal and Social Psychology,* 48 (1953), 327–35.

[33] C. E. Osgood and P. H. Tannenbaum, "The Principle of Congruity in the Prediction of Attitude Change," *Psychological Review,* 62 (1955), 42–55.

Having examined how the process of communications works and the various factors that influence communications effectiveness, we can appreciate the challenging task facing management. Management must make three major decisions in the communications arena:

1. What are the company's major communications objectives?
2. What total communications budget is necessary to accomplish these objectives?
3. How should the total communications budget be divided among the major communications tools?

Communications Objectives

Communications planning requires that the company has already developed its strategic management and marketing thrust, as discussed in chapter 4. It knows the business that it is in, the product/markets and market segments that it wants to reach, the product positions that it is aiming for, the resources and strengths that it has, and the basic marketing mix that it will use. It has analyzed the target markets with respect to awareness, knowledge, attitude, and buying behavior toward the company's and the competitors' products.

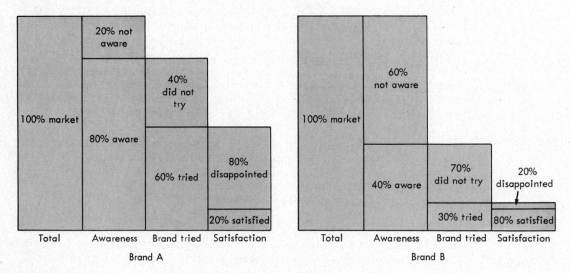

FIGURE 18–4
Current Consumer States for Two Brands

Communications objectives can be derived from analyzing how the target market is currently distributed over various states of readiness to buy the product. Consider a company that is preparing to set marketing communication objectives for two of its brands, A and B. For each brand the company has conducted marketing research to ascertain how many persons are in the market and the percentage distribution of these persons in three classes: awareness, brand trial, and satisfaction. The results are shown in Figure 18–4. As for brand A, 80 percent of the total market is aware of the brand, 60 percent have tried it and 20 percent of those who tried it are satisfied.[34] On the other hand, only 40 percent of the total market are aware of brand B, only 30 percent have tried it, and 80 percent of those who have tried it are satisfied. Clearly, these two profiles have very different implications for advertising objectives and strategy. The market is highly aware of brand A, but a substantial portion of those who have tried it are disappointed. This indicates that the advertising exposure schedule and creative message are effective in creating awareness but the product fails to live up to the claims. Brand B has the opposite problem. The advertising has produced only 40 percent awareness, and only 12 percent of the market have tried the product. But of those who have tried brand B, satisfaction runs in the order of 80 percent. In this case the entire advertising program, including the media, the message, and the level of expenditure may be much too weak to take advantage of the satisfaction-generating power of the brand.

Ottesen has suggested an alternative device called a *market map* for determining communication objectives (see Figure 18–5).[35] The horizontal dimension shows the current percentage of the market that has knowledge of the brand. This percentage increases through the life cycle of the brand, and in the illustration stands at 90 percent, indicating a mature brand. The vertical dimension shows the percentage of the market that has tried the brand. In this case, 80 percent of those who know the brand have tried it, another indication that the brand has been around for a while. There is a further breakdown of the knowers-triers into those who prefer (25 percent), are indifferent (50 percent), and have

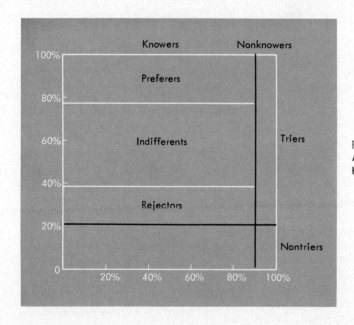

FIGURE 18–5
A Market Map Showing Percentage of Brand Knowers and Triers

[34] For a system for measuring these relationships, see John C. Maloney, "Attitude Measurement and Formation," a paper presented at the American Marketing Association Test Market Design and Measurement Workshop, Chicago, April 21, 1966.

[35] Otto Ottesen, "The Response Function," in *Current Theories in Scandinavian Mass Communications Research*, ed. Mie Berg (Grenaa, Denmark: G.M.T., 1977).

rejected (25 percent) the brand. We can imagine (not shown) a similar break-down of knower-nontriers into those who have a positive, indifferent, and nega-tive attitude toward the brand.

The task is to set communications objectives for this brand. Since 90 per-cent of the target market already know the brand, it would not make sense to devote a large effort to building awareness in the remaining 10 percent. Ninety percent is a fairly high awareness level in the population. The 10 percent who do not know this brand consist of many persons who are not in the mainstream, who are unaware of most things, and who don't have much income. It gets in-creasingly expensive to reach these people and usually is not worth it.

What about using communications to get more knower-nontriers to try the product? This is a worthy objective and can be best accomplished through sales promotion (free samples, cents-off coupons, and so on) rather than through addi-tional advertising or personal selling. Since 25 percent of the current triers pre-fer the brand, we cannot expect that more than 25 percent of the new triers will go for the brand. If so, the communicator should calculate whether achieving this number of new-trier preferers would be worth the cost of the contemplated sales promotion campaign.

Another possible communications objective is to try to increase the pro-portion of triers who prefer this brand to other brands. This is a difficult task since consumer attitude is largely a function of how the consumer experiences the value of the offer—e.g., performance and price rather than the commu-nications appeal. If the company wants to increase preference, that is better ac-complished through product improvement and lower prices.

Looking at the three trier attitude groups, the following conclusions can be drawn. Communication to those who already prefer the brand is usually not very productive unless there is high consumer forgetfulness or a high level of competitors' expenditure aimed at preferers. Communication directed to the re-jectors is probably wasted because the rejectors are not likely to pay attention to the advertising and probably would not re-try the brand. Communication di-rected to the indifferents will probably be effective in attracting a proportion of their purchases, especially if the advertising has some point to make to this audience.

The main conclusion is that the communications objectives depend very much on the state of the market. When a brand is new, there are few knowers and triers, and communication can be very effective in increasing their number. When the brand is in the mature stage of its life cycle, it makes sense to try to convert nontriers into triers through sales promotion and to fight for a normal share of the indifferent triers; it makes less sense to try to increase the percent-age of knowers, or reinforce preferers, or try to get rejectors to re-try the brand.

The Total Communications Budget

The total communications budget should be set at the level necessary to accom-plish the communications objectives. The budget can be established by using "objectives-and-tasks" thinking; that is, deciding on the tasks that have to be performed to accomplish the communication objectives and then estimating their costs. Here is an example:

1. We want to convince 100,000 people to try our brand.
2. This means getting our message into the attention set of 1,000,000 people since only 1 in 10 will try the product after hearing about it.

3. We will need 8,000,000 exposures because only 1 in 8 exposures gains attention.
4. The average cost-per-thousand exposures to the type of audience we want is $6. Therefore we can buy 8,000,000 exposures for a total budget of around $48,000 (= $6 × 8,000,000/1,000).

In this way, management is able to estimate a total budget to accomplish a specific communication task.

The Communications Mix

Most companies set their total communications budget first and then divide it among the alternative communications tools. The most striking fact about the various communications tools is that they can be interchanged with each other and with other marketing mix elements. It is possible to achieve a given sales level by increasing advertising expenditures, personal selling, or sales promotion. It is also possible to achieve the same sales level by product improvement, lower prices, or additional customer services. This substitutability explains why marketing departments are increasingly trying to achieve administrative coordination over all of the tools of communications and marketing.

In allocating the communications budget to the various tools, companies should pay attention to the following four factors: (1) the type of product—consumer versus industrial, (2) the communications task to be accomplished, (3) the stage of the product life cycle, and (4) the economic outlook.

Type of product—consumer versus industrial Historically, there has been a considerable difference in the communication mixes used by consumer and industrial marketers. The mix differences are illustrated in Figure 18–6A. Advertising is widely felt to be the most important promotool in consumer marketing, and personal selling the most important promotool in industrial marketing. Sales promotion is considered of equal, though smaller, importance in both markets. And publicity is considered to have even smaller, but equal, importance in both markets.

FIGURE 18–6
Communications Mix as a Function of Type of Market and Buyer Readiness Stage

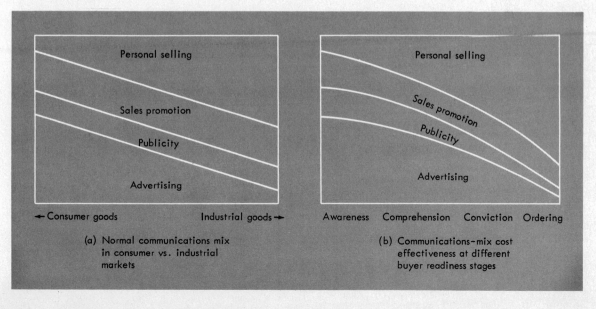

(a) Normal communications mix in consumer vs. industrial markets

(b) Communications-mix cost effectiveness at different buyer readiness stages

This view leads some marketers to act as if advertising is unimportant in industrial marketing and as if personal selling is unimportant in consumer marketing. Such conclusions are erroneous and can be refuted both in terms of common sense and by some recent studies.

While sales calls will normally have more impact than advertising in industrial marketing situations, especially where the product is complex, advertising can perform several useful functions:

1. *Awareness building.* Prospects who are not aware of the company or product may refuse to see the sales representative. Furthermore, the sales representative may have to use up a lot of time describing the company and its products.
2. *Comprehension building.* If the product embodies new features, some of the burden of explaining them can be effectively carried on by advertising.
3. *Efficient reminding.* If prospects know about the product but are not ready to buy, advertisements reminding them of the product would be much more economical than sales calls.
4. *Lead generation.* Advertisements carrying return coupons are an effective way to generate leads for sales representatives.
5. *Legitimation.* Sales representatives can use tear sheets of the company's advertisements to legitimatize their company and products.
6. *Reassurance.* Advertising can remind customers how to use the product and reassure them about their purchase.

A study by Theodore Levitt sought to determine the relative roles of the company's reputation (built mainly by advertising) and the company's sales presentation (personal selling) in producing industrial sales.[36] The experiment consisted of showing various groups of purchasing agents different filmed sales presentations of a new, but fictitious, technical product for use as an ingredient in making paint. The variables were the quality of the presentation and whether the sales person represented a well-known company, a less known but creditable company, or an unknown company. The reactions and ratings of the purchasing-agent groups were collected after the films and then again five weeks later. The findings were:

1. A company's generalized reputation (the source effect) has a positive influence on sales prospects in improving the chances of (a) getting a favorable first hearing and (b) getting an early adoption of the product. Therefore, to the extent that corporate advertising can build up the company's reputation (other factors also shape its reputation), the company's sales representatives will be helped.
2. Sales representatives from well-known companies have an edge in getting the sale, provided that their sales presentation is up to the expected standard. If, however, a sales representative from a less known company makes a highly effective sales presentation, that can overcome the disadvantage. To this extent, smaller companies may find it better to use their limited funds in selecting and training better sales representatives than in advertising.
3. Company reputations tend to have the most effect where the product is complex, the risk is high, and the purchasing agent is less professionally trained.

[36] Theodore Levitt, *Industrial Purchasing Behavior: A Study in Communications Effects* (Boston: Division of Research, Harvard Business School, 1965).

In general, the findings confirm the constructive role of both advertising and the source effect in the industrial marketing process.[37] Findings such as these have been developed by Cyril Freeman into a formal model for apportioning promotional funds between advertising and personal selling on the basis of the selling tasks that each performs more economically.[38]

In the same way that industrial marketers tend to play down the role of advertising, many consumer marketers tend to play down the role of the sales force. Many consumer companies use their inside sales force or an outside sales force mainly to collect weekly orders from dealers and to see that sufficient stock is on the shelf. The common feeling is that "salesmen put products on shelves and advertising takes them off." Yet even here, an effectively trained sales force can make three important contributions:

1. *Increased stock position.* Persuasive sales representatives can influence dealers to take more stock or devote more shelf space to the company's brand.
2. *Enthusiasm building.* Persuasive sales representatives can build dealer enthusiasm for a new product by dramatizing the planned advertising and sales promotion back-up.
3. *Missionary selling.* Sales representatives are crucial in any effort to sign up more dealers to carry the company's brands.

Within the same consumer industry, companies can be found that put quite different relative emphasis on the advertising, personal-selling mix. Nabisco and Kraftco rely very heavily on sales-force "push," while many of their competitors rely more heavily on advertising "pull." Revlon puts most of its promotional money into advertising, while Avon puts most of it into personal selling.

The communications task   The optimal communication mix also depends on the nature of the communications task or objective. Communications tools differ in their cost effectiveness in accomplishing different objectives. For example, although industrial marketers will generally spend far more on personal selling than on advertising, it would be inefficient to use the sales force for all communications purposes. Figure 18–6B shows the general findings that have come out of a number of studies.[39] Advertising, sales promotion, and publicity are the most cost-effective tools in building buyer awareness, more than "cold calls" from sales representatives. Advertising is highly cost effective in producing comprehension, with personal selling coming in second. Buyer conviction is influenced most by personal selling, followed by advertising. Finally, placing an order is predominantly a function of the sales call, with an assist from sales promotion.

[37] Also see John E. Morrill, "Industrial Advertising Pays Off," *Harvard Business Review*, March–April 1970, pp. 4ff.

[38] Cyril Freeman, "How to Evaluate Advertising's Contribution," *Harvard Business Review*, July–August 1962, pp. 137–48.

[39] "What IBM Found About Ways to Influence Selling," *Business Week*, December 5, 1959, pp. 69–70; and Harold C. Cash and William J. Crissy, "Comparison of Advertising and Selling," in vol. 12 of *The Psychology of Selling* (Flushing, N.Y.: Personnel Development Associates, 1965).

These findings have important practical implications. First, the company could effect promotional economies by cutting back on the involvement of salespeople in the early stages of the selling job so that they can concentrate on the vital phase: closing the sale. Second, when advertising is relied on to do more of the job, it should take different forms, some addressed to building product awareness and some to producing comprehension.

The stage of the product life cycle The effectiveness of communications expenditures varies at different stages of the product life cycle.

Promotion is particularly important in the introduction stage because the market is not aware of the product. This task is carried out best by advertising and sales promotion, both of which can be conducted on a low-cost-per-thousand-people-reached basis. Sales promotion, particularly trade and consumer deals, facilitates interest and trial of the new product.

In the growth stage, word-of-mouth processes begin to work hard for the new product and partially replace or supplement company promotion efforts. If the company wants to build its market share, it should continue to promote vigorously during the growth stage.

The maturity stage is marked by intensified promotional expenditures to meet competition and to advertise new-product uses and features. There is generally an increase in *dealing* effort relative to *advertising* effort.

In the decline stage, many companies reduce their promotion expenditures to improve their profit margins. Publicity is cut down to zero; salesmen give the product only minimal attention; and advertising is cut down to a reminder level. Dealing is probably the most exercised promotion tool at this stage.

The economic outlook Companies would do well to revise their communications mixes with shifts in the economic outlook. During inflation, for example, buyers become highly price conscious. They will be on the lookout for value. The enterprising company can do at least three things to respond: (1) it can increase its sales promotion relative to advertising, since people are looking for deals; (2) it can emphasize value and price in its communications; and (3) it can develop messages that help customers know how and where to buy intelligently.

Responsibility for Marketing Communications Planning Members of the marketing organization have strong and varied feelings about the proper proportions of the company's communications budget to spend on the different promotools. The sales manager finds it hard to understand how the company could get more value by spending $80,000 to buy a single exposure of a thirty-second television commercial than by hiring three or four additional sales representatives for a whole year. The public relations manager feels that the company can gain by transferring some of the advertising budget to publicity.

Historically, companies left these decisions to different people. No one was given the responsibility for thinking through the roles of the various promotional tools and coordinating the company's communication mix. Today companies are moving toward the concept of *integrated communications*. This concept calls for:

1. Developing a corporate position, such as marketing communications director, who has overall responsibility for the company's persuasive communications efforts
2. Working out a philosophy of the role and the extent to which the different promotools are to be used
3. Keeping track of all promotional investments by product, promotool, stage of product life cycle, and observed effect, as a basis for improving subsequent effective use of each tool
4. Coordinating the promotional activities and their timing when major campaigns take place

Integrated management of promotional activities promises more consistency in the company's *meaning* to its buyers and publics. It places a responsibility in someone's hand—where none existed before—to constructively unify and manage the company's image as it comes through the thousand activities the company carries on. It leads to the determination of a total marketing communications strategy aimed at showing how the company can help customers solve their problems.

SUMMARY

Marketing communications is one of the four major elements of the company's marketing mix. The instruments of marketing communications—advertising, personal selling, sales promotion, and publicity—have separate and overlapping capabilities, and their effective coordination requires careful definition of communications goals.

In preparing specific activities in marketing communications, the communicator has to understand the eight elements of any communication process: sender, receiver, encoding, decoding, message, media, response, and feedback. The communicator's first task is to identify the target audience, particularly to understand how they view the company and its product and how they process information. Next, the communicator has to establish the sought response, whether it is awareness, interest, desire, or action. Then a message must be constructed containing an effective content, structure, and format. Then media must be selected, for both person-to-person communication and mass communication. The message must be delivered by someone with good source credibility, particularly expertise, trustworthiness, and likability. Finally, the communicator must monitor how much of the market becomes aware and tries the product and is satisfied in the process.

The overall company planning of marketing communications requires establishing clear communications objectives, setting a communications budget that will achieve these objectives, and developing the most effective communications mix. In allocating the communications budget to different communications tools, the planner is guided by the type of product, the communications task, the stage of the product life cycle, and the economic outlook. Companies are increasingly coordinating the various departments that carry on communications work, in order to achieve a consistent and synergistic impact on their target markets.

1. Draw up a list of sales situations which can be aided by (a) atmospherics; (b) event management.

2. The dairy industry would like to interest teenagers in drinking more milk. Outline a nationwide promotion campaign using all the promotools and making use of the planning paradigm: audience, channels, message, and communicator.

3. An advertising agency is preparing a cake mix commercial. It is trying to choose between two copy versions. Version A allows the audience to share the entire product experience from the moment of purchase through the act of baking the cake and the family enthusiastically receiving it. Version B stops short of completing the process, hoping to involve the audience in imagining the rest. Which version do you think will be more effective and why?

4. A marketing research agency was asked to find out what consumers thought of the soft drink, Seven-Up. The agency found that most consumers regarded it as a wholesome drink. The company was pleased with this finding. Should they be?

5. The various mass media—newspapers, magazines, radio, television, and outdoor media—show striking differences in their capacity for dramatization, credibility, attention getting, and other valued aspects of communication. Describe the special characteristics of each media type.

6. Develop a set of thematic guidelines that laundry soap companies might follow in preparing soap ads aimed at upper-lower and lower-middle-class housewives in the 24–45 age bracket.

7. What types of consumer responses over time should be aimed for in communication strategies for the following products: legal services, frozen pizzas, veterinarian services, sewing machines, pianos, telephone answering services, hammers?

Advertising Decisions

19

If you think advertising doesn't pay—we understand there are twenty-five mountains in Colorado higher than Pike's Peak. Can you name one?
THE AMERICAN SALESMAN

Advertising is one of the four major tools companies use to direct persuasive communications to target buyers and publics. It consists of *nonpersonal forms of communication conducted through paid media under clear sponsorship.* This form of communication runs up a bill of over $33 billion a year in the United States. It is a tool by no means restricted to commercial firms. Advertising is used by the U.S. Army, museums, fund raisers, and various social-action organizations to bring messages about their causes and organizations to various target publics.

Within the commercial sector, the top 125 national advertisers account for as much as one-fifth of all national advertising. The five top spenders are Procter & Gamble ($460 million), General Motors ($312 million), General Foods ($300 million), Sears ($290 million), and K-Mart ($210 million). The highest absolute spenders are found in soaps and cleaners, drugs and cosmetics, autos, food, and tobacco. The highest relative advertising spenders (as a percentage of sales) are found in drugs and cosmetics (between 10 percent and 20 percent), gum and candy (12 percent), and soaps (6 to 12 percent).[1]

---

[1] For this information, see the special issue of *Advertising Age* on the one hundred leading national advertisers, August 28, 1978, esp. p. 29.

Purpose of Advertising

People have sought for years to define the purpose of advertising. In his *Madison Avenue, U.S.A.*, Martin Mayer sounded a skeptical note by saying: "Only the very brave or the very ignorant . . . can say exactly what advertising does in the marketplace." It is fairly clear, however, what advertising is *supposed* to do. In ultimate terms, advertising is undertaken to increase company sales and/or profits over what they otherwise would be. Advertising, however, is rarely able to create sales by itself. Whether the customer buys also depends upon the product, price, packaging, personal selling, services, financing, and other aspects of the marketing process.

More specifically, the purpose of advertising is to enhance potential buyers' responses to the organization and its offerings. It seeks to do this by providing information, by channelizing desires, and by supplying reasons for preferring a particular organization's offer.

What Are the Major Advertising Decisions?

This chapter will examine the following major decisions called for in the realm of advertising:

1. How much should be spent for overall company advertising? *(Money)*
2. What message should be used? *(Message)*
3. What media should be used? *(Media)*
4. How should the advertising be phased during the year? *(Motion)*
5. What are the best methods for knowing what the advertising is accomplishing? *(Measurement)*

SIZE OF THE ADVERTISING BUDGET

Common Methods for Setting the Advertising Budget

Each year the firm must decide how much to spend on advertising. Four of the more common methods are described below.[2]

"Affordable" method   Many companies set the advertising budget on the basis of what they think the company can afford. As explained by one advertising executive:

> Why it's simple. First I go upstairs to the controller and ask how much they can afford to give us this year. He says a million and a half. Later, the boss comes to me and asks how much we should spend, and I say "Oh, about a million and a half." Then we have an advertising appropriation.[3]

Setting budgets in this manner is tantamount to saying that the relationship between advertising expenditure and sales results is at best tenuous. If the company has enough funds, it should spend them on advertising as a form of insurance.

The basic weakness of the affordable approach is that it leads to a fluctuating advertising budget that makes it difficult to plan for long-range market development.

[2] See Joel Dean, *Managerial Economics* (Englewood Cliffs, N.J.: Prentice-Hall, 1951), pp. 363–75; and David L. Hurwood and James K. Brown, *Some Guidelines for Advertising Budgeting* (New York: Conference Board, 1972).

[3] Quoted in Daniel Seligman, "How Much for Advertising?" *Fortune*, December 1956, p. 123.

Percentage-of-sales method   Many companies set their advertising expenditures at a specified percentage of sales (either current or anticipated) or of the sales price. A railroad company executive said:

> We set our appropriation for each year on December 1 of the preceding year. On that date we add our passenger revenue for the next month, and then take 2 percent of the total for our advertising appropriation for the new year.[4]

Automobile companies typically budget a fixed percentage for advertising based on the planned price for each car, and oil companies tend to set the appropriation as some fraction of a cent for each gallon of gasoline sold under their own label.

A number of advantages are claimed for this method. First, the percentage-of-sales method means that advertising expenditures are likely to vary with what the company can "afford." This pleases the more financially minded members of top management, who feel that expenses of all types should bear a close relation to the movement of corporate sales over the business cycle. Second, this method encourages management to think in terms of the relationship between advertising cost, selling price, and profit per unit. Third, the method encourages competitive stability to the extent that competing firms spend approximately the same percentage of their sales on advertising.

In spite of these advantages, the percentage-of-sales method has little to justify it. It uses circular reasoning in viewing sales as the cause of advertising rather than as the result. It leads to an appropriation set by the availability of funds rather than by the opportunities. It discourages experimentation with countercyclical advertising or aggressive spending. The dependence of the advertising budget on year-to-year fluctuations in sales militates against the planning of long-range advertising programs. The method does not provide a logical basis for the choice of a specific percentage, except what has been done in the past, or what competitors are doing, or what the costs will be. Finally, it does not encourage the constructive development of advertising appropriations on a product-by-product and territory-by-territory basis but instead suggests that all allocations be made at the same percentage of sales.

Competitive-parity method   Some companies set their advertising budgets specifically to match competitors' outlays—that is, to maintain competitive parity. This thinking is illustrated by the executive who asked a trade source, "Do you have any figures that other companies in the builders' specialties field have used that would indicate what proportion of gross sales should be given over to advertising?"[5]

Two arguments are advanced for this method. One is that competitors' expenditures represent the collective wisdom of the industry. The other is that maintaining a competitive parity helps to prevent advertising wars.

Neither of these arguments is valid. There are no a priori grounds for believing that the competition is using more logical methods for determining outlays. Advertising reputations, resources, opportunities, and objectives are likely to differ so much among companies that their budgets are hardly a guide for an-

---

[4] Albert Wesley Frey, *How Many Dollars for Advertising?* (New York: Ronald Press Company, 1955), p. 65.

[5] *Ibid.*, p. 49.

other firm to follow. Furthermore, there is no evidence that appropriations based on the pursuit of competitive parity do in fact stabilize industry advertising expenditures.

Knowing what the competition is spending on advertising is undoubtedly useful information. But it is one thing to know this and another to follow it blindly.

Objective-and-task method The objective-and-task method calls upon advertisers to develop their budget by (1) defining their advertising objectives as specifically as possible, (2) determining the tasks that must be performed to achieve these objectives, and (3) estimating the costs of performing these tasks. The sum of these costs is the proposed advertising budget.

Advertising goals should be formulated as specifically as possible in order to guide the copy development, media selection, and results measurement. The stated goal, "to create brand preference," is much weaker than "to establish 30 percent preference for brand X among Y million housewives by next year." Colley listed as many as fifty-two specific communication goals, including:

Announce a special reason for "buying now" (price, premium, and so on).

Build familiarity and easy recognition of package or trademark.

Place advertiser in position to select preferred distributors and dealers.

Persuade prospect to visit a showroom, ask for a demonstration.

Build morale of company sales force.

Correct false impressions, misinformation and other obstacles to sales.[6]

The method has strong appeal and popularity among advertisers. Its major limitation is that it does not indicate how the objectives themselves should be chosen and whether they are worth the cost of attaining them.

Decision Models for Setting Advertising Budgets In recent years various researchers have proposed several decision models for setting the advertising budget. These models differ in the advertising situation to which they are addressed and the type and number of variables they include. We shall review four of the models here.

Sales response and decay models The earliest advertising-budgeting models attempted to measure the shape of the advertising sales response function. Given this function, the profit-maximizing advertising outlay can be determined. As for the shape itself, the evidence is mixed. Many analysts hold that the sales/advertising curve is S-shaped. This curve implies initial advertising economies of scale. According to Joel Dean:

Larger appropriations may make feasible the use of expert services and more economical media. More important than specialization usually are economies of repetition. Each advertising attack starts from ground that was taken in previous forays, and where no single onslaught can overcome the inertia of existing spending patterns, the hammering of repetition often overcomes skepticism by attrition.[7]

[6] See Russell H. Colley, ed., *Defining Advertising Goals* (New York: Association of National Advertisers, 1961); and H. D. Wolfe, J. K. Brown, and G. C. Thompson, *Measuring Advertising Results*, Studies in Business Policy, no. 102 (New York: Conference Board, 1962), pp. 62–68.

[7] Dean, *Managerial Economics,* p. 357.

Dean has also spelled out the reasons why diminishing returns to advertising can eventually be expected to set in:

> Presumably the most susceptible prospects are picked off first, and progressively stiffer resistance is encountered from layers of prospects who are more skeptical, more stodgy about their present spending patterns, or more attached to rival sellers. The rise may also be caused by progressive exhaustion of the most vulnerable geographical areas or the most efficient advertising media. Promotional channels that are ideally adapted to the scale and market of the firm are used first.[8]

Other studies of the advertising sales response function indicate that it is concave rather than S-shaped, which suggests that incremental advertising expenditures are increasingly less efficient. Simon, in a review of several studies, concluded that "there was no single piece of strong empirical support for the belief in *any* economies of scale in advertising, and . . . there was large evidence to the contrary."[9] From this he concluded:

> If diminishing returns rather than economies of scale are the case, then advertising expenditures should be dispersed rather than concentrated. That is, it would pay for a firm to: divide its advertising among several equally likely media buys rather than concentrate it in one; spread the advertising evenly over weeks and months, rather than concentrating in a few time periods; use two copy approaches if both are equally strong; disperse the advertising geographically (making allowance for variations in market potentials); use smaller-size ads; increase the number of brands marketed.[10]

One of the earliest and best models of the response of sales to advertising was developed by Vidale and Wolfe.[11] In their model, the change in the *rate of sales* at time *t* is a function of four factors: the *advertising budget*, the *sales response constant*, the *saturation level of sales*, and the *sales decay constant*. Their basic equation is

$$\frac{dS}{dt} = rA\,\frac{M - S}{M} - \lambda S \qquad (19\text{-}1)$$

where:

S = rate of sales at time t

$\dfrac{dS}{dt}$ = change in the rate of sales at time t $\left.\vphantom{\dfrac{dS}{dt}}\right\}$ *variables*

A = rate of advertising expenditure at time t

r = sales response constant (defined as the sales generated per advertising dollar when $S = 0$)

M = saturation level of sales $\qquad$ *parameters*

λ = sales decay constant (defined as the fraction of sales lost per time unit when $A = 0$)

[8] *Ibid.*, p. 358.

[9] Julian L. Simon, "New Evidence for No Effect of Scale in Advertising" *Journal of Advertising Research*, March 1969, pp. 38–41.

[10] Julian L. Simon, "Are There Economies of Scale in Advertising?" *Journal of Advertising Research*, June 1965, pp. 15–20.

[11] M. L. Vidale and H. B. Wolfe, "An Operations-Research Study of Sales Response to Advertising," *Operations Research*, June 1957, pp. 370–81.

The equation says that the change (increase) in the rate of sales will be higher, the higher the sales response constant, the higher the advertising expenditure, the higher the untapped sales potential, and the lower the decay constant. Suppose, for example, the sales response to advertising dollars is estimated at 4, current sales are $40,000, saturation-level sales are $100,000 and the company loses .1 of its sales per period if no advertising expenditure is made. In this case, by spending $10,000 in advertising, the company can hope to achieve an additional $20,000 of sales:

$$\frac{dS}{dt} = 4(10,000)\ \frac{100,000 - 40,000}{100,000} - .1(40,000) = \$20,000$$

If the profit margin on $20,000 is better than 50 percent, it pays to spend the $10,000 on advertising.

The Vidale-Wolfe model can be embedded in a long-run profit equation and used to estimate the profit consequences of alternative advertising-budgeting strategies. Its main significance is that it brings together and relates three useful concepts for determining the proper size of the advertising budget.

Some models of sales response to advertising go beyond the Vidale-Wolfe model in the number of factors they postulate. A notable example is Kuehn's model.[12] Here company sales are a function of the percentage of customers with brand loyalty and the rate of decay in this brand loyalty; the percentage of customers not committed to this firm or its main competitor; the size and rate of growth of the total market; the relative influence of product characteristics, price, advertising, and distribution as selling influences; the relative influence of the *interaction* of product characteristics and advertising as a selling influence; and the relative share and effectiveness of this company's advertising expenditure. Using this model to describe company sales for the case of two-firm competition, Kuehn derived an optimal formula for setting advertising expenditures.

Communication-stage models Communication-stage advertising models arrive at an advertising budget by noting its effects on several intermediate variables that link advertising expenditures to ultimate sales. Ule developed an example to show how a manufacturer of a brand new filter-tip cigarette, Sputniks (name fictitious), could establish the necessary advertising budget.[13] The steps are as follows:

1. *Establish the market-share goal.* The advertiser wants 8 percent of the market. There are 50 million cigarette smokers, which means the company wants to attract 4 million regular Sputnik smokers.

2. *Determine the percent of the market that should be reached by Sputnik advertising.* The advertiser hopes to reach 80 percent (40 million smokers) with the advertising campaign.

3. *Determine the percent of aware smokers that should be persuaded to try the*

---

[12] Alfred A. Kuehn, "A Model for Budgeting Advertising," in *Mathematical Models and Methods in Marketing,* ed. Frank M. Bass *et al.* (Homewood, Ill.: Richard D. Irwin, 1961), pp. 302–53.

[13] G. Maxwell Ule, "A Media Plan for 'Sputnik' Cigarettes," *How to Plan Media Strategy,* American Association of Advertising Agencies, 1957 Regional Conventions, pp. 41–52.

brand. The advertiser would be pleased if 25 percent of aware smokers, or 10 million smokers, tried Sputnik because it is estimated that 40 percent of all triers, or 4 million persons, would become loyal users. That is the market goal.

4. *Determine the number of advertising impressions per one percent trial rate.* The advertiser estimates that forty advertising impressions (exposures) for every one percent of the population would bring about a 25 percent trial rate.

5. *Determine the number of gross rating points that would have to be purchased.* A gross rating point is one exposure to one percent of the target population. Since the company wants to achieve forty exposures to 80 percent of the population, it will want to buy 3,200 gross rating points.

6. *Determine the necessary advertising budget on the basis of the average cost of buying a gross rating point.* To expose one percent of the target population to one impression costs an average of $3,277. Therefore 3,200 gross rating points would cost $10,486,400 (= $3,277 × 3,200) in the introductory year.

Ule's method is essentially an implementation of the objective-and-task method. It has the advantage of requiring management to spell out its assumptions about the relations between dollars spent, exposure levels, trial rates, and regular usage. Its major conceptual weakness is that the market-share goal is set arbitrarily without being derived from a profit-maximizing approach to sales.

Adaptive-control models Adaptive advertising-budgeting models make the assumption that the parameters of the advertising sales response function are not stable but change through time. If they were stable, it would pay the company to make a big effort to measure the functions as soon and as accurately as possible because the benefits in achieving optimization would extend far into the future. However, there is good reason to believe that the parameters are not stable because of continuously changing competitive activity, advertising copy, product design, and national economic activity. In this case it would not pay to invest heavily in learning the exact parameters of the sales response function in the current period. Suppose the parameters change slowly through time. Then the best research strategy would be to collect some new information each time about the current parameters and combine it with the old information to produce new estimated parameters for the sales response function on which the current outlay for advertising can be based.

The manner in which the periodic data can be collected and used to determine an optimal advertising expenditure has been described by Little.[14] Advertising expenditures should be set each period in such a way as to yield information about the current levels of the sales response parameters. Suppose the company has picked an advertising expenditure rate for the coming period on the basis of applying profit-maximization criteria to its most current information on the sales function. It then decides to spend this rate in all markets except a subset of $2n$ of them randomly drawn. In n of the test markets the company will spend a deliberately low amount of dollars, and in the other n it will spend a deliberately high amount of dollars. This experiment will yield information on the average sales created by the low, medium, and high rates of advertising, and this will provide the best estimate of the current sales response function. In turn,

---

[14] John D. C. Little, "A Model of Adaptive Control of Promotional Spending," *Operations Research*, November 1966, pp. 1075–97.

this estimate is used to determine the best promotional rate for the next period. If this procedure is carried out each period, actual advertising expenditures will track closely to the optimal advertising expenditures.

Competitive-share models The preceding models do not explicitly take competitors' expenditures into account. This omission is valid where there are many competitors, none of whom is large; or where it is difficult for companies to know what others are spending for advertising. In many situations, however, firms know what others are spending and try to maintain a competitive parity. In these situations a firm must take competitive reactions into account in determining its own advertising appropriation.

Under certain assumptions, the problem can be treated with some of the techniques of game theory. Friedman has developed some models to show how fixed advertising budgets should be allocated by two duopolists to different territories under the assumption that each is interested in taking maximum advantage of the other's mistakes.[15] He distinguishes between the case where resulting company sales are proportional to the company's share of advertising expenditures and the case where the company with 50-plus percent of the total advertising takes the whole market (as when a single customer is at stake).

MESSAGE DEVELOPMENT

Many studies of the effect of advertising expenditures on sales neglect the message factor. Some analysts rationalize this by arguing that all large advertising agencies are equally creative, and therefore differences in individual campaigns tend to "wash out." But it is precisely the differences in individual campaigns that advertisers want to note and exploit. The consequence of leaving out the creative factors is that a substantial part of the movement of market shares remains "unexplained."

One study claims to have overcome the neglect of the message factor.[16] A five-year study of sixty-seven different television campaigns led to the development of a multiple-regression formula that "explained" 73 percent of the fluctuations in market shares. What is most interesting is that one of the three independent variables was a measure of the effectiveness of the message. The study's major conclusion is that a campaign's quality is far more important than the number of dollars spent. Whether this is actually so, there is no doubt that differences in creative strategy are very important in advertising success.

Advertisers go through three stages to develop their message: message generation, evaluation and selection, and execution.

Message Generation Message generation is the activity of developing a number of alternative possible messages about the product. Many things can be said about any product. No ad should say more than a few things, and in fact, a case could be made that an ad, to gain distinctiveness, should emphasize one theme. This theme should

---

[15] Lawrence Friedman, "Game-Theory Models in the Allocation of Advertising Expenditures," *Operations Research*, September–October 1958), pp. 699–709.

[16] See "New Study Tells TV Advertisers How Advertising Builds Sales and Share of Market," *Printer's Ink*, May 8, 1964, pp. 27–38.

reinforce the product's positioning in the marketplace. The challenge is to develop a few major alternative messages that could be pretested to find the best one.

Creative people use different methods to generate possible advertising appeals. Many creative people proceed *inductively*. They talk to consumers, dealers, experts, and competitors to spot ideas. Consumers are by far the most important source of good ideas. Their feelings about the strengths and shortcomings of existing brands provide the most important clues to creative strategy. A leading hair-spray company, for example, carries out consumer research annually to determine consumer dissatisfaction with existing brands. If it turns out that consumers would like stronger holding power, the company would use this appeal, assuming that the company's brand promises good holding power or can be reformulated to meet this claim.

Today there is increasing interest in *deductive* frameworks for generating advertising appeals. Maloney proposed one possible framework.[17] He suggested that buyers may be expecting any of four types of reward from an offering: *rational, sensory, social,* or *ego satisfaction*. And they may visualize these rewards from *results-of-use experience, product-in-use experience,* or *incidental-to-use experience*. Crossing the four types of rewards with the three types of experience gives twelve different modes of buyer evaluation to be found concurrently in the marketplace. The advertiser can generate a theme for each of the twelve cells as possible messages for his product. For example, the appeal "gets clothes cleaner" is a rational reward promise following results-of-use experience; and the phrase "real gusto in a great light beer" is a sensory-reward promise connected with product-in-use experience.

Message Evaluation and Selection

The task of selecting the best message out of a large number of possibilities calls for the introduction of criteria for judging the communication potency of different messages. Twedt has suggested that the contending appeals be rated on three scales: *desirability, exclusiveness,* and *believability*.[18] He believes that the communication potency of an appeal is a function of a multiplicative relationship among the three named factors—multiplicative because if any of the three has a low rating, the appeal's communication potency will be greatly reduced. The appeal must first say something desirable or interesting about the product. That is not enough, however: many brands will be making the same claim. Therefore the statement must also say something exclusive or distinctive that does not apply to every brand in the product category. Finally, the statement must be believable or provable. By getting a sample of consumers to rate different product statements on the three scales of desirability, exclusiveness, and believability, these statements can be numerically rated for communication potency.

For example, the March of Dimes was searching for an advertising theme to raise money for its fight against birth defects.[19] A brainstorming session came

[17] John C. Maloney, "Marketing Decisions and Attitude Research," in *Effective Marketing Coordination,* ed. George L. Baker, Jr., (Chicago: American Marketing Association, 1961), pp. 595–618.

[18] Dik Warren Twedt, "How to Plan New Products, Improve Old Ones, and Create Better Advertising," *Journal of Marketing,* January 1969, pp. 53–57.

[19] See William A. Mindak and H. Malcolm Bybee, "Marketing's Application to Fund Raising," *Journal of Marketing,* July 1971, pp. 13–18.

up with more than twenty possible themes. A group of young married parents were asked to rate each theme for interest, distinctiveness, and believability, assigning up to 100 points for each. For example, the theme "500,000 unborn babies die each year from birth defects" scored 70, 60, and 80 on interest, distinctiveness, and believability, while the theme "your next baby could be born with a birth defect" scored 58, 50, and 70. The first theme dominates the second. If one theme does not dominate, then weights would be assigned to the three criteria to reflect their assumed importance.

Consumer ratings of ad appeals are not that reliable, however; they reflect opinion and not necessarily behavior. The advertiser should employ some pretest procedure to determine which final appeals are the strongest. For example, the Washington State Apple Commission was trying to decide which of two advertising themes for apples appealed more to housewives.[20] One theme stressed the various *uses* of apples; the other, the *healthful* qualities of apples. An experiment was carried out in seventy-two self-service food stores in six midwestern cities for sixteen weeks. An analysis of the final sales results revealed that the apple-use theme was significantly more effective in promoting sales than the health theme.

Message Execution

The impact of an advertisement depends not only upon what is said but also upon how it is said. In fact, message execution can be decisive for those products that are essentially the same as the competition, such as detergents, cigarettes, coffee, and beer. The advertiser has to put the message across in a way that will win attention and interest on the part of the target audience.

To guide the development of message execution, the advertiser usually prepares a *copy strategy statement* describing the objective, content, support, and tone of the desired ad. Here is a copy strategy statement for a Pillsbury product called 1869 Brand Biscuits:

The *objective* of the advertising is to convince biscuit users that now, for the first time, they can buy a canned biscuit that's as good as homemade—Pillsbury's 1869 Brand Biscuits.

The *content* consists of emphasizing the following product characteristics of the 1869 Brand Biscuits:
1. They look like homemade biscuits.
2. They have the same texture as homemade biscuits.
3. They taste like homemade biscuits.

Support for the "good as homemade" promise will be twofold:
1. 1869 Brand Biscuits are made from a special kind of flour (soft wheat flour) traditionally used to make homemade biscuits but never before used in making canned biscuits.
2. The use of traditional American biscuit recipes.

The *tone* of the advertising will be news announcement, yet tempered by a warm, reflective mood emanating from a look back at traditional American baking quality.

It is the task of the creative people in the advertising agency to find the *style, tone, words,* and *format factors* that make for effective message execution.

---

[20] See Peter L. Henderson, James F. Hind, and Sidney E. Brown, "Sales Effects of Two Campaign Themes," *Journal of Advertising Research*, December 1961, pp. 2–11.

Any message can be put across in different *execution styles,* such as:

1. *Slice-of-life.* This shows one or more persons using the product in a normal setting. A family might be shown at the dinner table expressing satisfaction with a new brand of biscuits.
2. *Life style.* This emphasizes how a product fits in with a life style. The Revlon ads of the Charlie fragrances show an adventuresome, rule-breaking young woman going after the things she wants in life and getting them.
3. *Fantasy.* This creates a fantasy about what might happen in connection with the use of the product. A woman sprays on a certain brand of perfume and suddenly becomes irresistible to every man she meets.
4. *Mood or image.* This builds an evocative mood or image around the product—beauty, love, or serenity. No claim is made about the product except through suggestion. Many cigarette ads, such as Salems and Newport, create moods.
5. *Musical.* This shows one or more persons or characters singing a song or jingle involving the product. Many cola ads have used this format.
6. *Personality symbol.* This creates a character that represents or personifies the product. The character might be *animated* (Green Giant, Cap'n Crunch, or Mr. Clean) or *real* (Marlboro man, Morris the Cat). The Chicago advertising agency of Leo Burnett has been very successful in creating memorable characters around mundane products.
7. *Technical expertise.* This features the care that the company exercises and the experience it has in selecting the ingredients for this product or in manufacturing the product. Thus Hills Brothers shows one of its buyers carefully selecting the coffee beans and Italian Swiss Colony emphasizes the many years of experience the company has in winemaking.
8. *Scientific evidence.* This presents survey or scientific evidence that the brand is preferred to or outperforms one or more other brands. For years, Crest toothpaste has featured scientfic evidence to convince toothpaste buyers of the superior cavity-fighting properties of Crest.
9. *Testimonial evidence.* This features a highly credible or likable source endorsing the product. It could be a celebrity like O. J. Simpson (Hertz Rent-a-Car) or ordinary people saying how much they like the product.

The communicator must also choose an effective *tone* for the ad. Procter & Gamble advertising, for example, is consistently positive in its tone: their ads say something superlatively positive about the product in the clearest possible way. Humor is avoided so as not to take attention away from the message. On the other hand, Volkswagen's ads for its famous "beetle" automobile typically took on a humorous and self-deprecating tone ("the Ugly Bug").

Words must be found that are memorable and attention getting. This is nowhere more apparent than in the development of headlines and slogans to lead the reader into an ad. There are six basic types of headlines: *news* ("New Boom and More Inflation Ahead . . . and What You Can Do About It"); *question* ("Have You Had It Lately?"); *narrative* ("They Laughed When I Sat Down at the Piano, but When I Started to Play!"); *command* ("Don't Buy Until You Try All Three"); *1-2-3 ways* ("12 Ways to Save on Your Income Tax"); and *how-what-why* ("Why They Can't Stop Buying").[21] Look at the care that airlines

[21] See "Powerful Headlines Uncover Basic Wants," *Marketing Insights,* May 19, 1969, pp. 16–17.

have lavished on finding the right way to describe their airline as safe without explicitly mentioning safety as an issue:

"The Friendly Skies of United" (United)
"The Wings of Man" (Eastern)
"The World's Most Experienced Airline" (Pan American)

Format elements such as ad size, color, and illustration can make a large difference in an ad's impact, as well as its cost. A minor rearrangement or alteration of mechanical elements within the advertisement can improve its attention-gaining power by several points. Larger-size ads gain more attention, though not necessarily by as much as their difference in cost. The use of four-color illustrations instead of black and white increases ad effectiveness and also ad cost.[22]

How Many Advertisements Should Be Created?

The client typically wants the advertising agency to create and test several alternative ideas before making a selection. The more ads created, the higher the probability that the agency will find a first-rate one. Yet the more time it spends creating alternative ads, the higher the costs. Therefore it would seem that there must be some optimal number of alternative ads that an agency should try to create and test for the client.

If the agency were reimbursed by the client for the cost of creating ads, the agency would create the optimal number. Under the present commission system, however, the agency does not like to go to the expense of creating and pretesting many ads. In an ingenious study, Gross concluded that agencies generally create too few advertisement alternatives for their clients.[23] The advertiser does not get a very good ad but only the best (one hopes) of the few that have been created.

Gross estimates that advertising agencies spend from 3 to 5 percent of their media income on creating and testing advertising, whereas he estimates they should be spending closer to 15 percent. He thinks agencies should devote a larger part of their budget to finding the best ad and somewhat less to buying media. He proposed splitting advertising agencies into two types, purely creative agencies and marketing agencies. The company hires a marketing agency, and this agency in turn hires several creative agencies to create advertisements, from which the best one is selected.

MEDIA SELECTION

Media selection is the *problem of finding the best way to deliver the desired number of exposures to the target audience.* But what do we mean by the desired number of exposures? Presumably the advertiser is seeking a certain response

---

[22] Twedt regressed the readership scores of 137 advertisements in *The American Builder* against a large number of variables and found that size of the advertisement, size of illustration, and number of colors accounted for over 50 percent of the variance in advertising readership. See Dik Warren Twedt; "A Multiple Factor Analysis of Advertising Readership," *Journal of Applied Psychology,* June 1952, pp. 207–15. Also see Daniel S. Diamond, "A Quantitative Approach to Magazine Advertisement Format Selection," *Journal of Marketing Research,* November 1968, pp. 376–87.

[23] Irwin Gross, "An Analytical Approach to the Creative Aspects of Advertising Operations" (Ph.D. dissertation, Case Institute of Technology, November 1967).

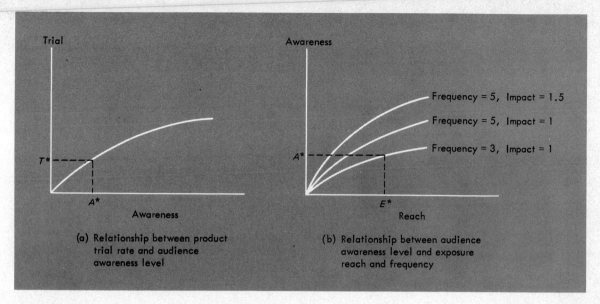

FIGURE 19–1
Relationship Between Trial, Awareness, and the Exposure Function

from the target audience, for example, a certain level of *product trial*. Now the rate of product trial will depend, among other things, on the level of audience brand awareness. Suppose the rate of product trial increases at a diminishing rate with the level of audience awareness, as shown in Figure 19–1A. If the advertiser wants to achieve a product trial rate of (say) T^*, it will be necessary to achieve a brand awareness rate of A^*.

Exposure Reach, Frequency, and Impact

The next task is to find out how many exposures, E^*, will be needed to produce a level of audience awareness of A^*. The effect of exposures on audience awareness depends on the exposures' reach, frequency, and impact. These terms are defined below:

Reach (R): the number of different persons or households exposed to a particular media schedule at least once during a specified time period

Frequency (F): the number of times within the specified time period that an average person or household is exposed to the message

Impact (I): the qualitative value of an exposure through a given medium (thus a food ad in *Good Housekeeping* would have a higher impact than in the *Police Gazette*)

Figure 19–1B shows the relationship between audience awareness and reach. Audience awareness will be greater, the higher the exposures' reach, frequency, and impact. The media planner recognizes important trade-offs between reach, frequency, and impact. Suppose the media planner has an advertising budget of $1,000,000 and the cost per thousand exposures of average quality is $5. This means that the advertiser can buy 200,000,000 exposures

509

(=$1,000,000 ÷ 1000/$5). If the advertiser seeks an average exposure frequency of 10, then the advertiser can reach 20,000,000 people (=200,000,000 ÷ 10) with the given budget. Now if the advertiser wants higher-quality media costing $10 per thousand exposures, the advertiser will be able to reach only 10,000,000 people unless he or she is willing to lower the desired exposure frequency.

The relationship between reach, frequency, and impact is captured in the following concepts:

Total number of exposures (E). This is the reach times the average frequency, that is, $E = R \times F$. It is also called the *gross rating points* (GRP). If a given media schedule reaches 80 percent of the homes with an average exposure frequency of 3, the media schedule is said to have a GRP of 240 (= 80 × 3). If another media schedule has a GRP of 300, it can be said to have more weight but we cannot tell how this weight breaks up into reach and frequency.

Weighted number of exposures (WE). This is the reach times the average frequency times the average impact, that is, $WE = R \times F \times I$.

The media planning challenge is as follows. With a given budget, what is the most cost-effective combination of reach, frequency and impact to buy? Suppose the media planner is willing to use average impact media. This leaves the task of deciding how many people to reach with what frequency. It would make sense to settle the issue of frequency first. How many exposures does an average member of the target audience need for the advertising to work? Once this target frequency is decided, then reach will fall into place.

Many advertisers have operated on the theory that members of the target audience need a large number of exposures for the advertising to work. Too few repetitions may be a waste, according to Lucas and Britt: "It can be reasoned that introductory advertisements make too weak an impression to initiate much interest in buying. Succeeding advertisements may sometimes be more effective by building up already established weak impressions to the action level."[24] Other advertising researchers doubt the value of many exposures. They feel that after people see the same ad a few times, they either act on it, get irritated by it, or stop noticing it. Krugman has made the case that three exposures may be enough:

The first exposure is by definition unique. As with the initial exposure to anything, a "What is it?" type of cognitive response dominates the reaction.

The second exposure to a stimulus . . . produces several effects. One may be the cognitive reaction that characterized the first exposure, if the audience missed much of the message the first time around. . . . More often, an evaluative "What of it?" response replaces the "What is it?" response. . . .

The third exposure constitutes a reminder, if a decision to buy based on the evaluations has not been acted on. The third exposure is also the beginning of disengagement and withdrawal of attention from a completed episode.[25]

[24] Darrell B. Lucas and Steuart Henderson Britt, *Measuring Advertising Effectiveness* (New York: McGraw-Hill Book Company, 1963), p. 218.

[25] See Herbert E. Krugman, "What Makes Advertising Effective?" *Harvard Business Review,* March–April 1975, pp. 96–103, here p. 98.

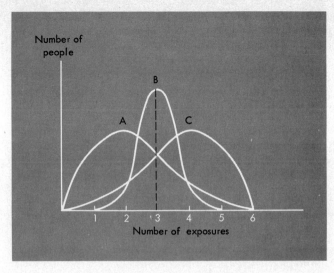

FIGURE 19–2
Exposure-Frequency Distributions

Let us assume for the moment that Krugman is right. Then advertisers should be concerned with the exposure-frequency distribution that a particular advertising campaign is achieving. An *exposure-frequency distribution* shows how many persons are receiving 0, 1, 2, . . . *n* exposures to the same ad in a given time period. Figure 19–2 shows three different exposure-frequency distributions. The media plan delivering the B distribution is the most efficient because most people are receiving three exposures. Distribution C overdoes repetition while distribution A underdoes the desired frequency of exposure.

Krugman's thesis favoring three exposures has to be qualified. He is using exposures to mean actual attention episodes on the part of the target audience. The advertiser would have to buy more exposures than three to insure that the audience actually sees three ads. Also, there is a forgetting factor that operates. The job of advertising repetition is partly to put the message back into memory. The higher the forgetting rate associated with that brand, product category, or message, the higher the warranted level of repetition.[26]

Choosing among Major Media Types

Given the reach, frequency, and impact objectives, the media planner has to review each major media type for its capacity to deliver the particular objectives. The major media types and the 1976 level of expenditures on each are as follows (in millions): newspapers, $9,910; television, $6,622; direct mail, $4,754; radio, $2,277; magazines, $1,789; outdoor, $383; and miscellaneous, $7,725. The total is $33,460.[27]

These major media types vary in their reach, frequency, and impact values.[28] For example, television typically delivers much more reach than maga-

[26] One of the best summaries of research in this area is *The Repetition of Advertising* (New York, N.Y.: Batten, Barton, Durstine, & Osborn, February 1967).

[27] *Statistical Abstract of the U.S., 1977*, p. 845.

[28] For a discussion of how the effectiveness of different media types might be compared, see Allan Greenberg, "Intermedia Comparisons," *Journal of Advertising Research*, October 1972, pp. 47–49.

zincs. Outdoor delivers much more frequency than magazines. Magazines deliver more impact than newspapers.

The experienced media planner knows the special characteristics of each media type. *Newspapers* have the advantages of flexibility, timeliness, good local market coverage, broad acceptance, and high believability. Their disadvantages are a short life, poor reproduction quality, and a small "pass-along" audience. *Magazines* have the advantages of high geographic and demographic selectivity, credibility and prestige, high-quality reproduction, long life, and good pass-along readership. They have the disadvantages of long ad-purchase lead time, some waste circulation, and no guarantee of position. *Radio* has the advantages of mass use, high geographic and demographic selectivity, and low cost. It has the disadvantages of audio presentation only, lower audience attention than television, nonstandardized rate structures, and fleeting exposure. *Television* has the advantages of combining sight, sound, and motion, appealing to the senses, high attention, and high reach. It has the disadvantages of high absolute cost, high clutter, fleeting exposure, and less audience selectivity. *Direct mail* has the advantages of audience selectivity, flexibility, no ad competition within the same medium, and personalization. It has the disadvantages of relatively high cost and a "junk mail" image. Finally, *outdoor* has the advantages of flexibility, high repeat exposure, low cost, and low competition. It has the disadvantages of no audience selectivity and creative limitations.

In choosing a combination of media types, the media planner will consider:

1. *Target audience media habits.* For example, the most effective medium for reaching stamp collectors is stamp collector magazines.
2. *Product.* A product like women's dresses might be shown to best advantage in color magazines, and Polaroid cameras might be best demonstrated on television. Media types have different potentialities for demonstration, visualization, explanation, believability, and color.
3. *Message.* A message announcing a major sale tomorrow will require radio or newspaper. A message containing a great deal of technical data might require specialized magazines or mailings.
4. *Cost.* Television is very expensive, and newspaper advertising is inexpensive. What counts, of course, is the cost per thousand exposures rather than the total cost.

Assumptions about media impact and cost must be reexamined from time to time. For a long time, television enjoyed the supreme position in the media mix, and magazines and other media were neglected. Then media researchers began to notice television's reduced effectiveness owing to increased clutter. Advertisers are beaming shorter and more numerous commercials at the television audience, resulting in poorer attention and registration. Furthermore, television advertising costs have been rising faster than other media costs. Several companies have found that a combination of print ads and television commercials often do a better job than television commercials alone. This illustrates how advertisers must reevaluate periodically what they are getting for their money from different media.

On the basis of these characteristics, the media planner has to decide on how to allocate the given budget to the major media types. For example, a firm launching a new biscuit mix may decide to allocate $6,000,000 in the following way:

MEDIA TYPES	AMOUNT	PERCENTAGE
Daytime network television	$3,000,000	50
Women's magazines	2,000,000	33
Daily newspapers in 20 major markets	1,000,000	17
	$6,000,000	100

Selecting Specific Media Vehicles

The next step is to choose the specific media vehicles within each media type that would deliver the desired response in the most cost-effective way. Consider for example, the category of women's magazines, which includes *Cosmopolitan, Family Circle, Good Housekeeping, Ladies' Home Journal, McCall's, Ms, Redbook, Seventeen,* and *Woman's Day.* The media planner turns to several volumes put out by Standard Rate and Data that provide circulation and costs for different ad sizes, color options, ad positions, and quantities of insertions. Beyond this, the media planner evaluates the different magazines on qualitative characteristics such as credibility, prestige, geographical editioning, reproduction quality, editorial climate, lead time, and psychological impact. The media planner makes a final judgment as to which specific vehicles will deliver the best reach, frequency, and impact for the money.

The cost-per-thousand criterion   Media planners calculate the *cost per thousand persons* reached by a particular vehicle. If a full-page, four-color advertisement in *Time* costs $50,000 and *Time's* estimated readership is 10 million persons, then the cost of reaching each one thousand persons is $5. The same advertisement in *Business Week* may cost $15,000 but reach only 2 million persons, at a cost per thousand of $7.50. The media planner would rank the various magazines according to cost per thousand and place advertisements in those magazines with the lowest cost per thousand.

The cost-per-thousand criterion, at least in its simple form, has come under increasing attack. Its major fault is that it uses the figure for the total readership of the magazine instead of weighing the different readership groups by their *exposure value.* For a baby lotion advertisement, the exposure value might be 1 million if all the readers are young mothers and zero if all the readers are old men.

The second weakness has to do with the varying probability of attention for different media. The media planner is interested in the number of persons who will see the ad, not the number who are exposed. Readers of certain magazines, such as *Vogue,* look at a higher percentage of the ads than readers of other magazines, say *Time.*

A third weakness of cost per thousand is that it neglects qualitative differences that might exist in the impact of different magazines. Even if two magazines reach the same number of target buyers, an advertisement may take on more believability, prestige, or other qualities in one magazine than the other.

A fourth weakness of cost per thousand is that it tends to be used in an average sense rather than in a marginal sense. If a magazine retains its lowest-cost-per-thousand standing independently of how much it is used, then logically the entire magazine budget should be spent on it. In reality, the magazine may quickly lose its cost-per-thousand advantage as more advertisements are placed in it. This is because successive-issue ads are seen largely by the same people, with diminishing impact in relation to what could be achieved by exposing new readers to the advertisement through new magazines.

Computerized Media Selection

An increasing number of agencies are using a computer program to develop their initial advertising media plan. At least three different basic types of models are in use.

Linear programming Linear programming seems like a natural format for analyzing the media-selection problem. The method can be used to discover the media mix that will maximize the number of effective exposures subject to a set of constraints—in this case the advertising budget, minimum and maximum media availabilities, and minimum desired exposure rates.

Figure 19–3 shows a linear programming statement of the media-selection problem. In the sample problem, the total advertising budget is $500,000, and at least $250,000 must be spent on medium 1. Medium 1 gives 3,100 (in thousands) effective exposures with each use and costs $15,000. It is possible to buy any-

FIGURE 19–3
Linear Programming Model for a Media Selection

Sample statement

$$\text{Maximize } E = e_1 X_1 + e_2 X_2 + \ldots + e_n X_n \quad \left.\right\} \text{effectiveness function}$$

$$\text{subject to } c_1 X_1 + c_2 X_2 + \ldots + c_n X_n \leq B \quad \left.\right\} \text{budget constraint}$$

$$c_1 X_1 + c_2 X_2 \leq B_1 \quad \left.\right\} \text{media category usage constraint}$$

$$X_1 \geq k_{1L}$$
$$X_1 \leq k_{1U}$$
$$X_2 \geq k_{2L}$$
$$X_2 \leq k_{2U}$$
$$\vdots \quad \vdots \quad \vdots$$
$$X_n \geq k_{nL}$$
$$X_n \leq k_{nU}$$

$\left.\right\}$ individual medium usage constraints

$$E = 3,100X_1 + 2,000X_2 + \ldots + 2,400X_n$$

$$15,000X_1 + 4,000X_2 + \ldots + 5,000X_n \leq 500,000$$

$$15,000X_1 \geq 250,000$$

$$X_1 \geq 0$$
$$X_1 \leq 52$$
$$X_2 \geq 1$$
$$X_2 \leq 8$$
$$\vdots \quad \vdots \quad \vdots$$
$$X_n \geq 6$$
$$X_n \leq 12$$

where:

E = total exposure value (number of rated exposures)

e_i = exposure value of one ad in medium i

X_i = number of ads placed in medium i

c_i = cost of one ad in medium i

B = total advertising budget

B_1 = part of advertising budget

k_{1L} = minimum number of units to purchase of medium i

k_{1U} = maximum number of units to purchase of medium i

where between zero and fifty-two advertisements in medium 1 over a year's time. The other values are similarly interpreted. Given these concrete values, a mathematical solution technique is used to find the precise optimum solution to the problems as stated.[29]

The problem, as stated, unfortunately contains a number of artificialities. The four most important limitations are: (1) linear programming assumes that repeat exposures have a constant marginal effect; (2) it assumes constant media costs (no discounts); (3) it cannot handle the problem of audience duplication; and (4) it fails to say anything about when the advertisement should be scheduled.

Heuristic programming An alternative technique proceeds with a sequential rather than a simultaneous selection of media. The basic idea is to start with the media available in the first week of the year and select the single best buy. After this selection is made, the remaining media choices are reevaluated to take into account audience duplication and potential media discounts. A second selection is made for the same week if the *achieved* exposure rate for the week is below the *optimal* rate. The latter is a complex function of several marketing and media variables. This process continues until the optimal exposure rate for the week is reached, at which point new media choices are considered for the following week. This cycling process continues until the year's schedule is completed.[30]

The sequential procedure has four advantages: (1) it develops a schedule simultaneously with the selection of media; (2) it handles the audience-duplication problem; (3) it handles the media-discount problem; and (4) it incorporates theoretically important variables such as brand-switching rates and multiple-exposure coefficients.

Simulation model A simulation model does not profess to find the "best" media plan but rather to estimate the exposure value of any given media plan. For example, the Simulmatics media model consists of a sample universe of 2,944 make-believe media users representing a cross section of the American population by sex, age, type of community, employment status, and education. Each individual's media choices are determined probabilistically as a function of the person's socioeconomic characteristics and location in one of ninety-eight American communities. A particular media schedule is exposed to all the persons in this hypothetical population. The computer tabulates the number and types of people being exposed. Summary graphs and tables are prepared at the end of the hypothetical year's run, and they supply a multidimensional picture of the schedule's probable impact. The advertiser examines these tabulations and decides whether the audience profile and the reach and frequency characteristics of the proposed media schedule are satisfactory.

Simulation complements rather than competes with the preceding models. Its major limitations are: (1) simulation normally does not include an overall effectiveness function; (2) it lacks a procedure for finding better schedules; and (3) the representativeness of the hypothetical population is always suspect.

---

[29] See James F. Engel and Martin R. Warshaw, "Allocating Advertising Dollars by Linear Programming," *Journal of Advertising Research*, September 1964, pp. 41–48.

[30] For an example, see William T. Moran, "Practical Media Decisions and the Computer," *Journal of Marketing*, July 1963, pp. 26–30.

Other models   Current media models have gone beyond these simple ones to incorporate additional variables and complexities. Little and Lodish created one of the best models, which they call MEDIAC.[31] MEDIAC handles in an analytical fashion a large number of marketing and advertising facets of the real media problem, such as market segments, sales potentials, exposure probabilities, diminishing marginal response rates, forgetting, seasonality, and cost discounts. It is programmed for on-line access in a conversational mode so that the user can follow the model's logic, supply the requested data, and receive in a matter of minutes an optimal media schedule. The user can easily change the data inputs and note the effect on the media schedule.

Computerized media-selection models should be thought of as an aid to, rather than a substitute for, executive judgment. The computer can produce or "test" in a matter of hours a media plan that formerly might have taken days or weeks. The plan itself must be regarded only as a starting point. This sounds paradoxical, because it may represent the optimum solution to a mathematical programming statement of the media problem. But it must be remembered that the programming statement is somewhat artificial in the weights used and the constraints set up. The media planner will want to bring judgment to bear on the quality of the plan as a whole as well as on its parts. The planner may want to revise some of the specifications in the programming statement of the problem. A great advantage of the computer is that new plans can be quickly generated to show the significance of changes made in problem specifications. The final media plan should be the joint product of the machine's ultralogical mind and man's imagination and judgment.

TIMING OF ADVERTISING EXPENDITURES

Another major advertising decision is the optimal timing of advertising expenditures throughout the year. We shall distinguish between the macroscheduling problem and the microscheduling problem.

Macroscheduling Problem   The macroscheduling problem involves deciding how to allocate advertising expenditures over the year in response to the seasonal pattern of industry sales. Suppose industry sales of a particular product peak in December and wane in March. Any individual seller in this market has three broad options. The firm can vary its advertising expenditures to follow the seasonal pattern; it can vary its advertising expenditures to oppose the seasonal pattern; or it can hold its expenditures constant throughout the year. The vast majority of firms tend to pursue a policy of seasonal rather than constant or counterseasonal advertising. Even here, the firm faces options. It has to decide whether its advertising expenditures should lead or coincide with seasonal sales. It also has to decide whether its advertising expenditures should be more intense, proportional, or less intense than the seasonal amplitude of sales.

Forrester has proposed using his "industrial dynamics" methodology to test alternative seasonal advertising policies.[32] He visualizes advertising as hav-

[31] John D. C. Little and Leonard M. Lodish, "A Media Planning Calculus," *Operations Research*. January–February 1969, pp. 1–35.

[32] See Jay W. Forrester, "Advertising: A Problem in Industrial Dynamics," *Harvard Business Review*, March–April 1959, pp. 100–110.

ing a lagged impact on consumer awareness; awareness in turn has a lagged impact on factory sales; and factory sales have a lagged impact on advertising expenditures. He suggests that these time relationships be studied for the individual company and formulated mathematically into a digital computer simulation model. The parameters for this model would be estimated from company data supplemented by executive judgment. Alternative timing strategies would be stimulated in an effort to assess their differential impacts on company sales, costs, and profits.

Kuehn developed a model to explore how advertising should be "timed" for frequently purchased, highly seasonal, low-cost grocery products. He adopted the following product and market assumptions for illustrative purposes:

> The long-run demand for the particular product is stable. The product, however, is subject to a seasonal demand. The timing and magnitude of industry advertising expenditures does not affect the seasonal demand. A company's advertising only influences the company's share of industry demand. Advertising has no effect on retailers. There are two dominant competitors, who develop their timing patterns independently of each other, but optimally. The gross margin from sales is constant throughout the year (no price or cost changes). Other brand merchandising variables, such as product characteristics, retail availability, and competing brand prices, maintain a constant relative appeal to consumers throughout the sales cycle.[33]

Kuehn showed that the appropriate timing pattern depends upon the *degree of advertising carry-over* and the *amount of habitual behavior in customer brand choice*. Carry-over refers to the rate at which the effect of an advertising expenditure decays with the passage of time. A carry-over of .75 per month means that the current effect of a past advertising expenditure is 75 percent of its level last month, whereas a carry-over of only .10 per month means that only 10 percent of last month's effect is carried over. Habitual behavior, the other variable, indicates how much brand holdover occurs by reason of habit, inertia, or brand loyalty, independently of the level of advertising. High habitual purchasing, say .90, means that 90 percent of the buyers repeat their purchase of the brand regardless of the marketing stimuli.

Kuehn found that in the case of no advertising carry-over and no habitual purchasing, the decision maker is justified in using a percentage-of-sales rule in budgeting advertising. The optimal timing pattern for advertising expenditures coincides with the expected seasonal pattern of industry sales. But, if there exists any advertising carry-over and/or habitual purchasing, the percentage-of-sales budgeting method is not optimal. In all these cases it would be better to time advertising to lead the sales curve. The peak in advertising expenditures should come before the expected peak in sales, and the trough in advertising expenditures should come before the trough in sales. Lead time should be greater, the higher the carry-over. Furthermore, advertising expenditures should be steadier, the greater the extent of habitual purchasing.

Microscheduling Problem

The microscheduling problem involves how to allocate a set of advertising exposures over a short period of time to obtain the maximum impact. Suppose the

---

[33] See Alfred A. Kuehn, "How Advertising Performance Depends on Other Marketing Factors," *Journal of Advertising Research*, March 1962, pp. 2–10.

firm has decided to buy thirty radio spot announcements in the month of September.

One way to classify the multitude of possible patterns is shown in Figure 19-4. The left side shows that advertising messages for the month can be concentrated in a small part of the month ("burst" advertising), dispersed continuously throughout the month, or dispersed intermittently throughout the month. The top side shows that the advertising messages can be beamed with a level frequency, a rising frequency, a falling frequency, or an alternating frequency. The advertiser's problem is to decide which of these twelve general patterns would represent the most effective distribution plan for the messages.

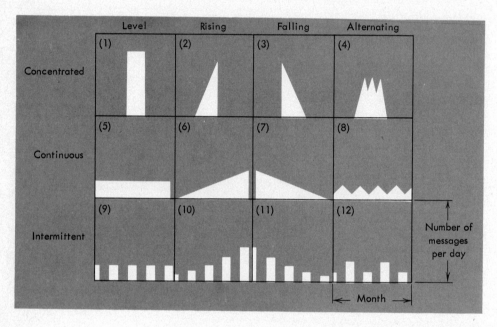

FIGURE 19-4
Classification
of Advertising
Timing Patterns

The most effective pattern depends upon the advertising communication objectives in relation to the nature of the product, target customers, distribution channels, and other marketing factors. Consider the following cases:

A *retailer* wants to announce a preseason sale of skiing equipment. She recognizes that only certain people will be interested in the message. Furthermore she recognizes that the target buyers need to hear the message only once or twice to know whether they are interested. Her objective is to maximize the *reach* of the message, not the *repetition*. She decides to concentrate the messages on the days of the sale at a level rate, but to vary the time of day to avoid the same audiences. She uses pattern (1).

A *muffler manufacturer-distributor* wants to keep his name before the public. Yet he does not want his advertising to be too continuous because only 3 to 5 percent of the cars on the road need a new muffler at any given time. He has therefore chosen to use intermittent advertising. Furthermore, he recognizes that Fridays are paydays for many potential buyers, and this would influence their interest in replacing a worn-out muffler. So he sponsors a few messages on a midweek day and more messages on Friday. He uses pattern (12).

The timing pattern should take into account three general factors. *Buyer turnover* expresses the rate at which new buyers appear in the market; the higher this rate, the more continuous the advertising ought to be to reach these new buyers. *Purchase frequency* is the number of times during the period that the buyer buys the product; the higher the purchase frequency, the more continuous the advertising ought to be to keep the brand on the buyer's mind. The *forgetting rate* is the rate at which the buyer forgets the brand in the absence of stimuli; the higher the forgetting rate, the more continuous the advertising ought to be to keep the brand in the buyer's mind.

In launching a new product, advertisers must make a choice between a campaign based on continuity versus flighting. *Continuity* is achieved by scheduling exposures evenly within a given time period. *Flighting* (or *pulsing*) refers to scheduling exposures unevenly over the same time period. Thus fifty-two exposures could be scheduled continuously at one a week throughout the year or flighted in bursts of thirteen exposures in each of four months, say January, April, July, October. Those who favor flighting feel that the resulting reduction in continuity is more than compensated for by the increased learning that takes place. They cite Ebbinghaus's finding that information learned more quickly is retained better than information learned more slowly.[34] However, the issue requires more research, and the decision model must take into account product, consumer, and competitive factors at the time of product introduction.[35]

When the decisions are made on the media vehicles and their timing, they should be displayed in a chart to give a bird's-eye view of the total media schedule. The media vehicles can be listed as rows and the months as columns, with the cells indicating when each media vehicle will be used.

MEASURING ADVERTISING EFFECTIVENESS

Good planning and control of advertising depend critically on measures of advertising effectiveness. Yet the amount of fundamental research on advertising effectiveness is appallingly small. According to Forrester:

> I doubt that there is any other function in industry where management bases so much expenditure on such scanty knowledge. The advertising industry spends 2 or 3 percent of its gross dollar volume on what it calls "research," and even if this were really true research, the small amount would be surprising. However, I estimate that less than a tenth of this amount would be considered research plus development as these terms are defined in the engineering and product research departments of companies . . . probably no more than 1/5 of 1 percent of total advertising expenditure is used to achieve an enduring understanding of how to spend the other 99.8 percent.[36]

Most of the measurement of advertising effectiveness is of an applied nature, dealing with specific advertisements and campaigns. Of the applied part, most of the money is spent by agencies on *pretesting* the given advertisement or

[34] Hermann Ebbinghaus, *Memory* (New York: Columbia University Press, 1913).

[35] See Ambar G. Rao, *Quantitative Theories in Advertising* (New York: John Wiley & Sons, 1970), pp. 60–79.

[36] Forrester, "Advertising," p. 102.

campaign before launching it into national circulation. Relatively less tends to be spent on *posttesting* the effect of given advertisements and campaigns.

The research techniques used to measure advertising effectiveness vary with what the advertiser is trying to accomplish. The behavioral change of ultimate interest to the advertiser is the act of purchase. One would expect to find that research on the "sales effect" of advertising predominates. Actually, sales-effect research tends to be meager in comparison with "communication-effect" research—research to determine the effect of given advertising on buyers' knowledge, feelings, and convictions. Many advertisers feel that the links between sales and advertising are too tenuous, complicated, and long-term to permit measuring the direct impact. They feel instead that the more short-term communication effects of given advertisements should be measured.

Communication-Effect Research

Communication-effect research seeks to discover whether the advertising is achieving the intended communication effects. There are various ways to evaluate the communication effectiveness of, say, an individual ad.[37] Called *copy testing,* it can be used both before and after an ad has been printed or broadcast. The purpose of *ad pretesting* is to make improvements in the advertising copy to the fullest extent possible prior to its release. There are three major methods of ad pretesting:

1. *Direct ratings.* Here a panel of target consumers or advertising experts examine alternative ads and fill out rating questionnaires. Sometimes a single question is raised, such as "Which of these ads do you think would influence you most to buy the product?" Or a more elaborate form consisting of several rating scales may be used, such as the one shown in Figure 19–5. Here the person evaluates the ad's at-

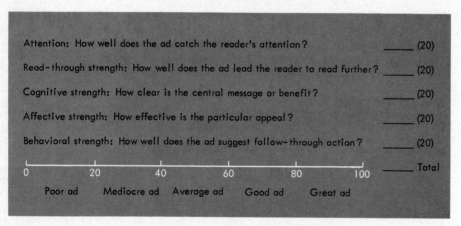

FIGURE 19–5
Rating Sheet for Ads

tention strength, read-through strength, cognitive strength, affective strength, and behavioral strength, assigning a number of points up to a maximum in each case. The underlying theory is that an effective ad must score high on all of these properties if it is ultimately to stimulate buying action. Too often ads are evaluated only on their attention- or comprehension-creating abilities. At the same

[37] For an excellent survey of research methods, see Lucas and Britt, "Measuring Advertising Effectiveness."

time, it must be appreciated that direct rating methods are less reliable than harder evidence of an ad's actual impact on target consumers. Direct rating scales help primarily to screen out poor ads rather than identify great ads.

2. *Portfolio tests.* Here respondents are given a dummy portfolio of ads and asked to take as much time as they want to read them. After putting them down, the respondents are asked to recall the ads they saw—unaided or aided by the interviewer—and to play back as much as they can about each ad. The results are taken to indicate the ability of an ad to stand out and of its intended message to be understood.

3. *Laboratory tests.* Some researchers assess the potential effect of an ad by measuring physiological reactions—heart beat, blood pressure, pupil dilation, perspiration—with such equipment as galvanometers, tachistoscopes, size-distance tunnels, and pupil-dilation-measuring equipment. These physiological tests at best measure the attention-getting power of an ad rather than any impact it has on beliefs, attitudes, or intentions.

There are two popular *ad posttesting* methods, the purpose of which is to assess the actual communication impact of the ad after it has appeared in media:

1. *Recall tests.* Recall tests involve finding persons who are regular users of the media vehicle and asking them to recall advertisers and products contained in the issue under study. They are asked to recall or play back everything they can remember. The administrator may or may not aid them in their recall. Recall scores are prepared on the basis of their responses and are used to indicate the power of the ad to be noticed and retained.

2. *Recognition tests.* Recognition tests call for sampling the readers of a given issue of, say, a magazine, asking them to point out what they recognize as having seen and/or read. For each ad, three different Starch readership scores (named after Daniel Starch, who provides the leading service) are prepared from the recognition data:

Noted. The percentage of readers of the magazine who say they have previously seen the advertisement in the particular magazine.

Seen/associated. The percentage of readers who say they have seen or read any part of the ad that clearly indicates the names of the product or service of the advertiser.

Read most. The percentage of readers who not only looked at the advertisement but say that they read more than half of the total written material in the ad.

The Starch organization also furnishes Adnorms, that is, average scores for each product class for the year, and separately for men and women for each magazine, to enable advertisers to evaluate their ads in relation to competitors' ads.

It should be noted that most of these efforts rate the attention and comprehension effectiveness of the ad and not necessarily its impact on attitude or behavior. Too many advertisers and agencies unfortunately stop short of investing the necessary money to really measure what the ad is accomplishing.

Sales-Effect Research

Communication-effect advertising research undoubtedly helps advertisers improve the quality of message content and presentation, but it reveals little about how much sales may be affected, if at all. What *sales* conclusion can the advertiser draw in learning that its recent campaign has increased brand awareness by

20 percent and brand comprehension by 10 percent? What has the advertiser learned about the sales productivity of its advertising dollars and therefore how much to spend?

The sales effect of advertising will generally be more difficult to measure than the communication effect. Advertising sales effectiveness is easiest to measure in mail-order situations and hardest to measure in brand or corporate-image-building advertising. Efforts to measure the sales impact of advertising usually follow one of two approaches.

The *historical approach* involves the researcher in fitting past company sales to past company advertising expenditures on a current or lagged basis using least-squares regression. One of the best studies of this type was conducted by Palda to estimate the effect of advertising expenditures on the sales of Lydia Pinkham's Vegetable Compound between 1908 and 1960. Fortunately, the marketing factors in this market were minimal:

> The firm spent a very high proportion (40–60 percent) of its sales on advertising. Furthermore, it did not employ many of the customary "parameters" of marketing action: sales force, credit, discounts, frequent changes in package, point of purchase efforts, special offerings, etc. The assumption thus could safely be made that advertising had a measurable effect on Pinkham's sales. The product itself, Lydia Pinkham's Vegetable Compound, had no close substitutes. Competitors' marketing action was not, therefore, a complicating factor to be coped with. By the same token certain allied issues, such as the geographic distribution of Pinkham's marketing effort, could be ignored.[38]

Palda's equation was shown in chapter 9, page 235. He was able to calculate both the short-term and long-term marginal sales effects of advertising. The marginal advertising dollar seemed to increase sales by only $.50 in the short term, seeming to suggest that Pinkham appropriated too much for advertising. But the long-term marginal sales effect was three times as large; the marginal advertising dollar increased sales by $1.63 in the long term. Palda went on to calculate the posttax marginal rate of return on the company's invested advertising dollar. He found it to be in the neighborhood of 37 percent over the whole period, not an implausible figure for a well-established monopolist.

A marketing communications study by Montgomery and Silk estimated the sales response to three different communication tools used in the pharmaceutical industry.[39] A particular drug company spent 38 percent of its communication budget on direct mail, 32 percent on samples and literature, and 29 percent on journal advertising. Yet the sales-effects research indicated that journal advertising, the least used communication element, had the highest long-run advertising elasticity, here .365; samples and literature had an elasticity of .108; and direct mail had an elasticity of only .018. It thus appeared that the company was overdoing direct mail and underdoing journal advertising.

Other investigators applying multiple-regression methods to historical data have also produced useful advertising impact-on-sales measures for such

[38] Kristian S. Palda, *The Measurement of Cumulative Advertising Effect* (Englewood Cliffs, N.J.: Prentice-Hall, 1964), p. 87.

[39] David B. Montgomery and Alvin J. Silk, "Estimating Dynamic Effects of Market Communications Expenditures," *Management Science*, June 1972, pp. 485–501.

items as cigarettes, branded gasoline, coffee, and other products.[40] In all cases, these investigators have had to cope with the following problems: (1) autocorrelation of annual advertising and sales series, respectively; (2) high intercorrelation among the explanatory variables; (3) confounding of the sales/advertising response coefficient by the fact that many companies set advertising as a percentage of sales; and (4) insufficient number of years of data to fit the required number of variables.

These problems have led a growing number of companies to rely on a second method of measuring the sales impact of advertising, that of *experimental design*. Du Pont, for example, was one of the earliest firms to use experimental design principles to measure the effects of varying levels of advertising expenditure on sales. In the case of one Du Pont brand, management thought that the advertising budget was too low.[41] There were fifty-six sales territories, and they were divided into three groups: high, average, and low market share. (See Figure 19–6.) In a third of the territories, Du Pont spent the normal amount for advertising in the next period; in another third, two and a half times the normal amount; and in the remaining third, four times the normal amount. At the end of the experimental period, Du Pont was able to estimate how much extra sales were created by higher levels of advertising expenditure. Du Pont found that higher levels of advertising expenditure led to increased sales at a diminishing rate; and that the sales response was less pronounced in the areas where Du Pont had a higher market share.

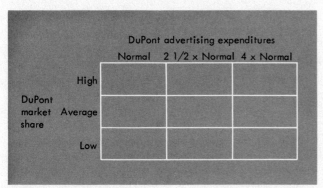

FIGURE 19–6

Experimental Design for Testing the Effect of Three Levels of Advertising Expenditure on Market Share

SOURCE: From p. 166, *Mathematical Models and Marketing Management,* by Robert Buzzell. Boston: Division of Research, Graduate School of Business Administration, Harvard University, 1968.

Anheuser-Busch uses advertising experiments in its beer markets to estimate sales response functions for different brands, market segments, and sales territories. This knowledge has enabled them to bring down their advertising ex-

[40] For a good review, see Nariman K. Dhalla, "Assessing the Long-term Value of Advertising," *Harvard Business Review,* January–February 1978, pp. 87–95.

[41] See Robert D. Buzzell, "E. I. Du Pont de Nemours & Co.: Measurement of Effects of Advertising," in his *Mathematical Models and Marketing Management* (Boston: Division of Research, Graduate School of Business Administration, Harvard University, 1968), pp. 157–79.

penditures per case while at the same time increasing their market share.[42] In general, a growing number of companies are striving to measure the sales effect of advertising expenditures rather than settling for lower-order measures such as ad recall or noting scores.

SUMMARY

Advertising—the use of paid media by a seller to communicate persuasive information about its products, services, or organization—is a potent promotional tool. American marketers spend over $33 billion annually on advertising. This includes many types of advertising (national, regional, local; consumer, industrial, retail; product, brand, institutional; and so on) designed to achieve a variety of objectives (immediate sales, brand recognition, preference, and so on).

The size of the advertising budget is commonly determined in a number of ways—according to what can be afforded, or as a regular percentage of the company's sales dollar, or to match competitors' expenditures, or by defining the cost of accomplishing specific communication goals. Four types of new decision models for setting the advertising budget are (1) sales response and decay models, (2) communication-stage models, (3) adaptive-control models, and (4) competitive-share models. The effectiveness of the advertising dollar will also depend upon the development of good message development and execution. The advertising copy must be placed in the most effective media, a problem that is increasingly being assisted by computerized media-selection models. The budget must be set over the business cycle, the seasons, the months, and even the days, with a careful consideration for delays in impact and the psychology of repetition. A continuous effort must be made to research the communication and sales effects of advertising programs before they are run, while they are running, and after they are terminated.

QUESTIONS AND PROBLEMS

1. Consider the following two statements: "The purpose of advertising is to create sales." "The purpose of advertising is to improve the buyers' disposition toward the company's products." Which comes closer to the truth?

2. The advertising manager of a large firm asks the executive committee to approve a $100,000 increase in the advertising budget. He submits that this extra money will probably increase company sales by $500,000 over what they would otherwise be. What other information would you want in order to judge the budget request?

3. A company's advertising expenditures average $5,000 a month. Current sales are $29,000, and the saturation sales level is estimated at $42,000. The sales response constant is $2, and the sales decay constant is 6 percent per month. Use the Vidale-Wolfe formula to estimate the probable sales increase next month.

4. A canned dog food manufacturer is trying to decide between media A and B. Medium A has 10,000,000 readers and charges $20,000 for a full page ad ($2.00 per 1,000). Medium B has 15,000,000 readers and charges $25,000 for a full page ad ($1.67 per 1,000). Is there any other calculation which might be made before assuming that B is the better medium?

5. A large oil company allocates its advertising budget to its territories according to current territorial sales. The advertising manager justifies using a constant advertising-to-sales ratio by saying that the company loses a certain percentage of its customers in

[42] See Russell L. Ackoff and James R. Emshoff, "Advertising Research at Anheuser-Busch, Inc. (1963–68)," *Sloan Management Review,* winter 1975, pp. 1–15.

each market each year and that advertising's most important job is to get new customers to replace them. What assumptions underlie this reasoning?

6. At one time, executives at Alberto-Culver expressed the following view about the relationship between increased advertising and sales: "We have found an astounding fact: the more we invest in advertising, the less our advertising-to-sales ratio becomes . . . once we get a brand off the ground, its ability to grow and return profits to the company accelerates at a much greater rate than the increased advertising expenditure." Is this plausible?

7. Hershey Foods for many years had the distinction of no consumer advertising. In spite of this, its candy bar sales continued to grow. Does this suggest that companies with excellent products may need little or no advertising?

8. Suggest some rules for developing effective advertising headlines and copy.

9. "The art department in an advertising agency is properly called the creative department. Media is not a creative function." Do you agree?

10. Is industrial advertising harder to measure for its communication effectiveness than consumer advertising?

11. Maloney's deductive scheme for generating advertising messages provides twelve ways to advertise a product. Develop an appeal illustrating each of the twelve types of messages.

Sales Promotion and Publicity Decisions

20

In this chapter, we turn to sales promotion and publicity. They are often viewed as playing a secondary role to the major tools of advertising and personal selling. Yet these tools can make a major contribution to marketing performance. They tend to be less well understood by marketing practitioners. Although some companies have created sales promotion departments, most companies do not have a sales promotion manager and leave it up to the individual product and brand managers to choose their own promotions. Many companies do not have a publicity director and borrow resources from the public relations department to help in product publicity. The recent high rate of inflation, however, has led companies to use these promotional tools more aggressively in showing customers ways to save money and gain more value in the marketplace.

SALES PROMOTION

Sales promotion comprises a wide variety of tactical promotion tools of a short-term incentive nature, designed to stimulate earlier and/or stronger target market response. Among the more popular ones are *coupons, premiums,* and *contests* for consumer markets; *buying allowances, cooperative advertising al-*

lowances, and *free goods* for distributors and dealers; *discounts, gifts,* and *extras* for industrial users; and sales contests and special bonuses for members of the sales force.

Sales promotion tools are used by a large variety of organizations, including manufacturers, distributors, retailers, trade associations, and various non-profit groups. As examples of the latter—churches sponsor bingo games, theatre parties, testimonial dinners, and raffles.

Rapid Growth of Sales Promotion

Sales promotion activities have grown rapidly in recent years. Between 1969 and 1976, sales promotion expenditures grew at an average rate of 9.4 percent per year, compared to 5.4 percent for advertising, and were estimated at over $30 billion in 1976.[1] Furthermore, sales promotion expenditures are expected to continue to grow faster than advertising. Consider the following:

> A technique of particularly high growth has been consumer couponing. The A. C. Nielsen Company reports that the number of consumer coupons distributed jumped from 23.4 billion in 1972 to 45.8 billion in 1976. The proportion of households using coupons rose from 58 percent to 77 percent between 1971 and 1977. However, redemption rates for coupons was relatively low in the 2.8 percent to 5.4 percent range for newspapers and magazines, 10.2 percent for direct mail, and up to 22.2 percent for "in" or "on" rack couponing.[2]

A number of factors contributed to the rapid growth of sales promotion in recent years, particularly in consumer markets.[3] Internal factors include: (1) promotion has become more acceptable to top management as an effective means to stimulate sales; (2) more product managers are qualified to use sales promotion tools; and (3) product managers are under greater pressure to obtain quick sales response. External factors include: (1) brands have increased in numbers; (2) competitors have become more promotion minded; (3) inflation and recession have made consumers more deal oriented; (4) trade pressure for more manufacturers' deals has grown; and (5) there is a belief that advertising efficiency has declined because of costs, media clutter, and government control.

Purpose of Sales Promotion

No single purpose can be advanced for sales promotion tools since they are so varied in form. A free sample stimulates consumer trial, while a free management-advisory service cements a long-term relationship with a retailer. Sales promotion techniques make three contributions to exchange relationships:

1. *Communication.* They gain attention and usually provide information that may lead the consumer to the product.
2. *Incentive.* They incorporate some concession, inducement, or contribution designed to represent value to the receiver.
3. *Invitation.* They include a distinct invitation to engage in the transaction now.

Incentive promotions are adopted by sellers to attract nonbrand users to

[1] Reprinted by permission of the *Harvard Business Review.* "Sales Promotion—Fast Growth, Faulty Management," by Roger A. Strang (July–August 1976). Copyright © 1976 by the President and Fellows of Harvard College; all rights reserved.

[2] "A Look At Sales Promotion," *The Nielsen Researcher,* no. 4, 1977, p. 8.

[3] Strang, "Sales Promotion," pp. 116–19.

527

try the brand and/or to reward brand-loyal users for their loyalty. Since both types of buyers will buy during the promotion period, both purposes are served, although the primary purpose is usually to attract nonbrand users to the brand. The nonbrand users are of two types, those who are loyal to other brands and those who are normal brand switchers. Incentive promotions primarily attract the brand switchers because the brand-loyal users of other brands do not always notice or act on the promotion. Since brand switchers are what they are, sales promotions are unlikely to turn them into loyal brand users. Incentive promotions used in markets of high brand similarity produce a high sales response in the short run but little permanent gain. In markets of high brand dissimilarity, incentive promotions are more likely to permanently alter market shares.

Incentive promotions essentially offer something extra to the customer and therefore attract the more price-conscious or premium-conscious customers. The extent to which the offer will be taken advantage of varies with the type of promotion, size of the incentive, ease of acting on the offer, and amount of advertising announcing the offer.

Sellers usually think of sales promotion as an activity designed to break down brand loyalty, and advertising as an activity designed to build up brand loyalty. Therefore an important issue for marketing managers is how to divide the budget between promotion and advertising. Companies can be found dividing their funds in ratios of anywhere from 20:80 to 80:20 on sales promotion and advertising respectively. This ratio has been rising over the past several years in response to the consumers' heightened sensitivity to price. Management should resist letting this ratio get too high. When a brand is on deal too much of the time, the dealing dilutes the brand image. The consumer begins to think of it as a cheap brand. No one knows when this happens but probably there is risk in putting a well-known brand on deal more than 30 percent of the time. In fact, dominant brands should use dealing infrequently, since most of it only gives a subsidy to current users.

Most observers feel that dealing activities do not build any long-term consumer franchise in contrast to advertising. Brown's study of 2,500 instant coffee buyers indicated that:

1. Sales promotions yield faster responses in sales than advertising.
2. Sales promotions do not tend to yield new, long-term buyers in mature markets because they attract mainly deal-prone consumers who switch among brands as deals become available.
3. Loyal brand buyers tend not to change their buying patterns as a result of competitive promotion.
4. Advertising appears to be capable of increasing the "prime franchise" of a brand.[4]

Prentice, however, has suggested that sales promotion tools can be divided into two groups, those that are "consumer franchise building" and those that are not.[5] The former imparts a selling message along with the deal, as in the case of

[4] Robert George Brown, "Sales Response to Promotions and Advertising," *Journal of Advertising Research,* August 1974, pp. 33–39, here pp. 36–37.

[5] See Roger A. Strang, Robert M. Prentice, and Alden G. Clayton, *The Relationship Between Advertising and Promotion in Brand Strategy* (Cambridge, Mass.: Marketing Science Institute, 1975), chap. 5.

free samples, coupons when they include a selling message, and premiums when they are related to the product. Sales promotion tools that are not consumer franchise building include price-off packs, consumer premiums not related to a product, contests and sweepstakes, consumer refund offers, and trade allowances. Sellers are urged to use consumer franchise-building promotions when possible because they enhance the brand's value in the mind of the consumers.

Ultimately, sales promotion seems most effective when used in conjunction with advertising.

> In one study, point-of-purchase displays related to current TV commercials were found to produce 15 percent more sales than similar displays not related to such advertising. In another, a heavy sampling approach along with TV advertising proved more successful than either TV alone or TV with coupons in introducing a product.[6]

Despite these research findings, there is a general lack of research studies to guide the sales promotion planner.[7] A systematic approach to sales promotion planning involves the following steps:

1. Establishing the sales promotion objectives
2. Selecting the sales promotion tools
3. Constructing the sales promotion program
4. Pretesting the sales promotion program
5. Implementing and controlling the sales promotion program
6. Evaluating the sales promotion results

Establishing the Sales Promotion Objectives

Sales promotion objectives are derived from basic *marketing communication objectives,* which in turn are derived from more basic *marketing objectives* developed for the product. Within this context, the specific objectives set for sales promotion will vary with the type of target market:

For *consumers,* objectives include encouraging more usage and purchase of larger-sized units by users, building trial among nonusers, attracting trial by other brand users.

For *retailers,* objectives include inducing retailer stocking of new items or larger volume, encouraging off-season buying, encouraging stocking of related items, offsetting competitive promotions, building brand loyalty of retailer, gaining entry into new retail outlets.

For *sales force,* objectives include encouraging support of a new product or model, encouraging more prospecting, stimulating sales in off-season.

Selecting the Sales Promotion Tools

A wide range of sales promotion tools are available to accomplish the various objectives. What is more, variations are continually being developed. The selection decision must take into account the type of market, sales promotion objec-

---

[6] Strang, "Sales Promotion," (1976), p. 124.

[7] For some interesting efforts, see *Promotional Decisions Using Mathematical Models* (Boston, Mass.: Allyn & Bacon, 1967); and Carl-Magnus Seipel, "Premiums—Forgotten by Theory," *Journal of Marketing,* April 1971, pp. 26–34.

tives, competitive conditions, and cost and effectiveness of each tool. The main tools for the markets and objectives are discussed below.

Use by manufacturers in consumer markets   If the objective is to offset a competitor's promotion, then *price-off packs* provide a quick, defensive response. On the other hand, if the objective is to generate initial trial of a product that is considered to have distinct competitive advantages, a *product sampling* program is an effective technique. For example, Lever Brothers had so much confidence in the superiority of its new mouthwash called Signal that it decided to distribute a free sample to two out of three American households at a cost of $15 million in 1978.

In launching a new consumer brand, the seller will typically use heavy sales promotion and advertising to achieve the objective of early and heavy trial. For example, P&G's plan for breaking into the Pittsburgh market in 1977 with its Folger brand included: (1) a 28 percent *discount* off wholesale price to retailers, (2) a thirty-five-cent *coupon* discount on a one-pound can mailed to area homes, (3) *coupon in can* for ten cents off, and (4) extensive area television advertising so the retailer couldn't refuse to carry the new brand.

In the case of mature brands, sales promotions are primarily designed to defend the current market share. Retailers often are unhappy about the form and amount of consumer deals they have to handle. They would much prefer to receive trade deals rather than handle consumer deals. According to Chevalier and Curhan:

> Retailers view promotional efforts initiated by manufacturers as encouraging profitless brand switching rather than increasing sales or profits. Manufacturers, on the other hand, complain that retailer-initiated promotions sometimes damage brand franchises which have been carefully and expensively nurtured over many years. Worse yet, manufacturers complain that retailers frequently take advantage of them by "absorbing" deals without passing their benefits along to consumers.[8]

Use by retailers in consumer markets   The retailer is concerned with building patronage and store traffic, and most sales promotion tools are selected with this objective in mind. The use of *specials* or *loss leaders* is prevalent in retailing, especially among food chains. *Trading stamps* emerged after World War II and boomed into the 1960s, only to fade in use when mass adoption of trading stamps removed competitive distinctiveness. *Sweepstakes*, and to a lesser extent *contests*, have emerged as popular techniques, with success being a function of factors such as the form and number of prizes.

Use by manufacturers for retailers and wholesalers   Manufacturers have a number of objectives for which sales promotions are usually effective. Basically, they are trying to secure the cooperation of wholesalers and retailers in carrying out their marketing strategy. These middlemen require some benefit, usually one that will be directly reflected in profit contribution. Manufacturers may offer a deal such as a *buying allowance* in order to stimulate middlemen to carry mer-

---

[8] Michel Chevalier and Ronald C. Curhan, *Temporary Promotions as a Function of Trade Deals: A Descriptive Analysis* (Cambridge, Mass.: Marketing Science Institute, 1975), p. 2.

chandise or to increase sales efforts. *Advertising allowances* and *display allowances* provide an indirect benefit to middlemen, since they contribute to promotional objectives. The manufacturer will normally want to run trade and consumer promotion in tandem. The use of promotions by manufacturers for the sole purpose of loading up the trade with merchandise is a short-sighted perspective. Trade deals must be coordinated with consumer promotional programs for long-run effectiveness.

Use by manufacturers for distributor salespersons Direct stimulation of the distributor's salespersons is often undertaken by manufacturers where these salespersons handle a large number of different brands and are in a position to recommend them to customers. *Sales bonuses* and *gift incentive programs* are two devices that can be used effectively to enlist brand support from salespersons working for distributors.

Use by manufacturers in industrial markets Industrial marketers use a whole range of sales promotion tools to stimulate sales and build stronger relationships with industrial customers. According to Shapiro:

> Technically oriented companies often offer design guides, or user brochures which provide a great deal of information. Some offer special calculation aids (e.g., specialized slide rules) or small pieces of equipment particularly suited to the industry (e.g., tape measure, magnifying glasses, magnets to detect iron and steel, and so on). Business gifts are perhaps more prevalent in the industrial area where buyer-seller relationships seem more permanent and are closer because of intimate design and production scheduling activities.[9]

Developing the Sales Promotion Program

A sales promotion program involves more than selecting the type of promotion. The marketer must make some additional decisions to define the full promotion program. The main decisions are size of incentive, conditions for participation, distributor vehicle for promotion, duration of promotion, timing of promotion, and overall budget for promotion.

Size of incentive The marketer has to determine the most cost-effective size of the incentive. We start with the assumption that sales response will increase with the size of the incentive. Thus a fifteen-cents-off coupon will bring about more consumer trial than a five-cents-off coupon. But we cannot say that there will be three times as much response. In fact, the sales response function is normally S-shaped. That is, if the incentive size is small, there may be very little response. A certain minimum incentive size must be reached for the promotion to start drawing sufficient attention. Beyond some point, higher incentives produce more sales response at a diminishing rate. By examining the relative rates of sales and cost increase, the marketer can determine the optimal size incentive to offer.

Some of the large consumer-packaged-goods firms have a sales promotion manager who keeps records on the effectiveness of different promotions used throughout the company and correlates their incentive value with the sales re-

[9] Benson P. Shapiro, "Improve Distribution with Your Promotional Mix," *Harvard Business Review*, March–April 1977, p. 123.

sponse in order to gain insight into the sales response function. As a result, the sales promotion manager can recommend incentive levels with a degree of expertise that would not normally be possessed by individual brand managers who carry out only one or two promotions a year.

Conditions for participation   Another decision in using a promotion is the conditions for participation. For example, a premium offer may be made available to anyone or only to those who turn in boxtops or other evidence of consumption. Sweepstakes may be limited to certain states and not made available to families of company personnel or to persons under a certain age. By carefully choosing conditions for participation, the seller can selectively discourage those who are unlikely to become regular users of the product. On the other hand, if the conditions are too restrictive, only the most loyal or deal-prone consumers will participate.

Distribution vehicle for promotion   The marketer must decide how to promote and distribute the promotion program to the target audience. Suppose the promotion is a coupon that will entitle the buyer to fifteen cents off the list price. The coupon could be made available to prospective customers in at least four ways: (1) in or on the package or related packages, (2) in the store, (3) in the mail, and (4) in advertising media. Each vehicle involves a different level of reach and cost. For example, in-pack coupons primarily reach current users, whereas mailed coupons can be directed at nonbrand users, although at a greater cost.

Duration of promotion   Another issue is the length of the period sales promotions should be run. If they are offered for too short a period, many prospects would not have a chance to take advantage, since they may not be repurchasing at the time or be too busy with other things. If the promotion runs for a long period, then the customers may begin to view this as a long-term price concession and the deal will lose some of its "act now" force and also raise questions about the brand's quality. Stern reports, on the basis of a number of studies, that an optimal frequency appears to be about three weeks per quarter and optimal duration is the length of the average purchase cycle.[10] This varies, of course, with the promotion objectives, customer buying habits, competitors' strategies, and other factors.

Timing of promotion   A schedule of sales promotion will usually be constructed by brand managers, subject to sales department requirements. This schedule will be studied and evaluated by divisional marketing management in terms of total divisional marketing strategy. The schedule is a planning instrument and requires careful timing to allow for production, salespersons, and distribution coordination. At the same time, some unplanned promotions will be needed under tactical pressure and will have to be prepared on short notice.

Overall sales promotion budget   The overall budget for sales promotion can be arrived at in two ways. It can be built from the ground up, where the marketer

[10] Arthur Stern, "Measuring the Effectiveness of Package Goods Promotion Strategies," a paper presented at a meeting of the Association of National Advertisers, Glen Cove, N.Y., February 1978.

decides on the various promotions to sponsor during the year and estimates the cost of each. The cost of a particular promotion consists of the total *administrative cost* (printing, mailing, and promoting the deal) and the *incentive cost* (cost of premium or cents-off, including rate of redemption), multiplied by the *expected number of units* that will be sold on deal.

> Suppose a brand of after-shave lotion will be marked down 9¢ for a limited period. The item regularly sells for $1.09, of which 40¢ represents a contribution to the manufacturer's profit before marketing expense. The brand manager expects a million bottles to be sold under this deal. Thus the incentive cost of the deal will be $90,000 (= .09 × 1,000,000). Suppose the administrative cost is estimated at $10,000. Then the total cost is $100,000. In order to break even on this deal, the company will have to sell 250,000 (= $100,000 ÷ .40) more units than would have occurred over the same period without the deal.

In the case of a coupon deal, the cost would take into account the fact that only a fraction of the consumers will redeem the coupons. In the case of an in-pack premium, the deal cost must include the costs of procurement and packaging of the premium offset by any price increase on the package.

The other, more common way to arrive at an overall budget for sales promotion is to resort to a conventional proportion of the total budget for advertising and sales promotion. For example, toiletries may get a sales promotion budget of 20 to 40 percent of the total promotion budget, whereas packaged goods may get as much as 30 to 60 percent. These proportions vary substantially for different brands in different markets and are influenced by the product stage of the life cycle and competitive expenditures on promotion.

Organizations with multiple brands should insure that brand budgets are coordinated in order to gain economies from sales promotion activities. Although not all sales promotion activities can be preplanned, coordination gives cost-saving advantages such as single mailings of multiple coupons to consumers.

Strang, in his study of sales promotion in seventeen leading U.S. consumer goods manufacturers and advertising agencies, found a number of inadequacies in budgeting proceedings.[11] These included:

1. Lack of consideration of cost effectiveness.
2. Use of simplistic decision rules, such as extensions of last year's spending, percentage of expected sales, maintenance of a fixed ratio to advertising, and the "leftover approach" where promotion gets what is left from a fixed percentage of sales after the advertising budget has been removed.
3. Advertising and promotional budgets being prepared independently.

Pretesting the Sales Promotion Program

Although sales promotion programs are designed on the basis of experience, pretests should be conducted whenever possible to determine if (1) the tools are appropriate, (2) the size of the incentive is optimal, and (3) the method for presentation is likely to be efficient. A survey by the Premium Advertisers Association indicated that fewer than 42 percent of premium offerers ever tested their effectiveness.[12] Strang maintains that promotions can usually be tested quickly and in-

[11] Strang, "Sales Promotion," p. 119.

[12] Russell D. Bowman, "Merchandising and Promotion Grow Big in Marketing World," *Advertising Age*, December 1974, p. 21.

expensively, and that some large companies test alternative strategies in selected market areas with each of their national promotions.[13]

Sales promotions directed at consumer markets can be readily pretested. Groups of consumers can be asked to rate or rank different possible deals according to their preference. Or trial tests can be run in limited geographical areas.

Implementing and Controlling the Sales Promotion Program

Effective control of sales promotions requires that specific goals and implementation plans for individual promotions be established. Program implementation must cover two critical time factors, lead time and sell-off time. Lead time is the time necessary to bring the program up to the point of announcing the deal.

> It covers initial planning, design, and approval of package modifications or material to be mailed or distributed to the home, preparation of conjunctive advertising and point-of-sale materials, notification of field sales personnel, establishment of allocations for individual distributors, purchasing and printing of special premiums or packaging materials, production of advance inventories and staging at distribution centers in preparation for release at a specific date, and, finally, the distribution to the retailer.[14]

Sell-off time begins at the date of release and ends when approximately 90 to 95 percent of the deal merchandise is in the hands of consumers, which may take one to several months, depending on the deal duration.

Evaluating the Sales Promotion Results

Evaluation is a crucial requirement for improving any program. Yet according to Strang:

> Evaluation of promotion programs receives . . . little attention. Even where an attempt is made to evaluate a promotion, it is likely to be superficial. . . . Evaluation in terms of profitability is even less common.[15]

Evaluation procedures vary with the type of market. For example, manufacturers usually measure the effectiveness of retail trade promotions by checking on store delivery volume, store shelf-space allocation, and cooperative advertising placed by retailers. Manufacturers measure the effectiveness of consumer promotions using any of four methods: sales performance movement, analysis of consumer-panel data, consumer surveys, and experimental studies.

The most common consumer promotion evaluation technique is to compare sales or market share before, during, and after a promotion. Increased sales are attributed to the impact of the sales promotion program, all other things being equal. Figure 20–1 shows the type of deal results that manufacturers would like to see. In the prepromotion period, the company's brand enjoyed a 6 percent share of the market. During the promotion period, the company's brand share rose to 10 percent. This share gain of 4 percent is made up of (1) deal-prone consumers who switched to this brand to take advantage of the deal and (2) brand-loyal customers who increased their purchases in response to the price

---

[13] Strang, "Sales Promotion," p. 122.

[14] Kurt H. Schaffir and H. George Trentin, *Marketing Information Systems* (New York: Amacom, 1973), p. 81.

[15] Strang, "Sales Promotion," p. 120.

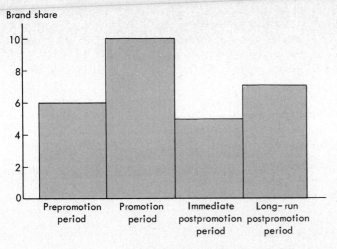

FIGURE 20–1
Effect of Consumer Deal on Brand Share

incentive. Immediately after the promotion ended, the brand share fell to 5 percent because consumers were overstocked and they were working down their inventory. After this stock adjustment period, brand share went up to 7 percent, showing a one percentage point increase in the number of loyal customers. This is likely to be the case when the brand has good qualities that many nonbrand users had not known about.

In many cases, the results are less satisfactory. We can imagine two different situations. In the first one, brand share jumps up to 10 percent in the promotion period, falls to 2 percent in the immediate postpromotion period, and then returns to 6 percent. This pattern suggests that the existing customers were the main buyers during the promotion period and they stocked up on this brand; then they consumed out of stock immediately after the promotion period; and they ultimately returned to their normal rate of purchase. Thus the effect of the deal was largely to alter the time pattern of purchase rather than the permanent level of purchase. This is not necessarily wasteful, especially if pipeline inventories are excessive and the company wants to clear them earlier and, in the meantime, cut production.

We can imagine another case where brand share rises little or not at all during the promotion period and falls and remains below the normal level after the promotion period. This situation suggests a brand that is basically on a downward sales trend, which the promotion simply slowed down but did not halt or reverse. Peckham reports some brands where the promotion slowed down the rate of decline, but did not stop it.[16]

Another way to measure the effect of a sales promotion program is to interview a sample of consumers in the target market, attempting to learn how many consumers recall the promotion, what they thought of it, how many took advantage of it, and how it affected their subsequent brand-choice behavior. This method would not be used for each promotion but only selectively to research the effect of that type of sales promotion on consumers.

Deals can also be studied through carefully arranged experiments that vary such deal attributes as incentive value, deal duration, and deal-distribution

[16] See James O. Peckham, Sr., *The Wheel of Marketing* (Chicago: A. C. Nielsen, 1973).

media. By varying the deal attributes offered to matched groups or matched geographical areas, inferences can be drawn on their sales impact. At the same time, experiments need some follow-up consumer study to understand the reasons why the deal attributes produced different levels of response.

Consumer-panel data can also be used to evaluate consumer response to sales promotion. A consumer-panel data study by Dodson, Tybout, and Sternthal found that deals generally enhance brand switching, the rate depending on the type of deal. Media-distributed coupons induce substantial switching, cents-off deals induce somewhat less switching, and package coupons hardly affect brand switching. Furthermore consumers generally return to their preferred brands after the deal.[17]

PUBLICITY

Another major marketing communications tool is *publicity*. Publicity has been defined as the activity of "securing editorial space, as divorced from paid space, in all media read, viewed, or heard by a company's customers or prospects, for the specific purpose of assisting in the meeting of sales goals."[18] To the extent that an organization can create events and news around a marketable entity, it is using publicity.

What kinds of entities can be publicized? Almost anything. Publicity is used to promote various brands, products, persons, places, ideas, activities, organizations, and even nations. For example, trade associations representing products whose primary demand has fallen—such as eggs, milk, potatoes—have developed publicity campaigns to renew interest in and increase use of these products. Publicity is commonly used in the launching of new products and brands as well as in efforts to rekindle interest in mature brands. Organizations suffering from low visibility have resorted to publicity to create more awareness, while organizations with poor public images have attempted to improve their image by engaging in and publicizing positive actions. Nations that are seeking more tourists, foreign investment, or international support often use publicity toward these purposes.

Publicity is part of a larger concept, that of public relations. Today's public relations practitioners perform the following functions:

1. *Press relations.* The aim of press relations is to place newsworthy information into the news media to attract attention to a person, product, or service.
2. *Product publicity.* Product publicity involves various efforts to publicize through news media and other means specific products and happenings related to products.
3. *Corporate communications.* This activity covers internal and external communications to give attention and understanding to the institution.
4. *Lobbying.* Lobbying refers to the effort to deal with legislators and government officials to defeat unwanted legislation and regulation and/or to promote wanted legislation and regulation.

[17] Joe A. Dodson, Alice M. Tybout, and Brian Sternthal, "Impact of Deals and Deal Retraction on Brand Switching," *Journal of Marketing Research*, February 1978, pp. 72–81, here p. 79.

[18] George Black, *Planned Industrial Publicity* (Chicago: Putnam Publishing, 1952), p. 3.

5. *Counseling.* Counseling is the provision of general advice to the company about what is happening in the society and what the company might do in the way of changing its ways or improving its communications.[19]

Since publicity is part of public relations, those skilled in publicity are usually found not in the company's marketing department but in its public relations department. The public relations department is typically located at corporate headquarters rather than in the various divisions; and its staff is so busy dealing with various publics—stockholders, employees, legislators, city officials—that publicity to support product marketing objectives may be neglected. One frequent solution is to establish a publicity unit within the marketing department.

Publicity is often described as a marketing stepchild because it is relatively underutilized in relation to the real contribution it can make. Publicity has created in many cases memorable impacts on public awareness that advertising alone could not have accomplished, at least not at the same low cost. The company does not pay for the space or time in the media. It does pay for the staff time used to develop the stories and induce the media to use them, but this cost is relatively small. If the company has a real story to tell, it could be picked up by all the news media and be worth millions of dollars in equivalent advertising. Furthermore, it would possess more credibility as news than if it had been delivered as advertising.

In considering when and how to use product publicity, management should approach the publicity function as it does any function. Management should define the publicity objectives; develop and carry out an effective publicity plan; and evaluate the results. We now turn to these decisions.

Establishing the Publicity Objectives

We will assume that an organization is engaged in developing a marketing plan for a brand, product, or other marketable entity. The organization has identified the target market and the target response that it wants in the coming period. It considers the role of different marketing communication tools in contributing to the target response. It decides to use advertising as the primary means of building or expanding market awareness and sales promotion as the primary means of stimulating trial. What can publicity contribute?

The first thing to recognize is that the usefulness of publicity varies from product to product. Publicity's potential contribution is stronger, the stronger the following variables:

1. *Newsworthiness.* Products that can support interesting stories that news editors will accept are the best candidates for publicity.
2. *Stimulus for sales force and dealers.* Publicity can be useful in boosting the enthusiasm of the sales force and dealers when it might be lacking. For example, news stories appearing about a new product before it is launched will help the sales force gain a hearing from retailers.
3. *Need for credibility.* Publicity introduces an element of credibility by virtue of communicating the message in an editorial context. Credibility is needed by new products as well as by mature products that the market has questioned.
4. *Small budget.* Publicity, while it is not without cost, tends to be low in cost for producing exposures in comparison with direct mail and media advertising. The

[19] Adapted from Scott M. Cutlip and Allen H. Center, *Effective Public Relations*, 3rd ed. (Englewood Cliffs, N.J.: Prentice-Hall, 1964), pp. 10–14.

smaller the company's marketing communications budget, the stronger the case for using imaginative publicity to neutralize the advantage of a competitor who has more money to spend on advertising.

If the product has one or more of these characteristics, publicity should be considered as a potentially useful tool in the marketing communications mix.

Now the task is to set specific objectives for the publicity. As an example, the Wine Growers of California hired the public relations firm of Daniel J. Edelman, Inc., in 1966 to create a publicity program to support two major marketing objectives: (1) to convince Americans that wine drinking is a pleasurable part of good living; and (2) to improve the image and market share of California wines among all wines. To contribute to these marketing objectives, the following publicity objectives were established: (1) to develop magazine stories about wine and get them placed in top magazines (*Time, House Beautiful*) and in newspapers (food columns, feature sections); (2) to develop stories directed to the medical profession on wine's many health values; and (3) to develop special programs for the young adult market, college market, governmental bodies, and various ethnic communities.

Where possible, objectives such as these should be translated into specific goals for audience response variables so that results can be evaluated at the end of the publicity campaign.

Choosing the Publicity Messages and Vehicles

After establishing the objectives, the publicist sets about determining whether there are any interesting stories to tell about the product. As an example, suppose a college with low visibility adopts the objective of achieving more public recognition. The publicist will review the college's various components to see whether any natural stories exist. Do any faculty members have unusual backgrounds or are any of them working on unusual projects? Are any novel courses being taught? Are any unusual students enrolled? Are any interesting events taking place on campus? Is there a story about the architecture, history, or aspirations of the college? Usually a search along these lines will uncover hundreds of stories that can be fed to the press with the effect of creating much more public recognition of the college. Ideally, stories should be chosen that symbolize the kind of college this college wants to be. The stories should support its desired market positioning.

If the number of good stories is insufficient, the publicist then dreams up newsworthy events that the college could sponsor. Here the publicist gets into *creating news* rather than *finding news*. Among the ideas are hosting major academic conventions, featuring well-known speakers, and developing news conferences. Each event is an opportunity to develop a host of stories directed to relevant media vehicles and audiences.

Event creation is a particularly important skill in publicizing fund-raising drives for nonprofit organizations. Fund raisers have developed a large repertoire of special events, including *anniversary celebrations, art exhibits, auctions, benefit evenings, bingo games, book sales, cake sales, contests, dances, dinners, fairs, fashion shows, parties in unusual places, telethons, rummage sales, tours,* and *walkathons.* No sooner does one type of event get created, such as a walkathon, than competitors spawn new versions such as read-a-thons, bike-a-thons, and jog-a-thons.

A publicist is able to find or create stories on behalf of even mundane products. Some years ago, the Potato Board, an association of more than fifteen thousand U.S. potato growers, decided to finance a publicity campaign to encourage more potato consumption.[20] A national attitude and usage study indicated that many consumers perceived potatoes as too fattening, not nutritious enough, and not a good source of vitamins and minerals. These attitudes were being disseminated by various opinion leaders, such as food editors, diet advocates, and doctors. In truth, potatoes have far fewer calories than people imagine and contain several important vitamins and minerals. The Potato Board decided to develop separate publicity programs for each major audience: consumers, doctors, dieticians, nutritionists, home economists, and food editors. The consumer program called for generating many stories about the potato for network television and national women's magazines, developing and distributing *The Potato Lover's Diet Cookbook,* and placing articles and recipes in food editors' columns. The food editors' program consisted of organizing seminars conducted by nutrition experts and a tour of major markets by a leading diet authority, who talked with food editors.

Publicity can also be highly effective in brand promotion. One of the top brands of cat food is Star-Kist Foods's 9-Lives. Its brand image revolves around one of the most famous felines in the world, the now-deceased Morris the Cat. The advertising agency of Leo Burnett, which created Morris for its ads, wanted to make him more of a living, breathing, real-life feline to whom cat owners and cat lovers could relate. They hired a public relations firm, which then proposed and carried out the following ideas: (1) launch a Morris "look-alike" contest in nine major markets, with Morris being booked for personal appearances, and extensive stories appearing about the search for a look-alike; (2) write a book called *Morris, An Intimate Biography,* describing the adventures of this famous feline; (3) establish a coveted award called The Morris, a bronze statuette given to the owners of award-winning cats selected at local cat shows; (4) sponsor Adopt-A-Cat Month with Morris as the official "spokescat" for the month, urging people to adopt stray cats as Morris once was; and (5) distribute a booklet called *The Morris Method,* on cat care. All of these publicity steps strengthened the brand's market share in the cat food market.

Implementing the Publicity Plan

Implementing publicity requires a great deal of care. Take the matter of placing stories in the media. A great story is easy to place, no matter who does the placing. But most stories are less than great and may not get through busy editors. One of the chief assets of publicists is the personal relationships they have established with media editors. Publicists are typically exjournalists who know a number of the media editors and know what they want. Media editors want interesting, well-written stories, and easy access to sources of further information. Publicists look at media editors as a market to satisfy so that in turn these editors will be inclined to "buy" their stories.

Publicity also requires extra care when it involves staging special events such as testimonial dinners, news conferences, and national contests. Publicists need a good head for detail and also for coming up with quick solutions when things go wrong.

---

[20] For details, see Joseph M. Coogle, Jr., "Media, Advertising, and Public Relations," in *Review of Marketing 1978,* eds. Gerald Zaltman and Thomas V. Bonoma (Chicago: American Marketing Association, 1978), pp. 481–84.

The most difficult thing about measuring publicity's contribution is that it is typically used with other marketing communication tools, and its contribution is
hard to separate out. If it is used before the other tools come into action, as often
happens in launching a new product, its contribution is easier to evaluate.

Publicity is designed with certain audience-response objectives in mind,
and these objectives form the basis of what is measured. The major response
measures are exposures, awareness/comprehension/attitude change, and sales.

Exposures   The easiest and most common measure of publicity effectiveness is
the number of exposures created in the media. Most publicists supply the client
with a clippings book, showing all the media that carried news about the product and a summary statement such as:

> Media coverage included 3,500 column inches of news and photographs in 350
> publications with a combined circulation of 79.4 million; 2,500 minutes of air
> time on 290 radio stations and an estimated audience of 65 million; and 660 min-
> utes of air time on 160 television stations with an estimated audience of 91 mil-
> lion. If this time and space had been purchased at advertising rates, it would have
> amounted to $1,047,000.[21]

The purpose of citing the equivalent advertising cost is to make a case for
publicity's cost effectiveness, since the total publicity effort must have cost less
than $1,047,000. Furthermore, publicity is usually more read and believed than
ads.

Still, this exposure measure is not very satisfying. There is no indication of
how many people actually read, saw, or heard the message, and what they
thought afterwards. Furthermore, there is no information on the net audience
reached since publications have overlapping readership.

Awareness/comprehension/attitude change   A better measure calls for finding
out what change in product awareness/comprehension/attitude occurred as a
result of the publicity campaign (after allowing for the impact of other marketing communications). This requires the use of survey methodology to measure
the before-after levels of these variables. The Potato Board carried out this type
of evaluation and learned, for example, that the number of people who agreed
with the statement "potatoes are rich in vitamins and minerals" went from 36
percent before the campaign to 67 percent after the campaign, a significant improvement in product comprehension.

Sales and profit contribution   Sales and profit impact is the most satisfactory
measure if obtainable. For example, 9-Lives sales had increased 43 percent at
the end of the Morris the Cat publicity campaign. However, advertising and
other marketing communications had been stepped up, and it was not possible
to attribute all the increased sales to publicity alone. It is necessary to make
some assumption as to the role that publicity played in the total impact. Sup-

---

[21] Arthur M. Merims, "Marketing's Stepchild: Product Publicity," *Harvard Business Review,*
November–December 1972, pp. 111–12. The value of "equivalent advertising" was arrived at by
summing the total number of publicity exposures, which is 235.4 million; then figuring that it costs
(at that time) approximately $4.45 per thousand exposures with advertising media, or a total adver-
tising cost of $1,047,000 (= $4.45 × 235,400).

pose total sales have increased $1,500,000, and management conservatively estimates that publicity contributed 15 percent of the total sales increase. Then the return on publicity investment is calculated as follows:

Total sales increase		$1,500,000
Estimated sales increase due to publicity (15%)		225,000
Contribution margin on product sales (10%)		22,500
Total direct cost of publicity program		−10,000
Contribution margin added by publicity investment		$ 12,500
Return on publicity investment	($12,500/$10,000) =	125%

SUMMARY

Sales promotion and publicity are two important tools of marketing communication that are often not as well understood by many marketing practitioners as advertising and personal selling. Yet their potential impact on sales and profit is substantial.

Sales promotion covers a wide variety of short-term incentive tools—such as coupons, premiums, contests, and buying allowances—designed to stimulate earlier and/or stronger market response. They can be used to stimulate consumer markets, the trade, and the organization's own sales force. Sales promotion expenditures now exceed advertising expenditures and have been growing at a faster rate than advertising in recent times. The effective use of sales promotion requires careful planning, consisting of six steps. The first step is to develop clear objectives for sales promotion that derive from the larger marketing communication objectives and still broader marketing objectives set for the product. The second step calls for choosing the sales promotion tools that can accomplish these objectives in the most cost-effective way. The third step calls for rounding out the sales promotion program by making decisions on the specific size of the promotion incentive, conditions for participation, distribution vehicles, duration and timing of promotion, and the overall budget for promotion. The fourth step calls for pretesting the proposed promotion in a limited geographical area or market group to assess its effectiveness. The fifth step calls for the careful implementation and control of the sales promotion program. Finally, the sixth step calls for evaluating the sales promotion results to improve the future use of this tool.

Publicity tends to be the least utilized of the major marketing communication tools, although it has great potential for building awareness and preference in the marketplace. Publicity resources in organizations tend to be located in public relations departments rather than in marketing departments, and this accounts for some of its relative neglect. Publicity is especially useful for organizations that have a good story to tell but have too limited a budget to support large-scale advertising. There are four steps in the effective use of publicity. The first step is to establish the objectives for publicity in support of the broader marketing objectives. The second step is to select the publicity messages and vehicles that would be most cost effective. The third step calls for implementing the publicity plan through seeking the cooperation of media people and arranging planned events. The final step is to evaluate the publicity results in terms of the number of exposures achieved, changes in awareness/comprehension/attitude in the target audience and, ultimately, increases in sales and profits.

1. A major basketball team has recently experienced a decline in home game attendance. The team's owner decided to hire a marketing person to stimulate attendance. What are some of the steps that can be taken?

2. A nationwide trucking company uses a combination of advertising and personal selling to stimulate demand for its services. Can you envision roles for publicity and sales promotion in the promotion of trucking services? What percentages of the total promotion budget should go into advertising, personal selling, publicity, and sales promotion?

3. Joe Pringle, a product manager at the XYZ Snacks Company, is concerned about falling sales in recent months. His inventory is high. He is contemplating a sales promotion to reverse the sales trend and reduce inventories. He is thinking of offering a case allowance to the trade. He expects sales to be 40,000 cases in the absence of promotion. The case price is $10 and the gross profit contribution is .40. He is currently thinking of offering a $1 case allowance. He expects increased sales of 20,000 cases during the promotion period. The estimated cost of developing this promotion is $12,000. (a) Will he make a profit on this promotion? (b) What is the breakeven sales increase that will justify this case allowance? (c) If he offered only a $.50 case allowance, he expects additional net sales of 12,000. Should he offer a $1 or $.50 case allowance?

4. Indicate how the movie industry is currently using publicity to promote its major new pictures. Give some examples.

5. Much of the public relations work done by business firms consists of miscellaneous and unrelated activities. Can you suggest an underlying public relations orientation a company could adopt that would provide a focus for many publicity activities?

6. Select a product or service of your choice and recommend which sales promotion tools should be used to build its consumer franchise.

SALES-FORCE DECISIONS

I don't know who you are.
I don't know your company.
I don't know your company's product.
I don't know what your company stands for.
I don't know your company's customers.
I don't know your company's record.
I don't know your company's reputation.

Now—what was it you wanted to sell me?

McGRAW-HILL PUBLICATIONS

21

Every organization contains one or more persons who have direct responsibility for contacting and dealing with prospects and customers. We call this group the sales force. Sales forces are found not only in commercial companies but in nonprofit organizations as well. College recruiters represent a sales-force arm of the college seeking to sell prospective students on coming to that college. Churches form membership committees, which are responsible for attracting new members. The U.S. Agricultural Extension Service consists of agricultural specialists who try to educate and sell farmers on using the latest technology. Hospitals, museums, and other organizations use a staff of fund raisers to contact prospective donors and sell them on supporting the organization.

The traditional term used to describe the persons in the sales force is *salesmen.* However, this term is becoming obsolete because of the increasing number of women who are taking on sales responsibilities. We will use *sales representatives* and *salespersons,* although *salesmen* will be used occasionally where appropriate. Many other terms have come into use to describe people who work in sales, including account executive, sales consultant, field representative, manufacturers' representative, agent, service representative, and marketing representative.

Organizations have a choice between engaging a direct and a contractual sales force. A *direct (or company) sales force* consists of full or part-time paid

543

employees who work exclusively for the company. This sales force may in turn consist of two groups: *inside sales personnel,* who conduct their business from their offices, using the telephone and receiving visits from prospective buyers, and *field sales personnel,* who travel and visit customers. A company can also use a *contractual sales force* such as manufacturers' reps, sales agents, or brokers, who are paid a commission on the sales they generate.

The sales force, to get its job done, requires the support of other personnel, such as:

1. *Top management.* Top management is increasingly getting involved in the sales process,[1] especially when *national accounts*[2] or *major sales*[3] are at stake.

2. *Technical sales personnel.* They are technical people who work with the sales representatives to supply technical information needed by the customer before, during, or after the purchase of the product.

3. *Customer service representatives.* They provide installation, maintenance, and other services to the customer.

4. *Office staff.* This group consists of sales analysts, order expediters, and secretarial personnel.

In 1976, American firms spent approximately $100 billion on personal selling compared with $33 billion on advertising. Over 5.4 million Americans work in sales and related occupations. Sales personnel serve as the company's unique link to the customers. The sales representative *is* the company to many of its customers. The sales representative tailors the company's offer to the individual customer and in turn brings back to the company much needed intelligence about the customer.

In this chapter, we will examine the major decisions involved in developing and managing personal selling resources. These decisions consist of defining tasks and objectives for the sales force, determining the size of the sales force, designing the sales organization and territories, and recruiting, selecting, training, compensating, supervising, and evaluating sales representatives.

SALES-FORCE TASKS AND OBJECTIVES

Sales-force objectives must be based on the character of the company's target markets and the company's sought position in these markets. The company must consider the unique role that personal selling can play in the marketing mix to serve customer needs in a competitively effective way. Personal selling happens to be the most expensive contact and communications tool of the company, costing companies an average of $59 a sales call in 1978.[4] Therefore it must be used

---

[1] "Executive Suite Salesmanship," *Business Week,* October 20, 1975, pp. 70, 74.

[2] Roger M. Pegram, *Selling and Servicing the National Account* (New York: Conference Board, Report No. 557, 1972).

[3] William H. Kaven, *Managing the Major Sale* (New York: American Management Association, 1971); and Benson P. Shapiro and Ronald S. Posner, "Making the Major Sale," *Harvard Business Review,* March–April 1976, pp. 68–78.

[4] John Steinbrink, *Compensation of Salesmen: Dartnell's 19th Biennial Survey* (Chicago: Dartnell Corp., 1978).

sparingly. Personal selling is also the most effective tool at certain stages of the buying process, such as the buyer-education, negotiation, and sales-closing stages. It is important that the company think out carefully when and how to use sales representatives to facilitate the marketing task.

Types of Sales Positions

There are probably more stereotypes about sales representatives than about any other group. The salesman is likely to conjure up an image of Arthur Miller's pitiable Willy Loman or Meredith Willson's ebullient Harold Hill from "The Music Man"—the latter a glib, boisterous character always ready with a glad hand and a racy story. Sales representatives are typically pictured as loving sociability—in spite of some recent evidence that many sales representatives actually dislike it. They are criticized for aggressively foisting goods on people—in spite of the fact that buyers often search out sales representatives.

Actually, the term *sales representative* covers a broad range of positions in our economy, within which the differences are often greater than the similarities. McMurry offered the following classification of sales positions:

1. Positions where the "salesperson's" job is predominantly to deliver the product, e.g., milk, bread, fuel, oil.
2. Positions where the salesperson is predominantly an inside order-taker, e.g., the haberdashery salesperson standing behind the counter.
3. Positions where the salesperson is also predominantly an order-taker but works in the field, as the packing-house, soap, or spice salesperson does.
4. Positions where the salesperson is not expected or permitted to take an order but is called on only to build goodwill or to educate the actual or potential user . . . the distiller's "missionary person" or the medical "detailer" representing an ethical pharmaceutical house.
5. Positions where the major emphasis is placed on technical knowledge, e.g., the engineering salesperson who is primarily a consultant to the "client" companies.
6. Positions which demand the creative sale of tangible products like vacuum cleaners, refrigerators, siding, and encyclopedias.
7. Positions requiring the creative sale of intangibles, such as insurance, advertising services, or education.[5]

The positions move along a spectrum ranging from the least to the most creative types of selling. The earlier jobs call primarily for maintaining accounts and taking orders, while the latter require hunting down prospects and creating new sales. Most of the discussion here will deal with the more creative types of selling.

Types of Selling Situations

Most people visualize selling as consisting of a single seller talking to a single buyer. This is really one of five types of selling situations. The five are:

1. *Sales representative to buyer.* Here a single sales representative talks to a single prospect or customer in person or over the phone.
2. *Sales representative to buyer-group.* Here a sales representative appears before a buying committee to make a sales presentation about a specific product.

[5] Robert N. McMurry, "The Mystique of Super-Salesmanship," *Harvard Business Review,* March–April 1961, p. 114.

3. **Sales team to buyer-group.** Here a sales team (such as a company officer, sales representative, and sales engineer) makes a sales presentation to a buying group.

4. **Conference selling.** Here the sales representative brings resource people from the company to meet with one or more buyers to discuss problems and mutual opportunities.

5. **Seminar selling.** Here a company team of technical people presents an educational seminar to a technical group in a customer company about recent state-of-the-arts developments. The aim is to enhance customer knowledge and loyalty rather than to make a specific sale.

Thus we see that the sales representative does not always do the whole selling job and may serve as a "matchmaker" bringing together company and customer personnel. The sales representative acts as "account manager" whose job it is to initiate and facilitate transactions between two companies.

The Buyer-Seller Relationship

Effective selling is in large part a matter of having the correct attitude toward the customer. *The customer wants help in solving problems. An effective sales representative recognizes the customer's problems and knows how to be of help.* A vice president of a major food company spent one week watching fifty sales presentations to a busy buyer for a major supermarket chain. Here are some of his experiences:

> I watched a soap company representative come in to the buyer. He had three separate new promotional deals to talk about with six different dates. He had *nothing* in writing. . . . After the salesman left, the buyer looked at me and said, "It will take me fifteen minutes to get this straightened out." I watched another salesman walk in to the buyer and say, "Well, I was in the area, and I want you to know that we have a great new promotion coming up next week." The buyer said, "That's fine. What is it?" He said, "I don't know . . . I'm coming in next week to tell you about it." The buyer asked him what he was doing there today. He said, "Well, I was in the area." Another salesman came [and] said, "Well, it's time for us to write that order now . . . getting ready for the summer business." The buyer said, "Well, fine, George, how much did I buy last year in total?" The salesman looked a little dumfounded and said, "Well, I'll be damned if I know. . . ." The majority of salesmen were ill-prepared, unable to answer basic questions, uncertain as to what they wanted to accomplish during the call. They did not think of the call as a studied, professional presentation. They didn't have a real idea of the busy retailer's *needs and wants*.[6]

Companies are striving to overcome these problems through better selection and training of their sales force. They are wary of "the old drummer type of salesman." Much of the old sales job has been taken over by mass media and nonpersonal retailing. The new breed of sales representative is better schooled and able to absorb a vast amount of information about many products and customers. He or she is likely to have technical training and be backed by a top-flight team of engineers and market researchers. The sales representative knows how to read the needs of customers and recognizes their growing interest in buying systems and service packages rather than single products. He or she goes after the *long-run relationship* rather than the *quick sale*. As technology grows

---

[6] From an address by Donald R. Keough at the 27th Annual Conference of the Super-Market Institute in Chicago, April 26–29, 1964.

more complex and competition more keen, one can expect to see more of this new type of sales representative.[7]

A Sales Representative's Tasks

Selling is only one of several tasks of the sales representative. He or she may perform as many as six different activities:

1. *Prospecting.* The company does its best to generate leads for the sales representative, but he or she is expected to search for additional prospects.
2. *Communicating.* Much of a sales representative's work consists of communicating information to existing and potential buyers about the company's products and services.
3. *Selling.* The sales representative engages in the "art of salesmanship"—approaching, presenting, answering objections, and closing sales.
4. *Servicing.* The sales representative provides various services to the customers—consulting on their problems, rendering technical assistance, arranging financing, and expediting delivery.
5. *Information gathering.* The sales representative conducts market research and intelligence work and is responsible for supplying regular reports on call activity.
6. *Allocating.* The sales representative helps evaluate customer profitability and advises on allocating scarce products to customers in times of product shortages.

The sales representative's actual mix of tasks varies with the character of the purchase decision process, company marketing strategy, and the economy. The nature of the purchase decision process establishes the kinds of activities that the sales representative must perform in order to develop and maintain satisfied customers. The sales activities required to handle straight rebuy situations are different from those required to "crack open" new accounts.

Sales-force strategy is also influenced by company marketing strategy. In the food industry, many manufacturers use a *pull strategy*, relying on massive consumer advertising to draw customers into the retailers' establishments to ask for their brands. The company sales representatives play a servicing role of seeing to it that the retailers carry a sufficient stock, give good shelf space, and cooperate in sales promotion programs. Other food manufacturers use a *push strategy*, primarily relying on their sales representatives to sell the trade on carrying their brands. Companies also will vary in how much time they want their sales representatives to spend on selling their established brands versus new ones and on calling on current customers versus prospects.

The sales representative's mix of tasks also varies with the state of the economy. When widespread product shortages appeared in 1973, sales representatives in many industries found themselves with nothing to sell. Some observers jumped to the conclusion that sales representatives were redundant and could be retrenched. But this thinking overlooked the other roles of the salesperson—allocating the product, counseling unhappy customers, communicating company plans on remedying the shortage, and selling the company's other products that were not in short supply.

Sales-Force Objectives

There are two schools of thought about what the sales force should be good at doing. The traditional view is that the job of sales representatives is to produce

---

[7] See Carl Rieser, "The Salesman Isn't Dead–He's Different," *Fortune*, November 1962, pp. 124ff; and "The New Supersalesmen: Wired for Success," *Business Week*, January 6, 1973, pp. 58–62.

sales volume. They must know the art of promoting the company's products and getting orders. The newer view says that the job of sales representative is to produce profit. They must know the cost and profit potential of various products and customers and manage their territories as profit centers.

These two views lead to different conceptions of the proper training of sales representatives. The traditional view emphasizes training sales personnel in the art of salesmanship. The new school emphasizes training sales personnel to use planning and marketing concepts. One marketing vice president complained recently: "It takes me about five years to train sales people to think like marketers. I want them to know how to find and solve customers' problems, bring intelligence back to the company, and make decisions that will maximize profit rather than sales volume."

At times, it seems that marketing management and sales management represent completely opposite cultures. Sales executives focus on sales volume planning, short-run sales goals, individual customers, customer contact work, and price as a marketing tool. Marketing executives focus on profit planning, long-run sales goals, market segments, analytical work, and perceived value as a marketing tool. Marketers believe that a marketing-oriented rather than a sales-oriented sales force will be most effective in the long run.

SALES-FORCE SIZE

Once the company clarifies the tasks and objectives of the sales force in the marketing mix, it is ready to consider the question of sales-force size. Sales representatives are among the most productive and expensive assets in a company. Increasing their number will increase both sales and costs. We shall describe two analytical approaches to determining the optimal sales-force size.

Productivity Approach Semlow proposed a solution to the problem of sales-force size that requires measuring the sales productivity of sales representatives in different-size territories.[8] He noted that sales representatives in territories rated as having higher sales potential produced more sales but that their sales were less than proportionate to the increase in sales potential. Citing a particular company's case, Semlow found that the sales in a territory with 1 percent of total national potential were $160,000 and sales in a territory with 5 percent of total potential were $200,000. In the latter case, there was only $40,000 in sales for every 1 percent of potential.

Now if the company employed one hundred sales representatives and wanted them all to work territories of equal potentials, it would create one hundred territories, each with 1 percent of total potential. This means that sales would average $160,000 in each territory, according to the previous analysis. Since there are one hundred sales representatives, total company sales would be $16 million.

If the company employed a sales force of only twenty, it would create twenty territories, each with 5 percent of the total potential. In this case, sales would average $200,000 in each territory, according to the previous analysis.

[8] Walter J. Semlow, "How Many Salesmen Do You Need?" *Harvard Business Review,* May–June 1959, pp. 126–32.

Since there were twenty sales representatives, total company sales would be only $4,000,000. Semlow applied the same reasoning to other possible sizes of the sales force. For each size, he projected to total sales volume, based on the estimated productivity of sales representatives in different-size territories.

His final step was to convert each sales volume into operating profit on investment. He first estimated the operating profit before variable selling cost on each sales volume. Then he deducted the variable selling cost, specifically the size of the sales force times the cost per sales representative. This left an estimate of operating profit on that sales volume. Then he estimated the working capital and plant investment required at alternative sales volumes. Finally, he expressed the estimated operating profit as a ratio to the required investment. In his example, the operating profit on investment was 11.6 percent with a sales force of one hundred and only 8.7 percent with a sales force of twenty. The optimal-size sales force called for sixty-five sales representatives, with the estimated rate of return of 22.0 percent.

Semlow's method depends on having a sufficient number of existing territories to allow making a statistical estimate of creating territories of equal sales potential. It also assumes that sales productivity is a function only of territory sales potential, neglecting the variations that might be produced by the mix of accounts in the territory, their geographical dispersion, and other factors.[9]

Workload Approach

Talley proposed an approach based on equalizing the workload of sales representatives rather than territory sales potential.[10] His method assumes that management has determined the economic number of calls to make on accounts of different sizes. The method consists of the following steps:

1. Customers are grouped into size classes according to their annual sales volume.
2. The desirable call frequencies (number of sales calls on an account per year) are established for each class.
3. The number of accounts in each size class are multiplied by the corresponding call frequency to arrive at the total workload for the country, in sales calls per year.
4. The average number of calls a sales representative can make per year is determined.
5. The number of sales representatives needed is determined by dividing the total annual calls required by the average annual calls made by a sales representative.

Suppose, for example, the company estimates that there are one thousand A-accounts and two thousand B-accounts in the nation; and A-accounts require thirty-six calls a year and B-accounts twelve calls a year. This means the company needs a sales force that can make sixty thousand sales calls a year. Suppose the average sales representative can make one thousand calls a year. The company would need sixty full-time sales representatives.

---

[9] For a criticism of Semlow's findings and an alternative method, see Henry C. Lucas, Jr., Charles B. Weinberg, and Kenneth W. Clowes, "Sales Response as a Function of Territorial Potential and Sales Representative Workload," *Journal of Marketing Research*, August 1975, pp. 298–305.

[10] Walter J. Talley, "How to Design Sales Territories," *Journal of Marketing*, January 1961, pp. 7–13.

SALES-FORCE DESIGN

**Sales-Force
Structure**

The effectiveness of a sales force depends a great deal on how it is organized. A sales force can be organized around company territories, products, customers, or some mixture of the three.

Territory-structured sales force   In the simplest sales organization each sales representative has an exclusive territory in which he or she represents the company's full line. This sales structure has a number of advantages. First, it results in a very clear definition of the salesperson's responsibilities. As the only salesperson working the territory, he or she bears the credit or blame for area sales to the extent that personal selling effort makes a difference. This tends to encourage a high level of effort, especially when management is able to gauge fairly accurately the area's sales potential. Second, responsibility for a definite territory increases the sales representative's incentive to cultivate local business and personal ties. These ties tend to improve the quality of the sales representative's selling effectiveness and personal life. Third, travel expenses are likely to be relatively small, since each sales representative's travel takes place within the bounds of a small geographical territory.

The territorial form of sales organization works quite well in companies with a relatively homogeneous set of products and customers. But these same companies, as their products and markets become diversified, find this form increasingly less effective. At the heart of the problem is the fact that the sales representative, to be effective, must know the company's products and markets. But there is a clear limit to how much knowledge a sales representative can acquire about different types of products and customers.

Product-structured sales force   The importance of sales representatives' knowing their products, together with the development of product divisions and management, has led many companies to structure their sales force along product lines. Specialization of the sales force by product is particularly warranted where the products are (1) technically complex, (2) highly unrelated, and/or (3) very numerous.

The mere existence of different company products, however, is not a sufficient argument for such specialization. A major drawback may exist if the company's separate product lines are bought by many of the same customers. For example:

> The *American Hospital Supply Corporation* has several divisions and subsidiaries, each with its own sales force. All of these sales forces call on the same hospitals. It is conceivable that as many as seven different sales representatives of the American Hospital Supply Corporation could call on the same hospital on the same day.[11]

This means that company sales personnel travel over the same routes, and each one uses up valuable time waiting in the outer office to see the customer's purchasing agents. These extra costs must be weighed against the benefits that may result from the higher level of customer service and more knowledgeable product representation.

[11] See Ralph Westfall and Harper C. Boyd, Jr., *Cases in Marketing Management* (Homewood, Ill.: Richard D. Irwin, 1961), pp. 376–83.

Customer-structured sales force   Companies often specialize their sales forces along customer lines. Separate sales forces may be set up for different industries, customer sizes, national accounts, and new business. The most obvious advantage of customer specialization is that each sales force can become more knowledgeable about specific customer needs. At one time General Electric's sales representatives specialized in specific products (fan motors, switches, and so forth), but later they changed to specialization in markets, such as the air conditioning market, because this is how the customer saw the problem of fan motors, switches, and so on. A customer-specialized sales force can also sometimes reduce total sales-force costs. A large pump manufacturer at one time used a single sales force of highly trained sales engineers to sell to both original equipment manufacturers (who needed to deal with technical representatives) and to jobbers (who did not need to deal with technical representatives). Later the company split its sales force and staffed the one selling to jobbers with less highly trained sales representatives.

The major disadvantage of customer-structured sales forces arises if the various types of customers are scattered evenly throughout the country. This means an overlapping coverage of territories, which is always more expensive.

Complex sales-force structures   When a company sells a wide variety of products to many types of customers over a broad geographical area, it often combines several principles of sales-force structure. Sales representatives may be specialized by territory-product, territory-customer, product-customer, or ultimately by territory-product-customer. A salesman may then be responsible to one or more line managers and/or one or more staff managers.

Territorial Design

The great majority of companies assign their sales representatives to specific territories whether or not they are further specialized by product or type of customers. The territories are aggregated into larger groupings called *districts,* and in turn these districts may be aggregated into major sales *regions.* Many of the larger companies, for example, utilize an eastern, southern, central, and western regional plan for field operations.

In designing a system of territories, the company generally tries to achieve the following territorial characteristics: the territories are easy to administer; their sales potential is easy to estimate; they keep down total travel time; and they provide a sufficient and equitable workload and sales potential for each sales representative. These characteristics are achieved through decisions about the size and shape of territorial units.

Territory size   One approach calls for forming territories of *equal sales potential,* and the other calls for forming territories of *equal workload.* Each principle offers advantages at the cost of some real dilemmas.

The logic of creating territories of *equal potential* is to provide each sales representative with the same income opportunities and to provide the company with a means of evaluating performance. Persistent differences in sales yield by territory are assumed to reflect differences in the ability or effort of individual sales representatives. Awareness of that will encourage salespersons to work at their top capacity.

But because customer geographical density almost always varies, territories with equal potential typically cover vastly different areas. For example, the potential for the sale of large drill presses is as large in Detroit as it is in a number of the western states. A sales representative assigned to Detroit can cover the same potential with far less effort than the sales representative who sells in the territory spanning the several western states.

The problem is that sales representatives assigned to the larger and sparser territories are either going to end up with fewer sales and less income for equal effort or with equal sales only through extraordinary effort. Is there any way around the problem? One possibility is to pay the western sales representatives more to compensate for the extra effort. But this reduces the profits on sales in the western territories. An alternative is to acknowledge that territories differ in attractiveness and assign the better or more senior sales representatives to the better territories.

The alternative principle for creating territories is to try to *equalize the sales workloads*. The objective is to permit each sales representative to cover his or her territory adequately. However, this principle generally results in some variation in territory sales potentials. That is not a concern when the sales force is on straight salary. But where sales representatives are compensated partly on the basis of their sales, territories definitely vary in their attractiveness even though the workloads are approximately equalized. The same solutions appear. A lower compensation rate can be paid to sales representatives in the territories with the higher sales potential, or the territories with the better potential can go to the higher performers.

Territory shape Territories are formed by combining smaller units, such as counties or states, until they add up to a territory of a given potential or workload. They are put together with reference to the location of natural barriers, the compatibility of adjacent areas, the adequacy of transportation, and so forth. Many companies also try to achieve a certain territory shape because this can influence the cost and ease of coverage and the sales representatives' satisfaction. The most common shapes are circular, cloverleaf, and wedge-shaped territories.

Computer models are being increasingly used to design sales territories that achieve some balance of workload, sales potential, compactness, and routing efficiency.[12] The efficient routing of sales calls through a territory to reduce travel time or cost is being assisted by computer programs based on the "traveling salesman problem."[13]

RECRUITING AND SELECTING SALES REPRESENTATIVES

Up to now, we have considered sales-force tasks and objectives, sales-force size, and sales-force structure. We now want to turn to the day-to-day concerns of sales management in operating an effective sales force. Sales management has to

[12] A computer-based method that creates territories that are compact and equal in workload is described in Sidney W. Hess and Stuart A. Samuels, "Experiences with a Sales Districting Model: Criteria and Implementation," *Management Science*, December 1971, pp. 41–54. Also see Leonard M. Lodish, "Sales Territory Alignment to Maximize Profit," *Journal of Marketing Research*, February 1975, pp. 30–36; and Andris A. Zoltners, "Integer Programming Models for Sales Territory Alignment to Maximize Profit," *Journal of Marketing Research*, November 1976, pp. 426–30.

[13] See John D. C. Little et al., "An Algorithm for the Traveling Salesman Problem," *Operations Research*, November–December 1963, pp. 972–89.

recruit, select, train, compensate, supervise, and evaluate sales representatives. Various strategies and policies guide these decisions.

Importance of Careful Selection

At the heart of a successful sales-force operation is the selection of good sales representatives. The performance levels of an average and a top sales representative are quite different. A survey of more than five hundred companies revealed that 27 percent of the sales force brought in over 52 percent of the sales.[14] Beyond the differences in sales productivity are the great wastes in hiring the wrong persons. Of the sixteen thousand sales representatives who were hired by the surveyed companies, only 68.5 percent still worked for their company at the end of the year, and only 50 percent were expected to remain through the following year. The cost of recruiting, training, and supervising an individual sales person for one year was estimated at the time at $8,730. As a result, the surveyed companies were expected to lose around $70 million, or half their investment. This loss would be much larger in today's dollars.

The financial loss due to turnover is only part of the total cost. The new sales representative who remains with the company receives a direct income averaging around half of the direct selling outlay. If he or she receives $14,000 a year, another $14,000 may go into fringe benefits, expenses for travel and entertainment, supervision, office space, supplies, and secretarial assistance. Consequently, the new sales representative should be capable of creating sales on which the gross margin at least covers the selling expenses of $28,000. If this margin was 10 percent, for example, he or she would have to sell at least $240,000 of product to constitute a breakeven resource for the company.

What Makes a Good Sales Representative?

Selecting sales representatives would not be such a problem if one knew the characteristics of an ideal salesperson. If ideal salespersons are outgoing, aggressive, and energetic, it would not be too difficult to check for these characteristics in applicants. But a review of the most successful sales representatives in any company is likely to reveal a good number who are introverted, mild-mannered, and far from energetic. The successful group will also include men and women who are tall and short, articulate and inarticulate, well groomed and slovenly.

Nevertheless, the search for the magic combination of traits that spells sure-fire sales ability continues unabated. The number of lists that have been drawn up is countless. Most of them recite the same qualities. McMurry wrote:

> It is my conviction that the possessor of *effective* sales personality is *a habitual "wooer," an individual who has a compulsive need to win and hold the affection of others.* . . . His wooing, however, is not based on a sincere desire for love because, in my opinion, he is convinced at heart that no one will ever love him. Therefore, his wooing is primarily exploitative . . . his relationships tend to be transient, superficial and evanescent.[15]

McMurry went on to list five additional traits of the supersalesperson: a high level of energy, abounding self-confidence, a chronic hunger for money, a well-

---

[14] The survey was conducted by the Sales Executives Club of New York and was reported in *Business Week*, February 1, 1964, p. 52.

[15] McMurry, "Mystique of Super-Salesmanship," p. 117.

established habit of industry, and a state of mind that regards each objection, resistance, or obstacle as a challenge.[16]

Mayer and Greenberg offered one of the shortest lists of traits exhibited by effective sales representatives.[17] Their seven years of field work led them to conclude that the effective salesperson has at least two basic qualities: (1) *empathy,* the ability to feel as the customer does; and (2) *ego drive,* a strong personal need to make the sale. Using these two traits, they were able to make fairly good predictions of the subsequent performance of applicants for sales positions in three different industries.

It may be true that certain basic traits may make a person effective in any line of selling. From the viewpoint of a particular company, however, these basic traits are rarely enough. Each selling job is characterized by a unique set of duties and challenges. One only has to think about insurance selling, computer selling, and automobile selling to realize the different educational, intellectual, and personality requirements that would be sought in the respective sales representatives.

How can a company determine the characteristics that its prospective sales representatives should "ideally" possess? The particular duties of the job suggest some of the characteristics to look for in applicants. Is there a lot of paperwork? Does the job call for much travel? Will the salesperson confront a high proportion of refusals? In addition, the traits of the company's most successful sales representatives suggest additional qualities to look for. Some companies compare the standing of their best versus their poorest sales representatives to see which characteristics differentiate the two groups.

Recruitment Procedures

After management develops general criteria for new sales personnel, it has the job of attracting a sufficient number of applicants. The recruiting is turned over to the personnel department, which seeks applicants through various means, including soliciting names from current sales representatives, using employment agencies, placing job ads, and contacting college students. As for college students, companies have not found it easy to sell them on selling. A survey of one thousand male students in 123 colleges indicated that only one in seventeen college students showed an interest in selling.[18] The reluctant ones gave as reasons the fear of insecurity and a dislike of travel and being away from their families. To counter these objections company recruiters emphasized starting salaries, income opportunities, and the fact that one-quarter of the presidents of large U.S. corporations started out in marketing and sales.

Applicant Rating Procedures

Recruitment procedures, if successful, will lead to the development of more applicants than jobs, and the company's task is to select the better applicants. The selection procedures vary in elaborateness from a single informal interview to prolonged testing and interviewing, not only of the applicant but also of her or his family.

An increasing number of companies are giving formal tests to applicants for sales positions. Although test scores are only one information element in a set

[16] *Ibid.,* p. 118.

[17] David Mayer and Herbert M. Greenberg, "What Makes a Good Salesman?" *Harvard Business Review,* July–August 1964, pp. 119–25.

[18] "Youth Continues to Snub Selling," *Sales Management,* January 15, 1965, p. 69.

that includes personal characteristics, references, past employment history, and interviewer reactions, they are weighed quite heavily by some companies, including IBM, Prudential, Procter & Gamble, and Gillette. Gillette claims that the use of tests has resulted in a 42 percent reduction in turnover and that test scores have correlated well with the subsequent progress of new sales representatives in the sales organization.

The choice of an appropriate battery of tests is not simple. Standard tests are available to measure intelligence, interests, personality, interpersonal skills and sales aptitude. There are also tailor-made tests for special selling situations. These tests vary considerably in reliability and validity. Furthermore, many of them are vulnerable to manipulation by the applicant. A person, for example, can spot a red-herring question such as "Do you prefer golf or reading?" Whyte laid down the following rules for the job applicant who takes company psychological tests: (1) Give the most conventional answer; (2) show that you like things as they are; (3) indicate that you never worry; and (4) deny any taste for books or music.[19]

TRAINING SALES REPRESENTATIVES

Not too long ago many companies sent their new salespeople out into the field almost immediately after hiring them. The sales representative would be supplied with a pack of samples, order books, and instructions to sell west of the Mississippi. Training programs were considered luxuries. A training program meant large outlays for instructors, materials, and space; the payment of a base salary to a person who was not selling; and lost opportunities because he or she was not in the field.

Nowadays new sales representatives can expect to spend from a few weeks to many months in the limbo state known as training. In industries such as steel or data processing new sales representatives are not on their own for two years!

IBM expects its sales representatives to spend 15 percent of their time each year in additional training. The sales-training bill for a major U.S. corporation can run into millions of dollars each year. Several factors have convinced sales management that extended training may add more value than cost. The sales representative of today is selling to more cost-conscious and value-conscious buyers. Furthermore, he or she is selling a host of products, often loosely related, and sometimes technically complex. More reports are expected of this person. The company wants to be represented by a mature and knowledgeable sales representative.

The purpose of the training is to instill certain information and attitudes in the sales force and teach certain skills:

The sales representative should know the company and identify with it. Most companies devote the first part of the training program to describing the history and objectives of the company, the organizational setup and lines of authority, the names of the chief officers, the company's financial structure and facilities, and the company's chief products and sales volume.

The sales representative should know the company's products. The sales trainee is shown how the products are produced and how they function in various uses.

[19] William H. Whyte, Jr., *The Organization Man* (New York: Simon and Schuster, 1956), pp. 405–10.

The sales representative should know customers' and competitors' characteristics. The sales representative is introduced to the different types of customers and their needs, buying motives, and buying habits. He or she learns about the company's and competitors' strategies and policies.

The sales representative should learn how to make effective sales presentations. The sales representative is trained in the basic principles of salesmanship. Part of the training time is used to develop the sales representative's personality and interpersonal skills. In addition, the company outlines the major sales arguments for each product, and some go so far as to provide a sales script.

The sales representative should be introduced to field procedures and responsibilities. The sales representative should know how to divide time between active accounts and potential accounts; how to use the expense account, prepare reports, and route effectively.

New methods of training are continually being sought to speed up and deepen skill development and understanding. Among the instructional approaches are role playing, sensitivity training, cassette tapes, videotapes, programmed learning, and films on salesmanship and company products.[20]

Does all this sales training pay off? Unless the sales training department of the company can show bottom-line results, they will be one of the first to have their budget cut in hard times. There is no one way to evaluate the training results, but training departments should make an effort to collect as much concrete evidence of improved sales performance as possible.[21] Besides a demonstrable change in the sales personnel's knowledge, skills, and attitudes, there should be a measurable impact on such variables as: (1) sales-force turnover, (2) sales volume, (3) absenteeism, (4) average sale size, (5) calls-to-close ratio, (6) customer complaints and compliments, (7) new accounts per time unit, and (8) volume of returned merchandise.

The substantial costs of company training programs raise the question of whether a company would be better off to hire experienced sales representatives away from other companies. The gain is often illusory, however, because the experienced salesperson is brought in at a higher salary, which sometimes may simply represent a capitalization of the equivalent training costs. From a national point of view, there is probably a net loss when an industry practices pirating on a large scale. Some of the representatives' specific training and company experience is wasted when he or she transfers to another company. Within some industries, companies tacitly agree not to hire sales personnel away from each other.

Principles of Salesmanship

One of the major objectives of sales-training programs is to train company sales personnel in the art of selling. The sales-training industry today involves expenditures of hundreds of millions of dollars in training programs, books, cassettes and other materials. Almost a million copies of books on selling are purchased every year, bearing such provocative titles as *How to Outsell the Born Salesman, How to Sell Anything to Anybody, The Power of Enthusiastic Selling, How Power Selling Brought Me Success in 6 Hours, Where Do You Go From No?*

[20] For a good overview, see Morgan B. MacDonald, Jr., and Earl L. Bailey, *Training Company Salesmen* (New York: Conference Board, 1967).

[21] See Ron Zemke, "Sales Training and the Bottom Line: Is There a Measurable Relationship?" *Training HRD*, October 1976, pp. 36–41.

and *1,000 Ways a Salesman Can Increase His Sales.* One of the most enduring books is Dale Carnegie's *How to Win Friends and Influence People.*

All of the sales-training approaches are designed to convert a salesperson from being a passive *order taker* to a more active *order getter.* Order taking is based on the notion that: (1) the customers are aware of their own needs; (2) they cannot be influenced or would resent any attempt at influence; and (3) they prefer salespersons who are courteous and self-effacing. An example of an order-taking mentality would be a Fuller Brush salesman who knocks on dozens of doors each day, simply asking if the consumer needs any brushes.

In training salespersons to be order getters, there are two basic approaches, a sales-oriented approach and a customer-oriented approach. The first one trains the salesperson to be adept in the use of *high-pressure selling techniques,* such as those used in selling encyclopedias or automobiles. The techniques include overstating the product's merits, critizing competitive products, using a slick, canned presentation, selling yourself, and offering some concession to get the order on the spot. The assumptions behind this form of selling are that: (1) the customers are not likely to buy except under pressure; (2) they are influenced by a slick presentation and ingratiating manners; and (3) they won't regret the transaction after signing the order, or if they do, it doesn't matter.

The other approach attempts to train sales personnel in *customer problem solving.* Here the salesperson studies the customers' needs and wants and proposes profitable solutions. An example would be a sales representative who examines a customer's situation and proposes a plan that would make or save the customer money. Here the salesperson does what is good for the customer, not what is immediately good for the salesperson. The assumptions behind this approach are that: (1) the customers have latent needs that constitute opportunities for the sales representative; (2) they appreciate good suggestions; and (3) they will be loyal to sales representatives who have their long-term interests at heart. Certainly the problem solver is a more compatible image for the salesperson, under the marketing concept, than is the hard seller or order taker.[22]

Blake and Mouton see the problem of selling in terms of two dimensions, the salesperson's *concern for the sale* and *concern for the customer.*[23] These two dimensions give rise to the *sales grid* shown in Figure 21–1A, which describes five types of salespersons. Type 1,1 is very much the order-taker mentality, and 9,1 is the hard-seller mentality. Type 5,5 is a soft-sell mentality, while type 1,9 is a sell-myself mentality. Type 9,9 epitomizes the problem-solving mentality, which is most consistent with the marketing concept.

Blake and Mouton go on to say that no one type of sales style is going to work with all buyers because buying styles are just as varied as salespersons. Figure 21–1B exhibits a *customer grid* and defines five types of customers based on their degree of *concern for the purchase* and *concern for the salesperson.*[24] One can begin to appreciate the difficulty—or low probability—of achieving com-

[22] The problem-solving salesperson is good at "consultative selling." See Mark Hanan, James Cribbin, and Herman Heiser, *Consultative Selling* (New York: American Management Association, 1970).

[23] Robert R. Blake and Jane S. Mouton, *The Grid for Sales Excellence: Benchmarks for Effective Salesmanship* (New York: McGraw-Hill Book Company, 1970), p. 4.

[24] *Ibid.,* p. 10.

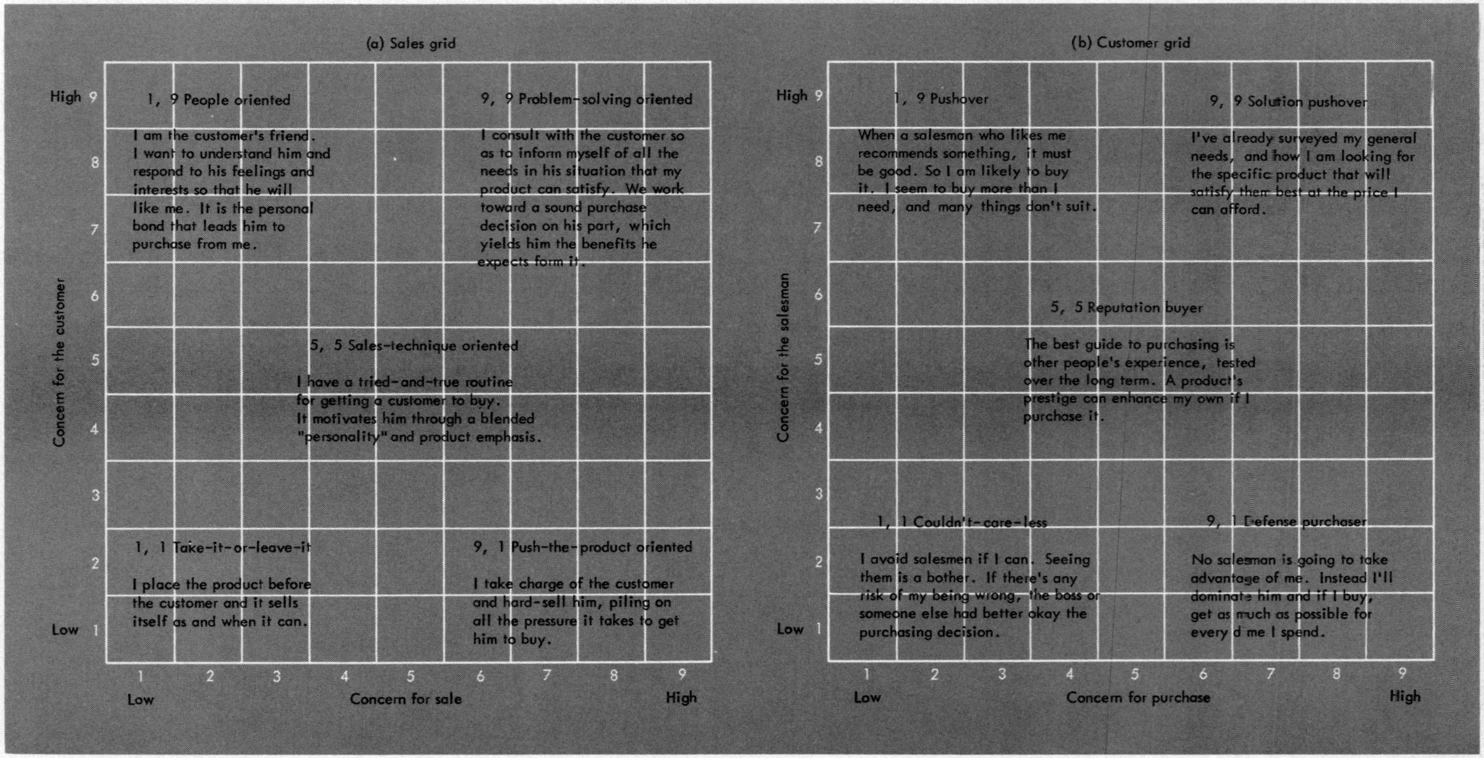

(a) Sales grid

Concern for the customer

High 9 — 1, 9 People oriented
I am the customer's friend. I want to understand him and respond to his feelings and interests so that he will like me. It is the personal bond that leads him to purchase from me.

9, 9 Problem-solving oriented
I consult with the customer so as to inform myself of all the needs in his situation that my product can satisfy. We work toward a sound purchase decision on his part, which yields him the benefits he expects from it.

5, 5 Sales-technique oriented
I have a tried-and-true routine for getting a customer to buy. It motivates him through a blended "personality" and product emphasis.

1, 1 Take-it-or-leave-it
I place the product before the customer and it sells itself as and when it can.

9, 1 Push-the-product oriented
I take charge of the customer and hard-sell him, piling on all the pressure it takes to get him to buy.

Low 1   Concern for sale   High

(b) Customer grid

Concern for the salesman

High 9 — 1, 9 Pushover
When a salesman who likes me recommends something, it must be good. So I am likely to buy it. I seem to buy more than I need, and many things don't suit.

9, 9 Solution pushover
I've already surveyed my general needs, and how I am looking for the specific product that will satisfy them best at the price I can afford.

5, 5 Reputation buyer
The best guide to purchasing is other people's experience, tested over the long term. A product's prestige can enhance my own if I purchase it.

1, 1 Couldn't-care-less
I avoid salesmen if I can. Seeing them is a bother. If there's any risk of my being wrong, the boss or someone else had better okay the purchasing decision.

9, 1 Defense purchaser
No salesman is going to take advantage of me. Instead I'll dominate him and if I buy, get as much as possible for every $ I spend.

Low 1   Concern for purchase   High

SOURCE: Robert R. Blake and Jane S. Mouton, *The Grid For Sales Excellence: Benchmarks for Effective Salesmanship* (New York: McGraw-Hill Book Company, 1970), p. 4.

FIGURE 21–1
Sales Types and Customer Types

patibility between a buyer and a seller. Consider, for example, the incompatibility of a 9,1 customer (defensive purchaser) and a 9,1 sales representative (product pusher). The purpose of these two grids is to provide diagnostics to the salesperson for analyzing a particular buyer and determining the best selling style to use.

The view that effective selling depends on matching *buyer and seller styles* is an alternative to the traditional view seeking to train salespersons in one particular selling style. It suggests that the buyer plays an active role in determining the outcome. Evans sees selling as a *dyadic process* where the outcome depends primarily on the match of *buyer and seller characteristics* even more than *buying and selling styles*.[25] He found, for example, that people tended to buy insurance from people very much like themselves. This was true for such factors as age, height, income, political opinions, religious beliefs, and smoking. What mattered was the perceived similarity more than the actual similarity. Evans proposed that insurance companies should hire all types of salespersons if they want to achieve broad market penetration. The only requirement is that they exhibit the intelligence and kinds of abilities effective in selling insurance.

Company sales-training programs differ depending on management's view of what constitutes an effective selling approach for the type of selling situation the company faces. Programs can be found that are based on stimulus-response thinking, formulated-steps thinking, or need-satisfaction thinking.[26] Regardless of the underlying model, most sales-training programs view the selling process as consisting of a set of steps that the salesperson has to carry out, each involving certain skills. The major steps are: *prospecting, preapproach, approach, demonstration, handling objections, closing,* and *follow-up.*[27]

Prospecting   The first step in the sales process is to identify prospects. Although the company can supply leads, the sales representatives also need skills in developing their own leads. Leads can be developed in the following ways:

1. Asking current satisfied customers for the names of other potential buyers
2. Cultivating other referral sources, such as suppliers, dealers, noncompeting sales representatives, bankers, and trade association executives
3. Joining organizations where there is a high probability of meeting or learning about new prospects
4. Engaging in speaking and writing activities that are likely to increase the salesperson's visibility
5. Examining various data sources (newspapers, directories) in search of names
6. Using the telephone and mail to track down leads
7. Dropping in cold on various offices (cold canvassing)

Sales representatives also need to know how to screen the leads to avoid wasting valuable time on poor leads. Prospects can be qualified by examining their finan-

[25] Franklin B. Evans, "Selling as a Dyadic Relationship—a New Approach," *The American Behavioral Scientist,* May 1963, pp. 76–79, at p. 76, 78. Also see Harry L. Davis and Alvin J. Silk, "Interaction and Influence Processes in Personal Selling," *Sloan Management Review,* winter 1972, pp. 59–76.

[26] See W. J. E. Crissy, William H. Cunningham, and Isabella C. M. Cunningham, *Selling: The Personal Force in Marketing* (New York: John Wiley & Sons, 1977), pp. 119–29.

[27] The following discussion draws in part from Crissy et al., *Selling.*

cial ability, volume of business, special requirements, location, and likelihood of continuous business. The salesperson should phone or write to prospects to see if they are worth pursuing further.

Preapproach   This step involves the salesperson's learning as much as possible about the company (what it needs, who is involved in the purchase decision) and the buyers (their personal characteristics and buying styles). The salesperson can consult standard sources (such as *Moody's, Standard and Poor, Dun and Bradstreet*), acquaintances, and others to learn about the company. The salesperson should determine *call objectives*, which may be to qualify the prospect, or to gather information, or to make an immediate sale. Another task is to decide on the best *approach*, which might be a personal visit (possibly with a respected intermediary), a phone call, or a letter. The best *timing* should be thought out because many prospects are especially busy at certain times of the year. Finally, the salesperson should give thought to an overall strategy to use in the approach stage.

Approach   This stage involves the salesperson's knowing how to meet and greet the buyer to get the relationship off to a good start. The salesperson's looks, opening lines, and follow-up remarks are all important factors. The salesperson's looks include his or her appearance, manner, and mannerisms. The salesperson is encouraged to wear clothes similar to the clothes buyers usually wear and is reminded to have a neat appearance, to show courtesy and attention to the buyer, and to avoid distracting mannerisms, such as pacing the floor or staring at the customer. The opening line should be positive and pleasant—"Mr. Smith, I am Bill Jones from the ABC Company. My company and I appreciate your willingness to see me. I will do my best to make this visit profitable and worthwhile for you and your company." This opener might be followed by some light talk to further the acquaintance, some key questions, or the showing of a display or sample to attract the buyer's attention and curiosity.

Demonstration   After getting acquainted and sizing up the buyer, the salesperson attempts to relate the company's products to the buyer's situation. The aim is to demonstrate the want-satisfying characteristics of the company and its products. The salesperson may follow the AIDA approach in presenting the product in a way that gains attention, holds interest, builds desire, and leads to purchase action. The salesperson covers the *features* of the product but concentrates on selling the *benefits*.[28] Emphasis is placed on how the product will save or make money for the buyer. The salesperson may use aids, such as attractive literature, an audiovisual presentation, or an actual physical demonstration. During the demonstration, the salesperson will apply a mix of five influence strategies.[29]

---

[28] A feature is a characteristic of a product, such as its portability. A benefit is any advantages the buyer obtains from this feature, such as less exertion or lower cost. A common mistake in selling is to dwell on product features (a product orientation) instead of user benefits (a marketing orientation). See the feature-benefit matrices in Crissy et al., *Selling*, pp. 247–50.

[29] See Rosann L. Spiro and William D. Perreault, Jr., "Influence Use by Industrial Salesmen: Influence Strategy Mixes and Situational Determinants," unpublished paper, Graduate School of Business Administration, University of North Carolina, 1976.

1. *Legitimacy.* The salesperson will attempt to convince the buyer of the relevant reputation and experience of the salesperson's company.

2. *Expertise.* The salesperson will attempt to demonstrate strong knowledge of the buyer's situation and of his or her own company's products, doing this without being overly "smart."

3. *Referent power.* The salesperson will attempt to build on any shared characteristics, interests, and acquaintances to deepen their personal relationship.

4. *Ingratiation.* The salesperson may attempt to provide personal favors (a free lunch, promotional gratuities) to the customer to strengthen affiliation and reciprocity feelings.

5. *Impression management.* The salesperson may manipulate impressions of self in order to achieve a more favorable response.

Handling objections   Customers will almost always pose objections during the demonstration or when asked to place an order. Their sales resistance could take a psychological or logical form. Psychological sales resistance includes: (1) resistance to interference, (2) preference for established habits, (3) apathy, (4) reluctance to give up something, (5) unpleasant associations with other person, (6) tendency to resist domination, (7) predetermined ideas, (8) dislike of making decisions, and (9) neurotic attitude toward money.[30] Logical resistance might consist of objections to the price, delivery schedule, or certain products or company characteristics. To handle these objections, the salesperson uses such techniques as maintaining a positive approach, trying to have the buyer clarify and define the objections, questioning the buyer in a way that the buyer has to answer his or her own objections, denying the validity of the objections, and turning the objection into a reason for buying. The salesperson needs training in the broader skills of negotiation, of which handling objections is a part.[31]

Closing   In this stage, the salesperson attempts to close the sale. Some salespeople do not handle this stage effectively. They lack confidence in themselves or their company or product; or feel guilty about asking for the order; or don't recognize the right psychological moment to close the sale. Salespersons have to be trained in recognizing specific closing signals from the buyer including physical actions, statements or comments, and questions signaling a possible readiness to close. Salespersons can then use one of several closing techniques. They can ask the prospect for the order (direct method), recapitulate the points of agreement (summative method), offer to help the secretary write up the order (assumptive method), ask whether the buyer wants A or B (positive-choice method), get the buyer to make minor choices such as the color or size (minor-decision method), or indicate what the buyer will lose if the order is not placed now (scare method). The salesperson may offer the buyer specific inducements to close, such as a special price, an extra quantity at no charge, or a gift.

Follow-up   This last stage is necessary if the salesperson wants to assure customer satisfaction and repeat business. Immediately after closing, the sales-

---

[30] Crissy et al., *Selling,* pp. 289–94.

[31] See Gerald I. Nierenberg, *The Art of Negotiation* (New York: Hawthorn Books, 1968); and Chester L. Karrass, *The Negotiating Game* (Cleveland, Ohio: World Publishing Co., 1970).

person should attempt to complete any necessary details on delivery time, purchase terms, and other matters. The salesperson should also consider scheduling a follow-up call when the initial order is received to make sure there is proper installation, instruction, and servicing. This visit is designed to detect any problems, to assure the buyer of the salesperson's interest and service, and to reduce any cognitive dissonance that might have arisen.

COMPENSATING SALESMEN

The major requirements for building a topflight sales force are (1) attracting good people, (2) motivating them, and (3) keeping them. In all three areas company compensation policies can make the crucial difference.

It is not easy to formulate a compensation plan that can be trusted to attract, motivate, and keep good sales personnel. Sales representatives and management tend to seek different, and often conflicting, objectives. Sales representatives would like a plan that offers the following features:

> *Income regularity.* Since sales are influenced by many factors beyond the sales representative's control, he or she wants to be assured of some regular base income regardless of sales. This minimum income will help pay bills in periods of poor sales.
>
> *Reward for above-average performance.* Most sales representatives think they can sell more than the average salesperson and want a compensation plan that provides superior income for superior performance.
>
> *Fairness.* Sales representatives want to feel that their pay is about right in relation to their experience and ability, the earnings of coworkers and competitors' sales representatives, and the cost of living.

On the other hand, an ideal compensation plan from management's point of view would emphasize:

> *Control.* Management likes a plan that facilitates its control over how sales representatives spend their time.
>
> *Economy.* Management wants to establish a level of pay that is reasonable in relation to the value of the sales representatives' efforts and the cost and value of company products.
>
> *Simplicity.* Management prefers a plan that is simple to administer from a payroll point of view, simple to explain to sales personnel, and simple to change as product situations and business conditions change.

Management is obviously hard pressed to reconcile all these objectives in one plan. Plans with good control features are generally not simple. Management objectives, such as economy, will conflict with sales representatives' objectives, such as financial security. In the light of these conflicting objectives, it is understandable why compensation plans exhibit a tremendous variety, not only among industries but among companies within the same industry.

The Level of Compensation

Management must determine the level, components, and structure of an effective compensation plan. The level must bear some relation to the "going market price" for the type of sales job and abilities required. For example, the average

562

earnings of the experienced salesperson in 1977 were $24,500.[32] If the market price for salespersons is well defined, the individual firm has little choice but to pay the going rate. To pay less would not bring forth the desired quantity or quality of applicants, and to pay more would be unnecessary. More often, however, the market price for salespersons is not well defined. For one thing, company plans vary in the importance of fixed and variable salary elements, fringe benefits, and expense allowances. And data on the average take-home pay of sales representatives working for competitive firms can be misleading because of significant variations in the average seniority and ability levels of the competitors' sales force. Published comparisons of industry-by-industry sales-force compensation levels are infrequent and generally lack sufficient detail.

The theoretical solution to the problem of the optimal compensation level is the same as shown in Figure 10–2, p. 259. Assume a company that is preparing to establish a specialized sales force of ten sales representatives to handle a new product. They will be paid on a straight salary. Higher salary levels would allow the company to recruit better applicants and lead to higher sales volumes. The sales curve can be assumed to be S-shaped with respect to the sales impact of greater total expenditures on the sales force. From the estimated sales curve would be deducted all costs before the total sales-force expenditures, to find gross profits. Then total sales-force expenditures would be deducted from gross profits, to find net profits. At the point where net profits are highest, the optimal total sales-force expenditure is found. This figure can be divided by the planned size of the sales force, here ten, to find the optimal salary level.

The Elements of Compensation

After a firm decides on the average pay level, it must determine the appropriate mix of the four basic elements of sales-force compensation—a fixed amount, a variable amount, expenses, and fringe benefits. The fixed amount, which might be salary or a drawing account, is intended to satisfy the sales representatives' need for some stability of income. The variable amount, which might be commissions, bonus, or profit sharing, is intended to stimulate and reward greater effort. Expense allowances are intended to enable the sales representatives to undertake selling efforts that are considered necessary or desirable. And fringe benefits, such as paid vacations, sickness or accident benefits, pensions, and life insurance, are intended to provide security and job satisfaction.

Top sales management must decide which elements should be in the compensation plan and their relative importance. A popular rule seems to favor making about 70 percent of the salesperson's total income fixed and allocating the remaining 30 percent among the other elements. But the variations around this average are so pronounced that it can hardly serve as a sufficient guide in planning. For example, fixed compensation should have more emphasis in jobs with a high ratio of nonselling duties to selling duties and in jobs where the selling task is technically complex. Variable compensation should have more emphasis in jobs where sales are cyclical and/or depend on the personal initiative of the sales representative.

Fixed and variable compensation taken alone give rise to three basic types of sales-force compensation plans—straight salary, straight commission, and

---

[32] John P. Steinbrink, "How to Pay Your Sales Force," *Harvard Business Review,* July–August 1978, pp. 111–22.

combination salary and commission. In one study, 28 percent of the companies paid straight salary, 21 percent paid straight commission, and 51 percent paid salary plus commission.[33] Figure 21–2 illustrates how the monthly compensation level of the sales representative is affected by his or her sales performance under four different plans. Clearly these different plans will have different effects on sales-force motivation and performance. More confident sales representatives will favor plans B and D because of the opportunity to earn more if they are high producers. More conservative sales representatives will favor plans A or C. The plans will also have different impacts on company costs and profits. Here we will examine the major strengths and drawbacks of each plan.

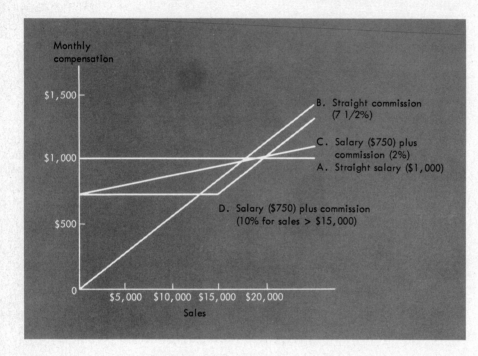

FIGURE 21–2
Sales-Force
Compensation
under Different
Compensation Plans

Straight salary   With this plan, the sales representative receives a fixed salary in total payment for services. Generally he or she also receives an amount to cover expenses incurred in performing various duties. Occasionally, this will be additional compensation in the way of discretionary bonuses or sales-contest prizes.

From management's point of view, a number of advantages are secured under a straight salary plan. The primary one is that management has more freedom to direct and alter sales duties without incurring strong opposition from the sales personnel affected. In addition, straight salary plans are generally less costly to administer and easier to explain. They also simplify the task of projecting the sales payroll for the coming year. Finally, by providing the sales

[33] *Ibid.*

force with security through stability of income, the straight salary plan may lead to a greater evenness in the morale of the sales force.

The chief weakness of the straight salary plan is that it does not present the sales force with any direct incentive to do a better-than-average selling job. This puts a greater supervision burden on management to control, evaluate, and reward the performances of individual sales representatives. Other problems posed by straight salary plans are an inflexible selling-expense burden during downswings in business; the danger that during upswings sales representatives on fixed salaries do not have sufficient incentive to exploit the increased business potential; thorny questions in salary adjustment for ability, rising living costs, length of service; and the probability that the more hard-driving type of salesperson will not be easy to attract.

Straight commission   This plan pays the sales representative some fixed or sliding rate related to his or her sales or profit volume. The sales representative may or may not also receive reimbursement for expenses incurred in performing the selling function. Straight commission plans are particularly prominent in the selling of insurance and investment securities, furniture, office equipment, small office machines, clothing, the textile and shoe industries, and drug and hardware wholesaling.

The straight commission plan offers at least three advantages. The most obvious one is that it provides a maximum financial incentive for the sales representative to work to capacity. A second advantage is that a straight commission plan leads to selling expenses more closely related to funds either currently available or becoming available through sales revenues. A third advantage is that commission plans enable management to employ financial incentives to direct sales representatives in their use of selling time.

These advantages come at a substantial price, however. The major difficulty is that management encounters great resistance when it tries to get the sales force to do things that do not generate immediate sales, such as following up leads, filling out reports, or providing sufficient customer service. Their personal financial involvement in getting the sale may lead them to use high-pressure tactics or price discounting, which in the long run may damage customer goodwill and company profits. Second, straight commission plans are generally more costly to administer. Third, straight commission plans provide little security and could have a deteriorative effect on the morale of sales representatives when sales fall through no fault of their own.

Management has several options regarding the commission base, the nature of commission rates, and the starting point for commissions. The *commission base* may be gross sales volume, net sales after returns, gross margins, or net profits. The *commission rates* may be identical for all sales or differentiated by customers and/or products; they may be constant with sales volume or vary in a progressive or regressive fashion. The *starting point for commissions* may be the first sale or sales beyond the established minimum quota. Most companies base sales commissions on sales volume because of administrative simplicity and because of sales management's traditional interest in promoting volume. But sales commissions based on sales volumes may not properly relate selling effort to company profitability. The payment of commissions on *gross margin* has been recommended as a better base and one that is practical to administer. Commissions tied to product gross margins should do a superior job of motivating sales representatives to improve their product and customer mix and, therefore, company profits.[34]

Combination salary and commission   The great majority of firms use a combination of salary and commission features in the hope of achieving the advantages of each while avoiding the disadvantages. The combination plan is especially appropriate where sales volume depends upon the sales representative's motivation and yet where management wants some control over the amount of nonselling duties performed by the sales representative. The plan also means that during downswings the company is not stuck with rigid selling costs, but neither does the sales representative lose his or her whole income.

Bonus   Many companies pay *bonuses* as a supplement or a substitute for commission-type incentives. Bonuses are noncontractual payments for extra effort or merit or for results beyond normal expectations. They are used to reward sales representatives for performing tasks that are desirable but not rewardable through commissions, for example, preparing prompt reports, supplying useful selling ideas, protecting the customer's inventory interests, and developing unusual product or market knowledge. The main problem with bonuses is that managerial judgment enters into their determination, and this can raise questions of fairness in the minds of individual sales representatives.

Other costs   Besides salary, commission, and bonus, the company's selling costs include the following additional elements:

1. *Selling expenses* (travel, lodging, telephone, entertainment, samples promotion, and office and/or clerical expenses)
2. *Fringe benefits* (hospitalization insurance, life insurance, pension plan, association memberships, and moving expenses)
3. *Special incentives* (contests, service awards)
4. *Staff back-up costs* (cost of technical and customer-service people, sales analysts, computer time, and sales-training programs)

Thus the cost of running a sales force adds up to much more than the direct compensation elements alone.

SUPERVISING SALES REPRESENTATIVES

The new sales representative is given more than a territory and a compensation package—he or she is given supervision. Supervision is the fate of everyone who works for someone else. It is the expression of employers' natural and continuous interest in the activities of their agents. Through supervision, employers hope to direct and motivate the sales force to do a better job.

---

[34] See Ralph L. Day and Peter D. Bennett, "Should Salesmen's Compensation Be Geared to Profits?" *Journal of Marketing Research,* May 1964, pp. 39–43; and John U. Farley and Charles B. Weinberg, "Inferential Optimization: An Algorithm for Determining Optimal Sales Commissions in Multiproduct Sales Forces," *Operational Research Quarterly,* June 1975, pp. 413–18.

| Directing Sales Representatives | Companies differ in the extent to which they try to prescribe to their sales representatives what they should be doing. Much depends upon the nature of the selling job. Sales representatives who are paid largely on commission and who are expected to hunt down their own prospects are generally left on their own. Those who are largely salaried and who must cover a definite set of accounts are likely to receive substantial supervision. |

A major purpose of supervision is to help the sales representatives use their major resource, which is *time*, effectively and efficiently. The effective use of time means that the sales representatives make good decisions as to which customers and prospects to spend the time on in the first place. The efficient use of time means that the sales representatives are able to plan their call time so as to maximize the ratio of selling to nonselling time.

Developing Customer Targets and Call Norms

Most companies classify their customers into a number of types, reflecting the sales volume or profit potential of the different accounts. They establish a certain desired number of calls per period that their sales force should make to each customer type. They might label the customer types A, B, and C. A accounts may receive nine calls a year, B six calls, and C three calls. The exact levels that are set depend upon competitive call norms and expected account profitability.

These call norms are to be taken as rough guidelines only.[35] The real issue is how much sales volume could be expected from a particular account as a function of the annual number of calls made to that account. In one current computer model for sales-call planning, the sales representative is asked to estimate sales for each account for five different possible call levels. The computer then calculates the optimal number of calls to make on each account, given these subjective sales response functions, the accounts' profit margins, and the total available sales call time.[36]

It may be possible to determine the sales-call response function experimentally. Magee described an experiment where sales representatives were asked to vary their call pattern in a particular way to determine what effect this would have on sales.[37] The experiment called first for sorting accounts into major classes. Each account class was then randomly split into three sets. The respective sales representatives were asked, for a specified period of time, to spend less than five hours a month with accounts in the first set, five to nine hours a month with the second set, and more than nine hours a month with the third set. The results demonstrated that additional call time increases sales volume, leaving only the question of whether the magnitude of sales increase was sufficient to justify the additional increase in call time.

[35] The story is told about a salesman who thought he literally had to make twelve prospect calls a day. At 4:45 P.M. he was still talking with the eleventh prospect, who was getting increasingly interested in the company's products. "Tell me more, young man," said the prospect. "I'm sorry, sir," replied the salesman. "There are only fifteen minutes left, and I must leave to make my last call."

[36] Leonard M. Lodish, "Callplan: An Interactive Salesman's Call Planning System," *Management Science*, December 1971, pp. 25–40. For company applications, see "Computers Route the Salesmen," *Business Week*, July 1, 1972.

[37] See John F. Magee, "Determining the Optimum Allocation of Expenditures for Promotional Effort with Operations Research Methods," in *The Frontiers of Marketing Thought and Science*, Frank M. Bass, ed. (Chicago: American Marketing Association, 1958), pp. 140–56. See also Arthur A. Brown, Frank T. Hulswit, and John D. Kettelle, "A Study of Sales Operations," *Operations Research*, June 1956, pp. 296–308.

Developing prospect targets and call norms Companies like to specify to their sales force how much time to spend prospecting for new accounts. For example, Spector Freight wants its sales force to spend 25 percent of their time prospecting and to stop calling on a prospect after three unsuccessful calls.

There are a number of reasons why companies try to set up a minimum requirement for the canvassing of new accounts. If left alone, many sales representatives will spend most of their time in the offices of current customers. Current customers are better-known quantities. The sales representatives can depend upon them for some business, whereas a prospect may never deliver any business or deliver it only after many months of effort. Unless the sales representative receives a bonus for opening new accounts, he or she may underdo new account development. Some companies have decided to rely on a salaried, missionary sales force to open new accounts.

The key issue in developing prospect call norms is to have a way to estimate the *value of any given prospect*. This problem is especially acute in situations where there are more prospects than time available for developing them. They must be ranked so that sales representatives can concentrate on the best prospects. A useful model can be formulated by looking at the value of an account in terms of investment theory. First the sales representative should estimate the value of the prospect's business if the prospect were converted to a customer. The value of the prospect's business may be represented in terms of a discounted income stream lasting so many years. Specifically,

$$Z = \sum_{t=1}^{\bar{t}} \frac{mQ_t - X}{(1 + r)^t} \tag{21-1}$$

where:

Z = present value of the future income from a new customer
m = gross margin on sales
Q_t = expected sales from new customer in year t
X = cost of maintaining customer contact per year
r = company discount rate
t = a subscript for year
$\bar{t}$ = number of years that this new customer is expected to remain a customer

Thus the sales representative estimates that this prospect, if converted to a customer, would annually purchase from the company Q_t units with a profit per unit of m less a customer-contact cost (X) and that this will last for t periods. Future income is discounted at an interest rate r.

The next step is to consider the investment necessary to convert this prospect to a customer. The investment can be described as:

$$I = nc \tag{21-2}$$

where:

I = investment in trying to convert the prospect to a customer
n = number of calls to convert the prospect into a customer
c = cost per call

The number of calls to the prospect will influence the probability of conversion—that is,

$$p = p(n) \qquad (21\text{--}3)$$

The value of the prospect's business should be scaled down by this probability. Putting the previous elements together, the following investment formula emerges for the value (V) of a prospect:

$$V = p(n) \sum_{t=1}^{\bar{t}} \frac{mQ_t - X}{(1 + r)^t} - nc \qquad (21\text{--}4)$$

According to this formula, the value of a prospect depends on the difference between the expected present value of the income stream and the investment made in prospect conversion. Both the expected present value and the investment depend in turn on the intended number of calls, n, upon the prospect. The intended number of calls should be the optimal number of calls, and this can be found mathematically if the probability-of-conversion function is known.

The formula could easily be incorporated into a computer program wherein the sales representative sits down at a terminal, types in a set of estimates for each prospect regarding the expected volume of the prospect's business, the maximum probability of conversion, and so on, and receives back a ranking of all the prospects in order of their investment value along with the suggested number of calls to make on each.

Using sales time efficiently The sales representative should also know how to schedule planned sales calls and use his or her time efficiently. One tool is the preparation of an annual call schedule showing which customers and prospects to call on in which months and which activities to carry out. The activities include such things as participating in trade shows, attending sales meetings, and carrying out marketing research projects. For example, the sales force in the various Bell Telephone Company subsidiaries plan their calls and activities around three concepts. The first is *market development*—various efforts to educate customers, cultivate new business, and gain greater visibility in the buying community. The second is *sales-generating activities*—direct efforts to sell particular products to customers on particular calls. The third is *market protection activities*—various efforts to learn what competition is doing and to protect relations with existing customers. The sales force is supposed to aim for some balance among these activities, so that the company does not achieve high current sales at the expense of long-run market development.

Sales representatives also have to be good at time management. They allocate their time to the following activities:

Travel. Travel time is the time spent in travel between rising in the morning and arriving at lodging in the evening. It can amount in some jobs to as much as 50 percent of total time. Travel time can be cut down by substituting faster for slower means of transportation, recognizing, however, that this will increase costs. More companies are encouraging air travel (commercial or private plane) for their sales force in order to increase their ratio of selling to total time. They are also encouraging the sales force to fill out reports while traveling or to listen to cassettes describing company products, customers, or policies.

Food and breaks. Some portion of the sales force's workday is spent in eating and breaks. If this involves dining with a customer, it will be classified as selling time, otherwise as food and breaks.

Waiting. Waiting consists of time spent in the outer office of the buyer. This is dead time unless the sales representative uses it to plan or fill out reports.

Selling. Selling is the time spent with the buyer in person or on the phone. It breaks down into "social talk," which is the time spent discussing other things, and "selling talk," which is the time spent discussing the company and its products.

Administration. This is a miscellaneous category consisting of the time spent in report writing and billing, attending sales meetings, and talking to others in the company about production, delivery, billing, sales performance, and other matters.

No wonder actual selling time may amount in some companies to as little as 15 percent of total working time! If it could be raised from 15 percent to 20 percent, it would be a 33 percent improvement. Companies are constantly seeking ways to help their sales representatives use their time more efficiently. They do so by training them in the effective use of the telephone ("phone power"), simplifying the record-keeping forms and requirements, using the computer to develop call and routing plans, and supplying marketing research reports on the customer.

Motivating Sales Representatives

A small percentage of sales representatives in any sales force can be expected to do their best without any special prompting from management. To them, selling is the most fascinating job in the world. They are ambitious and are self-starters. But the majority of sales representatives on nearly every sales force require personal encouragement and special incentives to work at their best level. This is especially true for creative field selling, for the following reasons:

The nature of the job. The selling job is one of frequent frustration. Sales representatives usually work alone, the hours are irregular, and they are often away from home. They confront aggressive competing sales representatives; they have an inferior status relative to the buyer; they often do not have the authority to do what is necessary to win an account; they lose large orders that they have worked hard to obtain.

Human nature. Most people operate below capacity in the absence of special incentive. They won't "kill themselves" without some prospect of financial gain or social recognition.

Personal problems. The sales representative, like everyone else, is occasionally preoccupied with personal problems, such as sickness in the family, marital discord, or debt.

Management can affect the morale and performance of the sales force through its organizational climate, sales quotas, and positive incentives.

Organizational climate   Organizational climate describes the feeling that the sales force get from their company regarding their opportunities, value, and rewards for a good performance. Some companies treat their sales force as being of minor importance. Other companies treat their sales representatives as the prime movers and allow unlimited opportunity for income and promotion. The company's attitude toward its sales representatives acts as a self-fulfilling prophecy: if they are held in low regard, there is much turnover and poor performance; if they are held in high regard, there is little turnover and high performance.

The quality of personal treatment from the sales representative's immediate supervisor is an important aspect of the organizational climate. An effective supervisor keeps in touch with the members of the sales force through regular correspondence and phone calls, personal visits in the field, and evaluation sessions in the home office. At different times the supervisor is the sales representative's boss, companion, coach, and confessor.

Sales quotas Many companies set sales quotas for their sales representatives specifying what they should sell during the year. Compensation is often, though not always, related to their degree of quota fulfillment.

Sales quotas are set each year in the process of developing the annual marketing plan. The company first decides on a sales forecast that is reasonably achievable. This becomes the basis of planning production, work-force size, and financial requirements. Then management establishes sales quotas for all of its regions and territories, which typically add up to more than the sales forecast. Sales quotas are set higher than the sales forecast in order to move the sales managers and sales representatives to their best effort. If they fail to make their quotas, the company nevertheless may make its sales forecast.

Each field sales manager takes his or her quota and divides it up among the sales representatives. Actually, there are three schools of thought on quota setting. The *high-quota school* sets quotas that are above what most sales representatives will achieve but that are possible for all. Advocates of this system are of the opinion that high quotas spur extra effort. The *modest-quota school* sets quotas that a majority of the sales force can achieve. The feeling is that the sales force will accept the quotas as fair, will be able to attain them, and will gain confidence from attaining them. Finally, the *variable-quota school* thinks that individual differences among sales representatives warrant high quotas for some, modest quotas for others. According to Heckert:

> Actual experience with sales quotas, as with all standards, will reveal that sales representatives react to them somewhat differently, particularly at first. Some are stimulated to their highest efficiency, others are discouraged. Some sales executives place considerable emphasis upon this human element in setting their quotas. In general, however, good men will in the long run respond favorably to intelligently devised quotas, particularly when compensation is fairly adjusted to performance.[38]

More formally, the variable-quota school will base quotas for the individual sales representative on a number of considerations, including the person's sales performance in the previous period, his or her territory's estimated potential, and a judgment of his or her aspiration level and reaction to pressure and incentive. Some propositions in this area are:

1. The sales quota for salesperson j at time t, Q_{jt}, should generally be set above his or her sales in the year just ending, $S_{j,t-1}$; that is,

$$Q_{jt} > S_{j,t-1}$$

[38] J. B. Heckert, *Business Budgeting and Control* (New York: Ronald Press Company, 1946), p. 138.

2. The sales quota for salesperson j at time t should be higher, the greater the positive gap between the estimated sales potential of the salesperson's territory, S_{Pjt}, and his or her sales in the year just ending; that is,

$$Q_{jt} \sim (S_{Pjt} - S_{j,t-1})$$

3. The sales quota for salesperson j at time t should be higher, the more positively he or she responds to pressure, E_j; that is,

$$Q_{jt} \sim E_j$$

These three propositions can be combined in an equation for setting a salesperson's quota:

$$Q_{jt} = S_{j,t-1} + E_j(S_{Pjt} - S_{j,t-1}) \qquad (21\text{--}5)$$

Thus, salesperson j's quota at time t should be at least equal to his or her actual sales in the previous period, plus some fraction, E_j, of the difference between estimated territorial sales potential and his or her sales last year; the more positively he or she reacts to pressure, the higher the fraction.

Positive incentives   Companies use a number of positive motivators to stimulate sales-force effort. Periodic *sales meetings* provide a social occasion, a break from routine, a chance to meet and talk with "company brass," a chance to air feelings and to identify with a larger group. Companies also sponsor *sales contests* when they want to spur the sales force to make a special selling effort above what would be normally expected. Other motivators include honors and awards, profit-sharing plans, and vacations with pay.

EVALUATING SALES REPRESENTATIVES

We have been describing the "feed-forward" aspects of supervision—the efforts of management to communicate to the sales representatives what they should be doing and to motivate them to do it. But good feed-forward requires good feedback. And good feedback means getting regular information from and about sales representatives to evaluate their performance.

Sources of Information   Management gains information about its sales representatives through a number of channels. Probably the most important source of information is the sales representative's periodic reports. Additional information comes through personal observation, through customers' letters and complaints, and through conversations with other sales representatives.

A distinction can be drawn between sales reports that represent *plans for future activities* and those that represent *write-ups of completed activities*. The best example of the former is the *salesperson's work plan*, which most sales representatives are required to submit for a specified future period, usually a week or a month in advance. The plan describes the calls they will make and the routing they will use. This report serves the purposes of encouraging the sales force to plan and schedule their activities, informing management of their whereabouts, and providing a basis for comparing their plans with their accomplishments. Sales representatives can be evaluated on their ability to "plan their work and work their plan." Occasionally, management contacts individual sales representatives after receiving their plans to suggest improvements.

Companies moving toward annual marketing planning in depth are beginning to require their sales representatives to draft an annual *territory marketing plan* in which they outline their program for developing new accounts and increasing business from existing accounts. The formats vary considerably, some asking for general ideas on territory development and others asking for detailed volume and profit estimates. This type of report reflects the conception of sales representatives as market managers and profit centers. The plans are studied by the immediate supervisors and become the bases for rendering constructive suggestions to sales representatives and developing branch sales objectives and estimates for higher-level management.

Several forms are used by sales representatives to write up their completed activities and accomplishments. Perhaps the best known is the *call report* on which the salesperson records pertinent aspects of his or her dealings with a customer, including competitive brands used, best time for calling, degree and type of resistance, and future account promise. Call reports serve the objectives of keeping sales management informed of the salesperson's activities, indicating the status of the customers' accounts, and providing information that might be useful in subsequent calls.

Sales representatives also report *expenses* incurred in the performance of selling duties, for which they are partly or wholly reimbursed. The objective from management's standpoint is primarily to exercise control over the type and amount of expenses and secondarily to have the requisite expense data for income-tax purposes. It is also hoped that the sales representatives will exercise more care in incurring expenses when they must report them in some detail.

Additional types of reports that some companies require from their sales representatives are:

A report on new business secured or potential new business. This alerts management to new accounts and new prospects for which it can formulate special marketing plans in the form of direct mail, team selling, and so on. It is also used to evaluate the extent and effectiveness of the sales representative's prospecting work.

A report on lost business. This report enables the company to keep abreast of competitive efforts and needed product or service improvements and, not the least important, to evaluate the effectiveness of the individual salesperson.

A periodic report on local business and economic conditions. This report aids the development of territory norms and sales programs, although it must be recognized that sales representatives sometimes distort the local picture to defend their own performance.

The reports that companies require their sales representatives to submit contain a wealth of information. Sales representatives, however, frequently complain that they have to devote too much time to writing when they should be selling and that their reports are not read. Management must guard against these criticisms by thinking through carefully the intended uses of the information. The forms should be brief and easy to fill out. Management should make a point of regularly responding to the information.

The sales force's reports along with other reports from the field and the manager's personal observations supply the raw materials for formally evaluating members of the sales force. Formal evaluation procedures lead to at least three benefits. First, they lead management to develop specific and uniform standards for judging sales performance. Second, they lead management to draw together all its information and impressions about individual sales representatives and make more systematic, point-by-point evaluations. Third, they tend to have a constructive effect on the performance of sales representatives. The constructive effect comes about because the sales representatives know that they will have to sit down one morning with their supervisor and explain certain facets of their routing or sales-call decisions or their failure to secure or maintain certain accounts.

Salesperson-to-salesperson comparisons One type of evaluation frequently made is to compare and rank the sales performance of the various sales representatives. Such comparisons, however, can be misleading. Relative sales performances are meaningful only if there are no variations from territory to territory in the market potential, workload, degree of competition, company promotional effort, and so forth. Furthermore, sales are not the best denominator of achievement. Management should be more interested in how much each sales representative contributed to net profits. And this cannot be known until the sales representatives' sales mix and sales expenses are examined. A possible ranking criterion would be the sales representative's *actual contribution to company net profits as a ratio to his or her territory's potential contribution to company net profits*. A ratio of 1.00 would mean that the sales representative delivered the potential sales in his or her territory. The lower a sales representative's ratio, the more supervision and counseling he or she needs.

Current-to-past-sales comparisons A second common type of evaluation is to compare a sales representative's current performance with his or her past performance. This should provide a more direct indication of progress. An example is shown in Table 21–1.

Many things can be learned by the sales manager about John Smith from the information in this table. One of the first things to note is that Smith's total sales increased every year (line 3). This does not necessarily mean that Smith is doing a better job. The product breakdown shows that he has been able to push further the sales of product B than product A (lines 1 and 2). According to his quotas for the two products (lines 4 and 5), his success in increasing sales of product B may be at the expense of product A. According to gross profits (lines 6 and 7), the company earns about twice as much on A as B. The picture begins to emerge that Smith may be pushing the higher-volume, lower-margin product at the expense of the more profitable product. In fact, although he increased total sales by $1,100 between 1978 and 1979 (line 3), the gross profits on his total sales actually decreased by $580 (line 8).

Sales expense (line 9) shows a steady increase, although total expense as a percentage of total sales seems to be under control (line 10). The upward trend in Smith's total dollar expense does not seem to be explained by any increase in the number of calls (line 11), although it may be related in part to his success in acquiring new customers (line 14). However, there is a possibility that in pros-

TABLE 21–1
Form for Evaluating Sales Representative's Progress

TERRITORY: MIDLAND SALES REPRESENTATIVE: JOHN SMITH	1976	1977	1978	1979
1. Net sales product A	$251,300	$253,200	$270,000	$263,100
2. Net sales product B	423,200	439,200	553,900	561,900
3. Net sales total	674,500	692,400	823,900	825,000
4. Percent of quota product A	95.6	92.0	88.0	84.7
5. Percent of quota product B	120.4	122.3	134.9	130.8
6. Gross profits product A	50,260	50,640	54,000	52,620
7. Gross profits product B	42,320	43,920	55,390	56,190
8. Gross profits total	92,580	94,560	109,390	108,810
9. Sales expense	10,200	11,100	11,600	13,200
10. Sales expense to total sales (%)	1.5	1.6	1.4	1.6
11. Number of calls	1,675	1,700	1,680	1,660
12. Cost per call	6.09	6.53	6.90	7.95
13. Average number of customers	320	324	328	334
14. Number of new customers	13	14	15	20
15. Number of lost customers	8	10	11	14
16. Average sales per customer	2,108	2,137	2,512	2,470
17. Average gross profit per customer	289	292	334	326

pecting for new customers, he is neglecting present customers, as indicated by an upward trend in the annual number of lost customers (line 15).

The last two lines show the level and trend in Smith's sales per customer and the gross profits on his sales per customer. These figures become more meaningful when they are compared with overall company averages. For example, if John Smith's average gross profit per customer is lower than the company's average, he may be concentrating on the wrong customers or may not be spending enough time with each customer. Looking back at his annual number of calls (line 11), it may be that Smith is making fewer annual calls than the average salesman. If distances in his territory are not much different, this may mean he is not putting in a full workday, he is poor at planning his routing or minimizing his waiting, or he spends too much time with certain accounts.

Qualitative appraisal of sales representatives   The appraisal usually includes an evaluation of the salesperson's knowledge, personality, and motivation. The salesperson can be rated on the extent of his or her knowledge of the company, products, customers, competitors, territory, and responsibilities. Personality characteristics can be rated, including general manner, appearance, speech, and temperament. The supervisor can also consider any problems in motivation or compliance. Since an almost endless number of qualitative factors might be included, each company must decide what would be most useful to know. It should also inform the sales representatives of these criteria so that they are aware of how their performance is judged.

SUMMARY

The great majority of companies utilize sales representatives, and many assign them the pivotal role in the creation of sales. Because sales representatives are capable of performing a wide variety of tasks, each company must decide exactly what it expects to accomplish through direct selling. The objectives set for the sales force influence the strategies and tactical decisions arising in the management of an effective sales operation.

At the strategic level, the company must decide on the size of its sales force and how it should be organized. In principle, the sales force should be expanded up to the point where an additional sales representative would impose more cost on the company than he or she generates in the way of a gross margin on sales. In practice, sales-force-size decisions are made on estimates of sales productivity in different territories or feasible territory workloads. Effective sales forces can be organized along territorial, product, or customer lines, and sales territories should be thoughtfully designed in terms of size and shape.

Sales representatives must be continuously recruited and selected on the basis of scientific procedures to hold down the high costs of hiring the wrong persons. Sales-training programs are growing more elaborate and are designed to familiarize the salesperson with the company's history, products, and policies, the characteristics of the market and competitors, and the art of selling. Compensation is probably the most important single element in sales-force motivation and should somehow provide a measure of both incentive and security to be maximally effective. The average salesperson needs supervision and continuous encouragement because he or she must make a large number of decisions and is subject to many frustrations. Periodically the person's performance must be formally evaluated to help him or her do a better job.

QUESTIONS AND PROBLEMS

1. A district sales manager voiced the following complaint at a sales meeting: "The average salesman costs our company $40,000 in compensation and expenses. Why can't we buy a few less $40,000 full-page advertisements in *Time* magazine and use the money to hire more men? Surely one man working a full year can sell more products than a one-page ad in one issue of *Time*." Evaluate this argument.

2. The text described some of the characteristics that might be looked for in sales representatives. What characteristics should be looked for in selecting district sales managers? What about the top sales manager?

3. (a) Show diagrammatically, in terms of distances traveled, why a product-structured sales force involves more total travel distance than an unspecialized sales force. (b) Show diagrammatically why a customer-structured sales force involves more total travel distance than an unspecialized sales force.

4. The sales manager of a large company would like to determine how many sales calls per month the sales force should make to average-size accounts. Describe how an experiment might be set up to answer the question.

5. A sales manager is trying to figure out the most that should be spent to win a particular account. This account would produce sales of $10,000 a year, and the company is likely to retain it for at least four years. The company's profit margin on sales is 15 percent. The company wants its various investments to earn 8 percent. What is the most that the company should spend to win this account?

6. Suppose a sales representative in a particular industry can make an average of 1,600 calls a year. If he or she has been writing $420,000 worth of business a year, how many calls can the sales representative afford to make to a $10,000-a-year account without diluting the total business written during the year?

7. Describe several types of selling situations where a straight salary plan seems appropriate.

8. A company regularly asks for its sales representatives' views on such questions as whether to introduce a new product or to raise the price on one of its products. How unbiased are the sales representatives' reactions likely to be?

9. Should individual sales representatives participate in the establishment of sales quotas for their territories? What would be the advantages and disadvantages of such participation?

10. Develop a formula showing Talley's method of determining the optimal size sales force.

Administering the Marketing PROGRAM

5

Marketing Organization

22

We now turn to the administrative side of marketing management to examine how firms organize and control their marketing activities. In this chapter we shall deal with marketing organization, and in the following two chapters, with the firm's marketing information and control systems.

We shall illustrate our discussion of marketing organization mainly in connection with manufacturing companies, where the marketing management function first emerged. The same organizational principles will also apply in such service industries as retailing, banking, and insurance. The marketing management function is even emerging in large nonprofit organizations, such as the U.S. Postal Service, U.S. Army, health maintenance organizations, and mass-transit companies.

THE EVOLUTION OF THE MARKETING DEPARTMENT

The modern marketing department is the product of a long evolution from very humble beginnings. It has evolved through the five stages, and companies can be found today in each of these stages.

Simple Sales Department (Stage One)	All companies start out with three simple functions. Someone must raise and manage capital (finance), produce the product or service (operations), and sell it (sales). The selling function is headed by a sales manager or sales vice president who basically manages a sales force and may do some selling. When the company needs some occasional marketing research or advertising, the sales vice president also handles these because they fall in the selling area. Nevertheless, the sales vice president's heart is in the sales force, and these other assignments are often handled halfheartedly.
Sales Department with Ancillary Functions (Stage Two)	As the company expands, it finds that it needs marketing research, advertising, and customer service on a more continuous and expert basis. The sales vice president hires a few specialists who can perform these functions. A marketing director might be appointed to manage these functions and report to the sales vice president.
Separate Marketing Department (Stage Three)	The continued growth of the company inevitably increases the importance of other marketing functions—marketing research, new-product development, advertising and promotion, customer service—relative to sales-force activity. Nevertheless, the sales vice president continues to give disproportionate time and attention to the sales force. The marketing director will argue that sales could be facilitated by more budget allocation for these other marketing activities. The company president or executive vice president will eventually see the advantage of establishing a marketing department with some independence from the sales vice president. The marketing department will be headed by a marketing director or marketing vice president and will report, along with the sales vice president, to the president or executive vice president. At this stage, sales and marketing are seen as separate and equal functions in the organization that are supposed to work together.
Modern Marketing Department (Stage Four)	Although the sales vice president and the marketing vice president are supposed to work together harmoniously, their relation is often characterized by rivalry and distrust. The sales vice president sees a conspiracy to make the sales force less important in the marketing mix; and the marketing vice president seeks to gain power over all the customer-impinging functions. The sales vice president tends to be short-run oriented and preoccupied with achieving current sales. The marketing vice president tends to be long-run oriented and preoccupied with planning the right products and marketing strategy to meet the customers' long-run needs.

At times it seems that the sales and marketing people represent two different cultures in the organization. The sales people usually have less education, are more practical and "street-wise," whereas the marketing people are younger, more educated, and less experienced in selling. Often the sales people don't trust or believe the marketing people's findings. Some companies arrange for the marketing people to get more selling experience and even hand them a few house accounts to keep them close to the selling situation.

If there is too much conflict between sales and marketing, the company president may (1) eliminate the marketing vice president's office and place marketing activities back under the sales vice president, (2) instruct the executive vice president to handle conflicts that arise, or (3) place the marketing vice president in charge of everything, including the sales force. The last solution is eventually chosen in many companies and forms the basis of the modern marketing department, a department headed by a marketing vice president with subordinates reporting from every marketing function, including sales management.[1]

Modern Marketing Company (Stage Five)

A company can have a modern marketing department and yet not operate as a modern marketing company. Whether it is the latter depends upon how the officers of the company view the marketing function. If they view marketing as primarily a selling function, they are missing the point. The vice president of marketing, no matter how well he or she runs the marketing department, meets frequent resistance from other vice presidents in the matter of carrying out a company-wide customer orientation. The manufacturing vice president holds to the logic of cost minimization and resents interrupting production schedules to please customers. The financial vice president is not sure about the returns from investments in marketing research, communication, and promotion and normally reacts to sales declines by recommending cuts in market-development expenditures. Other departments also resist cooperating to produce satisfied customers. Ultimately the job may call for increasing the power and authority of the marketing vice president over the other business functions. Only a few companies have attained the status of true marketing companies.

WAYS OF ORGANIZING THE MODERN MARKETING DEPARTMENT

An examination of modern marketing departments reveals innumerable arrangements. All marketing organizations must somehow accommodate to four basic dimensions of marketing activity: *functions, geographical units, products,* and *end-use markets.*

Functional Organization

The earliest and still most common form of marketing organization has various functional marketing specialists reporting to a marketing vice president, who is in charge of coordinating all of their activities. Figure 22–1 shows three such specialists, who bear the titles of advertising manager, sales manager, and marketing research manager, respectively. Additional functional specialties might also be present in the marketing department, such as *merchandising, sales promotion, new products, customer service, sales analysis, market planning,* and *marketing administration.*

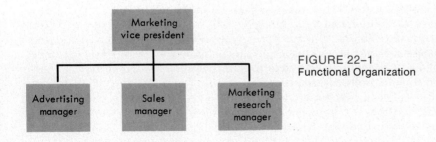

FIGURE 22–1
Functional Organization

---

[1] For job descriptions of the position of marketing vice president, see David S. Hopkins and Earl L. Bailey, *The Chief Marketing Executive* (New York: Conference Board, 1971), pp. 36–62.

If the number of functions reporting to the marketing vice president becomes large, they may be subgrouped into *operations* functions and *planning* functions. Reporting to the marketing vice president would be a manager of marketing operations responsible for sales, customer services, and advertising, and a manager of marketing planning responsible for marketing research, sales forecasting, and new-product planning. The marketing vice president then has two major functions to think about, planning and doing, instead of several specialties.

The main advantage of a functional marketing organization is its administrative simplicity. On the other hand, this organizational form suffers from certain disadvantages as the company's product line or number of markets increases. First, there is inadequate detailed planning for specific products and markets, since no one is assigned full responsibility for any product or market. Products that are not favorites with various functional specialists tend to get neglected. Second, each functional group develops its own subgoals, which include trying to gain more budget and status vis-a-vis the other functions. The marketing vice president has to constantly sift the claims of competing functional specialists and faces a difficult problem in coordination.

Geographical Organization

A company selling in a national market is likely to set up a vertically structured organization consisting of a sales vice president, regional sales managers, zone sales managers, district sales managers, and finally salespersons. The span of control increases as we move from the sales vice president, who supervises about four regional sales managers (East, West, North, South), to a district sales manager, who might supervise between six and fourteen salespeople. The shorter span allows the manager to give more time to subordinates and is warranted when the sales task is complex, the salespersons are highly paid, and the salespersons' impact on profits is high.

Some companies are now adding *local marketing specialists* to support the sales efforts in high-volume markets. The local marketing specialist for Cleveland, for example, would know everything there is to know about the Cleveland marketing environment. The specialist would prepare and implement a long-range and short-range marketing plan for developing the Cleveland market for the company's products.

Product Management Organization

Companies producing a variety of products and/or brands often establish a product management system (also called a brand management system). The product management system does not replace the functional management system but serves as another layer of management (see Figure 22–2). The functional managers are essentially *resource managers,* and the product managers are essentially *program managers.* This type of organization is called a *matrix organization* because each resource manager gets involved with each program manager. The organization can be visualized as a set of rows representing marketing functions and columns representing products.

The decision to establish a product management system is influenced by the extent of product heterogeneity and the sheer number of products. If the company product lines can benefit from specialized marketing programs, or if the sheer number of products is beyond the capacity of a functional marketing organization to handle, a product management organization is a natural recourse.

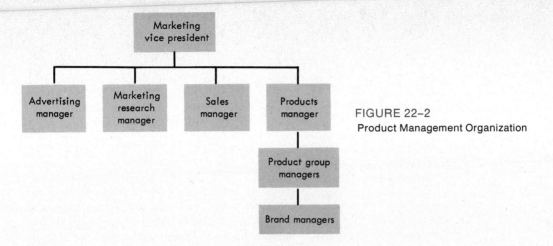

FIGURE 22–2
Product Management Organization

Product management first made its appearance in the Procter & Gamble Company in 1927. A new company soap, Camay, was not doing well, and one of the young men, Neil H. McElroy (later president of P&G), was assigned to give his exclusive attention to developing and promoting this product. This he did successfully, and the company soon afterward added other product managers. Since then a large number of firms, especially in the food, soap, toiletries, and chemical industries, have established product management systems. General Foods, for example, uses a product management system in its Post Division. There are separate product group managers in charge of cereals, pet food, and beverages. Within the cereal product group, there are separate product managers for nutritional cereals, children's presweetened cereals, family cereals, and miscellaneous cereals. In turn, the nutritional-cereal product manager supervises several brand managers.[2]

The product management system creates a focal point of planning and responsibility for individual products. The product manager's role is to create product strategies and plans, see that they are implemented, monitor the results, and take corrective action. This responsibility breaks down into the following six tasks:

1. Developing a long-range growth and competitive strategy for the product
2. Preparing an annual marketing plan and sales forecast
3. Working with advertising and merchandising agencies to develop copy, programs, and campaigns
4. Stimulating interest in and support of the product among the sales force and distributors
5. Gathering continuous intelligence on the product's performance, customer and dealer attitudes, and new problems and opportunities
6. Initiating product improvements to meet changing market needs

These basic functions are common to both consumer and industrial

[2] For details, see "General Foods Corporation: Post Division," in E. Raymond Corey and Steven H. Star, *Organization Strategy: A Marketing Approach* (Boston: Division of Research, Graduate School of Business Administration, Harvard University, 1971), pp. 201–30.

product managers. Yet there are some important differences in their jobs and emphases.[3] Consumer-product managers tend to manage fewer products than industrial-product managers. They spend considerably more time dealing with advertising and sales promotion. They spend most of their time working with others in the company and various agencies and little time in direct contact with customers. They tend to be younger and better educated. Industrial-product managers, by contrast, think more carefully about the technical aspects of their product and possible improvements in design. They spend more time with laboratory and engineering personnel in the company. They work more closely with the sales force and key buyers. They tend to pay less attention to advertising, sales promotion, and promotional pricing. They emphasize rational product factors over emotional ones.

The product management system introduces several advantages in the management of the firm's marketing activity. First, the product manager can balance and harmonize the various functional marketing inputs needed by a product. Second, the product manager is in a position to react quickly to problems in the marketplace without involving several different people in lengthy meetings. Third, smaller brands, because they have a product champion, are not as neglected in this system as they tend to be in functional marketing organizations. Fourth, product management is an excellent training ground for promising young executives, for it involves them in every area of company operations—marketing, production, and finance.

But a price is paid for these advantages. First, the product management system introduces many sources of conflict and frustration that might not otherwise be present.[4] Product managers are not given authority commensurate with their responsibility. They have to rely on persuasive methods to gain cooperation from various resource managers. They spend so much time importuning advertising, sales, and manufacturing for special support that they have little time for planning. They have been told by their superiors that they are minipresidents, but they are often treated like low-level coordinators. They solicit the help of specialists but often do not follow their advice. Sometimes they are forced to go over the heads of others. They are bogged down by a great amount of "housekeeping" paperwork. If this results in a rapid turnover of product managers, it can damage the sound long-range planning of products.

Second, product managers become experts in their product but rarely have a chance to become experts in any of the functions for which they are responsible. They vacillate between posing as an expert and being cowed by real experts. This is particularly unfortunate where the product basically depends on a particular type of expertise, such as advertising; here it would almost make more sense to put the product in the hands of an advertising specialist.

Third, the product management system often turns out to be costlier than anticipated. Originally, one person is appointed to manage each important product. Soon, product managers are appointed to manage even minor products. Each product manager, usually overworked, pleads for and gets an *assistant brand manager*. Later, both of them, still overworked, persuade management to

---

[3] See Elmer E. Waters, "Industrial Product Manager . . . Consumer Brand Manager: A Study in Contrast," *Industrial Marketing*, January 1969, pp. 45–49.

[4] See David J. Luck, "Interfaces of a Product Manager," *Journal of Marketing*, October 1969, pp. 32–36.

give them a *brand assistant.* Product managers who supervise the more important company products, in their frustration in having to coax time from advertising, packaging, and other specialists, next pressure to hire their own specialists. In one large brewery, the main brand manager has his own advertising department. With all this personnel, payroll costs climb. In the meantime the company continues to increase its number of functional specialists in copy, packaging, media, promotion, market surveys, statistical analysis, and so on. The company soon finds itself stuck with a costly superstructure of product-management people and a superstructure of specialists.

When a company has a product management system that breeds too much conflict or cost, it has four recourses. The first is to try to improve its functioning through better training and procedures. Although P&G managed to achieve over the years a smooth-working product management system, many of its imitators have installed the form without the substance. Pearson and Wilson have suggested five things that will make it work better:

1. *Clearly delineate the limits of the product manager's role and responsibility for the management of a product.* [They are essentially proposers, not deciders.]

2. *Build a strategy development and review process to provide an agreed-to framework for the product manager's operations.* [Too many companies allow product managers to get away with shallow marketing plans featuring a lot of statistics but little strategic rationale.]

3. *Take into account areas of potential conflict between product managers and functional specialists when defining their respective roles.* [Clarify which decisions are to be made by the product manager, which by the expert, and which will be shared.]

4. *Set up a formal process that forces to the top all conflict-of-interest situations between product management and functional line management.* [Both parties might be expected to put all issues in writing and forward them to general management for settlement.]

5. *Establish a system for measuring results that is consistent with the product manager's responsibilities.* [If product managers are to be held accountable for profit, they should be given more control over the factors that affect their profitability.][5]

A second alternative is to switch from a product manager to a product team approach. In fact, there are three types of product team structures in product management. The standard one is called the *vertical product team* and consists of a product manager, assistant product manager, and product assistant (see Figure 22–3A). The product manager is the leader and primarily interacts with other executives trying to gain their cooperation. The assistant product manager helps in these tasks and also does some of the paper work. The product assistant largely does the paperwork and runs various errands. Some companies have moved to a *triangular product team* consisting of a product manager and two specialized product assistants, one who takes care of (say) marketing research and the other, marketing communications (see Figure 22–3B). For example, this design is used at the Illinois Central Railroad where various three-person teams manage different commodities. As another example, the Hallmark Company uses a "marketing team" consisting of a market manager (the leader) and a mar-

---

[5] Andrall E. Pearson and Thomas W. Wilson, Jr., *Making Your Organization Work* (New York: Association of National Advertisers, 1967), pp. 8–13.

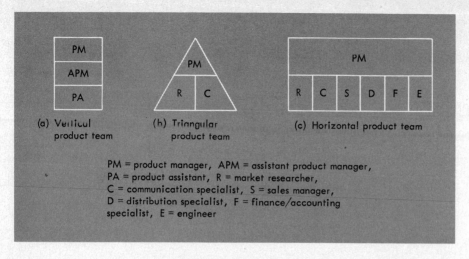

(a) Vertical product team

(b) Triangular product team

(c) Horizontal product team

FIGURE 22–3
Three Types of
Product Teams

PM = product manager, APM = assistant product manager,
PA = product assistant, R = market researcher,
C = communication specialist, S = sales manager,
D = distribution specialist, F = finance/accounting
specialist, E = engineer

keting manager and distribution manager. Still other companies have moved to a *horizontal product team* consisting of a product manager and several specialists from within and outside of marketing (see Figure 22–3C). Thus the 3M Company divided its commercial tape division into nine business planning teams, with each team further broken down into team leader and sales, marketing, laboratory, engineering, accounting, and marketing research members. Instead of a product manager's having to bear the entire responsibility for a product plan, the responsibility is shared by representatives from the various key parts of the company, and the opportunity for conflict is lessened. The ultimate step after a horizontal product team is organized is to form a product division around the product.

A third alternative is to eliminate product managers of minor brands and load two or more brands on the existing product managers. This is feasible especially where the company products appeal to a similar set of needs. Thus a cosmetics company does not need separate product managers as much because cosmetics serve one major need—beauty—whereas a toiletries company needs a different manager for headache remedies, toothpaste, soap, and hair shampoo because these products are very different in their use and appeal.

A fourth alternative is to establish divisions around the major company products or product groups and use functional arrangements within divisions. Pearson and Wilson feel that a functional marketing organization "is the oldest, simplest and, in many respects, the soundest form of organization for marketing."[6]

The position of product manager is undergoing important changes.[7] Three particular trends have been accelerated by recent company experiences with shortages, rapid inflation, recession, and consumerism. The first is the greater as-

[6] *Ibid.*, p. 5.

[7] See Richard M. Clewett and Stanley F. Stasch, "Shifting Role of the Product Manager," *Harvard Business Review*, January–February 1975, pp. 65–73; Victor P. Buell, "The Changing Role of the Product Manager in Consumer Goods Companies," *Journal of Marketing*, July 1975, pp. 3–11; and "The Brand Manager: No Longer King," *Business Week*, June 9, 1973.

sumption of profit responsibility by product managers. Cost inflation has led companies to be less satisfied with the sheer volume they sell and more concerned with the profits they make. The product manager is becoming more of a profit center and must put a profit test to the various items in his or her line and to the various marketing expenditures. Some companies are even holding their product managers responsible for excessive costs of inventory and receivables. The second trend is the closer working together of product managers with other managers in the company to find ways of securing scarce supplies, developing substitute ingredients, engineering product economies, smoothing production, and keeping total costs down. The third trend is for people in higher levels of marketing management to have more authority over brand managers. That is in response to the need for more coordinated planning of whole product lines rather than simply of brands and the need for greater responsiveness to consumerists' concerns with advertising truthfulness and product safety.[8]

Market Management Organization

Many companies will sell a product line to a highly diverse set of markets. For example, a paint firm will sell to the consumer, industrial, and government markets. A steel fabricator will sell to the railroad industry, construction industry, and public utilities. A soft-drink company will sell to retail and institutional markets. Where the company sells to customers who fall into distinct user groups having different buying practices or product preferences, some market specialization is desirable in the marketing organization.

The general structure of a market management organization is similar to the product management organization shown earlier in Figure 22–2, except with the substitution of market management for product management. Along with functional managers, there is a *markets manager* who supervises several *market managers* (also called *market development managers* or *market specialists*). The market managers draw upon functional services from the rest of the organization as needed. Market managers of important markets may even have some functional specialists reporting to them.

Market managers are essentially staff, not line, people with similar duties to product managers. Market managers develop long-range and annual plans for the sales and profits in their markets. They have to coax resource help from the other specialists in the organization. This system produces some of the same advantages and disadvantages as the product management system. Its strongest advantage is that the marketing activity is organized to meet the needs of distinct customer groups rather than focusing on marketing functions, regions, or products per se.

An increasing number of companies are reorganizing their management systems along market lines. Hanan calls these *market-centered organizations* and argues that "the only way to insure being market oriented is to put a company's organizational structure together so that its major markets become the centers around which its divisions are built."[9] Xerox has converted from geographical selling to selling by industry. The Mead Company is clustering its marketing activities around home building and furnishings, education, and leisure markets.

---

[8] See Joseph A. Morein, "Shift From Brand to Product Line Marketing," *Harvard Business Review*, September–October 1975, pp. 56–64.

[9] Mack Hanan, "Reorganize Your Company around Its Markets," *Harvard Business Review*, November–December 1974, pp. 63–74.

One of the most dramatic changes to market centeredness has occurred at the Heinz Company. Before 1964, Heinz was primarily organized around a brand management system, with separate brand managers for soups, condiments, puddings, and so on. Each brand manager, such as the ketchup brand manager, was responsible for both grocery sales and institutional sales. Then in 1964, Heinz created a separate marketing organization for institutional sales. Thus ketchup sales to institutions would be the responsibility of institutional product managers rather than the brand managers. More recently, Heinz split the marketing organization into three broad groups: groceries, commercial restaurants, and institutions. Each group contains further market specialists. For example, the institutional division contains separate market specialists for schools, colleges, hospitals, and prisons.

Product Management/ Market Management Organization

Companies that produce multiple products that flow into multiple markets face a real dilemma. They could utilize a product management system, which requires product managers to be familiar with highly divergent markets. Or they could utilize a market management system, which means that market managers would have to be familiar with highly divergent products bought by their markets. Or they could install both product and market managers, that is, a product/market organization.

Du Pont is an example of a company that has done the latter.[10] Its textile fibers department consists of separate product managers for rayon, acetate, nylon, orlon, and dacron; and also separate market managers for men's wear, women's wear, home furnishings, and industrial markets. The product managers have responsibility for planning the sales and profits of their respective fibers. They are primarily focused on short-run performance and uses of their fiber. Their job is to contact each market manager and ask for an estimate of how much material can be sold in each market. The market managers, on the other hand, have responsibility for developing profitable markets for existing and future Du Pont fibers. They take a long-view of market needs and care more about evolving the right products for their market than pushing specific fibers. In preparing their market plan, they contact each product manager to learn about planned prices and availabilities of different materials. The final sales forecasts of the market managers and the product managers should add to the same grand total.

It would seem that a product management/market management organization would be desirable in a multiple-product, multiple-market company. The rub, however, is that this system is both costly and conflictual. There is the cost of supporting a three-dimensional *matrix organization* (i.e., two layers of program management in addition to one layer of resource management). There are also serious questions as to where authority and responsibility should reside. Here are two of the many dilemmas:

1. How should the sales force be organized? In the Du Pont example, should there be separate sales forces for rayon, nylon, and each of the other fibers? Or should the sales forces be organized according to men's wear, women's wear, and other markets? Or should the sales force not be specialized?

2. Who should set the prices for a particular product/market? In the Du Pont

---

[10] For details, see Corey and Star, *Organization Strategy*, pp. 187–96.

example, should the nylon product manager have final authority for setting nylon prices in all markets? What happens if the men's wear market manager feels that nylon will lose out in this market unless special price concessions are made on nylon?

Some companies are adapting a product/market organization, and others using this organization are having second thoughts. Most agree that only the more important products and markets would justify separate managers. Some observers are not upset about the conflicts in this system on the argument that it provides the company with the benefit of both the short-run and the long-run view and the conflict is healthy.[11]

Corporate-Divisional Organization

As multiproduct companies grow in size, they have a tendency to turn their larger product groups into separate divisions. The larger divisions often set up their own marketing departments on the ground that this will give them more knowledgeable and controllable marketing resources. This poses the question as to what marketing services and activities should be retained at the corporate headquarters level.

Divisionalized companies have reached different answers to this question. Corporate marketing staffs seem to follow any of four models:[12]

1. *No corporate marketing.* Some companies do not have a corporate marketing staff. They don't see any useful function for marketing at the corporate level. Each division has its own marketing department.

2. *Minimal corporate marketing.* Some companies have a small corporate marketing staff that performs a few functions, primarily (a) assisting top management with overall opportunity evaluation, (b) providing divisions with consulting assistance on request, (c) helping divisions that are without marketing or that have weak marketing, and (d) attempting to promote the marketing concept to other departments in the company.

3. *Moderate corporate marketing.* Some companies have a corporate marketing staff that, in addition to the preceding activities, also provides various marketing services to the divisions. The corporate marketing staff might provide certain specialized *advertising services* (e.g., coordination of media buying, institutional advertising, review of division advertising from a taste and image standpoint, auditing of advertising expenditures), *sales promotion services* (e.g., company-wide promotions, central buying of promotional materials), *marketing research services* (e.g., advanced mathematical analysis, research on marketing developments cutting across divisional lines), *sales administration services* (e.g., counsel on sales organization and sales policies, development of common sales reporting systems, management of sales forces selling to common customers), and some miscellaneous services (e.g., counseling of marketing planning, hiring and training of marketing personnel).

4. *Strong corporate marketing.* Some companies have a corporate marketing staff that, in addition to the preceding activities, has the authority to participate strongly in the planning and control of divisional marketing activities.

[11] See B. Charles Ames, "Dilemma of Product/Market Management," *Harvard Business Review*, March–April 1971, pp. 66–74.

[12] See Watson Snyder, Jr., and Frank B. Gray, *The Corporate Marketing Staff: Its Role and Effectiveness in Multi-Division Companies* (Cambridge, Mass.: Marketing Science Institute, April 1971).

The question arises as to whether companies are tending to move toward a particular model of the corporate marketing department. There is no evidence of this. Some companies have recently installed a corporate marketing staff for the first time; others have expanded their department; others have reduced its size and scope; and still others have eliminated it altogether. The potential contribution of a corporate marketing staff varies in different stages of the company's evolution. Most companies begin with weak marketing in their divisions, and these companies often establish a corporate marketing staff whose primary purpose is to bring marketing into the various divisions through education and supplying various services. This begins to work, and some members of the corporate marketing staff join the divisions to head marketing departments. As the divisions grow strong in their marketing, corporate marketing has less to offer them. Some companies decide that corporate marketing no longer has a useful role to play, and it is eliminated.

All said, a corporate staff generally has three justifications. The first is to serve as a corporate focus for review and leadership of overall company marketing activities and opportunities. The second is to offer certain marketing services that could be provided more economically on a centralized basis than by being duplicated in the different divisions. The third is to take responsibility for educating divisional managers, sales managers, and others in the company on the meaning and implementation of the marketing concept.

MARKETING'S INTERFACE WITH OTHER DEPARTMENTS

In principle, business functions should mesh harmoniously to achieve the overall objectives of the firm. In practice, departmental interfaces are often characterized by deep rivalries and misunderstandings that profoundly impede the realization of the company's objectives. Some interdepartmental conflict stems from differences of opinion as to what lies in the best interests of the firm; some from real trade-offs between departmental well-being and company well-being; and some from unfortunate departmental stereotypes and prejudices.

Types of Interdepartmental Conflict

In the typical organization, made up of specialized departments charged with carrying out different company tasks, each department directly or indirectly has an impact on customer satisfaction through its own activities and decisions. Typically these impacts are uncoordinated. Under the marketing concept, it is desirable to coordinate them, because the satisfaction gained by the customer is a function of the *totality* of stimuli, not simply of the stimuli managed by the marketing department.

The marketing department is glad to accept this responsibility and use its influence. The reason for appointing a marketing vice president is twofold: (1) to bring about an integration and coordination of the formal marketing activities of the company, such as sales forecasting, marketing research, advertising, sales force, promotion, and customer service; and (2) to deal with the vice presidents of finance, operations, and so on, on a regular basis to try to develop a deeper appreciation by them of the value and benefits of a customer orientation. But there is little unanimity on how much influence and authority marketing should have over other departments to bring about coordinated marketing.

Other departments naturally resent having to bend their efforts to the will of the marketing department. Just as marketing stresses the customer's point of view, other departments wish to stress the importance of their tasks. Inevitably, departments and individuals define company problems and goals in terms slanted by self-interest. The reason is that each deals continuously with problems in a local portion of the overall system. The major departmental differences in point of view—or organizational conflicts—between marketing and other departments are summarized in Table 22–1. We will briefly examine the typical concerns of each department.

TABLE 22–1
Summary of Organizational Conflicts Between Marketing and Other Departments

DEPARTMENT	THEIR EMPHASIS	MARKETING'S EMPHASIS
R&D	Basic research	Applied research
	Intrinsic quality	Perceived quality
	Functional features	Sales features
Engineering	Long design lead time	Short design lead time
	Few models	Many models
	Standard components	Custom components
Purchasing	Narrow product line	Broad product line
	Standard parts	Nonstandard parts
	Price of material	Quality of material
	Economical lot sizes	Large lot sizes to avoid stockouts
	Purchasing at infrequent intervals	Immediate purchasing for customer needs
Manufacturing	Long production lead time	Short production lead time
	Long runs with few models	Short runs with many models
	No model changes	Frequent model changes
	Standard orders	Custom orders
	Ease of fabrication	Aesthetic appearance
	Average quality control	Tight quality control
Finance	Strict rationales for spending	Intuitive arguments for spending
	Hard and fast budgets	Flexible budgets to meet changing needs
	Pricing to cover costs	Pricing to further market development
Accounting	Standard transactions	Special terms and discounts
	Few reports	Many reports
Credit	Full financial disclosures by customers	Minimum credit examination of customers
	Low credit risks	Medium credit risks
	Tough credit terms	Easy credit terms
	Tough collection procedures	Easy collection procedures

R&D   The company's desire for successful new products is often thwarted by poor working relations between R&D and marketing. In many ways, these groups represent two different cultures in the organization. The R&D department is staffed with scientists and technicians who (1) pride themselves on scientific curiosity and detachment, (2) like to work on challenging technical problems without much concern for immediate sales payoffs, and (3) like to work without much supervision or accountability for research costs. The marketing/sales department is staffed with business-oriented persons who (1) pride themselves on a practical understanding of the world, (2) like to see many new products with sales points that can be talked about to customers, and (3) feel compelled to pay daily attention to the bottom line. Furthermore, each group often carries negative stereotypes of the other group. Marketers see the R&D people as impractical, long-haired, mad-scientist types who don't understand business at all, while R&D people see marketers as gimmick-oriented hucksters who are more interested in sales than in the technical quality of the product. These stereotypes interfere with achieving a good record of successful innovation.

Companies turn out to be either R&D dominated, marketing dominated, or balanced. In *R&D-dominated companies,* the R&D staff goes about researching fundamental problems, looking for major solutions, and striving for technical perfection in product development. In these companies, R&D expenditures tend to be high, and the new product success rate tends to be low, although R&D occasionally comes up with an important new product discovery. In *marketing-dominated companies,* the R&D staff is directed to design products for specific market needs, often involving product modification and the application of existing technologies. In these companies, a higher ratio of new products succeed, but they represent primarily product modifications with relatively short product lives.

A *balanced R&D/marketing company* is one in which effective organizational relations have been worked out between R&D and marketing to share responsibility for successful market-oriented innovation. The R&D staff takes responsibility not for invention alone but for successful innovation. The marketing staff takes responsibility not for new sales features alone but for supporting the discovery of new ways to satisfy needs. R&D/marketing understanding and communication is facilitated in several ways: (1) joint seminars are sponsored to build mutual understanding and respect for each other's goals, working styles, and problems; (2) each new project is assigned to both an R&D person and a marketing person who are in constant communication throughout the life of the project; (3) R&D and marketing personnel are interchanged so that they have a chance to experience each other's work situations. Some R&D people may travel with the sales force, while some marketing people might hang around the lab for a short time; (4) a liaison individual or committee is set up to work out problems that arise between the two groups.[13]

Engineering   Engineering has responsibility for finding practical ways to design new products and new production processes. Engineers are interested in achieving technical quality, cost economy, and manufacturing simplicity. They

---

[13] For further discussion, see William E. Souder, "Effectiveness of Nominal and Interacting Group Decision Processes for Integrating R&D and Marketing," *Management Science,* February 1977, pp. 595–605.

come into conflict with marketing personnel when the latter want several models to be produced, often with product features that require custom components rather than standard components. Engineers see marketers as wanting "bells-and-whistles" on the products rather than more substantial qualities. These problems are less pronounced in companies where the marketing executives have engineering backgrounds and can understand and communicate with the engineers more effectively.

Purchasing Purchasing executives are responsible for obtaining satisfactory materials and components at the lowest possible cost and in the right quantities from an inventory cost-control point of view. They see marketing executives as pushing for several models in a product line, which requires purchasing small quantities of many inventory items rather than large quantities of a few items. They may think that marketing insists on too high a quality of ordered materials and components. They dislike the inability of marketing to forecast sales accurately—it causes them to have to place rush orders at unfavorable prices and at other times to carry excessive inventories.

Manufacturing There are many occasions of conflict between manufacturing and marketing managers. Manufacturing people are responsible for the smooth running of the factory to produce the right products in the right quantities at the right time for the right cost. They have spent their lives in the factory, with its attendant problems of machine breakdowns, inventory stockouts, and labor disputes and slowdowns. They see marketers as having little understanding of factory economics or politics. Marketers will complain about insufficient plant capacity, delays in production, poor quality control, and poor customer service. Yet marketers often turn in inaccurate sales forecasts, design products that are difficult to manufacture and come in too many versions, and promise more factory service than is reasonable.

Marketers, being out in the marketplace, do not see the factory's problems but rather the problems of their customers who need the goods quickly, who receive defective merchandise, and who can't get factory service. Marketers show little concern with the extra factory costs of getting something done to make or save a customer. The problem is one not only of poor communication but of actual conflict of interest.

The conflict is settled by companies in different ways. Some companies are *manufacturing dominant,* in that everything is done to insure smooth production and low costs. The company chooses to produce narrow product lines in large quantities. Products are designed simply. Sales promotions calling for quick production are kept to a minimum. Customers on back order have to be patient and wait their turn. Other companies are *marketing dominant,* in that everything is done to serve and satisfy customers. In one large toiletries company, the marketing personnel call the shots, and the manufacturing people have to fall in line, including going overtime, producing short runs, and so on. This results in high and fluctuating manufacturing costs, as well as poor quality control.

Ideally, companies need to move toward a *balanced manufacturing/marketing orientation* in which policies and authority are defined, both sides feel important, and both participate in determining what is best for the company. Solutions take the form of joint seminars to understand each other's viewpoint, joint committees and liaison personnel, personnel exchange programs, and analytical methods to determine the most profitable course for the company to take when there is disagreement.[14]

Finance   Financial executives pride themselves on being able to evaluate the profit implications of different business actions. When it comes to marketing expenditures, they frequently feel frustrated. Marketing executives will ask for substantial budgets for advertising, sales promotion, and sales force, without providing dependable forecasts of how much sales will be produced by these different expenditures. Financial executives suspect that the marketers' forecasts are self-serving rather than arrived at by any solid scientific methodology. They think that marketing people don't spend enough time relating their expenditures to sales outcomes and shifting their budgets to more profitable areas. They think that marketers are too willing to slash prices in order to make sales, instead of pricing to make a profit.

In turn, marketing executives often see financial people as controlling the purse strings too tightly and refusing to invest in long-term market development. Financial people seem overly conservative and risk averse, causing many opportunities to be passed over. The solution lies in giving marketing people more training in financial concepts and giving financial people a better understanding of how the market works and responds to different types of marketing effort.

Accounting   Accountants see marketing people as lax in providing good sales reports and providing them on time. They also dislike the special deals sales people make with customers who require special accounting procedures. Marketers, on the other hand, are upset by the procedures used by accountants to allocate fixed-cost burdens to different products in the line. Thus brand managers may feel that their brand is more profitable than it looks if it were not for the high overhead assigned to it. They would also like the accounting department to prepare special reports on sales and profitability by different channels, territories, order sizes, and so on, only to hear that the accounting department is too busy to do it.

Credit   Credit officers are eager to check out the credit standing of potential customers and to deny or limit credit to the more doubtful ones. They think that marketers are too ready to sell to anyone, even to those from whom payment would be slow or doubtful. Marketers, on the other hand, often feel that credit standards are too high. They think that "zero bad debts" may look good on the credit officers' records but really means that a lot of sales and profits have been lost. They feel that they work too hard to find customers to hear that they are not good enough to sell to.

Strategies for Building a Company-wide Marketing Orientation   Only a handful of American companies—such as P&G, IBM, Caterpillar—are truly marketing oriented. A much larger number of companies are sales oriented, which they confuse with being marketing oriented. At some time in their history, something happens to create a disturbing awareness of their lack of a true marketing orientation. They may lose a major market, experience slow

---

[14] See Benson P. Shapiro, "Can Marketing and Manufacturing Coexist?" *Harvard Business Review*, September–October 1977, pp. 104–14.

growth or low profitability, or find themselves facing more sophisticated competitors. This has happened many times.

For years, General Motors prided itself on a marketing orientation and was able to point to its huge sales volume and market share as evidence. However, as management witnessed the growing share of small cars and foreign cars, they realized that they had not fully monitored the market and responded to consumer desires. They still have not yet learned to design small economy cars that Americans prefer as strongly as some foreign imports.

In the early 1970s, American Telephone and Telegraph (AT&T) suddenly found itself facing keen competition in the sale of switchboards and ancillary telephone equipment. AT&T was totally unprepared to make an effective marketing case to buyers to keep them from buying competitors' equipment selling at lower prices. They realized that they had been pushing sales when they should have been paying attention to changing market forces. They are now involved in a crash effort to acquire marketing know-how.[15]

American Hospital Supply Company enjoys market leadership in the hospital supplies business, based largely on their extensive distribution and sales coverage. They are now facing new sophisticated competitors, such as P&G, who are attacking their established markets. AHS is concerned and is rapidly transforming itself from a sales company to a marketing company.

The Chase National Bank of New York has watched Citibank, its main competitor, make one smart move after another, each time leaving Chase behind. Citibank has been systematically developing a marketing culture at the bank, while Chase has been running along traditional financial lines. Recently Chase has started to build new marketing resources at the bank.

All of these companies realized that they were weak in marketing and therefore at a great disadvantage when competing against topflight marketing companies. Old-fashioned sales responses are not enough. Sales managers, when faced with sales declines or stagnation, plea to top management for more resources and lower prices. They feel the answer lies in working harder. But top management is becoming less confident in pure sales power. They want those responsible for sales to get smarter, not work harder. They want more-advanced warnings and better analyses of the changing forces in the marketplace; they want better marketing strategies and plans; they want products that meet new and emerging customer needs.

Top management's problem is how to convert the company from a traditional sales company to a modern marketing company. Actually, there are several steps companies have to take to acquire a modern marketing orientation.

Presidential leadership Presidential leadership is a key prerequisite to establishing a modern marketing company. The vice president of marketing cannot unilaterally direct other company officers to bend their efforts to serve customers. The company president must understand marketing and its difference from sales, believe that it is the key to company growth and prosperity, and build it into his speeches and decisions.

---

[15] Bro Uttal, "Selling Is No Longer Mickey Mouse at A.T.&T.," *Fortune,* July 17, 1978, pp. 98–104.

Marketing task force   The president should appoint a marketing task force to develop a strategy for bringing modern marketing into the company. The task force should include the president, executive vice president, the vice presidents of sales, marketing, manufacturing, and finance, and a few other key individuals. They should examine the need for marketing, set objectives, anticipate problems in introducing it, and develop an overall strategy. For the next few years, this committee should meet from time to time to measure progress and take new initiatives.

Outside marketing consultant   The marketing task force would probably benefit from outside guidance and assistance in developing a plan for introducing marketing into the organization.

A corporate marketing department   A key step is to establish a corporate marketing department. The corporate marketing department should review each division's marketing resources and needs with the division's general manager. Often the division's general manager does not understand marketing and confuses it with sales. The division's sales operation is usually headed by a sales vice president who is not marketing oriented. To appoint a marketing vice president over this person would be asking for trouble. Alternative steps might be to add the outside marketer to the division as the executive vice president; or to add this person as a marketing vice president on a parallel level to the sales vice president; or to put this person in charge of divisional planning. Ultimately, each division will need a strong marketing vice president to make marketing headway.

In-house marketing seminars   The new corporate marketing department should develop an extensive program of in-house marketing seminars for top corporate management, divisional general managers, marketing and sales personnel, manufacturing personnel, R&D personnel, and so on. The seminars should start with the higher levels of management and move to lower levels. The aim of the marketing seminars is to bring about changes in the marketing beliefs, attitudes, and behavior of various executive groups.

Hiring marketing talent   The company should also hire marketing talent away from leading marketing companies and also hire new M.B.A.'s receiving their degrees in marketing. For example, when Citibank got serious about marketing some years ago, they hired away several brand managers from General Foods and other companies.

Promoting executives who are market oriented   The company should favor market-oriented individuals in selecting new division managers. A large public-accounting firm that is currently trying to become market-oriented has now sent out signals that it will give preference to marketing- rather than financially-oriented partners in promotions to branch manager.

Installing a modern marketing-planning system   An excellent way to train an organization to think marketing is to install a modern market-oriented planning system. This means that corporate planners will begin their thinking with market opportunity considerations and will formulate marketing strategies to capitalize on these opportunities. Other departments will do their planning around these marketing strategies and forecasts.

The job of implementing a marketing orientation throughout the company is an uphill and never-ending battle. The purpose is not to resolve every issue in favor of the customer, no matter what the cost, but rather to remind others that customers are the foundation of the company's business.[16]

SUMMARY

The modern marketing department evolved through several stages to reach its contemporary form. It started as a simple sales department consisting of only a sales force. Later the sales department took on some ancillary functions, such as advertising and marketing research. As the ancillary functions grew in importance, many companies created a marketing department separate from the sales department to manage these other marketing activities. But the heads of sales and marketing often disagreed on company marketing policy, and eventually the two departments were merged into a modern marketing department headed by the marketing vice-president. A modern marketing department, however, does not automatically create a modern marketing company unless the other officers accept a customer orientation as the hub of the enterprise.

Modern marketing departments are organized in a number of ways. The most common form is the functional marketing organization in which the various marketing functions are headed by separate managers who report to the marketing vice president. Another common form is the product management organization in which major products are the responsibility of product managers who work with the various functional specialists in the company to develop and achieve their plans for the product. Another, less common, form is the market management organization in which major markets are the responsibility of market managers who work with the various functional specialists to develop and achieve their plans for the market. Some large companies use a product management/market management organization, which combines both systems of management. Finally, multidivision companies normally develop a corporate marketing staff and separate marketing departments at the divisions, with some variations as to the division and authority for different services.

Marketing must work smoothly with the other functions in a company. In its pursuit of the customers' interests, marketing frequently comes into conflict with R&D, engineering, purchasing, manufacturing, finance, accounting, credit, and other functions that stress a cost minimization logic. These conflicts can be reduced when the company president commits himself and the company to a customer orientation and when the marketing vice president learns to work effectively with the other officers. Acquiring a modern marketing orientation requires presidential support, a marketing task force, outside marketing consulting help, the establishment of a corporate marketing department, in-house marketing seminars, marketing talent hired from the outside, and a market-oriented marketing-planning system.

[16] For further discussion, see Edward S. McKay, *The Marketing Mystique* (New York: American Management Association, 1972), pp. 22–30.

1. In order to carry out a proposed national sales promotion, describe some of the departments whose efforts must be coordinated with those of the marketing department. Through what kind of planning device might these efforts be integrated?

2. Does it make organizational sense to combine the company's marketing department and public relations department under one vice-president?

3. A major airline's marketing department is presently organized on a functional basis: advertising, field sales, customer services, and so on. The airline is considering setting up a route manager organization, with a manager assigned to each major route who would be to a route what a brand manager is to a brand. Do you think this is a good idea?

4. "In 1945 he had been brought back to Millburgh and made vice-president of sales. At fifty-three, J. Walter Dudley was probably the best-known man in the entire furniture industry. His memory for names and faces was phenomenal. At one Chicago Market . . . two bystanding salesmen had actually kept a count and heard him greet two hundred and eighteen furniture store owners and buyers by name before he was confronted by an individual whose name he did not know. There were hundreds of furniture merchants who would not have thought a market visit complete without having had the opportunity to shake hands with good old Walt Dudley."—Cameron Hawley, *Executive Suite* (Boston: Houghton Mifflin Company, 1952), pp. 133–34. Does J. Walter Dudley sound like the ideal vice-president of marketing?

5. You are being interviewed for the position of brand manager at the Blogg's Blotting Paper Company. Sales of blotters have been declining for several years. Develop a list of questions and suggestions that would reflect well on your qualifications for this position.

6. The General Electric Company does not have a corporate vice-president of marketing. Its vice-presidents of marketing are found in various sections, groups, and divisions. General Electric does have a corporate vice-president of strategic planning. Do you think a corporate vice-president of marketing should be added?

7. In large railroads, the operations department usually holds dominant power. The needs of freight customers were accorded less importance than sticking to schedules. Suggest a strategy for establishing a company-wide marketing orientation.

8. Describe some product and market situations where local marketing specialists would be of particular assistance to a company.

Marketing Research and the Marketing Information System

23

To manage a business well is to manage its future; and to manage its future is to manage information.
MARION HARPER, JR.

In the long history of business enterprise, management's overwhelming attention has been devoted to the problems of effectively managing *money, materials, machines,* and *men.* Through time, business has attained increased mastery over these resources. Less attention has been paid historically to the fifth critical resource of the firm: *information.* It is hard to find company executives anywhere who are substantially satisfied with their marketing information. Their complaints include:

There is too much marketing information of the wrong kind.

There is not enough marketing information of the right kind.

Marketing information is so dispersed throughout the company that usually a great effort must be made to locate simple facts.

Important marketing information is sometimes suppressed by subordinates if they believe it will reflect unfavorably on their performance.

Important information often arrives too late to be useful.

Information often arrives in a form that leaves no idea of its accuracy, and there is no one to turn to for confirmation.

The basic fact is that most companies have not yet adapted to the intensified information requirements for effective marketing in a modern economy. Three trends, in particular, render the needs for marketing information stronger than at any time in the past.

The first trend is the shift from local to national and international marketing. The concept of the national and international firm means that company decision makers must make their key decisions on the basis of secondhand information, since they are far removed from the scenes where their products are sold. *The second is the transition from buyer needs to buyer wants.* As the society becomes more affluent, its members' survival needs are increasingly satisfied. Buying becomes a highly expressive personal act, and sellers must depend on systematic research to understand the overt and latent wants of buyers. *The third is the transition from price to nonprice competition.* As sellers increase their reliance on competitive weapons such as branding, product differentiation, advertising, and sales promotion, they require great quantities of information on the effectiveness of these marketing tools. Not only markets but also the tools of marketing must be researched.

The explosive information requirements have been met on the supply side by impressive new information technologies. The last thirty years have witnessed the emergence of the computer, microfilming, closed-circuit television, copy machines, tape recorders, and many other devices that have created a veritable revolution in information-handling capacity.

Most business firms, however, do not operate at a high level of information sophistication. Many firms do not have a marketing research department. Many other firms have small marketing research departments whose work is limited to routine forecasting, sales analysis, and occasional surveys. Only a few firms have developed advanced marketing information systems that provide company management with up-to-date marketing information and analysis.

CONCEPT AND COMPONENTS OF A MARKETING INFORMATION SYSTEM

Every firm is the scene of many information flows affecting marketing management. Each firm has made some arrangements to systematize these flows. These arrangements constitute the firm's *marketing information system:*

> A structured, interacting complex of persons, machines, and procedures designed to generate an orderly flow of pertinent information, collected from both intra- and extra-firm sources, for use as the basis for decision making in specified responsibility areas of marketing management.[1]

Figure 23–1 presents a picture of the main components of a total marketing information system. The *marketing information system* is shown to stand between the *environment* and the *marketing executive-user.* There is a *marketing data flow* from the environment to the marketing information system of the company. The marketing information system turns this data flow into a *marketing information flow* that goes to its executives. On the basis of this information,

---

[1] Samuel V. Smith, Richard H. Brien, and James E. Stafford, eds., *Readings in Marketing Information Systems* (Boston: Houghton Mifflin Company, 1968), p. 7. Also see Kurt H. Schaffir and H. George Trentin, *Marketing Information Systems* (New York: American Management Association, 1973).

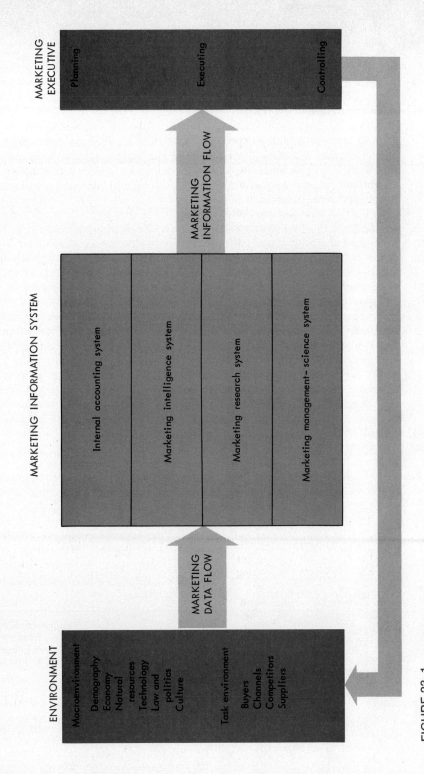

FIGURE 23-1
Components of the Marketing Information System

the executives develop plans and programs, which enter a *marketing decision flow* that goes back to the environment.

We now turn to the main components of the marketing information system.

INTERNAL ACCOUNTING SYSTEM

The earliest and most basic information system used by the marketing executive is the internal accounting system. It is the system that reports orders, sales, inventory levels, receivables, payables, and so on. Through this information the executives can spot opportunities and problems and can compare actual and expected levels of performance.

The Order-Shipping-Billing Cycle

The heart of the accounting system is the order-shipping-billing cycle. Sales representatives, dealers, and customers dispatch orders to the firm. The order department prepares multicopy invoices and dispatches them to various departments. Items that are out of stock are back-ordered. Items that are shipped are accompanied by shipping and billing documents that are also multicopied and go to various departments.

The company has a strong interest in carrying out these steps as quickly and accurately as possible. Sales representatives are supposed to send in their orders every evening, in some cases to phone them in when they are obtained. The order department should process them quickly. The warehouse should send the goods out as soon as possible. And bills should go out as soon as possible. The computer should be harnessed to expedite the order-shipping-billing cycle. Ringer and Howell reported a study of one company's order routine, which resulted in cutting down the elapsed time between the receipt and issuance of an order from sixty-two hours to thirty hours without any change in costs.[2]

Improving the Timeliness of Sales Reports

Marketing executives in many companies receive sales reports some time after the sales have taken place. In consumer food companies, warehouse withdrawal reports are issued with fair regularity, but actual retail purchase reports take about two months, based on special store or consumer panel audits. In the auto industry, executives wait with bated breath for a sales report that comes out every ten days; if sales are down, they can expect ten sleepless nights. Most marketing executives complain that they don't get the sales report fast enough, no matter how often they get it.

Here are three companies that have designed sophisticated sales-reporting systems to increase the value of sales information:

> *General Mills.* The executives at General Mills receive their information daily. The zone, regional, and district sales managers in the Grocery Products Division start their day with a teletype report on orders and shipments in their area the day before. The report also contains progress percentages to compare with target percentages and last year's progress percentages.

[2] Jurgen F. Ringer and Charles D. Howell, "The Industrial Engineer and Marketing," in *Industrial Engineering Handbook,* 2nd ed., ed. Harold Bright Maynard (New York: McGraw-Hill Book Company, 1963), pp. 10, 102–3.

Schenley. Schenley's system allows its key executives to retrieve within seconds, via video-display desk consoles and printers, current and past sales and inventory figures for any brand and package size for each of four hundred distributors; an executive can determine within seconds all areas where sales are lagging behind expectations.

Mead Paper. Mead Paper's system permits its sales representatives in buyers' offices to obtain on-the-spot answers to customers' queries about paper availability. The sales representative dials Mead Paper's computer center. The computer determines whether paper is available at the nearest warehouse and when it can be shipped; if it is not in stock, the computer checks the inventory at other nearby warehouses until one is located. If the paper is nowhere in stock, the computer program goes through a production-scheduling routine to determine where and when the paper can be produced and shipped. The sales representative gets an answer in seconds, and this places him or her in an advantageous position in relation to competitors.

Designing a User-Oriented Reports System

In designing an advanced sales information system, the company should avoid certain pitfalls. First, it is possible to create a system that delivers too much information to the executives. They arrive at their office each morning to face voluminous sales statistics. Second, it is possible to create a system that delivers information that is too current! Executives may end up reacting to sales movements that are essentially random; and their actions may in fact destabilize the market. Third, it is possible that the cost of supplying all of this information at some point will exceed its value.

Cox and Good noted that many companies had not taken advantage of all the existing modern information technology because they recognized the need for a system-manager balance.

> In a "steady state" . . . there usually seems to be a correspondence between management sophistication and information quality. . . . What happens when only the level of information quality is raised significantly? Our prediction is that this would not lead to better decisions. In fact, the reverse may be true, as the result of the confusion and resentment generated by the manager's inability to deal with the more sophisticated information.
>
> Information quality can be upgraded much more rapidly than management quality. It is easy to throw the management system out of balance by installing a sophisticated MIS. . . . A more positive approach is to develop a master plan for improving the system, but make the improvements gradually—say, over several years.[3]

The company's marketing information system should represent a cross between (a) what executives think they need, (b) what executives really need, and (c) what is economically feasible. A useful step is the appointment of a *marketing information-planning committee,* which interviews a cross section of marketing executives—product managers, sales executives, sales representatives, and so on—to find out their information needs. A useful set of questions is shown in Table 23–1. The information-planning committee will want to pay special attention to strong desires and complaints. At the same time, the committee will wisely discount some of the alleged information needs. Executives who have an appetite for information will list a great deal, failing to distinguish between *what is nice*

---

[3] Donald F. Cox and Robert E. Good, "How to Build a Marketing Information System," *Harvard Business Review,* May–June 1967, pp. 145–54.

TABLE 23–1
Questionnaire for Determining Marketing Information Needs

1. What types of decisions are you regularly called upon to make?
2. What types of information do you need to make these decisions?
3. What types of information do you regularly get?
4. What types of special studies do you periodically request?
5. What types of information would you like to get that you are not now getting?
6. What information would you want daily? weekly? monthly? yearly?
7. What magazines and trade reports would you like to see routed to you on a regular basis?
8. What specific topics would you like to be kept informed of?
9. What types of data-analysis programs would you like to see made available?
10. What do you think would be the four most helpful improvements that could be made in the present marketing information system?

to know and *what they need to know.* Other executives will be too busy to give the questionnaire serious thought and will omit many things they ought to know. This is why the information-planning committee must take another step, that of determining what executives *should know* to be able to make responsible decisions. For example, what should brand managers know in order to make truly informed decisions on the size of the advertising budget? They should know something about the degree of market saturation, the rate of sales decay in the absence of advertising, and the spending plans of competitors. The information system should be designed around models for making the key marketing decisions.

MARKETING INTELLIGENCE SYSTEM

Whereas the internal accounting system supplies executives with *results data,* the marketing intelligence system supplies executives with *happenings data.* We shall define the *marketing intelligence system* as *the way in which company executives are kept current and informed about changing conditions in the macroenvironment and task environment.*

All executives engage at different times in four modes of scanning the environment:

1. *Undirected viewing:* general exposure to information where the viewer has no specific purpose in mind.
2. *Conditioned viewing:* directed exposure, not involving active search, to a more or less clearly identified area or type of information.
3. *Informal search:* a relatively limited and unstructured effort to obtain specific information or information for a specific purpose.
4. *Formal search:* a deliberate effort—usually following a preestablished plan, procedure, or methodology—to secure specific information or information relating to a specific issue.[4]

[4] Francis Joseph Aguilar, *Scanning the Business Environment* (New York: Macmillan Company, 1967).

Marketing executives carry on marketing intelligence mostly on their own, being most interested in market news, keeping informed by reading newspapers and trade publications, relying on subordinates for search information, and getting some unsolicited information from outside sources. To the extent that their intelligence work is casual, valuable information will often come in too little or too late. Executives may learn of a competitive move, a new customer need, or a dealer problem too late to make the best response.

Improving Intelligence-Gathering Activity

A company can take three steps to improve the executives' intelligence system: (1) train the sales force to be better at intelligence gathering, (2) utilize additional intelligence resources, and (3) buy information from specialized marketing research services.

Sales representatives as intelligence agents Sales representatives have correctly been called the company's "eyes and ears to the marketplace." They meet the buyers, dealers, and occasionally the competitors. They are in a good position to pick up significant bits of information that would never appear in the usual summary statistics of company sales activity. When these bits and pieces of information are correlated at headquarters, they often yield a revealing picture.

The critical question is whether the sales force feels motivated to look for information and to pass it on to their superiors. In a telling experiment, Albaum arranged with a sample of company customers to pass on six fabricated pieces of market information to the company's sales representatives.[5] Of the six pieces of market information, only two were ever passed on by the sales representatives to their superiors. One arrived in three days but was seriously distorted; the other arrived in about ten days in fairly accurate form. Albaum concluded that there was not a free flow of market intelligence within this company and that, in general, most unmanaged intelligence systems are characterized by information disappearance, delay, and distortion.

The solution requires training sales representatives to be intelligence gatherers for the firm. Their job should be facilitated by designing call reports that are easy to fill out. Sales representatives should know who in the company can use various types of information, so that information does not always have to travel through several relay points before reaching the person who needs it. An intelligence office might be established to receive and disseminate intelligence. Sales managers should make a point of reviewing the intelligence performance of their sales representatives and make it a factor in pay raises.

Other means of gathering competitive intelligence Similar steps should be taken to motivate sales managers, dealers, the advertising agency, and others to pay more attention to gathering and passing along intelligence. It is sometimes desirable to hire one or more full-time specialists in marketing intelligence gathering. This does not necessarily mean industrial espionage agents. Many companies send out comparison shoppers to learn how various brands are selling and how helpful retail sales personnel are. Interviewing customers and dealers to learn about new opportunities and problems is a legitimate intelligence activity. Much can be learned about competitors' activities through such overt means as

---

[5] Gerald S. Albaum, "Horizontal Information Flow: An Exploratory Study," *Journal of the Academy of Management,* March 1964, pp. 21–33.

(1) pricing or purchasing competitors' products; (2) attending "open houses" and trade shows; (3) reading competitors' published reports and attending stock-holders' meetings; (4) talking to competitors' former employees and present employees, dealers, distributors, suppliers, and freight agents; (5) hiring a clipping service; and (6) reading the *Wall Street Journal,* the *New York Times,* and trade-association papers.

Purchase of special marketing intelligence services Many companies purchase information from outside suppliers. The A. C. Nielsen Company sells bimonthly data (based on a sample of sixteen hundred stores) on brand shares, retail prices, percentage of stores stocking item, and percentage of stock-out stores. The Market Research Corporation of America sells reports (based on the purchase diaries of a representative panel of seventy-five hundred households scattered throughout the country) on weekly movements of brand shares, sizes, prices, and deals. Clipping services may be hired to report on competitive advertising expenditures, media mixes, and advertising appeals.

Improving Intelligence-Processing Activity

The usefulness of gathered intelligence depends on its accuracy, retrievability, and speed in moving to higher management levels where it can be used. A centralized marketing intelligence center can offer several services to improve the processing and dissemination of intelligence.

The first service is intelligence *evaluation.* An analyst trained in data evaluation would be available to examine any information and render a technical opinion as to how much confidence can be placed in it. A second important service is intelligence *abstraction.* Trained abstracters can condense and edit incoming information to make it more useful for executives. *Dissemination* is a third important intelligence-processing service. Dissemination involves getting information to the right people in the right form in the shortest feasible time. Among the devices used are newsletters, telephone calls, cassettes, teletype services, and interconnected company computers. The fourth service is *storage and retrieval.* Each company should develop a master indexing system and organize all the existing information into easily accessible files. The fifth service is *purging,* where old information that is no longer useful is removed, to keep the amount of stored information within limits.

MARKETING RESEARCH SYSTEM

Besides internal accounting information and marketing intelligence, marketing executives need specific studies of problem and opportunity areas. They may need a market survey, a product-preference test, a sales forecast by region, or an advertising-effectiveness study. These studies require the talents of skilled researchers, who can apply principles of sample size, sample design, and questionnaire construction to the task. These researchers usually make up the marketing research department of the company.

Organizational Characteristics of Marketing Research

About 73 percent of all large companies have formal marketing research departments headed by a marketing research manager who reports normally to the marketing vice president and in some cases to top management or other officers. The marketing research manager is considered a major member of the marketing team and performs such roles as study director, administrator, internal company consultant, and advocate. In smaller companies, the department consists of a few professional researchers and in larger companies may comprise one to two dozen full-time employees. The department personnel may be specialized by skill (survey expert, statistician, behavioral scientist), by industry, or by type of project.

The department usually gets a budget anywhere from .01 to 3.50 percent of company sales. The department spends between one-quarter and one-half of this budget on outside services.[6] Bradford lists over three hundred fifty marketing research firms, falling into three major categories:

1. *Full-line marketing research firms.* These firms offer general marketing research services. Their clients range from companies that are too small to support their own marketing research department to large firms who subcontract a portion of their work to relieve backlog or to obtain an independent point of view.

2. *Specialty-line marketing research firms.* These firms specialize in particular marketing research services, such as market analysis and forecasting, survey research work, packaging research, product research, or brand-name testing. They may also specialize in either consumer or industrial goods.

3. *Syndicated information-selling firms.* These firms specialize in gathering continuous trade or consumer data, which they sell to clients on a fee-subscription basis. Well-known examples include A. C. Nielsen Company, Market Research Corporation of America, Daniel Starch, and Gallup-Robinson.[7]

The scope of marketing research Marketing research departments have been steadily expanding their activities and techniques. Table 23–2 lists thirty-three different marketing research activities and the percentage of companies carrying on each. The ten most common activities are determination of market characteristics, measurement of market potentials, market-share analysis, sales analysis, studies of business trends, competitive-product studies, short-range forecasting, new-product acceptance and potential, long-range forecasting, and pricing studies.[8]

These studies have benefited over the years from increasingly sophisticated techniques. Many of them—such as questionnaire construction and area sampling—came along early and were quickly and widely accepted in the corpus of marketing research practice. Others—such as motivation research and mathematical methods—came in uneasily, with prolonged and heated debates among practitioners over their practical usefulness. But they, too, settled in the corpus of marketing research methodology.

Management's use of marketing research In spite of the rapid growth of marketing research, there are many companies that are still without it or that use it poorly. Several factors stand in the way of its greater utilization.

A NARROW CONCEPTION OF MARKETING RESEARCH Many executives see marketing research as only a fact-finding operation. The marketing researcher is

---

[6] For specific statistics, see Dik Warren Twedt, ed., *1978 Survey of Marketing Research: Organization, Functions, Budget, Compensation* (Chicago: American Marketing Association, 1978).

[7] Ernest S. Bradford, *Bradford's Directory of Marketing Research Agencies and Management Consultants in the United States and the World*, 15th ed., 1973–1974 (Middlebury, Vt.: Bradford Co.).

[8] Twedt, *Survey of Marketing Research*, p. 41.

TABLE 23–2
Research Activities of 798 Companies

TYPE OF RESEARCH	PERCENT DOING
Advertising research:	
Motivation research	48
Copy research	49
Media research	61
Studies of ad effectiveness	67
Business economics and corporate research:	
Short-range forecasting (up to 1 year)	85
Long-range forecasting (over 1 year)	82
Studies of business trends	86
Pricing studies	81
Plant and warehouse location studies	71
Product mix studies	51
Acquisition studies	69
Export and international studies	51
MIS (management information system)	72
Operations research	60
Internal company employees	65
Corporate responsibility research:	
Consumers "right to know" studies	26
Ecological impact studies	33
Studies of legal constraints on advertising and promotion	51
Social values and policies studies	40
Product research:	
New-product acceptance and potential	84
Competitive-product studies	85
Testing of existing products	75
Packaging research—design or physical characteristics	60
Sales and market research:	
Measurement of market potentials	93
Market-share analysis	92
Determination of market characteristics	93
Sales analysis	89
Establishment of sales quotas, territories	75
Distribution channels studies	69
Test markets, store audits	54
Consumer-panel operations	50
Sales compensation studies	60
Promotional studies of premiums, coupons, sampling, deals, etc.	52

SOURCE: Dik Warren Twedt, ed., *1978 Survey of Marketing Research* (Chicago: American Marketing Association 1978), p. 41.

supposed to design a questionnaire, choose a sample, carry out interviews, and report results, often without being given a careful definition of the problem or of the decision alternatives before management. As a result, some of the fact finding fails to be useful. This reinforces management's idea of the limited good that can come from marketing research.

UNEVEN CALIBER OF MARKETING RESEARCHERS   Some executives view marketing research as little better than a clerical activity and reward it as such. In these cases, less able individuals are attracted into its ranks, and their weak training and deficient creativity are reflected in their output. The disappointing output reinforces management prejudice against expecting too much from marketing research. Management continues to pay low salaries, perpetuating the basic difficulty.

LATE RESULTS   Marketing research that is carefully designed may take a long time to carry out. Often the report is ready after the decision has had to be made, or when the issue has become less salient to the executives.

OCCASIONAL ERRONEOUS FINDINGS BY MARKETING RESEARCH   Many executives want conclusive information from marketing research, although usually marketing processes are too complex to yield more than tentative findings. The problem is complicated by the low budgets often given to marketing researchers to get the information. Executives become disappointed, and their opinion of the worth of marketing research is lowered.

INTELLECTUAL DIFFERENCES   Intellectual divergences between the mental styles of line managers and researchers often get in the way of productive relationships. All too often the marketing researcher's report is abstruse, complicated, and tentative, whereas the manager wants concreteness, simplicity, and certainty.

Marketing Research Procedure

Marketing research is undertaken in the effort to understand a marketing problem better. The value of the results depends upon the skill with which the marketing research project is designed and implemented. Effective marketing research involves the following five steps: *problem definition, research design, field work, data analysis,* and *report presentation and implementation.*

Problem definition   The first step in the conduct of research calls for a careful definition of the problem. If the problem is stated vaguely, if the wrong problem is defined, or if the uses of the research are not made clear, then the research results may prove useless to the manager.

The poor definition of the problem is often the fault of the manager requesting the study. Thus a top administrator in the U.S. Postal System might ask the marketing research manager to research public attitudes toward the postal system. The marketing research manager has a right to feel uneasy about the assignment. It is too general. It is not clear how much interviewing should be done of home users and business users or what aspects of the postal system they should comment on. This kind of research is called *exploratory research* and is mostly warranted in situations where the organization's ignorance of the marketplace is substantial. Yet research is generally more efficient when the problem and the alternatives are well defined—the cost of research is generally related to the total amount of information gathered, while the value of research is associated only with the proportion of information that is useful.

Research design   The problem definition stage should lead to the development of a clear set of research objectives, stated in writing if possible. The marketing research manager faces a choice among many alternative ways to collect the information that will satisfy the research objectives. The manager must decide on the *data collection method, research instrument,* and *sampling plan.*

DATA COLLECTION METHODS   In simple cases the data needed already exist in an accessible form and merely have to be found. This type of data is called *secondary data.* They might be present in the organization's internal records; in advertising agencies or trade associations; in government, commercial, or trade publications;[9] or purchasable from syndicated services. If the data are found in existing sources, the researcher has saved time and expense. However, the researcher must be careful to evaluate secondary data, since they were collected for a variety of purposes and under a variety of conditions that may limit their usefulness. Marketing researchers should check these data for relevance, impartiality, validity, and reliability.

When satisfactory secondary data are not available, the researcher must collect *primary data.* The data can be gathered from customers, middlemen, salesmen, competitors, or other information sources. There are three basic primary data collection methods.

The first is *observation,* in which case the researcher attempts to learn about the problem by observing the relevant actors. The observational method has been used to study such marketing behaviors: (1) the movement of shoppers through a department store; (2) the number of shoppers who stopped in front of a particular display; (3) the eye movements of the shoppers looking at the display; (4) the selling appeals used by the sales personnel with customers. Its main advantage is that it generally leads to a more objective picture of overt behavior than can be expected from relying on people's accounts of how they behave. On the other hand, this method yields no information about the state of mind, buying motives, or brand images of those being observed.

At the other extreme is *experimentation* as a method of gathering primary data. The experimental method consists of introducing selected stimuli into a controlled environment and systematically varying them. To the extent that extraneous factors are eliminated or controlled, the observed effects can be related to the variations in the stimuli. The purpose of control is to eliminate competing hypotheses that might also explain the observed phenomena. Marketers have applied this data-generation method to such marketing problems as finding the best sales-training method, the best sales promotion, the best price level, and the best ad campaign. Properly used, experimentation is the most reliable and fruitful way to find the answers. But it has rigorous requirements and can be costly. The cooperation of stores, sales forces, and other parties is necessary. There must be enough participating subjects to make a reliable inference. The treatments must be administered uniformly, and the subjects must react as they would under normal circumstances. When these and other conditions are lacking, the usefulness of the experimental results can be questioned.[10]

A third method of generating primary data, and the most common, is *survey research.* Compared with either direct observation or experimentation, surveys yield a broader range of information and are effective for a greater number of research problems. Surveys can produce information on socioeconomic characteristics, attitudes, opinions, motives, and overt behavior. Surveys are an effective way of gathering information for planning product features, advertis-

---

[9] For an excellent guide to major secondary sources in marketing, see Harper W. Boyd, Jr., Ralph Westfall, and Stanley F. Stasch, *Marketing Research: Text and Cases,* 4th ed. (Homewood, Ill.: Richard D. Irwin, 1977), pp. 150–62.

[10] See Seymour Banks, *Experimentation in Marketing* (New York: McGraw-Hill Book Company, 1965).

ing copy, advertising media, sales promotions, channels of distribution, and other marketing variables.

One of the most useful forms of surveys is called the *focus group interview.* From six to fifteen members of the target market are invited to gather for a few hours and discuss a product, service, organization, or other marketing entity. A trained leader probes the group's feelings and behavior toward the object, encouraging as much free discussion as possible. The comments are recorded and subsequently examined by marketing executives for clues about the market's thinking. Several focus group interviews might be held to sample the thinking of different market segments. The findings do not have sampling validity but provide a basis for effective questionnaire construction for a subsequent survey of the market.[11]

RESEARCH INSTRUMENT   The researcher has to use or design a reliable research instrument for gathering information. The observational method makes use of such instruments as tape recorders, cameras, and tally sheets. The experimental method might involve similar instruments if the subjects are put through a task. The survey method and, to some extent, the experimental method commonly rely on questionnaires.

The construction of good questionnaires calls for considerable skill. Every questionnaire should be pretested on a pilot sample of persons before being used on a large scale. A professional marketing researcher can usually spot several errors in a casually prepared questionnaire.

A common type of error occurs in the *types of questions asked:* the inclusion of questions that cannot be answered, or would not be answered, or need not be answered, and the omission of other questions that should be answered. Each question should be checked to determine whether it is necessary in terms of the research objectives. Questions should be dropped that are just interesting (except for one or two to start the interview on a good basis) because they lengthen the time required and try the respondent's patience.

The *form and wording of questions* can make a substantial difference to the response. An open-ended question is one in which the respondent is free to answer in his own words. A close-ended question is one in which the possible answers are supplied. The respondent may be asked to respond in one or two ways (dichotomous questions), to check one of several answers (multiple-choice questions), to place marks along a scale (scaling questions), and so forth. The choice between open-ended and close-ended questions affects the thoughtfulness of responses, the costs of interviewing, and the quality of the subsequent analysis.

The *choice of words* calls for considerable care. The designer should strive for simple, direct, unambiguous, and unbiased wording. A good rule is always to pretest the questions on a sample of respondents before they are used on a wide scale.

Other dos and don'ts arise in connection with the *sequencing of questions* in the questionnaire. The lead questions should create interest, if possible. Open questions are usually better here. Difficult questions or personal questions should be used toward the end of the interview, in order not to create an emotional reaction that may affect subsequent answers or cause the respondent to break off the interview. The questions should be asked in as logical an order as possible in

[11] See Keith K. Cox et al., "Applications of Focus Group Interviews in Marketing," *Journal of Marketing,* January 1976, pp. 77–80.

order to avoid confusing the respondent. Classificatory data on the respondent are usually asked for last, because they tend to be less interesting and are on the personal side.

SAMPLING PLAN   The third element of research design is a sampling plan. The sampling plan answers four questions: who is to be surveyed? (sampling unit); how many are to be surveyed? (sample size); how are they to be selected? (sampling procedure); and how are they to be reached? (sampling media).

Perhaps the basic issue is, Who is to be surveyed? The proper *sampling unit* is not always obvious from the nature of the information sought. In a survey designed to uncover attitudes toward breakfast cereals, should the primary sampling unit be the wife, the husband, the children, or some combination of the three? Where the roles of instigators, influencers, deciders, users, and/or purchasers are not combined in the same person, the researcher must determine not only what information is needed but also who is most likely to have it.

The next issue is *sample size.* Large samples obviously give more reliable results than small samples. However, it is not necessary to sample the entire universe or even a substantial part of it to achieve satisfactory precision. Samples amounting to less than 1 percent of a population can often provide good reliability, given a creditable sample procedure. In exploratory research, very small samples suffice. Much insight about marketing processes and attitudes can be gained from a sample of fewer than one hundred persons. In motivation-research studies, fewer than thirty depth interviews usually suffice to uncover significant attitudes.

Sampling procedure depends upon the research objective. For exploratory research, nonprobability sampling procedure may be adequate. However, to make an accurate estimate of population characteristics, a random (probability) sample of the population should be drawn. Random sampling allows the calculation of confidence limits for sampling error. One could say "the chances are ninety-five in a hundred that the interval '5 to 7 bottles' contains the true number of bottles purchased annually by the typical user of brand X." But random sampling is almost always more costly than nonrandom sampling. Some marketing researchers feel that the extra expenditure for probability sampling could be put to better use. Specifically, more of the money of a fixed research budget could be spent in designing better questionnaires and hiring better interviewers to reduce response and nonsampling errors, which can be just as fatal as sampling errors. This is a real issue, one that the marketing researcher and marketing executives must weigh carefully.

The final issue is *sampling method,* whether the target population should be reached by telephone, mail, or personal interviews. *Telephone interviewing* stands out as the best method for gathering information quickly. It permits the interviewer to clarify questions if they are not understood. The two main drawbacks of telephone interviewing are that only people with telephones can be interviewed, and only short, not too personal, interviews can be carried out. The *mail questionnaire* may be the best way to reach persons who would not give personal interviews or who might be biased by interviewers. On the other hand, mail questionnaires require simple and clearly worded questions, and the return rate is usually low and/or slow. *Personal interviewing* is the most versatile of the three methods. The personal interviewer can ask more questions and can supplement the interview with personal observations. Personal interviewing is the most expensive method and requires much more technical and administrative planning and supervision.

Field work   After the research design has been completed, the research department must supervise, or subcontract, the task of collecting the data. This phase is generally the most expensive and the most liable to error. Four major problems arise:

1. *Not-at-homes.* When no one is home, the interviewer must either call back later or substitute the household next door.
2. *Refusal to cooperate.* After finding the designated individual at home, the interviewer must interest the person in cooperating.
3. *Respondent bias.* The interviewer must encourage accurate and thoughtful answers.
4. *Interviewer bias.* Interviewers are capable of introducing a variety of biases into the interviewing process, through the mere fact of their age, sex, manner, or intonation. In addition, there is the problem of conscious interviewer bias or dishonesty.

Data analysis   The fourth step in marketing research procedure is to extract meaningful information from the data, and there are four steps in this process. The first is to calculate relevant averages and measures of dispersion. The second is to cross-tabulate the data to produce useful relationships. The third is to measure correlation coefficients and perform goodness-of-fit tests. The fourth is to apply *multivariate statistical techniques* to the data in the hope of discovering important relationships. The most important multivariate techniques are described below.[12]

MULTIPLE REGRESSION ANALYSIS   Every marketing problem involves a set of variables. The marketing researcher is interested in one of these variables, such as sales, and seeks to understand the cause(s) of its variation over time and/or space. This variable is called the dependent variable. The researcher hypothesizes about other variables, called independent variables, whose variations over time or space might contribute to the variations in the dependent variable. Regression analysis is the technique of estimating an equation showing the contribution of independent variables to variations in the dependent variable. When one independent variable is involved, the statistical procedure is called simple regression; when two or more independent variables are involved, the procedure is called multiple regression. An example of multiple regression was presented on page 235.

DISCRIMINANT ANALYSIS   In many marketing situations the dependent variable is classificatory rather than numerical. Consider the following situations:

An automobile company wants to explain brand preferences for Chevrolet versus Ford.

A detergent company wants to determine what consumer traits are associated with heavy, medium, and light usage of its brand.

A retailing chain wants to be able to discriminate between potentially successful and unsuccessful store sites.

In all these cases, two or more groups to which an entity (person or object) might belong are visualized. The challenge is to find discriminating variables

[12] See David A. Aaker, ed., *Multivariate Analysis in Marketing: Theory and Applications* (Belmont, Calif.: Wadsworth Publishing Co., 1971).

that could be combined in a predictive equation to produce better-than-chance assignment of the entities to the groups. The technique for solving this problem is known as discriminant analysis.

FACTOR ANALYSIS   One of the problems faced in many regression and discriminant analysis studies is multicollinearity—high intercorrelation of the independent variables. The idea in multiple regression is to use variables that are truly independent, both in the sense that they influence but are not influenced by the dependent variable and in the sense that each independent variable is independent of the others. The simple correlation coefficients for all pairs of variables will reveal which variables are highly intercorrelated, and the analyst has the option of dropping one from each pair. Another approach is to factor analyze the set of intercorrelated variables in order to derive a smaller set of factors that are truly independent of each other. Factor analysis is a statistical procedure for trying to discover a few basic factors that may underlie and explain the intercorrelations among a larger number of variables. In the marketing area, factor analysis has been applied to determining the basic factors underlying attitudes toward air travel, alcoholic beverages, and the clustering of media program types.[13]

Report presentation and implementation   The last step is the preparation, presentation, and implementation of a report presenting the major findings and recommendations coming from the study. The report should begin with a short statement of the problem and the major findings. This should be followed by an elaboration of the findings and technical appendices. The report should be discussed and decisions made on the basis of the findings.

Characteristics of Good Marketing Research

Having examined marketing research procedure, we can now advance five characteristics of good marketing research.

Scientific method   Competent marketing research is characterized by an attempt to follow the scientific method: careful observation, formulation of hypotheses, prediction, and testing. An example follows:

> A small mail-order house was suffering from a high rate (30 percent) of merchandise return. Management asked the marketing research manager to uncover the causes of the high return. The research manager proceeded to analyze various characteristics of the returned orders, such as the geographical locations of the customers, the sizes of the returned orders, and the type of merchandise. One hypothesis was that the longer the customer waited for ordered merchandise, the greater the probability of its return. The regression analysis confirmed this hypothesis. The researcher ventured the prediction that the return rate would fall if the company speeded up its delivery time. The company did this, and the prediction proved correct.[14]

[13] William H. Reynolds and George T. Wofford, "A Factor Analysis of Air Traveler Attitudes," *Proceedings of the American Marketing Association* (Chicago: American Marketing Association, June 1966), pp. 640–50; Jean Stoetzel, "A Factor Analysis of the Liquor Preferences of French Consumers," *Journal of Advertising Research*, December 1960, pp. 7–11; and Arthur D. Kirsch and Seymour Banks, "Program Types Defined by Factor Analysis," *Journal of Advertising Research*, September 1962, 29–32.

[14] Horace C. Levinson, "Experiences in Commercial Operations Research," *Operations Research*, August 1953, pp. 220–39.

Research creativity   At its best, marketing research develops innovative ways to solve a problem. A classic example of research creativity is described below:

> When instant coffee was first introduced, housewives complained that it did not taste like real coffee. Yet in blindfold tests, many of these same housewives could not distinguish between a cup of instant coffee and real coffee. This indicated that much of their resistance was psychological. The researcher decided to design two almost identical shopping lists, the only difference being that regular coffee was on one list and instant coffee on the other. The regular coffee list was given to one group of housewives and the instant coffee list was given to a different, but comparable, group. Both groups were asked to guess the social and personal characteristics of the woman whose shopping list they saw. The comments were pretty much the same with one significant difference; a higher proportion of the housewives whose list contained instant coffee described the subject as "lazy, a spendthrift, a poor wife, and failing to plan well for her family." These women obviously were imputing to the fictional housewife their own anxieties and negative images about the use of instant coffee. The instant-coffee company now knew the nature of the resistance and could develop a campaign to change the image of the housewife who serves instant coffee.[15]

Multiple methods   Competent marketing researchers shy away from over-reliance on any one method, preferring to adapt the method to the problem rather than the other way around. They also recognize the desirability of the simultaneous gathering of information in different ways to give greater confidence than any one method would provide.

Interdependence of models and data   Competent marketing researchers recognize that the facts do not speak for themselves but rather derive their meaning from models of the problem. They attempt to guide their search for information on the basis of a useful decision model to help the executive.

Value and cost of information   Competent marketing researchers show concern for measuring the value of information against its cost. Value/cost is a consideration when the marketing research department chooses which research projects to conduct, which research design to use, and whether to gather more information.[16]

MARKETING MANAGEMENT-SCIENCE SYSTEM

An increasing number of organizations have been adding a fourth information service to help their marketing executives—management science (also called operations research). A management scientist applies scientific methodology to organizational problems in the search for improved understanding, prediction, and control. Management scientists are often called model builders, and quite appropriately, because "model" is one of the central defining concepts in their

---

[15] Mason Haire, "Projective Techniques in Marketing Research," *Journal of Marketing*, April 1950, pp. 649–56.

[16] See James H. Myers and A. Coskun Samli, "Management Control of Marketing Research," *Journal of Marketing Research*, August 1969, pp. 267–77.

field. *A model is the specification of a set of variables and their interrelationships designed to represent some real system or process, in whole or in part.*

Although management science is a relative latecomer in marketing, it has already yielded useful insights and decision models in such areas as new-product development, competitive pricing, advertising budgeting and media selection, sales-call time allocation, and marketing-mix planning. Today some models are fully established and running in some larger companies.[17]

Basic Types of Models in Management Science

Marketing executives are in a much better position to understand and evaluate marketing management-science projects when they are aware of the major types of models. A description of model types is provided in Table 23–3.

TABLE 23–3
A Classification of Models

I. According to Purpose	*II. According to Techniques*
A. Descriptive Models	A. Verbal Models
1. Markov-process model	B. Graphical Models
2. Queuing model	1. Logical-flow model
3. Simulation	2. Network-planning model
B. Decision Models	3. Causal model
1. Differential calculus	4. Decision-tree model
2. Mathematical programming	5. Functional-relationship model
3. Statistical decision theory	6. Feedback-systems model
4. Game theory	C. Mathematical Models
	1. Linear vs. nonlinear model
	2. Static vs. dynamic model
	3. Deterministic vs. stochastic model

Descriptive models   Descriptive models are designed to communicate, explain, or predict. They can be built at three levels of detail. A *macromodel* consists of a few variables and a set of relationships among them. An example would be a sales model consisting of a single equation with total sales as the dependent variable and national income, average price, and company advertising expenditures as the independent variables. They are arrived at by fitting the "best" possible equation to the set of variables.

A *microanalytic model* postulates more detailed links between a dependent variable and its determinants. A good example is the DEMON model, in which the effect of total advertising expenditures on total sales is explained through the successive linking of total advertising expenditure, gross number of exposures, reach and frequency, advertising awareness, consumer trial, usage, and usage rate.[18]

[17] The factors affecting the likelihood that a marketing model will be used are examined in Jean-Claude Lerréché and David B. Montgomery, "A Framework for the Comparison of Marketing Models: A Delphi Study," *Journal of Marketing Research*, November 1977, pp. 487–98.

[18] David B. Learner, "Profit Maximization through New-Product Marketing Planning and Control," in *Applications of the Sciences to Marketing Management*, ed. Frank M. Bass et al. (New York: John Wiley & Sons, 1968), pp. 151–67.

A *microbehavioral model* creates hypothetical entities (consumers, dealers, and so on) who interact and produce a record of behavior, which is then analyzed. A good example is a consumer model built by Amstutz, in which a population of potential purchasers are exposed to weekly marketing stimuli, and some fraction of them purchase the product.[19]

Two descriptive models in the operations research literature have turned out to be particularly germane to marketing-type problems. The first is the *Markov-process model*, which is useful in describing systems whose next state is influenced by the current state and a set of transitional probabilities. Suppose there are three coffee brands, A, B, and C. Of those consumers who bought brand A last time, suppose 70 percent buy it again, 20 percent buy B, and 10 percent buy C. This information is represented in row one of Figure 23–2, along with further transitional probabilities associated with brands B and C. The brand-switching matrix provides information about:

The *repeat-purchase rate* for each brand, indicated by the numbers in the diagonal starting at the upper left. Under certain assumptions, the repeat-purchase rate can be interpreted as a measure of brand loyalty.

The *switching-in and switching-out rate* for each brand, represented by the off-diagonal numbers.

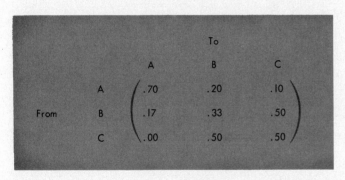

FIGURE 23–2
A Brand-Switching Matrix

If the switching rates are likely to remain constant, at least for the short run, the matrix becomes a useful tool in forecasting both the magnitude and the speed of change in future market shares on the basis of present market shares.[20]

A second descriptive model of relevance to many marketing situations is a *queuing model*. Queuing models are designed to represent waiting-line situations and answer two specific questions: What amount of waiting time may be expected in a particular system? How will this waiting time change as a result of given alterations in the facilities? These questions can be of particular importance to retailing institutions such as supermarkets, gasoline stations, and airline ticket offices. Wherever customers wait, there is the danger that waiting time will become excessive, leading to the loss of some customers to competitors.

[19] Arnold E. Amstutz, *Computer Simulation of Competitive Market Response* (Cambridge: MIT Press, 1967).

[20] See John U. Farley and Alfred A. Kuehn, "Stochastic Models of Brand Switching," in *Science in Marketing,* ed. George Schwartz (New York: John Wiley & Sons, 1965), pp. 446–64.

If the existing system breeds long queues, the decision maker can simulate the effects of different changes. In the case of a supermarket with a serious queuing problem on Saturdays, four possible attacks are indicated by the dimensions. The supermarket can try to influence its customers to do their shopping on other days. The supermarket can decrease the service time, by employing baggers to aid the cashiers. More service channels can be added. Or some of the channels can be specialized to handle smaller orders.

Decision models   Decision models are designed to evaluate alternative outcomes associated with different decisions and find the "best" decision. Decision models are subclassified into *optimization* and *heuristic* models. An *optimization model* is one for which computational routines exist for finding the best solution to the problem as stated. A *heuristic model* is one for which computational routines are not available for finding the best solution, but that offers other advantages. The heuristic model may be a much more flexible and complex statement of the problem. To use this model, the analyst applies heuristics, defined as rules of thumb that tend to shorten the time required to find a reasonably good solution. For example, in a model to determine good warehouse locations, the heuristic might be, "Consider locations only in large cities." This may exclude a perfectly good location in a small city, but the savings in having to check far fewer cities is expected to compensate for the omission.

The field of decision models contains four standard models that are of particular relevance to marketing-type problems. The first is *differential calculus,* a mathematical technique that can be applied to well-defined mathematical functions to determine whether the dependent variable has a maximum and/or minimum value(s), and if it does, to which value(s) of the dependent variable(s) it corresponds? Suppose a marketing analyst has determined the profit equation shown in Figure 23–3A. The task is to find the best price—that is, the value of P that will maximize the value of Z. One approach is to draw a picture of the equation and examine it for the profit-maximizing price, here $150. A quicker, more reliable procedure is to apply differential calculus to this equation without bothering to draw a graph.[21]

The second type of decision model is known as *mathematical programming.* Mathematical programming calls for expressing a decision maker's objective(s) in the form of a mathematical function whose value is to be optimized. Various constraints are also introduced in the form of equations and/or inequalities. Consider, for example, the problem in Figure 23–3B. Suppose the marketing analyst has found a profit function relating profits to the amount of funds spent on advertising and distribution. Note that a dollar of advertising appears to contribute $10 profit and a dollar of distribution appears to contribute $20. A set of policy constraints is also introduced. First the total marketing budget, as divided between advertising and distribution, should not exceed $100 (constraint 1). Of this, advertising should receive at least $40 (constraint 2) and no more than $80 (constraint 3); and distribution should receive at least $10 (constraint 4) and no more than $70 (constraint 5). Because of the simplicity of

---

[21] The calculus reader will know that the slope of a tangent to the curve is given by the first derivative of the equation: $dZ/dP = 1{,}200 - 8P$ But the maximum (or minimum) takes place where the slope is zero: $1{,}200 - 8P = 0$. Therefore profits are a maximum when $P = 150. (The sign of the second derivative must be checked to be sure that $P = 150 establishes a maximum and not a minimum.)

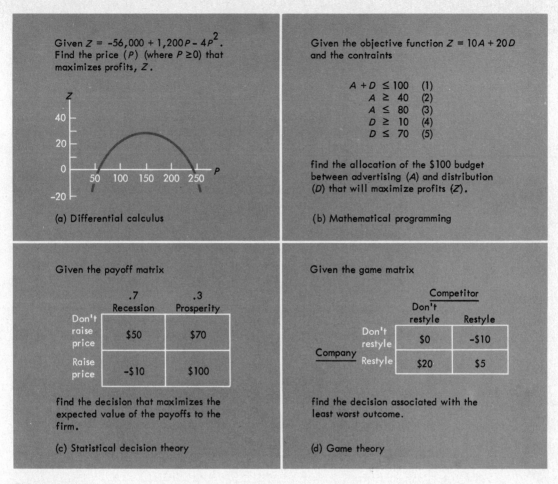

Given $Z = -56,000 + 1,200P - 4P^2$.
Find the price (P) (where $P \geq 0$) that
maximizes profits, Z.

(a) Differential calculus

Given the objective function $Z = 10A + 20D$
and the contraints

$$
\begin{array}{ll}
A + D \leq 100 & (1) \\
A \geq 40 & (2) \\
A \leq 80 & (3) \\
D \geq 10 & (4) \\
D \leq 70 & (5)
\end{array}
$$

find the allocation of the $100 budget
between advertising (A) and distribution
(D) that will maximize profits (Z).

(b) Mathematical programming

Given the payoff matrix

	.7 Recession	.3 Prosperity
Don't raise price	$50	$70
Raise price	-$10	$100

find the decision that maximizes the
expected value of the payoffs to the
firm.

(c) Statistical decision theory

Given the game matrix

		Competitor Don't restyle	Restyle
Company	Don't restyle	$0	-$10
	Restyle	$20	$5

find the decision associated with the
least worst outcome.

(d) Game theory

FIGURE 23–3
Four Decision Models

this problem, it is possible to find the best marketing program without invoking
an advanced solution technique. Since distribution dollars are twice as effective
as advertising dollars, it would make sense to spend all that is permitted within
the constraints on distribution. This would appear to be $70, leaving $30 for advertising. However, advertising must receive at least $40 according to constraint
2. Therefore, the optimal marketing-mix allocation would be $40 for advertising
and $60 for distribution; and with this solution, profits will be $10($40) +
$20($60) = $1,600. In larger problems, the analyst would have to resort to spe-
cific solution techniques.

The third type of decision model is called *statistical decision theory* (or
Bayesian decision theory). This model calls for (1) distinguishing major decision
alternatives facing the firm, (2) distinguishing the events (states of nature) that
might, in conjunction with each possible decision, bring about a distinct outcome, (3) estimating the probability of each possible state of nature, (4) estimat-

621

ing the value (payoff) of each possible outcome to the firm, (5) determining the expected value of each decision, and (6) choosing the decision with the highest expected value. Consider this in the context of the problem in Figure 23–3C. Suppose the product manager is trying to decide between raising the price on a product or leaving it alone. The outcome will be significantly affected by whether the economy moves into a recession, of which the product manager believes there is a .7 chance. If there is a recession and the price is not changed, the product manager estimates that profits will be $50; but if the price is raised, the product manager estimates a loss of $10. On the other hand, if the economy is prosperous in the coming year, the product manager estimates that leaving prices alone will yield $70 and raising prices will yield $100. These estimates are summarized conveniently in the payoff matrix.

Statistical decision theory calls for the product manager to estimate the expected value of each decision. Expected value is the weighted mean of the payoffs, with the probabilities serving as the weights. The expected value associated with not raising the price is .7($50) + .3($70) = $56, while the expected value of raising the price is .7(−$10) + .3($100) = $23. Clearly the extra gain with the best thing happening (a raised price and prosperity) is not worth the risk, and the product manager is better off leaving the price alone. This conclusion assumes that expected value is a satisfactory criterion for the firm to maximize. This criterion is a sensible one for the large firm that makes repeated decisions of this kind and is not going to go out of business with one or two adverse developments. It makes less sense for a smaller firm facing a major one-shot decision that could ruin it if things go wrong.[22]

Game theory is a fourth approach to evaluating decision alternatives. Like statistical decision theory, it calls for an identification of the decision alternatives, uncertain variables, and the value of different outcomes. It differs from statistical decision theory in that the major uncertain variable is assumed to be a competitor, nature, or some other force that is malevolent. The probability is 1.00 that each actor will do what is in its best interest. Consider the example in Figure 23–3D. An auto manufacturer is trying to decide whether to restyle its car or leave it alone. It knows that the competitor is also trying to make the same decision. The company estimates that if neither restyles, neither would gain anything over the normal rate of profit. If the company restyles and the competitor does not, the company will gain $20 over the competitor. (We will assume the competitor loses $20—that is, the gain to one company is a loss to the other.) If the company does not restyle and the competitor does, the company loses $10. (By the same token, the competitor gains $10.) Finally, if they both restyle, the company gains $5, and the competitor loses $5, because the company is assumed to be better at restyling.

A solution is possible if we assume that both opponents will want to take the course of action that will leave them *least worst off*. Called the *minimax criterion* (minimizing the maximum loss), it assumes that both opponents are conservative rather than adventurous. This criterion would lead the company to prefer the restyling alternative. If it does not restyle, it might lose as much as $10; if it does restyle, it will make at least $5. The competitor would also prefer

[22] See Frank M. Bass, "Marketing Research Expenditures: A Decision Model," *Journal of Business*, January 1963, pp. 77–90; and Rex V. Brown, "Do Managers Find Decision Theory Useful?" *Harvard Business Review*, May–June 1970, pp. 78–89.

to restyle. If it did not restyle, it might lose as much as $20; if it does restyle, it cannot lose more than $5. Hence, both opponents will decide in favor of restyling, which leads to a $5 gain for the company and a $5 loss for the competitor. Neither opponent can gain by switching unilaterally to a different strategy.[23]

Verbal models Models in which the variables and their relationships are described in prose are *verbal models*. Most of the great theories of individual, social, and societal behavior—theories such as those of Freud, Darwin, and Marx—are cast in verbal terms. Many models of consumer behavior are essentially in the verbal-model stage. Consider " . . . advertising should move people from *awareness . . .* to *knowledge . . .* to *liking . . .* to *preference . . .* to *conviction . . .* to *purchase.*"[24]

Graphical models Graphical models represent a useful step in the process of symbolizing a verbal model. Six graphical models can be distinguished.

Figure 23–4A shows a *logical-flow diagram*. A logical-flow diagram is a visual representation of a logical process or operation. The various boxes of such a diagram are connected in a sequential flow pattern and are related to each other through two fundamental operations. One of these is *branching*. Branching takes place when a question is posed at a certain step of the process, and its possible answers are expressed as alternative branches leading away from the box. The other operation is *looping*. Looping takes place if certain answers return the flow to an earlier stage. The flow diagram in Figure 23–4A describes a firm's efforts to determine how many competitors will cut their prices. The firm first considers competitor *i* and asks whether it is likely to cut its price. If the answer is yes, this result is tabulated, and then the firm asks whether there are any additional competitors to consider. If the answer is no, the firm goes directly to the next question. If there are more competitors to consider, the logical flow returns to the first box (that is, it loops back); otherwise, the flow ends. Logical-flow diagrams are coming into increasing use in marketing because of the clarity with which they illustrate a logical process.

Figure 23–4B shows a *network-planning diagram* (also called a critical-path diagram), which is used to portray the events that must occur to complete a project. The events, shown as circles, are connected by arrows indicating precedent relationships. In Figure 23–4B event 6 cannot occur until events 4 and 5 are completed; event 5 cannot occur until event 2 is completed; event 4 cannot occur until events 2 and 3 are completed; and so on. After going on to estimate the completion time of each task (and sometimes the optimistic and pessimistic completion times), the analyst can find the earliest date to completion of the entire project. Somewhere in the network there is a critical path that defines the earliest possible completion time; here it is fifteen weeks. Unless this critical path is shortened, there is no way to complete the project earlier. This diagram is the basis of planning, scheduling, and controlling projects.

Figure 23–4C shows a *causal-analysis diagram*, which is used to portray

---

[23] See R. Duncan Luce and Howard Raiffa, *Games and Decisions* (New York: John Wiley & Sons, 1957), pp. 453–55.

[24] Robert J. Lavidge and Gary A. Steiner, "A Model for Predictive Measurements of Advertising Effectiveness," *Journal of Marketing,* October 1961, pp. 59–62.

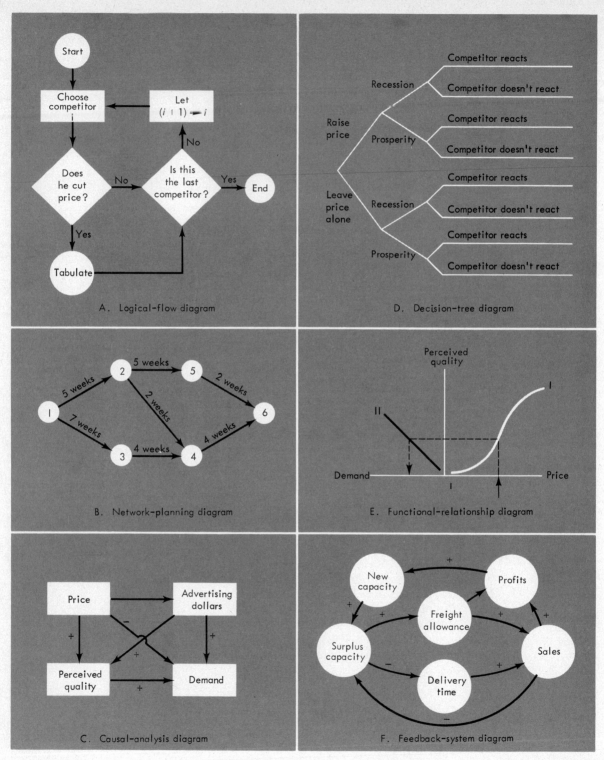

FIGURE 23–4
Six Graphical Models for Marketing Analysis

the directions of influence of various variables on each other. This diagram shows that price has a direct (negative) influence on demand, and an indirect influence also through its positive effects on advertising dollars and perceived quality. A high price leads to high perceived quality and leads the company to spend more on advertising. Both of these in turn have a positive effect on demand. (Not shown is the fact that the level of resulting demand will have a feedback influence on the level of advertising expenditures as well as on the perceived quality.) The value of causal-analysis diagrams is in exposing the complex relationships that the analyst should take into account. They remind us that single-equation relationships between variables may fail to capture the true structure of the phenomena.

Figure 23–4D shows a *decision-tree diagram,* which is used to portray the various decision alternatives and consequences found in a decision situation. The firm is trying to decide between raising its price and leaving it alone. The outcome will be influenced by whether the economy moves toward recession or prosperity, and further by whether or not competitors react. The tree could be extended still further to show other contingencies related to buyer reactions, inventory situations, and so on. By adding payoffs and probabilities to the various branches of the tree, the best decision can be found by using statistical decision theory.

Figure 23–4E is a *functional-relationship diagram*, which is used to portray functional relationship(s) between two or more variables. Quadrant I shows a positive relationship between price and perceived quality. Quadrant II shows a positive relationship between perceived quality and demand. The two quadrants enable the analyst to trace the effect of a *particular* price, through perceived quality, on a *particular* demand level. Thus one can generate a demand function from knowledge of two other functions. Functional graphs can be used to portray sales response functions, probability distributions, and many other relationships.

Figure 23–4F shows a *feedback-system diagram,* which is used to portray any system that yields outputs that return to earlier inputs and act as an influence. This process should not be confused with looping in logical-flow diagrams, which merely returns the procedure to an earlier point without implying any influence on that point. The example given here shows the interactions among sales, profits, capacity, and marketing variables. Surplus capacity leads the company to offer higher freight allowances to customers and reduced delivery time. These lead to higher sales. Increased sales lead to increased profits while drawing down surplus capacity. In the meantime the higher freight allowances reduce profits. If the net effect is a gain in profits, this leads to additional investment in capacity, which increases surplus capacity; and the cycle continues. Thus feedback-system diagrams are useful devices for representing variables that have interactive properties and feedbacks.[25]

Graphical models, in general, have all the virtues that are found in "pictures." A graph strips the phenomenon of inessentials; it allows a viewer to grasp the whole and select which relationships to examine. For marketing analysts, graphs improve exposition, facilitate discussion, and guide analysis.

[25] See Jay W. Forrester, "Modeling of Market and Company Interactions," in *Marketing and Economic Development,* ed. Peter D. Bennett (Chicago: American Marketing Association, 1965), pp. 353–64.

Mathematical models Mathematical models can be subclassified in many ways. A distinction can be drawn between *linear* and *nonlinear models*. In a *linear model* all the relationships between variables are expressed as straight lines. This means that a unit change in one variable has a *constant* marginal impact on a related variable. The advertising-sales relationship would be linear if every $100 increase in advertising created a $1,000 increase in sales, no matter how much had already been spent. This possibility, of course, is unlikely because increasing or diminishing returns to advertising are likely to occur at different points in the relationship. It is also likely that other marketing inputs, such as price and sales-call time, do not relate to sales in a thoroughly linear way. The assumption of linearity is generally useful only as a first approximation for mathematical convenience.

A second distinction can be drawn between *static* and *dynamic models*. A *static model* centers on the ultimate state (or solution) of a system, independent of time. A *dynamic model* brings time explicitly into its framework and allows the observation of the movement of the state (or solution) of the system over time. The elementary demand-supply diagram in beginning economics courses represents a static model of price determination in that it indicates where price and output will be in equilibrium without indicating the path of adjustment through time. Brand-switching models are dynamic in that they predict period-to-period changes in customer states.

A third distinction can be drawn between *deterministic* and *stochastic models*. A *deterministic model* is one in which chance plays no role. The solution is determined by a set of exact relationships. The linear-programming model for determining blends (oils, animal feeds, candies) is deterministic, because the relationships are exact and the cost data are known. A *stochastic model*, on the other hand, is one where chance or random variables are introduced explicitly. Brand-switching models are stochastic in that customer's brand choices are regulated by probabilities.

As marketing management scientists gain acceptance in companies, they will provide a set of statistical procedures and decision models that will greatly enhance the marketing manager's skill at making good decisions. The main need is that the scientists and managers move rapidly toward understanding each other's needs and capacities.

SUMMARY

Marketing information has become the critical element in effective marketing as a result of the trend toward national and international marketing, the transition from buyer needs to buyer wants, and the transition from price to nonprice competition. All firms have a marketing information system connecting the external environment with its executives, but the systems vary greatly in sophistication and the number and quality of services they provide.

Marketing information systems consist of four components. The internal accounting system reports orders, sales, inventory levels, receivables, payables, and so on. Several companies have made large investments in improving the speed, accuracy, and reporting potentials of their order-shipping-billing cycle.

The marketing intelligence system provides executives with current information about developments and changing conditions in the macro and task environments. Executives gather intelligence on their own, but their effectiveness can be augmented by improved training of salesmen in their intelligence responsibilities, the development of a marketing-intelligence center, and the purchase of information when appropriate from specialized intelligence services.

Marketing research provides specific studies of market opportunities, marketing effectiveness, and marketing problems. Marketing research procedure consists of five steps: problem definition, research design, field work, data analysis, and report preparation. Good marketing research is characterized by the scientific method, creativity, multiple methodologies, model building, and cost/benefit measures of the value of information.

The marketing management-science system is responsible for building models to explain, predict, or improve marketing processes. Marketing management scientists may build or use descriptive or decision models and verbal, graphical, or mathematical models to come to grips with marketing problems.

QUESTIONS AND PROBLEMS

1. You are a marketing director. Your boss comes in and wants to know how many stores carry your dry cereal. Since you sell through food brokers, you don't know the answer. He wants the answer in two days. How would you do it?

2. (a) Suggest how a liquor company might estimate the amount of liquor consumed in a legally dry town. (b) Suggest how a research organization might estimate the number of people who read given magazines in a doctor's office. (c) Suggest six different ways in which a sample of men can be gathered to be interviewed on their usage of hair tonics.

3. What is the major issue (impartiality, validity, reliability) that is likely to come up in the following use of secondary data: (a) using a time series of disposable personal income (in current dollars) to indicate the historical trend in consumer purchasing power; (b) using a local chamber of commerce study on the average income of the community; (c) using a man-in-the-street sample to estimate the proportion of men who own dinner jackets.

4. "A manufacturer of automobiles is testing a new direct-mail approach B versus a standard approach A. An experiment is conducted in which each of the two approaches is tried out on random samples of size n (sample size $2n$ in total) from a large national mailing list. Suppose that $n = 100,000$ so that $200,000$ is the total sample size of the experiment. During a three-month period, approach B has 761 sales and A has 753." What decision should be made? List the alternatives and the rationale of each.

5. Evaluate the following questions to be asked in a consumer survey: (a) What is your husband's favorite brand of golf balls? (b) What TV programs did you watch a week ago Monday? (c) How many pancakes did you make for your family last year? (d) Tell me your exact income. (e) Can you supply me with a list of your grocery purchases this month?

6. In obtaining estimates from company salesmen, product managers, and other personnel, one must discourage their supplying estimates that are self-serving. Give some examples of self-serving estimates by company personnel and suggest what might be done to discourage this.

7. List and discuss the major criteria for judging the usefulness of a mathematical marketing model.

8. Some marketing men view the emergence of mathematical model building in marketing with hostility. They will make the following statements: (a) we don't use models; (b) models are typically unrealistic; (c) anyone can build a model; (d) a model is of no help unless you can get the data. How would you answer these objections?

9. With the emergence of operations research in marketing, large companies are trying to determine the proper organizational relationship between marketing research activities (MR) and marketing operations research (MOR). Describe five alternative conceptions.

MARKETING CONTROL

Having lost sight of our objective, we redoubled our efforts.
OLD ADAGE

24

In spite of the growing need for better marketing control, many companies use less-than-satisfactory control procedures. This was the conclusion of a major recent private study of seventy-five companies of varying sizes in different industries. The main findings were:

1. Smaller companies have poorer controls than larger companies. They did a poorer job of setting clear objectives and establishing systems to measure performance.
2. Fewer than half of the companies knew the profitability of their individual product lines. About one-third of the companies had no regular review procedure for spotting and deleting weak products.
3. Almost half of the companies failed, on a regular basis, to compare their prices to competition, to analyze their warehousing and distribution costs, to analyze the causes of returned merchandise, to conduct formal evaluations of advertising effectiveness, and to review their sales-force call reports.
4. Management in many companies complained about four-to-eight-week delays in getting many control reports and frequent inaccuracies.

Marketing control, like marketing planning, is far from being a single process. Four different types of marketing control can be distinguished, and they are listed in Table 24–1.

TABLE 24–1
Types of Marketing Control

TYPE OF CONTROL	PRIME RESPONSIBILITY	PURPOSE OF CONTROL	APPROACHES
I. Annual-plan control	Top management Middle management	To examine whether the planned results are being achieved	Sales analysis Market share analysis Sales-to-expense ratios Financial analysis Attitude tracking
II. Profitability control	Marketing controller	To examine where the company is making and losing money	Profitability by: product territory customer group trade channel order size
III. Efficiency control	Line and staff management Marketing controller	To evaluate and improve the spending efficiency and impact of marketing expenditures	Efficiency of sales force advertising sales promotion distribution
IV. Strategic control	Top management Marketing auditor	To examine whether the company is pursuing its best opportunities with respect to markets, products, and channels	Marketing-effectiveness rating instrument Marketing audit

Annual-plan control refers to the steps taken during the year to check on-going performance against plan and to apply corrective actions when necessary. *Profitability control* consists of efforts to measure the actual profitability of different products, territories, end-use markets, and trade channels. *Efficiency control* involves searching for ways to improve the impact of different marketing tools and expenditures. Finally, *strategic control* consists of a systematic examination and appraisal of the overall fit of the company to its marketing environment and opportunities. The following sections will deal with each form of marketing control.

The heart of annual-plan control is the establishment of a system of *management by objectives,* which consists of four elements. First, the annual plan must establish a clear set of *goals* for each responsibility center in the firm. Second, provision must be made for periodic *performance measurement* against the goals to spot any serious performance gaps. Third, performance gaps should be subject to *causal analysis* to determine why they have occurred, that is, whether the environment has changed, the goals were set too high, or the implementers of the plan are not doing their job. Fourth, management must take *corrective action* to close the gap between goals and performance.

This model of control is applied to every level of the organization. Top management is committed to the attainment of certain sales and profit goals for the year. These goals have presumably been elaborated into specific goals for each successively lower level of management. Thus, each product and brand manager is committed to attaining specified levels of sales and costs. Each regional area and district sales manager and sales representative is also committed to specific goals. Each period top management receives summary reports indicating the results attained by the vice presidents, who in turn receive more-detailed reports of the results attained by their subordinates, down to the district sales manager, who observes the results of individual sales representatives in the district.

Managers use five performance tools to check on the progress in reaching the goals in the annual plan.

Sales Analysis   The first performance tool used by managers is sales analysis. *Sales analysis* is the effort to measure and evaluate the actual sales being achieved in relation to the sales goals set for different managers. There are two specific tools in this connection.

Sales variance analysis is an attempt to determine the relative contribution of different factors to a gap in sales performance. Suppose the annual plan called for selling 4,000 widgets in the first quarter at $1 a widget, or $4,000. At quarter's end, only 3,000 widgets were sold at 80¢ a widget, or $2,400. The sales performance variance is −$1,600, or −40 percent of expected sales. The question arises, How much of this underperformance is due to the price decline and how much is due to the volume decline? The following calculation answers this question:

Variance due to price decline = ($1 − .80)(3,000)   = $ 600   37.5%
Variance due to volume decline = ($1)(4,000 − 3,000) = $1,000   62.5%
                                                       $1,600   100.0%

Accordingly, almost two-thirds of the sales variance is due to a failure to realize the volume target. Since sales volume may be under more control than the price, the company should look closely into why its expected sales volume was not achieved.[1]

[1] For further discussion, see James M. Hulbert and Norman E. Toy, "A Strategic Framework for Marketing Control," *Journal of Marketing,* April 1977, pp. 12–20.

Microsales analysis may provide the answer. Microsales analysis is an attempt to determine the specific products, territories, and so forth, that failed to produce their expected share of sales. Suppose the company sells in three territories and expected sales were 1,500, 500, and 2,000 units, respectively, adding up to 4,000 widgets. The actual sales volume was 1,400, 525, and 1,075, respectively. Thus territory one showed a 7 percent shortfall in terms of expected sales; territory two, a 5 percent surplus; and territory three, a 46 percent shortfall! It is now clear that territory three is causing most of the trouble. The sales vice president can check into territory three to see which, if any, of the following hypotheses explains the poor performance: (1) territory three's sales representative is loafing or has a personal problem; (2) a major competitor has entered this territory; (3) GNP is depressed in this territory.

Market Share Analysis

A company's sales performance fails to reveal how well the company is performing relative to competitors. Suppose a company's sales increase. That could be due to a general improvement in the economy in which all firms are participating. Or it may be due to improved marketing by this company in relation to its competitors. The normal way to remove the influence of the general environment is to track the company's market share. If the company's market share goes up, it is gaining on competitors; if its market share goes down, it appears to be performing poorer relative to competitors.

Yet these conclusions from market share analysis are subject to certain qualifications.[2]

> ***The assumption that outside forces affect all companies in the same way is often not true.*** The surgeon general's report on the harmful consequences of cigarette smoking caused total cigarette sales to falter but not equally for all companies. The companies that had established a reputation for a better filter were hit less hard.
>
> ***The assumption that a company's performance should be judged against the average performance of all companies also is not always valid.*** A company with greater than average opportunities should register a growing market share. If its market share remains constant, this may imply deficient rather than average management.
>
> ***If a new firm enters the industry, then every existing firm's market share may fall (again, not necessarily equally).*** Here is a case where a fall in the company's market share does not mean that the company is performing below the average of the industry.
>
> ***Sometimes the decline in a company's market share is the result of a deliberate policy to improve profits.*** Management, for example, may drop unprofitable customers or products, with resulting decline in market share.
>
> ***Market share fluctuates for many reasons.*** For example, the market share in a particular period can be affected by whether a large sale is made on the last day of the period or at the beginning of the following period. A current shift in market share does not always have a significant marketing implication.

The first step in using market share measurement is to define clearly which measure of market share will be used. Four different measures are available:

[2] See Alfred R. Oxenfeldt, "How to Use Market-Share Measurement," *Harvard Business Review*, January–February 1959, pp. 59–68.

1. *Overall market share.* The company's overall market share is its sales expressed as a percentage of total industry sales. Two decisions are necessary to use this measure. The first is whether to use unit sales or dollar sales to express market share. Any changes in unit market share strictly reflect relative volume changes among competitors, whereas changes in dollar market share might reflect volume or price changes.

   The other decision has to do with defining the total industry. Defining the industry or market boundaries is always somewhat arbitrary. For example, suppose Harley Davidson wants to measure its share of the American motorcycle market. Does the motorcycle market include motor scooters and motorized bikes? If so, Harley Davidson's share of this market is lower than if these products are not included. The issue hinges on the degree of consumer perception of the difference between standard motorcycles and these lighter cycles.

2. *Served-market share.* The company's served-market share is its sales expressed as a percentage of the total sales to its served market. Its served market is the market (1) that would find the company's offering suitable and (2) that is reached by the company's marketing effort. For example, if Harley Davidson only sells motorcycles costing over $2,000 and sells them only on the East Coast, its served-market share would be its sales as a percentage of the total sales of expensive motorcycles sold on the East Coast. A company's served-market share is always larger than its overall market share. A company could have close to 100 percent of its served market and yet a relatively small percentage of the overall market. A company's first task is to try to get the lion's share of its served market, and as it approaches this, it should add new product lines and territories to enlarge its served market.

3. *Relative market share (to top three competitors).* This involves expressing the company's sales as a percentage of the combined sales of the three largest competitors. For example, if this company has 30 percent of the market and its three largest competitors have 20, 10, and 10 percent, then this company's relative market share is 75 percent (= 30/40). If all four companies each had 25 percent of the market, then any company's relative market share would be 33 percent. Relative market shares above 33 percent are considered to be strong.

4. *Relative market share (to leading competitor).* Some companies like to track their sales as a percentage of the leading competitor's sales. A relative market share greater than 100 percent suggests that the firm is the market leader. A relative market share of 100 percent means that the firm is tied for the lead. A rise in the company's relative market share means that it is gaining on its leading competitor.

After choosing which market share measure(s) to use, the company faces the task of finding the necessary data. Overall market share is normally the most available measure since it only requires total industry sales, and these are often available in government or trade association publications. Estimating served market share is harder in that the company will have to measure and keep track of its served market, which will be affected by changes in the company's product line and geographical market coverage, among other things. Estimating relative market shares is still harder, because the company will have to estimate the sales of from one to three specific competitors, who do their best to guard these figures. The company has to use indirect means, such as learning about competitors' purchase rate of raw materials, or the number of shifts they are operating. In the consumer-goods area, individual brand shares are measurable and available through syndicated store and consumer panels.

The final requirement is to be able to correctly interpret movements in market share. Market share analysis, like sales analysis, increases in value when the data are disaggregated along various dimensions. The company might watch the progress of its market share by product line, customer type, region, or other breakdowns.

A useful way to analyze market share movements is in terms of the following four components:

$$\begin{matrix}\text{Overall} \\ \text{market} \\ \text{share}\end{matrix} = \begin{matrix}\text{Customer} \\ \text{penetration}\end{matrix} \times \begin{matrix}\text{Customer} \\ \text{loyalty}\end{matrix} \times \begin{matrix}\text{Customer} \\ \text{selectivity}\end{matrix} \times \begin{matrix}\text{Price} \\ \text{selectivity}\end{matrix} \quad (24\text{--}1)$$

where:

Customer penetration is the percentage of all customers who buy from this company

Customer loyalty is the purchases from this company by its customers expressed as a percentage of their total purchases from all suppliers of the same products

Customer selectivity is the size of the average customer purchase from the company expressed as a percentage of the size of the average customer purchase from an average company

Price selectivity is the average price charged by this company expressed as a percentage of the average price charged by all companies

Now suppose the company's dollar market share falls during the period. Equation (24–1) suggests four possible factors:

1. The company has lost some of its customers (lower customer penetration).
2. The existing customers are buying a smaller share of their supplies from this company (lower customer loyalty).
3. The company's remaining customers are smaller in size (lower customer selectivity).
4. The company's price has slipped relative to competition (lower price selectivity).

By tracking these factors through time, the company can determine the underlying causes of market share changes. Suppose at the beginning of the period, customer penetration was 60 percent, customer loyalty 50 percent, customer selectivity 80 percent, and price selectivity 125 percent. According to (24–1), the company's market share was 30 percent. Suppose that at the end of the period, the company's market share fell to 27 percent. In checking on the market share components, the company finds customer penetration at 55 percent, customer loyalty at 50 percent, customer selectivity at 75 percent, and price selectivity at 130 percent. Clearly, the market share decline was due mainly to a loss of some customers (fall in customer penetration) who normally made larger-than-average purchases (fall in customer selectivity). The manager can now direct attention to finding out why these customers were lost.

Annual-plan control also requires checking on marketing expenses in relation to sales to make sure that the company is not overspending to achieve its sales goals. The key ratio to watch is *marketing expense to sales*. In one company, this ratio is normally 30 percent and is made up of five component expense-to-sales ratios: *sales force to sales* (15 percent); *advertising to sales* (5 percent); *sales promotion to sales* (6 percent); *marketing research to sales* (1 percent); and *sales administration to sales* (3 percent).

Management's job is to monitor the overall and component marketing expense ratios to detect whether any are getting out of control. These ratios will exhibit small random fluctuations that could well be ignored. Only fluctuations in excess of the normal range of variation are a cause for concern. The period-to-period fluctuations in each ratio can be charted on a *control chart* such as the one shown in Figure 24–1. This chart shows that the advertising expense-to-sales ratio normally fluctuates between 8 and 12 percent, say ninety-nine out of one hundred times. In the fifteenth period, however, the ratio exceeded the upper control limit. One of two opposing hypotheses can explain this occurrence:

> *Hypothesis A.* The company still has good control over sales, and this represents one of those rare chance events.
>
> *Hypothesis B.* The company has lost control over this cost as a result of some assignable cause.

If hypothesis A is accepted, no investigation is made to determine whether the environment has changed. The risk in not investigating is that some real change may have occurred, and the company will fall behind. If hypothesis B is accepted, the environment is investigated at the risk that the investigation will uncover nothing and be a waste of time and effort.

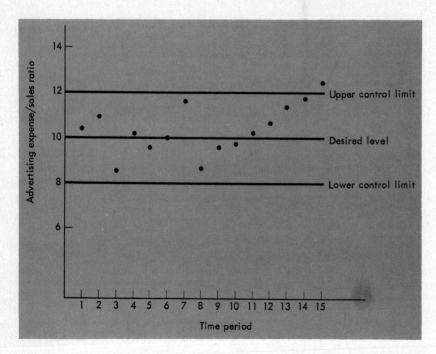

FIGURE 24–1
The Control-Chart Model

The behavior of successive observations even within the control limits should also be watched for patterns that seem difficult to explain by chance. In Figure 24–1 it should be noted that the level of the expense-to-sales ratio rose steadily from the ninth period onward. The probability of encountering a pattern of six successive increases in what should be a random and independent process is only one out of sixty-four.[3] This unusual pattern should have led to an investigation sometime before the fifteenth observation.

When an expense-to-sales ratio gets out of control, disaggregative data may be needed to track down the source of the problem. An *expense-to-sales deviation chart* can be used in this connection. Figure 24–2 shows the perform-

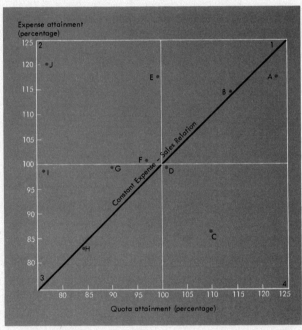

FIGURE 24–2
Comparison of Expense and Revenue
Deviations by District

SOURCE: Adapted from D. M. Phelps and J. H. Westing, *Marketing Management*, 3rd ed. (Homewood, Ill.: Richard D. Irwin, Inc., 1968), p. 754.

ances of different sales districts in terms of their quota attainment and expense attainment (in percentages). For example, district D has accomplished its quota nearly at the expected expense level. District B has exceeded its quota, and its expenses are proportionately higher. The most troubling districts are in the second quadrant. For example, district J has accomplished less than 80 percent of its quota and its expenses are disproportionately high. The next step is to prepare a similar chart for each deviant district that shows sales representatives' standings on percentage of quota attainment and expense attainment. Within

---

[3] There is a chance of ½ that any succeeding observation will be higher and the same chance that it will be lower (excluding the possibility that two successive values are identical). Therefore the probability of finding six successively higher values is given by $(½)^6 = \frac{1}{64}$.

district J, for example, it may turn out that the poor performance is associated with just a few sales representatives.

Financial Analysis The various expense-to-sales and other ratios should be analyzed by the marketer in an overall framework of financial analysis to determine how and where the company is making its money. Marketers are increasingly being trained to understand and apply financial concepts in the effort to improve their ability to find profitable strategies and not just sales-building strategies.

Financial analysis is directed to identifying the factors that affect the company's *rate of return on net worth*. The main factors are shown in Figure 24–3, along with some illustrative numbers, for a large chain store retailer. The retailer is earning a return on net worth of 12.5 percent. Many professional retailers would argue that this is too low and that retail organizations need at least a 15 percent return if they are to fully satisfy their profit requirements. Some successful retailers routinely earn returns of over 20 percent.

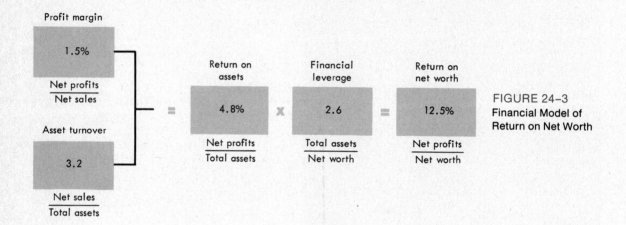

FIGURE 24–3
Financial Model of Return on Net Worth

Next, we notice that the return on net worth is the product of two ratios, the *return on assets* and the *financial leverage* of the company. In order for the company to improve its return on net worth, it must either increase the ratio of its net profits to its assets or increase the ratio of its assets to its net worth. The company should analyze the composition of its assets (i.e., cash, accounts receivable, inventory, and plant and equipment) and see if it can improve its assets management.

The return on assets is itself the product of two ratios, namely the *profit margin* and the *asset turnover*. We note that the profit margin is low, whereas the asset turnover is more normal for retailing. Given the low profit margin, the marketing executive's task is to find ways to increase sales and/or lower costs.

Customer-Attitude Tracking The preceding annual-plan control measures are largely financial and quantitative in character. They are important but not enough. They fail to give certain qualitative indications of marketplace developments and often come in too late for appropriate action to be taken.

Alert companies set up systems to track the attitudes of customers, dealers, and other marketing system participants as they are occurring. The assumption is that attitude change occurs first, it leads to purchasing behavior change, and then management eventually sees this in sales reports. By monitoring current customer attitudes toward the company and its products, management can take much earlier action.

Companies use the following major systems for tracking customer attitudes:

1. *Complaint and suggestion systems.* At a minimum, companies should record, analyze, and respond to any written or oral complaints that come in from customers. The complaints should be tabulated by types of complaint and the more serious and frequent ones should be given early attention. Many retailers, such as hotels, restaurants, and banks, have gone further and provide suggestion cards to encourage customer comments. In fact, the argument can be made that market-oriented companies should strive to maximize the opportunity for consumer complaints so that management can get a more complete picture of consumer reactions to their products and service.[4]

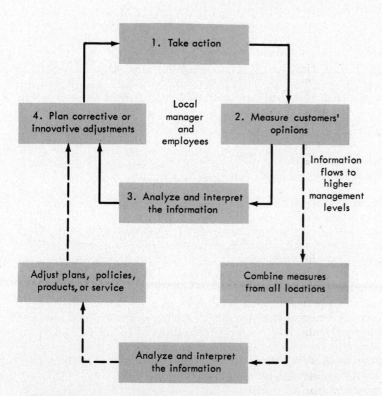

1. Local managers and employees serve customers' needs on a daily basis, using locally modified procedures along with general corporate policies and procedures.

2. By means of a standardized and locally sensitive questionnaire, determine the needs and attitudes of customers on a regular basis.

3. Comparing financial data, expectations, and past attitude information, determine strengths and weaknesses and their probable causes.

4. Determine where and how effort should be applied to correct weaknesses and preserve strengths. Repeat the process by taking action—Step 1—and maintain it to attain a steady state or to evolve in terms of customer changes.

5. A similar process can take place at higher levels, using aggregated data from the field and the existing policy flows of the organization.

SOURCE: Arthur J. Daltas, "Protecting Service Markets with Consumer Feedback," *The Cornell Hotel and Restaurant Administration Quarterly,* May 1977, p. 75.

FIGURE 24–4

A Consumer-Survey Feedback System

[4] See Claes Fornell, "Complaint Management and Marketing Performance," unpublished paper, Graduate School of Management, Northwestern University, Evanston, Ill., October 1978.

2. *Customer panels.* Some companies have created customer panels consisting of a cross-section of customers who have agreed to communicate their attitudes periodically through phone calls or mail questionnaires coming from the company. They are thought to be more representative of the range of customer attitudes than customer complaint and suggestion systems.

3. *Customer-survey systems.* A customer-survey system consists of periodically administering standardized questionnaires to a random sample of customers. Questions may be asked about the friendliness of the staff, the quality of the service, and so on. The customers check off their answers to these questions on a five-point scale (very dissatisfied, dissatisfied, neutral, satisfied, very satisfied). The responses are summarized and go both to local managers and to higher-management levels, as illustrated in Figure 24–4. Local managers receive back reports on how the various components of their service were rated in the current period compared to the last period, to the average of all the local units, and to the goal. Introducing this system has the beneficial effect of improving the staff's motivation to provide good customer service in the knowledge that their ratings will go to higher management.[5]

Corrective Action

We have mentioned corrective action several times. When actual performance deviates too much from the annual-plan goals, companies go through a well-known cycle of defensive maneuvers to correct the situation. Consider the following case:

> A large fertilizer producer found itself falling behind in its sales goals for the year. This was happening to its competitors as well, all of whom had built excess capacity. Some of the competitors were beginning to cut prices in order to achieve their planned sales volume.

In attempting to save and reverse the situation, this company was observed to go through several increasingly drastic steps:

1. *Production cutting.* The company found its inventories rising and proceeded to order cutbacks in production.

2. *Price cutting.* The company began to cut its prices selectively (higher discounts, freight allowances, and so on) to meet competition and retain its share of market.

3. *Increased pressure on sales force.* The company put more pressure on its sales force to meet their quotas. The sales representatives in turn started "beating down" doors, pressuring customers to buy more or buy before the end of the year.

4. *Fringe expenditure cutting.* The company proceeded to cut the budgets for personnel hiring and training, advertising, public relations, charities, and research and development.

5. *Manpower cuts.* The company began to lay off, retire, or fire personnel in various departments, particularly in staff services such as public relations, marketing research, and operations research.

6. *Bookkeeping adjustments.* The company undertook some fancy bookkeeping to bring about a better picture of profits, including changing the depreciation base, recording purchases wherever possible as capital items rather than as expenses, selling some company assets for leaseback in order to increase cash resources, and

---

[5] For an application to a hotel chain, see Arthur J. Daltas, "Protecting Service Markets with Consumer Feedback," *The Cornell Hotel and Restaurant Administration Quarterly,* May 1977, pp. 73–77.

recording sales to phantom buyers, revising them as returned merchandise in the following year.

7. *Investment cutting.* The company began to cut back on its investment in plant and equipment.

8. *Selling property.* The company started to consider selling some of its product lines or divisions to other companies.

9. *Selling the company.* The ultimate step this company considered was selling out or merging with another company that had good finances or some complementarities with this firm.

PROFITABILITY CONTROL

Besides annual-plan control, companies carry on periodic research to determine the actual profitability of their different products, territories, customer groups, trade channels, and order sizes. This task requires an ability to assign marketing and other costs to specific marketing entities and activities.

Methodology of Marketing-Profitability Analysis

Marketing-profitability analysis is a tool for helping the marketing executive determine whether any current marketing activities should be eliminated, added, or altered in scale.[6] The starting point for marketing-profitability analysis is the company's profit-and-loss statement. A simplified profit-and-loss statement is shown in Table 24–2. Profits are arrived at by subtracting cost of goods sold and other expenses from sales. The marketing executive's interest would be in developing analogous profit statements by functional marketing breakdowns, such as products, customers, or territories. To do this, the "natural" expense designations (such as salaries, rent, supplies) would have to be reclassified into "functional" expense designations. Consider the following example:

The marketing vice president of a lawn-mower firm wishes to determine the costs and profits of selling through three different types of retail channels: hardware stores, garden supply shops, and department stores. The company produces only one model of lawn mower. Its profit and loss statement is shown in Table 24–2.

Step 1: Identifying the functional expenses. Assume that the expenses listed in Table 24–2 are incurred to carry out the activities of selling the product, advertising the product, packing and delivering the product, and billing and collecting. The first task is to show how much of each natural expense was incurred in each of these activities.

Suppose that most of the salaries went to sales representatives and the rest went to an advertising manager, packing and delivery help, and an office accountant. Let the breakdown of the $9,300 be $5,100, $1,200, $1,400, and $1,600, respectively. Table 24–3 shows allocation of the salary expense to these four activities.

Table 24–3 also shows the rent account of $3,000 as allocated to the four activities. Since the sales representatives work away from the office, none of the building's rent expense is assigned to the selling activity. Most of the floor space and rental of equipment arises in connection with packing and delivery. A small portion of the floor space is taken up by the activities of the advertising manager and the office accountant.

[6] For a basic text, see Donald R. Longman and Michael Schiff, *Practical Distribution Cost Analysis* (Homewood, Ill.: Richard D. Irwin, 1955).

Finally, the supplies account lumps together promotional materials, packing materials, fuel purchases for delivery, and home-office stationery. The $3,500 in this account should be reassigned to the functional uses made of the supplies. The result of this and the previous breakdowns is that the total expenses of $15,800 are reclassified from a natural basis into a functional activity basis.

Step 2: Assigning the functional expenses to the marketing entities. The next task is to determine how much of each activity has gone into serving each type of channel. Consider the selling effort. The selling effort devoted to each channel is approximated by the number of sales calls made in each channel. This is given in the first column of Table 24–4. Altogether 275 sales calls were made during the period. Since the total selling expense amounted to $5,500 (see Table 24–3), then the selling expense per call averaged $20.

As for the advertising expense, Table 24–4 shows this allocated on the basis of the number of advertisements addressed to the different trade channels. Since there were 100 advertisements altogether, the advertising expense of $3,100 means that the average advertisement cost $31.

The basis chosen for allocating the packaging and delivery expense was the number of orders placed by each type of channel; this same basis also was used for allocating the expense of billing and collections.

Step 3: Preparing a profit-and-loss statement for each marketing entity. It is now possible to prepare a profit-and-loss statement for each type of channel. The results are shown in Table 24–5. Since hardware stores accounted for one-half of total sales ($30,000 out of $60,000), this channel is charged with half of the cost of goods sold ($19,500 out of $39,000). This leaves a gross margin from hardware stores of $10,500. From this must be deducted the proportions of the functional expenses that hardware stores consumed. According to Table 24–4 hardware stores received 200 out of 275 total sales calls. At an imputed value of $20 a call, hardware stores have to be charged with $4,000 of the selling expense. Table 24–4 also shows that hardware stores were the target of 50 advertisements. At $31 an advertisement, the hardware stores are charged with $1,550 of the advertising activity. The same reasoning applies in computing the share of the other functional expenses to charge to hardware stores. The result is that hardware stores gave rise to $10,050 of the total expenses. Subtracting this from the gross margin, the profit from the activities of selling to hardware stores is small ($450).

The same analysis is repeated for the other channels. It turns out that the company is losing money in selling through garden supply shops and makes virtually all of its profits from sales to department stores. Clearly, gross sales through each channel is not a reliable indicator of the net profits being made in each channel.

TABLE 24–2
A Simplified Profit-and-Loss Statement

Sales		$60,000
Cost of goods sold		39,000
Gross margin		$21,000
Expenses		
Salaries	$9,300	
Rent	3,000	
Supplies	3,500	
		15,800
Net profit		$ 5,200

TABLE 24–3
Mapping Natural Expenses Into Functional Expenses

NATURAL ACCOUNTS	TOTAL	SELLING	ADVERTISING	PACKING AND DELIVERY	BILLING AND COLLECTING
Salaries	$ 9,300	$5,100	$1,200	$1,400	$1,600
Rent	3,000	—	400	2,000	600
Supplies	3,500	400	1,500	1,400	200
	$15,800	$5,500	$3,100	$4,800	$2,400

TABLE 24–4
Bases for Allocating Functional Expenses to Channels

CHANNEL TYPE	SELLING NO. OF SALES CALLS IN PERIOD	ADVERTISING NO. OF ADVERTISE-MENTS	PACKING AND DELIVERY NO. OF ORDERS PLACED IN PERIOD	BILLING AND COLLECTING NO. OF ORDERS PLACED IN PERIOD
Hardware	200	50	50	50
Garden supply	65	20	21	21
Department stores	10	30	9	9
	275	100	80	80
Functional expense	= $5,500	$3,100	$4,800	$2,400
No. of units	275	100	80	80
Cost per unit	= $20	$31	$60	$30

TABLE 24–5
Profit-and-Loss Statements for Channels

	HARDWARE	GARDEN SUPPLY	DEPT. STORES	WHOLE COMPANY
Sales	$30,000	$10,000	$20,000	$60,000
Cost of goods sold	19,500	6,500	13,000	39,000
Gross margin	$10,500	$ 3,500	$ 7,000	$21,000
Expenses				
Selling ($20 per call)	$ 4,000	$ 1,300	$ 200	$ 5,500
Advertising ($31 per advertisement)	1,550	620	930	3,100
Packing and delivery ($60 per order)	3,000	1,260	540	4,800
Billing ($30 per order)	1,500	630	270	2,400
Total expenses	$10,050	$ 3,810	$ 1,940	$15,800
Net Profit (or loss)	$ 450	$ (310)	$ 5,060	$ 5,200

| Determining the Best Corrective Actions | The results of a marketing-profitability analysis do not constitute an adequate informational basis for deciding on corrective action. It would be naive to conclude that garden supply shops (and possibly hardware stores) should be dropped as channels in order to concentrate on department stores. Such information as the following would be needed first on each question: |

To what extent do buyers buy on the basis of the type of retail outlet versus the brand? Would they seek out the brand in those channels that are not eliminated?

What are the future market trends with respect to the importance of these three channels?

Have marketing efforts and policies directed at the three channels been optimal?

On the basis of this and other information, marketing management will want to define the major alternatives open to them:

Establish a special charge for handling smaller orders to encourage larger orders. This move is based on the assumption that small orders are the ultimate cause of the relative unprofitability of dealing with garden supply shops and hardware stores.

Give more aid to garden supply shops and hardware stores. This is based on the assumption that the managers of these stores could increase their sales with more training or promotional materials.

Reduce the number of sales calls and the amount of advertising going to garden supply shops and hardware stores. This is based on the assumption that some of these costs can be saved without reducing proportionately the level of sales to these channels.

Do nothing. This is based on the assumption that current marketing efforts are optimal and that either future marketing trends point to an imminent improvement in the profitability of the weaker channels or dropping any type of channel would reduce rather than improve profits because of repercussions on production costs or on demand.

Don't abandon any channel as a whole but only the weakest retail units in each channel. This is based on the assumption that a more detailed cost study would reveal many profitable garden shops and hardware stores whose profits are concealed by the poor performance of other stores in these categories.

To evaluate these alternatives, each would have to be spelled out in greater detail. In general, marketing-profitability analysis provides information on the relative profitability of different channels, products, territories, or other marketing entities.[7] It does not imply that the best course of action is to drop the unprofitable marketing entities, nor does it actually measure the likely profit improvement if these marginal marketing entities are dropped.

| Direct versus Full Costing | Like all information tools, marketing-profitability analysis is capable of leading or misleading marketing executives, depending upon the degree to which they understand its procedures and limitations. The example showed some arbitrariness in the choice of bases for allocating the functional expenses to the marketing entities being evaluated. Thus, the "number of sales calls" was used to allocate selling expenses, when in principle "number of sales man-hours" would |

---

[7] For another example, see Leland L. Beik and Stephen L. Buzby, "Profitability Analyses by Market Segments," *Journal of Marketing*, June 1973, pp. 48–53.

have been a more accurate indicator of cost. The former base was used because it generally involves less record keeping and computation. Such approximations may not involve the loss of too much accuracy, but marketing executives should be cognizant of this judgmental element in determining distribution costs.[8]

Far more serious may be another judgmental element affecting the computation of marketing costs. This is the matter of whether to allocate *full costs* or only *direct and traceable costs*. The example sidestepped this problem by assuming only simple costs that seemed to fit in with marketing activities. But it cannot be avoided in an actual analysis of marketing costs. Three classes of costs have to be distinguished:

> **Direct costs.** These are costs that can be assigned directly to the marketing entities that give rise to them. For example, sales commissions are a direct cost in a profitability analysis of sales territories, sales representatives, or customers. Advertising expenditures are a direct cost in a profitability analysis of products to the extent that each advertisement promotes only one company product. Other costs that are direct for some purposes are sales-force salaries, supplies, and traveling expenses.
>
> **Traceable common costs.** These are costs that can be assigned only indirectly, but on a plausible basis, to the marketing entities. In the example, rent was analyzed in this way. The company's floor space reflected the need to carry on three different marketing activities, and it was possible to estimate how much floor space supported each activity.
>
> **Nontraceable common costs.** These are costs whose allocation to the marketing entities is necessarily arbitrary. Consider "corporate image" expenditures. It would be arbitrary to allocate them equally among all products, since all products do not benefit equally from corporate image making. It would be arbitrary to allocate them proportionately to the sales of the various products, since relative product sales reflect many factors besides corporate image making. Other typical examples of common costs that are difficult to assign are management salaries, taxes, interest, and other types of overhead.

There is no controversy concerning the inclusion of direct costs in the marketing cost analysis. There is a small amount of controversy concerning the inclusion of traceable common costs. Traceable common costs lump together costs that would change with the scale of the marketing activity and costs that probably would not change in the near future. If the lawn-mower company drops garden supply shops, it is likely to continue to pay the same rent, for contractual reasons or through inertia. In this event its profits would not rise immediately by the amount of the present loss in selling to garden supply shops ($310). The profit figures are more meaningful when fixed traceable costs can be liquidated.

The major controversy concerns whether the nontraceable common costs should be allocated to the marketing entities. This is called the *full-cost approach*, and its advocates defend it on the grounds that all costs ultimately must be imputed in order to determine true profitability. But this argument tends to confuse the use of accounting for financial reporting with the use of accounting to provide a quantitative basis for decision making and profit planning. Full costing has three major weaknesses:

[8] For common bases of allocation, see Charles H. Sevin, *Marketing Productivity Analysis* (New York: McGraw-Hill Book Company, 1965).

The relative profitability of different marketing entities can shift quite radically when one highly arbitrary way to allocate nontraceable common costs is replaced by another. This tends to weaken confidence in the tool.

The arbitrariness leads to argument and demoralization, especially by those who feel that their performance or interest is being judged adversely as a result.

The inclusion of nontraceable common costs may weaken efforts at real cost control. Operating management is most effective in controlling direct costs and traceable common costs. Arbitrary assignments of nontraceable common costs may lead them to spend their time fighting the arbitrary allocations or may altogether discourage them in meeting their cost responsibility.

EFFICIENCY CONTROL

Suppose a profitability analysis reveals that the company is earning poor profits in connection with certain products, territories, or markets. The question is whether there are more efficient ways to manage the sales force, advertising, sales promotion, and distribution.

Sales-Force Efficiency

Sales managers at each level—regional, district, and area—should keep track of several key indicators of sales-force efficiency in their territory. They are:

1. Average number of sales calls per salesperson per day
2. Average sales-call time per contact
3. Average revenue per sales call
4. Average cost per sales call
5. Entertainment cost per sales call
6. Percentage of orders per 100 sales calls
7. Number of new customers per period
8. Number of lost customers per period
9. Sales-force cost as a percentage of total sales

An analysis of these statistics will raise useful questions such as: are sales representatives making too few calls per day? are they spending too much time per call? are they spending too much on entertainment? are they closing enough orders per hundred calls? are they producing enough new customers and holding onto the old customers?

There is much evidence of inefficiency in the way companies manage their personal selling resources. A survey of 257 Fortune-500 companies revealed the following:

- 54 percent have not conducted an organized study of sales representatives' use of time, even though most respondents felt that time utilization represents an area for improvement.
- 25 percent do not have a system for classifying accounts according to potential.
- 30 percent do not use call schedules for their sales force.
- 51 percent do not determine the number of calls it is economical to make on an account.
- 83 percent do not determine an approximate duration for each call.
- 51 percent do not use a planned sales presentation.

• 24 percent do not set sales objectives for accounts.
• 72 percent do not set profit objectives for accounts.
• 19 percent do not use a call report system.
• 63 percent do not use a prescribed routing pattern in covering territories.
• 77 percent do not use the computer to assist in time and territorial management.[9]

When a company becomes serious about improving sales-force efficiency, it often can effect a number of substantial improvements. General Electric was able to reduce the size of the sales force in one of its divisions without losing any sales after discovering that sales representatives were making an excessive number of calls on customers. A large airline found its sales representatives doing both selling and servicing, and took steps to transfer the servicing function to lower-paid clerks. Another company conducted time-and-duty studies and found ways to reduce the ratio of idle to productive time.[10]

Advertising Efficiency

Many managers feel that it is almost impossible to measure what they are getting for their advertising dollars. But an effort should be made to keep track of at least the following statistics:

1. Advertising cost per thousand buyers reached overall, for each media category, and each media vehicle
2. Percentage of audience who noted, saw/associated, and read most for each media vehicle
3. Consumer opinions on the ad content and effectiveness
4. Before-after measures of attitude toward the product
5. Number of inquiries stimulated by the ad
6. Cost per inquiry

Management can undertake a number of steps to improve advertising efficiency, including doing a better job of positioning the product, defining advertising objectives, pretesting messages, using the computer to guide the selection of advertising media, looking for better media buys, and doing advertising posttesting.

Sales Promotion Efficiency

Sales promotion includes dozens of devices for stimulating buyer interest and product trial. In order to improve the efficiency of sales promotion, management should keep records on each sales promotion, its costs, and its impact on sales. Such statistics should be watched as:

1. Percentage of sales sold on deal
2. Display costs per sales dollar
3. Percentage of coupons redeemed
4. Number of inquiries resulting from a demonstration

[9] Robert F. Vizza, "Managing Time and Territories for Maximum Sales Success," *Sales Management,* July 15, 1971, pp. 31–36.

[10] See Charles S. Goodman, *Management of the Personal Selling Function* (New York: Holt, Rinehart and Winston, 1971), pp. 78–80.

By establishing the job position of sales promotion manager, this person can observe the results of diffcrent sales promotion instruments and advise product managers on the most cost-effective promotions to use.

Distribution Efficiency

The area of distribution efficiency is one in which management has been active in searching for economies. Considerable work has been done in improving physical-distribution systems, particularly with regard to inventory levels, warehouse locations, and transportation modes. Work has also been done to improve local delivery methods, as the following example shows:

> *Wholesale bakers* face increased competition from chain bakers. They are especially at a disadvantage in the physical distribution of bread. The wholesale bakers must make more stops than the chain bakers and deliver a smaller average volume. Furthermore, the driver typically loads the store's shelf while the chain bakery leaves the bread at the chain's unloading platform to be placed on the shelf by store personnel. This led the American Bakers' Association to investigate whether more efficient bread handling procedures were achievable. A systems engineering study was instituted. The bread delivery operation was studied in minute detail from the time of truck loading to the time of shelving. As a result of riding with the drivers and observing procedures, the engineers recommended a number of changes. Economies could be secured from more scientific routing; from a relocation of the truck's door from the back of the trailer to the driver's side; and from the development of preshelved racks. The interesting thing is that these economies were always available but not recognized until competitive pressure increased the need for improved efficiency.[11]

STRATEGIC CONTROL

From time to time, companies must stand back and undertake a critical review of their overall marketing effectiveness. This goes beyond carrying out annual-plan control, profitability control, and efficiency control. Marketing is one of the major areas where rapid obsolescence of objectives, policies, strategies, and programs is a constant possibility. Because of the rapid changes in the marketing environment, each company should periodically reassess its overall approach to the marketplace. Two tools in this connection are a *marketing-effectiveness rating review* and a *marketing audit*.

Marketing-Effectiveness Rating Review

Consider the following actual situation. The president of a major industrial-equipment company was reviewing the annual business plans of various divisions and found several of the divisional plans lacking in marketing substance. He called in the corporate vice president of marketing and said:

> I am not happy with the quality of marketing in our divisions. It is very uneven. I want you to find out which of our divisions are strong, average, and weak in marketing. I want to know if they understand and are practicing customer-oriented marketing. I want a marketing score for each division. For each deficient division, I want a plan for improving its marketing effectiveness over the next few years. I want evidence next year that each marketing-deficient division is making progress toward a marketing orientation.

[11] See the study by Arthur D. Little, Inc., *Challenge of Distribution in the 60's* (Cambridge, Mass., March 1961).

The corporate marketing vice president agreed to do this, recognizing that it was a formidable task. His first impulse was to base the evaluation of divisional marketing effectiveness on each division's performance in sales growth, market share, and profitability. His thinking was that the high-performing divisions must have good marketing leadership and the poor-performing divisions have deficient marketing leadership.

Actually, marketing effectiveness is not so simple. Good results may be due to a division's being in the right place at the right time, rather than the consequence of effective marketing management. Improvements in that division's marketing might boost results from good to excellent. At the same time, another division might have poor results in spite of the best strategic marketing planning. Replacing the present marketing managers might only make things worse.

The marketing effectiveness of a company or division is reflected in the degree to which it exhibits five major attributes of a marketing orientation: *customer philosophy, integrated marketing organization, adequate marketing information, strategic orientation,* and *operational efficiency.* Each of these attributes can be measured. Table 24–6 presents a *marketing-effectiveness rating instrument* based on these five dimensions. This instrument is filled out by marketing and other managers in the division. The scores are then summarized.

The instrument has been tested in a number of companies, and very few achieve scores within the superior range of 26 to 30 points. The few include well-known master marketers such as Procter & Gamble, Avon, McDonald's, IBM, General Electric, and Caterpillar. Most companies and divisions receive scores in the fair-to-good range, indicating that their own managers feel there is much room for marketing improvement. The breakdown of the total score into the five dimensions indicates which elements of effective marketing action need the most attention. Divisional management can then establish a plan for correcting the major marketing weaknesses over time.[12]

TABLE 24–6
Marketing Effectiveness Rating Instrument
(Check one answer to each question)

CUSTOMER PHILOSOPHY

A. Does management recognize the importance of designing the company to serve the needs and wants of chosen markets?

Score

0 ☐ Management primarily thinks in terms of selling current and new products to whoever will buy them.

1 ☐ Management thinks in terms of serving a wide range of markets and needs with equal effectiveness.

2 ☐ Management thinks in terms of serving the needs and wants of well-defined markets chosen for their long-run growth and profit potential for the company.

---

[12] For further discussion of this instrument, see Philip Kotler, "From Sales Obsession to Marketing Effectiveness," *Harvard Business Review,* November–December 1977, pp. 67–75.

TABLE 24–6 continued

648

Marketing Control

B. Does management develop different offerings and marketing plans for different segments of the market?

0 ☐ No.

1 ☐ Somewhat.

2 ☐ To a good extent.

C. Does management take a whole marketing system view (suppliers, channels, competitors, customers, environment) in planning its business?

0 ☐ No. Management concentrates on selling and servicing its immediate customers.

1 ☐ Somewhat. Management takes a long view of its channels although the bulk of its effort goes to selling and servicing the immediate customers.

2 ☐ Yes. Management takes a whole marketing systems view recognizing the threats and opportunities created for the company by changes in any part of the system.

INTEGRATED MARKETING ORGANIZATION

D. Is there high-level marketing integration and control of the major marketing functions?

0 ☐ No. Sales and other marketing functions are not integrated at the top and there is some unproductive conflict.

1 ☐ Somewhat. There is formal integration and control of the major marketing functions but less than satisfactory coordination and cooperation.

2 ☐ Yes. The major marketing functions are effectively integrated.

E. Does marketing management work well with management in research, manufacturing, purchasing, physical distribution, and finance?

0 ☐ No. There are complaints that marketing is unreasonable in the demands and costs it places on other departments.

1 ☐ Somewhat. The relations are amicable although each department pretty much acts to serve its own power interests.

2 ☐ Yes. The departments cooperate effectively and resolve issues in the best interest of the company as a whole.

F. How well-organized is the new product development process?

0 ☐ The system is ill-defined and poorly handled.

1 ☐ The system formally exists but lacks sophistication.

2 ☐ The system is well-structured and professionally staffed.

ADEQUATE MARKETING INFORMATION

G. When were the latest marketing research studies of customers, buying influences, channels, and competitors conducted?

0 ☐ Several years ago.

1 ☐ A few years ago.

2 ☐ Recently.

H. How well does management know the sales potential and profitability of different market segments, customers, territories, products, channels, and order sizes?

0 ☐ Not at all.

1 ☐ Somewhat.

2 ☐ Very well.

I. What effort is expended to measure the cost-effectiveness of different marketing expenditures?

0 ☐ Little or no effort.

1 ☐ Some effort.

2 ☐ Substantial effort.

STRATEGIC ORIENTATION

J. What is the extent of formal marketing planning?

0 ☐ Management does little or no formal marketing planning.

1 ☐ Management develops an annual marketing plan.

2 ☐ Management develops a detailed annual marketing plan and a careful long-range plan that is updated annually.

K. What is the quality of the current marketing strategy?

0 ☐ The current strategy is not clear.

1 ☐ The current strategy is clear and represents a continuation of traditional strategy.

2 ☐ The current strategy is clear, innovative, data-based, and well-reasoned.

L. What is the extent of contingency thinking and planning?

0 ☐ Management does little or no contingency thinking.

1 ☐ Management does some contingency thinking although little formal contingency planning.

2 ☐ Management formally identifies the most important contingencies and develops contingency plans.

OPERATIONAL EFFICIENCY

M. How well is the marketing thinking at the top communicated and implemented down the line?

0 ☐ Poorly.

1 ☐ Fairly.

2 ☐ Successfully.

N. Is management doing an effective job with the marketing resources?

0 ☐ No. The marketing resources are inadequate for the job to be done.

1 ☐ Somewhat. The marketing resources are adequate but they are not employed optimally.

2 ☐ Yes. The marketing resources are adequate and are deployed efficiently.

O. Does management show a good capacity to react quickly and effectively to on-the-spot developments?

0 ☐ No. Sales and market information is not very current and management reaction time is slow.

1 ☐ Somewhat. Management receives fairly up-to-date sales and market information; management reaction time varies.

2 ☐ Yes. Management has installed systems yielding highly current information and fast reaction time.

TOTAL SCORE

The instrument is used in the following way. The appropriate answer is checked for each question. The scores are added—the total will be somewhere between 0 and 30. The following scale shows the level of marketing effectiveness:

0–5	= None	16–20	= Good
6–10	= Poor	21–25	= Very good
11–15	= Fair	26–30	= Superior

SOURCE: Philip Kotler, "From Sales Obsession to Marketing Effectiveness," *Harvard Business Review*, November–December 1977, pp 67–75. Copyright © 1977 by the President and Fellows of Harvard College; all rights reserved.

The Marketing Audit

Those companies and divisions that discover through applying the marketing-effectiveness rating instrument that their marketing operations need improvement should consider undertaking a more thorough study known as a *marketing audit*.[13] In its full form, a marketing audit has four basic characteristics.

1. *Comprehensive.* The term *marketing audit* should be reserved for a *comprehensive (or horizontal) audit* covering the company's marketing environment, objectives, strategies, organization, and systems. In contrast, a *functional (or vertical) audit* occurs when management decides to take an in-depth look into some key marketing function, such as sales-force management. A functional audit is called by the function that is being audited, such as a sales-force audit, an advertising audit, or a pricing audit. Although functional audits can be useful, they often blind management as to the real source of its problem. Excessive sales-force turnover, for example, may be a symptom not of poor sales-force training or compensation but of poor company products and promotion. A comprehensive marketing audit usually is more effective in locating the real source of the company's marketing problems.

2. *Systematic.* The usefulness of a marketing audit will normally increase to the extent that it follows an orderly sequence of diagnostic steps covering the organization's marketing environment, internal marketing system, and specific marketing activities. The diagnosis is followed by a corrective action plan involving both short-run and long-run actions to improve the organization's overall marketing effectiveness.

3. *Independent.* A marketing audit can be conducted in six ways:[14] (1) self-audit; (2) audit from across; (3) audit from above; (4) company auditing office; (5) company task-force audit; and (6) outsider audit. Self-audits, where managers use a checklist to rate their own operations, may be useful, but most experts agree that the self-audit lacks objectivity and independence.[15] The 3M Company has made good use of a headquarters-based auditing office, which provides marketing audit services to divisions on request.[16] Generally speaking, however, the best audits are likely to come from experienced outside consultants, who have the necessary objectivity and independence, broad experience in a number of industries, some familiarity with this industry, and the undivided time and attention to give to the audit.

4. *Periodic.* Typically, marketing audits are initiated only after sales have turned down sharply, sales-force morale has fallen, and other problems have occurred at the company. The irony is that companies are thrown into a crisis partly because they have failed to review their marketing operations during good times. A periodic marketing audit promises benefits for companies that are in good health as well as companies that are in trouble. "No marketing operation is ever so good that it cannot be improved. Even the best can be made better. In fact, even the best *must* be better, for few if any marketing operations can remain successful over the years by maintaining the status quo."[17]

---

[13] See Philip Kotler, William Gregor, and William Rodgers, "The Marketing Audit Comes of Age," *Sloan Management Review*, winter 1977, pp. 25–43.

[14] Some of these approaches are briefly discussed by Alfred Oxenfeldt and Richard D. Crisp in their respective articles in *Analyzing and Improving Marketing Performance*, Report No. 32 (New York: American Management Association, 1959).

[15] Many useful checklist questions for marketers are found in C. Eldridge, *The Management of the Marketing Function* (New York: Association of National Advertisers, 1967).

[16] Kotler, Gregor, and Rodgers, "Marketing Audit Comes of Age," p. 31.

[17] Abe Shuchman, "The Marketing Audit: Its Nature, Purposes, and Problems," in Oxenfeldt and Crisp, *Marketing Performance*, pp. 16–17.

The preceding ideas on a marketing audit can be brought together into a single definition:

> A *marketing audit* is a comprehensive, systematic, independent, and periodic examination of a company's—or business unit's—marketing environment, objectives, strategies, and activities with a view of determining problem areas and opportunities and recommending a plan of action to improve the company's marketing performance.

Marketing audit procedure   A marketing audit starts with a meeting between the company officer(s) and the marketing auditor(s) to work out an agreement on the objectives, coverage, depth, data sources, report format, and the time period for the audit. The bulk of the auditor's time is then spent in gathering data. A detailed plan as to who is to be interviewed, the questions to be asked, the time and place of contact, and so on, has to be carefully prepared so that auditing time and cost are kept to a minimum. The cardinal rule in data collection is not to rely solely on the company's executives for data and opinion. Customers, dealers, and other outside groups must be interviewed. Many companies do not really know how their customers and dealers see them and their competitors, nor do they fully understand customer needs.

When the data-gathering phase is over, the marketing auditor formally presents the main findings and recommendations. A valuable aspect of the marketing audit is the process that the managers go through to assimilate, debate, and develop new concepts of needed marketing action.

Components of the marketing audit   The marketing audit consists of examining six major components of the company's marketing situation. Each component has a semiautonomous status if a company wants less than a full marketing audit. The six components are described below and the major auditing questions are listed in Table 24–7.

1. *Marketing environment audit.* This audit calls for analyzing the major macro-environment forces that might impact on the company and major trends in the key components of the company's task environment: markets, customers, competitors, distributors and dealers, suppliers, and facilitators.

2. *Marketing strategy audit.* This audit calls for reviewing the company's marketing objectives and marketing strategy to appraise how well these are adapted to the current and forecasted marketing environment.

3. *Marketing organization audit.* This audit calls for evaluating the marketing organization's capability for developing and carrying out the necessary strategy for the forecasted environment.

4. *Marketing systems audit.* This audit involves examining the adequacy of the company's systems for analysis, planning, and control in the marketing area, as well as innovation.

5. *Marketing productivity audit.* This audit calls for examining data on the profitability of different marketing entities and on the cost-effectiveness of different marketing expenditures.

6. *Marketing function audits.* These audits involve carrying out in-depth evaluations of major marketing-mix components, namely products, price, distribution, sales force, advertising, promotion, and publicity.

TABLE 24–7
Components of a Marketing Audit

PART I. THE MARKETING ENVIRONMENT AUDIT

Macroenvironment

A. *Economic-Demographic*

1. What does the company expect in the way of inflation, material shortages, unemployment, and credit availability in the short run, intermediate run, and long run?
2. What effect will forecasted trends in the size, age distribution, and regional distribution of population have on the business?

B. *Technology*

1. What major changes are occurring in product technology? In process technology?
2. What are the major generic substitutes that might replace this product?

C. *Political-Legal*

1. What laws are being proposed that may affect marketing strategy and tactics?
2. What federal, state, and local agency actions should be watched? What is happening in the areas of pollution control, equal employment opportunity, product safety, advertising, price control, etc., that is relevant to marketing planning?

D. *Social-Cultural*

1. What attitudes is the public taking toward business and toward products such as those produced by the company?
2. What changes are occurring in consumer life styles and values that have a bearing on the company's target markets and marketing methods?

Task Environment

A. *Markets*

1. What is happening to market size, growth, geographical distribution, and profits?
2. What are the major market segments? What are their expected rates of growth? Which are high opportunity and low opportunity segments?

B. *Customers*

1. How do current customers and prospects rate the company and its competitors, particularly with respect to reputation, product quality, service, sales force, and price?
2. How do different classes of customers make their buying decisions?
3. What are the evolving needs and satisfactions being sought by the buyers in this market?

C. *Competitors*

1. Who are the major competitors? What are the objectives and strategy of each major competitor? What are their strengths and weaknesses? What are the sizes and trends in market shares?
2. What trends can be foreseen in future competition and substitutes for this product?

D. *Distribution and Dealers*

1. What are the main trade channels bringing products to customers?
2. What are the efficiency levels and growth potentials of the different trade channels?

E. *Suppliers*
1. What is the outlook for the availability of different key resources used in production?
2. What trends are occurring among suppliers in their pattern of selling?

F. *Facilitators*
1. What is the outlook for the cost and availability of transportation services?
2. What is the outlook for the cost and availability of warehousing facilities?
3. What is the outlook for the cost and availability of financial resources?
4. How effectively is the advertising agency performing? What trends are occurring in advertising agency services?

PART II. MARKETING STRATEGY AUDIT

A. *Marketing Objectives*
1. Are the corporate objectives clearly stated, and do they lead logically to the marketing objectives?
2. Are the marketing objectives stated in a clear form to guide marketing planning and subsequent performance measurement?
3. Are the marketing objectives appropriate, given the company's competitive position, resources, and opportunities? Is the appropriate strategic objective to build, hold, harvest, or terminate this business?

B. *Strategy*
1. What is the core marketing strategy for achieving the objectives? Is it a sound marketing strategy?
2. Are enough resources (or too much resources) budgeted to accomplish the marketing objectives?
3. Are the marketing resources allocated optimally to prime market segments, territories, and products of the organization?
4. Are the marketing resources allocated optimally to the major elements of the marketing mix, i.e., product quality, service, sales force, advertising, promotion, and distribution?

PART III. MARKETING ORGANIZATION AUDIT

A. *Formal Structure*
1. Is there a high level marketing officer with adequate authority and responsibility over those company activities that affect the customer's satisfaction?
2. Are the marketing responsibilities optimally structured along functional, product, end user, and territorial lines?

B. *Functional Efficiency*
1. Are there good communication and working relations between marketing and sales?
2. Is the product-management system working effectively? Are the product managers able to plan profits or only sales volume?
3. Are there any groups in marketing that need more training, motivation, supervision, or evaluation?

C. *Interface Efficiency*
1. Are there any problems between marketing and manufacturing that need attention?
2. What about marketing and R&D?

TABLE 24–7 continued

654

Marketing Control

3. What about marketing and financial management?
4. What about marketing and purchasing?

PART IV. MARKETING SYSTEMS AUDIT

A. *Marketing Information System*
1. Is the marketing intelligence system producing accurate, sufficient, and timely information about developments in the marketplace?
2. Is marketing research being adequately used by company decision makers?

B. *Marketing-Planning System*
1. Is the marketing-planning system well conceived and effective?
2. Is sales forecasting and market-potential measurement soundly carried out?
3. Are sales quotas set on a proper basis?

C. *Marketing Control System*
1. Are the control procedures (monthly, quarterly, etc.) adequate to insure that the annual-plan objectives are being achieved?
2. Is provision made to analyze periodically the profitability of different products, markets, territories, and channels of distribution?
3. Is provision made to examine and validate periodically various marketing costs?

D. *New-Product Development System*
1. Is the company well organized to gather, generate, and screen new product ideas?
2. Does the company do adequate concept research and business analysis before investing heavily in a new idea?
3. Does the company carry out adequate product and market testing before launching a new product?

PART V. MARKETING PRODUCTIVITY AUDIT

A. *Profitability Analysis*
1. What is the profitability of the company's different products, served markets, territories, and channels of distribution?
2. Should the company enter, expand, contract, or withdraw from any business segments and what would be the short- and long-run profit consequences?

B. *Cost-Effectiveness Analysis*
1. Do any marketing activities seem to have excessive costs? Are these costs valid? Can cost-reducing steps be taken?

PART VI. MARKETING FUNCTION AUDITS

A. *Products*
1. What are the product line objectives? Are these objectives sound? Is the current product line meeting these objectives?
2. Are there particular products that should be phased out?
3. Are there new products that are worth adding?
4. Are any products able to benefit from quality, feature, or style improvements?

B. *Price*
1. What are the pricing objectives, policies, strategies, and procedures? To what extent are prices set on sound cost, demand, and competitive criteria?

    2. Do the customers see the company's prices as being in line or out of line with the perceived value of its offer?

    3. Does the company use price promotions effectively?

C. *Distribution*

    1. What are the distribution objectives and strategies?

    2. Is there adequate market coverage and service?

    3. Should the company consider changing its degree of reliance on distributors, sales reps, and direct selling?

D. *Sales Force*

    1. What are the organization's sales force objectives?

    2. Is the sales force large enough to accomplish the company's objectives?

    3. Is the sales force organized along the proper principle(s) of specialization (territory, market, product)?

    4. Does the sales force show high morale, ability, and effort? Are they sufficiently trained and are there sufficient incentives?

    5. Are the procedures adequate for setting quotas and evaluating performances?

    6. How is the company's sales force perceived in relation to competitors' sales forces?

E. *Advertising, Sales Promotion, and Publicity*

    1. What are the organization's advertising objectives? Are they sound?

    2. Is the right amount being spent on advertising? How is the budget determined?

    3. Are the ad themes and copy effective? What do customers and the public think about the advertising?

    4. Are the advertising media well chosen?

    5. Is sales promotion used effectively?

    6. Is there a well-conceived publicity program?

Example of a marketing audit[18] O'Brien Candy Company is a medium-sized candy company located in the Midwest. In the last two years, its sales and profits have barely held their own. Top management feels that the trouble lies with the sales force; somehow they don't "work hard or smart enough." To correct this, management is considering introducing a new incentive-compensation system and hiring a sales-force trainer to train the sales force in modern merchandising and selling techniques. Before doing this, however, they decide to hire a marketing consultant to do a marketing audit. The auditor conducts a number of interviews with management, customers, sales representatives, and dealers and also examines various data. Here is what the auditor finds:

> The company's product line consists primarily of eighteen products, mostly candy bars. Its two leading brands are in the mature stage of their life cycles and account for 76 percent of total sales. The company has looked at the fast-developing markets of chocolate snacks and candies but has not made any moves yet.
>
> The company recently researched its customer profile. Its products appeal especially to lower-income and older people. Respondents who were asked to

---

[18] This case is adapted with permission from the excellent article by Dr. Ernst A. Tirmann, "Should Your Marketing be Audited?" *European Business*, autumn 1971, pp. 49–56.

assess O'Brien's chocolate products in relation to competitors' products described them as "average quality and a bit old-fashioned."

O'Brien sells its products to candy jobbers and large chains. Its sales force call on many of the small retailers reached by the candy jobbers to fortify displays and provide ideas; its sales force also call on many small retailers not covered by jobbers. O'Brien enjoys good penetration of small retailing, although not in all segments, such as the fast-growing restaurant area. Its major approach to middlemen is a "sell-in" strategy: discounts, exclusivity contracts, and stock financing. At the same time, O'Brien does not do too well in penetrating the various chains. Some of its competitors rely much more heavily on mass consumer advertising and store merchandising and are more successful with the large chains.

O'Brien's marketing budget amounts to about 15 percent of its total sales, compared with competitors' budgets of close to 20 percent. Most of the marketing budget supports the sales force and the remainder supports advertising; consumer promotions are very limited. The advertising budget is spent primarily in reminder advertising for the company's two leading products. New products are not developed often, and when they are, they are introduced to retailers by using a "push" strategy.

The marketing organization is headed by a sales vice president. Reporting to the sales vice president is the sales manager, the marketing research manager, and the advertising manager. Having come up from the ranks, the sales vice president is partial to sales-force activities and pays less attention to the other marketing functions. The sales force is organized by territorial responsibilities headed by area managers.

The marketing auditor came to the firm conclusion that O'Brien's problems would not be solved by actions taken to improve its sales force. The sales-force problem was symptomatic of a deeper company malaise. The auditor prepared and presented a report to management consisting of the findings and recommendations shown in Table 24–8.

TABLE 24–8

SUMMARY OF MARKETING AUDITOR'S FINDINGS AND RECOMMENDATIONS FOR O'BRIEN CANDY COMPANY

FINDINGS

1. The company's product lines are dangerously unbalanced. The two leading products accounted for 76 percent of total sales and have no growth potential. Five of the eighteen products are unprofitable and have no growth potential.
2. The company's marketing objectives are neither clear nor realistic.
3. The company's strategy is not taking changing distribution patterns into account or catering to rapidly changing markets.
4. The company is run by a sales organization rather than a marketing organization.
5. The company's marketing mix is unbalanced, with too much spending on sales force and not enough on advertising.
6. The company lacks procedures for successfully developing and launching new products.
7. The company's selling effort is not geared to profitable accounts.

SHORT-TERM RECOMMENDATIONS

1. Examine the current product line and weed out marginal performers with limited growth potential.
2. Shift some marketing expenditures from supporting mature products to supporting the more recent ones.
3. Shift the marketing-mix emphasis from direct selling to national advertising, especially for new products.
4. Conduct a market-profile study of the fastest growing segments of the candy market and develop a plan to break into these areas.
5. Instruct the sales force to drop some of the smaller outlets and not to take orders for under twenty items. Also, cut out the duplication of effort of sales representatives and jobbers calling on the same accounts.
6. Initiate sales-training programs and an improved compensation plan.

MEDIUM-TO-LONG-TERM RECOMMENDATIONS

1. Hire an experienced marketing vice president from the outside.
2. Set formal and operational marketing objectives.
3. Introduce the product manager concept in the marketing organization.
4. Initiate effective new-product development programs.
5. Develop strong brand names.
6. Find ways to market its brands to the chain stores more effectively.
7. Increase the level of marketing expenditures to 20 percent of sales.
8. Reorganize the selling function by specializing sales representatives by distribution channels.
9. Set sales objectives and base sales compensation on gross profit performance.

THE MARKETING CONTROLLER CONCEPT

We have examined how an outsider called a marketing auditor can contribute to strategic control. Some companies are also establishing inside job positions known as *marketing controllers* to monitor marketing expenses and activities. Marketing controllers are essentially individuals working in the controller office who have a specialization in the marketing side of the business. In the past, the controller's office concentrated on watching manufacturing, inventory, and financial expenses and did not contain individuals who really understood marketing very well. The new marketing controllers are trained in both finance and marketing and can perform a sophisticated financial analysis of past and contemplated marketing expenditures. A survey by Goodman showed that

> large sophisticated companies, such as General Foods, Du Pont, Johnson & Johnson, Trans World Airlines, and American Cyanamid, have all instituted financial control positions which directly oversee advertising and, in some selected cases, merchandising policies. The major functions of these individuals are to verify advertising bills, ensure the optimization of agency rates, negotiate agency contracts, and perform an audit function regarding the client's agency and certain of the suppliers.[19]

[19] Sam R. Goodman, *Techniques of Profitability Analysis* (New York: John Wiley & Sons, 1970), p. 2.

Goodman feels that this is a step in the right direction and advocates even a fuller role for the marketing controller. The marketing controller would:

1. Maintain record of adherence to profit plans;
2. Maintain close control of media expense;
3. Prepare brand manager's budgets;
4. Advise on optimum timing for strategies;
5. Measure the efficiency of promotions;
6. Analyze media production costs;
7. Evaluate customer and geographic profitability;
8. Present sales-oriented financial reports;
9. Assist direct accounts in optimizing purchasing and inventory policies;
10. Educate the marketing area to financial implications of decisions.[20]

The Nestlé Company took a step in this direction in 1965 when a specific segment of the controller operation was made available for marketing planning and control. Marketing-service analysts were assigned to each of Nestlé's six marketing divisions to work for the marketing head. They carried out diverse assignments designed to improve marketing efficiency and performance. Their reports proved helpful, and the position has served as a valuable training ground for future general managers because of their exposure to marketing, production, and finance.

The marketing controller concept is an intriguing one, particularly in organizations where marketing is still practiced with a primary eye toward sales rather than profits. The marketing controller can make a contribution by analyzing how and where the company is making its money. As future marketing managers come on the scene with greater training in financial analysis, they can be expected to do more of this work themselves, with marketing controllers continuing to provide a monitoring function of marketing expenditures.

SUMMARY

Marketing control is the natural sequel to marketing planning. Organizations need to exercise at least four types of marketing control.

Annual-plan control is the task of monitoring the current marketing effort and results to be sure that the annual sales and profit goals will be achieved. The main tools are sales analysis, market share analysis, marketing expense-to-sales ratios, financial analysis, and customer-attitude tracking. If underperformance is detected, the company can implement a variety of corrective measures, including cutting production, changing prices, increasing sales-force pressure, and cutting fringe expenditures.

Profitability control is the task of determining the actual profitability of different marketing entities, such as the firm's products, territories, market segments, and trade channels. Marketing-profitability analysis reveals the weaker marketing entities, although it does not indicate whether the weaker units should be bolstered or phased out.

[20] *Ibid.,* 17–18.

Efficiency control is the task of increasing the efficiency of such marketing activities as personal selling, advertising, sales promotion, and distribution. Managers regularly watch certain key ratios that indicate how efficiently these functions are being performed, and they also implement studies to find ways to improve performance.

Strategic control is the task of making sure that the company's marketing objectives, strategies, and systems are optimally adapted to the current and forecasted marketing environment. One tool, known as the marketing-effectiveness rating instrument, attempts to profile a company or division's overall marketing effectiveness in terms of customer philosophy, marketing organization, marketing information, strategic planning, and operational efficiency. Another tool, known as the marketing audit, is a comprehensive, systematic, independent, and periodic examination of the organization's marketing environment, objectives, strategies, and activities. The purpose of the marketing audit is to determine marketing problem areas and recommend a corrective short-run and long-run action plan to improve the organization's overall marketing effectiveness.

A growing number of companies have established marketing controller positions to monitor marketing expenditures and develop improved financial analyses of the impact of these expenditures.

QUESTIONS AND PROBLEMS

1. Do you foresee a professional marketing auditing association which licenses practitioners, on the model of professional certified public accountants? Why or why not? Do you think it is a good idea?

2. What are the main problems an outside marketing auditor is likely to encounter on a first-time assignment in a company?

3. A sales manager examined his company's sales by region and noted that the East Coast sales were about 2 percent below the quota. To probe this further, the sales manager examined district sales figures. He discovered that the Boston sales district within the East Coast region was responsible for most of the underachievement. He then examined the individual sales of the four salesmen in the Boston district. This examination revealed that the top salesman, Roberts, had filled only 69 percent of his quota for the period. Is it safe to conclude that Roberts is loafing or having personal problems?

4. Suppose a company's market share falls for a couple of periods. The marketing vice-president, however, refuses to take any action, calling it a "random walk." What does he mean? Is he justified?

5. Company XYZ produces five products, and its salesmen represent the full product line on each sales call. In order to determine the profit contribution of each product, salesmen costs (salary, commission, and expenses) have to be allocated among the five products. How should this be done?

6. A large manufacturer of industrial equipment has a salesman assigned to each major industrial city. Regional sales managers supervise the salesmen in several cities. The chief marketing officer wants to evaluate the profit contribution of the different cities. How might each of the following costs be allocated to the cities: (a) billing; (b) district sales manager's expenses; (c) national magazine advertising; (d) marketing research?

7. A company conducts a marketing cost study to determine the minimum size order for breaking even. After finding this size, should the company refuse to accept orders below this size? What issues and alternatives should be considered?

8. The idea of treating the marketing department as a profit center raises several difficult problems. Name them and suggest possible solutions.

9. What is the difference between marketing planning and marketing auditing?

10. What is the difference between the job of a marketing auditor and a marketing controller?

Special Marketing Topics

6

International Marketing

> *A traveller without knowledge is a bird without wings.*
> SA'DI, GULISTAN (1258)

25

Most American executives think of their market as consumers and business firms located in the United States. American exports, after all, account for only 6 percent of the U.S. gross national product. The American home market has been so large that American thinking has traditionally been directed inward.

When Belgian business executives think of selling their goods, they must include international markets in their thinking. Almost 50 percent of the Belgian national output is sold abroad. In other economies also, such as those of the Netherlands, Denmark, Sweden, and Venezuela, marketing thinking must cover international markets.

Ordinarily, most firms would prefer domestic marketing to foreign marketing. Domestic marketing is generally simpler and safer. The managers do not have to learn another language, deal with a different currency, face political and legal uncertainties, or adapt the product to a different set of needs and expectations. There are mainly two factors that might draw companies into international marketing. First, they might be *pushed* into it by the general lack of opportunity in the home market. The gross national product of the home country may be low or growing very slowly, or their government may be antibusiness or taxing heavily. Second, they might be *pulled* into it by growing opportunities for their product in other countries. Without necessarily abandoning their home market, they may find other markets an attractive place to make a profit, even after allowing for the extra costs and encumbrances they might face in operating abroad.

THE INTERNATIONAL MARKETING ENVIRONMENT

In deciding to sell abroad, a company will have to learn a great many new things. Although international marketing involves no new marketing principles, the company will have to acquire and maintain a good knowledge of the changing international marketing environment. The international marketing environment has undergone significant changes since 1945, creating both new opportunities and new problems. The most significant changes are:

1. The significant internationalization of the world economy reflected in the rapid growth of world trade and investment
2. The gradual erosion of the dominant position of the U.S. and its attendant problems of an unfavorable balance of trade and a falling value of the dollar in world markets
3. The rising economic power of Japan in world markets
4. The establishment of a working international financial system offering improved currency convertibility
5. The shift in world income since 1973 to the oil-producing countries
6. The increasing trade barriers put up to protect domestic markets against foreign competition.[1]

The company also has to know how to research specific foreign markets. American companies that are effective marketers domestically have often forgotten their marketing principles when going abroad, often resulting in costly blunders. They look at foreign markets from an ethnocentric point of view instead of the foreign consumer's point of view. Thus Campbell's bombed when it tried to sell its canned soup in Italy, a country where the way of life clearly rules out canned soup. When Italian housewives were asked, "Would you want your son to marry a canned-soup user?" 99 percent answered no. And the same company failed in some countries to vary the taste of its tomato soup sufficiently to meet varying national and regional taste preferences.

The hundred-odd nations of the world differ greatly in the kinds of goods and services they are ready to use. It would be as much a mistake for an American manufacturer of microwave ovens to seek a market in Nigeria as for Nigerians to seek a market for bullock carts here. On the other hand, American bicycles fetch a premium in Nigeria, and Nigerian palm oil is imported in large quantities into the United States. A nation's readiness for different products and services and its general attractiveness as a market to foreign firms depend on its economic, political-legal, cultural, and business environment.

Economic Environment The nations of the world exhibit great variation in *industrial structure* and *national income,* both of which critically influence the goods and services they are likely to need and their ability to buy.

[1] See Warren J. Keegan, "Multinational Product Planning: New Myths and Old Realities," in *Multinational Product Management* (Cambridge, Mass.: Marketing Science Institute, 1976), pp. 1–8.

Economies classified according to industrial structure   It is useful to distinguish among four types of industrial structure that a nation can have:

1. *Subsistence economies.* In a subsistence economy the vast majority of people are engaged in simple agriculture. They consume most of their output and barter the rest for simple goods and services. For obvious reasons, they offer few opportunities for exporters.

2. *Raw-material-exporting economies.* These economies are rich in one or more natural resources but poor in other respects. Much of their revenue comes from exporting these resources. Examples are Chile (tin and copper), the Congo (rubber), and Saudi Arabia (oil). These countries are good markets for extractive equipment, tools and supplies, materials-handling equipment, and trucks. Depending on the number of foreign residents and wealthy native rulers and landholders, they are also a market for Western-style commodities and luxury goods.

3. *Industrializing economies.* In an industrializing economy, manufacturing is beginning to play a role of some importance, probably accounting for somewhere between 10 and 20 percent of the country's gross national product. Examples include Egypt, the Philippines, India, and Brazil. As manufacturing increases, the country relies more on imports of textile raw materials, steel, and heavy machinery, and less on imports of finished textiles, paper products, and automobiles. The industrialization tends to create a new rich class and a small but growing middle class, both demanding new types of goods, some of which can be satisfied only by imports.

4. *Industrial economies.* Industrial economies have built up their industrial base to the extent that they become exporters of manufactured goods and investment funds. They trade manufactured goods among themselves and also export them to other types of economies in exchange for raw materials and semifinished goods. The large and varied manufacturing activities of these industrial nations and their sizable middle class make them rich markets for all sorts of goods.

Economies classified according to national incomes   The products and services consumed by a nation are also affected by its level and distribution of national income. These goods can be distinguished for five different national income profiles:

1. *Very low family incomes.* Subsistence economies tend to be characterized by very low family incomes. The families spend long hours at hard work eking out a bare living from the soil. Homegrown food and homemade clothing and simple services constitute the bulk of consumer goods and services.

2. *Mostly low family incomes.* Economies that are seeking industrialization along Marxist lines are characterized by low family incomes, to allow as much as possible for capital formation. Most consumer goods are produced domestically by state-owned enterprises. These nations present some opportunities for trade.

3. *Very low, very high family incomes.* Several countries of the world are characterized by extremes of income, where most of the population is very poor and a small minority is very rich. This makes the market for consumer goods very bizarre. The masses live on subsistence farming, supplemented by the import of needed foodstuffs and textiles, and the rich import expensive cars, appliances, and Western amenities.

4. *Low, medium, high family incomes.* Industrialization tends to be accompanied by the rise of a middle class. The very low and very high income classes tend to persist along with their distinct consumption patterns. The middle class is able to afford basic necessities and have something left over to purchase amenities.

5. ***Mostly medium family incomes.*** The advanced industrial nations tend to develop institutions that reduce the extremes of income. The result is a large and comfortable middle class confronted with a wide array of branded products, able to own automobiles and major appliances, as well as to enjoy leisure and take vacations.

Political-Legal Environment

Nations differ greatly in the favorableness of their political-legal environment for imports and foreign investment. At least four factors should be considered by the prospective marketer who is evaluating whether to do business in another country.

1. ***Attitudes toward international buying.*** Some nations are very receptive, indeed encouraging, to foreign firms, and others are very hostile. As an example of the former, Mexico for a number of years has been attracting foreign investment by offering investment incentives, site-location services, and a stable currency. On the other hand, India has required the exporter to deal with import quotas, blocked currencies, stipulations that a high percentage of the management team be nationals, and so on.

2. ***Political stability.*** One must consider not only the host country's present political climate but also its future stability. Governments change hands, sometimes quite violently. Even without a change in government, a regime may decide to respond to new popular feelings. At worst, the foreign company's property may be expropriated; or its currency holdings may be blocked; or import quotas or new duties may be imposed. Where political instability is high, international marketers may still find it profitable to do business with the host country, but the situation will affect their mode of entry. They will favor export marketing to direct foreign investment. They will keep their foreign stocks low. They will convert their currency rapidly. As a result, the people in the host country end up paying higher prices, have fewer jobs, and get less satisfactory products.

3. ***Monetary regulations.*** Sellers want to realize profits in a currency of value to them. In the best situation, the importer can pay either in the seller's currency or in hard world currencies. Short of this, sellers might accept a blocked currency if they can buy other goods in that country that they need or that they can sell elsewhere for a needed currency. In the worst case they have to take their money out of the host country in the form of relatively unmarketable products that they can sell elsewhere only at a loss. Besides currency restrictions, a fluctuating exchange rate also leads to unusual risks for the exporter.

4. ***Government bureaucracy.*** A fourth factor is the extent to which the host government runs an efficient system for assisting foreign companies: efficient customs-handling procedures, market information, and other factors conducive to doing business. Perhaps the most common shock to American business executives is the extent to which various impediments appear to stand in their way, all of which disappear if a suitable payment (bribe) is made to some official(s).

Cultural Environment

Perhaps the most difficult aspect of international markets is the consumer buying preferences and patterns, which are full of surprises:

The average Frenchman uses almost twice as many cosmetics and beauty aids as does his wife.

The Germans and the French eat more packaged, branded spaghetti than the Italians.

French and Italian housewives are not as interested in cooking as their counterparts in Luxembourg and Belgium.

666

Women in Tanzania will not give their children eggs for fear of making them bald or impotent.

Chevrolet's Nova would be an inappropriate brand name for Spain, where *no va* means "it doesn't go"!

Colors for packaging have varying connotations in different countries: green suggests illness in Malaysia, white indicates mourning in China, while blue connotes femininity in Holland and masculinity in Sweden.

And industrial buying styles vary tremendously:

South Americans are accustomed to talking business in close physical proximity with other persons, in fact almost nose to nose. The American business executive retreats, but the South American pursues. And both end up being offended.

In face-to-face communication Japanese business executives rarely say no to an American business executive. Americans are frustrated and don't know where they stand. Also, Americans tend to come to their point quickly and directly in business dealings. Japanese business executives tend to find this offensive.

In France, wholesalers just don't care to promote a product. They simply ask their retailers what they want today, and they deliver it. If an American company builds its strategy around the French wholesaler, it is almost bound to fail.

Each country (and even regional groups within each country) has cultural traditions, preferences, and taboos that must be carefully studied by the marketer.

In contemplating international marketing a company faces five major types of decisions. (1) The *international marketing decision* determines whether the foreign opportunities and the firm's resources are attractive enough to justify a general interest in marketing abroad. (2) The *market-selection decision* determines *which* foreign markets to enter. (3) The *entry and operating decision* determines the best way to enter and operate in an attractive foreign market. (4) The *marketing-mix decision* develops an appropriate product, price, distribution, and promotion program for that market. (5) The *marketing-organization decision* determines the best way for the firm to achieve and maintain control over its international business operations. We shall examine each of these decisions on the following pages.

THE INTERNATIONAL MARKETING DECISION

Companies initially get involved in international marketing in one of two ways. In some cases, someone—a domestic exporter, a foreign importer, a foreign government—approaches the company. In other cases, the company starts to think on its own about overseas marketing. It might face overcapacity or simply forecast better opportunities abroad than at home.

Before going abroad, the company should try to define its *international marketing objectives and policies*. This involves a number of component decisions.

1. *Proportion of foreign sales to total sales.* Most companies will start small when they venture abroad. Some will plan to stay small, seeing foreign operations as a small part of their business. Other companies will have more grandiose

international-expansion plans, seeing foreign business as ultimately equal to or even more important than their domestic business. Of the more than fifteen thousand American firms engaged in international trade, several companies sell more abroad than at home: Standard Oil (N.J.) (68 percent), United States Machinery Company (59 percent), Colgate Palmolive (55 percent), and Singer (50 percent). Other American companies selling over 30 percent of their output abroad are Pfizer, Kodak, Gillette, 3M, National Cash Register, International Harvester, Caterpillar, and Heinz.

2. *Few countries or many countries.* A company with a fixed budget for international expansion has a choice of entering only a few foreign markets and developing them well *(market concentration)* or entering several markets each on a smaller scale *(market diversification).* For example, Koor, a large Israel company, chose market diversification and set up sales offices in seven countries in one year with disappointing results. Ayal and Zif analyzed the product/market factors that favor market concentration versus market diversification.[2] Market concentration makes sense if market response is S-shaped rather than concave; each market has high growth potential and relative stability; each market needs high product and communication adaptation; each market has high constraints and needs high program control; each market has high economies of scale in distribution; the competitive lead-time is long; and the spillover effects on other markets are low. If the opposite conditions prevail, the firm should consider market diversification.

3. *Types of countries.* The types of countries that are attractive will depend on the product, geographical factors, income and population, political climate and numerous other factors. The seller may have a predilection for certain country groups or parts of the world. For example, the oil-producing countries are experiencing rapid growth and are key markets for construction equipment, luxury automobiles, electrical equipment, and other things. Mainland China is gradually opening its markets to foreign trade, and although trading arrangements are difficult, the gains would be very high.[3] Eastern European countries provide another growing market opportunity. Brazil is an example of a country with high potential. Other less-developed nations (LDNs) have the necessary population but often lack the incomes to be good markets for foreign manufacturers and in addition often impose severe manpower and currency requirements that lower profit opportunities. The company has to decide whether to cultivate opportunities in safe countries or in those countries that offer the chance for higher returns at somewhat high risks.

MARKET SELECTION DECISION

After developing a preliminary list of possible countries in which to market, the company will have to find some procedure for screening and ranking them. Consider the following example:

> CMC's market research in the computer field revealed that England, France, West Germany, and Italy offer us significant markets. England, France, and Germany are about equal-size markets, while Italy represents about two thirds the potential of any one of those countries. . . . Taking everything into consid-

[2] Igal Ayal and Jehiel Zif, "Market Expansion Strategies in Multinational Marketing," *Journal of Marketing,* Spring 1979, pp. 84–94.

[3] Bohdan O. Szuprowicz and Maria R. Szuprowicz, *Doing Business with the People's Republic of China: Industries and Markets* (New York: John Wiley & Sons, 1978).

eration, we decided to set up first in England because its market for our products is as large as any and its language and laws are similar to ours. England is
different enough to get your feet wet, yet similar enough to the familiar U.S.
business environment so that you do not get in over your head.[4]

The market choice seems relatively simple and straightforward. Yet one can
question whether the reason given for selecting England—the compatibility of
its language and culture—should have been given this prominence. Normally the
candidate countries should be ranked on several criteria, such as: (1) market size;
(2) market growth; (3) cost of doing business; (4) competitive advantage; (5) risk
level.

The core of the ranking procedure is to try to determine the probable rate
of return on investment in each market. Five steps are involved:

1. *Estimate of current market potential.* The first step is to estimate current market
potential in each candidate market. This *marketing research task* calls for using
existing published data supplemented by primary data collection through company surveys and studies of various kinds. The rub is that foreign marketing research is more difficult, as a general rule, than domestic market research, for at
least four reasons. (1) Published census and market data are usually scarce and
somewhat unreliable in several countries, especially the poorer ones. (2) Many
trade associations do not make their data public. (3) Marketing research firms are
not always of high quality. (4) Buyers in other countries are less used to cooperating in interviews. Yet there are some signs of improvement. The U.S. Department of Commerce and several large banks are increasing the amount of
information available about foreign markets. The United Nations publishes statistical data and market information. Foreign governments, banks, chambers of
commerce, and private companies are increasingly responding to the problem of
better market information.

2. *Forecast of future market potential.* The firm also needs a forecast of future market potential. This is complicated because the market analyst is usually insufficiently versed in the economic, political, cultural, and business currents of
another country. Many foreign countries do not show the stability of government,
currency, or law that permits reliable forecasting.

3. *Forecast of sales potential.* Estimating the company's sales potential requires
forecasting its probable market share. The normal difficulties of forecasting market shares are compounded in a foreign marketing environment. The foreign company will find itself competing against other foreign companies as well as against
home-country firms. It has to estimate how the buyers will feel about the relative
merits of its product, selling methods, and company. Even if the buyers are im-
partial, their government may put up barriers in the form of quotas, tariffs, taxes,
specifications, or even outright boycotts.

4. *Forecast of costs and profits.* Costs will depend on the company's contemplated
entry strategy. If it resorts to exporting or licensing, its costs will be spelled out in
the contracts. If it decides to locate manufacturing facilities abroad, its cost estimation will require an understanding of local labor conditions, taxes, trade practices, and stipulations regarding the hiring of nationals as key employees. After
estimating future costs, the company subtracts them from estimated company
sales to find company profits for each year of the planning horizon.

5. *Estimate of rate of return on investment.* The forecasted income stream must be

[4] James K. Sweeney, "A Small Company Enters the European Market," *Harvard Business Review*, September–October 1970, pp. 127–28.

related to the investment stream to derive an implicit rate of return. The estimated rate of return should be high enough to cover (1) the company's normal target return on its investment and (2) the risk and uncertainty of marketing in that country. The risk premium has to cover not only the chance that the basic estimates of sales and costs may be wrong but also the chance that unanticipated monetary changes (devaluation, blocked currency) and political changes (future discrimination against foreign business firms, or even expropriation) may occur.[5]

ENTRY AND OPERATING DECISION

Once a company decides that a particular foreign market represents an attractive opportunity, its task is to determine the best mode of entering that market. Here it has three major options: *exporting* (home production and selling abroad), *joint venturing* (joining with foreign companies in some way), or *direct investment* abroad.[6]

Export The simplest way for a company to get involved in a foreign market is to arrange to sell some of its present output abroad. Its manufacturing facilities remain located in the home country. The company may or may not modify its product for the foreign market. Exporting allows the company to enter foreign markets with a minimum of change in its product line, company organization, investment, or company mission.

A company can decide to export its product in two broad ways. It can hire independent international marketing middlemen (indirect export), or it can assume direct responsibility for selling to the foreign buyers or importers (direct export).

Indirect export Indirect export is the more popular of the two for the firm that is just beginning its exporting activity. First, it involves less investment. The firm does not have to develop an overseas sales force or set of contacts. Second, it involves less risk. International marketing middlemen presumably bring know-how and services to the relationship, and the seller will normally make fewer mistakes.

Three types of domestic middlemen arrangements are available to the exporting company:

1. *Domestic-based export merchant.* This middleman buys the manufacturer's product and sells it abroad on its own account. The exporting company makes its sales simply to the export merchant.

2. *Domestic-based export agent.* In this case the company retains some of the chores and all of the risk, because the agent simply agrees to seek foreign buyers for a commission. Within the agent class there are several variants: *export buying agents* reside in the manufacturer's country, represent foreign buyers, place orders with the manufacturer, take care of shipments, and make payment; *brokers*

[5] See David S. R. Leighton, "Deciding When to Enter International Markets," in *Handbook of Modern Marketing*, ed. Victor P. Buell (New York: McGraw-Hill Book Company, 1970), section 20, pp. 23–28.

[6] The discussion of entry channels in this section is indebted to the discussion in Gordon E. Miracle and Gerald S. Albaum, *International Marketing Management* (Homewood, Ill.: Richard D. Irwin, 1970), chaps. 14–16.

exist to find buyers, are paid a commission, and do not handle the products; and *manufacturers' export agents* represent several exporters whose interests are non-competing and carry out selling and other services.

3. ***Cooperative organization.*** A cooperative organization carries on exporting activities on behalf of several producers and is partly under the administrative control of the producers. This form is often used by producers of primary products—fruits, nuts, and so on—for foreign sales. Another form consists in piggyback arrangements between two or more domestic manufacturers trying to develop a complementary product line for a foreign market.

Direct export Sellers who are approached by foreign buyers will most likely undertake direct export instead of paying service charges to middlemen. So will larger sellers or those whose market has grown to sufficient size to justify undertaking their own export activity. The investment and risk are somewhat greater, but so is the potential return.

Here, too, there are several ways in which the company can carry on direct exporting activity.

1. ***Domestic-based export department or division.*** This consists of an export sales manager with some clerical assistants. They carry on the actual selling and draw on regular company departments for marketing assistance in such areas as advertising, credit, and logistics. It might evolve into a self-contained export department or sales subsidiary carrying out all the activities involved in export, and may possibly be operated as a profit center.

2. ***Overseas sales branch or subsidiary.*** This may be established in addition to, or instead of, a domestic export department. An overseas sales branch allows the manufacturer to achieve greater presence and program control in the foreign market. The sales branch handles sales distribution, and it may handle warehousing and promotion as well. It often serves as a display center and customer-service center.

3. ***Traveling export sales representatives.*** The company can decide to have one or more home-based sales representatives travel abroad at certain times to take orders or find business.

4. ***Foreign-based distributors or agents.*** Foreign-based distributors would buy and own the goods, foreign-based agents would sell the goods on behalf of the company. They may be given exclusive rights to represent the manufacturer in that country or only general rights.

Joint Venturing A second broad method of entering a foreign market is to join with nationals in the foreign country to set up production and marketing facilities. Joint venturing differs from exporting in that a partnership is formed that leads to some production facilities abroad, and it differs from direct investment in that an association is formed with someone in that country. Four types of joint venture can be distinguished.

Licensing Licensing represents a comparatively simple way for a manufacturer to become involved in international marketing. The licensor enters an agreement with a licensee in the foreign market, offering the right to use a manufacturing process, trademark, patent, trade secret, or other item of value for a fee or royalty. The licensor gains entry into the market at little risk; the licensee gains production expertise, or a well-known product or name, without having to start from scratch. Gerber introduced its baby foods in the Japanese market through a licensing arrangement. It did not have the staff to develop and operate its own production facility, nor did it want to risk the capital loss if the Japanese were not receptive to its products. Coca-Cola has carried out its international marketing activities by licensing bottlers around the world—or, more technically, *franchising* bottlers, because it supplies the syrup needed to produce the product.

Licensing has potential disadvantages in that the firm has less control over the licensee than if it had set up its own production facilities. Furthermore, if the licensee is very successful, the firm has foregone these profits, and if and when the contract ends, it may find it has set up a competitor. To avoid these dangers the licensor must establish a mutual advantage in working together, and a key to doing this is to remain innovative so that the licensee continues to depend on the licensor.

Contract manufacturing   Instead of licensing a foreign company to manufacture and market its products, the firm may wish to retain the marketing responsibility. But it may not be ready to invest in its own foreign production facilities. Under these conditions, an excellent option is to contract with local manufacturers to produce the product. Sears has used this method in opening up department stores abroad, as in Mexico and Spain. Sears enters into contracts with qualified local manufacturers to produce many of the products it sells. Procter & Gamble resorted to contract manufacturing of soap in entering the Italian market, where it faced Colgate and Unilever, who were not only longer entrenched but also owned their production facilities. Contract manufacturing allowed P&G to move in fast and get the feel of the market.

Contract manufacturing has the drawback of less control over the manufacturing process and the loss of potential profits on manufacturing. On the other hand, it offers the manufacturer a chance to get started faster, with less risk, and with the opportunity to possibly form a partnership or buy out the local company if its manufacturing facility operates efficiently.

Management contracting   Here the domestic firm agrees to supply the management know-how to a foreign company that is willing to supply the capital. Thus, the domestic firm is really exporting management services rather than its own products. This arrangement is used by the Hilton hotel system in undertaking to manage hotels throughout the world.

Management contracting is a low-risk method of getting into a foreign market, and it starts yielding income right from the beginning. The arrangement is especially attractive if the contracting firm is given an option to purchase some share in the managed company within a stated period. On the other hand, the arrangement is not sensible if the company can put its scarce management talent to better uses or if there are greater profits to be made by undertaking the whole venture. Management contracting prevents the company from setting up its own operations for a period of time.

Joint-ownership ventures   An increasingly popular arrangement is for foreign investors to join with local investors to create a local business in which they share joint ownership and control. The foreign investor may buy an interest in a local company, a local company may buy an interest in an existing operation of a foreign company, or the two parties may form a new business venture.

From the point of view of the foreign investor, a joint venture may be necessary or desirable for economic or political reasons. Economically, the firm may find it lacks the financial, physical, or managerial resources to undertake the venture alone. Or the foreign government may require joint ownership with local companies as a condition for entry.

Joint ownership can have certain drawbacks for the foreign firm. The partners may disagree over investment, marketing, or other policies. Whereas many American firms like to reinvest earnings for growth, local firms often like to pay out these earnings. Whereas American firms tend to accord a large role to marketing, local investors may see marketing as simply selling. If the American firm has only a minority interest, then its views are overruled in these disagreements. Furthermore, joint venturing can hamper the plans of a multinational company seeking to carry out specific manufacturing and marketing policies on a worldwide basis. The agreement may also make it difficult for the foreign firm to enter other markets where its partner already operates.

Direct Investment

The ultimate form of involvement in a foreign market is investment in foreign-based assembly or manufacturing facilities. Companies just starting out in the market would be well advised to avoid this scale of participation at the outset. However, as experience is gained through export channels, and if the foreign market appears large enough, foreign production facilities offer distinct advantages. The company may secure these advantages partially through licensing or joint-ownership ventures, but if it wants full control (and profits), it may give serious consideration to direct investment.

The advantages of direct investment are several. First, the firm may secure real cost economies in the form of cheaper labor or raw materials, foreign government investment incentives, freight savings, and so on. Second, the firm will gain a better image in the host country because it demonstrates its concern with that country's future. Third, the firm develops a deeper relationship with government, customers, local suppliers, and distributors, enabling it to make a better adaptation of its products to the local marketing environment. Fourth, the firm retains full control over the investment and therefore can develop manufacturing and marketing policies that serve its long-term international objectives.

The main disadvantage is that the firm has exposed a large investment to certain risks, such as blocked or devalued currencies, worsening markets, or expropriation. In some cases, however, the firm has no choice but to accept these risks if it wants to operate effectively in the host country.

Multinational Marketing

We have been examining the nature, advantages, and disadvantages of different modes of entry into a particular foreign market that appears attractive. If the company eventually gets involved in several foreign markets, it will want to begin thinking about its entire system for operating abroad rather than making ad hoc adaptations in each individual market. In fact, it may stop thinking of itself as a national marketer that ventures abroad and instead think of itself as a *global marketer* that operates in many countries, including the "home" country. At this point the company begins to think about developing a worldwide network of production facilities and serving a plurality of markets through a global marketing strategy. Such companies are called multinational corporations. According to Baker:

> The multinational corporation is defined as a company which has a direct investment base in several countries, which generally derives from 20–50 percent or more of its net profits from foreign operations, and whose management makes policy decisions based on the alternatives available anywhere in the world. Approximately 300 such companies are operating and most of these are American.[7]

Multinational corporations include such giants as Unilever, Philips Electric, the Beecham Group, Nestlé, Olivetti, IBM, and Massey-Ferguson. Such corporations must decide very carefully how standardized their marketing should be from country to country. For example, Nestlé strives for uniform quality, branding, labeling, and packaging of its chocolate products; however, its advertising policy is largely decentralized. Beecham, on the other hand, tries to make its advertising policy uniform: if a campaign or idea works well in one country, it will be used elsewhere. A recent survey of twenty-seven leading multinationals in consumer packaged-goods industries reached the following conclusion:

> To the successful multinational, it is not really important whether marketing programs are internationally standardized or differentiated; the important thing is that the *process* through which these programs are developed is standardized. At the heart of this process is the annual marketing-planning system they use.[8]

MARKETING-MIX DECISION

Companies that operate in one or more foreign markets must decide how much, if at all, to adapt their product and marketing mix to local conditions.

Product and Promotion

Keegan distinguished five possible strategies involving the adaptation of product and marketing communications to a foreign market (Figure 25–1).[9]

The first strategy, *straight extension*, means introducing the product in the foreign market in the same form and with the same communications that the company uses at home. It has been used successfully by Pepsi-Cola to introduce its soft drinks everywhere in the world, but it has failed for some other producers, for instance, Philip Morris in the Canadian market and Campbell's tomato soup in the British market. The strategy is a tempting one because it involves no additional expense of research and development, manufacturing retooling or setup, inventory control, or marketing communication reprogramming.

In the second strategy, *communication adaptation*, the company introduces its unchanged product but modifies its communications. For example,

[7] James C. Baker, "Multinational Marketing: A Comparative Case Study," in *Marketing in a Changing World*, ed. Bernard A. Morin (Chicago: American Marketing Association, 1969), p. 61.

[8] Ralph Z. Sorenson and Ulrich E. Wiechmann, "How Multinationals View Marketing Standardization," *Harvard Business Review*, May–June 1975, p. 54.

[9] This section relies heavily on Warren J. Keegan, "Multinational Product Planning: Strategic Alternatives," *Journal of Marketing*, January 1969, pp. 58–62.

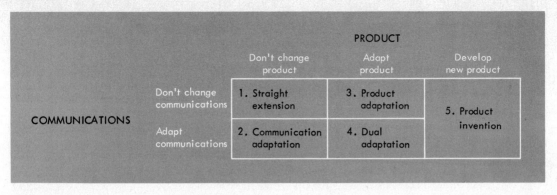

FIGURE 25–1
Five Multinational Product-Marketing Strategies

American bikes are advertised abroad for their transportation rather than pleasure qualities, since bikes are a basic mode of transportation in many other countries. Logic rather than fancy is used in advertising copy in Scandinavia; big, colored illustrations and terse copy in Spain; sex appeal is avoided in Pakistan; and a hundred other communication adaptations are made. The appeal of a communication-adaptation strategy is its relatively low cost of implementation.

The third strategy, *product adaptation*, involves altering the product to meet local conditions or preferences without altering the marketing communications. Thus Heinz varies its baby food products: in Australia, it sells a baby food made from strained lamb brains and in the Netherlands, a baby food made from strained brown beans. Many manufacturers vary the size or contents of their foods, fertilizers, clothing, or appliances to meet local conditions. This strategy involves extra engineering and production cost but may be better than introducing an unaltered product possessing less appeal.

The fourth strategy, *dual adaptation*, involves altering both the product and the communications to increase the product's acceptability. For example, the National Cash Register Company took an innovative step backward by developing and advertising a crank-operated cash register that could sell at half the cost of a modern cash register. This unit caught on greatly in the Philippines, the Orient, Latin America, and Spain. It confirms the existence of *international product life cycles* where countries stand at different stages of readiness to accept a particular product.[10] Dual adaptation is an expensive strategy but is worthwhile if the target markets are large enough.

The last strategy, *product invention*, involves creating a new product to meet a need in another country. For example, there is an enormous need in less-developed countries for low-cost high-protein foods. Companies such as Pillsbury, Swift, and Monsanto are researching the food needs of these countries, formulating new foods, and developing mass-communication programs to gain product trial and acceptance. Product invention would appear to be the costliest of all strategies, but the payoffs to the successful firm also appear to be the greatest.

[10] Louis T. Wells, Jr., "A Product Life Cycle for International Trade?" *Journal of Marketing*, July 1968, pp. 1–6.

Distribution Channels   The international company must take a *whole-channel* view of the problem of getting its products to the final users or consumers. It must see the channel of distribution as an integrated whole, from the manufacturer on one end to the final user or buyer on the other end.[11] Figure 25–2 shows the three major links between the seller and ultimate buyer. The first link, *seller's headquarters organization*, supervises the channels and is part of the channel itself. The second link, *channels between nations*, does the job of getting the products to the overseas markets. The third link, *channels within nations*, is extremely pertinent. Too many American manufacturers think of their channels as ending with the channels between nations, and they fail to observe what happens to their product once it arrives in the foreign market. If the channels within the foreign market are weak or inefficient, then the target customers fail to achieve satisfaction, and the company fails to achieve its international objectives.

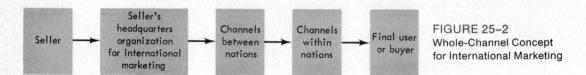

FIGURE 25–2
Whole-Channel Concept for International Marketing

With respect to consumer goods, within-country channels of distribution vary considerably from country to country. There are striking differences in the *size distribution of retailing units*. For example, food channels in the United States are dominated by the large supermarket chain; in France, supermarkets are growing in number, but food retailing is still dominated by small merchants with modest stores; in India, food is sold mainly through thousands of individual tradesmen squatting in open markets or selling in tiny shops. Second, the *services offered* by retailers vary considerably, with much more personal attention and bargaining in countries such as India as compared with the United States. Third, there tends to be greater specialization in the *assortment of goods* handled by retailers in the lower-income economies. Fourth, the retailing system in other countries tends to be more *stratified* according to class structure; thus selecting the retailer is tantamount to selecting the social class the product will reach.[12]

With respect to industrial goods, within-country channels in advanced countries resemble those found in the United States. In the less-developed countries, importers are strong, and the foreign company must often leave its products in their hands. If it seeks its own distributors, it must carefully sort out the good ones from the poor ones. Often the company has to offer exclusive distribution to a local distributor, and its fate in this market is tied up with how well it has chosen its distributor.

Pricing   Manufacturers often price their products lower for the foreign market than for the domestic market. This may be a response to lower incomes abroad, keener competition, or the use of the foreign market as a dumping ground for surpluses. Although the price quoted to merchants abroad may be lower, these merchants

[11] See Miracle and Albaum, *International Marketing Management*, pp. 317–19.

[12] These retailing variations are discussed in John Fayerweather, *International Marketing* (Englewood Cliffs, N.J.: Prentice-Hall, 1965), p. 63.

may not lower the retail price. Foreign middlemen often prefer high unit margins, even though they lead to a smaller volume. They also like to buy on credit, although that increases the manufacturer's cost and risk.

INTERNATIONAL-MARKETING-ORGANIZATION DECISION

Firms manage their international marketing activities in many different ways. The different organizational arrangements often parallel their degree of involvement and experience in international marketing and their international marketing objectives.

Export Department

A firm normally gets started in international marketing by responding to a few orders that come in fortuitously. At first it simply ships out the goods. If its international sales expand, the company usually organizes an export department consisting of a sales manager and a few clerical assistants. As sales increase further, the staff of the export department is expanded to include various marketing services so that it can go after business more aggressively and not depend on the domestic staff. If the firm moves beyond exports into a program of joint ventures or direct investment, the export department will no longer serve these purposes.

International Division

Many companies eventually become involved in a number of different international markets and ventures. A company may export to one country, license to another, have a joint-ownership venture in a third, and own a subsidiary in a fourth, and it may eventually create an international division or subsidiary with responsibility for all of its international activity. The international division is headed by a president (who usually ranks as one of the corporation's divisional vice presidents). The president has goals and budgets and is given total responsibility for the company's growth in the international market.

International divisions, like domestic divisions, are organized in a variety of ways. Usually the international division's corporate staff consists of functional specialists in marketing, manufacturing, research, finance, planning, and personnel. This staff will plan for, and provide services to, various operating units. The operating units may be organized according to one or more of three principles. First, the operating units may be *geographical organizations*. For example, reporting to the international division president (in addition to the division staff) may be vice presidents for different areas, such as North America, Latin America, Europe, Africa, and the Far East. Each area vice president is responsible for a sales force, sales branches, distributors, and licensees in his or her area. Or the operating units may be *product-group organizations*, with a vice president responsible for worldwide sales of each product group. The vice presidents may draw on corporate staff area specialists for expertise on different areas. Finally, the operating units may be *international subsidiaries*, each headed by a president. The various subsidiary presidents report to the president of the international division.

A major disadvantage of the international-division concept is that the corporation's top management may think of it as just another division and never really get involved enough to fully appreciate and plan for global marketing. Top management may not give the division the attention it deserves, and in difficult times may deprive it of adequate supplies or budget.

Multinational Organization

Several firms have passed beyond the international-division organization into a truly multinational organization. This means the top corporate management and staff are involved in the worldwide planning of manufacturing facilities, marketing policies, financial flows, and logistical systems. The various operating units around the world report directly to the chief executive or executive committee, not to the head of an international division. The company trains its executives in worldwide operations, not just domestic *or* international. Management talent is recruited from many countries; components and supplies are purchased where they can be obtained at the least cost; and investments are made where the anticipated returns are greatest.

There is good reason to believe that major companies will have to go multinational in the 1980s if they are going to grow. As foreign companies continue to invade the home market with some success, home companies will have to move aggressively into those international markets that are best suited to their distinctive products and competencies.

SUMMARY

International marketing does not involve any principles not found in domestic marketing, but nevertheless it deserves special attention because of (1) its growing importance as an area of marketing opportunity and (2) its greater level of risk and uncertainty stemming from the marketer's unfamiliarity with other cultures. Doing business abroad requires learning about quite different economic, political, and cultural environments. The company should make a decision in favor of international marketing only when the opportunities appear attractive relative to those at home and the resources are available for carrying out international marketing.

In moving abroad, the first step is to compare the various foreign markets and make market selections on the basis of a hard evaluation of the probable rate of return on investment. Given an attractive market, it can be entered in three ways: export, joint venturing, and direct investment. Many companies start as exporters, move to joint venturing, and finally undertake direct investment as their overseas business expands. A few become multinational corporations with worldwide markets and operating strategies. Companies must also decide on the extent to which their products, communications, distribution, and pricing should be adapted and individuated to individual foreign markets. Finally, they must develop an effective organization for pursuing international marketing. Most firms start with an export department and graduate to an international division. A few pass this stage and move to a multinational organization, which means that worldwide marketing is planned and managed by the top officers of the corporation.

QUESTIONS AND PROBLEMS

1. Develop a list of American products that might have a good reception in Greece. Select one of these and discuss the major problems you anticipate.

2. Pepsi-Cola has used the advertising theme "Now It's Pepsi for Those Who Think Young" quite successfully in the United States. Do you think the same theme makes sense in the Netherlands? Liberia? Hong Kong?

3. A U.S. heavy equipment manufacturer operating in Western Europe has been using Americans as salesmen. The company feels that it could reduce its costs by hiring and

training nationals for salesmen. What are the advantages and disadvantages of using Americans versus nationals for selling abroad?

4. A large American tire company decided to enter the French tire market some years ago. The company produced tires for medium-sized trucks designed to meet the official rear-axle weights. Its subsequent experience was bad, many of its tires blowing out. The company acquired a poor image in France as a result. What went wrong?

5. Select one of the following nations—Italy, Japan, or U.S.S.R.—and describe its marketing institutions and practices.

Nonbusiness Marketing

26

> *Man does not live by GNP alone.*
> PAUL SAMUELSON

Most of the examples of marketing presented in this book have been drawn from the business sector of the economy. That is because marketing theory and practice began and reached its highest level of development in this sector. Starting in the 1970s, however, there has been a "broadening of marketing" to cover all organizations, on the grounds that all organizations have marketing problems that can be aided by the application of marketing principles.[1] The public and nonprofit sectors in particular account for more than a quarter of the American economy and are badly in need of improved management and marketing practices.

Marketing in the public and nonprofit sectors, like marketing in the international economy, does not involve new marketing principles so much as new and challenging applications of these principles. Weinberg and Lovelock have

---

[1] See Philip Kotler and Sidney J. Levy, "Broadening the Concept of Marketing," *Journal of Marketing*, January 1969, pp. 10–15; David J. Luck, "Broadening the Concept of Marketing—Too Far," *Journal of Marketing*, July 1969, pp. 53–55; Philip Kotler, *Marketing for Nonprofit Organizations* (Englewood Cliffs, N. J.: Prentice-Hall, 1975); Christopher H. Lovelock and Charles B. Weinberg, *Cases in Public and Nonprofit Marketing* (Palo Alto, Calif.: Scientific Press, 1977); and Ralph M. Gaedeke, ed., *Marketing in Private and Public Nonprofit Organizations: Perspectives and Illustrations* (Santa Monica, Calif.: Goodyear Publishing Co., 1977).

identified four major characteristics of the nonbusiness sector that call for special attention in seeking to apply marketing principles.[2] They are:

1. *Multiple publics.* Nonbusiness organizations normally have at least two major publics to work with from a marketing point of view: their clients and their funders. The former pose the problem of resource allocation and the latter, the problem of resource attraction.[3] Besides these two publics, many other publics surround the nonbusiness organization and can be dealt with in marketing terms. Thus a college can direct marketing programs toward prospective students, current students, parents of students, alumni, faculty, staff, local business firms, and local government agencies. It turns out that business organizations also deal with a multitude of publics, but their tendency is to think about marketing only in connection with one of these publics, namely, their customers.

2. *Multiple objectives.* Nonbusiness organizations tend to pursue simultaneously several objectives rather than pursuing only one, such as profits. As a result, it is more difficult to evaluate strategic alternatives facing the organization. The management must do its best to explicate the organization's multiple objectives and their relative weight so that some useful evaluation of strategies and resource allocations can be made. Business organizations also have multiple objectives, but these tend to be dominated by the drive for profits.

3. *Services rather than physical goods.* Most nonbusiness organizations are engaged in the production of services rather than goods. As such, they need to draw primarily upon marketing principles used in the marketing of services.

4. *Public scrutiny and nonmarket pressures.* Nonbusiness organizations are usually subject to close public scrutiny because they provide needed public services, are subsidized, are tax exempt, and in many cases are mandated into existence. They experience political pressures from various publics and are expected to operate in the public interest. This means that any marketing activity they engage in will come under public scrutiny.

This chapter will examine how managers of nonprofit and public institutions can apply marketing thinking to the problems of their institutions. We will first examine major types of nonbusiness organizations, then examples of marketing problems and solutions facing colleges, hospitals, and other types of nonbusiness organizations, and finally steps that can be taken to introduce formal marketing responsibility into these nonbusiness organizations.

TYPES OF NONBUSINESS ORGANIZATIONS

Of the various ways to classify organizations in a society, we are primarily interested in two distinctions: (1) whether the organization is privately or publicly owned and operated and (2) whether the organization is organized for profit or nonprofit purposes. These two distinctions lead to the four types of organizations shown in Figure 26–1.

---

[2] Christopher H. Lovelock and Charles B. Weinberg, "Public and Nonprofit Marketing Comes of Age," in *Review of Marketing 1978*, ed. Gerald Zaltman and Thomas V. Bonoma (Chicago: American Marketing Association, 1978), pp. 413–52.

[3] See Benson P. Shapiro, "Marketing for Nonprofit Organizations," *Harvard Business Review*, September–October 1973, pp. 123–32.

FIGURE 26-1
Four Types of Organizations

In the figure:

Private | Public

Profit
I
Single proprietorships
Partnerships
Corporations

II
State-owned airlines
State-owned telephone co.

Nonprofit
IV
Private museums
Private charities
Private universities
Private associations
Private hospitals

III
Government agencies
Public schools
Public hospitals

Quadrant I shows private, for-profit firms and is called, at least in the United States, the *first sector* because it has been entrusted with doing most of society's economic work—producing food, clothing, shelter, and so on.

Quadrants II and III make up the *second sector* (or public sector) and include all of the government organizations set up to carry on residual societal functions that do not yield a profit, have to be performed, and warrant public control. Included are such classic governmental functions as defense, public works, public education, and justice. Most of the public sector organizations are in Quadrant III. However, the government may also own and operate a few enterprises for profit (or at least cost recovery), and these are shown in Quadrant II. Government organizations may be further classified into the following four types:[4]

1. *Business type.* Government organizations that perform economic work, such as the U.S. Post Office or a municipal bus company.

2. *Service type.* Government organizations that provide public services not normally provided by private enterprise, such as public schools, public libraries, police and fire departments, military service organizations, sanitation and water departments, parks and recreation departments, public health and hospital agencies, museums, and symphonies.

3. *Transfer type.* Government organizations that transfer income or aid from one group to another, such as social security administration, city and state welfare departments, and internal revenue service.

4. *Regulation type.* Government organizations that regulate the conduct of other organizations or individuals, such as penitentiaries, courts, and regulatory commissions.

Quadrant IV covers the remaining organizations in the society, those operated privately and not for profit. It is called the *third sector* (or nonprofit sector).

[4] For an alternative classification of government organizations, see William L. Shanklin, "New York City: A Portrait in Marketing Mania," *California Management Review*, winter 1975, pp. 34–40.

682

Nonprofits perform those societal functions that do not yield a profit, are desirable to perform, and need not be under public control. Third sector organizations represent a *middle way* for meeting social needs, without resorting to the profit motive on the one hand or government bureaucracy on the other. These organizations specialize in the delivery of societal services that are not adequately provided by either business or government. The third sector contains tens of thousands of private not-for-profit organizations, ranging from The Society for the Preservation and Encouragement of Barber Shop Quartet Singing in America to major foundations, colleges, hospitals, museums, charities, social agencies, and churches. In fact, nonprofit organizations can be classified into eight groups:

1. *Religious organizations.* Churches, church associations, evangelical movements.
2. *Social organizations.* Service clubs, fraternal organizations.
3. *Cultural organizations.* Museums, symphonies, opera companies, art leagues, zoos.
4. *Knowledge organizations.* Private grade schools, private colleges and universities, research organizations.
5. *Protective organizations.* Trade associations, trade unions.
6. *Political organizations.* Political parties, lobbyist groups.
7. *Philanthropic organizations.* Private welfare organizations, private foundations, charity hospitals, nursing homes.
8. *Social-cause organizations.* Peace groups, family-planning groups, environmental groups, racial rights groups, consumerist groups, women's rights groups, antivice groups.

ENTER MARKETING

Of all the classic business functions, marketing has been the last to arrive on the public and nonprofit scene. Some years earlier, managers of nonbusiness organizations began to get interested in accounting systems, financial management, personnel administration, and formal planning. As long as these organizations operated in the seller's market of the 1960s, marketing was largely ignored. This situation changed, however, when the same organizations began to experience a decline in clients, members, or funds. Consider the following developments:

More than 170 private colleges have closed their doors since 1965, unable to get either enough students or funds, or both. Tuition at the top private universities is now over $6,000. If college costs continue to climb at the current rate, the parents of a child born today will have to put aside $82,830 to buy that child a bachelor's degree at one of the better private colleges.[5]

Hospital costs continue to soar, leading to daily room rates of $300 or more in some large hospitals. Many hospitals are experiencing underutilization, particularly in the maternity and pediatrics sections. Some experts have predicted the closing of 1,400 to 1,500 hospitals in the next ten years.

The Catholic Church drew as many as 55 percent of all adult Catholics under

[5] See Donald L. Pyke, "The Future of Higher Education: Will Private Institutions Disappear in the U.S.?" *The Futurist*, December 1977, p. 374.

thirty years of age to church in a typical week in 1966. By 1975, the figure had fallen to 39 percent, and further declines in weekly attendance were expected.

Many performing-arts groups cannot attract large enough audiences. Even those that have seasonal sellouts, such as the Lyric Opera Company of Chicago, face huge operating deficits at the end of the year.

Many third-sector organizations that flourished in earlier years—the YMCA, Salvation Army, Girl Scouts, and Women's Christian Temperance Union—presently are reexamining their mission in an effort to reverse membership declines.

In a word, these organizations have marketplace problems. Their administrators are struggling to keep them alive in the face of rapidly changing societal needs, increasing public and private competition, changing client attitudes, and diminishing financial resources. Board members and supporters are asking administrators tough questions about the organization's mission, opportunities, and strategies. As a result, these organizations are now showing a growing interest in marketing. Here is what is happening in a few select "nonbusiness" industries.

Colleges   Colleges are facing an increasingly grim marketing scenario. (1) The annual number of high school graduates will decline from a peak of 3.2 million in 1977 to 2.8 million in 1982–83. (2) The proportion of high school students electing to go to college might decline. (3) A higher proportion of college-bound students are electing to attend community colleges instead of four-year colleges. (4) The absolute and relative future level of tuition will deter college going in general and hurt private colleges in particular.[6]

What are college administrators doing about these problems? One group is doing nothing. Either enrollment hasn't slipped, or if it has, the administrators believe the decline is temporary. Many believe it is "unprofessional" to go out and "sell" their colleges.

A second group has responded by increasing the budget of the admissions office, which serves as the college's sales department. The admissions office then dreams up new ways to attract more applicants. For example:

The admissions office at North Kentucky State University planned to release 103 balloons filled with scholarship offers.

The admissions staff of one college passed out promotional frisbees to high school students vacationing on the beaches of Fort Lauderdale during the annual Easter break.

St. Joseph's College in Renssalaer, Indiana, achieved a 40 percent increase in freshmen admissions through advertising in *Seventeen* and on several Chicago and Indianapolis rock radio stations. The admissions office also planned to introduce tuition rebates for students who recruited new students ($100 finder's fee) but this plan was cancelled.

Bard College developed a same-day-admission system for students who walk into their office and qualify.

Worcester Polytech offers negotiable admission in which credit is negotiated for previous study or work experience to shorten the degree period.

---

[6] See *A Role for Marketing in College Admissions* (New York: College Entrance Examination Board, 1976), p. 54 and elsewhere.

The University of Richmond has spent $13,000 to create a twelve-minute film for showings to high school students and other interested publics.

Drake University advertised on a billboard near O'Hare Airport in Chicago that "Drake is only 40 minutes from Chicago" (if one flies).

Promotional competition has not yet led to premiums given to students for enrollment (free radio, typewriter) or offers of "satisfaction guaranteed or your money back," but these may come.

In equating marketing with intensified promotion by the admissions office, these colleges may create new problems for themselves. Aggressive promotion tends to produce strong negative reactions among the school's constituencies, especially the faculty, who regard hard selling as offensive. Also, promotion may turn off as many prospective students and families as it turns on. Aggressive promotion can attract the wrong students to the college—students who drop out when they discover they don't have the ability to do the work or decide that the college is not what it was advertised to be. Finally, this kind of marketing creates the illusion that the college has undertaken sufficient response to declining enrollment—an illusion that slows down the needed work on "product improvement," which is the basis of all good marketing.[7]

A genuine marketing response has been undertaken by a relatively small number of colleges. Their approach is best described as *market-oriented institutional planning*. In this approach, marketing is recognized as much more than mere promotion, and indeed, the issue of promotion cannot be settled in principle until more fundamental issues are resolved. These institutions are analyzing their environment, markets, and consumer behavior; assessing their existing resources and resource needs; and developing a clear sense of mission, market targets, and market positioning. By doing its homework on market, resource, and missions analysis, a college is in a better position to make decisions that improve student and faculty recruitment and institutional fund raising.

As an example, the University of Houston recently completed an intensive institutional audit using several faculty task forces. The final report presented recommendations on the university's mission, strategy, and portfolio. The portfolio section recommended which components of the university's "product mix" (schools and departments) should be built, maintained, phased down, or phased out. The criteria included: (1) the centrality of that academic program to the mission of the university, (2) the program's academic quality, and (3) the program's market viability. Thus, a department of women's studies that is marginal to the mission of the school, of low national reputation, and unable to attract an adequate number of students would be slated for phasing down or out.

Hospitals   Hospitals are beginning to treat marketing as a "hot" topic. A few years ago, health professionals scorned the idea of marketing, imagining that it would lead to ads such as "This week's special—brain surgery—only $195." Hospital administrators also argued that patients didn't choose hospitals, their doctors did; so marketing, to be effective, would have to be directed to doctors.

Nevertheless, some hospitals began to take their first steps toward market-

[7] See "Rest in Pace," *Newsweek*, April 11, 1977, p. 96.

ing. A few rushed into marketing with more enthusiasm than understanding, believing it to consist of clever promotional gimmicks. For example:

> Sunrise Hospital in Las Vegas ran a large advertisement featuring the picture of a ship with the caption, "Introducing the Sunrise Cruise, Win a Once-in-a-Lifetime Cruise Simply by Entering Sunrise Hospital on Any Friday or Saturday: Recuperative Mediterranean Cruise for Two."
>
> St. Luke's Hospital in Phoenix introduced nightly bingo games for all patients (except cardiac cases), producing immense patient interest as well as a net annual profit of $60,000.
>
> A Philadelphia hospital, in competing for maternity patients, let the public know that the parents of a newborn child would enjoy a candlelight dinner with steak and champagne on the eve before the mother and child's departure from the hospital.
>
> A number of hospitals, in their competition to attract and retain physicians, have added "ego services," such as saunas, chauffeurs, and even private tennis courts.

Fortunately, some hospitals are now beginning to apply marketing to a broader set of problems. Where should the hospital locate a new branch or ambulatory care unit? How can the hospital estimate whether a new service will draw enough patients? How can the hospital attract more consumers to preventive care services, such as annual medical checkups and cancer-screening tests? How can a hospital successfully compete in the recruitment of highly trained specialists who are in short supply? What marketing programs can attract nurses, build community goodwill, attract more contributions?

The marketing naiveté of the typical hospital is illustrated in the following episode:

> A medium-size hospital in southern Illinois decided to establish an adult day-care center as a solution to its underutilized space. It designed a whole floor to serve senior citizens who required personal care and services in an ambulatory setting during the day, but who would return home each evening. The cost was $16 a day, and transportation was to be provided by the patient's relatives. About the only research that was done on this concept was to note that a lot of elderly people lived within a three-mile radius. The center was opened with a capacity to handle thirty patients. Only two signed up!

An increasing number of hospital administrators are now attending marketing seminars to learn more about marketing research and new-service development. The Evanston Hospital of Evanston, Illinois, a major 500-bed facility, appointed the world's first hospital vice president of marketing. Recently, MacStravic published a book devoted entirely to hospital marketing,[8] and many articles are now appearing on health-care marketing.[9]

Other Institutions In addition to colleges and hospitals, other institutions are paying more attention to marketing. The YMCA is taking a fresh look at its mission, services, and

[8] Robin E. MacStravic, *Marketing Health Care* (Germantown, Md.: Aspen Systems Corporation, 1977).

[9] See, for example, the special issue on marketing of *Hospitals, Journal of the American Hospital Association,* June 1, 1977.

clients in order to develop new services and markets for the 1980s. Major charities like the Multiple Sclerosis Society, the American Heart Association, and the March of Dimes are investigating marketing ideas that go beyond selling and advertising. Marketing successes have been reported by arts institutions.[10] It is likely that within ten years, most of the third sector and a good part of the second sector will have some understanding and appreciation of the marketing concept.

SOCIAL MARKETING

The term *social marketing* was first introduced in 1971 to describe the use of marketing principles and techniques to advance a social cause, idea, or practice.[11] More specifically:

> *Social marketing* is the design, implementation, and control of programs seeking to increase the acceptability of a social idea, cause, or practice in a target group(s). It utilizes market segmentation, consumer research, concept development, communications, facilitation, incentives, and exchange theory to maximize target group response.

Other names for social marketing are *social-cause marketing* or *idea marketing*.[12] Examples of social marketing would include public health campaigns to reduce smoking, alcoholism, drug abuse, and overeating; environmental campaigns to promote wilderness protection, clean air, and resource conservation; and a myriad of other campaigns, such as family planning, women's rights, and racial equality.

Social marketing, in contrast to ordinary business marketing, is more a change technology than a response technology. For example, an anticigarette-smoking group is attempting to get people to stop doing something they want to do. To this extent, social marketing seems to be based on the selling concept rather than the marketing concept. Yet the lesson of a consumer orientation is not lost on the social marketer. The social marketer tries to understand why smokers smoke, what pleasures they get, and what difficulties they have in trying to stop smoking. All of this is important in trying to formulate an effective marketing plan that will encourage people to give up smoking.

Social marketing may aim to produce one of four types of change in a target market. The first is a *cognitive change*, that is, a change in the target group's knowledge or understanding of something. An example would be a campaign to increase the public's understanding of the nutritional value of different foods. The second is an *action change*, that is, an effort to get a target market to carry out a specific action in a given period, such as showing up for a vaccination or

[10] See Danny Newman, *Subscribe Now! Building Arts Audiences through Dynamic Subscription Promotion* (New York: Theatre Communications Group, 1977). This book deals primarily with the use of promotion as a marketing tool rather than with overall marketing strategy.

[11] See Philip Kotler and Gerald Zaltman, "Social Marketing: An Approach to Planned Social Change," *Journal of Marketing*, July 1971, pp. 3–12.

[12] The term *social marketing* has subsequently acquired other usages. For instance, it is used in referring to "socially responsible marketing" by business firms or to any marketing done by nonprofit organizations. Hence more specific terms may be needed.

voting in a referendum. The third is a *behavioral change,* seeking to get the target market to change a certain pattern of behavior, such as using an auto seatbelt or giving up smoking. The fourth is a *value change,* that is, attempting to alter a target group's deeply felt beliefs or values toward some object or situation. An example would be to change people's ideas about family planning or abortion. Social marketing gets progressively more difficult as one goes from trying to produce a cognitive change to trying to produce a value change.

The following things should be noted about social marketing:

1. *Social marketing is more than social advertising.* There is a long history of ad campaigns to promote public-interest causes. But social marketing goes beyond communication efforts and incorporates other elements of the marketing mix, such as product, price, and place to increase the likelihood of achieving the desired response. Wiebe, in his study of four social campaigns, showed how their differential success was related to how closely they resembled the conditions of selling a normal product or service.[13] The great success of the Kate Smith radio marathon to sell bonds one evening during World War II was due, in Wiebe's opinion, to the presence of *force* (patriotism), *direction* (buy bonds), *mechanism* (banks, post offices, telephone orders), *adequacy and compatibility* (many centers to purchase the bonds), and *distance* (ease of purchase). These easily translate into such factors as product, price, place, and promotion. The other three social campaigns studied by Wiebe—recruiting Civil Defense volunteers, stimulating people to take steps to help juvenile delinquents, and arousing citizens against crime—met with much less success because of the lack or mishandling of product, price, place, or promotion variables.

2. *Social marketing can be carried out by any group or organization.* Any organization with a cause can approach its task through developing a marketing plan. Thus social marketing can be said to take place if Procter & Gamble sponsors a campaign in a developing nation aimed at encouraging people to take better care of their teeth or Coca-Cola sponsors a campaign calling upon people not to carelessly throw away their used soft-drink containers in public places.

3. *Social marketing is possible with any side of an issue.* The concepts and techniques making up social marketing are available to all sides of an issue. We cannot call it social marketing if we agree with the cause and propaganda if we disagree with it. Proabortion groups and antiabortion groups can both use social marketing.

Social marketing is only one of several strategies available to change agents. The other change strategies are: (1) violent action, (2) legal action, (3) social engineering, (4) social propaganda, (5) social advertising, and (6) economic action. Social marketing is substantially different in form and content from violent action, legal action, and social propaganda. On the other hand, it builds on the idea of social engineering, social advertising, and economic action. Social marketing is not a pure approach but rather a higher-order integration of the functions of incentivization, facilitation, and communication as applied to the problem of influencing the free and voluntary behavior of individuals and groups in an open society. It represents a democratic change technology that is positioned between the extremes of force on the one hand and brainwashing on the other.

---

[13] G. D. Wiebe, "Merchandising Commodities and Citizenship on Television," *Public Opinion Quarterly,* winter 1951–52, pp. 679–91.

The social marketer, in designing a social-change strategy, goes through a normal marketing-planning process. The first step is to define the social-change objective. Suppose the objective is "to reduce the number of teenage smokers from 60 to 40 percent of the teenage population within five years." The next step is to analyze the beliefs, attitudes, values, and behavior of the target group, here teenagers, and to identify key segments of the target market who would respond to different marketing approaches. An analysis is also made of the major competitive forces that support teenage smoking. This is followed by concept research in which the social marketer generates and tests alternative concepts that might be effective in dissuading teenagers from smoking. The next step is channel analysis, in which the social marketer identifies and assesses the most effective communication and distribution approaches to the target market. This is followed by the formal development of a marketing plan and a marketing organization to carry it out. Finally, provision is made to continuously monitor results and take corrective action when called for.

Social marketing is still too new to evaluate its effectiveness in comparison with other social-change strategies. Social change itself is hard to produce with any strategy, let alone one that relies on voluntary response. So far, the ideas of social marketing have been mainly applied in the areas of family planning,[14] environmental protection,[15] improved nutrition, auto driver safety, and public transportation, with some encouraging successes. Evaluating the full effects of social marketing campaigns is not an easy task.

Social-marketing campaigns, when completely successful, would have the following six attributes: (1) high incidence of adoption; (2) high speed of adoption; (3) high continuance of adoption; (4) no major counterproductive consequences; (5) low cost per unit of successful adoption; and (6) open and moral means.

IMPLEMENTING MARKETING IN NONBUSINESS ORGANIZATIONS

The interesting thing about marketing is that all organizations carry on marketing whether they know it or not. When this dawns on a nonprofit organization, the response is much like Moliere's character in *Le Bourgeois Gentilhomme* who exclaims: "Good Heavens! For more than forty years I have been speaking prose without knowing it." Colleges, for example, search for prospects (students), develop products (courses), price them (tuition and fees), distribute them (announce time and place), and promote them (college catalogs). Similarly, hospitals, social agencies, cultural groups, and other nonprofit organizations also carry on marketing in some fashion.

For nonbusiness organizations that would like to improve their marketing effectiveness, several alternatives are available, including appointing a marketing committee, setting up marketing task forces, hiring outside marketing specialists, and setting up an internal marketing position (see chap. 22, pp. 596–99).

For example, from time to time the organization should engage the

---

[14] Eduardo Roberto, *Strategic Decision-Making in a Social Program: The Case of Family-Planning Diffusion* (Lexington, Mass.: Lexington Books, 1975).

[15] Karl E. Henion, II, *Ecological Marketing* (Columbus, Ohio: Grid, 1976).

services of marketing specialist firms. A marketing research firm might be hired to survey the needs, perceptions, preferences, and satisfaction of the client market. An advertising agency might be hired to develop a corporate identification program or an advertising campaign. As a further step, the organization might hire a marketing consultant to carry out a comprehensive *marketing audit* on the problems and opportunities facing that organization.

Eventually the organization might be ready to appoint a director of marketing. The job is conceived as a middle-management position, created primarily to provide marketing services to others in the institution. A major issue is, What is the marketing director's relationship to those responsible for such related functions as planning, public relations, and fund raising? A good case could be made for locating the marketing director within the planning office, where he or she reports to the vice president of planning. It would not make sense for the marketing director to report to public relations or fund raising because that would overspecialize the use made of marketing.

The ultimate solution is the establishment of a vice president of marketing position in nonprofit organizations. This is an upper-level management position, which gives more scope, authority, and influence to marketing. A vice president of marketing not only coordinates and supplies analytical services but also has a strong voice in the determination of where the institution should be going in terms of its changing opportunities. The vice president of marketing would be responsible for planning and managing relations with several publics of the institution. The person's title may be altered to that of vice president of institutional relations or external affairs to avoid unnecessary semantic opposition.

SUMMARY

Marketing is beginning to attract the attention of nonbusiness administrators. There is a growing body of literature on college, hospital, and other nonbusiness marketing, as well as increased attendance at conferences on marketing for nonbusiness organizations. The interest is precipitated by changing societal needs, increasing public and private competition, changing client attitudes, and diminishing financial resources.

Nonbusiness marketing does not involve new principles so much as it challenges applications, given that nonbusiness organizations tend to have multiple publics, multiple objectives, a service rather than goods technology, and greater public scrutiny and nonmarket pressures.

In becoming interested in marketing, some nonbusiness organizations see it primarily as a promotion function and increase their budgets for advertising, sales promotion, and personal selling. Others recognize it as a planning approach calling for better competitive positioning, product development, and consumer-need satisfaction. Hospitals, colleges, YMCAs, art institutions, and churches are among those organizations currently showing the most interest in marketing.

Social marketing refers to the use of marketing principles to increase the acceptability of a social idea, cause, or practice in a target group(s). Social marketing may aim at producing a change in beliefs, action, behavior, or values. It differs from social advertising by utilizing all four elements of the marketing mix. It can be carried out by any group regardless of its ideological position. Social marketing is a higher-order integration of social engineering, social advertising, and economic action that is undertaken to effect a voluntary change in behavior by members of the target audience.

Nonbusiness organizations can introduce marketing through appointing a marketing committee or marketing task force, hiring outside marketing specialists, and setting up a position of marketing director or marketing vice president. A marketing audit will reveal the many opportunities for the application of marketing in that institution, and the marketing executive can proceed to tackle those problems that are most urgent, significant, and feasible.

QUESTIONS AND PROBLEMS

1. A major university has decided to hire a director of marketing. You are asked to prepare a job description for this position. Describe the scope, functions, and responsibilities of this position.

2. The Samaritan Hospital has appointed a new vice-president of marketing. The vice-president holds meetings with hospital physicians and nurses, describing his skills and inviting them to suggest projects. He receives more than enough suggestions and in fact has to prioritize them. What criteria might·he use to rank the proposed projects so that he can attend to the more "important" ones first?

3. An anti-smoking group is preparing to launch a major campaign to get people to quit smoking. A representative of the cigarette industry complained that the campaign, if it succeeds in getting people to quit smoking, will have the effect in many cases of shortening people's lives. What could he possibly have in mind?

4. In the early days of family planning in India, a commission was paid to "agents" who would find men who would be willing to be vasectomized. The commission rate was attractive enough to lead to certain abuses. What are some of the potential abuses and how can they be prevented?

5. In a million-dollar campaign to get people to snap on their auto seat belts while driving, it was estimated that the campaign saved one hundred lives, at a cost-per-life-saved of $10,000. This seemed like a very worthwhile use of public money. Do you agree that more public money should be put into seat belt campaigns?

6. The executive director of a private philanthropic organization saw an advertisement for a book entitled *Marketing for Nonprofit Organizations*. He decided against ordering a copy because his business is to give away money, not to market anything. Would you agree that a private philanthropic organization does not need to understand marketing concepts?

7. The conductor of a symphony orchestra states: "If we adopt a marketing orientation and give the audiences just what they want to hear, we'd be putting on some pretty conventional music. We'd never get a chance to play anything new and daring." Should the conductor adopt the marketing concept?

8. Develop a social marketing campaign to influence people to buy two-way bottles instead of the convenient throwaway bottles. What appeals would you use? What pricing mechanism? How much funding would you need? Do you think the campaign has much chance of success?

9. The New York Metropolitan Museum of Art is seeking to increase its membership, which begins at $15 a year. It believes that persons would respond more to selfish reasons for joining the museum than to broad social appeals. In this connection, the Met is trying to develop at least five tangible benefits that would go with museum membership. Can you suggest five benefits and prepare an ad that displays them?

Marketing in the Contemporary Environment

"Cheshire Puss," she [Alice] began . . . "would you please tell me which way I ought to go from here?" "That depends on where you want to get to," said the cat.
LEWIS CARROLL

27

Marketing is a constantly evolving craft and discipline. As society changes, so do our ideas of what constitutes effective and socially responsible marketing. Starting in the mid-1960s, several forces arose to challenge some of the major premises of marketing practice. These forces constitute a new marketing environment and pose challenging questions about the appropriate character of effective and socially responsible marketing in the years ahead. In this chapter we shall consider seven of these forces: consumerism, environmentalism, shortages, inflation, recession, government regulations, and marketing ethics.

CONSUMERISM

Starting in the 1960s, American business firms found themselves the target of a growing consumer movement.[1] Consumers had become better educated; products had become increasingly complex and hazardous; discontent with American institutions was widespread; influential writers accused big business of wasteful and manipulative practices; presidential messages of Kennedy and Johnson dis-

[1] The discussion in this section is adapted from the author's "What Consumerism Means for Marketers," *Harvard Business Review*, May–June 1972, pp. 48–57.

cussed consumer rights; congressional investigations of certain industries proved embarrassing; and finally Ralph Nader appeared on the scene to crystallize many of the issues.

Since these early stirrings, many private consumer organizations have emerged, several pieces of consumer legislation have been passed, and several state and local offices of consumer affairs have been created. Furthermore, the consumer movement has taken on an international character with much strength in Scandinavia and the Low Countries and a growing presence in France, Germany, and Japan.

But what is this movement? Put simply, *consumerism is an organized movement of concerned citizens and government to enhance the rights and power of buyers in relation to sellers.* The traditional sellers' rights include:

1. The right to introduce any product in any size and style, provided it is not hazardous to personal health or safety; or, if it is, to introduce it with the proper warnings and controls
2. The right to price the product at any level, provided there is no discrimination among similar classes of buyers
3. The right to spend any amount of money to promote the product, provided it is not defined as unfair competition
4. The right to formulate any product message, provided it is not misleading or dishonest in content or execution
5. The right to introduce any buying-incentive schemes they wish

The traditional buyers' rights include:

1. The right not to buy a product that is offered for sale
2. The right to expect the product to be safe
3. The right to expect the product to be what is claimed

Comparing these rights, many believe that the balance of power lies on the sellers' side. It is true that the buyer can refuse to buy any product. But it is generally felt that the buyer is really without sufficient information, education, and protection to make wise decisions in the face of highly sophisticated sellers. Consumer advocates therefore call for the following additional consumer rights:

4. The right to be adequately informed about the more important aspects of the product
5. The right to be protected against questionable products and marketing practices
6. The right to influence products and marketing practices in directions that will enhance the "quality of life"

Each of these proposed rights leads to a whole series of specific proposals by consumerists. The right to be informed includes such things as the right to know the true interest cost of a loan (*truth-in-lending*), the true cost per standard unit of competing brands (*unit pricing*), the basic ingredients in a product (*ingredient labeling*), the nutritional quality of foods (*nutritional labeling*), the freshness of products (*open dating*), and the true benefits of a product (*truth-in-advertising*).

The proposals related to additional *consumer protection* include the strengthening of consumers' position in cases of business fraud, the requiring of more safety to be designed into products, and the issuing of greater powers to existing government agencies.

The proposals relating to *quality-of-life* considerations include regulating the ingredients that go into certain products (detergents, gasoline) and packaging (soft-drink containers), reducing the level of advertising and promotional "noise," and creating consumer representation on company boards to introduce consumer welfare considerations in business decision making.

Implications for Marketing Management

A number of business firms at first balked at the consumer movement. They resented the power of strong consumer leaders to point an accusing finger at their products and cause their sales to plummet, as, for instance, when Ralph Nader called the Corvair automobile unsafe, when Robert Choate accused breakfast cereals of providing "empty calories," and when Herbert S. Denenberg published a list showing the wide variation in premiums different insurance companies were charging for the same protection. Businesses also resented consumer proposals that appeared to increase business costs more than they helped the consumer. They felt that most consumers would not pay attention to unit pricing or ingredient labeling and that the doctrines of advertising substantiation, corrective advertising, and counter advertising would stifle advertising creativity.[2] They felt that the consumer was better off than ever, that large companies were very careful in developing safe products and promoting them honestly, and that new consumer laws would only lead to new constraints and higher seller costs that would be passed on to the consumer in higher prices. Thus many companies opposed the consumer movement and lobbied vigorously against new legislation.

Many other companies took no stand and simply went about their business. A few companies undertook a series of bold initiatives to show their endorsement of consumer aims. Here are two examples:

> Giant Food, Inc., a leading supermarket chain in the Washington, D.C., area, took the initiative and introduced unit pricing, open dating, and nutritional labeling. They assigned home economists to their stores to help consumers buy and prepare food more intelligently. They invited Esther Peterson, formerly the president's advisor on consumer affairs, to join the board of directors and provide guidance on consumer-oriented retailing.
>
> Whirlpool Corporation adopted a number of measures to improve customer information and services. They installed a toll-free corporate phone number for consumers to use who were dissatisfied with their Whirlpool equipment or service. They improved the coverage of their product warranties and rewrote them in basic English.

In adopting a "we care" leadership role, these companies increased their market shares and profits substantially. Competitors were forced to emulate them, without, however, achieving the same impact enjoyed by the leader.

---

[2] *Advertising substantiation* is the requirement that advertisers should be able to prove any of their claims to the Federal Trade Commission. *Corrective advertising* is the ordering of an advertiser whose ad was deceptive or misleading to publicly announce this fact and make a correction. *Counter advertising* is the encouragement of parties of opposite persuasions to put out counter messages.

At the present time most companies have come around to accepting the new consumer rights in principle. They might oppose certain pieces of legislation on the ground that such measures are not the best way to solve a particular consumer problem. But they recognize the consumers' right to information and protection. Those who take a leadership role recognize that business's response to consumerism involves more than public relations and a few new products or services that meet neglected consumer needs. Consumerism involves a total commitment by top management, middle-management education and participation, new policy guidelines, marketing research, and company investment. Several companies have established consumer affairs departments to help formulate policies and deal with "consumerist" problems facing the company. All of these steps should improve customer satisfaction and company sales and profits.

Product managers are finding their role changing as a result of consumerism. They have to spend more time checking product ingredients and product features for safety, preparing safe packaging and informative labeling, substantiating their advertising claims, reviewing their sales promotion, developing clear and adequate product warranties, and so on. They have to check an increasing number of decisions with company lawyers. They have to develop a sixth sense about what the consumers really want and may feel about the product and various marketing practices.

On the other hand, consumerism is actually, in a profound way, the ultimate expression of the marketing concept. It will compel the product manager to consider things from the consumers' point of view. It will suggest needs and wants that may have been overlooked by all the firms in the industry. The resourceful manager will look for the positive opportunities implicit in the doctrine of consumerism rather than brood over its restraints.

ENVIRONMENTALISM

Whereas consumerists focus on whether the marketing system is efficiently serving consumer needs and wants, environmentalists focus on the impact of modern marketing on the surrounding environment and the costs that are borne in serving these consumer needs and wants. *Environmentalism is an organized movement of concerned citizens and government to protect and enhance man's living environment.* Environmentalists are concerned with strip mining, forest depletion, factory smoke, billboards, and litter; with the loss of recreational opportunity; and with the increase in health problems due to bad air, water, and chemically sprayed food.

Environmentalists are not against marketing and consumption; they simply want them to operate on more ecological principles. They do not think the goal of the marketing system should be the maximization of *consumption,* or *consumer choice,* or *consumer satisfaction* as such. The goal of the marketing system should be the maximization of *life quality.* And life quality means not only the quantity and quality of consumer goods and services but also the quality of the environment.

Environmentalists want environmental costs formally introduced into the decision calculus of producers and consumers. They favor the use of tax mechanisms and regulations to impose the true social costs of antienvironmental business activity and consumption. Requiring business to invest in antipollution devices, taxing nonreturnable bottles, banning high-phosphate detergents, and other measures are viewed as necessary to lead businesses and consumers to move in directions that are environmentally sound.

Environmentalists in some ways are more critical of marketing than are consumerists. They complain that there is too much wasteful packaging in the United States, whereas consumerists like the convenience offered by modern packaging. Environmentalists feel that mass advertising leads people to buy more than they need, whereas consumerists worry more about deception in advertising. Environmentalists dislike the proliferation of shopping centers, whereas consumerists welcome new stores and more competition.

Implications for Marketing Management

Environmentalism has hit certain industries hard. Steel companies and public utilities have been forced to invest billions of dollars in pollution-control equipment and costlier fuels. The auto industry has had to introduce expensive emission-control devices in cars. The soap industry has had to research and develop low-phosphate detergents. The packaging industry has been required to develop ways to reduce litter and increase biodegradability in its products. The gasoline industry has had to formulate new low-lead and no-lead gasolines. Naturally, these industries are inclined to resent environmental regulations, especially when those are formulated and imposed too rapidly to allow the companies to make the proper adjustments. These companies have had to absorb large costs and later pass them on to buyers.

Companies that did not experience direct environmental regulation found themselves paying more for their fuels and materials. Thus environmentalism touches everyone and reflects itself in higher costs. As a result, many business firms have attacked these regulations, using inflation, the energy crisis, and declining profits as their argument for a slower rate of implementation.

At the same time, many companies have taken positive steps to respond to the spirit and implications of environmentalism:

1. Companies have appointed plant-wide committees to review methods of production with an eye toward spotting wasteful procedures and identifying sources of polluton that critics or government agencies may point out.

2. Companies are introducing environmental criteria in their decision making on product ingredients, design, and packaging. Some companies direct their R&D toward finding ecologically superior products as the major selling point of the product. Sears developed and promoted a phosphate-free laundry detergent; Pepsi-Cola developed a one-way, plastic soft-drink bottle that is biodegradable in solid-waste treatment; and American Oil pioneered no-lead and low-lead gasolines.

3. Some companies moved directly into the rapidly expanding market for environmental products, such as pollution-control equipment and recycling plants.

4. Marketing managers are improving their research into buyer attitudes toward environmental issues to help guide their decisions.[3]

[3] For further reading on the implications of environmentalism for marketing, see George Fisk, "Criteria for a Theory of Responsible Consumption," *Journal of Marketing*, April 1973, pp. 24–31; Norman Kangun, "Environmental Problems and Marketing: Saint or Sinner?" in *Marketing Analysis for Societal Problems*, ed. J. N. Sheth and P. L. Wright (Urbana, Ill.: University of Illinois, 1974), pp. 250–70; and Karl E. Henion II, *Ecological Marketing* (Columbus, Ohio: Grid, 1976).

SHORTAGES

The gloomy predictions of the environmentalists that mankind would use up the earth's natural resources took on an air of frightening reality in 1973 when the world was plunged into alarming shortages of oil, various minerals, and even food. Business firms found themselves facing marked shortages of oil, chemicals, electricity, natural gas, cement, aluminum, copper, textiles, paper, glass, and furniture. Ironically, as late as 1972 most of these firms were spending the greater part of their time trying to dispose of surpluses.

One business columnist saw in shortages the possible end of marketing:

> There is little doubt that the energy crisis will force an alteration in the role of the marketing man. In some industries, it may alter him out of existence.... When demand exceeds supply marketing men can be replaced by order-takers. The art of selling is unnecessary. There also is no need for advertising, sales promotion, incentives, sweepstakes, trading stamps, free road maps or even windshield cleaning.[4]

What is the proper marketing response of companies to widening shortages? The two most common responses to shortages are both short-sighted.

The first is an *aggressive demarketing response.* The company rushes to buy supplies wherever it can get them, at any cost. It raises its own prices sharply, cuts product quality and new-product development, eliminates weaker customers, reduces customer services, allocates to the remaining customers according to ability to pay, cuts marketing budgets for research, advertising, and sales calls, and drops low-profit items. All of these steps have the positive effect of creating instant profits for the company. At the same time, the company is playing dangerously with its only asset, its customers. Their goodwill is sorely taxed, and when normal times return, many of them will have found other vendors and other ways to meet their needs.

The second is a *marketing-as-usual approach.* Here the company expects shortages to be temporary. The company continues to buy its supplies carefully. It maintains the same product line and sells to the same customers. It raises prices a little to keep up with cost increases. but not excessively. It maintains the same expenditures on advertising, sales force, and marketing research, with minor changes in its messages. These steps at best maintain the company's profit margins and customer goodwill. On the other hand, they smack too much of "Nero fiddling while Rome burns" and do not implement necessary steps to improve the company's position in the long run.

Implications for Marketing Management

A period of deep shortages calls for a third response, which can be characterized as *strategic remarketing.* It calls for the appointment of a top-management committee to review the company's basic policies on its *customer mix, product mix,* and *marketing mix,* and to make a set of recommendations. This committee studies the following questions:

[4] Joe Cappo, "Will Marketing Run Out of Energy?" *Chicago Daily News,* November 27, 1973, p. 34. The columnist makes the mistake of equating marketing with demand stimulation rather than demand management.

1. Which markets will be the most profitable in the coming years?
2. Which customers in these markets will be the best ones to serve?
3. What principles should be used to allocate scarce supplies to existing customers?
4. How many new customers can be cultivated without diluting the interest of present customers in receiving adequate supplies?
5. What products might the company drop from its line, and what products should the company try to add to its line?
6. How much price increase can the company take and justify to its customers?
7. What should the company be communicating to its customers, and what will this require in the way of an advertising and public relations budget?
8. How many sales representatives does the company need, and what kind of retraining should they receive?
9. What can be done to bring down costs to customers and assist them in solving their problems?

Although the answers to these questions will vary from company to company, the guiding principle should be one of customer orientation. The major asset that a firm has in the long run is its loyal customers. Loyal customers are not created by serving them royally during good times and charging what the traffic will bear during bad times. Loyal customers are created by companies that are considerate of their customers at all times. During a shortage period, the market-oriented company strives to help its customers solve their problems.

This philosophy can be translated into specific marketing tasks and activities:

1. *Sales representatives* will find their selling role diminished but their other roles increased: customer counseling, order expediting, and intelligence gathering. Even their *selling role* has not entirely vanished because they must turn some attention to selling slower-moving company products that are in adequate supply.
2. *Advertising* should probably be reduced somewhat but by no means abandoned. It can be redirected to building up demand for company products that are in oversupply: to create buying interest in new products and product modifications; to educate buyers in more economical uses of the scarce product; and to keep customers informed of steps the company is taking to solve the shortages.
3. *Marketing research* should be maintained at a level that permits the monitoring of competitive market changes and interpretation of evolving buyer practices and needs.
4. *Product development* should be alert to new-product opportunities created by the shortage. To a resourceful firm, a shortage means a need for substitute products. A shortage of gasoline expands the market for bikes and mass transportation; a shortage of heating oil expands the market for sweaters, fireplaces, and electric blankets.
5. *Purchasing* must be considerably strengthened as a company function. It must do a better job of finding alternative sources of supply and arranging long-term contracts. Purchasing departments need to utilize marketing principles to "sell" the company's neediness to the vendor's sales representatives. Some companies have transferred some sales representatives into the purchasing department to improve their effectiveness in attracting suppliers and supplies.[5]

[5] For additional steps, see the author's "Marketing during Periods of Shortage," *Journal of Marketing*, July 1974, pp. 20–29.

INFLATION

Ever since the Middle East war of 1973, with the attendant oil crisis, the nations of the world have experienced persistent inflation, sometimes at a double-digit rate and other times at a high single-digit rate. Several forces make it likely that inflation will continue to be a major economic and social problem for years to come. They include:

Raw-material-exporting countries are engaging in more price fixing of oil, coffee, cocoa, and various minerals and metals.

The rate of consumption of certain goods, such as energy, paper, and aluminum, is racing ahead of the level of supply.

Wage settlements are exceeding productivity gains in most developed countries. Industrial discipline is eroding in many countries. The trend toward a shorter workweek contributes to inflation.

Affluent economies with a growing services sector are subject to more inflationary pressure because of the greater difficulty in achieving productivity gains in service industries.

Increased government legislation and regulations covering antipollution investment, product liability, consumerism, and environmentalism raise the costs of doing business and are passed on to consumers in the form of higher prices.

The lengthening of the educational and life span tends to increase the proportion of nonproductive workers in an economy.

Implications for Marketing Management

High inflation poses a number of challenges to marketing management that have no easy answers. The company should establish a high-level *profit protection committee* to forecast the expected rate and duration of inflation, how their customers are responding to inflation, and the government's likely program. Then the company should consider the following possible moves:

1. An effort should be made to hold down purchase costs through such measures as considering new suppliers and searching for substitute ingredients.

2. Manufacturing processes should be reexamined for opportunities to increase efficiency.

3. The company should reexamine customer-account profitability and increase prices or reduce service to the smaller accounts.

4. The company should move more aggressively into those markets that are better able to absorb higher prices.

5. The company should place greater emphasis on its higher marginal products. It should also examine opportunities for improving profit margins on individual products through reducing packaging costs, ingredient costs, and other costs.

6. The company should consider introducing more economical versions of products for customers who need to save money.

7. Price increases should be sufficient but not so high as to drive away customers. The company should consider different ways of passing on price increases and explaining them to customers.

8. Advertising messages might incorporate price appeals, such as "more value for your money" or "buy now and save."

9. Companies should consider using price deals more aggressively, since customers are more responsive to them during high inflation.

10. The sales force should be trained to be effective in explaining price increases to customers and in helping customers find ways to economize.

11. The company should put more emphasis on lower-cost distribution channels, such as mass distributors and discount operations, since these will be increasingly favored by customers.

RECESSION

American consumers of the 1950s and 1960s believed in the American dream: continuous rising real income, a home in the suburbs, two cars, and money to travel. In the early 1970s this dream was shaken. American consumers confronted shortages, then inflation, and then recession. Their real incomes deteriorated.

Consumers exposed to income deterioration go through a number of stages in adjusting to the new economic realities:

1. At first they maintain their old spending patterns, refusing to take their real-income loss seriously.

2. As things get worse, they start to cut certain items from their budget and search for less expensive goods.

3. At a further point, they get angry and blame certain forces for the economic downturn: big business, unions, government.

4. Still later they start despairing because the situation continues to worsen, and no remedies seem to work.

5. Finally, consumers begin to take stock of their new situation and adopt consumer values matched to their economic realities.

Not all consumers pass through all these stages, but many of them make several adjustments of great importance to sellers. The dominant goal of consumers is to find ways to economize. That takes a number of forms:

1. Increased preference for *store brands* over manufacturer brands because of their lower prices, similar quality, and prominent display

2. Increased *multiple shopping* and *discount store patronage* to find lower prices

3. Increased *trading down* toward substitute products. Consumers go from steak to chicken to tuna fish to rice and beans

4. Increased *do-it-yourself* in the area of home repair services, clothing, and food production

5. Increased patronage of *secondhand markets* (used-clothing stores, flea markets, garage sales).

6. Increased interest in *functional product features* and *durability* and less in product aesthetics and convenience

7. Increased elimination of *impulse buying* and *nonnecessities*[6]

These changes result in the emergence of three distinct consumer life-style

---

[6] Industrial buyers go through similar changes. Their steps include (1) search for additional suppliers, (2) search for better terms, (3) movement toward self-production, (4) search for cheaper materials, and (5) product simplification. Industrial sellers must take these evolving customer needs into account in formulating their marketing program.

groups. The majority group, the *intense consumers*, still retain high consumption values. They want to spend freely, buy the latest products, and not worry about waste. The second group, the *sensible consumers*, concentrate on functional product values and economy. They buy small cars, practical clothes, simple appliances. The third and smallest group, the *austere consumers*, turn against material values and start "deconsuming." They may give up their cars, reduce the number of their appliances, wear simple clothes, make their own furniture, grow some of their own food, and eat less.

Implications for Marketing Management

Many of these consumer changes call for new marketing thinking. Traditional marketing is based on "more is better." At the same time, there is a growing market for goods that are less extravagant and conspicuous and more durable and economical. This market segment constitutes a growing market opportunity for manufacturers and retailers. It calls for a different emphasis in product design, distribution, pricing, and marketing communication. Companies may bemoan the decline of the old values, which were based on insatiable demand and never-ending product elaboration and replacement. But the alert marketer knows that there is always work to do as long as there are people, and it is only a question of finding out and offering what they need and want.[7]

GOVERNMENT REGULATIONS

All of the previous developments—consumerism, environmentalism, shortages, inflation, and recession—have increased the role of government in society. Businesses face an increasing number of government regulations affecting marketing practices, employee relations, manufacturing decisions, and a host of other things. Often laws of bewildering complexity are passed—such as OSHA legislation—that few people, including the lawyers, understand. This climate, combined with a growing propensity for people and business firms to sue other business firms for a variety of practices, is creating a highly litigious society. Managers are cautioned by their company not to make major decisions without clearing them with the company's lawyers.

Marketing executives, in particular, have to be keenly aware of the law as it affects marketing decisions in the areas of competitive relations, products, price, promotion, and channels of distribution. The major issues are reviewed here.

Competitive-Relations Decisions

The firm must be careful in the use of different competitive instruments to expand its market size or share. This includes attempts to grow through acquisition or merger, to develop cooperative relations with competitors, or to adopt certain hard tactics against competitors.

Expansion   In reviewing acquisitions, the law holds it is a question not of the good or bad intentions of the acquiring firm but only of the effects of the acquisition on competition. The courts have rejected such defenses as competitive intent, growth needs, declining position of acquiring company, lack of com-

---

[7] For further discussion of marketing under different economic climates, see Avraham Shama, "Management and Consumers in an Era of Stagflation," *Journal of Marketing,* July 1978, pp. 43–52.

petition, rapid expansion of an industry, ease of entry, and so forth. If there is a reasonable probability that the acquisition will substantially lessen competition "in any line of commerce in any section of the country," then the acquisition may be prevented by the government. The case hinges on how the relevant market is defined and how the acquisition will affect competition in this market.

Cooperative relations   The law also bears down hard on any signs of collusive relations between presumably competing companies. Such joint actions as price fixing, splitting up markets, excluding new competitors, agreeing on various customers, and so forth, would constitute a conspiracy. Price agreements are held to be illegal per se; that is, no defenses are acceptable. This applies to obvious violations, such as rigged bids or the use of common basing points in quoting price, and even such apparently minor actions as exchanging price lists for information purposes, or parallel pricing action.

Competitive tactics   The law will condemn a firm that uses hard or predatory tactics against its competitors. This includes cutting off a competitor's source of supply, disparaging a competitor's products or ability, or threatening or using actual intimidation.

Product Decisions   Marketing management must take cognizance of the law in making decisions respecting product additions and deletions, product design, product quality, and labeling.

Product additions and deletions   The firm's product mix changes through the process of adding new products and dropping old ones. Decisions to add products, particularly through acquisitions, may be prevented under the Antimerger Act if the effect threatens to lessen competition. Decisions to drop old products must be made with an awareness that the firm has legal obligations, written or implied, to its suppliers, dealers, and customers who have a stake in the discontinued product.

Product design   The firm must design its new product in the context of the complicated U.S. patent laws. The patent laws are both a constraint and an opportunity for any firm. They are a constraint in the sense that a firm is prevented from designing a product that is "illegally similar" to another company's established product. This may be quite difficult to determine, the definition of "similar" resting on whether consumers consider the design or outward appearance to be the same. After a patent is granted, the patent laws represent an opportunity, because the firm's new product is protected against "illegally similar" products for three and a half, seven, or fourteen years, depending on the patentable period. The firm may license manufacturing rights to others in return for a royalty but is under no legal compulsion to do so.

Product quality, safety, and labeling   Manufacturers of foods, drugs, cosmetics, and certain fibers must comply with specific laws in establishing product quality, safety, and labeling. The Federal Food, Drug, and Cosmetic Act was passed to protect consumers from unsafe and adulterated food, drugs, and cosmetics. Various acts provide for the inspection of sanitary conditions in the meat and poultry processing industries. Safety legislation has been passed to regulate fabrics, chemical substances, automobiles, toys, and drugs and poisons. In 1972, the Consumer Product Safety Act was passed, establishing a Consumer Product Safety Commission. As for labels, they must identify the manufacturer or distributor and the package contents and quality, and contain warnings if the product is dangerous or habit-forming.

Price Decisions

Pricing is one of the major marketing-decision areas where a knowledge of the law is essential. Management must avoid price fixing (except for resale price maintenance), price discrimination, charging less than the minimum legal price, raising prices unduly, or advertising deceptive prices.

Price fixing Price-fixing agreements among competitors, called horizontal price fixing, are prosecutable. The courts have even ruled that a company cannot fix the prices charged by its subsidiaries, where they may be in competition. The only exceptions occur where the price agreements are carried out under the supervision of a government agency, as is the case in many local milk industry agreements, in the regulated transportation industries, and in fruit and vegetable cooperatives.

Price discrimination Under the Robinson-Patman Act, management must be careful in developing its price differentials for different classes of customers and conditions of sale (as well as any differentials in advertising allowances, facilities, and services). Price differentials are justified to some extent where the products are not of like grade and quality, particularly in the buyers' minds. Otherwise, these differentials must be based on cost differences. Usually it is easiest to justify discounts based on the size of orders because of the obvious savings in the cost of manufacturing, selling, or delivering of larger orders. Discounts based on the amount purchased over a specified period, while not specifically outlawed, are harder to justify under the cost-savings argument. Marketing management may also employ price differentials where the purpose is to "meet competition" in "good faith," providing the firm is trying to meet competitors at its own level of competition and that the price discrimination is temporary, localized, and defensive rather than offensive.

Minimum prices Wholesalers and retailers face laws in over half the states requiring a minimum percentage markup over their cost of merchandise plus transportation. Called Unfair Trade Practices Acts, they are designed to protect smaller merchants from larger merchants who might otherwise sell certain items at or below cost for a while to attract customers.

Price increases In contrast to price floors, there is normally no legislation that places price ceilings on sellers' goods, except in times of price control. The company is generally free to increase the price of its goods to any level, the major hurdle being economic. The major exception occurs in the case of public-regulated utilities. Since they have monopoly power in their respective areas, their price schedules are regulated and approved in the public's interest. The executive branch of the government has used its influence from time to time to discourage major-industry price increases because of inflationary concerns.

Deceptive pricing   Deceptive pricing is a more common problem in the sale of consumer goods than business goods, because consumers typically possess less information and buying acumen. In 1958, the Automobile Information Disclosure Act was passed, requiring auto manufacturers to affix on the windshield of each new automobile a statement giving the manufacturer's suggested retail price, the prices of optional equipment, and the dealer's transportation charges. In the same year, the FTC issued its *Guides Against Deceptive Pricing,* admonishing sellers not to claim a price reduction unless it is a saving from the usual retail price, not to advertise "factory" or "wholesale" prices unless they are genuine, not to advertise comparable-value prices on imperfect goods, and so forth.

Promotion Decisions

The company must develop its promotion program in a way that does not invite charges of deception or of discrimination. Advertising is more vulnerable to legal action than personal selling because it leaves a clearer record of itself. Nevertheless, actions have been brought against sales representatives when the evidence indicated conscious deception of their customers.

False and misleading advertising   Marketing executives have to worry about false advertising and misleading advertising. They can avoid the former by refraining from deliberate misrepresentation. Misleading rather than false advertising is the major headache for sellers. The FTC can issue a temporary restraining order against any advertisement that seems to have the capacity to deceive, even though no one may be deceived. The problem is one of distinguishing between puffery in advertising, which is normal, and distortion.

Bait advertising   Bait advertising, where the seller attracts buyers' interest on false pretenses, comes under FTC surveillance. The seller offers or advertises an exceptionally good buy but then finds some excuse for not selling the advertised item and pushes something else instead. Tactics include refusing to sell the product, disparaging its features, demonstrating a defective one, or imposing unreasonable delivery dates or service terms.

Promotional allowances and services   In planning its promotional program, the company must be sure to make promotional allowances and services available to all customers on proportionately equal terms. However, it is difficult to establish what constitutes proportionately equal terms where small and large customers are involved.

Channel Decisions

By and large, manufacturers are free under the law to develop whatever channel arrangements suit them. In fact, much of the force of the law affecting channels is to make sure they are not foreclosed from using channels as the result of the exclusionary tactics of others. But this places them under obligation to proceed cautiously in their own possible use of exclusionary tactics. Most of the law is concerned with the mutual rights and duties of the manufacturer and channel members once they have formed a relationship.

Exclusive dealing   Many manufacturers and wholesalers like to develop exclusive channels for their products. The policy is called *exclusive distribution* when the seller enfranchises only certain outlets to carry its products. It is called *exclusive dealing* when the seller requires these outlets to agree to handle only its products, or conversely, not to handle competitors' products. Both parties tend to draw benefits from exclusive dealing, the seller enjoying a more dependable and enthusiastic set of outlets without having to invest capital in them, and the distributors gaining a steady source of supply and seller support. However, the result of exclusive dealing is that other manufacturers are excluded from selling to these dealers. This has brought exclusive-dealing contracts under the purview of the Clayton Act, although such contracts are not made illegal per se. They are illegal only if they tend to lessen competition substantially or create a monopoly.

Exclusive territorial distributorships Exclusive dealing often includes territorial agreements as well as exclusive-source agreements. The seller may agree not to sell to other distributors in the area, and/or the buyer may agree to confine sales to its own territory. The first practice is fairly normal under franchise systems, being regarded as a way to promote increased dealer enthusiasm and dealer investment in the area. The seller is under no legal compulsion to establish more outlets than it wishes. The second practice, where the manufacturer tries to restrain each dealer to sell only in its own territory, has become a major legal issue. This comes close to dividing up the market, even though in this case it is the market for a brand (vertical market division) rather than a product (horizontal market division).

Tying agreements Manufacturers with a brand in strong demand occasionally sell it to dealers on condition they take some or all of the rest of the line. In the latter case, this practice is called *full-line forcing*. Such tying arrangements are not illegal per se, but they do run afoul of the Clayton Act if they tend to lessen competition substantially. Buyers are prevented from exercising their free choice among competing suppliers of these other goods.

Dealers' rights Sellers are largely free to select their dealers, but their right to terminate dealerships is somewhat qualified. In general, sellers can drop dealers "for cause." But they cannot drop dealers, for example, if the latter refuse to cooperate in a dubious legal arrangement, such as exclusive-dealing or tying arrangements.

MARKETING ETHICS

The law defines what the company cannot do. This does not mean that everything else, because it is legal, is right. Here top management enters as an additional force in developing policies that define proper marketing conduct. Policies are "broad, fixed guidelines that everyone in the organization must adhere to, and that are not subject to exception."[8] They cover distributor relations, advertising standards, customer service, pricing, product development, and ethical standards.

There is little defense for the failure of a company's top management to develop formal policies. Their executives will inevitably face difficult moral di-

[8] Earl L. Bailey, *Formulating the Company's Marketing Policies: A Survey*, Experiences in Marketing Management, No. 19 (New York: Conference Board, 1968), p. 3.

lemmas. Even if they have the finest consciences, the question of the best thing to do is often unclear. Since not all of their executives will in fact have the finest moral sensitivity, the company is taking even more risk that its reputation may be compromised by improper executive behavior.

Even the best set of guidelines cannot anticipate or resolve all the ethically difficult situations that the marketer will face. Consider Howard Bowen's classic question about the responsibilities of marketers:

> Should he conduct selling in ways that intrude on the privacy of people, for example, by door-to-door selling? . . . Should he use methods involving ballyhoo, chances, prizes, hawking, and other tactics which are at least of doubtful good taste? Should he employ "high pressure" tactics in persuading people to buy? Should he try to hasten the obsolescence of goods by bringing out an endless succession of new models and new styles? Should he appeal to and attempt to strengthen the motives of materialism, invidious consumption, and "keeping up with the Joneses"? [9]

Table 27–1 lists fourteen ethically difficult situations that marketers could well face during their careers. If marketers decide in favor of the immediate sales-producing actions in all fourteen cases, their marketing behavior might well be described as immoral or amoral. On the other hand, if they refuse to go along with *any* of the actions, they might be ineffective as marketing managers and unhappy because of the constant moral tension. Obviously managers need a set of principles that will help them determine the moral gravity of each situation and how far they can go in good conscience.

TABLE 27–1
Some Morally Difficult Situations in Marketing

1. You work for a cigarette company and up to now have not been convinced that cigarettes cause cancer. A recent report has come across your desk that clearly establishes the connection between cigarette smoking and cancer. What would you do?

2. Your R&D department has modernized one of your products. It is not really "new and improved," but you know that putting this statement on the package and in the advertising will increase sales. What would you do?

3. You have been asked to add a stripped-down model to the low end of your line that could be advertised to attract customers. The product won't be very good, but the sales representatives could be depended upon to persuade buyers to buy the higher-priced units. You are asked to give the green light for developing this stripped-down version. What would you do?

4. You are interviewing a former product manager who just left a competitor's company. You are thinking of hiring him. He would be more than happy to tell you all the competitor's plans for the coming year. What would you do?

5. One of your dealers in an important territory has had family troubles recently and is not producing the sales he used to. He was one of the company's top producers in the past. It is not clear how long it will take before his family trouble

---

[9] Howard R. Bowen, *Social Responsibilities of the Businessman* (New York: Harper & Row, 1953), p. 215.

straightens out. In the meantime, many sales are being lost. There is a legal way to terminate the dealer's franchise and replace him. What would you do?

6. You have a chance to win a big account that will mean a lot to you and your company. The purchasing agent hinted that he would be influenced by a "gift." Your assistant recommends sending a fine color television set to his home. What would you do?

7. You have heard that a competitor has a new product feature that will make a big difference in sales. He will have a hospitality suite at the annual trade show and unveil this feature at a party thrown for his dealers. You can easily send a snooper to this meeting to learn what the new feature is. What would you do?

8. You are eager to win a big contract, and during sales negotiations you learn that the buyer is looking for a better job. You have no intention of hiring him, but if you hinted that you might, he would probably give you the order. What would you do?

9. You have to make a choice between three ad campaigns outlined by your agency for your new product. The first (A) is a soft-sell, honest informational campaign. The second (B) uses sex-loaded emotional appeals and exaggerates the product's benefits. The third (C) involves a noisy, irritating commercial that is sure to gain audience attention. Preliminary tests show that the commercials are effective in the following order: C, B, and A. What would you do?

10. You are a marketing vice president working for a beer company, and you have learned that a particularly lucrative state is planning to raise the minimum legal drinking age from 18 to 21. You have been asked to join other breweries in lobbying against this bill and to make contributions. What would you do?

11. You want to interview a sample of customers about their reactions to a competitive product. It has been suggested that you invent an innocuous name like the Marketing Research Institute and interview people. What would you do?

12. You produce an antidandruff shampoo that is effective with one application. Your assistant says that the product would turn over faster if the instructions on the label recommended two applications. What would you do?

13. You are interviewing a capable woman applicant for a job as sales representative. She is better qualified than the men just interviewed. At the same time, you suspect that some of your current salesmen will react negatively to her hiring, and you also know that some important customers may be ruffled. What would you do?

14. You are a sales manager in an encyclopedia company. A common way for encyclopedia representatives to get into homes is to pretend they are taking a survey. After they finish the survey, they switch to their sales pitch. This technique seems to be very effective and is used by most of your competitors. What would you do?

All ethical philosophies deal with one or more of three characteristics of the *act*. They judge either the act itself (moral idealism), the actor's motives (intuitionism), or the act's consequences (utilitarianism).

Moral idealism is the most rigid in that it postulates certain acts to be bad under all (or most) circumstances. Moral idealism gives marketing managers the most definitive answers to most of the questions raised in Table 27–1. They would refuse to hear privy information or spy on competitors, deceive customers, and so on. By refusing to let the ends justify the means, they would derive a greater feeling of right conduct.

Intuitionism is less rigid, leaving it up to the individual managers to sense the moral gravity of the situation. If managers feel their motives are good, that they are not out to hurt anyone, they are taking an intuitive approach to these morally difficult situations.

Utilitarianism is the most deliberative of the three systems, seeking to establish the moral locus not in the act or the motives but in the consequences. If the consequences of the act to the individual and society, both the good ones and bad ones, represent a net increase in society's happiness, the act is right.

Ultimately each executive must choose and work out a philosophy of proper behavior. Every moral system is predicated on some conception of the good life and the relation of one's welfare to that of others. Once the executive works out a clear philosophy and set of principles, they will help cut through the many knotty questions that marketing and other human activities pose.

Truly, marketing executives of the 1980s will find their job full of challenges. They will face abundant marketing opportunities opened up by technological advances in solar energy, home computers and robots, cable television, modern medicine, and new forms of transportation, recreation, and communication. At the same time, forces in the socioeconomic environment will increase the constraints under which marketing can be carried out. Those companies that are able to pioneer new values and practice societally responsible marketing will have a world to conquer.

SUMMARY

Marketing is an evolving discipline that must develop new answers as new problems arise. The marketing principles of the 1950s and 1960s are being challenged by new factors in the marketing environment—consumerism, environmentalism, shortages, inflation, recession, government regulation, and marketing ethics. *Consumerism* calls for a strengthening of consumers' rights and power in relation to sellers. Resourceful marketers will recognize it as an opportunity to serve consumers better through providing more information, education, and protection. *Environmentalism* calls for minimizing the harm done by marketing practices to the environment and quality of life. It calls for intervening in consumer wants when their satisfaction would create too much environmental cost. *Shortages* have made real the possibility of running out of resources in the absence of their wise use. Marketers must avoid responding to shortages with either aggressive demarketing or marketing-as-usual. Shortages call for strategic reprogramming of the customer mix, product mix, and marketing mix. *Inflation* raises the company's costs and the company has to determine how much to pass on to the buyer. Resourceful marketers will not simply pass on higher costs but will seek ways to offset them to hold customer costs down. *Recession* and the preceding developments lead to changing consumer life style, characterized by more sensible or austere consumption. Some firms recognize a marketing opportunity to serve the needs of the growing segment of sensible consumers. *Government regulation* continues to grow without any sign of abatement. This requires marketers to check many of their decisions on competitive relations, products, pricing, promotion, and distribution with the company's legal department. Finally, *marketing ethics* is a major concern in that company employees often have to choose between what is in their immediate self-interest, their long-run self-interest, and the interest of society as a whole. Companies have to formulate clear policies to guide the marketing decision making of their employees in socially responsible directions.

1. Consumerists have suggested that public schools should train students in how to view television commercials critically. Students should be taught to recognize objectively what the advertising is trying to do. As a business person, would you support this proposal? Why or why not?

2. The following products satisfy individual wants but at the same time have certain undesirable societal consequences: (a) detergents, (b) automobiles, (c) disposable paper diapers. Discuss what the manufacturers can or ought to do about each product.

3. Distinguish four alternative advertising strategies by an oil company in the event of another major fuel shortage.

4. Two companies, A and B, account for virtually 100 percent of the sales in a certain industry. Company A is the high-price, high-quality company and company B is the low-price, low-quality company. During the period of rising real incomes, company A enjoyed a 60 percent market share and company B had the rest. In the subsequent period of high inflation and recession, several buyers switched to company B because of their need to economize. What are some of the strategies available to company A to avoid losing further market share?

5. Suppose your company has sold 40,000 sets of a particular television set model. A company engineer has just discovered that a switch in the set will not stand up under constant use. There is a very small chance that the set could catch fire. You are the marketing vice-president. What would you do?

6. A group called Action for Children's Television is urging the following guidelines for children's television programs: (a) that there be no commercials on children's programs. (b) that hosts on children's shows should not sell. (c) that stations provide 14 hours a week of programs for children of different age groups. Suppose you are a marketing executive in a toy company. Would you lobby against guidelines?

Indices

Company Index

A. C. Nielson Company, 186, 527, 608–09
A&P, 184, 367, 371
Abbott Laboratories, 105
Alberto-Culver, 312, 524
Allis-Chalmers, 415
American Airlines, 36
American Bakeries, 421
American Bakers' Assoc., 646
American Cyanamid, 657
American Hospital Supply, 243, 550 597
American Motors, 171
American Oil, 696
American Optical, 354
American Telephone and Telegraph, 399–400, 569, 597
Anheuser-Busch, 283, 373, 523
Apeco, 365
Arco, 49
Armour, 371
Arthur D. Little, Inc., 646
Avis, 275, 281, 283, 426, 482
Avon, 6, 205, 413, 424, 429, 647

Bank of America, 12
Bard College, 684
Baskin's, 5
Bayer, 380
Beatrice Food, 310
Beecham Group, 674
Bell & Howell, 317, 410
Bell Laboratories, 114, 316
Bic, 275, 405
Bissell, 331, 354
Blatz, 373
Bobbie Brooks, 209
Boeing, 196, 274
Book-of-the-Month Club, 434
Booz, Allen & Hamilton, 312
Borden, 116, 186
Boston Consulting Group, 76, 80, 92, 356
Boston Globe, 427
Bristol-Myers, 282, 301, 405
Burger Chef, 92
Burger King, 31, 33, 426
Burroughs, 285, 464

Campbell's, 279, 367, 370, 425, 664, 674
Candy-of-the-Month, 434
Caterpillar, 6, 39–40, 273, 277–79, 288, 361, 596, 647, 668
Celanese, 242
Chase National Bank, 597
Chevron, 49

Chrysler, 171, 275
Citgo, 49
Citibank, 597–98
Clark Equipment, 415
Coca-Cola, 37, 207–08, 273, 279, 283–84, 672, 688
Colgate, 275, 281, 337, 347, 370, 668, 672
Conn Organ Company, 434
Continental Bank of Chicago, 12
Coors, 200, 288
Crown Cork & Seal, 285
Curtis Publishing Company, 7

Daniel J. Edelman, Inc., 538
Daniel Starch, 609
Data General, 361
Delta Airlines, 5
Digital Equipment, 361
Douglas, 146
Dow Chemical, 8, 315
Drake University, 685
DuPont, 114, 192, 201, 274–75, 311, 316, 332, 375, 387, 392, 523, 590, 657

Eastern Airlines, 508
Eastman Kodak, 6, 176, 203, 273, 275, 279, 282, 319, 333, 365, 405, 668
Elgin National Watch Company, 28–29
Endicott-Johnson, 319
Evanston Hospital, 8, 686
Exxon, 49

Falstaff, 373
Food Fair, 273
Ford, 31, 53, 92, 171, 200–01, 276, 281, 311, 363–64, 426, 429, 439
Fuji Film, 275, 282, 405
Fuller Brush, 424

Gallup-Robinson, 609
General Electric, 3, 6, 8, 76, 78–82, 102, 114, 177, 354, 356–57, 370, 425, 428, 458, 551, 645, 647
General Foods, 92, 120, 315, 333, 497, 585, 598, 657
General Mills, 13, 120, 311, 315, 604
General Motors, 8, 68, 81–82, 171, 208, 273–74, 276–77, 279, 286, 288, 319, 364, 371–72, 374, 380, 390, 397, 417, 429, 497, 597
Genesco, Inc., 370
Gerber, 104, 209, 671
Giant Food, 694
Gillette, 6, 273, 275, 279, 281, 405, 555, 668

Girl Scouts of America, 66, 684
Golden Crown Citrus Corp., 116
Gould, 313
Gulf, 49

Hallmark, 587
Hamm's, 373–74
Hanes, 333
Harley-Davidson, 632
Harris Bank of Chicago, 12
Harvard University, 66
Heinz, 46–47, 251, 254–55, 268, 282, 367, 370, 464, 590, 668, 675
Hendry, 197
Henkle, 244
Hershey Foods, 525
Hertz, 275, 277, 283, 426, 507
Heublein, 334, 405
Hewlett-Packard, 286, 304, 362–63
Hills Brothers, 507
Hilton, 672
Hippopotamus Food Stores, 421
Holiday Inn, 425, 429
Honda, 150, 284
Honeywell, 364
Howard Johnson, 426, 436
Hudson Institute, 102
Hunt Foods & Industries, 282, 354

IBM, 3, 5–6, 97, 273, 277, 279, 283, 319, 353, 361, 367, 413, 555, 596, 647, 674
Illinois Central Railroad, 587
Institute for the Future, 102
International Harvester, 7, 208, 278, 348, 362, 367, 668
Italian Swiss Colony, 508

J. C. Penney, 428
J. I. Case, 278
Jewel Food, 366
John Deere, 278, 361
John Smythe, 428
Johnson & Johnson, 105, 209, 274, 282, 315, 657

Kellogg, 120, 279, 367, 370
Kenmore, 288
Kentucky Fried Chicken, 5–6, 33, 81
K-Mart, 497
Kraftco, 92, 425, 427, 493

Leo Burnett, 507, 539
Lever Brothers, 530
Levi's, 332
Litton Industries, 310
Lockheed, 232

712

Name Index

Subject Index

721

ENCYCLOPEDIA OF
WORLD WRITERS
19TH AND 20TH CENTURIES

ENCYCLOPEDIA OF
WORLD WRITERS
19TH AND 20TH CENTURIES

Dr. Marie Josephine Diamond

GENERAL EDITOR
Department of Comparative English
Rutgers University

Dr. Maria DiBattista

ADVISER
Department of English
Princeton University

Julian Wolfreys

ADVISER
Department of English
University of Florida

Facts On File, Inc.

Encyclopedia of World Writers, 19th and 20th Centuries

Copyright © 2003 by BOOK BUILDERS LLC

Facts On File, Inc.
132 West 31st Street
New York NY 10001

Library of Congress Cataloging-in-Publication Data

Encyclopedia of world writers, 19th and 20th centuries [written and developed by Book Builders] ; Marie Josephine Diamond, general editor ; Maria DiBattista, Julian Wolfreys, advisers.
    p. cm.
  Includes bibliographical references and index.
  ISBN 0-8160-4675-1
    1. Authors—20th century—Bio-bibliography—Dictionaries. 2. Authors—19th century—Bio-bibliography—Dictionaries. I. Title: Encyclopedia of nineteenth and twentieth century world writers. II. Diamond, Marie Josephine. III. Book Builders LLC.

PN451.E53 2003
809'.04—dc21
[B]   2002192846

Text design by Rachel L. Berlin
Cover design by Cathy Rincon
Cover illustration by Smart Graphics

Printed in the United States of America

VB FOF 10 9 8 7 6 5 4 3 2 1

This book is printed on acid-free paper.

CONTENTS

PREFACE

The *Encyclopedia of World Writers, 19th and 20th Centuries* is an engaging survey of the changing map of world literature during the past 200 years, covering the world outside Great Britain, Ireland, and the United States. (British writers are covered in the *Encyclopedia of British Writers, 19th Century* and *20th Century,* Facts On File, 2003.) Our survey begins at the turn of the 19th century, a time of great change in Europe, catalyzed by the French Revolution of 1789 and the expansion of colonialism.

Literature in the 19th century, especially the dissemination of the novel, reflects the profound social, economic, and political changes that were taking place throughout Europe. By the end of the century, when colonialism had changed the map of the world through occupation and trade, Western literary movements and forms had deeply affected the ancient and traditional literatures of Asia and the Middle East and the post-Conquest literatures of South America and had marginalized the oral traditions of African and indigenous peoples.

The entries of the 19th century include the well-known European figures who have dominated the Western canon; lesser-known European writers who, for many reasons, have been rediscovered; and Asian, Latin American, and African writers or storytellers celebrated in their own cultures but often unfamiliar to the American reader. Entries include descriptions of major European literary movements, such as ROMANTICISM, REALISM, and SYMBOLISM, and their deployment and transformation, especially toward the end of the century, in the very different cultural contexts of Asia, the Middle East, and Latin America. These entries also show both the continuation and transformation of traditional genres and the growing importance of the novel in the context of modernization.

The entries of the 20th century include avant-garde writers, modernists, social realists, and writers responding to the traumas of world wars. They reflect the growing international importance and recognition of writers from Asia, the Middle East, Africa, and the Caribbean and of women writers who have made their voices heard in the wake of POSTCOLONIALISM and FEMINISM. They also include writers from nations that have asserted their independence since the collapse of the Soviet Union and writers responding in various ways to economic and cultural globalization and the revolution in electronic communications. Finally, in entries such as those on the ABORIGINAL MOVEMENT of Australia and the DALIT LITERATURE of India, they include writers from cultures in the process of reemergence or redefinition.

Directed to young scholars in high school and colleges, the entries encourage students to investigate further writers who, for the most part, have lived lives of passionate engagement with their craft and with the compelling, often disturbing historical events of their time. They include biographical information, descriptions of major works, cross-referencing, and suggestions for further reading and research. Most of the works mentioned have been translated into English. Where practical, titles are also provided in the original language. (Given the vast number of languages and alphabets involved, this is not always feasible or useful.) Definitions of traditions and movements from a wide variety of literatures make it possible for the American student to situate writers within the context of their literary cultures. A general bibliography suggests wider vistas for exploration.

This encyclopedia opens up worlds. It reveals how literature has been and continues to be not only a source of aesthetic pleasure and self-knowledge but also a means of responding to tyranny and injustice, to the alienation or suppression of identity, and to the loss of marginalized or indigenous cultures. For many writers in the last century, literature has been more than a quest for pleasure, success, or escape from the everyday. It has often been a matter of life and death.

We hope that for young researchers coming of age in the 21st century, a time of dramatic change on an international scale, the encyclopedia will be many things: an introduction to literary traditions from a wide diversity of cultures, an introduction to aesthetic experience and exploration in the global context, and an introduction to the extraordinary writers who have lived through and responded in their works to the social and political challenges of the past two centuries.

INTRODUCTION

World literature is as diverse as it is vast. From the turn of the 19th century to the present, different cultures and national literatures have followed unique and specific forms of development and change. However, it is possible to discern some major trends and patterns to suggest a way for American readers in particular to orient themselves among the more than 500 writers, literatures, and literary movements presented here.

The mapping of the world has undergone many transformations since the beginning of the 19th century, and it continues to be revised at an accelerated rate. This volume begins with literatures at the turn of the 19th century, a time of great change. The French Revolution of 1789 marked a watershed in Europe. Subsequently, many countries of the world were affected by both the ideals of the European Enlightenment and the expansion of colonialism.

In the modern age, beginning with the colonization of the Americas, countries of Western Europe—Spain, Portugal, France, the Netherlands, and England—have been the dominant colonial nations. They have exported their languages and cultures throughout the Americas, Africa, Asia, and the Pacific through conquest and occupation or, as in the case of China and Japan in the latter half of the 19th century, through trade wars and the imposition of trade agreements. During the last 200 years, there have been very few, if any, nations that have not been affected in one way or another by the cultures and values of Western Europe and, especially since World War II (1939–45), of the United States. With the breakdown of European colonialism after 1945, the liberation from Western influences has been a rallying cry for contemporary literary movements in many parts of the world. The map of the world in the 21st century has already begun to present a different, as yet undefined, literary landscape.

THE NINETEENTH CENTURY

In Europe, the values of the Enlightenment—freedom, scientific progress, the importance of the individual—expressed the needs of the rising middle class and the growing capitalist economy. These ideas challenged the principles of inherited power and the rule of an aristocratic and ecclesiastical elite traditionally dependent on ownership and exploitation of the land. They found political expression in the French Revolution of 1789. The Revolution was greeted as a new dawn by writers, musicians, and artists throughout Europe and by oppressed peoples, including many women. However, as the Revolution turned into the Terror and was followed by the dictatorial reign of Napoleon—who extended French dominion through much of Europe, including an incursion into Russia, and ventured into Egypt—many writers and artists lost faith in the future of the revolutionary ideal.

COLONIAL ENCOUNTERS

Colonialism flourished in the 19th century through a combination of new ideas and political projects. The confidence of Europeans in the superiority of their civilization reached its height as scientific discoveries produced new technologies and industrialization promised ever-expanding markets. It seemed an obvious good to impose European values on the rest of the world. Yet at the same time science was undermining religious faith, and people became aware of what was lost when cities and factories obliterated the old ways of life. Slaves, women, and the colonized discovered that people's rights as promised by the French Revolution did not apply to them. Although Haiti (San Domingo) won its independence from France in 1802, slavery continued in the French Caribbean until 1848, and France and England continued to fight for domination over India, Africa, and the Caribbean. Nevertheless, Enlightenment ideals continued to both support and challenge the colonial enterprise of trade and conquest.

Latin America

Financed by kings and queens vying for power and national prestige, European colonialism from the 16th century on had justified itself in the name of Christianity and civilization. Encountering people with predominantly oral cultures and animist beliefs, the first colonists of what now constitutes Latin America imposed their religion and assimilated or suppressed local cultural forms and languages, which they considered to be inferior. In the 19th century, colonialism in Latin America produced a unique pattern of cultural development. By that time, most countries were controlled by powerful elites who fought for their

independence from Spain and Portugal. The longing for freedom was expressed in literature. Fernandez de Lizardi (1776–1827), Mexico's first novelist, for example, satirized corrupt colonial officials and contributed to the movement for independence. Andrés Bello (1781–1865) of Venezuela argued that Latin America would be independent only when it had freed itself from forms of government modeled on those of Europe. On the other hand, Domingo F. Sarmiento (1811–88) of Argentina wished to eradicate traces of both native and Spanish cultures and replace them with northern European economic and cultural models. By the end of the century, most of Latin America underwent rapid modernization with varying consequences and produced varied, often cosmopolitan literatures.

Africa

When Europe colonized Africa, it encountered hundreds of different languages and diverse traditions. The north and northwest had long been influenced by Islamic and Arabic written culture, and East Africa, open to trade with Indonesia and India, had a rich multicultural history. Most of this vast continent had a rich oral tradition that included epics, legends, proverbs, genealogies, and praise poetry. When colonial schools were set up to produce local administrators and impose Western cultures, African languages were marginalized, but oral genres, many of which were then written down, continued to modify and contest imported European literary forms and ideas.

South Asia

European confrontations with ancient civilizations and literatures in Asia are complex in a different way. The establishment of the East India Company by the English, which took place in 1600, was the beginning of the colonization of India and the imposition of British cultural institutions. Until 1835, when English became the common language of instruction, Sanskrit, Arabic, and Persian were the dominant official languages. The British gave their preference to the Sanskrit tradition, with its Indo-European associations, and to Hindu culture, whose caste system approximated their own class system. Sanskrit epics, such as the *Ramayana* and the *Maharabata,* as well as Hindu spiritual texts, were translated by and also influenced many 19th-century European writers. However, the dozens of languages and cultures of the Indian subcontinent and Sri Lanka withstood assimilation and continued their own traditional forms of epic, drama, and lyrical and devotional poetry.

The introduction of English instruction coincided with the widespread dissemination of printing, and English literature and European literary forms were introduced to the subcontinent and a new reading public. With English as the official language, works in languages such as Urdu, Tamil, Bengali, Telegu, and Kannada were translated into English, giving South Asians easier access to each other's literatures. India had a strong epic and mythical narrative tradition. The European novel gave new direction to Indian writing. Rabindranath TAGORE, the great Bengali nationalist, was awarded the Nobel Prize in literature in 1913.

East Asia

Beginning with the Opium War (1840–42), China was exposed to Western influences when it was forcefully brought into the orbit of European financial interests. Western and Japanese incursions—including the sacking of Beijing in 1860, the Sino-Japanese War (1894–95), and the Boxer Rebellion (1900–01)—contributed to a critique of Chinese conservatism, Confucianism, and the power of the scholarly literati. In 1911, a thousand years of imperial rule came to an end with the establishment of the republic. May 4, 1919, became famous for a new realist literary movement (*see* REALISM) that broke with the past and turned toward the West for inspiration. The language of the common people, as opposed to the scholarly language of the imperial bureaucrats, was increasingly used as the language of literature, and under the influence of countless translations from European writers, particularly French, English, and Russian, the novel became popular. Such writers as

HU SHI and LU XUN turned away from traditional forms and looked to Western novels for inspiration and renewal.

Japan is famous for its distinctive forms of poetry, such as the complex linked forms of the *renga,* which developed into the haiku, and its indigenous forms of drama, such as the No and Kabuki. It also has a long narrative tradition and its own forms of the novel, the most famous of which is probably the classic *Tale of Genji* (ca. A.D. 1000) by Lady Murasaki. Japan did not open up to the West until it was forced to by the United States and Commodore Perry's warships in 1853. This event had a profound effect on Japanese literature. Japanese translations of European and Russian novels appeared and influenced new expressions of the Japanese novel, as in the works of NATSUME Sōseki. [Chinese, Japanese, Korean, and Vietnamese personal names are rendered in traditional East Asian order, with surnames followed by given names.]

The Middle East

Middle Eastern literature—Arabic, Persian, and Turkish—was dominated from its pre-Islamic beginnings by poetry, written by both men and women. With the spread of Islam, the Qur'an established a literary and aesthetic mood for Muslim writers. In the 19th century, Europeans began to look to the Middle East for literary inspiration: French and English translations of *The Thousand and One Nights,* a collection of stories from Persia with Indian influences, had a profound effect on the Western imagination.

At the same time, the growing imperial powers of Europe undermined the declining Ottoman Empire, which finally collapsed after World War I, and introduced to the Middle East Western liberal values such as equal rights and freedom of trade and travel, as well as new genres such as the novel. Modern and secular ideas were contentious from the beginning: European aesthetics and progressive ideas threatened traditional and national literary forms and were associated with political domination.

Australasia

An aboriginal culture had existed in Australia for at least 50,000 years before the arrival of the Europeans. It included songs, myths, and stories, which were orally transmitted. White settlement of Australia began in 1788 with the establishment of penal colonies by the British. Nineteenth-century Australian literature, produced both by convicts and free settlers, followed English models while exploring new experiences of life in the bush and outback. At the same time, aboriginal culture was threatened with extinction. It was not until 1901, when Australia won its independence, that a strong national literature emerged.

The first British missionary arrived in New Zealand in 1801, and the colony was formalized in 1841. The Treaty of Waitangi (1840) established an uneasy peace between the indigenous Maoris and the colonizers, but the oral language and culture of the aboriginal people inevitably declined. British models dominated 19th-century New Zealand literature.

EUROPEAN ROMANTICISM AND ITS DISCONTENTS

The literary movement that best expresses the aspirations, contradictions, and disappointments of the turn of the 19th century is romanticism. Romanticism began in Germany with writers such as GOETHE, SCHILLER, and HÖLDERLIN. It was influenced by Jean-Jacques Rousseau, the critic of the inequities of civilization, in his fiction and essays and by Immanuel Kant's ideas about the beautiful and sublime. His *Critique of Judgment* (1790) had a profound effect on romantic aesthetics. The German mystical and idealistic tradition competed with the more rational and scientific ideals of French thinkers and influenced writers throughout Europe. Germaine de STAËL, the Swiss/French intellectual and writer who introduced German literature and philosophy into France at the beginning of the 19th century, held that a nation's literature is reflective of its forms of government and its historical moment. Literature thus provides insight into national identity.

Because classical ideals were embedded in oppressive cultural institutions, romantic writers often turned to the myths and oral traditions of the Middle Ages, perpetuated in the folktales of the people, for inspiration and a redefinition of nationhood. Oral traditions seemed to offer a social cohesion missing in a society that was fragmented by revolution and strife. Folktales by German writers such as Benedikte NAUBERT and the brothers GRIMM were very popular. At the same time, the romantic love of freedom inspired subjugated nations, such as Greece, which was long dominated by the Turks, to struggle for liberation and revive their ancient cultural heritage. In both Germany and France, the theater of such dramatists as Schiller and HUGO threw off classical constraints and advocated passion and rebellion in the name of social justice.

Inspired by Enlightenment ideals of freedom, most romantic writers were critical of imperialism and slavery, but they were also fascinated by the exotic, especially the culture of the Orient. Even before the French Revolution, romantic writers, such as Goethe, were interested in the spiritual literature of India. After the Revolution, the development of romanticism coincided with a new phase of colonial expansion in the Middle East and North Africa. The Orient, often geographically vague and exoticized, came to represent the possibility of passion and escape from an increasingly utilitarian and secular world dominated by the pursuit of money and power. It provided not only luxury goods and cheap labor but also, in varying forms, a vision of sensuous fulfillment and respite from the pursuit of profits. Parallel to romantic exoticism was the romantic interest in nature as a source of inspiration. Many elements of the romantic movement were to reappear at the end of the century in countries outside Europe, including China and Latin America, as evidenced by the works of the Brazilian Antonio GONÇALVES DIAS, who wrote about NATIVIST issues, that is, the relation between indigenous peoples and the land.

A major theme of romantic writers, for example BALZAC and STENDHAL, is the struggle for survival of the sensibilities of the artist in a new world of industrialization, material values, and the brutal struggle for success. The defeat of romantic ideals, which sought refuge in an idealized imagination, is often embodied in the novel. The fate of the romantic hero who refuses the material values of the new bourgeois world is often suicide or madness.

THE NOVEL

Just as colonialism was facilitated in the 19th century by rapid advances in technology, engineering, and industrialization, improvements in printing techniques permitted cheaper and easier publication of books. At the same time, the growth of the urban population and extension of education and literacy provided a growing readership. The serialized novel, one of the great innovations of 19th-century European literature, established this literary form, variously defined by movements such as realism and NATURALISM, as the dominant genre. It became the place for discussion of every important social issue. Filled with energy and movement, novels by Stendhal, Balzac, Flaubert, and Zola place an individual within the social maelstrom and follow his or her development or destruction. The effects of modern Western values are more tragically explored in the Russian novels of DOSTOYEVSKY and TOLSTOY, both affected by and resistant to Westernization, who evolve an alternative to modernity through their different syntheses of their own culture and interpretations of Christianity.

The novel was one of the major exports of Western culture to other parts of the world. Its effects were felt, especially toward the end of the 19th century, in China, Japan, India, and the Middle East.

DECADENCE

By the late 19th century, the long advance of European modernity was accelerated by developments in technology and capital-driven imperialism. By 1914, the reach of Western civilization throughout the world was unprecedented. Although 19th-century colonialism had reached its heights in terms of appropriated land and affected cultures, the system at home was under pressure, and its crisis is evident in European literature. The great Scandinavian dramatists IBSEN and STRINDBERG explored the dilemmas of capitalist entrepreneurs and the tensions of bourgeois marriage. Symbolist poets (see SYMBOLISM) tried to lose themselves in an alternate linguistic world distilled of the dross of the everyday. The decadents (see DECADENCE) luxuriated in their disaffection with the bourgeoisie and espoused the artificiality of the aesthetic and technology. Misogyny and masculine symbols of power were glorified in the theories of FUTURISM.

Misogyny and racism flourished at the end of the 19th century in Europe, bringing to a crisis a process implicit in 19th-century social practice and ideology. Colonialism, of course, depended on racist beliefs in the superiority of white European civilization. The bourgeois family similarly supported a dichotomy between the pure domestic wife and mother and an inferior woman—working class or prostitute—identified with the fulfillment of base needs. There was no legitimate place in this schema for the woman writer.

If the expansion of education brought more literacy to Europeans and missionaries exported literacy to far reaches of the world, the institutions of literature were still owned and controlled by the male upper and middle classes. Literature was not considered an appropriate calling for a woman. It was common for women writers in the late 18th and early 19th centuries to disguise their identities in order to be published. Benedikte Naubert was successful in Germany when she published anonymously and was neglected when her female identity was revealed. George SAND took the name of a man. Still, women writers made a major mark on 19th-century literature, even though their contributions were not always recognized or acknowledged. With the crisis of the bourgeois family structure at the end of the century, there was a flurry of defiant women writers, such as COLETTE, who disregarded conventions and claimed their freedom.

However, the outbreak of World War I in 1914 severely challenged the hopes of the bourgeoisie for progress and enlightenment, and the Russian Revolution of 1917 signified the cataclysmic beginnings of a new era.

THE TWENTIETH CENTURY

Twentieth-century literature began in disillusion. Capitalism and the bourgeois family were in crisis, and an optimistic faith in progress through rationality and science was tested by the horrors of war. The avant-garde movements of DADA and SURREALISM, which emerged in the wake of the World War I, rejected bourgeois civilization as repressive and exploitative and gave value to the world of the unconscious and dreams, as explored by Sigmund FREUD. The war years and the 1920s also saw the emergence of MODERNISM.

The modernist movement in Europe, while celebrating the autonomous sphere of the aesthetic, had an acute sense that "the center does not hold." It sought carefully wrought and experimental forms with which to respond to what many writers saw as the chaos and cultural decline of the modern age. In their skepticism about civilization, modernists such as W. B. Yeats turned toward myth and the unconscious.

Although European modernism and the playful and iconoclastic surrealism may have expressed a crisis of Western civilization, both seemed out of touch with the social and economic lives of ordinary people, especially after the collapse of the stock market in 1929, a catastrophe felt throughout the world. The avant-garde movements that lamented the alienation of modern urban life were countered by a very different attitude to the future.

TOTALITARIANISM AND THE SECOND WORLD WAR

Revolutionary writers rejected the past and looked toward the liberation of the peasants and working classes with renewed hope. The 1920s in Russia, for example, saw a flowering of creativity among experimental poets and filmmakers. However, this euphoria was not to last. The lyrical poets Vladimir MAYAKOVSKY and Sergey YESENIN for example, frustrated by political imperatives, committed suicide. The 1930s saw the growth of fascism in Germany and Spain and the hardening of oppression in communist Russia. Both fascism and the communist SOCIALIST REALISM, the official aesthetic, condemned experimentation and modernist literature and art as decadent.

The totalitarian regimes of Japanese militarism, fascism and communism targeted writers whom they considered decadent or enemies of the people. Writing against the grain of oppressive political authority became, in the 20th century, a dangerous activity. The Korean writer YUN TONGJU, who spoke for Korean independence, was arrested by the Japanese in 1943 and died in prison. Jewish intellectuals and dissident writers were exterminated by the German fascists. Books that were considered dangerous were burned. For protesting against fascism, Thomas MANN and Hermann HESSE lost their German citizenship. Many others lost their lives, including Federico GARCÍA LORCA, one of Spain's most highly revered poets. Rafael ALBERTI, the Spanish surrealist poet, had to go into exile in Argentina after the victory of fascist general Francísco Franco.

Writers who lived during and after World War II had to confront the reality that modern civilization and technology had produced destruction and cruelty on an unprecedented scale. The Holocaust, in which millions of Jews and other civilians were exterminated; the mass destruction of cities; and the nuclear devastation visited on Hiroshima and Nagasaki seemed to defy the very possibilities of language. The critic Theodor Adorno (1903–69) suggested that after the Holocaust, lyric poetry might be impossible. However, the horrors of the Holocaust produced extraordinary poems and testimonials in the work of such writers as Primo LEVI, Nelly SACHS, and Elie WIESEL. With the establishment of the state of Israel in 1948, a new literature in Hebrew came into being. Fascist oppression also inspired an existential literature of engagement exemplified by the writings of Jean-Paul SARTRE, Simone de BEAUVOIR, and Albert CAMUS. The unspeakable suffering of the war, along with the stark reality of the cold war between the United States and the Soviet Union, created the climate for the THEATRE OF THE ABSURD of the 1950s.

The Soviet empire that emerged from World War II suppressed the national literatures of the countries under its sway and, particularly during the Stalinist era, imprisoned and killed its dissident writers. Among many others, Varlam SHALAMOV, Andrei AMALRIK, and Aleksandr SOLZHENITSYN were imprisoned; Osip MANDELSTAM died during imprisonment; and Isaak BABEL was summarily executed. Similarly in China, during the Cultural Revolution, such writers as DING LING and Hu Feng (1903–85), who resisted the restrictions of socialist realism, were imprisoned.

Throughout these periods of repression, writers have been remarkably resilient. Some, like the exiled novelist Vladimir NABOKOV, reinvented themselves in exile. Surviving imprisonment, illness, and forced exile, Solzhenitsyn returned to acclaim in Russia after the fall of the Soviet Union. Paris, after the war, became a particular magnet for exiled writers from Russia, Central Europe, Latin America, and Greece. At the same time, writers who remained in the Soviet Union used their creative resources to develop a genre of dissident literature, *samizdat,* which was often distributed underground at great risk and depended on humor, irony, obliqueness, and allegory. Literary movements affirming freedom and national identity emerged—as in Poland, Hungary, and Czechoslovakia—surreptitiously to challenge both socialist realism and Soviet domination.

THE AFTERMATH OF COLONIALISM

One of the more inspiring effects of the postwar years was the end of colonialism and the emergence of cultures, albeit changed, that colonialism had tried to destroy or assimilate. The NÉGRITUDE movement, for example, united French-speaking African and Caribbean writers in an effort to forge a new self-expression from the colonial language they had learned in French schools and universities and the language they spoke at home. This produced the extraordinary writings of Léopold SENGHOR, Birago DIOP, and Aimé CÉSAIRE, among others, and revitalized a sense of African identity. Similarly, the independence of India in 1947 had a profound effect on definitions of Indian identity and catalyzed a resurgence of regional writers.

Even within Europe, up until World War II, marginalized cultures such as Breton, Provençal, Welsh, Irish, and Scottish Gaelic were disappearing because, within a centralized educational system, only the dominant, official language was encouraged. Increasingly, these cultures have resisted such internal colonization, and their languages are now included in the curriculum of some schools. This trend has continued under the aegis of the institution of the European Common Market. In Canada, the revival of the Québecois identity and the emergence of major authors writing in French, as a response to the dominant Anglophone culture, have been other remarkable examples, in a different context, of renewed cultural self-determination.

Postcolonialism has produced a strong immigrant and diasporic literature. For economic and political reasons, South Asians, Indonesians, Africans, Turks, and Caribbeans have established themselves in the West and have produced a new definition of what constitutes, for example, English, French, German, or Dutch literature.

WOMEN WRITERS

Feminist movements in America and Europe since the 1970s have had an equally transformative effect on world literature. They have revealed the difficulties of women writers in the past who, for the most part, had no legal or civil rights and were not supposed to participate in public life or have their work published. They have also brought to light works that had once been influential (when published anonymously or with male pseudonyms) but were later excluded from the literary canon. They have questioned the conventional notions of what is considered literary—the priority given to poetry, drama, and the realistic novel—and have given value to "inferior" forms of expression, such as letters, memoirs, and diaries, often pejoratively described as "women's literature." Above all, the women's movement has inspired women writers throughout the world. Even in cultures that have hardened against the engagement of women in public life, as in some nations of North Africa and the Middle East, women writers such as Assia DJEBAR from Algeria and Nawal SADAWI from Egypt have changed the political and literary map. Confronting very different social and economic conditions, women in Latin America, Africa, and South Asia are engaging in the complex issues of liberation, modernization, and their roles in traditional patriarchal, religious communities.

Many women writers have been recipients of the Nobel Prize. Swedish novelist Selma LAGERLÖF, became the first woman to receive the Nobel Prize in 1909. Chilean poet Gabriela MISTRAL became the first Latin American woman to receive the prize in 1945.

LITERATURE AFTER THE COLLAPSE OF THE SOVIET UNION

In the last 15 years, the borders of the map of literature have become almost unrecognizable. The fall of the Soviet Union has meant the reconfiguration of social and national identities in Eastern and Central Europe. This has brought about the revival of national traditions and the creation of new ones. Economic disorder and political unrest, especially due to the war in the former Yugoslavia and neighboring states, have also created a new wave of national consciousness as well as increased immigration of writers to Western Europe and the United States.

EFFECTS OF GLOBALIZATION

Despite revivals of national identities, the technological revolution of the Internet and the globalization of markets pose the threat of cultural homogenization. Although it is now possible for diverse cultures to interact on an unprecedented scale, during the last two centuries, languages of aboriginal peoples have been disappearing at an alarming rate, and new forms of globalization have brought fear of domination by a Western culture identified as secular and materialistic. Fundamentalist religious authorities, in particular, have instituted the persecution of writers whom they consider to be disrespectful of religious beliefs and customs.

The persecution of writers and artists by political or religious groups for blasphemy or obscenity is nothing new in the history of world literature. During the last 200 years, some of the iconic texts of Western culture, such as Flaubert's *Madame Bovary,* Baudelaire's *Les Fleurs du mal,* and Joyce's *Ulysses,* were put on trial. The Catholic Church has long placed many writers, admired by readers and literary critics alike, on its "Index" of what should not be read. In the face of fundamentalist Islamic interdictions, the very lives of writers considered to be blasphemous are at risk. A death threat by religious decree was imposed on Salman Rushdie for his *Satanic Verses.*

Nevertheless, under the most difficult circumstances, writers have shown extraordinary capacity for transformation. The 21st century promises to be just as challenging. At a recent discussion among world writers in the small Welsh village of Hay-on-Wye, the Irish writer and playwright Sebastian Barry suggested that writers write to create equilibrium. It remains to be seen, given the intensification of political and economical instability, what new balancing acts will be performed on the high wire of world literature.

—M. Josephine Diamond
New York City, August 2002

AUTHORS' TIMELINE

Dates	Author	Dates	Author
1749–1842	Goethe, Johann Wolfgang von	1798–1837	Leopardi, Giacomo
1756–1819	Naubert, Benedikte	1798–1855	Mickiewicz, Adam Bernard
1759–1805	Schiller, Friedrich	1799–1837	Pushkin, Aleksandr
1764–1842	Fischer, Caroline Auguste	1799–1850	Balzac, Honoré de
1765–1820	Nguyen Du	1802–1885	Hugo, Victor
1766–1826	Karamzin, Nikolai	1804–1876	Sand, George
1766–1877	Staël, Germaine de	1805–1875	Andersen, Hans Christian
1767–1830	Constant de Rebecque, Benjamin	1807–1893	Pavlova, Karolina
		1808–1842	Espronceda y Delgado, José de
1768–1848	Chateaubriand, François-René de	1808–1852	Gogol, Nikolay
		1808–1855	Nerval, Gérard de
1770–1843	Hölderlin, Friedrich	1808–1889	Barbey d'Aurevilly, Jules-Amédée
1776–1820	Ho Xuan Huong		
1776–1822	Hoffmann, E. T. A.	1810–1857	Musset, Alfred de
1777–1828	Duras, Claire de	1811–1872	Gautier, Théophile
1778–1827	Foscolo, Ugo	1812–1870	Herzen, Aleksandr
1783–1842	Stendhal	1812–1891	Goncharov, Ivan
1785–1859	Arnim, Bettina von	1813–1837	Büchner, Georg
1785–1863	Grimm, Jacob and Wilhelm	1814–1841	Lermontov, Mikhail
1785–1873	Manzoni, Alessandro	1818–1883	Turgenev, Ivan
1786–1859	Desbordes-Valmore, Marceline	1819–1898	Fontane, Theodor
1790–1869	Lamartine, Alphonse de	1821–1867	Baudelaire, Charles
1797–1856	Heine, Heinrich	1821–1880	Flaubert, Gustave
1797–1863	Vigny, Alfred-Victor de	1821–1881	Fyodor Dostoyevsky
1797–1869	Ghālib, Mirzā Asadullāh Khān	1822–1896	Goncourt, Edmond
		1823–1864	Gonçalves Dias, Antônio

Dates	Author	Dates	Author
1828–1889	Chernyshevsky, Nikolai	1862–1922	Mori Ōgai
1828–1906	Ibsen, Henrik	1862–1946	Hauptmann, Gerhardt
1828–1910	Tolstoy, Leo	1862–1949	Maeterlinck, Maurice
1829 1877	Alencar, José Martiniano de	1863–1933	Cavafy, Constantine P.
1830–1870	Goncourt, Jules	1863–1938	D'Annunzio, Gabriele
1832–1910	Bjørnson, Bjørnstjerne	1864–1925	Rosas, Oscar
1836–1870	Bécquer, Gustavo Alfonso	1864–1936	Unamuno y Jugo, Miguel de
1837–1885	Castro, Rosalía	1867–1900	Nobre, António
1838–1889	Villiers de L'Isle-Adam,	1867–1902	Masaoka Shiki
	Auguste de	1867–1916	Darío, Rubén
1838–1894	Cattopadhyay, Bankim-	1867–1916	Natsume Sōseki
	Chandra	1867–1922	Lawson, Henry
1839–1908	Machado de Assis, Joachim	1867–1928	Blasco Ibáñez, Vicente
	Maria	1867–1936	Pirandello, Luigi
1840–1902	Zola, Émile	1868–1933	George, Stefan
1840–1922	Verga, Giovanni	1868–1936	Gorky, Maxim
1842–1891	Quental, Antero Tarquínio de	1868–1955	Claudel, Paul
1842–1898	Mallarmé, Stéphane	1869–1945	Lasker-Schüler, Else
1843–1920	Pérez Galdós, Benito	1869–1948	Gandhi, Mohandas K.
1844–1900	Nietzsche, Friedrich	1869–1951	Gide, André
1845–1900	Queiroz, José Maria Eça de	1869–1952	Hamsun, Knut
1846–1870	Lautreamont, Comte de	1870–1953	Bunin, Ivan
	(Isidore-Lucien Ducasse)	1871–1905	Fin de siècle
1846–1916	Sienkiewicz, Henryk	1871–1922	Proust, Marcel
1848–1907	Huysmans, Joris-Karl	1871–1945	Valéry, Paul
1849–1912	Strindberg, August	1871–1950	Mann, Heinrich
1850–1893	Maupassant, Guy de	1872–1896	Higuchi Ichiyō
1851–1896	Verlaine, Paul	1872–1956	Baroja y Nessi, Pío
1851–1921	Pardo Bazán, Emilia	1873–1907	Jarry, Alfred
1852–1915	Peretz, Isaac Leib	1873–1924	Bryusov, Valery Yakovlevich
1853–1900	Solovyov, Vladimir Sergeyevich	1873–1954	Colette
1854–1891	Rimbaud, Arthur	1874–1929	Hofmannstahl, Hugo von
1856–1939	Freud, Sigmund	1874–1947	Machado y Ruiz, Manuel
1857–1909	Liu E	1875–1926	Rilke, Rainer Maria
1858–1940	Lagerlöf, Selma	1875–1939	Machado, Antonio
1859–1916	Akhmatova, Anna	1875–1955	Mann, Thomas
1859–1916	Aleichem, Shalom	1876–1938	Chatterji, Sarat Chandra
1860–1900	naturalism	1876–1944	Marinetti, Filippo
1860–1904	Chekhov, Anton	1877–1938	Iqbāl, Muhammad
1860–1943	Roberts, Charles	1877–1962	Hesse, Hermann
1861–1913	Johnson, Pauline	1878–1942	Yosano Akiko
1861–1928	Svevo, Italo	1878–1957	Döblin, Alfred
1861–1941	Tagore, Rabindranath	1879–1944	Han Yongun

Dates	Author	Dates	Author
1879–1949	Naidu, Sarojini	1891–1970	Sachs, Nellie
1880–1918	Apollinaire, Guillaume	1891–1974	Lagerkvist, Pär
1880–1934	Bely, Andrei	1892–1923	Södergran, Edith
1880–1936	Premchand, Munshi	1892–1927	Akutagawa Ryūnosuke
1880–1942	Musil, Robert von	1892–1938	Storni, Alfonsina
1880–1967	Arghezi, Tudor	1892–1938	Vallejo, César
1881–1936	Lu Xun (Lu Hsün)	1892–1941	Tsvetaeva, Marina
1881–1958	Jiménez, Juan Ramón	1892–1975	Andrić, Ivo
1882–1944	Giraudoux, Jean	1893–1930	Mayakovsky, Vladimir
1882–1949	Undset, Sigrid	1893–1980	Collymore, Frank A.
1883–1923	Hašek, Jaroslav	1893–1984	Guillén, Jorge
1883–1924	Kafka, Franz	1894–1941	Babel, Isaac
1883–1955	Ortega y Gasset, José	1894–1953	Tuwim, Julian
1883–1956	Takamura Kotaro	1894–1961	Céline, Louis-Ferdinand
1883–1957	Kazantsakis, Nikos	1895–1925	Yesenin, Sergey Aleksandrovich
1883–1971	Shiga Naoya	1895–1952	Éluard, Paul
1884–1937	Zamyatin, Yevgeny	1895–1976	Satyanarayana, Visvanatha
1885–1962	Dinesen, Isak	1895–1998	Jünger, Ernst
1886–1921	Gumilev, Nikolai	1896–1948	Artaud, Antonin
1886–1942	Hagiwara Sakutarō	1896–1957	Lampedusa, Giuseppe di
1886–1951	Broch, Hermann	1896–1963	Tzara, Tristan
1886–1956	Benn, Gottfried	1896–1966	Breton, André
1886–1965	Tanizaki Jun'ichirō	1896–1981	Montale. Eugenio
1886–1978	Madariaga, Salvador de	1897–1962	Bataille, Georges
1886–1980	Kokoschka, Oskar	1897–1982	Aragon, Louis
1887–1914	Trakl, Georg	1898–1936	García Lorca, Federico
1887–1966	Arp, Hans	1898–1956	Brecht, Bertolt
1887–1975	Perse, Saint-Jean	1898–1970	Remarque, Erich Maria
1888–1923	Mansfield, Katherine	1899–1950	Langgässer, Elisabeth
1888–1935	Pessoa, Fernando	1899–1966	Lao She
1888–1970	Agnon, Shmuel Yosef	1899–1972	Kawabata Yasunari
1888–1970	Ungaretti, Giuseppe	1899–1977	Nabokov, Vladimir
1889–1957	Mistral, Gabriela	1899–1984	Michaux, Henri
1889–1963	Cocteau, Jean	1899–1986	Borges, Jorge Luis
1889–1965	Alberti, Rafael	1899–1988	Ponge, Francis
1889–1975	Gunnarsson, Gunnar	1900–1944	Saint-Exupéry, Antoine de
1890–1960	Pasternak, Boris	1900–1971	Seferis, George
1890–1979	Rhys, Jean	1900–1987	Freyre, Gilberto de Mello
1891–1938	Mandelstam, Osip	1900–1999	Bing Xin (Ping Hsin)
1891–1940	Bulgakov, Mikhail	1900–1999	Sarraute, Nathalie
1891–1958	Becher, Johannes Robert	1901–1956	Fadeyev, Aleksandr Aleksandrovich
1891–1962	Hu Shih		
1891–1967	Ehrenburg, Ilya	1901–1968	Quasimodo, Salvatore

Dates	Author	Dates	Author
1901–1974	Kaschnitz, Marie-Luise	1910–1986	Genet, Jean
1901–1976	Malraux, André	1910–1987	Anouilh, Jean
1901 -1986	Seifert, Jaroslav	1910–	Queirós, Raquel de
1901–1988	Ausländer, Rose	1911–1996	Elytis, Odysseus
1901–1990	Leiris, Michel	1911–2001	Curnow, Allen
1902–1963	Hikmet, Nazim	1911–	Frisch, Max
1902–1974	Torres Bodet, Jaime	1911–	Mahfouz, Naguib
1902–1983	Stead, Christina	1911–	Milosz, Czeslaw
1902–1989	Guillén, Nicolás	1911–	Rinser, Luise
1903–1937	Rabéarivelo, Jean-Joseph	1912–1980	White, Patrick
1903–1951	Hayashi Fumiko	1912–1984	Faiz, Faiz Ahmed
1903–1976	Queneau, Raymond	1912–1994	Ionesco, Eugène
1903–1981	Huchel, Peter	1912–2001	Amado, Jorge
1903–1982	Sargeson, Frank	1913–1960	Camus, Albert
1903–1987	Yourcenar, Marguerite	1913–1995	Davies, Robertson
1903–1988	Paton, Alan	1913–	Césaire, Aimé
1903–1989	Simenon, Georges	1913–	Simon, Claude
1904–1936	Ostrovsky, Nikolai	1914–1950	Kanik, Orhan Veli
1904–1969	Gombrowicz, Witold	1914–1984	Cortázar, Julio
1904–1973	Neruda, Pablo	1914–1987	Abbas, K.A.
1904–1980	Carpentier, Alejo	1914–1996	Duras, Marguerite
1904–1986	Ding Ling	1914–1998	Paz, Octavio
1904–1991	Singer, Isaac Bashevis	1914–	Dağlarka, Fazil Hüsnü
1904–	Ba Jin		
1905–1980	Sartre, Jean-Paul	1915–1986	Allfrey, Phyllis
1905–1984	Sholokhov, Mikhail	1915–2000	Wright, Judith
1905–1986	Enchi Fumiko	1915–2001	Hwang Sun-won
1905–1993	Feng Zhi (Feng Chih)	1915–2001	So Chông-ju
1905–1994	Canetti, Elias	1915–1991	Chugtai, Ismat
1905–	Anand, Mulk Raj	1916–1920	Dada
1906–1989	Beckett, Samuel	1916–1978	Pak Mogwol
1906–1989	Diop, Birago	1916–1985	Tian Jian
1906–2001	Narayan, R. K.	1916–1991	Ginzburg, Natalia
1906–2001	Senghor, Léopold Sédar	1916–2000	Hébert, Anne
1907–1972	Eich, Günter	1916–	Cela, Camilo José
1907–1982	Shalamov, Varlam	1917–1945	Yun Tongju
1907–1988	Char, René	1917–1985	Böll, Heinrich
1907–1990	Moravia, Alberto	1918–1985	Morante, Elsa
1908–1950	Pavese, Cesare	1918–1998	Dudintsev, Vladimir
1908–1986	Beauvoir, Simone de	1918–	Solzhenitsyn, Aleksandr
1909–1973	Brasch, Charles Orwell	1919–1987	Levi, Primo
1909–1994	Onetti, Juan Carlos	1919–	Abrahams, Peter
1910–1983	Sri Sri	1919–	Bennett, Louise

Dates	Author	Dates	Author
1920–1970	Celan, Paul	1927–	Frame, Janet
1920–1977	Lispector, Clarice	1927–	Grass, Günter
1920–1993	Noonuccal, Oodgeroo	1927–	Jhabvala, Ruth Prawer
1920–	Memmi, Albert	1927–	Lamming, George
1920–	Rin Ishigaki	1928–1953	Capécia, Mayotte
1921–1988	Fried, Erich	1928–1996	Miron, Gaston
1921–1990	Dürrenmatt, Friedrich	1928–	Fuentes, Carlos
1921–1996	Habibi, Emile	1928–	Garcia Márquez, Gabriel
1921–	Aichinger, Ilse	1928–	Wiesel, Elie
1921–	Harris, Wilson	1928–	Yu Guanzhong (Yü Kwang-chung)
1921–	Okara, Gabriel		
1922–1975	Pasolini, Pier Paolo	1929–1981	Bâ, Mariama
1922–1979	Neto, António Agostinho	1929–1989	Yacine, Kateb
1922–1991	Popa, Vasko	1929–1995	Müller, Heiner
1922–	Burkart, Erika	1929–	Cabrera Infante, Guillermo
1922–	Höllerer, Walter	1929–	Enzensberger, Hans Magnus
1922–	Robbe-Grillet, Alain	1929–	Kundera, Milan
1922–	Saramago, José	1929–	Kunert, Günter
1923–1985	Calvino, Italo	1929–	Maillet, Antonine
1923–1998	Kabbani, Nizar	1929–	Munonye, John
1923–	Bonnefoy, Yves	1929–	Saleh, Tayyib
1923–	Gordimer, Nadine	1929–	Wolf, Christa
1923–	Kemal, Yaşar	1930–1986	Pagis, Dan
1923–	Mala'ika, Nazek al-	1930–	Adonis
1923–	Sembène, Ousmane	1930–	Brathwaite, Edward Kamau
1923–	Szimborska, Wislawa	1930–	Fallaci, Oriana
1924–1993	Abe Kōbō	1930–	Hayashi Kyoko
1924–1997	Donoso, José	1930–	Kunene, Mazisi
1924–2000	Amichai, Yehuda	1930–	Mro˙zek, Slawomir
1924–	Skvorecky, Jozef	1930–	Ōba Minako
1925–1970	Mishima Yukio	1930–	Ogot, Grace
1925–1974	Castellanos, Rosario	1930–	Walcott, Derek
1925–1985	La Guma, Alex	1931–1982	p'Bitek, Okot
1925–	Astley, Thea	1931–1989	Bernhard, Thomas
1925–	Gomringer, Eugen	1931–1993	Nwapa, Flora
1925–	Jaccottet, Philippe	1931–	Munro, Alice
1925–	Toer, Pramoedya Ananta	1931–	Sadawi, Nawal
1926–1973	Bachmann, Ingeborg	1931–	Tanikawa Shuntaro
1926–	Dépestre, René	1932–	Appelfeld, Aharon
1926–	Devi, Mahasweta	1932–	Chen Yuan-tsung
1926–	Fo, Dario	1932–	Eco, Umberto
1927–1960	Diop, David	1932–	Naipaul, V.S.
1927–1991	Idris, Yūsuf	1932–	Voinovich, Vladimir

Dates	Author	Dates	Author
1933–	Yevtushenko, Yevgeny	1942–1970	Nortje, Arthur
1934–1984	Johnson, Uwe	1942–	Aidoo, Ama Ata
1934–	Condé, Maryse	1942–	Allende, Isabel
1934–	Fraire, Isabel	1942–	Bitton, Erez
1934–	Malouf, David	1942–	Darwish, Mahmud
1934–	Soyinka, Wole	1942–	Ferré, Rosario
1935–1989	Kiš, Danilo	1942–	Handke, Peter
1935–	Brink, André	1942–	Hasluck, Nicholas
1935–	Keneally, Thomas	1942–	Sammam, Ghada
1935–	Kirsch, Sarah	1943–1990	Arenas, Renaldo
1935–	Kogawa, Joy	1943–	Carey, Peter
1935–	Kurahashi Yumiko	1943–	Mehta, Gita
1935–	Ōe Kenzaburō	1943–	Ondaatje, Michael
1935–	Wittig, Monique	1944–1988	Nichol, b. p.
1936–1980	Amalrik, Andrey	1944–	Emecheta, Buchi
1936–1982	Perec, Georges	1944–	Lim, Shirley Geok-Lin
1936–	Djebar, Assia	1944–	Serote, Mongane Wally
1936–	Havel, Václav	1944–	Yathay Pin
1936–	Nkosi, Lewis	1945–	Farah, Nuruddin
1936–	Ravikovitch, Dahlia	1945–	Laird, Christopher
1936–	Vargas Llosa, Mario	1946–	Al-Jayyusi, Salma al-Khadra
1937–1986	Head, Bessie	1946–	Cliff, Michelle
1937–	Akhmadulina, Izabella	1946–	Laing, B. Kojo
1937–	Arrabal, Fernando	1947–1967	Gruppe 47
1937–	Cixous, Hélène	1947–	Anyidoho, Kofi
1937–	Desai, Anita	1947–	Dhammachoti, Ussiri
1938–1960	Theatre of the Absurd, the	1947–	Dhasal, Namdeo
1938–	Hwang Tonggyu	1947–	Goodison, Lorna
1938–	Karnad, Girish	1947–	Rushdie, Salman
1938–	Ngugi wa Thiong'o	1947–	Tsushima Yuko
1938–	San Juan, Epifanio	1947–	Yáñez, Mirta
1938–	Schwarz-Bart, Simone	1948–	Achebe, Chinua
1939–	Atwood, Margaret	1948–	Espinet, Ramabai
1939–	Braun, Volker	1948–	Ndebele. Njabulo, S.
1939–	Breytenbach, Breyten	1948–	Wicomb, Zoë
1939–	Huang Chunming (Huang Ch'un-ming)	1949–	Bei Dao
		1949–	Cronin, Jeremy
1939–	Oz, Amos	1949–	Hayslip, Le Ly
1940–1975	Brinkmann, Rolf Dieter	1949–	Kincaid, Jamaica
1940–	Coetzee, J. M.	1949–	Murakami Haruki
1940–	Gao Xingjian	1951–1999	Kauraka, Kauraka
1940–	Souza, Eunice de	1951–	De Kok, Ingrid
1941–	Maron, Monika	1951–	Falkner, Gerhard

Dates	Author	Dates	Author
1951–	Ipellie, Alootook	1956–	Bhatt, Sujata
1952–	Grünzweig, Dorothea	1956–	Ghosh, Amitav
1952–	Mistry, Ronhinton	1956–	Mo Yan
1952–	Pamuk, Orhan	1959–	Chatterjee, Upamanyu
1952–	Seth, Vikram	1959–	Köhler, Barbara
1953–	Busia, Abena	1959–	Menchú, Rigoberta
1953–	Chamoiseau, Patrick	1959–	Yamada Eimi
1953–	Meeks, Brian	1960–	Malange, Nise
1953–	Suleri, Sara	1961–	Roy, Arundhati
1954–	Braschi, Giannina	1962–	Flanagan, Richard
1954–	Gunesekara, Ramesh	1962–	Grünbein, Durs

WRITERS COVERED, BY GEOGRAPHICAL AREA

AFRICA

Abrahams, Peter
Achebe, Chinua
Aidoo, Ama Ata
Anyidoho, Kofi
Bá, Mariama
Breytenbach, Breyten
Brink, André
Busia, Abena
Coetzee, J. M.
Cronin, Jeremy
De Kok, Ingrid
Diop, Birago
Diop, David
Emecheta, Buchi
Farah, Nuruddin
Gordimer, Nadine
Head, Bessie
Kunene, Mazisi
La Guma, Alex
Laing, B. Kojo
Malange, Nise
Munonye, John
Ndebele. Njabulo, S.
Neto, António Agostinho
Ngugi wa Thiong'o
Nkosi, Lewis

Nortje, Arthur
Nwapa, Flora
Ogot, Grace
Okara, Gabriel
p'Bitek, Okot
Paton, Alan
Rabéarivelo, Jean-Joseph
Saleh, Tayyib
Sembène, Ousmane
Senghor, Léopold Sédar
Serote, Mongane Wally
Soyinka, Wolo
Wicomb, Zoë
Yacine, Kateb

THE AMERICAS

Canada

Atwood, Margaret
Davies, Robertson
Hébert, Anne
Ipellie, Alootook
Johnson, Pauline
Kogawa, Joy
Maillet, Antonine
Miron, Gaston
Munro, Alice
Nichol, bp

Kawabata Yasunari
Kurahashi Yumiko
Masaoka Shiki
Mishima Yukio
Mori Ōgai
Murakami Haruki
Natsume Sōseki
Oba Minako
Ōe Kenzaburō
Shiga Naoya
Takamura Kotarō
Tanikawa Shuntaro
Tanizaki Jun'ichirō
Tsushima Yukō
Yamada Eimi
Yosano Akiko

Korea

Han Yongun
Hwang Sun-won
Hwang Tonggyu
Pak Mogwol
So Chông-ju
Yun Tongju

South Asia

Abbas, K.A.
Anand, Mulk Raj
Bhatt, Sujata
Cattopadhyay, Bankim-Chandra
Chatterjee, Upamanyu
Chatterji, Sarat Chandra
Chugtai, Ismat
Dalit literature
Desai, Anita
Devi, Mahasweta
Dhasal, Namdeo
Faiz, Faiz Ahmed
Gandhi, Mohandas K.
Ghālib, Mirza Asadullah Khan
Ghosh, Amitav
Gunesekara, Ramesh
Iqbal, Muhammad
Jhabvala, Ruth Prawer
Karnad, Girish

Mehta, Gita
Mistry, Rohinton
Naidu, Sarojini
Narayan, R. K.
Premchand, Munshi
Roy, Arundhati
Rushdie, Salman
Satyanarayana, Visvanatha
Seth, Vikram
Souza, Eunice de
Sri Sri
Suleri, Sara
Tagore, Rabindranath

Southeast Asia and the Pacific

Dhammachoti, Ussiri
Hayslip, Le Ly
Ho Xuan Huong
Kauraka Kauraka
Lim, Shirley Geok-Lin
Nguyen Du
San Juan, Epifanio
Toer, Pramoedya Ananta
Yathay Pin

AUSTRALIA AND NEW ZEALAND

Aboriginal movement
Astley, Thea
Brasch, Charles Orwell
Carey, Peter
Curnow, Allen
Flanagan, Richard
Frame, Janet
Hasluck, Nicholas
Keneally, Thomas
Lawson, Henry
Malouf, David
Mansfield, Katherine
Noonuccal, Oodgeroo
Sargeson, Frank
Stead, Christina
White, Patrick
Wright, Judith

EUROPE

Eastern and Central Europe
Arghezi, Tudor
Canetti, Elias
Gombrowicz, Witold
Hašek, Jaroslav
Havel, Václav
Kiš, Danilo
Kundera, Milan
Mickiewicz, Adam
Milosz, Czeslaw
Mrożek, Slawomir
Peretz, Isaac Leib
Popa, Vasko
Seifert, Jaroslav
Sienkiewicz, Henryk
Singer, Isaac Bashevis
Škvorecký, Jozef
Socialist realism
Szimborska, Wislawa
Tuwim, Julian
Wiesel, Elie

French-Speaking Europe
Anouilh, Jean
Apollinaire, Guillaume
Aragon, Louis
Artaud, Antonin
Balzac, Honoré de
Barbey d'Aurevilly, Jules-Amédée
Bataille, Georges
Baudelaire, Charles
Beauvoir, Simone de
Beckett, Samuel
Bonnefoy, Yves
Breton, André
Camus, Albert
Céline, Louis-Ferdinand
Char, René
Chateaubriand, François-René de
Cixous, Hélène
Claudel, Paul
Cocteau, Jean
Colette

Constant, Benjamin
Desbordes-Valmore, Marceline
Duras, Claire de
Duras, Marguerite
Éluard, Paul
Flaubert, Gustave
Gautier, Théophile
Genet, Jean
Gide, André
Giraudoux, Jean
Goncourt brothers, Edmond and Jules
Hugo, Victor
Huysmans, Joris-Karl
Ionesco, Eugène
Jaccottet, Philippe
Jarry, Alfred
Lamartine, Alphonse de
Lautreamont, Comte de (Isidore-Lucien Ducasse)
Leiris, Michel
Maeterlinck, Maurice
Mallarmé, Stéphane
Malraux, André
Maupassant, Guy de
Michaux, Henri
Musset, Alfred de
Naturalism
Nerval, Gérard de
Perec, Georges
Ponge, Francis
Proust, Marcel
Queneau, Raymond
Rimbaud, Arthur
Robbe-Grillet, Alain
Saint-Exupéry, Antoine de
Sand, George
Sarraute, Nathalie
Sartre, Jean-Paul
Simenon, Georges
Simon, Claude
Staël, Germaine de
Stendhal
Tzara, Tristan
Valéry, Paul
Verlaine, Paul
Vigny, Alfred-Victor de

Elytis, Odysseus
Hikmet, Nazim
Kanik, Orhan Veli
Kazantsakis, Nikos
Seferis, George

Italy
Calvino, Italo
D'Annunzio, Gabriele
Eco, Umberto
Fallaci, Oriana
Fo, Dario
Foscolo, Ugo
Ginzburg, Natalia
Lampedusa, Giuseppe di
Leopardi, Giacomo
Levi, Primo
Manzoni, Alessandro
Marinetti, Filippo
Montale, Eugenio
Morante, Elsa
Moravia, Alberto
Pasolini, Pier Paolo
Pavese, Cesare
Pirandello, Luigi
Quasimodo, Salvatore
Svevo, Italo
Ungaretti, Giuseppe
Verga, Giovanni

Russia
Akhmadulina, Izabella
Akhmatova, Anna
Amalrik, Andrey
Babel, Isaac
Bely, Andrei
Bryusov, Valery Yakovlevich
Bulgakov, Mikhail
Bunin, Ivan
Chekhov, Anton
Chernyshevsky, Nikolay
Dostoyevsky, Fyodor
Dudintsev, Vladimir
Ehrenburg, Ilya
Fadeyev, Aleksandr Aleksandrovich

Gogol, Nikolai
Goncharov, Ivan
Gorky, Maxim
Gumilev, Nikolai
Herzen, Aleksandr
Karamzin, Nikolai
Lermontov, Mikhail
Mandelstam, Osip
Mayakovsky, Vladimir
Nabokov, Vladimir
Ostrovsky, Nikolai
Pasternak, Boris
Pavlova, Karolina
Pushkin, Aleksandr
Shalamov, Varlam
Sholokhov, Mikhail
Solovyov, Vladimir Sergeyevich
Solzhenitsyn, Aleksandr
Tolstoy, Leo
Tsvetaeva, Marina
Turgenev, Ivan
Voinovich, Vladimir
Yesenin, Sergey
Yevtushenko, Yevgeny
Zamyatin, Yevgeny

Spain and Portugal
Alberti, Rafael
Arrabal, Fernando
Baroja y Nessi, Pío
Bécquer, Gustavo Alfonso
Blasco Ibáñez, Vicente
Castro, Rosalía
Cela, Camilo José
Espronceda y Delgado, José de
García Lorca, Federico
Generation of 98
Guillén, Jorge
Jiménez, Juan Ramón
Machado y Ruiz, Antonio
Machado y Ruiz, Manuel
Madariaga, Salvador de
Nobre, António
Ortega y Gasset, José
Pardo Bazán, Emilia

Abbas, K(hawaja) A(hmad) (1914–1987)
novelist, short-story writer, screenwriter

Khawaja Ahmad Abbas was born in Panipat, India, into a privileged, upper-middle-class family. After graduating from the University of Aligarh, Abbas became a journalist and went on to write novels and screenplays. While studying law, Abbas founded a fledgling newspaper called *Aligarh Opinion*. He was also a major Hindi movie director and screenwriter. Throughout his career, Abbas used films because of their accessibility to the uneducated and poor to promote his views on social castes and class conflicts. Abbas was also one of the founders and a member of the Indian People's Theatre Association (IPTA), which produced two of his plays.

Like many other writers, Abbas was concerned with national politics and wrote from a Marxist, sociopolitical perspective. This attitude was fostered and grew under the influence of Sri Aurobindo (1872–1950) and Mohandas GANDHI (1869–1948). Some of Abbas's most famous English works are *Tomorrow Is Ours: A Novel of the India of Today* (1943) and *Inquilab: A Novel of the Indian Revolution* (1955). These novels are good examples of Abbas's treatment of the oppressed as they struggle against social and political systems such as untouchability, fascism, and imperialism.

His screenplay for the classic Hindi movie *Awara* (Vagabond, 1952) is perhaps one of Indian cinema's most lyrical and compelling compositions on the irrepressible human spirit against the shadow of colonial capitalism.

In 1951, Abbas established his own film production company. His movie *Pardesi* (Foreigner) was selected for screening at the 1958 Cannes Film Festival in France. In 1968, Abbas was awarded the Padma Shri in recognition of his contribution to Indian literature.

Another Work by K. A. Abbas
The World Is My Village: A Novel with an Index. Columbia, Mo.: South Asia Books, 1984.

Abe Kimifusa
See ABE KŌBŌ.

Abe Kōbō (Abe Kimifusa) (1924–1993)
novelist, short-story writer, playwright

Abe Kōbō was born in Tokyo to Abe Asakichi and Yorimi. He moved to Manchuria with his family in 1925 but returned to Tokyo to finish high school. In 1943, he entered the medical department of Tokyo Imperial University, graduating in 1948.

Abe's first work was reflective of his experiences in Manchuria. In *On the Sign at the End of the Road* (1948), an opium addict relates his story of flight and imprisonment in Manchuria at the end of World War II. The narration is conveyed through a series of notebooks that the protagonist kept during the war as he mused over the nature of his native country and the loss of his home.

Abe's writing quickly became more surrealistic. The novel *The Crime of S. Karma* (1951) portrays a man who wakes up one morning to find that he has lost his identity. When he arrives at work, he finds that his business card has stolen his identity and, with the help of his fountain pen, wristwatch, and glasses, is making a play for his secretary. Like many of Abe's stories, *The Crime of S. Karma* combines logic and fantasy. The story won the Akutagawa Prize for new writers.

In the 1950s, Abe joined the Japanese Communist Party (JCP) and wrote for publications associated with the party. However, by the late 1950s, Abe was writing articles critical of the JCP's restrictive policies, which earned his expulsion in 1962.

During this period, Abe also began writing science fiction stories. As a genre, science fiction was new to Japan, but Abe broke open the field with his novel *Inter Ice Age 4,* serialized in the journal *Sekai* from 1958 to 1959. In the story, the scientist Katsumi uses a computer to predict the future and discovers that a future race of gilled underwater dwellers has condemned him because he cannot adapt to the changes that are in store for society.

Abe's most acclaimed writing was published in the 1960s: *The Woman in the Dunes* (1962), *The Face of Another* (1964), and *The Ruined Map* (1967). All three novels explore the theme of alienated protagonists who must overcome or accept change. For example, in *The Face of Another,* the protagonist's face has been disfigured, so he creates a latex mask to hide his scars. However, with the mask, he assumes a new identity, and the mask eventually forms its own identity and threatens to take over the wearer. *The Ruined Map* follows suit with a detective who searches for a missing husband and, during the process, becomes jealous of the freedom the escaped husband has found. The most well known of the three novels, *The Woman in the Dunes,* portrays the kidnapping of a man who collects insects as a hobby. Held in a dwelling beneath the sand dunes, he must come to terms with his new life.

In the next decade, Abe founded an experimental theater troupe called the Abe Kōbō Studio. For nine years, he directed plays, adapted a number of his stories and wrote several plays for the troupe. Notably, one of these adaptations—*Friends* (1967)—has been translated into several languages and performed internationally. It tells the story of a man whose life is invaded by a family who adopts him, moves into his apartment, and basically takes over his life.

Following the closing of the troupe in 1979, Abe wrote only three major novels: *Secret Rendezvous* (1977), *The Ark Sakura* (1984) and *Kangaroo Notebook* (1991). Unlike his earlier stories, these novels were not greeted with acclaim because they are difficult to interpret. For example, in *Secret Rendezvous,* a man searches for his missing wife in a hospital. During his investigation, he meets a man with a horse's body as well as a cavalcade of other strange characters. The reader is bombarded not only with bizarre visual images but also with a cacophony of sound imagery.

Abe died of heart failure while writing his final novel, *The Flying Man,* which was published posthumously in 1993.

Other Works by Abe Kōbō

Beyond the Curve. Translated by Juliet Winters Carpenter. New York: Kodansha International, 1991.

The Box Man. Translated by E. Dale Saunders. New York: Knopf, 1974.

Three Plays. Translated by Donald Keene. New York: Columbia University Press, 1993.

Works about Abe Kōbō

Currie, William. *Metaphors of Alienation: The Fiction of Abe, Beckett and Kafka.* Ann Arbor, Mich.: University Microfilms, 1973.

Yamanouchi, Hisaki. "Abe Kōbō and Ōe Kenzaburō: The Search for Identity in Contemporary Japanese Literature." In *Modern Japan: Aspects of History, Literature and Society*. Edited by W. G. Beasley. Berkeley: University of California Press, 1975.

Aboriginal movement

Aboriginal people have inhabited Australia for between 40,000 and 100,000 years. Prior to English settlement in 1788, Aboriginal people had minimal contact with other peoples. Their culture was very diversified, with more than 200 different languages spoken, but they shared a commonality of territoriality, kinship, family structures, the Dreamtime, spirituality, and ceremonies. The Dreamtime and dream songs of the Aborigines reveal their sense of sacred interrelation with the land and all other living creatures. They also explain the group's spiritual life and history and are the traditional source of their music, painting, and storytelling. Dreamtime connects the past, present, and future in a sacred spiritual reality.

A well-known musical form is the *corroboree,* a singing of life stories, rich in rhyme, rhythm, repetition, and poetry. This is part of a translation of a corroboree called *Moonbone:* "Now the moon is changing, having cast away his bone/ Gradually he grows larger, taking on new bone and flesh." Rock paintings and engravings also show the richness of the imagination in Aboriginal culture. Sacred rituals include singing, music, dance, and performance.

After colonization, European settlers appropriated Aboriginal lands and, through conquest and policies of forced assimilation (children were stolen from their parents and placed in European families), almost wiped out Aboriginal culture. However, beginning in 1938, an Aboriginal movement emerged that began to demand civil rights. This movement, influenced by the American Civil Rights movement, became stronger in the 1960s and again in the 1990s when Aborigines won some land rights and an apology from the Australian government for past abuses.

Aboriginal storytelling and poetry is very strongly influenced by traditional oral narratives. The storyteller Pauline McCleod, for example, has revived and created dream songs for a modern Aboriginal audience that had largely forgotten them. The following few lines of a typical modern poem, by Stephen Clayton, express the Aboriginal loss of a connectedness to nature:

> I am born of the land, my soul is the sun
> Nature is my mother,
> I am Mother Nature's son
> The wind is my spirit, running wild,
>   running free
> Water is my mirror, reflecting visions in me
> I am like a great river that slowly runs dry
> Polluted and abused, I am the River
>   slowly—I die. . . .

Anthropologists such as Robert Louis Nathan and Kingsley Palmer have revealed Aboriginal culture to the rest of the world, but it was not until the 1960s that the world heard the voice of the Aborigines speaking for themselves about their lives. Monica Clare's *Karobran: The Story of an Aboriginal Girl* (1978) is the first novel ever written by an Aboriginal woman. It was completed, edited, and published by Jack Horner because Monica Clare died in 1973 before she could finish the book. *Karobran* means "togetherness." The book is a moving autobiographical novel about Isabelle, an Aboriginal girl who was removed from her family and ill-treated as a domestic servant.

Several other Aboriginal writers followed Monica Clare. Hyllus Maris (1934–   ) wrote *Women of the Sun* in the early 1950s, but the book was not published until 1985. It is a collection of stories of the lives of strong Aboriginal women who looked to the ancestors for guidance. Jack Davis (1917–2000), a noted poet and playwright, belonged to the Nyoongarah people of southwest Australia and later became the editor of the Aboriginal Publications Foundation. His first play, *Kullark* (1982), was popular as a documentary on the history of the Aboriginals in western Australia.

He also wrote *The Dreamers* (1982) and *No Sugar* (1986), both known for their depth and closeness to the reality of the Aboriginal experience. *No Sugar* was voted the best stage play of the year by the Australian Writers Guild.

Oodegeroo NOONUCCAL, commonly known as Kath Walker, started writing in the 1950s. Her poems were about the struggles of the Aboriginal people and their demands for land rights and education. Noonuccal combined social issues with literature, thus revealing her depth of experience and a unique skill with the English language. She is one of Australia's greatest poets. Faith Bandler (1920–   ) wrote *Wacvie* (1977), in which she retraces her father's history as a forced worker on a sugar plantation in Queensland. Writers such as Noonuccal and Bandler also built political coalitions to lobby for positive changes for the Aborigines.

Holding up the Sky: Aboriginal Women Speak (1999) is a collection of powerful stories by Aboriginal women. They talk about issues concerning displacement from their homelands, forced removal from families, physical abuse, and lost identities. Collections like this one and *Writing Us Mob: New Indigenous Voices* (2000) are of great value because these are the voices of the Aborigines.

B. Wongar's *The Track to Bralgu* (1977) is a collection of 12 short stories that portray the barrenness of the once fertile land of the Aborigines and the exploitation by the white world of all the Aborigines' resources.

Several writers of mixed origin emerged to tell the stories of the Aboriginal experience because the government considered them to be Aborigines. One such writer is Sally Morgan (1951–   ), who wrote *My Place* (1987), an autobiography tracing the lives of her ancestors of the Nyoongal people of southwest Australia. Morgan captures their struggles to be educated and find jobs to sustain their families. She emphasizes the importance of the family roots that kept her family together. She also talks about the deep Aboriginal spirituality that believes in the spirits of the ancestors protecting future generations.

Today, there are institutions that specifically promote Aboriginal art and literature, such as the Aboriginal Center in Perth, the Aboriginal Publications Foundation, the Australian Institute of Aboriginal and Torres Strait Islander Studies in Canberra, and the Aboriginal Arts Board of the Australian Arts Council.

The Aboriginal literary movement emerged from autobiographies and life experiences. Memoirs written by women are often referred to as "herstories." They reveal a strong sense of the writers' connection with the land and the spirit world. Herstories are self-presentations, an expression of the self as part of others, even across generations. They were also a means of resisting government control. Aboriginal writings are seen by some scholars as political acts in themselves, as the writers fight against the oblivion imposed on Aborigines by the white culture to identify, recognize, and recapture some of the social, spiritual and literary elements of the Aboriginal past.

Works about the Aboriginal Movement

Brock, Peggy, ed. *Women, Rites and Sites: Aboriginal Women's Cultural Knowledge.* Boston: Allen and Unwin, 1900.

Clayton, Stephen. "I Am-Aborigine." Available online at www.dreamtime.auz.net/StoryAbor.htm.

Nathan, Robert Louis. *The Dreamtime.* Woodstock, N.Y.: Overlook Press, 1975.

Simms, Norman. *Silence and Invisibility: A Study of the New Literature from the Pacific.* Washington, D.C.: Three Continents Press, 1986.

Abrahams, Peter Henry (Peter Graham)
(1919–   ) *novelist, short-story writer, journalist*

When Peter Abrahams was five years old, his father, an Ethiopian, died. Abrahams was sent to live with relatives in Johannesburg, South Africa, far from his mixed-race mother. Although he returned three years later, the family's desperate financial situation forced young Abrahams to go to work for a metal worker. This nine-year-old boy was to grow up to become one of South Africa's best-known writers.

When Abrahams was still a young man, an office worker took him under her wing and read Shakespeare to him, awakening a lifelong love of learning. Throughout many years of menial employment, Abrahams held fast to his educational dreams, going to school when he could. At one point, Abrahams even tried to start a school for poor, black and colored South Africans, one where native languages could be spoken.

When Abrahams was 20, he took a job as a stoker on a freighter bound for England. Abrahams wrote regularly, publishing his first books during World War II: a collection of short stories, *Dark Testament* (1942), and a novel, *Song of the City* (1945), which begins to examine the costs of urbanization for black South Africans, a theme he took up again more successfully two years later in *Mine Boy*. His growing professional reputation made it possible for him to return to South Africa in 1952, when he took a job as a reporter for *The London Observer*.

His work as a journalist, including employment as a scriptwriter for the BBC, provided the opportunity to write creatively. Of Abrahams's eight novels, the two that have most solidified his reputation are *Mine Boy* (1946) and *Wild Conquest* (1951). Both novels deal with the great movements of peoples within South Africa during its several centuries of settlement and development. *Wild Conquest* focuses on the Great Trek of the Boers in the 19th century. These descendants of Dutch settlers spread north from Cape Province in search of a religious and secular paradise. They inevitably encountered indigenous peoples, including the Matabeles, who challenged the Boers' sense of mission. Because the descendants of the Boers were to set the foundation for the next century's apartheid laws, Abrahams's focus on these interactions combines historical perspective with contemporary focus. This type of novelistic approach made him something of a literary spokesperson for the developing antiapartheid movement in the 1950s and 1960s. *Mine Boy* follows a migration of a different sort: the economic movement of people in search of jobs in mines and in urban areas. Such economic migrations led to the dissolution of families and the creation of company and industry-controlled living areas. Although this novel calls for a multiracial coexistence as the only possible future for South Africa, the story ends with the deaths of many characters who embraced this noble goal.

Critical reception of Abrahams's many essays, novels, and autobiographical writings has been mixed, in part because of the contradictory messages of novels such as *Mine Boy*. However, his fusion of a European narrative style with a focus on African themes and tendencies made Abrahams one of the first voices from South Africa to question the divisiveness of apartheid from the perspective of a person of color.

Other Works by Peter Abrahams

The Black Experience in the 20th Century: An Autobiography and Meditation. Bloomington: Indiana University Press, 2001.
A Night of Their Own. New York: Knopf, 1965.
The View from Coyaba. London: Faber and Faber, 1985.
A Wreath for Udomo. London: Faber and Faber, 1956.

Works about Peter Abrahams

Lindfors, Bernth. "Exile and Aesthetic Distance: Geographical Influences on Political Commitment in the Works of Peter Abrahams." *International Fiction Review* 13 (Summer 1986).
Wade, Michael. *Peter Abrahams.* London: Evans Bros., 1972.
———. "Peter Abrahams at 70." *Southern African Review of Books* (June/July 1989). Available online at http://www.uni-ulm.de/~rturrell/antho4html/Wade.html.

Achebe, Chinua (1948–) *novelist*

Albert Chinualumogu Achebe (ah CHAY bay) was born in Ogidi, eastern Nigeria, when Nigeria was a

British colony. His father, Isaiah Okafor Achebe, was raised according to the traditions of the Ibgo people but converted to Christianity and became a church teacher. His mother, Janet Achebe, told him traditional folktales as he was growing up. Achebe learned to respect the old ways even as his country was adopting new ones.

After studying at University College in Ibadan, Achebe received a B.A. from London University in 1953. He became a producer and eventually a director for the Nigerian Broadcasting Company. In 1961, he married Christie Chinwe Okoli, with whom he had four children. After establishing his reputation as a writer, he left broadcasting in 1966. When civil war broke out the following year—eastern Nigeria, the Igbo homeland, attempted to secede from the Nigerian federation as a new country called Biafra—he traveled abroad to promote the Biafran cause. *Beware, Soul Brother* (1971) describes his war experiences, including his family's narrow escape when their apartment was hit by a bomb. In 1976, he became professor of English at the University of Nigeria. A serious car accident in 1990 left him paralyzed from the waist down. He is now professor of literature at Bard College in New York's Hudson Valley.

In *Home and Exile* (1988), Achebe writes that he decided to become a writer after reading Joyce Cary's *Mr. Johnson*. Critics praised the book's realistic portrayal of Africa, but Achebe thought its Nigerian hero was "an embarrassing nitwit." He decided that "the story we had to tell could not be told for us by anyone else, no matter how gifted and well-intentioned." His novels tell the story of Nigeria "from the inside," from Igbo resistance to British colonization through the coup that established the commander of the Nigerian army, General Ironisi, as head of state in 1966.

Critical Analysis

Achebe's first novel, *Things Fall Apart* (1958), tells the story of Okonwo, a great man among his people but someone who cannot adapt to the changes brought by colonization. Achebe does not idealize the old ways, but he presents them as worthy of respect. However, as Okonkwo's son Obierika tells him, "he [the white man] has put a knife on the things that held us together, and we have fallen apart." Okonkwo's refusal to adapt leads him to violence and ultimately to destruction. As Achebe explained in a 2000 interview in *Atlantic*, "With the coming of the British, Igbo land as a whole was incorporated . . . with a whole lot of other people with whom the Igbo people had not had direct contact before. . . . You had to learn a totally new reality, and accommodate yourself to the demands of this new reality, which is the state called Nigeria."

Things Fall Apart established Achebe as "the founding father of modern African literature," according to Harvard philosopher K. Anthony Appiah. Achebe was the first novelist to present colonization from an African point of view. He also introduced what he calls a "new English," using Igbo proverbs and pidgin English to express the African oral tradition in English. As editor of the journal *Okike*, which he founded in 1971, Achebe continues to promote new African writing.

The most influential of his works, *Things Fall Apart* has been translated into more than 50 languages. In the *Atlantic* interview, Achebe explains its appeal: "There are many, many ways in which people are deprived or subjected to all kinds of victimization—it doesn't have to be colonization. Once you allow yourself to identify with the people in a story, then you might begin to see yourself in that story."

At the beginning of Achebe's second novel, *No Longer at Ease* (1960), Okonkwo's grandson Obi is on trial for accepting bribes. Obi is one of the educated elite to whom the British plan to turn over the government when Nigeria becomes independent. "Like his grandfather, Obi was another victim of cultural conflict," notes Bernth Lindfors. "Obi had been weaned away from traditional values but had not fully assimilated Western ideals; having no firm moral convictions, he was confused by his predicament and fell." Torn between tradition and modern ways, Obi—and his generation—are "no longer at ease."

Arrow of God (1964) is set in the 1920s. Enzelu, chief priest of the patron god of his Igbo village, finds himself caught in a conflict between his people and British colonial administrators, who want to make him village chieftain. Gerald Moore, in *Seven African Writers,* notes that "As in Achebe's other novels, it is the strong-willed man of tradition who cannot adapt, and who is crushed by virtues in the war between the new, more worldly order, and the old conservative values of an isolated society."

The narrator of Achebe's fourth novel, *A Man of the People,* is involved in a fictional coup that foreshadows the actual coup the occurred the year the novel was published. Odili, a schoolteacher, at first supports M. A. Nanga, a villager who has become minister of culture, but runs against him when he realizes that Nanga abuses his power. Although set in the fictional Republic of Kangan, the satire has obvious parallels to present-day Nigeria. The novel reflects the conviction Achebe expressed in *The Trouble with Nigeria* (1983): "Hopeless as it may seem today, Nigeria is not absolutely beyond redemption. Critical, yes, but not entirely hopeless. Nigerians are what they are only because their leaders are *not* what *they* should be."

In 1979, Achebe received the Order of the Federal Republic for his contributions to African literature. "I would be quite satisfied if my novels (especially the ones I set in the past) did no more than teach my readers that their past—with all its imperfections—was not one long night of savagery from which the first Europeans acting on God's behalf delivered them," he reflected in *Morning Yet on Creation Day* (1975). Today, he is recognized as the first African to adapt the conventions of the European novel successfully and is Africa's most widely translated writer.

Works about Chinua Achebe

Ezenwa-Ohaeto. *Chinua Achebe: A Biography.* Bloomington: Indiana University Press, 1997.
Innes, C. L. *Chinua Achebe.* New York: Cambridge University Press, 1992.
Lindfors, Bernth. *Conversations with Chinua Achebe.* Jackson: University Press of Mississippi, 1997.

Moore, Gerald. *Seven African Writers.* New York: Oxford University Press, 1960.

acmeism

Acmeism (a term derived from the Greek word meaning "perfection") was a Russian poetic movement established in St. Petersburg in 1913. In a sense, acmeism was a reactionary movement that opposed the mystical elements of SYMBOLISM. The poets Nikolai GUMILEV, Sergey Gorodetsky (1884–1967), Anna AKHMATOVA, and Osip MANDELSTAM were the leaders of the movement and regularly contributed to *Apollon,* the main literary journal of acmeism. According to the acmeists, poetry should contain concrete ideas about culture and human experience rather than abstract and, often, solipsistic notions that are found in symbolist poetry. At the same time, however, the acmeists incorporated the symbolist emphasis on the role of mythical and religious figures in poetry. The mythical figures found in acmeist poetry stressed continuity of history and culture.

The movement lasted until the early 1920s and eventually disintegrated with the advent of SOCIALIST REALISM. The role of the acmeists, however, is enormous in terms of their influence on the later generations of poets and writers. The acmeists attempted to provide verse with significance that extended the bounds of social and political reality. Their revolution was of linguistic kind. The acmeists treated the individual as a being of cosmic significance rather than a dispossessed creature, tethered to a landscape grown ungovernably hostile.

A Work about Acmeism

Doherty, Justin. *The Acmeist Movement in Russian Poetry: Culture and the Word.* New York: Oxford University Press, 1997.

Adonis (Ali Ahmad Sa'id; Adunis)
(1930–) *poet, critic*

Adonis is one of the fathers of modernism in Arabic literature and is its leading proponent of avant-garde verse. *Songs of Mihyar the Damascene* (1960) is his most important book of poems, combining his concern for history and politics with his demand for a new kind of poetic language and a radically experimental poetic form. *The Static and the Dynamic in Arabic Culture* is one of his many books of cultural theory and literary criticism that earned a key, if controversial, place on the Arabic bookshelf. In it, Adonis describes cycles of change and stagnation in the history of Arabic culture, defining moments of MODERNISM as those times when creative new ways of looking at the world emerge and challenge habitual ways. These breakthroughs, themselves, gradually become habitual and inhibit creativity until the next moment breaks with tradition. In other volumes of theory, such as *The Time of Poetry* (1972), *The Shock of Modernity* (1978), and a massive work entitled simply *The Book* (1995), Adonis continues his philosophical task of clearing away what he sees as stagnant Arabic literary traditions and calling for an embrace of modernism.

Adonis is a proponent of intellectual poetry, opposing the traditional connection of Arabic poetics to musicality and *tarab,* the state of being entranced by a poem, typically a goal of Arabic poetry. "A Grave for New York" is a long, important political poem that cites Walt Whitman as an influence and also demonstrates the influence on Adonis of SYMBOLISM and surrealism, and a cryptic, almost mystical use of language. So contrary are many of his poetic methods to Arabic expectations that his readership tends to be small, though refined. Adonis's literary criticism, on the other hand, has had considerable weight in the world of Arabic literature, through his books as well as his founding and editorship of two literary magazines, *Shi'r* (Poetry) with poet Yusuf al-Khal (1957), and *Mawaqif* (Stances) (1968).

Born in the Syrian mountains and educated in Syria, Adonis moved to Beirut and took Lebanese citizenship. Influenced in his belief in the importance of myth and symbol by Anton Sa'ada, founder of the Syrian Nationalist Socialist Party, Adonis changed his name to that of a figure from ancient Syrian myth. He has taught at the Sorbonne and other European and American universities and is translated most extensively in French. His wife of many years, Khalida Sa'id, is an important literary critic.

Other Works by Adonis

The Blood of Adonis. Translated by Samuel Hazo. Pittsburgh, Pa.: University of Pittsburgh Press, 1971.

Introduction to Arabic Poetics. Translated by Catherine Cobham. Austin: University of Texas Press, 1991.

The Pages of Day and Night. Translated by Samuel Hazo. Evanston, Ill.: Marlboro Press/Northwestern University Press, 1994.

Victims of a Map: A Bilingual Anthology of Arabic Poetry by Samih al-Qasim, Adonis, and Mahmud Darwish. Translated by Abdullah al-Udhari. London: Al-Saqi Books, 1984.

Adunis

See ADONIS.

Agnon, Samuel Joseph (Shmuel Yosef Czaczkes) (1888–1970) *novelist, short-story writer*

Samuel Joseph Agnon was born Shmuel Yosef Czaczkes in the Jewish town of Buczacz, in the Austro-Hungarian Empire (now Poland). Agnon began writing at eight years old in both Hebrew and Yiddish and published his first poems in a newspaper at age 15. Though he did not attend school, he was educated by both his father, a fur trader with rabbinical training, and his mother, who taught him German literature. In 1907, he left home for Palestine (now Israel), where he changed his surname from Czaczkes to Agnon. He remained there his entire life, with the exception of 11 years spent in Germany from 1913 to 1924.

His folk-epic *The Bridal Canopy* (1931), an allegory on the decline of the Jewish religious life in Poland, is considered a classic in modern Hebrew literature. The plot chronicles the travels and the inner religious turmoil of a Hasidic Jew who seeks a dowry for his daughters in early 19th-century Europe. Agnon's greatest novel, however, is *The Day Before Yesterday* (1945), which is set in the period of the second *aliyah*, the wave of Jewish emigration to Palestine between 1907 and 1913. The novel is considered a cornerstone of modern Hebrew literature.

Nearly all of Agnon's symbolic and folkloric writing is set in Palestine. Many of his stories are influenced by the Jewish emigration to Palestine, Jewish assimilation into Western culture, and the contrasts between a traditional Jewish life and a modern Jewish life.

Agnon secured his place as one of the central figures of modern world literature for bringing the conflicts of Jewish culture to life. He won the Nobel Prize for literature in 1965 and is widely considered the greatest writer of modern fiction in Hebrew.

Other Works by Shmuel Yosef Agnon

Days of Awe. New York: Schocken Books, 1995.
Only Yesterday. Princeton, N.J.: Princeton University Press, 2002.
Shira. New York: Syracuse University Press, 1996.
A Simple Story. New York: Syracuse University Press, 1999.

A Work about Shmuel Yosef Agnon

Shaked, Gershon. *Shmuel Yosef Agnon: A Revolutionary Traditionalist.* Translated by Jeffrey M. Green. New York: New York University Press, 1989.

Aichinger, Ilse (1921–) *poet, short-story writer, novelist*

Ilse Aichinger was born in Vienna, Austria. Her father, Leopold, was a Jewish doctor, and her mother, Berta Kremer, was a gentile teacher. Aichinger grew up in Vienna and Linz, graduating from high school in 1939. The Nazis prevented her from attending medical school because of her Jewish heritage. During World War II, many of her relatives were killed in concentration camps. Aichinger became fiercely antifascist, a trait that would characterize her postwar writing.

Following the war, Aichinger enrolled in medical school in Vienna. She quit after five semesters to devote herself full time to a writing career. In 1948, she worked as a reader for Fischer Publishing Company and wrote *Die Größere Hoffnung* (*The Greater Hope*, 1948), a novel about a Viennese girl who sympathizes with her Jewish friends after the Nazi takeover of Austria. The following year, Aichinger cofounded the Hochschule für Gestaltung (Academy for Arts and Designs) in Ulm, West Germany. She married poet Günter EICH in 1953. The couple occasionally attended the annual meetings of the German writers' association, GRUPPE 47.

Aichinger wrote numerous short stories, radio plays, and poems in the second half of the 20th century. Influenced by the Holocaust, Aichinger's writings often take the perspective of the victims of German-Austrian society. Literary scholar James Alldridge explains that "her appeal is to a humanity deep within each of us, addressed in a language unadorned by flourishes and unadorned by experiments in usage." Aichinger won numerous German and Austrian awards, including the Georg Trakl Prize for Poetry and the Literature Prize of the Bavarian Academy of Fine Arts.

Other Works by Ilse Aichinger

The Bound Man and Other Stories. Translated by Eric Mosbacher. New York: Noonday Press, 1956.
Herod's Children. Translated by Cornelia Schaeffer. New York: Atheneum, 1963.

A Work about Ilse Aichinger

Alldridge, James C. *Ilse Aichinger.* Chester Springs, Pa.: Dufour Editions, 1969.

Aidoo, Christina Ama Ata (1942–)
short-story writer, novelist, poet, dramatist

Ghana gained its independence from Britain in 1957 when Christina Ama Ata Aidoo was 15; thus, in a sense, Aidoo came of age at the same time as her country. Her very name, with its combination of Christian and indigenous elements (she dropped her Christian name in the early 1970s), speaks to Aidoo's lifelong passion for exploring the fusion of elements that makes her people unique. Aidoo's works speak to the synthesis of traditional and Christian beliefs inherent in Ghana. Her family has a tradition of resistance to oppression, including a grandfather who was killed by the British. Aidoo is descended from the Fante, a group that was particularly active in their resistance to the British during the colonial period in Ghana. The Fante are part of a larger group of people, the Akan, whose traditionalist values are explored—and questioned—in many of her texts.

Aidoo won a short-story competition sponsored by a prestigious publisher at an early age. This led her to have confidence in herself as a voice for her people, but especially as a voice for women of color in Ghana and throughout the world. Because very few women in developing countries have easy access to educational opportunities, Aidoo has often written from the perspective of one who has succeeded against the odds. She voices the belief that education can lead to an awareness of a culture's limitations. In short-story collections such as *No Sweetness Here* (1970), poems such as those collected in *An Angry Letter in January and Other Poems* (1992), and in novels such as *Our Sister Killjoy* (1977), Aidoo voices a fierce resistance to gender subjugation—the oppression of women—and class domination. Her essay, "To Be a Woman," published in 1980, bemoans the traditional Akan degradation of women. As such, Aidoo challenges both the vestiges of the British colonial presence and the ingrained attitudes of Africans.

Aidoo was Ghana's minister of education for a brief time in the early 1980s, until her controversial views led to her removal from office. She now lives primarily in Zimbabwe and the United States, where she has had a series of academic appointments. Aidoo is a regular speaker at African literary gatherings throughout the United States and the world, where she continues to influence those interested in issues of gender, race, and class.

Another Work by Ama Ata Aidoo
Someone Talking to Sometime. Harare, Zimbabwe: College Press, 1985.

A Work about Ama Ata Aidoo
Nasta, Susheila, ed. *Motherlands: Black Women's Writing from Africa.* New Brunswick, N.J.: Rutgers University Press, 1992.

Akhmadulina, Izabella Akhatovna
(1937–   ) *poet*

Izabella Akhmadulina was born in Moscow, Russia. She graduated from high school in 1954 and began her literary career working for a small newspaper *Metrostroevets*. In 1955, Akhmadulina began her studies at the prestigious Gorky Institute of Literature and published her first poem. During her studies, she was briefly expelled from the university for the apolitical focus of her verse. She was allowed to return only when Pavel Antokolsky, a respected Russian writer (1896–1978), intervened on her behalf. In 1958, she married the poet Yevgeny YEVTUSHENKO, but they were later divorced.

Akhmadulina is often associated with the "New Wave" of Russian poets that emerged after Stalin's death. The New Wave poets often focused on themes outside the political agenda of SOCIALIST REALISM. Akhmadulina, in particular, addressed the craft of poetry in her verse, often exploring metapoetics as a subject in itself. Akhmadulina considers Marina TSVETAEVA and Anna AKHMATOVA to be the greatest influences on her own work.

With the publication of her first poetry collection, *Strings* (1962), Akhmadulina established her position among the major contemporary poets of Russia. Her careful attention to the poetic form and diction made her enormously popular with both the Russian public and critics. During Akhmadulina's prolific career, she has published eight books of verse: *Chills* (1968), *Music Lessons* (1969), *Poems* (1975), *Candle* (1977), *Dreams of Georgia* (1977), *The Secret: New Poems* (1983), *The Garden* (1987), *Poems* (1987), and *Selected Works* (1988). Virtually all of these books were critically acclaimed and celebrated for their lyrical beauty and impressive poetic form. These lines from "Autumn" are an example:

> Not working, not breathing,
> the beehive sweetens and dies.
> The autumn deepens, the soul
> ripens and grows round . . .

As Sonia I. Ketchian points out, "Akhmadulina's poetry has been lauded for forcefulness of expression and masterful execution of form, in its finesse and sentient approach to her subject and its underlying surroundings, the product of Izabella Akhmadulina's pen bears the unmistakable signature of a woman."

Akhmadulina was elected a member of the American Academy of Arts and Literature in 1977, but at home she often faced government criticism, and she was not permitted to publish any works in between 1977 and 1983. This government mandate, however, was completely reversed by 1989, when Akhmadulina was awarded the State Prize in Literature—the highest prize for literature in the Soviet Union. The mother of two daughters, Akhmadulina currently resides in Moscow with her husband Boris Messerer, an artist and stage designer. She gives readings throughout Europe and is also known as a translator, especially of works by Georgian poets. Her work is continuously acclaimed both in Russia and abroad.

Works by Izabella Akhmadulina

Fever & Other New Poems. With an introduction by Yevgeny Yevtushenko. Translated by Geoffrey Dutton and Igor Mezhakoff-Koriakin. New York: William Morrow, 1969.

The Garden: New and Selected Poetry and Prose. Translated by F. D. Reeve. New York: Henry Holt, 1990.

A Work about Izabella Akhmadulina

Ketchian, Sonia I. *The Poetic Craft of Bella Akhmadulina.* University Park: Pennsylvania State University Press, 1993.

Akhmatova, Anna (Anna Andreyevna Gorenko) (1889–1965) *poet*

Anna Akhmatova was born in a small town near Odessa, Russia, into a family of minor nobility. Her father, Andrey Gorenko, was a retired navy engineer, and her mother, Inna Gorenko, was in charge of the family affairs. The Akhmatovs moved to Zarskoye Selo, the birthplace of Aleksandr PUSH-KIN, when Anna was one year old. Akhmatova began writing poetry when she was 11. While in school, Akhmatova was an academically average student, more concerned with writing poetry than studying. Her father disapproved of her writing and told her that it brought shame to the family's name. From then on, Anna Gorenko signed her work as Anna Akhmatova. Akhmatova was an intense reader, and she particularly loved the poetry of Aleksandr Pushkin.

In 1907, Akhmatova began to study law at the university in Kiev. In 1910, she married the poet Nikolai GUMILEV, whom she had known since her school days. These years of intense work and passionate personal relationships produced two collections of lyrical poems, *Evening* (1912) and *Chiotki* (1914), notable for their striking images and skillful use of rhyme and meter. In all her work, Akhmatova cared more about the craft of poetry and its personal implications than about social issues. Both volumes received favorable reviews from the critics. During this time, Akhmatova adhered to ACMEISM, a poetic movement that opposed SYMBOLISM and emphasized clarity of expression and concrete imagery. Along with Gumilev, Akhmatova became the leading figure of this movement.

In 1918, Akhmatova divorced Gumilev, but his political difficulties (he was executed in 1921 for alleged involvement in an anti-Soviet plot) affected her standing with the authorities, who were already uncomfortable with her poetic preoccupation with love and religion. Between 1923 and 1940, none of her work was published in book form, although a few poems were published in journals. She worked as an assistant librarian at the Agricultural Institute and lived in poverty. In the

1930s, she faced personal tragedy when her son and her second husband were arrested for espionage. They were released only after personal intervention by Stalin. Her lyric cycle *Requiem* was composed during this period; inspired by her grief over her son's absence, the poems memorialize the suffering of the entire Russian people under Stalin. They were not published in Russia until 1989, but Akhmatova developed an enormous underground following in Russia, as well as a large audience abroad. During World War II, when Germany invaded Russia and laid siege to Leningrad, Akhmatova was enlisted to help boost public morale with radio addresses and readings.

Akhmatova refused to conform to the standards of SOCIALIST REALISM, and for this she was ostracized by many in the Soviet Writers' Union. She criticized the Stalinist regime and paid dearly for her honesty when, in 1946, she was publicly humiliated and expelled from the Writers' Union. In addition, in 1949, her son was sent to Siberia as a political prisoner, remaining there until 1956. Even after Stalin's death in 1953, Akhmatova continued to be criticized by government officials because her work supposedly did not address the needs and reality of the Soviet people. In spite of these adversities, however, Akhmatova became one of Russia's most famous poets. Small volumes of her poems and translations and her critical essays on Pushkin began to be issued in Russia after 1958.

Akhmatova did not break with the rich tradition of Russian poetry but rather enriched it. She also introduced Russian readers to a larger world with her translations of such great poets as Victor HUGO, Rabindranath TAGORE, and Giacomo LEOPARDI. Today, she is one of the most widely read and quoted poets in Russia. In addition to its extraordinary lyrical beauty, Akhmatova's poetry is associated with personal freedom, the expression of emotions, and political liberty.

During her lifetime Akhmatova received a number of awards, particularly from European countries, including the Etna-Taormina literary prize from the Italian government in 1964 and an honorary doctorate from Oxford University in 1965. She established a reputation as a "Russian Sappho" in many countries.

Other Works by Anna Akhmatova

Kunitz, Stanley, ed. *Poems of Akhmatova: Izbrannye Stikhi*. Translated by Max Hayward. Boston: Houghton Mifflin, 1997.

Meyer, Ronald, ed. *My Half-century: Selected Prose*. Evanston, Ill.: Northwestern University Press, 1997.

Reeder, Roberta, ed. *The Complete Poems of Anna Akhmatova*. Translated by Judith Hemschemeyer. Tucson, Ariz.: Zephyr Press, 1998.

Works about Anna Akhmatova

Dalos, Gyorgy. *The Guest from the Future: Anna Akhmatova and Isaiah Berlin*. Translated by Antony Wood. New York: Farrar, Straus & Giroux, 1999.

Reeder, Roberta. *Anna Akhmatova: Poet and Prophet*. New York: Picador, 1995.

Akutagawa Ryūnosuke (1892–1927)
short-story writer, poet, essayist

Akutagawa Ryūnosuke was born in Tokyo to Niihara Toshizō and Fuku. Shortly after his birth, his mother went insane, so Akutagawa was adopted by his uncle, Akutagawa Dōshō. He was an excellent student and took lessons in English and Chinese in addition to doing his regular schoolwork. In 1913, he entered the English department of Tokyo Imperial University. After graduating in 1916, he took up teaching at a naval school in Yokosuka and soon married Tsukamoto Fumiko. Three years later, he resigned to write stories full-time for the *Osaka Mainichi Newspaper*. In 1921, the newspaper sent him to China as a correspondent; however, health problems prevented him from writing any articles until he had returned home. At the age of 35, he committed suicide by drinking poison.

While still at university, Akutagawa began publishing short stories in a school literary magazine called *Shinshichō* (New tides) and he published a short story collection called *Rashōmon* (1915), set in medieval Kyoto. In 1916, the respected novelist

NATSUME Sōseki promoted his story "The Nose" for publication. The short story achieved widespread popularity, establishing Akutagawa as a writer. "The Nose" draws on the classical stories of *Tales of Times Now Past* (ca. 1107) for its main character, a priest who is troubled by a long, dangling nose. Akutagawa's best-known work, "Hell Screen" (1918), portrays the madness of an artist inspired to depict hell's burning fires. Toward the end of his short life, Akutagawa's style shifted sharply from well-plotted historical tales. In works such as "A Fool's Life" (1927), he wrote stories that were more confessional in style, set in the modern period, and narrated in the first person.

Akutagawa is known as a master craftsman. He commonly drew on traditional stories for his tales, in part to provide a believable setting for his fantastic subject matter. In all, he wrote about 150 stories in a variety of styles and diction with strikingly evocative precision. He achieved international renown as one of the earliest Japanese authors to be translated into European languages.

Other Works by Akutagawa Ryūnosuke

The Essential Akutagawa. Edited by Seiji Lippit. New York: Marsilio, 1999.
Tales Grotesque and Curious. Translated by Glen W. Shaw. Tokyo: Hokuseido, 1948.

A Work about Akutagawa Ryūnosuke

Yu, Beongsheon. *Akutagawa: An Introduction.* Detroit, Mich.: Wayne State University Press, 1972.

Alberti, Rafael (1902–1999) *poet*

Rafael Alberti was born in Puerto de Santa María near the Mediterranean city of Cadíz, Spain. After moving with his family to Madrid when he was 15, he began to study painting and had his first show in 1922. Soon afterward, he contracted tuberculosis and left Madrid for Sierra de Guadarrama to recover. It was then that he began writing poetry, and within several years, he published his first collection, *Landlocked Sailor* (1925), a group of folkloric poems that won that year's National Prize for Literature.

With the publication of other poetry collections, including *Passion and Form* (1927) and *Concerning the Angels* (1928), which differ from his earlier work in their more anguished and emotional themes, Alberti's reputation as a poet grew. He was considered part of the Generation of 1927, a group of surrealist Spanish poets influenced by the language and imagery used by the 17th-century Spanish poet, Luis de Góngora.

Like many other surrealist writers and artists, Alberti became much more political in the 1930s, first joining the Communist Party, then being expelled from it, and finally fighting on behalf of the republic when the Spanish civil war broke out in 1936. Being on the losing side, he was forced to flee Spain in 1939, settling in Argentina, where he wrote poetry, painted, and worked for a publishing house. During his exile, Alberti continued to publish, including two collections, *Between the Carnation and the Sword* (1941) and *On Painting* (1945), the latter of which reflects his love of that medium, and an autobiography, *The Lost Grove* (1942). Far from his native Spain, he experienced loss, as seen in his poignant 1952 poem, "The Coming Back of an Assassinated Poet," translated by poet Mark Strand, in which the speaker mourns the death of his dear friend GARCÍA LORCA: "You come back to me older and sadder in the drowsy / light of a quiet dream in March."

In 1961 Alberti moved to Italy, and after the death in 1975 of Franco, dictator of Spain, he finally returned to Spain, where he lived from 1977 until his death. His later poems, in *The Eight Names of Picasso* (1970), reflect his long friendship with the Spanish artist Pablo Picasso. Alberti is considered one of Spain's greatest 20th-century poets.

Another Work by Rafael Alberti

The Owl's Insomnia: Poems Selected and Translated by Mark Strand. New York: Athenaeum, 1973.

A Work about Rafael Alberti

Nantell, Judith. *Rafael Alberti's Poetry of the Thirties: The Poet's Public Voice.* Athens: University of Georgia Press, 1986.

Alcayaga, Lucila Godoy
See MISTRAL, GABRIELA.

Aleichem, Shalom (Sholem Rabinowitz)
(1859–1916) *novelist, short-story writer, playwright*

Shalom Aleichem was born in Pereyaslavl in the Poltava area of what is now Ukraine. His father was a religious scholar and wealthy man, but the family fell on hard times when Aleichem was 12. His mother died of cholera soon after. At this time, Jews in western Russia faced the increasing threat of pogroms (organized persecution or massacres). Throughout these difficult times, Aleichem attended a traditional *cheder,* an elementary Jewish school in which children are taught to read the Torah and other books in Hebrew. His father encouraged him to write and, when his family again achieved stability, he sought additional schooling at the Russian district school.

As a young man, Aleichem joined the army and then worked as a government rabbi for three years. He began his writing career in the 1880s, rejecting his mother tongue, Yiddish (considered, in that place and time, an inappropriate language for literature), to write in Hebrew and Russian. He published his first short stories under his pen name in 1883 at age 20.

When Aleichem turned to writing in Yiddish, "for the fun of it," he said, he described the impoverishment and oppression of Russian Jews with surprising, yet appropriate, humor. These stories are set in eastern Europe and in New York in the late 19th and early 20th centuries. Aleichem's themes are apparent most notably in *Fiddler on the Roof* (1964), the popular musical based on his stories in *Tevye the Dairyman,* (1918). Humor, combined with insight, have led many to compare Aleichem with the American writer and humorist Mark Twain.

A combination of the pogroms of 1905 and World War I convinced Aleichem and his family to abandon their home and relocate in the United States, where he attempted to establish himself as a playwright. He helped found, through his plays, the Yiddish theater in New York City.

Today, Shalom Aleichem is recognized as having been one of the greatest Yiddish writers. His five novels, many plays, and some 300 short stories illustrate universal themes of wisdom, humiliation, pride, and humor that find their voice in the poverty of the Jews of his era. His tales have touched generations of readers around the world. Known as the "bard of the poor," he said, "Life is a dream for the wise, a game for the fool, a comedy for the rich, a tragedy for the poor" ("Putting Sholom Aleichem on a Belated Pedestal," The *New York Times,* January 5, 2002).

Other Works by Shalom Aleichem
Letters to Menakhem. New Haven, Conn.: Yale University Press, 2002.
Nineteen to the Dozen. Syracuse, N.Y.: Syracuse University Press, 2002.
Tevye the Dairyman. New York: Random House, 1988.

A Work about Shalom Aleichem
Samuel, Maurice. *The World of Shalom Aleichem.* New York: Dramatists Play Series, 1948.

Alencar, José Martiniano de
(1829–1877) *novelist*

José Martiniano de Alencar was born on May 1 in Mecejana in the state of Ceará in Brazil. He came from a well-to-do family of the northeastern region of Brazil, and he pursued his higher education in Rio de Janeiro and São Paulo. After completing his studies, he moved to Rio de Janeiro in 1850 to begin his career as a lawyer and a journalist. In 1856, he rose to literary fame through his critiques of the sentimental poetry of a famous Brazilian author, Domingos José Gonçalves de Magalhães. That same year, Alencar published his first novel, *Five Minutes,* which came out as a serial in a daily newspaper.

Alencar also wrote plays, biographies, political analyses, and journalistic works, but he is best known as a novelist. He was one of the earliest novelists in Brazil, and his goal was to create novels that were unique to Brazil's situation as a newly independent nation and that could represent the Brazilian national identity. He wrote historical novels and novels about modern Brazilian life in urban and rural areas, but his most famous works are three novels whose main characters are indigenous Brazilians: *O Guarani* (*The Guaraní Indian,* 1857), *Iracema* (1865), and *Ubirajara* (1874). Alencar's image of Brazil's identity as a new nation was based on the mix of cultures between native Brazilians and Portuguese colonialists. Alencar's representation of miscegenation between Indians and white Portuguese colonialists as the root of the Brazilian race predicts the theories of an important Brazilian author of the 20th century, Gilberto FREYRE, who defined Brazil as a racial democracy. For Alencar, it was this mix that made Brazil's cultural identity unique. He valorizes the noble Indian characters in his romantic novels, and his work is considered part of the INDIANIST movement in Brazilian literature. Because he was the only novelist from that movement (all of the other Indianist writers were poets), and because he was one of the earliest Brazilian novelists, his work is especially important in the history of Brazilian literature.

In addition to being a novelist, Alencar had a long career in public affairs, which influenced his social ideals and his writing. Following his success as a lawyer and a journalist, Alencar was a deputy in the legislature and then minister of justice from 1868 to 1870. He ran for the senate in 1869 and received the highest number of votes. However, Pedro II, the emperor, had the constitutional privilege to select from three finalists, and he chose a different candidate because Alencar had previously criticized him. In spite of this disappointment, Alencar participated in public affairs throughout his life, in addition to his career as a journalist and later as a university professor. He was considered one of the greatest orators of his day. Alencar died on December 12 of tuberculosis.

Other Works by José de Alencar

Iracema: A Novel. Translated by Clifford E. Landers. Los Angeles: Getty Center for Education in the Arts, 2000.
Senhora: Profile of a Woman. Translated by Catarina Feldmann Edinger. Austin: University of Texas Press, 1994.

Works about José de Alencar

Haberly, David. *Three Sad Races: Racial Identity and National Consciousness in Brazilian Literature.* New York: Cambridge University Press, 1983.
Schwarz, Roberto. "The Importing of the Novel to Brazil and its Contradictions in the Work of Alencar." In *Misplaced Ideas: Essays on Brazilian Culture.* New York: Verso, 1992.
Treece, David. *Exiles, Allies, Rebels: Brazil's Indianist Movement, Indigenist Politics, and the Imperial Nation-State.* Westport, Conn.: Greenwood Press, 2000.

Alepoudelis, Odysseus
See ELYTIS, ODYSSEUS.

Allende, Isabel (1942–) *novelist*
Born in Lima, Peru, Allende is the daughter of Chilean diplomat Tomas Allende and Francisca Llona Barros. Her parents divorced when Allende was two, and she, her mother, and two brothers moved in with her mother's parents in Santiago, Chile. It was while living with her grandparents, spending many hours in their library, that Allende developed her passion for the written word. Her grandparents were the inspiration behind the characters Clara del Valle and Esteban Trueba in *The House of the Spirits* (1982).

Allende began her career working for the United Nations but soon found herself drawn to journalism. She wrote for the women's magazine *Paula* and also edited *Mampato,* a children's magazine. During this time she also experimented with writing short stories for children and producing plays. She finally turned to novel writing, which allowed a free range of expression. In 1962, she married Miguel Frias, an engineer, with whom she had two children, Paula and Nicolas. In 1973 her uncle, President Salvador Allende, was assassinated, and she and her family were moved to Venezuela for safety. The assassination had a profound effect on her: "I think I have divided my life [into] before that day and after that day," she told *Publisher's Weekly.* "In that moment, I realized that everything was possible, that violence was a dimension that was always around you." While in Venezuela, Allende learned that her grandfather was dying in Chile, and, unable to go to him, she wrote him a letter that evolved into her first novel, *The House of the Spirits* (1982).

Set in an unnamed South American country, the novel traces the experiences of four generations of the del Valle–Trueba family through 75 years of social change and politics in the 20th century. The novel employs MAGIC REALISM (a literary technique that allows fantasy and magic to intrude on otherwise realistic depictions of settings or characters) to tell a story of power relations and passion. It became an international best-seller and inspired a 1994 American film version starring Jeremy Irons and Meryl Streep.

Allende's next novel, *Of Love and Shadows* (1984), also set in an unnamed South American country (one that clearly resembles Chile in the 1970s), treats topics that are prominent in all Allende's novels: love, politics, violence, death, and strong women. Her third novel, *Eva Luna* (1989), is a first-person narrative by a heroine who tells stories first to save her own life and then to find love and fortune. Written after her divorce from Frias, the novel mirrors aspects of Allende's life.

In 1988, Allende married American lawyer William Gordon and moved to California. Her new home did not distract her from writing about Latin America, and her next work, *The Stories of Eva Luna* (1990), is a collection of 23 short stories that contain many of the characters first introduced in the novel *Eva Luna.* Allende followed this with *The Infinite Plan* (1991), a novel inspired by the life of her second husband.

Although all of Allende's novels draw deeply on personal experience and historical events, none of her works is more poignant than *Paula* (1995). Written in a Madrid hospital at the bedside of her dying daughter, this autobiographical work is a "collage of memories," tracing Allende's life, profession, and beliefs. The book ends on the day of Paula's death at Allende's home in California.

Allende found it difficult to contemplate writing again after the wrenching work of *Paula;* yet, by 1998, she had come back joyously into print with *Aphrodite: A Memoir of the Senses,* a memoir that celebrates the connections between eroticism and food and includes more than 100 recipes. Her subsequent novels, *Daughter of Fortune* (1999) and *Portrait in Sepia* (2001), reflect their creator's journey, telling sweeping stories set both in Chile and in California, involving characters first encountered in *The House of the Spirits.*

Allende's books, all of which are written in Spanish, have been translated into 27 different languages. She has received numerous literary prizes, including the Panorama Literio Award (Chile) in 1983, Author of the Year and Book of the Year Awards (Germany) in 1984, Colima Award for Best Novel (Mexico) in 1985, Mulheres Best Foreign Novel Award (Portugal) in 1987, Library Journal's Best Book Award (United States) in 1988, Bancarella Literature Award (Italy) in 1993. Allende is the most widely read Latin American author in the world.

A Work about Isabel Allende

Rojas, Sonia Riguelme, and Edna Aguirre Rehbeim, eds. *Critical Approaches to Isabel Allende's Novels.* New York: Peter Lang, 1991.

Allfrey, Phyllis (1915–1986) *novelist, poet, politician, journalist*

Phyllis Allfrey was born in Dominica, West Indies, to Francis Byam Berkeley Shand, former crown attorney of Dominica, and Elfreda Nicholls, daughter of Doctor H. A. A. Nicholls (later Sir Henry Alford Nicholls). She was educated by tutors and started writing poems, short plays, and short stories at a young age, publishing her first short story in *Tiger Tim's Weekly* at age 13.

Many years passed before Allfrey published her first collection of poems, *Palm and Oak I* (1950), which foregrounds one of Allfrey's self-expressed themes, her ancestry's "tropical and Nordic strains." Having her poem, "While the young sleep," win second prize in the Society of Women Writers and Journalists' 1953 contest, and hearing a literary agent's encouragement prompted Allfrey to finish her first novel, *The Orchid House* (1953). The novel's antichurch sentiment and its focus on a white family's decreasing powers rather than black empowerment distinguishes it from preceding West Indian literature.

Subsequent political involvement with the Dominica Labour Party, which she cofounded to assist the island's tropical-fruit workers, diverted Allfrey's attention from literary work. After the West Indies Federation (a political organization of Caribbean islands) dissolved in 1962, Allfrey worked as the editor for *The Dominica Herald,* an opposition newspaper, and the *Star,* a weekly newspaper that encouraged local writers, while writing poems, short stories, political essays, and editorials. As Elaine Campbell writes in a 1986 essay in *Fifty Caribbean Writers,* recent republications and critical examinations of Allfrey's works might enable her to "enjoy an overdue appreciation of her role as one of the few West Indian women to participate in the early growth of West Indian literature."

Other Works by Phyllis Allfrey

Contrasts. Bridgetown, Barbados: Advocate Press, 1955.

Palm and Oak II. Roseau, Dominica, West Indies: The Star Printery, 1974.

Works about Phyllis Allfrey

Paravisini-Gerbert, Lizabeth. "Jean Rhys and Phyllis Shand Allfrey: The Story of a Friendship." *Jean Rhys Review* 9, nos.1–2 (1998): 1–24.

———. *Phyllis Shand Allfrey: A Caribbean Life.* New Brunswick, N.J.: Rutgers University Press, 1996.

al-Malaika, Nazik
See MALAIKA, NAZIK AL-.

al-Sa'dawi, Nawal
See SADAWI, NAWAL.

Amado, Jorge (1912–2001) *novelist*

Born in 1912 in Bahia, the northeastern province of Brazil, Jorge Amado was educated in Salvador and Rio de Janeiro. He began to work as a journalist for a local paper at 15, and he was 19 when his first novel, *O Pais do Carnival (Land of Carnival,* 1931), was published. It has never been translated into English. *Jubiabá* (1935) is a picaresque novel about the childhood and youth of a black hero, set in the slums of a Brazilian city. *Sea of Death* (1936) examines the lives of the mulatto families who run small transport boats out of Salvador. *Captains of the Sands* (1937), the most commercially successful of all his novels, describes the daily existence of a band of homeless children led by a white boy.

By 1936 Amado had joined the Communist Party and had been arrested for his participation in a attempted coup backed by the Kremlin. As a result of his political activities, he spent much of the 1940s in exile in Paris and Prague. When he settled in Brazil again in 1952, he adopted a softer tone in his work, employing rich sensuality and a sometimes outrageous humor, but his novels still focus on the difficulties faced by the poor and by Brazilians of color. Two of the many novels of this later period are *Gabriela, cravo e canela (Gabriela, Clove and Cinnamon,* 1958) and *Dona Flor and Her Two Husbands: A Moral and Amorous Tale* (1966). Both of these were adapted for Brazilian TV, and he became in his lifetime the most famous of all Brazilian writers.

Brazilians took pride in Amado's international reputation. He was awarded France's Legion of Honor and Portugal's Camoens Prize and was a perpetual nominee for the Nobel Prize, though he never won. His death in Salvador in August 2001 was an occasion for national mourning.

Other Works by Jorge Amado

Dona Flor and Her Two Husbands: A Moral and Amorous Tale. Translated by Harriet De Onis. New York: Avon, 1998.

Gabriela, Clove and Cinnamon. Translated by William Grossman. New York: Bard Books, 1998.

Showdown. Translated by Gregory Rabassa. New York: Bantam Books, 1989.

The War of the Saints. Translated by Gregory Rabassa. New York: Bantam Books, 1995.

Works about Jorge Amado

Brower, Keith H., Earl E. Fitz, and Enrique Martínez-Vidal, eds. *Jorge Amado: New Critical Essays.* New York: Routledge, 2001.

Chamberlain, Bobby J. *Jorge Amado.* Boston: Twayne, 1990.

Amalrik, Andrey (1936–1980) *publicist, dramatist*

Andrey Amalrik, a playwright who had achieved modest success, caused an enormous scandal for the government of the Soviet Union when his essay, *Will the Soviet Union Survive to 1984?* (1969) was published in the West. Andrey Amalrik was sentenced to three years of hard labor on charges of "parasitism." On the day of his release, the Soviet officials added another three years to his sentence. The extended sentence caused an uproar around the world, and Amalrik went on a hunger strike for 117 days. In light of the protests, Amalrik's sentence was reduced to two years of exile in Siberia.

Will the Soviet Union Survive to 1984? painted a realistic and gloomy picture of Soviet reality. Amalrik recognized that the Soviet government's policies encouraged in the Soviet people a perverted psychology of mediocrity, in which the main goal was not to stand out from one's peers. He predicted that the Soviet Union would fall as a result of a great war with China and a massive revolt by different ethnic groups within Russia. Many of his predictions were realized when the Soviet Union finally collapsed in 1991.

On his release from exile, Amalrik emigrated to Western Europe in 1976, settling in Spain, where he died in a car accident in 1980. His other work of great importance, *Involuntary Journey to Siberia* (1971), describes the hardships that he faced in the Soviet labor camp for political prisoners.

Andrey Amalrik was one of the first Soviet dissidents to be seen on U.S. television when an interview he and his colleagues Vladimir Bukowsky and Pyotr Yakir gave to a United States correspondent was broadcast in July 1970. He is remembered today as one of the dissidents who exposed the dark side of the Soviet system to people around the world.

Other Works by Andrey Amalrik

Nose! Nose? No-Se and Other Plays. New York: Harcourt Brace, 1973.

Notes of a Revolutionary. Translated by Guy Daniels. New York: Knopf, 1982.

Amichai, Yehuda (1924–2000) *poet, novelist, short-story writer, playwright*

Yehuda Amichai, one of Israel's most widely esteemed poets in modern Hebrew, was born in Wurzburg, Germany, into a religiously observant family. By the time he and his family emigrated to Palestine (now Israel) in 1935, Amichai was able to read Hebrew fluently. He settled in Jerusalem but left to fight with the Jewish brigade of the British army in World War II. When he returned, he joined the elite Palmach unit to fight with the Israeli defense forces in the 1948 Arab–Israeli war. He also attended Hebrew University, where he studied literature and biblical studies and trained as a teacher.

Amichai is best known for his revolutionary style that helped create modern Israeli poetry. He evoked contemporary images—tanks, airplanes, and fuel—and used an accessible, nontraditional voice—charged with puns, idioms, and colloquialisms—that was new to Hebrew verse in the 1950s.

With his first volume of poetry, *Now and in Other Days* (1955), Amichai began to establish himself as a leading contemporary Hebrew poet and national treasure. His poems are now recited at weddings and funerals and by schoolchildren. He has published volumes of poetry, novels, a book of short stories, and a number of plays that have been produced in Israel. His poetry has been translated into more than 30 languages, including Chinese and Arabic, and, in 1982, Amichai received the prestigious Israel Prize for poetry.

Other Works by Yehuda Amichai

Amen. New York: Harper & Row, 1977.

Even a Fist Was Once an Open Palm with Fingers. New York: Harper Perennial, 1991.

Songs of Jerusalem and Myself. New York: Harper & Row, 1973.

Works about Yehuda Amichai

Abramson, Glenda. *The Writing of Yehuda Amichai: A Thematic Approach.* Albany: State University of New York Press, July 1989.

Cohen, Joseph. *Voices of Israel: Essays on and Interviews with Yehuda Amichai, A.B. Yehoshua, T. Carmi, Aharon Applefeld, and Amos Oz.* Albany: State University of New York Press, 1990.

Anand, Mulk Raj (1905–) *novelist, short-story writer, essayist*

Mulk Raj Anand was born in Peshawar, in what is now Pakistan. Educated in Lahore, Pakistan, and in London, Anand's fiction has been influenced by the literary traditions of both countries. Anand first began writing while in England as a book critic for T. S. Eliot's *Criterion.* After spending a number of years in England, he returned to India in 1945.

Anand used the structural techniques of the Western novel to write about India's social issues. He is often compared to R. K. NARAYAN, but Anand is different because of his choice of subject, which was the poor communities of rural India. His decision to write in English about people who could not read the language is the basis of much criticism against him. Anand claims, however, that he had to write in English because of practical necessity. Punjabi and Hindustani (his mother tongues)

publishers would not accept his books because of their "unpopular" themes; English language publishers were far more supportive.

His novels *Untouchable* (1935) and *Coolie* (1936) represent the struggles of the poor and underprivileged in British India. *Coolie* explores the life of an indentured laborer, Munoo, as he must travel across northern India to keep a job. *Untouchable* approaches the national problem of "untouchability" as it is revealed in a day in the life of an 18-year-old man, Bakha. Symbolically, the characters' growth in these narratives catalogues humanity's struggle against social abuse and represents the underprivileged state of an oppressed nation, such as India under British colonialism.

Untouchable leads up to a moment in Bakha's life when class and caste barriers cease to matter. This occurs when Bakha climbs up a tree to listen to GANDHI'S speech. Slowly gathering courage to enter the crowd, his fears of touching other people evaporate. As the novel progresses, Bakha finds that he must decide between Christianity and following Gandhi if he is to be free from social injustices. It becomes clear, however, that these choices do not offer Bakha any real escape from the evils of his own life. Either option would only negate the specificity of Bakha's struggles. Through Bakha, Anand tries to show that untouchability is not just a problem of casteism in India but a global problem whenever a powerful force seeks to oppress a weaker one.

Along with Munshi PREMCHAND, Anand was involved in forming DALIT literature, a genre addressed exclusively to the oppressed sections of Indian society. Because he wrote exclusively in English, his unwavering focus on the downtrodden helped bring their social issues into the international literary world for the first time in Indian literary history. In 1971, Anand was awarded India's National Academy of Letters Award for his novel *Morning Face* (1968).

Other Works by Mulk Raj Anand

The Road. New Delhi: Sterling Publishers, 1974.

Two Leaves and a Bud. New York: Liberty Press, 1954.

Works about Mulk Raj Anand

Cowasjee, Saros. *So Many Freedoms: A Study of the Major Fiction of Mulk Raj Anand.* Delhi: Oxford University Press, 1977.

Dhawan, R. K. *The Novels of Mulk Raj Anand.* New York: Prestige Books, 1992.

Andersen, Hans Christian (1805–1875)

fiction writer, poet, dramatist

It is believed that Hans Christian Andersen was born near Odense, Denmark. His father, Hans Andersen, was a poor shoemaker, and there is no record of his mother's name or occupation. Despite poverty and harsh living conditions, Andersen's father devoted much of his time to his son: He made him a wooden theater and other toys and read to him every evening. The time Andersen spent with his paternal grandmother also provided some of his most important childhood experiences, including going with her to Greyfriars Hospital, an asylum for the elderly, where she worked as a gardener. Andersen listened to the traditional stories of Denmark told by the old women in the spinning rooms of the hospital.

Andersen was as apt and studious a student as he was a voracious reader. Although his family could not afford books, Andersen borrowed them from the people in his neighborhood. He was fascinated by theater, reading Shakespeare and Danish dramatists. In 1819, he left Odense for Copenhagen in hopes of becoming an actor. He held various minor acting jobs at the Royal Theater, performing as a ballet dancer and a singer in an opera choir. He was dismissed by the management after three years. His years as an actor were not a complete failure: He attended the theater every night, acquired a knowledge of drama, and was befriended by several important figures of the Danish cultural community. He began writing plays, and his talent was recognized by Jonas Collin, a senior civil servant in the Danish government, who arranged a grammar-school scholarship for Andersen. At age 17, Andersen was placed in a class with 10-year-old students. He studied hard and passed his final exams in 1828.

Andersen began his literary career as a poet. Between 1827 and 1828, he published minor poems in newspapers and periodicals and won public favor. By 1832, he had produced two collections of poems, written lyrics for two operas, and created adaptations of two French plays for the Danish stage. In 1831, he traveled to Germany, where he established contacts with some of the leading figures of the romantic movement (*see* ROMANTICISM). In 1833, he received a grant from the Danish government that allowed him to travel throughout Europe.

Andersen wrote three novels between 1835 and 1837: *The Improvisator* (1835), *O.T.* (1836), and *Only a Fiddler* (1837). Surprisingly, Andersen's works were better received in Germany and France than they were in Denmark. Although his novels were popular, he achieved his status as a great figure of world literature by writing his famous fairy tales, the first volume of which was published in 1835. Written at the height of the romantic movement, Andersen's fairy tales were praised throughout Europe. He was treated as an equal by Victor HUGO and Alexandre DUMAS. In Germany, the reading public raved over Andersen's latest works, and publishing companies engaged in bidding wars over the rights to them. In 1844, Andersen finally received recognition in Denmark: He was personally invited to be the guest of King Christian VIII. In 1845, he visited England, where his works were enormously popular. He made numerous acquaintances, including a lifelong friendship with Charles Dickens.

During the late 1840s, Andersen wrote some of his best fairy tales, including "The Nightingale," "The Ugly Duckling," "The Snow Queen," and "The Story of a Mother." In his tales, Andersen often celebrated the common people, whom he portrayed as ingenious, diligent, and brave. The fantastic element accentuated emotion and imagination, qualities cherished by romanticism. In conjunction with his work on the fairy tales, Andersen also wrote numerous travel books and plays.

By the time of his death in 1875, Andersen was considered a national monument. He enjoyed personal visits from the king, numerous public awards, and appreciative letters from readers throughout the world. His fairy tales are as popular today as they were during his lifetime, and they have been translated into virtually every major language. As one obituary remarked, Andersen had known how "to strike chords that reverberated in every human breast."

Another Work by Hans Christian Andersen
Hans Christian Andersen: The Complete Fairy Tales and Stories. Translated by Erik Christian Haugaard. New York: Anchor, 1983.

Works about Hans Christian Andersen
Lederer, Wolfgang. *The Kiss of the Snow Queen: Hans Christian Andersen and Man's Redemption by Woman.* Berkeley: University of California Press, 1990.
Wullschlager, Jackie. *Hans Christian Andersen: The Life of a Storyteller.* New York: Knopf, 2001.

Andrézel, Pierre
See DINESEN, ISAK.

Andric, Ivo (1892–1975) *novelist, poet, short-story writer*
Ivo Andric was born in Doc, near Travnik, Bosnia, to a family of artisans. As a college student, he worked to help achieve unity and independence for the South Slavic peoples by joining Mlada Bosnia (Young Bosnia), a revolutionary nationalist student organization. During World War I, Andric was arrested and spent three years in prison, where he read the works of Sören Kierkegaard and Fyodor DOSTOYEVSKY. After his release, Andric held a number of diplomatic posts for the Yugoslav government. He was the ambassador in Berlin when World War II broke out, narrowly escaping when the city was bombed by German planes.

In the shadow of war, Andric wrote the historical series for which he received the Nobel Prize for literature in 1961. Commonly referred to as the Bosnian Trilogy, *The Bridge on the Drina* (1945; translated 1959), *Bosnian Story* (1945; translated 1959), and *Woman from Sarajevo* (1945; translated 1965) examine life in a country where multiple nationalities and religions meet and often clash. Influenced by both the war and a Kierkegaardian sense of isolation and pessimism, Andric wrote primarily about the misery of man and his struggle to maintain his existence. *The Bridge on the Drina,* Andric's most famous work, for example, tells the history of Bosnia from 1516, when the bridge was first built, to 1914, when it was partially destroyed in World War I. The bridge is Andric's metaphor for sorrow born out of struggle, particularly that between Christians and Muslims. Although the bridge was originally built to connect the eastern and western sides of the Ottoman Empire, in actuality it both united and divided people along cultural, religious, and generational lines. As the novel shows, it was Andric's hope, like the original purpose of a bridge, that people would someday live in peace.

After World War II, Andric continued to write short stories, essays, and travel memoirs about Bosnia. He wrote continuously until his death in Belgrade on March 13.

Another Work by Ivo Andric
The Day of the Consuls. Translated by Celia Hawkesworth. New York: Defour Editions, 1993.

A Work about Ivo Andric
Vucinich, Wayne, ed. *Ivo Andric Revisited: The Bridge Still Stands.* Berkeley Calif.: UC Regents, 1996.

Anouilh, Jean (1910–1987) *playwright*
Jean Anouilh, one of the most popular French dramatists of the post-World War II era, was born on June 23 in Bordeaux, France. Anouilh began writing plays at age 12. He briefly studied law at the Sorbonne while writing comic scenes for the cinema and working as a copywriter. In 1929 he collaborated with Jean Aurenche on his first play, *Humulus the Mute,* and by age 25 dedicated himself to a career as a writer. His best-known plays are *Antigone* (1944) and *Becket* (1959), both of which explore the individual's resistance to state oppression.

Anouilh's works, ranging from serious drama to absurdist farce, are too diverse to be considered a part of any one literary movement, but he was influenced by both SARTRE's existentialism and the plays of Jouvet, COCTEAU, GIRAUDOUX and Molière. He often blended choreography and music into his plots, and used the theater itself as the setting of his plays; yet, beneath the farce and spectacle, the tone was almost always serious and pessimistic.

Anouilh titled the collections of his plays with adjectives that described their dominant tone. The "black" plays, such as *Eurydice* (1941) and *Antigone* (1944), are his tragedies and realistic pieces. The "pink" pieces are dominated by fantasy and include *Thieves' Carnival* (1938; translated 1952) and *Time Remembered* (1939; translated 1955). The "brilliant" pieces, such as *Ring Round the Moon* (1947; translated 1950), *Colombe* (1951; translated 1952), and *The Rehearsal* (1950; translated 1961), are a blending of both "pink" and "black" plays set among the aristocracy. There are only four "jarring" or "grating" plays, black plays with bitter humor: *Ardele* (1949; translated 1959), *The Waltz of the Toreadors* (1952; translated 1956), *Ornifle* (1955; translated 1970), and *Poor Bitos,* or *The Masked Dinner* (1956; translated 1963). His "costumed" or "history" plays, including *The Lark* (1953; translated 1955), about Joan of Arc, and the Tony Award–winning *Becket* (1959; translated 1962), were especially popular in the United States.

In 1936, Anouilh began to collaborate on screenplays, directed two films, and wrote ballets. In the 1980s, he directed productions of several plays, both his own works and those of other authors. He died in Switzerland on October 3.

Other Works by Jean Anouilh

The Collected Plays. London: Methuen, 1966.
Ornifle. Translated by Lucienne Hill. New York: Hill and Wang, 1970.

A Work about Jean Anouilh

Falb, Lewis W. *Jean Anouilh.* New York: F. Unger, 1977.

Antschel, Paul

See CELAN, PAUL.

Anyidoho, Kofi (1947–   ) *poet*

Anyidoho was born at Wheta, a small town on the Keta lagoon in the Volta region of Ghana. His mother, Abla Adidi Anyidoho, was a composer and cantor of traditional poetry, as was his uncle, Kodzovi Anyidoho, who was responsible for the poet's early education. The region's rich poetic tradition became an important resource for Anyidoho's work. Anyidoho trained as a teacher at Accra Teacher Training College, where he began to submit poetry for publication. He graduated with honors in 1977 from the University of Ghana with a degree in English and linguistics. He then left for the United States to study at Indiana University for an M.A. in folklore and later received a Ph.D. in comparative literature from the University of Texas at Austin. His experiences in America provided material for *A Harvest of Our Dreams with Elegy for the Revolution* (1984), a collection of poems written as a series of letters home.

Although America may have served as subject matter for a series of poems, Anyidoho's work always seems to turn home. He uses the oral tradition of the Ewe people in many of his poems. He retranslates English to fit the cadences and rhythms of the Ewe people and uses many of the images and idioms of traditional Ewe poetry in his own verse. He draws on traditional poetic genres such as the funeral dirge and the halo, the song of abuse. He also uses the spiritual imagery of invocation, a calling upon the spirits. Yet, his poetry is aware of the fractures and challenges caused by globalization. "Slums of Our Earth" (1983) includes the lines:

> The darkness of the slums
> is the shadow side of
> proud structures on Wall Street

Anyidoho is committed to writing in both English and Ewe. He has won many awards: His first collection of poems, *Earthchild, with Brain Surgery* (1985), won the Valco Fund Literary Award for Poetry in 1976 while still in manuscript, the BBC Poetry Award for "Arts in Africa" in 1981, and the Poet of the Year in Ghana in 1984.

Other Works by Kofi Anyidoho

Ancestral Logic and Caribbean Blues. Trenton, N.J.: Africa World Press, 1993.

Elegy for the Revolution. New York: Greenfield Review Press, 1978.

Apollinaire, Guillaume (Wilhelm Apollinaris de Kostrowitski) (1880–1918)
poet

Guillaume Apollinaire was a major figure in early 20th-century French avant-garde literary movements. He was one of the innovators of the THEATRE OF THE ABSURD and as a critic, with his publication of *The Cubist Painters* (1913), established cubism as an artistic movement. He is best known, however, for his poetry.

Most of Apollinaire's personal history remains unknown. He was most likely born in Rome, the illegitimate son of the Swiss-Italian aristocrat Francesco Flugi d'Aspermont and Angelica de Kostrowitzky, a notoriously rebellious and adventurous Polish girl. He was raised by his mother, a heavy gambler, and they resided at various times in Italy, in Monaco, on the French Riviera, and in Paris.

A highly intelligent child, Apollinaire managed to pursue a solid education at the Collège Saint-Charles in Monaco and later at schools in Cannes and Nice by assuming the identity of a Russian prince. In 1900, he moved to Paris where he took a position working in a bank and became friends with artists such as Pablo Picasso and André Derain, playwright Alfred JARRY, and painter Marie Laurencin, who was also his lover. He traveled to Germany in 1921, which was where he received his introduction to two of his major influences: German romantic poetry and the torments of unrequited love.

Bold, forward-thinking, and often controversial, Apollinaire began his career as a writer by editing a number of reviews and publishing both satirical and semipornographic texts. He quickly gained a reputation as a dangerous foreigner and a thief, and in 1911, he was imprisoned for a week under suspicion of having stolen the *Mona Lisa* (it was missing, but Apollinaire was not involved). As a poet, Apollinaire began his career with the publication of a collection called *L'enchanteur pourrissant* (*The Rotting Magician,* 1909). The poems depict a vision of Merlin the Enchanter who, entombed by love, creates a new world of poetry from the depths of his suffering. The work was illustrated by André Derain.

It was not until the publication of Apollinaire's second collection, however, that he began to gain true critical notice as a promising young poet.

Critical Analysis

Alcools (*Alcohols,* 1913) was a breakthrough work in form and content, combining elements of classical verse with modern imagery. The poems were transcriptions of overheard street conversations and were often devoid of punctuation. The poem "Zone," for instance, which opens the collection, focuses on a period of time in the life of a tormented poet as he wanders through the streets, lamenting the recent loss of his mistress.

The beginnings of the cubist movement had a profound effect on Apollinaire. In *The Cubist Painters,* a collection of essays, Apollinaire explores cubism as a theoretical concept and as a psychological phenomenon. However, he was not one to hold to any school of thought for long. Shortly after the publication of his work on the cubists, he deserted cubism altogether for orphism, a movement which he created and described, as quoted by William Bohn, as "the art of painting new structures out of elements that have not been borrowed from the visual sphere but have been created entirely by the artist himself, and have been endowed by him with the fullness of reality."

When World War I broke out in 1915, Apollinaire enlisted in the army. A wound he sustained left him in fragile health. Nonetheless, he kept writing. *The Poet Assassinated* (1916), written from his hospital bed, is a novella in the form of a tribute to the life of the fictional great poet Croniamantal, from his birth to his life as a poet and ultimately his death at the hands of an angry mob.

Apollinaire's one play, *Les mamelles de Tirésias* (*The Breasts of Tiresias*), was staged in 1917. Apollinaire subtitled the work "Drame surréaliste" ("surrealist drama")—thus laying ground for yet another avant-garde movement, surrealism. The play combines the playwright's own sexual obsessions with a satirical exploitation of Greek legend. It also focuses, in a farcical manner, on the low birthrate in France during the late 19th and early 20th centuries. It tells the story of Thérèse, a discontented housewife who decides to give up being a woman. She lets her breasts (red and blue balloons) float out over the audience and becomes Tiresias, named for the Greek seer who, in the legend, was granted the opportunity to experience life as a woman. In 1947, the play was made into an opera by Francis Poulenc.

For several years beginning in 1913, Apollinaire worked on a collection of experimental poems that form visual images on the page. The result, *Calligrammes*, was published in 1918, shortly before the poet's death.

After a series of well-known and often high-profile affairs, Apollinaire married Jaqueline Kolb in 1918. He succumbed to influenza that same year, dying on November 9 in Paris.

Other Works by Guillaume Apollinaire

Calligrammes: Poems of Peace and War (1913–1916). Translated by Anne Hyde Greet. Berkeley: University of California Press, 1991.

Les onze mille vierges (The eleven thousand virgins) and *Les Mémoires d'un jeune Don Juan* (Memoirs of a young Don Juan). In *Flesh Unlimited*. Translated by Alexis Lykiard. London: Creation, 2000.

The Poet Assassinated. Translated by Matthew Josephson. Cambridge, Mass.: Exact Change, 2000.

Selected Writings of Guillaume Apollinaire. Translated by Roger Shattuck. New York: Norton, 1971.

A Work about Guillaume Apollinaire

Bohn, William. *Apollinaire and the International Avante-Garde*. Albany: State University of New York Press, 1997.

Appelfeld, Aharon (1932–) *novelist, essayist, short-story writer*

Aharon Appelfeld was born in Czernowitz, Romania (now Chernivtsi, Ukraine). When he was eight, his mother was killed by the Nazis, and his father was sent to a Nazi work camp. Appelfeld himself was deported to a concentration camp but managed to escape and spent the next three years hiding and wandering in the nearby forests and villages of the Ukraine on his own. In a 1998 interview with the *New York Times* he said, "I lived with marginal people during the war—prostitutes, horse thieves, witches, fortune tellers. They gave me my real education."

Eventually, Appelfeld became a kitchen boy in the Russian army. He found his way to refugee camps in Yugoslavia and Italy and, in 1948, at age 16, went to the new state of Israel. It was there, at age 28, that he reunited with his father and began to teach at a kibbutz.

Much of Appelfeld's writing explores themes of the Holocaust. Yet, he says, "Mainly, I write Jewish stories, but I don't accept the label Holocaust writer. Of my 20 books, perhaps one-third are on the Holocaust period, one-third on Israel, and one-third on Jewish life in general." In his highly acclaimed novels, such as *Badenheim 1939* (1979), Appelfeld rejects literalism and instead uses abstract symbolism —creating dreamlike scenes—and fable to examine the inner workings of his characters. In both *Badenheim*, and another novel, *To the Land of Cattails* (1987), he employs an almost hallucinatory sense of the Holocaust that is evident in much of his work.

Appelfeld is one of Israel's preeminent novelists, largely due to his literary style of exploring the Holocaust and his ability to bring the enormous dimensions of the Holocaust to a human scale. His works have received critical and popular acclaim. He has served as professor of Hebrew Literature at Ben-Gurion University and has held visiting professorships at Boston University, Brandeis, and Yale. He has been a visiting scholar at Oxford and Harvard. Among his many awards and honors are the Bialik Prize, the Harold U. Ribelow Prize, and the Israel Prize.

Other Works by Aharon Appelfeld

The Age of Wonders. Boston: Godine, 1990.
Katerina. New York: Norton, 1992.
To the Land of Reeds. New York: Grove Atlantic Monthly Press, 1994.
TZILI: The Story of a Life. New York: Grove Press, 1996.

A Work about Aharon Appelfeld

Cohen, Joseph. *Voices of Israel: Essays on and Interviews with Yehuda Amichai, A.B. Yehoshua, T. Carmi, Aharon Applefeld, and Amos Oz.* Albany: State University of New York Press, 1990.

Aragon, Louis (1897–1982) *poet, novelist, essayist*

Louis Aragon was born in Paris. He studied medicine at the University of Paris and served as an auxiliary doctor in World War I. During this time, he met the poet André BRETON, who introduced him to surrealism and DADA.

In 1919, Aragon, Breton, and fellow writer and activist Philippe Soupault (1897–1990) founded the literary review *Littérature*. Aragon wrote his first collection of poems, *Feu de joie* (1920), to echo the dadaist desire to destroy traditional institutions and values. He also published *Anicet; ou, Le Panorama* (1921), a novel that parodies Picasso's success through the career of its cynical hero, Bleu; *Le Libertinage* (1924), a surrealist short-story collection; *Le Mouvement perpetual* (*Perpetual Movement,* 1925), a novel; and *Le paysan de Paris* (*The Paris Peasant,* 1926), in which the city's parks and cafés are the setting for a series of intense encounters.

Aragon broke from Breton and Soupault in 1931 and joined the Communist Party. He visited the Soviet Union and returned to France to write "The Red Front," a poem influenced by the Russian poet Vladimir MAYAKOVSKY that calls for revolution in France. In the 1930s and 1940s, Aragon advocated SOCIALIST REALISM in his works.

During World War II, Aragon was taken prisoner but managed to escape to the Unoccupied Zone. When the Nazis occupied France, he became a key figure in the resistance. *Le Crève-Coeur* (1941) was one of five poetry collections Aragon wrote, detailing the Nazi occupation of France. His poetry took on a nationalistic sentiment, and he helped form a network of writers for the Resistance journals.

After the liberation, Aragon attempted a new form of novel that was almost journalistic in style. He also edited a French literary magazine and served as a member of the French Communist Party. In 1957, he was awarded the Lenin Peace Prize. He began to express a dislike for socialist realism and in 1968 attacked the Soviet Union for its intervention in Czechoslovakia. His later works include criticism and several autobiographical poems and novels. He died in Paris on December 24.

Other Works by Louis Aragon

The Adventures of Telemachus. Translated by Renee Riese Hubert and Judd D. Hubert. Cambridge, Mass.: Exact Change, 1997.
Le Con d'Irène. In *Flesh Unlimited.* Translated by Alexis Lykiard. London: Creation, 2000.
Paris Peasant. Translated by Simon W. Taylor. Cambridge, Mass.: Exact Change, 1995.

Works about Louis Aragon

Adereth, Max. *Elsa Triolet and Louis Aragon: An Introduction to Their Interwoven Lives and Works.* Lewiston, N.Y.: Edwin Mellen Press, 1994.
Becker, Lucille F. *Louis Aragon.* Boston: Twayne, 1971.

Arenas, Reinaldo (1943–1990) *novelist,*
poet, essayist, short-story writer, playwright

Reinaldo Arenas was born in Holguín, Cuba, to Oneida Fuentes Rodríguez and Antonio Arenas Machín. Because of his family's impoverished condition, Arenas received virtually no formal education and had little access to books, but his active imagination drove him to begin writing at an early age. After joining Fidel Castro's revolutionary army at age 15 and serving for a short time, he completed a degree in agricultural accounting.

Published when he was 21, Arenas's first book, *Singing from the Well,* (the first of a series of autobiographical novels) brought him some recognition, but because relatively few copies were printed, it remained unknown outside of Cuba. As Arenas began to speak out in his writings against Castro's regime and about his own homosexuality, his books were increasingly censored and suppressed in Cuba. He was, however, able to publish some works overseas, including *The Ill-Fated Peregrinations of Fray Servando,* which first appeared in a French translation in 1968. A first-person account of the title character's fantastic travels through Europe and the Americas, the novel may represent Arenas's best-known and most widely read book. Here and elsewhere, Arenas writes about homosexuality, as well as the more encompassing issue of the individual's right to self-determination and self-expression. After escaping Cuba and establishing residence in the United States, Arenas went on to publish an extensive amount of fiction, drama, poetry, and criticism. Among the works he wrote in exile are *The Color of Summer* (1993) and *The Assault* (1994), both part of his fictional autobiography and published posthumously.

Arenas was and continues to be a controversial but much celebrated author in Latin America and the rest of the world. His confrontation of issues related to sexuality and societal stereotypes and his vivid depiction of life under the Castro regime set him apart as one of the most important Cuban writers of the 20th century. Terminally ill with AIDS, he committed suicide on December 7.

Another Work by Reinaldo Arenas
Before Night Falls. Translated by Dolores M. Koch. New York: Viking, 1993.

A Work about Reinaldo Arenas
Soto, Francisco. *Reinaldo Arenas.* Boston: Twayne, 1998.

Arghezi, Tudor (Ion N. Theodorescu)
(1880–1967) *poet, novelist, nonfiction writer*

Tudor Arghezi was born in Bucharest, Romania. He took the pseudonym Arghezi because of its similarity to Argesis, the ancient name of the river Arges, of which he was very fond. As a teenager, Arghezi was rebellious and was often involved in political youth movements. He turned to writing as a focus for his ideas and began to publish in 1896, signing his works as Ion Theo. In his early 20s, Arghezi began to travel abroad, spending four years in the Cernica Monastery and a brief period at a monastery in Paris, where he converted to Catholicism. He ultimately moved to Geneva, where he wrote poetry, much of which was influenced by religion and Arghezi's own thoughts on the nature of life and death.

In 1912, Arghezi returned to Romania, where he published pamphlets and lyrics, many of which aggressively advocated the neutrality of Romania. For this, Arghezi was imprisoned, along with 11 other writers and journalists, and spent from 1918 to 1920 at Vacaresti Penitentiary.

Arghezi's first volume of poetry, *Cuvinte Potrivite (Arranged Words),* was published in 1927. This work gained him celebrity status among the Romanian people. He continued to publish other volumes, including *Flowers of Mould* (1931), inspired by his years in prison, *Notebook for the Night* (1935), and *Choirs* (1939). The artistic novelty of these collections shocked readers. Arghezi did not conform to any preexisting poetic formulas. Instead, his writing showed a restlessness, and a bold and innovative combination of often crude, forceful language, and a traditional reliance on folklore and mythology. Mainly religious in theme, Arghezi focused on life, love, humanity, death, and the nature of God.

In 1931, the same year in which Arghezi published *Flowers of Mould,* he turned his attention to writing poetry and prose for children. *Cartea cu Jucarii* (1931) was the first of several of his works for children that are still used in Romanian schools today. Between 1931 and 1967, Arghezi was at his most prolific, writing, in addition to the children's works, the poetry collections *Notebook for the Night* and *Choirs,* and three novels: *Mother's Love and Filial Devotion* (1934), *Cimitrul Buna-Vestire* (1936), and *Lina* (1942), which was actually an extended poem in prose form.

Alongside his work as a writer, Arghesi also managed the Romanian newspaper, *Bilete de Papagal.* Because of the sarcastic and often satirical political pamphlets it published, Arghezi once again came under police scrutiny. The paper was ultimately confiscated, and he was imprisoned for a year in Bucharest.

After his release from prison, Arghezi was considered to be rehabilitated. Under the Communist regime, he was awarded numerous prizes for his work, was elected as a member of the Romanian Academy, and twice was celebrated as the National Poet of Romania. He began to collaborate with political officials, writing poetry that supported the goals of the regime. He was buried in the garden of his house, which is managed today as a museum in his honor.

Other Works by Tudor Arghezi

Poems: Tudor Arghezi. Translated by Andrei Bantas. Bucharest: Minerva Publishing House, 1983.
Selected Poems of Tudor Arghezi. Translated by Michael Impey and Brian Swann. Princeton, N.J.: Princeton University Press, 1976.

Arnim, Bettina von (Catarina Elisabetha Ludovica Magdalena Brentano, Bettine)
(1785–1859) *poet, fiction writer*

Bettina von Arnim was one of 20 children fathered by the wealthy Italian merchant Peter Anton Brentano. She was the seventh child of her mother, Maximiliane von La Roche. Bettina was born in the German city of Frankfurt am Main. Her early influences included her grandmother Sophie von La Roche and brother Clemens Brentano, both well-known writers. Like her grandmother and mother, Bettina developed a friendship with Johann Wolfgang von GOETHE. In 1811, Bettina married Clemens's friend, Ludwig Achim von Arnim, an editor of folk song collections. Although she published a few songs for her husband's company, Bettina did not work full time as a writer until after Achim's death in 1831.

Bettina's first book, *Goethe's Briefwechsel mit einem Kinde* (*Goethe's Correspondence with a Child,* 1835), was based on her correspondence with Goethe and his mother. Arnim edited these letters and poems to provide a fictionalized description of events, dreams, and thoughts. Although controversial for its erotic content, the book was a literary success. Arnim used her correspondence with two friends and a brother to produce three more books exploring the topics of love and friendship.

Arnim's other writings include musical compositions and fairy tales that she wrote with her daughters. As a widow, she was actively involved in the political causes of opposing censorship and governmental abuse. Arnim also used her works to promote social reforms to help the poor and the sick. Her biographers Arthur Helps and Elizabeth Jane Howard explain that Arnim "had a talent for social satire" and was "a penetrating observer" of life in early 19th-century Europe.

Other Works by Bettina von Arnim

Goethe's Correspondence with a Child. Boston: Tichner and Fields, 1859.
The Life of High Countess Gritta von Ratsinourhouse. Gisela von Arnim Grimm, coauthor. Translated by Lisa Ohm. Lincoln: University of Nebraska Press, 1999.

A Work about Bettina von Arnim

Helps, Arthur, and Elizabeth Jane Howard. *Bettina: A Portrait.* London: Chatto and Windus, 1957.

Arp, Hans (Jean Arp) (1887–1966) *poet*

Hans Arp was born in Strasbourg, Alsace. Now part of France, Alsace belonged to Germany at the time of Arp's birth. His father, Pierre-Guillaume Arp, operated a cigar and cigarette factory. Arp's mother, Josephine, was French, and the family sympathized politically with France. Arp grew up speaking German, French, and the Alsatian dialect. His childhood daydreams translated into an early literary creativity. Arp published his first poem, written in Alsatian, at age 15. Two years later, he published three more poems.

Although a gifted poet, Arp would achieve his greatest fame as a painter and sculptor. He studied art in Strasbourg, Weimar, and Paris. After moving to Switzerland, Arp produced abstract painting and in 1916 helped found the DADA movement in art. In 1921, he married the artist Sophie Taeuber. Five years later, he changed his name from Hans to Jean.

Arp published his first collection of poetry, written in German, in 1920. His poems gained a wider audience in 1948 when a New York firm published his collection *On My Way: Poetry and Essays, 1912–1947*. Arp's early verse was conventional but amusing and inventive. In the 1940s and 1950s, his poems were written as a series of dreamlike word associations and had more emotional depth. The historian Hermann Boeschenstein explains that Arp was a pioneer in "freeing the word from the task of relating to and disclosing the meaning of outer and inner realities. Language as such is advanced to the central position in poetry and forms its theme."

Other Works by Hans Arp

The Isms of Art. 1925. Authorized Reprint Edition. New York: Arno Press, 1968.

Jean, Marcel, ed. *Arp on Arp: Poems, Essays, Memories*. Translated by Joachim Neugroschel. New York: Viking Press, 1972.

A Work about Hans Arp

Last, Rex W. *German Dadaist Literature: Kurt Schwitters, Hugo Ball, Hans Arp*. Boston: Twayne, 1973.

Arp, Jean

See ARP, HANS.

Arrabal, Fernando (1937–   ) *playwright, novelist*

Fernando Arrabal was born in Melilla, Spanish Morocco. His childhood was extremely traumatic. In the Spanish civil war his father was an officer in the liberal republican army, and his mother was a fascist sympathizer. At the end of the war, she betrayed his father to the authorities, and he was condemned to death. The violent loss of his father, combined with Arrabal's knowledge of his mother's betrayal, permanently scarred him.

When Arrabal was four years old, his family moved to Spain, where he attended school. As a young boy, he would entertain himself by constructing puppet theaters and putting on plays. These experiences play an important role in some of his later works. Arrabal was also fascinated by Charlie Chaplin movies; later in life, he used slapstick and the stylized acting techniques of Chaplin in the context of his Panic Theater movement.

Unable to find attractive career opportunities in Franco's Spain, Arrabal moved to Paris to pursue his career as a playwright. Ironically, around the same time he arrived in Paris, he discovered he had tuberculosis. Nevertheless, he persisted in working arduously at his writing and, in 1958, his efforts paid off when a Paris publisher gave him a lifetime contract.

The Labyrinth (1956), one of Arrabal's early plays, reflects the depressing and daunting quality of his early life. It resembles to some degree the dark fantasies of Franz KAFKA. A nightmarish play, it portrays the horrors of the modern world as a sort of absurd hell. As Arrabal developed as a writer, he persisted in his use of absurdity. In his later plays, however, the effect was more often black humor rather than terror or angst.

In the 1960s, Arrabal emerged as one of the central writers of the THEATRE OF THE ABSURD, a movement pioneered by such writers as Antonin ARTAUD and Samuel BECKETT. The movement had many subcategories of playwrights who shared a common use of absurd elements as a method to revitalize the stolid conventions of traditional Western theater.

Arrabal's particular subcategory was a style of theater he called Panic Theater. The Greek god of surprise and confusion, Pan, for whom the movement was named, brings both pleasure and terror when he appears. It is important to remember that the scope of Panic Theater extends beyond the simple definition of fear that we normally associate with panic.

Critical Analysis

Arrabal's play *The Architect and the Emperor of Assyria* (1965) is an example of the height of Panic Theater. The play begins when the emperor of Assyria's plane crashes on a desert island and he is the only one who survives. He finds on this island an architect who is not quite human. He is a supernatural creature who is able to control night and day and the seasons. The emperor nevertheless is unimpressed and begins to try to educate the architect in the manners of bourgeois society. The two men fall into a sadomasochistic relationship that involves acting out plays in which they assume opposite roles, such as a pair of fiancés, mother and son, a nun and her confessor, and a doctor and his patient. As the play progresses, the two actors switch roles, behave like each other, and act out scenes by themselves playing two people. It becomes obvious that they are each other's double and part of the same mind.

The use of games and ritualized behavior to structure the action of the play in lieu of a plot is one of Arrabal's major innovations. In addition, the absurd sequence of events creates confusion and incomprehensibility that embodies one of the main aspects of Panic Theater. Arrabal believed that to be accurate to life, art must be confusing and filled with chance or absurdity. *The Architect and the Emperor of Assyria* can be seen as a psy-chological drama that, perhaps, takes place within a single mind, a kind of dream projected onto the stage.

In the late 1960s, after being censored and arrested in Spain, Arrabal began to become more political in his drama. He wrote a series of plays that he called Guerrilla Theater, many of which were meant to be performed impromptu on the street. *And They Put Handcuffs on the Flowers* (1969), the culmination of this period in Arrabal's work, is performed in a theater; however, the actors sit with the audience, and the staging is highly unconventional. Arrabal continues to use many of the methods of Panic Theater, but now his purpose was to convey a public, political message.

Arrabal is primarily a dramatist, but he has also had success in a number of other genres. His novel *The Tower Struck by Lightning* (1988) is a semiautobiographical work structured entirely around the game of chess, at which Arrabal is an expert. He has made several films, including a film for children, *Pacific Fantasy* (1981), starring Mickey Rooney. He has also exhibited his dreamlike paintings. Although under the Franco regime his plays were banned in Spain, in 1986 King Juan Carlos of Spain awarded him the Medalla d'Oro de las Bellas Artes. His other awards include France's Prix du Centre National du Livre. Arrabal lives and works in Paris. In a review of the La Mama (New York) production of *The Architect and the Emperor of Assyria*, Clive Barnes wrote: "Mr. Arrabal, with his perceptions, absurdities, loves and understanding, is a playwright to be honored, treasured and understood. In this play he is saying something about the isolation, the solitariness and the need of 20th-century man that, so far, as I can see, no other playwright has quite gotten on stage before."

Other Works by Fernando Arrabal

Baal Babylon. Translated by Richard Howard. New York: Grove, 1961.

Selected Plays: Guernica; The Labyrinth; The Tricycle; Picnic on the Battlefield; And They Put Handcuffs on the Flowers; The Architect and the Emperor of

Assyria; Garden of Delights. New York: Grove Press, 1986.

A Work about Fernando Arrabal

Donahue, Thomas John. *The Theater of Fernando Arrabal: A Garden of Earthly Delights.* New York: New York University Press, 1980.

Artaud, Antonin (1896–1948) *poet, dramatist*

Antonin Artaud was born in Marseille, France. In 1920, he moved to Paris to become an actor. His work, both on stage and as a writer, was influential to the development of experimental theater. In particular, he visualized a new form of theater, both for stage and screen, known as the Theater of Cruelty, in which traditional forms of representation would be cast aside in favor of new actions and spectacles and in which language would be all but abandoned in a carefully choreographed new creation. His efforts to produce his visions, however, failed, not so much as a result of a lack of vision but because he spent most of his life destitute, addicted to numerous drugs and hampered by both physical and mental illness. His book *The Theatre and Its Double* (1938; translated 1958), however, was later used as the basis for much of the ensemble-theater movement as well as for identifying characteristics that would be linked to the THEATRE OF THE ABSURD.

A prime example of this type of work was his play *The Cenci* (1935), which was produced at the Théâtre Alfred Jarry, a theater cofounded by Artaud himself. An illustration of the Theater of Cruelty, it was performed without a traditionally constructed set and featured minimal spoken dialogue, relying instead on movement, gestures, and incoherent sounds. The goal of this form of art was to force the audience to confront a "primal self" devoid of the trappings of civilization.

A pioneer, Artaud first began to publish his texts, complete with detailed instruction on lighting, violent gestures, and a noisy cacophony of sound in place of music, in 1924, almost 40 years

before Andy Warhol introduced the trend of multimedia spectacle. He initially aligned himself with the SURREALISTS, but he was expelled from their group in 1926 because he was unwilling to follow the movement's mission. Finding himself with few artistic allies, he focused his creative energies on writing essays and poetry, as well as taking small roles in mainstream films, something he felt was degrading to him as an artist.

In 1936 and 1937, Artaud traveled to Mexico (where he studied the rituals of the Tarahumaras Indians), Belgium, and Ireland (where he became increasingly disillusioned with the social restrictions placed on creative artists). He suffered a mental breakdown that involved episodes of violent behavior and hallucinations. On his return from Ireland, Artaud was placed in a psychiatric hospital. Institutionalized from 1937 to 1946, he was subjected to various experimental forms of therapy, including 51 electric shock treatments, coma-inducing insulin therapy, and periods of starvation. As a result, his health declined rapidly.

The final two years of Artaud's life, after his release from the asylum, were unquestionably his most productive. He sought desperately to give voice to his vision. His final work was *To Have Done With The Judgment Of God* (1947), a radio script in which Artaud sought revenge against those who had kept him in the asylum. Billed as vicious, obscene, anti-American and anti-Catholic, the script did not air until 30 years after Artaud's death; it was eventually banned. In the script itself, the United States is presented as a baby factory and war machine. Death rituals are depicted, and excrement is revered as symbolic of life and mortality. Questions about reality are answered with more questions, leading to the final scene in which God takes the stage as a dissected organ on an autopsy table.

Artaud died of cancer, shortly after suffering the disappointment of having his radio broadcast banned, but he left behind a legacy that would influence many generations of artists. As recently as 1982, the punk musical group

Bauhaus recorded a song in tribute to the genius of Antonin Artaud.

Another Work by Antonin Artaud

Artaud on Theatre. Edited by Claude Schumacher. London: Methuen Drama, 1991.

Works about Antonin Artaud

Bermel, Albert. *Artaud's Theatre of Cruelty.* New York: Taplinger, 1977.

Plunka, Gene A., ed. *Antonin Artaud and the Modern Theatre.* Cranbury, N.J.: Associated University Presses, 1994.

Astley, Thea (1925–) *novelist*

Thea Astley was born in Brisbane, Australia. Almost all of her novels are set in south Queensland. She studied for 12 years in the University of Queensland, graduated with an arts degree, and has taught in several schools and institutions in Queensland, New South Wales, and Sydney. Astley has won several prizes for her works, including the Miles Franklin Award on three occasions. She has published several novels and a few short stories, and edited an anthology of short stories in 1971. She is married and has one son.

Astley's writings are marked by a unique blend of comedic wit and biting sarcasm. Her novels reflect her constant struggle to come to terms with Queensland society and with Catholicism. Her characters come from a variety of backgrounds, and her settings are usually small towns. Astley believes that the closely knit community of a small town allows her to express the depths of her characters fully. Her novel *Reaching Tin River* (1980), for example, is set in a rural town whose economic life is centered on the sugar industry.

The most intriguing aspect of Astley's novels is the point of view from which she writes. She often chooses to write from the perspective of the misfits or outsiders of a society. In *A Boat Load of Home Folk* (1968), Astley relates how the inability of a group of elderly Australians to cope with the strange environment of a tropical island reveals their inadequacies. In another novel, *The Slow Natives* (1965), she examines relationships between the elders and the young in the Leverson. She exposes the estrangement between generations and laments the way the aged are marginalized and neglected within the community. This novel won both a Miles Franklin Award and a Moomba Festival prize and is considered to be one of Astley's best novels for the way it finds the depths in shallow, constricted lives.

Astley's poetic prose explores the depth of experience and emotions of her flawed characters. She mixes her chastisement and mockery with humor, as in her depiction of Paul Vesper in *The Acolyte.* This penchant for injecting humor in her narrative makes a deeper impact on her readers. In the view of the Australian writer and critic Brian Matthews, Astley is "one of the most impressive of major Australian novelists currently writing."

Other Works by Thea Astley

A Descant for Gossips. St. Lucia: University of Queensland Press, 1986.

Girl With A Monkey. New York: Viking Press, 1987.

Hunting the Wild Pineapple. New York: Penguin USA. 1982.

An Item from the Late News. New York: Viking Press, 1984.

It's Raining in Mango: Pictures from a Family Album. New York: Penguin USA, 1988.

A Kindness Cup. New York: Penguin USA, 1989.

The Well Dressed Explorer. New York: Penguin USA, 1988.

A Work about Thea Astley

Matthews, Brian. "Life in the Eye of the Hurricane: The Novels of Thea Astley." *Southern Review* 5 (1973): 148–73.

Atwood, Margaret (1939–) *novelist, poet*

Margaret Atwood was born in Ottawa, Ontario, to Carl Atwood, an entomologist, and Margaret Killam, a nutritionist. She spent her childhood accompanying her father on his researches in the wilderness of Quebec. Graduating from the University of Toronto with a B.A. in 1961, she received an M.A. from Radcliffe in 1962 and did some graduate work at Harvard University, beginning a thesis on Gothic fiction.

Atwood's first published work, *Double Persephone* (1961), was a book of poetry exploring the mythological figure Persephone. Her most important collection of verse, *The Circle Game* (1966) uses Gothic imagery to explore issues of gender; for example, the first poem, "This is a Photograph of Me," is narrated by a dead woman: "The photograph was taken / the day after I drowned." Atwood's first novel, *Edible Woman* (1969) is a darkly comic tale of a woman who fears marriage and stops eating.

Her most celebrated novel, *The Handmaid's Tale* (1985), is set in a horrifying future society, Gilead, where women are condemned to illiteracy and servitude. The novel purports to be the recorded narration of Offred, a servant: "Where the edges are we aren't sure, they vary, according to the attacks and counterattacks; but this is the centre, where nothing moves. The Republic of Gilead, said Aunt Lydia, knows no bounds. Gilead is within you." Critic Sandra Tomc sees the novel as a critique not merely of male oppression but also of United States domination over Canada: "In the nightmare future she imagines, women have succumbed to a totalizing patriarchy. Appropriately, given Atwood's conflation of feminism and nationalism, Canada, in some analogous gesture, has succumbed to its totalizing southern neighbor."

The Robber Bride (1993), focuses on the demonic Zenia's haunting of her three friends, robbing them of their money and men, and has dark Gothic undertones: "Zenia, with her dark hair sleeked down by the rain, wet and shivering, standing on the back step as she had done once before, long ago. Zenia, who had been dead for five years." *Alias Grace* (1996) continues Atwood's exploration of gender and power, based on the story of Grace Marks, a servant accused of murdering her master in 1843. Her most recent novel, *Blind Assassin* (2000), contains three interconnected stories, be-

ginning with a woman, Iris Griffin, telling of her sister's death in 1945. It won the Booker Prize. Fellow Canadian writer Alice MUNRO comments: "It's easy to appreciate the grand array of Margaret Atwood's work—the novels, the stories, the poems, in all their power and grace and variety. This work in itself has opened up the gates for a recognition of Canadian writing all over the world."

Other Works by Margaret Atwood

Cat's Eye. New York: Doubleday, 1989.
Power Politics. New York: Harper & Row, 1973.

A Work about Margaret Atwood

Cooke, Nathalie. *Margaret Atwood: A Biography.* Toronto: ECW Press, 1998.

Ausländer, Rose (Rosalie Scherzer)
(1901–1988) *poet*

Rose Ausländer was born in Czernowitz, Austria-Hungary, a city now situated in Ukraine. Her father Sigmund Scherzer, a former rabbinical student, ensured that the family practiced traditional Jewish customs and rituals. As part of her upbringing, she learned both Hebrew and Yiddish and later attended the University of Czernowitz where she studied literature, EXPRESSIONISM, and philosophy. After her father died in 1920, she emigrated to the United States in 1921 to relieve some of the financial strain on her mother, Etie Scherzer, and was joined by another student from the university, Ignaz Ausländer, whom she married in 1923. The couple divorced after three years, and she moved back to Czernowitz in 1931.

Rose Ausländer started writing poetry in German while in the United States. After returning to Czernowitz, she published her first book-length collection of poetry, *Der Regenbogen (The Rainbow,* 1939). Although it received positive reviews, the Nazis prevented the book from achieving a wide circulation because Ausländer was Jewish. During World War II, Ausländer and her mother avoided Nazi death camps by hiding in a cellar. Ausländer composed poetry to cope with the traumatic situation. During this time, she met Paul CELAN, a poet who would influence Ausländer's works after 1957.

Following World War II, Ausländer published 12 volumes of poetry while living in West Germany and the United States. Her best poems describe her personal experiences in Czernowitz and the fear and suffering of the Holocaust. As the literary scholar Kathrin Bower writes, "Ausländer's poems evidence a dialogue of remembrance and mourning at once historical and redemptive."

Ausländer thus became a voice for a shattered generation of German Jews.

Another Work by Rose Ausländer

Selected Poems of Rose Ausländer. Translated by Ewald Osers. London: London Magazine Editors, 1977.

A Work about Rose Ausländer

Bower, Kathrin M. *Ethics and Remembrance in the Poetry of Nelly Sachs and Rose Ausländer.* Rochester, N.Y.: Camden House, 2000.

B

Ba Jin (Pa Chin; Li Feigan) (1904–)
novelist

Li Feigan was born on November 25 in Chengdu and received a private education. He studied English at Chengdu Foreign Languages School, participating in antifeudal activity and studying Russian writers and anarchist philosophers. He adopted a pen name from syllables of the Chinese names of Russian anarchists Mikhail Bakunin (1814–76) and Pyotr Kropotkin (1842–1921).

After moving to France in 1927, Ba Jin wrote autobiographical essays and articles on anarchism, as well as his first novel, *Destruction* (1929), about the life of a young anarchist, Du Daxin. He produced many works, mostly political in nature, with clear-cut moral lessons. His subjects were frequently the Chinese gentry class or intellectuals. In 1931, he published his best-known work, *Family,* a sentimental melodrama of several generations living in one compound. The novel chronicled a family's rise and fall and charted the fate of feudalism after the May Fourth Movement (1919 student demonstrations against the weak Chinese concessions of the imperialist Versailles Treaty). *Family* became part of Ba Jin's *Torrent* trilogy, which included *Spring* (1938) and *Autumn* (1940).

The three-year period between 1931 and 1933 brought a novella companion to *Destruction* called *New Life,* as well as two novels about mining life, *The Antimony Miners* and *The Sprouts.* In 1935, Ba Jin also completed the *Trilogy of Love,* which followed the revolutionary activities of a group of intellectuals.

Ba Jin was active in many aspects of literary and political life. He published two manifestos on behalf of and with other Chinese artists and writers, including LU Xun, for freedom of speech and against imperialism. He actively urged a united front against Japanese aggression during the Sino-Japanese War and continued his literary output with the novelettes *The Garden of Repose* (1944), *Ward No. 4* (1946), and *Cold Nights* (1946). As a Korean War correspondent, he wrote two books about the battlefields, *Living Amongst Heroes* (1953) and *Defenders of Peace* (1954).

Ba Jin has earned many awards and distinctions, including France's Legion of Honor. He holds an honorary doctorate from the Chinese University of Hong Kong and is a fellow of the American Academy of Arts and Letters. He is one of China's most prominent writers.

Other Works by Ba Jin
Family. Translated by Sidney Shapiro. Boston: Cheng & Tsui, 1992.

"My *J'accuse* Against this Moribund System: Notes on a Crumbling Landlord Clan of Western Sichuan." In Helmut Martin and Jeffrey Kinkley, eds., *Modern Chinese Writers: Self-Portrayals.* Armonk, N.Y.: M. E. Sharpe, 1992.

Random Thoughts. Translated by Geremie Barmé. San Francisco: China Books & Periodicals, 1984.

Selected Works of Ba Jin. Beijing: Foreign Language Press, 1988.

Ward Four: A Novel of Wartime China. Translated by Haili Kong and Howard Goldblatt. San Francisco: China Books & Periodicals, 2001.

Bâ, Mariama (1929–1981) *novelist, essayist, activist*

Mariama Bâ was born into a prominent family in Dakar, Senegal. At a time when only Europeans maintained political positions in Senegal, Bâ's father became the first Senegalese minister of health. Her maternal grandparents raised her in the Muslim tradition. Against her grandparents' wishes, she graduated from the Teacher's College in 1947 and taught for 12 years. Bâ was married to Obèye Diop, a member of Parliament, with whom she had nine children. After they divorced, she remained single, becoming an advocate for women in Senegal.

Bâ's first novel, *So Long a Letter* (1979), was an international success that illuminated the complex lives of African women. Although the critics have mostly viewed the novel as a criticism of polygamy, exposing the inequalities between men and women, it addresses multiple women's issues. The story centers on two educated women who had happy, loving marriages until their husbands took second wives. Each woman responds in her own way: One stays and one leaves. The book reveals the limited choices for women and also presents the strong bonds and support systems between women. Writing in letter format, Bâ gives the reader an intimate look at a woman's internal reflections. This novel received the Noma Award for Publishing in Africa in 1980.

Bâ died prior to the publishing of her second novel, *Scarlet Song* (1981), which tackles the diffi-culties of interracial marriage. Today, she is considered one of the most important French West African feminists.

Works about Mariama Bâ

Cham, Mbye B. "Contemporary Society and the Female Imagination: A Study of the Novels of Mariama Bâ." *African Literature Today* 15 (1987): 89–101.

d'Almeida, Irene Assiba. "The Concept of Choice in Mariama Bâ's Fiction." In Carole Boyce Davies and Anne Adams Graves, eds., *Nagambika: Studies of Women in African Literature.* Trenton, N.J.: Africa World Press, 1986.

Edson, Laurie. "Mariama Bâ and the Politics of the Family." *Studies in Twentieth Century Literature* 17.1 (1993): 13–25.

Babel, Isaac (1894–1941) *short-story writer, novelist, dramatist*

Isaac Emmanuelovich Babel was born in Odessa, Russia, into a Jewish family. Emmanuel Babel, his father, was a sales representative for an agricultural firm. At the time, Odessa had the largest Jewish population in Russia, and Babel grew up in the city's Jewish ghetto, Moldavanka. He was constantly faced with anti-Semitism from teachers and peers, a fact that played a substantial role in his development as a writer.

Babel's father was a domineering patriarch who forced young Isaac to practice violin for hours every day and sent him, when he was 11, to study business in Kiev, where he stayed until 1914. Although Babel excelled in all areas as a student, literature was his only passion.

Babel began his career as a writer while studying at Kiev, often drawing upon his experience growing up in the Jewish ghetto. His first published story, "Old Shloyme" (1913), explores anti-Semitism directly; in the story, a Jewish family faces a choice between renouncing their religion and losing their home.

In 1914, Babel moved to St. Petersburg to pursue writing professionally. He had difficulty publishing his material until a meeting with Maxim GORKY in 1916. Gorky assisted Babel with the publication of two stories in the prestigious literary journal *Letopis*.

Babel supported the Bolshevik cause during the Russian Revolution. Like many other Jews in Russia faced with persecution, Babel was intrigued by the Bolshevik promises of freedom and equality for all. Between 1917 and 1919, Babel served in the Red Army. His most famous collection of stories, *Red Cavalry* (1926), reflects his experiences during the war. The work raises issues of violence, anti-Semitism, and political ideology, as well as the themes of friendship, love, and compassion. The success of *Red Cavalry* firmly established Babel as one of the leading writers in Russia.

In 1929, Babel left Russia and traveled throughout Europe, visiting France, Italy, Belgium, and Germany. When he returned to Russia, he became skeptical of the Communists. During the same period, he began writing drama, completing his most notable play, *Sunset*, in 1928. Set in Odessa in 1913, the play explores the social interactions of the Jewish ghetto. In the play, the reader notices a duality that persistently appears throughout Babel's works: He embraces his Jewishness and at the same time intellectually opposes Judaism. The play was criticized by the authorities for its lack of socialist themes.

During the 1930s, Babel was repeatedly criticized by the government. Arrested in 1939, Babel was executed in 1940 after a 20-minute trial for allegedly spying for France and Austria. The charges were false, as the records, released in 1954, confirm.

Babel made an enormous contribution to Russian literature, emerging as one of the first writers to discuss openly and positively the cultural and social position of the Jews in Russia. As Natalie Babel, his wife, later pointed out, "His life centered on writing, and it can be said without exaggeration that he sacrificed everything to his art, including his relationship with his family, his liberty, and finally even his life."

Other Works by Isaac Babel

Babel, Natalie, ed. *The Collected Stories of Isaac Babel*. Translated by Peter Constantine. New York: Norton, 2002.

The Complete Works of Isaac Babel. Translated by Peter Constantine. New York: Norton, 2001.

Works about Isaac Babel

Bloom, Harold, ed. *Isaac Babel: Modern Critical Views*. Broomall, Pa.: Chelsea House, 1987.

Ehre, Milton. *Isaac Babel*. Boston: Twayne, 1986.

Bachmann, Ingeborg (1926–1973) *poet, novelist, dramatist*

A daughter of a teacher, Ingeborg Bachmann was born in Klagenfurt, Austria. She grew up in a disturbing political atmosphere, as Nazi Germany was gaining control of Austria, and at the age of 12 she watched Nazi troops march into her town. Bachmann studied philosophy at the universities of Innsburg, Graz, and Vienna; she completed a dissertation on Ludwig Wittgenstein under the direction of the famous philosopher Martin Heidegger in 1950.

Bachmann began her career as a professional writer in the early 1950s, writing radio plays. In 1953, Bachmann published her first collection of poetry, *The Deferred Time*. The collection was critically praised and received the prestigious GRUPPE 47 award. In 1953 she spent a year in the United States as a visiting scholar at Harvard University, and she later moved to Italy, where she wrote a number of political articles for Austrian and German newspapers. In 1959, Bachmann was appointed to the newly created position as chair of poetics at the University of Frankfurt, where she lectured on philosophy and literature.

Her poetry is influenced by many sources, including CLASSICISM, surrealism, and the avant-garde movement. The somber tone of her poetry lyrically and precisely describes the anguish of a personal experience. Bachmann's dark, powerful, and complex imagery is thematically juxtaposed against simple individual emotions such as love, guilt, and failed aspirations. Her use of imagery is exemplified by these lines from "In the Storm of Roses": "Wherever we turn in the storm of roses,/ the night is lit up by thorns. . . ." Unlike her prose, which is often read as social and feminist fiction, her poetry centers on deeply personal observations.

In 1961, Bachmann published her highly influential autobiographical work, *The Thirtieth Year,* which was awarded the Berlin Critics Prize and the Georg Büchner Prize in 1964. Her first published novel, *Malina* (1971), deals with a number of feminist issues. Malina, the protagonist of the novel, has a relationship with Ivan, a younger man of Hungarian descent. The relationship becomes psychologically complex as Malina has recurrent nightmares of her father as a Nazi who kills her in a gas chamber, nightmares that seem to contribute to the deterioration of her relationship with Ivan. *Malina* also confronts the theme of national memory and national identity in postwar Europe. The issues of ego and alter ego and with the subtle influence of the memory of genocide create a powerful combination. The novel was highly praised and remains an excellent representative work of German POSTMODERNISM.

Just before her death, Bachmann visited Auschwitz in Poland and gave a series of readings. She died under mysterious circumstances in a fire in her apartment. Bachmann was awarded numerous prizes, including the Austrian Medal of Honor, the highest prize in literature an Austrian citizen can receive from the government. Her works continue to be of great social and literary importance.

Other Works by Ingeborg Bachmann

Selected Prose and Drama. New York: Continuum, 1998.

Songs in Flight: The Collected Poems of Ingeborg Bachmann. Translated by Peter Filkins (bilingual edition). New York: Marsilio Publications, 1995.

The Book of Franza and Requiem for Fanny Goldman. Translated by Peter Filkins. Evanston, Ill.: Northwestern University Press, 1999.

Three Radio Plays. Translated by Lilian Friedberg. Riverside, Calif.: Ariadne Press, 1999.

A Work about Ingeborg Bachmann

Redwitz, Eckenbert. *The Image of the Woman in the Works of Ingeborg Bachmann.* New York: Peter Lang, 1993.

Balzac, Honoré de (1799–1850) *novelist*

Honoré de Balzac, one of the creators of REALISM in literature, was born in Tours, France, to a middle-class family. Originally from Paris, the family had moved to Tours during the French Revolution because of their royalist opinions. In 1814, however, they were able to return to Paris. Balzac, neglected by his mother, spent his early years in boarding schools. After graduating from the Collège de Vendôme he went on to the Sorbonne, where he read the works of the mystical philosophers Jakob Böhme (1575–1624) and Emanuel Swedenborg (1688–1772) and was particularly interested in Franz Anton Mesmer's lectures on animal magnetism. These influences are detectable in his early fiction. After graduation, he began to work in a law office. When, in 1819, his family was forced by financial setbacks to move to the small town of Villeparisis, Balzac decided that he would return to Paris alone and embark on a career as a writer.

Balzac rented a shabby room in Paris, a room he later described in the novel *Le Peau de chagrin* (*The Wild Ass's Skin,* 1831), and began what would become a habit of late night writing and excessive consumption of caffeine. In his lifetime, he wrote more than 100 novels, mostly between the hours of midnight and six in the morning, always on blue paper and by candlelight, while drinking large quantities of thick Turkish coffee. By 1822 Balzac, using a variety of pseudonyms, had written several plays and novels, all of which were ignored. Undaunted, he continued to write.

A compulsive spender, Balzac had a difficult time staying ahead of his creditors. He attempted to run a publishing company and also bought a printing house. Both of these endeavors left him with large debts that would stay with him throughout his life. Destitute at 29, he accepted an invitation to stay at the home of Général de Pommereul in

Fougères in Brittany, where he worked on his novel *Le Dernier chouan, ou la Bretagne en 1800* (1829), a historical work that he eventually published under his own name. Finally, with this work, Balzac began to gain some recognition and popularity, although not enough to release him from debt.

In 1833, Balzac developed the idea of collecting all of his previously written novels under one name and linking them together as a series of works which, when taken as a whole, would encompass all the customs, atmosphere, and habits of French society. This idea eventually led to the collection of more than 2,000 characters appearing in 90 novels and novellas. The works were eventually collected under the title *La Comédie humaine,* or *The Human Comedy,* a name Balzac borrowed from Dante's *The Divine Comedy.*

Critical Analysis

Included in *La Comédie humaine* were well-known works such as *Le Père Goriot* (*Father Goriot,* 1834–35), *Les Paysans* (*The Peasants,* 1844), and *Illusions perdues* (*Lost Illusions,* 1837–43). The settings for these works include all levels of society in Paris and the provinces. The characters include a mix of old aristocracy and new money, set alongside middle-class tradespeople and professionals, servants, young intellectuals, and criminals. Some of the characters, such as Eugène de Rastignac, the poor provincial man who comes to Paris with big dreams and makes good on them through gambling, affairs, and connections with the nobility, recur throughout the works. Balzac inserted himself in his works as well, alluding to incidents and adventures in which he participated side by side with his characters who grew to exist not only on paper but in his imagination outside of his novels as if they were actual acquaintances. It is said that Balzac once interrupted a conversation in which a friend of his was telling him about his sister's ill health by saying, "That's all very well, but let's get back to reality: to whom are we going to marry Eugénie Grandet?"

During the height of his productivity, Balzac was known to spend anywhere from 14 to 16 hours a day writing. He would eat a large meal each evening, sleep for a few hours, and then wake at midnight to continue writing. There are reports that once he consumed 100 oysters and 12 lamb chops in a single meal. His few free hours were spent having amorous affairs and pursuing the joy of life. One of his affairs was with Eveline Hanska, a wealthy Polish woman who had been among his friends for 15 years. He based several of his female characters on her, such as Mme. Hulot in *La Cousine Bette* (*Cousin Bette,* 1846). She was married throughout most of their acquaintance, but after her husband passed away in 1841, Balzac spent increasing amounts of time in her company. Already in poor health, he eventually married her and brought her back to Paris in the spring of 1850, only five months before his death in August, when his excesses got the better of him and he died, reportedly of caffeine poisoning.

Other Works by Honoré de Balzac

The Girl with the Golden Eyes. Translated by Carol Cosman. New York: Carroll and Graf, 1998.

The Unknown Masterpiece; and, Gambara. Translated by Richard Howard. New York: New York Review of Books, 2001.

Works about Honoré de Balzac

Graham, Robb. *Balzac: A Biography.* New York: Norton, 1994.

Kanes, Martin. *Pere Goriot: Anatomy of a Troubled World.* Boston: Twayne, 1993.

Kanes, Martin, ed. *Critical Essays on Honoré de Balzac.* Boston: G. K. Hall, 1990.

Barbey d'Aurevilly, Jules-Amédée

(1808–1889) *novelist*

Jules-Amédée Barbey d'Aurevilly was born in Saint-Sauveur-le-Vicomte on November 2 into an aristocratic family, was well educated, and was accustomed to privilege. In 1833, he moved to Paris, where he had numerous love affairs and led the unprincipled life of a "dandy," supporting his activities through journalism. In 1841, he converted to strict Catholicism and eventually became, as would be apparent in his novels, a strong Christian moralist.

Barbey d'Aurevilly wrote numerous works of criticism and articles, but it was his novels that brought him acclaim. He was influenced by BALZAC and greatly admired BAUDELAIRE. As well as harshly criticizing NATURALISM, his novels and stories are notable for their highly moralistic but sadistic portrayals of the struggles and tragedies associated with life in the provinces of France.

Barbey d'Aurevilly is perhaps best known for his work *Les Diaboliques* (1874; *The Diabolic Ones*, 1925), a collection of six stories, all having some basis in fact and all carrying a similar satanic motif. This shocking work achieved great success both critically and popularly. He died in Paris, 15 years after its publication, at the age of 81.

Another Work by Jules Barbey d'Aurevilly

Dandyism. Translated by Douglas Ainsley. New York: PAJ Publications, 1988.

Works about Jules Barbey d'Aurevilly

Chartier, Armand B. *Barbey d'Aurevilly.* Boston: Twayne, 1977.

Eisenberg, Davina L. *The Figure of the Dandy in Barbey D'Aurevilly's "Le Bonheur Dans Le Crime".* New York: Peter Lang, 1996.

Baroja y Nessi, Pío (1872–1956) *novelist*

Pío Baroja y Nessi was born in San Sebastian, Spain. His father was a mining engineer, and the family moved frequently during his childhood, relocating from town to town, following his father's professional career. Baroja y Nessi studied to be a doctor, and when he graduated from school, he began a medical practice in the town of Cestona in northern Spain. The medical profession did not suit him. His practice was a disaster; after a short time, he gave it up and moved to Madrid, a cosmopolitan city, where he ran a bakery that was owned by his aunt.

It was at this time that he began to publish his novels. He was successful as an author and quickly gave up the management of the bakery to write full time.

Baroja y Nessi was a member of the GENERATION OF 1898. He shared with the other writers of the Generation of '98 a strong sense of Spanish nationalism and a need to reform society. However, Baroja y Nessi was particularly individualistic. As a youth, he had briefly been an anarchist but found even this ideology too constraining. Because of an aversion to any societal structure that limited his freedom, he never married. This individualism was the main theme of his novels.

In his trilogy *The Struggle for Life* (1903–04), Baroja y Nessi depicts the slums of Madrid and a collection of characters who, by living outside the norms of society, manage to achieve personal freedom. Though the books are distinctly melancholy and terse, written in what critics call Baroja y Nessi's gray style, they are optimistic in that some of the characters do achieve a degree of freedom by opposing society. In later novels, such as *The Tree of Knowledge* (1911), Baroja y Nessi depicts the same scenario but in a more pessimistic manner. At the end, the protagonist is unable to realize his goal of personal freedom and is crushed by society.

Baroja y Nessi was a formal innovator. He did not believe in the "closed" novel, the standard model of the 19th century, because he felt its carefully planned plot, structure, and resolution of every conflict did not accurately reflect reality. Instead he wrote in a style of apparent aimlessness. For example, he creates scenes in which suspense is carefully built but never resolved. His stark tone and innovative structure had a great effect on many 20th-century writers, most notably Ernest Hemingway.

Baroja y Nessi is one of the greatest Spanish novelists of the early 20th century. His work, along with that of the other members of the Generation of '98, revitalized Spanish literature. His influence on later Spanish writers is widespread, but it can be particularly seen in the works of Camilo José CELA. His innovative style, as well as his theme of the struggle of the individual in modern society, has secured his place among other great writers of world literature.

Another Work by Pío Baroja y Nessi

The Restlessness of Shanti Andia and Other Writings. Translated by Anthony Corrigan. Ann Arbor: University of Michigan Press, 1959.

A Work about Pío Baroja y Nessi

Patt, Beatrice P. *Pío Baroja y Nessi.* Boston: Twayne, 1971.

Bastida, Gustavo Adolfo Dominguez

See BÉQUER, GUSTAVO ADOLFO.

Bataille, Georges (1897–1962) *novelist, essayist*

Often called the "metaphysician of evil" because of his interests in sex, death, and the obscene, Georges Bataille was born in Billon, Puy-de-Dôme, France. His childhood was difficult because his mother repeatedly attempted suicide, and his father, whom Bataille dearly loved, became both blind and paralyzed as a result of syphilis before he died.

Bataille converted to Catholicism just prior to World War I and served in the army from 1916 to 1917. Troubled by poor health throughout his life as well as by recurring periods of depression, he was discharged from the army as a result of tuberculosis. He joined a seminary, thinking of becoming a priest, and spent time with a Benedictine congregation, but he soon experienced a profound loss of faith. He continued his education at the École des Chartres, writing his thesis in 1922 on 13th-century verse.

Bataille aligned himself early on with surrealism, but he considered himself to be the "enemy from within." André BRETON officially excommunicated Bataille from the movement. After a period of psychoanalysis, Bataille began to write. He founded several journals and was the first to publish innovative thinkers such as Barthes, Foucault, and Derrida.

Bataille rejected the traditional, believing that all artistic and intellectual pursuits should ultimately focus on the violent annihilation of the rational individual. His work was greatly influenced by both Friedrich NIETZSCHE and Gilles de Rais, a 15th-century serial killer. All of Bataille's writings deal with violence and sexuality. His best known erotic works are *The Story of the Eye* (1928), *Blue of Noon* (1945), and *The Abbot C.* (1950). Bataille believed pornography was a means of understanding the relation between life and death. *The Story of the Eye,* which he wrote under the pseudonym Lord Auch, for example, is the story of a young couple who test the boundaries of sexual taboos, escalating to extreme playing out of sexual fantasies. The novel quickly gained and still maintains a cult status decades after Bataille's death in Paris on July 8.

Other Works by Georges Bataille

Eroticism: Death and Sensuality. Translated by Mary Dalwood. San Francisco: City Lights Books, 1991.
The Unfinished System of Nonknowledge. Translated by Michelle Kendall and Stuart Kendall. Minneapolis: University of Minnesota Press, 2001.

Works about Georges Bataille

Champagne, Roland A. *Georges Bataille.* Boston: Twayne, 1998.
Surya, Michel. *Georges Bataille: An Intellectual Biography.* Translated by Krysztof Kijalkowski and Michael Richardson. New York: Verso, 2002.

Baudelaire, Charles (1821–1867) *poet, critic*

Considered one of the greatest 19th-century French poets, Charles-Pierre Baudelaire was born on April 9. He was the son of Joseph-François Baudelaire and Caroline Archimbaut Dufays. His father had been an ordained priest who left the ministry during the French Revolution to work as a tutor for the duc of Choiseul-Praslin's children. During this time, he met a number of influential people and amassed a small financial fortune. A modestly talented poet and painter, he taught his son an early appreciation for art.

Considered by many to be a revolutionary even in his own time, Baudelaire was often given to depression and cynicism. His father died when Baudelaire was only six years old. For a short time, he received a great deal of attention from both his mother and his nurse, Mariette, until his mother's remarriage, this time to a man much closer to her own age, Major Jacques Aupick. Aupick was an intelligent and self-disciplined man who served as a military general, an ambassador, and ultimately as a senator. Baudelaire's relationship with his stepfather was not a good one, although he did not reveal his dislike of the man until later in life, at which point he attributed much of his depression and dual personalities to his mother's remarriage.

In 1833, the family moved to Lyons, and Aupick enrolled Baudelaire in a strict military boarding school. The influence of the education and discipline he received there had a great impact on his outlook on life; it also increased his dislike for his stepfather. He continued his education at Louis-le-Grand, a respected French high school in Paris. His growing behavior problems led to his expulsion in 1839. It was at this point that he announced his decision to become a writer. To appease his family, he also agreed to study law at the École de Droit, but his attention was never focused on his studies. He led a bohemian life, going deeply into debt and becoming an increasingly radical thinker. During these years, he also made his first contacts in the literary world and discovered the use of hashish and opium.

In 1841, hoping to encourage him to change his way of life, Baudelaire's parents sent him by boat on a trip to India. Throughout the voyage, he remained depressed and sullen; therefore, when the ship was forced to stop for repairs after a terrible storm, he decided to return to France. Although he did not enjoy the journey, it did have a strong influence on his writing by giving him a unique perspective on the world that few other writers of his time could claim. On his return, he collected a large inheritance that allowed him to immerse himself in art and literature, paying particular attention to the satanic-based and horror literature that was popular at the time. However, in only two years, he had spent almost half of his money. He was placed by his family under a legal guardianship and was forced to live on a controlled income for the duration of his life.

A series of amorous affairs provided much of the impetus for Baudelaire's erotic poetry. The Martinican Jeanne Duval, whom Baudelaire met in 1842, held perhaps the greatest influence. Her exotic black hair provided the erotic imagery for his poem "La Chevelure" ("The Head of Hair"). A dark-haired, dark-skinned beauty, she was referred to quite derogatorily by Baudelaire's mother as the "Black Venus." Marie Daubrun, an actress and his mistress from 1855 to 1860, as well as Apollonie Sabatier, who presided over a salon for artists and writers, were also the objects of Baudelaire's poetic and as well as romantic attentions.

In 1845, Baudelaire's depression caused him to unsuccessfully attempt suicide. Soon after, he published *La Fanfarlo* (1847), an autobiographical novella that anticipated his experimentation with prose poetry. In 1848, French workers against social injustice minimally involved him in the revolution: He fired a few shots through the barricades and worked on radical political publications.

Baudelaire turned to literary and art criticism, for which he became well respected. His admiration for Delacroix and Constantin Guys influenced his own modern aesthetics. He translated Edgar Allan Poe's works into French, publishing five volumes of these translations from 1856 to 1865. He became greatly influenced by the dark melancholic brooding nature of Poe's works and began to incorporate the ideas into his own writing. He was particularly interested in the transformation of life in the modern city.

Critical Analysis
The first edition of Baudelaire's collected poems, *Les Fleurs du mal* (*Flowers of Evil*) was published in

1857. Focusing on erotic, satanic and often lesbian themes, the work was not well received by the public. Scathing reviews of the work published in literary journals had a profoundly negative effect on Baudelaire's writing career, and both he and the publisher were ultimately prosecuted and heavily fined for offending public morality. Six poems from the collection were expressly banned as too radical for public consumption.

Baudelaire became more depressed as a result of this seeming failure and, after the death of his stepfather, he returned in 1859 to live once again with his mother. He wrote 35 new poems for the second edition of *Les Fleurs du mal* (1861), including one of his best-known poems, "Le Voyage," first published in 1857. He also published a book of essays on the use of drugs, *Les Paradis artificiels* (*Artificial Paradises,* 1860). He had often used opium and hashish as a means of inspiring creativity. He began to become convinced, however, of the dangers inherent in this habit.

Baudelaire's life, however, was plagued by tragedies. He was financially unable to assist his publisher, who had been jailed for debt from the first edition of Baudelaire's poems, and he learned that his mistress Jeanne Duval had been living with another man. He also began to experience severe headaches and suffered from nightmares, most probably as a result of syphilis, which caused him to think he was becoming insane. He moved to Brussels in 1863, hoping to find a new publisher, but his health steadily declined until a series of strokes left him partially paralyzed. He returned once again to Paris, where he died in his mother's arms on August 31.

Baudelaire's works, including his critical essays *Curiosités esthétiques* (*Aesthetic Curiosities,* 1868) and his collections of prose poems *Les Petits poemes en prose* (*Little Prose Poems,* 1868) and *l'Art romantique* (*Romantic Art,* 1869) were major influences on the symbolist and modernist movements (*see* MODERNISM). Through his use of irony and his depiction of the scenes of modern life, he transformed poetic language, and his criticism founded an aesthetics of modernism.

Another Work by Charles Baudelaire

Baudelaire: Poems. Translated by Laurence Lerner. London: J. M. Dent, 1999.

Works about Charles Baudelaire

Benjamin, Walter. *Charles Baudelaire: A Lyric Poet in the Era of High Capitalism.* Translated by Harry Zohn. London: New Left Books, 1973.

Hyslop, Lois Boe. *Charles Baudelaire Revisited.* New York: Twayne Publishers, 1992.

Richardson, Joanna. *Baudelaire.* New York: St. Martin's Press, 1994.

Beauchamp, Katherine Mansfield

See MANSFIELD, KATHERINE.

Beauvoir, Simone de (Simone Lucie-Ernestine-Marie-Bertrand de Beauvoir) (1908–1986) *novelist, essayist*

Simone de Beauvoir was born in Paris, France, on January 9. A leading feminist and existentialist (*see* EXISTENTIALISM), her works bear a clear resemblance to those of her lifelong friend, mentor, colleague, and lover Jean Paul SARTRE. Best known for her two-volume work *The Second Sex* (1949), a work in which de Beauvoir calls for the abolition of the myth of the "eternal feminine," she is considered by many scholars working in the field of cultural studies to be the primary voice for early feminist studies. This work quickly became a classic among feminist theorists and scholars and is considered to be the founding text of gender studies.

De Beauvoir's life history is well known, largely as a result of the publication of numerous autobiographical works such as *Memoirs of a Dutiful Daughter* (1958), *The Prime of Life* (1960), *Force of Circumstance* (1963), and *All Said and Done* (1972). In these texts, she also documents the life of Sartre, Albert CAMUS, and other influential philosophers, novelists, and intellectuals from the 1930s to the 1970s.

Educated first at private schools and then at the Sorbonne, where she received a degree in philosophy and first became acquainted with Sartre, de Beauvoir pursued a career as a teacher after receiving her degree. She left this occupation to become a full-time writer in 1943, the same year that she published her first novel, *She Came to Stay* (1943), which explores existential themes by examining the ways in which a relationship between two people is destroyed as a result of a guest, a young girl, who stays for an extended period of time in a young couple's home. Although purportedly fictional, this work was based largely on de Beauvoir's own relationship with Sartre and Olga Kosakiewicz, a former student, who came to stay with them in occupied Paris during the war. Her presence created many difficulties for Sartre and de Beauvoir within their own relationship, but it gave de Beauvoir much inspiration in her work.

Critical Analysis

Although intellectual and existential issues are a concern of all de Beauvoir's works, she is best known for her application of existentialism to an understanding of the oppression of women. In *The Second Sex* she makes known her firm belief that an individual's choices must be made on the basis of equality between the male and female, not on the basis of any essential differentiation between the sexes. The importance of choice—free will—is also a prevalent theme in many of de Beauvoir's other works. Her *Ethics of Ambiguity* (1947) is devoted largely to the study of individual choices and the resultant anxieties associated with the ramifications of those choices, an underlying theme of existentialism.

In addition to feminist issues and free will, de Beauvoir was also interested in the theme of aging. She first covers this topic in *A Very Easy Death* (1964), in which she addresses the issue of her own mother's death. She returns to this theme again in *Old Age* (1970), a work that details the indifference and lack of respect that the elderly receive from society.

Political activism is another theme in de Beauvoir's writings, particularly those works written after World War II when she and Sartre both worked on a leftist journal. She published two novels, *The Blood of Others* (1945), exploring the life of members of the wartime resistance to the Nazi occupation, as well as *The Mandarins* (1954), which describes the struggles faced by middle-class intellectuals as they attempt to enter into the sphere of political activism. Her political views tended increasingly toward the left, and by the 1950s, she was defending communism and criticizing U.S. and Western European capitalism regularly in her works. This attitude becomes even clearer after de Beauvoir visited the United States and, on returning to France, published her observations. Her *America Day by Day* (1948) is a critique of the social problems caused by capitalism in the United States. While there, she also fell in love with fellow writer Nelson Algren, complicating her existing love affair with Sartre. Elements of *The Mandarins* reflect this new development in her life.

De Beauvoir's final years were marked by Sartre's death and her attempts to write about the nature of their relationship, the end result of which she eventually published in *Adieux: A Farewell to Sartre* (1981). It was her desire to remain as honest and true as possible in her examination of their life together. To the critics and to members of Sartre's family, however, it seemed as if she was attacking the late philosopher.

De Beauvoir passed away on April 14. After her death, several additional works were published, including *Letters to Sartre* (1990), *Journal of a Resistance Fighter* (1990), and, in 1997, her passionate *Letters to Algren*. Most important, *The Second Sex* is still considered a primary text for feminist studies.

Other Works by Simone de Beauvoir

All Men Are Mortal. Translated by Euan Cameron. London: Virago, 1995.

When Things of the Spirit Come First: Five Early Tales. Translated by Patrick O'Brian. New York: Pantheon Books, 1982.

Works about Simone de Beauvoir

Bauer, Nancy. *Simone de Beauvoir, Philosophy and Feminism.* New York: Columbia University Press, 2001.

Pilardi, Jo-Ann. *Simone de Beauvoir Writing the Self: Philosophy Becomes Autobiography.* Westport, Conn.: Praeger, 1999.

Scholz, Sally. *On de Beauvoir.* Belmont, Calif.: Wadsworth/Thomson Learning, 2000.

Simons, Margaret A. *Beauvoir and "The Second Sex": Feminism, Race and the Origins of Existentialism.* Boston: Lanham, Rowman and Littlefield Publishers, 1999.

Becher, Johannes Robert (1891–1958)
poet, novelist

Johannes Robert Becher was born into an upper-middle-class Catholic family in Munich, Germany. His father was a high-ranking Bavarian judge. Although Becher studied philosophy and medicine, he favored poetry as the creative outlet for his political views. His early poems were radical and rooted in EXPRESSIONISM. He published his first collection of verse in 1914. During World War I, Becher refused to join the German military and became a pacifist. He joined the left-wing Spartacus League in 1918 and the German Communist Party in 1919.

Becher emerged as a leader among German communists and radical writers in the 1920s. The literary historian Adolf D. Klarmann noted that, at this time, Becher wrote revolutionary poetry that "literally bursts and scatters the traditional shackles of sentence, logic, and grammatical structure." Becher served as a deputy to the Reichstag (German legislature) in 1925 and became head of the League of Proletarian–Revolutionary Writers in 1928. His book of poetry *Der Leichnam auf dem Thron* (*The Corpse on the Throne*, 1925) and his novel *Levisite oder der einzig gerechte Krieg* (*The Only Just War,* 1926) led to accusations of treason against the German government. The rise of the Nazis to power in 1933 made Germany too dangerous for left-wing writers like Becher. He fled the country and eventually settled in Moscow.

After the defeat of Nazi Germany in 1945, Becher moved to Communist East Berlin. He soon became president of the East German Academy of Arts. He won several awards for his works, including the Lenin Peace Prize in 1952. Becher's poem "Auferstanden aus Ruinen" ("Risen from the Ruins", 1949) was used as the text for his country's national anthem. In 1954, Becher was appointed cultural minister of East Germany. His support for modernist authors, such as Bertolt BRECHT, created tension with his government, which officially favored SOCIALIST REALISM. Becher's efforts to promote cooperation with noncommunist German intellectuals earned him a reprimand from his party. He had already lost much of his political power when he died in 1958.

Another Work by Johannes Robert Becher
Farewell. Translated by Joan Becker. Berlin: Seven Seas Publishers, 1970.

A Work about Johannes Robert Becher
Haase, Horst. *Johannes R. Becher, Leben and Werk.* West Berlin: Das Europäische buch, 1981.

Beckett, Samuel (1906–1989) *playwright, novelist, poet*

Samuel Beckett was born on April 13 in Dublin, Ireland. He was educated at Earlsfort House in Dublin and later in Enniskillen at Portora Royal School, the alma mater of writer Oscar Wilde. Although Beckett came from an Anglo-Irish Protestant family, he wrote most of his work in French. He received a degree from Trinity College in Dublin in Romance languages. During this time, he also began to enjoy the vibrant theater scene that was emerging in a postindependence Ireland. He was particularly influenced by the plays of J. M. Synge, the arrival of American silent movies, and the vaudeville antics of performers such as Charlie Chaplin and Buster Keaton, which he would later incorporate in his plays.

After graduation, Beckett spent two years, from 1928 to 1930, as an exchange lecturer in Paris. While there, he met and became lifelong friends with writer James Joyce. He acted as one of Joyce's assistants while the author was working on

Finnegan's Wake and, at the same time, began his own career as a writer. He published his first poem, "Whoroscope," which concerns time and the ideas of the philosopher René Descartes, in 1930. That same year, he returned to lecture at Trinity College and began to work on a series of stories about the life of a Dublin intellectual that later formed the collection *More Pricks Than Kicks* (1934). After only four terms at Trinity, Beckett left to pursue a career as a freelance writer, traveling throughout Europe and finally settling in Paris, which was to be his primary home for the rest of his life. He also began work on his first novel, *Dream of Fair to Middling Women* (1932), which was highly autobiographical.

Beckett was seriously injured one night when, as he was walking home, he was stabbed. It was during his hospitalization and recuperation that he cemented his friendship with Joyce, who became his caretaker. He also began a long-term association with Suzanne Deschevaux-Dusmesnil, whom he married in 1961. In 1941, when Paris was invaded, Deschevaux-Dusmesnil joined the resistance with Beckett and they narrowly escaped the arrival of the Gestapo at their apartment. Fleeing to a small town in the south of France, Beckett worked on a farm in exchange for living quarters and continued his writing. After the defeat of the Germans in 1945, he returned to Paris and, at this point, made the decision to write all of his works in French.

Critical Analysis

Taken as a whole, Beckett's works attempt to reduce basic existential problems to a minimalist structure where only the most essential elements are considered. His concerns are commonplace in that they reflect the shared worries of society as a whole, but they are never simple. He ponders such large-scale issues as the nature of life itself, the question of time and its relevance, the concept of eternity, and the sense of isolation, alienation, and loneliness of the individual self.

Beckett's early works are composed of a series of internal monologues: *Molloy* (1951; translated 1955), *Malone Meurt* (1951; translated as *Malone*

Dies, 1956), and *L'Innomable* (1953; translated as *The Unnameable,* 1958). These pieces reflect one of the many paradoxes Beckett explores: the dilemma associated with the fact that the self can never truly know itself. The act of self-observation leads to a split in which the self becomes two individual entities: the observer and the observed. The self is only able to perceive itself through narration, a monologue. This same theme is returned to later in his essentially two-character play, *Fin de partie* (*Endgame,* 1958).

Best known as a playwright, Beckett's major dramatic works, all considered pioneering plays in the emerging tradition of the THEATRE OF THE ABSURD, are *En attendant Godot* (*Waiting for Godot,* 1952), *Endgame, Krapp's Last Tape* (1959), *Happy Days* (1961), *Play* (1964), *Not I* (1973), *That Time* (1976), and *Footfalls* (1976). Beckett also wrote a series of radio and television dramas, as well as adaptations of his stage works for film.

Beckett is best known for the play *Waiting for Godot,* an absurdist piece that was first performed on January 5, 1953, in Paris. Two derelict-looking characters, Vladimir and Estragon, sit by the side of a road throughout the two acts, waiting for the mysterious Godot, who never appears (is he to be identified with God? Critics do not agree), and aimlessly discuss possible action. Each of the two acts ends with the same words, except that the roles are reversed. This is the end of Act II:

> **VLADIMIR:** Well, shall we go?
> **ESTRAGON:** Yes, let's go.
> *They do not move.*

The play won worldwide acclaim and was followed by a series of critical successes of plays and novels, some of which he had written much earlier in his life.

Beckett's novels and short stories, such as *Murphy* (1938; translated 1957); *Watt* (1953), which was his last novel initially written in English; and *Texts for Nothing* (1955; translated 1967), also examine the self trapped and isolated in its quest for understanding of identity. The situations are often grotesque, and the overall tone is one of anguish and suffering, lightened by gallows humor.

In 1969, Beckett was awarded the Nobel Prize for literature. He continued to write and to be involved in literary and dramatic projects, publishing his last major work *Stirrings Still* in 1986. Emphysema forced his hospitalization, and, bedridden, he wrote his last poem, "What Is the Word." Shortly after, his declining health kept him from writing and forced him into a nursing home, where he remained until his death on December 22. Death, however, was not the end of Beckett's publishing career. His first play, the previously unpublished *Eleutheria* (1947), which depicts the author's search for freedom through the character of a young man, was rediscovered and published in English translation in 1995, six years after his death. Beckett had not allowed the play to be printed during his lifetime because he considered it to be a failure. Its publication was the result of a long dispute between Beckett's American publisher and close friend, Barney Rosset, and his family and his French publisher. Critically, this work is of great importance because it shows the beginnings of the ideas that would define Beckett's works and predates, as well as predicts, the beginnings of the Theater of the Absurd movement.

Other Works by Samuel Beckett

Gontarski, S. E., ed. *The Theatrical Notebooks of Samuel Beckett, Volume 4: The Shorter Plays.* New York: Grove Press, 1999.

Nohow On: Company, Ill Seen Ill Said, Worstward Ho: Three Novels. Introduction by S. E. Gontarski. New York: Grove Press, 1996.

Works about Samuel Beckett

Bair, Dierdre. *Samuel Beckett: A Biography.* New York: Harcourt Brace Jovanovich, 1978.

Cronin, Anthony. *Samuel Beckett: The Last Modernist.* London: HarperCollins, 1996.

Gordon, Lois. *The World of Samuel Beckett.* New Haven: Yale University Press, 1996.

Knowlson, James. *Damned to Fame: The Life of Samuel Beckett.* New York: Simon & Schuster, 1996.

Bécquer, Gustavo Adolfo (Gustavo Adolfo Dominguez Bastida)
(1836–1870) *poet, prose writer*

Gustavo Adolfo Bécquer was born in Seville, Spain. The son of José Dominguez Bécquer, a somewhat successful painter, Bécquer was orphaned at the age of 11. Apprenticed to be a painter, as was his brother, he eventually gave up the art when his uncle informed him that he had no talent and would be better off as a writer. His brother continued to paint and, although Bécquer turned to writing, he remained deeply interested in visual art throughout his life. One of his major literary innovations was the way he used striking visual descriptions.

For most of his adulthood, Bécquer lived hand-to-mouth in Madrid, publishing his poems and short stories in small journals and magazines. Toward the end of his life, he was given a government position as a censor, which helped improve his quality of living. By this time, he had contracted tuberculosis.

Most of Bécquer's work was never published in book form during his life, only in periodicals. After his death, his friends collected his published and unpublished manuscripts and put out a two-volume book simply titled *Works* (1871). It was only then that, for the first time, Bécquer received critical acclaim.

Bécquer's works can be divided into three major components. The poems or *Rimas* (*Rhymes*, (1860–61), the short stories or *Leyendas* (*Legends*, 1864), and a series of autobiographical literary essays, *Cartas desde Mi Celda* (*Letters from My Cell*), which he wrote while convalescing at the monastery of Veruela in 1864.

Bécquer called his poems *Rhymes* to indicate his break with earlier traditions of Spanish verse and to show his poems' relationship to folk ballads. His simple but very visual language gives the impression that he is expressing true emotions and getting to the essence of things. He has been compared to the GERMAN ROMANTIC poet HEINE, although the two writers were probably not familiar with each other's work.

His *Legends* are rich with magical imagery and descriptions of nature and the supernatural. Frequently they take the form of fables and have morals at the end. In his *Legends,* Bécquer is exploring a typical romantic tendency to bring folklore and popular stories into the realm of high art.

Finally, *Letters From My Cell* is a collection of essays in which Bécquer explores his moral, artistic, and spiritual beliefs. Written as he was approaching death, they serve as a kind of psychic autobiography.

Bécquer, underappreciated during his life, went on to become one of the most influential Spanish poets of the 19th century. He was the central figure of Spanish ROMANTICISM. The great Latin American poet Ruben DARIO openly acknowledged Bécquer's powerful effect on him. Bécquer died at age 34 from tuberculosis, never knowing the lasting influence his work would have.

See also COSTUMBRISMO.

Another Work by Gustavo Adolfo Bécquer

Legends and Letters. Translated by Robert M. Fedorchek. Cranbury, N.J.: Bucknell University Press, 1995.

A Work about Gustavo Adolfo Bécquer

Bynum, Brant B. *The Romantic Imagination in the Works of Gustavo Adolfo Bécquer.* Chapel Hill: University of North Carolina, Department of Romance Languages, 1993.

Bei Dao (Zhao Zhenkai) (1949–) *poet, novelist*

Bei Dao was born in Beijing, China, and received a good education until the Cultural Revolution, when the Communist Chinese government sent intellectuals to the countryside to be "reeducated" with revolutionary ideas. Bei Dao was assigned to labor in a construction company outside of Beijing and wrote poetry in his spare time.

He adopted the pen name Bei Dao, which means "north island," and began to write poetry and short stories. In 1979, he published the short novel *Waves,* in China's first underground literary journal, *Today,* which he cofounded in 1978. The novel was characterized as modern because it interweaves five separate narrative voices to create a subjective point of view.

Bei Dao is best known for his political poems, such as "The Answer" and "Declaration," in which he addresses the oppressiveness of the government regime, using thinly veiled, nihilistic language. Bei Dao's poetry was also criticized for its Western roots, impenetrable and sparse language, and confusing metaphors. One critic dubbed it "misty" in the 1980s, when Communist Party leadership and traditional voices in the literary community took modernism to task. *Today* was shut down in 1980; during a 1983 campaign to wipe out literary "pollution" by modernist and avant-garde writers, Bei Dao and the *Today* poets were among the first denounced. Many poets were suspended from their official jobs, and their poetry banned from publication.

The Communist Party just as quickly revised its thinking on modernism, however, and Bei Dao and his colleagues were rerecognized by the party in 1985. Bei Dao even participated in the Beijing Writers Association, and some of his poems were published in state-sponsored magazines that year, including "The Answer."

Bei Dao continued to write against the mainstream, both in a literary and a political sense. When the prodemocracy movement gained momentum in 1989, he was a leader and activist. Quotations from his poems were chanted and posted at Tiananmen Square. Shortly afterward, he went into exile in Sweden.

Bei Dao currently lives in Davis, California. His works are widely translated, many in English, including *The August Sleepwalker* (1990), *Old Snow* (1991), and *Forms of Distance* (1995).

A Work about Bei Dao

Gleichmann, Gabi. "An Interview with Bei Dao." Translated and edited by Michelle Yeh. In *Modern Chinese Literature* 9 (1996): 387–93.

Bely, Andrey (Boris Nikolayevich Bugaev) (1880–1934) *novelist, poet*

The only child of Nikolai Vasilevich Bugaev, a Moscow University mathematician, and Aleksandra Dmitrivna Egorova, a musician, Andrey Bely was born in Moscow, Russia. Bely's parents had different attitudes about the relative importance of natural sciences and the arts, and he was constantly caught in their conflict. Aiming to please his father, Bely successfully pursued a degree in natural sciences at Moscow University and graduated in 1903.

Bely began to write poetry as a university student. The main support for his initial efforts came from Mikhail Solovyov, the Bugaevs' neighbor and a younger brother of the famous Russian philosopher Vladimir Solovyov. Solovyov provided financial support for Bely's first published collection of poems, *Second Symphony,* in 1902 and suggested the pseudonym Andrey Bely. After the death of his father in 1903, Bely decided to abandon science and devote himself to writing.

Between 1903 and 1910, Bely wrote for *Vesy,* a major journal of the symbolist movement. In his articles, Bely desperately attempted to define and synthesize some kind of philosophy of SYMBOLISM. Bely wrote more than 200 articles, reviews, and essays during this period, as well as another two volumes of *Symphonies.*

In 1905, Bely left Russia and traveled to Munich and Paris, where he was befriended by Jean Jaurès, the famous socialist leader. When he returned to Russia, Bely established a relationship with Asya Turgeneva, who was to be his lover for many years, and in 1910, they went abroad together. They were drawn to Rudolf Steiner's mystical philosophy, anthroposophy. From 1914 to 1916, when Bely was recalled by the Russian government for military duty, the couple were with Steiner in Switzerland.

Although Bely firmly established himself as a poet, he is mostly known for his prose. In *Petersburg* (1913), Bely explores the social and political turmoil of the Russian Revolution of 1905. The novel centers on a plot to deliver a bomb to a high government official. It is a commentary on family, the role of the individual, and spiritualism.

In the Joycean autobiographical novel *Kotik Latayev* (1922), Bely incorporates the story of his own childhood, exploring emotional conflicts between parents and the delicate psyche of a child. Bely's intricate prose brilliantly captures intensity of time, translating the sensory experiences into intriguing and powerful works of fiction.

Bely broke with both Steiner and Turgeneva in 1921 and lived in Moscow from 1923 until his death, producing three more novels and three volumes of memoirs.

Most critics today agree on the literary genius and immense impact of Bely's work. Vladimir Nabokov (quoted in Malmstad and Maguire's introduction to their translation of *Petersburg*) ranked *Petersburg* with James Joyce's *Ulysses,* Franz KAFKA's *The Castle,* and Marcel PROUST's *In Search of Lost Time,* as one of the great books of the 20th century.

Other Works by Andrey Bely

Kotik Letayev. Translated by Gerald J. Janacek. Evanston, Ill.: Northwestern University Press, 1999.
Petersburg. Translated by Robert A. Maguire and John E. Malmstad. Bloomington: Indiana University Press, 1978.

Works about Andrey Bely

Janecek, Gerald. *Andrey Bely: A Critical Review.* Lexington: Kentucky University Press, 1978.
Keys, Roger. *The Reluctant Modernist: Andrey Belyi and the Development of Russian Fiction.* Oxford: Clarendon Press, 1996.

Benn, Gottfried (Kurt Wolff) (1886–1956) *poet, novelist, playwright*

Gottfried Benn was born in the German village of Mansfield. His father was a Lutheran minister and his mother was a French-speaking native of Switzerland. Benn attended the Gymnasium at Frankfurt an der Oder. He studied theology and philosophy at the University of Marbach and in 1905 was accepted at Kaiser Wilhelm Akademie, a prominent military medical school. He earned his doctorate in 1912 and married actress Edith Brosin two years later.

Benn had a private practice in Berlin specializing in skin diseases and served in the German army's medical corps in both world wars. He performed numerous autopsies in his career and frequently wrote about morgues in his early poetry. Benn's scientific background instilled a skepticism and self-criticism that often appeared in his literary work.

Benn published five books of poetry between 1910 and 1925. He also wrote a series of works called the "Rönne novellas," which earned critical praise for demonstrating the concept of "absolute prose." In this unique style, Benn replaced a descriptive, psychologically oriented narrative with a blend of associative and visionary elements. In the 1930s, Benn briefly embraced the Nazis before becoming disillusioned with their barbarism. His popularity increased after World War II with the publication of *Statische Gedichte* (*Static Poems*, 1948), a volume of apolitical modernist poems. In 1951, Benn received the Georg Bücher Prize, one of Germany's most prestigious literary awards. At the age of 67, he finally earned enough money from his writing career to quit his medical practice.

Benn's influences included Friedrich NIETZSCHE and his friend Else LASKER-SCHÜLER, the expressionist poet. Benn's poetry is melancholy and elegiac, conveying cultural despair. His writings were both praised and denounced for challenging established German literary traditions. Critics are also divided on his significance: Edgar Lohner described Benn as "one of the foremost modern European lyric poets," while Michael Hamburger concluded that "Benn was too restricted in tone to be described as a major writer" in *Gottfried Benn: The Unreconstructed Expressionist* by J. M. Ritchie. As an embodiment of the contradictions of literary modernism, Benn will likely remain a debated German literary figure.

Another Work by Gottfried Benn

Prose, Essays, Poems. Edited by Volknar Sander. New York: Continuum, 1987.

A Work about Gottfried Benn

Ritchie, J. M. *Gottfried Benn: The Unreconstructed Expressionist.* London: Oswald Wolff, 1972.

Bennett, Louise (Louise Bennett–Coverley, Miss Lou, Mrs. Eric Coverley) (1919–   ) *poet, folklorist*

Louise Bennett was born in Kingston, Jamaica, to Augustus Cornelius Bennett, a bakery owner, and Kerene Robinson, a dressmaker. English poetry influenced the writing she did as a schoolgirl; she wrote poems in standard English until she overheard a country woman on a Kingston tramcar and wrote the first of many poems in Jamaican dialect. Bennett published her first collection of poems, *(Jamaica) Dialect Verses* (1942), in her early twenties.

Bennett primarily writes in Jamaican dialect about Jamaican people's "now" experiences. One speaker usually uses literary techniques—such as allusions to Jamaican folksongs, the Bible, and English literature—and oral performance techniques—such as rhetorical lists—to address an audience. In a 1968 interview with Dennis Scott, Bennett said that people thought of her "as a performing artist primarily" but added, "I did start to write before I started to perform," and "I felt I wanted to put on paper some of the wonderful things that people say in dialect." *Jamaica Labrish* (1966), her most substantial collection of poems, shows Bennett as performer, poet, and social commentator.

Bennett's work as a journalist, actress, folk singer, radio- and television-show host, and drama and folklore lecturer helped generate a large audience for her poetry. But her poetry did not start to receive critical acceptance until the late 1960s. Many distinguished awards followed, and in "Proverb as Metaphor in the Poetry of Louise Bennett" (1984), Carolyn Cooper called Bennett "the quintessential Jamaican example of the sensitive and competent Caribbean artist consciously incorporating features of traditional oral art into written literature."

Other Works by Louise Bennett

Anancy and Miss Lou. Kingston: Sangster's Book Stores, 1966.

Collected Poems. Kingston: Sangster's Book Stores, 1982.

Jamaican Humour in Dialect. Kingston: Jamaica Press Association, 1943.

Laugh with Louise. Kingston: City Printery, 1961.

Miss Lula Sez. Kingston: Gleaner, 1949.

Works about Louise Bennett

Cooper, Carolyn. "Noh Lickle Twang: An Introduction to the Poetry of Louise Bennett." *World Literature Written in English* vol. 17 (April 1978).

———. *Noises in the Blood: Orality, Gender and the "Vulgar" Body of Jamaican Popular Culture.* Durham, N.C.: Duke University Press, 1995.

Erwin, Lee. "Two Jamaican Women Writers and the Uses of Creole." In A. L. McLeod, ed., *Commonwealth and American Women's Discourse: Essays in Criticism.* New Delhi: Sterling, 1996.

Bernhard, Thomas (1931–1989) *playwright, novelist*

Thomas Bernhard was born in Heerlen, Netherlands, to Hertha Bernhard. He moved with his mother to Austria at age four; Thomas never met his father, an Austrian carpenter. Hertha's father, Johannes Freumbichler, a novelist, was one of Thomas's earliest influences. Bernhard grew up in poverty and did poorly in school, eventually dropping out at age 15. He studied voice at this time and hoped to start a career in music; however, pneumonia and tuberculosis nearly killed him a few years later. His grandfather and mother died while he struggled to recover from his own health problems. These experiences with death and illness created a pessimism that characterized Bernhard's literary work.

Bernhard studied music and drama in Vienna and Salzburg as a young adult. He published three books of poetry in the late 1950s but received little acclaim until he published his first novel, *Frost* (1963). His first drama *Ein Fest Für Boris* (*A Party for Boris,* 1968) premiered on stage in 1970. A tasteless farce about demented invalids who abuse each other, the play reflects Bernhard's vision of humanity's wretchedness. In the following two decades, Bernhard solidified his reputation as a novelist with works such as *Korrektur* (*Correction,* 1975), a novel about a man's increasing obsession with the manuscripts written by a brilliant mathematician friend who committed suicide. Bernhard also gained fame as a playwright for dramas such as *Die Macht der Gewohnheit* (*The Force of Habit,* 1976), a commentary about the empty rituals of high culture. He won numerous literary awards, including the Georg Büchner Prize (1970).

Bernhard was obsessed with insanity, death, and the wretchedness of the human condition. He sharply criticized the moral failures of Austria's history. His works stirred controversy in their attack on the complacency of German theater and their criticism of modern life. Despite his dark themes, Bernhard was illuminating in his use of language and, as literary scholar J. J. Long comments, "a writer of considerable diversity, who was profoundly concerned with both the problems and potential of storytelling."

Other Works by Thomas Bernhard

Gargoyles. Translated by Richard and Clara Winston. New York: Knopf, 1970.

The Force of Habit: A Comedy. Translated by Neville and Stephen Plaice. London: Heinemann, 1976.

A Work about Thomas Bernhard

Long, J. J. *The Novels of Thomas Bernhard: Form and Its Function.* Rochester, N.Y.: Camden House, 2001.

Bernstein, Ingrid

See KIRSCH, SARAH.

Bhatt, Sujata (1956–) *poet, translator*

Sujata Bhatt was born in Ahmedabad, India, and grew up in Pune in a large household with her extended family. Her paternal grandfather was a poet, and two of her uncles were famous Gujarati poets. Hearing their stories and listening to their poetry as a child, Bhatt was inspired to write. As a child, she was very proud that she could compose poetry in English, which her family could not do. Her father, a virologist, moved to America in 1968 with the family and wanted Bhatt to become a scientist, too. In school, she obediently took classes in science but slowly gained interest in philosophy, creative writing, and English literature.

Though Bhatt left India at an early age, her childhood years in Gujarat are constantly referred to in almost all her poetry. Written in English, her poetry unabashedly translates sounds of Gujarati words in play with English ones, creating a language-based tension and highlighting the contradictions inherent in translating concepts or ideas from one language to another. Works such as *Brunizem* (1988), however, display her agility in synthesizing the East with the West, a tribute to the positive rewards of a multicultural existence.

In an interview with *PN Review,* Bhatt said that she writes poetry to "break [the] historical silence" surrounding female sexuality, but she also brings out the sensual aspects of seemingly ordinary objects. *Stinking Rose* (1995) is a journey through the myth and history of garlic—its medicinal, herbal, and erotic uses in different cultures through the ages. Her studies in the sciences and her interest in visual arts add dimension to her imagery in matters of light, form, and texture. Her forthcoming work *A Color for Solitude* is said to be inspired by the self-portraits of the German painter Paula Modersohn-Becker (1876–1907) during her relationship with poets such as Rainer Maria RILKE.

Bhatt was briefly a professor of writing at the University of British Columbia, Canada, but left when she moved to Germany. She now works as a freelance writer and also translates other Gujarati poetry into English. Her collection *Brunizem* won the Commonwealth Poetry Prize (Asia), and in 1991, she won the Cholmondeley Award for Poetry (U.K.)

Other Works by Sujata Bhatt
Augatora. Manchester, U.K.: Carcanet Press, 2000.
Monkey Shadows. Manchester, U.K.: Carcanet Press, 1988.

A Work about Sujata Bhatt
Pandey, M. S. "The Trishanku Motif in the Poetry of Sujata Bhatt and Uma Parameswaran." *The Literature of the Indian Diaspora: Essays in Criticism.* Edited by A. L. McLeod. New Delhi: Sterling Publishers Private Ltd., 2000.

Bing Xin (Ping Hsin; Xie Wanying; Hsieh Wan-ying) (1900–1999) *short-story writer, poet*

Bing Xin, the daughter of a naval officer, was born on October 5 in Fuzhou, the capital of China's Fujian province. She was raised in Chefoo in Shandong province and moved to Beijing in 1914 where she attended a Congregational missionary school. She then attended Yanjing University in Beijing. In 1919, during the May Fourth Movement against foreign imperialism, Bing Xin changed her major from medicine to literature, believing that writing fiction would have a positive social impact on Chinese society.

In 1923, she published *Superman,* a collection of short stories, and two poetry collections, *The Stars* and *Waters of Spring.* After these works received critical acclaim, Bing Xin traveled to Massachusetts, where she attended Wellesley College and began to write columns for children that were collected in *Letters to My Little Readers* (1926), which was published in China and was immensely popular. She received her master's degree in 1926 and returned to Yanjing to teach literature. In 1929, she married Wu Wenzao, a sociologist, with whom she had three children. The family moved at the onset of the Sino-Japanese War to Kunming in 1937 and then to Chongqing in 1941.

Bing Xin's short stories are widely known for their sentimental depictions of motherly love and family life. Some modernist critics have written that her work is old-fashioned and too traditional.

Nonetheless, most of her stories, such as "Loneliness" (1922), are well observed and address the dilemmas of life and love faced by younger Chinese women. In other stories, such as "Our Mistress' Parlor" (1933), a sarcastic indictment of a shallow Shanghaiese woman, Bing Xin depicts different types of women.

In the 1950s and 1960s, Bing Xin focused on writing children's literature and translating the Indian poet Rabindranath TAGORE. Like all artists, she was sent to Hubei for manual labor reeducation during the Cultural Revolution but was reinstated to the party in 1980. She continued to write articles and stories and to serve the party in a number of official positions until her death. Although she was often criticized for being overly traditional, her acutely observed stories of young womanhood earned her a reputation as one of China's foremost women writers.

Other Works by Bing Xin

"Autobiographical Notes" and selected poems. In Special Section on Bing Xin, *Renditions* 16, no. 32 (Fall 1989).

Bingxin Shi Quan Pian = Bing Xin's Complete Poems. Hangzhou: Zhejiang Wen Yi Chu Ban She, 1994.

A Work about Bing Xin

Cayley, John. "Birds and Stars: Tagore's Influence on Bing Xin's Early Poetry." *Renditions* 16, no. 32 (Fall 1989).

Bitton, Erez (Erez Biton) (1942–) *poet*

Erez Bitton was born in Algeria. As a child, playing in an abandoned orchard, he discovered an old grenade. The explosion blinded him and cost him partial use of an arm. Ironically, it was this childhood accident that brought him to an institution for the blind where he received an education not previously available to him.

Bitton's poetry often deals with people who are classified as "other" by a dominant culture, as can be seen in the poem "Summary of a Conversation." As a *Mizrahi,* a Jew who emigrated to Israel from other parts of the Middle East, Bitton had first-hand knowledge of what it meant to be "other."

While the critical establishment views his work as an authentic expression of Middle Eastern Jewry, his poetry defies categorization. He is one of the first poets to weave Middle Eastern themes that explore the question of what actually constitutes an authentic or genuine expression of Middle Eastern Jewry. Bitton even challenges the very notions of such categorization. In "Summary of a Conversation," Bitton asserts that the resolution to the dilemma faced by those classified as "other" is found within the self.

Bitton lives in Tel Aviv, Israel, where he edits *Aperion,* a literary journal dedicated to Mediterranean and Middle Eastern culture. He also performs dramatic recitals of his work to musical accompaniment as an expression the condition of the Mizrahi experience.

A Work about Erez Bitton

Alcalay, Ammiel. *Keys to the Garden, New Israeli Writing.* New York: City Light Books, 1996.

Bjørnson, Bjørnstjerne (1832–1910)
writer, editor

Bjørnstjerne Bjørnson was born in Kvikne, Norway, to Peder Bjørnson, a Lutheran minister, and Elise Nordraak, a daughter of an affluent merchant. Bjørnson was at first educated by his father and at various country schools. In 1849, to prepare for the university entrance exams, he moved to Oslo where he was planning to study religion, following in his father's footsteps. Bjørnson entered the university in 1852 but soon abandoned his study for the bustling cultural life of Oslo.

He began his literary career as a theater and literary critic for several daily newspapers in Oslo. He later became an editor of the daily *Norsk Folkeblad.* In 1857, Bjørnson took over the management of the Norske Theater in Bergen from Henrik IBSEN. He returned to Oslo in 1859 and continued to work for newspapers. Bjørnson's liberal editorials, however, finally led to his resignation. In collaboration with Henrik Ibsen, Bjørnson organized the Norwegian Society for Theater, Music, and Language to promote more liberal notions about drama and theater in general.

Bjørnson began writing fiction in the late 1850s, and published several short stories. His short stories were often set in an idyllic, rural environment and idealized the lives of simple peasants. The conflict in the stories is often created when something new or unexpected disrupts the existing order. In "The Railway and the Churchyard" (1858), Knut Aakre, a chairman of the parish and a member of an old and influential family, protects the interests of the village. His neighbor, Lars Hogstad, decides to build a savings bank, which initially brings prosperity to the village. Lars soon realizes that a railroad is necessary to preserve the savings bank. This railroad must go through the old churchyard, and Knut firmly opposes the idea. When the railroad is finally built, a disaster happens: Lars's house is set on fire by sparks from the train. Knut is the first one to help his neighbor. The opposition between the old and the new is the source of tension in the story, but the reader finally sees the synthesis of the two opposing points.

Bjørnson also created a number of historical dramas that were quite popular; however, the political and social issues introduced in these works, along with his staunch atheism, produced charges of high treason. Bjørnson then went abroad, spending several years in Italy, the United States, and Finland. He also completed several novels that centered on social themes such as education, inheritance, dogmatism, and the state of peasantry in Norway. Bjørnson also opposed industrialization and joined Emile ZOLA in protest against the bigotry involved in the Dreyfus affair in France.

Despite declining health which left him paralyzed on one side, Bjørnstjerne Bjørnson continued working until his death in Paris in 1910. His work contributed to the formation of modern drama in Norway; his social and political articles eventually prompted change and caused an upheaval in artistic circles; his short stories and novels promoted understanding of the traditional Norwegian culture. Bjørnson's stories and novels are still popular in Norway and are considered to be among the classics of Scandinavian literature.

Other Works by Bjørnstjerne Bjørnson

Captain Mansana, and Other Stories. Translated by Rasmus B. Anderson. North Stratford, N.H.: Ayer Co. Publishing, 1980.

Heigen, Einar, ed. *Land of the Free: Bjørnstjerne Bjørnson's America Letters, 1880–1881.* Translated by Eva Lund Haugen. Northfield, Minn.: Norwegian American Historical Association, 2001.

The Bridal March, and Other Stories. Translated by Rasmus B. Anderson. North Stratford, N.H.: Ayer Co. Publishing, 1969.

Three Plays. New York: Howard Fertig, 1989.

A Work about Bjørnstjerne Bjørnson

Cohen, Georg. *Henrik Ibsen: A Critical Study. With a 42-Page Essay on Bjørnstjerne Bjørnson.* New York: Classic Books, 1964.

Blasco Ibáñez, Vicente (1867–1928)
novelist

Born in Valencia, Spain, Blasco Ibáñez first began writing about life in that Mediterranean seaport. His is the "regional" novel, and his works depict life in his "patria chica," or place of birth. Blasco Ibáñez writes in the naturalist style: He believes that our behavior is controlled by instinct, emotion, and environment and that we have no free will. His best novel, *La barraca* (1898), takes place in the lovely farmlike regions of Valencia. It presents the animosity held by the half-Moorish peasants toward a stranger in their land.

Around 1902, after writing several novels situated in Valencia, Blasco Ibáñez attempted to describe other areas of Spain, but these works lack the power of his earlier works. His writing became more propaganda than literary expression as he attacked the church, the government, and the military. He carries the reader across Spain, visiting the religious capital, Toledo; Bilbao, an industrial city, and Andalusia in southern Spain, where he describes the hardships suffered by the peasants. His novel, *Sangre y arena* (*Blood and Sand,* 1906) has been called the most complete portrayal of bullfighting ever presented in fiction. Far from an idealistic account, it is a description of all the blood and gore of the fight and depicts the spectators as monsters.

In 1910, in trouble for his unpopular political opinions and his radical journal, *El Pueblo,* Blasco Ibáñez went to South America, where he hoped to devote a novel to each country. After he wrote *Los argonautas* (1914) about Argentina, the outbreak of World War I caused him to return to Europe. He fought for the Allies, earning the French Légion d'Honneur. His later novels deal with the war, for example, *Los cuatro jinetes del Apocalipsis* (*The Four Horsemen of the Apocalypse,* 1916).

Some critics say Blasco Ibáñez has received more recognition than he deserves. His popularity is partly due to his forceful style. His novels are not delicate. It is the powerful descriptions of his hometown, Valencia, in his earlier novels that most attract his readers.

A Work about Blasco Ibáñez
Day, A. Grove, and Edgar C. Knowlton, Jr. *Vicente Blasco Ibáñez.* Boston: Twayne, 1972.

Blixen, Baroness Karen Christence
See DINESEN, ISAK.

Böll, Heinrich (1917–1985) *novelist, short-story writer*
Heinrich Theodor Böll was born in Cologne to Victor and Marie Hermanns Böll. His father was a carpenter, and his mother was from a farming and brewing family. Böll attended a Catholic elementary school and later graduated from the Kaiser Wilhelm-Gymnasium in Cologne. He studied German and philology for a semester at the University of Cologne before the German army drafted him in 1939. Böll was wounded four times, fighting in World War II. He married Annemarie Cech in 1942.

The postwar years were lean for Böll and his family. He worked in a carpentry shop and as a temporary employee for the city of Cologne. It was not long, however, before he published several short stories. One of these works received the prize from the German authors' association GRUPPE 47. The success of Böll's novel on generational reckoning, *Billard um halb zehn* (*Billiards at Half-Past Nine,* 1959), helped Gruppe 47 become a stronger voice in German literature. His novel criticizing the government and the church, *Ansichten eines Clowns,* (*The Clown,* 1965), marked the start of a new German literary phase in which blunt political reasoning took precedence over formal artistic expression.

Böll's writing career lasted four decades and produced a host of popular and critically acclaimed novels. In a poll taken in the 1970s, West Germans selected him as the fourth-most-influential person in their country. He received the Nobel Prize in literature in 1972, in part for his novel *Gruppenbild mit Dame* (*Group Portrait with Lady,* 1971), about an "author" researching the war experiences of a woman whom he gradually comes to love.

Several themes emerge from Böll's writings. He portrays war as senseless and absurd, refuting the notion of heroism. Böll's opposition of postwar materialism is another common theme. He often challenged authority and criticized the abuses of the Catholic Church. Böll strongly promoted human rights and was considered by many to be the conscience of West Germany. In the words of literary scholar Heinrich Vormweg, "Heinrich Böll created a literary oeuvre which reflects the true history of the Federal Republic as no other has done."

Other Works by Heinrich Böll
Adam, Where Art Thou? Translated by Mervyn Savill. New York: Criterion Books, 1955.
The Lost Honor of Katharina Blum. Translated by Leila Vennewitz. New York: McGraw-Hill, 1975.
The Train Was on Time. Translated by Richard Graves. New York: Criterion Books, 1956.

Works about Heinrich Böll

Heinrich Böll, on His Death: Selected Obituaries and the Last Interview. Bonn: Inter Nationes, 1985.

Schwarz, Wilhelm. *Heinrich Böll: Teller of Tales.* New York: Ungar, 1968.

Bonnefoy, Yves (1923–   ) *poet, critic*

Yves Bonnefoy was born in Tours, France, on June 24 to a working-class family. His father was a railroad worker, and his mother was a teacher. He received his degree in mathematics and philosophy from the University of Descartes in Tours and then studied mathematics, history, and philosophy at both the University of Poitiers and the Sorbonne.

In 1953, Bonnefoy published his first collection, *Of the Movement and the Immobility of Douve* (1953; translated 1968). These poems were chiefly concerned with human beings' struggle to establish a firm connection among themselves and with the world. Six other collections of poetry followed, including *Ce qui fut sans lumière* (*What Was Without Light*, 1987); *Début et fin de la neige* (*Beginning and End of Snow*, 1991); and *La vie errante* (*The Wandering Life*, 1993) about Helen of Troy, the image of beauty threatened by violence.

In addition to poetry, Bonnefoy has written numerous historical and critical texts, such as *The Art and the Place of Poetry* (1989), and is concerned with the connection between poetry and the visual arts.

Bonnefoy has taught at several universities, both in France and abroad, and has been involved in the translation from English to French of 10 Shakespearean plays as well as an edition of the poetry of Yeats. He is also the editor of *Mythologies* (1991), a two-volume scholarly work: One volume explores and reproduces African, American, and Ancient European myths and the histories of religious traditions; the second volume explores the same themes from Greek and Egyptian traditions, as written by French authors. Bonnefoy has received several awards for his poetry, including the Montaigne prize in 1978 and Grand National Prize for Poetry in 1993.

Other Works by Yves Bonnefoy

In the Shadow's Light. Translated by John Naughton. Chicago: University of Chicago Press, 1991.

Naughton, John, and Anthony Rudolf, eds. *New and Selected Poems.* Chicago: University of Chicago Press, 1995.

Yesterday's Wilderness Kingdom. Translated by Anthony Rudolf. London: MPT Books, 2000.

A Work about Yves Bonnefoy

Naughton, John. *The Poetics of Yves Bonnefoy.* Chicago: University of Chicago Press, 1984.

Borges, Jorge Luis (1899–1986) *poet, short-story writer, essayist*

Born in Buenos Aires, Argentina, Borges was the son of Jorge Guillermo Borges and Leonor Acevedo de Borges. The Borgeses were a prominent Argentinean family descended from Juan de Garay, the founder of Buenos Aires.

Borges's father, a lawyer and professor of psychology, had Borges tutored at home until the age of 10 by a British governess. The family also had a large library with many works in English, and Borges read, at a very early age authors such as Stevenson, Wells, Kipling, and Poe. These writers influenced him dramatically, tempering his bookishness with a love of adventure stories and fantasy. His first publication was a translation into Spanish of Oscar Wilde's fairy tale *The Happy Prince,* which Borges wrote when he was nine.

At the beginning of World War I, Borges's family moved to Switzerland, where he attended high school and became fluent in French, German, and Latin in addition to English and his native Spanish. After graduating from high school, Borges traveled to Spain where he thrust himself into the avant-garde literary discussions in the cafés and befriended a Spanish poet, Cansinos-Assens, a minor but extremely learned poet. Borges's experience during these years sparked his interest in literary experimentation and solidified his desire to become a writer.

Borges returned to Argentina in his mid-20s, and during the next 20 years, he steadily published volumes of poetry, essays, and short stories. His "fictions," as he called them, exhibit his extraordinary literary originality. At their best, his stories are a kind of philosophic science fiction. They have a broad popular appeal and have also received the highest literary respect. Borges was one of the first authors in the 20th century to take popular genres, like the science-fiction tale or the hardboiled detective story, and use them to investigate metaphysical ideas that were traditionally explored only in poetry, philosophy, and "serious" prose fiction. This can be seen in the story from *Fictions* (1962), "The Garden of Forking Paths"—a detective story that is also an intricate exploration of the limits of language.

Many of Borges's stories have little or no plot. They explore instead the different possibilities of an idea. For example, in "The Library of Babel," also from *Fictions,* the narrator explains to the reader how the Library in which he lives works. The Library is infinite and there is no way out. On the shelves are books filled with random letters. Most of the books are filled with nonsense. However, because there is an infinite number of books, sometimes by chance the letters form words or even whole books that make sense. In fact, simply by the laws of mathematics, every possible book in the world must exist in the Library. The trouble is trying to find the important books among the millions of meaningless ones. Borges, who himself spent many years working as a librarian, thus presents his audience with a symbolic tale about the human condition, his message being that if we had enough time, it would be possible to know everything about the world and ourselves, but time is exactly what is limited.

Death and the Compass, another tale from *Fictions,* is the best example of the "other kind" of Borges short story. It is, in essence, a mystery with an intricate and perfectly constructed plot. However, the hero, Lonnrot, is a kind of anti-Sherlock Holmes, a master of logical deduction. In Borges's world, Lonnrot uses this very quality, as he is led to his doom, to solve his own murder. The story can be read as a parable concerning the dangers to the human soul in our highly rational and scientific culture.

In his later life, Borges received many honorary degrees from such universities as Oxford and Harvard, where he also taught. He was the first Latin-American prose writer to become an internationally recognized literary figure. He has had a strong influence on many of the greatest Latin American authors of the 20th century, for example Gabriel GARCÍA MÁRQUEZ, Carlos FUENTES, and Julio CORTAZAR, who follow Borges in the art of irony and prose filled with verbal invention and intellectual game playing, rather than the psychological and social drama of REALISM.

Other Works by Jorge Luis Borges

Coleman, Alexander, ed. *Selected Poems.* New York: Penguin, 2000.

Collected Fictions. Translated by Andrew Hurley. New York: Penguin, 1999.

Dreamtigers. Translated by Mildred Boyer and Harold Moreland. Austin: University of Texas Press, 1985.

Irby, James, and Donald Yeats, eds. *Labyrinths: Selected Stories and Other Writings.* New York: Norton, 1988.

Works about Jorge Luis Borges

Barnstone, Willis, ed. *Borges at Eighty: Conversations.* Bloomington: Indiana University Press, 1982.

Bell-Villada, Gene H. *Borges and His Fiction.* Austin: University of Texas Press, 1999.

Brasch, Charles (1909–1973) *poet, critic, translator*

Charles Brasch was born in Otago, New Zealand, the only son of Jewish parents. His father was an established businessman, but from an early age Brasch, to his father's disappointment, aspired to be a poet and writer. Unlike some of his peers, Brasch had little confidence in his innate lyrical gift, and he spent most of his life learning and perfecting the technical aspects of writing poetry. He studied history at Oxford University and worked in the Foreign Office in London before returning to New Zealand permanently in 1945.

In 1947 the journal *Landfall* began publication, with Brasch as its founding editor. For 20 years, Brasch nurtured the talent of young New Zealand writers through his intense editorial scrutiny as well as through contributions from his personal wealth. In addition, each issue of the journal contained an editorial essay by Brasch. *Landfall* is still an important part of New Zealand literary life.

The poems in his first published collection, *The Land and the People, and Other Poems* (1939), betray his preference for accuracy of sense over rhythm; metrically they are a little awkward. Brasch's later poetry finally achieves an impeccable balance between expression in terms of words and cadence. This, however, is the result of a lifetime of hard work.

Brasch's poems deal prominently with his life and travels. Nature and its interaction with human beings constitute an important theme in Brasch's poetry. In the title sequence "The Land and the People," Brasch recounts the past through the reenactment in four poems of the first arrival of people on the islands of New Zealand. The initial arrival is compared to the "original sin," a destruction of nature's paradise. In another poem, "Letter from Thurlby Domain," Brasch sees the ruins of a house as a payment of a debt by human beings to the natural environment they had tried to alter.

Four more collections appeared during his lifetime, including *The Estate and Other Poems* (1957), whose lengthy title poem was written in memory of a friend who died in an accident, and *Ambulando* (1964), in which he began to focus more on his own experience rather than on philosophical subjects and the issue of national identity. As he states in "Cry Mercy":

> Getting older, I grow more personal,
> Like more, dislike more
> And more intensely than ever . . .

His final collection, *Home Ground* (1974) was published after his death, as was an unfinished autobiography, *Indirections: A Memoir* (1980). Brasch's extensive and valuable collection of books and paintings was bequeathed to the Hocken Library in Dunedin, New Zealand.

Other Works by Charles Brasch

Roddick, Alan, ed. *Collected Poems: Charles Brasch.* New York: Oxford University Press, 1991.

Watson, J. L., ed. *The Universal Dance: A Selection from the Critical Prose Writings of Charles Brasch.* Otago, New Zealand: University of Otago Press, 1991.

Works about Charles Brasch

Bertram, James. *Charles Brasch.* New York: Oxford University Press, 1976.

Daalder, Joost. "'Disputed Ground' in the Poetry of Charles Brasch." *Landfall* 26 (September 1972).

De Beer, Mary, et al. "Charles Brasch 1909–73: Tributes and Memories from his Friends." *Islands* 2 (Spring 1973).

Braschi, Giannina (1954–   ) *poet, novelist, professor*

Giannina Braschi was born in San Juan, Puerto Rico, and lived in Madrid, Rome, Paris, and London before settling in New York in the late 1970s. Braschi earned a Ph.D. from the State University of New York. In 1994, her selected works in Spanish were published in English as *Empire of Dreams,* a collection that explores gender and linguistic boundaries. *Yo-Yo Boing!* (1998), a work written in Spanish and English, juxtaposes themes of identity, ethnicity, and globalization with artistic innovations. A *Publisher's Weekly* reviewer wrote, "Braschi's melange of prose and poetry, English and Spanish, is admirable for its energy, its experimental format." *Yo-Yo Boing!* was nominated for the Pulitzer Prize and the American Library Association's Notable Book Award.

Another Work by Giannina Braschi

"Three Prose Poems." Translated by Tess O'Dwyer. *The Literary Review: An International Journal of Contemporary Writing* 36, no. 2 (Winter 1993): 147–49.

Works about Giannina Braschi

"Giannina Braschi." *The Literary Review* 36, no.2 (Winter 1993): 14.

"*Yo-Yo Boing!.*" *Publishers Weekly* 245, no. 35 (August 1998): 49.

Brathwaite, Edward Kamau (Lawson Edward Brathwaite) (1930–) *poet, critic, short-story writer, teacher, historian*

Born in Bridgetown, Barbados, Brathwaite was educated at Harrison College in Barbados. He won a Barbados scholarship in 1949 to Pembroke College, Cambridge, where he read history. After graduating in 1953, Brathwaite stayed on one more year to earn a Certificate in Education.

In 1955, Brathwaite left England for Ghana and worked as an education officer for seven years. There he founded a children's theater and wrote plays, later published as *Four Plays for Primary Schools* (1964) and *Odale's Choice* (1967). He also published multiple poems in Cambridge University journals and West Indies periodicals, such as *Bim* and *Kyk-Over-Al*. In "Timehri" (1970), Brathwaite remarked on his Ghanaian experiences: "Slowly, ever so slowly, I came to a sense of identification of myself with these people, my living diviners. I came to connect my history with theirs, the bridge of my mind was linking Atlantic and ancestor, homeland and heartland." The historical and geographical themes expressed in these statements reappear in many of Brathwaite's works.

Returning to the Caribbean in 1962, Brathwaite worked as a tutor for the University of the West Indies in St. Lucia. One year later he became a lecturer in history at Mona, Jamaica. He completed his first book of poetry, *Rights of Passage*, during his first year there, and it was published in 1967 as the first volume of a trilogy. The *Rights of Passage*, Brath-

waite states on the record sleeve, is "based on my own experience of that old triple journey: in my case, from the Caribbean to Europe, to West Africa and back home again. . . . It is a rite and the possession of the Negro peoples of the New World." *Masks* (1968) and *Islands* (1969) soon followed. In the deluge of reviews and commentaries generated by the publication of *Islands,* the trilogy was named one of the most ambitious aesthetic and ethical poetic projects from the Antilles. A *Sunday Times* review of *Islands* positioned Brathwaite as "one of the finest living poets of the Western Hemisphere."

Published as *The Arrivants: A New World Trilogy* in 1973, all three volumes examine African roots to recover West Indian identity. The trilogy explores many themes examined in later works—community, tribal concerns, spiritual growth, and history. Later works, many in dialect, incorporated musical elements of popular culture, such as folk music, jazz, and religious hymns, as well as speech rhythms. Some claimed Brathwaite inadequately recorded intended rhythms in his verse but admit he reads his verse brilliantly.

In subsequent years, Brathwaite successfully published scholarly as well as creative writing. Interested in the relationship of jazz to Caribbean writing, he published *Jazz and the West Indian Novel* in *Bim* in 1967. Other notable scholarly works include *The Folk Culture of Jamaican Slaves* (1969) and *The Development of Creole Society in Jamaica 1770–1820* (1971). Brathwaite's work positioned him as one of the Antilles' most consistent and important English-speaking critics.

Multiple collections of poetry followed, but they received less critical attention than *The Arrivants*. Dissatisfied, some critics said *Other Exiles* (1975) merely collected poems not included in *The Arrivants*. Brathwaite's use of violent demonic imagery to explore Rastafarian subculture and urban slum experiences in *Black and Blues* (1976) earned him a prize at the Cuban Casa de las Americas poetry competition. Critics also quickly recognized Brathwaite's poetic talent in *Mother Poem* (1977). As Brathwaite writes in the preface, "This poem is about porous limestone, my mother, Barbados."

Like *Mother Poem, Sun Poem* (1982) is autobiographical: Brathwaite universalizes his cyclical masculine experiences. One year after publishing *Sun Poem,* Brathwaite was appointed professor of social and cultural history at the University of the West Indies. Lecturing and reading his poetry allowed him to travel widely in Europe, Africa, North America, and the Far East.

More recent works, including *The Zea Mexican Diary* (1993), *Trench Town Rock* (1994), and *Dream-Stories* (1994), employ what Brathwaite calls the Sycorax writing style. They alter font, type size, and margins, "allowing [Brathwaite] to write in light and to make sounds visible as if [he is] in video," as stated in an interview with Kwame Dawes in *Talk Yuh Talk: Interviews with Anglophone Caribbean Poets* (2001). Although Brathwaite's poetry has been translated into Spanish, French, German, and the Sranantongo language of Suriname, he recently admitted, "My big regret is that Caribbean criticism has almost totally disregarded my work since *The Arrivants* as long ago now as 1973."

A comparative-literature professor at New York University, Brathwaite divides his time between New York and Barbados. To quote editor and interviewer Kwame Dawes, Brathwaite's "critical work is virtually foundational to an examination of a Caribbean aesthetic; his experimentation with music, popular culture, and various forms of poetic expression has proved influential for a significant number of writers. Brathwaite's work is challenging because its meaning resides as much in the sounds of his words as in their semantic construction."

Other Works by Edward Kamau Brathwaite

Ancestors: A Reinvention of Mother Poem, Sun Poem, and X/Self. New York: New Directions, 2001.
Third World Poems. London: Longman, 1983.
Words Need Love Too. Philipsburg, St. Martin: House of Nehesi, 2000.

Works about Edward Kamau Brathwaite

Brown, Stewart, ed. *The Art of Kamau Brathwaite.* Bridgend, Mid Glamorgan, Wales: Seren, 1995.
Reiss, Timothy J. *For the Geography of a Soul: Emerging Perspectives on Kamau Brathwaite.* Trenton, N.J.: Africa World Press, 2001.
Savory, Elaine. "The Word Becomes Nam: Self and Community in the Poetry of Kamau Brathwaite, and its Relation to Caribbean Culture and Postmodern Theory." In *Writing the Nation: Self and Country in the Postcolonial Imagination.* Edited by John C. Hawley. Amsterdam: Rodopi, 1996: 23–43.

Brathwaite, Lawson Edward
See BRATHWAITE, EDWARD KAMAU.

Braun, Volker (1939–) *poet, playwright*
Volker Braun was born in Dresden, Germany, less than four months before the start of World War II. His father, a soldier in the German army, was killed in the last year of the war. After completing his schooling, Braun worked as a printer's assistant, a machine engineer, and a construction worker. In 1960, he joined the Communist Party in East Germany and enrolled at the University of Leipzig, where he studied philosophy for four years. After college, Braun worked as a writer and producer for the Berlin Ensemble, the City Theater of Leipzig, and the Deutsches Theater in Berlin.

Braun wrote several works of poetry and prose but achieved his greatest fame as a playwright. His influences include Bertolt BRECHT and Friedrich SCHILLER. Braun frequently portrayed the individual's struggle for identity in the face of contrary societal expectations. As an idealist, Braun sought to promote a greater acceptance of socialism with his early plays. He opposed reunification in 1989, hoping for the continuance of an East Germany committed to social justice and the environment. Braun's awards include the Heinrich Heine Prize, the Heinrich Mann Prize, and Germany's National Prize.

Another Work by Volker Braun

Das Wirklichgewallte. Frankfurt am Main: Suhrkamp, 2000.

A Work about Volker Braun

Bothe Kathrin. *Die Imaginierte Natur des Sozialismus: eine Biographie des Schreibens und der Texte Volker Brauns (1959–1974)*. Würzburg: Konigshausen & Neumann, 1997

Brecht, Bertolt (1898–1956) *dramatist, playwright*

Bertold Brecht was born in Augsburg, Germany. His father was an administrator of a paper company. Brecht began writing while he was very young and published a few poems at the age of 16. In school, he developed a reputation as a hooligan and a troublemaker. Despite the constant disciplinary problems, he graduated from school and entered the University of Munich in 1917 to study medicine. His studies were interrupted by the outbreak of World War I, and Brecht enlisted in the German army as a medical orderly. After the war, Brecht briefly resumed his studies but eventually abandoned them to pursue a writing career.

In 1919, Brecht joined the Independent Social Democratic Party and began his lifelong association with communism. Starting in 1920, he began to work as a dramatist and playwright at various theaters throughout Germany. Although his early plays were not directly engaged with politics, Brecht often mocked the conventions of bourgeois sensibility and lifestyle. His political engagement, his indictment of capitalism, and his epic style established Brecht as one of the most radical playwrights in Germany.

After Brecht officially joined the Communist Party of Germany in 1929, his works assumed an even more radical stance and directly addressed important political issues. Brecht's affiliation with the Communist Party made him an unpopular figure with government censors and other officials. Many of Brecht's works were banned in Germany even in the years before Hitler came to power.

The political atmosphere in Germany became dangerous for Brecht during the 1930s because of the rise of the Nazis, who were opposed to communism. His works were banned throughout the country, and he was forced into exile. Brecht lived in Denmark, Finland, Russia, and finally the United States. While living in the United States, Brecht tried to write screenplays for the movies, but he had difficulty getting his work accepted. He also found the atmosphere in Hollywood intellectually stifling. In 1947, Brecht was investigated by the anti-Communist congressional Committee on Un-American Activities. Although the committee did not establish any definitive charges against Brecht, his reputation was damaged and he could no longer produce any work in the United States.

In 1948, Brecht returned to Germany, settling in Communist East Germany. Brecht founded his own Marxist theater in East Berlin, where many of his plays were produced. Brecht also experimented with many theatrical conventions, such as lighting, sound, and set. Brecht's reputation spread beyond the borders of Germany, and he became an internationally renowned dramatist. In 1955, he was awarded the Stalin Peace Prize, the highest recognition in the Soviet Union, for his contribution to drama.

Critical Analysis

Brecht's drama reflects his view that theater should provide a forum for social and political change, rather than serve a purely aesthetic function geared toward entertainment. Brecht formulated a new style of acting based on the "alienation effect." He wanted his audience to become objective spectators by disassociating themselves from the characters of the play. Moreover, Brecht argued that actors should disassociate themselves from the characters they portray. Instead of creating an illusion of reality, Brecht wanted his audience to understand that the play is not a reality but a forum for social debate. Brecht believed his style of production would make the political lesson more apparent to the masses.

Mother Courage and Her Children (1941), one of Brecht's most famous historical plays, set during the Thirty Years' War, presents a series of conflicts that occurred between Catholics and Protestants in central Europe between 1618 and 1648. Mother Courage is a woman who depends on the continuation of the war for her economic survival. She is nicknamed Mother Courage for courageously protecting her merchandise under enemy fire. She has three children who die in the war, one by one. Yet, she continues her career as a war profiteer. Staged in East Berlin, the play attracted instant critical attention for its controversial portrayal of war and its dehumanizing effects on people.

The Caucasian Chalk Circle (1948), an adaptation of a medieval Chinese play based on the parable of the chalk circle, centers on a land dispute in a small commune in the Soviet Union after World War II. The main action revolves around the conflict of two women over a child. It is similar to the biblical tale of King Solomon who must resolve a dispute between two women, both of whom claim to be the mother of a child. The play was warmly greeted by audiences and received international recognition.

Among Brecht's most famous plays was *The Threepenny Opera* (1928). This adaptation of John Gay's *Beggar's Opera* presents a universe of beggars, thieves, and prostitutes, a world bereft of honor or trust. Kurt Weill's inventive score adds to the experience of this brittle world, an allegory of Germany's Weimar Republic, the period before Hitler took power. The popular song "Mack the Knife" is from this play.

The Good Woman of Setzuan (1940) tells the tale of three gods who are in search of a truly good person. Their choice is Shen Te, a prostitute. They give her money to start a new life, but she finds that a truly good person cannot survive, so she creates a nasty alter ego, her "cousin" Shu Tai.

Galileo (1939) deals with the historical figure of the famous astronomer, Galileo, who discovers that Earth is not the center of the universe. He holds his findings for eight years but finally reveals them to the pope. The pope subjects Galileo to the Inquisition, and Galileo recants his theory. The play dealt with many political and social issues. The freedom of the individual is juxtaposed against oppressive society, which is dominated by the religious leaders who are not interested in scientific truth because it threatens to overturn their supremacy.

Brecht is also among the finest poets of the 20th century, a talent overshadowed somewhat by his success as a playwright. Brecht published more than 1,500 poems that span more than 30 years, including both world wars. Brecht's poetry combines lyricism with an epic and Marxist view of society and history. In the poem "1940," for example the speaker says that his young son asks him why he should learn mathematics, French, or history, and the speaker wonders why indeed when "two pieces of bread are more than one's about all you'll end up with" and language is unnecessary to convey hunger—a groan will do—and history does not teach us how to survive. Still he tells his son, with false optimism, to study.

Bertolt Brecht is considered to be among the most influential writers of the 20th century. His theoretical works changed the face of the modern theater, and his emphasis on social responsibility of the individual inspired many playwrights to write works of social significance.

Other Works by Bertolt Brecht

Baal. Translated by Peter Tagel. New York: Arcade, 1998.

Brecht on Theater: The Development of an Aesthetic. Translated by John Willett. New York: Hill and Wang, 1994.

Drums in the Night. New York: Methuen Drama, 1988.

Works about Bertolt Brecht

Esslin, Martin. *Brecht, a Choice of Evils: A Critical Study of the Man, His Works, and His Opinions.* New York: Methuen Drama, 1984.

Munsterer, Hans. *The Young Brecht.* New York: Paul and Co., 1992.

Brentano, Catarina Elisabetha Ludovica Magdalena

See ARNIM, BETTINA VON.

Breton, André (1896–1966) *poet, novelist, essayist*

André Breton was born in Tichenbray, France. He studied medicine in Paris and was assigned to a military hospital, where he worked primarily in the psychiatric wards during World War I.

Breton studied the works of Sigmund FREUD, and Freud's notion of free association greatly influenced Breton's experiments with automatic writing. Aided by French poet Philippe Soupault, he began to work with this concept. He was searching for a higher form of reality that, he assumed, was present at the point where dreams and reality converged. Together, he and Soupault founded the journal *Littérature*, in which they published the works of such writers as Louis ARAGON. Breton also used the journal as a vehicle to express his own views, which he went on to publish in a series of three surrealist manifestos in 1924, 1930, and 1942.

The first of Breton's surrealist manifestos is considered to be the founding text of the surrealist movement. Breton assumed a position of leadership within the movement as a result of this text, and he was joined by numerous talented poets and visual artists, all of whom shared the beliefs he had set forth in his text, causing the movement to gain momentum and eventually to spread beyond Europe.

Critical Analysis

In the middle of this creative tempest, Breton published what is considered critically to be his finest work, *Nadja* (1928), which is based, in part, on firsthand experiences. Breton met and spent time with an unknown girl who was living her life in the same manner that Breton had advocated: She made no distinction between factual reality and fictional reality. Her behavior, however, was not socially acceptable, and she was ultimately placed in an asylum.

Surrealism as a movement was eclipsed after World War II by EXISTENTIALISM and was vehemently attacked by such new voices as SARTRE and CAMUS. Breton was subjected to political derision for having denounced the 1936 Moscow trials, thus making himself an enemy of the Communist Party as well as forcing him into conflict with several of his former friends and colleagues, such as Aragon and Paul ÉLUARD, who rejected surrealism and fervently promoted communism.

Breton continued to proclaim his theme of the need for artists to focus on individual freedom, to develop an anarchist regime in the arts that functions as the exact antithesis of Stalinism and SOCIALIST REALISM and their attempts to harness creativity under totalitarian rule. In particular, he viewed socialist realism, as enforced by Stalin, to be the negation of freedom and was angered and disheartened to see that it could be supported by someone he had respected as much as Aragon. He denounced the idea of artists falling victim to a blind allegiance to repressive ideology. His essay "The Tower of Light" (1952) is solid evidence of Breton's continuing detachment from materialism and his increasing move toward utopian philosophy. He expresses the idea that revolution, to effect change on society, must first promote change in the mind of the individual.

Breton believed that very little had actually been learned as a result of World War I. In a 1942 address to French students at Yale University, Breton expressed these concerns. He also expressed his hope that the outcome of World War II would be different. This vision was shattered, however, by the emergence of the cold war and the added potential of nuclear weaponry to annihilate the human race. In response, Breton's essay "The Lamp in the Clock" (1948) called for a radical reconsideration of exactly what was at stake: the continued survival of humanity.

Breton also expressed his views through poetry. These works, collected as *Selected Poems* (1948; translated 1969), reflect the influence of other poets such as Paul VALÉRY and Arthur RIMBAUD. Breton continued, throughout his life, to focus on the importance of revelation and the links that can be made through the arts between that which is concrete reality and that which exists solely in the realm of the imagination.

Other Works by André Breton

Break of Day. Translated by Mark Polizzotti and Mary Ann Caws. Lincoln: University of Nebraska Press, 1999.

Poems of André Breton: A Bilingual Anthology. Translated by Jean-Pierre Cauvin and Mary Ann Caws. Austin: University of Texas Press, 1982.

Works about André Breton

Caws, Mary Ann. *André Breton.* Boston: Twayne, 1996.

Polizzotti, Mark. *Revolution of the Mind: The Life of André Breton.* New York: Farrar, Straus & Giroux, 1995.

Breytenbach, Breyten (1939–) *poet, novelist, short-story writer, essayist*

One of the most controversial figures in South African literary history, Breytenbach was born to an affluent Afrikaner family in the Cape Province. His ancestors settled in South Africa in the early 1700s.

Breytenbach has written wistfully about the poignant beauty of Cape Province. In several of his works, he has written about childhood memories and about the ancestral memory of his people. For example, his great-grandmother, his father, and his mother figure prominently in the retrospective novel *Dog Heart: A Travel Memoir* (1998). His eventual rejection of the Afrikaner tradition echoes all the more loudly because of the depth of his family's connections to the Dutch-settler heritage Afrikaners treasure.

He was seen, even at a young age, to possess great literary and immense talents. His early writings, all written in Afrikaans, such as those in his collection *Catastrophes* (1964), explore his sense of himself as distant from his own people and their traditions. While he was in college in Cape Town in the early 1960s, he was troubled by the encroaching control of the many apartheid laws and chose to go to Europe, where he met and married an Asian woman named Yolande Lien, who figures prominently in his poetry. Breytenbach was trying to return to South Africa in 1965 to accept a literary award when he was told that his marriage was a serious breach of South Africa's law against interracial marriage. His general distaste for apartheid had become personal, and Breytenbach became a founder and organizer of a group called *Okhela,* meaning to "set fire to." The goal of this group was to persuade white South Africans that the apartheid regime could only be brought down from within.

Issues of personal identity, especially regarding the relationship between art and life intrigued Breytenbach even before the frankly autobiographical writings that would develop from his experiences in the 1970s and 1980s. In poetry written during the 1960s, Breytenbach used only lowercase letters, referred to himself in his own poems, and used profanity. All of his writings stress the fictional nature of "real" life.

Since 1961, he has made his home primarily in Paris. Breytenbach entered South Africa illegally in 1975, using the name Christian Jean-Marc Galaska, and was arrested as a terrorist. His trial was an international event, although most of the proceedings occurred within the limitations and secrecy imposed by the Nationalist government. He was sentenced to nine years in prison, and he served seven. His imprisonment became the subject of some of his major works: a loosely structured collection of fragmentary narratives entitled *Mouroir: Mirror Notes to a Novel* (1984) and the autobiographical novel *The True Confessions of an Albino Terrorist* (1984). Another novel, *A Season in Paradise* (1980), and several collections of poetry, notably *Judas Eye* (1988), also investigate Breytenbach's time in South African prisons, although they are not all specifically concerned only with his prison experiences. Pressure from the international community, especially by the then-president of France, François Mitterrand, led to Breytenbach's early release from prison, with the provision that he leave South Africa.

Breytenbach has returned to South Africa since the institution of democratic elections, and he has recently championed the cause of the Afrikaner in South Africa as a political minority. In this way, one can see a consistency in Breytenbach's political ideology: The oppression of dissident groups, whether that of a minority holding a minority in check or that of a willful majority, should not be allowed to pass unremarked.

Critical Analysis

Breytenbach occupies a unique position in the African literary tradition. Like André BRINK and Nadine GORDIMER he has often written of political oppression and his distaste for the apartheid regime in South Africa. Breytenbach and Brink are also the most well-known writers who publish in Afrikaans, the language of the Dutch settlers, and those most often, and sometimes unfairly, vilified for all of apartheid's wrongs. Like another countryman, J. M. COETZEE, Breytenbach often plays with language at multiple levels. Their willingness to experiment with language, reveling in the multiplicity of possibilities for confusion and misunderstanding, is referred to as "postmodernism": a celebration of fragmentary, rather than unified, meaning, the purpose of which is meant to make readers think about not only what they read but also what they believe. This "playfulness" has often been criticized and stands as one end of the spectrum of opinion on Breytenbach. Ultimately, Breytenbach stands alone, like so many of the protagonists of his novels. Isolation, introspection, scathing self-analysis, and a refusal to use fictions as a crutch for existence mark both his poetry and his prose. For example, in *Dog Heart: A Memoir* (1999), he writes that he needs to see the child he once was to determine how he has become the man he is: "Why, after all these years, do I feel the urge to go and look for the other one, the child I must have been?"

J. M. Coetzee has commented on *Dog Heart* in his collection, *Stranger Shores: Literary Essays 1986–1999* (2001). He sees Breytenbach's text as typical of those narratives which mine his, and South Africa's, past: "Like Breytenbach's other memoirs, *Dog Heart* is loose, almost miscellaneous, in its structure. Part journal, part essay on autobiography, part book of the dead, part what one might call speculative history, it also contains searching meditations on the elusiveness of memory and passages of virtuoso writing . . . breathtaking in the immediacy of their evocation of Africa."

Even in what are recognizably novels, Breytenbach melds the real with the fantastic. For example, *Memory of Snow and Dust* (1989) concerns itself with fables of identity and the uncertainty that lies underneath our solid sense of who we are. The plot involves an Ethiopian journalist who meets and impregnates a mixed-race South African woman while they are in Switzerland for an arts festival, a "neutral" cultural and political space carved out by both custom and art. The journalist agrees to act as a spy for an antiapartheid group and goes to South Africa under an assumed name. But the identity under which he is traveling is accused of murder, and the would-be spy and absentee father cannot clear himself without revealing his own identity and betraying his political comrades. Fictions such as *Memory of Snow and Dust* call into question the seemingly simple injunction that the lives and works of artists are cleanly and clearly separate.

Breytenbach's contributions and importance to world literature are linked to the combination in his works of the personal, political, and cultural in ways that force readers to acknowledge the naturalness of the connections.

Other Works by Breyten Breytenbach

In Africa Even the Flies are Happy: Selected Poems, 1964–1977. London: Calder, 1978.

Return to Paradise: An African Journal. New York: Harcourt Brace, 1993.

A Work about Breyten Breytenbach

Jolly, Rosemary. *Colonization, Violence, and Narration in White South African Writing: André Brink, Breyten Breytenbach, and J. M. Coetzee.* Athens: Ohio University Press, 1996.

Brink, André (1935–   ) *novelist, essayist, playwright*

André Brink, a white South African, writes in Afrikaans, a national South African language derived from Dutch. His first two novels, *A Dry White Season* (1969) and *Looking on Darkness* (1973), were banned because of their political implications, which prompted Brink to write in English as well.

Brink is part of the Sestiger group (also known as the Sixtyers), a loose network of Afrikaans writers who began their careers in the 1960s and whose works combine Afrikaans literature with European literary trends and an antiapartheid political consciousness. The Sestigers depicted sexual and moral matters and examined the political system in a way that rapidly antagonized the traditional Afrikaner reader. The group opposed the rising authoritarianism of South Africa and provided a voice against racism in the language of the dominant National Party. Brink's works are the most politically committed of the group's collective writings, which led to many of his works being banned until the end of apartheid in the early 1990s.

Much of Brink's work deals with the structures that informed apartheid, such as slavery, interracial relationships, and abuse of police power. In *Cape of Storms* (1992), he uses allegory and myth, which he calls "African magical realism," to depict a historical relationship and the social transition of South Africa. Some critics saw this book as a confused search for identity. His later book, *On the Contrary* (1993), seemed to have an easier time finding its voice within history, perhaps because of Brink's narrative technique, which is based in the oral tradition of African culture. The narrator, Estienne Barbier, speaks to an imaginary woman— an escaped slave whose name might be Rosette and who might or might not exist. The doubt and lack of permanence inherent in the narrator's tale determines the reader's perception of Barbier's life. Her stories, as Brink tells them, seem to determine the content and style of human lives.

Another of Brink's texts, *The Rights of Desire* (2001), deals with racial conflicts. The protagonist, Ruben Olivier, a 65-year-old librarian, is cared for by his black housekeeper, Magrieta, and Antje of Bengal, the ghost of a 17th-century slave who was executed for murdering her master and his wife. Olivier's children force him to take in a lodger, who appears to bring Olivier out of the books and into life. Olivier, thus, represents an Africa that needs to be brought out of the past and into the present.

Brink is a professor of Afrikaans and Dutch literature. In April of 2000, he received two literary awards: the Hertzog Prize for Afrikaans Literature and the National Book Journalist of the Year award. Brink had previously won the Hertzog Prize in 1994, but turned it down because, he said, "at the time the Akademie appeared to be wholly 'untransformed' and unrepentant about it [apartheid]. To accept the prize seemed like allowing myself to be co-opted into an establishment (the cultural wing of the apartheid regime) with which I could not accept to be identified" (*Monday Paper*). He has now accepted the award because the academy can no longer represent the "old Africaner establishment because that establishment no longer exists" (*Monday Paper*).

Other Works by André Brink

A Chain of Voices. New York: Morrow. 1982.
A Dry White Season. New York: Morrow. 1980.
Writing in a State of Siege. New York: Summit Books. 1983.

Works about André Brink

"André Brink Wins Literary Double." *Monday Paper* (University of Cape Town) 19:12, May 8–15, 2000.
Jolly, Rosemary Jane. *Colonization, Violence, and Narration in White South African Writing: André Brink, Breyten Breytenbach, and J. M. Coetzee.* Athens: Ohio University Press, 1996.

Brinkmann, Rolf Dieter (1940–1975)
poet, short-story writer

Rolf Dieter Brinkmann was born in Vechta, Germany. After completing high school, he worked in a variety of temporary jobs. He began writing at a young age and published his first collection of poems in 1962. He studied at the Teachers' College in Cologne for two years before dropping out. In the late 1960s, Brinkmann edited and translated three anthologies of American post–beat-generation poets. He studied at the Villa Massimo in Rome from 1972 to 1973 with a scholarship from the German government and in 1974 was a visiting lecturer at the University of Texas. The following year, he was killed in London by a hit-and-run driver.

American beat and underground poetry were Brinkmann's heaviest literary influences. The leading German-language pop poet of his day, he helped introduce American pop culture to his country. Brinkmann hoped to free German society from inhibitions and constraints. His poems exhibit a thematic and stylistic break from German tradition. Brinkmann used everyday speech geared to the senses to describe the transitory occurrences of daily life. Scholar Peter Demetz explains that Brinkmann "wanted to quicken the demise of old forms and metaphysical attitudes by a new kind of imagism 'catching momentary impressions' in 'snapshots,' precise, firm, and 'translucent'; he advocated 'no more big emotions,' but 'small momentary excitations.'"

Largely ignored in his lifetime, Brinkmann attained fame after his death. His last collection of poems *Westwärts 1 & 2* (*Westward 1 & 2*, 1975), published posthumously, won the Petrarca Lyric Prize and became a best-seller. In the 1980s, critics recognized Brinkmann as a precursor of postmodernism and an articulator of his generation's consciousness.

Another Work by Rolf Dieter Brinkmann

Keiner weiß mehr. Berlin: Kiepeheuer & Witsch, 1968.

A Work about Rolf Dieter Brinkmann

Schafer, Jorgen. *Pop-literatur: Rolf Dieter Brinkmann und das Verhaltnis zur Popularkultur in der Literatur der Sechziger Jahre.* Stuttgart: M & D Verlag fur Wissenschaft und Forschung, 1998.

Broch, Hermann (1886–1951) *novelist, dramatist*

Herman Broch was born to Jewish parents in Vienna, Austria. His father Josef Broch, a flannel merchant, and his mother Johanna Schnabel were both wealthy. In 1904, Broch graduated from the kaiserlich-königlich Staats-Realschule (Imperial and Royal State Secondary School). Acceding to his father's wishes, Broch studied to be a textile engineer at the Spinning and Weaving School in Alsace. He also studied philosophy and mathematics for a semester at the University of Vienna. In 1909, he converted to Catholicism to marry Franziska von Rothermann, a sugar heiress. He became director of his father's Teesdorf textile factory that same year.

As part of the Vienna intellectual scene, Broch became concerned with the disintegration of values. Influenced by Friedrich NIETZSCHE and Immanuel KANT, Broch published his first articles on philosophy in 1913. In 1925, he resumed his study of mathematics and philosophy at Vienna University. Three years later, he left the Teesdorf factory to write full time. His first major work was the trilogy *Die Schlafwandler* (*The Sleepwalkers,* 1930–32). He wrote several novels, dramas, and essays in the 1930s, but his works did not fare well financially, due to opposition from the anti-Semitic government. Broch was arrested by Nazis in 1938, but influential friends arranged for his emigration to the United States. In America, Broch wrote his best-known novel, *Der Tod des Vergil* (*The Death of Virgil,* 1945), a lyrical prose recounting of the last hours of the famous poet's life.

Broch's powerful works address the issues of mass psychology, moral decay, ethics, and death. Although an industrialist, he had socialist tendencies and worked to help laborers, needy children, and refugees. He wrote didactic fiction, hoping to improve the condition of humanity and society. In the words of German literary scholar Theodore Ziolkowski, Broch "was conscious of a mission in life, to which he devoted himself with absolute consistency and an almost messianic zeal" (*Herman Broch,* 1964).

Other Works by Herman Broch

The Guiltless. Translated by Charles Wharton Stark. New Haven, Conn.: Yale University Press, 1974.

The Unknown Quantity. Translated by Willa and Edwin Muir. Marlboro, Vt.: Marlboro Press, 1988.

Works about Herman Broch

Lützeler, Paul Michael. *Hermann Broch: A Biography.* Translated by Janice Fureness. London: Quarter, 1987.

Ziolkowski, Theodore. *Herman Broch.* New York: Columbia University Press, 1964.

Bruman, Simone

See SCHWARZ-BART, SIMONE.

Bryusov, Valery (1873–1924) *poet, novelist, critic*

Valery Yakovlevich Bryusov was born in Moscow, Russia, to an affluent middle-class family. He was educated at Moscow University and could speak and write fluently in several European language, including French, English, and German. He was a fundamental figure in the establishment of the Russian symbolist movement (*see* SYMBOLISM), outlining the movement's aesthetic goals in his book *The Russian Symbolists* (1894). Despite being a prolific poet and novelist, Bryusov today is mostly remembered for his role as the editor of the symbolist publication *Vesy* between 1904 and 1909.

Bryusov's verse has often been described as sophisticated and graceful, yet marked by frequent use of cryptic language that praises sensuous delights and bodily pleasures. *Stephanos* (1906) is perhaps the best known of his poetry collections. In addition to composing his own poetry, Bryusov produced a number of magnificent translations of American, French, and Armenian poets into Russian.

Bryusov wrote two novels, *The Fiery Angel* (1908), a mystical novel that depicts a cult of practitioners of black magic in 16th-century Germany, and *Altar of Victory* (1911–12), an obscure post-symbolist novel.

In 1908, after a bitter disagreement with other symbolist writers, Bryusov disassociated himself from the movement. He devoted himself to teaching and to writing a number of respected scholarly works. After the communist revolution, Bryusov indirectly joined the Bolshevik cause and worked for the Soviet literary establishment as a director of several artistic and educational institutions, mainly as a bureaucratic administrator.

Today, Valery Bryusov is mostly remembered for his initial guidance of the symbolist movement and as a literary scholar. His own works are mainly forgotten and only studied in the context of the symbolist movement. His corpus of literary criticism and translations is still respected and used in Russian academic institutions.

Other Works by Valery Bryusov

Diary of Valery Bryusov, 1893–1905. Translated by Joan Delaney Grossman. Berkeley: University of California Press, 1980.

The Republic of the Southern Cross and Other Stories. Translated by Stephen Graham. New York: Hyperion Press, 1977.

A Work about Valery Bryusov

Grossman, Joan Delaney. *Valery Bryusov and the Riddle of Russian Decadence.* Berkeley: University of California Press, 1985.

Büchner, Georg (1813–1837) *dramatist*

Georg Büchner was born in the Hessian village of Goddelau. At the age of three, he moved to Darmstadt with his father, Ernst Karl Büchner, a physician, and his mother, Caroline Louis Reuß Büchner. In 1831, Büchner graduated from the Darmstädter Großherzogliches Gymnasium, one of the finest schools in Hesse, and then studied medicine and natural sciences at the University of Strasbourg. In 1833, he continued his studies at the University of Gießen. Sympathetic with the social misery of the peasant class, he founded a student group committed to radical democratic reform. Büchner anonymously published a pamphlet, *Der Hessische Landbote* (*The Hessian Courier,* 1834), which called for a peasant revolt to end the oppressive rule of the elite class. To avoid arrest, Büchner had to flee to Darmstadt in 1834 and to Strasbourg in 1835.

While at Darmstadt, Büchner wrote the complex historical drama, *Dantons Tod* (*Danton's Death,* 1835). Considered a masterpiece of German literature, this work displays many levels of meaning in its study of the French Revolution and the purpose of history. He later translated two of Victor HUGO's works. Büchner's last work, *Woyzeck* (1877), is a drama about an army barber who murders his unfaithful lover. Noted for its originality, the play was a precursor to both expressionism and naturalism in German theater. In 1836, Büchner took a position as a lecturer in comparative anatomy at the University of Zurich. He soon became ill and died in February 1837 from typhoid.

Aside from *Dantons Tod,* all of Büchner's works were published posthumously. His melancholy writing addressed the conflict between the ideals of human freedom and the circumstances of history. Büchner captured the contradictions of his age and in the 20th century became an important influence in the development of German modernism. In his book *Georg Büchner: The Shattered Whole,* scholar John Reddick explains that Büchner's genius stems in part from "the sheer subtlety and complexity of his poetic vision" and "his compulsion to explore questions rather than present answers." The Georg Büchner Prize for literature created by the city of Darmstadt in 1923 is one of the most coveted German literary awards.

Another Work by Georg Büchner

Leonce and Lena. Translated by Hedwig Rappolt. New York: Time and Space Limited, 1983.

A Work about Georg Büchner

Reddick, John, *Georg Büchner: The Shattered Whole.* Oxford: Clarendon Press, 1994.

Bulgakov, Mikhail (1891–1940) *novelist, short-story writer, dramatist*

Mikhail Afanasievich Bulgakov was born in Kiev, Ukraine, to Afanasy Bulgakov, a professor of history of religion and a censor, and Varvara Pokrovskaya, a teacher. He was the youngest of six children. When Bulgakov was 16 years old, his father died unexpectedly. Bulgakov studied medicine at the Imperial University of St. Vladimir in Kiev, married Tatiana Lappa in 1913, and received his degree in 1916.

Russia was in the middle of World War I when he volunteered to work as a doctor at the front line for the Russian Red Cross. Along with his wife, a trained nurse, Bulgakov worked in the army for several months. Between 1916 and 1919, he intermittently worked as a doctor in villages and towns throughout Russia. After the Bolshevik revolution in 1917, Russia was engulfed by civil war. Bulgakov served as an army doctor in the forces opposing the revolutionary regime and witnessed firsthand the horrors of war. Discharged in 1919, he settled in the city of Vladikavkaz.

Between 1919 and 1920, Bulgakov gave up his medical career to work as a journalist and dramatist. He wrote feuilletons (short literary articles or sketches that appear in the entertainment section of a newspaper), gave lectures on literature, and produced his first plays. Despite these efforts, Bulgakov and his wife lived in poverty. They survived by cutting and selling Bulgakov's golden chain, given to him by his father, piece by piece. During the summer of 1921, Bulgakov attempted to emigrate from Russia, now controlled by the Communist regime, but health and money problems prevented him from leaving the country. He moved to Moscow, where he lived for the rest of his life.

In 1924, Bulgakov published the first part of *White Guard,* a novel largely based on the experiences during his service in the army at the time of the Russian civil war. Set in Kiev, the novel describes the war's effect on a middle-class family. *White Guard* was not published in its entirety in the Soviet Union until the 1960s, but the complete text, edited by Bulgakov, was published in Paris in

1929. He also published his first collection of short stories, *Diaboliad,* during the same period. Between 1925 and 1927, Bulgakov also published individual short stories based on his experiences as a doctor before and during the war. These stories were later compiled as *Notes of a Young Doctor.*

In 1925, Bulgakov published a novella, *Heart of a Dog.* Bulgakov tells a tale of a stray dog that gains human intelligence when a Moscow professor transplants human glands into the animal's body. The work's elements of surrealism were offensive to Communist orthodoxy of the time and brought Bulgakov under close government scrutiny.

From 1927 until his death in 1940, Bulgakov was in constant conflict with government censors. According to the official Big Soviet Encyclopedia, Bulgakov was considered as a "slanderer of Soviet reality" because of his satirical treatment of the Soviet regime and government officials. Bulgakov continued to work in various theaters in spite of the censorship, but by 1929 his plays *Days of the Turbins, Zoya's Apartment,* and *The Crimson Island* were officially banned. In despair, Bulgakov burned all of his manuscripts. Ill and poverty stricken, he wrote a letter to Joseph Stalin, the leader of the Soviet Union, requesting permission to leave the country, stating, "there is no hope for any of my works" in Russia. His petition was denied; instead, he was granted a minor position in a Moscow theater.

Between 1928 and 1940, Mikhail Bulgakov wrote his most famous and complex novel *The Master and Margarita.* Now considered a major masterpiece of Russian literature, the novel remained unpublished until 1966, more than 25 years after its completion.

After an extended illness that resulted in kidney failure, Bulgakov died in 1940 at the age of 49. Shortly before his death, Bulgakov suffered a nervous breakdown. He eventually lost his sight and his ability to speak and communicated with his wife through gestures. Bulgakov completed *The Master and Margarita* on his deathbed. He did not achieve his current reputation as one of the most influential Russian writers until after his death.

Critical Analysis

As Bulgakov admitted in his diaries, *The Master and Margarita* was mostly influenced by Nikolai GOGOL, an earlier master of Russian mysticism. Besides being a devastating political satire, the novel is an allegory of good and evil. The work's main character, Satan, appears in the guise of a foreigner and self-proclaimed black magician named Woland. Along with a talking black cat and a "translator" wearing a jockey's cap and cracked pince-nez, Woland wreaks havoc throughout literary Moscow. The parallel narrative in the work centers on Master, a writer driven to insanity by criticism and political persecution, and his unpublished book about Pontius Pilate. Irreducible to a single theme, *Master and Margarita* comments on authorship, religion, spirituality, politics, and the role of an individual in a socially repressive society.

During the early 1950s, the monument of Nikolai Gogol's grave was renovated by the government. Bulgakov's widow purchased the original headstone and placed it on the grave of her husband. Bulgakov had referred to Gogol as a teacher, writing in one of his letters, "Teacher, cover me with your heavy mantle." The request came true after Bulgakov's death.

Other Works by Mikhail Bulgakov

Black Snow. Translated by Michael Glenny. New York: Harvill Press, 1999.

The White Guard. Translated by Michael Glenny. Chicago: Academy Chicago Publishers, 1995.

Works about Mikhail Bulgakov

Curtis, J. A. E. *Mikhail Bulgakov: A Life in Letters and Diaries.* New York: Overlook Press, 1992.

Proffer, Ellendea. *A Pictorial Biography of Mikhail Bulgakov.* Ann Arbor, Mich.: Ardis, 1984.

Bunin, Ivan (1870–1953) *poet, novelist, short-story writer, translator*

Ivan Alexeyevich Bunin was born in Voronezh, Russia, to poor provincial aristocrats Alexei and Ludmila Bunin. The family situation of the Bunins was in constant jeopardy because of the father's heavy drinking and gambling. In 1881, Bunin was accepted into a small grammar school where he received a classical education suitable for entry into the civil service. Bunin's brother, Julian, joined the socialist cause, for which he was sent into exile by government authorities. Bunin briefly joined his brother's revolutionary clique, but he was ultimately disenchanted with politics and left revolutionary circles to concentrate on his writing.

Bunin first published his poems in 1887 and released his first volume of poetry in 1891. To earn money, Bunin worked as a translator. In 1899, he completed translations of the English poet George Gordon, Lord Byron and the American poet Henry Wadsworth Longfellow that were so successful that Bunin was awarded prestigious Pushkin Prize in 1903. Inspired by his friendships with Anton CHEKHOV and Maxim GORKY, Bunin turned to prose. Bunin's fiction, influenced by Ivan TURGENEV and Leo TOLSTOY, often addresses the dynamics of family and the social position of an individual in rapidly changing Russia. The revolution of 1905 had a dramatic effect on Bunin: He saw the growing power of the Bolsheviks as a threat to Russian social and cultural traditions.

Despite Bunin's aversion to radical reform, his prose often exposes social injustices. In the internationally acclaimed novel *The Village* (1910), Bunin reveals the horrors of peasant life in Russia. In *Dry Valley* (1911), Bunin analyzes the degeneration of family order and economic stability among the aristocratic gentry in provincial Russia. Bunin's themes, however, are not limited to a social agenda. In his collection of short stories, *The Gentleman from San Francisco* (1915), Bunin's thematic focus explores moral decay, death, and pride. Bunin's fiction is marked by a delicate understanding of human nature, as well as by a keen awareness of the social environment.

As a result of the Bolshevik revolution, Bunin left Russia for France in 1919. In France, he continued his prolific output of prose. *The Well Days* (1930), Bunin's autobiographical novel, was hailed as a masterpiece by a number of critics. In 1933, Bunin was awarded the Nobel Prize in literature.

Bunin lived the rest of his life in Paris, where he died in 1953. His contribution to Russian literature is immeasurable. His elegant prose, combined with lively poetic diction, is remarkable for its literary value, as well as for its social commentary and insight.

Other Works by Ivan Bunin

Edited and translated by Thomas Gaiton Marullo. *Cursed Days: A Diary of Revolution.* Chicago: Ivan R. Dee, 1998.

The Life of Arseniev: Youth. Translated by Gleb Struv and Hamish Miles. Evanston, Ill.: Northwestern University Press, 1994.

Sunstroke: Selected Stories of Ivan Bunin. Translated by Graham Hettlinger. Chicago: Ivan R. Dee, 2002.

Works about Ivan Bunin

Marullo, Thomas Gaiton. *If You See the Buddha: Studies in the Fiction of Ivan Bunin.* Evanston, Ill.: Northwestern University Press, 1998.

Woodward, James B. *Ivan Bunin: A Study of His Fiction.* Chapel Hill: University of North Carolina Press, 1980.

Burkart, Erika (Erika Halter)
(1922–) *poet, novelist*

Erika Burkart was born in Aarau, Switzerland. Her father was a writer, hunter, and adventurer. Burkart became a schoolteacher and taught at a primary school from 1942 to 1952. At age 30, however, she gave up teaching to write full time and lived in isolation to better connect with nature—the inspiration for her writing.

Burkart's early volumes of poetry include *Der dünkel Vogel* (*The Dark Bird*, 1953) and *Die gerettete Erde* (*The Saved Earth*, 1960). These collections convey her belief in the divinity of nature and her empathy with the natural world. Burkart's reputation increased after she won the Annette von Droste-Hülshoff Prize in 1957. Her poems in the

1960s express her anxiety about the threats to nature. Her first novel *Moräne* (1970) vividly describes the Swiss countryside and, with its attention to the beauties of nature, reflects the influence of the French writer Marcel PROUST. Burkart's works in the 1980s and 1990s show her continued affinity and concern for the landscape. She is widely admired for her commitment to ecology and her efforts to heal the rift between humanity and nature.

Another Work by Erika Burkart
Der Weg zu den Schaffen. Zurich: Artemis, 1979.

A Work about Erika Burkart
Rudin-Lange, Doris. *Erika Burkart, Leben und Werk.* Zurich: Juris Druck and Verlag, 1979.

Busia, Abena (1953–) *poet, essayist, scholar*

Abena Busia was born in Ghana, daughter to the former prime minister. As a youth her family was forced into exile following a coup d'état. Her personal history is marked by the experience of exile, as she traveled the world encountering other people of African descent in the Americas and Europe. Her focus became the points of cultural connection within the African Diaspora (the scattering of African peoples throughout the world through slavery). She received her Ph.D. from Oxford writing her dissertation on images of Africa in the colonial imagination.

Her collection of poems, *Testimonies of Exile* (1990), speaks to multiple experiences of exile. Her poetry expresses the complexity of her cultural experience: She dresses in traditional Ghanaian attire and speaks with a British accent that reveals the history of colonization yet never betrays the pulsating rhythms and culture of her native Africa.

As a professor she has taught at Yale, UCLA, and University of Ghana and is currently an associate professor at Rutgers University. Much of her recent work focuses on black feminism, exploring the issues of identity, race, and politics. She is currently the codirector of *Women Writing Africa*, a Ford Foundation literary project of the Feminist Press that publishes African women's written and oral narratives.

Another Work by Abena Busia
"What Is Your Nation? Reconnecting Africa and Her Diaspora through Paule Marshall's *Praisesong for the Widow.*" In Cheryl Wall, ed., *Changing Our Own Words: Essays on Criticism, Theory, and Writing by Black Women.* London: Rutgers University Press, 1989.

Cabrera Infante, Guillermo (G. Cain)
(1929–) novelist, essayist

Cabrera Infante was born in Gibara, Cuba. His father was a journalist and typographer. Both of his parents were leaders in the then-underground Cuban Communist Party. When Cabrera Infante was 14 years old, his parents were arrested for holding secret political meetings in their home and spent three months in jail. This infringement on their freedom gave Cabrera Infante a strong dislike for authority. Even after the Cuban revolution, when he was given a number of prestigious literary appointments, he was still unable to abide government censorship and control.

Because his father had lost his job, after Cabrera Infante's parents were released from jail, the family was forced to move to Havana. The urban culture and nightlife of Havana affected Cabrera Infante enormously, and the city at night became the setting for his most famous novel, *Three Trapped Tigers* (1971).

When he was 18, he read *El Señor Presidente* by Guatemalan novelist Miguel Angel Asturias (1899–1974). Cabrera Infante decided that if Asturias was considered a writer, he could be one too, and he began to write short stories and sketches. During the next few years, he published his writing in and founded several small magazines. At age 23,

he was jailed for what the government called "publishing profanities in English." When he was forbidden to publish anything using his name, he assumed the pseudonym G. Cain and continued to write and publish until the Cuban revolution.

It was not until Cabrera Infante was sent to Brussels as a cultural attaché at the Cuban embassy that he completed and published *Three Trapped Tigers* (1970), which gained him international attention. In this book, Cabrera Infante uses humor and wordplay to challenge every type of authority, even the authority of language itself. The book is written using a great deal of Cuban slang, undermining the authority of standard literary Spanish. Cabrera Infante's idiomatic language captures the flavor of nightlife in prerevolutionary Havana one evening in 1958. On first reading, the book appears to be a series of unrelated episodes that are unified only by their setting. However, on careful examination, it becomes obvious that the book is carefully structured so that each episode corresponds to a biblical story, beginning with a creation story and moving on to stories that correspond to the fall from the Garden of Eden, the events related to the Tower of Babel, and the apocalypse. This structuring is both profound, giving depth to the frivolous scenes of nightlife, and irreverent, proposing a highly unorthodox commentary on the Bible and society.

Infante's Inferno (1984), his second novel, centers on a single character. The book follows a young boy growing up in Havana and is semiautobiographical. It focuses on the loves and erotic adventures of the narrator, who claims to be a modern-day Don Juan. The book begins when the boy is 12 years old and follows him, as he matures, through a series of frivolous relationships. Finally, as an adult, he finds an exalted and ideal form of love. Like Cabrera Infante's other works, this book is filled with game playing, literary allusion, and humor. However, it also established that he is one of the great erotic writers of Latin America.

Cabrera Infante has been a major proponent of interpreting books based on the text alone, without relying on historical context. He believes that once a fact is placed into a work of fiction, it is no longer connected to the reality that may have inspired its author to create it. This idea, combined with his playful literary style, has made him one of the major proponents of "art for art's sake" in 20th-century Latin American literature.

Other Works by Guillermo Cabrera Infante

Guilty of Dancing the Chachacha. Translated by the author. New York: Welcome Rain Publishers, 2001.
Holy Smoke. New York: Harper & Row, 1985.
View Of Dawn in the Tropics. Translated by Suzanne Jill Levine. New York: Harper & Row, 1978.

Works about Guillermo Cabrera Infante

Hall, Kenneth E. "Cabrera Infante as Biographer" in *Biography* 19:4 (Fall 1996): 394–403. Hawaii: University of Hawaii Press, 1996.
Souza, Raymond D. *Guillermo Cabrera Infante: Two Islands, Many Worlds.* Austin: University of Texas Press, 1996.

Caeiro, Alberto

See PESSOA, FERNANDO.

Cain, G.

See CABRERA INFANTE, GUILLERMO.

Calvino, Italo (1923–1985) *novelist, short-story writer, journalist*

Born in Santiago de las Vegas, Cuba, Italo Calvino is the son of Mario Calvino and Eva (Mameli) Calvino, both tropical agronomists. Calvino grew up on the family farm in San Remo, where his father grew tropical fruit for experimentation and acted as a curator for a botanical garden. Early on, Calvino was enchanted by Rudyard Kipling's stories. He enrolled in the University of Turin with plans to study agronomy, but his plans changed in the early 1940s when he joined the Italian resistance in World War II to fight against the Nazis and fascists.

After the war, Calvino resumed studies at the University of Turin in 1945, this time focusing his attention on literature. He wrote his thesis on novelist Joseph Conrad. In 1945, Calvino combined writing with his wartime efforts by contributing to leftist newspapers such as *Il Politecnico*. He produced his first novel, *The Path to the Nest of Spiders* (1947), two years later. The book, which won him the Premio Riccione award, is based on his time as a partisan fighter, yet it retains an innocence that is part of much of his early narratives. "The problems of our time appear in any story I write," Calvino told the *New York Times Book Review* in 1983.

The Path to the Nest of Spiders lacks the grimness of much of Italian neorealism, both in fiction and in films, partly because of an exuberant, picaresque flavor for which Calvino is indebted to his boyhood reading of Robert Louis Stevenson's *Kidnapped* and *Treasure Island*.

Other notable works followed, including the collection, *Short Stories* (1958) and a three-volume edition of *Italian Folktales* (1956). In his introduction to the latter, Calvino states, "Folktales are real. These folk stories are the catalog of the potential destinies of men and women, especially for that stage in life when destiny is formed, i.e., youth." Calvino's stories and novels use elements of fantasy and fable, displaying the influence of Italian folktales and other traditional narratives. In one of his best-known novels, *Invisible Cities* (1972), for example, an imaginary Marco Polo describes the cities of his empire to Kublai Khan.

One of his most popular novels with readers in the United States was *If on a Winter's Night a Traveler* (1979). In this work, the protagonist is the reader. Calvino's characters are highly self-conscious, and his novels are self-referential. Irish author Silas Flannery, one of the characters in *If On a Winter's Night a Traveler,* states, "I have had the idea of writing a novel composed only of beginnings of novels. The protagonist could be the reader who is continually interrupted."

At his death in 1985, Italo Calvino was the best-known and most-translated contemporary Italian writer. He has accumulated numerous honors and accolades through the span of his career, earning the Italian equivalent of the Pulitzer Prize in literature in 1972.

Other Works by Italo Calvino

Mr. Palomar. Translated by William Weaver. San Diego: Harcourt Brace Jovanovich, 1985.

Under the Jaguar Sun. Translated by William Weaver. Harvest Books, 1990.

Works about Italo Calvino

McLaughlin, Martin. *Italo Calvino.* Edinburgh: Edinburgh University Press, 1998.

Weiss, Beno. *Understanding Italo Calvino.* Columbia: University of South Carolina Press, 1995.

Campos, Alvaro de

See PESSOA, FERNANDO.

Camus, Albert (1913–1960) *novelist, essayist, playwright*

Albert Camus was born in Mondovi, Algeria, on November 7. Perhaps because he was born to a poverty-stricken family, his education was taken seriously. He attended the university in Algiers, where he became interested in both sports and the theater. He was forced to end his education early, however, by an acute bout with tuberculosis, a disease that continued to plague him throughout his life. The experience of poverty and the fear of death take on major significance in Camus's series of Algerian essays, collected in *L'Envers et l'endroit* (*The Wrong Side and the Right Side,* 1937), *Noces* (*Nuptials,* 1938), and *Été* (*Summer,* 1954).

Recovered from his illness, Camus went to work in the early 1950s as a journalist for the anticolonialist newspaper *Alger-Républicain,* for which he wrote daily articles on the impoverished lives of Arabs in the Kabyles region. He later collected these works in *Actuelles III* (1958). His journalistic background proved invaluable when he went to France during World War II. While working for the combat resistance network, he began to edit a clandestine journal. The subject of his editorials showed a strong desire to integrate political activism with strict morality.

During the war years, Camus also began to explore what came to be known as his doctrine of the absurd. It was his view that all things in life become meaningless as a result of the fact that the human mind has no rational capacity to understand the experience of death. His novel *L'Étranger* (1942; translated as *The Stranger,* 1946), for example, explores the concept of alienation. *The Myth of Sysiphus* (1942; translated 1955) and two plays published in 1944, *Cross Purpose* (1944; translated 1948) and *Caligula* (1941; translated 1948), all explore the idea of nihilism.

Although considered an absurdist, Camus had difficulty with the idea that the absurd entailed a lack of morality. His own life and his experiences in occupied France during the war would not allow him to abandon all concepts of moral responsibility. This idea became the focus of *Letters to a German Friend* (1945). Camus began to rebel against the absurd, seeking ways to create a greater strength of humanity guided by morality. His novel *The Plague* (1947; translated 1948), for example, details the struggle of those who fight against the bubonic plague, an allegory for the struggle against the evils of war. Instead of focusing on whether or not the battle against evil can be successful, he chooses instead to glorify dignity, as exemplary of humanity's strength in the face of devastation.

Camus also became embroiled in a bitter controversy with fellow philosopher Jean Paul SARTRE as a result of the publication of his controversial essay *L'Homme Révolté* (1951; translated as *The Rebel,* 1954). In this essay, Camus criticized the absolutism of the Christian belief in eternal life in heaven and of the Marxist belief in political utopia. He argued instead that the more moral concept was that of Mediterranean humanism, a doctrine that placed value on nature and temperance in behavior over blind belief and the descent into violence as an acceptable solution to problems. Camus further explores the concept of modern amorality in his novel *La Chute* (*The Fall,* 1956).

As a playwright, Camus published two political dramas, *State of Siege* (1948; translated 1958) and *The Just Assassins* (1950; translated 1958), as well as adaptations of Faulkner's *Requiem for a Nun* (1956) and DOSTOYEVSKY's *The Possessed* (1959).

In 1957, Camus was awarded the Nobel Prize for literature. He had become the leading voice for morality and for writing as a means to achieve social change in his generation. He was at the height of his popularity when he died in an automobile accident near Sens, France, on January 4.

Other Works by Albert Camus

Between Hell and Reason: Essays from the Resistance Newspaper "Combat," 1944–47. Translated by Alexandre de Gramont. Middletown, Conn.: Wesleyan University Press, 1991.
The First Man. Translated by David Hapgood. New York: Knopf, 1995.

Works about Albert Camus

Bronner, Stephen Eric. *Camus: Portrait of a Moralist.* Minneapolis: University of Minnesota Press, 1999.
Camber, Richard. *On Camus.* Belmont, Calif.: Wadsworth/Thompson Learning, 2002.

Canetti, Elias (1905–1994) *novelist, essayist, playwright*

Elias Canetti was born in Ruse, Bulgaria, to a wealthy Jewish merchant family. After the sudden death of his father, he moved with his mother to Vienna, where he learned German, the language he would ultimately choose for his writing.

Canetti produced his first play *Junius Brutus* while studying in Zurich between 1916 and 1921. However, it was during a visit to Berlin in 1928 when, influenced by the ideas of Bertold BRECHT, George Grosz, and Isaac BABEL, Canetti developed the idea for a series of works that would explore human madness. This later became the basis of his novel *Die Blendung* (1935; *The Tower of Babel,* translated 1947 and 1964). The tale of a madman who only feels at home with his books and shuns human contact in any form, the novel was banned by the Nazis as subversive but was well received internationally after World War II.

In 1927, another event influenced Canetti's writing: A crowd of angry protestors burned down the Palace of Justice in Vienna, and Canetti was caught up in the mob. Later, he turned this incident into the basis for his best-known book, *Crowds and Power* (1960), a fictional study of death, disordered society, and mass movements. Drawing not only on his own experience but also on history, folklore, and mythology, this work received critical acclaim that culminated in Canetti's receipt of the Nobel Prize for literature in 1981.

In his later years, Canetti returned to his focus on death. He wrote three largely autobiographical works, including *Die Gerettete Zunge* (1978; *The Rescued Tongue,* translated 1980) about his father's death. He lived modestly in Hampstead, England, avoiding critical attention as much as possible to the point of writing his own diary in a code so that intrusive readers would not be able to understand it after his death.

Other Works by Elias Canetti

Crowds and Power. Translated by Carol Stewart. New York: Continuum Pub Group, 1982.
The Play of the Eyes. Translated by Ralph Manheim. New York: Farrar Straus & Giroux, 1986.

The Wedding. Translated by Gitta Honegger. New York: PAJ Publications, 1986.

A Work about Elias Canetti

Falk, Thomas II. *Elias Canetti*. Boston: Twayne, 1993.

Capécia, Mayotte (1928–1953) *novelist*

Mayotte Capécia was born in Carbet, Martinique, but spent most of her adult years in France. Barely able to read when she arrived in Paris in 1946, Capécia published her first novelette, *Je suis Martiniquaise* (*I Am a Martinican Woman*) in 1948. According to *Mayotte Capécia ou l'Alienation selon Fanon* (1999), Capécia drew on a lover's manuscript and used several ghostwriters and editors to construct her novelettes.

Je suis martiniquaise and *La Négresse blanche* (*The White Negress*, 1950), her second novelette, explore themes of miscegenation, racial identity, and exile. They also examine people in Martinique and Guadeloupe during the German occupation of France in World War II. Frantz FANON criticized both works for exemplifying the hatred of blacks and used them as examples of Caribbean alienation. Others have also criticized the novels for positioning whites as superior.

Counterattacks in defense of Capécia's work have since surfaced, acclaiming their exploration of race relations in the West Indies. In a 1998 review in *World Literature Today*, Robert P. Smith Jr., asserts, "in spite of their date, Capécia's novelettes remain contemporary in today's complex world of illusion and reality."

Another Work by Mayotte Capécia

I Am a Martinican Woman & The White Negress. Translated by Beatrice Stith Clark. Pueblo, Colo.: Passeggiata Press, 1997.

Works about Mayotte Capécia

Hurley, E. Anthony. "Intersections of Female Identity or Writing the Woman in Two Novels by Mayotte Capécia and Marie-Magdeleine Carbet." *The French Review*, 70, no. 4 (1997): 575–86.

Sparrow, Jennifer. "Capécia, Conde and the Antillean Woman's Identity Quest." *Journal of the Association of Caribbean Women Writers and Scholars*, 1 (1998): 179–87.

Stith Clark, Beatrice. "Who was Mayotte Capécia? An Update." *CLA Journal*, 39, no. 4 (1996): 454–57.

Carey, Peter (1943–) *novelist*

Peter Carey was born in Bacchus Marsh, Victoria, Australia. He studied chemistry at Monash University but failed his first-year examinations and dropped out of college. Carey then found work as an apprentice writer in an advertising agency in Melbourne, and this became the turning point in his life. At the agency, Carey met writers and playwrights, especially Barry Oakley, who would forever influence him. Oakley introduced Carey to the works of writers such as James Joyce, William Faulkner, and Samuel BECKETT, which had a powerful influence on Carey's writings. Carey next worked in advertising agencies in London and Sydney before settling down in New York in the late 1980s.

Carey's novels are often described as a mix of seriousness and surrealism. His preference for the macabre and the unusual is exemplified by the assortment of strange and tormented characters in his stories, such as the minister in the grip of a gambling compulsion in *Oscar and Lucinda* (1988). The absurdity of the characters' internal world is complicated by their actual situations in the external world in which they live. Through the clever twisting of his tales, Carey is able to communicate the phantasmagoric but realistic situations of ordinary human experiences. His stories are sardonic commentaries on the bittersweet and inextricably welded relationship between the individual and the society. The often seedy and shadowy nature of Carey's actors makes it hard for some readers to empathize with their tragic and unfortunate experiences. This controversial nature of Carey's novels makes them compelling and thought-provoking to read.

Carey sees himself as an Australian writer, and his works are predominantly set in Australia, either in the countryside or on the streets of big cities. His characters, however, have a variety of backgrounds and origins. They range from the average man on the street to infamous outlaws. Though most of Carey's characters are fictional figures, he has also used historical materials to reconstruct the life and exploits of certain historical figures, such as Ned Kelly in *The True History of the Kelly Gang* (2000). Ned Kelly was a celebrated outlaw who eluded the police for many years before he was captured and hanged in 1880. An unlikely hero, Kelly is a powerful legendary figure who is admired and respected for his filial piety and loyalty. Many of Carey's protagonists share a similar characteristic—they are social failures and misfits. By narrating their stories, Carey attempts to show that these characters, through their unconventional behavior and personality, challenge a society that does not endorse difference; it is society's inflexible institutions that make the characters victims within their own societies.

Critical Analysis

Carey is an accessible writer whose works appeal to a mass audience. Carey wrote several short stories before the publication of his first novel (*Bliss*, 1981). These stories won Carey a large following of fans in Australia, especially among the younger generation. One of these stories is "Crabs," a powerful depiction of the sense of alienation. "Crabs" tells the tale of a young man who transforms himself into a tow truck after he realizes that he and his girlfriend are marooned at the drive-in theater. The young man finally realizes in the end that although he has successfully escaped, he is all alone in the world as is everyone else who is still at the drive-in theater.

Carey's later short stories also examine the theme of estrangement. In "The Fat Man in History," for instance, a fat man finds himself caught in a world that favors slim and muscular bodies. In a postrevolutionary era, where humanity is reduced to forms and shapes of its bodies, the protagonist declares obesity to be subversive and challenges the status quo. Through his misfit cen-

tral characters, Carey is able to poke fun at the mindless fashion trends of contemporary society where men and women are reduced to mere objects. "The Fat Man in History" was published in a collection of short stories of the same title in 1980.

Bliss, which won the Miles Franklin Award in 1982, is a nightmarish and surrealistic tale of a man who dies three times but is resurrected each time to face new challenges. This novel combines light comedy with cynical jabs at the contemporary situation. The story has a political message, as it laments the role of American companies and popular culture in influencing and changing Australia.

Carey's second novel, *Illywhacker* (1985), which is set in Australia's bushwhacking country, conveys a bleak view of Australian society. The narrator, the 139-year-old Herbert Badgery, represents the first generation of Australia's inhabitants whose desire to make good and succeed in society is not fulfilled. Badgery's failure to market the plow he has invented is an allegory of Australia's own failure to extract itself from its economic crisis. The poignancy of Badgery's experiences is worsened by his observation that, two generations later, his descendants, now pet-shop owners, find themselves imprisoned within metaphorical cage similar to those in which the pets are kept constrained.

The most influential of all Carey's books are those that examine the history of Australia's social outcasts, such as the convicts, the poor, and the gang members. *Jack Maggs* (1997), which won the 1998 Commonwealth Writers Prize, is the tale of a young man who inherits money from a convict. It critiques the oppressive influence of English literary writing on Australian literature and represents an attempt to break free of the English conventions of writing.

Carey gains more recognition with every publication. *The True History of the Kelly Gang* won the 2001 Commonwealth Writers' Prize and 2001 Booker Prize and was shortlisted for the Miles Franklin Award. Anthony J. Hassall, after describing a harrowing death by drowning in the final scene of *Oscar and Lucinda*, remarks, "All of Carey's stories offer such fierce and dangerous pleasures, and despite the terrors they also enact and arouse, they create a wild, apocalyptic beauty." He sums up Carey as "a tribal teller of tales, whose stories strive to articulate an indigenous Australian mythology needed to replace the cultural narratives of successive colonial masters."

Other Works by Peter Carey

Collected Stories. St. Lucia: University of Queensland Press, 1994.

The Big Bazoohley. Illustrated by Abira Ali. New York: Henry Holt, 1995.

The Tax Inspector. New York: Vintage, 1993.

The Unusual Life of Tristan Smith: A Novel. New York: Vintage, 1996.

30 Days in Sydney: A Wildly Distorted Account. London: Bloomsbury USA, 2001.

Works about Peter Carey

Hassall, Anthony J. *Dancing on Hot MacAdam: Peter Carey's Fiction.* St. Lucia: University of Queensland Press, 1998.

Huggan, Graham. *Peter Carey.* New York: Oxford University Press, 1997.

Woodcock, Bruce. *Peter Carey.* Manchester: Manchester University Press, 1997.

Carpentier, Alejo (1904–1980) *novelist*

Alejo Carpentier was born in Havana to European parents. His father, a French architect, and his Russian mother, a medical student, had been living in Cuba for only two years when Carpentier was born. Carpentier's first language was French, and the family returned to Paris while he was still young, so he received both his elementary and secondary education in French schools. Nevertheless, Carpentier felt very strongly attached to his Cuban roots. All of his literature was inspired by what he felt to be the inner spirit of the indigenous Cuban culture.

Carpentier was obsessed with music and was particularly influenced and inspired by the experimental techniques of Igor Stravinsky. Stravinsky's ballet *The Rite of Spring*, which employs tribal rhythms, awakened Carpentier to the creative re-sources that Afro-Cuban music and culture offered for use as raw material by avant-garde literature. Carpentier went on to become a distinguished musicologist, and his interest in music guided his literary development throughout his career.

When he returned to Cuba in his early 20s, he did not have much time to write fiction because of his political activities. He joined the resistance against Cuban dictator Machado and, in 1927, was arrested. He spent seven months in jail, which ironically gave him time to begin his first novel, *Ecue-Yamba-O!* (1933), which means "God be praised" in the language of the native Cuban religion of Lucumi. This realistic historical novel depicts the struggles of Africans in the new world; however, the book also includes many scenes of mythic and religious rituals that prefigure MAGIC REALISM, one of Carpentier's key contributions to world literature.

Carpentier was released from jail but was not allowed to leave Cuba. Using forged papers, he escaped and returned to France, where he became involved in surrealism and contributed frequently to André BRETON's journal *Révolution Surréaliste*. However, he later rejected the shocking absurdity of surrealism for a literary style that was closer to myth.

Carpentier's historical novel, *The Kingdom of This World* (1949), takes place in early 19th-century Haiti under the rule of the Emperor Henri Christophe, a Haitian man who became ruler of the island after the French were overthrown. It is based on research that Carpentier did when he visited Haiti in 1943. While *The Kingdom of This World* still follows many of the conventions of traditional historical novels, in this book Carpentier first displays his particular style of magic realism, using historical facts as a backdrop for a narrative filled with myth and magic.

In his collection of short stories *War of Time* (1958), Carpentier used the same musical and mythological style to tell four vaguely autobiographical tales in which he explores the theme of how individuals interact with the larger forces of history around them. These stories examine how everyday reality can take on mythic force. For example, in "The Pursuit," which takes place in a Havana concert hall during a Beethoven symphony, a young man listens to the music and waits to be assassinated for betraying the Cuban Communist Party to Machado's forces. The story, which has the plot of an espionage tale, is told in a kind of symbolic montage that is itself a sort of symphony.

After the Cuban revolution, Carpentier became an active member of Castro's government and continued to write lyrical novels that, most important, saw individuals as capable of determining their own fate through acts of everyday magic.

Other Works by Alejo Carpentier

Explosion in a Cathedral. Translated by John Sturrock; introduction by Timothy Brennan. Minneapolis: University of Minnesota Press, 2001.

The Lost Steps. Translated by Harriet de Onis; introduction by Timothy Brennan. Minneapolis: University of Minnesota Press, 2001.

A Work about Alejo Carpentier

Gonzalez Echevarria, Roberto. *Alejo Carpentier: The Pilgrim at Home.* Ithaca, N.Y.: Cornell University Press, 1977.

Castellanos, Rosario (1925–1974)
diplomat, novelist, poet, short-story writer, playwright, critic

Born in Mexico City, Rosario Castellanos grew up in the town of Comitán, Chiapas, Mexico, close to the Guatemalan border. She was educated at the University of Mexico, where she eventually taught literature, although her work as a novelist and poet was the major source of her income. Her familiarity with the lives of the Indians of Chiapas and Guatemala caused her to focus on their plight in many of her works.

Castellanos began her writing career as a poet, publishing her first book of poems, *Trajectory of Dust,* in 1948. She continued to write many volumes of poetry, including *Poetry Is Not You* (1972), which focused on human frailty, the limitations of love, and the problems generated by social injus-

tice. Her first novel, *The Nine Guardians,* first appeared in 1958 and was translated into English in 1970. The story tells of a seven-year-old girl who fights the prevailing exploitation of the indigenous (native) people, as well as social and gender prejudice prevalent in the 1930s in Chiapas. *The Nine Guardians* won the 1958 Chiapas Prize.

Castellanos's involvement in the arts and her efforts on behalf of the Mexican feminist movement and indigenous Mexican women led her to be a cultural promoter at the Institute of Science and Arts in Tuxtla Gutiérrez, Chiapas. Her play, *The Eternal Feminine,* published posthumously in 1975, was first performed in Mexico in 1976 and is considered among the most original and important feminist works of literature in Latin America today.

Castellanos's 1960 collection of short stories, *City of Kings,* which focuses on the deceitful treatment of the Chiapa people by white landowners, won the Xavier Vaillaurrutia prize, and her novel, *Labors of Darkness* (1962), earned the 1962 Sor Juana Inés de la Cruz prize, the 1967 Carlos Trouyat Prize in Letters, and the 1972 Elías Sourasky Prize in Letters. When she accidentally died of electrocution while serving as Mexico's ambassador to Israel, Rosario Castellanos was regarded as Mexico's major 20th-century female novelist, a title she continues to hold.

Another Work by Rosario Castellanos

A Rosario Castellanos Reader. Translated by Maureen Ahern et al. Austin: University of Texas Press, 1988.

A Work about Rosario Castellanos

Bonifaz Caballero, Oscar. *Remembering Rosario: A Personal Glimpse into the Life and Works of Rosario Castellanos.* Translated by Myralyn F. Allgood. Potomac, Md.: Scripta Humanistica, 1990.

Castro, Rosalía de (1837–1885) *poet, novelist*

Rosalía de Castro was born in Santiago de Compostela, a region in the northwest of Spain where

Galician, similar to Portuguese, was the dominant dialect. She was illegitimate, the child of Teresa de Castro y Abadía, a Galician from a well-off family, and José Martínez Viojo, a seminarian who eventually rose to become the chaplain of Iria. Castro was raised in the countryside with a peasant family and then "reclaimed" by her mother when she was 13. Thus, her early years gave her the opportunity to learn the folklore and songs of Galicia, while her adolescence introduced her to a more traditional education typical for women of her time: learning how to play music, draw, and speak a foreign language.

At the age of 21, Castro married another Galician, Manuel Murguía, a dwarf who had favorably reviewed her first book of poems, *The Flower* (1857). After returning with her husband to her native Santiago in 1859, she bore six children and lived to bury three of them. Her life was difficult, characterized by illness, poverty, and the frustrations associated with being a woman writer in a male-dominated society.

Although her early work is written in the more widely read Castilian, the Spanish language, Castro later chose to write in her beloved Galician, the musical language in which Spanish medieval poetry was written. However, by the 19th century, Galicia was a poor region that provided many of the servants employed by wealthy Castilians, so her work was not appreciated or read by the majority of people. Critics now believe that writing in Galician most likely limited Castro's audience and postponed her current recognition as one of Spain's major 19th-century poets.

Rosalía de Castro was the author of four novels. The first, *Daughter of the Sea,* was published in 1859, and the last, *The First Madman,* was published in 1881, both touching on the pain experienced by children. During this period she published two volumes of poetry written in Galician, *Galician Songs* (1863) and *New Leaves* (1880), with themes of nature, solitude, and the plight of women and the poor. Her final volume of poems, *On the Shores of the Saar* (1884), expressing the disillusionment of adulthood, was written in

Spanish and appeared shortly before she died of cancer.

Although Castro's novels contributed to her fame, her poetry established her talent and success. As noted by Salvador de Madariaga, quoted in *The Defiant Muse: Hispanic Feminist Poets from the Middle Ages to the Present,* Castro's poetry can be considered "the best written in Spain in the nineteenth century."

Another Work by Rosalía de Castro

Poems. Translated by Anna-Marie Aldaz and Barbara N. Gantt. Albany: State University of New York Press, 1991.

Works about Rosalía de Castro

Dever, Aileen. *Radical Insufficiency of Human Life: The Poetry of R. de Castro and J. A. Silva.* Jefferson, N.C.: McFarland & Company, 2000.

Stevens, Shelley. *Rosalía de Castro and the Galician Revival.* London: Tamesis Books Ltd., 1986.

Cattopadhyay, Bankim-Chandra
(Bankim Chandra Chatterji) (1838–1894)
novelist

Bankim-Chandra Cattopadhyay was born in Kantalpara, West Bengal, India. His father worked as a tax collector for the government. Cattopadhyay was the first Indian to graduate from Calcutta University (in 1858) at a time when only British people were enrolled. He worked for the government for 30 years while also writing literature. He founded the literary magazine *Bangadarsan* (Mirror of Bengal) in 1872 and was always very involved in supporting Bengali journalism.

Cattopadhyay started to write poetry but soon turned to the novel. His attempt at the novel was written in Bengali and submitted for a writing contest; it did not win and has never been published. Cattopadhyay's first published novel, *Rajmohan's Wife* (1864), was written in English and is considered to be a reworking of his earlier unpublished novelette. He published numerous romance novels, which display his ability to rewrite historical moments within romantic and melodramatic contexts. His development of the novel in India had an immense impact, as he rejected the conventional Sanskritized literary movement, which supplanted Perso-Arabic words with Sanskrit ones and developed a more Westernized approach to Indian themes. Western ideas, such as romance and sensibility, were seen to be more important than the Indian sense of duty. This shift comes out most strongly in his depiction of women who are often compelled to transgress convention in the pursuit of love. Their love is tragic, however, because it can never be fully realized. In *Durgesnandini* (1865), for instance, the volatile politics between Pathans and Mughals in 16th-century Bengal is offset by a Pathan princess's refusal to accept racial boundaries in her love. Famous for such historical novels, Cattopadhyay is today viewed as the "father of the Indian novel."

Cattopadhyay is also seen as a national poet. The patriotic poem "Vande Materam" ("I Worship Mother") from his novel *Ānandamāth* (*The Abbey of Bliss*, 1882) was adopted throughout India as its unofficial national anthem in the early decades of the 20th century. It was adopted into a song by another famous Bengali poet Rabindranath TAGORE. The novel is a powerful story based on the 1773 resistance against Muslim and British conquerors of India by a group of Hindu hermits.

Cattopadhyay's work has been translated into every major Indian language. In 1884, his novel *Bishabriksa*, was translated into English for publication outside India. In 1892, the British government awarded Cattopadhyay the title of *Ray Bahadur* (Brave leader) in honor of his worldwide literary achievements.

Another Work by Bankim C. Cattopadhyay

Krishnakanta's Will. Norfolk, Conn.: New Directions, 1962.

Cavafy, Constantine P. (1863–1933) *poet*

Constantine P. Cavafy was born in Alexandria, Egypt, on April 29. He died in Alexandria on the same date. The son of a wealthy English businessman, he moved with his mother to England after his father's death in 1870. He stayed there for seven years, until the family business folded, causing Cavafy and his family to return to Alexandria in poverty. During his time in England, Cavafy became fluent in English and developed a love of English literature that would ultimately influence his decision to become a poet.

Cavafy's first job in 1885 was as a journalist. During this time, he began to publish a few poems on conventional romantic themes. Eventually, he gained steady employment and continued to write poetry. Between 1891 and 1904, he distributed his poetry exclusively to friends. His collected works did not emerge until two years after his death and did not become well known among English audiences until 1952.

After his death, Cavafy's reputation grew, and his poetry, often referred to as disturbing yet beautiful, began to influence other Greek poets. His poetry is known primarily for its themes of love and longing, as well as for its open expression of homosexuality. Often filled with a sense of nostalgia and regret at the decay of culture and the failure of human aspirations, his works are unsentimental.

Cavafy spent most of his life alone. He developed two short-lived relationships, both with men, which shaped the sense of longing in his poems. He also had a long-term acquaintance with the English novelist E. M. Forster. Cavafy died of cancer in Alexandria. It was reported that his final action was to draw a circle on a sheet of paper and enclose within it a period.

Another Work by Constantine P. Cavafy

Before Time Could Change Them: The Complete Poems of Constantine P. Cavafy. Translated by Theoharis Constantine Theoharis. New York: Harcourt Brace, 2001.

A Work about Constantine P. Cavafy

Keeley, Edmund. *Cavafy's Alexandria.* Princeton, N.J.: Princeton University Press, 1995.

Cela, Camilo José (1916–   ) *novelist, short-story writer, essayist*

Camilo José Cela was born in Iria Flavia, Spain, the eldest of seven children in a conservative upper-middle-class home. When he was 20, the Spanish civil war erupted and he was caught in the siege of Madrid. The horrors he saw at that time became the source for much of the imagery he uses in his later novels. He joined Franco's army and, after the fascists' victory, was given a number of important literary and political positions. His work, however, can be seen as an ironic subversion of some of the regime's principles.

Cela's first novel, *The Family of Pascual Duarte* (1942), has been compared to Albert CAMUS's novel *The Stranger. The Family of Pascual Duarte* tells the story of a peasant, Pascual Duarte, who is waiting in jail to be executed. Pascual relates, in a distant and emotionally flat tone, a series of horrible acts that he has committed. Cela uses this contrast to explore existential feelings of disconnection. The novel shows the influence of Pío BAROJA Y NESSI in its terse style and complicated structure, and it has inspired many imitators in modern Spanish prose. It is also one of the precursors of OBJECTIVISMO.

Cela went on to write a number of innovative novels that experimented with structure. *San Camilo 1936* (1969), written entirely in the second person, is a long monologue that depicts life in Madrid just before the outbreak of war.

In 1989, Cela won the Nobel Prize in literature. His novels and essays walk a fine line between representing traditional literary and political modes and ironically undermining them. His address to the Nobel Committee expresses his respect both for tradition and for the need to push against its limits: "Let us never forget that confusing procedure with the rule of Law, just as observing the letter rather than the spirit of the Law, always leads to injustice which is both the source and consequence of disorder."

Another Work by Camilo José Cela

The Hive. Translated by J. M. Cohen in consultation with Arturo Barea. New York: Noonday Press, 1990.

A Work about Camilo José Cela

Kirsner, Robert. *The Novels and Travels of Camilo José Cela.* Chapel Hill: University of North Carolina Press, 1964.

Celan, Paul (Paul Antschel) (1920–1970) *poet, essayist, translator*

Paul Celan was born Paul Antschel, the only child of German-speaking Jewish parents, in Cernauti, Romania. Young Celan attended German-speaking school and Hebrew school in his childhood. He shared a passion for German poetry with his mother, Fritzi Antschel, especially the ROMANTICISM of Novalis. Celan went to Paris in 1938 to study medicine and then to the University of Czernowitz to learn romance philology. He was particularly attracted by the poetry of Georg TRAKL and Rainer Maria RILKE. During World War II, Celan's parents were killed by the Nazis in a concentration camp. Celan was able to survive by working in a forced labor camp until it was liberated by Russian troops in 1943.

In 1944, Celan moved to Bucharest, Romania, where he worked as a translator and editor for a publishing company. In 1947, he emigrated to Vienna, and the following year, he permanently settled in Paris, where he taught German language and literature at the École Normale Superieure. Celan began writing poetry in the late 1940s to relate his experiences of the Holocaust. He was published in several magazines and newspapers throughout West Germany.

Celan gained critical recognition and acclaim in 1952 with the publication of *Poppy and Memories,* a collection that thematically focused on the Holocaust and the Jewish experience under the Nazi regime. The imagery in the collection is nightmarish and surreal, marked by the underlying violence of the place and time, as can be seen in "Death Fugue," the most famous poem in the collection: "Black milk of morning we drink at you at dusktime . . ./We scoop out a grave in the sky where it is roomy to lie."

During the 1960s, Celan extensively translated French poetry into German. In 1960, he was awarded the prestigious Georg Büchner Prize for his poetry. Celan's mental health deteriorated rapidly during these years; apparently, he could not reconcile his Jewish origins and the Holocaust experience with his love for the German language. Although he visited Israel and frequently introduced Jewish themes in his work, the memory of his suffering and the medium of his poetic expression (German) proved to be utterly irreconcilable. He entered a psychiatric hospital in 1965. After being accused of plagiarism, seemingly without grounds, Celan suffered a complete nervous breakdown. He killed himself at the age of 49.

Paul Celan made a tremendous contribution to the German language and the expression of the Jewish experience during and after the Holocaust. The fragmented syntax and minimalism often found in his verse represents the violence and the shattered world of the Holocaust survivor. He is widely read and studied throughout the world.

Other Works by Paul Celan

Glottal Stop: 101 Poems. Translated by Nikolai Popov. Boston: University of New England Press, 2000.

Selected Poems and Prose of Paul Celan. Translated by John Felsteiner. New York: Norton, 2000.

A Work about Paul Celan

Felsteiner, John. *Paul Celan: Poet, Survivor, Jew.* New Haven, Conn.: Yale University Press, 2001.

Céline, Louis-Ferdinand (1894–1961)
novelist

Louis-Ferdinand Céline was born Louis Ferdinand Destouches on May 27 in Courbevoie to a working-class family. He grew up in Paris, where his mother ran a lace shop. In 1912, he enlisted in the army and served in World War I, where he was severely wounded and left with permanent disabilities. He returned to France to study medicine, going on to become a doctor.

Céline became famous as a writer with the publication of his first novel, *Journey to the End of the Night* (1932; translated 1943). Praised by right-wing extremists, the work was largely based on Céline's own adventures: in the trenches during World War I, running a trading post in Africa, working in a factory in the United States, and returning to Paris to practice medicine. His second novel, *Death on the Installment Plan* (1936; translated 1938), which continues the protagonist's story from *Journey to the End of the Night,* was also a critical success. Céline's popularity stemmed largely from the contemporary nature of his writing and its relevance to the understanding of current events and world situations.

In the late 1930s, Céline traveled to the Soviet Union, where he wrote the first of several notorious anti-Semitic, pacifist pamphlets, declaring his disenchantment with war. He began to focus his writing in an attempt to prevent his country from entering World War II. After the war, Céline was accused of having Nazi sympathies. He fled to Germany, where he remained in exile until 1951.

In all of Céline's works, his characters' lives are filled with failure, anxiety, and nihilism. He had difficulty communicating during his life and sank progressively into depression, madness, and rage. His novels display this through their depictions of giants, paraplegics, and gnomes, as well as graphic visions of dismemberment and murder.

Céline died on July 1 of a ruptured aneurysm. Though his works remain controversial, his attacks against war have influenced such writers as Henry Miller and Kurt Vonnegut, Jr. His influence on world literature stems largely from his willingness to write about controversial subjects and his innovative style (his use of first-person narrative and slang).

Another Work by Louis-Ferdinand Céline

Ballets Without Music, Without Dancers, Without Anything. Translated by Thomas and Carol Christensen. Los Angeles: Green Integer, 1999.

A Work about Louis-Ferdinand Céline

Hewitt, Nicholas. *The Life of Céline: A Critical Biography.* Malden, Mass.: Blackwell, 1999.

Césaire, Aimé (1913–) *poet, teacher, playwright, politician*

Aimé Césaire was born into a family of seven children in Basse-Pointe, Martinique. Césaire's father worked as an accountant for the colonial internal-revenue service, and his mother was a seamstress. After earning a scholarship in 1924, Césaire left his local elementary school to attend the Lycée Schoelcher in Fort-de-France, the capital of Martinique. There Césaire met classmate Léon Damas, who later contributed to NÉGRITUDE, and instructor Octave Manoni, whose theories of colonization Césaire later critiqued.

The top student at Lycée Schoelcher in 1931, Césaire earned a scholarship to Paris's prestigious Lycée Louis-le-Grand. There Césaire read widely, including the works of Marx, FREUD, and the precursors of surrealism, LAUTREAMONT and RIMBAUD. With Léopold Sédar SENGHOR, head of the African students, and Damas, Césaire published *L'Étudiant Noir* (*The Black Student*) in 1934 "for all black students, regardless of origin." Now considered the cofounder of négritude with Senghor, Damas claimed that Césaire first used the word *négritude* in a *L'Étudiant Noir* editorial. The small student newspaper appeared five or six times during the next two years until funding difficulties and French authorities stopped publication.

After taking and passing entrance exams to L'École Normale Supérieure in 1935, Césaire went to Yugoslavia with classmate Peter Guberina. A visit to Martinska, or St. Martin's Island, contributed to notes which became *Cahier d'un retour au pays natal* (*Return to My Native Land*), published in 1939, near the time Césaire became a teacher of classical and modern literature at the Lycée Schoelcher. Themes of black West Indian identity run through this and subsequent works, including *Tropiques,* a quarterly journal founded in 1941 with his wife Suzanne and other Martinican intellectuals. Reading *Cahier d'un retour au pays natal* prompted André BRETON to publish "Un grand poèt noir" in a 1943 New York–based French-English review. This essay served as the preface to subsequent editions of the original text.

Césaire lived in Haiti and lectured on French poetry after the Provisional French government, which took over in 1943, sent him there as a cultural ambassador. Working in Haiti gave Césaire enough material to write a celebratory historical study on Haiti and his first play written for the stage, *La Tragédie du roi Christophe* (*The Tragedy of King Christophe,* 1963). The play draws on the life of Henri Christophe, one of Haiti's earliest leaders, and employs Shakespearean style and tone.

In 1945 Césaire became Mayor of Fort-de-France on a Communist ticket and the following year was the deputy for Martinique in the French National Assembly. In response to criticism of his critiques of French government, Césaire published *Discours sur le colonialisme* (*Discourse on Colonialism,* 1950). The pamphlet critiques racist tendencies in French government and "universal" values based on white civilization, and it calls for political change.

Césaire continued combining literary endeavors with political activism. The surrealistic style of his poetry prompted praise from Jean-Paul SARTRE and criticism from Communist Party members, who called it "decadent." Frustrated with attitudes and actions of the French Communist Party, which Césaire accused of "empire building" in the Third World in a *Lettre a Maurice Thorez* (*Letter to Maurice Thorez*), Césaire founded the Martinican Progressive Party in 1958.

Plays published during the 1960s caused some to consider Césaire one of the leading black dramatists of French expression. *Une saison au Congo* (*A Season in the Congo,* 1966) focuses on the demise of Congolese premier Patrice Lumumba and was not as well received by critics or audiences as Césaire's first play, *La Tragédie du roi Christophe.* Césaire's radical adaptation of Shakespeare's *The Tempest* as *Une tempête* (*A Tempest,* 1969) focuses on the relationship between the colonizer and the colonized and uses modern language and three acts instead of five. *Une tempête* initially generated much negative commentary by Western critics but was well received by international audiences when performed.

The younger generation of Martinican writers, including Bernabé, CHAMOISEAU, and Confiant, disagree with Césaire's allegiance to writing black literature in French. As Ernest Moutoussamy remarks in *Aimé Césaire, Député à l'Assemblée Nationale, 1945–1993* (1993), "His poetic discourse is that of a prophet, his political discourse is that of a realist and as such makes room for compromise."

Other Works by Aimé Césaire

Aimé Césaire: The Collected Poetry. Translated by Clayton Eshleman and Annette Smith. Berkeley: University of California Press, 1983.
Lyric and Dramatic Poetry, 1946–82. Translated by Clayton Eshleman and Annette Smith. Charlottesville: University Press of Virginia, 1990.

Works about Aimé Césaire

Davis, Gregson. *Aimé Césaire.* Cambridge: Cambridge University Press, 1997.
Hale, Thomas, ed. *Critical Perspectives on Aimé Césaire.* Washington, D.C.: Three Continents Press, 1992.
San Juan, E. *Aimé Césaire: Surrealism and Revolution.* Bowling Green, Ohio: Bowling Green State University Press, 2000.

Chamoiseau, Patrick (1953–   ) *nonfiction and fiction writer*

Patrick Chamoiseau was born in Fort-de-France, Martinique. Educated as a lawyer in Martinique and France, Chamoiseau worked as a full-time probation officer for 15 years. In an interview with James Ferguson, Chamoiseau said, "It sounds terrible, but understanding these people's experiences has helped me hugely as a writer, as it has allowed me to look into aspects of life that you wouldn't normally encounter." By writing evenings, weekends, and holidays, Chamoiseau managed to publish prolifically—novels, memoirs, literary criticism, and a collection of short stories.

Chamoiseau sees himself as a "word scratcher" —novelist or writer—who communicates traditions of *créolité.* To Chamoiseau, "Créolité tries to restore to the modern-day writer that status of storyteller by breaking down the barrier between the written and spoken French and Creole. If a writer can use Creole, then he's much more in touch with the thoughts and expressions of ordinary people."

Chamoiseau's own multivocal novels explore sociolinguistic realities by juxtaposing French and Creole, producing what Pierre Pinalie calls "Fréole," a nonspoken, partially invented, and playful language. In his first published novel, *Chronique des sept misères* (*Chronicle of the Seven Sorrows,* 1986), he examines the lives and stories of Martinican workers. His second novel, *Solibo Magnifique* (*Solibo Magnificent,* 1988), a murder suspense story, allegorizes the Creole oral culture. Themes of slavery, class, and colonialism run through Chamoiseau's fictional works.

Inspired by Edouard Glissant's *Discours Antillais,* Chamoiseau collaborated with Raphaël Confiant and Jean Bernabé on "Éloge de la Créolité." Published in 1989, the first sentence reads, "Neither Europeans, nor Africans, nor Asians, we proclaim ourselves Creoles." The literary manifesto sparked the French-Antillean Créolité movement by challenging many ideas proposed by another Martinican writer, Aimé CÉSAIRE, including the NÉGRITUDE literary movement.

"Éloge de la Créolité" generated much controversy, but it was the novel *Texaco,* published in French in 1992, that more staunchly positioned Chamoiseau as an exceptionally talented, internationally significant writer. In *Texaco,* the character Marie-Sophie Laborieux tells the history of the village of Texaco to save it from an urban planner's intended alterations. *Texaco* won France's prestigious Prix Goncourt the year it was published, prompting the translation of a number of Chamoiseau's works into multiple languages.

Apart from novels, Chamoiseau has published two autobiographical narratives on his childhood in Fort-de-France: *Antan d'enfance* (*Childhood,* 1993) and *Chemin-d'école* (*School Days,* 1994). *Antan d'enfance* explores Chamoiseau's magical experience of childhood and foregrounds his mother, who raised five children amidst poverty. The sequel *Chemin-d'école* introduces readers to Chamoiseau's Francophile and Africanist teachers, as well as the imaginative Big Bellybutton, who tells fantastical stories. Like Chamoiseau's other works, *Chemin-d'école* received accolades: "Imaginative and moving," said the *Washington Post.*

In the 1999 afterword to the English translation of the *Chronicle of the Seven Sorrows,* Linda Coverdale asserted, "Chamoiseau is a free-range writer who tries to keep his language 'open' so that readers will feel its humble, questing flexibility, a kind of remarkable mongrelism that proves perfect for the task at hand: presenting a deftly self-conscious form of Creoleness in this chronicle of 'mouth-memory' telling stories to a word scratcher."

Other Works by Patrick Chamoiseau

Creole Folktales. New York: New Press, 1994.
Seven Dreams of Elmira: A Tale of Martinique. Nashville, Tenn.: St. Albans, 2001.
Strange Words. London: Granta Books, 1998.

Works about Patrick Chamoiseau

Milne, Lorna. "From Creolite to Diversalite: The Postcolonial Subject in Patrick Chamoiseau's *Texaco.*" In Paul Gifford and Johnnie Gratton, eds., *Subject Matters: Subject and Self in French Literature from Descartes to the Present.* Amsterdam, Netherlands: Rodopi, 2000.
———. "Sex, Gender and the Right to Write: Patrick Chamoiseau and the Erotics of Colonialism." *Paragraph: The Journal of the Modern Critical Theory Group* 24, no. 3 (2001): 59–75.
Shelly, Sharon L. "Addressing Linguistic and Cultural Diversity with Patrick Chamoiseau's *Chemin-d'école.*" *French Review: Journal of the American Association of Teachers of French* 75, no. 1 (October 2001): 112–26.

Char, René (1907–1988) *poet*

One of the early surrealists, René Char was born in Provence and educated at the University in Aix. A controversial figure, he had a great many admirers and an equal number of detractors. As a writer, Char was a key figure in the surrealist movement, from which he later branched off to pursue his own unique direction. His poetry was marked by its extreme economy of language. As a political figure, he was very active in the French Resistance movement.

Char was most deeply affected and inspired by his experience as the leader of a resistance group in Provence during World War II. He understood the tragic nature of war and the difficult attempts of humanity to achieve freedom. These themes are reflected in his works, such as the poems in his collection *Hypnos Waking* (1956). Unlike the majority of his contemporaries, however, Char does not focus on the disillusionment and despair inherent in war. Instead, he is more concerned with humanity's capacity to hope and to love. What bothered him most was immobility, the lack of change that allowed for the acceptance of the status quo.

Char's major contribution to world literature stems from his use of the written word as a means of bringing about positive solutions to social change. In his introduction to *Hypnos Waking,* Jackson Matthews say that Char "has faced the difficult conditions of human freedom, and understood the role of the imagination in the life of man."

Other Works by René Char

Leaves of Hypnos. Translated by Cid Corman. New York: Grossman, 1973.
Poems of René Char. Translated and annotated by Mary Ann Caws and Jonathan Griffin. Princeton, N.J.: Princeton University Press, 1976.

Works about René Char

Caws, Mary Ann. *René Char.* Boston: Twayne, 1977.
Matthews, Jackson. "Introduction." In René Char, *Hypnos Waking: Poems and Prose.* New York: Random House, 1956.
Piore, Nancy Kline. *Lightning: The Poetry of René Char.* Boston: Northeastern University Press, 1981.

Chateaubriand, François-René de (1768–1848) *novelist, nonfiction writer*

François-René de Chateaubriand and Jean Anthelme Brillat-Savarin once met at a restaurant to celebrate the publication of Chateaubriand's *The Genius of Christianity*. The chef surprised the diners by already having prepared a new recipe and named it in honor of the author, thus giving birth to the famous Chateaubriand steak.

Chateaubriand was born to nobility, and he grew up in the castle of Combourg, his family's isolated estate in Brittany. His world was devastated by the French Revolution, which forced him into exile. An avid adventurer with a great interest in American Indians, Chateaubriand visited the United States in 1791 to do research for a book on the massacre of the Natchez and to search for the Northwest Passage. However, his journey took him only as far as Niagara Falls, at which point he returned briefly to France before becoming an émigré and living in England until 1800. While there, Chateaubriand decided to pursue a career as a writer and published his first book, *Essai historique, politique, et moral sur les révolutions anciennes et modernes* (*Historical, Political, and Moral Essays on the Ancient and Modern Revolutions*, 1797). The publication of his book *The Genius of Christianity* (1802; translated 1856), with its frank and honest treatment of its subject matter, brought Chateaubriand's name to the forefront of French literature. In spite of his upper-class background, Chateaubriand worked diligently during the French Revolution to eradicate religious barriers, which he viewed as directly responsible for the severe restrictions levied against the poor and the uneducated. *The Genius of Christianity* was his attempt to restore a lost religion to his people. His *The Martyrs* (1809; translated 1812) celebrates Christianity's triumph over paganism.

In addition, two tragic love stories, the unfinished *Atala* (1801) and *René* (1802), stand as prime examples of the ways in which Chateaubriand utilized the melancholy and exotic descriptions of nature and the language of nostalgia that came to characterize the ROMANTIC movement in French literature. Other works that fall under this style of writing include *Les Aventures du dernier des Abencérages* (*The Adventures of the Last of the Abencérages,* 1826), a romance novel set in Spain.

In addition to his writing career, Chateaubriand was also politically active. He was appointed by Napoleon in 1803 as secretary of the legation to Rome and promoted, in 1804, as minister to Valaise. However, on hearing of the execution of the duc d'Enghien, he became outraged and resigned from his position. He channeled his anger into becoming a bitter anti-Bonapartist, going on to support the Bourbons. He served as ambassador to London in 1822 and as the minister of foreign affairs from 1823 to 1824.

Chateaubriand abandoned political activity in 1830 to devote the final years of his life to composing his own personal history, which he collected as *Memoirs from Beyond the Tomb* (1849). Although he was often accused of plagiarism and exaggeration by scholars, particularly in his purportedly factual travel narratives, his richly detailed and evocative language greatly enhanced and influenced the romantic movement. In response to this criticism, Chateaubriand once said, "The original writer is not he who refrains from imitating others, but he who can be imitated by none."

Another Work by François-René de Chateaubriand

Travels in America. Translated by Richard Switzer, Lexington: University of Kentucky Press, 1969.

Works about François-René de Chateaubriand

Painter, George Duncan. *Chateaubriand: A Biography.* New York: Knopf, 1978.

Smethurst, Colin. *Chateaubriand, Atala and René.* London: Grant and Cutler, 1995.

Chatterjee, Upamanyu (1959–)
novelist

Upamanyu Chatterjee was born in India. He comes from a family of civil servants, and after completing a degree in English Literature, he joined the Indian Administrative Services (IAS) in 1983. This professional move, however, signifies not only the beginning of Chatterjee's career in writing but also the source behind much of the content of his novels.

While in high school, Chatterjee wrote a play adopted from a Hitchcock story called *Dilemma*. It was never published but won the school drama competition despite its open caricaturing of school rules and regulations. Since then, he has written three novels, all of which have received similar critical and political approval in spite of a style that parodies the state legal systems, in which he also holds a job, and its effect on human behavior.

The novel *English, August: An Indian Story* (1988) and its sequel *The Mammaries of the Welfare State* (2000) are based on a civil servant's experiences working in small-town politics. The adventures of the protagonist, Augustya, take him from a position of naïveté to cynicism after initiation into the politics of the real world. The sequel continues with the life of Augustya, further exposing the parasitic nature of civil servants and the political system of which they are a part. In addition, *mammaries* is a common "Hinglish" (Hindi-English) mispronunciation of the word *memories*. Thus, Chatterjee begins with a joke by teasing the reader from the moment one encounters the title of his book.

Chatterjee's novels are told in a relentlessly satirical style that is intended to broaden the concept of comedy. He wishes to go beyond satire, parody, and burlesque. His intent is to provide comic relief from the hypocrisies that are inherent in society by revealing the idiosyncrasies produced when idealism meets with reality.

Another Work by Upamanyu Chatterjee

The Last Burden. New York: Penguin, 1997.

Chatterji, Bankim Chandra

See CATTOPADHYAY, B(ANKIM)-C(HANDRA).

Chatterji, Sarat Chandra (Sarat Chandra Chattopadhyay) (1876–1938)
novelist

Sarat Chandra Chatterji was born in Bengal, India. He was born into a very poor family and did not have the opportunity to pursue a higher education. As a young adult, he spent a number of years wandering all over India dressed as a beggar. Despite these trying early years, Chatterji did eventually reclaim his family responsibilities and started to work as a clerk. During his posting in Burma, he began writing and was eventually able to achieve enough financial stability to return to India.

Chatterji's writing was influenced by Bengali renaissance literature by Bankim-Chandra CATTOPADHYAY and Rabindranath TAGORE. Their focus on the beauty of human life and nature can be found in Chatterji's works. In addition, he was an early proponent of women's rights, and many of his works offer unflinching criticism of the gender inequalities of his time. His novel *Palli Samaj* (Village Society, 1915–16) caused a sensation because of its open acknowledgment of a woman's desire for a man after the death of her husband. His "feminist" novels, however, eventually conformed to social norms despite the revolutionary thoughts expressed in his prose work. Chatterji continued his criticism, however, in such essays as "Narir Mulya" (1922–23) that denounce society's maltreatment of women, especially in middle-class Bengal.

Chatterji also wrote numerous political novels. He wrote *Pather Dabi* (*The Right Way*, 1926) while he was president of the Congress Committee of Howrah District in West Bengal, India. Based on the rebel forces in Burma and Singapore, this novel prescribed violence as the only path for a free India and upheld anti-British sentiments. Much controversy surrounded this work, especially because Chatterji then held a post in the Congress Party, which was then still subject to British authority.

Chatterji's romance novels were a sensational success all over India. Much of his national popularity had to do with the fact that his stories were so often adapted for commercial Hindi (not just Bengali) movies. His first novel *Devadas* (1917) introduces a new type of character in Chandramukhi, a "noble" prostitute. This is a story about the suppression of love and desire by those whom society rejects. Her story also reveals social patriarchy's hypocritical views on female chastity. In *Srikanta* (1917–33), Chatterji's most famous work, the union of a singer-dancer and her lover serves to criticize the institution of marriage by examining its social and ethical definition. *Srikanta* is a partly autobiographical collection of episodes in four volumes.

Even today, Chatterji's Bengali novels are the most often translated works into almost all mainstream Indian languages.

Another Work by Sarat Chandra Chatterji

Devdas and Other Stories. Translated by V. S. Naravane. Ottawa: Laurier Press Ltd., 2000.

A Work about Sarat Chandra Chatterji

Naravane, Vishwanath S. *Sarat Chandra Chatterji: An Introduction to His Life and Work.* New Delhi: Macmillan Company of India, 1976.

Chattopadhay, Sarat Chandra

See CHATTERJI, SARAT CHANDRA.

Chekhov, Anton (1860–1904) *short-story writer, dramatist*

Anton Pavlovich Chekhov was born in Taganrok, a small provincial town in Russia. His father, Pavel Yegorovich, owned a small grocery where Anton worked after school. Taganrok was on an important commercial route, and Chekhov had an opportunity to meet a variety of people from all walks of life—an invaluable experience for a developing writer. In school, Chekhov particularly excelled in German and scripture. When Chekhov was 16, his father, facing bankruptcy and imprisonment, escaped to Moscow. Eventually, his wife and the younger children joined him, leaving Chekhov behind in Taganrok, where he worked as a tutor and sent most of his money to help his family.

In 1879, Chekhov rejoined his family in Moscow. In that same year, he entered Moscow University to study medicine. While there, Chekhov began to write to help support the family. His first story appeared in 1880 in a comic magazine called *Fragments*. While working for *Fragments*, Chekhov developed a keen ability to capture the speech patterns of characters from all levels of society. Chekhov's characters ranged from thieves to wealthy landowners and every type in between. Chekhov also honed his narrative technique during the five years he worked for *Fragments*. In the typical Chekhov story, the narrative begins in the present, and the characters' motives are seldom explicitly explained. Everyday life is not simply background in Chekhov's fiction; it forms the dynamic center of the narrative.

Chekhov graduated in 1884 and began to practice medicine. He also continued to write. In 1886, *New Time*, one of the most prestigious and popular newspapers in Russia, began to publish his work. Chekhov developed a warm relationship with the editor of *New Time*, Alexey Suvorin, who encouraged Chekhov and often helped him financially.

In 1887, Chekhov received the prestigious Pushkin Prize for *At Dusk*, a collection of short stories, and completed his first play, *Ivanov*, the story of a young man, very like Chekhov himself, who commits suicide. Chekhov's second play, *The Wood Demon*, was a failure and caused him to stop writing for a period. His first great success in the theater came with *The Seagull* (1896), a tragic tale of love gone awry.

The popularity of his works was such that Chekhov finally achieved financial independence and was able to buy a country estate in Melikhovo and spend money on philanthropic pursuits, such as a free medical clinic he ran between 1892 and 1893 during a devastating outbreak of cholera. Instead of fully concentrating on his writing career, Chekhov extended his medical practice and treated as many as 1,500 patients a year.

In 1897, Chekhov was diagnosed with tuberculosis, and his health deteriorated rapidly. On doctor's orders, Chekhov moved to the small tourist town of Yalta on the Black Sea where the salt air was supposed to help his lungs recover. He found Yalta to be dull and depressing; however, it was there that he created some of his most famous works, including the *The Cherry Orchard*. In Yalta, Chekhov was often visited by his famous friends, such as the writer Maxim GORKY, the poet Ivan BUNIN, and the composer Sergey Rakhmaninov, which helped alleviate his loneliness and sense of isolation. Despite his doctors' warnings, Chekhov continued to work throughout his long illness. He died on July 14, 1904, at a German health resort.

Critical Analysis

In most of Chekhov's work, one notices a complete absence of an authorial view. A contemporary critic, Aleksandar Chudakov said that other "Critics called into question his narrative patterns in the short stories, the absence of extended introductions, of definite conclusions, of the elaborately detailed pre-histories for his characters, or clear-cut motives for their actions." Chekhov's short-story technique was thus innovative not only in terms of subject matter but also style. Eventually, most critics came to recognize the genius of Chekhov's prose, although belatedly, and he was ranked among the giants of Russian literature during his lifetime.

Chekhov's ground-breaking dramatic techniques were not very well received in 1896, and *The Seagull*, one of his most famous plays, was essentially a failure the first time it was performed. When it was later performed by the Moscow Art Theater, however, the play was a critical and popular success because this troupe used realistic acting techniques and an ensemble cast, which were perfectly suited to Chekhov's drama. The Moscow Art Theater eventually staged all of Chekhov's plays. Unlike his fiction, Chekhov's major dramatic work focused on the politics and psychology of bourgeois life. One often finds the same feeling of hopelessness and claustrophobia in the conflicts of the middle-class families in Chekhov's plays as one does in the works of French naturalist writer Emile ZOLA.

The Seagull focuses on such diverse themes as family life, suicide, love, and the mother–son relationship in the context of middle-class dynamics. The action of the play revolves around Arkadina, a famous actress with an established household in the country, whose son, Konstantin, kills a seagull one day. The plot is complicated by the presence of Trigorin, a novelist who is writing a story about Arkadina's household.

Chekhov's last play, *The Cherry Orchard*, was a tremendous success when it was first staged in 1904. The play delineates the tragic downfall of the Ranevskaya family. Madame Ranevskaya, driven by financial despair, reluctantly decides to cut down the cherry orchard on her family estate. In *Cherry Orchard*, Chekhov explores the results of social change on the Russian aristocracy and on the freed serfs. A major theme of the play is independence and the meaning of freedom as it applies to each of the characters.

Chekhov's legacy as a writer and dramatist extended beyond the borders of Russia. His innovative narrative techniques, which contributed to the development of MODERNISM, influenced later generations of writers. His plays, still widely popular today, are produced all over the world. Chekhov taught future generations of writers to present life without authorial commentary—in all its complexity, and in all of its absurdity—and to avoid omniscient explanations and pat answers to life's dilemmas.

Other Works by Anton Chekhov

Five Plays: Ivanov, The Seagull, Uncle Vanya, Three Sisters, and Cherry Orchard. Oxford: Oxford University Press, 1998.
Forty Stories. New York: Vintage Press, 1991.

Works about Anton Chekhov

Gottlieb, Vera, and Paul Allain, eds. *The Cambridge Companion to Chekhov*. Cambridge: Cambridge University Press, 2000.
Rayfield, Donal. *Anton Chekhov: A Life*. Chicago: Northwestern University Press, 2000.

Chen Yuan-tsung (1932–   ) novelist

Chen Yuan-tsung was born in Shanghai, China, was raised in a wealthy household, and received a Western-style education at a missionary school. During the Sino-Japanese War, she lived in Chongqing but returned to Shanghai, where she lived in 1949, the year of the Communist takeover. Chen stayed in China because of her idealistic belief in the revolutionary cause.

In 1950, at age 18, she acquired her first job at the Film Bureau of Beijing, but this did not last long. The Communist Party leadership began to "send down" young people from cities to the countryside to participate in the so-called agrarian revolution. In 1951, Chen left Beijing for Gansu province in northwestern China to join this revolution and manually work the land. She became a young revolutionary, known as a *cadre*. She worked at land reform and endured extreme hardships, such as starvation, during Mao Zedong's failed industrial and agrarian initiative known as the Great Leap Forward. She wrote and read as much as possible during this time but suffered during the Cultural Revolution when the oppressive regime persecuted writers, artists, and intellectuals as counter-revolutionaries.

Chen immigrated to the United States in 1972 with her husband, Jack Chen, an artist and writer, and their son and later taught at Cornell. She determined to publish her story from writings she had hidden during her cadre years, which was the tale of millions of young people who came of age in Communist China. She fictionalized her life in her only work—the 1980 novel, *The Dragon's Village*. The novel follows Guan Ling-ling, a young woman from a wealthy family who becomes swept up in the revolutionary fervor of pre-Communist China and joins the Red Guards. She encounters both corrupt officials and cadres, but she finds kindness among comrades and endures the same hardships that Chen herself did. Chen lives with her husband in El Cerrito, California.

Works about Chen Yuan-tsung

Grunfeld, A. Tom. "The Dragon's Village: An Autobiographical Novel of Revolutionary China." In *Focus* (Spring 1993).

Stone, Judy. "A Talk with the Author/An Author's Ordeal." *New York Times Book Review*, May 4, 1980.

Chernyshevsky, Nikolay (1828–1889)
essayist, fiction writer

Nikolay Gavrilovich Chernyshevsky was born in Saratov, Russia. At first educated by his father, a priest of the Russian Orthodox Church, Chernyshevsky was admitted into a seminary, an institution that prepared students for careers in the clergy. While in the seminary, he demonstrated great ability as a scholar, and his parents decided to send him to a university in St. Petersburg, where he enrolled in the department of philology.

Socially awkward and financially destitute, Chernyshevsky isolated himself from his fellow students. He was an avid reader and dreamed of becoming a great social reformer and philosopher. Between 1855 and 1862, Chernyshevsky worked for a political publication, *The Contemporary,* where he published translations, criticism, and political articles. He was greatly influenced by European socialist thinkers, such as Hegel. Chernyshevsky advocated agrarian reform, emancipation of the serfs, and establishment of communal agrarian communities, which he viewed as a transition to socialism. His politically radical thinking and attacks on government policies, particularly on the institution of serfdom, resulted in almost 20 years of exile to Siberia, where he was sent in 1864. He continued to attack government policies relentlessly and became a member of several underground radical organizations that wanted to reform Russia by any means necessary, including violence against representatives of the government.

Although Chernyshevsky is remembered as a forerunner of the Russian revolutionary movement, he is also noted for his novel, *What Is To Be Done?* (1863). This polemical novel explores the social inequalities of Russian society. The plot concerns a group of young, idealized intellectuals who go to the countryside to ease the lives of peasants through scientific means. The novel condemns moderates for their seeming inability to engage in social transformation and calls for a swift, radical movement. The novel was generally praised by the radical reformers but was condemned by government officials.

Chernyshevsky left a radical legacy for Russian socialism. His works influenced a number of historical figures, including Vladimir Lenin, who participated in the Russian Revolution. Chernyshevsky is considered to be one of the greatest social philosophers of Russia.

Other Works by Nikolay Chernyshevsky

Prologue: A Novel for the 1860's. Translated by Michael J. Katz. Evanston, Ill.: Northwestern University Press, 1995.

Selected Philosophical Essays. Moscow: Foreign Languages Publishing House, 1953; reissued 2002.

A Work about Nikolay Chernyshevsky

Paperno, Irina. *Chernyshevsky and the Age of Realism.* Stanford: Stanford University Press, 1988.

Chughtai (Chugtai), Ismat (1915–1991)
poet, dramatist, novelist, short-story writer, scriptwriter

Ismat Chughtai was born in Aligarh, India. Though she was one of 10 children, Chughtai spent most of her time alone, climbing trees, running after chickens in her backyard and watching the world go by. From an early age, Chughtai collected mental pictures of everyday life whose simplicity underlies the complex emotional portraits of her characters.

Her father worked at court and played a seminal role in allowing Chughtai to pursue a freedom in thought and deed that was denied to most women of her time. In her autobiographical essay, "My Autobiography," she calls herself "Ismat the rebel," perhaps the best description of both her personality and her work. Her unflinching, interrogative look at social rules helped to pave the way for much of the Indian fiction that was written by women in the second half of the 20th century.

Chughtai constantly used the freedoms allowed to her brothers as the model for her own rights. When her parents decided that she would get married when she turned 13, she threatened to renounce Islam. Her father sent her to school, which she entered in fourth grade and received a double promotion immediately. She then left her home to continue her education in Lucknow and finally gained financial independence by becoming a headmistress of a school for girls.

All of Chughtai's work is written in Urdu. The quality and success of her poems changed the previously held conception that only men could write good Urdu poetry. After Munshi PREMCHAND, who is considered the father of the Urdu short story ("Afsara"), Chughtai is one of the most popular and prodigious writers of Urdu fiction. She wrote about the lives of the middle class, national politics, and gender at a time when such topics were not explored in popular fiction, especially by women writers. Her works confuse the private realm of a person's mind with the moral codes of the social world. The story *The Quilt* (1942) uses the context of a loveless marriage to question assumptions surrounding female sexuality. The quilt becomes a metaphor for all that is hidden behind the words society uses to construct meaning.

Chughtai's legacy is not limited to the book world. Her husband, a film producer, took her stories to directors and producers who adopted her work for cinema. Chughtai won several National Awards for her Hindi films. She wrote for 11 films and is one of the few female scriptwriters ever to have written for Hindi cinema.

Another Work by Ismat Chughtai

The Quilt and Other Stories. Translated by Tahira Naqvi. New York: Sheep Meadow Press, 1994.

Cixous, Hélène (1937–) *poet, nonfiction writer*

A feminist and theorist, Hélène Cixous was born in the French colony of Oran, Algeria, and grew up in a German-Jewish household. She received a degree in English from the Lycée Bugeaud in Algiers in 1959 and a doctorate in 1968. After graduation, Cixous held teaching posts at several French universities, including the University of Bordeaux, the Sorbonne, and Nanterre, before finally establishing herself at the University of Paris VIII–Vincennes. At the Sorbonne, Cixous participated in the 1968 student uprisings. Later, at Vincennes, she instituted several courses in experimental literature, particularly the significance to women of the relationship between psychoanalysis and language. She also established a center for women's studies at the University at Vincennes and cofounded the structuralist journal *Poétique.*

Cixous was greatly influenced by the progressive ideologies of such intellectuals as Heinrich von Kleist, Franz KAFKA, Arthur RIMBAUD, Clarice LISPECTOR, Jacques Derrida, Jaques Lacan, Sigmund FREUD, and Heidegger. In the 1970s, Cixous, along with other theorists, such as Kristeva, Barthes, and Derrida, began to explore the complex relationships that exist between sexuality and writing. From this study, she produced several influential feminist texts, including "Sortie" (1975) and "The Laugh of the Medusa" (1975).

Critical Analysis

The essay "Sortie" is of particular importance in that she uses it to establish a basic understanding of the hierarchy of opposites, such as in culture/nature; head/heart; colonizer/colonized; and speaking/writing. She then proceeds to link these opposites to the differences that exist between the male and the female genders in a discussion that calls for the abolition of such dichotomies as a means of empowering women.

"The Laugh of the Medusa" discusses feminine repression as a direct result of male-dominated cultural discourse. Cixous depicts this repression through the image of a dark, unexplored room that stands, metaphorically, for the largely unexplored area of female language and sexuality. It is Cixous's belief that women do not explore these areas of the self out of a deep-rooted fear that has been placed in them by a language deeply rooted in

male dominance. She goes on to theorize that women can shed light on this darkened existence simply by questioning their fears. Through this questioning, they will come to find that there is nothing about which to be frightened and that all of their preconceived fears were created by male images and standards that must be viewed as obstacles that can and must be overcome. Cixous also insists that the only way in which women can overcome the obstacles placed before them is to learn to speak with their bodies, using the body as a medium from which they can regain their inner voice. In the absence of a true feminine discourse, as language itself is historically the realm of the masculine, the language of the body takes on significance in its power to change and to reclaim.

In both "The Laugh of the Medusa" and "Coming to Writing" (1977), Cixous tackles many difficult ideas. She explains the idea of feminine discourse, a concept that eludes definition, by arguing convincingly that any attempt to define the term using the language of masculinity would destroy its inherent beauty; therefore, it must be left undefined. She relies heavily on Freudian concepts mingled with certain feminist ideas, such as a rereading of the Medusa myth as an analogy for female empowerment, rediscovered from Greek mythology. She also fervently expresses the idea that the only escape from masculine discourse is to understand and use the link between language and sexuality. Freedom of language results directly from freedom of sexuality. This freedom leads to what Cixous refers to as *jouissance,* a term that relates to a fulfillment of desire that fuses the erotic, the mystical, and the political in a way that goes beyond mere physical satisfaction. It is through this fulfillment, which can be found specifically in writing, that feminine discourse is discovered.

Since her emergence as a strong voice on the literary scene in the 1970s, Cixous has developed even greater complexity in her style and has become somewhat more mysterious in her thinking; however, her radical feminist ideology has softened somewhat as she seeks to explore the idea of collective identities. Cixous continues to lecture at the

University of Paris VIII–Vincennes, where she is active in women's studies. Her major contribution to world literature lies in her advancement of feminist ideas.

Other Works by Hélène Cixous

Cixous and Jacques Derrida. *Veils.* Translated by Geoffrey Bennington with drawings by Ernest Pignon-Ernest. Stanford: Stanford University Press, 2001.

The Third Body. Translated by Keith Cohen. Evanston, Ill.: Hydra Books/Northwestern University Press, 1999.

A Work about Hélène Cixous

Penrod, Lynn. *Hélène Cixous.* Boston: Twayne, 1996.

classicism

Classicism as a term is generally accepted as indicative of clarity in style, adhering to principles of elegance and symmetry, and created by attention and adherence to traditional forms. It has often been used synonymously with generic terms such as excellence or artistic quality. The term has its basis in the study, reverence for, and imitation of Greek and Roman literature, art, and architecture. Because the principles of classicism are deeply rooted in the history, rites, rituals, and practices of specific ancient cultures, the term also came to apply to specific cultural, literary, artistic, and academic canons.

The first full-scale revival of classicism occurred during the Renaissance when intensified interest in Greek and Roman culture, especially the literary works of Plato and Cicero, influenced a renewal of classical standards in literature. In the 18th and 19th centuries, following the archaeological discovery of the remains of Pompeii and Herculaneum, there was again a revival of interest first in the culture of Rome and later in the ideas of ancient Greece. This period, generally referred to as neoclassicism, was actually the start of the larger romantic movement (*see* ROMANTICISM). The revival was closely linked to the American and French Revolutions and draws parallels between ancient and modern forms of government.

In Central Europe, during the early part of the 20th century, there was again a spirit of revolution that coincided with a revival of interest in Greek literature. The classical models were somewhat reinvented. This was particularly apparent in the renewed interest in Greek literature and in a tendency among many Greek writers to look to the past—to history, myth, and folklore—as a means of understanding the present situation.

The Greek poet and Nobel laureate George SE-FERIS was particularly interested in awareness of the past and the ways in which history can be used to understand the present. His collection of poems, *Mythistorema* (1935; translated 1960) applied the Odyssean myths to modern situations and circumstances. Homer's *Odyssey* became the symbolic basis for many of his works.

Other poets and novelists, such as Tudor ARGHEZI and Nikos KAZANTSAKIS, based elements of their works on principles of classicism and turned their attention to myth as an allegory for modern times. Although his writing was modern in its sense of restlessness and was bold and innovative in its use of often crude, forceful language, Arghezi leaned toward the traditional elements of classicism in his tendency to rely on folklore and mythology. Kazantsakis's epic poem *Odyssey: A Modern Sequel* (1938) picks up Ulysses' tale where Homer leaves off and brings it to a more solid conclusion.

Although classicism cannot be said to have ever been abandoned completely during any period of literary history, its resurgence is cyclical and responsive to historical circumstances. As a result of the early 20th-century interest in revolution and change, similar to the spirit of Greek and Roman times as well as that of the Renaissance, classicism experienced a literary resurgence throughout 20th-century Central Europe.

Works about Classicism

Buxton, John. *The Grecian Taste: Literature in the Age of Neo-Classicism 1740–1820.* New York: Barnes & Noble, 1978.

Knox, Bernard. *Backing into the Future: The Classical Tradition and its Renewal.* New York: Norton, 1994.

Claudel, Paul (1868–1955) *poet, playwright, essayist*

A prominent figure in the early 20th-century French Catholic renaissance, Paul Claudel was born in Villeneuve-sur-Fère-en-Tardenois, in Aisne, France. He came from a family of farmers, Catholic priests, and landed gentry. A profound religious experience at the age of 18 changed not only his view of the world but also impacted his future as a writer. On Christmas day, during services at Notre Dame cathedral, he heard a distinct voice above him proclaim, "There is a God." He became a fervent Catholic and turned to the Bible as his source of inspiration.

As a poet, Claudel's most influential work is his *Five Great Odes* (1910). Claudel uses this poem in five parts to relate poetic inspiration as a gift from God, describing the mystery and wonder of the universe.

As a journalist and literary critic, Claudel also based his beliefs and impressions in his strong religious faith. He regularly attacked musician Richard Wagner, stating that, while he admired Wagner's music, he disliked what it expressed in Wagner's *Der Ring des Nibelungen.* He also wrote on the subject of French literature, particularly admiring BAUDELAIRE and RIMBAUD.

Claudel debuted as a playwright with *Tête d'or* (1889), a drama largely influenced by his own religious experiences. This work was followed by the trilogy of plays, *L'otage* (*The Hostage,* 1911), *Le Pain dur* (*Crusts,* 1918), and *Le Père humilié* (*The Humiliation of the Father,* 1920), which trace the degeneration the nobility. Another dramatic work, *Break at Noon* (1906), dealt with the theme of adultery and was based on an experience in Claudel's own life in which, for a four-year period in the early 1900s, he had engaged in a passionate affair with a married Polish woman. This episode caused him to contemplate the complexities inher-ent in the theme of forbidden love. One of Claudel's best-known dramas is *The Satin Slipper* (1924), about the epic adventures of Rodrique and the woman he loves.

On May 1, 1950, as a result of his contributions to literature in the form of religion, Claudel was honored by the pope. He died five years later in Paris on February 23.

Another Work by Paul Claudel

Claudel on the Theatre. Translated by Christine Trol-lope. Coral Gables, Fla.: University of Miami Press, 1972.

Works about Paul Claudel

Caranfa, Angelo. *Claudel: Beauty and Grace.* Lewisburg, Pa.: Bucknell University Press, 1989.
Knapp, Bettina L. *Paul Claudel.* New York: Ungar, 1982.

Cliff, Michelle (1946–) *novelist, poet, short-story writer, teacher, critic, editor*

Michelle Cliff was born in Kingston, Jamaica. As a young child, she moved to New York City with her family. After attending public schools and graduating from Wagner College in 1969 with a B.A. in European History, she worked for the New York publisher W. W. Norton from 1970 to 1971. Then she studied at the Warburg Institute in London, earning a master of philosophy degree in 1974. She returned to W. W. Norton as a copy editor and then as a manuscript and production editor. She resigned in 1979 to focus on writing, and in 1980, she published her first book, the prose poem *Claiming an Identity They Taught Me to Despise.*

Themes of race, gender, and power run through Cliff's internationally known poetry, novels, essays, articles, lectures, and workshops. In "Clare Savage as a Crossroads Character" (1990), Cliff acknowledges the autobiographical strands present in her prose poem and earliest novels, *Abeng* (1984) and *No Telephone to Heaven* (1987). *Abeng,* the African word for "conch shell," alludes to Caribbean, United States, and world history. The novel narrates how two runaway slaves, Nanny and Cuffee, lead raids to liberate other slaves. Both *Abeng* and its sequel, *No Telephone to Heaven*, were critically acclaimed for their dexterous linguistic shifts from Jamaican creole to standard English.

Critics name *Free Enterprise* (1993) her strongest novel. In it, female protagonists Annie Christmas and Ellen Pleasant work with freedom fighters to liberate slaves. To quote *Booklist,* "In tall tales and legends, cherished memories, and regrettable misunderstandings, *Free Enterprise* explores the multiple meanings of freedom and enterprise and of a society that enshrines selected meanings of both."

In *Writing in Limbo* Simon Gikandi claims, "The uniqueness of Cliff's aesthetics lies in her realization that the fragmentation, silence and repression that mark the life of the Caribbean subject under colonialism must be confronted not only as a problem to be overcome but also as a condition of possibility—as a license to dissimulate and to affirm difference—in which an identity is created out of the chaotic colonial and postcolonial history."

Other Works by Michelle Cliff

Bodies of Water. New York: Dutton, 1990.
The Land of Look Behind: Prose and Poetry. Ithaca, N.Y.: Firebrand Books, 1985.
The Store of a Million Items: Stories. Boston: Houghton Mifflin, 1998.

Works about Michelle Cliff

Berrian, Brenda F. "Claiming an Identity: Caribbean Women Writers in English." *Journal of Black Studies* 25 (December 1994): 200–16.
Edmonson, Belinda. "Race, Privilege, and the Politics of (Re)Writing History: An Analysis of the Novels of Michelle Cliff." *Callaloo* 16, no. 1 (1993): 180–91.
Gikandi, Simon. *Writing in Limbo: Modernism and Caribbean Literature.* Ithaca, N.Y.: Cornell University Press, 1992.

Schwartz, Meryl F. "An Interview with Michelle Cliff." *Contemporary Literature* 34, no. 4 (Winter 1993): 595–619.

Cocteau, Jean (1889–1963) *poet, novelist, dramatist*

Jean Cocteau was born in Maisons-Lafitte, France. His father, a lawyer and amateur painter, committed suicide when Cocteau was nine. This experience left him with an intense awareness of human frailty and an almost uncanny ability to identify with the world of the dead, as is seen in his earlier poetry such as *L'Ange Heurtebise* (1925).

A mediocre student who failed several attempts to pass the secondary-school graduation examination, poetry was Cocteau's first artistic outlet. He published his first volume of poems, *Aladdin's Lamp,* at the age of 19. Influenced by surrealism, psychoanalysis, cubism, and Catholicism, coupled with a frequent use of opium, Cocteau promoted the avant-garde in his works. He counted among his closest friends prominent artists such as Pablo Picasso, composer Erik Satie, and Russian stage director Sergey Diaghilev.

Cocteau met Pablo Picasso and Sergey Diaghilev in 1915. They challenged Cocteau to write a ballet, which is the collaborative work *Parade* (1917), produced by Diaghilev, with scenic design by Picasso and music by Erik Satie. Cocteau went on to firmly establish himself as a writer with the prose fantasy *Le Potomak* (1919) about a creature trapped in an aquarium.

Another close and influential friend was the poet and novelist Raymond Radiguet, whose death from typhoid fever caused Cocteau to experiment with opium. Under influence of the drug, he began to write psychological novels such as *Thomas the Impostor* (1923) and his masterpiece, *Les Enfants terribles* (*The Incorrigible Children,* 1929) about a group of children trapped in their own scary world.

In 1929, Cocteau was hospitalized for opium addiction, the experience of which he recounts in *Opium* (1930). On his release, he began to work on a series of films that often depicted mirrors as doors to alternate realities. He also befriended the young actor Jean Marais in 1937 and thereafter designed and wrote roles especially for him, producing such works as *Orphée* (*Orpheus*, 1950), a one-act tragedy about death's connection to inspiration, and *Le Testament d'Orphée* (*The Testament of Orpheus*, 1961), whose theme was death.

Branded a decadent during World War II, Cocteau continued to lead an active literary life. Always seeking to shock, he had a facelift and began to wear leather trousers and matador's capes in his declining years. He died on October 11, 1963.

Another Work by Jean Cocteau

Tempest of Stars: Selected Poems. Translated by Jeremy Reed. Chester Springs, Pa.: Dufour Editions, 1992.

Works about Jean Cocteau

Knapp, Bettina L. *Jean Cocteau.* Boston: Twayne, 1989.

Saul, Julie, ed. *Jean Cocteau: The Mirror and the Mask: A Photo-Biography.* Introduction by Francis Steegmuller. Boston: David Godine, 1992.

Coetzee, J(ohn) M. (1940–) *novelist and essayist*

John M. Coetzee was born to a middle-class family in South Africa. His parents were of African and German heritage, but he writes only in English. Like the narrator of his 1997 memoir, *Boyhood*, he spoke both Afrikaans and English fluently as a boy but was an outsider in both communities.

J. M. Coetzee studied undergraduate English in Cape Town but found old, canonized British literature dull. He turned to mathematics for comfort and worked for IBM as a computer systems designer in England in the early 1960s. He returned to literature, however, and came to the United States to study at the University of Texas at Austin, where he received his doctorate in literature in 1969. Coetzee's graduating thesis studied the work of Irish playwright Samuel BECKETT, a major influence on his own writing. Also while at the university, he started historical research into the life of explorer and ancestor Jacobus Coetzee, the results of which became his first novel, *Dusklands* (1974).

Critical Analysis

Dusklands simultaneously tells the stories of two main characters, an American bureaucrat in 1970s war-torn Vietnam and an Afrikaner explorer moving into 18th-century South Africa. The book compares America's involvement in Vietnam with the Dutch colonization of South Africa. Coetzee, in essence, explores the imperialist mentality of believing one's own culture superior to others.

In his next novel, *In the Heart of the Country* (1976), Coetzee uses a woman's point of view to tell the story of Magda, who cannot recover from the tragedy of her father's death and her own rape. The book ends with Magda in a state of hysterical loneliness. In his 1980 book, *Waiting for the Barbarians,* Coetzee turns the colonial experience into allegory, telling the story of an imaginary country being overrun by barbarians.

Coetzee received worldwide recognition with *The Life and Times of Michael K.,* which won England's Booker Prize in 1983. The story introduces another important subject matter of Coetzee's works: the relationship between parents and their children. The narrator, Michael K., escapes from the civil strife and violence of apartheid Cape Town to his mother's farm. He is a simple-minded gardener who lives with his dying mother until their farm is destroyed in the ongoing civil war. Michael and his mother are innocent victims of their political surroundings, but Michael has a simple attitude: He says, "one can live."

Coetzee wrote three more works of fiction in the late 1980s and early 1990s before taking home the Booker Prize again for his 1999 *Disgrace*. In two of these, *Foe* (1986) and *The Master of Petersburg* (1994), he responds to and rewrites great works of European literature. *Foe* is the story of an unnamed woman who tells the story of *Robinson Crusoe* to author Daniel Defoe. This woman, like the colonized people of South Africa, loses her voice in the great machine of colonial history and is unrecognized and forgotten.

Russian author Fyodor DOSTOYEVSKY is the hero of *The Master of Petersburg,* a fictional account of Dostoyevsky tracing the steps of his recently dead stepson, Pavel, around the city of St. Petersburg. The novel is Coetzee's most postmodern work in that it explores the act of writing and the power of language. The character of Dostoyevsky does not use writing's power to help the Russian revolutionaries, however, but to understand and come closer to his dead stepson.

Coetzee's novel *Disgrace* is similar to *The Life and Times of Michael K,* in that its main character, David Lurie, like Michael K., suffers greatly to achieve a small amount of clarity and redemption. David Lurie loses his job as a professor, becomes a caretaker for dying animals, is refused by prostitutes, and considers castrating himself.

Disgrace is Coetzee's first book to deal with postapartheid South Africa directly. Political change does little to improve the lives of the individuals in the novel. Andrew O'Hehir writes that in Coetzee's novels "political and historical forces blow through the lives of individuals like nasty weather systems" (www.salon.com). Again and again, Coetzee presents characters who are tossed about violently but who, in every novel, pick up and move on.

The major influences on his work are Franz KAFKA and Samuel BECKETT. Like Kafka and Beckett's characters, the people in Coetzee's books have a troubled existence in which suffering seems to be the defining characteristic of life.

Coetzee's books have been translated into more than 20 languages. Coetzee has held visiting professorships across the United States, including Harvard, the University of Chicago, and Johns Hopkins University. Besides fiction, he has written many books of essays, including *White Writing: On the Culture of Letters in South Africa* (1988) and *The Lives of Animals* (1999).

J. M. Coetzee's work eloquently deals with South Africa's political history; the nature of writing, language, and power; and how human relationships are divided by the gap between the powered and the powerless.

Other Works by J. M. Coetzee

Giving Offence: Essays on Censorship. Chicago: University of Chicago Press, 1996.

A Land Apart: A Contemporary South African Reader. New York: Viking, 1987.

Works about J. M. Coetzee

Atwell, David. *J. M. Coetzee: South Africa and the Politics of Writing.* Berkeley: University of California Press, 1993.

O'Hehir, Andrew. "'Disgrace' by J. M. Coetzee." *Salon Books* 5, November 1999. www.salon.com/books/review/1999/11/05/coetzee

Viola, Andre. "An Interview with J. M. Coetzee." *Commonwealth Essays and Studies* 14, no. 2 (Spring 1992): 6–7.

Colette (Sidonie-Gabrielle Colette)
(1873–1954) *novelist*

Considered one of the leading French novelists of the 20th century, Colette was born in the village of Saint-Saveur-en-Puisaye, Burgundy. She was the daughter of a retired army captain, Jules-Joseph Colette, who had lost a leg in the Italian campaign, and the highly unconventional Adèle Eugénie Sidonie Landoy, known as "Sidonie" or "Sido." Her mother's down-to-earth personality, devotion to animals, reading, and gardening greatly influenced Colette.

Colette's career as a novelist began when she was in her early 20s and continued into her mid-70s, during which time she wrote more than 50 books, numerous short stories, and articles for major newspapers and magazines. Always in some way autobiographical in nature, her works blur the boundaries between reality and fiction in an attempt to explore love and female sexuality in a masculine world.

Colette was first encouraged to write by her first husband, writer and music critic Henri Gauthier-Villars. According to some sources, he locked her in her room and would not let her leave until she had completed a requisite number of pages. Regardless of how she started, however, Colette published four of what came to be known as her *Claudine* novels in rapid succession between 1900 and 1903, using her husband's pen name Willy. The novels, all recounting the often prurient adventures of a teenage girl, became so successful that they inspired other products, including a musical adaptation, costumes, soap, cigars, and perfume.

Becoming disillusioned by her husband's repeated adultery, Colette separated from him in 1905 and was divorced in 1906. She went to work as a music-hall performer, doing such memorable things as baring her breasts and simulating sex on stage, an act that resulted in a riot at the Moulin Rouge.

During this period, Colette found a protector, a woman known as "Missy," the niece of Napoleon III, and who was instrumental in establishing Colette's image as a writer, an actress, and a lesbian. "Missy" committed suicide in 1944. Colette was later known, at various points in her life, to have become friends and, most likely, lovers with noted American lesbian Natalie Clifford Barney and Italian author Gabriele D'ANNUNZIO. Such an independent and gregarious lifestyle eventually filtered into Colette's writing. She remained devoted to her independence, however, and published *La Vagabonde* (1910), a story about an actress who decides to reject the man she loves to protect her ability to live her life as she pleases.

In 1912, Colette married newspaper editor Henri de Jouvenel des Ursins. She wrote theater articles and short stories for his paper and bore him one child, Colette de Jouvenel. Colette had not wanted children and, consequently, neglected her daughter. She also began a questionable relationship with her stepson, Bertrand de Jouvenel, which resulted in much gossip. She depicts this affair in her novel *Chéri* (1920), as told from the point of view of a sexually naive young man.

Critical Analysis

Colette's works are generally divided into four phases. Her early works are the Claudine novels, followed by a time when she wrote predominantly about life in the theater, followed by works about the politics of love, and ultimately followed by her more mature works depicting reminiscences of youth and family. Her fame began to expand in the 1920s, and by 1927 she was often referred to as France's leading female writer. Her mature works, written during this time, depict a peaceful world and the delicate nature of the mother–daughter bond. *La Maison de Claudine* (*My Mother's House*, 1922), *La Naissance du jour* (*A Lesson in Love*, 1928) and *Sido* (1929) all celebrate her carefree rural childhood and her mother's strength and vitality. This period marks a distinction from the darker world depicted in her earlier works. Her use of the character/narrator "Colette" in works such as *L'Étoile vesper* (1946) and *Le Fanal bleu* (1949) further blurred her distinctions between fiction and reality.

Colette received many awards throughout her lifetime. She was the first woman to be granted admission to the prestigious Goncourt Academy, and in 1953, she was elected a grand officer of the Legion of Honour. A crippling form of arthritis haunted the last 20 years of her life; however, she still managed to publish *Gigi* (1945) at the age of 72. The novel was later made into a film in 1948 and into a musical in 1958, directed by Vincente Minnelli.

Colette died on August 3 in Paris. Because of her popularity, she was granted a state funeral that was attended by thousands of her admirers but was denied Catholic rites because she had been divorced.

Another Work by Colette
Break of Day. New York: Ballantine Books, 1983.

A Work about Colette
Thurman, Judith. *Secrets of the Flesh: A Life of Colette.* New York: Knopf, 1999.

Collymore, Frank (Colly) (1893–1980)
poet, short-story writer, teacher, lexicographer, editor

Frank Collymore was born in St. Michael, Barbados, to Joseph Appleton Collymore, a government customs officer, and Rebecca Wilhelmina, née Clark. Collymore attended Combermere School, a grammar school for boys, from 1903 to 1910 and taught at the same school from 1910 until 1963. George LAMMING, the West Indian novelist, poet, and critic, was one of his many students.

Collymore did not publish his first book of poetry, *Thirty Poems,* until 1944. Poems in this and other collections both humorously and seriously examine a variety of topics—landscape, love, war, conformity, and history. After the productive poetry years of the 1940s when he published three books containing 103 poems, Collymore shifted his attention to writing short stories. Eighteen of his short stories appeared in *Bim,* a magazine started by the Young Men's Progressive Club of Barbados. Many of these stories have a dark, even morbid edge, and the mind appears as a recurring theme. In his story *Shadows,* published in *Bim* in December 1942, for example, the narrator asks:

> "The mind. What do you and I know of the mind, and of the vast forces which lie around us, in us and yet not wholly of us, secret, prowling, mysterious, fraught with such power as is beyond our knowledge, watching and waiting to encompass us, to overthrow what we call the seat of the reason—the mind whose powers and weaknesses we can never hope to comprehend?"

Working with the editing and publishing of *Bim* from 1942 to 1975 enabled Collymore to influence the production and consumption of West Indian literature significantly, as explained by Lamming in a special introduction to the June 1955 issue:

> "There are not many West Indian writers today who did not use *Bim* as a kind of platform, the surest, if not the only avenue, by which they might reach a literate and sensitive reading public, and almost all of the West Indians who are now writers in a more professional sense and whose work has compelled the attention of readers and writers in other countries, were introduced, so to speak, by *Bim.*"

Collymore also used other avenues to introduce readers to West Indian writers; he introduced a 19-year-old Derek WALCOTT as a true poet in *Savacou* (1949). In a 1986 essay in *Fifty Caribbean Writers,* Edward Baugh asserts, "Collymore earned his reputation as a doyen and godfather of West Indian Literature." In a 1971 essay in *West Indian Poetry 1900–1970,* Baugh goes on to say that Collymore's poetry marked "something of an advance in West Indian poetry," his influences having been "more twentieth-century than those of his coevals [contemporaries]."

Other Works by Frank Collymore
The Man Who Loved Attending Funerals and Other Stories. Edited by Harold Barratt and Reinhard Sander. Portsmouth, N.H.: Heinemann, 1993.
Rhymed Ruminations of the Fauna of Barbados. Bridgetown, Barbados: Advocate, 1968.
Selected Poems. Bridgetown, Barbados: Coles Printery, 1971.

Works about Frank Collymore
Baugh, Edward. "Frank Collymore: A Biographical Portrait." *Savacou: A Journal of the Caribbean Artists Movement* 7–8 (1973): 139–48.
Sander, Reinhard W., Esmond D. Ramesar, and Edward Baugh. *An Index to Bim 1942–1972.* St. Augustine, Trinidad: University of West Indies Extra-Mural Studies Unit, 1973.

Condé, Maryse (1934–　) *novelist, playwright, essayist, critic, professor*

Maryse Condé was born in Pointe-à-Pitre, Guadeloupe. A bright student with a penchant for reading, Condé attended school in Guadeloupe before continuing her education in France. Studying black stereotypes in Caribbean literature, she earned a doctorate in comparative literature in 1975 from the Université de Paris III (Sorbonne Nouvelle).

Condé taught French in multiple countries, including Guinea, Accra, and Sénégal, from 1960 to 1968. After working as a program producer for the French Services of the BBC from 1968 to 1970, she became an editor at the Paris publishing house Présence Africaine and, in 1973, began to teach Francophone literature at Paris VII (Jussieu), X (Nanterre), and III (Sorbonne Nouvelle).

While teaching, Condé also wrote. She published numerous novels after the release of her first, *Hérémakhonon* (*Welcome Home*) in 1976. In *Hérémakhonon*, Veronica, a young Guadeloupian woman who was educated in Paris, goes to West Africa to examine her history. Although multiple similarities exist between Veronica's and Condé's life experiences, Condé denies that Veronica is an autobiographical character. Like the first novel, *Une Saison à Rihata* (*A Season in Rihata*, 1981) follows a Guadeloupian female protagonist to a fictional West African country repressed by postcolonial regimes. Both novels use multiple points of view to reconstruct history.

Ségou (*Segu*, 1984, 1985), Condé's third novel and written in two volumes, positioned her as a premier contemporary Caribbean writer. Set in the African kingdom of Segu between 1797 and 1860, the novel follows four sons of a royal family to Brazil and the Caribbean while addressing religion, slavery, corruption, incest, and rape. Some criticized the novel as soap-operaesque, but in *The New York Times Book Review,* May 31, 1987, Charles Larson called *Ségou* "the most significant historical novel about black Africa published in many a year." It weaves relatively unknown fragments of African history with compelling personal narratives.

Between *Hérémakhonon* and *Ségou,* Condé published numerous theoretical essays on Antillean culture and literature, but afterward she focused on creative writing. The focus of her fiction also shifted from Africa to the African diaspora after *Ségou. Moi, Tituba, sorcière noire de Salem* (*I, Tituba, Black Witch of Salem,* 1986) uses first-person narrative to tell the story of an obscure historical figure, Tituba—a black slave from Barbados arrested for witchcraft in the United States during the 17th century. Subsequent works, such as *La Vie scélérate* (*The Tree of Life,* 1987) and *Les Derniers Rois Mages* (*The Last Magi,* 1992) continue to explore themes of exile, psychological dislocation, race, class, gender, and history. An indication of Condé's widespread acclaim, her novels have been translated into English, German, Dutch, Italian, Spanish, Portuguese, and Japanese.

In 1990, Condé took a position at the University of California, Berkeley. Since then, she has worked at the University of Virginia, the University of Maryland, and Harvard. Condé, at the University of Columbia since 1995, now chairs the new Center for French and francophone studies. Her multifaceted writing techniques and narrative strategies, as well as her work's political and cultural themes, make her one of the most important Caribbean francophone writers.

Other Works by Maryse Condé

Crossing the Mangrove. Translated by Richard Philcox. New York: Anchor Books, 1995.

Land of Many Colors & Nanna-ya. Translated by Nicole Ball. Lincoln: University of Nebraska Press, 1999.

Tales from the Heart: True Stories from My Childhood. Translated by Richard Philcox. New York: Soho, 2001.

Works about Maryse Condé

Apter, Emily S. "Crossover Texts/Creole Tongues: A Conversation with Maryse Condé." *Public Culture* 13, no. 1 (Winter 2001): 89–96.

Arowolo, Bukoye. "The Black Caribbean Woman's Search for Identity in Maryse Condé's Novels." In *Feminism and Black Women's Creative Writing: Theory, Practice, and Criticism.* Edited by Aduke Adebayo. Ibadan, Nigeria: AMD, 1996.

Suk, Jeannie. *Postcolonial Paradoxes in French Caribbean Writing: Césaire, Glissant, Condé.* Oxford: Clarendon, 2001.

Constant de Rebecque, Benjamin
(1767–1830) *nonfiction writer, novelist*

Henri-Benjamin Constant de Rebecque was born on October 25 in Lausanne, Switzerland. His mother died from complications in childbirth one week after Constant was born. Tutored as a young child, he read daily for eight to 10 hours. He was sent at a young age to the University of Erlangen in Bavaria, where he learned German, one of three languages in which he was proficient by the time he was 18. He later transferred to the University of Edinburgh where he studied under distinguished proponents of freedom, including Adam Smith, Adam Ferguson, and Dugald Stewart. He subsequently moved to Paris to study with the intellectual Jean-Baptiste-Antoine Suard. While there, he became close friends with the great Lafayette, among other influential thinkers.

In 1794, he met Germaine de STAËL, whose influence piqued his interest in politics. He began to publish political pamphlets and was appointed a member of the Tribunal under Napoleon. But Constant was critical of Napoleon's policies, especially his project to make himself consul for life (and later emperor), and when in 1802 Napoleon banished de Staël, Constant accompanied her in her exile from France.

Constant's works of political theory include *De l'esprit de conquête et de l'usurpation* (*On the Spirit of Conquest and Usurpation*, 1814) and *Principes de politique* (*Political Principles*, 1816). One of his principles was the importance of protecting individual liberty against both government and the encroachments of the majority. He also wrote a five-volume treatise, *De la religion* (*On Religion*, 1824–31). Unlike many French thinkers of his time, he believed that religion was a positive force in society and a necessary balance to the power of government.

In 1816, a short novel Constant had written 10 years previously, *Adolphe,* was published. With great economy of style, the work tells the story of a young man's involvement with an older woman and his painful efforts to disentangle himself from the affair. It is presumed that the story has autobi-ographical elements, though whether the unfortunate Elleanore is based on Madame de Staël or on one of the other women in Constant's life has not been established. Ironically, Constant is better remembered for *Adolphe,* a work to which he attached no great value but which is seen as an important forerunner of the psychological novel than for his immense work on religion, which occupied decades of his life.

Constant produced dozens of works that defied laws limiting freedom of speech and freedom of the press. He campaigned against the African slave trade and fought for civil liberties alongside Lafayette. Constant's health began to decline rapidly in 1830, and he died on December 8. At his funeral service, people lined the streets to wave the tricolor flags of the Liberal Party in his honor.

Other Works by Benjamin Constant
Adolphe. Translated by Margaret Mauldon. New York: Oxford University Press, 2001.
Political Writings. Translated by Biancamaria Fontana. New York: Cambridge University Press, 1988.

Works about Benjamin Constant
Holmes, Stephen. *Benjamin Constant and the Making of Modern Liberalism.* New Haven, Conn.: Yale University Press, 1984.
Todorov, Tszvetan. *A Passion for Democracy: Benjamin Constant.* New York: Algora, 1998.
Wood, Dennis. *Benjamin Constant: A Biography.* New York: Routledge, 1993.

Cortázar, Julio (1914–1984) *novelist, short-story writer, translator*

Julio Cortázar was born in Brussels, Belgium, to Argentinean parents. He moved to Argentina with his family after World War I when he was four years old, having learned by then to speak French as well as Spanish. Not long after returning to Argentina, his father abandoned his family, leaving Cortázar to be raised by his mother. As a student, Cortázar was interested in literature, attending the

Teacher's College in Buenos Aires from which he received a degree in literature in 1935. His earliest jobs were as a secondary school teacher in various towns in Argentina.

In 1945, Cortázar left teaching to become a translator of both English and French writers for various publishing houses in Argentina, but by 1951 he was so much against the Perón regime in Argentina that he turned down the opportunity to have a chair at the University of Buenos Aires and instead went to live in France, where he remained until his death. While in France, he also worked as a translator for UNESCO, dividing each year so that he would translate for six months and write fiction and play jazz trumpet the remaining six months. He lived part of the time in Paris and the rest at his home in the Provençal village of Saignon in the south of France. Cortázar was committed to the revolutionary political movements in Latin America, as witnessed by his visit to Cuba in 1961, his support of the United Chilean Front, and his visit to Nicaragua in 1983.

By his own admission, Cortázar was influenced by SYMBOLIST and surrealist writers such as Comte de LAUTREAMONT, Arthur RIMBAUD, Stéphane MALLARMÉ, Alfred JARRY, Jean COCTEAU, and Jorge Luis BORGES. He was also influenced by Edgar Allen Poe, John Keats, and Virginia Woolf. Both his fiction and interviews with him reveal his belief that reality is actually a collage of the rational and the irrational, the linear and the nonlinear, fantasy and what we generally tend to consider "real," all existing on different planes at the same time. In his humorous and satirical book *Cronopios and Famas* (1962), for example, Cortázar divides the world between *cronopios,* imaginary creatures who represent the magical in life, and *famas,* those who represent conventional reality. In addition, his novel *The Winners* (1960) is composed of various disparate characters who, after winning a lottery, find themselves together on a holiday cruise, their prize. This external voyage becomes a metaphor for the internal, metaphysical confrontation that each character has with himself or herself.

Of all that Cortázar has written, however, he is best known for being the author of the short story "Blow-Up" (which inspired Michelangelo Antonioni's famous film of the same name) and of the novel *Hopscotch,* which first appeared in 1963. A novel that works on a number of levels, *Hopscotch* consists of a series of numbered chapters that can be read "in normal fashion" or in an entirely different sequence, which Cortázar provides, informing the reader, "In its own way, this book consists of many books, but two books above all." Like a labyrinth or the actual game of hopscotch, the reader who follows the nonlinear "sequence" jumps around while trying to keep his or her balance as the characters search for heaven or hell or the center of the labyrinth. Considered to be one of the major novels written by a Latin American in the 20th-century, *Hopscotch* has been called an "antinovel" in its methods of breaking with traditional form and content while maintaining a comical sense of the absurd.

Julio Cortázar is now considered one of the most important 20th-century Latin American writers, known for his experimentalism and MAGIC REALISM. His short stories and novels, written with wit and a startling sense of fantasy, portray complex characters faced with metaphysical anguish.

Other Works by Julio Cortázar

62: A Model Kit. Translated by Gregory Rabassa. New York: New Directions, 2000.

Blow Up and Other Stories. Translated by Paul Blackburn. New York: Pantheon, 1985.

Final Exam. Translated by Alfred J. MacAdam. New York: New Directions, 2000.

Works about Julio Cortázar

Moran, Dominic. *Questions of the Liminal in the Fiction of Julio Cortázar.* Oxford: European Humanities Research Centre, 2001.

Standish, Peter. *Understanding Julio Cortázar.* Columbia, S.C.: University of South Carolina Press, 2001.

Stavans, Ilan. *Julio Cortázar: A Study of the Short Fiction.* New York: Twayne, 1996.

Costumbrismo

Costumbrismo was a main feature of Spanish romanticism. It was, in the most general of terms, the practice of creating literary sketches that captured realistic details about local life and customs. The word *costumbrismo* comes from the Spanish *costumbres,* which means "customs."

Although this practice was a feature in all of Europe's romantic traditions, such as French ROMANTICISM and German Romanticism, it was so pronounced and so central to the Spanish romantics that it deserves notice.

Romanticism in Spain in the late 18th and early 19th centuries was a reaction to the previous century's domination by the aesthetic ideas of the Enlightenment. The Enlightenment proposed that there were universal standards for beauty and harmony and that the arts should always follow neoclassical models. Spanish Costumbrismo is a reaction against this sort of subtle cultural imperialism. By concentrating on the aesthetic value of the extremely local and idiosyncratic elements of Spanish culture, the writers of the Spanish romantic movement, for example Gustavo Alfonso BÉCQUER, were rebelling against the tyranny of the ideal in favor of their own experiences.

Other romantic writers used Costumbrismo for other purposes. For example, the author Mariano José de Larra (1809–37) used Costumbrismo as a mode to satirize peculiar Spanish customs and point out the absurdity and barbarity of his contemporaries.

Costumbrismo used slang and local dialects to such a degree that a literary portrait written in Seville was unlikely to be understood by a citizen of Barcelona.

In Enlightenment thought, the individual is always subservient to a norm that may be discovered empirically. The consequence of this line of thinking is that the individual artist is discouraged from expressing idiosyncratic points of view in favor of attempting to express values and ideas that are universally applicable to all humanity. Costumbrismo challenges these ideas by focusing on art's relationship to the specific and immediate environment in which it is made. As a result many works of Costumbrismo are not portable to other times and are not easily translated or understood. On the other hand, Costumbrismo has a nuance and a level of vivid, sensuous detail that is often lacking in the didactic works of Enlightenment literature, which are mostly philosophical treatises.

Costumbrismo reintroduced the more personal dramas of everyday life into Spanish literature. In addition, the roots of the 19th-century novel and even of MODERNISM may be seen in Costumbrismo.

A Work about Costumbrismo

Tully, Carol Lisa. *Creating a National Identity: A Comparative Study of German and Spanish Romanticism.* Stuttgart, Germany: H. D. Heinz, 1997.

Coverley, Mrs. Eric

See BENNETT, LOUISE.

Crayencour, Marguerite de

See YOURCENAR, MARGUERITE.

Cronin, Jeremy (1949–) *poet and essayist*

Jeremy Cronin was born in Durban, South Africa, and studied at the University of Cape Town and the Sorbornne. He was arrested under the 1976 Terrorism Act for participating in underground work for the banned African National Congress in 1976 and spent seven years in a maximum-security prison, three of those years among inmates on death row. While he served his sentence, his wife unexpectedly died. He was released in 1983, the same year that his first collection of poems, *Inside,* was released.

Inside was translated into many languages and won the 1984 Ingrid Jonker Prize. The collection chronicles the relationship between the public life of political struggle and the private life and feelings that accompany this struggle.

Cronin spent three years in exile from South Africa, returning in 1990. His poetry has appeared in many magazines and anthologies, and his collection *Even The Dead* received much critical acclaim after its publication in 1997. The collection is a marked departure from his earlier work and attempts to defy the "amnesia" that prevents people from remembering South Africa's past. Cronin says of his eponymous poem, "Even The Dead," "I am not sure what poetry is. I am not sure what the aesthetic is. Perhaps the aesthetic should be defined in opposition to the anesthetic. . . . Art is the struggle to stay awake" (De Kock). Cronin's pieces determinedly fight the urge to forget the past—he uses the past to forge the trail to the future. His most recent work, *Inside and Out* (1999) a compilation of poems from his previously published volumes, revisits these themes.

Cronin has served as deputy general secretary of the South African Communist Party and lives in Johannesburg. His reinvention of poetic form and style shows the changing landscape of South Africa both physically and politically.

Works Edited by Jeremy Cronin

The Ideologies of Politics. With Anthony de Crespigny. New York: Oxford University Press, 1975.

Thirty Years of the Freedom Charter. With Raymond Suttner. Athens: Ohio University Press, 1987.

Works about Jeremy Cronin

De Kock, Leon. "A Different Cronin." *Electronic Mail and Guardian Review of Books.* August 1997.

Gardner, Susan. *Four South African Poets: Robert Berold, Jeremy Cronin, Douglas Reid Skinner, and Stephen Watson—Interviews.* Grahamstown, South Africa: National English Literary Museum, 1986.

Curnow, Allen (1911–2001) *poet, dramatist, editor*

Allen Curnow was born in Timaru, New Zealand. Although his mother was born in England, on his father's side he was a fifth-generation New Zealander. After studying at Christchurch BHS and the universities of Canterbury and Auckland, Curnow made the decision not to be ordained as an Anglican clergyman, as his father was. Instead, he began his career as a journalist and, between 1951 and 1976, taught English at Auckland University. Curnow edited the first collections of New Zealand poetry, *A Book of New Zealand Verse: 1923–45* (1945, 1951) and *The Penguin Book of New Zealand Verse* (1960).

A MODERNIST poet, Curnow was a friend of the British-American poet W. H. Auden, for whom he named his son Wystan (Auden's first name). For a short period of time, while overseas in 1949, he stayed with the Welsh poet, Dylan Thomas, with whom he became friends. Curnow's early poetry focuses on social and physical aspects of New Zealand, its landscape, and its place in the larger world, but by the time World War II broke out, Curnow was more concerned with personal as well as universal themes, as reflected in *At Dead Low Water and Sonnets* (1949).

Throughout the 1950s and 1960s, Curnow was considered one of New Zealand's most important poets. His reputation only increased with the 1972 publication of *Trees, Effigies, Moving Objects,* a highly acclaimed sequence of 18 poems. The style of his writing was becoming more open and contemporary as he began to focus on the wild landscape of Lone Kauri Road and Karekare Beach on Auckland's west coast, where he had been spending vacations.

During his long career, Curnow was awarded the New Zealand Book Award for Poetry six times, the Commonwealth Poetry Prize (1988), the Queen's Gold Medal for Poetry (1989), a Cholmondeley Award (1992), the A. W. Reed Lifetime Achievement Award of the Montana New Zealand Books Awards (2000), and the 2001 Montana New Zealand Award for his last book of poems, *The Bells of Saint Babel's.*

Works about Allen Curnow

Stead, C. K. *Kin of Place: Essays on New Zealand Writers.* Auckland: Auckland University Press, 2002.

Wieland, James. *Ensphering Mind: A Comparative Study of Derek Walcott, Christopher Okigbo, A. D. Hope, Allen Curnow, A. M. Klein and Nissim Ezekiel.* Pueblo, Colo.: Passeggiata Press, 1988.

Czaczkes, Shmuel Yosef

See AGNON, SAMUEL JOSEF.

Dada (1916–1920)

Dada or dadaism, taken from the French word for hobby-horse, was a nihilistic movement in the arts that spread primarily throughout France, Switzerland, and Germany, and the United States between 1916 and 1920. It was founded on principles of anarchy, intentional irrationality, cynicism, and the rejection of social organization.

The origin of the name, like the movement itself, lacks any formal logic. The most widely accepted theory is that, at a meeting in 1916 at the Café Voltaire in Zurich, a group of young artists and war resisters inserted a letter opener into a French–German dictionary. The letter opener pointed to the word *dada.*

The basis of the movement was more substantive than the origin of its name. It was founded as a protest against bourgeois values and as a direct result of mounting sentiments of despair about World War I. One of the chief ambitions of the movement was to discover authentic reality by abolishing traditional culture and values. Comprised of painters, writers, dancers, and musicians, the dadaists were often involved in several art forms simultaneously and sought to break down the boundaries that kept individual art forms distinct. The dadaists did not only want to create art; they wanted to promote revolutionary changes.

They were not interested in public admiration but sought to provoke the public into action. To the dadaists, a violently negative reaction was better than a passive acceptance.

Although as a movement dadaism concerned all forms of the arts, including visual and performance modes, in France it was predominately literary in emphasis, taking the lead from one of its founders, the poet Tristan TZARA. The most noted French publication was the journal *Littérature,* which was published from 1919 to 1924 and contained works by André BRETON, Louis ARAGON, Philippe Soupault (1897–?), and Paul ÉLUARD.

The dada movement began to decline in 1922 as many of its proponents began to develop an interest in surrealism.

Works about Dada

Erickson, John D. *Dada: Performance, Poetry and Art.* Boston: Twayne, 1984.

Matthews, J. H. *Theatre in Dada and Surrealism.* Syracuse: Syracuse University Press, 1974.

Dağlarca, Fazil Hüsnü (1914–) *poet*

Fazil Hüsnü Dağlarca was born in Istanbul, Turkey, shortly after the start of World War I. He was the fifth child of an army officer, completed his higher education at a military college, and received his own commission as second lieutenant in 1935.

Although Dağlarca received a military education and was an army officer from 1935 to 1950, he showed an aptitude for writing at an early age, publishing his first poems while he was still in middle school. His first complete book of poetry was published in 1935, but he had been publishing poetry in various literary magazines since 1933. He first gained public attention in 1933 for his poem *Slowing Life,* but it was his book *Child of God* (1940) that actually provided the basis of the questions about the universe and God that the bulk of his poetry would attempt to answer. The book's major theme is humanity's amazement at the universe, expressed through the psychological viewpoint of a child who constantly asks questions and searches for answers, while at the same time both admiring and fearing the world itself. God and the nature of God are recurring themes in much of Dağlarca's work.

Dağlarca's military career also provided useful ideas on which he would ultimately focus his poetry. Toward the end of his time as an officer, Dağlarca began to use his writing in an attempt to answer diverse questions on the relationship of humanity to nature in poems such as *The Stone Age* (1945) and *Mother Earth.* Other areas of interest included humanity's relationship to one's own history (in *The War of Independence* [1951], *The Conquest of Istanbul* [1953], and *The Epic of Gallipoli* [1963]) and people's struggles with other people (in *The Agony of the West* [1951], *Song of Algeria* [1961] and *Our Vietnam War* [1966]). Dağlarca's poetry is highly patriotic and firmly entrenched in the ideals of Turkish nationalism.

Dağlarca is one of the Turkey's most prolific and most frequently translated poets. Throughout his career, Dağlarca successfully has tried virtually every form of poetry, including lyric, epic, and inspirational verse; he has also written satire and social criticism. His early poems, in particular, were focused on inspiration and are exemplified by visions of a soul at peace, ready to embrace God. Because Dağlarca watched and lived during a time of conflict, love of God and of the universe were ultimately replaced in his works by a deeper concern for the tragedy of humanity as a whole and a love for all of mankind. His epic poems fall under this category, celebrating the heroic spirit of his nation. Dağlarca's *Epic of the Three Martyrs* (1949) exemplifies and glorifies the Turkish people's struggles.

Dağlarca's style, particularly in his inspirational works, is influenced by a form of Turkish folk poetry known as divan, which has its basis in mysticism and elements of both Islam and Sufism. Folk poets concentrated primarily on native forms and vernacular in much the same manner as the oral literary tradition of the early minstrels. In conjunction with this, early in the 20th century, a nationalist movement sought to create a "Turkish" literature free of borrowed words. This combination of military precision, nationalist sentiment, and mystical allusion is a driving force behind Dağlarca's popularity.

After resigning from the military in 1950, Dağlarca began to concentrate solely on literature and its impact on Turkish culture. Particularly since the Turkish Revolution of 1960, he became increasingly disillusioned by humankind and the failure of intellectuals to contribute adequately to social change. Starting with the publication of *Mother Earth* (1950), his works focus on civic responsibility. Along with a friend, he opened a bookstore in Istanbul that he managed until 1970. On the storefront window glass, he displayed a variety of poems dedicated to current events and social change. Printed in large letters, these poems attracted much attention. When one of his poems of social protest, *Horoz* (1965), prompted legal action against him, Dağlarca responded to his persecutors in yet another poem, *Savci'ya* (1965), which is translated as *To the Public Prosecutor,* thus proving that the literary form can be as viable a weapon as military force.

Another Work by Fazil Hüsnü Dağlarca

Seçme Siirler. Selected Poems. Translated by Talât Sait Halman. Pittsburgh, Pa.: University of Pittsburgh Press, 1969.

dalit literature

The term *dalit* literally means "oppressed" and is used to refer to the "untouchable," casteless sects of India. Dalit literature, therefore, is not only about but also written by the educated of this social group. Unlike literature that is defined by its affiliation to a particular style or structure, such as MODERNISM or DADA, dalit fiction and its literary movement is based on the common ground of social oppression. This movement puts all importance on the lived experience of the writer. Only those who have undergone the trials of being socially ostracized can be said to write dalit literature of any political or moral relevance. Predictably, such a framework allowed newfound opportunities among women to voice their rebellion against gender oppression.

Dalit writers belong to a historical, social, and political background that spreads throughout India from Gujarat, Tamil Nadu, Maharashtra, and Andhra Pradesh to Punjab. It could be said that dalit literature achieved a firm foundation in the mid-20th century, but its framework was established in the early 19th century. Today, dalit writers have their own literary foundations and publish numerous journals. They also have a number of political organizations. The most prominent of these is the Dalit Panthers (begun in the 1970s), which has borrowed much of its ideology from America's Black Panthers.

The form or style of dalit literature covers a wide range of literary genres. In content, however, there are similarities between authors and their works. The overall message is about community not individuality, revolt not passivity, progress not backwardness. The shared political position of these authors is against the hegemony of upper- and middle-class Hindu beliefs and for the power of the human being against oppressive social rules. Because of this, cultural concepts such as religion and identity are called into question. The language of these texts is very faithful to local, spoken dialects, and high-flown language is not seen to have adequate political power.

Many national leaders have based their reform on the social cause of the lower castes. For the dalits, the most famous of these leaders was Dr. Bhimrao Ramji Ambedkar (1891–1956). The emancipation of the dalits was due in large part to Ambedkar's foundation of educational institutions in the 1960s. These schools were havens where dalit professors and educated, middle-class, dalit students could come together intellectually. Some famous dalit writers are Mulk Raj ANAND and Namdeo DHASAL.

Dalit literature has, since its inception, been translated into several Indian and European languages without compromising on the quality of rebellion that first characterized it. Such literature defies the idea that practice and theory remain separate. The strength of the term *dalit,* originally used to ostracize a section of Indian society, enabled a successful literary movement that has overthrown social prejudice and won worldwide acclaim.

Works about Dalit Literature

Anand, Mulk Raj. *Anthology of Dalit Literature.* Columbia, Mo.: South Asia Books, 1992.
Moon, Vasant. *Growing up Untouchable in India: A Dalit Autobiography.* Translated by Gail Omvedt. New Delhi: Vistaar, 2002.

D'Annunzio, Gabriele (1863–1938) *poet, novelist, dramatist*

Renowned as a writer and a military hero who strongly supported fascism, Gabriele D'Annunzio was born in Pescara, a town in central Italy. The son of a wealthy landowner, he received his education in Prato at Liceo Cicognini, one of the best schools in Italy during that period.

D'Annunzio published his first collection of poems while he was still in his teens. *Primo Vere* (*First Spring,* 1879) was inspired by the works of the aristocratic, elitist, classical scholar Giosue Carducci, who sought a humanistic approach to literary studies.

In 1881, D'Annunzio enrolled at the University of Rome. Life in the capital city exposed him to a variety of cultural, artistic, and literary stimulation. He contributed articles to several newspapers and became a member of several literary groups. He also married Maria Hardouin di Galese. The daughter of a duke, she expected a specific standard of living, and D'Annunzio produced large quantities of hack writing to maintain her. The works he produced during this time, however, also included some notable pieces strongly influenced by Guy de MAUPASSANT and the French DECADENCE movement. In particular, the short stories *Canto novo* (1882), *Terra Vergine* (1882), and *L'Intermezzo di rime* (1883) express a sensual awareness of life.

D'Annunzio's first novel, *The Child of Pleasure* (1889), was a parody of decadence. He followed this highly successful work with *The Victim* (1891), a novel about sexual depravity. The same year as this work came out, his marriage ended. He moved to Naples and began a series of affairs, the most influential of which was his long-term liaison with the actress Eleonora Duse. He was so deeply inspired by her that he began to produce dramatic works specifically for her, including *La Gioconda* (1899) and *Francesca Da Rimini* (1901).

Beginning in 1897, D'Annunzio served a three-year term in parliament, but he was not reelected at the end of his term. Having just purchased an expensive villa in anticipation of maintaining his position, he was able to live off of his savings for only a short period before being forced to flee to France to avoid his debts. He returned to writing during this period, staying away from his native Italy until the start of World War I.

Ever the nationalist, D'Annunzio was prompted by the war to return to Italy. He also began his military career. He wrote powerful speeches and articles, urging his fellow countrymen to support the Allied cause. He began a series of correspondences with Mussolini that provided the leader with much insight into potential military tactics. At one point, however, during 1919, D'Annunzio began to lose faith in Italy and its lack of determination. He took his troops and occupied the town of Fiume, ruling as its dictator for 18 months and professing a desire to declare war against Italy. Ultimately, however, he was forced to retreat.

After losing one eye in a flying accident, D'Annunzio retired to once again work on his writing. He was given the title of Prince of Monte Nevoso in 1924 and was elected president of the Italian Royal Academy in 1937. On March 1, 1938, he suffered a stroke and died the same day. Mussolini, in honor of his contributions to the cause, ordered that he be given a state funeral.

A Work about Gabriele D'Annunzio

Woodhouse, John. *Gabriele D'Annunzio, Defiant Archangel.* New York: Oxford University Press, 2001.

Darío, Rubén (Félix Rubén García Sarmiento) (1867– 1916) *poet, short-story writer*

Rubén Darío was born in Metapa, Nicaragua (now called Ciudad Darío). While still an infant, his parents divorced, and he was adopted by his godfather, Colonel Félix Ramírez. Though he showed writing talent and ability as a teenager, he was denied a scholarship to study in Europe because his youthful writing was too liberal in its religious views. Instead, after he finished school, he traveled to El Salvador, where he met the poet Francisco Gavidia.

Gavidia introduced Darío to French literature. Darío was particularly interested in Victor HUGO and briefly imitated his style. Unable to go to France, he absorbed French culture through its novels and poems. This immersion, first in Hugo and then in the writers of the French symbolist movement (*see* SYMBOLISM), particularly the poet VERLAINE, was a key factor in Darío's development and led to his founding of the movement of Latin American MODERNISM.

Before Darío, Latin American literature was completely dominated by antiquated modes of writing inherited from Europe. In addition, the subject matter was almost exclusively limited to descriptions of local life and scenery. By introducing modernist ideas such as making art for art's sake and developing a unique poetic voice, Darío succeeded in creating a literature of international scope.

In 1888, while living in Chile, Darío published *Blue,* a book of short stories and poems that investigate again and again the role of an artist in an industrial society where all value is based on monetary worth. In the poem "Queen Mab's Veil," Darío uses strong metaphors and symbolic imagery to depict how the artist's inner life can be filled with beauty, even when his or her outer reality is cold and unfeeling. The title of the poem alludes to a speech from Shakespeare's play *Romeo and Juliet* in which Mercutio speaks about the magical quality of dreams.

In *Songs of Life and Hope* (1905), a book of poems, Darío reached another stage in his poetic development. While his earlier books freely use nostalgic images that traditionally represented beauty in poetry, for example, the nightingale, *Songs of Life and Hope* reshapes those images and questions what they mean in a Latin American social and political context. His long poem *To Roosevelt,* written to United States president Theodore Roosevelt, is a meditation on the United States. In it Darío both admires the United States as a model of modern democracy and worries about the possible threat of U.S. imperialism.

In the final years of his life, the poet would write increasingly about politics, his fear of death, and the uncertainty of the fate of humanity. These are the themes that occupy his haunting and beautiful poem "Fatalities," the final poem in *Songs of Life and Hope.*

Darío was the central figure in Latin American MODERNISM and was a forerunner of the cosmopolitan tendencies of such later Latin American authors as Jorge Luis BORGES, Julio CORTÁZAR, and Octavio PAZ. He introduced idiomatic language, original metaphors, and formal innovations to the Latin American literary scene. Finally, his body of work stands as a testament to a highly learned and expressive mind, struggling with the great themes of history, spirituality, and art.

Another Work by Darío

Selected Poems. Translated by Lysander Kemp. Austin: University of Texas Press, 1965.

A Work about Darío

Ellis, Keith. *Critical Approaches to Rubén Darío.* Toronto: University of Toronto Press, 1974.

Darwish, Mahmud (Mahmoud)
(1942–   ) poet

Foremost Palestinian poet Darwish emerged as one of the "Resistance Poets," Palestinians who, in the aftermath of the 1967 Israeli occupation, wrote poetry of struggle. The poem "Identity Card" (1964), an impassioned cry from an Arab quarryman who is determined to keep his dignity despite Israeli occupation, typifies Darwish's early voice. In the 1970s, Darwish's poetry became the definitive expression of the pain of Palestinian exile. He has evolved beyond being keeper of Palestine's spiritual flame, and editor Munir Akash calls him the "poet of human grief." Darwish's broad vision embraces the literary heritage not only of Arabs but also of Jews and the many other peoples who inhabit the land of his birth. His creative scope encompasses ancient Near Eastern, Native American, and European mythology. A giant in his significance for modern Arabic literature, Darwish remains such a literary icon for Palestinians that when he writes personal poetry, such as the volume of love poems, *Bed of a Stranger* (1999), some Arab critics respond as if he were turning his back on the plight of his people.

Darwish was born in Barweh, a Palestinian town that was attacked by Israel in its 1948 campaign. Darwish grew up, in Salma K. Jayyusi's words, "as a refugee in his own country." He became active in the Israeli Communist Party and, in 1964, published his first book of poetry, *Leaves of Olive.* In 1971, he resettled in Beirut, where he lived until 1982, when Palestinians were driven out of Lebanon. His memoir, *Memory for Forgetfulness,* is about being trapped in the 1982 Israeli siege of Beirut. In 1996, Darwish was allowed to return to the land of his birth.

Darwish's awards include the Lenin Prize (1983) and France's Knighthood of Arts and Belles Lettres (1997). He served on the Palestinian National Council, founded the prestigious literary magazine *al Karmel,* has written 30 books, and is translated into 35 languages. In 1999, Israeli authorities finally permitted five Darwish poems to be included in schoolbooks.

Other Works by Mahmud Darwish

Adam of Two Edens. Edited by Munir Akash and Daniel Moore. Syracuse, N.Y.: Syracuse University Press, 2000.

Psalms. Translated by Ben Bennani. Boulder, Colo.: Passeggiata Press, 1995.

Victims of a Map: A Bilingual Anthology of Arabic Poetry by Samih al-Qasim, Adonis, and Mahmud Darwish. Translated by Abdullah al-Udhari. London: Al-Saqi Books, 1984.

Davies, Robertson (1913–1995) *novelist, playwright, essayist*

Robertson William Davies was born in Thamesville, Ontario, Canada, to a newspaper owner. He attended Oxford, receiving a degree in literature in 1938. From a young age, he was drawn to the theater, playing small roles outside London; in 1940, he acted at the Old Vic Repertory Company in London and married Brenda Matthews, who was the stage manager for the company. He returned to Canada with his wife soon after to work as a journalist. He was the editor of the *Peterborough Examiner* for 15 years and its publisher from 1955 to 1965.

Davies's love of theater was evident from the many plays he wrote, and he said that he considered his plays comedies rather than tragedies that criticized Canada's provincial attitudes. He won the 1948 Dominion Drama Festival Award for best Canadian play for *Eros at Breakfast,* which made use of allegory (using symbols rather than direct representation) and was more theatrical than realistic. In a similar style, *King Phoenix* is a fantasy based on the mythical King Cole, while *General Confession* is a historical comedy of ideas with the main characters serving as Jungian (derived from Carl Jung) archetypes of self, persona, shadow, and anima. These three plays, with their elaborate costumes and settings and magic transformations, reveal Davies's inclination for spectacle and extravagance.

Although Davies wrote plays, essays, and criticism, it is for his many novels that he is best known and admired. His first trilogy, the Salterton trilogy—*Tempest-Tost* (1951), *Leaven of Malice* (1954), and *A Mixture of Frailties* (1958)—is an ongoing social comedy set in a small Ontario university town. The novel that begins the Deptford trilogy, *Fifth Business* (1970), is considered by most critics to be his finest work with its blend of myths, magic, freaks, evil, and theatrical elements. A snowball with a stone concealed in it opens the novel, which then proceeds through the life of a magician whose life is linked through that stone to that of the protagonist, Boy Staunton. The other Deptford novels are *The Manticore* (1972) and *World of Wonders* (1975).

Davies's work often plays with traditional themes and tropes from the Western literary canon. He often works with classical themes set in a modern context, making frequent allusions to works like Milton's *Paradise Lost.* The influence of Shakespeare and Milton is immediately evident. (In fact, Davies's B.Lit. thesis at Oxford was on Shakespearean Theatre.) Davies's work also reflects his interest in Freudian and subsequently Jungian psychology, especially *The Manticore.*

During the course of his career, Davies won a number of major awards for his work, including the Lorne Pierce Medal, the Stephen Leacock Medal for Humour, and the Governor General's Award for *The Manticore.* Davies was the first Canadian to become an Honorary Member of the American Academy and Institute of Arts and Letters. He was a Companion of the Order of Canada.

Reviewer S. A. Rowland writes in *Contemporary Novelists* that Davies "delights in paradox and is himself an example: Among the most innovative of contemporary novelists, he stresses our deep roots in old cultures and 'magical' beliefs."

Other Works by Robertson Davies

The Cunning Man: A Novel. New York: Viking, 1995.

The Lyre of Orpheus. New York: Viking Penguin, 1988.

The Mirror of Nature. Toronto: University of Toronto Press, 1983.

The Rebel Angels. New York: Viking Press, 1982.

The Well-tempered Critic: One Man's View of Theatre and Letters in Canada. Toronto: McClelland and Stewart, 1981.

Works about Robertson Davies

Grant, Judith Skelton. *Robertson Davies: Man of Myth.* New York: Viking, 1994.

Peterman, Michael. *Robertson Davies.* Boston: Twayne, 1986.

decadence

Decadence is a literary and artistic movement that began in Europe during the final decades of the 19th century. Although France produced the most notable of all decadent authors, Joris-Karl HUYSMANS, whose *À Rebours* (*Against Nature,* 1884) epitomizes the movement, decadence was not confined to France. It spread to Belgium with writers such as Rodenbach, to Germany, with the early works of Thomas MANN and the writings of Stefan GEORGE, and Austria, with Hugo von HOFMANNSTHAL. It was also evidenced in Britain and Ireland in the works of Oscar Wilde, particularly his novel *The Picture of Dorian Gray* (1890). Huysmans's influence on Wilde seems apparent in that Wilde refers to *A Rebours,* calling it the *The Yellow Book* that corrupts Dorian Gray. Other notable members of the French decadent movement include Charles BAUDELAIRE and Stéphane MALLARMÉ and Arthur RIMBAUD.

Characteristic of the decadence movement as a whole, and symptomatic of the obsessions of FIN-DE-SIÈCLE Europe, elements such as decapitation, vampirism, and images of women as evil predators and temptresses were common throughout decadence texts. The themes in these writings are, therefore, inherently diverse and include tales of the supernatural and occult, science fiction, romance, and "faits divers" or "slice of life" sensational crimes.

Seeking to speak out against scientific progress and democracy, decadent authors created their own paradise, often drug induced, and reveled in the poetics of necrophilia. Self-centered and egomaniacal almost to the point of self-annihilation, they tended to be members of the aristocracy who were antidemocratic in politics, misanthropic, and misogynistic (hating or fearful of women). They were often members of the occult, and their lifestyles tended to be as flamboyant as their writings were insolent. Many members of the decadent movement ultimately died from their excesses.

A Work about Decadence

McGuinness, Patrick, ed. *Symbolism, Decadence and the Fin de Siècle: French and European Perspectives.* Exeter: University of Exeter Press, 2000.

De Kok, Ingrid (1951–) poet

Ingrid De Kok was raised in South Africa, whose geography influenced her later work. She says, "Growing up in a hard, flat, dry place, a demanding physical environment has probably influenced the way I see a great number of things as well as the way I respond to landscape. I'm interested in geography and space insofar as it relates to the notion of home" (Rich). This image of home appears in much of her poetry. Her work has appeared in many anthologies and numerous journals in South Africa, England, the United States, and Canada.

De Kok's poetry blends the languages of Afrikaans and English to create images of the South African landscape. In a move that she calls unconscious, she weaves into her poetry the political subjects of loss and apartheid alongside the very personal lives of the people; for example, in her poem, "Mending," from her collection *Familiar Ground* (1988), the narrator says, "The woman plies her ancient art, / Her needle sutures as it darts, / scoring, scripting, scarring, stitching, / the invisible mending of the heart." By blending the traditional sewing metaphor with images of scarring and scoring, De Kok shows not only a garment or body being mended but also a nation.

Her notion of the community in her poetry is influenced by authors such as Seamus HEANEY and Jeremy CRONIN, while her interest in form is more influenced by traditional English and American writers such as Emily Dickinson, John Donne, and Robert Frost. De Kok's work has been described as having "fearlessness, guts to transgress, an unfailing ear for the alternation of consonants on the tongue, a turn of thinking and the ability to capture in the most delicate and individual terms a devastating phenomenon."

A Work about Ingrid De Kok

Krog, Antjie. "Defenceless in the Face of De Kok's Poetry." *Electronic Mail and Guardian.* Johannesburg, South Africa. January 19, 1998.

Dépestre, René (1926–   ) *poet, novelist, essayist, journalist, professor, editor*

René Dépestre was born and educated in Jacmel, Haiti, before attending the Lycée Pétion in Port-au-Prince. There he worked with the revolutionary magazine *La Ruche.* At 19, Dépestre published his first revolutionary volume of verse, *Étincelles* (*Sparks,* 1945). He became a leading voice for young Haitian radicals by, for example, criticizing the Haitian government's exploitative acts in *La Ruche.* After a Haitian student revolution sparked by *La Ruche*'s prohibition in 1946, Dépestre was exiled to France. He published *Traduit du grand large* (*Translated from the High Sea,* 1952), a volume of poetry, before returning to Haiti in 1958. Dissatisfied with Haitian dictator François Duvalier, Dépestre moved to Cuba in 1959 and worked as an editor and professor. After Cuba expelled him in 1978, Dépestre returned to France. He worked for UNESCO during the 1980s and became a French citizen in 1991.

Although Dépestre has lived much of his adult life outside Haiti, he is one of Haiti's most celebrated contemporary poets. His poetry voices Haitian and Caribbean values and explores the relationships between and among identity and ethnicity, slavery, and exploitation. His articles and essays grapple with similar issues, as seen in *Bonjour et adieu à la négritude* (*Hello and Goodbye to Negritude,* 1980), a collection of essays that marks Dépestre's ideological shift from embracing authentic identity to embracing more-open concepts of cultural and personal identities.

Alléluia pour une femme-jardin (*Hallelujah for a Garden-Woman,* 1973) marks an erotic shift in Dépestre's writing. There, for example, Dépestre employs erotic and allegorical representations of women. In *Éros dans un train chinois* (*Eros in a Chinese Train,* 1993), Dépestre develops a new, imaginative, erotic aesthetic called erotic-magical realism that would ideally re-create Haiti. Dépestre's work not only focuses on revolution, but his innovative aesthetics also redefine how to write about revolution.

Other Works by René Dépestre

The Festival of the Greasy Pole. Translated by Carrol F. Coates. Charlottesville: University Press of Virginia, 1990.
A Rainbow for the Christian West. Translated by Jack Hirschman. Fairfax, Calif.: Red Hill Press, 1972.
Vegetations of Splendor. Translated by Jack Hirschman. Chicago: Vanguard, 1981.

Works about René Dépestre

Dayan, Joan. "France Reads Haiti: An Interview with René Dépestre." *Yale French Studies* 83 (1994): 136–53.
Ferdinand, Joseph. "The New Political Statement in Haitian Fiction." In *Voices from Under: Black Narrative in Latin American and the Caribbean.* Edited by William Luis. Westport, Conn.: Greenwood Press, 1984.

Desai, Anita (Mazumdar, Anita)
(1937–   ) *novelist*

Anita Desai was born in Mussoorie, a tiny hill station on the outskirts of Delhi, India, to a German mother and an Indian father. Though her novels are in English, Desai is fluent in several languages. It has been noted that she spoke German at home, Hindi with friends, and English at school. In addition to being a professor of writing at Massachusetts Institute of Technology (MIT), Desai is also involved in education in India and is a member of the Advisory Board of English in New Delhi. She is currently a Fellow of the Royal Society of Literature in London.

Desai's novels are preoccupied with the theme of alienation. Her novel *In Custody* (1985) is set during the fraught political tensions between India and Pakistan during the Partition War and traces the daily lives of middle-class women at home. What unfolds is a female narrative of political struggle that occurs outside of and simultaneous to the one fought in the public space dominated by men. One of the main characters, Nur, is a budding poet whose talent is silenced and hidden by her husband. Her story is one example of the novel's concern with the effects historical events have on family relations and how women are denied public recognition.

Although Desai's earlier novels are based on the question of women's roles in Indian and Pakistani societies, Desai's later novel, *Baumgartner's Bombay* (1988), goes beyond the problem of gender. It is the story of a businessman's search across continents to escape Western anti-Semitism, only to discover traces of it even in India. This novel is more global in perspective in its exploration of the aftereffects of World War II in an Indian context.

Desai has also written numerous children's books, of which *The Village by the Sea* (1982) won the Guardian Prize for Children's Fiction in 1983. Her first novel, *Fire on the Mountain,* (1977) won the Indian National Academy of Letters Award. In 1988, she was awarded the Padma Shri by the president of India for her outstanding contribution to Indian literature.

Other Works by Anita Desai
Clear Light of Day. New York: Houghton Mifflin, 2000.
Journey to Ithaca. New York: Knopf, 1995.

Works about Anita Desai
Bande, Usha. *The Novels of Anita Desai.* Prestige Books, 1992.
Buruma, Ian, ed. *India: A Mosaic.* New York: New York Review of Books, 2000.

Desbordes-Valmore, Marceline
(1786–1859) *poet*

Marceline Desbordes-Valmore was born in Douai, France, to a lower-middle-class family whose lives had been ruined by the French Revolution. She left with her mother for the Antilles in 1801 only to find the conditions there horrible. Faced with riots and an epidemic of yellow fever, her mother died only a few days after their arrival. Desbordes-Valmore returned to Douai in 1802 to embark on a career as a professional singer and actress.

Desbordes-Valmore's life was fraught with tragedy. In 1809, she fell in love with a writer who left her shortly after she gave birth to their child. The child lived only five years. In 1817, she married the actor Prosper Valmore, with whom she had three children, Hippolyte, Ondine, and Inês. The family lived a precarious existence, fleeing the dangers of revolution throughout Europe. Her daughter Inês died in 1846; Ondine's daughter died in 1852, followed by Ondine herself in 1853; and in 1858 Desbordes-Valmore lost her best friend, the musician Pauline Duchambge.

Desbordes-Valmore's poetry was the one reliable source of satisfaction in her life. In it, her griefs found memorable expression and perhaps catharsis. In "Les Séparés ("Apart"), for example, the poet addresses an absent lover with a constant refrain: "Do not write!":

> *Do not write. Let us learn to die, as best we may.*

Did I love you? Ask God. Ask yourself. Do
  you know?
To hear that you love me, when you are far
  away,
Is like hearing from heaven and never to go.
  Do not write!

Between 1819 and 1843, she published several collections of poetry and received recognition from critics such as Charles Augustin Sainte-Beuve (1804–69) and Victor HUGO as one of the leading poets of her time. She also wrote a number of works for children. Her poetry is characterized by sincerity, spontaneity, grace, and melancholy.

Another Work by Marceline Desbordes-Valmore

Simpson, Louis, ed. and trans. Selections in *Modern Poets of France: A Bilingual Anthology.* Ashland, Ore.: Story Line Press, 1997.

Works about Marceline Desbordes-Valmore

Boutine, Aimee. *Maternal Echoes: the Poetry of Marceline Desbordes-Valmore and Alphonse de Lamartine.* Newark: University of Delaware Press, 2001.

Johnson, Barbara. *The Feminist Difference: Literature, Psychoanalysis, Race, and Gender.* Cambridge, Mass.: Harvard University Press, 2000.

Sainte-Beuve, Charles Augustin. *Memoirs of Madame Desbordes-Valmore, with a selection from her poems.* Translated by Harriet W. Preston. New York: AMS Press, 1980.

Devi, Mahasweta (1926–) *novelist, short-story writer, dramatist, journalist*

Mahasweta Devi was born into a literary family in Dacca, Bangladesh (previously known as East Bengal). As a young child, she migrated to West Bengal (India) with her parents. The local politics of West Bengal and the Bengali language are to this day the source and inspiration for Devi's literature. Her early involvement with the local political theater group "Ganantaya" formed her ambition to spread social and political awareness through her writing. Since then, she has used her prodigious talent to champion the cause of suppressed Indian tribal societies. Most of her work is written in Bengali and has been translated into several Indian languages and into English. In a 1998 interview, she said that her goal is to "fight for the tribals, downtrodden, underprivileged, and write creatively if and when I find the time."

Devi's feminist tone comments on the traditional view of women in Indian society. Female characters in her works are borrowed from an older literary tradition but are transformed to reveal a profound political self-awareness. In the short story "Dopadi," Devi evokes the central female character from the classical epic *Mahabharata,* Draupadi, to tell a story of a fugitive tribal woman, also of the same name, who outwits the local police. Another short story, "Breast-Giver" (1993), is a symbolic comparison between a woman's physical illness and the social illnesses extant in postindependent India.

Mahasweta Devi gave up her position as a professor in English literature at a Calcutta university in 1984. This decision allowed her to begin a new life devoted to social work and writing. In 1997, she was a recipient of the Magsaysay Award (Asia's equivalent to the Nobel Prize) for a lifetime spent in creating literature that extends beyond the literary and intellectual to the social.

Another Work by Mahasweta Devi

Imaginary Maps: Three Stories by Mahasweta Devi. Translated by Gayatri Spivak. New York: Routledge, 1994.

Works about Mahasweta Devi

"Mahasweta Devi." Available online at http://www.emory.edu/ENGLISH/Bahri/Devi.html.

Spivak, Gayatri. *In Other Worlds: Essays in Cultural Politics.* New York: Routledge, 1987.

Dhammachoti, Ussiri (Atsiri Thamma-choat) (1947–   ) *novelist*

Ussiri Dhammachoti was born in the Hua Hin district, Prachuap Khiri Khan, Thailand. His father was a fisherman who owned several fishing trawlers. Dhammachoti received his primary and secondary education at Sathukan School. When he failed to pass the entrance exams for Chulalongkorn University, he applied to work for the National Statistical Office and was assigned to draw maps for the national population census. In 1970, he reapplied and was admitted to Chulalongkorn University. He graduated with a bachelor's degree in communications arts in 1974 and started a magazine, which lasted less than a year. He worked for various newspapers, including the *Siam Rath*, for many years before finally quitting his post as publisher in 1998. He is now a freelance writer and writes only in Thai.

Dhammachoti's writings are deeply influenced by his life experiences. His mother's death greatly affected Dhammachoti, whose initial interest in literature was motivated by his mother's love for old Thai literature and poetry. His travels to the northern provinces of Thailand during the years he worked for the National Statistical Office opened the opportunity for him to collect ideas that formed the basis of his works. Dhammachoti's works deal with a variety of themes, such as the impact of the modern world on traditional societies located in the hilly outskirts of Thailand. These themes are often represented in his TV plays, such as *Khun Det* and *Mae Nak Phra Khanong*. His fascination with the local folklore and cultural and religious practices can be observed in his short stories. Dhammachoti also possesses a nostalgic empathy for the people who live in the remote regions of the country. His goal to better their lives is intermixed with his desire to preserve some aspects of their way of life. He sees richness in the traditional history of many of the tribes, like the Miao and Hmong, that should be preserved.

Dhammachoti's stories, such as "Samnuk Khong Pho Thao" ("The Old Man's Conscience,"

1972), reflect his compassion for and understanding of not only the poor and downtrodden in Thai society but also the various ethnic groups that live at the borders of the Thai nation. His characters consist of a variety of personality types, ranging from the elite group to the marginalized peoples who lived in the northern region of Thailand. Their differences in background, philosophy, and status, however, do not hinder their attempts to gain a mutual understanding of each other's cultures and tradition.

When Dhammachoti was still an undergraduate, he won the Phlubphla Mali Literary Award from the Literary Circle of Chulalongkorn University for his short story "Samnuk Khong Pho Thao" in 1972. His collection of short stories *Kuntong . . . Chao Cha Khlab Ma Mua Fa Sang (Kuntong . . . You Will Return at Dawn)* was published in 1978 and won the Southeast Asian Writer Award in 1981. On November 3, 2000, Dhammachoti was awarded the honor of National Artist in Literature.

Another Work by Ussiri Dhammachoti
Of Time and Tide: A Thai Novel. Bangkok: Thai Modern Classic Series, 1985.

Dhasal, Namdeo (Namdev) (1947–   ) *poet, novelist*

Namdeo Dhasal was born in a small village outside Pune, India. He is a DALIT, which means "casteless" or "untouchable," and grew up very poor. Dhasal had almost no formal education but educated himself on the literature of other dalit writers who also wrote about the conditions of the oppressed. Because of this focus, at no time can the voice of the poet be distinguished from that of the political rebel. Dhasal's poetry directly addresses the sources of human unhappiness such as poverty, prostitution, and underworld politics of Bombay. His famed knowledge of the city caught the attention of Trinidadian author V. S. NAIPAUL, who used Dhasal as his guide to Bombay and made him an important figure in his book *India: A Million Mutinies Now* (1990).

The city of Bombay is the subject of Dhasal's first collection of poems called *Golpitha* (1973). When the famous Indian playwright Vinay Tendulkar offered to write the introduction to Dhasal's collection, Dhasal insisted that he first come on a walking tour of Golpitha, a red-light district, before writing anything. Dhasal's portraits of the inhabitants in Golpitha vividly capture "life gone wrong" in a world of poverty, filth, and violence. Paradox, however, is a defining feature of Dhasal's style and the harsh realism of his poetry is coupled with images that are both alluring and hopeful. In an untitled poem from *Khel* (*Play*, 1983), for example, "Butterflies of hibiscus" dance under the sun that throws love over a "wounded dog" turning in circles.

Since *Golpitha,* Dhasal has written two novels and several collections of poetry. Dhasal writes in Marathi and a hybrid of Hindi and Urdu. His work, written in the language of the streets, has been called a translator's nightmare. In spite of this, Dhasal's poetry has been translated into numerous European languages, and he has traveled widely to read his poetry.

Dhasal was one of the founders of the Dalit Panthers in 1972. In 1990, he joined mainstream politics and became a member of the Indian Republican Party. He received the Padma Shri from the president of India for his outstanding contribution to Indian literature and was chosen to represent India at the first International Literary Festival in Berlin in 2001.

Another Work by Namdeo Dhasal

"The Poems of Namdeo Dhasal," in *An Anthology of Dalit Literature.* Edited by Mulk Raj Anand and Eleanor Zelliot. Columbia, Mo.: South Asia Books, 1992.

Dinesen, Isak (Karen Christence Dinesen, Baroness Karen Blixen, Osceola, Pierre Andrézel) (1885–1962)
short-story writer, novelist

Isak Dinesen was born in Rungsted, Denmark, to wealth and privilege. Her father, Wilhelm Dinesen, was an army officer and a writer. Her mother, Ingeborg Westenholz Dinesen, was from a prominent business family. Dinesen studied painting at the Royal Academy of Fine Arts in Copenhagen from 1903 to 1906. In 1907, she published several short stories in a Danish monthly, but these works attracted little attention. In 1914, Dinesen married Swedish nobleman Baron Bror Blixen-Finecke and settled on a coffee plantation in Kenya. They later divorced, and Dinesen moved back to Denmark after the plantation went bankrupt in 1931.

Dinesen's writing career thrived after she returned to Rungsted. Critics in Great Britain and the United States praised her first major work, *Seven Gothic Tales* (1934), for its sophistication and imaginative use of fantasy. Dinesen's description of her experiences in Africa, *Den africanske farm* (*Out of Africa,* 1937), was later made into a movie. During World War II, she wrote *Sorg-Acre* (*Sorrow Acre,* 1942), a story set in a rural Denmark that many consider to be her masterpiece.

Dinesen's influences included her father, the Bible, Danish romantic writers, the *Arabian Nights,* and the Icelandic sagas. Many of her works, including *Sorrow Acre,* reflect Dinesen's belief that an individual's fate is in the hands of God. She wrote about the topics of love and dreams in her many imaginative tales of fantasy. However, irony destroys romanticism in many of Dinesen's stories, which critic Curtis Cate describes as "sophisticated," "psychologically subtle," and "philosophically speculative."

Another Work by Isak Dinesen

Last Tales. New York: Vintage Books, 1991.

Works about Isak Dinesen

Cate, Curtis. "Isaac Dinesen: The Scheherazade of Our Times." In Olga A. Pelensky, ed., *Isak Dinesen: Critical Views.* Athens: Ohio University Press, 1993.

Thurman, Judith. *Isak Dinesen: The Life of a Storyteller.* New York: St. Martin's Press, 1982.

Ding Ling (Jiang Bingzhi) (1904–1986)
novelist, short-story and nonfiction writer

Jiang Bingzhi was born on October 12 in Hunan Province's Linli County in China. After her father's death, she lived with her uncle in Changde. She was introduced to ideas of revolution and democracy at a young age because Changde was a focal point for the 1911 republican revolution to overthrow the Qing dynasty. At 17, she attended a Communist school in Shanghai and later Shanghai University. In 1923, she left for Beijing, where China's "new culture" was developing. She could not afford to attend lectures at Beijing University, so she read Western and Eastern writers. She also learned to paint, and in 1925, she married Hu Yepin, a revolutionary writer.

In 1927, Ding Ling published to great acclaim her first short story, "Meng Ke," based on her own experience at an unsuccessful film audition. Its publication was quickly followed by "Miss Sophie's Diary," a story about a girl with tuberculosis and her fruitless desire to find love. The next year, she published her first short-story collection, *In the Dark.*

In 1930, Ding Ling and her husband joined the proletarian literary movement in Shanghai, where they joined the newly formed League of Left-wing Writers headed by LU Xun. Hu Yepin was executed by the Nationalists for his involvement in the Chinese Communist Party (CCP) underground, an event that plunged Ding Ling into the revolution. Ding Ling herself was later kidnapped by the Guomingdang (GMD) Nationalist Party.

Amidst her political activity, Ding Ling was also busy writing. She edited *The Dipper,* the league's literary magazine, and published *Flood,* a major revolutionary work of social realist (*see* SOCIALIST REALISM) fiction about peasants exploited by local despots during a disaster. In 1933, she also published the first part of the novel *Mother,* about a spirited heroine during the 1911 revolution, a character based loosely on her own mother.

After her release from Nationalist prison in 1936, Mao Zedong welcomed her with two poems he wrote in her honor at the Yan'an Communist base. She began to work on the *Liberation Daily's* literary supplement. When the Sino-Japanese War broke out in 1937, Ding Ling performed field and propaganda work and wrote stories from the front. An outspoken woman yet a loyal servant of both literature and communism, she voiced opinions on inequities within the supposedly egalitarian party, especially in regard to women, at the Yan'an Forum on Literature and Art in 1942.

During the next decade, Ding Ling continued her literary endeavors, writing, among other pieces, a novel about land reform, *The Sun Shines over the Sanggan River* (1949), which won the Stalin Prize for literature. She also traveled extensively abroad, lecturing on literature and producing essays, literary criticism, and speeches. She frequently wrote about women, both in her stories and in essays, advocating feminist thought, women's sexual freedom, and the rights to seek divorce and not to marry. Her writing was frequently considered scandalous, but it also explored the new dimensions of Chinese womanhood under China's rapidly changing sociopolitical landscape.

In 1955, Ding Ling came under fire from the party leadership. She was accused of heading an antiparty clique and was criticized for the sexual content of her stories. During the brief open period of the Hundred Flowers Campaign in 1956, her plea to make literature independent earned her the label of rightist, as well as party expulsion in 1957. She was "sent down" to do physical labor in a reclamation area in the Great Northern Wilderness in Heilongjiang Province.

When the Cultural Revolution began in 1966, Ding Ling did not escape persecution. She was imprisoned from 1970 to 1975 in Beijing and then removed to a commune in Shanxi. After the revolution, she was officially restored in a 1979 verdict and again became a respected member of the establishment.

As part of the "scar" literature by writers who survived the Cultural Revolution, Ding Ling published essays and stories about her experiences and those of her friends. In 1981, she and her second husband, Chen Ming, moved to a convalescent home in Fukien. Although she was in poor health, she started the literary magazine *China* in 1985. She died on March 4.

Another Work by Ding Ling

I Myself Am a Woman: Selected Writings of Ding Ling. Barlow, Tani E., and Gary J. Bjorge, eds. Boston: Beacon Press, 1990.

A Work about Ding Ling

Feuerwerker, Yi-tsi Mei. *Ding Ling's Fiction: Ideology and Narrative in Modern Chinese Literature.* Cambridge, Mass.: Harvard University Press, 1982.

Diop, Birago (1906–1989) *poet, folklorist*

Birago Diop was born into an influential family in Dakar, Senegal. His father died prematurely leaving him to be raised by his mother's family. He attended high school in the old capital before going to France to earn his degree as a veterinarian at the University of Toulouse. In Paris, Diop met many of the founders of NÉGRITUDE, an intellectual and artistic movement that was begun in Paris by black students from the French colonies. The movement celebrated a global African identity, while taking a political stance against colonialism and assimilation. Diop met his compatriot Léopold Sédar SENGHOR, a founder of Négritude, who influenced him to write about African cultural values. Diop used his own cultural background as a resource, recounting the stories he was told as a child. In addition, his experience as a veterinarian allowed him to travel throughout remote areas of French West Africa, giving him access to the rural life and values of traditional Africa.

He is most famous for his work *Tales of Amadou Koumba* (1966), an award-winning collection of folk tales that he translated from Wolof, the most prevalent indigenous language in Senegal. He is noted for maintaining its rhythm, imagery, and subtleties in his transcription of these stories and for giving the French world access to these ethnic treasures.

In his poetry, Diop concentrated on the mystical elements in African culture. He released a poetry anthology called *Lures and Glimmers* (1960) that captures the spiritual belief system of many African religions. In 1960, Senghor, the president of Senegal at the time, appointed Diop ambassador to Tunisia. Today, Birago Diop is considered a central contributor of traditional ethnic resources to the Négritude movement.

Works about Birago Diop

Gibbs, James. "The Animal Trickster as Political Satirist and Social Dissident." In Edris Makward et al. *The Growth of African Literature.* Trenton, N.J.: Africa World Press, 1998.

Tollerson, Marie. *Mythology and Cosmology in the Narratives of Bernard Dadie and Birago Diop.* Washington, D.C.: Three Continents Press, 1984.

Diop, David (1927–1960) *poet*

David Diop was born in Bordeaux, France, to a Senegalese father on tour of duty and a Cameroonian mother. In his teens, he was deeply impressed by the poetry of Aimé CÉSAIRE, the cofounder of NÉGRITUDE, an intellectual movement started by black students in Paris. These students were writers from the French colonies who celebrated the essence of being African while also criticizing colonialism and assimilation.

As a youth, Diop battled tuberculosis, spending months in hospitals. These solitary moments gave rise to many of his most tender poems. While attending high school, he met Léopold SENGHOR, another founder of the Négritude movement, who later published some of Diop's poems. Diop traveled between Africa and Europe, and many of his poems express a longing for a return to his ancestral land of Africa. In "Africa," for example, he creates nostalgic images of Africa before colonialism, but this was an Africa with which he was not familiar. His only memories were of the aftermath of slavery and assimilation. When Senegal was close to gaining its independence in the late 1950s, Diop moved back to take part in the rebuilding of the country. His revolutionary poems and teachings were his tools of change. Ellen Kennedy, a Négritude historian, quotes Diop as writing that his poems were meant "to burst the eardrums of those who do not wish to hear."

Unfortunately, Diop's life came to a tragic end in a plane crash that also destroyed much of his last, unpublished work. Only 22 of his poems still exist; yet these clearly established him as a powerful contributor to the Négritude movement and to world literature.

Another Work by David Diop

Hammer Blows and Other Writings. Translated and edited by Simon Mpondo and Frank Jones. Bloomington: Indiana University Press, 1973.

Djebar, Assia (Fatima Zohra Imalayen)
(1936–) *novelist, playwright, filmmaker, short-story writer*

An Algerian writing in French, Djebar has produced compelling novels that express Arab women's voices in the postcolonial world. She launched her writing career with the acclaimed novel, *La Soif* (1957; published in English as *The Mischief,* 1958). She and her ex-husband, Walid Garn, wrote a play, *Rouge l'aube* (1969) (*Red Dawn*), about the Algerian war of independence. During the 1960s, Djebar taught history at the University of Algiers. In the 1970s, she embarked on a filmmaking career, in part to reach Algerian women who could not read her work in French, but she returned to fiction writing in the 1980s.

Her intense, lyrical, often sensual prose articulates the voices of Arab women, as individuals and as members of a community with a specific political history. In *Far from Medina* (trans. 1994; originally published as *Loin de Medine: filles d'Ismael,* 1991), she tells of the participation of Muslim women in the first days of Islam. Her rich, intricate historical novel, *L'amour, la fantasia* (1985; *Fantasia: An Algerian Cavalcade,* 1993), tells the history of Algeria from the French colonial onslaught in 1830 to the war of independence, ending in 1961.

In this book, Djebar alternates between formal French accounts and oral histories that are based on her field interviews in Arabic with Algerian women who participated in the independence struggle but whose voices are not included in any official history. Djebar conceived the story as part of a quartet that includes its prequel novel, *Ombre Sultane* (1987; *A Sister to Scheherazade,* 1993). "If Algerian Woman in all her complexity and historical reality is the protagonist of Assia Djebar's most ambitious and original work of fiction," writes her translator Dorothy S. Blair in the introduction to *Fantasia,* "this is also an attempt to wrest her own identity as an Algerian woman from the warring strands of her Arabo-Berber origins and her Franco-European education."

Djebar went to primary school in Algeria, attended college in France, and lives in Paris and Baton Rouge, Louisiana, where she directs the Center for French and Francophone Studies at Louisiana State University. She won the Venice Biennale Critics Prize for her film *La Nouba des femmes du Mont Chenoua* (1979), Prix Maurice Maeterlinck (1995), Neustadt Prize for Contributions to World Literature (1996), and the Yourcenar Prize (1997).

Other Works by Assia Djebar

Algerian White. Translated by Marjolijin De Jager and David Kelley. New York: Seven Stories Press, 2001.

So Vast the Prison. Translated by Betsy Wing. New York: Seven Stories Press, 1999.

Women of Algiers in Their Apartment. Translated by Marjolijin De Jager. Charlottesville, Va.: University Press of Virginia, 1992.

Works about Assia Djebar

Merini, Rafika. *Two Major Francophone Women Writers: Assia Djébar and Leila Sebbar: A Thematic Study of Their Works.* New York: Peter Lang, 1999.

Mortimer, Mildred P. *Journeys Through the French African Novel.* Westport, Conn.: Heinemann, 1990.

———., ed. *Maghrebian Mosaic: A Literature in Transition.* Boulder, Colo.: Lynne Rienner Publishers, 2001.

Döblin, Alfred (Linke Poot, Hans Fiedeler) (1878–1957) *short-story writer, novelist, playwright*

Alfred Döblin was born in Stettin, Germany. His father, a tailor, left the family when Alfred was 10, and his mother was from a lower-middle-class Jewish family. Döblin had difficulty in school and did not pass the Arbitur (school-leaving exam) until age 22. Döblin studied medicine from 1900 to 1905 in Berlin and Freiburg and, in 1911, opened a practice as a family doctor and neurologist. In 1912, he married Erna Reiss and served as an army medical officer during World War I.

Döblin began to write in 1900 and by the early 1910s earned critical acclaim for his expressionist (*see* EXPRESSIONISM) short stories that appeared in the journal *Der Stürm.* His first novel *Die drei Sprünge des Wang-lun* (*The Three Leaps of Wang-lun,* 1915) describes a tragic rebellion in China. Following the war, Döblin wrote theater reviews and plays in addition to his novels. Döblin's novel, *Berlin Alexanderplatz* (1929), was a popular and critical success, inspiring a radio play and a film. The story uses an omniscient anonymous narrative voice, montage, and parody—techniques inspired by James Joyce (1882–1941)—to describe the exploits of an ex-convict in the Berlin underworld.

In 1928, Döblin was elected to the Prussian Academy of the Arts. He and his friend Bertolt BRECHT were members of a leftist discussion group called Group 1925. After the Nazis gained power in 1933, Döblin lived in France and the United States. In 1941, he converted to the Roman Catholic faith, and in 1945, he returned to West Germany. Although Döblin achieved some critical acclaim for his substantive explorations of human relationships and relationships with God, most of his works were not popular. His novels were complicated, unconventional, and, according to the scholar David Dollenmayer, reflective of Döblin's

"deep sense of unease about himself and his place in society, and about modern man and society in general."

Other Works by Alfred Döblin
Destiny's Journey. Translated by Edna McCown. New York: Paragon House, 1992.
Tales of a Long Night: A Novel. Translated by Robert and Rita Kimber. New York: Fromm International Publishing Corporation, 1984.

A Work about Alfred Döblin
Dollenmayer, David. *The Berlin Novels of Alfred Döblin.* Berkeley: University of California Press, 1988.

Donoso, José (1924–1997) *novelist, short-story writer, poet*

José Donoso was born to Dr. José Donoso and Alicia Yáñez in a suburb of Santiago, Chile. Educated by private teachers as a young child, he later attended the prestigious Grange School. Donoso was inspired to write at an early age by uncles who were authors, as well as by the novels of such writers as Jules VERNE and Alexandre DUMAS. After dropping out of school and working for some time on a sheep farm, he completed his education at Princeton University, where he published his first short stories, in English.

It was not until Donoso's first novel, *Coronation,* was released in 1957 that his work began to receive serious critical attention. The least experimental of his novels, it relates the transformation of the conservative, middle-class Andrés, as he is drawn out of his orderly, sterile existence and into the realm of obsession and desire. In *Coronation,* the most important themes of Donoso's fiction are already present: insanity, the complex nature of identity, and the conflict between the demands of instincts and the expectations of society. These same themes are central to *The Obscene Bird of Night* (1970), which represents Donoso's best-known and perhaps most mature work. This book tells the story of the decline of an aristocratic family, as seen through the eyes of Humberto Peñaloza, the private teacher of the family's last offspring. The plot is not presented in any kind of logical sequence, as the disorder of Peñaloza's narrative is intended to reflect the narrator's psychic instability and to question traditional notions of time, space, and reality.

Donoso is a difficult writer to categorize in Latin American and Chilean literature. Although the unorthodox structure of his novels connect them to the phenomenon known as the Boom (a movement in Latin-American fiction involving such authors as Gabriel GARCÍA MÁRQUEZ and Carlos FUENTES, who employed experimental narrative techniques in their novels and stories), the domestic settings of his works tie them to the realist tradition.

Donoso has received such recognition for his fiction as the Chilean National Prize for Literature and the William Faulkner Foundation Prize. His stories and novels have been translated into many languages and adapted for film and theater. His work has exercised a critical influence on Spanish-language fiction and represents one of the most varied and compelling attempts to come to terms with the complex history and sociology of Latin America.

Another Work by José Donoso

A House in the Country. Translated by David Pritchard. New York: Knopf, 1984.

A Work about José Donoso

Magnarelli, Sharon. *Understanding José Donoso.* Columbia: University of South Carolina Press, 1993.

Dostoyevsky, Fyodor Mikhaylovich
(1821–1881) *novelist, short-story writer*

Fyodor Mikhaylovich Dostoyevsky was born in Moscow, Russia, to Mikhay Dostoyevsky, an army surgeon, and Maria Nechaeva, a daughter of a prominent Moscow merchant. Dostoyevsky had a traumatic childhood. His father was an alcoholic and constantly terrorized the family. When Dos-

toyevsky was only nine years old, his best friend was raped and murdered, a tragic incident he remembered throughout his life. In 1834 Dostoyevsky entered a prestigious private school in Moscow, where he concentrated on literary studies. He made very few friends and spent most of his time reading. He particularly admired the works of Aleksandr PUSHKIN and Nikolai KARAMZIN.

At the insistence of his father, Dostoyevsky enrolled in a school for military engineers in St. Petersburg in 1837. That same year, Dostoyevsky's studies were briefly interrupted by the death of his mother. In 1839, his father died; it was rumored that he had been murdered by his own serfs. Both events had a deep impact on Dostoyevsky and later reemerged in his novels.

On completion of his studies in 1845, Dostoyevsky briefly entered the civil service as an engineer but resigned after only a few months to pursue writing. The publication of *Poor Folk* in 1846 immediately gained critical attention, launching his literary career.

Fascinated with French social philosophy, Dostoyevsky began to attend meetings of a radical, utopian group. This group included several prominent figures, mostly artists and intellectuals who were interested in the reformation of Russian society. In 1849, 39 members, including Dostoyevsky, were arrested by the police. After months of interrogation and torture (three members of the group were confined to an insane asylum after their release), Dostoyevsky and other members of the group were sentenced to death. Minutes before the execution, however, Dostoyevsky was pardoned and his sentence reduced to five years of hard labor in Siberia.

The period of exile was perhaps the most crucial experience in Dostoyevsky's life. Spiritually and mentally distraught, Dostoyevsky passionately embraced the doctrines of the Russian Orthodox Church. Deeply affected by his experience as a prisoner, Dostoyevsky became politically reactionary and a staunch supporter of the czar.

As a result, Dostoyevsky was allowed to return to St. Petersburg in 1857, but his exile had taken its toll. He developed epilepsy, and his physical health was very fragile. Along with his brother Mikhail, Dostoyevsky began to edit *Times,* a literary journal that serialized a number of Dostoyevsky's early novels. Among works published during the early 1860s was *The House of the Dead* (1862), a fictional account of prison life based on Dostoyevsky's experiences in Siberia, and *The Insulted and Injured* (1861), a novel that analyzes the shortcomings of naïve utopianism.

Dostoyevsky married Maria Isaev in 1857, but she died in the early 1860s, as did his brother. In 1862, Dostoyevsky left Russia to tour Europe, where he was introduced to gambling, especially roulette, which became an irresistible passion. Gambling compounded his financial troubles, and he returned to Russia in 1864 virtually penniless. Dostoyevsky examined the psychological implications of gambling in his fascinating novel *The Gambler* (1866).

In 1866, Dostoyevsky began working on *Crime and Punishment,* which—harried by debt and desperately in need of money—he completed in a month with the help of a stenographer, Anna Snitkina. Dostoyevsky and Snitkina were married in 1867. With his epilepsy and obsessions, Dostoyevsky was not the easiest of companions, but the intimacy and love between Dostoyevsky and his wife sustained them for the rest of their lives. The couple traveled extensively throughout Europe but once again had to return to Russia in 1871 because of financial troubles caused by Dostoyevsky's gambling.

Critical Analysis

Dostoyevsky's fiction is notable for its deep and intense understanding of human psychology. In *Notes from the Underground* (1864), Dostoyevsky began his literary experiments with the human psyche through a detailed account of neurotic dementia. In the novel, a minor government official describes his hatred of the society he sees from his "underground" viewpoint. The novel also explores the spiritual conflict between the individual and society. It is also a reaction against the optimistic rationalism of CHERNYSHEVSKY's *What Is to Be Done?*.

In *Crime and Punishment,* Dostoyevsky portrays the spiritual and philosophical struggle of Raskolnikov, a young student who murders a pawnbroker. The novel explores the themes of spiritual suffering, psychosis, and redemption, set against the dark, nauseating background of the slums of St. Petersburg. Dostoyevsky examines the terms of formation of philosophical concepts and their subsequent effect on the individual. Many critics consider *Crime and Punishment* to be the most seminal psychological drama in literary history.

The Idiot (1868) is an indictment of the materialism of the governing classes of Russia. In this striking, realistic portrayal of 19th-century Russian society, Dostoyevsky juxtaposes the ethical idealism of a young man against the crass materialism of the drawing rooms of the middle class. The novel amplifies the growing spiritual unrest of Russian society that attempts to emulate the material values of Western Europe. Dostoyevsky denounces the society in which moral idealism is labeled as mental incompetence. *The Idiot* marks the growing philosophical crises of the realist literature of 19th-century Russia. Yet, though he saw so clearly the flaws in the society that surrounded him, Dostoyevsky denounced political violence and extremism as a way to reform society.

In *The Possessed* (1871), Dostoyevsky comments upon the responsibility of an individual in social matters. The story is about Stavrogin, a charismatic intellectual and atheist, who attracts a group of fanatics who wreak havoc on a small provincial town. It was based on the life of a revolutionary named Sergey Nechayev but may have reminded readers of several radical movements that were current at the time. *The Possessed* was ambivalently received in Russia: With its unflattering picture of political activism, it was hailed as a masterpiece by conservatives, while revolutionary circles denounced it as reactionary.

The Brothers Karamazov (1880) was Dostoyevsky's last and arguably finest novel. As a pioneering work in psychological realism, the novel engages a number of powerful themes: love, hate, patricide, and the search for God, to name a few. *The Brothers Karamzov* follows the destiny of Fyodor Karamazov and his three sons. The most famous chapter of the novel, "The Legend of the Grand Inquisitor," dramatizes the inner struggle between heart and mind in the context of religion. The profound psychological and social implications of the plot assured the everlasting significance of the novel, which was hailed as a great masterpiece virtually from its first publication.

Fyodor Dostoyevsky received unprecedented critical acclaim during the last years of his life. He finally achieved financial solvency and turned his attention to family life. After his death, his widow and children were given a government pension by the czar. Dostoyevsky's funeral was attended by thousands of people. He was hailed as a literary genius, the father of Russian REALISM, and a master of psychological realism. The contribution of Feyodor Dostoyevsky to world literature is almost immeasurable, as his works transformed entire generations of writers and created new dimensions in the world of fiction.

Other Works by Fyodor Dostoyevsky

The Best Short Stories of Dostoyevsky. Translated by David Magarshack. New York: Modern Library, 1992.

Winter Notes on Summer Impressions. Translated by Kyril Fitzlyon. London: Quartet Books, 1986.

Works about Fyodor Dostoyevsky

Amoia, Alba della Fazia. *Feodor Dostoyevsky.* New York: Continuum Press, 1993.

Frank, Joseph. *Dostoevsky: The Seeds of Revolt, 1821–1849.* Princeton, N.J.: Princeton University Press, 1976.

———. *Dostoevsky: The Years of Ordeal, 1850–1859.* Princeton, N.J.: Princeton University Press, 1984.

———. *Dostoevsky: The Years of Liberation, 1860–1865.* Princeton, N.J.: Princeton University Press, 1986.

———. *Dostoevsky: The Miraculous Years, 1865–1871.* Princeton, N.J.: Princeton University Press, 1996.

———. *Dostoevsky: The Mantle of the Prophet, 1871–1881.* Princeton, N.J.: Princeton University Press, 2002.

Leatherborrow, William J. *Feodor Dostoevsky: A Reference Guide.* Boston: G. K. Hall, 1990.

Du, Nguyen

See NGUYEN DU.

Ducasse, Isadore-Lucien

See LAUTREAMONT, COMTE DE.

Dudintsev, Vladimir Dmitrievich

(1918–1998) *novelist*

Vladimir Dudintsev was born in Kupyansk, Ukraine. After his graduation from the Moscow Law Institute, Dudintsev briefly served in the Soviet army at the outbreak of World War II. Although he wrote a number of short works during the Stalinist era, most of them, as Dudintsev later admitted, were lackluster and mediocre. His real publishing debut came in 1956 with the publication of the novel *Not by Bread Alone.*

Not by Bread Alone tells the story of Lopatkin, a brilliant inventor who was hindered by government red tape. In the West, the novel was hailed for its candid portrayal of negative aspects of the Soviet Union. The work was harshly criticized at a notorious 1957 meeting of the Soviet Writers' Union. (That meeting became the topic of a poem by Yevgeny YEVTUSHENKO, "Again a Meeting": "Again a meeting, noisy, dying / half colloquium / half co-lying . . ." —translation by Albert C. Todd.) For a long period of time, he was shunned by most of the "official" Soviet writers. Dudintsev found ready support for his work among the political dissidents, but he encountered enormous difficulties publishing in the Soviet Union. His second work, *A New Year's Fairy Tale* (1957), was a science-fiction novel set in a Soviet Union of the future.

Dudintsev published his final novel, *White Clothes,* in 1987 at the height of the perestroika movement. *White Clothes* once again criticized government corruption and endless circles of bureaucracy. He also blamed a number of careless, greedy government officials for the environmental disasters in Russia. The novel was widely read and hailed as a work of great social significance.

When Dudintsev died in 1998, he was considered one of the best writers of the Soviet era. He often took great personal risks to expose the social problems of the Soviet Union, and his well-crafted prose is much admired.

Another Work by Vladimir Dudintsev

A New Year's Fairy Tale. In Robert Magidoff, ed., *Russian Science Fiction: An Anthology.* Translated by Doris Johnson. New York: New York University Press, 1964.

Dupin, Amandine-Aurore-Lucile

See SAND, GEORGE.

Duras, Claire de (ca. 1777–1828) *novelist*

Claire de Duras was born to a French noble family. Her father, a count, was a member of the liberal French aristocracy. A supporter of radical ideas, he was executed for failing to support the execution of Louis XVI. After her father's death, de Duras fled with her mother to the United States where they spent some time in Philadelphia, Pennsylvania, with family. She also took a journey to Martinique to receive an inheritance. In both America and Martinique, she saw the realities of slavery. They then traveled to Switzerland and to London, where de Duras met her future husband, Amédée-Brittany-Malo de Durfort, the duke of Durfort and the future duke of Duras. They were married in 1797.

In 1808, de Duras moved to France with her husband where, as a result of changes brought about by the Restoration, he became an active member of the court in 1814. While her husband was busy with his duties, de Duras held gatherings of thinkers, poets, and intellectuals who discussed their thoughts and ideas about the unjustness of life. It was during these meetings that de Duras began to relate the story of a Senegalese girl, rescued from slavery by a French aristocratic family, whose life of privilege does not protect her from the alienation of racism. The story became popular in the group, and de Duras was encouraged to write it down. This became her first novel, *Ourika* (1823).

Initially published anonymously, *Ourika* grew to become a national obsession. The work opposed the prevailing attitude that slavery was a natural thing and denounced it as an evil institution. The work was also unique in that the narrator was a black woman, which was almost unheard of in French literature at this time. As John Fowles says in the introduction to his translation, it is "the first serious attempt by a white novelist to enter a black mind."

In 1822, de Duras became sick and depressed. She withdrew to her country house, where she wrote two more novels on the subjects of sex and class: *Olivier* (1822) and the epistolary novel *Edouard* (1825), both of which feature gentle heroes with feminine characteristics. She was never interested in writing for money or fame; instead, she hoped that her works would promote change. Only after her death did her works and their frank depiction of social concerns begin to gain recognition.

Another Work by Claire de Duras

Ourika: An English Translation. Translated by John Fowles. New York: Modern Language Association of America, 1995.

Works about Claire de Duras

Crichfield, Grant. *Three Novels of Madame de Duras.* The Hague: Mouton, 1975.

Kadish, Doris Y., and Françoise Massardier-Kenney, eds. *Translating Slavery: Gender and Race in French*

Women's Writing, 1783–1823. Kent, Ohio: Kent State University Press, 1994.

Duras, Marguerite (1914–1996) *novelist, playwright, screenwriter*

Born Marguerite Donnadieu in Gia Dinh, Indochina, the area which is now Vietnam, she took her pseudonym, Duras, from the name of a French village near where her father had once owned land. Her father died when Duras was only four years old, and her mother, a teacher, struggled to support her three children on her own. Duras spent most of her childhood in Indochina and, when she was still a teenager, had an affair with a wealthy Chinese man. She returns to this period of life repeatedly in her novels.

When Duras was 17, she moved to France to study law and political science at the Sorbonne. After graduating in 1935, she went to work as a secretary at the Ministry of Colonies. In 1939, she married Robert Antelme. With the arrival of World War II, she became a member of the French Resistance. Antelme became a Resistance leader and was captured and imprisoned. He survived Buchenwald, Gandersheim, and Dachau. After his release, Duras, who had been planning to leave him before his capture, nursed him back to health, living with him in a ménage à trois with Dionys Mascolo. She joined the Communist Party in that period but in 1950, after the Prague Uprising, was expelled for revisionism.

Duras published her first novel, *Les Impudents* (1942), in a style greatly influenced by American author Ernest Hemingway. She gained the most recognition, however, during the 1950s with her novels *Un Barrage Contre le Pacifique* (*The Sea Wall,* 1950) about an impoverished family living in Indochina, and the psychological romance novel *Le Marin de Gibralter* (*The Sailor from Gibraltar,* 1952). Her novel *Le Square* (1955) earned her both respect as an author and association with what was known as the NEW NOVEL group. However, in her next novel, *Moderato Cantabile* (1958), Duras shifts her writing style

from traditional topics and themes to what would become her prevailing themes of death, memory, sexual desire, and love.

Toward the end of the 1950s, Duras turned her attention to writing screenplays. The film for which she is best known internationally is *Hiroshima, Mon Amour* (1959). Directed by Alain Resnais, the film focuses on the theme of complications arising from the love between two people who have experienced the trauma of war. It tells of the brief love affair between Emmanuelle Riva, a married French actress, and Eija Okada, a Japanese architect, during which Riva tells Okada of her forbidden love affair with a German soldier and her subsequent mental breakdown. Innovative in its use of flashbacks and montages, the film received mixed reviews. It earned an Academy Award nomination for best screenplay but failed miserably in the box offices in Japan.

Duras's work became increasingly experimental in the 1960s, especially after the 1968 student revolts. She became interested in the power of language, memories, and alienation. Feminist critics tie her shift in style directly to the concept of feminine writing with its increasing sparseness and suggestiveness. Love, for Duras's characters, becomes an escape that is often linked with alcohol and madness.

In the 1970s, Duras continued to focus on writing screenplays, including the film *Camion* (1982) with French actor Gérald Depardieu. She returned to the novel format in the 1980s with the semiautobiographical *The Lover* (1984), for which she won France's most cherished literary honor, the Prix Goncourt. The novel, made into a film by the same name in 1992, focuses on the sexual initiation of a young girl in Indochina. Duras's works were often associated with events in her life. Her collection of short stories *La Doleur* (1985) was based on her relationship with Antelme and Mascolo.

In 1980, Duras met Yann Andréa Steiner. The two lived together until Duras's death. Duras's creativity during this period was often shadowed by her increasing abuse of alcohol. In *Practicalities* (1987), she wrote about her relationship with

Steiner, her alcoholism, and her 15-year addiction to aspirin. Steiner finally encouraged her to enter a hospital for treatment in 1982, but when Duras returned home, she began to suffer from hallucinations and a fear that her house had been invaded by strangers. Steiner stayed with her until her death.

Other Works by Marguerite Duras

No More. Translated by Richard Howard. New York: Seven Stories Press, 1998.

The North China Lover. Translated by Leigh Hafrey. New York: The New Press, 1992.

The Ravishing of Lol Stein. Translated by Richard Seaver. New York: Pantheon Books, 1986.

Writing. Translated by Mark Polizzotti. Cambridge, Mass.: Brookline Books, 1998.

Works about Marguerite Duras

Adler, Laure. *Marguerite Duras: A Life.* Translated by Anne-Marie Glasheen. Chicago: University of Chicago Press, 2000.

Schuster, Marilyn R. *Marguerite Duras Revisited.* Boston: Twayne, 1993.

Dürrenmatt, Friedrich (1921–1990)
dramatist, novelist

Friedrich Dürrenmatt was born in Konolfingen, Switzerland, to Reinhold and Hulda Zimmermann Dürrenmatt. His father was the pastor of the Konolfingen church. Dürrenmatt attended secondary school in Großhochstetten and spent his spare time painting, a lifelong interest. After his family moved to Bern in 1935, he attended Freies Gymnasium, a Christian secondary school, and then Humboldtianum, a private school. After graduating in 1941, he studied philosophy, literature, and natural sciences at the University of Zurich and the University of Bern. He served for a year in the Swiss military during World War II and married actress Lotti Geißler in 1946.

Dürrenmatt's first drama, *Es steht geschrieben* (*It Is Written,* 1947) succeeded with critics but not audiences. He attracted more popular success with his play *Romulus der Große* (*Romulus the Great,* 1949). Dürrenmatt wrote three detective novels and his first work of essays, *Theaterprobleme* (1955), in the 1950s. His most popular plays, *Der Besuch der alten Dame* (*The Visit,* 1956, translated 1958) and *Die Physiker* (*The Physicists,* 1962), examine the themes of power, responsibility, and guilt. Dürrenmatt later served on the board of directors of the Zurich Schauspielhaus and continued writing plays until 1988.

Dürrenmatt adapted the satire of Jonathan Swift (1667–1745) and the dramatic technique of Bertolt BRECHT to his works. He is best known for comic-grotesque satires that explore religious and philosophical issues. He was a pessimist who, according to biographer Roger Crockett, "did not believe that humanity had a promising future on this planet, and he created scenario after scenario to demonstrate this conclusion." Dürrenmatt's numerous awards include the Georg Büchner Prize and the New York Theater Critics' Prize. Even after his death in 1990, *The Visit* and the *The Physicists* were among the most performed plays in Germany.

Other Works by Friedrich Dürrenmatt

The Assignment. Translated by Joel Agee. New York: Random House, 1988.

The Execution of Justice. Translated by John E. Woods. New York: Random House, 1989.

A Work about Friedrich Dürrenmatt

Crockett, Roger A. *Understanding Friedrich Dürrenmatt.* Columbia, S.C.: University of South Carolina Press, 1998.

E

Eco, Umberto (1932–) *novelist, literary critic*

Born in Alessandria, Italy, Umberto Eco is the son of Giralio Eco, an office worker for an iron-bathtub manufacturer, and Giovanna (Bisio) Eco. He grew up amid World War II, dodging bombs in the countryside as a young teen but also embracing American literature and popular music.

Eco received a doctorate of philosophy from the University of Turin in 1954 at age 22. His thesis on St. Thomas Aquinas and his later work, *The Development of Medieval Aesthetics* (1959), helped stir his passion for the medieval world. His research was invaluable when he wrote his signature work, the novel *The Name of the Rose* (1980).

After his 1954 graduation, Eco worked in Milan preparing cultural programs for RAI, a new state television network. This exposure to television gave him insights into the world of mass media, a subject about which he wrote extensively later in his career. From 1956 to 1964, Eco held a lecturing post at the University of Turin and from 1964 to 1965 at the University of Milan.

In the late 1950s, Eco began to contribute to such Italian daily newspapers and magazines as *L'Espresso*, but it was the publication of his first novel, *The Name of the Rose*, that won Eco worldwide critical acclaim. The novel uses semiotics (the study of signs, codes, and clues) to tell the story of a murder mystery set in a medieval monastery. Eco founded a journal on semiotics in 1971 and has written several books on the subject. In *The Name of the Rose*, he employs semiotic techniques such as using the 10-part Sefirot or Cabbalic system as an underlying structure. The novel became popular with a cross-section of readers from lovers of bestsellers to scholars and set records for world sales of an Italian book. In 1986, the novel was made into a major motion picture starring Sean Connery and also received the Strega and Viareggio Prizes, as well as the Medici Prize in France. Eco told *Contemporary Authors* in 1979, "I think that the duty of a scholar is not only to do scientific research but also to communicate with people through various media about most important issues of social life from the point of view of his own discipline."

Eco is also well known for *Foucault's Pendulum* (1988), a novel set in Milan, Paris, and Brazil. It tells the story of a search for a plan of the universe that involves the medieval religious order the Knights Templar and their plans for world domination. The story comes to this conclusion: "There is no map. There is no plan: the secret, he has come to see, is that there is no secret; the answer is that there is no answer."

Umberto Eco is a significant Italian literary figure. Much more than a best-selling novelist, Eco has made his name, say scholars Norma Bouchard and Veronica Pravadelli, as "a theorist of avant-gardist aesthetics, a scholar of popular culture, a leading semiotician and philosopher of language, [and] a highly respected journalist."

Another Work by Umberto Eco

The Island of the Day Before. Translated by William Weaver. New York: Harcourt Brace Jovanovich, 1995.

Works about Umberto Eco

Bondanella, Peter. *Umberto Eco and the Open Text: Semiotics, Fiction, Popular Culture.* New York: Cambridge University Press, 1997.

Bouchard, Norma, and Veronica Pravadelli, eds. *Umberto Eco's Alternative.* New York: Peter Lang, 1998.

Ehrenburg, Ilya Grigoryevich

(1891–1967) *novelist, short-story writer, poet, travel writer, essayist*

Ilya Grigoryevich Ehrenburg was born in Kiev, Ukraine, into the family of a middle-class Jewish brewer. Facing rapidly growing anti-Semitism in Ukraine, the Ehrenburgs moved to Moscow, Russia, in 1896. Ehrenburg briefly attending the First Moscow gymnasium (high school) but was expelled for participating in revolutionary activities. In 1908, Ehrenburg decided to leave Russia to avoid a trial for his political activities that could, despite his youth, have resulted in a lengthy prison term. Living in Paris, Ehrenburg participated in the artistic circles of French society.

Ehrenburg started his prolific career with a publication of a poetry collection in 1910. During World War I, he briefly served as a war correspondent. Between 1921 and 1924, he lived in Germany and Belgium. His first novel, *The Extraordinary Adventures of Julia Jurenito and His Disciples* (1921) was a political satire that ridiculed both the capitalist and Communist political systems. In 1928,

Ehrenburg published *The Stormy Life and Lazar Roitschwantz,* a novel that depicts wanderings through Europe of a Jewish tailor who barely escapes the anti-Semitism of Russia. Both novels combined sensitivity for the nuances of the plot with biting social commentary.

From 1925 to 1945, Ehrenburg lived in Paris, working for Soviet newspapers and returning to Russia on occasion. In the 1930s, his writings became markedly less radical as he accepted the official doctrines of the Communist Party. In *Out of Chaos* (1934), for instance, he ardently defends the aesthetic goals of SOCIALIST REALISM. In his novel *The Fall of Paris* (1941), he criticizes the capitalist system of France and delineates the social degeneration of French society.

Ehrenburg was honored on several occasions in the Soviet Union. In 1942 and 1948, he was awarded the Stalin Prize and, in 1952, the International Lenin Peace Prize. He also served as a deputy of the Supreme Soviet of the USSR from 1950 and as a vice president of the World Peace Council until his death in 1967. Ehrenburg spent his last days campaigning to publish the works of writers who were suppressed under Stalin's regime. Ehrenburg's fiction, although deeply politicized, reveals a high level of narrative control and a deep understanding of human nature. Despite his positions in the Soviet regime, Ehrenburg was highly respected by Western intellectuals and artists.

A Work about Ilya Ehrenburg

Goldberg, Anatol. *Ilya Ehrenburg, Revolutionary, Novelist, Poet, War Correspondent, Propagandist: The Extraordinary Epic of a Russian Survivor.* New York: Viking Press, 1984.

Eich, Günter (Erich Günter) (1907–1972)
dramatist, poet

Günter Eich was born in Lebus an der Oder to Otto and Helen Heine Eich. Otto, an accountant, moved the family to Berlin in 1918. Eich finished his secondary education in Leipzig in 1925. He studied Chinese, law, and economics at universities in Leipzig, Berlin, and Paris. Eich published his first poems in an anthology in 1927 and his first volume of poems in 1930. In the 1930s, he worked as a freelance writer and was a pioneer in the writing of German radio plays. In 1940, he married Else Anna Burk, a singer who died a few years later. Eich served in the German air force during World War II. The Americans captured him in 1945 and released him the following year. Starting in 1947, Eich regularly attended the annual meetings of the German literary association, GRUPPE 47. He married the poet Ilse AICHINGER in 1953.

While in a POW camp, Eich wrote "Inventur," a poem that is considered the epitome of the *Kahlschlag* (Clean Sweep) movement. Popular in the 1950s, *Kahlschlag* symbolized the break with past ideologies. German writers embracing this movement sought to address material facts, such as hunger and disease, while cutting corrupt ideals, ideas, and language out of their writing.

Eich's lyric poetry was inspired by Chinese poets such as Li Tai Pe. Favoring the audible over the visual, he attained his greatest notoriety for his radio plays. Eich's best-known play is *Träume* (*Dreams*, 1953). It contains some of his best poetry and addresses his favorite themes: dreams, death, and the divide between reality and unreality. According to the literary scholar Egbert Krispyn, Eich displayed an "uncompromising creative honesty" in his work, which won several awards, including the Munich Grant Prize for Literature and the Friedrich Schiller Memorial Prize of Mannheim.

Another Work by Günter Eich

Pigeons and Moles: Selected Writings of Günter Eich. Translated by Michael Hamburger. Columbia, S.C.: Camden House, 1990.

Works about Günter Eich

Cuomo, Glenn R. *Career at the Cost of Compromise: Günter Eich's Life and Work in the Years 1933–1945.* Atlanta: Rodopi, 1989.

Krispyn, Egbert. *Günter Eich.* Boston: Twayne, 1971.

El Saadawi, Nawal

See SADAWI, NAWAL.

Éluard, Paul (Eugène-Emile-Paul Grindel)
(1895–1952) *poet*

Paul Éluard was born Paul Grindel in Saint-Denis on the outskirts of Paris. When he was 18, he was confined to a sanatorium in Switzerland to recover from a bout of tuberculosis. During this time, he discovered his love for poetry and published his first collection of poems.

Éluard was deeply affected by the tragedy of World War I. He became a pacifist militant and wrote *Poèmes pour la paix* (1918), which details both the need for conflict and the desire to temper it with peace. He also met Tristan TZARA, André BRETON, and Louis ARAGON, who encouraged him in 1920 to become an active participant in the DADA movement. He later joined the surrealists, becoming one of its major influences. But, simultaneously, he remained true to his own visions of literary integrity, questioning the validity of certain ideas such as automatic writing, a belief that the spiritual realm could convey itself through the writing implement, without the judgment of the writer.

Alongside his opposition to violence and war, Éluard's personal life, in particular his marriage to Maria Benz, became one of the focal points of his writing. She was the inspiration for the passionate celebration of love in his collections *Capitale de la douleur* (1926), *L'Amour, la poésie* (1929), and *La Vérité immédiate* (1932). These works are notable in that they mark a departure from his focus on passive militarism.

Éluard was barred from the Communist Party as a result of a conflict with Aragon. He joined the Resistance, continuing his creative work with collections such as *La victoire de Guernica* (1938) and *Poésie et vérité* (1942). The latter collection contains his most often studied poem "Liberté." Shortly after the liberation and the traumatic death of his wife in 1946, Éluard began to focus his writing on the hope that one day humanity would leave behind its murderous tendencies. He became an impassioned humanist, as evidenced in his works. He died in Charenton-le-Pont.

Other Works by Paul Éluard

Last Love Poems of Paul Éluard. Translated by Marilyn Kallet. Baton Rouge: Louisiana State University Press, 1980.
Selected Poems. Translated by Gilbert Bowen. New York: River Run Press, 1987.

A Work about Paul Éluard

Nugent, Robert. *Paul Éluard.* Boston: Twayne Publishers, 1974.

Elytis, Odysseus (Odysseus Alepoudelis)
(1911–1996) *poet*

Odysseus Elytis was born in Iraklion on the island of Crete. The son of a wealthy manufacturer, he shunned the privileged life and devoted himself entirely to seeking truth in his works.

Elytis's first poetry dates back to 1929 and celebrates his childhood visits to the Aegean Sea. He established his reputation as a poet in the 1930s, a decade haunted by the threat of war, by focusing on the intrinsic beauty of humanity and nature. In *Orientations* (1940), Elytis's first and largest collection, he combines elements of the surrealist movement with free association and pagan nature worship. During World War II, Elytis served on the front lines in Albania, fighting against Italian and German forces. This struggle particularly affected him, as did the subsequent horrors of the Nazi occupation of Greece. It was the barbaric nature of war that led him to continue writing poetry that glorified the beauty of his homeland and sought to maintain its integrity against the threat of human destruction. His long poem *Heroic and Elegiac Song of the Lost Second Lieutenant of Albania* (1945) gave voice to Elytis's experiences and feelings. The novel celebrates life and the invisible forces that bind humankind to the natural world while, simultaneously, confronting the very basic conflict of good versus evil.

Elytis is most remembered, however, for *Axion Esti* (1959), a three-part celebration of Greek folklore and history. Translated as *Worth It Be,* this epic poem draws on elements of the Byzantine mass in conjunction with the history of Greece and the biblical creation story. It was later set to music by Theodorakis, who also composed the film score for *Zorba the Greek.* Theodorakis described the poem as a "Bible for the Greek people," which, in a sense, it was, as it later became an anthem for Greek youth.

Elytis spent much of his life in seclusion, focusing only on his poetry. He considered himself to be neither a patriotic poet nor a nature poet. He felt that his duty as a poet was to transform the images offered him by nature to a level where they could exist as reminders to all humanity of the possibility of perfection and beauty in this world. In 1979, he was awarded the Nobel Prize in literature and became a cultural ambassador for the Greek people. He began to travel to give lectures; however, three years later, he confessed to being so busy traveling that he had no time to write. Returning to semiseclusion, he resumed writing, publishing his final collection *West of Sorrow* (1995).

Elytis was so important to the Greek people that radio and television programs were interrupted to announce his death in 1966. Elytis's own definition of death perhaps explains his significance as a writer: "Death is where words no longer have the power to generate, right from the start, the things that they name." For Elytis, poetry was not simply an art; it was also a social responsibility.

Other Works by Odysseus Elytis

The Collected Poems of Odysseus Elytis. Translated by Jeffrey Carson and Nikos Sarris. Baltimore: Johns Hopkins University Press, 1997.
Odysseus Elytis: Analogies of Light. Edited by Ivar Ivask. Norman: University of Oklahoma Press, 1981.
What I Love: Selected Poems of Odysseas Elytis. Translated by Olga Broumas. Port Townsend, Wash.: Copper Canyon Press, 1986.

Emecheta, Buchi (1944–   ) *novelist*

Buchi Emecheta was born of Ibuza parents in Nigeria. Orphaned at an early age, she spent her childhood in a missionary school. In 1960, at age 16, she married Sylvester Onwordi, to whom she had been engaged since she was 11. In 1962, the couple moved to London; the marriage lasted six years and produced five children.

Many of Emecheta's earliest novels draw on her experiences in Africa and England. Emecheta's early writing style is based on oral tradition. She speaks from her own experiences and vividly describes the people and places encountered by her characters on their journey to self-awareness. Her first novel, *In the Ditch* (1972), tells the story of her life as a struggling immigrant and single mother in London through the character of Adah, a young woman who leaves her husband to find out who she is. In a strange land, she is seen as an outsider. With children in tow, Adah negotiates the welfare system, the job market, and what it means to be deemed a social "problem."

In Emecheta's second novel, *Second Class Citizen* (1974), she continues to chronicle Adah's life, but this time she steps back to see how she arrived in "the ditch." This story concentrates on the inequalities within her culture that manifest themselves as discrimination against women. Adah encounters strict tribal customs that deny education to women. As she bends under the workload of supporting her family and caring for her children, she witnesses the privileges of her student husband. "Second Class Citizen" reveals how gender roles are maintained through culture.

The last novel of Emecheta's trilogy is *Head Above Water* (1986), in which Adah continues to confront the poor social conditions of blacks in London while simultaneously emerging as a writer.

Emecheta has come under fire from some critics for her refusal to support the pastoral ideas of Africa and Europe. Her raw views often expose the dark side of tribal relations, colonialism, and male/female relations.

She was raised at a time in Nigeria when traditional structures were being challenged by a society that was shifting from rural to urban living. It was also a time when immigration to colonial centers, such as London, presented another test of maintaining or adapting one's identity. Emecheta's novels reflect both the chaos and the opportunities of this unrest and uprooting. Emecheta does not write about an idyllic Africa of the past but instead about contemporary Africa with painstaking accuracy.

She centers the majority of her stories on gender relations and the conflicts between modernity and tradition. These topics often serve as metaphors for the relationship between Africa and the Diaspora (the scattering of people of African descent through slavery) and for the relationship between colonizer and the colonized; for example, in *The Family* (1989), she chronicles the life of an impoverished Jamaican girl who negotiates familial abuse, which is one of slavery's legacies. Emecheta's brave approach to writing about the unspoken has set her apart from other African writers. She has won several literary prizes including her selection in 1983 as one of the Best Young British Writers Award. Emecheta is a strong postcolonial writer who witnesses with a feminist lens; as a result, she has diversified traditional Western feminism by adding a voice that speaks to the specific issues of women from developing countries.

Other Works by Buchi Emecheta

The Bride Price. New York: George Braziller, 1980.
In the Ditch. Westport, Conn.: Heinemann, 1994.
The Joys of Motherhood. New York: George Braziller, 1980.
The New Tribe. Westport, Conn.: Heinemann, 2001.
Second Class Citizen. New York: George Braziller, 1983.
The Slave Girl. New York: George Braziller, 1980.

Works about Buchi Emecheta

Fishburn, Katherine. *Reading Buchi Emecheta: Cross-Cultural Conversations.* Westport, Conn.: Greenwood Publishing Group, 1995.

Uraizee, Joya F. *This Is No Place for a Woman: Nadine Gordimer, Nayantara Sahgal, Buchi Emecheta, and the Politics of Gender.* Lawrenceville, N.J.: Africa World Press, 2000.

Enchi Fumiko (Fumi Ueda) (1905–1986)
playwright, novelist

Enchi Fumiko was born in Tokyo to Ueda Kazutoshi and Tsuruko. Kazutoshi was a well-known linguistics professor who helped put together a major Japanese-language dictionary in 1902. As a young child, Enchi was reclusive and sickly, spending more time in her father's extensive library than at play with other children. Enchi attended Japan Women's University but did not earn a degree. In 1930, she married the journalist Enchi Yoshimatsu and had a child, Motoko, two years later. In 1935, she joined a group of novelists known as Nichireki to learn more about writing. In the 1930s and 1940s, she suffered from breast cancer, uterine cancer, and tuberculosis. At the end of World War II, Enchi's home in Tokyo was destroyed during an air raid.

When Enchi was at university, she developed plays for a Tokyo theater founded by a leader in the modern drama-theater (*shingeki*) movement, Kaoru Osanai (1881–1928). However, by the mid-1930s, she could not find publishers for her plays, so she switched to writing novels. At first, the literary world was receptive to her work; however, for most of the 1940s, she had difficulty finding publishers. Her first major success was *The Starving Years* (1953), about a woman trapped in marriage to a womanizing, chauvinistic man. The novel, however, that won her international acclaim was *Masks* (1958), based on the story of Lady Rokujō from *The Tale of Genji.*

Enchi is known for combining elements from classical Japanese works from the Heian (794–1185) and Edo (1600–1867) periods into modern settings. Many of her stories center on women navigating patriarchal Japan. She has won numerous literary awards, including the Tanizaki Prize in 1969, the Japanese Literature Grand Prize in 1972, and the Order of Culture in 1985.

Other Works by Enchi Fumiko
A Tale of False Fortunes. Translated by Roger K. Thomas. Honolulu: University of Hawaii Press, 2000.
The Waiting Years. Translated by John Bester. Tokyo: Kodansha International, 1971.

A Work about Enchi Fumiko
Vernon, Victoria V. *Daughters of the Moon: Wish, Will and Social Constraint in Fiction by Modern Japanese Women.* Berkeley: Institute of East Asian Studies, University of California Press, 1988.

Enzensberger, Hans Magnus (1929–)
poet, novelist, essayist

Hans Magnus Enzensberger was born in Kaufbeuren, Germany, to middle-class parents and grew up in Nuremberg. As a teenager during World War II, Enzensberger served in the *Volksstürm* (Home Guard). After the war, he worked as an interpreter for the occupying British and American armies, tended bar, and traded on the black market. Enzensberger studied philosophy, literature, and languages at several universities, including the Sorbonne in Paris. After completing his dissertation, he spent two years in radio work and traveled extensively.

Enzensberger's first book of poetry, *Verteidigung der Wölfe* (*Defense of the Wolves,* 1957), sharply criticized West Germany's government and culture, establishing his reputation as one of Germany's most controversial poets. His important influences include Bertolt BRECHT. He was a member of the literary association GRUPPE 47 and won the Georg Büchner Prize in 1963. In 1965, Enzensberger founded *Kursbuch* (*Coursebook*), a progressive magazine that provided a forum for political and literary debates. He used his essays, poems, and novels to voice his social criticisms and to call for revolutionary change. Literary scholar Peter Demetz describes Enzensberger, in *Postwar German Literature* (1970), as "a highly gifted intellectual" who "wants his reader to think."

Other Works by Hans Magnus Enzensberger

Politics and Crime. New York: Seabury Press, 1974.

The Sinking of the Titanic: A Poem. Translated by the author. Boston: Houghton Mifflin, 1980.

A Work about Hans Magnus Enzensberger

Fischer, Gerhard, ed. *Debating Enzensberger: Great Migration and Civil War.* Tübingen, Germany: Stauffenburg, 1996.

Esenin, Sergey

See YESENIN, SERGEY.

Espinet, Ramabai (1948–   ) *poet, researcher, professor, activist, social commentator*

Born in Trinidad, Ramabai Espinet grew up in a largely creolized, Christian-Indian community in San Fernando. She started reading the works of the English romantics, along with those of Alfred, Lord Tennyson and Henry Wadsworth Longfellow, at an early age. By her late teens, when she moved to Toronto, Espinet had read most of William Butler Yeats's and Derek WALCOTT's works. These poets, as well as the calypso music from her childhood, have significantly influenced her writing.

Poets Barbara Jones and Gabriela MISTRAL, who both wrote about women's issues, shaped Espinet's perception of women's poetics, and Espinet subsequently became active in the women's movement in the Caribbean and Canada. In 1990, she published *Creation Fire,* a Caribbean poetry anthology containing a wide range of female Caribbean poets' works in English, French, Dutch, and Spanish.

Themes of identity, gender, and spirituality run through Espinet's own imagistic poetry, which has been published in *CAFRA News, Trinidad and Tobago Review, Woman Speak, Fireweed,* and *Toronto South Asian Review. Nuclear Seasons,* published in 1991, contains her collected poems. In an interview with Kwame Dawes in *Talk Yuh Talk: Interviews with Anglophone Caribbean Poets,* (2001)

Espinet said, "In *Nuclear Seasons* the narrative line, for the most part, comes second to the metaphor. But I find myself writing a series of poems more directly now."

Apart from poetry, Espinet has published children's fiction: *The Princess of Spadina: a Tale of Toronto* (1992) and *Ninja's Carnival* (1993). Her essays and short fiction have appeared in journals and anthologies. *The Swinging Bridge* (forthcoming), Espinet's first novel, examines an Indo-Caribbean woman's experiences in Trinidad and Canada.

After dividing her time between Canada and the Caribbean since the 1970s, Espinet now lives in Toronto, where she teaches English and Caribbean studies. She weaves one of her unique projects, "the invention or the renewal of lost myths, especially Caribbean feminist myth," through her varied but connected academic, literary, and activist pursuits.

Other Works by Ramabai Espinet

"Indian Cuisine." *The Massachusetts Review* 35, no. 3–4 (Fall 1994): 563.

"The Invisible Woman in West Indian Fiction." *World Literature Written in English.* 29, no. 2 (Autumn 1989): 116–26.

Works about Ramabai Espinet

Birbalsingh, Frank. *Indo-Caribbean Resistance.* Toronto: TSAR, 1993.

Mehta, Brinda J. "Indo-Trinidadian Fiction: Female Identity and Creative Cooking." *Alif: A Journal of Comparative Poetics* 19 (1999): 151–84.

Puri, Shalini. "Race, Rape, and Representation: Indo-Caribbean Women and Cultural Nationalism." *Cultural Critique* (Spring 1997): 119–63.

Espronceda y Delgado, José de (José Ignacio Javier Oriol Encarnación de Espronceda) (1808–1842) *poet*

Born in western Spain, Espronceda was the son of a soldier. He had three brothers, all of whom died shortly after birth. During the first several years of his life, Espronceda and his family were constantly on the move due to the Napoleonic Wars. Espronceda witnessed many of the atrocities of war; his poems are moving, painful, bitter, and tender, reflecting his life experience.

At age 15, Espronceda formed and became president of *Los Numantinos,* a secret patriotic organization. Shortly thereafter, he was arrested and sentenced to prison. The intervention of his father, then a colonel, resulted in his release just weeks later.

In 1826, he traveled to the Portuguese capital of Lisbon, then a center for Spanish liberals. Espronceda tried to enlist in the National Guard but was exiled instead because one of his published poems proved to be too liberal. During this exile, he wrote his only novel, *Sancho Saldaña o el castellano de Cuéllar (Sancho Saldaña or the Spaniard of Cuéllar,* 1834). He returned to Madrid, where he founded several liberal/democratic newspapers and wrote one of the most popular Spanish poems of all time, "The Pirate's Song" (1835), which celebrates its antisocial narrator's love of liberty. Other poems of the 1930s that raise questions of social justice include "Under Sentence of Death," "The Executioner," and "The Beggar." In 1840, he published "To Jarifa in an Orgy," a sympathetic address to a prostitute by a disillusioned idealist. After traveling as a delegate to the Spanish embassy, Espronceda took ill and died at age 34.

His two major works were written in his last two years. *The Student from Salamanca* is a narrative poem about a Don Juan-like character. *The Godforsaken World,* which includes the celebrated "Canto a Teresa," addressed to Teresa Mancha, Espronceda's mistress of 10 years, remained unfinished at his death. José de Espronceda's poetry is the epitome of Spanish ROMANTICISM. It is lyrical, patriotic, and youthful. It portrays doubt, sorrow, pleasure, death, pessimism, and disillusion.

Another Work by José de Espronceda y Delgado

The Student of Salamanca/El estudiante de Salamanca. Translated by C. K. Davies, with introduction and notes by Richard A. Cardwell. Warminster, U.K.: Aris & Phillips, 1998.

Works about José de Espronceda y Delgado
Ilie, Paul. "Espronceda and the Romantic Grotesque." *Studies in Romanticism II* (1972): 94–112.

Landeira, Ricardo. *José de Espronceda.* Boulder: University of Colorado, 1984.

Pallady, Stephen. *Irony in the Poetry of José de Espronceda.* Lewiston, N.Y.: Edwin Mellen Press, 1991.

existentialism
Existentialism is a philosophical, artistic, and literary movement that emphasizes individual existence and freedom of choice. Although difficult to define precisely because it encompassed a wide array of diverse elements, certain themes are consistent in works by writers associated with the movement, most particularly the theme of individual existence. Although existentialism is linked explicitly to the 19th and 20th centuries, elements of existentialism can also be found in Socrates' works and in the Bible.

The literary form of the novel became one of the most prominent modes of expression for the movement in the 19th century. Russian novelist Fyodor Dostoyevsky was considered the most prominent existentialist literary figure as exemplified in his novel, *Notes from the Underground* (1864), which focuses on the alienated antihero who must fight against the optimism inherent in rationalist humanism. Logic is eventually shown to be self-destructive. Only Christian love, which cannot be understood through reason and logic, can save humanity. This and other existentialist works found a base in strong Christian theology, as can be seen in the works of German Protestant theologians Paul Tillich and Rudolf Karl Bultmann, French Roman Catholic theologian Gabriel Marcel, the Russian Orthodox philosopher Nikolay Aleksandrovich Berdyayev, and the German Jewish philosopher Martin Buber (existential theists). However, the movement itself encompassed equally strong proponents of atheism, agnosticism, and paganism (existential atheists), all sharing the common theme of individual choice.

Examined historically, existentialism was first anticipated by the 17th-century French philosopher Blaise Pascal, who rejected the rigorous rationalism of his contemporary René Descartes. Pascal contends, in his *Pensées* (1670), that any attempt to explain systematically and rationally concepts as broad as God and humanity must be rooted in arrogance. Like the existentialists, he viewed human existence as a series of paradoxes, the ultimate of which was the human self, a combination of mind and body that inherently contradicts itself.

The 19th-century Danish philosopher, Søren Kierkegaard, was the first writer to refer to himself actually as an existentialist. Regarded as the founder of modern existentialism, he insisted in his works that the highest good for the individual is to find his or her own true path in life. Writing in response to and in negation of G. W. F. Hegel, who claimed to have discovered a way to understand and explain humanity and history rationally and absolutely, Kierkegaard focused on the ambiguity and absurdity of life. He also stressed the importance of committing completely to the choices that are made, often forsaking established societal norms, in the ultimate quest for personal validity. He advocated faith and the Christian way of life as the only means of avoiding despair. Kierkegaard also examined the concept of fear or dread as crucial to greater understanding.

Other existentialist writers and artists went on to echo Kierkegaard's ideas, focusing on the belief that the individual must be allowed to pursue his or her own path, free from the constraints of imposed moral standards. Existentialists argue that there is no objective or rational basis for moral decisions. The German existential philosopher Friedrich NIETZSCHE, for example, theorized that individual choice has a basis in subjectivity and that it is the individual's responsibility to choose the actions that constitute a moral decision. Nietzsche criticized traditional moral assumptions, citing free will as existing in direct opposition to moral conformity. Unlike Kierkegaard,

whose ideas led to radically individualistic Christianity, Nietzsche rejected Judeo-Christian ideals, proclaiming the "death of God" and espousing the pagan ideal.

French existentialism grew and flourished independently from German existentialism. Jean Wahl (1888–1974) is considered to be the founder of the French existentialist movement, which was later expanded and brought to greater attention under Jean Paul SARTRE. Sartre adopted the term *existentialism* for his own philosophy and became the leader of the movement in France. It was through his works that, after World War II, existentialism began to gain recognition and followers on an international scale. Sartre's philosophy is atheistic and decidedly pessimistic. He asserts that, although human beings desire a rational basis for their existence, no such foundation exists. Therefore, human life seems contingent and futile. His negativity notwithstanding, he also insisted that existentialism is tied directly to humanism with its emphasis on freedom, choice, and responsibility. Other French writers were profoundly influenced by Sartre and Nietzsche. The works of André MALRAUX and Albert CAMUS are generally associated with existentialist ideas because of their focus on the absurdity of life and the apparent indifference of the universe to human suffering. The French THEATRE OF THE ABSURD also reflects existentialist ideals, as seen in the plays of Samuel BECKETT and Eugène IONESCO.

Works about Existentialism

Giles, James, ed. *French Existentialism: Consciousness, Ethics and Relations with Others.* Atlanta, Ga.: Rodopi, 1999.

Gordon, Haim, ed. *The Dictionary of Existentialism.* Westport, Conn.: Greenwood Press, 1999.

Guignon, Charles, and Derk Pereboom, eds. *Existentialism: Basic Writings.* Indianapolis, Ind.: Hackett Publishing Company, 2001.

MacDonald, Paul S., ed. *The Existentialist Reader: An Anthology of Key Texts.* New York: Routledge, 2001.

expressionism

Expressionism refers to a literary and artistic movement that emerged in Germany in the late 19th century and reached its pinnacle in the late 1920s. Expressionists generally believed that an individual's thoughts and experiences cannot be rendered in objective terms because such representation would distort and sterilize subjective, emotional experience. Under this premise, expressionists rejected REALISM and aimed to depict the world artistically through personal vision. To achieve this, expressionists portray their subjects as experience or emotion rather than through realistic detail. In general, expressionists tended either to simplify or to distort their subjects to expose extreme and fragmented states of human consciousness. Expressionist works are often set in a nightmarish atmosphere to emphasize the dramatic gap between subjective and objective reality.

Expressionism has a more precise meaning in art criticism than it does in literary criticism. In art, the term refers to a school of German and Scandinavian painters of the early 20th century who claimed that human condition cannot be mimetically represented through exact depiction of reality. In the visual arts, one of the most famous examples of a work that depicts expressionistic ideals is Edvard Munch's painting *The Cry* (1893).

Expressionism also found a fertile ground in film: Fritz Lang's expressionist film *Metropolis* (1927), for example, presents a dystopian vision of the future in which the workers are oppressed and held under control by the machines and the elite that controls the machines. *Metropolis* established itself as the foundational classic of world cinema.

In literature, expressionism also originated in Germany. Most literary scholars identify the emergence of expressionism with the works of dramatists Frank Nedekind, Carl Stranheim, and August STRINDBERG. Expressionism also took root in the poetry of Franz Werfel and the fiction of Franz KAFKA. Eventually, literary critics began to refer to every work of literature of the period in which reality is purposefully distorted as expressionist.

Consequently, it has become difficult to demarcate the literary expressionists precisely. Although some critics limit the use of the term to the German literary movement of the 20th century, some critics apply the term more liberally to any work that manifests expressionist characteristics.

The German expressionist movement had an intriguing influence on psychology as well, particularly in the works of the Austrian psychoanalytic theorist Sigmund FREUD. Expressionism tended to explore the dark corners of the human mind, often illuminating anxieties, fears, and secret fantasies. Many critics have attributed this interest to the historical conditions following World War I and the subsequent disillusionment with humanity. Expressionism, thus, also artistically revealed the repressed fears and anxieties of the human psyche.

The expressionist movement was brutally suppressed by the Nazi government. The Nazis viewed the expressionists as a degenerate and subversive group and organized an exhibition of confiscated works of expressionists to demonstrate their "decadence" and "absurdity"; ironically, the exhibition backfired, and thousands of people flooded in to appreciate the works of the famous expressionist artists.

German expressionism influenced a number of writers and artists around the world, including James Joyce and T. S. Eliot. Many modern and POSTMODERN writers, including Tennessee Williams, the Beat writers, and Joseph Heller, were all influenced by the expressionism, which questioned accepted ideas about "objective" reality and brought to literature and art a new psychological dimension—one that is often dark, disturbing, and thought-provoking.

Works about Expressionism

Barron, Stephanie, and Wolf-Dieter Dube, ed. *German Expressionism: Art and Society.* New York: Rizzoli, 1997.

Polcari, Stephen. *Abstract Expressionism and the Modern Experience.* New York: Cambridge University Press, 1993.

Fabian

See LAGERKVIST, PÄR.

Fadeyev, Aleksandr Aleksandrovich

(1901–1956) *novelist, short-story writer*
Aleksandr Aleksandrovich Fadeyev was born in Krimy, Russia. His father was a village teacher, and his mother a nurse. Fadeyev's family moved to Sarovka, in the far eastern region of Russia, in 1908. Fadeyev attended a small village school where he learned the basic skills, and went on to the Commercial Academy of Vladivostok. After becoming involved in the Communist cause in 1918, he left school without graduating. He joined the partisans to defend the Vladivostok region against invading Japanese forces and eventually joined the Red Army, where he was quickly promoted. Fadeyev started his writing career as a journalist for *Soviet South,* a small newspaper in the Russian city of Rostov. He also established a literary journal called *Lava.*

The Communist regime assigned Fadeyev as the representative of the Writers' Association. In this capacity, Fadeyev traveled throughout Europe, including Spain during its civil war. When World War II broke out, he worked as a frontline reporter for the two major newspapers in Russia, *Pravda* and *Izvestya.* After the war, he served as the general secretary of the Union of Soviet Writers from 1946 to 1954, editor of several literary journals, and member of the party's Central Committee. He was awarded two Orders of Lenin for his work with the Communist Party.

Fadeyev's fiction often glorifies the struggle of the Soviet Union, specifically of its workers and soldiers, during the Russian civil war and World War II. *The Birth of the Amgunsky Regiment* (1934) describes the war efforts of Communist partisans in Far East during the early 1920s. His most seminal work was *The Young Guard* (1945), which deals with the resistance efforts of the young Communist workers of Krasnodon during the Nazi occupation.

During the last years of his life, Fadeyev suffered from a number of physical and psychological disorders that were a result of alcoholism. He committed suicide in 1956, leaving a note that revealed his disillusionment with the party and with Stalin. Fadeyev's vivid description of the war experience contributed to the discourse of the Soviet national identity. The heroes of his novels, although highly politicized, display heroism and patriotism in their commitment to defend their homeland.

Another Work by Aleksandr Fadeyev

The Nineteen. New York: Hyperion Press, 1973.

Faiz, Faiz Ahmed (1912–1984) poet

Faiz Ahmed Faiz was born in Sialkot, modern Pakistan. His father was a successful lawyer. Faiz studied extensively in the humanities and earned his master's degrees in English and Arabic literatures from Punjab University. Next to Muhammad IQBĀL, he is perhaps Pakistan's best-known poet. He is regarded as the cofounder of the progressive movement in Urdu literature and wrote exclusively in Urdu, a language similar to Arabic.

Faiz was editor of *The Pakistan Times,* a leftist English daily, and of *Imraz,* an Urdu daily. In the 1930s, he was introduced to marxism and became increasingly involved in politics. Through the course of his life, Faiz spent several terms in jail for alleged sabotage against the government. His poetry, however, is a unique intermingling of romantic, sublime, and political themes. He uses traditional images of Urdu love poetry in *ghazal* form, a conventional prose form of the Mughal courts, to address contemporary politics. The customary representation of the *bulbul* (nightingale), the *gul* (rose), and the *baghban* (gardener) in Faiz's *ghazals* were reconfigured to represent the poet, the poet's ideals, and the political system, respectively. At a time when the tensions between Hindus and Muslims in India were rising, Faiz was able to address the state of Muslims in India in this manner.

Faiz's politically motivated works, such as *Zindan Namah* (Prison narrative, 1956) and *Naqsh-e Faryadi* (Image of complaint, 1941), are written in protest against the government, but Faiz never excludes the power of human love in these verses. This can also be seen in the collection of poems, *Zindan Naman,* which Faiz wrote while in prison. It contains a poem called "Come, Africa" that unites the beating of the heart of the poet with Africa's, evoking a life force that will free the poet and his nation from political and religious intolerance.

Despite being viewed as a militant and subversive by the government of Pakistan, Faiz won the Soviet Lenin Peace Prize in 1962 for his commitment to people's struggles through his poetry.

Other Work by Faiz Ahmed Faiz

The True Subject: Selected Poems of Faiz Ahmed Faiz. Translated by Naomi Lazard. Princeton, N.J.: Princeton University Press, 1988.

Zakir, Mohammed, and Menai, M. N., trans. *Poems of Faiz Ahmad Faiz: A Poet of the Third World.* South Asia. Print House, 1998.

Falkner, Gerhard (1951–) poet, dramatist, essayist

Gerhard Falkner was born in Schwabuch, Germany. He prepared for a career as a book dealer before moving to London and the United States. Falkner published his first volume of poetry, *so beginnen am körper die tage* (so begin the days along your body), at the age of 30. After publishing two more poetry collections and a work of prose in the 1980s, he expanded his focus in the following decade to include works for the stage. Falkner wrote the libretto for the opera, *A Lady Dies* (2000), which is based on the death of Princess Diana.

Falkner's influences include critic T. W. Adorno, poet Oskar Pastior, and the DADA movement. Falkner takes a critical view of society in his poems, which reflect a synthesis of several postwar trends in German poetry. His verse is sensual, intellectually full, and written with a disorienting dissection of syntax. In his review of *Voice and Void* by Neil H. Donohue, critic Jerry Glenn describes Falkner as "one of the most talented and explosive poetic voices to have emerged from Germany in recent decades." Although not widely recognized by scholars and critics, Falkner's influence is already evident in the work of younger German poets such as Durs GRÜNBEIN.

Another Work by Gerhard Falkner

Seventeen Selected Poems. Translated by Mark Anderson. Berlin: Qwert, 1994.

A Work about Gerhard Falkner

Donahue, Neil. *Voice and Void: The Poetry of Gerhard Falkner.* Heidelberg, Germany: Universitätsverlag G. Winter, 1998.

Fallaci, Oriana (1930–) *novelist, journalist*

An accomplished journalist who has had the opportunity to interview some of the most remarkable political figures of the 20th century, Oriana Fallaci was born in Florence, Italy, on June 29. The daughter of a cabinetmaker and liberal political activist, her childhood coincided with Mussolini's rise to power. Growing up under a fascist regime, she became interested in power and the ways in which it can be both used and abused.

By the time Fallaci was 10 years old, Italy was deeply involved in World War II. One of her greatest influences throughout her life came from this period and the political views of her very liberal father, who opposed Mussolini. Fallaci joined her father as a member of the underground resistance movements that were dedicated to fighting the Nazis, who were allied with Italy. During this period, her father was captured, sent to jail, and tortured. Fallaci continued to fight in his absence, receiving, at age 14, an honorable discharge from the Italian army. The war ended when she was 15, but the effects of having been so directly involved with the struggle remained ingrained in her mind and formed the background for her future work as an author and journalist.

Fallaci began writing at age 16. She received a degree from the University of Florence and went on to become an award-winning writer for several newspapers. Her first journalistic assignment was to a crime column at a daily paper, but she rapidly progressed and soon was interviewing such political figures as U.S. Secretary of State Henry Kissinger, CIA director William Colby, and Iranian leader Ayatollah Khomeini. She has also interviewed actors and scientists and conducted intensive research on the U.S. space program.

Aside from her accomplishments as a journalist, Fallaci is also an accomplished novelist. Her works of fiction also address the subject of power, particularly in terms of resistance. *Letter to a Child Never Born* (1976), for example, tackles the subject of an unwed pregnant woman who is faced with the difficult choice between having an illegal abortion or keeping the child and facing the social stigma. In this case, the power struggle comes in the form of cultural perceptions and the control they exert on the individual's decision-making processes.

Fallaci maintained a long-term relationship with political activist and Greek resistance leader Alexandros Panagoulis. His death in 1976 prompted her novel *A Man* (1980). Although fictional, this work expresses the challenges of confrontation and resistance to political power structures. Similarly, her novel *Inshallah* (1992) tackles these themes by restructuring the setting to illuminate the same challenges with regard to the civil war in Lebanon.

Fallaci continues to write. Her works are important for their contemporary social and political implications and the glimpse they provide at social conditions.

Other Works by Oriana Fallaci

Interview with History. New York: Liveright, 1976.
The Egoists: Sixteen Surprising Interviews. Chicago: Henry Regnery Company, 1963.

Works about Oriana Fallaci

Arico, Santo L. *Oriana Fallaci: The Woman and the Myth.* Carbondale: Southern Illinois University Press, 1998.
Gatt-Rutter, John. *Oriana Fallaci: The Rhetoric of Freedom.* Washington, D.C.: Berg, 1996.

Farah, Nuruddin (1945–) *novelist, playwright, essayist*

When Nuruddin Farah was born, his section of what is now called Somalia, located on the eastern coast of Africa, was a colony of Italy. In 1960, the nation of Somalia was formed by the merger of this Italian colony with what had been known as British Somaliland. He is descended from nomadic peoples who wandered far to feed their herds. His father was a merchant, and his mother was a poet who spoke several languages. Today, Farah has married an exile's nomadic life to a narrative style that wanders far from any conception of "traditional" REALISM. His travels throughout the world mirror his experiments in language use: His novels tend to use fantastic, improbable elements, what some critics refer to as MAGICAL REALISM.

Young Farah grew up speaking Somali, Arabic, and Amharic. English is his fourth language. From his mother, he gained a love of the sounds of words, of the power of language, and of the need to use the tapestry of cultures that language represents as a political tool. In many countries like Somalia that have a history of colonialism, the language one uses has political implications. Because English (and Italian and French) are reminders of a time when racism and oppression were the order of the day in such countries, many writers have chosen to avoid what they saw as the "language of the conqueror." Unlike the Kenyan writer, NGUGI WA THIONG'O, however, Farah chooses to write in English for pragmatic reasons. As Charles Larson has observed in *The Ordeal of the African Writer* (2001), relatively few Africans in any country are able to read literary works in any language. Farah is not, however, unaware of the political implications of this choice. His novels often deal with political themes, including language usage.

For example, Farah's third novel, *A Naked Needle* (1976), so infuriated Somali dictator Mohamed Siyad Barre that Farah has lived in exile for more than 20 years. Among other issues, *A Naked Needle* deals with the corruption of those who have ruled the country since independence.

Farah has continued to speak for his country and his people, most notably in his trilogy, *Sweet and Sour Milk* (1979), *Sardines* (1981), and *Close Sesame* (1983), known collectively as *Variations on the Theme of an African Dictatorship*. This trilogy is the fullest and most complex treatment that Farah has yet attempted on his most important theme: the oppression of Somalia's various groups by a succession of despots.

Farah is Somalia's first novelist and its most renowned international literary figure. In addition to his focus on racial inequality and the problems of POSTCOLONIALISM, he has also focused extensively on gender inequities and the problems women face in the Third World. In 1998, he received the Neustadt Prize for literature, one of the most prestigious literary awards in the world. The Neustadt Prize is awarded by the University of Oklahoma and its international quarterly journal *World Literature Today*. It carries a $50,000 award and is often seen as a precursor for consideration for the Nobel Prize.

Other Works by Nuruddin Farah
From a Crooked Rib. London: Heinemann, 1976.
Maps. New York: Pantheon, 1986.

A Work about Nuruddin Farah
Alden, Patricio, and Louis Tremaine. *Nuruddin Farah.*
    New York: Twayne, 1999.

feminism

The term *feminism,* with regard to literature, has a number of distinct associations. Largely grouped under the interdisciplinary field of gender studies, and arising out of increasing understanding of women's issues, different branches of the discipline focus on divergent ideas. The oldest identifiable form of literary feminism grew out of 18th-century liberal philosophy such as that found in Mary Wollstonecraft's *A Vindication of the Rights of Women* (1792), which emphasized female autonomy and self-fulfillment. In the 20th century, liberal feminism worked to achieve economic and social equality for women. More a revisionist than a revolutionary movement, feminism's literary aim was to reform existing structures by getting people to learn and read about women's issues, not to break down those structures to create new ones.

The movement eventually broadened to encompass radical feminism, which accused liberal feminism of not having high enough goals. Arising out of the Civil Rights movement and the surge of Leftist activism in the late 1960s, radical feminism's goal of addressing the women's oppression was revolutionary. As the 1970s progressed, the movement gained a more cultural perspective, the one most widely adopted by feminist writers.

Cultural feminism celebrates women's culture and community. Its goal is to seek out those qualities that are traditionally associated with women, such as compassion, subjectivity, intuition, and closeness to nature, and to claim them as desirable, positive, and even superior traits. Proponents of cultural feminism, including the writers Elizabeth Gould Davis and Ashley Montagu, also believe that these qualities are not innate but are learned.

In France, the feminist social movement began in April 1944 when French women obtained the right to vote. It was advanced greatly by the 1949 publication of Simone de BEAUVOIR'S *The Second Sex,* in which she states "One is not born, but rather becomes, a woman. No biological, psychological or economic fate determines the figure that the human female presents in society; it is civilization as a whole that determines this creature."

Simone de Beauvoir was not alone in her support of the emerging feminist trend in France. Other writers soon began to follow her example. Hélène CIXOUS and her "écriture feminine," developed in her essay "The Laugh of the Medusa" (1975), established a new form of women's writing whereby women could learn to "write from the body" to break free of the bonds of male-dominated rhetoric. Theories of the body became particularly important for feminist thinkers, as a woman's body was traditionally the source of such male-defined constructs as physical weakness, immorality, and unseemliness. One of the main goals of feminism as a literary movement was to redefine the body and society's view of it.

In reference to the concept of the body, many feminist critics turn to the work of writer Julia Kristeva. Although she does not consider herself a feminist writer, her theories linking the mind to the body and linking biology to representation have been pivotal to the movement. Kristeva emphasizes the maternal function of a woman's body and its significance to the development of language and culture. As a result of this function, Kristeva purports, ideals of feminism as espoused by de Beauvoir should be rejected because they negate the importance of motherhood. She also insists that early feminism, which sought total equality, is remiss in its attempts to ignore the inherent differences between genders. She further argues that a unique feminine language, as proposed by Cixous, is impossible. However, in rejecting existing feminisms, Kristeva paves the way for another form of feminism, one grounded in the exploration of multiple identities, arguing that there are as many sexualities as there are individuals.

In the 1990s, the trend toward gender studies, encompassing not only feminism but also lesbian criticism and queer theory, has shifted the focus once again to a more inclusive philosophy.

Some Works by Feminist Writers

Gilbert, Sandra M., and Susan Gubar. *The Madwoman in the Attic: The Woman Writer and the Nineteenth-Century Literary Imagination.* New Haven, Conn.: Yale University Press, 2000.

Kristeva, Julia. *The Kristeva Reader.* Edited by Tori Moi. New York: Columbia University Press, 1986.

Millet, Kate. *Sexual Politics.* Champaign: University of Illinois Press, 2000.

Moers, Ellen. *Literary Women.* Indianapolis, Ind.: Doubleday, 1976.

Moi, Tori. *Sexual/Textual Politics: Feminist Literary Theory.* New York: Routledge, 2002.

Woolf, Virginia. *A Room of One's Own.* Fort Washington, Pa.: Harvest Books, 1990.

Works about Feminism

Richardson, Angelique, and Chris Willis, eds. *The New Woman in Fiction and in Fact: Fin de Siècle Feminisms.* New York: Palgrave, 2001.

Warhol, Robyn R., and Diane Price, eds. *Feminisms: An Anthology of Literary Theory and Criticism.* Piscataway, N.J.: Rutgers University Press, 1977.

Feng Zhi (Feng Chih; Feng Chengzhi)
(1905–1993) *poet*

Feng Zhi was born in China's Hebei Province on September 17. At age 12, he was sent to Beijing to study. He entered Beijing University in 1921 and produced a high volume of poems. In 1924, his first work appeared in *Hidden Grass*, a journal he published with friends in Shanghai. From 1925 to 1932, he edited another journal, *The Sunken Bell*. He graduated from Beijing University two years later and published his first collection, *Songs of Yesterday*. He then moved to Harbin to teach secondary school but returned to Beijing a year later to rejoin the literary community.

Feng Zhi's second collection, *The Northern Journey and Other Poems* (1929), is one of the most famous examples of modern Chinese lyric poetry. Written in melodic, romantic vernacular, it is a lengthy narrative poem about Feng Zhi's social education and his encounters with decadent and morally destitute warlords, prostitutes, and foreign invaders.

The next year, Feng Zhi traveled to Germany to study philosophy and literature in Heidelberg and Berlin. He earned a Ph.D. and translated German poets such as Rainer Maria RILKE. When he returned to China in 1936, he taught at Tongji University until 1939, when he joined the faculty at South-West United University in Kunming.

In 1941, Feng Zhi published *Sonnets* (1942), a collection of 27 sonnets that earned him fame as the Chinese practitioner of the poetic form. The sonnets are mostly contemplative reflections on life and nature, and because of their tone and internal direction, Feng Zhi is sometimes referred to as a metaphysical poet.

After the 1949 communist revolution, Feng Zhi wrote mostly patriotic poems (in *Collected Poems,* 1955) and focused on scholarship. He joined the Communist Party in 1956 and became director of the Foreign Literature Institute at the Academy of Social Sciences, where he continued his translations and studies of German literature.

Feng Zhi was considered one of modern China's great poets and also was honored with several German literary prizes, such as the Medal of Brothers Green from the German Democratic Republic and the Prize for the Arts by the Center for International Exchanges. He died on February 22.

A Work about Feng Zhi

Cheung, Dominic. *Feng Chih*. Boston: Twayne, 1979.

Ferré, Rosario (1942–) *novelist, short-story writer, poet, critic*

Rosario Ferré was born in Ponce, Puerto Rico, to Luis Ferré, politician and eventual governor of the island, and Lorenza Ramírez Ferré. Although Ferré received a conventional, aristocratic education, her childhood nanny, a vivid storyteller, introduced her early on to the worlds of fantasy, legend, and myth. Later in life, she studied under the Peruvian novelist Mario VARGAS LLOSA and the Uruguayan critic Ángel RAMA, both of whom encouraged her to write.

Ferré's early work, including *The Youngest Doll* (1976), a series of short stories set in Puerto Rico, established her as one of the first Puerto Rican feminist writers. In it, one finds the criticism of feminine stereotypes and an implicit call for the end of the repression of women, both of which themes have come to characterize much of her work. Her writing also deals with the cultural and historical heritage of Puerto Rico. To explore such themes, she incorporates elements of local myth and legend as well as realistic depictions of characters and settings. The title story of one of her best-known books, *Sweet Diamond Dust* (1986), relates the rise and fall of the aristocratic De la Valle family. The alternation of colloquial and formal language and the incorporation of different narrative perspectives in this work are typical of her fiction.

For Ferré writing has been and continues to be a manner of breaking through the societal constraints placed on her as a woman and as an individual. In this sense, she has followed in the tradition of such feminine writers as Simone de BEAUVOIR and Virginia WOOLF. Her questioning of restrictive gender and class divisions in Puerto Rico and the West in general, as well as her sensitive and profound character portrayals, have made her an important figure in contemporary Hispanic and world literature.

Another Work by Rosario Ferré

Ferré, Rosario. *The House on the Lagoon.* New York: Plume, 1996.

A Work about Rosario Ferré

Hintz, Suzanne S. *Rosario Ferré, A Search for Identity.* New York: Peter Lang, 1995.

Fiedeler, Hans

See DÖBLIN, ALFRED.

fin de siècle

French for "end of the century," fin de siècle first came about as a literary movement in 1871 when German troops withdrew from Paris after the Franco-Prussian War. French anarchists were able to establish the Commune of Paris briefly, which, although it did not last for an extended period of time, was instrumental in creating an atmosphere in French culture in which radical ideas in literature, theater, and the visual arts began to thrive. Paris, at this time, became one of the centers of avant-garde culture. DECADENCE, drug abuse, degradation, and surrealism are commonly associated with the era, as were the fascination with prostitution by male writers, the development of lesbianism as an artistic trend, and an increased focus on sexuality, both heterosexual and homosexual.

Among the most influential writers of this period was Victor HUGO, whose works, including *Les Misérables* (1862), were published in the middle of the century and greatly influenced the next generation of artists. In particular, his portrayal of bohemians and student revolutionaries was consistent with fin de siècle dark idealism. Other writers, such as Guy de MAUPASSANT (whose works dealt chiefly with the Franco-Prussian war and

fashionable life in Paris) and the prominent SYMBOLIST poets Stephan MALLARMÉ and Charles BAUDELAIRE and their often dark and unconventional ideas flourished at the turn of the century as well.

The tone of the fin de siècle movement was dark without the expected, accompanying melancholy. It was a time of political scandal, the most notable of which was the Dreyfus affair in which Captain Alfred Dreyfus was falsely accused and convicted of spying for the Germans during the war. He was sentenced to serve time on Devil's Island, French Guiana. Angered by this, and feeling that the charges were largely a result of anti-Semitism, the writer Emile ZOLA wrote a letter that openly criticized Dreyfus's conviction and subsequent imprisonment. Titled *J'Accuse* (January 13, 1898), Zola's letter passionately defended Dreyfus. As a result, the case was reopened and the conviction ultimately overturned. The situation, however, was typical of the prevailing mood of the time, and art was used to effect for social change and rebellion.

Another fin de siècle scandal involved the poet Arthur RIMBAUD. He had already caused quite an artistic commotion with his dark, introspective *A Season in Hell* (1873; translated 1932), in which he described his own intense and often tortured existence. He had further scandalized Parisian society when he left his wife for a man, poet Paul VERLAINE. This affair was an integral part of *A Season in Hell* and also typical of the tumultuousness of the age.

The social, literary, and artistic changes that were occurring at this time affected the theater as well. Actresses began to interpret the works of writers such as COLETTE, whose simulated sexual performance on stage caused a riot at the Moulin Rouge. Women, in particular, began to display their sensuality openly. Bored aristocrats, such as lovers Natalie Barney and poet René Vivien, often gave private yet elaborate shows in their own homes. The concept of *lesbian chic* emerged and flourished in these venues.

As a movement, the fin de siècle officially came to an end in 1905. It had achieved such momentum that it ultimately reached a breaking point; however, many of the influences that came out of the movement and other avant-garde and experimental art forms continued into the next century, shaping future trends in literature, culture, and the arts, not just in France but also internationally.

Works about the Fin de Siècle

Chadwick, Kay, and Timothy Unwin, eds. *New Perspectives on the Fin-de-Siècle in Nineteenth- and Twentieth-Century France.* Lewiston, N.Y.: E. Mellen Press, 2000.

McGuinness, Patrick, ed. *Symbolism, Decadence and the Fin de Siècle: French and European Perspectives.* Exeter, England: University of Exeter Press, 2000.

Fischer, Caroline Auguste (Karoline Auguste Fernandine Fischer)
(1764–1842) novelist, short-story writer

Little is known about Caroline Auguste Fischer's childhood and youth. Her father, Karl Heinrich Ernst Venturini, was a court violinist at the Duchy of Brunswick. Her mother, Charlotte Juliane Wilhelmine Köchy Venturini, was the daughter of a local tailor. Fischer married Christoph Johann Rudolph Christiani in the early 1790s and moved to Copenhagen. The couple separated in 1798, and Fischer moved back to Germany the following year. In 1803, she had a child with the writer Christian August Fischer (1771–1829). The couple married in 1808 but separated after only seven months.

Fischer used Christian's literary contacts to publish her first novel, *Gustavs Verirrungen* (*Gustav's Aberrations,* 1801). She quickly followed up with two more novels, *Vierzehn Tage in Paris* (*A Fortnight in Paris,* 1801) and *Die Honigmonathe* (*The Honeymoons,* 1802). These works sold well and made her a popular author. After Fischer's second marriage ended, she tried to support herself by running a girls' school in Heidelberg and a library in Würzburg, but these ventures failed. Fischer had only limited success with her later novels and short stories before she quit writing in 1820.

She spent her last years in and out of mental institutions and died penniless in 1842.

Fischer often wrote about the incompatibility between pursuing happiness and pursuing virtue. Her stories often portray women forced to choose between creativity and a stifling home life. Fischer's powerful works expose the destructiveness that stereotypes and gender roles had on women in the 1800s. Largely forgotten until the late 20th century, Fischer is now viewed as a significant precursor to modern women's literature in Germany.

Works about Caroline Auguste Fischer

Purver, Judith. "Passion, Possession, Patriarchy: Images of Men in the Novels and Short Stories of Caroline Auguste Fischer." *Neophilologus* 79 (1995).

———. "Caroline Auguste Fischer: An Introduction." In Margaret C. Ives, ed., *Women Writers of the Age of Goethe* IV. Lancaster, U.K.: Lancaster University Press, 1991.

Flanagan, Richard (1962–) novelist, filmmaker

Richard Flanagan was born in Australia to an Irish Catholic family. He grew up in a mining town on the west coast in the state of Tasmania and left school at 16 to be a bush laborer. In his life since that time, he has been a construction worker at a hydroelectric plant, a Rhodes scholar, and a river guide. He began his writing career by concentrating on history, but his ambition from an early age was to be a fiction writer.

Flanagan considers his major literary influences to be Henry LAWSON, CAMUS, DOSTOYEVSKY, KAFKA, Faulkner, South American novelists, and, most recently, Toni Morrison. Supported by a grant from Ars Tasmania, he wrote his first novel, *Death of a River Guide* (1994); it was an unexpected success. As Flanagan states in an interview with Giles Hugo, he is interested in writing about Tasmania not as a nostalgic regional novelist but to find new forms for the richness and complexities of Tasmania's past and present. He draws on oral traditions from his own Irish culture, aboriginal myths, the landscape, and migrant experience, particularly since World War II. Married to a Slovenian, he is particularly interested in how immigrants from Central Europe have redefined themselves, through many trials, as Tasmanians.

Flanagan's first film, "Sound of One Hand Clapping," is situated in a community of mostly Central European migrant workers. He uses music as an integral role in the film, not as background but as a component of character and action. "Sound of One Hand Clapping" was shown at both the Berlin and Cannes film festivals.

Flanagan's most recent novel, *Gould's Book of Fish* (2002), supported by a grant from the Australia Council, is a best-seller and a critical success in Australia and internationally. It has won the Commonwealth Writers Prize for 2002, establishing Richard Flanagan as one of the most imaginative and innovative of contemporary novelists.

Flaubert, Gustave (1821–1880) *novelist*

Gustave Flaubert was born in Rouen, France. His father was the chief of surgery at the hospital in Rouen, and his mother, who went on to become the most important and influential person in his life, was the daughter of a physician. Flaubert was never satisfied with his bourgeois background and often rebelled against it; these rebellions ultimately led to his expulsion from school and to his finishing his education privately in Paris.

Flaubert's school years, aside from aiding in the development of his rebellious personality, also introduced him to his love of writing. As a teenager, he fell in love with a married woman, Elisa Schlésinger. The relationship was destined to end in disappointment, but his idealized love for Elisa provided the inspiration and subject matter for much of his writing.

While studying law in Paris in the early 1840s, Flaubert suffered from what was diagnosed at the time as a nervous attack, probably a form of epilepsy. He subsequently failed his law exams and decided to devote himself full time to writing.

In 1846, he was introduced to another writer, Louise Colet. This was the start of a relationship that lasted many years. Although they spent very little time together, they corresponded regularly, and she became his mistress. He broke off the relationship in 1855 when she attempted to visit him at his country retreat. Her novel, *Lui* (1859), gives a vengeful account of their relationship.

Although he was living outside of Paris at the time, Flaubert maintained close contact with family and friends in the city and was a witness to the Revolution of 1848. Afterward, he took up an acquaintance with the writer Maxime du Camp. Together, the pair traveled for three years, visiting North Africa, Greece, Syria, Turkey, Egypt, and Italy. On his return to France, Flaubert began work on what would become his greatest achievement, *Madame Bovary*, a novel that took five years to complete.

Critical Analysis

Madame Bovary is a shocking tale of adultery, based on the unhappy affair of the title character, Emma Bovary. The novel was first published in the *Revue de Paris* in 1856 and appeared as a two-volume book in 1857. Like many of his contemporaries' works, Flaubert's novel was attacked for its vivid depiction of what was considered morally offensive behavior. Flaubert was prosecuted for the work on charges of immorality and on the grounds that it was offensive to religion. He came before the same judge who later found Charles BAUDELAIRE guilty on a similar charge. Flaubert, however, was not convicted.

Madame Bovary is more than a simple tale of adultery. The protagonist, Emma Bovary, is a dreamer who, as a child, read the works of Sir Walter Scott and the romantics and, as an adult, longs for a life of romance and adventure. She is stuck, instead, in an unhappy marriage to Charles Bovary, a physician, who fails to recognize how miserable his wife is. Seeking escape from her boredom, she turns to extramarital affairs as a source of happiness and adventure. Her pursuit of another life ultimately causes her to fall deeply into debt and leads to her decision to commit suicide. The character was important to Flaubert, who felt her choices exemplified the problem of women who lived in a society trapped in materialism.

As a result of his success with *Madame Bovary,* Flaubert enjoyed much fame as a writer during the 1860s in the court of Napoleon III. He counted among his close friends Emile ZOLA, George SAND, Hippolyte Taine, and Ivan TURGENEV. All of these writers shared with him similar aesthetic ideals and a dedication to the realistic and nonjudgmental representation of life through literature.

His later works included *Salammbô* (1862), about the siege of Carthage, and *L'Éducation sentimentale* (1869), a novel of forbidden romance between a young man and an older married woman set against the backdrop of the 1848 revolution. With his concern for precise form and for detailed observation of human nature, Flaubert began to be associated with a new school of naturalistic writers. He took the approach that it was the goal of the novelist to remain neutral, explaining and teaching but never judging. Many younger writers, such as Guy de MAUPASSANT and Anton CHEKOV adopted this outlook.

Although Flaubert was highly respected as a writer, his personal life was shadowed by financial difficulties. After the death of his father, he took up residence with his mother and young niece, who was forced to declare bankruptcy. Flaubert spent much of his fortune assisting her and her family. During his final years, Flaubert lived as a virtual hermit, working on a collection of three stories, *Trois contes,* and on the long novel *Bouvard et Pécuchet.* Before completing the novel, he died from a cerebral hemorrhage.

Other Works by Gustave Flaubert

Early Writings. Translated by Robert Griffin. Lincoln: University of Nebraska Press, 1991.
Flaubert–Sand: The Correspondance. Translated by Francis Steegmuller and Barbara Bray. New York: Knopf, 1993.
The First Sentimental Education. Translated by Douglas Garman. Berkeley: University of California Press, 1972.
The Temptation of St. Anthony. Garden City, N.Y.: Halcyon House, 1950.

Works about Gustave Flaubert

Berg, William J., and Laurey K. Martin. *Gustave Flaubert.* Boston: Twayne, 1997.
Sartre, Jean-Paul. *The Family Idiot: Gustave Flaubert, 1821–1857.* Chicago: University of Chicago Press, 1991.
Wall, Geoffrey. *Gustave Flaubert: A Life.* London: Faber and Faber, 2001.

Fo, Dario (1926–   ) *playwright*

Dario Fo was born in San Giano, Italy, to Pina (Rota) Fo, an author, and Felice Fo, who divided his time between acting in an amateur theater company and work as a railway station master. As a child, Fo spent vacations with his grandparents on a farm and traveled around the countryside with his grandfather, selling produce from a wagon. His grandfather told imaginative stories infused with local news to attract customers. This was Fo's introduction to the narrative tradition. In his youth, he sat for hours in taverns, listening to glassblowers and fishermen spin tall tales filled with political satire, planting the seeds of his own satirical work.

Fo moved to Milan in 1940 to study art at the Brera Art Academy. During this time, he began to write stories and sketches that were influenced by traveling storytellers. "Nothing gets down as deeply into the mind and intelligence as satire," Fo said in a statement cited by James Fisher. "The end of satire is the first alarm bell signaling the end of real democracy."

Much of Fo's satire focuses on political-religious issues. His one-man show *Comical Mystery* (1969), for example, was a mockery of Catholic hierarchy. The play, considered a cornerstone of his collective work, is his own version of the Gospels with commentary on church corruption.

Sketches in his play include one about a man without legs who shuns a healing from Christ and another depicting a wedding feast at Cana told from the perspective of a drunkard. The show was presented on television in 1977. According to Tony Mitchell in *Dario Fo: People's Court Jester,* the Vatican described the program as the "most blasphemous show in the history of television."

In 1970, Fo performed *I'd Die Tonight If I Didn't Think It Had Been Worth It* (1970), a play comparing Palestinian freedom fighters and Italian partisans. He followed this the same year with *Accidental Death of an Anarchist* (1970), a play about an anarchist who dies while in police custody. The play closed at the Cinema Rossini when police pressured the theater owners.

More than 40 of Fo's plays have been translated into dozens of languages. Fo himself has also performed on radio and film and once hosted a controversial Italian television program in 1962. In 1997, he won the Nobel Prize in literature for his theatrical contributions, which emphasized international topics ranging from AIDS to the Israeli-Palestinian conflict.

Another Work by Dario Fo

We Won't Pay! We Won't Pay! and Other Plays. Translated by Ron Jenkins. New York: Theatre Communications Group, 2001.

Works about Dario Fo

Fisher, James. "Images of the Fool in Italian Theatre from Pirandello to Fo." Available online at http://persweb.wabash.edu/facstaff/fisherj/new/ItalianTheatre.html

Mitchell, Tony. *Dario Fo: People's Court Jester.* London: Methuen, 1999.

Fontane, Theodor (Henri Théodor Fontane) (1819–1898) *novelist, balladeer*

Theodor Fontane was born in Neurippen, Prussia. His parents, Louis Henri and Emilie Labry Fontane, descended from French Huguenots who moved to Prussia in the 1600s. Fontane's education consisted of private tutors and public schools in Swinemünde and Neurippen. As a youth, he joined literary clubs and wrote poems and historical tales. Pursuing the profession of his father, Fontane served as an apprentice to an apothecary from 1836 to 1844. After serving in the Prussian military, Fontane operated his own pharmacy in Berlin until 1849. In 1850, he married Emilie Rouanet-Kummer.

During his lifetime, Fontane achieved his greatest recognition as a balladeer. He published his first two books of ballads in 1850. In 1852, he started to work as a newspaper correspondent. He traveled extensively in the 1860s and 1870s and wrote five travel books based on his experiences, also wrote theater reviews and briefly served as secretary of the Berlin Academy of Arts in 1876 before he started to write novels. His first novel *Vor dem Sturm: Roman aus dem Winter 1812 auf 1813 (Before the Storm: A Novel of the Winter of 1812–1813,* 1878) is considered one of the finest historical novels in German literature for its artistic portrayal of the Prussian aristocracy, bourgeoisie, and peasantry during the Napoleonic Wars. He wrote three more historical novels before turning his attention to Berlin society.

Fontane's greatest literary influence was Scottish writer Sir Walter Scott. An accomplished writer of dialogue, Fontane helped pioneer the modernist trend of emphasizing conversation rather than plot. His ironic observations are critical of the prejudices and conventions of society, but his works still exhibit spontaneity, charm, and wit. His novels engage the themes of money, morality, guilt, retribution, and class hierarchy. His biographer Helen Chambers concludes that Fontane made a "unique and refined contribution to world fiction."

Other Works by Theodor Fontane

Effi Briest. Translated by Hugh Rorrison and Helen Chambers. London: Penguin, 2000.

Journeys to England in Victoria's Early Days. Translated by Dorothy Harrison. London: Massie, 1939.

A Work about Theodor Fontane

Chambers, Helen. *The Changing Image of Theodor Fontane.* Columbia, S.C.: Camden House Inc., 1997.

Foscolo, Ugo (Niccolò Foscolo)
(1778–1827) *playwright, novelist, poet, essayist*

Ugo Foscolo was born on the island of Zante in Greece to Andrea Foscolo, a ship's physician, and Diamanatina Spathis. He was brought up speaking both Italian and Greek. Young Ugo changed residences at least twice when his father was named a ship's physician in the Levant and then again when he was made hospital director in Spalato.

Stability was not a big part of Foscolo's life. When his father died in 1788, Foscolo was forced to live with relatives in Zante. When his family was reunited in 1792 in Venice, Foscolo was enrolled in the San Capriano school in Murano, where he mastered Greek and Latin.

In about 1794, Foscolo began to experiment with poetry and to visit Venetian salons. Isabella Teotochi, also Greek, ran a salon that attracted great intellectuals. Teotochi eventually became Foscolo's lover, benefactor, and muse. Her decision to annul her marriage and secretly wed another seemed to be the catalyst for Foscolo's 1802 novel *Last Letters of Jacopo Ortis,* a novel in letters modeled after the works of Samuel Richardson and Jean-Jacques Rousseau that depicts the doomed love of Ortis for Teresa.

One of Foscolo's most famous collections of poems is *On Sepulchres* (1807), which speaks about the struggle of civilization and displays the ROMANTIC fascination with ruins: "Even the last ruins, the Pierian sisters gladden / The desert wastes with their singing, and harmony."

Foscolo was one of the major voices of his generation. From his precocious youth to the end of his life, he held tight to romantic ideals.

A Work about Ugo Foscolo

Radcliff-Umstead, Douglas. *Ugo Foscolo.* Boston: Twayne, 1970.

Fraire, Isabel (1934–) *poet, translator*

Isabel Fraire was born in Mexico City and raised in New York. A student of philosophy at the Autonomous National University of Mexico, by the early 1960s, she was writing poetry, literary criticism, reviews, and translations, and she became a member of the editorial council of the prestigious review, *Revista Mexicana de Literatura* (Mexican Review of Literature). Although her earliest poems appeared in 1959 in *15 Poems of Isabel Fraire,* her first published book of poems is generally considered to be *Only This Light,* which appeared in 1969.

Fraire's translations from English to Spanish of such American poets as Ezra Pound, T. S. Eliot, Wallace Stevens, E. E. Cummings, William Carlos Williams, and W. S. Auden have been collected in *Seis poetas de lengua inglesa* (Six Poets Writing in English, 1976) and have appeared in many Latin American journals and anthologies. In 1978, she was awarded the Xavier Villaurrutia Prize for her third collection of poetry, *Poems in the Lap of Death* (1977). Of her work, Mexican poet and critic Octavio PAZ has said, "Her poetry is a continual flight of images that disappear, reappear, and return to disappear" (quoted at www.columbia.edu/~gmo9/poetry/fraire/fraire-bio.html).

Other Works by Isabel Fraire

Isabel Fraire: Poems. Translated by Thomas Hoeksema. Athens, Ohio: Mundus Artium Press, 1975.

Poems in the Lap of Death. Translated by Thomas Hoeksema. Pittsburgh, Pa.: Latin American Literary Review Press, 1981.

Frame, Janet (1924–) *novelist*

Janet Frame was born in Dunedin, South Island, New Zealand, and grew up in Oamuru, South Island. The daughter of a railway-worker father and an encouraging mother who wrote poetry and fiction, she studied to be a teacher at Dunedin Teachers' College and the University of Otago. Her early life was a happy one, despite poverty, her brother's epilepsy, and the drowning of two of her sisters. Before she was able to work as a teacher, however, she was incorrectly diagnosed as being schizophrenic and hospitalized in mental wards for almost 10 years. During this time, she wrote her first collection of short stories, *The Lagoon* (1951), which saved her from being lobotomized when the book won a literary award shortly before the surgery was scheduled. Finally able to leave the hospital, Frame then lived in a friend's garden shed, where she completed her first novel, *Owls Do Cry* (1957), which established her as an important novelist. As Prudence Hockley notes in her review in *500 Great Books by Women* (1994), "The special quality of this novel lies in its poetic, hallucinatory, perceptive voice, imbued with the surreal vision of childhood and madness."

Afraid that she might be forced back to a mental hospital, Frame then left New Zealand in 1956, living in England and Spain until she finally returned to New Zealand in 1963. She is the author of numerous novels, including *Faces in the Water* (1982), a first-person narrative told in the voice of Estina, a woman incarcerated in a mental institution, and a three-volume autobiography, *To The Island* (1982), *An Angel at My Table* (1984), and *The Envoy from Mirror City* (1985). Her style of writing is considered unique, moving between realism and a more nonlinear exploration of the nature of reality. Although her earlier novels focus on the inner world of children, outcasts, and the insane, her later novels are considered poetic and POSTMODERN, with a freshness of language and voice that makes them unique. She has been awarded every major New Zealand literary prize and is considered New Zealand's best-known contemporary novelist.

Other Works by Janet Frame

The Adaptable Man: A Novel. New York: George Braziller, 1965, 2000.
The Edge of the Alphabet. New York: George Braziller, 1992.

Works about Janet Frame

King, Michael. *Wrestling with the Angel: A Life of Janet Frame.* Washington, D.C.: Counterpoint Press, 2000.

Panny, Judith Dell. *I Have What I Gave: The Fiction of Janet Frame.* New York: George Braziller, 1993.

Freud, Sigmund (1856–1939) *philosopher, psychologist*

Sigmund Freud was born in Freiberg, today in the Czech Republic, to Jewish parents, Jacob Freud, a small-time textile merchant, and Amalia Freud. Although the family was Jewish, Jacob Freud was not at all religious, and Sigmund Freud grew up an avowed atheist. When he was four years old, the family moved to Vienna, Austria, where Freud lived for most of his life. He was a brilliant student, always at the head of his class; however, the options for Jewish boys in Austria were limited by the government to medicine and law. As Freud was interested in science, he entered the University of Vienna medical school in 1873. After three years, he became deeply involved in research, which delayed his M.D. until 1881. Independent research was not financially feasible, however, so Freud established a private medical practice, specializing in neurology. He became interested in the use of hypnosis to treat hysteria and other mental illnesses, and with the help of a grant, he went to France in 1885 to study under Jean-Martin Charcot, a famous neurologist, known all over Europe for his studies of hysteria and various uses of hypnosis. On his return to Vienna in 1886, Freud married and opened a practice specializing in disorders of the nervous system and the brain. He tried to use hypnosis to treat his patients but quickly abandoned it, finding that he could produce better results by placing patients in a relaxing environment and allowing them to speak freely. He then analyzed whatever they said to identify the traumatic effects in the past that caused their current suffering. The way his own self-analysis contributed to the growth of his ideas during this period may be seen in letters and drafts of papers sent to a colleague, Wilhelm Fliess.

After several years of practice, Freud published *The Interpretation of Dreams* (1900), the first major statement of his theories, in which he introduced the public to the notion of the unconscious mind. He explains in the book that dreams, as products of the unconscious mind, can reveal past psychological traumas that, repressed from conscious awareness, underlie certain kinds of neurotic disorders. In addition, he attempts to establish a provisional matrix for interpreting and analyzing dreams in terms of their psychological significance.

In his second book, *The Psychopathology of Everyday Life* (1901), Freud expands the idea of the unconscious mind by introducing the concept of the *dynamic unconscious.* In this work, Freud theorizes that everyday forgetfulness and accidental slips of the tongue (today commonly called Freudian slips) reveal many meaningful things about the person's unconscious psychological state. The ideas outlined in these two works were not taken seriously by most readers, which is not a surprise considering that, at the time, most psychological disorders were treated as physical illnesses, if treated at all.

Freud's major clinical discoveries, including his five major case histories, were published in *Three Essays on the Theory of Sexuality* (1905). In this work, he elaborates his theories about infantile sexuality, the meanings of the id, the ego, and the superego, and the Oedipus complex (the inevitable but tabooed incestuous attraction in families, and the associated fear of castration and intrafamilial jealousy).

In 1902, Freud was appointed full professor at the University of Vienna and developed a large following. In 1906, he formed the Vienna Psychoanalytic Society, but some political infighting resulted in division among members of the group (Carl Jung, for instance, split from the group with bitter feelings). Freud continued to work on his theories and, in 1909, presented them internationally at a conference at Clark University in Massachusetts. Freud's name became a household word after the conference. In his later period, in *Beyond the Pleasure Principle* (1920) and *The Ego and the Id* (1923), he modified his structural model of the psychic apparatus. In *Inhibitions, Symptoms and Anxiety* (1926), he applied psychoanalysis to larger social problems.

In 1923, Freud was diagnosed with cancer of the jaw as a result of years of cigar smoking. In 1938, the Nazi party burned Freud's books. They also confiscated his passport, but the leading intellectuals around the world voiced their protest, and he was allowed to leave Austria. Freud died in England in 1939.

Freud made an enormous contribution to the field of psychology: He established our basic ideas about sexuality and the unconscious and also influenced, to some extent, the way we read literary works by establishing premises for psychoanalytic criticism. His own case studies are often interpreted for their literary merit.

Other Works by Sigmund Freud

Civilization and Its Discontents. Translated by Peter Gay. New York: W. W. Norton, 1989.
The Future of an Illusion. Translated by Peter Gay. New York: W. W. Norton, 1989.

Works about Sigmund Freud

Bernheimer, Charles, and Claire Kahane, eds. *In Dora's Case: Freud-Hysteria—Feminism.* New York: Columbia University Press, 1985.
Erwin, Edward. *The Freud Encyclopedia: Theory, Therapy, and Culture.* New York: Garland Press, 2002.
Mitchell, Stephen. *Freud and Beyond: A History of Modern Psychoanalytical Thought.* New York: Basic Books, 1996.

Freyre, Gilberto de Mello (1900–1987)
nonfiction writer, sociologist

Born on March 15 in the city of Recife in the state of Pernambuco in the northeast of Brazil, Gilberto de Mello Freyre is one of the country's leading intellectual figures. After completing his B.A. in Brazil, he continued his studies in the United States where he earned an M.A. at Columbia, studying under anthropologist Franz Boas. After further studies in Portugal, he returned to Brazil and immersed himself in life in his region of origin, becoming good friends with other northeastern writers such as José Lins do Rego.

Freyre is known for his sociological and anthropological texts about Brazilian life. His argument that the specific nature of Portuguese colonization led to a mixed-race society in its colonies is where the concept of Brazil's status as a racial democracy originates. Freyre's most important texts are *The Mansions and the Shanties: The Making of Modern Brazil* (1936) and *The Masters and the Slaves: A Study in the Development of Brazilian Civilization* (1933). His works have left an indelible mark on Brazilian intellectual and popular history.

Another Work by Gilberto Freyre

The Gilberto Freyre Reader. Translated by Barbara Shelby. New York: Knopf, 1974.

Fried, Erich (1921–1988) *poet, short-story writer*

Erich Fried was born in Vienna, Austria, to Hugo and Nellie Stein Fried. In the mid-1920s, his father's shipping company went bankrupt, and the family survived on the money his mother earned selling porcelain figures. After the Nazis sent his father to a concentration camp in 1938, Fried fled to London where he settled permanently. During World War II, he helped his mother and other Jews escape from Nazi-controlled Europe. Fried held many jobs after the war, including dairy chemist, librarian, and worker in a glass factory. He was a commentator for the British Broadcasting System from 1952 to 1968.

Fried published his first collection of poems in 1944. From the 1950s through the 1980s, he published more than 25 volumes of verse and established his reputation as a lyric poet. Fried also translated the works of Dylan Thomas (1914–53), T. S. Eliot (1888–1965), and William Shakespeare (1564–1616) into German. He published the novel *Ein Soldat und ein Mädchen* (*A Soldier and a Girl*, 1960) and wrote Kafkaesque short stories (see

Franz Kafka). His awards include the Schiller Prize (1965) and the Bremen Literature Prize (1983).

Fried used terse language laced with aphorisms and epigrams to address contemporary issues and events, such as the Vietnam War. National background had little influence on his opinions. Stuart Hood, who translated many of his works into English, stated in an interview, "Fried did not have a problem with nationality. He did not want to be British, German, or Jewish." Fried's positions were thus often paradoxical: He was a German language writer who criticized the policies of West Germany, a Jew who opposed Israel's fight against the Palestinians, and a leftist who was critical of Marxist practice.

Another Work by Erich Fried

Children and Fools. Translated by Martin Chalmers. London: Serpent's Tail, 1992.

A Work about Erich Fried

Lawie, Steven W. *Erich Fried: A Writer Without a Country.* New York: Peter Lang, 1996.

Frisch, Max (1911–1991) *playwright, novelist*

Max Frisch was born in Zurich, Switzerland, to Franz and Lina Wildermuth Frisch. He wrote several unpublished plays as a teenager and studied German literature at the University of Zurich from 1930 to 1933. He then supported himself as a freelance journalist and wrote his first novel, *Jürg Reinhart* (1934). In 1936, Frisch decided to pursue his father's profession and enrolled in the Eidgenössische Technische Hochschule in Zurich to study architecture. He received his degree and opened an architectural firm in 1941. Frisch served intermittently in the Swiss army during World War II and married Gertrud Anna Constance in 1942.

Frisch established his reputation as a dramatist soon after the war with a series of plays that captured the mood of the time. Staying neutral during the cold war, Frisch remained in contact with the literary worlds on both sides of the iron curtain. East German writer Bertolt BRECHT became one of his most important influences. Frisch traveled extensively throughout his life and gained a reputation as a notable diarist. His novels and plays made him one of the most respected German language writers. The novel *I'm Not Stiller* (1954) deals with the issue of individual freedom and displays the experimental narrative prose that made him famous. His novel *Homo Faber* (1957) is a commentary on the uncontrollable nature of technology. Frisch's later works, such as *Montauk* (1975), reflect a concern with aging and death. He won numerous American, Swiss, and German literary awards, including the Georg Büchner Prize.

Frisch was an original writer with integrity and a concern for truth and relevance. He continually used new contexts to address his common themes: male-female relationships, reality and imagination, social responsibility, and the quest for self-fulfillment. Frisch also had a piercing insight into contemporary life. German literary scholar Wulf Koepke wrote that Frisch's works "exemplify the struggle for survival of the human individual in the face of a society blindly intent on its own extinction."

Another Work by Max Frisch

Sketchbook 1946–1949. Translated by Geoffrey Skelton. New York: Harcourt Brace Jovanovich, 1977.

A Work about Max Frisch

Koepke, Wulf. *Understanding Max Frisch.* Columbia: University of South Carolina Press, 1991.

Fuentes, Carlos (1928–) *novelist, short-story writer, dramatist, essayist*

Carlos Fuentes was born in Panama City, Panama, where his father, Rafael Fuentes Boettiger, was the Mexican ambassador. Being the son of a career diplomat, Fuentes spent his childhood moving from city to city, following his father's assignments. He lived in Washington, D.C., where he became acutely aware of his Mexican nationality, in part because of being ostracized and harassed by his schoolmates.

Fuentes received an excellent and international education and is fluent in Spanish, English, and French. At first, it seemed that he would follow his father into the world of diplomacy. He returned to Mexico City to attend law school, but after graduating, he began to dedicate more and more of his time to literary pursuits. His early exposure to the inner workings of the Mexican government and his studies of economics and law gave his later literature a keen political sense and an ability to depict and criticize aspects of the Mexican upper classes.

Though Fuentes began to write as early as the 1940s, it was not until the late 1950s that he became well known. His second novel, *The Death of Artemio Cruz* (1962), received a shocked and confused reaction from its first critics, followed by an almost immediate wave of praise for its groundbreaking style and depth. The book's stream-of-consciousness style evokes the last thoughts of a powerful capitalist, Artemio Cruz, on his deathbed. The book is written in first-person, second-person, and third-person sections that represent the different points of view that Cruz has on his own life.

The use of the fragmented and musical language associated with stream-of-consciousness writing as well as the use of multiple points of view indicate a clear influence by James JOYCE, Virginia WOOLF, and particularly William Faulkner. The book also is clearly structured on Orson Welles's film *Citizen Kane,* which Fuentes saw in New York at an early age.

Another of Fuentes's novels, *Terra Nostra* (1975), pushes the envelope of a novel's experimental possibilities even further. It is, essentially, a meditation on Spanish and Latin-American history that uses fiction as its medium. It has no cohesive plot of which to speak and ranges from ancient Rome to the imagined end of the world. The main characters are barely human; they are, in fact, allegorical representations of the primal forces that drive human history.

Fuentes has also written a large number of essays. *La Nueva Novela Hispanoamericana (The*

New Hispanic-American Novel, 1969), a study of the "new" Latin American novel of the 1960s, is a profound account of what distinguishes the novels of the cultural boom that occurred in Latin America at that time. It delves into the significance of the new style of MAGIC REALISM and thoughtfully examines the strengths and tendencies of what was, at the time, a newly emerging force in world literature.

Along with Octavio PAZ, Fuentes stands as one of the foremost Mexican authors of the 20th century. His erudition and refined intelligence, combined with the gifts of an epic storyteller, earned him in 1987 the Cervantes Prize, the most prestigious award given to a Spanish language author.

Other Works by Carlos Fuentes

The Crystal Frontier: A Novel in Nine Stories. Translated by Alfred MacAdam. New York: Farrar, Straus & Giroux, 1997.

The Hydra Head. Translated by Margaret Sayers Peden. New York: Farrar, Straus & Giroux, 1978.

A Work about Carlos Fuentes

Williams, Raymond Leslie. *The Writings of Carlos Fuentes.* Austin: University of Texas Press, 1996.

futurism

Having its origins in literature and poetry, the futurist movement began in Europe on February 20, 1909, when the front page of the French newspaper *Le Figaro* published the *Founding and Manifesto of Futurism* by artist and lawyer Emilio Filippo Tommaso Marinetti. Marinetti's manifesto glorified technology, particularly the speed and power of the newly developed automobile, while at the same time promoting violence and aggression and calling for the destruction of traditional culture. This wide-scale obliteration of the past, according to Marinetti, was to also include the physical demolition of cultural institutions that were linked to traditional society, such as museums and libraries. Marinetti referred to these institutions as "those cemeteries of wasted efforts, those calvaries of crucified dreams, those catalogues of broken impulses!" He also encouraged his followers to "Let the good incendiaries come with their carbonized fingers! . . . Here they are! Here they are! . . . Set the library stacks on fire! Turn the canals in their course to flood the museum vaults!" (*The Futurist Cookbook*) At the time of the publication, Marinetti was the only member of the movement, but he soon gained a large literary and artistic following.

The name *futurism* was coined by Marinetti as a celebration of the change and growth of the future. Futurism stood in contrast to the sentimentality inherent in ROMANTICISM. Futurists openly and intentionally defied tradition and constantly questioned the accepted concepts of art and even the standard definitions of what constitutes art. They embraced technology, particularly anything relating to speed or power, and glorified the energy and violent nature of 20th-century urban life. The power of machinery and a fascination with speed were focal points of the movement, as was the renunciation of the "static" art of previous generations. Futurist literary theory, for example, focused on the ability of language to express. A futurist poet, for example, might frame words so that they would project from the page like gunfire.

Although it began as an Italian movement, futurism quickly spread throughout the world during the early part of the 20th century to places such as Hungary, Poland, the Ukraine, Holland, Portugal, and America. In Poland, Czechoslovakia, and other Eastern bloc countries, futurism was adopted quickly as a movement of protest against established cultural values and political hierarchy.

Futurism not only promoted destruction of cultural institutions; it also glorified war. It favored fascism and aimed to destroy artistic tradition. The motivation behind futurism was largely political. Marinetti and many other futurists were heavily involved in demonstrations urging Italy to enter World War I.

Futurism was also characterized by the numerous manifestos written and published simply for the purpose of explaining the movement itself.

These documents took the form of pamphlets and illustrated books of poetry. The rules of futurism as it applied to the arts were defined in these manifestos long before they were actually seen in the arts themselves. The tone of Marinetti's initial manifesto and many others that followed was intentionally inflammatory and, like the movement itself, designed to inspire anger, arouse controversy, and attract attention.

One of the reasons that Italian futurism is not better known today is its relationship to fascism. After World War II, futurism was viewed in a negative light because of this association; however, although Marinetti was a friend of the young fascist Benito Mussolini and both were ardent supporter of fascism, Futurism was never, as it has sometimes been claimed, "the official art of fascism." Mussolini was politically active in promoting the futurists, especially during the years 1918 to 1920. He ultimately turned against them, using his political clout to silence them. Many futurists then became disillusioned by the political situation and drifted away from political activism.

Futurism officially ended in 1944 with the fall of Italy and Marinetti's death; however, the legacy of futurism to modern art, including literature, is enormous. Futurism was the first attempt to focus art on technology and machines. Remnants of futurism can be found throughout 20th-century avant-garde art, particularly with regard to many aspects of modern science fiction.

Works about Futurism

Marinetti, F. T. *The Futurist Cookbook.* Translated by Suzanne Brill, edited and introduction by Lesley Chamberlain. San Francisco: Bedford Arts, 1989.

Tisdall, Caroline, and Angela Bozolla. *Futurism.* Oxford: Oxford University Press, 1978.

Gabo

See GARCÍA MÁRQUEZ, GABRIEL.

Gandhi, Mohandas K(aramchand)

(1869–1948) *writer, political leader*

Mohandas Karamchand Gandhi was born in Kathiawar, Gujarat, India. He was the youngest son of Karamchand Gandhi, a politician, and Putlibai Gandhi. His mother was an extremely devout Hindu, and Gandhi often said his own beliefs on pacifism were based on his mother's religious teachings. In 1883, at age 13, Gandhi was wedded to Kasturba. Five years later, he was sent to England to study law and, in 1891, was called to the bar but decided to return to India.

After a brief period at work as a lawyer for the Bombay High Court in 1893, Gandhi went to South Africa to work for a Muslim law firm and spent the next 20 years fighting against the maltreatment of South African Indians, a fight that led to the formation in 1894 of the Natal Indian Congress. He later wrote about his experiences in South Africa in *Satyagraha in South Africa* (1924). In this work, Gandhi describes the idea behind *Satyagraha* (Truth Force), which later became the *Satyagraha* movement. This movement was a form of "peaceful resistance" against British colonial rule

and was the most powerful political tool in India's struggle for independence.

By the time he was 45, Gandhi had become an international figure. His wide-ranging influence and prodigious social work gave him the title of "Bapu" (Father) in India and "Mahatma" (Great Soul) all over the world. His teachings on the importance of combining spiritual healing with political struggle have been adopted by international leaders such as America's Martin Luther King and Malcolm X. These ideas are passionately and candidly expressed in his autobiography, *An Autobiography or The Story of My Experiments with Truth* (1929). His experiments with truth, he explains, are a lifelong commitment to achieve purity in mind and action. For Gandhi, however, purity also had political power. His political career was dedicated to encouraging Indians to be nonviolent in their struggle against the violent and oppressive power of the British.

Gandhi's most important contribution to Indian history was his leadership in helping India and Pakistan gain independence from British colonial rule in 1947. His political legacy often overshadows his literary talent, but he wrote prodigiously in both English and Gujarati (his mother tongue). Gandhi wrote numerous essays on topics ranging from vegetarianism to anticasteism to passive disobedience to spiritual healing to religious tolerance. His most important work, *Hind Swaraj* or *Indian Home Rule* (1909), is a compilation of essays on his philosophies and political goals. He was also an editor and contributor to several journals, including an English weekly called *Young India* and a Gujarati monthly called *Navajivan* (*New Life*).

Gandhi spent his later years in and out of prison. In 1948, on his way to evening prayers, he was assassinated by a Hindu fanatic. This event seems, even today, an ironic and tragic end to a life spent spreading the cause for peace and nonviolence.

Other Works by Mohandas K. Gandhi

All Men Are Brothers. New York: Columbia University Press, 1969.

Mahatma Gandhi: Selected Political Writing. Edited by Dennis Dalton. Indianapolis: Hackett Pub. Co., 1996.

A Work about Mohandas K. Gandhi

Wolpert, Stanley. *Gandhi's Passion: The Life and Legacy of Mahatma Gandhi.* New York: Oxford University Press, 2001.

Gao Xingjian (Kao Tsing–jen) (1940–   )
novelist, playwright

Gao Xingjian was born on January 4 in Ganzhou in China's Jiangxi Province. Although he was not formally educated, both his parents were interested and educated in the arts, and his mother taught him to read and write. When he entered Nanjing High School in 1951, he wrote prolifically. He graduated with a degree in French from Beijing Foreign Studies University in 1962 and took a job translating books.

Like most Chinese youth of the period, Gao Xingjian became a Red Guard under Mao Zedong's Communist rule and entered cadre schools in Henan and Anhui in 1969. Although China was in the middle of Mao's Cultural Revolution, Gao Xingjian continued to write, largely for psychological relief from the politically oppressive envi-

ronment, although he later burned all his work from that period.

After the Cultural Revolution, Gao Xingjian was able to publish essays and short stories. In 1975, he was asked to head the French section for the magazine *China Reconstructs,* which helped him build important contacts in the French and Western literary worlds. He made further connections while handling external liaison affairs for the Chinese Writers Association in 1977.

During this time, Gao Xingjian also focused on his own literary endeavors, becoming a playwright for the Beijing People's Art Theater. *Absolute Signal,* his first play, about a thief and his girlfriend, takes place in a train car. It was performed in 1982 and combined traditional dramatic methods with methods used by modern Western playwrights. His 1983 absurdist play *Bus Stop* is based on Samuel BECKETT's *Waiting for Godot* and is about a bus that never comes and the hapless passengers who eventually wait years for it. Also interpreted as a critique of the Communist leadership, the play placed Gao Xingjian squarely in the middle of China's debate over MODERNISM. He also authored a piece of critical theory, "A Rough Study of Techniques in Modern Fiction Writing," (1981) which further raised controversy about his sympathy with modern and Western influences. In 1986, Gao Xingjian's plays were banned by the Chinese government from being performed after uproar over the staging of his avant-garde play, *The Other Shore,* essentially a conversation between ambiguous actors struggling to use a rope to cross from one side of water to another. The dialogue is vague and fluid, a characteristic critics found pointless and subversive.

The next year, Gao Xingjian was diagnosed with terminal lung cancer. The diagnosis turned out to be incorrect, but the brush with mortality and his fear of further persecution by the government drove him to seek spiritual renewal by journeying into the wild, mountainous forests of the Sichuan province. After his wilderness travels, he journeyed to Europe on the invitation of a German organization and became a Chinese exile. He moved to

France, of which he is now a citizen. He has been the recipient of France's prestigious Chevalier d'Ordre des Arts et des Lettres award and has frequently worked on government commissions. He recorded his Sichuan-mountain experiences in his novel, *Soul Mountain* (1990), which fictionalizes his journey through the wilderness and his quest for truth and spiritual rebirth. The novel is also known for its innovative voice: The narrator's voice alternately assumes the use of different pronouns—*I, you, he,* and *she*—to create multiple perspectives.

Gao Xingjian is also an accomplished painter. While he has been the recipient of much critical attention and acclaim in the West for his literary work, he has earned his living with his misty and evocative brush paintings that often grace the covers of his volumes.

In 2001, Gao Xingjian became the first Chinese writer to win the Nobel Prize in literature. He accepted the prize as a Chinese writer in exile, and the Chinese government denounced the Swedish Academy for its choice of a writer unknown in China. In awarding the prize, the academy praised Gao Xingjian's "oeuvre of universal validity, bitter insights, and linguistic ingenuity."

Another Work by Gao Xingjian

The Other Shore: Plays by Gao Xingjian. Translated by Gilbert Fong. Hong Kong: The Chinese University Press, 1999.

A Work about Gao Xingjian

Tam, Kwok-kan. *Soul of Chaos: Critical Perspectives on Gao Xingjian.* Hong Kong: The Chinese University Press, 2001.

García Lorca, Federico (1898–1936) *poet, playwright*

Federico García Lorca was born in Fuente Vaqueros, Spain, to a well-to-do family. He was given an excellent education and the opportunity to pursue his artistic interests, which included painting, music, and, most of all, poetry. He spent his child-hood in the Andalusian city of Granada, which instilled in him a love of that region's folk traditions. This folk influence would later be seen in his plays and poetry and a series of folksongs he collected and anthologized.

In 1919, he moved to Madrid and, within a short time, earned a reputation as one of the most talented young poets in Spain. His reputation spread throughout the Spanish-speaking world, and such Latin American poets as Pablo NERUDA were inspired and influenced by him.

García Lorca's international reputation had been established, and his career was progressing in Spain. However, personal conflicts and politics within the Spanish literary world caused him to travel to the United States for a year, where he attended Columbia University.

He found New York to be a nightmare, if an exciting one, and he wrote the surrealistic and expressionistic work *Poet in New York* (1940), which was not published until after his death. A castigation of the inhumanity of the modern world, *Poet in New York* remains one of García Lorca's most popular poems in the English-speaking world. It uses surrealist techniques, but unlike the French surrealism of André BRETON, it is filled with emotion and passion.

When García Lorca returned to Spain, he became increasingly involved in theater and wrote a series of plays that reveal the folkloric influences of his youth, creating a theater of strong emotions and symbolism. He also directed a traveling theater company called *La Barraca*, which performed Spanish theater classics in rural areas that had little exposure to culture. This project was one of many liberal political activities in which García Lorca was engaged during the period of the Spanish republic and before the Spanish civil war.

It was also at this time that García Lorca became particularly interested in the emerging women's rights movement. His reputation and fame grew exponentially during this period.

In 1936, while on a trip to Granada to visit his family, García Lorca was trapped by the outbreak of the Spanish civil war and went into hiding. He was captured within a few weeks and executed without trial. The presumed reason was his homosexuality, a crime at the time. However, his liberal agenda was undoubtedly a strong factor as well.

Critical Analysis

García Lorca was obsessed with expressing the intense, vital energy of life, which he did by using subconscious images and strong musical language. In his works, he constantly examined the struggle of opposing forces and the power of dialectical opposites such as good and evil or freedom and repression. These themes interact with his politics to create three major trends in his work: examinations of individuals oppressed by the need to conform to social norms, minorities oppressed by uncaring majorities, and life oppressed by death itself.

In the play *The House of Bernarda Alba* (1936), García Lorca recounts the power relationship between a controlling mother, Bernarda Alba, and her daughter Adela. Bernarda Alba's attempts to separate Adela from her lover end tragically, as do all García Lorca's plays, with her daughter's suicide. Bernarda Alba is a larger-than-life figure who ends up destroying everything she seeks to preserve. The play has distinctive feminist overtones and, along with IBSEN's *Hedda Gabler,* is one of the great early works of feminist literature.

Blood Wedding (1933) recounts the struggle between Leonardo and the citizens of the village in which he lives who react to his nonconformity with murderous rage. The villagers are not given proper names but called only Mother, Father, and so on, indicating that they are not real people but symbols of the rigid conventions of an unjust social morality. Like *The House of Bernarda Alba, Blood Wedding* ends with the tragic death of its most noble character.

In García Lorca's collection of poems *Gypsy Ballads* (1928), he explores the problematic cultural identity of the gypsies in Spain. These poems critique Spanish society for its unfair marginalization of the gypsies. *Gypsy Ballads* also celebrates the beauty and poetry of gypsy culture, pointing out that many things that are quintes-

sentially Spanish, in fact, originated with the gypsies.

Dirge for Ignacio Sánchez Mejías (1937) brings García Lorca's celebration of the power of life into a confrontation with its opposite, the power of death. Ignacio Sánchez Mejías was a friend of García Lorca's who was tragically killed in a bullfight. In the dirge, García Lorca celebrates the matador's vitality and emphasizes the beauty of living on the tightrope between life and death.

García Lorca is one of the most influential poets of the 20th century. NERUDA, PAZ, and many other 20th-century Spanish-speaking poets owe García Lorca a tremendous debt as the central figure of a type of surrealism that is uniquely expressive of emotions. His tragic death at the hands of fascists also stands as an important historical symbol for the need for freedom of expression. He may be seen as a forerunner of the Civil Rights and women's movements of the latter 20th century, but more important, he was a writer of exquisite poems and plays that truly reveal the preciousness of human life on the edge of death.

Other Works by García Lorca

A Season in Granada: Uncollected Poems & Prose. Edited and translated by Christopher Maurer. London: Anvil Press Poetry, 1998.

Four Major Plays. Translated by John Edmunds; introduction by Nicholas Round; notes by Ann MacLaren. New York: Oxford University Press, 1997.

A Work about García Lorca

Wellington, Beth. *Reflections on Lorca's Private Mythology: Once Five Years Pass and the Rural Plays.* New York: Peter Lang, 1993.

García Márquez, Gabriel (Gabo)
(1928–) *novelist, short-story writer, screenplay writer, journalist*

Gabriel García Márquez was born in Aracataca, Colombia, a small town near a banana plantation called Macondo. His father, Gabriel Eligio García, was a telegraph operator who had courted his mother in secret by telegraph when she would write home from school. García Márquez lived in Aracataca until the age of eight. During that time, his closest connections were to his maternal grandparents, who had initially tried to prevent their daughter from marrying Gabriel Eligio García because of his conservative political affiliations.

García Márquez's grandmother was a highly superstitious woman and also a brilliant storyteller. She would tell García Márquez the most incredible, exaggerated, and impossible things with the deadpan manner of someone explaining that Earth has a north and a south pole. As a child, García Márquez believed everything she told him and, on some level, never stopped believing. This early experience of blending the real with the fantastic later led García Márquez to develop his unique style of MAGIC REALISM.

His grandfather, who had been a colonel in the Colombian civil war, was a local official. He would spend a great deal of time with his young grandson and often took him to the circus. García Márquez has stated that his grandfather was the most important person in his life and his best friend. The colonel died when García Márquez was eight years old, but García Márquez drew more inspiration for his books from these eight years than from any other period of his life.

García Márquez was sent to boarding school and won a scholarship to go to college in Bogotá, the capital of Colombia. After studying law, he worked as a journalist, traveling throughout South America, Europe, and the United States, eventually settling in Mexico City in 1961.

In Mexico City, he wrote film scripts, including a western in collaboration with Carlos FUENTES titled *Tiempo de Morir* (*A Time to Die*), to support himself and his wife Mercedes, whom he had married in 1958.

García Márquez had written an unsuccessful first novel called *Leaf Storm* (1955) about life in Macondo, a fictionalized version of García Márquez's birthplace. The novel spans the period from the turn of the century to the 1930s. Though it contains many of the themes in García Márquez's later works, the novel is poorly structured and remains flat.

No One Writes to the Colonel (1961), however, is in many ways García Márquez's first masterpiece. It is a novella that depicts an elderly colonel who waits for a government pension that never arrives. The colonel, lovingly based on García Márquez's grandfather, is a magnificent literary character filled with humor and vitality. It is in this work that García Márquez's control of language and his stylistic innovations caught up with his psychological perception. The combination created a new sort of literature, which was fantastic in its details and yet deeply true in its emotions.

Critical Analysis

The imaginary town of Macondo is the setting of most of García Márquez's novels and stories. In this way, Macondo is a literary device like the Yoknapatawpha County of William Faulkner. Both places are imaginary worlds, closely based on the setting of the author's childhood, that by being written about repeatedly become literary microcosms, self-contained realities. García Márquez has often spoken of his sense of kinship with Faulkner. He has even said that Faulkner, who grew up in Mississippi near the Gulf of Mexico, is a fellow Caribbean writer.

It was in 1965 that García Márquez began to write his single greatest work *One Hundred Years of Solitude* (1967). He was driving to the beach with his family when suddenly all of the themes that he had been developing since he was a boy solidified into a clear structure. He returned home immediately and began to write.

One Hundred Years of Solitude revisits all of the themes of García Márquez's earlier work as episodes within the epic story of six generations of the Buendia family, the founding family of the town of Macondo.

The book is subtly structured in four sections of five unnumbered chapters each. Each section corresponds to an abstract historical category.

The first section explores the mythic and utopian prehistory of the town. Mythical narratives from both the biblical and classical traditions are woven with local superstitions and García Márquez's own inventions. Macondo, though it is a place that seems full of promise, has been founded by José Arcadio Buendia because of a murder he has committed and is trying to forget. This evokes the story of Cain and Abel and shows that Macondo is a place created by an act of transgression.

The second section of the book moves into what could be called historical time. The events in this section closely parallel the history of the actual Columbian civil war in which García Márquez's grandfather fought. However, García Márquez continues to write in his magical style. This combination of historical fact and fantasy has an extraordinarily dramatic effect and is, above all, what makes *One Hundred Years of Solitude* the quintessential example of magic realism.

The third section is an account of how, after the Columbian civil war, a U.S. company comes to Macondo to exploit its banana industry. Though this section can also be said to take place in historical, as opposed to mythic, time, it is different from the previous section. History in the third section has been corrupted by language, particularly the propaganda and media manipulation the banana company uses to exploit the citizens of Macondo. By the time the company is finished, Macondo has been reduced to a wasteland, barely holding on to what is left of its previous vitality.

In the fourth section, the book returns to mythic time, not the utopian time of the beginning but the apocalyptic time of the true end of the world. The final Buendia, the great-great-grandson of the first José Arcadio, lives in Macondo disconnected from history. He does not even know his origins or that he is a Buendia by blood. He spends his time trying to decipher a magical manuscript that holds the secret of his origins and his fate.

García Márquez went on to write multiple novels of the highest literary merit, including *Love in the Time of Cholera* (1988) and *Chronicle of a Death Foretold* (1981). In 1982, he was awarded the world's highest literary award, the Nobel Prize. In his acceptance speech, he spoke of his hopes for a positive political future for Latin America. He emphasized that magic realism is merely an accurate depiction of the miraculous occurrences that take place in Latin American life, occurrences of superhuman wonder and terror.

Other Works by Gabriel García Márquez

Collected Novellas. Translated from the Spanish by Gregory Rabassa and J. S. Bernstein. New York: HarperPerennial, 1991.

The General in His Labyrinth. Translated from the Spanish by Edith Grossman. New York: Knopf, 1990.

A Work about Gabriel García Márquez

Miller, Yvette E., and Charles Rossman. *Gabriel García Márquez.* Pittsburgh, Pa.: Department of Hispanic Languages and Literatures, University of Pittsburgh, 1985.

Gautier, Théophile (1811–1872) *poet, novelist*

Théophile Gautier was born in Tarbes on August 31. He moved as a young child to Paris with his family, where he studied to become a painter. In June 1829, however, Gautier met with the great novelist Victor HUGO, which prompted him to change his aspirations and become a writer. Five months later, his first collection, *Poetries* (1836), was published on the same day that the barricades were erected in Paris.

For financial reasons, Gautier took a position as a journalist in 1836, working as an art critic while continuing to write fiction. His novel *Mademoiselle de Maupin* (1835) caused quite a scandal when it first appeared on account of its description of sexual ambiguity. It is also credited for founding the concept of *art for art's sake*, a phrase Gautier uses in his prologue to the book. The next year, he wrote *La Mort amoureuse* (translated into

English as *Clarimonde*), about a priest who becomes obsessed with a beautiful vampiress. Gautier also continued to write poetry, publishing the collection *The Comedy of Death* (1838), which shows influences of Shakespeare, GOETHE, and Dante.

In 1839, Gautier decided to try to write for the theater. He created numerous tales of fantasy, but the one for which he is most remembered is his libretto for the ballet *Giselle,* which opened in Paris on June 28, 1841, to overwhelming popular and critical acclaim. *Giselle* continues to be performed frequently in the 21st century.

Gautier was a proponent of the idea of art for art's sake, which is evident in the fact that he originally wanted to be a painter. His love of the visual has transferred to his written works as well.

Others Works by Théophile Gautier

Gautier on Dance. Translated by Ivor Guest. London: Dance, 1986.

Gentle Enchanter: Thirty-Four Poems. Translated by Brian Hill. London: R. Hart Davis, 1960.

A Work about Théophile Gautier

Tennant, Philip E. *Théophile Gautier.* London: Athlone Press, 1975.

Generation of 1898

A group of writers who shared a common concern for Spain's national identity and who worked to revitalize the social, political, and aesthetic structures of their country. The Spanish-American War of 1898 brought an end to the period of Spanish imperialism in the New World. Spain, which had been a world power for hundreds of years, had to face the new reality of being a small provincial nation. The Generation of 1898 urged their fellow compatriots to turn away from the trappings of empire and to search for the "true" Spain of their medieval and Arabic heritage.

ORTEGA Y GASSET, the Spanish philosopher and critic, attributes a span of 15 years to the generation as a movement and further divides it into two groups. The first group includes the forerunners Miguel de UNAMUNO and Ángel Ganivet y García (1865–98); the second group includes the secondary members of the movement such as Pío BAROJA.

Perhaps the difficulty of conclusively saying who is and is not a member of this movement comes from the fact that one of the main characteristics that members of the Generation of 1898 shared is a strong sense of individuality and nonconformism. The central figures, however, would unquestionably include Baroja, Unamuno, Ganivet, Antonio MACHADO, and the Latin American poet Rubén DARÍO, who spent a great deal of time traveling in Europe. Other members include Azorín (José Martínez Ruiz, 1873–1967), who was the first to identify the Generation of '98 as a group; Ramón Maria del Valle-Inclán (1866–1936); Juan Ramón Jiménez (1881–1958), who won the Nobel Prize in literature in 1956; and Ramón Pérez de Ayala (1880–1962).

These authors, in addition to individualism, shared strong national feelings mixed with literary and formal experimentation. Out of their rejection of the decedent features of Spanish culture, they embraced MODERNISM in hope that it would cleanse the dead tissue from Spanish art. In politics, they shared a sense of apathy and a mistrust of government control over the individual. In society, they rejected refined manners and taboos. They called for bringing Spanish culture down to earth and embracing Arab and flamenco influences. They wanted a return to the culture of the people rather than the aristocrats. Finally, in art, they introduced new structures and difficult but vital modes of expression.

The writers of the Generation of 1898 opened up the structures of literature and showed the exciting possibilities of experimentation. They influenced 20th-century authors as diverse as GARCÍA LORCA and Ernest Hemingway.

A Work about the Generation of 1898

Shaw, Donald Leslie. *The Generation of 1898 in Spain.* New York: Barnes & Noble, 1975.

Genet, Jean (1910–1986) *novelist, playwright*

A convicted felon who went on to become one of the leaders in the avant-garde theater movement, Jean Genet was born in Paris as the illegitimate son of a woman who abandoned him shortly after birth. Raised in state institutions, he embarked on a life of crime, turning to theft at age 10. He spent time at the Mettray Reformatory, escaping from there at age 19 to join the foreign legion, a position he soon abandoned. From there, Genet wandered throughout Europe spending time in several prisons on charges of vagrancy, theft, homosexuality, and smuggling.

In 1939, Genet began to write about his experiences. His subsequent novels detailed and glorified the underworld, homosexuality, male prostitutes, convicts, and other social outcasts. He wrote his first novel, *Our Lady of the Flowers* (1943; translated 1963), a fictional creation based on the events in his life while he was in prison.

In 1948, Genet was once again convicted of burglary. This, his 10th offense, resulted in an automatic sentence of life imprisonment. By this time, however, his works had gained the attention of fellow writers Jean Paul SARTRE, André GIDE, and Jean COCTEAU. On hearing of Genet's sentence, they petitioned the president of the republic for Genet's release. His parole was granted, after which his life changed dramatically.

Encouraged by the show of support from such prominent writers, Genet determined to dedicate his life to writing and to abandon crime permanently. He continued to glorify the underworld in which he had lived in his works, but he also began to focus on the beauty and sadness of homosexual love.

In the 1940s, Genet turned his attention to the theater, writing several plays that, at the time, were considered too controversial to be performed in France. His first play, *The Maids* (1947; translated 1954), made a significant impact on the rising trend toward the THEATRE OF THE ABSURD. It was based on a true story of two sisters, both maids for the same woman, who murder their mistress. This play was followed by *Deathwatch* (1949; translated 1954), which takes the prison setting so commonly seen in his novels and uses it as a backdrop from which to explore despair and loneliness.

Genet began to abandon traditional ideas of what should constitute acceptable character, plot, and motivation within a theatrical piece. He began to focus on conflicts within society—between illusion and reality, good and evil, and other cultural oppositions—with a fervor that can almost be described as religious. His plays are ritualistic in structure, aimed at arousing the audience's innermost feelings and then offering them the opportunity to undergo a transformation or to reach a catharsis alongside the characters on the stage. Filled with an energy largely created by violence and cruelty, his plays, while shocking, were never vulgar and were diverse in both setting and subject. *The Balcony* (1956; translated 1957), for instance, was set in a brothel; *The Blacks* (1959) in a fantastical court; and *The Screens* (1961; translated 1962) in the middle of the French–Algerian war. All three works, however, focused on the inherent paradoxes of an imperfect life.

Genet's autobiography, *The Thief's Journal* (1949; translated 1964), is a record of his remarkable life and the misery and degradation he suffered at the hands of a bourgeois society. He gave up writing in the 1960s to devote himself to lecturing and supporting the emerging radical activist fervor of the decade. He continued to support radical causes until his death on April 15.

Other Works by Jean Genet

Funeral Rites. Translated by Bernard Frechtman. New York: Grove Press, 1969.

Prisoner of Love. Translated by Barbara Bray. Hanover. Mass.: University Press of New England, 1992.

Rembrant. Translated by Randolph Hough. New York: Hanuman Books, 1988.

Works about Jean Genet

Knapp, Bettina. *Jean Genet.* Boston: Twayne, 1968.

Sartre, Jean-Paul. *Saint Genet: Actor and Martyr.* New York: Pantheon Books, 1983.

White, Edmund. *Genet: A Biography.* New York: Knopf, 1993.

George, Stefan (1868–1933) *poet*

Stefan George was born in the German village of Rüdesheim to Stephan and Eva George. His father was a prosperous wine merchant. George attended secondary school in Darmstadt and graduated in 1888. He studied modern languages at the University of Berlin for three semesters. Deciding early in life to be a poet, George never engaged in another profession or trade. He rarely remained in one place, frequently traveling to the countries of central and western Europe. While in Paris, he found formative influences in Stéphane MALLARMÉ and other French symbolist poets.

George published his first volume of poetry in 1890. In 1892, he founded the journal *Blätter für die Kunst* (*Journal of the Arts*). George formed many close friendships among the literati, including the Austrian writer Hugo von HOFMANNSTHAL. He soon attracted a group of disciples known as the George Circle. After the turn of the century, George increasingly saw himself as an educator to lead the reform of a decadent culture. A brief friendship with a 15-year-old boy, Maximin, further focused George's attention on the beauty and the renewing potential of an elite group of youth. By the 1910s, George's poetry had moved into a prophetic phase. His volume *Der neue Riech* (*The Kingdom Come,* (1928) revealed his vision for a new Germany. The Nazis sought to use George as a symbol of their state, but he refused their honors and awards. He moved to Switzerland, where he died in December 1933.

George became famous for writing beautiful lyrical poems on such themes as landscape, friendship, and art. He sometimes used terse and forceful language but still produced balladesque works. Early in his career, George wrote of the artist's isolation from nature, but he later sought to teach that man was divine and capable of perfection. He left a lasting influence on German lyrical poetry and expressionist writers. His biographers, Michael and Erika Metzger, explain that George's works "bear witness to the unremitting striving of a man of unique poetic and intellectual powers to find a higher meaning in his existence and ours."

Another Work by Stefan George

The Works of Stefan George. Translated by Olga Marx and Ernst Morwitz. Chapel Hill: University of North Carolina Press, 1974.

A Work about Stefan George

Metzger, Michael M., and Erika A Metzger. *Stefan George.* Boston: Twayne, 1972.

Ghālib, Mirzā (1797–1869) *poet*

Mirzā Asadullāh Khān Ghālib was born in Agra, India. His grandfather immigrated to India from Asia Minor and belonged to a long line of soldiers. Ghālib's father was also a soldier and was killed in battle when Ghālib was five years old. After his father's death, he grew up with his mother's family, who were wealthy landowners. Ghālib was given a private education in languages and sciences and, at age 13, was married and moved to Delhi, where he spent the rest of his life.

Much of Ghālib's finest poetry is in Persian, though he also wrote in Urdu. Ghālib started writing poetry at a very young age and was already moving among literary circles by the time of his marriage. When he was young, he used the name *Asad* and later adopted the name *Ghālib*. He was always hesitant about his choice to become a poet, and he was the first male in his family who did not want to be a soldier. In one of his letters, he describes this decision by comparing his poetic words with the weapons of war. He states that his poetry will be "his ship upon the illusory sea of verse . . . and the broken arrows of my ancestors become my pens." Characteristically witty, Ghālib's allusions are often obscured by the strict rhyme and rhythm constraints of the *ghazal*. (A *ghazal* is defined as a short poem consisting of up to a dozen couplets in the same meter, with a specific rhyme scheme.) Often, however, this necessity only further liberated Ghālib's deliberate play with words and sounds.

Ghālib was never rich, but in middle age, he was invited to join the court of Bahādur Shāh Zafar, the last of the Moghul emperors. Under Bahādur Shāh Zafar's patronage, he began to make a comfortable living from his poetry. The British takeover of India from the Moghuls after the Sepoy Mutiny in 1857 (also known as the First War of Indian Independence) had a tremendous impact on Ghālib's life and work: He lost his position as court poet and instead began writing copious letters to his friends, who were now spread across the subcontinent. Although they were written for private reading, they were collected and published, the first volume of them in the year before he died. Written in Urdu in a colloquial style, these letters are his subjective responses to current events and allow modern readers a glimpse into his time, while taking Urdu literature into a new direction by showing that profound literature could exist outside of the formal *ghazal* and its emphasis on idealism, romance, and universalism.

Another Work by Mirzā Ghālib

Ghazals of Ghālib. Translated by Aijaz Ahmad. New York: Columbia University Press, 1971.

A Work about Mirzā Ghālib

Russell, Ralph. *Ghālib.* Cambridge, Mass.: Harvard University Press, 1969.

Ghosh, Amitav (1956–) *novelist*

Amitav Ghosh was born in Calcutta, India, but grew up in Bangladesh (formerly East Pakistan). As a child, and while on fieldwork research, Ghosh spent much of his time living in many countries, including Sri Lanka, Iran, England, Egypt, and the United States. Despite his diverse interests (he has studied and taught philosophy, literature, and social anthropology), Ghosh has said that his creative work best captures his ideas. As a child, during summer holidays in Calcutta, Ghosh would spend hours reading books from his uncle's library in his grandfather's house. Because of this initiation into reading and literature, he has acknowledged the lasting influence of Rabindranath TAGORE and the Bengali literary tradition in his own writing. Today, Ghosh is a writer, a journalist, and a teacher at Columbia University.

After graduation in India, Ghosh went to Oxford University to study social anthropology, where he received a masters, and a doctorate in philosophy in 1982. On his return to India, he began to work for the *Indian Express* newspaper in New Delhi while working on his first novel, *The Circle of Reason* (1986). This and his next novel, *Shadow Lines* (1988), are about the seamlessness of geographical boundaries, and much of the plot of *Shadow Lines* hinges on the question of national identity. The main character suffers from a sudden identity crisis after he is thrown into a situation where he must decide which country (India or Bangladesh) is his, which culture defines him, and which place he can ultimately call his own. This novel won Ghosh India's prestigious Sahitya Akademi Award in 1990.

Many of Ghosh's novels have been the result of years spent in different countries while conducting field research for his college degrees. *In an Antique Land* (1993), for instance, comes out of his research in 1980 while living in a small village in Egypt. Ghosh's latest novel, *The Glass Palace* (2000), tells the story of an orphaned Indian boy, developed alongside the story of the royal family's exile in India after the British invasion of the kingdom of Mandalay (Burma) in 1885.

Ghosh refused the Commonwealth Writers Prize for this novel in 2001 in protest against being classified as a "commonwealth" writer. Accepting the award, he said in his letter to the Commonwealth Foundation, would have placed "contemporary writing not within the realities of the present day . . . but rather within a disputed aspect of the past." His works reflect the elements of universal humanity. The cross-cultural references he makes to different nations and cultures render insignificant physical or political boundaries.

Another Work by Amitav Ghosh

The Calcutta Chromosome: A Novel of Fevers, Delirium, and Discovery. New York: HarperCollins, 1998.

Works about Amitav Ghosh

Bhatt, Indira, and Indira Nityanandan, eds. *The Fiction of Amitav Ghosh.* New Delhi: Creative Books, 2001.

Dhawan, R. K. *The Novels of Amitav Ghosh.* New York: Prestige Books, 1999.

Gide, André (1869–1951) *novelist*

André Gide was born in Paris on November 22. His father, a law professor at the University of Paris, died when André was 11. Gide was subsequently raised by his wealthy mother on her family's estate near Rouen. Overly protective of her son and concerned over what she believed to be his delicate health, she withdrew him from school and hired private tutors. He was brought up in a strict Protestant tradition, memorizing passages from the Bible at an early age, and undergoing periods of religious fervor. He also developed an abiding affection for his cousin, Madeleine Rondeux, whom he married in 1895. The two stayed married 42 years in what is, according to some accounts, the longest unconsummated marriage in recorded history.

In 1889, after completing his studies and passing his required exams, Gide, never needing to worry about supporting himself financially, decided to devote his life to writing and traveling. He published his first work, *The Notebooks of André Walter* (1891), in the style that was to become his signature: the intimate confessional. He also began to attend gatherings of intellectuals at the Paris apartment of symbolist poet Stéphane MALLARMÉ. This was followed by a trip to North Africa in 1893 with a young painter, Paul Albert Laurens. The effect of this journey proved critical to both Gide's life and his works.

Liberated from the confinement of the society in which he was born and raised, he began to examine certain truths about himself, including his homosexuality. When he returned to Paris, however, he quickly began to deny many of these revelations. He took a second trip to North Africa, during which he met Oscar Wilde, an intellectual experience that would forever shape his life and his work. The result of these sexual and intellectual awakenings was the novel *The Fruits of the Earth* (1897).

Although Gide had begun to make discoveries about himself, he was unable to reconcile the reality of his life with his strict moral religious upbringing. On returning to Paris once again, he married his cousin Madeleine Rondeux. The marriage was largely a pretense and fraught with difficulties, as is revealed in his novels *The Immoralist* (1902) and *Strait Is the Gate* (1909). Both works examine the tension between social responsibility and the desire to remain true to the self.

During World War I, Gide worked with the Red Cross in Paris, where he met and fell in love with Marc Allegret. When Madeleine learned of this, she destroyed all the letters Gide had ever sent to her, an act that greatly hurt Gide. In response, he published *Corydon* (1924), a defense of homosexuality, and *If I Die* (1924), his autobiography. These two works shocked and scandalized his closest friends and resulted in Gide's alienation from his previously close social groups. Gide, however, felt personally vindicated by his decision to admit openly his homosexuality and sold his estates to move with Allegret to French Equatorial Africa.

In the 1930s, Gide began to look favorably on principles of marxism and by 1932 had embraced communism largely because of Lenin's decriminalization of homosexuality. However, a visit to the Soviet Union in 1934 left him disillusioned.

A firm antifascist, he spent most of World War II living in North Africa. He was awarded the Nobel Prize in literature in 1947 and, at the time of his death in 1951, he was one of only two authors whose entire collection of works appeared on the Index Liborum Prohibitorum, a listing of books forbidden to be read by Roman Catholics.

André Gide's life was complicated by many facets, and his writing, which reflects the circumstances of his life, is based on an intense scrutiny of himself and the world around him.

Other Works by André Gide

Amyntas. Translated by Richard Howard. New York: Ecco Press, 1988.

The Counterfeiters. New York: Random House, 1973.

Works about André Gide

Fryer, Jonathan. *André and Oscar: Gide, Wilde and the Gay Art of Living.* London: Constable, 1997.

Sheridan, Alan. *André Gide: A Life in the Present.* London: Hamish Hamilton, 1998.

Ginzburg, Natalia (Alessandra Tornimparti) (1916–1991) *novelist, essayist, nonfiction writer*

Natalia Ginzburg, well known for her autobiographical novels detailing her unconventional family and its fight against fascism, was born Natalia Levi in Palermo to a middle-class family. Her religious background was mixed, being Jewish on her father's side and Catholic on her mother's side, and she was raised as an atheist. Because of this, she spent her childhood removed from other children, isolated for her differences. In 1919, she moved to Turin, where her father had accepted a position as a professor at the University of Turin. There, she was immersed in the culture of the time, particularly the activities centered around antifascism. Intellectuals, all opponents of Benito Mussolini, would gather regularly at her family's home to discuss opposition.

Ginzburg graduated from the University of Turin in 1935. Three years later, she married editor and political activist Leone Ginzburg. The couple had two children and spent much of their life together in seclusion in the region of Abruzzi, where they were involved in numerous antifascist activi-

ties. Eventually, they were forced into hiding, alternately in Rome and in Florence, until Leone Ginzburg was arrested in 1944. Imprisoned at the Regina Coeli prison, he died after being subjected to extreme torture.

Ginzburg had begun her career as a writer of short stories. Many of these were published in the Florintine magazine *Solaria.* Her first major work to appear in the magazine was "Un'assenza" (1933), a tale about an unhappy marriage. It was printed when she was only 17 years old. Her first short novel, however, was not written until almost a decade later. She published *The Road to the City* (1942) under the pseudonym of Alessandra Tornimparti while she and her husband were still in hiding.

In 1944, after the death of her husband and the Allied liberation, Ginzburg returned to Rome where she gained employment with the publishing house of Guilio Einaudi. While working as an editorial consultant, she continued to produce novels of her own, including *The Dry Heart* (1947), another tale of unhappy marriage, and *A Light for Fools* (1952), the story of a family's struggles to survive in an era of fascism.

Ginzburg remarried in 1950, this time to Gabriele Baldini, an English literature professor from the University of Rome. While married to him, she produced her humorous and well-known autobiographical work, *Family Sayings* (1963). After his death in 1969, she continued to write, producing essays, biographies, and translations, as well as fiction. She was elected to the Italian Parliament in 1983 and later published more works including *The City and the House* (1984) and *True Justice* (1990). Ginzburg died of cancer on October 7, leaving behind works that show in vivid detail the social implications of fascism and the history and culture of her world.

A Work about Natalia Ginzburg

Jeannet, Angela M., and Giuliana Sanguinetti Katz, eds. *Natalia Ginzburg: A Voice of the Twentieth Century.* Toronto: University of Toronto Press, 2000.

Giraudoux, Jean (1882–1944) *playwright*

Hippolyte-Jean Giraudoux was born in France in the village of Bellac. He was educated at the École Normale Supérieure. As a child and young man, he traveled extensively to Germany, Italy, the Balkans, Canada, and finally to the United States, where he spent a year as an instructor at Harvard. He returned to France to serve in World War I; he was wounded twice and became the only writer ever to be awarded the Wartime Legion of Honor.

Giraudoux began his literary career as a novelist, with *Suzanne et le Pacifique* (1921), and he wrote several other works of fiction. He also wrote literary studies such as *Racine* (1930) and political works, including *Full Powers* (1939). But he gained recognition for his stage plays, 15 in all, most of which were initially staged in France by actor-director Louis Jouvet.

Like the great 17th-century French dramatist Racine, whom he deeply admired, Giraudoux often chose classical themes. He titled one of his plays *Amphitryon 38* (1929; translated 1938) in acknowledgement of the 37 versions of the story (about a man whose wife gives birth to twins, of whom one has been fathered not by Amphitryon but by the sky god Zeus) that preceded his own. *Judith* (1931) revisits the biblical story of Judith's outwitting of Holofernes. But unlike Racine, who grandly presents his characters as consumed by fatal passions, Giraudoux treats his characters informally and ironically. He believed that he was living in an age when grandness could not be appreciated, and he adjusted his art accordingly.

Giraudoux's last play, *The Madwoman of Chaillot* (1946; translated 1949), was completed in 1943 but produced and published posthumously. Written during the German occupation of France, it tells an inspirational story of a group of greedy prospectors whose search for oil threatens to destroy a small town and of the "madwoman" who thwarts their plans.

Giraudoux's work is rich in allegory and fantasy and has strong political and psychological undertones. His playful anachronisms and his wit helped release the inhibitions that REALISM had placed on French theater.

Other Works by Jean Giraudoux

Choice of the Elect. Translated by Henry Bosworth Russell. Evanston, Ill.: Northwestern University Press, 2002.

The Five Temptations of La Fontaine. Translated by Richard Howard. New York: Turtle Point Press, 2002.

Lying Woman: A Novel. Translated by Richard Howard. New York: Winter House, 1972.

Plays. Translated by Roger Gellert. London: Methuen, 1967.

Three Plays. Translated by Phyllis La Farge with Peter H. Judd. New York: Hill and Wang, 1964.

The Trojan War Will Not Take Place = La Guerre de Troie n'aura pas lieu. Translated by Christopher Fry. London: Methuen, 1983.

Works about Jean Giraudoux

Body, Jacques. *Jean Giraudoux: The Legend and the Secret.* Translated by James Norwood. Madison, N.J.: Fairleigh Dickinson University Press, 1991.

Korzeniowska, Victoria B. *The Heroine as Social Redeemer in the Plays of Jean Giraudoux.* New York: Peter Long, 1991.

Nagel, Susan. *The Influence of the Novels of Jean Giraudoux on the Hispanic Vanguard Novels of the 1920s–1930s.* Lewisburg, Pa.: Bucknell University Press, 1991.

Goethe, Johann Wolfgang von (1749–1842) *poet, novelist, playwright, essayist*

Johann Wolfgang von Goethe was born in Frankfurt, Germany, to Johann Caspar Goethe, an attorney, and Katherine Elizabeth Goethe, a daughter of Frankfurt's mayor. Goethe's early interest in literature was wholeheartedly encouraged by his mother, an extremely well-educated woman. His childhood was marked by academic brilliance, as well as constant conflict with authority figures in school. Emotionally, Goethe's adolescence was shaped by several unsuccessful love affairs, which greatly contributed to his development as a writer.

At age 16, Goethe enrolled in Leipzig University to study law. During an interruption of his education due to illness, he studied drawing. He transferred to the University of Strasbourg where, in 1771, he obtained a degree in law. Between 1771 and 1774, he practiced law in Frankfurt and Wetzlar, until he was hired by Duke Karl August of Weimar. During his career as an administrator at the Weimar court, Goethe acted as the duke's councilman, a member of the war commission, and director of roads and services, and he directed the financial affairs of the court. A true member of the Enlightenment—the 18th-century movement of confidence in the capacities of human reason—Goethe dedicated his spare time to scientific research, mostly in anatomy. Between 1791 and 1817, Goethe acted as the director of court theaters. He also became an expert on mining, and under his influence and directorship, Jena University enjoyed the status as one of the most prominent and prestigious academic institutions in Europe, particularly in history and philosophy.

Critical Analysis

Goethe's first major work, *The Sorrows of Young Werther*, appeared in 1774. The novel delineates Werther's hopeless love for Lotte Buff, the wife of his close friend. Driven to self-alienation and psychological breakdown, no longer able to live without his beloved, Werther commits suicide. Werther expresses his misery in terms that resonated widely, especially with young readers: "My creative powers have been reduced to a senseless indolence. I cannot be idle, yet I cannot seem to do anything either. When we are robbed of ourselves, we are robbed of everything." Goethe explained his motivation for writing the novel in terms of his heightened spiritual and emotional awareness: "I tried to release myself from all alien emotions, to look kindly upon what was going on around me and let all living things, beginning with man himself, affect me as deeply as possible, each in its own way." The emotions and local color are placed in the foreground of his work. *The Sorrows of Young Werther* is considered to among the most influential texts of German ROMANTICISM.

In Goethe's second major novel, *Wilhelm Meister's Apprenticeship* (1795–96), Goethe continues to explore themes of love and alienation. However, the novel presents a more optimistic outlook on life. Like Werther, Wilhelm suffers a tragic blow after an unsuccessful courtship. Unlike Werther, however, Wilhelm begins to seek out actively other values in life. He dedicates himself to work and becomes a playwright and an actor. In the end, Wilhelm is spiritually satisfied with his newfound outlet for passion. The novel remains thematically consistent with the Romantic school; however, critics have noted the emergence of the conservative side of Goethe's thinking. Unlike many of his contemporaries, Goethe was not impressed by the uprising and violence of the French Revolution. He supported liberty and progress but also maintained that the aristocracy had an important role in society. Many younger readers began to criticize Goethe for what they saw as subservience to the upper classes.

The first part of Goethe's dramatic masterpiece, *Faust*, appeared in 1808. This drama became his passion and he worked on it for more than 30 years. Based on the play by the English Renaissance dramatist Christopher Marlowe, it tells a chilling story of a man who sells his soul for knowledge. Faust makes a contract with Mephistopheles to die as soon as his thirst for knowledge is satisfied. Faust is driven to despair when Margaret, an innocent woman, is condemned to death for giving birth to Faust's illegitimate child. He finally realizes that his lust for knowledge has led to tragic mistakes.

The second part of *Faust* appeared in 1838. Faust marries the beautiful Helen of Troy and creates a happy community of scholars. The bliss of his good deeds brings satisfaction in old age, and Mephistopheles is about to demand satisfaction. But Faust's changed attitudes and good heart are rewarded, as angels descend from the sky in the final scene of the play and take Faust to heaven. The play brought Goethe international success and had a profound influence on modern drama.

During his illustrious career, Goethe produced, in addition, a number of important poetical works. He also provided literary guidance to his close friend Friedrich SCHILLER and produced several of his plays. After his death, he was buried next to Schiller in Weimar.

Although it is difficult to measure the influence of Johann Wolfgang von Goethe, he is certainly among the giants of world literature. His novels, poems, and plays are still widely read and studied. He is a dominant figure of German Romanticism.

Other Works by Johann Wolfgang von Goethe

Italian Journey. Translated by Elizabeth Mayer. New York: Penguin, 1992.

The Sorrows of Young Werther and Selected Writings. Translated by Catherine Hutter. New York: New American Library, 1987.

Theory of Colors. Cambridge, Mass.: MIT Press, 1970.

Vaget, Hans R., ed. *Erotic Poems.* Translated by David Luke. New York: Oxford University Press, 1999.

Works about Johann Wolfgang von Goethe

Eckermann, Johann. *Conversations of Goethe.* Translated by John Oxenford. New York: Da Capo Press, 1998.

Wagner, Irmgard. *Goethe.* Boston: Twayne, 1999.

Williams, John. *The Life of Goethe: A Critical Biography.* Malden, Mass.: Blackwell Publishers, 2001.

Gogol, Nikolay (1808–1852) *novelist, short-story writer, dramatist*

Nikolay Vasilyevich Gogol was born in Sorochinez, Ukraine, into a family of minor aristocrats. He was a mediocre student in school and avoided other people. After graduation, he moved to St. Petersburg in search of a position in the civil service. More interested in writing than in a government career, Gogol worked as a minor official for only a brief period of time, quitting his job for a higher-paying position as a history professor at the St. Petersburg University.

In 1831, Gogol published his first collection of short stories, *Evenings on a Farm Near Dikanka.* Based on Ukrainian folk tales, the stories combine elements of the supernatural, humor, and romance. Gogol's first collection was greeted with acclaim from both critics and readers. Fired from his university position for incompetence, Gogol continued his literary work. In *Mirgorod* (1835), he produced more short stories that were based on Ukrainian folklore and history. It was with this collection that Gogol established himself as the father of Russian REALISM. In his famous story "The Overcoat," he explores the psychology of a clerk who must make enormous sacrifices to buy a new overcoat. It was the first work of Russian literature to bring sympathetic attention to the plight of a social misfit, who would previously have been seen only as a comic character.

In 1836, Gogol presented his first comic play, *The Inspector General,* to an enormous audience that included the czar of Russia. In the play, the officials of a small town expect an important visit from a governor. They mistake Hlestakov, a petty government official en route to his father's estate, for the inspector general. The play, with its hilarious satire on provincial officials, was a huge success in St. Petersburg, but certain censors in the government viewed it as politically dangerous. Afraid of losing his freedom, Gogol left Russia for Europe to continue his work away from government oversight.

Gogol traveled throughout Europe, staying for extended periods in Germany, Switzerland, France, and Italy. While in Paris, he lost one of his closest friends to a cholera epidemic. This tragic event prompted Gogol's return to Russia in 1839. Contrary to his expectations, Russia celebrated his return, and a version of *The Inspector General* was produced in Moscow to mark the occasion. Facing serious health problems, Gogol returned to Europe, became a complete recluse, and turned to studying the sacred texts of the Russian Orthodox Church. His newly found religious sentiments, which some contemporaries described as zeal, eventually surfaced in his work.

Critical Analysis

In 1842, Gogol published the first volume of his masterpiece, *Dead Souls*. Even before publication, it attracted negative attention from the censors, and it came into print only after the personal intervention of the czar. The novel centers on a small time provincial bureaucrat named Chichikov and satirizes both middle-class greed and the institution of serfdom in Russia. Gogol's critique of serfdom, which essentially consigned peasants to a form of slavery, skillfully portrays the moral decay of Russian society. In hope of advancing his social position and his opportunities for a profitable marriage, Chichikov falsifies his economic status by purchasing "dead souls"—the names of dead serfs. In the second volume, Gogol apparently attempted to incorporate strong elements of spirituality and religion; however, spiritually and psychologically troubled, he destroyed the manuscript. In 1848, he departed on a pilgrimage to Jerusalem, but the journey proved quite unsuccessful in terms of providing the religious consolation Gogol was seeking.

In many respects, Gogol's life translated into his works of fiction. Characters are often mentally distraught, almost to the point of grotesquerie, centering their lives on seemingly insignificant, worldly goals. By the same token, Gogol's critique of Russian society extends far beyond social issues and often illuminates the individual's struggle for spiritual fulfillment.

The last years of Gogol's life were marked by deep physical and psychological suffering. As many experts concur today, Gogol suffered from acute forms of depression and anxiety. Gogol spent the last three days of his life praying. He died in 1852, reportedly from a stroke.

In Russia, Gogol is viewed as one of the major figures of the literary canon. His prose shows a deep understanding and sensitivity, not only to the social order but also to individual psychological dimensions.

Other Works by Nikolay Gogol

Arabesques. Translated by Alexander Tulloch. Ann Arbor, Mich.: Ardis, 1982.

The Collected Tales of Nikolai Gogol. Translated by Richard Pevear and Larissa Volokhonsky. New York: Pantheon, 1998.
Gogol: Three Plays. Translated by Stephen Mulrine. London: Methuen, 2000.

Works about Nikolay Gogol

Fanger, Donald. *Creation of Nikolai Gogol.* Cambridge, Mass.: Harvard University Press, 1982.
Nabokov, Vladimir. *Nikolai Gogol.* New York: W. W. Norton, 1961.
Stilman, Leon. *Gogol.* New York: Columbia University Press, 1990.

Gombrowicz, Witold (1904–1969)
novelist, playwright

Witold Gombrowicz was born on his family's estate in Maolsczyce and then moved to Warsaw, Poland. As a boy, he was introverted and sickly. He felt alienated by the nationalist sentiment of the time and ultimately rejected orthodox culture in favor of the company of peasants, such as maids and stablehands.

Attempting to follow a career that would be accepted by his family, Gombrowicz studied law at the University of Warsaw but began, in secret, to write short stories, which were later published in the collection *Memoirs of a Time of Immaturity* (1933). Although his writing was attacked by critics for its rejection of contemporary viewpoints, it was moderately successful with readers who shared his discontent. Gombrowicz eventually gave up law and began writing full time. In 1938, he published his first play, *Yvonne, the Princess of Burgundy,* and followed it with his first novel, *Ferdydurke* (1938), which is a satirical comment on the absurdities of Polish society in the 1930s with elements of mystery and eroticism.

Gombrowicz was commissioned in 1939 to write a series of articles about Argentina. Two days after he arrived in Buenos Aires, World War II began and Poland was invaded. He stayed in Buenos Aires, working for several small newspapers. There, he published his second play *The*

Marriage (1947) and the novel *Trans-Atlantic* (1953).

During a brief respite from censorship in 1956, several of his works were reprinted in Poland, but Gombrowicz did not return to his homeland. His third novel, *Pornografia* (1960), an account of a relationship between two teenagers in rural Poland as viewed by fascinated old men, was followed in 1963 by his receipt of a Ford Foundation Fellowship, which allowed him to leave Argentina. He settled in Berlin, where he wrote his fourth novel, *Cosmos* (1964), an absurdist mystery that has been compared to Franz KAFKA's *The Castle*, as well as his final play, *Operetta* (1966), before dying of heart failure in Vence, France.

Gombrowicz's popularity was largely posthumous. His books had been banned, once again, in Poland in the 1960s. After his death, the ban was partially lifted, but Gombrowicz specified in his will that his works were not to be published in Poland unless they were reprinted in their entirety. As a result, an underground movement was formed to smuggle foreign editions of his work into Poland. His plays were performed in Polish theaters, but their texts could not be bought in official stores. This contributed to a rise in Gombrowicz's popularity. It was not until 1988, after the collapse of Communist Party rule, that the first full edition of his books was published in Poland.

Other Works by Witold Gombrowicz

Cosmos and Pornografia: Two Novels. Translated by Eric Mosbacher and Alastair Hamilton. New York: Grove Press, 1994.

Diary. Translated by Lillian Vallee. Evanston, Ill.: Northwestern University Press, 1988.

Ferdydurke. Translated by Danuta Borchardt, with a foreword by Susan Sontag. New Haven, Conn.: Yale University Press, 2000.

Works about Witold Gombrowicz

Milosz, Czeslaw. *Who Is Gombrowicz?* New York: Penguin, 1986.

Thompson, Ewa M. *Witold Gombrowicz.* Boston: Twayne, 1979.

Gomringer, Eugen (1925–   ) poet

Born in Cachuela Esperanza, Bolivia, Eugen Gomringer was raised in Switzerland by his grandparents. He studied art history and economics at colleges in Bern and Rome and later worked as a graphic designer. In 1952, Gomringer cofounded the magazine *Spirale*. From 1954 to 1958, he worked as a secretary for Max Bill, the director of the Academy of Art in Ulm, Germany. Since the 1960s, Gomringer has worked as a business manager for the Schweizer Werkbund in Zurich, an artistic adviser for the Rosenthal concern, and as a professor of aesthetic theory at the Art Academy in Düsseldorf.

Gomringer published his first poems in *Spirale* in 1953. His verse helped initiate the concrete movement in poetry. These poems create a concrete reality by using words as building blocks to form three-dimensional semantic, phonetic, and visual explorations. Conventional syntax, description, and metaphor are ignored. The poet Jerome Rothenberg explained that concrete poetry is "a question of making the words cohere in a given space, the poem's force or strength related to the weight & value of the words within it, the way they pull & act on each other." Gomringer's "schweigen" ("Silence") is his most famous concrete poem. The word *schweigen* is printed 14 times to form a rectangle, with the empty space in the middle representing silence.

In addition to poetry collections, Gomringer wrote theoretical tracts explaining his style and calling for a simple, universal language devoid of irrationality. His influence was strong in the 1950s and 1960s, inspiring a range of linguistic experiments. The concrete poetry movement waned in 1972, however, as critics found it too simplistic. Gomringer then gave up poetry to write about art and artists.

Another Work by Eugen Gomringer

The Book of Hours and Constellations. Translated by Jerome Rothenberg. New York: Something Else Press, 1968.

Gonçalves Dias, Antônio (1823–1864)
poet, dramatist

Born in 1823, Antônio Gonçalves Dias was the most important romantic poet to write in the Brazilian literary tradition. He was educated in Portugal at the University of Coimbra but felt strong ties to Brazil. He celebrates Brazil in his poetry collections, such as *Primeiros cantos* (1846) and *Ultimos cantos* (1851), focusing on themes of nature. Specifically, Dias wrote extensively about nativist issues. His glorification of indigenous peoples places him among the many writers of the Indianist movement (*see* INDIANISM) of the 19th century in Brazil, along with the novelist José de ALENCAR. Gonçalves Dias's work *Song of Exile* (1843), with its nostalgic first line, "My land has palm trees, where the nightingale sings," is Brazil's best known poem. He is often thought of as Brazil's national poet, although he published only three collections of poetry. He was killed in a shipwreck while returning to Brazil from Portugal.

Works about Antônio Gonçalves Dias

Haberly, David. *Three Sad Races: Racial Identity and National Consciousness in Brazilian Literature.* New York: Cambridge University Press, 1983.

Treece, David. *Exiles, Allies and Rebels: Brazil's Indianist Movement, Indigenist Politics, and the Imperial Nation-State.* Westport, Conn.: Greenwood Press, 2000.

Goncharov, Ivan (1812–1891) *novelist*

Ivan Aleksandrovich Goncharov was born in Simbirsk, Russia. His father, a wealthy grain merchant, died when Goncharov was only seven. Young Ivan was raised by his godfather, Nikolay Tregubov. An average student, Goncharov studied business at the University of Moscow. After he graduated in 1834, he worked in the civil service for nearly 30 years.

In 1847, Goncharov published his first novel, *An Ordinary Story,* which focuses on the conflict between Russian nobility and the newly emergent merchant class. The novel examines the moral implications of income and how it affected social position of the two classes.

Between 1852 and 1855, Goncharov traveled around the world as a personal secretary for Admiral Putyatin. He published his account of the journey as *Frigate Pallada* (1858). His observations about the nations he visited, which included England, parts of Africa, and Japan, are often unflattering, and he expresses his sense of Russian superiority and his distrust of social reform.

In 1859 Goncharov published his most famous novel, *Oblomov,* a masterpiece of Russian REALISM. In the novel, Goncharov satirizes the character of Oblomov, a young aristocrat who is indecisive and apathetic. Goncharov presents the aristocracy as an obsolete class that no longer contributes to the welfare of the state. The novel was so successful that it introduced a new word into the Russian language: *oblomovshina,* meaning "indecision and inertia."

Goncharov's talent was readily acknowledged in Russia by such personages as Fyodor DOSTOYEVSKY. Goncharov, however, was a quarrelsome figure. He accused Ivan TURGENEV and Gustave FLAUBERT of plagiarizing his ideas for their own novels. Goncharov never married. He published his last novel, *The Precipice,* in 1869. The work tells of a sentimental love affair between three men and a mysterious woman. Critical response to the novel was devastating, and Goncharov never published another. He spent the rest of his life virtually alone, writing short stories and essays.

Goncharov died in St. Petersburg in 1891. Through his works, Goncharov depicted the emergent class conflict between aristocracy and the rising middle class. He is mostly remembered for his contribution to realism and his mastery of social satire.

Another Work by Ivan Goncharov

An Ordinary Story: Including the Stage Adaptation of the Novel. Translated by Marjorie L. Hoover. New York: Ardis Publishers, 1994.

Works about Ivan Goncharov

Diment, Galya. *The Autobiographical Novel of Co-Consciousness: Goncharov, Woolf, and Joyce.* Gainesville: University of Florida Press, 1994.

Diment, Galya, ed. *Goncharov's Oblomov: A Critical Companion.* Evanston, Ill.: Northwestern University Press, 1998.

Ehre, Milton. *Oblomov and His Creator: The Life and Art of Ivan Goncharov.* Princeton, N.J.: Princeton University Press, 1974.

Goncourt, Edmond (1822–1896) and Jules (1830–1870) *novelists*

The Goncourt brothers, Edmond and Jules, are most notable for their long history of collaboration as a team of novelists writing in the tradition of naturalism. Edmond was born in Nancy, France, and Jules in Paris eight years later. Close as children, they retained their special bond throughout their lives.

In 1849, "les deux Goncourts," as they would come to be known, began to travel throughout France as artists, painting watercolor sketches and ultimately keeping detailed notes of their travels in a journal. This journal, published as *Journal des Goncourts* (nine volumes, 1887–96; translation of selections by Lewis Galantière, 1937), which they began together in 1851, contains 40 years of detailed accounts of French social and literary life.

The brothers also became successful as art critics and art historians. After a failed attempt at writing for the theater, they began to collaborate on a series of novels, including *Sœur Philomène* (1861), *Renée Mauperin* (1864; translated 1887), *Germinie Lacerteux* (1864), and *Mme. Gervaisais* (1869), all of which became well known as representations of the naturalist school. Their elaborate and often convoluted style as well as their selection of subjects based on their sensational value anticipated naturalist ideas.

After Jules died, Edmond continued to write, publishing three more novels, among them *La Fille Élisa* (1877; translated 1959), a tragic story of a girl who becomes a prostitute. As a condition of his will, Edmond provided funding for the establishment of the Goncourt Academy to award and encourage excellence in fiction. The Goncourt Prize for literature is awarded annually to an outstanding French author.

Other Works by Edmond and Jules Goncourt

Pages from the Goncourt Journal. Translated by Robert Baldick. New York: Penguin USA, 1984.

Paris and the Arts, 1851–1896; from the Goncourt Journal. Translated by George J. Becker and Edith Philips. Ithaca, N.Y.: Cornell University Press, 1971.

Paris Under Siege, 1870–1871; from the Goncourt Journal. Translated by George J. Becker. Ithaca, N.Y.: Cornell University Press, 1969.

Works about Edmond and Jules Goncourt

Brookner, Anita. *The Genius of the Future: Diderot, Stendhal, Baudelaire, Zola, the Brothers Goncourt, Huysmans: Essays in French Art Criticism.* Ithaca, N.Y.: Cornell University Press, 1988.

Heil, Elissa. *The Conflicting Discourses of the Drawing-Room: Anthony Trollope and Edmond and Jules de Goncourt.* New York: Peter Lang, 1997.

Goodison, Lorna (1947–   ) *poet, short-story writer, professor, painter, illustrator*

Lorna Goodison was born in Kingston, Jamaica, to Vivian Goodison, a Jamaica Telephone Company technician, and Dorice Goodison, a dressmaker. She was educated at St. Hugh's High School for girls and read the major English writers at an early age. V. S. NAIPAUL's *Miguel Street,* which she read as a teenager, sparked Goodison's appetite for Caribbean literature. In an interview with Kwame Dawes, Goodison said she started writing to read her own writing because so many of the characters she had been reading about differed from those of her experiences.

Goodison wrote while attending the Jamaica School of Art and the Art Students League of New York during her early 20s, but she did not begin to write seriously until the 1970s. Many of her poems juxtapose standard English and Jamaican dialect, and a variety of musical traditions, including rhythm and blues and reggae, influence her writing style. "For Don Drummond," a notable poem in Goodison's first collection, *Tamarind Season: Poems* (1980), reproduces the sound of Drummond's voice and trombone to mourn the influential Jamaican musician's death.

The poetry collections *I Am Becoming My Mother* (1986) and *Heartease* (1988) explore women's experiences, and *To Us, All Flowers Are Roses: Poems* (1995) focuses on common Jamaican experiences. The poet Andrew Salkey commented in the journal *World Literature Today,* "The evocative power of Lorna Goodison's poetry derives its urgency and appeal from the heart-and-mind concerns she has for language, history, racial identity, and gender."

Other Works by Lorna Goodison

Guinea Woman: New and Selected Poems. Manchester, U.K.: Carcanet, 2000.

Travelling Mercies. Toronto: McClelland & Stewart, 2001.

Works about Lorna Goodison

Dawes, Kwame, ed. *Talk Yuh Talk: Interviews with Anglophone Caribbean Poets.* Charlottesville: University Press of Virginia, 2001.

Kuwabong, D. "The Mother as Archetype of Self: A Poetics of Matrilineage in the Poetry of Claire Harris and Lorna Goodison." *Ariel* 30, no. 1 (1999): 105–29.

Gordimer, Nadine (1923–   ) *novelist, short-story writer, essayist*

Nadine Gordimer published her first short story when she was 13. Since that first publication in 1937, she has published eight collections of short stories and more than a dozen novels. She has also written extensively on political, literary, and cultural issues. She is one of Africa's, and the world's, premier literary talents.

Gordimer was born in a small mining town in South Africa outside of Johannesburg. Her father, Isidore, a Jew, was a jeweler from Lithuania, and her mother, Nan Myers, helped him to become a shopkeeper in the conservative suburban town where Nadine was raised. Her first novel, *The Lying Days* (1953), evaluates the growth and development of a young woman as she confronts the conformity of a comfortable, middle-class existence.

While still a young girl, Gordimer had an experience that was to forever change her life. As she related the incident to Bill Moyers in a 1992 videotaped interview entitled "On Being a Liberal White South African," Gordimer's mother had removed the 11-year-old Gordimer from school "on the pretext of a heart ailment." She was to have little contact with other children until she was 16. Her enforced isolation led to a life filled with reading, writing, and observing. One of the novels she read during this period was Upton Sinclair's *The Jungle,* which recounts the horrible living conditions of workers in Chicago's meat-packing plants in the early 20th century. In the Bill Moyers interview, Gordimer said that the reading of this book changed her life because she saw, clearly, that literature could change the world, that it could open people's eyes to inequity and foster change.

Critical Analysis

Many of Gordimer's stories and novels examine the status and responsibilities of white, liberal intellectuals in both South Africa and abroad. Novels such as *The Late Bourgeois World* (1966), *A Guest of Honor* (1970), and *Burger's Daughter* (1979) examine the difference between engaging with the world and withdrawing from it. For example, the plot of *Burger's Daughter* concerns the reflections of a young woman whose father had led a life of active political resistance to the inequities of South African culture. His daughter struggles with his legacy and her own wavering commitment to confrontation. The novel raises an issue that is very important in Gordimer's work: Can white South Africans be a part of the world that will come when majority rule becomes a reality? Will "liberalism" alone create a space for whites in the new South Africa? Rosa Burger, the daughter of the title, seems to find her only real fulfillment outside of South Africa and outside of politics. The story that unfolds on her return to South Africa, however, shows that an embrace of the political is necessary, even if the end result is tragic.

Gordimer has been quoted by critic Stephen Clingman, in *The Novels of Nadine Gordimer* (1986), as saying, "If you want to read the facts of the retreat from Moscow in 1812, you may read a history book; if you want to know what war is like and how people of a certain time and background dealt with it as their personal situation, you must read *War and Peace*." In this and other statements, Gordimer has insisted that the novelist's job is to convey human truth as regards historical events. As Clingman explains, she makes a case for the value of literature in a world of facts and incidents: "This . . . is the primary material that a novel offers: not so much an historical world, but a certain *consciousness* of that world." Gordimer's novels attempt to present complete worlds in which characters are faced with conflicts of class, race, and gender, all of which exist within the dynamics of personal relationships. In other words, she presents the consciousness of a culture by dealing with both the larger political and "smaller" interpersonal relationships that make up her characters' lives. She has, throughout her career, incorporated the historical reality of the South African situation into her work. She has also written many essays that examine the relationship between writers and their worlds, such as those collected in *The Essential Gesture: Writing, Politics, and Places* (1988). Her essays examine many of the ideological implications of what it means to be a writer living in a politically charged environment.

Her first published novel, *The Lying Days* (1953), focuses on the small Jewish world of the Aaron family and its relationship to the various Afrikaners around it. The young woman at the center of the tale, Helen Shaw, views the different cultures (Afrikaner, or Dutch settler, Jewish, and others) with which she interacts as exotic and distinct. The story of this early work also deals with those Jews who sold goods to the black mineworkers in the area outside of Johannesburg.

Her next novel, *A World of Strangers* (1958), was more pointedly political. It deals with the developing anti-apartheid forces of the African National Congress (ANC) in their resistance to the apartheid policies of the increasingly severe Nationalist government. Johannesburg in the mid-1950s was a hotbed of political activity, and writers, such as Lewis NKOSI and others, were agitating in magazines, such as *Drum*, about active resistance to apartheid. Gordimer's novel details the connection between writing and political engagement, and this early work's insistence on that connection—between the personal and the political—is at the heart of most of her work.

But Gordimer's works are not only political treatises. Her writing is lyrical, and she uses detail to great effect. For example, in *A Sport of Nature* (1987), which tells the story of a white woman who becomes completely immersed in black revolutionary politics, she describes a woman walking through an embassy: "through ceremonial purplish corridors she walked, past buried bars outlined like burning eyelids with neon, reception rooms named for African political heroes holding a silent assembly of stacked gilt chairs. . . ." The images this description evoke are of a "silent," or ineffective, government built on the foundations of "gilt," or pomp.

Her ability to combine rich description, sharply observed dialogue, knowledge of human nature, and political situations has made Gordimer one of the most respected novelists in the English-speaking world. In her own country, she has been consistently controversial in her ongoing literary analysis of the failure of the politics of liberalism, as South Africa has attempted to deal with its multiracial reality. Her international reputation has led to many awards, including Britain's prestigious Booker Prize (for her novel *The Conservationist*) in 1974, and the Nobel Prize in 1991.

Other Works by Nadine Gordimer

July's People. New York: Viking, 1981.
Jump and Other Stories. New York: Penguin USA, 1992.

Living in Hope and History: Notes from Our Century.
New York: Farrar, Straus & Giroux, 2000.
My Son's Story. New York: Farrar, Straus & Giroux,
1990.
The Pick Up. New York: Penguin, 2002.
Writing and Being. Cambridge, Mass.: Harvard University Press, 1995.

Works about Nadine Gordimer

Clingman, Stephen. *The Novels of Nadine Gordimer: History from the Inside.* Amherst: University of Massachusetts Press, 1992 (1986).
Cooke, John. *The Novels of Nadine Gordimer: Private Lives/Public Landscapes.* Baton Rouge: Louisiana State University Press, 1985.
Kamanga, Brighton J. Uledi. *Nadine Gordimer's Fiction and the Irony of Apartheid.* Lawrenceville, N.J.: Africa World Press, 2002.
Newman, Judie, ed. *Nadine Gordimer's Berger's Daughter: A Casebook (Casebooks in Criticism).* New York: Oxford University Press, 2003.
Smith, Rowland, ed. *Critical Essays on Nadine Gordimer.* Boston: G. K. Hall, 1990.

Gorenko, Anna Andreyevna

See AKHMATOVA, ANNA.

Gorky, Maxim (Aleksei Maksimovich Peshkov) (1868–1936) *novelist, playwright, short-story writer*

Maxim Gorky was born in Nizhnii Novgorod, Russia, to an extremely poor family. His father, a boatyard carpenter, died of cholera when Gorky was only three years old. Gorky's mother died of tuberculosis in 1879. At eight, Gorky began a series of menial jobs in terrible conditions, working as an icon painter, a baker, a watchman, a clerk, and a cabin boy on a Volga steamer—where luckily a kind cook taught him to read. Reading soon took up all his spare time. The pseudonym *Gorky* (Russian for "bitter"), with which he signed his first published short story, "Makar Chudra," in 1892, seems to reflect the pain of his childhood.

The death of his grandmother had a devastating effect on Gorky, and at 21, he attempted suicide. When he recovered from the gunshot wound, he took up wandering, in a period of two years walking all the way to the southern Caucasus and back again to his native city, associating with tramps, prostitutes, and thieves, who became the subjects of his fiction.

At 24, Gorky settled into a job as a reporter for a provincial newspaper and began to publish his stories, which became extremely popular. He was arrested a number of times in this period for his involvement in radical politics. His politics surface in his work as SOCIALIST REALISM.

Gorky admired and was influenced by Leo TOLSTOY and Anton CHEKHOV, although whereas Tolstoy and Chekhov focused their works on the upper and middle classes, Gorky concentrated almost exclusively on depicting the social injustices faced by the millions of Russia's workers and peasants. Chekhov also admired Gorky and introduced him to colleagues at the Moscow Art Theater, who persuaded Gorky to write a play for them. Two plays, *The Smug Citizen* and *The Lower Depths,* were produced by the Moscow Art Theater in 1902. Both were very successful with the public, and both brought Gorky negative attention from the czarist authorities. An outcry against inhumanity, *The Lower Depths* is based on outcasts Gorky had met on his travels.

In 1905, Gorky was imprisoned for his involvement in the events of Bloody Sunday (a peaceful demonstration of workers asking the czar for democratic reforms, which ended with dozens dead from gunfire from government troops). He wrote one of his most famous plays, *Children of the Sun*—a satirical look at the ineffective middle classes—while imprisoned. After his release, Gorky traveled to the United States and tried to raise support for the Marxist cause. He lived in exile in Italy until 1913, when he was granted an amnesty by the government. While in Italy, Gorky was visited by Lenin and other radical revolutionaries.

Gorky's *My Childhood* (1913–14) is considered one of the best autobiographical works of Russian literature. In it, Gorky juxtaposes his grandfather's brutality against his grandmother's tender love, skillfully creating individual portraits and demonstrating his great descriptive power. *My Childhood* was followed by two other autobiographical volumes, *In the World* (1915–16) and *My Universities* (1923).

After the Russian Revolution, Gorky often found himself as odds with the hard-line Bolsheviks. Gorky maintained an oscillating position on the Bolshevik policy: He was a spokesman for the Soviet view of art and literature and also worked to preserve Russia's cultural heritage. In 1922, he went back to Italy to live for several years but returned to Russia in 1928 in response to the appeals of his public. There is a question as to whether his death eight years later was from the tuberculosis that had plagued him since his youth or whether Stalin may have been behind it. His funeral in Red Square was a state event.

Gorky achieved tremendous respect and recognition during his lifetime. He not only described social injustice but also acted against it. He did not simply contribute to socialist realism but also left a literary legacy to support it.

Other Works by Maxim Gorky

The Lower Depths and Other Plays. Translated by Alexander Bakshy. New Haven, Conn.: Yale University Press, 1973.

Untimely Thoughts: Essays on Revolution, Culture and the Bolsheviks, 1917–1918. New Haven, Conn.: Yale University Press, 1995.

Yarmolinsky, Avram, and Baroness Moura Budberg, eds. *The Collected Short Stories of Maxim Gorky.* Secaucus, N.J.: Citadel Press, 1988.

Works about Maxim Gorky

Levin, Dan. *Stormy Petrel: The Life and Work of Maxim Gorky.* New York: Schocken Books, 1986.

Yedlin, Tova. *Maxim Gorky: A Political Biography.* New York: Praeger, 1999.

Graham, Peter

See ABRAHAMS, PETER HENRY.

Grass, Günter (1927–) *novelist, poet, playwright*

Günter Grass was born in Danzig, Germany (now Gdansk, Poland). His father, a descendent of German Protestants, owned a grocery store, and his mother was of Slavic origin. Grass entered Conradinum High School in 1937 but was never able to finish his education because of the outbreak of World War II. When the Nazis came to power, Grass joined the Hitler Youth Movement. At 16, he was drafted into the German army as a tank gunner. After being wounded, he was interned by the U.S. forces stationed in Bavaria. The reeducation program provided by the U.S. Army had a profound influence on Grass: He was taken on a tour of a Nazi concentration camp at Dachau, near Munich, where he witnessed the horrors of the Holocaust that had been inflicted by the Nazi regime. This experience would be reflected later in Grass's fiction.

After his release, Grass worked as a stonemason, a farmworker, and a potash miner. In 1948, he enrolled in the Düsseldorf Academy of the Arts to study sculpture. He worked as a sculptor for several years, but his interests shifted, and he began to write poetry. In 1955, he officially entered the literary world by winning the third prize in poetry competition sponsored by a German radio station. The prize included the right to attend the meetings of GRUPPE 47, Germany's most important literary circle at the time. Grass then lived in Spain and Paris, where he developed a friendship with Paul CELAN. He published a volume of poems in 1956, followed by several plays and another book of verse, and he had an exhibition of his art works. His work was well known to a small group of connoisseurs.

With *Die Blechtrommel* (*The Tin Drum*, 1959), the first book of what has came to be known as the Danzig trilogy, Grass was suddenly famous. The novel instantly made Grass into one of the most prominent figures of the German and international literary scenes. The second book of the trilogy, *Katz und Maus* (*Cat and Mouse*), appeared in 1961, and the third, *Hundejahre* (*Dog Years*), in 1963. All the novels in the trilogy achieved critical and popular success. Between 1960 and 1965,

Grass received the prestigious Berlin Critics' Prize and the Georg Büchner Prize and was elected into the German Academy of the Arts. In the 10 years following its publication, *The Tin Drum* was translated into more than 15 languages. The book caused offense, too: It was publicly burned in Düsseldorf by an organization of religious youth. Grass faced more than 40 civil lawsuits—all eventually unsuccessful—against the Danzig trilogy. The charges ranged from blasphemy to obscenity. The books, however, remained major best-sellers in Germany and around the world.

In the mid-1960s, Grass spent less time writing as he used his acclaim and recognition to campaign for the Social Democratic Party of Germany. The party supported moderate reform, normalization of relations with East Germany, and easing of tensions with the Communist states. *Ortlich Betaubt* (*Local Anesthetic*) was published in 1969, but Grass did not produce another major novel until 1977, when *Das Butt* (*The Flounder*) appeared. It aroused more excitement than any of Grass's works since *The Tin Drum*. Grass's international fame was increased by the appearance of Volker Schlöndorff's film of *The Tin Drum,* which won the Academy Award for Best Foreign Picture in 1979, but, like the novel, it offended some people: The film was banned in Oklahoma, in a decision that was subsequently overturned by a higher court.

Die Rättin (*The Rat,* 1986) is perhaps even more ambitious than *The Flounder,* but Grass continues to be politically involved. In the late 1980s, he was among the few Germans in the political sphere to oppose the reunification of East and West Germany, claiming irreconcilable political, social, and economic differences. Grass also loudly campaigned against the neo-Nazi groups in Germany and actively supported the defense of Salman RUSHDIE when Rushdie's book *The Satanic Verses* made him the subject of a death threat.

Critical Analysis

The Tin Drum presents an irreverent and colorful account of 20th-century German history through the eyes of a mental patient, Oskar Matzerath. A midget, Oskar refuses to grow as a protest against the cruelties of German people, and he communicates with other characters through his drum.

Cat and Mouse, a much shorter work, relates the story of Joachim Mahlke through the voice of Pilenz, a 32-year-old social worker. The story takes place between 1939 and 1944 and essentially recounts the relationship between the life of a self-conscious teenager (the mouse of the title is Mahlke's enormous Adam's apple) and the fearful historical events unfolding around him. Guilt, with its attendant psychological implications, is the predominant theme running throughout the novel.

Dog Years, a novel with similar thematic concerns, examines the crimes of the Nazis and their acceptance by the German society after the World War II. The story is presented in terms of an ambiguous friendship between Amsel, a son of prosperous Jewish merchant who becomes a Protestant to escape persecution, and Walter Matern, the son of a Catholic miller. In the trilogy, Grass forced his readers to confront the truth about the Nazi past. By using blasphemous Christian imagery, grotesque sexuality, and ribald scatological humor, he made it impossible to subsume the unspeakable in a featureless tragic view.

Die Plebejer Proben den Aufstand (*The Plebeians Rehearse the Uprising,* 1966) is Grass's fifth play. It is set in Berlin in 1953 in Bertolt BRECHT's theater. Brecht is directing a rehearsal of his adaptation of Shakespeare's *Coriolanus;* outside, workers are protesting unfair government labor practices. When the workers appeal to Brecht to help their cause, he lets them down by failing to respond: He chooses to perfect the artistic representation of revolution rather than involve himself in real life. The play is both an homage to and a critique of the artist Grass acknowledges as his master.

The Flounder is written on an epic scale, encompassing 4,000 years of European history, with an elaborate narrative technique that has room for poems, recipes, historical documents, autobiographical accounts of Grass's political campaigns and a version of the GRIMM brothers' "Tale of the Fisherman and His Wife."

The Rat is another massive work, this time looking toward the future, examining what hope there is for a world threatened by nuclear disaster and ecological devastation. There are two narrators: a rat who has already witnessed and survived, with her family, the nuclear winter that has obliterated humanity; and a human "I" who still hopes, against the evidence, that people can escape the final catastrophe. The characters, of whom there are many, include some familiar to Grass's readers, among them Oskar Matzerath, 30 years older, and the talking flounder of The Flounder.

Günter Grass has received innumerable awards for his contribution to world literature from governments and organizations in Germany, the United States, the United Kingdom, Italy, France, and Russia, including the Nobel Prize in literature in 1999. He is recognized today as perhaps the most important German writer of the second half of the 20th century. His works have been translated into more than 20 languages and still enjoy international status as best-sellers. Grass continues his productive career as a writer and a public figure. As the American novelist John Irving said in a 1982 review of Headbirths, or the Germans Are Dying Out, "You can't be called well-read today if you haven't read him. Günter Grass is simply the most original and versatile writer alive."

Other Works by Günter Grass

The Call of the Toad. Translated by Ralph Manheim. New York: Harvest Books, 1993.

The Flounder. Translated by Ralph Manheim. New York: Harcourt Brace, 1989.

Four Plays. Translated by Ralph Manheim and A. Leslie Wilson. New York: Harvest Books, 1968.

My Century. Translated by Michael Henry Heim. New York: Harvest Books, 2000.

Novemberland: Selected Poems 1956–1993. Translated by Michael Hamburger. New York: Harvest Books, 1996.

On Writing and Politics 1967–1983. Translated by Ralph Manheim. New York: Harcourt Brace, 1985.

Too Far Afield. Translated by Krishna Winston. New York: Harcourt Brace, 2000.

Works about Günter Grass

Irving, John. "Günter Grass: King of the Toy Merchants." In Patrick O'Neill, ed., Critical Essays on Günter Grass. Boston: G. K. Hall, 1987.

O'Neill, Patrick. Günter Grass Revisited. Boston: Twayne, 1999.

Preece, Julian. The Life and Work of Günter Grass: Literature, History, Politics. New York: St. Martin's Press, 2001.

Grimm, Jacob (1785–1863) and Wilhelm (1786–1859) collectors of folklore and writers of folktales

Jacob and Wilhelm Grimm were born in Hanau, Germany, to Philipp Wilhelm Grimm, an administrative court official and lawyer, and Dorothea Grimm. After the untimely death of their father in 1796, the Grimm brothers lived with their aunt in Kassel, their mother's hometown, and entered secondary school. Jacob and Wilhelm shared many interests, including reading and listening to German folktales. They entered the University of Marburg within a year of each other to study law. There, the Grimm brothers became interested in folklore, linguistics, and the history of medieval Germany.

Influenced by the sweeping force of German ROMANTICISM, the Grimm brothers began to compile a collection of folktales, many of which existed only as oral accounts passed from generation to generation. They listened carefully to the stories and transcribed them in their journals. They sometimes altered the plots and changed the language of the tales, transforming them into cautionary tales for a new bourgeois readership. In 1812, the Grimm brothers published their first collection of stories, known simply as Children's and Household Tales. This collection of 86 stories and went virtually unnoticed by the critics. The second volume, published in 1814, added 70 stories to the original 86 and was far more successful. This two-volume work went through several editions during the Grimms' lifetime. The final version of the work contained more than 200 stories and became one of the best-known works in German and world literature. Unfortunately, writing did not provide a steady income for the brothers, so both worked as librarians in Kassel until 1830.

Today, the brothers Grimm are primarily remembered for their versions of classic fairy tales, such as "Cinderella," the story of a downtrodden young girl who marries a prince; "The Frog Prince," the story of a girl whose kiss turns a frog into a prince; "Snow White," the tale of a girl who eats a poisoned apple and is saved by a prince; and "Rapunzel," the tale of a girl who is rescued from a tower by a prince. Their tales not only capture the innocent magic of folklore, but they also reflect the realistic political and social concerns of German society in the period in which the brothers were writing. In fact, their tales were actually intended for adults. The brothers were in favor of a unified, democratically ruled Germany and were on the side of the emerging middle class against oppressive princes who ruled a loosely knit confederation of states. By capturing the folklore of the German people, the brothers hoped to create a sense of a common past and pride in a German heritage. As they began to realize that many of their readers were children, they changed some of the stories to emphasize many of the domestic values of the emerging middle class; for example, the Grimms changed the original version of "Rapunzel" to eliminate any suggestion of premarital sex.

In 1819, the Grimm brothers were awarded honorary doctorates from the University of Marburg for their influential work in German folklore. In 1830, they resigned from the library and accepted positions as professors at the University of Göttingen. They lost their positions in 1841, however, when they joined a protest against King Ernst August II, who had revoked the constitution and dissolved parliament on his ascension to the throne of Hannover. Fortunately, their scholarly reputations were such that they immediately received offers from other universities in Germany. The two brothers finally settled at the University of Berlin, where they worked as professors and librarians.

The works of Wilhelm and Jacob Grimm are still widely read today by children and adults alike.

Their contribution to German literature as writers and scholars is simply immeasurable; not only did they collect folklore that might otherwise have been lost, but they also made lasting contributions to studies of the German language and linguistics in general. Even more impressive, however, is the successful collaborative effort that existed for three decades. Their tales are known all over the world and have been translated into more than 20 languages. The Grimm brothers influenced entire generations of writers as well as modern poetry in Germany, England, France, and Russia.

Another Work by Wilhelm and Jacob Grimm

The Complete Fairy Tales of the Brothers Grimm. Translated by Jack Zipes. New York: Bantam, 1992.

Works about Wilhelm and Jacob Grimm

Hettinga, Donald. *The Brothers Grimm: Two Lives, One Legacy.* London: Clarion Books, 2001.

Zipes, Jack. *The Brothers Grimm: From Enchanted Forests to the Modern World.* New York: Routledge, 1988.

Grünbein, Durs (1962–) *poet, essayist*

Durs Grünbein was born in Dresden and lived in East Germany prior to reunification. In the 1990s, he became a professional poet and traveled throughout the world. He also worked as an essayist and translator. Grünbein is considered one of the most innovative and intellectual of contemporary German poets. The collection of poems *Schädelbasislektion: Gedichte* (*Basal Skull Lesson: Poems,* 1991) is one of his best-known works. He has received many literary awards, including the Marburger Literature Prize (1992) and the prestigious Georg Büchner prize (1995). Grünbein's verse reveals an influence from the German poets Gottfried BENN and Gerhard FALKNER.

Science is the prevailing theme in Grünbein's poems and essays. His specific topics include human biology, laboratories, formaldehyde, X-rays, and radioactive decay. Many of his poems portray the exposure of human organs through sonar imaging or autopsies. Although Grünbein views modern science as the dominant power of the present era, he presents it as a threat that diminishes the worth of human beings and reveals the meaninglessness of life. German literary scholar Ruth J. Owen observed that Grünbein portrays the poet as a scientist and successfully challenges "the assumption that science could be an area of human knowledge cordoned off from the poem."

Another Work by Durs Grünbein

Falten und Fallen: Gedichte. Frankfurt am Main: Suhrkamp Verlag, 1994.

A Work about Durs Grünbein

Winkler, Ron. *Dichtung Zwischen Grossstadt und Grosshirm: Annaherungen an das lyrische werk Durs Grünbeins.* Hamburg: Kovac, 2000.

Grünzweig, Dorothea (1952–) *poet*

Dorothea Grünzweig was born in Stuttgart, Germany. She attended colleges in Tübingen, Germany, and Bangor, Wales, where she majored in German studies and English studies. After a research stay at Oxford, she was a lecturer for the University of Dundee in Scotland. Grünzweig later taught at a German boarding school and a German school in Helsinki, Finland. She also wrote reviews and translated Finnish and English literature.

Grünzweig's first collection of poetry, *Mittsommerschnitt* (*Midsummer Cut,* 1997), won the poetry prize of the Neidersachsen/Wolfenbüttel foundation. The next year she contributed poems to *Das verlorene Alphabet* (*The Lost Alphabet,* 1998) anthology. In 2000, Grünzweig gained international exposure after her poems appeared in the English language journals *The Massachusetts Review* and *Arc.* Her other honors include Finland's P.E.N. Club prize (1999) and the Heinrich Heine stipend (2000).

Grünzweig, who divides her time between Germany and Helsinki, frequently writes poems that have a geographical frame of reference. Inspired by

her own experience, she often covers the concepts of original homeland and adopted country. The poems "Spell," "Beginning," and "Insel Seili" ("The Island of Seili") address her other recurring themes of language and speechlessness, and the freezing cold. Her poetry is syntactically complex but creates clear pictures to help illuminate the meaning of her words.

Another Work by Dorothea Grünzweig

Vom Eisgebreit: Gedichte. Göttingen: Wallstein, 2000.

Gruppe 47 (Group 47) (1947–1967)

Following World War II the German writers Hans Werner Richter (1908–93) and Alfred Andersch (1914–80) edited a left-wing journal *Der Ruf* (*The Call*). In 1947, the American military government banned the magazine and upset many German literati. In September, these writers joined Richter and Anderson at Bannwaldsee, Bavaria, to discuss plans for another journal. This became the first meeting of Gruppe 47, a loose association of authors whose regular attendees came to include Wolfgang Weyrauch (1904–80), Ilse AICHINGER, Heinrich BÖLL, Günter EICH, and Günter GRASS. Gruppe 47 met in the autumn of each year through 1967 to discuss and read new literary works. Its only official function was to award the Gruppe 47 Prize, one of Germany's most coveted literary awards at the time.

The German literary scholar Siegfried Mandel described Gruppe 47 as a paradox: "It is one man, Hans Werner Richter, and at the same time an expanding and contracting constellation identifiable by several constant stars." The group avoided an inflexible ideology. Although right-wing writers did not join the group, it had no official social or political program and usually did not initiate new trends. Gruppe 47 was instead more like a barometer of changing literary tastes and social conditions. In general, its members were critical of the values of the West German "economic miracle" and of East German socialism. The 1968 meeting scheduled for Prague was cancelled after Soviet troops invaded Czechoslovakia. Although Richter hosted an informal meeting in 1972, Gruppe 47 never again held a full conference after 1967.

A Work about Gruppe 47

Mandel, Siegfried. *Group 47: The Reflected Intellect.* Edwardsville: Southern Illinois University Press, 1973.

Guan Moye

See MO YAN.

Guillén, Jorge (1893–1984) *poet*

Jorge Guillén was born in Valladolid in the Spanish province of Castile. His poetry reflects the austerity of the region, known for its harsh winters and gray landscape. He was a teacher of Spanish his entire life, on the faculty of such institutions as the Sorbonne, Oxford University, Wellesley College, and Harvard University.

Guillén is generally considered the most intellectual and classic of modern Spanish poets. His poems are terse and lyrical; his work is sober, and he employs more nouns than adjectives. He has been compared to the French poet Paul VALÉRY, whose works he translated. Guillén tries to describe objects through their "poetic presence" rather than through metaphor, making his work difficult for many to comprehend.

In 1976, the Spanish government honored Guillén with the Cervantes Prize, the highest literary honor of the Spanish-speaking world.

Other Works by Jorge Guillén

Affirmation: A Bilingual Anthology 1919–1966. Translated by Julian Palley. Norman: University of Oklahoma Press, 1971.
Guillén on Guillén: The Poetry and the Poet. Translated by Reginald Gibbons. Princeton, N.J.: Princeton University Press, 1979.
Horses in the Air and Other Poems. Translated by Cola Franzen. San Francisco, Calif.: City Lights Books, 1999.
Our Air/Nuestro Aire: Canticle/Cántico. Translated by Carl W. Cobb. Lewiston, N.Y.: Edwin Mellen Press, 1997.

Guillén, Nicolás (1902–1989) *poet, novelist, editor*

Nicolás Guillén was born and educated in Camagüey, Cuba, and later studied law at the University of Havana. In 1919, the magazine *Camagüey Gráfico* published Guillén's first poems. After meeting the American writer Langston Hughes (1902–67) in January 1930, Guillén published "en negro de verdad" (in an authentic African voice) for the first time when his eight *Motivos de son* (Sound motifs) poems appeared in the *Diario de la Marina* newspaper in April. Later, Guillén dedicated his powerful poem "Sabás" to Hughes.

The publication of *Sóngoro cosongo* (1931) marks what Amilcar Cabral calls the Revitalization Phase. In the prologue, Guillén names his "born again" poetry "versos mulatos," filled with *"color cubano." West Indies, Ltd.* (1934) marks Guillén's shift into the "Radicalization Phase," or fighting phase, during which he wrote *Cantos para soldados y sones para turistas* (Songs for soldiers and sounds for tourists, 1937). In 1938, Guillén joined the National Committee of the Cuban Communist Party and worked on its journal, *Hoy,* until authorities closed it in 1950. He received the International Lenin Peace Prize in 1954 and the Cuban National Prize for Literature in 1983.

Although Guillén used literature for political ends, he argued that writers should also make "art" when striving to express revolutionary ideas. In *Un poeta en la historia* (n.d.), Alfred Melon, a Universidad de Sorbonne–Nouvelle literature professor, describes Guillén as "one of the major contemporary poets of the world." His work has been translated into more than 30 languages, and it couples experimental aesthetics, such as a conversational tone and free verse, with distinctively Afro-Caribbean experiences.

Other Works by Nicolás Guillén

The Great Zoo and Other Poems. Translated by Robert Marquez. New York: Monthly Review Press, 1981.

New Love Poetry: In Some Springtime Place: Elegy. Edited and translated by Keith Ellis. Toronto: University of Toronto Press, 1994.

The Daily Daily. Translated by Vera M. Kutzinski. Berkeley: University of California Press, 1989.

Works about Nicolás Guillén

Smart, Ian Isadore. *Nicolás Guillén, Popular Poet of the Caribbean.* Columbia: University of Missouri Press, 1990.

White, Clement A. *Decoding the Word: Nicolás Guillén as Maker and Debunker of Myth.* Miami, Fla.: Ediciones Universal, 1993.

Gumilev, Nikolay (1886–1921) *poet*

Nikolay Stepanovich Gumilev was born in Ekaterinburg, Russia, to Stephan Gumilev, a navy doctor, and Anna Lvova, a sister of a navy admiral. The family soon moved to Tsarskoe Selo, where Gumilev would later meet his future wife, Anna AKHMATOVA. Gumilev grew up playing with his brothers in the countryside. He was sent away to a boarding school in 1900: Academically, he performed very poorly—instead of studying, Gumilev avidly read adventure stories and books about travels to exotic lands. In 1902, Gumilev published his first poem in a small provincial newspaper. He felt triumphant, despite the fact that the publication misspelled his name. After Gumilev graduated, he traveled to Paris where he met several Symbolist poets, and where he also published *Romantic Poems,* his first collection of lyric poetry.

In 1909, Gumilev founded a literary journal, *Apollon,* which eventually published some of the best poetry of the period and was the main organ of the ACMEIST movement. In 1910, he and Anna Akhmatova were married. The marriage was stormy from the start; soon afterward, Gumilev left for an extended journey to Africa. By the time he returned, Akhmatova had published many of the poems that went into her first collection, and her fame had begun to exceed her husband's.

Gumilev resumed his position as one of the leaders of the acmeists. Gumilev supported and wrote lyrical poetry that relied on concrete images and opposed the mysticism of SYMBOLISM. In many ways, acmeist poetry, including Gumilev's, was conservative because it relied on rhyme, meter, and traditional poetic devices. Gumilev strove to uphold and advance the literary tradition of Russia, rather than replace it.

In 1913, Gumilev returned to Africa. He explored exotic places, visited local mystics and healers, and was even attacked by a crocodile. The trip to Africa provided Gumilev with vivid images and exotic metaphors that appear throughout his poetry. At the outbreak of World War I, Gumilev returned to Russia and joined the army; he was decorated twice for bravery in combat. After the war, Gumilev returned to St. Petersburg and divorced Akhmatova in 1918. The association of the acmeists was dissolved. Akhmatova's and Gumilev's son, Lev Gumilev, was raised mainly by Gumilev's mother.

Gumilev was recruited by Maxim GORKY to help with a project in world literature, working with an editor to select important works from other literatures, to write introductory essays for them, and to translate them for publication in Russian. But he was in trouble politically: After the Russian Revolution of 1917, Gumilev had supported the provisional government against the Bolsheviks. When in 1921 the sailors at the Kronstadt naval base, who had helped sweep the Bolsheviks to power, protested against the loss of political freedoms under the Bolshevik government, Gumilev supported their uprising, which was brutally put down. A short time afterward, he was arrested and executed, despite Lenin's intervention. His grave was never found.

Although Gumilev produced a number of notable collections throughout his career, his last work, *The Pillar of Fire* (1921), is considered by most to be his best. *The Pillar of Fire* is marked by exotic and foreign elements. The poems in the collection are explorations of personal experiences of the poet during his travels, as well as the emotional dramas of his personal life. "The Streetcar Gone Astray" imagines a derailed streetcar careering past the landmarks of Russian history and Gumilev's life. This is an example of its imagery (in Carl Proffer's translation):

> *A sign . . . letters poured from blood*
> *Announce—"Vegetables." I know this is*
> *   where,*
> *Instead of cabbages, instead of rutabagas,*
> *Corpses' heads are being sold.*

Gumilev left a profound and long-lasting influence on Russian poetry. His images were as unique as they were strange and refreshing. Gumilev's personal life, filled with tragedy, despair, and, at the same time, love and adventure, in many ways reflected the passion of his verse.

Other Works by Nikolay Gumilev

Lapeza, David, ed. *Nikolai Gumilev on Russian Poetry*. Ann Arbor, Mich.: Ardis, 1977.
Selections in Proffer, Carl R., and Elledea Proffer, eds. *The Silver Age of Russian Culture* (anthology). Ann Arbor, Mich.: Ardis, 1975.
Selected Works of Nikolai Gumilev. Translated by Burton Raffel and Alla Burago. Albany: State University of New York Press, 1972.
The Pillar of Fire: And Selected Poems. Translated by Richard McKane. Chester, Pa.: Dufour Editions, 1999.

Works about Nikolay Gumilev

Eshelman, Ralph. *Nikolaj Gumilev and Neoclassical Modernism: The Metaphysics of Style*. New York: Peter Lang, 1993.
Sampson, Earl. *Nikolai Gumilev*. Boston: Twayne, 1979.

Gunesekara, Romesh (1954–) *poet, novelist, short-story writer*

Romesh Gunesekara was born in Sri Lanka and moved to the Philippines with his family in the 1960s. When he was 17, he went to England, which became his adopted home, but the spirit of travel has not left him, and he continues to visit both Asia and Europe as a writer-in-residence. Gunesekara's poetry is especially popular in Europe, where it has been translated into almost every major European language. His poems are widely anthologized and are a recurring favorite on BBC radio.

Constantly traveling from a young age, Gunesekara's fiction privileges the role of exile. During his years in the Philippines, for example, he was exposed to writers of the 1960s U.S. Beat Generation, such as Jack Kerouac and Allen Ginsberg, whom he would not have met otherwise.

Gunesekara started writing when he was 14, beginning with short stories and poetry. Poetry, in fact, is a medium he continues to write in and explore, even when he is working on a novel. His first novel *Reef* (1994), set in the Sri Lanka of the 1950s and 1960s, is an exploration into the memories of the protagonist who leaves Sri Lanka for England to stay with his master, a marine biologist. Their story of relationships, cooking, and domesticity is set against the rise of rebel terrorism between the Sinhalese and the Tamils in Sri Lanka during this time. The other essential character is the reef itself: Its precarious existence serves as a metaphor for the fragile political condition of the nation.

In addition to his two novels, a collection of short fiction, and poetry, Gunesekara also writes children's poems. His novel *Sandglass* (1998) won the BBC Asia Award for Achievement in Writing and Literature, and in 1997 he won the Premio Mondello Five Continents Award, Italy's highest literary prize.

Another Work by Romesh Gunesekara

Monkfish Moon. New York: New Press, 1992.

Gunnarsson, Gunnar (1889–1975) *novelist, dramatist, poet, playwright*

A son of a farmer, Gunnar Gunnarsson was born in Fljotsdalur, Iceland. The death of his mother when he was nine years old was a deeply traumatic experience that he remembered for the rest of his life. Gunnarsson grew up in Vopnafjorour, where his family moved while he was still a boy. Until the age of 18, he was educated at various country schools. In 1907, he moved to Denmark, where he studied at Askov Folk High School for two years.

Gunnarsson started his career as a writer at the age of 17, and by 1910 he was devoting all his time to writing. Many of Gunnarsson's early works were written in Danish because Denmark provided a wider audience for his poetry and fiction; however, his works were always set in his native Iceland. During his career as a writer, Gunnarsson published more than 40 novels, as well as short stories, articles, and translations. Although he is very well known in the Scandinavian countries, only a small margin of his works were ever translated into English. Unfortunately, currently no work of Gunnar Gunnarsson is in print in the United States.

Gunnar Gunnarsson's works depict the courage of the common people of Iceland. His first important work, *Guest the One-Eyed*, a four-volume family saga about three generations of an Icelandic family, was published in 1912 and instantly became a best-seller throughout Scandinavia. Recalling the biblical Cain and Abel story, the work describes the parallel lives of a virtuous son, torn between his art and familial obligations to the farm, and an evil son. The work received critical praise in virtually every publication that reviewed it.

World War I deeply affected Gunnarsson's sensibility, and for many years after the war, his fiction reflected a deep, oppositional tension. *Seven Days Darkness* (1920), for example, is about war and the conflicts that it creates within a person, particularly the conflict between national identity and the self.

Between 1920 and 1940, Gunnarsson dedicated his writing to history and culture of the Nordic countries. He gave lectures throughout Scandinavia and Germany and wrote numerous articles on social and cultural problems of unification of the Nordic countries. In many respects, Gunnarsson recognized certain common cultural attributes throughout Scandinavia, but he also insisted on the singularity of particular regions. In 1939, he returned to Iceland, and from then on he only wrote in Icelandic.

Many critics consider *Church on the Mountain* (1923–1928), a five-volume semiautobiographical novel, to be Gunnarsson's masterpiece. The work describes the various twists in the life of an Icelandic farming family. It truly demonstrates Gunnarsson's skill as a storyteller, as well as his rich use of poetic language to portray everyday life. The work has only been partially translated into English, appearing in 1938 as two volumes, *Ships in the Sky* and *The Night and the Dream.*

Gunnar Gunnarsson remains one of the most popular and respected writers not only in Iceland but throughout Europe. He was given honorary degrees by the University of Iceland and the University of Heidelberg. Gunnarsson was instrumental in the formation of Icelandic national identity and was a giant cultural figure in his beloved country.

Other Works by Gunnar Gunnarsson

"A Legend." In Sven Hakon Rossel et al., eds., *Christmas in Scandinavia.* Translated by David W. Colbert. Lincoln: University of Nebraska Press, 1996.

The Black Cliffs. Madison: University of Wisconsin Press, 1967.

The Good Shepherd. New York: The Bobbs-Merrill Company, 1940.

Günter, Erich

See EICH, GÜNTER.

Habibi, Emile (Imil Habibi) (1921–1996)
novelist, short-story writer, political essayist
Acclaimed experimental novelist Habibi writes about Palestinians who, like him, live within Israel after its 1948 statehood and are marginalized and displaced in the land of their birth. *The Secret Life of Sa'eed, the Ill-Fated Pessoptimist* (1974; translated by Salma K. Jayyusi and Trevor LeGassick, 1982), about a Palestinian who becomes an overzealous informant for the Israeli government, is considered his greatest novel, engaging Habibi's typical black humor and cynical wit. The novel's hapless antihero, Sa'eed, faces bewildering choices between Zionist exploitation and Arab stupidities in an Arabic text studded with puns and witty wordplay. The protagonist's name means "happy;" of course, he is profoundly not happy. Among Habibi's novels are *Sudasiyat al-ayyam al-sitta* (*Sextet on the Six Days*, 1968), about the 1967 Six Day War; *Luka' ibn Luka'* (1980; the title is a nonsensical name combined with its patronymic, which is difficult to translate); and *Ikhtayyi* (*Such a Pity*, 1986), which remembers Palestinian community life before it came into conflict with Israel in 1948.

Habibi helped found the Israeli Communist Party and was elected to three Knesset terms on its platform. His decision to accept the 1992 Israeli Prize for Literature from the Israeli prime minister surprised some among both Arabs and Israeli Jews because his principled opposition to Israel's policies seemed to preclude his acceptance of such an award. A humanist with a broad vision that transcended the sad specifics of his condition as a Palestinian living in Israel, Habibi donated the award money to a Palestinian clinic.

Another Work by Emile Habibi
The Secret Life of Sa'eed, the Ill-Fated Pessoptimist, a Palestinian Who Became a Citizen of Israel. Translated by Salma K. Jayyusi and Trevor LeGassick. Brooklyn N.Y.: Interlink Publishing Group, 1982.

A Work about Emile Habibi
Boullata, Issa J., and Roger Allen. *The Arabic Novel Since 1950: Critical Essays, Interviews, and Bibliography.* Cambridge, Mass.: Dar Mahjar Publications, 1992.

Hagiwara Sakutarō (1886–1942) *poet*
Hagiwara Sakutarō was born in Maebashi, Gumma Prefecture, in Japan. While a student at Maebashi Middle School, he began to show interest in poetry and in 1908 entered the German literature course at the Sixth High School; how-

ever, due to illness, he withdrew. In addition to academics, Hagiwara studied the mandolin and guitar, hoping at one time that he might become a professional musician.

Hagiwara's literary career did not take root until 1913, when he published tanka in the magazine *Zamboa*. He experimented with colloquial language, onomatopoeia, and free verse and, in 1917, published his first collection, *Howling at the Moon,* which is regarded as the model for modern lyric poetry. In 1922, he published *The Blue Cat,* a collection of poems that was more reflective and less imagistic than *Howling*. His last collection, *The Iceland* (1934), received mixed reviews. In writing the *Iceland* poems, Hagiwara abandoned the modern, colloquial style of his earlier collections and wrote in classical Japanese. After *The Iceland,* he retired from writing poetry, turning to poetic criticism and studies on Japanese culture.

Hagiwara is known as the father of modern Japanese poetry. He established a new style of poetry that incorporated free verse, colloquial language, and onomatopoeia. His poems are often dark, containing elements of morbid fantasy and FIN-DE-SIÈCLE decadence. He is often contrasted to poet TAKAMURA Kotarō.

Other Works by Hagiwara Sakutarō

Face at the Bottom of the World and Other Poems. Translated by Graeme Wilson. Paintings by York Wilson. Rutland, Vt.: C. E. Tuttle Co., 1969.

Principles of Poetry. Translated by Chester C.I. Wang and Isamu P. Fukuchi. Ithaca, N.Y.: East Asia Program, Cornell University, 1998.

Rats' Nests: The Poetry of Hagiwara Sakutarō. Stanwood, Wash.: UNESCO Publishing, 1999.

Ten Japanese Poets. Translated by Hiroaki Sato. Hanover, N.H.: Granite Publications, 1973.

Works about Hagiwara Sakutarō

Gaffke, Carol. *Poetry Criticism: Vol. 18.* Detroit: Gale Research, 1997.

Keene, Donald. *Dawn to the West: Japanese Literature of the Modern Era: Poetry, Drama, Criticism.* New York: Columbia University Press, 1999.

Halter, Erika
See BURKART, ERIKA.

Hamsun, Knut (pseudonym of Knut Pederson) (1859–1952) *novelist, poet, playwright*

Knut Hamsun was born in Lom, Norway, to Peder Petersen, a tailor, and Tora Petersen. The family moved to Hamaroy, a small town 100 miles north of the Arctic Circle, where they took charge of the farm of Hans Olsen, Peder's brother-in-law, who was afflicted with a paralytic illness. Olsen accused the Petersens of owing him money, and as a child, Hamsun was forced to work for his uncle, keeping accounts in the post office, chopping wood, and running the small library in the village. Hamsun read the few books available at the library but had no formal schooling. His father taught him to read and write, and Hamsun occasionally attended a traveling school for a few weeks a year. Hamsun ran away to Lom in 1873 but returned the following year, working small jobs around the village. Hamsun's works reflect the bitterness and hardships of his childhood.

Somehow, Hamsun managed to produce his first novel and have it published in 1877 when he was 18. The same year, Hamsun was hired as a schoolteacher in the small town of Vesteralen. The following year, he published his second novel to no great acclaim. Driven by literary aspirations, he moved to Oslo, where he lived in poverty and worked as a highway construction worker. Destitution forced Hamsun to move to the United States, where he resided between 1882 and 1888, working as a farmhand in North Dakota and as a streetcar attendant in Chicago. These experiences greatly contributed to the formation of Hamsun's literary style.

Hamsun's experiences in the United States inspired him to compose a satirical piece, *Fra det Moderne Amerikas Aandsliv* (*Cultural Life in Modern America*, 1889), which described numerous religions and religious outlooks that Hamsun discovered during his stay. His first breakthrough work, however, appeared in 1890: *Sult* (*Hunger*), which depicts the life of a starving writer in Oslo, became a literary sensation. This sudden success resulted in Hamsun giving a series of lectures in which he criticized such literary figures as Henrik IBSEN and Leo TOLSTOY for their sentimentality. His next novel, *Mysterier* (*Mysteries*) followed in 1892. *Pan* (1894) was written in Paris, where Hamsun lived from 1893 to 1895.

In 1911, Hamsun relocated to a small farm in Norway. For much of the rest of his life, he divided his time between writing and farming and virtually isolated himself from the outside world. *Markens Grøde* (*The Growth of the Soil,* 1917) tells a story of Isak, a simple man who commits his life to the natural rhythms of rural life and combines the mythological and historical aspects of the Norwegian culture. The novel was well received, not only in Norway but also in Germany, where Hamsun's work developed a huge following. In 1920, Hamsun was awarded the Nobel Prize in literature.

During World War I, Hamsun, unlike most Norwegians, supported the German cause, and before and during World War II, he was a vocal supporter of the Nazi party. During the Nazi occupation of Norway, Hamsun wrote a series of pro-Nazi articles and met with Adolf Hitler and Josef Goebbels, the Nazi propaganda minister, on whom Hamsun bestowed his Nobel Prize medal as a sign of admiration.

After World War II, Hamsun was arrested by the Norwegian government for his collaboration with the Nazi regime. After spending some time in a psychiatric hospital, he was placed on trial in 1947. He did not rescind his opinions and showed support for Hitler's military policies throughout the trial. Hamsun was heavily fined by the court and censured by the public; sales of his work fell after the trial. Yet, when Hamsun attempted to explain his political views in *På Gjengrodde Stier* (*On Overgrown Paths,* 1949), the work sold out in Norway almost instantly.

Critical Analysis

Despite the controversy about Knut Hamsun's political affiliations, his work has been rediscovered in recent years. Most critics concur that his best work was written before the turn of the century, though *The Growth of the Soil* has its advocates. *Hunger* retains its capacity to shock with its intense depiction of the psychological degeneration of the young writer, whose thoughts become more and more incomprehensible as time passes. This passage is an example of Hamsun's close focus:

> If one only had something to eat, just a little, on such a clear day! The mood of the gay morning overwhelmed me, I became unusually serene, and started to hum for pure joy and for no particular reason. In front of a butcher's shop there was a woman with a basket on her arm, debating about some sausage for dinner; as I went past, she looked up at me. She had only a single tooth in the lower jaw. In the nervous and excitable state I was on, her face made an instant and revolting impression on me—the long yellow tooth looked like a finger sticking out of her jaw, and as she turned toward me, her eyes were full of sausage. I lost my appetite instantly, and felt nauseated.

Hamsun's narrative innovations in this novel, such as the way he shifts between first and third person, have been much imitated, and his anxious, alienated artist prefigures many 20th-century literary heroes.

By the time he wrote *Pan* (1894), Hamsun had become an admirer of Friedrich NIETZCHE's work, especially Nietzsche's notions about the superman. Written in the form of a hunter's diary, it tells the story of Lieutenant Thomas Glahn's doomed obsession with a mysterious woman. Its stress on the need to escape from urban civilization into the wilderness of nature strongly demonstrates the influence of Nietzsche in its emphasis on the individual.

Undeniably, Hamsun served an important role in presenting the Norwegian culture and struggles to the world in his writings. The focus of Hamsun's work always rested on the relationship between individuals and their respective environments. In terms of style, Hamsun's work was simply exceptional and groundbreaking in its irreverence for the established epistemology of the novel, for the all too readily accepted conventions of fiction. Isaac Bashevis SINGER has observed that Hamsun "is the father of the modern school of literature in his every aspect—his subjectiveness, his fragmentariness, his use of flashbacks, his lyricism. The whole modern school of fiction in the twentieth century stems from Hamsun."

Other Works by Knut Hamsun

Dreamers. Translated by Tom Geddes. New York: New Directions, 1996.

Mysteries. Translated by Sverre Lyngstadt. New York: Penguin, 2001.

Victoria. Translated by Oliver Stallybrass. New York: Green Integer, 2001.

Works about Knut Hamsun

Ferguson, Robert. *Enigma: The Life of Knut Hamsun.* New York: Noonday Press, 1988.

Naess, Harold. *Knut Hamsun.* Boston: Twayne, 1984.

Singer, Isaac Bashevis. Introduction to Knut Hamsun, *Hunger.* New York: Farrar, Straus, 1967.

Han Yongun (Han Yu-chon; Manhae)
(1879–1944) *poet*

Han Yongun was born in Hongsong, Chungchong province, Korea, on August 29. A voracious reader, he taught himself the Chinese classics as a youth. Like many young people of the period, he entered into an arranged marriage at age 13. Later, he entered Komajawa College, where he studied Buddhist philosophy.

In 1904, he became a monk at Paektamsa temple. He hoped to rebuild Buddhism radically in Korea with modern reforms such as a choice for celibacy, establishing a solid economic base, and taking Buddhism to the masses. As president of the Buddhist Studies Association in 1913 and in 1918, he established the Buddhist monthly, *Mind.* His poem of the same name is considered by some to be the first modern poem, written in free verse, and highly metaphysical.

Han Yongun was an active leader of the 1919 Korean Independence Movement, which culminated in a demonstration against Japanese colonial rule on March 1, 1919. His works were frequently patriotic, invoking Buddhist themes to reiterate Korean culture and to inspire resistance against Japanese rule. Examples of such poems are "Submission" and the title poem from his most famous work, a collection of 88 poems titled *The Silence of Love* (1926). In these free-verse Buddhist poems addressing a *nim,* or love, the object of love is ambiguous. Critics believe that the *nim* is alternately a woman ("And You"), the Korean people ("To My Readers"), or a Buddhist object of nature ("Preface"). Although the *nim* itself may remain nameless, themes of patriotism, devotion, and a pantheistic love are evident. One of the most famous poems from the collection, "Ferryboat and Traveler," examines the relationship between joining and parting in love.

Han Yongun wrote in the Chinese style, in *sijo,* or the traditional Korean verse, and in free verse. The poems from *The Silence of Love* are known for their innovative free verse. Another literary innovation was using poetry as a vehicle for social and political change, a marked departure from the lyrical and apolitical Korean literary tradition.

Han Yongun died of neuralgia on June 29 at age 65, just one year before Korea gained liberation from Japanese rule.

Another Work by Han Yongun

Love's Silence and Other Poems. New York: Ronsdale Press, 1999.

A Work about Han Yongun

Yu, Beongcheon. *Han Yong-un and Yi Kwang-su: Two Pioneers of Modern Korean Literature.* Detroit: Wayne State University Press, 1992.

Handke, Peter (1942–) *playwright, novelist, critic*

Peter Handke was born in Altenmarkt, Austria, to Maria Handke, an impoverished farmer, and was raised by his stepfather, Bruno Handke, a soldier in the German army and later a carpenter. Handke attended a standard Austrian elementary school. Between 1954 and 1959, he lived and studied at a Roman Catholic seminary, intending to become a priest. The admission to the seminary of a poor country boy, gained through a rigid examination, was a source of pride for Handke and his parents. Handke, however, was extremely unhappy at the seminary and later expounded on the state-sponsored lies taught by the priests.

Between 1961 and 1965, Handke studied law at the Karl-Franzens University in Graz. When Handke's first novel was accepted for publication by a prestigious publishing company, he immediately quit the law, leaving the school before the final exam. Handke began his writing career as a literary critic and writer for the Austrian radio. In 1966, shortly after the publication of his first major work, *Die Hornissen* (*The Hornets*), the 23-year-old Handke publicly criticized contemporary German literature and GRUPPE 47, the group of leading German writers, at a literary seminar held at Princeton University. He claimed that Group 47 established a codified set of aesthetics that rigidly defined what literature should be. Handke has remained a controversial figure in literature for much of his career. In 1969, he started Verlag der Autoren, a publishing house that supported radical writers and filmmakers.

Critical Analysis

Handke established himself as a renovator of the German theater with the production of *Publikumsbeschimpfung* (1966; translated as *Offending the Audience*, 1971). The play completely departs from traditional theatrical conventions, such as plot, theme, and character. The four actors literally set about offending the audience by lecturing the spectators about their expectations, naïveté, and conventional role. The play caused a sensation, but many critics saw Handke's gesture as pretentious and concluded that his drama would never gain a wide appeal in Germany.

The Hornets has not been translated into English. Instead of using the traditional units of demarcations, the novel is structured into 67 free-standing, episodic parts that seemingly have no connection, narrative or otherwise, among them. At the center of the convoluted narrative is the blind narrator, Gregor Benedikt, who attempts to reconstruct the events leading to his blindness. Instead of using visual images, Handke relies on imitation of words and sounds to recreate Gregor's environment. While deconstructing the traditional conventions of the novel, *The Hornets* comments on the structure of the traditional novel. Although the novel brought critical recognition to Handke, it baffled and surprised most of its readers.

Der Hausierer (*The Peddler*, 1967) further challenges the traditional methodology of the novel. The novel is divided into chapters, which are further subdivided into theoretical and narrative sections. The theoretical sections present the theory behind the detective novel. The narrative parts elusively delineate a fragmented murder mystery but do not present a motivation for the murder, nor is the crime solved in the end. Indeed, the only clues to reading the narrative are provided in the theoretical parts of the work. *The Peddler* was called unreadable by many critics and never achieved wide success with the general reading public.

A prolific writer, Peter Handke has produced more than 20 plays, several screenplays, and several works of fiction. He has also directed and acted in films. He currently lives in Chaville, France, after having lived in Berlin, Paris, and the United States, as well as in Austria. He has received numerous prizes for his writing, including the Corinthian Culture Prize in 1983, the Franz Kafka Prize in 1979, and the Great Austrian State Prize in 1988.

By the 1980s, Handke had achieved recognition as a leading contemporary author in Austria. Many of his plays were translated into French and English. In the mid–1990s, however, his name once again became controversial when he wrote a series of articles supporting Serbia in the Balkan Wars and condemning the NATO bombings. Despite the controversial political stance, Handke's work is still praised and read throughout the world. Peter Handke has established himself as one of the leading figures of POSTMODERNISM.

Other Works by Peter Handke

On a Dark Night I Left My Silent House. Translated by Krishna Winston. New York: Farrar, Straus & Giroux, 2000.

Once Again for Thucydides. Translated by Tess Lewis. New York: New Directions, 1998.

A Sorrow Beyond Dreams: A Life Story. Translated by Ralph Manheim. New York: Farrar, Straus & Giroux, 1975.

Works about Peter Handke

Demeritt, Linda C. *New Subjectivity and Prose Forms of Alienation: Peter Handke and Botho Strauss.* New York: Peter Lang, 1987.

Firda, Richard. *Peter Handke.* Boston: Twayne, 1993.

Konzett, Matthias. *The Rhetoric of National Dissent: In Thomas Bernhard, Peter Handke, and Elfriede Jelinek.* Rochester, N.Y.: Camden House, 2000.

Harris, Wilson (Kona Woruk) (1921–)
novelist, critic, poet

Wilson Theodore Harris was born to a middle-class family in New Amsterdam, a colony of British Guiana that is now the independent country of Guyana. He studied English literary classics and classical literature while attending Queen's College in Georgetown, the capital of Guyana, from 1934 to 1939. Harris also studied and practiced land surveying, which informed his fiction; the surveyor is one of Harris's recurring fictional characters. He also uses the land as an innovative fictional tool.

While working as a land surveyor, Harris began to publish poems, stories, critical essays, and reviews in the literary journal *Kyk-over-al*. He published two small books of poems, *Fetish* (1951) and *Eternity to Season* (1954), before leaving Guyana for Britain in 1959 to become a full-time writer. His first novel, *Palace of the Peacock* (1969), one of his best known, is an exploration of intercultural and interracial relationships, as well as of history and mythology in Guyana.

Harris continues to explore these intercultural, interracial, and transhistorical themes in Guyana in subsequent novels: *The Far Journey of Oudin* (1961), *The Whole Armour* (1962), *The Secret Ladder* (1963), and *Heartland* (1964). Commenting on Harris's poetry and novels in *New World Guyana Independence Issue*, Louis James asserts, "For Harris, time and space are exploded, and as in atomic physics, matter is transformed into energy and vice versa, a person may turn into a place, a place into an aspiration."

Harris's own comments in *Explorations* (1981), a collection of critical writings, explain what motivates the symbols, mythological allusions, nonlinearity, imagistic juxtaposition, and multiple speakers that reappear in his novels. He states that, "Within the art of fiction we are attempting to explore . . . it is a 'vacancy' in nature within which agents appear who are translated one by the other and who . . . reappear through each other, inhabit each other, reflect a burden of necessity, push each other to plunge into the unknown, into the translatable, transmutable legacies of history." In other words, Harris's literary devices require the reader to participate actively with him in exploring culture and history.

In his next novels, Harris focuses on memory and the mind, still using the setting of Guyana, and explores the land's symbolic potential. Some of these novels include *The Eye of the Scarecrow* (1965) and *The Waiting Room* (1967), both of which were written in the form of a diary or journal. *Tumatumari* (1968) and *Ascent to Omai* (1970) explore the female and male consciousness, respectively.

In Harris's later novels, he begins to use different settings, such as London, Mexico, Edinburgh, and India. Themes of resurrection, metaphors of painting, and characters reoccur in these novels: *Companions of the Day and Night* (1975), *Da Silva da Silva's Cultivated Wilderness* (1977), *Genesis of the Clowns* (1977), *The Tree of the Sun* (1978), and *The Angel at the Gate* (1982). *Da Silva da Silva's Cultivated Wilderness* exemplifies the autobiographical traces found in his other works, such as the *Genesis of Clowns;* like Harris, Da Silva is a South American artist of mixed racial background who lives in London.

While writing, Harris worked as a lecturer and writer-in-residence at different universities, including the University of the West Indies, the University of Texas at Austin and Yale University in the United States, and New Castle University in Australia. His critical works include *Fossil and Psyche* (1974), *The Womb of Space: The Cross-Cultural Imagination* (1983), and *The Radical Imagination* (1992). In *Wilson Harris and the Caribbean Novel* (1975), Michael Gilkes asserts, "The work of Wilson Harris deserves serious attention for this reason above all: it suggests the possibility of a response to the West Indian cultural and historical reality which is neither a revolt against, nor a passive acceptance of, a divisive situation."

Other Works by Wilson Harris

Bundy, A. J. M., ed. *Selected Essays of Wilson Harris: The Unfinished Genesis of the Imagination.* New York: Routledge, 1999.

Resurrection at Sorrow Hill. London: Faber & Faber, 1993.

The Four Banks of the River of Space. Boston: Faber, 1990.

Works about Wilson Harris

Cribb, Timothy J. "Toward the Reading of Wilson Harris." *Review of Contemporary Fiction* 17, no. 2 (Summer 1997): 59–62.

Johnson, Kerry L. "Translations of Gender, Pain, and Space: Wilson Harris's *The Carnival Trilogy, Meddelanden fran Strindbergssallskapet*" 44, no. 1 (Spring 1998): 123–43.

Kutzinski, Vera M. "New Personalities: Race, Sexuality, and Gender in Wilson Harris's Recent Fiction." *Review of Contemporary Fiction* 17, no. 2 (Summer 1997): 72–76.

Hašek, Jaroslav (1883–1923) *novelist*

Jaroslav Hašek was born in Prague in 1883 to a middle-class family. His childhood was uneventful, but his later years were fraught with alcoholism and mental instability. He is best known for his satiric masterpiece *The Good Soldier Schweik* (1921). He also created the Party of Peaceful Progress Within the Limits of Law, a political party, the financial proceeds from which he spent at the local pub.

At the start of his literary career, Hašek was widely published in political journals. In 1907, he became the editor of *Komuna,* a noted anarchist magazine. He married, but his wife later left him when he became involved in stealing dogs and forging pedigrees. After attempting suicide, Hašek spent a brief period in a mental institution. In 1915, he began to work as a cabaret performer but was called to serve in the Austrian army during World War I. All of these experiences were used to create the character of Schweik, a drunkard and a liar who ultimately outwits the army. Other exploits from Hašek's own life that found their place in his work include his imprisonment in camps in Ukraine and the Urals during the war, his work as a propagandist with the Czech Legion, and his ultimate return to Prague and nationalist politics.

Critically acclaimed as one of the world's greatest satires, *The Good Soldier Schweik* was first rejected by the literary establishment because the character of Schweik was considered too low class. An incompetent soldier, Schweik is arrested for making snide remarks about the assassination of Archduke Ferdinand and, in another escapade, is thrown out of an insane asylum when the doctors suspect him of merely feigning madness. The general public, however, responded favorably to his antics. Four volumes of Schweik's adventures were completed, the last published posthumously and finished by Hašek's friend Karel Vanek.

Another Work by Jaroslav Hašek

The Bachura Scandal and Other Stories and Sketches. Translated by Alan Menhennet. Chester Springs, Pa.: Dufour Editions, 1992.

A Work about Jaroslav Hašek

Parrott, Cecil. *The Bad Bohemian: The Life of Jaroslav Hašek, Creator of The Good Soldier Svejk*. London: Bodley Head, 1978.

———. *Jaroslav Hašek: A Study of Svejk and the Short Stories*. Cambridge: Cambridge University Press, 1982.

Hasluck, Nicholas (1942–   ) *novelist, poet*

Nicholas Hasluck, born in Canberra, Australia, was the son of Sir Paul and Dame Alexandra Hasluck, both established writers. His father served on numerous missions to the United Nations and was governor-general of Australia between 1969 and 1974. His parents' achievements in writing and their involvement in public life have influenced Hasluck's own writing career. After studying law at the universities of Western Australia and Oxford in 1963 and 1966, respectively, Hasluck worked briefly as an editorial assistant in London before returning to Australia in 1967 to become a barrister.

Hasluck's literary works reflect his concerns with political and social issues within Australian society. In his 1982 novel, *The Hand That Feeds You,* a cynical commentary on contemporary Australian society, Hasluck observes that the push for development and progress meets reluctance because people prefer easy options, such as reliance on the welfare system. His literature presents a world of espionage and subversion. The characters of his novels, such as Dyson Garrick, are compelling figures whose goals are usually hampered by external factors that lead them to choose between their dreams and their lives. His poetry, however, is diffuse and slightly satirical. In the poem "Anchor" (1976), the "anchor" refers to turning points or moments suspended in time at which a person's life arrives and departs from a new juncture, departing from the old path. This poem illuminates Hasluck's awareness of the transient nature of life and the importance of events in determining changes in one's life.

The newspaper *The West Australian* refers to Hasluck as "A writer who obviously thinks the truth and the relationship between art and life are important matters . . . one of those rare writers who can meditate on these issues and at the same time write highly entertaining stories." Hasluck's novel *Our Man K* (1999) shows most aptly his desire to achieve a balance between reality and fiction. Drawing on historical materials, Hasluck recreates Egon Kisch (1855–1948), a Czech reporter who went to Australia in the 1930s to address an antiwar congress, as his central character. Kisch was a key figure during the war years, and his controversial character and his satirical writings form the basis for Hasluck's fictional novel. Hasluck's *The Bellarmine Jug,* a detective thriller set in Holland, won the *Age* Book of the Year Award in 1984. *The Country Without Music,* a fiction that examines the earlier history of Australia when it was still a penal colony, was the joint winner of the 1990 Western Australia Premier's Award for Fiction.

Other Works by Nicholas Hasluck

Anchor and Other Poems. Fremantle, Australia: Fremantle Arts Center Press, 1976.

The Blue Guitar. New York: Holt, Rinehart and Winston, 1980.

A Grain of Truth. Melbourne, Australia: Penguin, 1987.

The Hat on the Letter O. (Revised Edition) Fremantle, Australia: Fremantle Arts Center Press, 1990.

Quarantine. Melbourne and Sydney: Macmillan Press, 1978.

Truant State. Victoria: Penguin, 1987.

Hauptmann, Gerhart (1862–1946)

playwright, novelist

Gerhart Hauptmann was born in Obersalzbrunn, Germany, a fashionable resort town, to Robert and Marie Hauptmann, owners of a small hotel. Hauptmann entered a gymnasium in Breslau but had to leave because of conduct problems and poor academic performance. Hauptmann was artistically inclined from an early age and initially rejected formal education. Disturbed by the attitudes of young Hauptmann, his family sent him to live with his uncle, a pious estate owner. Hauptmann spent several years living and working alongside the peasants on his uncle's estate, learning their simple way of life and their deep religious devotion. Hauptmann eventually changed his attitude toward formal education but remained adamant in his goal of becoming an artist. He attended an art academy in Breslau, initially intending to become a sculptor. Hauptmann's artistic goals changed, however, and he briefly studied history at the University of Jena between 1882 and 1883.

Hauptmann studied art in Rome but was forced to return to Germany because of ill health in 1884. While in Rome, Hauptmann decided to become a writer. In 1885, Hauptmann married Marie Thienemann, an attractive heiress. Thienemann's wealth provided the financial support for Hauptmann's artistic goals. After settling in Berlin, Hauptmann immersed himself in the literary and intellectual currents of the day.

Gerhardt Hauptmann's early influences were derived from the works of German ROMANTICISM. In Berlin, however, Hauptmann came into a contact with progressive intellectuals who rejected romanticism and fervently advocated REALISM. Indeed, Hauptmann's early plays reflect the profound influence of Henrik IBSEN, the master of dramatic realism. Consequently, Hauptmann's themes are often related to the social and political conditions of German society.

Critical Analysis

In 1889, Hauptmann's debut play, *Vor Sonnenaufgang* (*Before Dawn*) attracted attention from many and shocked its audiences with its candid realism. The play depicts the relationship between Alfred Loth, a young socialist who studies the working conditions in the Silesian coal mines, and Helene Kraus, a sister-in-law of his former college comrade who takes control of the mines. Helene's family is corrupted by the power and money that the coal mines bring. Alfred Loth leaves Helene after an intense emotional struggle that results in her suicide. Hauptmann highlights the intense opposi-

tion and conflict created by corruption and exploitation of workers.

Die Weber (*The Weavers,* 1892) dramatizes a revolt of the Silesian weavers that occurred in 1844. The audience was amazed to find no leading hero in the cast of more than 70 characters. Hauptmann wrote the play without a leading character to dramatize the struggle of ordinary people. Viewed as politically dangerous, *The Weavers* was at first banned by the authorities. When the play was finally performed, it established Hauptmann's reputation as one of the world's leading dramatists.

Another play, *The Beaver Coat* (1893), is a broad comedy in Berlin dialect about a woman who cleverly tricks pompous bureaucrats; it was a great hit with the public. But Hauptmann began to withdraw from realism and to focus on the destiny of individual characters rather than tackling social problems with *Hanneles Himmelfahrt* (*The Assumption of Hannele,* 1894), about a peasant girl's visionary dream life, and *Die versunkene Glocke* (*The Sunken Bell,* 1897), a mystical verse drama. In many respects, this shift is associated with turmoil in Hauptmann's personal life. He developed a romantic relationship with a 14-year-old girl, Margaret Marschalk. In 1904, Hauptmann divorced his wife and married Marschalk after she became pregnant. The deep spiritual and psychological conflict of this relationship is reflected in such tragedies as *Fuhrman Henschell* (*Drayman Henschell,* 1898), which shows the psychological deterioration brought about in its central hero by domestic conflict.

Although mainly remembered as a dramatist, Hauptmann was also a prolific novelist. *Der Narr in Christo, Emanuel Quint* (*The Fool in Christ, Emmanuel Quint,* 1910), Hauptmann's most famous novel, reflects in the story of a Silesian carpenter Hauptmann's fascination with the figure of Christ. Indescribable in terms of a single thematic focus, the novel combines elements of mysticism, fantasy, symbolism, and folklore to create a complex world of religious and spiritual ambiguity.

Gerhardt Hauptmann was recognized for his contributions to world literature when he was awarded the Nobel Prize in 1912. He remained in Germany throughout the Nazi period, his adherence to the principles of social justice and socialism remaining strong in the face of the Nazi harassment and threats. Despite constant recommendations by Hauptmann's peers, the Nazi regime adamantly denied him the Schiller Prize, the most prestigious prize for literature in Germany. By the time he died, his Silesian homeland had been annexed by the Russian army.

Other Works by Gerhart Hauptmann

Lineman Thiel and Other Tales. Translated by Stanley Radcliffe. Chester Springs, Pa.: Dufour Editions, 1989.

Plays: Before Daybreak, The Weavers, The Beaver Coat. Edited by Reinhold Grimm and Caroline Molina y Vedia. New York: Continuum, 1994.

Three Plays: The Weavers, Hannele, The Beaver Coat. Translated by Horst Frenz and Miles Waggoner. New York: Ungar, 1977.

Works about Gerhart Hauptmann

Maurer, Warren G. *Understanding Gerhart Hauptmann*. Columbia: University of South Carolina Press, 1992.

Osborne, John. *Gerhart Hauptmann and the Naturalist Drama*. London: Routledge, 1998.

Havel, Václav (1936–   ) *nonfiction, playwright*

Best known internationally as the former president of the Czech Republic, Václav Havel was born in Prague. The son of intellectuals who were closely tied to political uprisings, Havel was prohibited by the Communist government from finishing school after his compulsory education. Havel, therefore, apprenticed as a lab technician and continued taking night classes.

After serving two years in the military, Havel took a job as a stagehand at the ABC Theater and later at The Balustrade, where he became resident playwright and where his first plays, including his well-known *The Garden Party* (1963) were produced. *The Garden Party* was a satire of modern bureaucratic routines.

Havel enrolled at the Academy of Dramatic Arts and graduated in 1967. He also joined the editorial board of *Tvárin*, a literary magazine that conflicted with the conservative Writers' Association. The magazine disappeared in 1969, the same year Havel's passport was confiscated because of his supposed subversive writings.

In many of his plays, Havel used satire to comment on social and political issues. In *The Memorandum* (1965), for example, the creation of an improved language results in a breakdown of human relationships. *The Increased Difficulty of Concentration* (1968), moreover, attacks sociological terminology. After the Soviet invasion in 1968, Havel wrote a series of one-act plays, *Audience* (1978), *Private View* (1978), and *Protest* (1978), in which the main character is a playwright in trouble with the authorities.

Throughout the 1970s, a period of political unrest, Havel helped start the human-rights organization Charter 77 and the Committee for the Defense of the Unjustly Prosecuted. His plays were banned, but the manuscripts circulated privately and were printed in Western Europe, bringing attention to the Czechoslovakian struggle. As a result, Havel was subjected to police harassment and numerous arrests.

After the fall of communism, Havel was president of Czechoslovakia from 1989 to 2003. His contribution to politics having grown directly from his active participation in politically motivated literature. His lifelong dedication to human rights and democratic reforms are reflected in his plays, which serve as inspiration to others that the power of one person can change history.

Another Work by Václav Havel

The Garden Party and Other Plays. New York: Grove Press, 1993.

Works about Václav Havel

Kriseova, Eda. *Vacláv Havel: The Authorized Biography*. New York: St. Martin's Press, 1993.

McRae, Robert. *Resistance and Revolution*. Ottawa: Carleton University Press, 1997.

Hayashi Fumiko (Miyata Fumiko)
(1903–1951) *novelist, poet, children's story writer, reporter*

Hayashi Fumiko was born to Hayashi Assatarō Miyata and Kiku in Shimonoseki, Yamaguchi Prefecture, in Japan. Her schooling was sporadic until she entered Onomichi Girls High School in Hiroshima Prefecture. However, because her family could not pay her school fees, Hayashi worked nights at a canvas-sail factory to pay for her own education. After graduating, Hayashi had a number of unsuccessful relationships with men until she settled down with Rokutoshi Tezuka in 1926. She was obsessive about her writing, often sacrificing her health for her work. She died of a heart attack.

While Hayashi was attending high school, she contributed poems to local newspapers. Her aspirations to become a professional writer took her to Tokyo, Japan's literary center, in 1924, and she began to publish children's stories. However, she achieved greater success as a poet, producing her first collection, *I Saw a Blue Horse,* in 1929. A year later, she published one of her best received works, the fictional diary *Vagabond's Song,* which was based on her early life. During the war, Hayashi became a war correspondent and witnessed the fall of Nanking. The war became a source of inspiration, and afterward she entered her most productive period, writing numerous short stories, essays, and novels about people struggling against the adversity of war. Her final novel, *Drifting Clouds* (1951), follows in this vein, portraying a young woman trying to navigate the changing social structure of postwar Japan.

Hayashi gained special fame for the quantity of literature she produced and for her ability to capture subtle emotions in her writing. Her stories typically portray the lives of the underdogs struggling in prewar and postwar Japan.

Other Works by Hayashi Fumiko
"Narcissus." Translated by Kyoko Selden. In Noriko Lippit and Kyoko Selden, eds., *Stories by Contemporary Japanese Women Writers*. Ardsley, N.Y.: M. E. Sharpe, 1982.

"Tokyo." Translated by Ivan Morris. In Donald Keene, ed., *Modern Japanese Literature,* New York: Grove Press, 1956.

Works about Hayashi Fumiko
Ericson, Joan E. *Be a Woman: Hayashi Fumiko and Modern Japanese Women's Literature*. Honolulu: University of Hawaii Press, 1997.

Tanaka, Yukiko, ed. *To Love and to Write: Selections by Japanese Women Writers 1913–1938*. Seattle: Seal Press, 1987.

Hayashi Kyōko (Miyazaki Kyōko)
(1930–) *novelist, essayist*

Hayashi Kyōko was born in Nagasaki but spent her first 14 years in Japanese-occupied Shanghai. In 1945, a few months before Japan's defeat, Hayashi moved to Nagasaki, where she attended high school and worked in a munitions factory. When the atomic bomb was dropped on Nagasaki, Hayashi fell victim to severe radiation sickness. After several months, she had recovered enough to re-enter high school, graduating in 1947. She then studied nursing but shortly abandoned it and moved to Tokyo. There, she met and married a journalist in 1951 and gave birth to a son.

Hayashi began her writing career in 1962 when she was hired by the magazine *Bungei Shuto* (*Literary Capital*). Her first story, "Ritual of Death," based on her experiences on August 9, 1945, appeared in the magazine in 1975. Three years later, she published a short-story collection, *Cut Glass and Blown Glass,* which depicts atomic bomb experiences. In her next collection, *Michelle's Lipstick* (1980), the stories are narrated by a girl in Shanghai. Developing her concerns about the long-term effects of war, Hayashi published her third collection, *Home in Three Worlds,* in 1984.

As a *hibakusha* (a survivor of the atomic bombing), Hayashi lives with fears about the effect of radiation on her son, her health, and the human race. Her writing usually focuses on the atomic bombing and her experiences in Shanghai and reflects a personal belief that the past exists in the present. She has won the Gunzō New Writer's Prize, the Akutagawa Award, the Kawabata Yasunari Literary Award, and the Woman Writer's Award.

Other Works by Hayashi Kyōko

"The Empty Can." Translated by Margaret Mitsutani. In *The Crazy Iris and Other Stories of the Atomic Aftermath.* Edited by Kenzaburō Ōe. New York: Grove Press, 1985.

"Yellow Sand." Translated by Kyoko Iriye Selden. In *Stories by Contemporary Japanese Women Writers.* Edited by Noriko Mizuta Lippit and Kyoko Selden. New York: M. E. Sharpe, 1982.

Works about Hayashi Kyōko

Bhowmik, Davinder L. "Temporal Discontinuity in the Atomic Bomb Fiction of Hayashi Kyōko." In *¯Oe and Beyond: Fiction in Contemporary Japan.* Edited by Stephen Snyder and Philip Gabriel. Honolulu: University of Hawaii Press, 1999.

Treat, John Whittier. "Hayashi Kyōko and the Gender of Ground Zero." In *The Woman's Hand: Gender and Theory in Japanese Women's Writing.* Edited by Paul Schalow and Janet Walker. Stanford, Calif.: Stanford University Press, 1996.

Hayslip, Le Ly (1949–) *novelist*

Le Ly Hayslip was born in Ky La, a village near Da Nang, Vietnam. She was the seventh child in a peasant farm family, grew up during the Vietnam War, and received only a third-grade education. When she turned 14, she was accused of sympathizing with the revolutionaries by the South Vietnamese government and of being a government spy by the Vietcong. Originally sentenced to death by the Vietcong revolutionaries, her life was spared and Hayslip fled to Saigon, where she met her first

husband, Ed Munro, an American civilian working in Vietnam. They married when she turned 21 and escaped to the United States in 1970.

Hayslip's first memoir, *When Heaven and Earth Changed Places,* is a heartrending account of her life beginning with her turbulent childhood and ending with her return to Vietnam after an absence of 16 years. The book, published in 1989 and well received, explores the ironic balance between the bittersweet anguish of Hayslip's past and her renewed hope and forgiveness for her homeland. Hayslip published her second memoir, *Child of War, Woman of Peace,* in 1993. Her eldest son, James, was her coauthor. The memoir relates the author's life after she moved to the United States.

Hayslip's literary success lies in her ability to blend both Eastern and Western values. Her poignant story became the setting for the award-winning film *Heaven and Earth* (1993), directed by Oliver Stone. Stone was so moved by Hayslip's account that he funded the building of a clinic in Hayslip's home village in Da Nang.

Hayslip, who now lives in California, continues to encourage both Vietnamese and Americans to overcome the stigma of the Vietnam War by engaging in projects to build schools and medical facilities in impoverished parts of Vietnam. Her East Meets West Foundation, formed in 1988, continues to give humanitarian relief to individuals and groups to help them rebuild their lives.

Head, Bessie (1937–1986) *novelist*

Bessie Head was born in Pietermaritzburg, South Africa. She was the illegitimate daughter of a wealthy white Scottish woman and a South African stablehand. Head was born in the mental institution where her mother died. She was taken from her mother at birth and raised in a foster home in the colored community of Cape Province. When she turned 13, she began six years of study at St. Monica's Home, an Anglican missionary school for colored girls.

Head received a teaching certificate in 1955 and taught in an elementary school for two years. She then worked for a succession of newspapers in Cape Town, Johannesburg, and Port Elizabeth. Though married in 1960, she soon divorced in 1964. Her involvement in the Pan Africanist Congress, a political party that emerged around the same time as the African National Congress, led to her brief arrest and constant surveillance by the government. She left South Africa for Botswana in 1964 and remained in exile until her death. Although Head always felt a sense of nostalgia for South Africa, she never wanted to return to her homeland, dreading the prospect of fighting apartheid.

Head's writings are epitomized by tumultuous emotions, unsettling trauma, and hope, as seen through the optimism and resilience of her characters. Her works deal with issues of alienation, racial discrimination, poverty and interpersonal relationships. Her ability to convey a variety of perspectives through her characters is a testimony to her creativity and talent. Head's most renowned novel is *Question of Power,* published in 1973. The story revolves around an expatriate named Elizabeth who lives in Botswana. Elizabeth's various imagined encounters with a lover land her in a mental hospital, and her hellish experiences are metaphorical allegories of racism and gender discrimination. Bessie Head's greatest contribution to world literature lies in her ability not only to examine the problems related to the issue of gender discrimination in South Africa but also to offer solutions to the problems.

Other Works by Bessie Head

The Collectors of Treasures. London: Heinemann, 1992.

Daymond, M. J., ed. *The Cardinals: With Meditations and Short Stories.* London: Heinemann, 1996.

Maru. London: Heinemann, 1996.

Tales of Tenderness and Power. London: Heinemann, 1989.

When Rain Clouds Gather. London: Heinemann, 1996.

A Woman Alone: Autobiographical Writings. London: Heinemann, 1991.

Works about Bessie Head

Abrahams, C., ed. *The Tragic Life: Bessie Head and Literature in Southern Africa.* Trenton, N.J.: Africa World Press, 1990.

Eilersen, Gillian. *Bessie Head: Thunder Behind Her Ears: Her Life and Writing.* Cape Town: David Philip, 1995.

Garrett, James. "Writing Community: Bessie Head and the Politics of Narrative." *Research in African Literature* 30:2 (Summer 1999).

Hébert, Anne (1916–2000) *poet, novelist*

Anne Hébert was born in Quebec. Her earliest influences include her father, a civil servant, and her cousin, the poet Hector de Saint-Denys Garneau. Though Hébert moved to Paris in the 1950s, she made several trips back to Canada. She died of cancer in the city of Montreal.

Hébert's work began to receive critical attention in the 1940s and 1950s with the publication of her first book of poetry in 1942, *Les Songes en Equilibre;* her next book of poems appeared in 1953, titled *Le Tombeau des rois.* Her first novel, *Kamouraska,* about a 19th-century murder, appeared in 1970 and was translated into English in 1974. Another of Hébert's novels, *Héloïse* (1980), concerns a vampire in Paris. *Les Fous de Bassan* (1982, translated as *In the Shadow of the Wind*) tells the story of a double rape and murder from multiple points of view. Hébert won the Governor General's Literary Award twice, for *Poèmes* in 1960 and for the novel *Les Enfants du Sabbat* (*The Children of the Sabbath*) in 1975, and received many other awards. She is one of the best-known and most translated Québecois writers.

Another Work by Anne Hébert

Anne Hébert: Selected Poems. Translated by A. Poulin, Jr. Brockport, N.Y.: BOA Editions, 1987.

A Work about Anne Hébert

Knight, Kelton, W. *Anne Hébert: In Search of the First Garden.* New York: Peter Lang, 1998.

Heine, Heinrich (1797–1856) *poet*

Heinrich Heine was born in Düsseldorf, Germany, to a Jewish family. Heine's father was a merchant who provided prospects for other Jews in Düsseldorf during the French occupation. After the failure of his father's business, Heine went to live with his uncle Solomon in Hamburg to train for a career in commerce. Heine disliked commerce and decided to study law, which he did at the universities of Bonn, Berlin, and Göttingen, finally taking a degree in 1825. To enter civil service, which was closed to Jews at that time in Germany, Heine converted to Protestantism; however, he never practiced law or held a government post of any sort.

Heine's own writing was deeply influenced by the philosophy of G. W. F. Hegel, who was a professor at the University of Berlin. Heine was fascinated with the early ideas of socialism and with the improvement of workers' conditions and frequently corresponded with Friedrich Engels and Karl Marx, both admirers of Heine's work. In 1831, he embarked for Paris as a journalist.

Heine found the bustling, artistic world of Paris a startling contrast to the repressive atmosphere in Germany. In Paris, Heine reported on French cultural life, wrote travel books, and reviewed German works on politics and philosophy. His affinity for socialism and vocal criticism of German politics quickly brought him to the attention of censors. In 1835, the Federal German Diet attempted to enforce strictly a ban on all of his works throughout Germany. Heine was surrounded by government spies, and his stay in Paris eventually became a permanent exile.

Heine's poems range from bitter political satires to love lyrics. *The Book of Songs* (1827), one of the early lyrical collections, established Heine's success in Germany. The collection reveals a heavy influence of traditional folk poetry but also a stylistic shift from the lyrical traditions of the romantic movement to a dimension of social criticism. *Germany: A Winter's Tale* (1844) presents a satire in verse that attacks reactionary aspects of German society. At the end of the long narrative poem, the Goddess of Hamburg reveals a gloomy vision of Germany's future to the narrator, who is half submerged in a chamber pot.

The death of Heine's uncle in 1844 left him with a small pension; the French government also subsidized him. The same year, Heine was overcome by a terrible disease that left him paralyzed and partially blind. Heine continued to work and, in 1851, produced one of his finest collections of verses, *Romanzero*. The collection was different from anything he had done before. In *Romanzero*, Heine attempted to reconcile and combine the elements of Christianity and paganism. Thematically, Heine attempted to avoid the political controversy that his previous collections caused in Germany.

Heinrich Heine remained a controversial figure long after his death. A proposal to erect a statue commemorating his works caused riots in Germany. The works have been closely identified with German national identity, and he had an enormous influence on later poets, such as Rainer Maria RILKE. The Nazis allowed publication of Heine's works; they did not reveal the identity of the author, however, because of his Jewish background. Although Heine contributed to German romanticism, his later works clearly show a deviation from the traditional themes and motifs of this movement. Today, Heinrich Heine is included in the canon of German literature as an influential poet crucial to the development of national literature, as well as an important social thinker.

Other Works by Heinrich Heine

The Harz Journey. Translated by Charles Leland. New York: Marsilio Publishers, 1995.

The Romantic School and Other Essays. New York: Continuum, 1985.

Songs of Love and Grief. Translated by Arndt Walter. Chicago: Northwestern University Press, 1995.

Works about Heinrich Heine

Hermand, Joest. *Heinrich Heine's Contested Identities: Politics, Religion, and Nationalism in Nineteenth Century Germany.* New York: Peter Lang, 1999.

Kossoff, Philip. *Valiant Heart: A Biography of Heinrich Heine.* London: Cornwall Books, 1983.

Herzen, Aleksandr Ivanovich
(1812–1870) *philosopher, essayist*

Aleksandr Herzen was born in Moscow, Russia, as an illegitimate child of Luisa Gaag, a German immigrant, and Ivan Yakovlev, a retired army officer and minor aristocrat. His father paid for Herzen to receive an excellent education from private tutors, and Herzen became fluent in several European languages. He was particularly interested in the history of the French Revolution and the poetry of Aleksandr PUSHKIN. In 1829, he began to attend the Moscow University in preparation for a job in civil service.

In 1834, Herzen was implicated in an antigovernment conspiracy. Placed under arrest and, after months of interrogations, exiled to Perm, Herzen did not return to Moscow until 1840. During his years in exile, Herzen began his prolific career as a writer, but most of the works written during this period could not be published in Russia because of their politically incendiary, liberal content. Influenced by the French socialist philosophers, particularly Claude Saint-Simon (1760–1825), Herzen often criticized the institution of serfdom and dominant autocracy in Russian government. Unable to continue his work in Russia, Herzen moved to Paris in 1847, never to return.

That year, Herzen published a novel, *Who Is to Blame?* (1847), about a young liberal who becomes disillusioned with Russia and its political institutions. After his relocation abroad, Herzen abandoned fiction writing in favor of social and political works. During his brief stay in France, Herzen supported the French revolution of 1848. After the failure of the revolution, Herzen wrote *From the Other Shore* (1850), an analysis and critique of the European revolutionary movements of the time.

In 1852 Herzen moved to London, where he founded the Free Russian Press, which published a series of journals. Herzen was finally able to express freely his political opinions. Between 1857 and 1862, Herzen published a liberal journal, *Kolokol* (*The Bell),* which was banned in Russia but smuggled in. For a time, the journal acquired tremendous popularity and wide readership in Russia. It may have been influential in Czar Aleksandr II's 1860 liberation of the serfs. Herzen supported the traditional, communal institutions of Russia, which he considered as precursor for a free, socialist society—contrary to the government's agenda. However, by the 1860s, Herzen's views seemed conservative to many Russian political factions, and *The Bell*'s influence waned. Herzen turned to writing his autobiography, *My Past and Thoughts* (1852–55), in which he included an account of Russia under serfdom and the attendant social-resistance movements of the period.

British playwright Tom Stoppard has made Herzen the subject of a trilogy, *The Coast of Utopia.* In a 2002 article in the *Observer,* Stoppard says:

> Herzen had no time for the kind of mono-theory that bound history, progress and individual autonomy to some overarching abstraction like Marx's material dialecticism. What he did have time for . . . was the individual over the collective, the actual over the theoretical. What he detested above all was the conceit that future bliss justified present sacrifice and bloodshed.

Works by Aleksandr Herzen
From the Other Shore. Translated by Moura Budberg. New York: Oxford University Press, 1989.
My Past and Thoughts: The Memoirs of Alexander Herzen. Translated by Constance Garnett. Berkeley: University of California Press, 1999.
Who Is to Blame? A Novel in Two Parts. Translated by Michael R. Katz. Ithaca, N.Y.: Cornell University Press, 1984.

Works about Aleksandr Herzen
Acton, Edward. *Alexander Herzen and the Role of the Intellectual Revolutionary.* New York: Cambridge University Press, 1979.

Partridge, Monica. *Alexander Herzen*. Paris: Unesco, 1984.

Hesse, Hermann (1877–1962) *novelist, poet*

Hermann Hesse was born in Calw, Germany, to Johannes and Marie Hesse, Pietist missionaries and religious publishers. Hesse's parents traveled to India on several occasions to conduct missionary work. The travels to India provided a profound formative experience for young Hesse, one that deeply influenced his writings. At first, Hesse was educated by his parents and was expected to follow their path. In 1891, he entered a Protestant seminary at Maulbronn to prepare for life as a missionary and preacher. Hesse, however, found himself spiritually and psychologically unfit for a religious career, and he left the seminary without taking a degree.

Hesse became a professional writer in 1904 when he published *Peter Camenzind,* a novel about a man who—like Saint Francis of Assisi—leaves a big city to devote his life to meditation. The novel was a great success, and Hesse was subsequently able to dedicate his time to writing. After a visit to India in 1911, Hesse began to study Eastern religions. *Siddhartha* (1922), a novel about young Guatama Buddha who rebels against the repressive traditions of his Brahmin father and ultimately finds enlightenment, reflects Hesse's interests in Eastern philosophy. *Siddhartha* remains the most widely read work of Herman Hesse.

In 1912, Hesse moved to Switzerland, where he remained throughout World War I. He openly attacked the attitudes of militarism and nationalism that beleaguered Europe and promoted the rights of prisoners of war. Because of Hesse's antiwar attitudes, he was regarded as a traitor by many in Germany. *Demian* (1919), a novel published by Hesse under the pseudonym of Emil Sinclair, reflected Hesse's personal crises during the years of World War I. In the novel, Demian, a young man, is torn between the world of sensuality and pleasures and the orderly, restrained world of middle-class existence. The novel also revealed Hesse's

interest in psychoanalysis and the works of Carl Jung, a pupil of Sigmund FREUD. The work was well received, particularly by veterans of World War I.

Der Steppenwolf (1927) tells a story of Harry Haller, a man undergoing a midlife crisis, who recognizes another personality within himself called Hermine. Hermine introduces Haller to a sensuous life of drinking, sex, and drugs. The novel's psychological complexity and the problematic treatment of spiritual persona appealed to many readers. *Der Steppenwolf* became a seminal text for the American Beat poets, and the famous American rock band Steppenwolf is named after the novel.

During the Nazi regime, Hesse's works were still published in Germany and were privately defended by Joseph Goebbels, the Nazi propaganda minister; however, after Hesse refused to remove the brutal scenes of anti-Semitism and violence against the Jews from the reprint of *Narcissus and Goldmund* (1930) in 1941, he was blacklisted by the Nazis. Hesse also assisted political refugees during World War II. He wrote *The Glass Bead Game* (1943), a novel about a futuristic, imaginary community in which wisdom is communicated through a series of complex games, in response to the Nazi regime in Germany.

Hermann Hesse was awarded the Nobel Prize in literature in 1946. He wrote more than 50 poems and essays between 1945 and 1962 for several Swiss newspapers. His works remain popular throughout the world. During the 1970s, Hesse was a cult figure for many young readers because of his focus on Eastern religions and his criticism of middle-class attitudes and values. He influenced many contemporary writers. He is one of the most popular writers of the German-speaking world.

Other Works by Hermann Hesse

Gertrude. Translated by Hilda Rosner. New York: Noonday, 1998.

Poems. Translated by James Wright. New York: Farrar, Straus & Giroux, 1970.

Soul of the Age, Selected Letters of Hermann Hesse. New York: Noonday, 1992.

A Work about Hermann Hesse

Mileck, Joseph. *Hermann Hesse: Life and Art.* Riverside: University of California Press, 1981.

Higuchi Ichiyō (Higuchi Natsuko)
(1872–1896) *short-story writer*

Higuchi Ichiyō was born in Tokyo to Higuchi Noriyoshi and Taki. When Higuchi was very young, she was sent to private school, where she learned the Chinese classics and developed her writing skills; in addition, her father taught her Japanese classical poetry at home. When her father died, however, the family fell on hard times. They moved to the Yoshiwara pleasure district and opened a shop that eventually failed. Higuchi died of tuberculosis at age 24.

During her time in school, Higuchi developed a passion for writing. In 1892, the novelist and magazine publisher Tōsui Nakarai launched Higuchi's career by helping her publish articles in well-regarded literary magazines. She quickly earned the esteem of established writers and critics. Higuchi began to publish short stories in a variety of literary journals; however, she produced her greatest writing after she had moved her family to the Yoshiwara district in 1893. Her most enduring works— "Child's Play," "Troubled Waters," and "Separate Ways" (1895)—bring to life the characters and lifestyles of the district in the late 19th century.

Higuchi is the only woman whose works have been consistently included among the great works of the Meiji period (1868–1912). She is particularly known for her short stories that depict life in the Yoshiwara district and for her revival of the written style of Ihara Saikaku (1642–1693).

Other Works by Higuchi Ichiyō

"Muddy Bay." Translated by Hisako Tanaka. *Monumenta Nipponica* 14 (1958): 173–204.

"The Thirteenth Night" and "Child's Play." In *In the Shade of Spring Leaves: The Life and Writings of Higuchi Ichiyō, a Woman of Letters in Meiji Japan.* Translated by Robert Lyons Danly. New Haven, Conn.: Yale University Press, 1981.

Works about Higuchi Ichiyō

Copeland, Rebecca L. *Lost Leaves: Women Writers of Meiji Japan.* Honolulu: University of Hawaii Press, 2000.

Danly, Robert Lyons. *In the Shade of Spring Leaves: The Life and Writings of Higuchi Ichiyō, a Woman of Letters in Meiji Japan.* New Haven, Conn.: Yale University Press, 1981.

Hikmet, Nazim (1902–1963) *poet, playwright, novelist, memoirist*

Nazim Hikmet was born in Salonica, Greece, where his father was serving in the foreign service. His mother was an artist, his grandfather a poet. Introduced to poetry at an early age, Hikmet published his first poems at age 17. In 1922, attracted to the ideas of social justice promised by the Russian Revolution, he went to Moscow. There he met Vladimir MAYAKOVSKI, the FUTURIST poet who became one of his greatest influences.

Hikmet's life from this point on was fraught with political conflict as a result of the leftist political views that were contained in his writings. In 1924, after the Turkish War of Independence, he returned to Istanbul but was soon arrested and sentenced to 15 years of hard labor for working with a "leftist" magazine. He managed to escape in 1926 by fleeing, once again, to Russia. He continued to write in exile and attempted to return home in 1928, hoping for political amnesty. Instead, he was immediately arrested and sentenced to six years in prison; in 1933, he was released. During this period, Hikmet established himself as a major poet and playwright, publishing, among other works, *The Epic of Sheik Bedrettin* (1936). It was this poem, based on a rebellion by Turkish peasants against the Ottoman Empire in the 15th century, that led to another arrest; this time Hikmet was sentenced to 61 years in prison.

Hikmet continued to write in prison, sending out manuscripts secretly in letters to family and friends. Most of his poetry was inspired by universal humanism, compassion, and a love for the country that had exiled him. Among these works was his epic masterpiece, *Human Landscapes* (1941–45). In 1950, he was awarded the World Peace Prize and granted his freedom. This freedom was illusory, however: Two attempts were made on his life as he tried to flee the country. He escaped to Russia aboard a Romanian freighter and remained as a political refugee until his death from a heart attack in 1963.

Other Works by Nazim Hikmet

The Epic of Sheik Bedreddin and Other Poems. Translated by Randy Blasing and Mutlu Konuk. New York: Persea Books, 1977.

Poems of Nazim Hikmet. Translated by Randy Blasing and Mutlu Konuk. New York: Persea, 1994.

A Work about Nazim Hikmet

Goksu, Saime, and Edward Timms. *Romantic Communist.* New York: St. Martin's Press, 1999.

Hiraoka Kimitake

See MISHIMA YUKIO.

Ho Xuan Huong (1776–1820) *poet*

Ho Xuan Huong was born in Quynh Doi village, Nghe An province, Vietnam. Her father, Ho Phi Dien, was a member of the Hanoi scholar–gentry class. Her first husband was the prefect of the Vin Tuong district and encouraged her to write poetry. Ho had a good understanding of Chinese and Vietnamese writing that allowed her to write well in both classical Chinese and popular *nom* genres. Scholars of Vietnamese literature believed that Ho was a woman ahead of her time. With verve, Ho attacked the hypocrisy of Confucian Vietnamese society by showing her contempt for social conventions. She was seen not only as a feminist but also as a courageous defender of women's rights in early conservative Vietnam. Her simple yet forceful language appealed to a wide audience.

Sexuality is a dominant theme in Ho's poems. Her casual and playful exploration of sensual pleasures attracted and infuriated the conservative members of Vietnamese society. Ho was simultaneously seen as a wanton female and a heroine who stood steadfast to her own beliefs and values. Her poem "Jackfruit" is a compelling tale about the panic of an unmarried girl who discovers she is pregnant. In "Sharing a Husband," Ho describes the suffering of girls who are resigned to a subsidiary status in their husbands' homes. Ho's subversive attacks on the social hierarchy ironically won her the respect of those in power. She was respected for her fearlessness in criticizing the injustice of Vietnamese society, an action that few men, even those in power, would dare to undertake. Ho triumphed as a heroic female poet in a society that was overwhelmingly dominated by men.

Other Works by Ho Xuan Huong

"On Being a Concubine." In Jacquelyn Chagnon and Don Luce, eds., *Quiet Courage: Poems from Viet Nam.* Washington, D.C.: Indochina Mobile Education Project, 1974.

"The Man-and-Woman Mountain." In Jacquelyn Chagnon and Don Luce, eds., *Quiet Courage: Poems from Viet Nam.* Washington, D.C.: Indochina Mobile Education Project, 1974.

"Poking Fun at a Bronze." In Jacquelyn Chagnon and Don Luce, eds., *Quiet Courage: Poems from Viet Nam.* Washington, D.C.: Indochina Mobile Education Project, 1974.

Hoffmann, E. T. A. (pen name of Ernst Theodor Hoffmann) (1776–1822)
novelist, fairy-tale writer

Ernst Theodor Amadeus Hoffmann was born in Köningsberg, Prussia (today Kaliningrad, Russia), to Christoph Ludwig and Lovisa Hoffmann. Ludwig left Lovisa while Ernst was still an infant. Responsibility for raising young Hoffmann fell on the shoulders of his maternal uncle, Otto Wilhelm Doerffer, a jurist. Young Hoffmann shared two passions: music and literature. Hoffmann was particularly influenced by the novels of Johann Wolfgang von GOETHE and the plays of Friedrich SCHILLER and William Shakespeare. In music, Hoffmann adored the operas of Wolfgang Amadeus Mozart (Hoffmann added the letter *A* to his first name in honor of Mozart).

Hoffmann studied law at Köningsberg's university but seemingly without inspiration. On graduation, Hoffmann moved to Głogów in Silesia to study law under the guidance of his uncle Johann Ludwig Doerffer, an established provincial judiciary. Between 1798 and 1800, Hoffmann served as an intern in the high court of Berlin. Hoffmann was quite successful in his law career, and he was promoted to supervise the jurisdiction of Posen in South Prussia. In 1816, Hoffmann attained a high position in the Supreme Court at Berlin.

Hoffmann began his artistic career as a composer rather than as a writer. He worked as a musical director, composer, and theatrical critic until 1814 when he finally recognized that he would never be a great composer. Many of Hoffmann's stories, however, reflect his passion for music. In "Don Juan" (1813), for instance, a hotel guest undergoes a supernatural transformation while watching a performance of Mozart's opera *Don Giovanni*. In "Councilor Krespel" (1816), a young girl dies when she is forced to produce the perfect voice.

Hoffmann's themes often deal with the magical, grotesque, or supernatural experience. His fiction is considered to be among early works of horror and fantasy. Furthermore, it was difficult for Hoffmann to reconcile his two seemingly conflicting roles as bureaucrat and artist, and this internal conflict is often reflected in his works. "The Golden Pot" (1816) presents the conflict between the world of the artist and the mundane, spiritually destructive world of the bourgeoisie. In another tale, "Das Fräulein von Scuderi" (1819), Hoffmann depicts a respectable goldsmith who becomes a heartless criminal at night.

In time, Hoffmann was seen as the heart of late German romanticism. Quite ironically, many of Hoffmann's literary masterpieces were transformed into musical masterpieces. The best known of these is the "Nutcracker and the Mouse King" (1816). The famous German composer Offenbach composed an opera based on the life and tales of Hoffmann, *The Tales of Hoffmann*, which is still widely popular.

Of his longer works, *The Devil's Elixir* (1816), the most popular, depicts the travels and adventures of an 18th-century Capuchin monk, Brother Medardus. This strange tale combines Gothic and grotesque elements and portrays several shocking situations, such as rape and scandalous murder–intrigues of the pope's court. The work was praised for its intricate plot and psychological complexity.

E. T. A. Hoffmann was perhaps one of the most influential writers in the world. Many of the psychological theories of Carl Jung and Sigmund FREUD are based on Hoffmann's work, specifically Freud's theory of the uncanny. Furthermore, Hoffmann was one of the most influential figures for Russian romanticism, inspiring numerous writers and composers to the present day. In the United States, Hoffmann became the main inspiration for the dark, nightmarish fiction of Edgar Allan Poe. Despite his failure as a composer, Hoffmann's work as a writer inspired some of the world's greatest and most remembered musical masterpieces. His work has been translated into more than 20 languages.

Other Works by E. T. A. Hoffmann

The Life and Opinions of the Tomcat Murr. Translated by Anthea Bell. New York: Penguin, 1999.

The Tales of Hoffmann. Translated by R. J. Hollingdale. New York: Penguin, 1990.

A Work about E. T. A. Hoffmann

McGlathery, James. *E. T. A. Hoffmann*. Boston: Twayne, 1997.

Hofmannsthal, Hugo von (Loris, Loris Melikow, Theophil Morren) (1874–1929)
poet, dramatist, essayist

Hugo von Hofmannsthal was born in Vienna, Austria, to Hugo August Peter Hofmann, the director of a large investment bank, and Anna

Maria Josefa Fohleutner, a brewing heiress. Hofmannsthal studied with private tutors and attended the Akademisches Gymnasium, one of Vienna's most prominent schools. There, he published poetry and wrote his first play at age 16. Hofmannsthal studied law and French at Vienna University and earned a doctorate in romance literature in 1899. Two years later, he married Gerty Schlesinger, the daughter of the general secretary of the Anglo-Austrian Bank.

Hofmannsthal's early poems and essays made him a literary sensation in Vienna. In the early 1890s, Hofmannsthal became part of a prominent circle of young writers known as Young Vienna. For a short time, he had close ties with the poet Stefan GEORGE. Hofmannsthal wrote his best poems in the mid-1890s. His early works, such as *Der Tor und der Tod* (*Death and the Fool*, 1893), were characterized by Viennese aestheticism and FIN-DE-SIÈCLE melancholy.

After the turn of the century, Hofmannsthal abandoned aestheticism and turned from poetry to plays and essays. The composer Richard Strauss (1864–1949) used Hofmannsthal's play *Elektra* (1904) for the libretto, or text, of an opera. Hofmannsthal later wrote five more librettos for Strauss. After World War I, Hofmannsthal's increasing anxiety over the decline of Western civilization can be seen in his play *Der Turm* (*The Tower*, 1925), in which Hofmannsthal addresses the question of whether a decaying society can be renewed through revolutionary violence.

Although Hofmannsthal's later critics saw him as an elitist defender of outdated conservative values, his works still command popular and critical attention. German literary scholar Claude Hall described Hofmannsthal as "a great theatrical showman who aimed at reproducing the macrocosm of the world and his dreams in the microcosm of the stage."

Other Works by Hugo von Hofmannsthal
The Lyrical Poems of Hugo von Hofmannsthal. Translated by Charles Wharton Stark. New Haven, Conn.: Yale University Press, 1918.

Selected Plays and Libretti. Michael Hamburger, ed. New York: Pantheon Books, 1963.

Works about Hugo von Hofmannsthal
Coghlan, Brian. *Hofmannsthal's Festival Dramas.* Cambridge: Cambridge University Press, 1964.
Vilain, Robert. *The Poetry of Hugo von Hofmannsthal and French Symbolism.* New York: Oxford University Press, 2000.

Hölderlin, Friedrich (1770–1843) *poet, novelist*

Friedrich Hölderlin was born in Lauffen am Neckar, Germany. His father, an administrator at a local monastery, died when Hölderlin was two years old. His mother, Johanna Christina Hölderlin, married the mayor of Nürtingen, Johann Christoph Gok, a few years later. In childhood, Hölderlin read intensely, including the classics and was fluent in Greek and Latin by the age of 12. At 14, he began to write poems. In 1788, under the guidance of his stepfather, Hölderlin entered the University of Tübingen to pursue studies in theology. He graduated with a master's degree.

During Hölderlin's studies at the university, his interests in theology began to fade away. He became a close friend of Friedrich Wilhelm Hegel (1770–1831), an important philosopher whose theories became the foundation for revolutionary thinking. Hölderlin also became involved in liberalism and passionately admired the ideals of the French Revolution. In 1793, Hölderlin met Friedrich von SCHILLER, one of the most important literary figures of German ROMANTICISM, who agreed to publish several of Hölderlin's poems.

In 1793, Hölderlin began work as a private tutor. Employed by Jacob Gontard, a wealthy Frankfurt banker, he fell in love with Gontard's wife, Susette. Although the love affair was platonic, it had a deep impact on the psyche of the young poet. In many of his famous poems, Susette appears as the mysterious "Diotima." Hölderlin eventually left Frankfurt in 1798, but the two continued to meet secretly and to corresponded frequently with each other.

Hölderlin briefly worked in France as a private tutor. During this period, his mental health was becoming unstable. In 1802, Hölderlin returned to Germany in the advanced stages of schizophrenia. After learning about Susette's death in 1805, Hölderlin suffered a complete psychological breakdown and spent the last 36 years of his life in an unstable state of mind. He died in poverty and virtual obscurity.

Critical Analysis

Combining the elements of classicism and ROMANTICISM, Hölderlin did not exclusively belong to either of the two dominant literary movements of his day. He tended to use classical verse form and syntax in his poetry, following the teachings of Friedrich Klopstock (1724–1803), who attempted to perfect the German language by modeling it to a classical form. From the Romantics, Hölderlin borrowed a rich but convoluted tradition of mystical nature, pantheism, and Christianity. He referred to notions of the cosmos and history to assign some poetic meaning to a world that was collapsing before his eyes. By following and enriching the German philosophical tradition, he greatly contributed to the formation of German idealism, a term usually used to define liberal, philosophical trends during and after the French Revolution.

Hölderlin's most famous novel, *Hyperion* (1797–99), focuses on the young Greek of ancient mythology who takes up arms to fight the Turkish oppression in his homeland. The novel virtually has no plot; *Hyperion*'s beauty rises from its lyrical, dithyrambic (highly emotional) language combined with a deep knowledge of Greek antiquity. The romance of the novel is developed in the form of letters between Hyperion and his beloved. *Hyperion* has often been celebrated as a masterpiece of German literature. It certainly impressed Friedrich Schiller when the young Hölderlin presented the manuscript of the novel to the famous poet, who encouraged Hölderlin to continue his work.

The vast majority of Hölderlin's work deals with heroic themes or subjects. In his poetry, he preferred to maintain classical verse measures. He dedicated an ode to French emperor Napoleon Bonaparte (titled "Bonaparte" (1798), in which he compares Bonaparte to a poet:

> *Poets are holy vessels*
> *In which the wine of life,*
> *The spirit of heroes is preserved.*
> *But this young man's spirit,*
> *The quick—would it not burst,*
> *Any vessel that tried to contain it?*

Hölderlin's verse, especially in its attention to the preservation of classical Greek measures, seems, at the same time, both heroic and rugged. The lyricism is achieved through carefully selected images and irregular lines. Hölderlin's verse became popular, especially among students of philosophy for its liberal inclinations and romantic celebration of life.

In a series of poems to his beloved Diotima, Hölderlin reveals a delicate control of the classical image. In "Diotima" (1797), Hölderlin reveals the full potential of his poetic mind: "Beautiful thing, you live as do delicate blossoms in winter / In a world that's grown old hidden your blossom, alone." The Diotima poems are considered among the greatest lyrical poems in the German language. Hölderlin dedicated the last years of his life to translating Sophocles' works into German. His translations are still considered superb.

Friedrich Hölderlin did not achieve the recognition that his works enjoy today until the early part of the 20th century. Hölderlin was the favorite poet of Friedrich NIETZSCHE, and Martin Heidegger referred to Hölderlin as "a poet's poet." Today, Hölderlin is considered second only to GOETHE. In many respects, Hölderlin is still being rediscovered for the beauty of his poetic form and the magnificent control of his poetic lines.

Other Works by Friedrich Hölderlin

Hymns and Fragments. Princeton, N.J.: Princeton University Press, 1984.

Selected Poems and Fragments. New York: Penguin, 1998.

Works about Friedrich Hölderlin

Fioretos, Aris. *The Solid Letter: Readings of Friedrich Hölderlin*. Stanford, Calif.: Stanford University Press, 2000.
Unger, Richard. *Friedrich Hölderlin*. Boston: Twayne, 1984.

Höllerer, Walter (1922–   ) *poet, critic*

Walter Höllerer was born in the Bavarian town of Sulzbach-Rosenberg. During World War II, he served in the German military on the Mediterranean front. After the war, he studied at universities in Erlangen, Göttingen, and Heidelberg, earning a doctorate in 1949 in comparative literature. Höllerer then began a long career as a professor of German and comparative literature at Frankfurt University, the Technical University of Berlin, and the University of Illinois. He co-founded and edited the journals *Akzente* (*Accents*) and *Sprache im technischen Zeitalter* (*Language in the Technological Age*). In 1977 he founded the Archives for Contemporary German Literature in Sulzbach-Rosenberg.

Höllerer's first collection *Der andrere Gast* (*The Other Guest,* 1952) contains many poems written in classical meters. Four years later, he edited *Transit* (1956), a significant anthology of German poetry. Höllerer published three more volumes of verse in the 1960s. During the following decade, he wrote the novel *Die Elephantenuhr* (*The Elephant Clock,* 1973), a complicated work that reflects his perception of chaos in the contemporary world. His comedy *Alle Vögel alle* (*All the Birds,* 1978) is a composition that was influenced by his conception of semiology.

In addition to his writing and editing, Höllerer attained recognition in his versatile career as a scholar, critic, and literary theorist. He was also a prominent member of the German writers' association GRUPPE 47. Although his early poetry contained traditional forms, Höllerer later became more progressive, writing experimental lyrical poems. His view of literature emphasized its role in communicating art, science, and everyday life. Because he has spent much time and energy promoting the careers of young authors, Höllerer's influence in German literature will likely remain strong well into the 21st century.

Another Work by Walter Höllerer

Gedichte 1942–1982. Frankfurt am Main: Suhrkamp, 1982.

A Work about Walter Höllerer

Frisch, Max. *Dramaturgisches: ein Briefwechsel mit Walter Höollerer*. Berlin: Literarisches Colloquium, 1976.

Hsieh Wan-ying

See BING XIN.

Hu Shih (Hu Hongxin) (1891–1962) *poet, scholar, critic*

Born on December 17 in Shanghai, Hu Shih was educated first by private tutors and then in Shanghai schools. He entered China College in 1906, where he published essays and poems in a school paper, *Emulation,* which he later edited. Hu Shih traveled to the United States to study agriculture at Cornell University in 1910 but soon switched to literature and philosophy. He completed his Ph.D. in philosophy at Columbia University under the department head, John Dewey.

Greatly influenced by his studies of imagist poetry, American literature, and his experiences in the United States, Hu Shih wrote an article considered by many to have brought about the era of modern Chinese literature. "Suggestions for a Reform of Literature" was published in 1919 in the popular journal *New Youth* and made him one of the leading intellectuals of the anti-imperialist May Fourth Movement. In his article, Hu Shih encouraged writing that addressed substantive and timely issues and that was innovative and fresh and used accessible language, particularly *baihua,* the Chinese vernacular.

Hu Shih himself was one of the first to attempt *baihua* poetry in a 1920 volume titled *Experiments.* Although the literary quality of the poems is considered only fair, the style was, nonetheless, a pioneering work in modern poetry. Hu Shih incorporated innovations such as writing without traditional meters, transcribing Western names into verse, and writing in a pragmatic and impersonal style.

As one of the leading literary intellectuals in the 1920s and 1930s, Hu Shih criticized official corruption and vice in the ranks of leadership. He also expressed grave concern over the condition of workers, especially the particularly disadvantaged—women, rural poor, and factory laborers. He was known as a radical for being a Confucian realist who combined classical Confucian and Daoist thought with modern pragmatism, individualism, and secular humanism. He also supported opening China to Western ideas and influence while maintaining China's classical traditions and thought.

At the time, Hu Shih was considered China's foremost man of letters, as well as a cultural icon. As a result, he enjoyed prestige and acclaim. After serving as ambassador to the United States from 1938 until 1942, he presided over the prestigious Beijing University from 1946 until 1949 when he moved to the United States to direct the Gest Oriental Library at Princeton.

Hu Shih continued his focus on scholarship, studying the 18th-century Chinese classic by Cao Xueqin, *Dream of the Red Chamber,* praising its autobiographical angle. His studies prompted the onset of his own persecution in China because officials felt that his scholarship that addressed the novel's literary form undermined its political importance as an exposé of feudal society and the traditional family system. Party conservatives also viewed him as overly Westernized. As he was politically moderate, Hu Shih was also reviled for his increasing distance from revolutionary thought.

Hu Shih, however, remained undeterred. Throughout his career, he produced reference and scholarly works, including *An Outline of the History of Chinese Philosophy* in 1919. He also translated a wide selection of writers from the Americans Bret Harte and John Dewey to the French writer Alphonse Daudet. Hu Shih moved to Taiwan in 1958 to serve as the president of the country's highest cultural institution, the Academia Sinica. He remained in Taiwan until his death.

Another Work by Hu Shih
A Hu Shi Reader. New Haven, Conn.: Yale Far Eastern Publications, 1991.

Works about Hu Shih
Goldman, Merle. *Modern Chinese Literature in the May Fourth Era.* Cambridge, Mass.: Harvard University Press, 1977.
Grieder, Jerome B. *Hu Shih and the Chinese Renaissance: Liberalism in the Chinese Revolution, 1917–1937.* Cambridge, Mass.: Harvard University Press, 1970.

Huang Chunming (Huang Ch'un-ming)
(1939–) *short-story writer, satirist*
Huang Chunming was born in Yilan, a small coastal town in Taiwan on February 13. He ran away from home after his mother's death and wandered from place to place, performing odd jobs. This pattern continued with his schooling as he drifted from college to college until he graduated from Pingtung Normal College and as he worked at various jobs, as schoolteacher, freelance musicologist, radio program editor, television producer, and documentary filmmaker. As a writer, he has created a small but distinctive body of work that is known for its national and popular appeal.

In the late 1960s, Huang Chunming's main theme is the agrarian fight against the disintegrating effects of modernization on their communities. Because he traveled frequently through the countryside, he was in tune with the particular trials of agrarian workers. Although concerned with the fate of individuals who were faced with a rapidly changing and increasingly modern society, he was not a traditionalist; he simply objected to the often dehumanizing aspects of progress. One of his most famous stories, "His Son's Big Doll" (1968), illustrates how commercialization undermines individual dignity—a father accepts a job as a walking costumed advertisement and dreads being discovered by his young son. Other stories, such as "The Drowning of an Old Cat" (1967), directly address official corruption.

Huang Chunming's literary style is simple, similar to folk writing, and although it largely portrays realistic images of rural life, it is modern. His views—universal and anti-imperialistic—and his progressive politics render him a modern teller of folk stories.

A self-described vagabond and free spirit, Huang Chunming presently spends most of his time as a scholar and practitioner of folk culture. He researches and compiles Taiwanese folk songs and documents Taiwanese festivals on film, in addition to writing stories that celebrate the common people and folk life.

Another Work by Huang Chunming

The Drowning of an Old Cat and Other Stories. Translated by Howard Goldblatt. Bloomington: Indiana University Press, 1980.

Works about Huang Chunming

"Father's Writings Have Been Republished: Or, The Sexuality of Women Students in a Taibei Bookstore." In Helmut Martin and Jeffrey Kinkley, eds., *Modern Chinese Writers: Self-Portrayals.* Armonk, N.Y.: M.E. Sharpe, 1992.

Goldblatt, Howard. "The Rural Stories of Huang Chunming." In Jeannette L. Faurot, ed., *Chinese Fiction from Taiwan: Critical Perspectives.* Bloomington: Indiana University Press, 1980.

Huchel, Peter (1903–1981) *poet*

Peter Huchel was born in Berlin to Friedrich Huchel, a civil servant, and Marie (Zimmermann) Huchel. He grew up in Mark Brandenburg and studied literature at Humboldt University, the University of Freiburg, and the University of Vienna. Huchel supported himself as a writer and translator before serving in the German army during World War II. From 1945 to 1948, he edited, produced, and directed for East German radio and in 1948 edited *Sinn und Form* (*Meaning and Form*), making it one of the most respected liberal European literary journals. He was fired in 1962, however, for not following the government's SOCIALIST-REALISM principles in his editorial policy. Huchel later moved to West Germany and married Nora Rosenthal in 1953.

Huchel published his early poems in journals in the 1920s. In 1932, he won the literary prize of the leftist journal *Die Kolonne* (*The Column*). After World War II, he published many of his early poems in *Gedichte* (*Poems,* 1948). His later collections included *Chausseen Chausseen* (*Highways Highways,* 1963) and *Die Neunte Stunde* (*The Ninth Hour,* 1979). Huchel won numerous literary awards, including the National Prize in 1951.

His influences included the poets Oskar Loerke and Wilhelm Lehmann. Many of his poems about nature describe the magic and mystery of the landscape near his hometown of Mark Brandenburg, and critics have praised the effective use of rhyme, meter, assonance, and alliteration in his early verse. After falling out of favor with the East German government, Huchel became withdrawn and isolated. His later writing used less rhyme and meter, and his poems were elegiac, melancholy, and pessimistic. Despite the opposition he faced, Huchel retained his principles and integrity. Literary scholar Ian Hilton wrote that "Huchel swam against the tide to remain stubbornly independent—and survived, albeit with difficulty."

Another Work by Peter Huchel

Selected Poems. Translated by Michael Hamburger. Manchester, U.K.: Carcanet Press, 1974.

A Work about Peter Huchel

Hilton, Ian. *Peter Huchel: Plough a Lonely Furrow.* Dundee, Scotland: Lochee Publications, 1986.

Hugo, Victor (1802–1885) *novelist, poet, dramatist*

Now best known internationally for his novels on which the acclaimed Broadway musicals *Les Misérables* and *Notre Dame de Paris* were based, Victor Hugo was born in Besançon on February 22. His father, an army general, taught him a great admiration of Napoleon, as a young child; however, as a result of his parent's separation, he moved to Paris to live with his mother and her lover, Hugo's father's former commanding officer. The lover was executed in 1812 for plotting against Napoleon, an event that set up a conflicting ideology within the impressionable young Hugo.

As a youth, Hugo's views tended toward the conservative, but he grew to become deeply involved in republican politics, the essence of which provided the theme for many of his works. From 1815 to 1818, while attending the lycée Louis-le Grand in Paris, he began to write poems and tragic verses. He also translated the works of Virgil and, in 1819, with the help of his brothers, founded the literary review *Conservateur Littéraire.* Inspired by François René de CHATEAUBRIAND, Hugo began to publish poetry, gaining both recognition and a pension from Louis XVIII. His debut novel *Han d'Islande* (1823) appeared shortly thereafter.

Hugo married Adèle Foucher in 1822. Their wedding was eventful because Hugo's brother, distraught over losing a longtime rivalry for her affections, went insane on the day of the ceremony and spent the remainder of his life institutionalized. This event had a profound effect on the psychological motivations for several of Hugo's characters.

Critical Analysis

Hugo came into contact with a number of liberal writers in the 1820s, and his own political views began to shift from criticizing Napoleon to glorifying him. He also became involved in the literary debate between French CLASSICISM and ROMANTICISM. Although he was not directly involved in political movements at this time, Hugo nevertheless expressed his admiration for romanticism and its values in his works. The preface to his drama, *Cromwell* (1827), placed him at the forefront of the romanticists. His play *Hernani* (1830), about two lovers who poison each other, caused a riot between classicists and romanticists.

Hugo gained lasting fame with *Notre-Dame de Paris* (1831; translated 1833), the story, set in 15th-century Paris, of a deformed and hunchbacked bell-ringer, Quasimodo, who falls deeply in love with a beautiful gypsy girl, Esmeralda. His love, however, is a tragic one: Esmeralda is in love with another man, Captain Phoebus, and an evil priest, Claude Frollo, seeks after her. When Frollo discovers that Esmerelda loves Phoebus, he murders his rival, and Esmeralda is accused of the crime. Quasimodo provides sanctuary for his distraught love in the cathedral, but Frollo finds her. When she rejects him, he leaves her to be executed. Grief-stricken, Quasimodo throws the priest from the cathedral tower and vanishes. Later, it is discovered that there are not one but two skeletons in Esmeralda's tomb, locked in an eternal embrace, a beautiful gypsy and the hunchback who loved her. The story was well received and has since become a prominent cultural myth.

Following the success of *Notre-Dame de Paris,* Hugo published several volumes of lyric poetry, all of which were also successful. He was considered by many to be the greatest poet of the day. These poems were inspired by an actress, Juliette Drouet, with whom Hugo had an affair that lasted until her death in 1882. His principal poetic works include *Les Orientales* (1829), *Feuilles d'automme* (*Autumn's Leaves,* 1831), *Chants du crépuscule* (*Twilight Songs,* 1835), and *Voix intérieures* (*Inner Voices,* 1837). The poems in these collections are rich in language and intensely sexual, but they also carry a trace of Hugo's growing bitterness toward life.

Becoming disillusioned with the political and cultural values of France, Hugo finally took a stand

and became involved in republican politics. In 1841 he was elected to the prestigious Académie Française, an achievement largely overshadowed a few short years later by the death of his beloved daughter Léopoldine. So distraught was Hugo over her loss that it was a full decade before he began to publish again. Instead, he devoted his time and energy to politics and the promotion of social justice.

In 1851, Napoleon III claimed complete power in France. Fearing for his life as a result of his openly republican beliefs, Hugo fled with Juliette Drouet first to Brussels and then to the Channel Islands. This exile, which was to last 20 years, provided him with the opportunity to produce some of his best-known works including, most notably, *Les Misérables* (1862; translated 1862). An epic tale of social injustice told from the perspective of Jean Valjean, imprisoned and labeled a criminal for life because he stole a loaf of bread, the novel spectacularly depicts the conditions of post-Napoleonic France.

The political upheaval in France after Napoleon III fell from power and the proclamation of the Third Republic allowed Hugo to return to France in 1870. Labeled a national hero, he was elected as member of the National Assembly and then as a senator of the Third Republic. The last two decades of Hugo's life, however, were marked by tragedy that included the deaths of his sons, his wife, and his mistress. He continued to write poetry and remained active in politics until his health began to fail 1878. Hugo died in Paris on May 22. His funeral was a national event attended by 2 million people. Hugo is buried in the Panthéon.

Other Works by Victor Hugo

The Distance, The Shadows: Selected Poems. Translated by Harry Guest. London: Anvil Press Poetry in association with Wildwood House, 1981.

History of a Crime. Translated by Huntington Smith. New York: T. Y. Crowell and Co., 1888.

The Last Day of a Condemned Man. Translated by Geoff Woollen. London: Hesperus Press, 2003.

La Légend des Siécles. Mamaroneck, N.Y.: Gerard Hamon, 1965.

Oeuvres Poetiques, Vol. 2 Avec: Les Châtiments et Les Contemplations. New York: French and European Publications, 1987.

Things Seen. Translated by David Kimber. London: Oxford University Press, 1964.

Works about Victor Hugo

Frey, John Andrew. *A Victor Hugo Encyclopedia.* Westport, Conn.: Greenwood Press, 1999.

Porter, Laurence M. *Victor Hugo.* Boston: Twayne, 1999.

Huysmans, Joris-Karl (Charles-Marie-Georges Huysmans) (1848–1907) *poet, novelist, essayist*

Joris-Karl Huysmans, a writer and art critic first associated with the NATURALIST movement who became prominent in the French decadent movement (*see* DECADENCE), was born in Paris on February 5. His father died when Huysmans was eight years old, a traumatic experience that would influence his later works, many of which, such as *À Rebours* (*Against Nature,* 1884), *Là-bas* (*Down There,* 1891), and *La Cathédrale* (*The Cathedral,* 1898), trace the author's conversion to Catholicism through satanism.

Huysmans's first work, *Le Drageoir aux épices* (*A Dish of Spices,* 1874), was comprised of a series of prose poems that were stylistically similar to those of Charles BAUDELAIRE. He published it at his own expense, taking on the pseudonym of Joris-Karl Huysmans. The work captured the attention of writer Emile ZOLA and was followed by Huysmans's publication of several naturalistic novels, including *Marthe, histoire d'une fille* (*Martha, the story of a girl,* 1876), *Les Soeurs Vatard* (*The Vatard Sisters,* 1879), and *En ménage* (1881). He also served in the Franco-Prussian War and wrote *Sac au dos* (1880) about his experiences.

In 1877, Huysmans began to turn away from naturalism. *À Rebours* explores decadence. This misogynistic work, while important in its own right, was also influential in the decadent movement. Oscar Wilde refers to it as the "poisonous yellow book" that causes the downfall of his famous protagonist Dorian Gray. The dark comedy tells of a wealthy aristocrat, Des Esseinres, who experiments with exotic, often erotic, pleasures to the point at which he cannot face the real world for fear that it will be mediocre in comparison. He attempts to overcome nature by turning it into an object of art.

Huysmans's later novels, including *Là-bas,* are highly autobiographical and trace the spiritual search of a man named Durtal, who experiments with satanism and attends a Black Mass. The work went on to become prominent for its depiction of satanic rites and for its mention of several well-known occultists of the FIN DE SIÈCLE in Paris.

In the early 1890s, Huysmans experienced a crisis of faith and returned to the Catholic Church. His novels *En route* (1895) and *La Cathédrale* trace his spiritual journey. Taken as a whole, his works are both erotic and spiritual in nature and rich and intoxicating in language. Huysmans remained a staunch Roman Catholic until his death from cancer on May 12.

Another Work by Joris-Karl Huysmans

The Road from Decadence: From Brothel to Cloister: Selected Letters of J. K. Huysmans. Translated by Barbara Beaumont. Columbus: Ohio State University Press, 1989.

A Work about Joris-Karl Huysmans

Ridge, George Ross. *Joris-Karl Huysmans.* Boston: Twayne, 1968.

Hwang Sun-won (1915–2001) *poet, fiction writer*

Hwang Sun-won was born on March 26 in Taedong, a county in modern-day North Korea. He published his first poem in 1931 while he was still in high school; by the end of the 1930s, he was regularly publishing poems and short stories. Graduating from Waseda University in Japan with a B.A. in English in 1939, he published his first short-story collection, *The Swamp,* in 1940. The volume is largely comprised of nostalgic stories of country folk that focus on childhood or the loss of innocence. Hwang Sun-won wrote in the dialect of his home province of Pyongannam and in a sparse and minimalist style that would become his trademark.

Hwang Sun-won is known for his reverence for life and humanity and for maintenance of an optimistic outlook even when writing critically. Although he began his career with the sentimental stories of rural Korea, the content of his work changed as Korea moved through history. In 1945, Korea was liberated from Japanese colonial rule and the postliberation period provided the backdrop for his first novel, *Living with the Stars* (1945). The next year, Hwang Sun-won and his family moved to Seoul, where he taught high school.

Affected by the outbreak of civil war in 1950, Hwang Sun-won wrote pieces, such as the novel *Trees on a Cliff* (1960), that reflect upon the tragic consequences of war for humanity. After the war divided Korea into north and south, he wrote *The Descendants of Cain* (1959), a novel featuring characters on a farm and highlighting the class disparity between landowners and tenant farmers. Although a traditional love story, it primarily criticizes the Communist North Korean regime's land-reform policies. Eventually, Hwang Sun-won turned his attention to the dehumanizing urban areas, where an increasing number of Koreans had settled.

Hwang Sun-won taught at Kyung Hee University from 1955 to 1993. He has received many prizes and awards for his work, including the Freedom Literary Award in 1955 and the Republic of Korea Literary Award in 1983. His son, HWANG TONGGYU, carries on his literary legacy as a respected poet.

Other Works by Hwang Sun-won

The Book of Masks. Translated by Martin Holman. London: Readers International, 1976.

The Stars. Translated by Edward W. Poitras. Singapore City: Heinemann Asia, 1980.

A Work about Hwang Sun-won

Epstein, Stephen J. "Elusive Narrators in Hwang Sun-won." In *Korean Studies*, 19 (1995).

Hwang Tonggyu (Hwang Tong-gyu)
(1938–   ) *poet*

Hwang Tonggyu was born on April 9 in Seoul to one of Korea's most famous writers, HWANG SUN-WON. He studied English literature at Seoul National University, graduating in 1961, and continued his graduate studies at Dongguk University. He completed further scholarship abroad, first at Scotland's Edinburgh University (1966–67) and then at the University of Iowa (1970–71).

Hwang Tonggyu's extensive training abroad affected his writing style. He blends the lyricism of traditional Korean poetry with Western modernism. As a result, his works are both contemplative and critical. He published his first volume of poems, *One Fine Day,* in 1961, followed by *Sad Songs* in 1965, moving from the abstract to concrete examinations of daily life. By the time he released *Snow That Falls on the Three Southern Provinces* in 1975, he had shifted from writing about daily life to Korea's social and political climate in quiet protest poems, such as "Song Under Martial Law." This shift evolved into a growing search for self that often manifested itself in dark and harrowing verse, such as "Lips." These poems in turn, evolved into a deep examination of metaphysics and death ("Flight").

Hwang Tonggyu continues to write, and his works are widely translated into many languages, especially English, German, and French. As a specialist in English-language poetry, he also translates Western works such as Robert Lowell and T .S. Eliot. He currently teaches English and American poetry at Seoul National University. In 1987, he served as an exchange professor at New York University. He lives in Seoul with his wife and two children.

Other Works by Hwang Tonggyu

Strong Winds at Mishi Pass. Groveport, Ohio: White Pines Press, 2001.
Wind Burial: Selected Poems of Hwang Tonggyu. Laurenberg, N.C.: St. Andrew's Press, 1990.

Ibsen, Henrik (1828–1906) *dramatist, playwright, poet*

Henrik Ibsen was born in Skien, Norway, into a wealthy merchant family. While Ibsen was very young, his father suffered financial losses, and the family verged on poverty, no longer able to afford Ibsen's solid education. Young Ibsen developed a deep distrust for society and engaged in drunkenness and gambling. He also fathered an illegitimate child at the age of 18. To evade the social repercussions of his relationship with a servant girl, he was forced to support the child financially.

In 1850, Ibsen moved to Oslo to prepare for entrance into the university, but he failed to pass the entrance examinations. Becoming involved in radical politics, he joined a revolutionary group, but after the group was broken up by the government, Ibsen disengaged himself from politics for the rest of his life. During these years in Oslo, Ibsen began to write articles for various journals. He also wrote poetry and a play, neither of which was successful.

In 1851, Ibsen was appointed "stage poet" for a small provincial theater in Bergen. Ibsen wrote several early plays based on the history and folklore of Norway. Although these works were by no means Ibsen's greatest efforts, the theater management soon recognized Ibsen's talent as a playwright. In 1852, the theater sent Ibsen on a study tour to Denmark and Germany.

Returning to Norway in 1857, Ibsen was appointed director of the newly formed Norwegian Theater in Oslo. After several unsuccessful productions, the theater went bankrupt. Ibsen was reappointed to the Oslo Theater, where he attempted to establish his reputation as a playwright with a series of historical dramas. They were poorly received, and Ibsen was often publicly humiliated by their criticism.

The Norwegian government provided Ibsen with a grant to study in Italy and Germany. He left in 1863 and lived abroad until 1891. Ibsen's reputation as a playwright was established in the late 1860s with production of several successful pieces, including *Brand* (1866), in which a minister takes his calling too seriously, and *Peer Gynt* (1867), in which a man lacking in character finds redemption in the love of a woman. In 1866, Ibsen was granted an annual pension from the Norwegian government. When Ibsen returned to Norway in 1891, he was known as one of the world's greatest dramatists.

Critical Analysis

Henrik Ibsen's drama often focused on the realistic psychological complexities of the individual, and his work was much more focused on character than on plot. One of the central conflicts in Ibsen's drama is between characters who seek to realize themselves emotionally and spiritually and the barriers that have been created by outdated conventions of bourgeois society. Ibsen was often seen as a progressive, liberal thinker by younger generations outside Norway; in Norway, however, Ibsen was generally viewed as a conservative playwright, writing against the tide of increasing pressures of modern times. The themes of Ibsen's work are still debated by contemporary audiences and scholars.

Peer Gynt (1867) tells the story of a young man raised on the traditional fairy tales of Norway. Peer leads an irresponsible life, drinking, lying, and ruining young women's reputations. The epic play describes Peer's fantastical journey through the world. Peer becomes a slave dealer and a prophet and finally finds himself alone, wandering through the desert. When Peer returns home, he finds himself spiritually ruined because of the immoral life that he led in the past. In the end, Peer is saved by the love of Salvig, one of the women he abandoned. The play is a combination of psychological realism and folklore. This popular play was set to music by the famous Norwegian composer Edvard Grieg (1843–1907).

Ibsen's most famous work of realism, *A Doll's House* (1879), presents a tragic conflict in a middle-class family. Nora, the mother of three children, is treated like a doll by her husband. Faced with a familial conflict, Nora suddenly matures, realizing that she needs to leave her family to fulfill herself spiritually. The play created much controversy throughout Europe: Ibsen's representation of a woman who leaves her family in pursuit of spiritual fulfillment was seen as disturbing and unconventional. The realistic portrayal of the middle-class household also hurt bourgeois sentimentality. Despite the criticism, the play caused quite a sensation, and it toured Europe and America. The play remains Ibsen's most widely read and produced work.

Hedda Gabler (1890), the story of a woman who cannot resolve a conflict between her inner self and what society demands of her, was roundly condemned by many when it was first produced. A contemporary critic, Hjalmer Boyeson, called her "a complete perversion of womanhood." But Hedda is a character of tremendous complexity who continues to intrigue audiences.

Ibsen's most controversial play, however, was *Ghosts* (1881), which tells the story of the wife of a terrible drunk who sacrifices herself to the undesirable marriage because of social conventions. Their son is unknowingly engaged in a love affair with his half-sister, an illegitimate child of the father and a servant woman. The mother sends her son away, hoping that he will change. The son returns years later, the very picture of his father. He begins to suffer from syphilis, which he inherited from his father. The mother is faced with the difficult choice of administering poison to her son at his request or watching him go through complete psychological and physical degeneration. The subject of venereal disease was not seen as appropriate for theater. The play was bitterly criticized by the conservative segments of the public. *Ghosts* attacks the accepted social conventions of marriage and presents them as destructive to individual happiness.

Although Henrik Ibsen's talent was recognized during his lifetime, today his works enjoy the unanimous acclaim of the critics. Some of Ibsen's topics are still seen as controversial by many audiences. Ibsen is probably among the most influential playwrights in the development of modern drama. He anticipates the modern themes of alienation and the smothering pressure to conform that society exerts on individuals.

Other Works by Henrik Ibsen

Brand. Translated by Robert David McDonald. New York: Theater Communications Group, 1997.

Four Great Plays: Ghosts, An Enemy of the People, The Wild Duck, A Doll's House. Translated by R. Sharp. New York: Bantam, 1981.

Hedda Gabler and Other Plays. Translated by Una Ellis-Fermor. New York: Penguin, 1988.

Works about Henrik Ibsen
Clurman, Harold. *Ibsen.* New York: Da Capo Press, 1989.
Rose, Henry. *Henrik Ibsen: Poet, Mystic, and Moralist.* New York: Haskell, 1972.

Idris, Yūsuf (1927–1991) *novelist*

Yūsuf Idris was born in a small Egyptian village in the district of Sharqiyyah. His father was a middle-class farmer, and Idris's family moved frequently in the 1930s. He was brought up in his grandmother's house, where he was the only child in the household. When Idris was five years old, he attended primary school in a nearby village. He was the youngest student in the school, and his inability to relate to the other students or to his grandmother led Idris to seek consolation in reading folktales and popular stories. His interest in storytelling increased when he was sent to live with his elderly uncle, who had a rich supply of stories.

The outbreak of World War II forced Idris to move to different schools to avoid the violence. When the war ended, he studied medicine at Cairo University, becoming increasingly involved in the students' nationalist movement, which had its center in the department of medicine. Idris's political activities led to his arrest and exposed him to the political turmoil following the war.

In the 1940s, he became friends with the Chekhovian writer Muhammad Yusri Ahmad, who recognized and encouraged Idris's gift for storytelling. In 1950, Idris published his first short story. During the next 10 years, he wrote prolifically. In his first collection of short stories, *Arkhas layali* (*The Cheapest Nights,* 1954), Idris focuses mainly on people from impoverished and oppressed backgrounds, and he examines different character types from various occupations, social classes, and age groups. Idris did not write with the intention to shock readers with the oppressive circumstances of his characters' existence but rather to illuminate the subtle optimism and endurance that his characters possessed. For example, in "The Cheapest Nights," the title story of his collection, the main protagonist, besieged with increasing problems that exacerbate his poverty, eventually discovers that his only means of finding salvation is to try and create peace from his situation.

Idris's works resonate with vivid depictions, bold ideas, and intelligible presentation. His creative imagination, which he developed as a child, is artistically mixed with his sharp observation and understanding of the human situation. Idris's writings are celebrated because he presents familiar characters and situations from new perspectives. His writing style is powerful and provocative, and his novels and short stories explode with energy. Idris's political views and his determination to revolt against injustice remained strong, and his views often found expression in the stories he wrote.

Other Works by Yūsuf Idris
In the Eye of the Beholder: Tales of Egyptian Life. Edited by Roger Allen. Minneapolis: Bibliotheca Islamica, 1978.
Rings of Burnished Brass. Translated by Catherine Cobham. Cairo: American University in Cairo Press, 1992.
The Piper Dies and Other Stories. Translated by Dalya Cohen-Mor. Potomac, Md.: Sheba Press, 1992.
Three Egyptian Short Stories. Translated by Saad al-Gabalawy. Timonium, Md.: York Press, 1991.

Works about Yūsuf Idris
Allen, Roger M. A., ed. *Critical Perspectives on Yūsuf Idris.* Boulder, Colo.: Lynne Rienner, 1994.
Cobham, Catherine. "Sex and Society in Yūsuf Idris: 'Qa al-Madina'." *Journal of Arabic Literature* 6 (1975).
Cohen-Mor, Dalya. *Yūsuf Idris: Changing Visions.* Potomac, Md.: Sheba Press, 1992.
Kurpershoek, P. M. *The Short Stories of Yūsuf Idris: A Modern Egyptian Author.* Leiden, Netherlands: E. J. Brill, 1981.

Ihenfeld, Christa
See WOLF, CHRISTA.

Imalayen, Fatima Zohra
See DJEBAR, ASSIA.

Indianism

Indianism, or the valorization of the native peoples of the Americas, was a popular sentiment in Latin American literature. Although Indianism can be seen as far back as the 17th century in the poetry of Diogo Garção Tinoco of Brazil and even earlier in the writings of Bartolomé de Las Casas, a defender of the Indians in the Americas who wrote extensively during the early 1500s, the movement reached its height in the 19th century. One reason for this may be that the newly independent countries of Latin America were searching for a way to distinguish their literary history from that of Europe. In doing so, many authors looked to the continent's indigenous past as a source. In Brazil, Antônio Gonçalves DIAS (1823–64) was the first great Indianist writer of this period. He wrote romantic literature often with Indianist themes, such as his first major work, *First Cantos,* and his later novel *Memories of Agapito Goiaba.* He also wrote a dictionary of the Tupi language, that of the native people of Brazil. Additionally, another major Brazilian author of the period, novelist José Martiniano de ALENCAR wrote historical novels with Indian main characters that celebrated the native peoples as the defining origin of the Brazilian nation. Alencar's three major Indianist novels are *The Guarani Warrior* 1857), *Iracema* (1865), and *The Ubirajara. Iracema* is the only work available in English; and it is a love story of an Indian princess and a Portuguese officer. Dominican author Manuel de Jesús Galván (1834–1910) also used the historical novel as a vehicle for Indianist writing. His novel, *Enriquillo,* written between 1879 and 1882, is a fine example of this genre.

Works about Indianism

Haberly, David. *Three Sad Races: Racial Identity and National Consciousness in Brazilian Literature.* New York: Cambridge University Press, 1986.

Tapia, John Reyna. *The Indian in the Spanish-American Novel.* Durango, Colo.: University Press of America, 1981.

Treece, David. *Exiles, Allies, Rebels: Brazil's Indianist Movement, Indigenist Politics, and the Imperial Nation-State.* Westport, Conn.: Greenwood Press, 2000.

Ionesco, Eugène (1912–1994) *playwright*

Considered by critics as the founding father of the French THEATRE OF THE ABSURD, Eugène Ionesco was born in Slatina, Romania, on November 26. His beginnings as a writer came when he received a grant to study in Paris, where he wrote his thesis on "Sin and Death in French Poetry since Baudelaire" in 1938. He remained in France, where he began to concentrate on writing for the theater.

Ionesco was a staunch anti-Communist and a fervent believer in human rights. His plays dramatize the theme of the individual's struggle against conformity. Although more openly humorous and less despairing, his works are often compared to those of Samuel BECKETT. His best-known and often-produced play, *La Cantatrice chauve* (1949; *The Bald Soprano,* 1965), takes its initiative from the empty clichés that Ionesco found while trying to learn English from a language textbook. He used the nonsensical sentences to illustrate the emptiness of a life that is stifled by the formalities of language and custom.

Ionesco referred to his works as "antiplays" that fuse tragedy and comedy. *The Lesson* (1951; translated 1958) tells of a teacher who dominates and ultimately kills his student through his oppressive mastery of language. *The Chairs* (1952; translated 1958) relates the tale of an old couple who attempt to pass on their life experience to a gathering of invited guests. With the exception of a deaf mute, the guests never arrive. The couple, however, believing that the audience is assembled, say their piece and then kill themselves, reflecting the lack of attention given to the playwright's message by a non-thinking audience.

Ionesco's breakthrough work in the English-speaking theater was *Rhinoceros* (1959; translated 1960), a play that depicts totalitarianism as a disease that ultimately turns human beings into savage rhinoceroses. Ionesco's protagonist, Bérenger, an ordinary man who holds onto his humanity, reappears in several of Ionesco's other works.

Aside from writing plays, Ionesco also wrote about the theater in his *Notes and Counternotes* (1962; translated 1964). He published his memoirs in *Present Past, Past Present* (1968; translated 1971), and wrote one novel, *The Hermit* (1973). He was elected to the prestigious Académie française in 1970 and died at the age of 84.

Another Work by Eugène Ionesco

A Hell of a Mess. Translated by Helen Gary Bishop. New York: Grove, 1975.

A Work about Eugène Ionesco

Hayman, Ronald. *Eugène Ionesco.* New York: Ungar, 1976.

Ipellie, Alootook (1951–) *poet*

Born in Nunavit in northern Canada, Alootook Ipellie is one of the foremost Inuit writers and artists today. He began his career as an announcer for CBC radio, moving to Ottawa, Ontario, in 1973. Since that time, he has written poetry and essays, contributed to Inuit newspapers and magazines such as *Nunavut* and *Nunatsiaq News,* and edited the *Inuktitut,* a quarterly magazine published by the Inuit Tapirisat of Canada that features articles on traditional ways of life and current issues of interest to Inuit readers and is published in English and Inuktitut.

Published in 1993, Ipellie's major work, *Arctic Dreams and Nightmares,* is a collection of 20 short stories that celebrate the Inuit way of life. The book also includes Ipellie's drawings—he is a celebrated

artist and illustrator as well as a writer—and an introductory essay.

A Work by Alootook Ipellie

"The Igloos Are Calm in the Camp." *Canadian Literature* Issue 167 (Winter 2000), 43.

Works about Alootook Ipellie

Kennedy, Michael P. J. "Alootook Ipellie: The Voice of an Inuk Artist." *Studies in Canadian Literature* 21, no. 2 (1996): 155–64.
———. "Review of Arctic Dreams and Nightmares by Alootook Ipellie." *Canadian Journal of Native Studies* 14, no. 1 (1994): 181–83.

Iqbāl, Muhammad (1877–1938) *poet, essayist*

Muhammad Iqbāl was born in Sialkot, India (now modern Pakistan), into a middle-class orthodox Muslim family. Iqbāl was an exceptional student and won numerous scholarships that allowed him to complete his advanced education in England and Germany. In 1905, Iqbāl left for England, intending to become a lawyer. He quit his position as a lecturer at Government College, Lahore, and after three years obtained a master's degree in philosophy from Cambridge University and a doctoral degree from the University of Munich. He returned to India in 1908 and started to teach philosophy again but quit after only two years, saying that the government did not allow enough freedom of expression to Muslims.

Iqbāl began writing poetry for personal satisfaction. His peers saw his talent and convinced him to submit his poems to a journal for young writers called *Makhzan,* which was published by a close friend of his. The admiration of the older poets for his poetry encouraged Iqbāl to contribute to every single issue.

Critical Analysis

Though never actively involved in political events, Iqbāl's works are a testimony to his deep concern for Muslims around the world. Troubled by the mounting tension between Indian Muslims and Hindus in prepartition India, much of his poetry was written based on his own desire to find a solution to end India's religious conflicts. He often attended large political gatherings in Lahore, where people united with the common goal of leading India to freedom from British colonial rule. Later, prior to his death, Iqbāl's poetry played a pivotal role in the years leading to Pakistan's freedom from Britain and India.

The influence of religion at home and his studies in Persian mysticism and philosophy, however, are as important as religious politics in the formation of Iqbāl's unique poetic voice, which is at once extremely mystical, bombastic, and patriotic. It gracefully navigates between religious zealousness and the sublime in nature and humanity. In Iqbāl's poetry, the idea of love, or *Ishq* in Urdu, is deeply connected to the principles of *self* and *personality*. These concepts illustrate Iqbāl's views on the close relationship between poetry and pan-Islamism.

Iqbāl believed that the affirmation of an individual's intellect, desires, and ambitions would lead directly to the progress of the international Islamic community. In his opinion, the slower progress of the East, compared to Western civilization, resulted from blindly believing in systems of thought that had refused to recognize the power of the self in the individual. To remedy this, Iqbāl's poetry sought to teach that the act of loving the self would give birth to individual personality. An individual, therefore, is not a passive follower of fate or faith but the chief protagonist in his or her own life.

As with all his poetry, however, the theme of unity is essential. This reflects Iqbāl's involvement with the modernist school of Islam, which sought to create a bridge between the older traditions of Islam and the new one being shaped under current cultural influences. In *Rumuz-i-Bekhudi* (*Mysteries of Selflessness*, 1914–18), the poet calls life a "wave of consciousness," which can "thread between the past and now, / And the far future." For Iqbāl this thread is always the message of God as prescribed in the Qur'an.

Iqbāl's vision of Islam was multifaceted in that he sought to bring science, philosophy, psychology, and politics under one rubric. His poems embody many different Western and non-Western philosophical, political, and religious concepts. The central point, however, is the need to believe in personal action and its role in aiding the betterment and progress of the world's Muslim community. Although Iqbāl's use of the concept of freedom evokes the Renaissance belief in a universal humanity, he wrote primarily for a Muslim audience.

The connection of the terms *progress* and the *individual* can be traced to Iqbāl's admiration of Western philosophies where the emphasis is on the self, its role in the freedom of expression, and its potential as a source of power against oppression. In one of his Urdu poems from *Bang-i-Dira* (*The Sound of the Caravan Bell*, 1925) he highlights the importance of capitalizing on the gift of human intellect. Only nature is passive and that is only because it does not have intellect. In this collection, the bell serves to symbolically awaken readers to the accomplishments of Islam. Islam, therefore, is projected as the timeless answer to personal freedom and religious salvation.

The element of revival was already begun in Iqbāl's first prose work *Asrar-i-Khudi* (*Secrets of the Self,* 1911–12). This Persian masterpiece was unlike anything Iqbāl had written before because of its profound psychological and philosophical message. In this work, Iqbāl proposes that the awakening of the soul and the self must happen before Islam itself can undergo any changes. Its publication bewildered his contemporaries because it was radically different from his earlier, nationalist poetry.

Though less political in its approach, *Asrar-i-Khudi* does not detract from Iqbāl's prescription that change and advancement will bring harmony to the world. This theme is continued in a later work, *Rumuz-i-Bekhudi,* where individual selflessness is shown to be an expression of one's social duty. This idea is best captured in the lines "A common aim shared by the multitude / Is unity which, when it is mature, / Forms the Community; the many live / Only by virtue of the single bond."

During Iqbāl's adulthood, Muslims were facing religious crises across the globe. The precarious, double-edged positioning of Muslims in India reinforced Iqbāl 's collaboration with the international Muslim Nationalism Movement, which worked under the slogan: "Freedom and Unity, Pan-Arabism and Pan-Islamism." Many critics, in fact, have claimed that Iqbāl's decision (in the 1910s) to write almost exclusively in Persian was a gesture to join with the wider Islamic community for whom Persian was the true language of Islam.

Stylistically, GHĀLIB and Iqbāl have a lot in common and are regarded as Urdu literature's greatest poets. Both wrote *ghazals,* which are metrical poems similar to the Western sonnet. While Ghālib's *ghazals* are extremely metaphysical and obscure in tone, Iqbāl writes almost like an orator. When he started writing in Urdu again in 1935, Iqbāl began to address the cause of Indian Muslims with new vigor. Even the element of lyricism is absent in his poems, and his tone more didactic than ever before.

The fiery spirit behind his later work marked the final stage in Iqbāl's contribution to bridging the gap between the Middle Ages and the modern in Urdu poetry. The new emphasis given to freedom, personal achievement, individual action, and self-development transformed the traditional Islamic belief in the negation of earthly life. Iqbāl, however, was not a reactionary and did not completely eschew previous Islamic ideas or the poetic conventions of older Urdu poetry: He highlighted existent ones and was able to show that the future for the Islamic world could be changed because the past supported it. As Muhammad Sadiq points, "Iqbāl gave [Islamic Internationalism] a new edge. . . . He does not think ahead of his day, therefore, he thinks in terms of it . . . to meet the challenge of the present." Iqbāl's value as a poet, therefore, lies in his ability to use his heritage to help his contemporary world envision its future.

In 1922, despite his open criticism of British rule, Iqbāl accepted the offer of knighthood by the queen of England. The highly mystical and philosophical undertones in his poetry explain why a poet who favors one religion and expounds one political path is still read by people of all religions and all political beliefs. In 1930, Iqbāl became president of the Muslim league. He was one of the first Muslim leaders to propose the possibility of an independent Muslim country called Pakistan. This idea was Iqbāl's solution for ending religious dissent in India, and it became a reality after his death in 1947.

Other Works by Muhammad Iqbāl

Complaint and Answer: Iqbāl's Dialogue with Allah. Translated by Khuswant Singh. Delhi: Oxford University Press, 1981.

Tulip in the Desert: A Selection of the Poetry of Mohammad Iqbāl. Translated by Mustansir Mir. London: Hurst & Co., 2000.

A Work about Muhammad Iqbāl

Malik, Hafeez, ed. *Iqbāl, Poet-Philosopher of Pakistan.* New York: Columbia University Press, 1971.

Ishigaki Rin (1920–) *poet, short-story writer*

Ishigaki Rin was born in Tokyo. When she was four, her mother died, which led to an unstable home life. During this early period, she contributed poems to girls' magazines. After graduation from Akasaka Higher Elementary School, she began to work at Nihon Kyōgyō Bank in 1934, where she remained until 1975.

While working at the bank, Ishigaki began to publish poems in union periodicals. In 1944, together with a number of other women writers, she launched the poetry magazine *Dansō,* under the guidance of poet Fukuda Masao. During this period, she also tried her hand at short-story writing. In the postwar period, she composed poetry in the style of REALISM, leading to her first poetry collection *Watashi no Mae ni Aru Nabe to Okama to Moeru Hi to* (The pots, pans and burning fire before me) (1959). In a poem of the same name, she wrote about cooking as an expression of love for the people around her. Her second poetry collection, *Hyōsatsu nado* (Nameplates, etc.)(1968), focused on the pain of life as one of its themes; for example, in the poem "Cliff," she wrote about the women who committed suicide in Saipan at the end of World War II by leaping from a cliff into the sea. The collection won the H-shi Award, named after modern poet Hirazawa Teijirō. She has also won the Toshiko Tamura Prize for a general collection, *Ishigaki Rin Shishū* (Ishigaki Rin's poetry anthology) (1971), and the Globe Award for the poetry collection *Ryakureki* (An abbreviated history) (1979). Other publications include *Yūmoa no Sakoku* (The national isolation of humor) (1973), a collection of essays and early short stories, and the poetry collection *Yasashii Kotoba* (Sweet words) (1984).

Ishigaki's poetry is renowned for its frankness and sympathy for humankind while exercising humorous social criticism. She is also unique in her frank portrayal of Japan's defeat in World War II.

Another Work by Ishigaki Rin

Anthology of Modern Japanese Poets. Edited and translated by Alexander Besher, Hiroaki Sato, and Yoichi Midorikawa. Chicago: University of Chicago Press.

J

Jaccottet, Philippe (1925–) *poet, novelist*

Philippe Jaccottet was born in Moudon, Switzerland, was educated in Lausanne, and developed an early enthusiasm for poetry, beginning his career by publishing French translations of Homer, Góngora, HÖLDERLIN, LEOPARDI, and UNGARETTI.

Jaccottet met his literary mentor, Gustave Round, in 1941 and, after a trip to Italy where he met Ungaretti, settled in Paris. He made friendships in the literary community with such writers as Francis PONGE, Yves BONNEFOY, André du Bouchet (1924–) and Jacques Dupin (1927–). Their influence caused him to be wary of EXISTENTIALISM and surrealism, and he took refuge in his own works in the more coherent and traditional style of CLASSICISM.

Jaccottet's first published poetry collection was *Requiem* (1947), but his first significant collection was *Frightens and Other Poetries* (1953), whose poems deal with the passage of time, the anguish of death, and the loss of love. His first prose work, *A Walk Under the Trees* (1957), established his fascination with landscapes.

Several other prose works followed these early successes. *The Ignoramus* (1958) and *Elements of a Dream* (1961) explore the tenuous nature of human existence. With *Airs* (1967), he returned to poetry, focusing on lighter themes. A passage from his latest work, *Cahier de verdure* (*Notebook of Green,* 1990), gives a sense of the intensity with which he endows encounters with the natural world:

> This time it was a cherry tree. Not a cherry tree in full bloom, referring to some kind of clear approach, but a cherry tree loaded with fruits, caught sight of one evening in June, on the other side of a huge cornfield. It was once more as if someone had appeared there and were talking to you without really talking to you, without even pointing at you: someone or, rather, somebody, and a "beautiful thing" indeed . . .

Jaccottet has also written several works of criticism, as well as poetry and prose dealing with significant events in his life. He continues to write and work as a translator.

Other Works by Philippe Jaccottet

Selected Poems. Translated by Derek Mahon. Winston-Salem, N.C.: Wake Forest University Press, 1988.

Under Clouded Skies; and, Beauregard. Translated by David Constantine and Mark Treharne. Newcastle upon Tyne: Bloodaxe Books, 1994.

A Work about Philippe Jaccottet

Cady, Andrea. *Measuring the Visible: The Verse and Prose of Philippe Jaccottet.* Atlanta, Ga.: Rodopi, 1992.

Jarry, Alfred (1873–1907) *playwright, poet, novelist*

Best known for his play *Ubu roi* (*King Ubu*, 1896), Alfred Jarry was an eccentric whose fantastic works are considered to be forerunners of the THEATRE OF THE ABSURD. Born in Lavalle, Mayenne, he inherited much of his eccentricity and a trace of insanity from his mother. By age 15, he had already collaborated with several classmates to write *Ubu roi* as a means of ridiculing a disliked mathematics professor. Originally performed with marionettes, the play was later produced in Paris where its anarchist themes and coarse language incited a riot.

Jarry created his own absurdist logic, which he called Pataphysics, a science governing the laws of exceptions and reaching beyond metaphysics to encompass that which cannot be defined. He attributed his logic to a science-fiction type character known as Dr. Faustoll. He even invented a Pataphysical calendar, which begins on September 8, 1873, Jarry's birthdate.

Inspired by H. G. Wells's novel *The Time Machine,* Jarry turned to science fiction and wrote the essay "How to Build a Time Machine" (1900). His final novel, *Le Surmâle* (*The Supermale*, 1902), was a comic fantasy of a superman who ate superfood and performed feats of erotic endurance before dying in the embrace of a machine.

Jarry's life eventually began to mirror his art. From Père Ubu, his protagonist in *Ubu roi,* he picked up eccentric and destructive habits. Referring to himself frequently in the third person, he drank excessively, hallucinated frequently, and shouted orders and obscenities at friends and acquaintances.

By the time Jarry was 34, he had become a familiar figure in Paris, where he walked the streets and carried a green umbrella, a symbol of middle-class power in *Ubu roi.* He also wore cycling clothes and brandished two pistols, which he often used to threaten fellow pedestrians.

Jarry's way of life ultimately took its toll. He died on All Saint's Day from alcoholism and tuberculosis, leaving behind a legacy to modern science fiction, as well as two sequels to *Ubu roi,* one of which, *Ubu echaîné* (*Ubu Bound,* 1900) was not performed until 1937. *Ubu cocu* (*Ubu Cuckolded,* 1944) was published posthumously.

Another Work by Alfred Jarry

Adventures in Pataphysics. Translated by Paul Edwards. London: Atlas, 2001.

A Work about Alfred Jarry

Lennon, Nigey. *Alfred Jarry: The Man with the Axe.* Los Angeles: Panjandrum Books, 1984.

Al-Jayyusi, Salma al-Khadra (1946–) *anthologist, literary critic, poet*

Salma al-Khadra Al-Jayyusi was born in East Jordan to a Palestinian father and a Lebanese mother. She spent most of her childhood in Acre and Jerusalem. After graduating from the American University of Beirut with a B.A. in Arabic and English literature, she went to London for her Ph.D. Jayyusi has traveled widely and lived in many places around the globe. She has taught at various universities in the Middle East and the United States and founded the Project of Translation from Arabic Literature in 1980. This project stemmed from Al-Jayyusi's discovery that Arabic literature was not widely known around the world, and in cases where translations could be found, they were poorly done.

Al-Jayyusi is best known for her literary critique of Arabian literature and poetry. Having traveled widely during her life, she is able to interpolate in her poems the richness of her experiences within other cultures. Despite her ability to immerse herself in other traditions, Al-Jayyusi is committed to presenting the essence of Arabic literary tradition to the literary world. Her first collection of poems, *Return from the Dreamy Fountain,* was first published in 1960. Even though it was well received by readers, Al-Jayyusi decided to focus her next efforts on collecting rarely known Arabic works and bringing them to the attention of the world. In 1977, she published a two-volume critical literary history of Arabic poetry, *Trends and Movements in Modern Arabic Poetry.* She hopes that by continuing to introduce books such as the above to the world, readers can gain a better understanding of the richness of Arabic literature.

Other Works Edited by Salma al-Khadra Al-Jayyusi

Anthology of Modern Palestinian Literature. New York: Columbia University Press, 1992.
The Legacy of Muslim Spain. Leiden; New York: E. J. Brill, 1992.

Jhabvala, Ruth Prawer (1927–)

novelist, short-story writer, scriptwriter

Born in Cologne to Polish parents, Ruth Prawer Jhabvala possesses a triple or quadruple heritage—European (Jewish), British, Indian, and now American; she has made her home on three continents and absorbed several cultures. She was educated in England at Hendon County School and at the University of London's Queen Mary College, where she obtained an M.A. In 1951, she married Cyrus Jhabvala, a Parsi architect, and she lived with him in New Delhi from 1951 to 1975. (The Jhabvalas have three daughters.) In 1975 she emigrated to the United States, but she visits England frequently and spends winters in India.

In addition to a dozen novels and a half-dozen volumes of short stories, Ruth Prawer Jhabvala has written many film scripts. In 1962, she met Ismail Merchant and James Ivory; theirs has proved a long-lasting team, responsible for such films as *Shakespeare Wallah* (1965), *A Room with a View* (1986), *Howard's End* (1992), and *The Remains of the Day* (1993). For *A Room with a View,* Jhabvala won an Academy Award. Two of her own novels, *The Householder* and *Heat and Dust,* have also been filmed.

Critical Analysis

Jhabvala's literary career spans 40 years and exhibits several phases. Often compared with Jane AUSTEN and E. M. FORSTER because she writes comedies of manners, her influences include Charles DICKENS, George ELIOT, Thomas HARDY, Tolstoy, Turgenev, and Proust. Her early novels are more narrowly focused than her later ones and often center on joint or extended Indian families and their problems. East/West conflict is another major theme and the chief reason for comparing her with Forster.

Esmond in India (1957) tells of a philandering British civil servant who has an Indian wife and a British mistress, befriends a number of middle-class Indian women, and exhibits a love/hate relationship with the subcontinent. *The Householder* (1960) focuses on the marriage of Prem and Indu; Prem discovers he must defeat his mother-in-law and rise above himself to fulfill his marriage. *Heat and Dust* (1975), which won the BOOKER PRIZE, is one of this author's most complex, sophisticated works, interweaving two love stories 50 years apart—that of Olivia, who runs off with an Indian prince, and that of her granddaughter. The novel raises the question "What is identity?" and probes the relations between history and reality, history and fiction, and fiction and reality. *A New Dominion* (1971) is experimental, employing omniscient narration (like Jhabvala's earlier fiction) but supplementing this by shifting from one character's viewpoint to another's. This novel and *Heat and Dust* are both reminiscent of Forster's *A Passage to India.*

Later novels are more complex in narration, more detached, and darker in mood. They exhibit film techniques learned from scriptwriting. The first Jhabvala novel to be written in the United States, *In Search of Love and Beauty* (1983), is a quest novel exploring all three of its author's heritages—German, British, and Indian—against an American background. The later novels also handle another favorite Jhabvala theme: the fraudulent guru or swami who cheats his devotees. In *Three Continents,* American female twins turn over their lives and fortunes to sham gurus with disastrous results.

Jhabvala's fiction has received mixed reviews. A craftswoman whose every word counts, she is prized as such in the Western world; Indians, however, are often nettled by her outsider's "inside" view of them and the subcontinent, and they chafe at her detachment—which is really self-defense, as she makes clear in the introduction to *Out of India.* She admits that, while immersed in India, she was never of it. After reviewing differing oriental and occidental evaluations of Jhabvala, Ralph Crane observes simply, "She is a writer whose work will stand the test of time."

Another Work by Ruth Prawer Jhabvala

East into Upper East: Plain Tales from New York and New Delhi. Washington, D.C.: Counterpoint Press, 2000.

Works about Ruth Prawer Jhabvala

Crane, Ralph J. *Ruth Prawer Jhabvala.* New York: Twayne, 1992.
Sucher, Laurie. *The Fiction of Ruth Prawer Jhabvala: The Politics of Passion.* New York: St. Martin's Press, 1989.

Jiang Bingzhi

See DING LING.

Jiménez, Juan Ramón (1881–1958) *poet*

Juan Ramón Jiménez was born in southern Spain but spent most of his life in Madrid. He devoted his life to poetry, publishing his first volume at age 20. In about 1916, when he fell in love and married, he stopped writing in fixed meters and switched to free verse. He wanted to remove everything but the pure poetic essence from his verse. His constant inspiration came from his wife.

Jiménez was a member of the GENERATION OF 1898, a literary and cultural movement in the first two decades of the 20th century. Each author of the movement had his own idea of how to write "well," but all agreed that the improvisation, pomp, and regionalism of earlier Spanish literature must be replaced by a more modern, simpler literature that seeks its inspiration abroad. Jiménez's poetry is an example of the move toward this simplicity. Much of his work, such as *Arias tristes* (*Sad Arias,* 1903) and *Melancolía* (*Melancholy,* 1912), is very sad.

Although known for his voluminous output of poetry, Jiménez is also the author of the beautiful story of a little donkey called *Platero y yo.* It was first published in 1917 and has been translated into English. Jiménez was awarded the Nobel Prize for literature in 1956.

Other Works by Juan Ramón Jiménez

Florit, Eugenio, ed. *Selected Writings of Juan Ramón Jiménez.* Translated by H. R. Hays. New York: Farrar, Straus & Giroux, 1999.
Light and Shadows: Selected Poems and Prose. Translated by James Wright and Robert Bly. Buffalo, N.Y.: White Pine Press, 1987.
The Complete Perfectionist. Translated by Christopher Maurer. New York: Doubleday, 1997.

Works about Juan Ramón Jiménez

Kluback, William. *Encounters with Juan Ramón Jiménez.* New York: Peter Lang, 1995.
Wilcox, John. *Self and Image in Juan Ramón Jiménez.* Champaign: University of Illinois Press, 1987.

Johnson, Pauline (Tekahionwake) (1861–1913) *poet*

Pauline Johnson was born on the Six Nations Reserve near Brantford, Ontario, Canada. Her mother was a nonnative who came to Canada from

Ohio, and her Mohawk father was a chief of the Six Nations Reserve. Johnson had two older brothers and a sister. She was influenced at early age by such canonical writers as John Milton (1608–74) and Sir Walter Scott (1771–1832) but was also exposed to native stories by her father and grandfather. This combination of influences had a great impact on her development as a writer.

When Johnson's father died, the family moved to Brantford, Ontario, where Johnson began to write poems and short stories. She published these stories in local newspapers to make money. In addition, Johnson became famous for her poetry recitals, her gift for performing poetry, a legacy of the storytelling she learned from her father and grandfather. She toured Canada and the United States and also traveled abroad, performing her work and often sharing the bill with famous musicians or comedians.

Johnson's popular books of poetry include *The White Wampum* (1895), *Canadian Born* (1903), and *Flint and Feather* (1912). In all her work, Johnson celebrates her native heritage: "My aim, my joy, my pride is to sing the glories of my own people." In 1911, Johnson published *Legends of Vancouver,* a collection of stories and legends of the Squamish people as told to her by her friend Squamish chief Joe Capilano. Johnson died at the age of 52 of breast cancer. The monument to her grave can be found in Vancouver's Stanley Park.

Another Work by Pauline Johnson

Ruoff, LaVonne Brown, ed. *The Moccasin Maker.* Norman: University of Oklahoma Press, 1998.

A Work about Pauline Johnson

Strong-Boag, Veronica Jane, and Carole Gerson. *Paddling Her Own Canoe: The Times and Texts of E. Pauline Johnson (Tekahionwake).* Toronto: University of Toronto Press, 2000.

Johnson, Uwe (1934–1984) *novelist, critic*

Uwe Johnson was born in Cammin, Poland, to Erich Johnson, an administrative official of the

Nazi Party, and Erna Johnson. Johnson attended an elite elementary school that provided intensive training in the Nazi ideology for its students. After the end of World War II, the Johnsons moved to Rechnitz, Germany, to avoid the advancing Soviet army. Johnson's father was arrested in 1946 by Soviet officials for participation in the Nazi regime. The family never saw him again.

Between 1952 and 1954, Johnson studied German language and literature at University of Rostock, East Germany. Johnson joined the junior ranks of the Free German Youth, an East German Communist organization for high school and college students. Johnson was expelled from the university when he refused, despite strong pressure from the Communist officials, to make false claims during a public speech at a Free German Youth meeting about the Young Congregation, a movement of Christian youth. Later, Johnson was allowed to continue his studies at Karl Marx University of Leipzig, where he finished his bachelor's degree in 1956. He was not allowed to pursue doctoral studies.

Johnson began his literary career translating English works into German. He also worked for various publishing houses in East Germany, appraising the merit of proposed projects. Johnson constantly struggled to find employment and had several altercations with the Communist regime of East Germany, which prevented any possibility of a teaching career. Completely disenchanted, Johnson moved to West Berlin in 1959.

Uwe Johnson's work definitely has political dimensions; however, it is not easy to assess what these exactly are. His work has been criticized by the government and some writers of West Germany as procommunist and has been similarly derogated in East Germany as anticommunist: It seems that Johnson opposed the regimes of both countries. He saw the government of East Germany as socially oppressive, dictatorial, and dominated by Stalinism. At the same time, Johnson was disgusted with the government of West Germany, which he frequently characterized as fascist. Indeed, the national government of West Germany was dominated by ex-Nazis and was in many ways as repressive as the government of East Germany. Johnson lived in West Berlin because it was not under the direct jurisdiction of the national government in Germany.

Critical Analysis

Johnson's first novel, *Mutmassungen über Jakob* (*Speculations about Jacob,* 1959), was an instant success when it appeared in West Germany. The plot of the novel centers on Rohlfs, a member of the East German Security Force, who enters the life of the Cresspahl family. Heinrich Cresspahl's daughter, Gesine, left for West Germany and works for NATO. Throughout the novel, Rohlfs attempts to influence the family to recruit Gesine as a spy for East Germany. By no means a one-sided perspective, the novel discusses the personal and political challenges brought about by the division of Germany. The novel also gained popularity in East Germany and was not censored by government officials.

Das dritte Buch über Achim (*The Third Book about Achim,* 1961) tells the story of Karsch, a West German journalist who travels to East Germany to visit his ex-lover Karin, a successful actress. While in East Germany, Karsch meets Achim, Karin's boyfriend, a professional biker and a star in East Germany. Karsch faces a difficult decision when a publishing company approaches him to write Achim's life story in a way that would glorify socialist life in East Germany. Once again, the book does not provide a clear political message and seems to present an objective reflection of a divided Germany. The work was hailed as an achievement in contemporary German literature and especially was praised by Günter GRASS, another controversial and famous German writer.

Uwe Johnson lived for a time in the United States and finally settled in the United Kingdom. He found the environments of both Germanys stifling and not conducive to his work. He continued to write novels and received numerous awards, including the Fontane Prize in 1960, the Wilhelm Raabe Prize in 1975, the Georg Büchner Prize in 1971, and the Thomas Mann Prize in 1978. Johnson was a member of the Academy of Arts in West Berlin and of the German Academy for Language and Literature. After the reunification of Germany in 1990, interest in Johnson's work dramatically increased. Gary Baker remarks,

> Uwe Johnson is significant not only for his unique literary style and linguistic creativity but also for the thematic issues addressed in his works. He was the first German author to treat, in fiction, the division of Germany after the war. He explored its psychological, political, and cultural manifestations in a network of characters and places unmatched in complexity and authenticity.

Other Works by Uwe Johnson

Anniversaries: From the Life of Gesine Cresspahl. Translated by Leila Vennewitz and Walter Arndt. New York: Harcourt Brace, 2000.
A Trip to Klagenfurt: In the Footsteps of Ingeborg Bachmann. Translated by Damion Searls. New York: Hydra Books, 2002.

A Work about Uwe Johnson

Baker, Gary. *Understanding Uwe Johnson.* Columbia: University of South Carolina Press, 1999.

Jünger, Ernst (1895–1998) *novelist, essayist*
Ernst Jünger was born in Heidelberg, Germany, and grew up in Hannover. The son of a pharmacist, he ran away from home in 1913 to look for more exciting possibilities in life. Joining the French Foreign Legion and serving in North Africa, he joined the German army at the outbreak of World War I and served as an officer on the Western front. Between 1919 and 1923, Jünger continued his military career and served as an officer in the Weimar Republic army. After retirement, he studied entomology at Leipzig, Germany, and Naples, Italy. He eventually became a famous entomologist (several insects were named after him).

During the 1920s, Jünger joined the pro-Nazi movement and contributed to several right-wing publications. His first book, *The Storm of Steel* (1920), argued that Germany's suffering during World War I was a prelude to a rebirth of a powerful nation and great victory ahead. In *Adventurous Heart* (1929) and *The Workers* (1933), Jünger examined the social and emotional structure of the worker. In these works, Jünger rejects humanism and claims that struggle for power among world nations is imminent. Although Jünger supported the right-wing movement, he rejected offers of friendship from Adolf Hitler during the 1920s, refused to serve as the head of the Nazi Writers' Union in 1933, and vocally opposed anti-Semitism. For these reasons, the Nazi government prohibited further publication of his work in 1938.

During World War II, Jünger served as a captain in the German army. Stationed in Paris, he associated with several artists, including the famous painter Pablo Picasso. After the death of his son at the Italian front, he became completely disenchanted with war.

After the war, Jünger published a number of works in which he supported European unity and promoted the rights of the individual. In *The Glass Bees* (1957), for example, he paints a world in which machines threaten the rights of individuals. In his books, Jünger often dispassionately painted historical and social developments that resulted in violation of human rights; hence, he was sometimes accused of indifference and elitism. Despite criticism, he achieved a reputation as a great German writer.

He was awarded numerous prizes, including the Great Order of Merit (1959), the Immermann Prize (1964), and the Goethe Prize (1982), as well as an honorary degree from the University of Bilbao, among others. By the time of his death at the age of 103, Jünger had published more than 20 books. His works have been translated into more than a dozen languages.

Other Works by Ernst Jünger

Aladdin's Problem. Translated by Joachim Neugroschel. New York: Marsilio, 1992.
A Dangerous Encounter. Translated by Hilary Barr. New York: Marsilio, 1993.

A Work about Ernst Jünger

Nevin, Thomas. *Ernst Jünger and Germany: Into the Abyss, 1914–1945.* Durham, N.C.: Duke University Press, 1997.

Kabbani, Nizar (Qabbani) (1923–1998)
poet, essayist

Born in Damascus, Syria, to a respected middle-class Muslim family, Kabbani published his first volume of poetry in 1944. He immediately gained fame for his bad-boy erotic daring and his "hip" language that expressed Arabic youth culture. Kabbani's poetry often incites rebellion against what he saw as repressive political and social morés. In 1954, the Syrian parliament considered demoting him from his diplomatic post for the disrespect to religion some found in his poem, "Bread, Hashish, and the Moon," but the motion failed.

At the height of his literary career, from the 1950s to the 1970s, Kabbani, often writing in a female voice, expressed the joys of love and eros for a generation of men and especially women. He saw himself as a champion of women's liberation and sexual freedom.

In the 1980s, Kabbani wrote three volumes of poetry, titled "Trilogy of the Children of the Rocks" (1988), celebrating the teenage rebels of the Palestinian *intifadah*. His poetry conveys deep Arab pride as well as sharp criticism of many aspects of Arab life and culture, such as the sexual double standard for men and women. His most scathing poetic attacks, such as "Scribblings in the Margins of the Notebook of Defeat," are aimed at repressive Arab governments that curtail the human rights of the Arab peoples. He also wrote strident poems against Israeli and American policies toward Arabs, such as the poem "I Am a Terrorist" in which he says that Arab men are labeled terrorists by the Western media for defending their homes and their people's dignity.

Kabbani graduated from the University of Damascus with a law degree in 1945 and joined Syria's diplomatic corps. He was posted in Egypt, Turkey, Britain, Lebanon, Spain, and China before he resigned in 1966 and moved to Beirut, where he established his own publishing company.

From a brief early marriage in Syria, he had two children, one of whom died in a car accident as a young man; Kabbani eulogized him in poetry. Kabbani married again, this time to an Iraqi schoolteacher, Balqis al-Rawi. His poem, "Choose," was widely considered by the Arabic reading public to be Kabbani's marriage proposal to Balqis. The handsome poet—he was nicknamed "the blond rebel"—and the beautiful woman who was his muse captivated public attention. They had two children. Kabbani wrote some of his finest poetry of love and sensuality in the 1970s. The poem "I Bear Witness That There Is No Woman But You," for example, provocatively turns the Muslim testimony of faith in one God into a testimony of a man's love for one woman. When Balqis was killed at her office in a Beirut bombing in 1981, he publicly mourned her in several anguished poems.

After her death, Kabbani left the Arab world for Europe, living in Geneva, Paris, and London, where he settled down to a life of exile. In 1997, a street was named after him in his old neighborhood in Damascus. When he died, his body was flown back to Damascus for burial, as he had requested in his will.

Kabbani wrote more than 50 books of poetry as well as several volumes of essays and one drama, a political satire. During his lifetime, his readings drew crowds in the tens of thousands. Many Kabbani poems were adopted as song lyrics by some of the most popular figures in Arabic music so that his words continue to be heard through song. In today's pop music scene, Iraqi icon Kazem al-Saher has acquired rights to sing many of Kabbani's poems. Kabbani's work has been translated into Spanish, French, Italian, Persian, and English. In 1994, he was awarded the Oweiss Prize for Cultural Productivity in the United Arab Emirates.

Other Works by Nizar Kabbani

Arabian Love Poems: Full Arabic and English Texts. Translated by Bassam K. Frangieh and Clementina Brown. Boulder, Colo.: Lynn Rienner, 1999.

On Entering the Sea: The Erotic and Other Poetry of Nizar Qubbani. Translated by Lena Jayyusi et al. New York: Interlink, 1996.

Kafka, Franz (1883–1924) *novelist, short-story writer*

Franz Kafka was born in Prague, Czech Republic, to Hermann Kafka, a dry-goods merchant, and Julie Kafka. Kafka's family spoke German and belonged to a small but old community of German-speaking Jews in Prague. Hermann Kafka was a domineering, almost tyrannical figure in the Kafka household. He took out his anger and frustration on young Franz, who recalled the terrifying experiences later in his life. Indeed, many biographers

and critics of Kafka note that Kafka's work often deals with a conflict between father and son or with people pleading innocence in front of authority figures. Kafka's childhood was marked by the constant domestic conflicts and by the social atmosphere of Prague that branded Jews as second-class citizens and outcasts. Kafka's attitude toward his Jewish heritage was ambiguous and is an obliquely expressed conflict in his works.

Kafka was educated in German elementary schools. In 1901, he enrolled in Ferdinand-Karls University to study law, graduating with a doctorate in 1906. Kafka's career as a writer began about 1904 when he was working as a legal clerk. At work, Kafka composed mundane reports on industrial health hazards and the legal implications of industrial injuries; at night, however, Kafka composed elaborate, sometimes fantastic tales. Between 1907 and 1923, Kafka worked in the insurance business and achieved remarkable success; indeed, he was so valued by his employers that they arranged a deferment from the draft during World War I.

In 1917 Kafka was diagnosed with tuberculosis. He continued to work but suffered a serious setback when he contracted influenza in 1919. Kafka also met constant disappointment from publishers who rejected his work. After several turbulent but unsuccessful relationships with women, in 1922 Kafka finally married Dora Diamant, a young woman from a respected Orthodox Jewish family in Prague. The couple moved to Berlin, where Kafka, by then confined to bed, worked on his journals and wrote numerous letters to his friends and family. By 1924, Kafka was moved to a sanatorium just outside of Vienna. He died of tuberculosis in obscurity and poverty.

Kafka asked his friend and fellow writer Max Brod to destroy all manuscripts after his death. Fortunately, Brod disobeyed the last wish of his friend. Thus, with the exception of few short stories, most of Kafka's major work was published posthumously.

Critical Analysis

"The Metamorphosis" (1915) is probably Kafka's best-known and most critically acclaimed short story. In the story, Gregor Samsa, a traveling salesman, awakes one day to discover himself transformed into a giant grotesque insect. No longer able to communicate with his parents or the outside world, Gregor physically degenerates day by day; mentally, however, he does not seem to change. Gregor is finally killed by his father. "The Metamorphosis" presents a range of themes found in the works of MODERNISM, such as alienation of the individual, failure of communication, and attachment to a landscape that has grown ungovernably hostile. At the time of its publication, however, most readers did not know how to interpret the strange allegorical plot of the story. Today, the story is often cited as central to the modernist movement, and it reflects the ideas that the movement embodied.

Kafka's novel *The Trial* (1925) depicts the suffering and psychological torment of Josef K., who is arrested one morning without reason. Throughout his "trial," Josef never discovers the crime of which he is accused. He is dragged through a seemingly endless investigation in a court system that reveals nothing. Josef does not confront an identifiable authority figure, but he is constantly burdened by laws he cannot comprehend. At the end of the novel, Josef becomes a martyr to the law when he is stabbed to death. Truth is no longer relevant in the faceless system of law that delivers arbitrary judgment and punishment. Kafka addressed a similar theme in the short story "The Penal Colony" (1919); here, truth becomes an instrument of punishment, as the victims of truth are killed by a machine that inscribes the nature of their crimes on their bodies.

The protagonist of Kafka's novel, *The Castle* (1926), is simply identified as K. K arrives in a small village, claiming to be a land surveyor and bears the official authority of the government. K seeks to meet Klamm, the ruler of the mysterious castle that supposedly has sovereignty over the village. K develops a strange relationship with Arthur and Jeremiah, Klamm's assistants, who refuse to arrange a meeting with their supervisor. K finally befriends and uses Frieda, a former mistress of the castle, who leaves K after discovering his true intents. *The Castle* focuses on several important themes, including bureaucracy, love, guilt, and law. All these themes are strangely interconnected in the landscape where the individual is incapable of retaining a stable identity. Although Kafka never finished *The Castle,* it remains as one of his most important works.

Franz Kafka received no recognition for his incredible talent during his lifetime. Today, however, Kafka is considered one of the leading figures of modernism and of world literature in general. He left a body of works of great complexity and literary genius, and one that continues to enrich readers and critics today. Kafka was rediscovered in the 1950s and is among the most admired of modern writers. Perhaps more than any other writer, Kafka captures the nightmare reality and absurdity of modern existence and the strange, alienated feel of a world without reason.

Other Works by Franz Kafka

Amerika. Translated by Willia Muir. New York: Schocken Books, 1996.

The Complete Stories. New York: Schocken Books, 1995.

Franz Kafka: The Diaries, 1921–1923. New York: Schocken Books, 1989.

Works about Franz Kafka

Adler, Jeremy. *Franz Kafka.* New York: Overlook Press, 2002.

Brod, Max. *Franz Kafka: A Biography.* New York: Da Capo Press, 1995.

Kanik, Orhan Veli (1914–1950) *poet*

Orhan Veli Kanik was born in Istanbul, Turkey. The son of a conductor for the Presidential Symphony Orchestra, he received a diverse and liberal education but withdrew from the University of Istanbul before completing his degree. His talent as a writer was nurtured at a young age, and he was fortunate to have among his mentors the leading poet, literary critic, and historian Ahmet Hamdi Tapinar.

Tapinar encouraged Kanik to write, leading him to publish his poetry in the school paper *Sesimiz* (*Our Voice*) while Kanik was in his early teens. Kanik served with the armed forces during World War II and obtained a job as a translator after the war, but he left this position to lead a bohemian life, more in tune with his poetry and his philosophy.

Kanik was born into a family of writers and artists. His younger brother, Adnan, was also a writer until he was sent to prison in 1949 for a political offense. Orhan, however, was able to avoid conflicts with the authorities and to publish *Leaf*, a literary journal. The journal ran for 28 issues and ceased publication with a special memorial edition on Kanik's death.

Kanik was never a prolific writer, but he had a great influence on the development of Turkish poetry. His own work was more influenced by Japanese haiku than by traditional Turkish or Western forms. Kanik believed that a strict adherence to traditional forms had made much of Turkish poetry sterile. He sought to reinvent tradition with a sense of vibrancy that would resonate with the needs of common humanity. He broke free of conventional modes, discarding rhyme and meter, and focused instead on an almost nihilistic viewpoint that, simultaneously, managed to incorporate a reaffirmation of the joy of life. He wrote entirely in free verse, tackling the issues relevant to everyday life in plain language that was devoid of metaphors and clichés.

Although Nazim HIKMET had earlier brought the use of free verse to Turkish poetry, it was Kanik who established its relevance by introducing ideas of the French modernist movement to his poetry. Alongside fellow poets Oktay Rifat and Melih Cevdet Anday, he started the artistic movement POETIC REALISM, which focuses on the emergence of the common man as hero. By stripping away the traditional adornments of poetry, the poet is free to use everyday life as subject matter.

Kanik died from a cerebral hemorrhage after collapsing in Istanbul on November 14. Many believed that his death was a result of his love of alcohol, citing a famous line from one of his poems,

"I wish I were a fish in a bottle of booze." Kanik's death came as a shock to the people of Turkey. After a well-attended funeral ceremony, he was buried on a hill where he could rest forever, "Listening to Istanbul."

Another Work by Orhan Veli Kanik

I, Orhan Veli: Poems by Orhan Veli. Translated by Murat Nemet-Nejat. Brooklyn, N.Y.: Hanging Loose Press, 1989.

Kao Tsing-jen

See GAO XINGJIAN.

Karamzin, Nikolai Mikhailovich
(1766–1826) *historian, short-story writer, novelist*

The birthplace of Nikolai Karamzin is uncertain, but most research suggests a small village along the Volga River in Russia. Karamzin's mother died when he was very young, and he was raised by his father, Mikhail Karamzin, a retired army captain and minor aristocrat. A village priest taught him to read and write. When Karamzin was 13, his father send him to study in Moscow. He was a brilliant student, and attended university lectures when he was just 16. Although he was eager to study at the university, Karamzin's father insisted that he pursue an army career. Karamzin enlisted as an officer in the Preobrozhentsky regiment in St. Petersburg in 1783.

In St. Petersburg, Karamzin spent his time in literary circles and eventually became a translator. He published his first translation at the age of 17 and was paid with two volumes of the English novelist Henry Fielding's works. He left the army in 1784 after the death of his father. In 1789, he left Russia and traveled across Europe, visiting Germany, Switzerland, France, and England. On his return to Russia in 1790, Karamzin established a literary journal, *Moscow Journal,* in which he published his *Letters of the Russian Traveler* (1792), a collection that was based on his travels in Europe, and "Poor Liza" (1792), a short novel about a peasant girl. Several other stories that Karamzin wrote at this time brought French sentimentalism to Russia and were widely imitated.

Karamzin was not particularly interested in politics, but when he established a new journal in 1801, *Vestnik Evropy* (*The Messenger of Europe*), it became the leading political journal in Russia. It was the most widely read publication in Russia during the early 1800s. The journal's popularity brought financial success, which freed Karamzin to begin his enormous historiographic work, *History of the Russian State* (1819–29). This 12-volume work, which covered Russian history up to 1613, was the most complete history of Russia of the time. The Russian emperor, Aleksandr I, appointed Karamzin official historiographer in 1803 with a pension of 2,000 rubles a year, a considerable sum.

Between 1810 and 1811, Karamzin worked on *Memoir on Ancient and Modern Russia* (1811). In this work, Karamzin related his political beliefs, as well as his personal conversations with Aleksandr I. He believed that autocracy was the appropriate form of government for Russia, making a careful distinction between autocracy and despotism, based on the importance of the law.

Karamzin left a long-lasting legacy when he died in 1826. He had become one of the closest friends of the emperor and remained a defender of the monarchy. More important, Karamzin's work influenced such important writers as Aleksandr PUSHKIN and Mikhail LERMONTOV. He also established a historiographic tradition that did not previously exist in Russia, and his account of Russian history was an important part of the Russian self-image into the 20th century.

Works about Nikolai Karamzin

Black, Joseph Lawrence. *Nicholas Karamzin and Russian Society in the Nineteenth Century: A Study in Russian Political and Historical Thought*. Toronto: University of Toronto Press, 1976.

Hammarberg, Gitta. *From the Idyll to the Novel: Karamzin's Sentimentalist Prose*. New York: Cambridge University Press, 1991.

Lewis, S. Mark. *Modes of Historical Discourse in J. G. Herder and N. M. Karamzin*. New York: Peter Lange, 1995.

Karnad, Girish (1938–   ) *playwright*

Girish Ranghunath Karnad was born in Maharashtra, India, but has lived most of his life in the southern state of Karnataka. Most of Karnad's work is written in Kannada, the language spoken in Karnataka, but he has translated all his major plays into English. He is a playwright, story writer, poet, and director of films.

After completing his college studies in math and statistics in 1958 at Karnataka University, Karnad went to Oxford University to earn a master's degree in philosophy, politics, and economics. It is here that Karnad first started to explore his artistic talents and began writing poetry.

When Karnad returned to India, he started to work at Oxford University Press in 1963. After the success of his second play *Tughlaq* (1964), he decided to quit the press and has since devoted his life to writing drama. At one point (1974–75), he was the director of the Film Institute of Pune, India.

Karnad has written 10 plays, all of which are extremely politically driven but read like folktales. His very first play *Yayati* (1961), written while studying at Oxford, is taken from a story in the great Hindu epic *The Mahabharata*. It recounts the events that follow a son's attempt to rescue his father from a curse, thus throwing the entire family into a moral dilemma. There is a strong sense of the past in Karnad's work, and he borrows extensively from Indian mythology and history. His play *Tughlaq*, for instance, shows the transformation of the old Mughal emperor (Mohammad bin Tughlaq) from a sensitive ruler into an unjust oppressor. His folktale *Cheluvi* (1992), which was also made into a movie, is about a girl who turns into a tree, thus becoming a symbolic vehicle of nature's outcry against humanity's inconsiderate actions.

Karnad's plays have always carried social messages. At a time when most of his peers were switching to the more-lucrative film industry, Karnad steadfastly stuck to writing about social reform for the theater. In 1994, he won the Sahitya Akademi Award for his social drama, *Taledanda* (1990), and the Jnanpith Award in 1999 for his contribution to modern Indian drama.

Another Work by Girish Karnad

Three Plays: Naga-Mandala; Hayavadana; Tughlaq. New York: Oxford University Press, 1996.

A Work about Girish Karnad

Dodiya, Jaydipsinh. *The Plays of Girish Karnad: Critical Perspectives.* New Delhi: Prestige Books, 1999.

Kaschnitz, Marie Luise (pseudonym of Freifrau Marie Luise von Kaschnitz-Weinberg) (1901–1974) *poet, short-story writer*

Marie Luise Kaschnitz was born in Karlsruhe, Germany. Her parents were Max Freiherr von Holzing-Berstett, a general and nobleman, and Elsa von Seldenek. Kaschnitz grew up in Berlin and Potsdam. She trained to be a book dealer and later worked at a publishing house in Munich. In 1925, she married Guido von Kaschnitz-Weinberg, an archaeology professor. They traveled extensively and lived for several years in Rome.

Although best known as a poet, Kaschnitz's first work was a novel, *Liebe beginnt* (*Love Begins,* 1933). After World War II, she emerged as a lyric poet with her first collection *Gedichte* (*Poems,* 1947). Starting in the 1950s, she also published short-story collections and radio plays based on biblical legends. After Kaschnitz's husband died, she wrote *Wohin denn ich* (*Where Do I Go Now?* 1963), a moving collection of poems inspired by her loss.

A central theme in Kaschnitz's writings is the search for self. She often describes the plight of the individual in an impersonal, alien world. Influenced by her Christian faith and World War II, she frequently dealt with the issues of guilt and death. She used traditional forms but also experimented, developing her own unique style. Kaschnitz

received the guest chair for poetry at the University of Frankfurt and won numerous awards, including the prestigious Georg Büchner Prize.

Other Works by Marie Luise Kaschnitz

Circe's Mountain: Stories by Marie Luise Kaschnitz. Translated by Lisel Mueller. Minneapolis: Milkweed Editions, 1990.

Selected Later Poems of Marie Luise Kaschnitz. Translated by Lisel Mueller. Princeton, N.J.: Princeton University Press, 1980.

A Work about Marie Luise Kaschnitz

Pulver, Elsbeth. *Marie Luise Kaschnitz.* Munich: C. H. Beck, 1984.

Kauraka Kauraka (1951–1999) *poet*

Kauraka Kauraka was born in the village of Avatiu, Rarotonga, the Cook Islands. Kauraka's poetry reflects the interesting cultural roots of his heritage. His mother was a descendant of the Manihiki, and his father was part Manihiki, Mangaian, and Chinese. Kauraka went to New Zealand for his high school and college education and later went to Japan as a professional singer and musician for the Betela Dance Troupe. Kauraka graduated from the University of the South Pacific in Fiji in 1980 and became the language curriculum adviser to the Education Department in Rarotonga. He received his M.A. degree from the Anthropology Department in the University of Hawaii at Manoa in 1987. He became a full-time writer retelling, translating, and writing stories of the Pacific Islands. Kauraka founded Sunblossom Press in the Cook Islands and devoted his life to writing about the richness of Polynesian cultural tradition.

Kauraka's poetry reflects the ancient beliefs and traditions of his rich heritage. The images and metaphors in his poems are essentially Polynesian in nature. His talent for music shows distinctly in his poetry, which has a sing-song quality. Nature imagery (such as gardenias and coconut trees) and animal symbols (such as snakes, dolphins, and birds) constitute important elements of his poems.

In "Return to Havaiki" (1985), Kauraka uses the images of the *ngoio* (black noddy tern) and "great sky mushrooms" to reflect the natural richness of his Polynesian home, Manihiki.

Kauraka's experiences while traveling also give his poetry a unique blend of cross-cultural elements that reveal his desire to share cultural complexities, especially those of Polynesia. He often questions the abandoning of traditional culture to embrace unquestionably the cultural practices of modern Western society. In "Darkness within the Light" (1985), Kauraka beseeches the New Zealander of indigenous descent not to forsake his traditional roots. In another poem, "Children of Manuhiki, Arise" (1985), he laments the powerful influence of modernity on the younger generation of Polynesians who no longer heeds the oral traditions of their ancestors.

Kauraka's poems also bespeak the need to use the past to understand the future. All of these characteristics can be seen in the poems in Kauraka's collection, *Dreams of a Rainbow* (1987), which he wrote when he was still a graduate student in Hawaii. His respect for the traditional past was most aptly described in "Po, The Great" and "Three Warriors." In "Po, The Great", he celebrates the power of Po, the parent of all mythical gods of the Pacific Islands; in "Three Warriors," he personifies the three virtues of Polynesian heroes.

Kauraka's most important contribution lies in his ability to create a dialogue between different groups of people. Through poetry, he establishes a platform on which the older and more traditional generation interacts with the younger, modern one. His poetry leads to a better understanding of world culture and interaction between not only two different cultures but also two generations within a culture.

Other Works by Kauraka Kauraka

Manakonako = reflections. Auckland: Mana Publications, 1991.

Manihikian traditional narratives = Na fakahiti o Manihikian. New Zealand: Te Ropu Kahurangi, 1988.

Taku Akatauira = My dawning star: poems. Suva, Fiji: Mana Publications, 1999.

A Work about Kauraka Kauraka

Simpson, Michael, and John Untfrecker. *Dreams of the Rainbow: Poems by Kauraka Kauraka.* Honolulu: University of Hawaii at Manoa, East–West Center, 1986.

Kawabata Yasunari (1899–1972) *novelist and short-story writer*

Kawabata Yasunari was born to Kawabata Eikichi and Gen in Osaka. When he was young, his father, mother, grandmother and sister died, leaving him in the care of his nearly blind and terminally ill grandfather. In 1915, having also lost his grandfather, Kawabata moved to a middle-school dormitory, and then, having determined to become a writer, he studied Japanese literature at Tokyo Imperial University. In the 1930s, Kawabata became actively involved in the literary community, supporting young writers, working for magazines, and becoming a member of the censorious Literary Discussion Group, organized by the government as Japan entered World War II. Kawabata went into semiretirement in the late 1960s. In 1972, he was found dead, an apparent suicide, in his seaside apartment.

In 1921, Kawabata published his first story, "A View of the Yasukuni Festival," which garnered the attention of influential writer Kan Kikuchi (1888–1948). Even with his support, however, Kawabata's early stories were largely unsuccessful, perhaps due to their experimental style. In 1926, however, he published a novella written with more traditional literary idioms. The success of *The Izu Dancer,* about a walking tour of the Izu Peninsula near Tokyo, established Kawabata as a writer. A distinctive feature of his novels is the theme of unrequited longing. In *Snow Country* (1947), the protagonist Shimamura engages in an unfulfilling love affair with a geisha while secretly longing for a woman involved with another man. In 1950, Kawabata published one of his best works, *Sound of the Mountain* (1950), which won the literary prize of the Japanese Academy. The story, which catalogs the rambling thoughts of an aging patriarch, is distinctive for its stream-of-consciousness narrative.

Kawabata was a member of the literary movement called Shinkankakuha (Neo-Perceptionists). The movement attempted to find methods of bringing individual senses to life, chiefly through stream-of-consciousness narrative. Typically, his stories lack a traditional plot structure but excel in lyrical quality. His unique narrative style garnered attention internationally, and in 1968 Kawabata was the first Japanese writer to receive a Nobel Prize in literature.

Other Works by Kawabata Yasunari

Beauty and Sadness. Translated by Howard Hibbett. New York: Knopf, 1975.

The House of the Sleeping Beauties and Other Stories. Translated by Edward Seidensticker. Tokyo: Kodansha International, 1969.

A Work about Kawabata Yasunari

Gessel, Van C. *Three Modern Novelists: Sōseki, Tanizaki, Kawabata.* Tokyo: Kodansha International, 1993.

Kazantzakis, Nikos (1883–1957) *poet, philosopher, novelist*

Nikos Kazantzakis was born in Iráklion, Crete, and is considered one of the most important 20th-century Greek philosophers. He graduated from Athens Law School in 1906 and fought as a volunteer for the Greek army during the Balkan wars. After the wars ended, he traveled to Spain, Egypt, China, Japan, and Russia, publishing travelogues of his journeys.

Kazantzakis is much better known as a philosopher than as a writer. His work was influenced by the writings of NIETZSCHE, elements of marxism, and the basic philosophical beliefs of Christianity and Buddhism. He attempted to combine and harmonize these different ideas in his book *Askitiki*

(1927), which is considered the basis of his own philosophy. His epic poem *Odyssey: A Modern Sequel* (1938) is also among his well-known earlier works. It picks up Ulysses' tale where Homer left off and brings it to a more solid conclusion.

It was in the later years of his life, however, that Kazantzakis became famous for his novels, including *Zorba the Greek* (1946) and *The Last Temptation of Christ* (1955). Both of these works have since been made into films. The controversial nature of *The Last Temptation of Christ,* in which Jesus must face the greatest temptation of all, led to the Roman Catholic Church's banning of the book and to Kazantzakis's excommunication from the Greek Orthodox Church in 1955. The film version, produced in 1988, also caused much protest from conservative Christian organizations.

In 1956, Kazantzakis was awarded the International Peace Award. He died one year later in Germany, the same year that the first of his novels to be made into a film, *He Who Must Die* (1957) was presented at the Cannes Film Festival.

Other Works by Nikos Kazantzakis

At the Palaces of Knossos: A Novel. Translated by Themi and Theodora Vasils. Athens: Ohio University Press, 1988.

Buddha. Translated By Kimon Friar and Athena Dallis-Damis. San Diego, Calif.: Avant Books, 1983.

Works about Nikos Kazantzakis

Bien, Peter. *Nikos Kazantzakis, Novelist.* Bristol: Bristol Classical Press, 1989.

Dombrowski, Daniel. *Kazantzakis and God.* Albany: State University of New York Press, 1997.

Kemal, Yaşar (1923–) *novelist, poet*

Yaşar Kemal was born in Hemite, a hamlet in the province of Adana in southern Turkey. When Kemal was five, his father was murdered while praying in the mosque. Kemal found solace in his love of music and poetry. When he turned nine, he attended a school in the neighboring village. He completed his primary education in Kadirli where his family resettled, becoming the first villager from Hemite to complete his primary education.

Kemal wrote his first story in 1947 and worked as a public letter writer for the next three years. In 1950, he moved to Istanbul, where he found a job as a reporter for the daily newspaper *Cumhuriyet (Republic)*. Kemal's unique style of writing won him not only national but also international recognition. He was a fervent activist for human rights in Turkey, and his works and activities enhanced his fame as a spellbinding storyteller.

Kemal's enchantment with the Anatolian tradition of folk minstrels features prominently in his writings such as *Salman the Solitary* (translated 1998), in which the traveling bard assumes the narrator's role. Kemal's love of music and creativity allow him to enhance his talent as an animated and powerful storyteller. He writes with energy and devotion, drawing on the rich tradition of his Turkish heritage and the literary tradition of Anatolia. His works, though heavily imbued by his strong leftist political views, still preserve a certain idyllic quality, which bespeaks of optimism and romanticism.

In an interesting way, Kemal represents the romantic bard of the Anatolian past who writes and sings of social injustice. He has found balance between his appropriation of the genre of traditional literature and his concern with modern issues. His best-known novel is the epic *Memed, My Hawk* (1955), which won the Varlik Prize 1996 for Best Novel. Kemal has been short-listed for the Nobel Prize in literature many times, and his collection of articles won the annual Journalists' Association Prize.

Other Works by Yaşar Kemal

Anatolian Tales. Translated from the Turkish by Thilda Kemal. New York: Mead, 1969.

Iron Earth, Copper Sky. Translated from the Turkish by Thilda Kemal. London: Collins and Harvill Press, 1974.

Seagull. Translated from the Turkish by Thilda Kemal. New York: Pantheon Books, 1981.

A Work about Yaşar Kemal

Bosquet, Alain. *Yaşar Kemal on His Life and Art: Yaşar Kemal with Alain Bosquet.* Translated from the French by Eugene Hibert and Barry Tharaud. Albany, N.Y.: Syracuse University Press, 1990.

Keneally, Thomas (1935–   ) *novelist, playwright*

Thomas Keneally was born at Kempsey on the north coast of New South Wales, Australia. His father was a postman. He attended a Christian Brothers' school for his primary and high school education, and, at 17, he began to study for the Catholic priesthood. He abandoned this vocation in 1960 before his official ordination. Keneally taught for two years at the University of New England at Armidale before becoming a full-time writer. He was one of the few Australians who could rely on his writing to support himself and his family. Keneally has received three Commonwealth Literary Fund Awards, and his books have won two Miles Franklin Awards. He was awarded the Order of Australia in 1983 for his contributions to Australian literature. Keneally now lives in New York and Sydney.

Keneally's writing appeals to both Australian and international audiences because it deals with human issues that transcend all geographical and social boundaries. Using a mixture of humor and tragic irony, Keneally is able to capture the constant struggle of society to come to terms with its actions, its relationships with others, and its uncertainty. Keneally's past clearly influences his works. His first novel, *The Place at Whitton* (1964), is a mystery tale set in a Catholic seminary, while *Blood Red, Sister Rose* (1974) involves a female heroine character who resembles Joan of Arc. These two novels highlight the importance influence of the Catholic vocation as a phase in his past.

One of the major subjects represented in Keneally's works is his concern with history and its lessons. Using historical materials, he is able to examine historical events and their impact through the perspectives of his central characters in novels such as *Schindler's Ark* (1982) and *Bring Larks and Heroes* (1967). *Schindler's Ark* tells the true story of Oskar Schindler, a German industrialist who saved thousands of Jews from death during the Holocaust. This book was adapted and made into a movie, *Schindler's List,* in 1993. *Bring Larks and Heroes* narrates the story of Australians who fought in Vietnam during World War II.

Keneally's earlier novels tend to have a predominantly Australian setting. Books such as *The Fear* (1965) and *The Chant of Jimmie Blacksmith* (1972) are set in Australia. In *The Fear,* Keneally examines the experiences of a young boy growing up during World War II. The fears of war reaching Australian shores loom heavy in the imaginative mind of the boy as he begins to conjure imaginary visions of war atrocities and prisoner-of-war camps. *The Chant of Jimmie Blacksmith,* however, is a study of a history of interracial relations between the Aborigines and the Europeans. His later novels, beginning with *Blood Red, Sister Rose,* are set in locations including France, England, Yugoslavia, and the United States.

Keneally's novels cover a wide range of genres from fables to macabre murders and mysteries. His versatility can be observed in his writings from concise and didactic parables to ornately elaborate narratives. In all Keneally's novels, he is concerned with the connection between the past and the present. His motivation to write stems from his curiosity regarding the irony that human beings often find themselves in conflict with the conventions and values of the systems of authority that they help create. For instance, Schindler in *Schindler's Ark* tries to do the humane thing by assisting many Jews to escape even though the fear of being discovered by the fanatical Nazi government hovers constantly over his head.

Keneally's heroes and heroines act with integrity and honor despite their individual flaws. They are tragic figures trapped between the demands of unsympathetic institutions of authority and their own personal desires. In their attempts to do the right thing, they often flounder either in the seas of their guilt or under the destructive claws of the authority. Examples of these can be found in two of Keneally's characters, Ramsey and Maitland. Ramsey, in *The Survivor* (1969), finds himself caught in a vicious abyss of guilt and remorse for 40 years after he deserted his close friend and companion during an Antarctic expedition. Maitland, a priest–teacher in *Three Cheers for the Paraclete* (1968), finds himself the subject of a series of religious hymns poking fun at the absurdity of religious rules. The tragic nature of the characters' experiences is partially alleviated by Keneally's injections of humor into the harsh reality of their experiences. The message that Keneally clearly sends across to his readers is the recognition that in spite of their poignant experiences, these heroic characters are active shapers of their own worlds. This is perhaps a main reason that Keneally's novels are so appealing to readers all over the world: Readers are able to empathize with Keneally's protagonists. The human condition is a complex web, and people are victims as well as active participants in their destinies.

Keneally also writes in other genres such as drama, children's stories, nonfiction, and film scripts. His plays include *Halloran's Little Boat* (1968), which is an adaptation of his book *Bring Larks and Heroes,* and *Bullie's House* (1981), which examines early interactions between Australian Aborigines and the European settlers. In *Bullie's House,* the Aborigines show the white settlers their precious totems hoping that the latter would in return share their knowledge and technology, which the whites never quite do on equal terms. Keneally's greatest contribution lies in his ability to capture in essence and intensity the dramatic clash of two cultures, which constitutes an important theme in world literature.

Other Works by Thomas Keneally

The Great Shame: and the Triumph of the Irish in the English-speaking World. New York: Nan A. Talese, 1999.

The Playmaker. London: Sceptre, 1988.

A Season in Purgatory. New York: Harcourt Brace Jovanovich, 1977.

Three Cheers for the Paraclete. New York: Viking, 1969.

Towards Asmara. London: Hodder and Staughton, 1989.

Victim of the Aurora. New York: Harcourt Brace Jovanovich, 1978.

Works about Thomas Keneally

Beston, John. "Novelist's Vital Professionalism," *Hemisphere* 17, no. 10 (1973): 23–26.

Breitinger, Eckhard. "Thomas Keneally's Historical Novels," *Commonwealth News (Aarhus)* 10 (1976): 16–20.

Kincaid, Jamaica (Elaine Potter Richardson) (1949–   ) *novelist, short-story writer*

Jamaica Kincaid was born in St. John's, Antigua, and named Elaine Potter Richardson by her mother, Annie Richardson. Shortly after Kincaid's birth, Annie married David Drew, a carpenter and cabinetmaker, after whom Kincaid models her fictional fathers, not her biological father, Roderick Potter. Annie Richardson taught her daughter how to read and sent her to the Moravian school. Shortly after her 17th birthday, Kincaid traveled to the United States to work and study.

Elaine Potter Richardson officially changed her name to Jamaica Kincaid in 1973, partially to heighten her anonymity as a writer. In 1976, she started to work as a staff writer for *The New Yorker,* after George W. Trow, the *New Yorker*'s "Talk of the Town" editor, introduced Kincaid to the magazine's editor, William Shawn. Before long, Kincaid began to write the "Talk of the Town" column and by 1992 was using the metaphor of gardening to write about the effects of colonialism.

Critics have praised Kincaid's lyrical originality, her characterization, and the modernist narrative techniques in her depiction of Caribbean life, including colonialism, separation, and mother-child relationships. Kincaid voiced a lack of interest in First World approval, assuming a self-exiled literary position (in a 1990 interview with Donna Perry).

Ironically enough, critical attention and acclaim from First World critics—especially for her short-story collection, *At the Bottom of the River* (1983), and her novels, *Annie John* (1985) and *Lucy* (1990)—steadily increased. To quote R. B. Hughes in *Empire and Domestic Space in the Fiction of Jamaica Kincaid,* "Kincaid's novels illustrate alternative, conceptual, emancipatory spaces within idealised colonial territory. Her doing so depends upon her '. . . displacing the discursive structures of the (colonial) master subject,' and depends too '. . . on a sense of possibilities and self-representation beyond the territory defined by the dominant [culture].'"

Other Works by Jamaica Kincaid

Annie, Gwen, Lilly, Pam and Tulip. New York: Whitney Museum of Modern Art, 1986.

Autobiography of My Mother. New York: Farrar, Straus & Giroux, 1995.

A Small Place. New York: Farrar, Straus & Giroux, 1988.

Works about Jamaica Kincaid

Covi, Giovanna. *Jamaica Kincaid and the Resistance to Canons.* In Carole Boyce Davies and Elaine Savory Fido, eds., *Out of the Kumbla: Caribbean Women and Literature.* Trenton, N.J.: Africa World Press, 1990: 345–354.

Paravisini-Gebert, Lizabeth. *Jamaica Kincaid: A Critical Companion.* Westport, Conn.: Greenwood, Press, 1999.

Kirsch, Sarah (Ingrid Bernstein) (1935–   ) *poet, short-story writer*

Sarah Kirsch was born in Limlingerode, a village in the Harz Mountains. Her father worked in telecommunications for the East German government. Kirsch became a socialist at a young age. She earned a diploma in biology from the University of Halle and attended the Johannes R. Becher Institute for Literature in Leipzig from 1963 to 1965. Participating in the East German effort to build solidarity between workers and writers, Kirsch worked in factories and collective farms during the

1960s. She married the writer Rainer Kirsch in 1958.

Kirsch's first publication was a radio play for children that she cowrote with her husband in 1963. They also collaborated on her first poetry collection, *Gesprach mit dem Saurier* (*Conversation with a Dinosaur*, 1965), a volume of children's poems with a political edge. Her poems in *Landaufenthalt* (*A Stay in the Country*, 1967) combine descriptions of nature with political commentary. In the late 1960s, Kirsch defended the value of lyric poetry in the socialist state. Although her stand drew government criticism, the debate started a "lyric boom" among poets. In 1976, she protested when East Germany revoked the citizenship of the singer Wolf Biermann. As a result, she lost her membership in the Communist Party and moved to West Berlin.

Kirsch is known for her unique style that combines musicality and facility of language. She used intense nature images to describe human experiences and to bridge the gap between love poetry and the poetry of social production. She was especially concerned about the role of women in modern society in both private and public realms. Kirsch's influences include Bettina von ARNIM and the Russian poet Anna AKHMATOVA. Despite her political difficulties, Kirsch won numerous awards for her poetry and short-story collections in the 1970s and 1980s, including the Friedrich Hölderlin Prize.

Another Work by Sarah Kirsch

The Panther Woman: Five Tales from the Cassette Recorder. Translated by Marion Faber. Lincoln: University of Nebraska Press, 1989.

A Work about Sarah Kirsch

Hopwood, Mererid, and David Basker, eds. *Sarah Kirsch.* Cardiff: University of Wales Press, 1997.

Kiš, Danilo (1935–1989) *novelist, poet*

Danilo Kiš was born in Subotica, on the border of Yugoslavia and Hungary. His father, a Hungarian Jew, died in Auschwitz. Most of his family was killed during World War II except his mother, a Christian from Montenegro. Raised in Hungary and Montenegro, Kiš studied literature at the University of Belgrade and eventually worked as a teacher in France.

Kiš's work was greatly influenced by the loss of his family. His novels *Garden, Ashes* (1965) and *Hourglass* (1972) are monuments to his father's life and death. *A Tomb for Boris Davidovic* (1976) is a collection of stories about victims of Communist terror set in a politically oppressed Eastern Europe. In the title story of this collection, Boris repeatedly flees from prison and changes his name, only to be recaptured. The frequency of this pattern is both comic and tragic. This and the rest of the stories in the volume are short biographical sketches of a victim as hero, fighting against history and a pervasive sense of doom. The characters range from idealistic to opportunistic, from sadistic to compassionate, and the stories themselves from the absurd to the horrific.

Another of Kiš's works, based largely on personal narrative, is *Early Sorrows* (1969), a collection of stories about the often tragic childhood experiences of a Jewish boy in a small Serbian town near the Hungarian border during World War II. Kiš illustrates the dramatic change in the boy's life from peaceful serenity to horror and brutality after soldiers enter his village.

Kiš's work gained large international audiences primarily because noted writer Susan Sontag introduced Kiš to English-speaking readers. He has also been compared with Jorge Luis BORGES, to whom he explicitly admitted a debt, once indicating that the history of the short story can be divided into two distinct eras: before Borges and after Borges.

Other Works by Danilo Kiš

The Encyclopedia of the Dead. Translated by Michael Henry Heim. New York: Farrar, Straus & Giroux, 1989.
Hourglass. Translated by Ralph Manheim. Evanston, Ill.: Northwestern University Press, 1997.

A Work about Danilo Kiš

Birnbaum, M. D., and R. Trager-Verchovsky, eds. *History, Another Text*. Ann Arbor: University of Michigan Press, 1988.

Klausner, Amos

See OZ, AMOS.

Kogawa, Joy (1935–   ) *poet, novelist*

Joy Kogawa was born in Vancouver. As a second-generation Japanese-Canadian, or *nisei*, her work, including poetry, fiction, children's literature, and nonfiction, often reflects the perspectives of Japanese-Canadians. Kogawa and her family were evacuated to Slocan, British Columbia, and later to Coaldale, Alberta, during World War II. Kogawa received her education at the University of Alberta and taught elementary school in Coaldale. She also studied at the University of Toronto and at both the Anglican Women's Training College and the University of Saskatchewan. She married in 1957, had two children, and divorced in 1968.

Joy Kogawa has published several collections of poetry, essays, children's literature, and novels. Among her more notable works are the novels *Obasan* (1981), which focuses on the lives of Japanese-Canadians during World War II, and *The Rain Ascends* (1995), about a Protestant clergyman who abuses children. Kogawa has been active in lobbying the Canadian federal government to acknowledge and redress its decision to intern 20,000 Japanese Canadians during World War II.

Another Work by Joy Kogawa

Itsuka. Toronto: Viking, 1992.

Köhler, Barbara (1959–   ) *poet, essayist*

Barbara Köhler was born in Burgstädt, Germany. After passing the Arbitur (school-leaving exam), she studied literature at the Johannes R. Becher Institute in Leipzig. Her first collection of verse, *Deutsches Roulette* (*German Roulette*, 1991), es-tablished her as one of Germany's most innovative young poets. She followed up with a second collection, *Blue Box* (1995), and published internationally in journals such as *Poetry* magazine. She has also written for several newspapers. Köhler's several literary awards include the Leonce and Lena Prize (1991), the Else Lasker-Schuler Prize (1994), and the Clemens–Brentano Prize (1996).

Köhler's verse displays a restless yet precise passion, as seen in the poem "Self-portrait" (1991), and also combines traditional and contemporary forms. Her poems "Gedicht" ("Poem," 1991), "Ingeborg Bachmann Stirbt in Rom" ("Ingeborg Bachmann Dies in Rome," 1991), and "IV" (1991) reveal Köhler's common themes of yearning, mourning, and the memories of unhappy women, respectively. Köhler's writing shows an understanding of poetry's potential in bringing out the richness and fullness of language.

A Work about Barbara Köhler

Paul, Georgina, and Helmut Schmitz, eds. *Entgegenkommen: Dialogues with Barbara Köhler.* Atlanta: Rodopi, 2000.

Kokoschka, Oskar (1886–1980) *painter, poet, playwright*

Oskar Kokoschka was born in Pochlarn, Austria, to Gustav Kokoschka, a goldsmith, and Romana Loidl, a great storyteller who inspired his love for nature. Kokoschka graduated from state school, but he dreamed of becoming an artist and entered the Vienna School of Arts and Crafts, where he studied from 1905 to 1909. The revolutionary nature of his art was deemed scandalous by some instructors and administrators, and he was expelled after painting a particularly controversial painting.

Kokoschka's work often openly expressed sexual themes and other controversial motifs; indeed, the imagery in Kokoschka's poetry often resembled the strange and unusual images found in his graphic works. In 1908, Kokoschka published his first book of poetry, *The Dreaming Youth*. Along with the poems, the book contained reproductions of paintings that he specifically completed for the book. Kokoschka's early work was heavily influenced by SYMBOLISM; however, he is often credited with the foundation of EXPRESSIONISM.

The aim of the movement was to represent the subjective psychological experience through literature and other forms of art. *Murder, the Women's Hope* (1916), a short play completed by Kokoschka in 1907, became the basis for expressionist drama. In the play, first performed in 1909, the nameless Man confronts his impulsive sexual drives and attempts to free himself from the physical dependence associated with bodily functions. In a kind of crude sexual fantasy, the Man strangles the nameless Woman and then slaughters her female companions. The clearly demarcated antagonism between the male and female, violence, and sexual submission were persistent themes of Kokoschka's work. *Orpheus and Eurydice* (1923) pursues similar themes and comments on the turbulent relationship between Kokoschka and Alma Mahler, the widow of the famous composer Gustav Mahler (1860–1911). In many instances, however, his work was simply too overwhelming for the sensibility of the general public, and it never gained a wide appeal.

Kokoschka's painting became renowned for its surreal, dreamlike images, and it gained some popularity. He held an appointment as an art instructor between 1911 and the outbreak of World War I in Vienna and Berlin. Kokoschka served in the cavalry of the Austrian army during World War I and was wounded several times. After retiring from the army, Kokoschka continued working extensively on his paintings.

During the 1930s, Kokoschka's works were openly attacked by pro-Nazi newspapers in Austria and Germany. Kokoschka left Austria for Czechoslovakia in 1931 and then emigrated to England after the fall of Czechoslovakia to the Nazis. In Nazi Germany, Kokoschka's work was banned and was ridiculed by the authorities as an example of "degenerate art." During this time of turmoil,

Kokoschka mostly wrote essays on art and expressionist aesthetics.

After the end of World War II, Kokoschka returned to Austria and worked as an art instructor and theater designer. His gained international popularity by the 1950s, and his works were exhibited throughout the world. In 1971, Kokoschka published *My Life*, an autobiography in which he also presents his views on art and culture and provides engaging accounts of his personal relationships with famous artists of the expressionist movement.

Oskar Kokoschka is mainly remembered today for his paintings; however, his work in literature laid the ground for the seminal expressionist movement. His striking, often disturbing works challenge our epistemological notions about art and aesthetics. Today, Kokoschka's visual art and literary works are considered to be among the masterpieces of the 20th century.

Other Works by Oskar Kokoschka

Oscar Kokoschka Drawings, 1906–1965. Miami: University of Miami Press, 1970.
Plays and Poems. Translated by Michael Mitchell. New York: Ariadne Press, 2001.

Works about Oskar Kokoschka

Calvocaressi, Richard, and Katharina Schultz. *Oskar Kokoschka, 1886–1980*. New York: Solomon R. Guggenheim Foundation, 1986.
Whitford, Frank. *Oskar Kokoschka: A Life*. New York: Atheneum, 1986.

Kostrowitsky, Wilhelm Apollinaris de

See APOLLINAIRE, GUILLAUME.

Kumagai Yumiko

See KURAHASHI YUMIKO.

Kundera, Milan (1929–   ) *novelist*

Milan Kundera was born on April 1 in Brno, Moravia. The son of a concert pianist and musicologist, Kundera studied music and was a jazz musician in his youth. He soon turned to writing, publishing his first volume of poetry, *Clovek Zahrada Sirá* (*Man: A Broad Garden*) in 1953. This work, as well as two later poetry collections— *Poslední Máj* (*The Last May*, 1955) and *Monology* (*Monologues*, 1957)—were condemned by Czechoslovakian officials because of their ironic tone and erotic imagery. Kundera has repeatedly denied any political motivation behind his works.

Kundera was a Communist Party member twice, from 1948 to 1950 and from 1956 to 1968. Both times, he was expelled from the party for his supposedly unorthodox or anticommunist opinions. During this time, he also studied and taught in the Film Faculty of Prague's Academy of Music and Dramatic Arts. His political entanglements and disagreements with the Communist Party, however, ultimately led to the threat of a loss of his employment. Kundera was involved in the liberalization of Czechoslovakia in 1967 to 1968. After the Soviet occupation, he was attacked by the authorities for his liberal beliefs and ousted once again. In 1969, he was fired from his job, and his works were banned from legal publication in Czechoslovakia.

Kundera is best known internationally for his novel *The Unbearable Lightness of Being* (1984), which was made into a film of the same name in 1988 by American film director Philip Kauffman. The novel tells the story of four relationships. It primarily focuses on the character of Thomas, a man torn between loving his wife and sustaining his erotic adventures and extramarital affairs. At the beginning of the novel, Kundera asks, "What then shall we choose? Weight or lightness?" The lives of these characters are shaped not only by the choices they make but also by the desires and demands of society and history; thus, Kundera looks at the ways in which history and choice shape life and identity.

Kundera is a prolific writer. In his early career, several volumes of short stories, as well as a successful one-act play, *The Owners of the Keys* (1962), were followed by the publication of his first novel,

The Joke (1967; translated 1982). This comedic work takes an ironic look at the private lives of various people in Czechoslovakia during the years of Stalinism. It has been translated into numerous languages and has achieved international acclaim. This was followed by a second novel, *Life Is Elsewhere* (1969; translated 1974), about a hopeless romantic who embraces the 1948 Communist takeover. This novel was banned immediately from Czech publication. Kundera's subsequent novels, including *The Farewell Party* (1976), *The Book of Laughter and Forgetting* (1979; translated 1980), and *The Unbearable Lightness of Being* were banned in Czechoslovakia but were published in France and other countries. *The Book of Laughter and Forgetting* was among his most successful novels, perhaps because it pointed to one of the harsher truths of Kundera's homeland: humankind's propensity to deny or erase historical truths.

In a collection of essays titled *The Art of the Novel* (1988), Kundera writes that a novel must be "autonomous," that it should be created independently of any political belief system. In 1975, in response to the suppression of his work, Kundera was allowed to emigrate to France. He took a teaching post at the University of Rennes, where he remained on the faculty until 1978. In 1979, the Czech government revoked his citizenship. Kundera continues to write works that are humorous yet skeptical and pessimistic in their depictions of humanity, whether under Communist rule or elsewhere.

Other Works by Milan Kundera

Identity. Translated by Linda Asher. New York: Harper Flamingo, 1998.

Slowness. Translated by Linda Asher. Boston: Faber and Faber, 1996.

Testaments Betrayed. Translated by Linda Asher. Boston: Faber and Faber, 1996.

Works about Milan Kundera

Misurella, Fred. *Understanding Milan Kundera: Public Events, Private Affairs.* Columbia: University of South Carolina Press, 1993.

Petro, Peter, ed. *Critical Essays on Milan Kundera.*
New York: G. K. Hall, 1999.

Kunene, Mazisi (1930–) *poet*

Mazisi Kunene was born in Durban, South Africa.
He began writing poetry as a boy and by the age of
10 was already submitting poems to local newspapers and magazines. Kunene taught for four years
in Natal, where he obtained his master's degree. In
1959, he went to London to further his studies in
the School of Oriental and African Studies at the
University of London. In London, he founded the
Anti-Apartheid Movement and became the director of education for the South African United
Front. Kunene spent 34 years in exile in England
and the United States for his leadership in the antiapartheid movement. He finally returned to
South Africa in 1993 and became a professor in the
Department of Zulu Language and Literature in
the University of Natal, where he still works today.
In the same year, he was appointed Africa's poet
laureate in the United Nation's Education, Science
and Cultural Organization.

Kunene's poetry shows how the concerns and
themes of his Zulu heritage can be used to enhance
an understanding of South African history and society. His poems, such as "Encounter with the Ancestors" (1982), draw on the rich images and
symbols of Zulu myths. They reveal ideas such as
the virtues and wisdom of ancestors, which have
been transmitted from generation to generation in
Zulu oral tradition. His poetry expresses the relevance of these motifs in South African society today.

Kunene's intimate involvement in the political
movement against apartheid is also an essential element of his works, which, perhaps, explains why
his first volume of poems, *Zulu Poems* (1970), was
banned for many years in South Africa. One of his
two epic poems, *Emperor Shaka the Great,* celebrates the heroism and strength of Shaka Zulu, the
founder of the Zulu nation. Kunene's favorable depiction of Shaka as a hero challenges the Eurocentric portrayal of the man as a tyrannical despot.
His other epic poem *Anthem of the Decades* was

published in 1981. Both poems were first published in the Zulu language and later translated
into English.

In recognition of Kunene's contributions to
African literature, the Mazisi Kunene Library was
jointly established by Create Africa South and the
Kunene family. Its aims are to fund study in the
Zulu language, to publish and distribute Kunene
and other writers' works in the Zulu language, and
to provide research facilities for scholars interested
in South African history and society. Kunene's
writing stands apart from other African voices that
speak of alienation and anger. His works, especially
the two epic poems, showcase the glory and
richness of the African traditions and challenge
Western readers to accept and appreciate the importance of African cultures. His use of Zulu language and style also provides a medium through
which African cultural symbols and thought are
effectively transmitted without appropriating English or other European diction.

Another Work by Mazisi Kunene

The Ancestors and the Sacred Mountain. London:
Heinemann, 1982.

Works about Mazisi Kunene

Barnett, Ursula. *A Vision of Order: A Study of Black
South African Literature in English (1914–1980).*
Amherst: University of Massachusetts Press/London: Sinclair Browne, 1983.

Goodwin, K. L. *Understanding Poetry: A Study of Ten
Poets.* London: Heinemann, 1982.

Haynes, John. "Kunene's Shaka and the Idea of a Poet
as Teacher." *Ariel* 18, no. 1 (1987): 39–50.

Maduka, Chidi. "Poetry, Humanism and Apartheid: A
Study of Mazisi Kunene's *Zulu Poems,*" *Griot* 4,
nos. 1–2 (1985): 57–72.

Kunert, Günter (1929–) *poet, short-story writer*

Günter Kunert was born in Berlin four years before the Nazi rise to power. Because his mother was
Jewish, he faced discrimination and was prevented

from completing grammar school. After the war, he attended Berlin Kunsthochschule, an art institute. While a teenager, he switched his focus from art to literature and published his first poems and prose in the *Ulenspiegel* (*Joker*) magazine. An idealistic socialist at an early age, Kunert joined the Socialist Unity Party in East Germany in 1949. Three years later, he married Marianne Todten, whose critical assistance greatly benefited his writing career.

Kunert's first collection of poetry, *Wegschilder und Mauerinschriften* (*Road Signs and Wall Writings*, 1950), made a significant literary impact. In 1952, the German poet Bertolt BRECHT, one of Kunert's influences, praised him as a gifted young poet. During the following three decades, Kunert published more than 20 works of poetry, prose, and essays as well as one novel. In the mid-1960s, he became critical of East Germany's socialist government. In the 1970s, he joined Sarah KIRSCH and Christa WOLF in protesting the revoking of the singer Wolf Biermann's citizenship. Kunert was then harassed and lost his party membership. He moved to West Germany in 1979.

Kunert is considered a master of the epigram, the parable, the satire, and the use of aphoristic form to express a principle in a short work. His writing was serious, ironic, and grotesque. He took a firm stand against misuse of the language. Kunert frequently dealt with contemporary concerns— such as greed, poverty, and injustice—and was committed to remembering the victims of past persecutions. Although his writing became increasingly pessimistic after the mid-1960s, Kunert is known for the integrity of his work. His many awards include the Johannes R. Becher Prize.

Another Work by Günter Kunert

Windy Times: Poems and Prose. Translated by Agnes Stein. New York: Red Dust, 1983.

Kurahashi Yumiko (Kumagai Yumiko)

(1935–) *novelist, short-story writer*

Kurahashi Yumiko was born in Kōchi, Shikuoka Prefecture, to dentist Kurahashi Toshirō and his wife, Misae. Kurahashi entered Kyoto Women's College in 1953 and, in 1955, enrolled in Japanese Women's Junior College of Hygiene in Tokyo to become a dental hygienist at her father's practice. However, she surprised her family when, upon graduation, she enrolled as an undergraduate in the French Department of Meiji University. Upon completing the program, she started graduate school but returned home when her father died in 1962. Two years later, she married photographer Kumagai Tomihiro and later attended the University of Iowa's creative-writing program under a Fulbright Fellowship in 1966.

Kurahashi's writing garnered notice while she was still an undergraduate. Her short story "Party" (1960) won both the Meiji University Chancellor's Award in 1960 and the Women's Literary Award in 1961. She quickly followed with her first novel, *Blue Journey* (1961), a story about a woman's search for the man to whom she is engaged. In 1969, Kurahashi published *The Adventures of Sumiyakist Q*, which portrays the attempts of a man to convert people secretly to an imaginary ideology called Sumiyakism. Shortly after her return from studying in the United States, Kurahashi initiated a series of novels centered on the life of a woman named Keiko with the publication of *A Floating Bridge of Dreams* (1969). In this ongoing series, Kurahashi creates a parallel fictional world that continues through several generations of Keiko's family.

Kurahashi is known both for writing complex stories that are presented with striking clarity and for her inclusion of controversial subjects, such as incest and partner swapping, in her stories. In addition to her prizes for "Party," she won the Tamura Toshiko Award in 1963 and the Izumi Kyōka Memorial Prize in 1987.

Other Works by Kurahashi Yumiko

"The Monastery." Translated by Carolyn Haynes. In Van C. Gessel and Tomone Matsumoto, eds., *The Shōwa Anthology: Modern Japanese Short Stories.* Tokyo: Kodansha International, 1985.

The Woman with the Flying Head and Other Stories of Kurahashi Yumiko. Translated by Atsuko Sakaki. Armonk, N.Y.: M. E. Sharpe, 1998.

A Work about Kurahashi Yumiko

Sakaki, Atsuko. "(Re)canonizing Kurahashi Yumiko: Toward Alternative Perspectives for 'Modern' 'Japanese' 'Literature.'" In Stephen Snyder and Philip Gabriel, eds., *Ōe and Beyond: Fiction in Contemporary Japan.* Honolulu: University of Hawaii Press, 1999.

L

La Guma, Alex (1925–1985) *novelist, short-story writer*

One of South Africa's premier chroniclers of life under apartheid in South Africa, Justin Alexander La Guma was born into a trade-unionist household. This early involvement with socialist politics combined with his status as a Cape Town "coloured" (a person of mixed race ancestry according to apartheid laws established in 1948) conspired to make of La Guma a writer concerned with issues of class and race in all his writings.

His parents made him aware of his mixed-race heritage by stressing the various cultures that were his heritage. His maternal grandmother had come to South Africa from Indonesia; his maternal grandfather came from Scotland. His father was originally from what is now known as the Malagasy Republic. When La Guma was only 13 years old, he tried to get to Spain to fight against the fascists in the Spanish civil war, but he was turned down. Two years later, in 1940, he tried to enlist as a soldier to fight against Nazi Germany, but he was refused because of his slight build and unhealthy appearance. At 17, he went to work doing manual labor in a box factory where he developed a life-long awareness of the real concerns of working people.

In 1955, La Guma worked for a left-wing newspaper in Cape Town as a journalist until the apartheid government banned his work; he wrote political columns, reported on the absurdities of apartheid laws, and even penned a regular political cartoon. After the murders of unarmed blacks in 1960 by white policemen, an event since referred to as the Sharpeville Massacre, all antigovernment groups were banned, and La Guma himself was jailed for more than six months. He was later sentenced, in 1962, to five years under house arrest. The punishment meant that he could not leave his home, meet with any of his friends, or in any way communicate with those whose ideology he shared. In his novel, *The Stone Country* (1967), La Guma fictionalizes this experience, and several stays in prison in 1960 and 1961 when South Africa was under a state of emergency and many people were detained without being formally charged.

La Guma was banned from employment as a journalist during the early 1960s, and he turned to writing fiction as a result. The publication, in 1962, of a collection of short stories entitled *A Walk in the Night and Other Stories* marked the advent of something truly different in the South African literary tradition. In the lead story in the collection, the novella from which the collection takes its name, La Guma allows his characters to speak in a sanitized version of the Cape Town dialect that the real underclass spoke. Another story in the collection, "Tattoo Marks and Nails," focuses on a prison cell and is a precursor to *The Stone Country*. Although he was not the first South African writer to focus on working people and their problems, La Guma's concentration on the realistic representation of the poorest and most vulnerable of his culture's people marked him as a uniquely South African voice. For example, although Peter ABRAHAMS can very easily be seen as a literary pioneer for his focus on the poorest of South Africa's noncitizens in *Mine Boy* (1946) and other texts, La Guma allows the streets to speak for themselves. In many ways, he signals a resistance to the forms of the European literary tradition that had, to that date, influenced the vast majority of South African works written in English.

La Guma is an important figure in the literary tradition of South Africa because he points up something about the way people in the United States understand places like South Africa. Important critics such as Lewis NKOSI and J. M. COETZEE observed long ago that those of us who read about foreign cultures often view foreign texts as "sociological" documents; for example, a 1974 essay by Coetzee examines the reduction of the literary text to an example of an exotic culture. These astute critics also have observed that—worse—"weak" literature all too often is celebrated because its politics are right. But La Guma's works have both a deceptive, realist style and true literary merit. He is rightly read as much for the quality of his writing as for his content. As Cecil Abrahams states "He [La Guma] sees his task as similar to that of the African storyteller, namely that of recording events as told to him and fashioning the tale in such a manner that there is both a moral and an entertaining purpose involved."

Other Works by Alex La Guma

In the Fog of the Season's End. London: Heinemann, 1972.
Time of the Butcherbird. London: Heinemann, 1979.

Works about Alex La Guma

Abrahams, Cecil. *Alex La Guma.* Boston: Twayne, 1985.
Coetzee, J. M. "Man's Fate in the Novels of Alex La Guma." *Studies in Black Literature* 5.1 (Spring 1974).

Labrunie, Gerard
See NERVAL, GERARD DE.

Lagerkvist, Pär (Fabian) (1891–1974) *poet dramatist, novelist, short-story writer*

Pär Lagerkvist was born in Växjö, Sweden, to Anders Johan, a railway linesman, and Johanna (Blad) Lagerquist. Although he embraced Darwinism and political radicalism at a young age, Lagerkvist was influenced throughout his life by his parents' pietistic Christian faith. He attended the University of Uppsala in 1911 and 1912. In addition to writing, he briefly worked as a theater critic for a Stockholm newspaper in the late 1910s. He married Karen Dagmar Johanne Soerensen in 1918 and, after they divorced, married Elaine Luella Hallberg in 1925.

Lagerkvist first emerged on the literary scene as a poet. The second of his nine collections, *Ångest* (*Anguish,* 1916), described the despair and pain of World War I. The volume challenged the Swedish romantic tradition in verse and is considered the beginning of poetic modernism. Lagerkvist continued his search for aesthetic revolt and renewal in his dramas. He wrote 13 plays, including *Himlens Hemlighet* (*The Secret of Heaven,* 1919), which addressed the search for meaning in life. In the 1930s, Lagerkvist's dramas, plays, and short stories dealt with the issues of evil and fascism. After 1940, he focused on writing novels. *Dvärgen* (*The Dwarf,* 1944), considered by many to be his best work, explores the evil and creativity of humans.

Lagerkvist wrote more than 40 major works and has been translated into 34 languages. He was elected to the Swedish Academy of Literature in

1940 and won the Nobel Prize for Literature in 1951. His influences include the dramatist August STRINDBERG, and naivism, cubism, and fauvism in French painting. His literary career lasted a half-century and encompassed all major genres but still displayed a remarkable internal consistency. Lagerkvist wrote about faith, skepticism, death, and evil, and explored the mysteries of existence. The scholar Robert Donald Spector observed that in Lagerkvist's works "his major theme is a quest for a god who will replace the deity of his youth."

Another Work by Pär Lagerkvist

Guest of Reality. Translated by Robin Fulton. New York: Quartet, 1989.

A Work about Pär Lagerkvist

Spector, Robert Donald. *Pär Lagerkvist.* Boston: Twayne, 1973.

Lagerlöf, Selma (1858–1940) *novelist*

Selma Lagerlöf was born in Marbacka, Sweden. She was educated at home by her father, a retired army officer, and her grandmother. Lagerlöf's grandmother told her traditional tales of Sweden, which played an important role in the formation of her artistic imagination. In 1882, Lagerlöf went to the Royal Women's Superior Training Academy in Stockholm to prepare for a career as a teacher. After graduation, she taught in a school for girls for 10 years.

While teaching, Lagerlöf began writing her first novel. She sent early chapters to a literary contest in a local magazine and was awarded a publishing contract for the entire novel. Financially supported by her lifelong friend, the Baroness Sophie Aldesparre, Lagerlöf completed her first novel, *The Story of Gösta Berling* (1891). Gösta, a young adventurous hero, suffers a series of ordeals before he marries the dashing heroine, Countess Elizabeth, and finds peace in his life. The story was significant in the Swedish romantic revival of the late 1890s.

Lagerlöf's work appealed to people of all ranks. Her work was founded on the rich tradi-tions and deep cultural history of the Swedish people. With financial assistance from the Swedish Academy and a pension from Sweden's King Oscar, Lagerlöf resigned from teaching to concentrated on her writing. A journey to Egypt and Palestine between 1899 and 1900 inspired the publication of her first major and critically ac-claimed work, *Jerusalem.* The collection of stories describes the destructive effects of a conserva-tive, religious revival on a small Swedish commu-nity. The Ingmar family takes a journey to Jerusalem, and one of the family members is sold into slavery by another. Still another Ingmar re-nounces his engagement to the love of his life so he can marry a rich woman. The collection placed Lagerlöf on a prominent level in the literary world of Sweden.

In 1906, Lagerlöf published her best-known work, *The Wonderful Adventures of Nils.* The work was commissioned by the Swedish board of educa-tion to teach geography in the primary school. It tells the story of a naughty but courageous young boy, Nils, who is magically reduced to the size of a gnome. He travels throughout Sweden on the back of a gander who escapes the farm to join the flock of wild geese. From them, Nils learns courage, companionship, and commitment. Although this story is a fairy tale, it also provides, as it was meant to do, useful information about Swedish geogra-phy and life in Sweden. The story is loved and ad-mired throughout the world.

In 1909, Selma Lagerlöf became the first female writer to win the Nobel Prize for literature. When the Soviets invaded Finland in 1939, Lagerlöf do-nated the Nobel medal to raise money for the Finnish army. A truly amazing and courageous person, she helped a great number of German writers and artists to escape Nazi persecution by arranging to smuggle them into Sweden. This re-markable woman is not only a national writer of Sweden but also its national hero. She used her artistic talent to depict the cultural history and customs of her country. Selma Lagerlöf's work is still widely read throughout the world today, with the sad exception of the United States.

Other Works by Selma Lagerlöf

Girl from the Marsh Croft, and Other Stories. Translated by Greta Andersen. Iowa City: Penfield Press, 1996.

Invisible Links. Translated by Greta Andersen. Iowa City: Penfield Press, 1995.

Memories of Marbacka. Translated by Greta Andersen. Iowa City: Penfield Press, 1996.

A Work about Selma Lagerlöf

Edstrom, Vivi Bloom. *Selma Lagerlöf.* Boston: Twayne, 1982.

Laing, B. Kojo (1946–) *novelist, poet*

B. kojo Laing was born in Kumasi in the Ashanti region of Ghana. He was the eldest son of six children and was baptized Bernard Ebenezer, but he later dropped his Christian name in favor of his African identity. Laing's father was the first African rector of the Anglican Theological College in Kumasi. Although Laing's family belonged to the educated middle class, they were by no means rich. Laing had to sell snacks on the street in Accra when he was a child. His disgust with this experience influenced his perception of the city and is distinctly expressed in his writings. Laing spent the first five years of his early education in Accra and was later sent to Scotland in 1957, where he had both his primary and secondary education. In 1968, he graduated from Glasgow University with a master's degree, then returned to Ghana to join the civil service. Laing left the service in 1979 to work as an administrative secretary of the Institute of African Studies for five years and then headed Saint Anthony's School in Accra in 1984, where he still works today.

Laing emerged as an important poet in the 1970s but did not become very widely known until 1986 when he published his first novel, *Search Sweet Country* (1975). His search for spiritual meaning is most intensely expressed in this novel, which is an analogy of his own experience as a civil servant in the Ashanti region. In the novel, Laing explores the complexities of human relationships and the different responses of people from different backgrounds to the reign of a corrupt military government. The bittersweet flavor of Laing's writing reveals his continuous attempt, through language, to bridge the differences between physical reality and spiritual ideals.

Laing's love of nature is also clearly reflected in his writing. One of his favorite pastimes is hunting, which provides him with a source of imagery. In *Woman of the Aeroplanes* (1988), for example, Laing uses images that symbolize the natural, surreal, and human worlds. An example of Laing's use of nature imagery in the novel is his humorous personification of the lake, which becomes extremely jealous of the ducks that swim in its waters and refuses to ripple.

Laing was also deeply influenced by his life experiences, such as his father's religious devotion and early death and his own journeys and failed relationships. His poem "Funeral in Accra" commemorated his father's death and marked his rite of passage from youth to adulthood. This poem was published in 1968 together with two other poems, "African Storm" and "Jaw." These poems contain the metaphors of his psychological struggle between alienation and dislocation.

Laing's main contribution to world literature is his ability to create a hybrid of languages and images from both the traditional African and modern Western worlds. His works, such as *Godhorse* (1989), appropriate the common symbol of technology, such as the car, and by simplifying its locomotive movements, compare it with daily human actions, such as walking or transplanting crops in the fields. By carefully and cleverly blending mixed symbols and language, Laing reveals the complexity of interdependent relationships within society.

Another Work by B. Kojo Laing

Major Gentl and the Achimota Wars. London: Heinemann, 1992.

Laird, Christopher (1945–) *poet, writer, editor, producer, director*

Born in Trinidad, Christopher Laird is the author of poetry that has appeared in *The New Voices,* the *Caribbean Writer,* and *Kairi.* As editor of *Kairi,* he has striven to increase the visibility of writers from and about Trinidad and Tobago. Laird has also done a number of extensive interviews with cultural personalities, including novelist George LAMMING, carnival artist Peter Minshall, and actor and dramatist Slade Hopkinson.

Laird's poetry has been anthologized in *Voiceprint: An Anthology of Oral and Related Poetry from the Caribbean* (1989). In "Hosay," a seven-part poem published in *Voiceprint,* the speaker draws attention to himself with speech and musical rhythms, but then concludes the poem saying,

> I am silent now.
> I done talk.
> Until a mounting fire
> stretches me taut
> to move the air again.

As video producer, director, writer, and editor, Laird examines the Caribbean culture. One of Laird's projects, the *Caribbean Eye* videos, explores regional Caribbean philosophies, celebrations, and styles of music and drama. *Caribbean Carnivals* (1991), *Dramatic Actions* (1991), and *Women in Action* (1991) are three of the 13 half-hour, made-for-television *Caribbean Eye* videos from Trinidad's Banyan Studios.

Released in 1992, Laird codirected *And the Dish Ran Away with the Spoon* with Tony Hall. Produced as part of the BBC/TVE Developing World Series, the video uses poetry, interviews, music, and clips from television shows to highlight effects of American television broadcasts on local Caribbean cultures. It won best documentary and best video at Images Caraibes, the Caribbean Film & Video festival, and also best documentary at the Prized Pieces competition of the National Black Programmers Consortium of the United States. Laird's varied projects significantly facilitate the exploration and appreciation of Caribbean culture.

Other Works by Christopher Laird

Brown, Stewart, Mervyn Morris, and Gordon Rohlehr, eds. Selections in *Voiceprint: An Anthology of Oral and Related Poetry from the Caribbean.* Harlow, U.K.: Longman, 1989.
"Faith, Beauty and Blood." *Caribbean Writer* 5 (1991): 49–50.
"Jamestown Beach, Accra." *Caribbean Writer* 3 (1989): 44–45.

Lamartine, Alphonse de (1790–1869) *poet, novelist*

Alphonse Marie Louis de Lamartine was born to a family of minor nobility in Mâcon on October 10. He received a traditional education and, after spending a brief period of time in the army, traveled to Italy where he discovered much of the aesthetics of love and nature that would prevail in his works and that tie him closely to French ROMANTICISM.

His first published work, *Méditations Poétiques* (1820), met with immediate success. Within the 24 poems that compose this collection, Lamartine expressed his feelings about religion, love, and nature. Subsequent works, such as *Harmonies* (1830), developed his theme of lyricism and his musical tones. He also expressed his religious views in such works as *Jocelyn* (1836), a novel in verse, and *La Chute d'un Ange* (*An Angel's Fall,* 1838), an epic poem that describes an evil tyranny.

Politically, Lamartine tried to remain distant from party conflicts; however, his idealist philosophy tended toward democracy and the campaign for social justice. His *Histoire des Girondins* (*History of the Girondists,* 1847), a work that promoted and glorified the aims of a political group of moderate Republicans known as the Girondists during the French Revolution met with immense popular success. After competing unsuccessfully against Napoleon III for the presidency, Lamartine left politics to devote his life to writing.

Another Work by Alphonse de Lamartine

Poetical Meditations/Méditations Poétiques. Translated by Gervase Hittle. Lewiston, N.Y.: Edwin Mellen Press, 1993.

Works about Alphonse de Lamartine

Boutin, Aimee. *Maternal Echoes: The Poetry of Marceline Desbordes-Valmore and Alphonse de Lamartine.* Cranbury, N.J.: University of Delaware Press, 2001.

Fortescue, William. *Alphonse de Lamartine: A Political Biography.* New York: St. Martin's Press, 1983.

Lombard, Charles M. *Lamartine.* Boston: Twayne, 1973.

Lamming, George (William) (1927–)
novelist, poet, critic, teacher, lecturer, broadcaster, trade-union activist

George Lamming was born and raised in Carrington's Village, a former sugar estate on the outskirts of Barbados's capital, Bridgetown. Although Lamming's mother married after his birth, Lamming said, "it was my mother who fathered me." Lamming attended Combermere High School on a scholarship. There, teacher and writer Frank COLLYMORE encouraged his writing. When Lamming's courses ended in 1946, Collymore helped Lamming obtain a teaching position at El Colegio de Venezuela, a boarding school for boys of South American origin, in Port of Spain, Trinidad. That year Lamming also started publishing poetry in *Bim,* a literary magazine edited by Collymore. From 1947, the BBC's "Caribbean Voices" series broadcast Lamming's poems and occasional short prose pieces. Themes Lamming explored during this period—frustration with West Indian cultural life and artists' preference for imported culture—reappear in later works as well.

In 1950, Lamming sailed to England with other West Indian immigrants, including the novelist Samuel Selvon, and briefly worked in a factory and hosted a book program for the BBC West Indian Service while writing. Lamming dedicated his first novel, *In the Castle of My Skin* (1953), to his mother and Frank Collymore. This fictional account of the West Indian experience quickly garnered critical acclaim in the United States and England. In the preface, U.S. novelist Richard Wright describes Lamming's prose as "quietly melodious," and in an essay entitled "George Lamming's *In the Castle of My Skin*" (1954), the novelist NGUGI WA THIONG'O calls the work "one of the great political novels in modern 'colonial' literature."

Lamming's subsequent works explore West Indian history, culture, and politics. After completing *The Emigrants* (1954), a novel that follows a group of young men of Lamming's generation from the West Indies to London, Lamming returned to the Caribbean to gather material for his third novel, *Of Age and Innocence* (1958), set on the fictitious island of San Cristobal. This novel examines relationships formed during colonial history, as does Lamming's fourth novel, *Season of Adventure* (1960). In a 1989 interview archived online by *Banyan Limited,* Lamming said that *Season of Adventure* was "probably the first" and "only" novel "which is in a sense devoted to the elevation of the steelband not only as a moment of great culture and triumph, but also showing the way in which cultural activity can be so decisive in political life." Published the same year as *Season of Adventure, The Pleasures of Exile* (1960), a collection of essays, examines West Indian colonialism.

Two more novels published in the early 1970s, *Water with Berries* (1971) and *Natives of My Person* (1972), use allegory to examine guilt produced by colonialism and carried by English and Caribbean characters. Some critics consider the latter work as Lamming's major work, while others criticize its ideological representation of characters. In 1974, Lamming edited *Cannon Shot and Glass Beads: Modern Black Writing,* an anthology examining black responses to white racism.

In later years, Lamming devoted his attention to lecturing and essays, regularly contributing to the journal *Casa de las Américas,* published in Havana. Since entering academia as a writer-in-residence and lecturer at the University of the West Indies in

1967, Lamming has been a visiting professor at the University of Texas at Austin and the University of Pennsylvania, a teacher at the University of Miami's summer Institute for Caribbean Creative Writing, and a lecturer in Denmark, Tanzania, Kenya, and Australia. Regarded as one of the most perceptive commentators on the West Indies, Lamming is also considered one of the most important Caribbean West Indian novelists.

Other Works by George Lamming

Coming, Coming Home: Conversations II: Monographs. Philpsburg, St. Martin: House of Nehesi, 2000.

"Concepts of the Caribbean." In Frank Birbalsingh, ed., *Frontiers of Caribbean Literatures in English.* New York: St. Martin's Press, 1996.

Drayton, Richard, and Andaiye, eds. *Conversations: George Lamming Essays, Addresses and Interviews, 1956–1990.* London: Karia Press, 1992.

Works about George Lamming

Hulme, Peter. "Reading from Elsewhere: George Lamming and the Paradox of Exile." In Peter Hulme and William H. Sherman, eds., *The Tempest and Its Travels.* Philadelphia, Pa.: University of Pennsylvania Press, 2000.

Phillips, Caryl. "George Lamming." *Wasafiri: Journal of Caribbean, African, Asian and Associated Literatures and Film* 26 (Autumn 1997).

Silva, A. J. Simoes da. *The Luxury of Nationalist Despair: George Lamming's Fiction as Decolonizing Project.* Atlanta, Ga.: Rodopi, 2000.

Lampedusa, Giuseppe Tomasi di
(1896–1957) *novelist*

Giuseppe Tomasi di Lampedusa was born in Palermo, Italy, to Prince Guilio di Lampedusa and his wife, Beatrice. He grew up in a palace and had a great fondness for his upbringing, which he was able to capture in his writing. He had an extremely close, nearly suffocating relationship with his mother through much of his life. From age 16 to 18, he attended the Liceo-Ginnasio Garibaldi school, where he proved to be an excellent scholar in philosophy, history, and Italian. He went on to study law at the University of Rome.

From 1916 to 1918, Lampedusa fought in the Italian Alps in World War I and was wounded and captured. After the war, he traveled extensively in Italy as well as to London, Paris, and other European cities. In the 1920s, he immersed himself in a self-directed course of study in European history and literature. His favorite writers included William Shakespeare, John Keats, and Charles BAUDELAIRE.

In 1954, Lampedusa began a course of lectures on literature, one of which was published as the book, *Lessons on Stendahl* (1977). He then turned to novel writing and began *The Leopard,* a book about the Italian aristocracy, which was published posthumously in 1958. As a diversion from this book, Lampedusa began his autobiography. It was a chance to write about his beloved family palace, which had nearly been destroyed in an air attack during World War II.

Lampedusa had an active and varied life that contributed to the richness of his work. He left his mark in the worlds of education, literature, and history. David Gilmour, his biographer, writes, "his work will survive because he wrote about the central problems of the human experience."

A Work about Giuseppe Tomasi di Lampedusa

Gilmour, David. *The Last Leopard: A Life of Giuseppe di Lampedusa.* New York: Pantheon, 1988.

Langgässer, Elisabeth (1899–1950) *poet, novelist, short-story writer*

Elisabeth Langgässer was born in Alzey, Germany, to Eduard and Eugenie Dienst Langgässer. Her father, an architect, was a Jew, but she was raised as a Catholic. After Eduard's death in 1909, the family moved to Darmstadt, where Langgässer attended the Viktoria-Schule. After passing the school-leaving exam in 1918, she taught at a primary school in Grieshein. In 1935, she married the theologian Wilhelm Hoffmann.

Langgässer wrote book and theater reviews before publishing her first poetry collection, *Der Wenderkreis des Lammes* (*The Tropic of the Lamb,* 1924). Her first novel, *Proserpina* (1933), won the Literary Prize of the Association of Women's Citizens. In 1936, the Nazis forbade her from further publication because she was of Jewish descent; she defied the ban with a short-story collection in 1938. After World War II, she gained wider popularity and critical acceptance. Her novel *Das Unauslöschliche Siegel* (*The Indelible Seal,* 1946) earned praise from writers Thomas MANN and Hermann BROCH.

The influence of Franz KAFKA and James Joyce is evident in Langgässer's works. Many considered her a religious writer, but she often included nonreligious aspects such as war and economic hardship in her writing. Langgässer's poems explore the conceptions of *soul* and *psyche* and investigate the evil side of human nature. Not afraid of paradoxes, she also dealt with the irrationality, beauty, and brutality of human passions. The literary scholar Hermann Boeschenstein writes that Langgässer "is able to do what has often been termed the prerequisite to the revitalization of modern religious literature; she repeats the old truths in an exciting new way."

Another Work by Elisabeth Langgässer

The Quest. New York: Knopf, 1953.

A Work about Elisabeth Langgässer

Gelbin, Cathy S. *An Indelible Seal: Race, Hybridity and Identity in Elisabeth Langgässer's Writings.* Essen: Die Blaue Eule, 2001.

Lao She (Shu Qingchun) (1899–1966)
novelist

Shu Qingchun was born Shu She-yü on February 3 in Beijing. When foreign allied forces attacked Beijing in the 1900 Boxer Rebellion, his father was killed. His mother did laundry so that Shu Qingchun could be privately tutored. He graduated from Beijing Normal in 1918 and became headmaster of a primary school, managing it so efficiently that he was appointed a government post in 1920. He returned to teaching and did social work with various Beijing organizations while studying English at Yenching University. In 1924, he taught Chinese at the Oriental School of London University and assisted in translating a 16th-century Chinese novel.

Inspired by the writing of Charles Dickens, Shu began to write (under the pseudonym Lao She), completing his first novel, *The Philosophy of Lao Zhang* (1926), while in London. The book was published as a serial in Shanghai to critical and popular acclaim because of its patriotism and realistic portrayal of a civil servant, two students, and a contemptible schoolmaster.

In 1930, Lao She returned to China and taught Chinese at Qilu and Shandong Universities, where he continued to write prolifically. His most popular work was the social critique *Lo-t'o Hsiang-tzu* (*Rickshaw Boy,* 1936), a novel about making a living in Beijing. In 1940, he completed the trilogy about Japanese-occupied Beijing, *Four Generations Under One Roof.*

As one of the country's foremost patriotic writers, Lao She was active in the anti-Japanese movement during the Sino-Japanese War. He was elected director of general affairs of the All-China Resist-the-Enemy Federation of Writers and Artists. In 1946, he traveled to the United States as a visiting lecturer and wrote his last novel, *The Drum Singers,* published in the United States in 1952. He returned to celebrate China's new Communist regime in 1949 and wrote plays, all of which became classics of socialist literature, including *Dragon Beard Ditch* (1950), *Teahouse* (1956), *All the Family Are Blessed* (1959), and *Beneath the Red Banner* (1964).

Although he served high posts in the Chinese Writers Association, Lao She was no exception to the suppression of writers during the Cultural Revolution. Unable to contend with the disgrace of public denunciations and criticisms, he committed suicide on August 24. He was posthumously "rehabilitated" by the Communist Party in 1979, and his complete works were published.

Other Works by Lao She

Blades of Grass: The Stories of Lao She. Honolulu: University of Hawaii Press, 1999.

Cat Country: A Satirical Novel of China in the 1930s. Translated by William A. Lyell. Columbus: Ohio State University Press, 1970.

Heavensent. Translated by Xiong Deni. San Francisco: China Books and Periodicals, 1986.

Teahouse: A Play in Three Acts. Translated by John Howard-Gibbon. Beijing: Foreign Languages Press, 1980.

Works about Lao She

Vohra, Ranbir. *Lao She and the Chinese Revolution.* Cambridge, Mass.: East Asian Research Center, Harvard University, 1974.

Wang, David Der-Wei. *Fictional Realism in Twentieth-Century China: Mao Dun, Lao She, Shen Congwen.* New York: Columbia University Press, 1992.

Lasker-Schüler, Else (1869–1945) *poet, novelist*

Else Lasker-Schüler was born in Elberfeld, Germany, to Aron Schüler, a banker, and Jeanette Schüler. The youngest of six children, Else was deeply devoted to her mother, who encouraged Else's early interest in poetry. Paul, Lasker-Schüler's older brother, also helped develop her strong passion for poetry. As a Jewish family, the Schülers had difficulty in the social environment of Germany. Because of constant teasing by the Catholic and Lutheran children, Else had to quit elementary school and was tutored at home by her parents.

In 1890, Lasker-Schüler suffered the painful loss of her mother. Four years later, she married Jonathan Lasker. Lasker-Schüler separated from her husband in 1899 after refusing to acknowledge him as the father of their son Paul. Along with her son, she moved to Berlin in 1899 where she immediately became immersed in the artistic and cultural life of the city. Lasker-Schüler frequented various literary cafés throughout Berlin where she composed poetry, made sketches, and conversed with other artists. For the next 10 years, although she associated with various literary groups, such as the expressionists (*see* EXPRESSIONISM), her work does not appear to have been influenced by them.

In 1913, Lasker-Schüler traveled to Russia with the goal of securing the release of her longtime friend Johannes Holzmann, who had been arrested for revolutionary activities and leadership in anarchist circles. Her mission was unsuccessful, but it provided plenty of material for her writings. During World War I, Lasker-Schüler lost many friends, such as the Austrian poet Georg TRAKL. As a result of these experiences, she became deeply committed to pacifism.

In 1932 Lasker-Schüler received the Kleist prize, one of the highest literary honors in Germany. The atmosphere in German society, however, was becoming dangerous for her with the rise of the National Socialists (Nazi) Party. One of the newspapers controlled by the Nazis commented on Lasker-Schüler's award: "The pure Hebrew poetry of Else Lasker-Schüler has nothing to do with us Germans." Fearing for her life, Lasker-Schüler promptly left Germany for Switzerland. Arriving without luggage, she spent six nights sleeping on a bench in a Zurich park but survived by giving poetry readings and selling her drawings and sketches, as well as on generous gifts from her friends and readers. She spent several years living in Switzerland and Jerusalem, where she died in 1945.

Lasker-Schüler's early poetry was first published about 1899. Through the years, her poetry became more and more complex, often treating concrete ideas with abstract images. Her first collection of poetry, *Styx* (1902), reveals some qualities of the Expressionist school that are characterized by decorative and emotional imagery, as seen in "Coolness" (1902): "In the white blaze / Of bright roses / I want to bleed to death." As Ruth Schwertfeger notes, "Preoccupation with spiritual reality dominates Lasker-Schüler's thinking."

Lasker-Schüler clearly considered herself a Jewish poet: In the poem "My People," published in *The Seventh Day* (1905), she openly identifies herself with the Jewish people: "I have traveled the diaspora / From my blood's fermentation / Constantly over in me again." Lasker-Schüler's fascination with her Jewish roots also led to her constant longing for Jerusalem, which she visited five times during her life.

Lasker-Schüler's banishment from Germany was a painful experience and one to which she returns over and over in her poetry. In "Banished" (1934) she longs for Germany, which she always considered her homeland: "Where is the breath my life exhaled? / Exiled dreamer I glide between pale hours / Companion to wild game. I used to love you." Lasker-Schüler considered herself a German to the end of her life.

Else Lasker-Schüler's poetry did not become widely popular until the end of the World War II. Today, she is considered to be among the best poets of Germany. In 1953, at a poetry reading dedicated to the memory of Else Lasker-Schüler, the poet Gottfried Benn referred to her as "the greatest lyric poet Germany ever had." Lasker-Schüler's work is not well known outside of German-speaking countries because, as many critics and scholars claim, the complexity of her verse renders it virtually untranslatable. Recent translations, however, have been more successful, and her works are now available in more than 12 languages.

Other Works by Else Lasker-Schüler

Selected Poems. Translated by Jeanette Demeestere-Litman. New York: Green Integer, 2000.
Star in my Forehead. Translated by Janine Canan. New York: Consortium, 1999.

A Work about Else Lasker-Schüler

Yudkin, Leon I. *Else Lasker-Schueler: A Study in German Jewish Literature.* Washington, D.C.: B'nai B'rith Book Service, 1991.

Lautreamont, Comte de (Isadore-Lucien Ducasse) (1846–1870) *poet*

Isadore Ducasse, who adopted the pen name and title of Comte de Lautreamont, was born in Uruguay on April 4, 1846, to French parents. His father was a consular officer; his mother died when he was 18 months old. When he was 10 years old, his father left him with relatives in France, where he attended school and earned a reputation as a sullen, introverted student who disliked math and Latin. Lautreamont, however, became interested in literature and, as an independent thinker, developed ideas and attitudes that would eventually earn him a permanent place in French literary history.

After leaving school at age 19, Lautreamont traveled abroad, made some literary contacts, and then returned to Paris to begin his first major work, *Les Chants de Maldoror* (1869). The title of this work has been subject to various interpretations, ranging from "dawn of evil" to "evil from the beginning." It is a macabre prose poem in which the main character celebrates evil with religious fervor. Themes within the work include rebellion against God, the image of Christ as a rapist, and a bitter protagonist whose decomposing and disfigured body is a haven for animals who have taken up residence in it while he still lives.

For the publication of *Maldoror,* he assumed the pseudonym Lautreamont, a name that is taken perhaps from Eugène Sue's novel *Lautreamont,* whose protagonist is similar in attitude to the main character in *Maldoror.* Part of the work was first printed privately in 1868, most likely with financial assistance from Lautreamont's father. The entire work was printed in 1869, but the publishers, fearing prosecution because of the blasphemous nature of the piece, opted not to make the text available for purchase.

Lautreamont tried in vain to convince the publishers to make his work available. He also began another collection, this time celebrating hope and faith, but he died before completing it.

Nine years after his death, Lautreamont's works were finally published. They met with little notice, however, until members of the surrealist movement in the 1920s began to focus on Lautreamont as a thematic forerunner of their own ideals.

Another Work by Comte de Lautreamont

Maldoror; and Poems. Translated by Paul Knight. Hardmonsworth, U.K.: Penguin, 1978.

A Work about Comte de Lautreamont

Bachelard, Gaston. *Lautreamont.* Translated by Robert S. Dupree. Dallas, Tex.: Dallas Institute of Humanities and Culture, 1986.

Lawson, Henry (Larsen, Henry Hertzberg; Henry Archibald)
(1867–1922) *short-story writer, poet*

Henry Lawson was born on the goldfields of Grenfell, New South Wales, Australia. He was the eldest son of a Norwegian sailor, Peter Lawson, and his wife, Louisa. His mother was actively involved in publishing and was a famous leader of the women's rights movement in Australia. Lawson's early life was difficult: His family was poor, and an ear infection caused him to lose his hearing by the time he turned 14. His parents eventually separated, and his mother moved to Sydney. Lawson later moved to Sydney as well and became deeply influenced by his mother's radical friends.

Lawson's writings reflect his bitter life experiences. His inability to communicate because of the deafness led him to develop a keen habit of observing people. Lawson's works are about watching people and observing their actions. He used his powers of observation and his past experiences to enhance his writing. The major themes of Lawson's poems revolve around the Australian bush. Growing up in the bushland, Lawson knew the hardships of bush life and drew inspiration from the lessons learned coping and living with nature and the land, as can be seen in most of his short stories, including "The Drover's Wife," published in his collection *While the Billy Boils* (1896). Lawson found an affinity with the bush that he could not feel from human company. The celebratory tone of such poems as "The Roaring Days" (1889) and "Andy's Gone with Cattle" (1888) contrasts with the estrangement that the poet clearly felt in observing people.

Lawson's writings also reflect his deep concern for political and social issues. Some of his major poems of political and social protest include "The Watch on the Kerb" (1888) and "The Men Who Made Australia" (1901), which highlight the alienation and despair that are shared among most of Australia's struggling population. These same themes can be seen in his short stories "In the Storm That Is to Come" (1904) and "The Union Buries Its Dead" (1896).

Lawson's isolation increased as he failed to find happiness in marriage. He resorted to heavy drinking and spent most of his later life in a state of delirium and mental instability. His writing declined as his health collapsed. He began to write autobiographical works as he sought to hang on to his sanity. At his death, he was the first Australian writer to be granted a state funeral. Lawson's contribution to Australian and world literature lies in his accurate but starkly depressing portrayal of the difficult lives of the Australian lower classes, especially the much neglected regions of the Australian countryside and bush areas.

Other Works by Henry Lawson

The Bush Undertaker and Other Stories. Sydney: Angus and Robertson, 1994.
Henry Lawson: Short Stories. Edited by John Barnes. New York: Penguin, 1986.

Works about Henry Lawson

Philips, A. A. *Henry Lawson.* Boston: Twayne, 1970.
Wright, Judith. *Henry Lawson.* Melbourne, Australia: Oxford University Press, 1967.

Léger, Alexis Saint-Léger
See PERSE, SAINT-JOHN.

Leiris, Michel (1901–1990) *novelist, nonfiction writer*

Noted for his work as anthropologist and writer, Michel Leiris was born in Paris to an upper-class family. He became a serious student of chemistry but was soon drawn to the Bohemian world of Parisian cafés and cabarets where he first encountered and then became enamored with the growing surrealist, and DADA movements.

Leiris was first introduced to surrealism by his close friend André Masson. He focused for a time on writing poetry in the surrealist fashion but by the 1920s abandoned the movement. With Georges BATAILLE and others, Leiris formed the College de Sociologie. Leiris had an abiding interest in the cultures of Central America, Africa, and the Caribbean, and the college formed a launching point for his extensive fieldwork in Ethiopia and the Sudan. Many of his writings come from his experiences there, including *L'Afrique fantôme* (1933), a travel account of his voyages.

Leiris's other writings include a four-volume autobiography, *La Règle du jeu*, the first volume of which was originally published in English as *Manhood*. The entire work was eventually translated and titled *Rules of the Game*. He also wrote a detailed biography of Francis Bacon and conducted several anthropological studies.

Leiris lived out his life in Paris with his wife, the owner of Galérie Louise Leiris, a prominent art institution of the postwar era. It is because of her interest in the arts that Leiris also wrote extensively on the modern artists of the period, such as Miró, Giacometti, Bacon, Lam, and Duchamp.

Other Works by Michel Leiris

Aurora: A Novel. Translated by Anna Warby. London: Atlas, 1990.
Broken Branches. Translated by Lydia Davis. San Francisco: North Point Press, 1989.
Nights as Day, Days as Night. Translated by Richard Sieburth. New York: Rizzoli, 1988.
Rules of the Game. Translated by Lydia Davis. Baltimore: Johns Hopkins University Press, 1997.

A Work about Michel Leiris

Hand, Sean. *Michel Leiris: Writing the Self.* New York: Cambridge University Press, 2002.

Leopardi, Giacomo　(1798–1837)　*poet, essayist, philosopher*

Giacomo Leopardi was born in Recanti, now Marche, Italy, to Count Monaldo Leopardi and Marchesa Adelaide Antici. His upbringing was so sequestered that he was 20 years old before he left his home unaccompanied. Leopardi was a precocious youth and at 12 had surpassed the educational level of his tutors. He was a bibliophile and a polyglot who learned seven languages, including, Greek, Latin, and German. As a young man, he made translations and wrote commentary on the classics and at age 15 produced his first book, *History of Astronomy.* Although he grappled with blindness and a hunchback, his passion for writing saw him through his maladies.

Leopardi's crowning masterpiece was the book of poetry *I Canti* (1831). His poems were very personal statements of his life, loves, and loneliness. In his poem "To Italy," he states, "If but the gods be willing / Endure as long as your renown endures." In his poem "The Solitary Life," he strikes a more despairing note: "On earth, unhappy people find no friend / Or refuge left for them except cold steel."

Giacomo Leopardi is considered the greatest literary figure of 19th-century Italy for his poetry, essays, and translations. According to Leopardi's biographer J. H. Whitfield, no Italian poet aside from Dante has attracted such a circle of devoted admirers as Leopardi. Whitfield summarizes Leopardi's contribution to Italian literature: "[he] sees the poet as potentially a philosopher, and the philosopher as potentially a poet; and though it has been fashionable, especially in Italian criticism, to set the two as opposites, the marriage of the terms is most nearly achieved in the case of Leopardi."

Other Works by Giacomo Leopardi

The Canti: With a Selection of His Prose. Manchester, U.K.: Carcanet, 1998.
Leopardi: Selected Poems. Translated by Eamon Grennan. Princeton, N.J.: Princeton University Press, 1997.

Works about Giacomo Leopardi

Nisbet, Delia Fabbroni-Gianotti. *Heinrich Heine and Giacomo Leopardi: The Rhetoric of Midrash.* New York: Peter Lang, 2000.

Press, Lynne, and Pamela Williams. *Women and Feminine Images in Giacomo Leopardi*. Lewiston, N.Y.: Edwin Mellen Press, 1999.

Whitfield, J. H. *Giacomo Leopardi*. Oxford: Blackwell, 1954.

Lermontov, Mikhail (1814–1841) *poet, novelist*

Mikhail Yuryevich Lermontov was born in Moscow, Russia, to Yuri Lermontov, a retired army captain, and Maria Lermontov, a descendent of an aristocratic family. After the death of his mother in 1817, Lermontov was sent to his affluent grandmother, Elizabetha Stolypin. He received an excellent education from private tutors, and in 1827, he enrolled in a prestigious academy in Moscow that was sponsored by the royal family. Young Lermontov, surrounded by the most prominent intellectuals and writers in Russia, began to compose poetry in 1828. In 1830, he traveled with his grandmother to the family estate outside Moscow, where, in idyllic surroundings, he read intensively and wrote poetry.

Lermontov was heavily influenced by ROMANTICISM. George Gordon, Lord Byron (1788–1824) and Aleksandr PUSHKIN were his favorite poets. After a few unsuccessful years at the Moscow University, Lermontov joined the army as a junior officer in 1832. After the death of Aleksandr Pushkin in a duel in 1835, Lermontov wrote a commemorative poem, "On the Death of the Poet," in which he suggested that the government had been involved in the scandal that led to the duel and may even have paid Pushkin's opponent. The poem was widely popular but was considered incendiary by the authorities. Lermontov was demoted and exiled to the Caucasus, an isolated, mountainous region of Russia. The material for most of Lermontov's prose came from his experiences in the Caucasus. Lermontov composed a heroic poem, "The Song of the Merchant Kalashnikov" (1837), about a man whose heroism consists in following his inner principles rather than the pressures of society. Lermontov returned to St. Petersburg in 1838, after his grandmother made numerous petitions on his behalf. In 1840, Lermontov was sent back to the Caucasus, as a punishment for dueling.

Lermontov enlisted in a regiment that was responsible for putting down a violent rebellion by Chechen forces. After receiving an award for bravery in combat, he was allowed to return to St. Petersburg in 1841. While in St. Petersburg, he published a collection of poems and completed *Demon* (1828–41), a long narrative poem about a love affair between a fallen angel and a mortal. The poem reveals Lermontov's aversion to religion and his love for rugged, primitive landscape.

Shortly before his death, Lermontov completed one of the greatest novels in Russian literature, *A Hero of Our Time* (1840). Based on Lermontov's experiences in the Caucasus, this classic work of psychological realism examines the psyche and emotions of the disenchanted aristocrat Pichorin.

Nearly all of Lermontov's works were critically acclaimed and widely popular during his lifetime, but his personal relationships were often turbulent and dramatic. He made many enemies during his short life, largely because of his cynical and, at times, cruel disposition. Like his hero Aleksandr Pushkin, Lermontov was shot and killed in a duel.

Lermontov's reputation as a poet is only second to Pushkin's in Russia. His stirring poetry is remarkable for its lyricism and for its skillful and ingenious use of metaphor. Lermontov made a dramatic contribution to the poetic tradition of Russia, revealing new ways in which the Russian language could be extended, molded, and shaped into a dramatic lyrical form. He is not very well known outside Russia because his poetry is extremely difficult to translate; today, however, he is recognized as one of the most influential and seminal figures of the Russian literary landscape.

Other Works by Mikhail Lermontov
A Hero of Our Time. Translated by Vladimir Nabokov. New York: Knopf, 1992.

Major Poetical Works. Translated by Anatoly Liberman. Minneapolis: University of Minnesota Press, 1984.

Works about Mikhail Lermontov

Garrard, John. *Mikhail Lermontov.* Boston: Twayne, 1982.

Golstein, Vladimir B. *Heroes of Their Times: Lermontov's Representation of the Heroic Self.* New Haven, Conn.: Yale University Press, 1992.

Levi, Primo (1919–1987) *novelist, nonfiction writer*

Best known for his autobiographical *If This Is a Man* (1947), an account of survival in a Nazi concentration camp, Primo Levi was born in 1919 to a middle-class Jewish family in Turin. Growing up under Benito Mussolini and his fascist, anti-Semitic regime, Levi learned little about his heritage as a child. He was able to enter the University of Turin to study chemistry just before laws were enacted in 1938 to prohibit Jews from academic study. He graduated in 1941 at the top of his class, one year after Italy allied with Germany during World War II.

During the war, Levi began to write articles for *Giustizia e Liberata,* a resistance magazine. He was captured in December 1943 while attempting to make contact with a partisan group in northern Italy. He was first interred at a transitional camp in Fossoli but was soon deported to the major concentration camp at Auschwitz. Traveling to the camp in a convoy of 650 prisoners, he was one of only 24 survivors. Forced to work in one of the laboratories, he was spared the gas chambers but not the memory of those around him who did not survive.

After the camp was liberated by the Soviets in 1945, Levi returned to Turin where he secured work as a chemist. He returned to his family's old manor home and began to write. *If This Is a Man* was written in the form of a memoir documenting his internment at Auschwitz. Although the subject matter was gruesome and intense, part of Levi's appeal was his ability to abstract himself from his surroundings and take on the role of an objective, scientific observer. The work was not without compassion, but neither did it seek to capitalize on the tragedy of life in a concentration camp. The book was an instant success, selling more than a half-million copies in Italy before being translated into eight languages as well as being adapted for radio broadcast and theatrical production. A sequel to the book, *The Truce* (1963), detailed Levi's eight months spent wandering the remains of a war-torn Europe immediately after his liberation. The focus of the work is the difficulty a survivor faces when he or she is allowed to return, after great trauma, to a normal life.

By 1961, Levi had become the general manager of a paint factory, which enabled him to save enough money to retire in 1977 and devote himself full time to his writing. All of his works are in some way autobiographical. *The Periodic Table* (1975) uses the elements as a background; each element represents an event that is then recorded in memoir form as a meditation on the past. In all, the work is comprised of 21 separate entries, ranging from his encounter with an official from Auschwitz to a homage to his Jewish heritage. *If Not Now, When* (1989) focuses on the emerging sense of Jewish pride, coupled with an historical account of Russian action against the Nazis.

Levi's final work, *The Drowned and the Saved* (1986), is a collection of essays relating the ever-present memory of the Holocaust to the fact that anti-Semitism still exists even though the war is over. It was published one year prior to Levi's death, an apparent suicide. He struggled for much of the last 40 years of his life to reconcile the fact that he had survived life in a concentration camp.

Levi's greatest contribution to world literature is the legacy he left behind. His works give great insight into the life of a Jew and a survivor.

Another Work by Primo Levi

The Voice of Memory: Interviews, 1961–1987. Translated by Robert Gordon. New York: New Press, 2001.

A Work about Primo Levi

Kremer, Roberta S., ed. *Memory and Mastery: Primo Levi as Writer and Witness.* Albany: State University of New York Press, 2001.

Li Feigan

See BA JIN.

Lim, Shirley Geok-Lin (1944–) *novelist, poet*

Shirley Geok-Lin Lim was born in historic Malacca, a small town on the west coast of Malaysia. Lim's childhood was marked by feelings of abandonment, deprivation, and suffering, caused by her mother's abandoning her and her five brothers when they were still young. As the only girl in the family, Lim often felt neglected and marginalized; she nevertheless completed her high school education in a Catholic convent and went on to the University of Malaya. She taught for two years before going to the United States to obtain graduate degrees at Brandeis University in Massachusetts. Lim taught briefly at Westchester College before moving to Santa Barbara in 1990. She is currently professor of English and Women's Studies at the University of California and professor of English and head of the English Department at the University of Hong Kong.

Lim is an animated writer who is able to draw on her rich cultural origins and experience to elevate her poetry and prose. Her writings bespeak the emotional longing she holds for her homeland, even as they dramatize her grappling with issues of ethnicity, gender, and identity as an Asian American living in the United States. In her poem, "Bukit China" (Malay name for "Chinese Hill") (1994), for example, Lim examines the theme of displacement and loss as experienced by her Chinese forefathers who crossed the South China Sea in the distant past to seek fortune in the reputedly rich "Southern Ocean" in Southeast Asia. Issues of ethnicity and identity are most poignantly expressed in her collection *Life's Mysteries: The Best of Shirley Lim* (1995). In one poem in the collection, "A Pot of Rice," Su Yu reaffirms her own identity as she cooks a pot of rice in her New York apartment to offer to her dead father. In another poem, "Transportation in Westchester," the subject of interracial relationships takes on a new

shape when the Asian-American protagonist realizes her own prejudice through her interactions with African Americans.

Lim has received many awards, honors, and prizes for her critical and literary contributions. Her first book, *Crossing the Peninsula and Other Poems* (1980), won the Commonwealth Poetry Prize in 1980; a work she edited, *The Forbidden Stitch: An Asian-American Women's Anthology* (1989), was the recipient of the 1990 American Book Award.

Other Works by Shirley Geok-Lin Lim

Among the White Moon Faces: An Asian-American Memoir of Homelands. New York: The Feminist Press, 1996.
Another Country and Other Stories. Singapore: Times Books International, 1982.
Joss and Gold. New York: The Feminist Press, 2001.
What the Fortune-Teller Didn't Say. Albuquerque, N. Mex.: West End Press, 1998.
Writing Southeast Asia in English: Against the Grain, Focus on Asian English Language Literature. London: Skoob Books Publications, 1994.

Lispector, Clarice (1920–1977) *novelist*

Clarice Lispector was born in Ukraine on December 10 but moved to Recife, Brazil, when she was only two months old and remained there for the rest of her life. Although it is likely that her parents, Ukrainian Jews, spoke Yiddish at home, she often denied it because she so strongly identified herself as Brazilian. The family later moved to Rio de Janeiro where she eventually completed her college studies. At the age of 23, she married her former classmate, Maury Gurgel Valente, who had become a diplomat. As a result of his career, they traveled widely, allowing her the opportunity for many new experiences, which certainly contributed to her career as a writer.

One year after her marriage, Lispector published her first novel, *Near to the Wild Heart.* The book was very well received, and she wrote several novels throughout her lifetime, including among the best-known, *Family Ties* and *The Passion of G.H.* In addition she wrote short stories. Her final book, a short novel, *The Hour of the Star*, recounts the life story of a poor Brazilian girl and considers the issues of otherness and understanding.

Lispector's work has been more popularized outside of Brazil than that of many other female Brazilian authors who remain mostly unknown in the United States. This is largely because of Hélène CIXOUS, a French writer who is currently a university professor in the United States. She has written several books of criticism and even a novel inspired by Clarice Lispector's work. Lispector's novels tend to concern family relationships, moral uncertainty, and social isolation that so many 20th-century novelists have focused on. Lispector died in Rio de Janeiro, Brazil, on December 9, one day short of her 57th birthday, having made extraordinary contributions to Brazilian literature.

Other Works by Clarice Lispector

Family Ties. Arlington: The University of Texas Press, 1972.

The Hour of the Star. New York: New Directions, 1977.

The Passion of G.H. Minneapolis: University of Minnesota Press, 1989.

Works about Clarice Lispector

Cixous, Hélène. *Reading with Clarice Lispector.* Minneapolis: University of Minnesota Press, 1990.

Peixoto, Marta. *Passionate Fictions: Gender, Narrative, and Violence in Clarice Lispector.* Minneapolis: University of Minnesota Press, 1994.

Liu E (Liu Tieh Yun) (1857–1909) *poet, novelist*

Liu E was born the son of a scholar official in Liuhe in the Jiangsu Province. He was a good student with diverse interests and was very open to new ideas. He worked variously as a doctor, a merchant, and a government administrator, in addition to writing. He had friends in high places but was also adaptive to Western influ-

ences during the late Qing (Ch'ing) dynasty when China was especially guarded against them. This would ultimately damage his career and reputation.

Liu E wrote and published poetry and fiction throughout his life but is known primarily for writing one of the first Chinese novels in a vernacular language, *The Travels of Lao Can (Ts'an)*. As a serial that began publication in 1903, and as a complete book in 1907, it is considered to be one of the first modern novels because of its accessible vernacular language and its satiric and pointed critique of official corruption. The novel opens with the title character Lao Can's allegorical dream that equates China with a leaking, sinking ship. Lao Can offers potential solutions in his dream, including the use of new technical instruments and other Western innovations. After the dream ends, the novel then follows Lao Can, an itinerant and eccentric doctor, on his travels through the country. Inspired by his dream to effect change, Lao Can encounters cruel officials who are insensible to the plight of the Chinese people and closed to the possibility of improvements.

Liu E suffered at the hands of official corruption himself, and the parallels to Lao Can are many; in fact, many of the officials in the novel bear names very similar to Liu E's own colleagues. When Liu E suggested building a railway in the city of Zhili, he was attacked by conservative officials. Eventually, in 1908, he was banished to Xinjiang, China's western barren lands, for associating with foreign merchants during the Boxer Rebellion. He died in exile.

A Work about Liu E

Holoch, Donald. "The Travels of Laocan: Allegorical Narrative." In M. Dolezelova-Velingerova, ed., *The Chinese Novel at the Turn of the Century.* Toronto: University of Toronto Press, 1980.

Lorca, Federico García

See GARCÍA LORCA, FEDERICO.

Lu Xun (Lu Hsün; Zhou Shuren)

(1881–1936) *short-story writer, essayist*

Zhou Shuren, who adopted the pen name Lu Xun, was born September 25 into a family of declining social status in Shaoxing, Zhejiang province. His grandfather directed his schooling, which was less rigid than a traditional education. By age 11, he was an avid reader of popular literature and nonfiction but lacked interest in classical Confucian texts.

In 1893, when Zhou Shuren's grandfather was charged for taking bribes in the examination system and imprisoned, he went to live with his mother's family. He was deeply affected by the shift from a wealthy lifestyle to a poor one, later writing that it illuminated his understanding of the world.

In 1902, Zhou Shuren moved to Japan. Eager to better the conditions of China's people, he studied medicine at Sendai Medical College but maintained interests in literature and philosophy and read Western publications. He was especially influenced by Russian writers such as GOGOL and CHEKHOV. However, when he watched a newsreel from the Russo-Japanese War of 1904–05 of a captured Chinese spy being tortured, he changed his course of study; the inhumanity in the footage affected Lu Xun deeply. Subsequently, he participated in democratic and nationalistic activities and focused on writing as a means to effect social change, believing that literature would uplift the collective Chinese "spirit."

While still in Tokyo, Lu Xun edited the journal *New Life* and published essays in the Communist journal *Henan* on Western philosophy, sometimes collaborating with his brother, the writer Zhou Zuoren. In 1909, he returned to China and taught middle-school biology in Hangzhou and Shaoxing. After the Nationalist Revolution in 1911, Lu Xun accepted a position with the education ministry, where he studied and compiled Buddhist sutras. He began to publish poems and fiction in the popular journal *New Youth* in 1918, including "The Diary of a Madman," a short story about a man who suffers from paranoid delusions of the widespread practice of cannibalism. It is considered the first Chinese modernist short story because of its subjective, first-person narrative. He also submitted "random essays" and "random thoughts," which were published as such in the magazine. He accepted a lectureship at National Beijing University in Chinese literature in 1919 but soon returned home to take care of personal matters. There, he was moved to write stories about the debilitating effects of the old Chinese way of life on conditions in his hometown.

By 1921, back in Beijing and teaching at Beijing Normal University, he became established as a fiction writer and one of the leading writers of the May Fourth Movement, with more than 50 stories published in *New Youth*. He also wrote his first collections of stories, *The Outcry* (1923) and *Hesitation* (1926). The stories in these collections were inspired by the folk tales and myths of Lu Xun's childhood, but they were often dark and brooding. Perhaps his most famous work is the novella *The True Story of Ah Q* (1922), about a lonely laborer from a poor village. Despite failing at all his endeavors, Ah Q blindly interprets each failure as a victory and is eventually unfairly executed because of his foolishness. The story demonstrates Lu Xun's contempt for the similar myopia of Chinese society toward its sociopolitical and economic plight.

Lu Xun left Beijing in 1926 for Guangdong and Macau and often engaged in debates with the new breed of communist writers who advocated SOCIALIST-REALISM in literature. He grew disillusioned with the Nationalist Party and became a Communist in 1929. He was active as a founder of the League of Left-Wing Writers in 1930 but never joined the Communist Party itself. He turned to translating Soviet theory and attacking Nationalists, antileftists, and Western writers. He became one of the leading socialist intellectuals, teaching at various universities, including Xiamen and Zhongsan, and editing numerous journals, including *Wilderness, Tattler,* and *Torrent.* Even when he contracted pulmonary tuberculosis in 1933, he continued to contribute articles on a near-daily basis to the newspaper *Shen Pao.* He died on October 19 in Shanghai. At his funeral, he was eulogized as the "national soul," and the Communist

Party canonized him posthumously. Today, he is revered as one of China's greatest writers whose contributions to modernism and communist literature are held up as the highest literary ideals.

Other Works by Lu Xun

Call to Arms (Chinese/English Edition). Beijing: Foreign Language Press, 2000.

Diary of a Madman and Other Stories. Translated by William Lyell. Honolulu: University of Hawaii Press, 1990.

Lu Xun: Selected Poems. Translated by W. J. F. Jenner. Beijing: Foreign Languages Press, 1982.

Selected Stories of Lu Xun (Chinese/English Edition). Beijing: Foreign Language Press, 2000.

Works about Lu Xun

Lee, Leo Ou-fan. *Voices from the Iron House: A Study of Lu Xun.* Bloomington: Indiana University Press, 1987.

Lyell, William A. *Lu Hsun's Vision of Reality.* Berkeley: University of California Press, 1976.

Machado de Assis, Joaquim Maria
(1839–1908) *short-story writer*

Machado de Assis was born in Rio de Janeiro, Brazil, on June 21. The son of a mulatto father and a white mother, Machado de Assis's racial background has often been remarked upon. He lost his mother when he was very young and became extremely attached to his stepmother, who encouraged his education and put him through public school. After his father died in 1851, she accepted a job in a local college, and Machado de Assis was forced to leave school and work, but it is likely that he continued attending some classes intermittently at her place of employment. Machado de Assis published his first poem, "Ela," in a journal at age 16, thus beginning a long and prolific literary career. He became one of the most important Brazilian literary figure of the second half of the 19th century.

Machado de Assis published 200 short stories in newspapers and magazines and chose 68 to be published in anthologies. Many critics consider him to be the master of the Brazilian short story, and his influence on other writers has been widespread. In his short stories, he takes up many themes from Brazilian life and also addresses various areas of the human psyche; for example, in "The Fortune-teller," published in a collection titled *Various Stories*, from 1897, he writes about the question of destiny. The story tells about three friends: a couple and their single male friend. The wife and the male friend are having an affair, and they are afraid the husband may have found out. Each goes separately to see a fortune-teller about their destiny, with surprising results. In an earlier story, "The Mirror," from an 1882 collection, he writes about the interior and exterior life of one man. The story is told in the first person; the main character recounts the process of his realization that all humans are actually two people. The person we are inside is not the person we dress in the mirror. His narrative is psychologically compelling, again with a startling finish. Although Machado de Assis rarely touches on the issue of race in his stories (something for which Gilberto FREYRE criticized him, stating that his style was too Europeanized), he does treat the question of slavery in some of his short stories. Brazil was the last country in the Northern Hemisphere to abolish slavery in 1888, so this was a public question that marked the author's lifetime. In an 1899 collection of short stories, Machado de Assis published the story "Father against Mother" that examines the struggle between a poor man and a mulatto slave woman. He and his wife will be forced to give up their baby because of lack of finances if he cannot raise money. He is a slave catcher by profession. At the last moment, he sees a mulatto slave woman whose reward price is very high. However, she is pregnant and begs him not to take her back. In the conclusion, he is forced to make a difficult choice in this ethical dilemma.

Machado de Assis was friendly with many great literary figures of his day. He enjoyed meeting with these friends and discussing intellectual issues. From this, came the idea of founding the Brazilian Academy of Letters. He and his circle of peers founded the academy in 1897. At the initial meeting, they elected him as the academy's first president, a position he held until his death. Because of his great importance to Brazilian literature, the Brazilian Academy of Letters is also called the House of Machado de Assis.

Other Works by Joaquin Maria Machado de Assis

The Devil's Church and Other Stories. Arlington: University of Texas Press, 1977.
The Posthumous Memoirs of Brás Cubas. New York: Oxford University Press, 1997.

A Work about Joaquin Maria Machado de Assis

Schwarz, Roberto. *Misplaced Ideas: Essays on Brazilian Culture.* New York: Verso, 1992.

Machado y Ruiz, Antonio (1875–1939)
poet

Born in Seville, Spain, the son of liberal intellectuals, Antonio Machado y Ruiz became a French teacher and lived in the province of Castile, where he found the somewhat stark landscape more in keeping with his seriousness than that of Andalusia, the more verdant province of his birth. His poems portray the sober, dramatic Castilian landscape, and it is its nature that guides him. Machado, like Juan Ramón JIMÉNEZ, was a member of the GENERATION OF 1898, a group of writers who sought a moral and cultural rebirth for Spain. They analyzed the problems of the social

framework of Spain and prescribed cures. A fondness for simplicity and landscape characterizes Machado's work. With his brother, the poet Manuel Machado (1874–1947), he also wrote plays.

Machado attended the Institución Libre de Enseñanza, considered the best learning institution of its kind in Spain at that time. The education he received there had a profound influence on his work. There, he developed his love of nature and adopted tolerance, respect, patriotism, and austerity as his way of life.

In 1888, he and his brother began to attend theater, befriending actors and even doing a little acting. In 1893 his father died. The subsequent death of his grandfather left the family in a precarious financial situation and interrupted Machado's education. He then tried unsuccessfully to work in a bank and, in 1898, moved with his brother to Seville, where he began to write poetry.

The principal influences on his poetry were Juan Ramón Jiménez, Gustavo Adolfo BÉCQUER, and Rosalía de CASTRO. In his first book of poems, *Soledades* (1903), the poet searches for himself in time, in love, and in death. An important theme in all his work is time, something that he perceives as alive and personal. He often searches for love and lost youth.

Machado was forced to leave Spain in 1936 because of his political beliefs. He crossed the Pyrenees on foot and died a month later in France.

Other Works by Antonio Machado y Ruiz

Barnstone, Willis S., ed. and trans. *Six Masters of the Spanish Sonnet: Francisco de Quevedo, Sor Juana Inés de la Cruz, Antonio Machado, Federico García Lorca, Jorge Luis Borges, and Miguel Hernández.* Carbondale: Southern Illinois University Press, 1993.
The Landscape of Soria. Translated by Dennis Maloney. Fredonia, N.Y.: White Pine Press, 1985.
Trueblood, Alan S., ed. *Antonio Machado: Selected Poems.* Cambridge, Mass.: Harvard University Press, 1988.

Works about Antonio Machado y Ruiz

Cobb, Carl. *Antonio Machado.* Boston: Twayne, 1971.

Johnston, Philip G. *The Power of Paradox in the Work of Spanish Poet Antonio Machado.* Lewiston, N.Y.: Edwin Mellen Press, 2002.

Machado y Ruiz, Manuel (1874–1947)
poet, playwright, critic

Manuel Machado y Ruiz was born in Seville, Spain. His family were prominent and wealthy members of the city's middle class. His grandfather was a university professor and an expert in Spanish music and folklore. The Arabic inflections of Seville and his grandfather's studies of folk traditions led Machado y Ruiz to emphasize Arab imagery in his poetry.

Though he published few poems, he was one of the central figures of Spanish MODERNISM. His poetry resembles the work of Rubén DARÍO, the key figure of Latin American Modernism, but with more emphasis on the cultivation of aesthetic pleasure and less on inner anguish.

Machado y Ruiz was a member of the GENERATION OF 1898 and, like other members of that movement, he was concerned with revitalizing Spain's national identity. He believed this would be achieved by celebrating Spain's inner Arab spirit, which had been repressed by hundreds of years of Catholic rule.

His use of symbolism shows a clear influence of the poet VERLAINE, whose works he read when he was a young man studying in Paris. By combining modern trends from Europe and Spanish folk traditions, Machado y Ruiz was a forerunner to the poet GARCÍA LORCA.

Machado y Ruiz also modernized a number of plays by the Spanish dramatist Lope de Vega in collaboration with his brother Antonio MACHADO Y RUIZ. Machado y Ruiz had a sophisticated literary sensibility, and his literary style influenced lyric poetry in Spain and the world into the 20th century.

A Work about Manuel Machado y Ruiz

Brotherston, Gordon. *Manuel Machado: A Revaluation.* Cambridge, U.K.: Cambridge University Press, 1968.

Madariaga, Salvador de (1886–1978)
historian, essayist

Born in La Coruña, Spain, to a Spanish colonel, Madariaga held many jobs during his lifetime. He studied engineering in Paris and returned to his homeland to work for the Spanish railways. Then he went to London, was an editor for the *Times,* and wrote articles about World War I that were later published as *La Guerra Desde Londres* (*The War from London,* 1917).

In 1922, he was named head of the disarmament section of the League of Nations. He taught at Oxford (1928–31) and then was Spanish ambassador to the United States and France. He resigned in 1936 but did not participate in the Spanish civil war (1936–39). In disagreement with the Spanish dictator, Generalísimo Francisco Franco, he never returned to Spain while Franco was in power. During World War II, he worked for the BBC, broadcasting in Spanish, French, and German to Europe. He visited Spain in 1976 and was received into the Academia Española 40 years after his election into it, the ceremony having been postponed until after Franco's death.

Madariaga wrote in Spanish, French, and English. His works include historical works (biographies of Hernán Cortés, Columbus, and Simón Bolívar) and literary criticism (*Guía del lector del Quijote,* 1926). In *Englishmen, Frenchmen, Spaniards* (1928), he comments on national characteristics. His book *España* (1930) is an important historical interpretation of Spain and exemplifies Madariaga's ambition to familiarize the rest of the world with Spain.

Other Works by Salvador de Madariaga

Anarchy or Hierarchy. New York: Macmillan, 1978.

Don Quixote: An Introductory Essay in Psychology. Westport, Conn.: Greenwood, 1980.

Latin America between the Eagle and the Bear. Westport, Conn.: Greenwood, 1976.

A Work about Salvador de Madariaga

Preston, Paul. *Salvador de Madariaga and the Quest for Liberty in Spain.* Oxford: Clarendon Press, 1987.

Maeterlinck, Maurice (1862–1949) *poet, playwright, novelist, essayist*

Count Maurice-Polydore-Marie-Bernard Maeterlinck was born in Ghent, Belgium, to an affluent family. Educated at a Jesuit college, he originally studied to be a lawyer but practiced law only for a brief time before turning his interests and talents to writing.

During a trip to Paris, Maeterlinck came in contact with several members of the literary community, such as Villiers de l'Isle Adam, who became one of Maeterlinck's greatest literary influences. Maeterlinck eventually moved to Paris to pursue his writing career.

Although his later works were mostly dramatic in nature, his earliest published efforts were poetic, his first published work being the collection of poems *Ardent talons* (1889). He published his first play, *La Princesse Maleine,* in 1899, and it was well received, particularly by Octave Mirbeau, the literary critic of *Le Figaro,* whose praise of the work transformed Maeterlinck into an almost overnight success.

Maeterlinck's works are characterized by symbolist (*see* SYMBOLISM) themes, including a concern with the metaphysical, mysticism, and an awareness of death. This is particularly evident in *The Intruder* (1890) and *The Blind* (1890). Even his ostensibly love-themed works such as *Pelléas et Mélisande* (1892), *Alladine et Palomides* (1894), and *Aglavaine et Sélysette* (1896) share this same bleak undertone, as do the works in which he developed his mystical ideas: *The Treasure of the Humble* (1896), *Wisdom and Destiny* (1898), and *The Buried Temple* (1902). Even some of Maeterlinck's later works, such as *Joyzelle* (1903) and

Marie Magdeleine (1909), focus prevalently on death, but by World War I, he began to dwell on an almost fantasylike optimism. This optimism can be found in his play *The Burgomaster of Stilemonde* (1918). His *Oiseau bleu* (*The Blue Bird,* 1908), intended for children, also struck a positive note. His best-known play, however, is *Monna Vanna* (1902), set in an exotic 15th-century Pisa, which deals with a moral dilemma of a beautiful wife.

In 1911, Maeterlinck was awarded the Nobel Prize in literature. In his later years, he turned his attention to writing philosophical essays and, in 1932, was awarded the title of count in Belgium.

Another Work by Maurice Maeterlinck

The Life of the Bee. Translated by Alfred Sutro. New York: Dodd, Mead, 1970.

A Work about Maurice Maeterlinck

Knapp, Bettina. *Maurice Maeterlinck.* Boston: Twayne, 1975.

magic realism

Magic realism is a style of fiction writing that combines elements of fantasy and reality without any clear delineation between the two. Though elements of fantasy in literature can be found throughout history, it is the particular relationship between the fantastic and the real that characterizes magic realism's unique flavor. Though it had some precedent in European literature, particularly in the work of Franz KAFKA, magic realism was primarily developed in post–World War II Latin America.

The Latin-American literary ancestor of magic realism was Jorge Luis BORGES, who used fantasy in his short stories as a means of exploring philosophical mysteries. In the 1960s, the generation after Borges—Gabriel GARCÍA MÁRQUEZ, Carlos FUENTES, Mario VARGAS LLOSA, and Alejo CARPENTIER, all important contributors to the development of the magical-realist style—came to the world's attention. It was clear there was a Latin-American renaissance in progress and that magic realism would make an important contribution to world literature.

Critical Analysis

Magic realism demonstrates the presence of a hidden layer of reality behind the appearance of the natural world and human society. This effect is achieved both by presenting the incredible in a straightforward manner and by describing the commonplace as mysterious. Both Gabriel García Márquez and Alejo Carpentier have said that magic realism is an effect that is based not in fantasy but in Latin-American reality.

A humorous example of this can be found in García Márquez's novel *One Hundred Years of Solitude* (1967), in which a child is born with the tail of a pig. García Márquez chose this particular "stigma" specifically because of its unreality. The episode reinforces the carefully balanced themes of what is real versus the absurd and fantastic. After the book was published, people from all over Latin America came forward, admitting to having been born with a pig's tail. Having read *One Hundred Years of Solitude,* they realized that it was only natural and that they were no longer embarrassed to admit it. The outrageousness of the incident and the readers' reactions to it force readers to consider the absurdity in everyday life and society.

Many of the Latin-American magic-realist writers spent time in Europe, particularly France, and were exposed to surrealism and its use of the absurd. Though the influence of surrealism on magic realism is unquestionable, it is magic realism's relationship to truth that sets it apart. The surrealists used fantasy and absurdity to attack conventional ideas of reality; the magic realists created substitute ideas of reality in hope of coming closer to psychological and metaphysical truths.

In this way, the fantastic elements of magic realism take on the stature of myths. Myths, although not able to be proved by science or history, have a kind of accuracy about the nature and needs of humanity and the world. Because of their connection to some inner aspect of human consciousness, myths have a power beyond that of mere

fantasy. Magic realism attempts to use this mythic force.

Another distinguishing feature of magic-realist novels is their relationship to history. Carlos Fuentes and Mario Vargas Llosa, as well as García Márquez and Carpentier, combine specific details of Latin-American history with fantastical elements in their works.

In *Terra Nostra* (1975), Fuentes uses magic realism as a means to recount and analyze the history of Spain and Latin America. The book is unquestionably about the history of the Hispanic world, but the use of the fantastic allows Fuentes to give the events a sense of universality.

Vargas Llosa, however, embellishes history with fantasy for the purpose of making an ideological critique in a dramatic and nondidactic way. To a lesser degree, this is also García Márquez's strategy in *One Hundred Years of Solitude,* in which he combines the actual events of Columbian history with a mythical story of the imaginary town Macondo to critique Latin-American politics and U.S. imperialism. Perhaps it is this perfect synthesis of the two powers of magic realism that makes *One Hundred Years of Solitude* the generally acknowledged masterpiece of the genre.

Isabel ALLENDE, though not one of the inventors of magic realism, adopted a style similar to García Márquez's. In her novel *The House of the Spirits* (1982), Allende uses magic realism to convey a feminist perspective on Latin-American history and culture. Some readers have even seen in Allende's novels a feminist critique of magic realism itself.

American writer Toni Morrison has also been called a magic realist. Her work, particularly her novel *Beloved* (1987), employs the characteristic use of the fantastic to reveal metaphysical truth and confront the historical injustice of slavery.

Magic realism, when it is most successful, goes beyond itself to penetrate into unrecognized truths. It engages history in a way that REALISM cannot. Realism, our sense of what is subjective and what is objective in reality, is, in a certain sense, determined by history. The extraordinary success of magic realism demonstrated, both in Latin America and throughout the world, that traditional realism, dominant into the 20th century, is no longer necessarily the best mode for expressing the drama of contemporary life.

Works about Magic Realism

Angulo, María-Elena. *Magic Realism: Social Context and Discourse.* New York: Garland, 1995.

Mellen, Joan. *Magic Realism.* Detroit: Gale Group, 2000.

Mahfouz, Naguib (1911–) *novelist*

Naguib Mahfouz was born in the al-Jamaliyyah district of Cairo, Egypt, the youngest child of a civil servant. When Mahfouz was six years old, his father moved the family to a more prosperous suburb. Mahfouz read extensively as a child. His father's wealth allowed him to acquire many translated books that were not part of his school curriculum. When the 1919 revolution in Egypt took place, Mahfouz was only eight years old. The revolution had broken out because the British colonial government prevented an Egyptian nationalist from traveling to the Versailles Conference to demand Egypt's independence. Despite Mahfouz's young age, he was greatly affected by the event, and he idolized the heroes of the revolution for their bravery and courage.

After completing his secondary education, Mahfouz studied philosophy at the University of Cairo. He was invited after his graduation to continue his studies in the master's program. By the 1930s, Mahfouz was writing articles about the intellectual ideas and issues of the time, such as the pursuit of science in conjunction with socialist ideology to foster a better future for Egypt and the replacement of the absolutist monarchic government with a social-democratic one. He eventually turned away from his university career and entered the civil service, where he remained until his retirement in 1971. His work gave him time to pursue his writing, which was his first love. Throughout his writing career, Mahfouz

continued to read avidly the works of many European and Russian writers such as Albert CAMUS, Feyodor DOSTOYEVSKY, Leo TOLSTOY, and Marcel PROUST.

Mahfouz's writings were clearly affected by the turmoil caused by the political changes in Egypt. A supporter of the political revolution of the 1960s, Mahfouz found many kindred spirits in revolutionary movement of this time but was deeply disturbed by the methods activists employed to achieve their goals. He attempted to represent the spirit of the revolution and its ideals through his works. His stories bespeak the uncertainty of the 1960s, which peaked with the outbreak of the war between Egypt and Israel in 1967. The war signaled the final failure of the ideas and structures of the Egyptian government and also prompted many writers, including Mahfouz, to engage in more reflective writings.

In 1988, Mahfouz became the first Arab author to win the Nobel Prize in literature. The award recognized Mahfouz's contribution to developing the novel in the Arab literary world, but it also put Mahfouz and his family under intense scrutiny by the news media. His worsening health led him to seek medical care in London, and when he returned, he narrowly escaped an attempt on his life by a group of Islamic fundamentalists in 1994. Although he suffered a stab wound in the attack, he remained a faithful advocate of free expression.

Critical Analysis

The early stage of Mahfouz's writing was marked by his deep concern with philosophical issues such as class struggle, identity, poverty, and colonial oppression. These themes are represented in his works of the 1940s and 1950s, such as *Kifah Tiba* (*Struggle at Thebes*, 1944), *Al-Qahirah al-jadidah* (*Modern Cairo*, 1946), and the Cairo trilogy *Al-Thulathiyya: Bayn al-Qasrayn* (*Palace Walk*, 1956), *Qasr al-Shawq* (*Palace of Desire*, 1957), and *Al-Sukkariyya* (*Sugar Street*, 1957). In *Kifah Tiba*, he examines the significance of the country's early history during the time of its struggle for independence. By reflecting on the character and rash actions of the youthful pharaoh, Mahfouz was able to compare his pharaoh protagonist with the young King Farouk of Egypt. In *Al-Qahirah al-jadidah,* on the other hand, Mahfouz analyzes the lives of various characters whose continuous quest for better lives brings them into conflict with the dominant British colonial class. Themes such as the exploitation of the lower classes by the colonial rulers are further elaborated and portrayed in another of Mahfouz's novels, *Zuqaq al-Midaqq* (*Midaq Alley,* 1947).

In his early work, Mahfouz masterfully portrays the varied view of many different characters. In the Cairo trilogy, a monumental work of 1,500 pages, he traces the major events of Egyptian history through his narrative about the 'Abd al-Jawwad family. He explicates a complex web of relationships set against the background of Egypt's bitter struggle against British colonialism. The novel examines complicated and fragile human relationships against the backdrop of major political events such as the political revolution of 1919. It also explores important themes, such as generational differences, tradition versus modernity, and sexual equality. Mahfouz's protagonists continued to find their own identities as they faced and reacted to the changes of the times. In a certain way, Mahfouz's life was a reflection of this haplessness of humanity to change.

In the second phase of Mahfouz's literary career, he became more outspoken, especially when expressing his political views. This stage was clearly influenced by his reaction to the political events from the 1960s to the 1980s. Between 1961 and 1967, he published six novels, in which he began to enhance his narration to convey the complexities and urgency of colonial oppression and the disillusionment that accompanied this period of chaos and disorder. He also began to write from the point of view of the protagonists of his stories. In tersely realistic style, he expressed his characters' emotional estrangement from their peers and their community. As a result, his explicitness brought a new dimension to Mahfouz's stories. He was able to showcase his talent in creating a variety of human characters with varied and complex personalities and points of view. In *Miramar* (1967), for example, Mahfouz conjures a setting in which characters from different occupational backgrounds and age groups come together. The story focuses on the character of Zahra, a lovely peasant girl who exudes innocence, simplicity, and optimism. Zahra personifies the optimism of Egypt in the postwar period, which is marred by the harsh reality of corruption and vice that leads to the suicide of one main character and the continuous impoverishment of the others.

Mahfouz's works reflect his personality and his experiences in Egypt where he spent most of his life. His concern with the human condition and other philosophical issues clearly influenced his writings. The major themes in his works include the constant human need for acceptance and solace, the vicious cycle of social oppression from which the poor could never escape, and the irreconcilable differences between the ideologies of the upper and lower classes. Even though Mahfouz wrote of the struggle and suffering of the poor, his stories are mostly narratives of the urban middle class, especially the lives and problems of intellectuals. In addition, Mahfouz's middle-class background and his long-term residence in cities gave him the experience and knowledge with which to create familiar settings.

Other Works by Naguib Mahfouz

Arabian Nights and Days. Translated by Denys Johnson-Davies. New York: Doubleday, 1995.
The Beggar. Translated by Kristin Walker Henry and Nariman Khales Naili al Warrah. Cairo: American University in Cairo Press, 1986.
Children of the Alley. Translated by Peter Theroux. New York: Doubleday, 1996.
The Thief and the Dogs. Translated by Trevor Le Gassick and Mustafa Badawi. Cairo: American University in Cairo Press, 1984.
The Time and the Place. Translated by Denys Johnson-Davies. New York: Doubleday, 1991.

Works about Naguib Mahfouz

Gordon, Haim. *Naguib Mahfouz's Egypt: Existential Themes in his Writings*. Westport, Conn.: Greenwood Press, 1990.

Le Gassick, Trevor, ed. *Critical Perspectives on Naguib Mahfouz*. Washington, D.C.: Three Continents Press, 1991.

Peled, Mattityahu. *Religion My Own: The Literary Works of Naguib Mahfouz*. New Brunswick, N.J.: Transaction Books, 1983.

Somekh, Sasson. *The Changing Rhythm: A Study of Naguib Mahfouz's Novels*. Leiden, The Netherlands: Brill, 1973.

Maillet, Antonine (1929–   ) poet, playwright, novelist

Antonine Maillet was born in the Acadian community of Bouctouche, New Brunswick. Her work often draws on her Acadian upbringing and employs a particular Acadian dialect. In 1950, she received a B.A. from the University of Moncton and, nine years later, completed an M.A. She continued her studies at Laval, earning a Ph.D. in literature in 1970. She taught literature and folklore, first at Laval and then at Montreal. She also worked for Radio-Canada in Moncton as a scriptwriter and host. She is currently the chancellor of the University of Moncton.

While in school, Maillet worked on her writing, producing her first play, *Poire-acre,* in 1958. That same year, her first novel, *Pointe-aux-Coques* was published. Since that time, she has published close to 50 novels, plays, and poems and has become one of the most important living French-Canadian writers. Her novel *The Tale of Don L'Original* (1972) won the Governor General's Award for Fiction. In 1979, Maillet became the only Canadian author to win France's most prestigious literary award, the Prix Goncourt, for her novel *Pélagie-la-Charette* (1979), a historical novel about the British army's destruction of Acadian settlements in 1755.

Another Work by Antonine Maillet

The Devil is Loose! New York: Walker & Co., 1987.

Works about Antonine Maillet

Aresu, Bernard. "Pélagie la Charette and Antonine Maillet's Epic Voices." In Makoto Ueda, ed., *Explorations: Essays in Comparative Literature*. Lanham, Md.: University Press of America, 1986.

Briere, Eloise A. "Antonine Maillet and the Construction of Acadian Identity." *Postcolonial Subjects: Francophone Women Writers*. Edited by Mary Jean Green et al. Minneapolis: University of Minnesota Press, 1996, 3–21.

Mala'ika, Nazik al– (1923–   ) poet, critic

Al-Mala'ika was born in Baghdad to a literary family; her mother was a nationalist poet in the independence movement against British rule. She earned a B.A. in Arabic at the Teacher's Training College, Baghdad (1944), and an M.A. in comparative literature from the University of Wisconson (1956). With her husband, she helped found the University of Basra in Iraq. Al-Mala'ika taught at the University of Kuwait from 1970 to 1982 and thereafter lived in Iraq until living conditions, affected by the Gulf War (1991), deteriorated so much that she could not maintain her health, so she moved to Cairo.

Al-Mala'ika's literary criticism and poetry helped to break the hold of traditional forms on modern Arabic poetry. Her first collection, *Ashiqat al-lail* ("Lover of night," 1947) offered poetry of highly sensitive emotion, idealism, despair, and disillusion, themes typically associated with Arabic literary romanticism of the 1930s and 1940s. In the introduction to her second collection, *Shazaya wa ramad* ("Shards and ashes," 1949) she suggests a break with the centuries-old rhyme patterns of Arabic poetry and proposes that the "poetic foot" be cut loose from the two-hemistitch verse form that has anchored Arabic poetry since its beginnings. Her belief is that this form and the poetic conventions associated with it have come to inhibit rather than spur creativity. *Shazaya wa ramad* and subsequent poetry collections depart from traditional forms. "Cholera" was her first poem to demonstrate what is considered, in Arabic literature, to be "free verse." Her 1962 book of literary criticism *Qadaya al-shi'r al-mu'asir*, (the title means "Issues in Contemporary Arabic Poetry"), in which she refines and elaborates the proposal for modern verse begun in the introduction to *Shazaya wa ramad*, is a milestone text and is hotly debated. Al-Mala'ika continued to write poetry into the 1970s, departing from the dark, romantic tendencies of her early work to a more philosophical stance. Religious and spiritual themes enter her later poetry; her recent work is often marginalized, as very few modern Arab poets and critics take religious inspiration seriously.

Only a small amount of her work is available in English, in anthologies such as Kamal Boullata's *Women of the Fertile Crescent* (1981).

Another Work by Nazik al-Mala'ika

Jayyusi, Salma, ed. Selections in *Modern Arabic Poetry*. New York: Columbia University Press, 1987.

A Work about Nazik al-Mala'ika

Jayyusi, Salma. *Trends and Movements in Modern Arabic Poetry*. Boston: Brill, 1977.

Malange, Nise (1960–   ) *poet, screenwriter*

Nise Malange was born in Cape Town, South Africa. She went to the United States, where she obtained a degree from the University of Iowa. Malange specialized in scriptwriting and film and video production while she was in Zimbabwe. She is currently the director of the Culture and Working Life Project at the University of Natal in Durban. She is also the national vice president of the Congress of South African Writers. In addition, Malange works as a consultant within the labor movement and writes to forward the cause of women's rights in South Africa. Malange writes poetry and plays and has presented papers on African arts and cultures at international conferences. She won the prestigious Norwegian Award for Poetry in 1987.

Malange's poems are inspired by her personal experiences as a disenfranchised black woman in South Africa. Her turbulent youth, spent during the years of apartheid, has had a distinct impact on her writing. Issues such as domestic violence, disenfranchisement, and education for girls are common themes in her works. Her play *Pondo Women Cleaners* (1987) addresses the pain and suffering of a marginal group of disenfranchised women. Malange believes that literature can be used for the mobilization of the masses, and her poetry examines the oppression and struggle of women in a male-dominated society. Through her poetry, Malange also reaches out to her readers, imploring them to derive strength from their common experiences. She believes that literature has the power to influence and help them to improve their lives.

Malange represents one of the prominent members of a new generation of African poets known as the "oral poets." Her desire to inspire ordinary people to voice their opinions against social evils such as oppression and class differences is most effectively carried out in her active participation in community work and workshops that she helps organize.

Other Works by Nise Malange

"Ditsela! Ditsela," *Pathways* 1 (May 1997).

"Nightshift Cleaner, Nightshift Mother," *Illuminations: An International Magazine of Contemporary Writing* 8 (Summer 1989).

Mallarmé, Stéphane (1842–1898) *poet*

A Symbolist (*see* SYMBOLISM) poet whose works are often considered by critics to be the best example of "pure poetry," Stéphane Mallarmé was born in Paris into a family of French civil servants. As a student, he distinguished himself in the study of languages. After graduation, he visited England, was married in London, and then returned to France, where he accepted the first in a series of teaching posts. He taught English in several provincial schools in Tournon, Besançon, Avignon, and Paris until his retirement in 1893.

Mallarmé made many close contacts within the artistic community. Chief among these was his sustained friendship with Manet, which began in 1873 and continued until the artist's death in 1883. He wrote two articles on Manet, which are considered to be incisive symbolist analyses of impressionism.

In the 1880s, Mallarmé became the center of a group of French writers who lived and worked in Paris. This group, which included André GIDE and Paul VALÉRY, met to share ideas on poetry and art. Mallarmé's ideas often contradicted each other. According to Mallarmé, nothing lies beyond reality; however, within this state of nothingness, there exists that which is the essence of perfection. This takes the shape of what he refers to as the "perfect form." He believed it was the poet's task to find these essences within the void of nothingness and to clarify them with the language of poetry.

Mallarmé's ideas were not always well received. Readers and critics alike found him to be unnecessarily complicated and often obtuse. He would challenge his readers to use their minds when they read his works by, among other things, looking up common words in the dictionary to find archaic meanings for them. He would then employ these words in their long-lost form within his poems.

Critical Analysis

Mallarmé began to write poetry in his early teens. His first poems were published in magazines in the 1860s, and his first important poem, "L'Azur," was published when he was only 24. He was profoundly influenced by the works of Charles BAUDELAIRE, particularly by Baudelaire's advocacy of the obscure and his emphasis on the element of mystery within a poetic work. Mallarmé, however, went beyond this concept, stressing the inherent magical quality and the sacredness of poetry. He spent long periods of time obsessing over the minute details of each of his poems, reveling in the importance of even the smallest and seemingly most insignificant details of language and imagery. His poetry was allusive and often hard for readers to grasp. His language was compressed in such a way that a finished poem often seemed more an interpretation than a poem that could be easily de-

fined, which demanded an awareness of the process of poetic creation.

Language and art held a close association in many of Mallarmé's works. His association with the visual arts is readily evident in his poetry collection, *The Afternoon of a Faun* (1876), his best-known work. It was illustrated by Manet and inspired both Dubussy's 1894 musical composition of the same name and the subsequent ballet by Nijinsky. The poems in the collection were written while Mallarmé was working at Tournon, a town he found both ugly and unpleasant. In contrast to the author's own surroundings, the poem presents the rambling erotic thoughts of a faun as it whiles away the hours of a drowsy summer afternoon in a place of great beauty.

Perhaps Mallarmé's greatest achievement came in his contribution to those writers who came after him. This influence was not restricted to French poetry but spread internationally among a diverse group of writers. Wallace Stevens credits Mallarmé as a source of great inspiration, as does T. S. Eliot. His influence is readily apparent in James Joyce's *Finnegans Wake.*

The condensed figures and unorthodox syntax of Mallarmé's poetry set it apart from much of the rest of the works of his time. He framed each of his poems around one central symbol, idea, or metaphor. All of the additional imagery simply served to help illustrate and develop the main idea. His use of free verse was influential on the FIN DE SIÈCLE movement in France, the 1890s Decadent movement (see *decadence*), and 20th-century MODERNIST poetry.

Mallarmé's other works include *Hérodiade* (1896) and *A Funeral Toast,* the latter of which was written as a memoriam to the French author Théophile GAUTIER, whose works Mallarmé greatly admired. He also wrote an experimental poem *Un Coup de dés Jamais n'aboliva le hasard* (1897), which was published posthumously. In his later years, he became close friends with Whistler and devoted himself to creating what he referred to as his "grand oeuvre" or "great work." Unfortunately, Mallarmé died in Paris on September 9 before he could complete this impossible masterpiece.

Other Works by Stéphane Mallarmé

Collected Poems. Translated by Henry Weinfield. Berkeley: University of California Press, 1994.

Mallarmé in Prose. Translated by Jill Anderson. New York: New Directions, 2001.

Works about Stéphane Mallarmé

Lloyd, Rosemary. *Mallarmé: The Poet and His Circle.* Ithaca, N.Y.: Cornell University Press, 1999.

Stafford, Hélène. *Mallarmé and the Poetics of Everyday Life: A Study of the Concept of the Ordinary in His Verse and Prose.* Atlanta, Ga.: Rodopi, 2000.

Malouf, David (1934–) *poet, novelist, playwright*

David Malouf was born in Brisbane, Australia, to a Lebanese father and an English mother. He attended the Brisbane Grammar school and later received an honors degree in language and literature at the University of Queensland, where he taught English until 1962. His expertise and skill in the use of the English language inspired him to write poems. He published his first poem, "Interiors," in *Four Poets* in 1962.

Malouf is considered both a primitive and a romantic for his uses of nature. His themes include nature, the use of language as a transforming device across cultures, identity, isolation, unity, and belonging. He uses imagery, metaphor, symbolism, and analogy to express these themes.

In "Twelve Night Pieces" from *Poems 1975–76* (1976), he writes, "From wetness of earth and earth rot morning / Glory climbs to the sun . . ." to reveal the morning glory as a symbol of human connection with nature. In "The Bicycle" from *The Bicycle and Other Poems* (1970), he uses the analogy of the mechanical bicycle and the natural human experience of traveling through life: "Now time yawns and its messengers appear/ like huge stick insects, wingless, spoked with stars. . . ."

Malouf's novels carry the theme of identity for which the hero longs through union with another. In Malouf's first novel, *Johnno* (1975), Johnno and Dante long for their fathers' love. In *Conversations at Curlow Creek* (1996), Michael Adair wants to be united with his brother and his love, Virgilia. *An Imaginary Life* (1978), *Remembering Babylon* (1993), *Child's Play* (1982), and *Flyaway Peter* (1982), the novels for which Malouf won the Australian Literature Society's Gold medal, all talk about the predicament of isolation.

Malouf is celebrated as a poet, essayist, novelist, and playwright. He won the Australian Literature Society gold medal for the verse collection *Neighbours in a Thicket* (1974). He also won the Townsville Foundation for Australian Literary Studies Award and the Grace Leven Poetry Prize. The novel *Remembering Babylon* was nominated for the 1993 Booker Prize. Malouf speaks about his passion for writing in his autobiography, *12, Edmonstone Street* (1985).

Other Works by David Malouf

Dream Stuff: Stories. New York: Pantheon, 2000.

Selected Poems, 1959–1989. London: Chatto and Windus, 1994.

A Work about David Malouf

Indyk, Ivor. *David Malouf.* New York: Oxford University Press, 1993.

Malraux, André (1901–1976) *novelist, nonfiction writer*

André Georges Malraux was born in Paris, France, on November 3, into a wealthy family. His parents separated when he was a child and he was brought up by his mother. His father was a stockbroker who committed suicide in 1930. As a youth, Malraux studied a wide variety of subjects, such as archaeology, art history, and anthropology. However, what interested him the most was oriental languages, histories, and cultures, which he studied at the École des Langues Orientales.

At the age of 21, Malraux married Clara Goldsmidt, also a writer, and together they traveled to Cambodia and spent time in Indochina, attempting to rediscover the Khmer statuary. He was arrested, however, for taking bas-reliefs from a temple. His three-year sentence was rescinded, and he returned briefly to France. It was during this period that he became highly critical of French colonial authorities governing Indochina. As a result, Malraux began the first of many political endeavors that, alongside and often directly linked to his literary achievements, eventually distinguished his remarkable life. He helped to first organize the Young Annam League, an anticolonial organization in Saigon in 1925. He also founded and edited the politically active and outspoken anticolonial Saigon newspaper *Indochina in Chains.*

On returning to France, Malraux published his first novel, *The Temptation of the West* (1926). The work, set in the early stages of the Chinese revolution and revolving around letters exchanged between a young European and an Asian intellectual, focuses on the parallels between Eastern and Western culture. He followed this work with two novels, *The Conquerors* (1928), which dealt with a revolutionary strike in Canton, and *The Royal Way* (1930), a successful adventure story set in the jungles of Indochina.

Malraux supported himself by working as an art editor in Paris for Gallimard Publishers. He was able to take several archaeological expeditions to Afghanistan and Iran, which led to his discovery of the lost city that may have been home to the Queen of Sheba. He continued to write, with death and revolution two of his major themes. *Man's Fate* (1933), one of his best-known novels, earned for him the prestigious Goncourt Prize, as well as much deserved recognition as an author. The novel depicts a communist uprising in Shanghai and focuses on the dignity of human solidarity in both life and death.

In the 1930s, Malraux became known politically for his support of antifascist and leftist organizations. He fought for the Republicans during the Spanish civil war and wrote about these experiences in his novel *L'Espoir* (*Days of Hope,* 1937). The book, published prior to the end of the war, stops with the March 1937 battle at Guadalajara. In 1938, *L'Espoir* was revised as a screenplay under the title *Sierrade Teruel;* however, the film was not released in France until after the conclusion of World War II.

The 1940s marked a shift in Malraux's life. He divorced his wife and broke away from communism, as he did not agree with the Nazi–Soviet pact. He began to concentrate on writing nonfiction and was openly opposed to Stalin's ideas. He served with a French tank unit during World War II and, though twice captured by the Gestapo, managed to escape both times.

After the war, Malraux became a vocal supporter of Charles de Gaulle. He wrote a number of books on art and aesthetics and married a concert pianist. When De Gaulle came into power, Malraux was appointed minister of cultural affairs, and his first act in office was to order the cleaning of the Louvre. This act was highly controversial in that many people saw it not as an improvement but as an act of vandalism. Malraux eventually retired from the forefront of politics to write his memoirs, including the autobiographical *The Fallen Oaks* (1971). He wrote regularly until his death on November 23.

Another Work by André Malraux

The Walnut Trees of Altenburg. Translated by A. W. Fielding. Chicago: University of Chicago Press, 1992.

A Work about André Malraux

Cate, Curtis. *André Malraux: A Biography.* New York: Fromm International, 1998.

Mandelstam, Osip Yemilyevich
(1891–1938) *poet*

Osip Mandelstam was born in Warsaw, Poland, but grew up in St. Petersburg, Russia. His father was a successful leather merchant, and his mother a piano teacher. Although the Mandelstams were

Jewish, the family was not very religious. Mandelstam received an excellent education at home from various tutors and later from the Tenishev Academy. He traveled extensively throughout Europe between 1907 and 1910 and studied French literature at the University of Heidelberg. Between 1911 and 1917, Mandelstam studied philosophy at the University of St. Petersburg. He published his first poem in 1910 in the journal *Apollon*. With the advent of revolution, Mandelstam abandoned his studies to concentrate on poetry.

Influenced by his close relationship with Anna AKHMATOVA and Nikolay GUMILEV, Mandelstam readily joined the Acmeists (*see* ACHEMISM) and established his reputation as a poet with his collection *Kamen* (*Stone,* 1913). Like Akhmatova, Mandelstam often mixed classical images with those of contemporary Russian culture. Mandelstam's poetry also exalted the architectural and literary achievements of classical Greece and Rome. In his next two collections, *Tristiya* (1922) and *Poems 1921–25* (1928), he reaffirmed his position as one of the best poets in Russia. Although both collections contained images and themes previously found in *Stones,* Mandelstam, influenced by political upheaval in Russia, expanded his poetic perspective to more universal themes of life, death, and exile.

In 1918, Mandelstam began to work for the education ministry of the new communist regime, but his support for the regime soured and stopped completely after the 1921 execution of his friend Gumilev. In the 1920s, he supported himself by writing children's books and translating works by English and French writers. He married Nadezhda Kazin in 1922 and in 1928 published three books: a poetry collection, entitled simply *Poems,* and two collections of critical essays. After a trip to Armenia in 1930, Mandelstam published his last major collection of poetry, *Journey to Armenia,* in 1933. An epigram about Stalin he wrote in 1934—"And every killing is a treat / For the broad-chested Ossete"—resulted in Mandelstam's being arrested and exiled to Voronezh. Nadezhda accompanied him and helped transcribe the agonized poems he composed there. In 1938, he was arrested again for "counterrevolutionary" activities. This time he was sentenced to five years of hard labor. Mandelstam died that year in the Gulag Archipelago and was buried in a common grave.

International acclaim for Mandelstam's work did not come until the 1970s, when his works were published in Russia and the West. Mandelstam's poems of exile were not published until 1990 in *The Voronezh Notebooks.* Their lyrical approach to almost unimaginable pain is astonishing, as in the poem "Black Candle" (1934):

> It is your fate, for your narrow shoulders to
>   turn red
> under the lashes,
> red under the lashes, to burn in the frost . . .
> And as for me, I burn after you like a black
>   candle,
> burn like a black candle and dare not pray.

The magnificence of Mandelstam's verse is still being rediscovered today. He is now considered to be one of the best Russian poets of the 20th century. The critic Simon Karlinsky, for example, remarked in a review of Bruce McClelland's translation of *Tristiya* in the *New York Times Book Review:* "In Mandelstam, Russian poetry at last has a poet of stature comparable to Pushkin's—a claim that even the most fanatical admirers of Blok, Mayakovsky or Pasternak would not dream of making."

Other Works by Osip Mandelstam

50 Poems/Osip Mandelstam. Translated by Bernard Meares, with an introduction by Joseph Brodsky. New York: Persea Books, 2000.

The Noise of Time: The Prose of Osip Mandelstam. Translated by Clarence Brown. San Francisco: North Point Press, 1986.

Osip Mandelstam's Stone. Translated and introduced by Robert Tracy. Princeton, N.J.: Princeton University Press, 1981.

Tristia. Translated by Bruce McClelland. Barrytown, N.Y.: Station Hill Press, 1987.

The Voronezh Notebooks: Poems 1935–1937. Translated by Richard McKane and Elizabeth Mc-Kane. Chester Springs, Pa.: Dufour Editions, 1998.

Works about Osip Mandelstam

Cavanagh, Clare. *Osip Mandelstam and the Modernist Creation of Tradition*. Princeton, N.J.: Princeton University Press, 1995.

Harris, Jane Garry. *Osip Mandelstam*. Boston: Twayne, 1988.

Mandelstam, Nadezhda. *Hope Against Hope*. Translated by Max Hayward. New York: Modern Library, 1999.

———. *Mozart and Salieri: An Essay on Osip Mandelstam and the Poetic Process*. New York: Vintage, 1994.

Manhae
See HAN YONGUN.

Mann, Heinrich (1871–1950) *novelist, playwright, essayist*

Luiz Heinrich Mann was born in Lübeck, Germany. His father, Thomas Johann Heinrich Mann, was a successful grain merchant. His mother, Julia da Silva-Bruhns Mann, was of Brazilian descent. As a teenager, Mann became an apprentice to a bookseller and worked for a publishing house. After an inheritance made him financially independent, he started his literary career in 1891. He lived in Italy, Munich, Berlin, and France before moving to the United States in 1940 to escape the Nazis. He married the actress Maria Kanová in 1914 and, after their divorce, married Nelly Kroeger in 1939.

Mann, a prolific essayist, was one of the few German writers to oppose his country's participation in World War I. He attained literary fame with his novel *Der Untertan* (*The Patrioteer*, 1918), a satirical critique of Germany under Kaiser Wilhelm. His novel *Professor Unrat* (1905) was translated as *The Blue Angel* and made into a popular movie in 1928. In the 1930s, Mann wrote two successful historical novels on King Henry of Navarre. In 1949, he won the National Prize of East Germany and died a year later after accepting the presidency of that country's Academy of Arts.

Mann's influences included Friedrich NIETZSCHE and 19th-century French writers such as Gustave FLAUBERT. He and his brother Thomas MANN criticized, supported, and influenced each other's writing careers. Mann employed caricature and sarcasm in his works to convey his social and political criticisms. A socialist, he used his novels and plays to oppose authoritarianism, militarism, and fascism. Less successful than his brother, Mann was sometimes an uneven and impatient writer who lacked precision and polish. Nonetheless, as the scholar Rolf Linn points out, Mann's work represents "an almost complete intellectual and political history of Germany in the first half of the twentieth century" and "through it the best thought of nineteenth century France entered German thinking."

Another Work by Heinrich Mann
Henry, King of France. Translated by Eric Sutton. New York: Knopf, 1939.

A Work about Heinrich Mann
Linn, Rolf N. *Heinrich Mann*. Boston: Twayne, 1967.

Mann, Thomas (1875–1955) *novelist, critic, essayist*

Thomas Mann was born in Lübeck, Germany. His father was a wealthy, prominent citizen who was twice elected as mayor of Lübeck. His mother, Julia da Silva-Bruhns, was born in Brazil of mixed German and Portuguese ancestry. After the death of Mann's father in 1891, his family relocated to Munich. Mann was an avid reader during childhood and particularly admired realistic literature. Mann attended the University of Munich; on graduation, he worked for the German Fire Insurance Company.

While at university, Mann immersed himself in the writings of Arthur SCHOPENHAUER and Friedrich NIETZSCHE, two very influential German philosophers and cultural critics. Mann also became obsessed with the musical works of Richard Wagner, a composer whose operas and orchestral works were inspired by German myth and legend. Mann's early literary influences, were Leo TOLSTOY and Fyodor DOSTOYEVSKY, whose psychological realism Mann particularly admired.

In 1929, Mann won the Nobel Prize in literature. When Adolf Hitler came to power in Germany, Mann, along with his family, moved to Switzerland, where Mann worked as an editor for various literary journals. In 1938, Mann moved to the United States, working as a visiting professor at Princeton University. While at Princeton, Mann completed several critical works, including a study of Dostoevsky. Mann eventually moved to California but left the United States in 1952, bitterly disappointed by the persecution of communists and communist sympathizers by the U.S. government.

Critical Analysis

Mann's first major work, *Buddenbrooks* (1900), shows the influence of Richard Wagner in its use of leitmotif, using a word or an image over and over again in the work as a thematically unifying element. The novel follows several generations of the Buddenbrook family, a wealthy and powerful German family that disintegrates and degenerates with each successive generation. The novel especially focuses on the last Buddenbrook, the decadent artist Hanno. The work demonstrates Mann's affinity for the epic quality of the novel, which he inherited from early Tolstoy works. *Buddenbrooks* was well received throughout Germany and established Mann as a prominent writer.

In 1912, Mann completed a much shorter but also less conventional work, *Death in Venice*. The story recounts a strange relationship between Tadzio, a 14-year-old boy, and Gustav von Aschenbach, a mature German writer. Aschenbach becomes obsessed with the boy, who falls ill during an epidemic. Aschenbach decides to brave the epidemic and nurse the boy but contracts the disease himself and dies. Throughout the story the narrator asks this question:

[D]o you believe, my dear boy, that the man whose pass to the spiritual passes through the senses can ever achieve wisdom and true manly dignity?

Aschenbach, who has never before allowed himself to experience passion, literally dies for it and of it. The ambiguities in the relationship between Aschenbach and the boy, as well as the story's multilayered symbolism, have made *Death in Venice* a frequent subject of debate among scholars and critics.

During World War I, Mann adamantly supported the policies of the kaiser, the leader of Germany, and vehemently attacked liberalism. After the end of World War I, however, Mann's political opinions changed, and he vocally supported parliamentary democracy and the newly formed Weimar Republic.

The Magic Mountain (1924), Mann's second great work, reflects the political conflict found in the writer's contemporary world. In the novel, Hans Castorp visits his cousin at a fashionable tuberculosis sanatorium and decides to stay there even though he is not ill. The stay spans more than seven years, during which time Castorp talks with the other patients in the sanatorium and learns valuable lessons about the meaning of life and death. Castorp is caught in a conflict between two opposing political forces represented by two characters: a young Italian liberal humanist, Settembrini, and Naptha, a radical reactionary figure who supports faith beyond reason. The differences between the two men culminate in a duel: Settembrini fires into the air, and Naptha, overwhelmed by rage, kills himself. The duel between the two opposing forces symbolically reflects the conflict in Mann's own society. The work also reflects Mann's concern about fascism and the growing popularity of the Nazis in his native Germany. The novel received tremendous critical acclaim and became a best-seller in Germany.

Joseph and His Brothers appeared as a trilogy written between 1933 and 1943. Set in the biblical world, the story emerges as a religious and political allegory of conflict between individual liberty and political oppression. The story describes the progress of Joseph who matures into a wise political leader ready to lead his people to freedom. The novel was written during the height of the Nazi regime and reflects Mann's personal hatred for fascism and oppression.

Mann's last great novel, *Doctor Faustus* (1947), delineates the life of a famous composer, Adrian Lewerkuhn. The work is set against the grim background of crumbling German culture and society between the First and the Second World Wars. Mann's exploration of the roots of fascism in Germany was well received around the world but was resented by some in Germany itself.

When Thomas Mann returned to Europe in 1953, he refused to live in Germany—the government of which had deprived him of his citizenship in 1936—and settled in Switzerland. In 1949, Mann was awarded the Goethe Prize, the highest literary honor in Germany. Mann's exploration of the relationship of the extraordinary person to the society has never been surpassed.

Other Works by Thomas Mann

Confessions of Felix Krull: The Confidence Man. New York: Vintage Press, 1992.
Death in Venice and Other Stories. Translated by David Luke. New York: Bantam Books, 1988.

Works about Thomas Mann

Heilbut, Anthony. *Thomas Mann: Eros and Literature.* Riverside: University of California Press, 1997.
Robertson, Ritchie. *The Cambridge Companion to Thomas Mann.* Cambridge: Cambridge University Press, 2002.

Mansfield, Katherine (Kathleen Mansfield Beauchamp) (1888–1923)
short-story writer, poet

Katherine Mansfield was born Kathleen Mansfield Beauchamp in Wellington, New Zealand, to an affluent, middle-class family, but in 1909 she left for London to pursue a career as a writer. There,

she met and married George Bowdon, a music teacher, but left him a few days after the wedding. Her first complete volume of short stories was published in 1911, under the title *In a German Pension*. These stories were based on Mansfield's stay at a Bavarian health resort, where she lived for a time after she left her husband and where she suffered a miscarriage.

Shortly after her return to London, she met John Middleton Murry, a critic, poet, and editor, whom she married in 1918. In that same year, she was diagnosed with tuberculosis. In London, she met a number of artists and writers, including D. H. Lawrence, who modeled one of his characters in his novel *Women in Love* after Mansfield, and Virginia Woolf. The painter Dorothy Brett described Mansfield as having "a sort of ironic ruthlessness toward the small minds and less agile brains. . . . Katherine had a tongue like a knife, she could cut the very heart of one with it." (She was much more subtle and ambiguous in her writing.) In fiction writing, Virginia Woolf treated Mansfield as such a serious rival that, after her death, Woolf said there was "no point in writing. Katherine won't read it."

When her brother Leslie was killed during World War I, Mansfield began to write stories about her family and growing up. Some of her best stories, such as "The Garden Party," are set in New Zealand at the turn of the century.

"The Garden Party," published in 1922, deals with social class, death, and the artist's sensibility. The Sheridan family is hosting an elaborate garden party when a delivery man brings the news that a worker who lived in one of the little cottages near the Sheridan house has been killed in an accident. Mrs. Sheridan, once assured that the man did not actually die in her garden, insists that the party go on, telling her daughter, Laura, "People like that don't expect sacrifices from us." Later, Mrs. Sheridan sends Laura to the Scott house with the leftovers from the party, and at the "pokey little hole . . ." she accidentally enters the room where the body is laid out. Gazing at the dead man, she thinks, "He was given up to his dream. What did garden parties . . . matter to him?" The story exemplifies Mansfield's delicate, poetic style, her tendency to focus on a life-changing moment, and her habit of ending on a note of ambiguity.

In "The Fly" (1923), a businessman is reminded by a visitor of the death of his son six years earlier in World War I. Unable to summon up the grief he wants to feel, he picks up a photograph of his son. At this moment, he notices a fly that has fallen into the inkpot. He rescues the fly and watches as it begins the tedious process of cleaning itself off. Just as it is "ready for life again," the man drops more ink on it. He repeats the process, amazed at the fly's courage and resilience, until the final blot of ink kills the fly, at which point the man is seized by "a grinding feeling of wretchedness." He calls for fresh blotting paper but cannot remember what he had been thinking about before he began to torment the fly. Although the man cannot remember, the reader knows that the fly stands for all those who are helpless victims of a cruel fate.

Although *Poems* (1923) and *The Letters of Katherine Mansfield* (1928) were published posthumously, Mansfield is primarily remembered for her seven books of short stories, and she has exerted a lasting influence on modern short-story writers. She crafted her stories very carefully, writing and rewriting. Her writing is always subtle and often ironic and witty. As she defied conventions in her life, so her stories question conventional ideas about social class, family life, and marriage.

Katherine Mansfield died of tuberculosis in 1923 near Fontainebleau, France. The first significant writer to emerge from New Zealand, she is claimed by nationalist critics in both New Zealand and Britain but is best thought of as a product of colonialism. Her biographer Antony Alpers says of her New Zealand stories:

> They were really insights into the social isolation that used to be common in New Zealand . . . and they were written in a cultural isolation that was total for their author: no one who read them in London could have known what they in fact achieved. . . . The stories were something that only a New Zealander could have written at that time. They succeeded in relating character to environment in a land of "no tradition."

Other Works by Katherine Mansfield

Bliss and Other Stories. London: Wordsworth, 1996.
Something Childish. North Pomfret, Vt.: Trafalgar Square, 2000.

Works about Katherine Mansfield

Alpers, Antony. *The Life of Katherine Mansfield.* New York: Viking Press, 1980.
Kobler, J. F. *Katherine Mansfield: A Study of the Short Fiction.* Boston: Twayne, 1990.
Tomalin, Claire. *Katherine Mansfield: A Secret Life.* New York: Knopf, 1988.

Manzoni, Alessandro (1785–1873) *poet, novelist*

Italian patriot Alessandro Manzoni, best known for his fiercely nationalistic novel *The Betrothed* (1827) was born on March 7 in Milan. His father was a wealthy landowner, and his mother was the daughter of Cesare Beccaria, a well-known jurist and author of an influential treatise on crime and punishment. His parents separated in 1792, and, as a child, he moved with his mother to Paris where he received his education at several Catholic schools. His earliest works are characterized by a deeply anticlerical sentiment, as well as by strong support for Jacobean and democratic ideologies. He later rejected deism for an equally fervent devotion to Roman Catholicism. Manzoni returned to Italy in 1810, where he met and married Enrichetta Blondel.

Although he published several early works, Manzoni's most prolific period as a writer came between the years of 1812 and 1815. During this time, he began the poetry collection *Inni Sacri*, which he concluded 10 years later with the final piece, *La Pentacoste* (1822). His poetry is noted for its warmth of religious feeling. He also wrote two tragic dramas, *Il Conte di Carmagnola* (1820) and *Adelchi* (1822), as well as an ode to Napoleon upon his death, "Il Cinque Maggio" (1822).

Manzoni's best-known work, *I promessi sposi* (1827; translated *The Betrothed* 1951), was written between 1821 and 1827, during which the author was influenced by Sir Walter Scott. Developed from a series of theoretical writings, the historical novel is set in 17th-century Milan and provides a lavishly detailed and fiercely patriotic look at life in Italy. In Lombardy, a local tyrant thwarts the love between two peasants. After initial publication of the work, Manzoni continued to make revisions to create a stylistically superior version of the text, publishing the final revised edition in 1840. It now stands as a prime example of modern Italian prose. In revising, Manzoni sought to remove all traces of non-Tuscan idiom. This act revived the age-long conflict as to which dialect should be the standard for Italian prose, an issue in which Manzoni was interested. Manzoni was convinced that Tuscan should be the standard, national Italian literary language.

Beginning in 1842, Manzoni turned away from writing fiction and concentrated on theoretical works and as well as his involvement in politics. In 1860, he was elected senator of the new Italian kingdom. He was also assigned as president for the commission for the unification of the Italian language. For his work in this capacity, he was granted Roman citizenship.

Manzoni died on May 22 in Milan. He is best remembered for his constant contribution to improving the Italian prose style, as well as for his patriotic ideology and religious fervor. His legacy is such that, on the first anniversary of his death, the composer Verdi wrote his *Requiem* in honor of Manzoni.

A Work about Alessandro Manzoni
Barricelli, Gian Piero. *Alessandro Manzoni.* Boston: Twayne, 1976.

Marinetti, Filippo Tommaso
(1876–1944) *nonfiction writer*

Emilio Filippo Tommaso Marinetti, one of the founders and a leading proponent of the Italian futurist movement (*see* FUTURISM), was born in Alexandria, Egypt. The son of a wealthy lawyer, he was educated in a strict French Jesuit school in Alexandria. He completed his studies in Paris and then studied law at Pavia and Genoa universities. His devotion to literature soon overshadowed his plan for a career as a lawyer.

At 16, while still at the Jesuit College, Marinetti began to develop his skills as a writer, publishing a literary magazine from 1892 to 1894. He experimented with the emerging poetic form of free verse, publishing his first poems in that style in 1898. By 1900, he had abandoned all pretense of aspiring to the legal profession and devoted himself full time to the study of French and Italian poetry and literature. In 1905, he founded another literary magazine, *Poesia,* which was published in Milan until 1909. Through this journal, he embarked on a crusade to liberate poetry from the traditional constraints of language, form, and meter by providing an outlet for emerging nontraditional writers. Still a virtual unknown, Marinetti gained instant recognition with a single publication in *Le Figaro* on February 20, 1909. His essay *Foundation and Manifesto of Futurism* initiated a controversial shift in the nature of literature. In the work, he glorified the rapid pace of the future—machines, danger, speed, violence, and war. Other artists, unaware that Marinetti was not only the movement's leading theorist but also its sole member, soon joined the trend so that by 1910, a small but vocal group of artists, writers, and musicians were known as the first wave of futurists.

A brilliant publicist, Marinetti spurred the growth of the movement by inundating the public with a series of manifestos, each one progressively more vehement and filled with promises of the future. His earliest manifestos were published in *Poesia,* but subsequent works were printed in his new journal *Lacerba* after its inception in 1913.

Alongside his manifestos, Marinetti was also hard at work as a novelist. His works, which followed the tenets set forth by his own concept of futurism, most particularly the denigration of women, often caused controversy. The publication of his experimental novel, *Marfarka the Futurist* (1910), resulted in his arrest and imprisonment on charges of pornography.

Marinetti continued to work to expand the goals of futurism to encompass all areas of the arts, including literature, music, painting, architecture, costume design, and photography. Two years after meeting his future wife, Benedetta Cappa, he published another manifesto, *Against Marriage* (1919); however, he broke from his own reasoning and the two were finally wed in 1923.

The end of futurism and the end of Marinetti's life coincide. Italy's defeat in the war changed the popular opinion of violence and conflict, and, with the loss of Marinetti in 1944, the movement was unable to sustain its brief but explosive momentum.

A Work about Filippo Tommaso Marinetti

Blum, Cinzia Sartini. *The Other Modernism: F. T. Martinetti's Futurist Fiction of Power.* Berkeley: University of California Press, 1944.

Maron, Monika (1941–) *novelist, short-story writer*

Monika Maron was born in Berlin during World War II. Her father was a Communist who served as East Germany's minister of the interior. Her mother was a Pole of Jewish descent. After Maron completed grammar school, she studied drama and art history. She worked at a factory and for East Berlin television before spending six years as a journalist for *Für Dich* and *Wochenpost.* She became a full-time writer in 1976.

Maron's first novel, *Flugasche* (*Flying Ash*, 1981), was banned in East Germany for its critical portrayal of conditions there; it was, however, successful in the West. The novel describes the efforts of a journalist to shut down a power plant that is poisoning residents of an industrial city. *Flugasche* is the first book to address the problems of pollution in East Germany. Maron's second novel *Die Überläuferin* (*The Turncoat,* 1986) continues her theme of criticizing the East German state. In this work, she describes a woman's psychological collapse while living in dehumanizing conditions. Maron wrote a third novel in 1991 to form a trilogy about East Berlin. Part of a rebellious and critical generation of German writers, her criticism of East Germany also appears in her short stories and essays. In 1992, Maron won the coveted Kleist Prize.

Another Work by Monika Maron

Silent Close No. 6. Translated by David Newton Marinelli. Columbia, La.: Reader's International, 1993.

Masaoka Shiki (Masaoka Tsunenori) (1867–1902) *poet, diarist, critic*

Masaoka Shiki was born in Matsuyama in present-day Ehime Prefecture to Masaoka Hayata and Yae. He began to write prose and poetry while still in grade school there. He left Matsuyama in 1883 to attend University Preparatory College in Tokyo. In 1890, he entered the Literature Department of Tokyo Imperial University but left in 1893 to devote himself to literature. During his university period, he traveled around Japan, and in 1895, he volunteered to become a war correspondent in China during the Sino–Japanese War (1894–95). In the last years of his life, tuberculosis virtually confined Masaoka to a sickbed. He succumbed to this illness in 1902.

While still at university, Masaoka published three analytical books that were highly critical of modern haiku poetry, in particular attacking the stature of widely acclaimed haiku master Bashō Matsuo (1644–94). By 1896, he had softened his perspective and published *Buson the Haiku Poet,* which praised the style of Buson Yosa (1716–83). In 1897, he started the magazine *Hototogisu* to provide an outlet for modern haiku. He then wrote a critique of tanka poetry called *Letters to the Tanka Poets,* published in 1898. His most highly regarded poetry was written from his sickbed toward the end of his life and published posthumously in a volume called *Poems from the Bamboo Village* (1904).

Masaoka is known more for revitalizing the haiku and tanka forms of poetry than for writing poetry. He espoused a new style of poetry based on *shasei* (copying life). He claimed the traditional poetic conventions that restricted haiku and tanka were killing them as art forms.

Other Works by Masaoka Shiki

Masaoka Shiki: Selected Poems. Translated by Burton Watson. New York: Columbia University Press, 1997.

Peonies Kana. Translated by Harold J. Isaacson. New York: Theatre Arts, 1972.

A Work about Masaoka Shiki

Beichman, Janine. *Masaoka Shiki.* New York: Kodansha International, 1986.

Maupassant, Guy de (1850–1893)
novelist

Although some accounts vary, Henri-René-Albert-Guy de Maupassant was most likely born at the Château de Miromesnil in Dieppe, France, to a noble family. He spent his childhood in Normandy, where, graced with an almost photographic memory, he began to gather the rich and vivid details that he would later use in his stories about the Norman people.

In 1869, Maupassant went to Paris, where he began to study law, but he left school at age 20 to serve in the Franco–Prussian War. When he returned to Paris, he became obsessed with the idea of becoming a writer and sought out the company of other writers including Gustave FLAUBERT, from whom he learned much about the writer's craft. He also began to search his memories for ideas of his own and soon published the short story "La Main ecorchée" (1875), in which he richly details the

haunting image of a mummified hand. The story was based on an experience Maupassant had as a teenager when he actually saw a mummified hand up close. The details of his description reveal not only the vividness of Maupassant's memories but also his adherence to accuracy.

Aligning himself with the naturalist school (see *naturalism*), Maupassant published collections of poetry, the first of which was *Des Verse* (1880). It was his short stories, however, that gained critical and popular acclaim. In a journal edited by Émile ZOLA, Maupassant published what has come to be regarded as one of his greatest works, "Boule de Suif" ("Ball of Fat," 1880). Set during the Franco-Prussian War, it is the sad tale of a prostitute and her inhumane treatment by the bourgeois passengers with whom she must travel on a coach. She is forced to spend the night with a Prussian officer so that he will allow the coach to proceed. The next day, she is scorned by her fellow travelers, even though it is her action that allows them to complete their journey.

Throughout the 1880s, Maupassant wrote more than 300 short stories, six novels, and three travel books. All of his works are marked by his attention to detail, objectivity, and a remarkable sense of comedic timing. Most often, they focus on everyday events in the lives of common people, while revealing the hidden sides of human nature. Two of his best-known works include *A Woman's Life* (1883), which details the frustrating and unhappy existence of a Norman wife, and *Pierre et Jean* (1888), a psychological tale of two brothers. The latter inspired debate about its morality, as the hero of the tale is successful only because he commits acts that are morally questionable.

Another of Maupassant's works, *Le Horla* (*The Hallucination,* 1887), established him as a master of the horror tale. The main character, probably suffering from syphilis, believes he has summoned the Horlas, invisible cousins to vampires, and, in an attempt to get rid of them, burns down his house, killing his servants. When this does not work, he commits suicide. Maupassant himself suffered from syphilis, contracted at age 20, and the increasing madness brought on by the disease is readily apparent in his later works. One-tenth of his total literary output is in the form of horror stories and, of these, the main recurring theme is madness.

Maupassant attempted to end his own life on January 2, 1892. The attempt was unsuccessful but did lead to his admission to a private asylum, where he died one year later.

Other Works by Guy de Maupassant

A Life: The Humble Truth. Translated by Roger Pearson. New York: Oxford University Press, 1999.

The Necklace. Translated by Jonathan Sturges. London: Pushkin, 1999.

A Work about Guy de Maupassant

Lerner, Michael G. *Maupassant.* New York: George Braziller, 1975.

Mayakovsky, Vladimir (1893–1930) *poet*

Vladimir Vladimirovich Mayakovsky was born in Bagdadi, Georgia. Vladimir Konstantinovich, Mayakovsky's father, was employed as a forest ranger. Mayakovsky started school in 1902 but was not very interested in his studies. His older sister Ludmila, a student in Moscow, brought home political pamphlets, which Mayakovsky read avidly. When Mayakovsky's father died in 1906, his mother, Alexandra Alexeevna, moved her family to Moscow. Mayakovsky was instantly absorbed by the political situation of Moscow: At age 14, he was a full member of the Moscow Bolshevik Party.

Expelled from school in 1908 for nonpayment of tuition, Mayakovsky served as a messenger and lookout for the Bolsheviks. He was arrested for his activities but soon was released on probation. A year later, he was again placed in jail for his association with the revolutionaries. He wrote his first poem in solitary confinement. In 1911, he decided to study art and was admitted to the Moscow Institute for the Study of Painting, Sculpture, and Architecture. Painter David Burliuk introduced Mayakovsky to modern painting and poetry and was the first person to read Mayakovsky's poetry.

Mayakovsky joined the futurist movement, denouncing the rich literary tradition of Russia. He labeled Aleksandr PUSHKIN and Maxim GORKY, for instance, "insignificant." He did not rebel against only the literary canon but also against the conventional use of language. Many of Mayakovsky's poems contains words that do not actually exist in the Russian language. Mayakovsky published his first two poems, "Night" and "Morning," in 1912; they were published the same year in a collection with other poems and some prose pieces entitled *A Slap in the Face of Public Taste.*

In 1913, Mayakovsky produced his first play, *Vladimir Mayakovsky: A Tragedy.* The play consists of a number of poetic monologues that explore the self-perception of the poet, and the leading part was played by Mayakovsky himself. It was not big success with the public. Mayakovsky's first major poem, "A Cloud in Trousers," appeared in 1915. The poem is a tale of love and uses unusual images to denounce the traditional romantic representation of the poet in such lines as: "I am spit of the filthy night on a palm of a beggar."

Between 1915 and 1918, Mayakovsky produced a number of poetic works that dealt mostly with political ideology and were clearly propaganda for the Communist Party, which took control of the country in October 1917. He was an enthusiastic supporter of the Bolshevik regime and wrote in 1924 a poem in praise of Lenin.

In 1925, Mayakovsky visited the United States, attending meetings of labor unions, giving lectures about workers' rights, and sometimes joining the picketers during a strike. Mayakovsky described these experiences in two collections of poems, *Poems of America* and *My Discovery of America* (1926). In 1927, Mayakovsky established a literary journal, *Novy Lef,* in which he attacked Maxim Gorky. The short-lived journal published purely political poems that criticized capitalism, the West, and the "vices of the bourgeoisie." After a trip to Europe in 1929, Mayakovsky produced *Poems About a Soviet Passport,* a collection that recounted the reactions produced by his passport as he traveled across Europe. During 1928 and 1929, he also produced a number of propaganda pieces that dealt with various mundane issues of the proletariat, such as the joys of electricity, the advantages of running hot water, and the necessity of five-year plans. But his political verse alternated through the 1920s with much more personal love poems.

Mayakovsky received numerous awards from the Soviet government. Yet, he wrote two plays, *The Bedbug* (1928) and *The Bathhouse* (1930), that satirized Soviet bureaucracy and were suppressed by the authorities. His most successful play, *Moscow on Fire* (1930), appeared just a few days after his death, and recounted the events of the revolution of 1905.

In 1930, Mayakovsky shot and killed himself in his Moscow apartment. He seems to have been motivated by disappointment in love as well as by anxiety about the reception of his work. After his death, his body was placed on display for three days, and more than 150,000 mourners came to say their farewells. Stalin eulogized him, and generations of Soviet students memorized his poems. Today, critical opinion his works remains mixed, as it was during his lifetime. Mayakovsky completely broke away from literary tradition, establishing his own unique style for poetry and drama; at the same time, he attacked and denounced a number of writers and poets who did not adhere to the principles of SOCIALIST REALISM.

Other Works by Vladimir Mayakovsky

The Bedbug and Selected Poetry. Translated by Max Hayward. Bloomington: Indiana University Press, 1975.

For the Voice. Cambridge, Mass.: MIT Press, 2000.

Listen! Early Poems. Translated by Maria Enzberger. San Francisco: City Lights Books, 1991.

Mayakovsky: Plays. Translated by Guy Daniels. Evanston, Ill.: Northwestern University Press, 1995.

Works about Vladimir Mayakovsky

Bowra, C. M. "The Futurism of Vladimir Mayakovsky." In *The Creative Experiment.* New York: Grove Press, 1958.

Terras, Victor. *Vladimir Mayakovsky.* Boston: Twayne, 1983.

Mazumdar, Anita

See DESAI, ANITA.

Meeks, Brian (1953–) *nonfiction writer, poet, fiction writer*

Born in Montreal, Canada, to a Trinidadian mother and Jamaican father, Meeks grew up in Jamaica. There he attended Jamaica College before doing undergraduate work at the University of the West Indies, St. Augustine, Trinidad, during the politically turbulent early 1970s. After earning a doctorate from the University of the West Indies, Mona, Meeks acted as a media and political education consultant for the People's Revolutionary Government of Grenada. He also edited *The Free West Indian* during the early 1980s. Musicians Bob Marley, John Coltrane, and Miles Davis significantly influenced Meeks's work. In the acknowledgments to *Radical Caribbean: From Black Power to Abu Bakr* (1996), Meeks thanked Gordon Rohlehr and Kamau BRATHWAITE for teaching him "the importance of rigorous study and appreciation of popular culture as both central cause and effect of the political process."

Themes of human agency, revolution, and radical Caribbean activism reappear in Meeks's intellectual works. *Caribbean Revolutions and Revolutionary Theory: an Assessment of Cuba, Nicaragua and Grenada* (1993) traces revolutionary concepts from the French Revolution to reconsider revolutionary meaning. In *Radical Caribbean: From Black Power to Abu Bakr,* Meeks maps two decades of radical movements in the Caribbean to examine why revolutions occur. An *International Affairs* reviewer wrote, "In the case of Grenada [Meeks's] account of the tragic fall of the revolution goes beyond anything which has been written before."

Before returning to the University of the West Indies, Mona, where he is currently a senior lecturer in comparative politics and political theory and head of the Department of Government, Meeks taught at James Madison College, Michigan State University. In addition, Meeks has written poetry, which has been published in many anthologies. His recent and consistent intellectual contributions foreground significant revolutionary issues, making him one of the most influential contemporary Caribbean political theorists.

Other Works by Brian Meeks

Narratives of Resistance: Jamaica, Trinidad, the Caribbean. Kingston, Jamaica: University of West Indies Press, 2000.

"NUFF at the Cusp of an Idea: Grassroots Guerrillas and the Politics of the 1970s in Trinidad and Tobago." *Social Identities* 5, no. 4 (1999).

"The Political Moment in Jamaica: The Dimensions of Hegemonic Dissolution." In Manning Marable, ed., *Dispatches from the Ebony Tower.* New York: Columbia University Press, 2000.

A Work about Brian Meeks

Allahar, Anton, ed. *Caribbean Charisma: Reflections on Leadership, Legitimacy, and Populist Politics.* Boulder, Colo.: L. Rienner Publishers, 2001.

Mehta, Gita (1943–) *novelist*

Gita Mehta was born in Delhi, India. Her parents were deeply involved in India's political struggle for independence against the British. Her father, Biju Patnaik, is one of India's most famous freedom fighters who went on to become the political leader of the state of Orissa, India. Mehta was sent to boarding school at an early age, as both her parents were constantly in and out of jail due to their political activities.

Mehta was educated in India and England, and her novels reflect her preoccupation with the ongoing relationship between Western and Eastern cultures. She explores this theme in her nonfiction book *Karma Cola: Marketing the Mystic East* (1979) in which she looks into the fascination that Eastern cultures hold for "hippies" from the West. As the title suggests, the novel is based on global economy and explores the commodification of one culture by the other.

Her first fictional work, *Raj: A Novel* (1989), is a historical novel about a young girl from a noble family who comes of age during the British Raj. Through her experiences, it becomes obvious that the roots of British and Indian culture cannot be easily untangled in colonial India, especially among the privileged classes who have benefited from British education. What develops alongside the maturity of the heroine is India's own birthing process into independence from the British. Mehta's latest work, *Snakes and Ladders: Glimpses of Modern India* (1997), further explores aspects of India's change after its independence.

In addition to writing novels, Mehta is a journalist and documentary filmmaker. She has directed four films on the Bangladesh war and one on the Indo–Pakistan war for the BBC and NBC.

Another Work by Gita Mehta

A River Sutra. New York: Vintage Books, 1994.

A Work about Gita Mehta

Byer, Kathleen Collins. "The Lama and the Vanaprasthi: Rudyard Kipling's *Kim* and Gita Mehta's *A River Sutra.*" In A. L. McLeod, ed., *The Literature of the Indian Diaspora: Essays in Criticism.* New Delhi: Sterling, 2000.

Memmi, Albert (1920–) *novelist*

Albert Memmi was born in the Jewish quarter of Tunis, Tunisia. His father was a Jewish-Italian skilled saddler, and his mother was a Berber (a member of the non-Arab minority of North Africa). When Memmi was four years old, he went to rabbinical school and studied there for three years. In 1927, he attended the school of the Alliance Israélite Universelle in the rue Malta Srira in Tunis. Memmi would often help his father in his workshop where he listened to stories told by an old family friend. While attending school, Memmi was actively involved with local Jewish youth groups; this strongly influenced his perceptions, which would later surface in his writings, especially those relating to colonial issues. Memmi graduated from the Lycée Carnot in 1939 and was awarded the honor prize in philosophy. From 1941 to 1942, he studied philosophy at the University of Algiers. After the invasion of France by Nazi Germany when anti-Semitic laws were implemented by the collaborationist Vichy government of France, Memmi was expelled from the university and sent to a forced labor camp until 1945. After World War II, he moved to Paris and continued his studies at the Sorbonne. After Tunisia gained full independence, Memmi settled in Paris, where he took on various professorial positions. He retired from teaching in 1987.

Memmi's works were heavily influenced by the political and social situations that shaped his life, and his dual position as a member of the French educated elite as an impoverished and marginalized Jew also influenced his writings. In his first novel, *La Statue de sel* (*The Pillar of Salt,* 1953), Memmi's main protagonist, Mordecai, pours out his despair and sorrow. He is plagued by poverty and solitude, living as an estranged "outsider" who tries to make sense of his existence in a foreign land. Memmi's political views, his sociological training, and his own experiences, especially during World War II, allow him to discuss and explore the complexity of colonialism, particularly in his 1957 work, *The Colonizer and the Colonized,* in which he examines the social and psychological foundations of the views held by the colonizer and the colonized. To Memmi, the two groups constitute a framework in which neither group can exist without the other: The colonizer and the colonized are interdependent, but each group is a complex organization.

Memmi's works clearly show his genius as one of the leading intellectuals in postcolonial theory and thinking. He wrote all of his works in French, but many have been translated and published in English.

Other Works by Albert Memmi

Dependence: A Sketch for a Portrait of the Dependent. Translated by Philip A. Facey. Boston: Beacon, 1984.

Desert. Pueblo, Colo.: Passeggiata Press, 1992.

Jews and Arabs. Translated by Eleanor Levieux. Chicago: J. P. O'Hara, 1975.

The Liberation of the Jew. Translated by Judy Hyun. New York: Viking Press, 1966.

Racism. Translated by Kwame Anthony Appiah. Minneapolis: University of Minnesota Press, 1999.

The Scorpion. Translated by Eleanor Levieux. New York: Orion, 1971.

A Work about Albert Memmi

Roumani, Judith. *Albert Memmi.* Philadelphia: Temple University Press, 1987.

Menchú, Rigoberta (1959–) *memoirist*

Rigoberta Menchú was born in the village of Uspanadan in the western highlands of Guatemala to Vicente Menchú, a Quiche Maya Indian and an organizer of the Committee of Peasant Unity, and Juana Menchú Tum, also a Quiche Indian. She began to work at age five to help her mother pick coffee beans. At age nine, she was helping her father hoe and plant maize, and at 12, she joined in the communal work of her people by participating in the harvesting of maize. By then, her eldest and youngest brothers had died, the former from having breathed in the fumes of pesticide that had been sprayed at the farm where he worked, and the latter from malnutrition.

At age 13, Menchú, who was eager to learn to read and speak Spanish, the language of her oppressors, decided to accept a position as a maid in the distant capital. The exploitation she experienced as a maid, as well as her father's imprisonment at this time for his efforts at organizing against the landowners who were intent on depriving the Quiche Indians of their land, contributed to her later transformation into a leader of her people. Menchú's political activism began when she was still a teenager, involving herself in social reform through the Catholic church, the women's rights movement, and a local guerrilla organization. In 1979, she joined the Committee of Peasant Unity (CUC), as her father had recently done. Yet, it was not until the Guatemalan army brutally killed her father, her brother, and her mother in separate incidents in 1980 and 1981 that she became prominent in the CUC. Aware of the horrendous torture each of her family members received before being burned to death, Menchú was forced to go into hiding in 1981, first in Guatemala then in Mexico.

Since then, Menchú has dedicated her life to resisting oppression in Guatemala and fighting for the rights of all its Indian peasant groups. She was one of the founders of the United Representation of the Guatemalan Opposition (RUOG) in 1982, and the following year, she recounted the story of her life and the ways of her people to the anthropologist, Elisabeth Burgos-Debray, who proceeded to transcribe the tapes and edit them into the internationally known book, *I, Rigoberta Menchú* (1983), which was translated into English by Ann Wright and published in 1984. However, an unexpected controversy erupted in 1999 after anthropologist David Stoll raised questions concerning the authenticity of Menchú's autobiography in *Rigoberta Menchú and the Story of All Poor Guatemalans*. In response to Stoll's book, Arturo Arias edited *The Rigoberta Menchú Controversy* (2001), a compilation of the various newspaper reports, articles, and letters—including one by Stoll—written in response to this ongoing controversy.

After the publication of her autobiography, Menchú continued her activism, becoming a member of the National Committee of the CUC in 1986 and, in 1987, participating as the narrator of *When the Mountains Tremble*, a film protesting the suffering of the Maya people. Menchú was awarded the Nobel Peace Prize in 1992 and, in 1996, became a Goodwill Ambassador for UNESCO.

Another Work by Rigoberta Menchú

Crossing Borders. Translated by Ann Wright. New York: Verso, 1998.

A Work about Rigoberta Menchú

Schulze, Julie. *Rigoberta Menchú Tum: Champion of Human Rights.* New York: John Gordon Burke, 1997.

Michaux, Henri (1899–1984) *poet*

An accomplished painter and poet, Henri Michaux was born on May 24 to a bourgeois family in Namur, Belgium. As a student, he was indifferent at best and held himself apart from his peers. He found comfort in art, languages, and literature, all of which helped him through World War II and the German occupation of Belgium.

Although Michaux attempted to write poetry while he was still in school, he concentrated mostly on reading everything from the works of the saints to avant-garde poetry. He considered entering the priesthood but instead followed the advice of his father and embarked on the study of medicine. Dissatisfied, he left to work as a sailor on a merchant vessel, disembarking only two days before the ship capsized. He returned to Belgium where, after a series of miserable jobs, he discovered the works of the Comte de LAUTREAMONT.

Inspired, Michaux moved to Paris, where he began to paint and secured a job in a publishing house while developing himself as a writer. After the death of his parents in 1929, he traveled extensively and became fascinated by Eastern religion. His writing career was firmly established due to favorable criticism from André GIDE. Among his best-known collections are *My Properties* (1929), a work that explores the imagination and consciousness, and *Plume* (1930), a comic exploration of self-identity.

Michaux married during World War II but lost his wife in a house fire. After this, he began to experiment with drugs. He became a French citizen in 1955, abandoned drugs, and began to focus his writing on the themes of drug addiction, human anguish, and despair; in *Miserable Miracle* (1956), for example, he details the journeys of the imagination as it searches for self-knowledge while under the influence of mescaline.

Michaux was admired by both the surrealists and the U.S. beat poets. Toward the end of his life, he turned more and more to Eastern meditation as he focused on the study of the human spirit. Michaux died on October 18, having contributed greatly to both the origins of the surrealist movement and U.S. beat literature.

Another Work by Henri Michaux

Tent Posts. Translated by Lynn Hoggard. Los Angeles: Sun and Moon Press, 1997.

A Work about Henri Michaux

Broome, Peter. *Henri Michaux.* London: Athlone Press, 1977.

Mickiewicz, Adam (1798–1855) *poet, playwright*

Adam Bernard Mickiewicz was born in Nowo-gródek, Poland. Regarded as one of the greatest Polish poets and activists for Polish independence, much of his past remains a mystery, including the possibility that he might have been of Jewish descent on his mother's side. Biographical data, particularly regarding his relationships with women and his interest in mysticism, were kept quiet during the years of Communist rule in Poland. Spirituality of any kind was looked on unfavorably, and much of Mickiewicz's history was deliberately hidden to maintain his flawless public image. After his death, Mickiewicz's son, Władysław, destroyed documents that might have negatively affected his father's public image. Mickiewicz's actions and writings, however, reveal not only a romantic poet and great artist but also a political activist. Mickiewicz's major poetic and dramatic works were written during a three-year period before his attention shifted to political writing.

Mickiewicz received a government-sponsored education in Polish literature and history. He made friends with many fellow students who were members of secret youth organizations. On graduating, he took a high-school teaching position in Kovno to repay his government scholarship, but when authorities discovered secret student organizations at the school, an investigation resulted in a six-month prison term and a five-year exile in Russia.

Mickiewicz's banishment had a positive influence on his career as a writer and activist. He befriended Russian poet Aleksandr PUSHKIN and traveled to Germany where he attended Hegel's lectures and met GOETHE. Hearing news of the No-vember uprising in 1830, he attempted unsuccessfully to return to Poland. When the uprising failed, Mickiewicz, along with many other Polish artists, moved to France.

In Paris, he began to focus on political journalism, appealing to Polish emigrants to unite in the common cause. In 1839, he took a position as lecturer on Roman literature at the University of Lausanne and, in 1840, on Slavonic literatures at the Collège de France. He was suspended from his post in 1844 for his antichurch attitude and mystic or supernaturally oriented ideas.

Mickiewicz's poetry was first collected in two volumes called *Vilna* (1822–23) and reflected his love of Polish folklore and tradition, particularly folk songs and legends. This love is evident in his plays *The Forefathers Eve* (1823) and *Grazyna* (1825). Mickiewicz's poetic novel *Konrad Wallen-rod* (1828) is based on the history of the Teutonic knights. His work always contains a sense of patriotism and a desire for Poland to one day regain its independence.

Mickiewicz was also a poet of prophecy, a trend held in high regard in Poland throughout the 18th and 19th centuries. He linked his patriotism and nationalism to mysticism and spirituality. Influenced by Andrzej Towianski, a known mystic, Mickiewicz came to believe that Israel was a fellow sufferer of Poland and that Poland was the "Christ" of all nations. He believed that the kingdom of God would prevail in the middle of the 19th century and that the chosen nations would be the Poles, French, and Jews. This commitment to Judaism is often linked to his mother's ancestry and is evident as well in his positive representation of Jewish characters such as Jankiel, the patriotic Jew in *Pan Tadeusz* (1834). Written while he was in exile, this epic poem, his last strictly poetic work, attempts to recapture the Poland of his childhood as an idealized place and time. After the publication of this work, Mickiewicz made what he referred to as a "moral decision" to commit himself to prophecy and political activism, viewing the writing of poetry as trivial in light of Poland's tragic political situation.

More than just a poet and playwright, Mickiewicz was a spiritual leader to the Polish nation. His writings provided hope to not only the people of his native Poland as they struggled under Russian, Prussian, and Austrian rule but also to his many fellow exiles in the emigré circles in Paris.

Other Works by Adam Mickiewicz

Forefathers. Translated by Count Potoki of Montalk. London: Polish Cultural Foundation, 1968.

The Great Improvisation. Translated by Louise Varèse. New York: Voyages, 1956.

Olzer, Krystyna, ed. *Treasury of Love Poems by Adam Mickiewicz.* New York: Hipprocrene Books, 1998.

Works about Adam Mickiewicz

Gardner, Maria. *Adam Mickiewicz, the National Poet of Poland.* New York: Arno Press, 1971.

Welsh, David J. *Adam Mickiewicz.* Boston: Twayne, 1970.

Midang

See SO CHONG-JU.

Milosz, Czeslaw (1911–   ) *poet, novelist*

Czeslaw Milosz was born on June 30 in Seteksniai, Lithuania. Recipient of the Nobel Prize in literature in 1980, he is considered one of the leading figures of contemporary Polish poetry, though his works, like many of his contemporaries', were once banned in his native land.

Milosz received his early education in Roman Catholic schools. In 1917, at the start of the October Revolution, he left war-torn Russia to live with his grandparents in Szetejnie. He earned a law degree from King Stefan Batory University, where he became politically active, cofounding a leftist literary group called Zagary. On graduation, he began working for a Polish radio station but was ultimately fired from his position for associating with Jews.

Milosz's greatest early influence was his uncle, Oscar Milosz, a noted French Lithuanian metaphysical poet. He published his first collection of poetry, *Poemat O Czasie* (*Poem in Frozen Time*, 1933) at age 22. A second volume followed shortly thereafter, and in 1934 he received an award from the Union of Polish Writers for his poetry. World War II intervened and Milosz served as a radio operator. He returned home only to be captured in the Russian occupation of his city. He managed to escape to Poland where he joined the resistance in Warsaw.

Although he was ultimately exiled from Poland, Milosz became well known as a poet in literary circles but suffering greatly, however, from government censorship. He assembled an anthology of English and American poetry that he was not allowed to publish; in addition, so many changes were made to a screenplay he cowrote that he refused to allow his name to appear in the credits. In 1945, he joined the Polish diplomatic service, serving in New York and Washington. A year later, his works were banned in Poland, and the government withheld his passport in 1950 as a result of his leftist views and his critical stance against the Communist regime in Poland.

Milosz was allowed to leave Poland in 1951 to seek political asylum in Paris. He obtained refuge at "Kultura," a haven for exiled political writers and artists, with other influential Polish émigrés. Alone and financially destitute, he wrote *The Captive Mind* (1953), in which he harshly criticized Stalinism and "The vulnerability of the twentieth century mind . . . and its readiness to accept totalitarian terror for the sake of a hypothetical future" (Milosz). Although officially banned in Poland and viewed with much negativity by French left-wing intellectuals, the book was astoundingly successful. It was printed by Kultura's underground publishing house, and copies were shipped secretly to Poland.

For five years after the publication of *The Captive Mind,* Milosz did not produce any works. His exile left him feeling alone. He wrote his second novel *Issa Valley* (1955), which tells of childhood in Lithuania, as a means of reconnecting to his past. He was finally able to reunite with his family and, in 1960, moved once again, this time to the United

States, where he took a post in Slavic languages and literature at the University of California at Berkeley.

In 1981, Milosz returned home for the first time since 1951. Martial law was declared, however, in December of that same year, and his works were once again banned in Poland. After winning the Nobel Prize, his recognition grew to the point that his poem *You Who Wronged a Simple Man* was used on Solidarity flyers and also inscribed on a monument to Gdansk shipyard workers who had been killed during the 1970 protests. Milosz continues to write and lecture in California and is still active in his support for the future of Solidarity in his native land.

Other Works by Czeslaw Milosz

Milosz's ABCs. Translated by Madeline G. Levine. New York: Farrar, Straus & Giroux, 2001.

Road-side Dog. Translated by Czeslaw Milosz and Robert Haas. New York: Farrar, Straus & Giroux, 1998.

The History of Polish Literature. Berkeley: University of California Press, 1983.

A Work about Czeslaw Milosz

Nathan, Leonard, and Arthur Quinn. *The Poet's Work: An Introduction to Czeslaw Milosz.* Cambridge, Mass.: Harvard University Press, 1991.

Miron, Gaston (1928–1996) *poet*

Gaston Miron was born in Sainte-Agathe-des-Monts, Québec. He is one of most famous contemporary Québecois poets and has played a significant role in fostering Québecois writing. He cofounded *Hexagon,* which he directed from 1953 to 1983, and he has lectured on Québecois writing and has read his work throughout Europe and North America.

Miron's poems are rich in rhythms, melodies, and evocative words; yet at the same time, they convey an impassioned militant independence. In 1954, he began his major poetic cycle with "Agonique Life," "Walk with Love," and "Bateche." Fragments of these works were eventually pub-

lished in the early 1960s, and in the 1970s, university presses continued to publish collections of the cycle. Miron's work is today regularly reprinted, translated, and anthologized, reaching a wide and diverse audience. For his work as an editor and essayist, in addition to his work as a poet, he received numerous awards, including the Academy of Letters of Quebec Medal (which recognized Miron's role in celebrating Québecois culture). In 1995, he received an honorary doctorate from the University of Montreal. Miron is considered one of the most significant poets of Quebec.

Another Work by Gaston Miron

The March to Love: Selected Poems, Gaston Miron. Edited and translated by Douglas J. Jones. Pittsburgh, Pa.: International Poetry Forum, 1986.

Mishima Yukio (Hiraoka Kimitake) (1925–1970) *novelist, short-story writer, playwright*

Mishima Yukio was born in Tokyo to Hiraoka Azusa and Shizue Hashi. Shortly after his birth, Mishima's paternal grandmother, Natsuko, took him to raise. In accordance with his grandmother's wishes, he attended the elitist Gakushūin, a school founded to educate the imperial family. Mishima was a good student and displayed a talent for writing even while he was young.

While still at Gakushūin, he published his first prose work, *A Forest in Full Bloom* (1941), a historical novel. Mishima disclaimed this story as imitative of Austrian poet Rainer Maria RILKE, but critics received it favorably. Having made a literary entrance, Mishima widened his literary circles, becoming associated with the Japanese romantics.

As World War II raged, Mishima prepared himself to go to war. However, when he went for his final physical, he was misdiagnosed with tuberculosis. As a result, he sat out the war, working in a navy library, and was accepted to Tokyo Imperial University in 1944.

After World War II, the romantics were out of favor in a world dominated by the struggle to recover from the war. Mishima's work was regarded as too introspective, so he had difficulty publishing his stories. However, in 1946 he met KAWABATA Yasunari, who helped him publish two stories. The first of these—"The Middle Ages" (1946)—was a portrayal of the grief the historical figure Ashikaga Yoshimasa felt over the death of his son, Shogun Ashikaga Yoshihisa. The second story—"Cigarettes" (1946)—was based on Mishima's experiences at Gakushūin. The protagonist becomes a target of members of a rugby club when he reveals that he has joined the literary club. Shortly thereafter, Mishima received his degree from Tokyo Imperial University and went to work for the finance ministry. After less than a year, he left the ministry and joined a group of leftist writers, who helped him once again to publish his work.

In 1948, he published his first novel, *Thieves,* a story of love among a group of upper-class youth. The novel was not well received but demonstrated the development of a romantic style that reached its fulfillment in Mishima's next novel.

Confessions of a Mask (1949) established Mishima as a writer of merit. The story is about a man who struggles with a growing awareness of his homosexuality and attempts to throw off the mask of heterosexuality. In this novel, Mishima tackles for the first time the issue of false appearances, a theme that recurs in his later works.

Although *Confessions of a Mask* launched Mishima's career, the stories that followed were not of the same caliber. Two years passed before he published his next major work, *Forbidden Colors,* a novel that describes the homosexual subculture of Tokyo in the immediate postwar period.

In 1956, Mishima published his best-received work, *The Temple of the Golden Pavilion.* The story centers on a temple acolyte who is handicapped by a stutter. Frustrated by the inaccessibility of beauty, he decides to destroy the temple, a symbol of beauty, and burns it to the ground. This novel won Mishima the Yomiuri Prize for literature.

Mishima married Yōko Sugiyama, the daughter of a well-known painter, in 1958 and settled into a comfortable life. During this period his nationalistic beliefs began to resurface, and he wrote "Patriotism" (1956), a short story based on an attempted coup d'état by imperial army officers in 1936. "Patriotism" was the first in a series of stories that deal with characters who either betray or uphold ideals.

These nationalistic stories helped build to the climax of Mishima's life—his ritualistic suicide within the compound of Japan's Self-Defense Forces in Tokyo in protest of the demilitarization of Japan. On November 25, 1970, Mishima and three members of the militaristic group he organized, the Shield Society, took Gen. Kanetoshi Mashita hostage. After a publicized speech from a rooftop in which Mishima called for a return of the emperor to power, he retired into the building and committed *seppuku* (a ritualistic suicide using a sword).

Other Works by Yukio Mishima

After the Banquet. Translated by Donald Keene. New York: Knopf, 1963.

Madame de Sade. Translated by Donald Keene. New York: Grove Press, 1967.

The Sailor Who Fell from Grace with the Sea. Translated by John Nathan. New York: Knopf, 1965.

Works about Yukio Mishima

Nathan, John. *Mishima: A Biography.* Cambridge, Mass.: Da Capo Press, 2000.

Scott-Stokes, Henry. *The Life and Death of Yukio Mishima.* New York: Farrar, Straus & Giroux, 1974.

Yourcenar, Marguerite. *Mishima: A Vision of the Void.* Translated by Alberto Manguel. New York: Farrar, Straus & Giroux, 1986.

Miss Lou

See BENNETT, LOUISE.

Mistral, Gabriela (Lucila Godoy Alcayaga) (1889–1957) *poet, essayist*

Gabriela Mistral was born in a rural community in northern Chile to Jerónimo Godoy Villanueva (former schoolteacher, guitar player, and songwriter) and Petronila Alcayaga Rojas. As a child Mistral was falsely accused by her schoolmaster, also her godmother, of stealing paper from a supply cabinet. After the incident, she never returned to the local school and received most of her early education from her mother and an older sister. By age 15, she had completed her teacher training and had begun to teach reading and writing to Indian children and adults in remote villages.

In 1914, Mistral began to publish poems in various journals in Chile and overseas. It was at this time that she adopted her pseudonym as a tribute to two writers she admired: the Italian Gabriele D'ANNUNZIO and the Frenchman Frédéric Mistral. As she devoted much of her energies to her career as a school administrator, which she considered her real vocation, it was not until 1922 that she published a larger selection of her poems under the title *Desolation*. Her first book drew immediate praise from critics, other writers, and audiences. In it, the poet addressed many of the themes that would preoccupy her throughout her life: maternal affection, the joys and trials of love, the suffering of the poor. Her second book, *Tenderness* (1925), includes much of the children's verse that originally appeared in *Desolation* and that Mistral strove to develop as a genre in its own right. *Felling* (1938) represented a break from the style of her earlier works: While the poetry remains essentially simple, the stanzaic structure of poems in this and the last book Mistral published, *Wine Press* (1954), tends to be more variable and complex. It is the simplicity, emotive force, and subtle profundity of Mistral's poetry that make it so moving and unique. The poem "Mourning" from *Wine Press* begins, "In one single night there burst from my breast / the tree of mourning; it heightened and grew."

Later in life Mistral received international recognition as a poet, an educator, and an ambassador, and in 1945, she was awarded the Nobel Prize in literature. She is considered one of the most important figures in early 20th-century Chilean and Latin-American poetry, and her influence has proven extensive. Both as an educator and as a poet, she made poetry accessible to all classes of society and, in this way, has contributed directly and indirectly to much of the great poetry that has appeared in Chile and other Hispanic countries in the last several decades.

Other Works by Gabriela Mistral

Agosin, Marjorie, ed. *A Gabriela Mistral Reader.* Translated by Maria Jacketti. Fredonia, N.Y.: White Pine Press, 1992.
Selected Poems. Translated and edited by Doris Dana. Baltimore: Johns Hopkins University Press, 1971.

Works about Gabriela Mistral

Arce de Vázquez, Margot. *Gabriela Mistral: The Poet and Her Work.* Translated by Helene Masslo Anderson. New York: New York University Press, 1964.
Fiol-Matta, Licia. *A Queer Mother for the Nation: The State and Gabriela Mistral.* Minneapolis: University of Minnesota Press, 2002.

Mistry, Rohinton (1952–) *novelist*

Rohinton Mistry was born in Bombay, India, and is of Parsi descent (a community exiled after the Islamic conquest of Iran and one of the smallest existing ethnic minorities in India). After his studies in mathematics and economics at Bombay University, Mistry left India and immigrated to Canada in 1975. He joined the University of Toronto, where he graduated with a bachelor's degree in English and philosophy. This blend of interests may explain the recurring commentary on class status that is an important theme in his works, which are strongly expressive of his upbringing in Bombay and Zoroastrian beliefs.

Mistry's future with writing was sealed after he won first prize in a writing contest held at the University of Toronto. Following this success, Mistry wrote two collections of short stories, later compiled together in *Swimming Lessons and Other Stories from Feroz Shah Baag* (1987). These works portray both the problems and tribulations of being a Bombay Parsi. Most of the characters are Bombay Parsis who are under pressure to find a balance between their split identities as Zoroastrian Parsis and Indian Parsis.

Mistry's first novel, *Such a Long Journey* (1991), is a continuation of these issues, and it won the Commonwealth Writers Prize. His novels are written in English but are saturated with a multilingual (English–Hindi–Parsi) colloquialism that is peculiar to Bombay city-talk. Mistry's characters are harmonious hybrids out of the clash between histories and communities. His second novel, *A Fine Balance* (1995), for example, traces the lives of four characters of different castes and religions who must defy social, even individual, prejudices to help each other survive the 1947 partition of India and Pakistan.

Unlike other Indian authors living abroad who, because of distance or exile from India, write about problems surrounding migration or postcolonial subjectivity (*see* POSTCOLONIALISM), Mistry's works are remarkably free of these perspectives. The India of his books is equally recognizable to Indian readers for its authenticity as it is rewarding to an international audience that has little opportunity to read Parsi authors in English.

Another Work by Rohinton Mistry

The Tales of Ferozsha Baag. London: Faber, 1992.

A Work about Rohinton Mistry

Dodiya, Jaydipsing, ed. *The Fiction of Rohinton Mistry: Critical Studies.* London: Sangam, 1998.

Mo Yan (Guan Moye) (1956–   ) *short-story writer, novelist*

Mo Yan was born on February 17 in Gaomi township in China's Shandong province, a poor rural community. He often went without food and clothing in the harsh northern climate. Like most young people of his generation, he joined the People's Liberation Army (PLA) in 1976, at age 20, serving as a police commissar and a propaganda officer. He also began writing, publishing his first story, "Rain Falling Thick and Fast in the Spring Night," in 1981.

Mo Yan often describes his writing as an outgrowth of the extreme poverty and isolation of his childhood, as well as of his family's strong oral tradition. He chose an ironic pen name that belied his desire to express himself (*Mo Yan* means, "don't speak"). In 1986, he graduated from the PLA's Armed Forces Cultural Academy's literature department and joined the Chinese Writers Association. By then, he had completed his first book of stories, *The Crystal Carrot* (1986). He also finished *Red Sorghum* (1987), his best-known work, which addresses the plight of China's rural poor while describing an unusual love story set among the sorghum fields of his hometown. Taking place during the Japanese occupation of China, *Red Sorghum* contains patriotic themes. Zhang Yimou's film version won the top prize at the Berlin Film Festival in 1987.

Mo Yan's second novel, *The Garlic Ballads* (1987), addresses corrupt practices by Chinese officials. He writes in *World Literature Today* that it is "a book about hunger, and it is a book about rage." His third novel, *The Republic of Wine,* is both an examination of greed and a reflection upon Mo Yan's own struggles with alcoholism.

Mo Yan's writings are vividly rendered and are often exceedingly graphic in their portrayal of human excess, desire, decadence, and waste. However, his compassion for the Chinese peasant is always present. Most criticisms of Mo Yan's works are aimed at the continuation of patriarchal themes in his work.

Mo Yan remained an employee of the PLA until 1997 when he joined the editorial staff of the *Beijing Procuratorial Daily*. His latest book of short stories, *Shifu, You'll Do Anything for a Laugh,* was published in English in 2001; the English translation of his novel *Big Breasts and Wide Hips* (2003) is forthcoming. He lives in Beijing.

Another Work by Mo Yan

"My American Books." In *World Literature Today* 74:3 (Summer 2000).

Works about Mo Yan

Goldblatt, Howard. "'The Saturnicon': Forbidden Food of Mo Yan." In *World Literature Today* 74:3 (Summer 2000).

Inge, M. Thomas. "Mo Yan through Western Eyes." In *World Literature Today* 74:3 (Summer 2000).

Wang, David Der-Wei. "The Literary World of Mo Yan." In *World Literature Today* 74:3 (Summer 2000).

modernism

The term *modernism* generally refers to the literary and cultural movements associated with the early part of the 20th century from the start of World War I in 1914 to the start of World War II, though there are claims that it began in the middle of the 19th century with the publication of BAUDELAIRE's *Les Fleurs du mal* and FLAUBERT's *Madame Bovary* in 1857, as a response to urbanization, the increasing commodification of life, and the devaluation of art. The modernist movement in literature was created by a change in the way writers looked at the world around them. Influenced by the horrors of World War I and the rise in societal materialism, as well as socioeconomic and religious suppression, these writers' perceptions, not only of the world as a whole but also of humanity's place in that world shifted radically. They needed new ways to express their shifting perceptions.

Modernist writers experimented, often radically, with form. In poetry, formalized rhymes and meters became free verse. Novelists began to write more loosely, for example, forsaking a logical sequence of thoughts for a stream-of-consciousness style. In particular, the conventions of REALISM were discarded in favor of distorted time sequences and collages of imagery. These new forms and styles were often complex and posed a challenge to readers, who then had to struggle to find their own positions relative to the fragmented nature of the works. This creation of a feeling of isolation and dislocation in the reader was one of the main ideas behind modernism.

Modernist writers wanted their readers to think differently about the cultural and political changes occurring throughout Europe and America at the start of the 20th century. The horrors of World War I as well as the discovery of hidden forces motivating and governing human behavior (made by thinkers such as Karl Marx, Sigmund FREUD, and Friedrich NIETZSCHE) led to a search for hidden meanings elsewhere in society. There was also a shift towards mysticism as an alternative to traditional ideology.

A widespread loss of confidence in the concept of identity was also foremost among the philosophical questions that plagued modernist writers. Longstanding scientific beliefs about the origin of humanity were challenged. The industrialization and mechanization of society was rapidly displacing people from their jobs. Christianity was becoming widely associated with capitalism and with an oppressive, often hypocritical, view of morality. At the same time, the critical study of biblical texts and the rising popularity of Darwin's theory of evolution gave rise to further religious challenge. Finally, a growing awareness of other cultures also influenced modernist concepts and world views, leading to changes in the perception of reality, which began to seem like an external concept rather than an innate one.

Like many other eras of social and political upheaval, the early 20th century found its expression through the arts, with modernism at the heart of that ideology. World War II brought a new period of social change, thus marking the end of this particular movement and paving the way for other trends.

Latin-American Modernism

Modernismo, or Latin-American modernism, was a mostly poetic literary movement, distinct from European and American modernism, that began at the end of the 19th century and lasted until the end of World War I. It resembles French SYMBOLISM and borrowed extensively from the ideas of Charles

BAUDELAIRE, especially those concerning art for art's sake.

Modernism rose in a cultural framework defined by a disillusionment with ROMANTICISM and a desire for a renewal of spiritual ideals. Its central figure is poet Rubén DARÍO, who, in the 1880s, revitalized Latin-American poetry through his unique diction and his upholding of artistic beauty as life's ultimate ideal.

The modernist poem valued sensations over ideas. This was a revolutionary position in Latin America where, up until that time, most poetry had been either didactic or sentimental. Modernist writers also employed a collection of symbols, borrowed from the French and from antiquity, to represent their ideas in a more visceral fashion. The swan was the most prominent of these symbols. White and graceful, it was a symbol of ideal beauty; at the same time, its neck—hooked in the form of a question mark—represented the doubts of modern humanity.

The erotic, which earlier Latin-American writers had avoided, was embraced by modernists. The sensual aspects of love were celebrated, and erotic passion was equated with the artist's desire to create.

The modernists proposed that artists were in contact with a higher being and were able to unlock life's mysteries by the powers of art. To this end, they concentrated a great deal of effort on developing formal virtuosity and inventing new kinds of versification.

The high modernism of Darío and his followers, with its French influences, was a highly aestheticized movement, cosmopolitan, and not tied to national or patriotic issues. Modernism took a different turn in Brazil, where writers such as Mario de Andrade (1893–1945) and Oswald de Andrade (1890–1954) sought to create a new nation by assimilating the eclectic influences of its history, including indigenous and African cultures, in a new tapestry of national identity. Avant-garde movements in Nicaragua, Mexico, and Cuba also incorporated indigenous and African-based popular cultures.

The modernist movement, and Darío in particular, prepared the way for such poets as Pablo NERUDA and Octavio PAZ. It is important to note, however, that modernists had not yet completely accepted the idea of a world without absolute values and meanings as their 20th-century descendents would. Their poetry was rigorously structured in imitation of their conception of reality. It remained logical and was essentially neoclassical in its ambitions. Unlike their descendents, modernists reacted to the uncertainty of the world by trying to create an art form that reassured them that a moral order could exist. As the 20th century progressed this idea became more and more untenable.

Chinese Modernism

Modernism in China had a more progressive meaning than in Europe and Latin America. Its beginnings can be dated to 1899, when Liang Qichao (Liang Ch'i-ch'ao) (1873–1929), a leading intellectual, called for a "revolution in poetry" and the overthrow of traditional literature, which was written in a formal literary language. He advocated the use of both old and new vernacular mixed with literary Chinese. Other writers, such as Huang Zunxian (Huang Tsun-hsien) (1848–1905), advocated further reforms, such as the addition of colloquial vocabulary and references to modern life in poetry. These reforms were augmented by an increased number of translations of foreign works that had a modernity all their own.

By 1916, despite China's political chaos, writers found unprecedented freedom to experiment and modernize. The decade saw the birth of many literary journals. One of the most influential was Chen Duxiu's *New Youth*, which he founded in 1915 and which served as a focal point in the modernist movement. Chen Duxiu blamed the Confucian classics, which formed the foundation of Chinese literary tradition, for China's inability to modernize.

1917 marks a milestone in the development of China's literary modernism: In January, Chen Duxiu published HU SHIH's "Some Tentative Suggestions for the Reform of Chinese Literature." Its suggestions were indeed modest, but the article was held up as a modernist manifesto. Hu Shih advised against the use of clichés and advocated timeliness in topics, but the most important innovation he urged was to write in the Chinese vernacular language, known as *baihua*, that is, to use the national language to create a national literature. Hu Shih insisted that the use of a "dead" language produced a "dead" literature.

Hu Shih's article took the literary world by storm. By the time that the second beginning of modernism rolled around on May 4, 1919, experiments in *baihua* literature were already underway. Hu Shih published several *baihua* poems in January 1918, and in May, LU Xun published what is regarded as the first Chinese modernist short story, "Diary of a Madman." A vicious satire that attacks the old Chinese morality, the story is about a paranoid man who suspects all of conspiring to kill and eat him.

The political climate in China urged further change in its literature. After World War I, the 1919 Treaty of Versailles awarded parts of China in concession to Japan. This outraged the Chinese people, and many began to turn their attention to China's weaknesses in the new world and to mobilize in protest. A demonstration on May 4, 1919, drew thousands, including many students and scholars. The task of rectifying China's humiliation instilled literary modernism with a sense of political urgency; writers committed to writing with a cause—that of national pride.

Some of the main themes of modernism were to write in an accessible and truthful language (*baihua*), to think and write critically as a means for change in society and government, to celebrate individualism, and to experiment with new forms. The short story rose to prominence as a vehicle for modernism. The May Fourth era had begun, and it was a time of great productivity, openness to foreign literature and ideas, and a deep commitment to social change. Writers such as DING LING used modernism to explore modern ideas, such as feminist independence.

Eventually, the May Fourth era gave way to the ascendancy of SOCIALIST REALISM under the Communist regime. Modernism experienced a revival after the easing of restrictions in the 1970s and 1980s, and it is still currently as much the subject of examination and debate in China as is POST-MODERNISM, as Chinese writers reexamine history through literary innovation. Since the Cultural Revolution, modernism has focused on form, such as SYMBOLISM in poetry (as in the writing of BEI DAO) and the avant-garde in theater (as in the plays of Nobel laureate GAO Xingjian). Also, a number of writers have turned to explorations of MAGIC REALISM, satire, and stream-of-consciousness writing. Much of the writing that is done in China and in exile by Chinese writers continues the modernist experiment.

Works about Modernism

Ellison, David Richard. *Ethics and Aesthetics in Modernist Literature: From the Sublime to the Uncanny.* New York: Cambridge University Press, 2001.

Fekkema, Douwe, and Elrud Ibsch. *Modernist Conjectures: A Mainstream in European Literature, 1910–1940.* New York: St. Martin's Press, 1988.

Goldman, Merle, ed. *Modern Chinese Literature in the May Fourth Era.* Cambridge, Mass.: Harvard University Press, 1985.

Gross, John, ed. *The Modern Movement: A TLS Companion.* Chicago: University of Chicago Press, 1993.

Larson, Wendy, and Anne Wedell-Wedellsborg. *Inside Out: Modernism and Post-Modernism in Chinese Literary Culture.* Aarhus, Denmark: Aarhus University Press, 1993.

Lee, Leo Ou-fan. "Beyond Realism: Thoughts on Modernist Experiments in Contemporary Chinese Writing." In Howard Goldblatt, ed., *Worlds Apart: Recent Chinese Writing and its Audiences.* Armonk, N.Y.: M. E. Sharpe, 1990.

Login Jrade, Cathy. *Rubén Darío and the Romantic Search for Unity: The Modernist Recourse to Esoteric Tradition.* Austin: University of Texas Press, 1983.

Montale, Eugenio (1896–1981) *poet*

Winner of the 1975 Nobel Prize in literature, Eugenio Montale was born in Genoa, Italy. The youngest of five children born to Domenico Montale, an import businessman, Montale's formal education was cut short by poor health, but summers spent observing the harsh landscape surrounding his family's villa on the Ligurian Riviera soon affected the tone and vision of his poetry. He had originally aspired to a career as an opera singer, but a brief tour as an infantry officer during World War I caused him to set his plans aside.

Montale continued to read fervently, devouring the works of philosophers such as Benedetto Croce and Henri Bergson but also delighting in the classics of both Italian and French fiction. Returning from the war, he again began to sing, but the death of his voice teacher in 1923 caused him to abandon his desire to pursue an operatic career and to look instead toward a literary career.

In 1927, Montale moved to Florence where he secured employment with a publishing house before moving on, in 1928, to accept the position as director of the Gabinetto Viesseux research library. He worked primarily as a critic and is best known in this field for assisting James Joyce in promoting Italo SVEVO as an emerging Italian voice. At the same time, Montale also began to establish his own literary voice as a poet; he published his first collection of poems, *Bones of the Cuttlefish* (1925), in which he focused on the scenery of his childhood summers in Liguria. Subsequent collections, such as *The Occasions* (1939), became increasingly introspective and focused on personal emotions set against a background of current events.

In 1938, Montale, who had always vocally opposed fascism, was dismissed from his cultural position because of his refusal to join the Fascist Party. He withdrew from public circles and ceased to write, working instead on translations of other writers. In particular, he became very much affected by T. S. ELIOT's poem *The Waste Land*. Montale believed that this work expressed succinctly the confusion and pessimism felt by people living in the time between World War I and World War

II. Eliot, in turn, knew of Montale's works and translated his poem *Arsenio* into English at the same time that Montale was working on Eliot's piece. The two writers, separated by vast cultural and geographic distances, seemed to share a similar view of the world. Much of Montale's poetry, like Eliot's, focuses on the dilemma of everyday life and explores modern history, philosophy, and the nature and effect of love on the human condition.

Montale's third collection, *The Storm and Other Poems* (1956), engaged similar themes. His fourth collection, however, took on a slightly more autobiographical tone, containing elements drawn directly from the author's life. This work, *Satura* (1962; translated 1971), also experimented with dialogue and nontraditional form. Some of the poems are satirical in nature, particularly in their look at the empty promises made by certain proponents of ideologies.

In 1967, Montale was made a member for life in the Italian Senate. Shortly thereafter, in 1975, he was awarded the Nobel Prize. His two final works were both diaries written in verse. *Diaro del '71 e del '72* (1973) and *Diaro di Quattro Annini* (1977) both express aspects of Montale's own life as an artist and as a human being. He died in Milan on September 12, four years after his final publication.

Another Work by Eugenio Montale

Collected Poems: 1920–1954. Translated by Jonathan Galassi. New York: Farrar, Straus & Giroux, 1998.

A Work about Eugenio Montale

Ó Ceallacháin, Éanna. *Eugenio Montale: The Poetry of Later Years.* Oxford: Legenda, 2001.

Morante, Elsa (1918–1985) *novelist*

Elsa Morante, best known for her critically acclaimed novel *La Storia* (1974), was born in Rome. She left home at the age of 18 to live with an older man, her education incomplete. A year later, however, she met the writer Alberto MORAVIA, whom she married after a brief affair with a younger man. Moravia recognized Morante's natural gift as a writer and introduced her to many of the leading Italian writers and intellectuals of the time.

Morante's first published work, *Il Gioco Segreto* (1941), was a collection of short stories, several of which she had already published in magazines and journals. She followed this with a children's book, *La Bellissime Avventure di Cateri Dalla* (1942). Although both works were well received, they received little critical attention. She spent the latter half of World War II hiding from fascist authorities in the countryside. This rural environment later played a great role in her fiction.

Late in the 1940s, William Weaver, an American translator, befriended both Morante and Moravia and introduced their works to an American audience. Simultaneously, Morante began to translate the works of writer Katherine Mansfield. Influenced by Mansfield's style, Morante wrote *Menzogna e Sortilegio* (1948; translated 1951) which, with the help of Weaver, was translated into English as *House of Liars*. The work presented what would come to be Morante's common themes of memory, dreams, and obsessions, and the novel gained immediate critical success.

Morante was never a prolific writer and was critical of her own work, much of which she destroyed. Her major work, *La Storia* (1974), translated into English as *History*, was set in Rome during and after World War II and dealt with the impact of historical events on the individual human beings who lived them. Each of the work's eight sections begins with an omniscient narrator who relates the events of the war as they are happening and then describes how these events affect the lives of individuals, both physically and psychologically. The novel was awarded the Viareggio Prize and was adapted to film in 1985.

Morante's final novel, *Aracoeli* (1982), a sensitive treatment of homosexuality, was also highly acclaimed. She continued to write, publishing essays and short stories, until her death in Rome.

Another Work by Elsa Morante

Arturo's Island: A Novel. Translated by Isabel Quigley. South Royalton, Vt.: Steerforth Press, 2002.

Moravia, Alberto (Alberto Pincherle)
(1907–1990) *novelist, short-story writer, essayist, playwright*

Alberto Moravia was born in Rome to Carlo Pincherle Moravia, an architect and painter, and Teresa DeMarsanich, a countess. At age 9, Moravia's health deteriorated when he became ill with coxitis, tuberculosis of the bone. After several months in bed, he recovered somewhat and was taken to Viareggio on vacation. In *Life of Moravia* (1990), a book he wrote with Alain Elkann, Moravia said, "In Viareggio, many things happened: I found out what sex was. More or less the basic experience I narrated in *Agostino,* though the situations and characters there are the fruit of invention."

Moravia published his first novel, *The Time of Indifference,* in 1929, which gained him recognition. This existentialist (*see* EXISTENTIALISM) novel is the story of siblings who explore the themes of alienation and a society that they perceive as shallow and false. Moravia won more praise for his two novels *Agostino* (1944) and *Luca* (1948). He fused the two works and published them in English under the title *Two Adolescents.* The story of Agostino, depicting themes of a teen's sexual exploration, loss of innocence, and disillusionment with the world, melds into the story of Luca, a 15-year-old boy, chronicling the angst and rebellion of the teen. It follows him through his sexual initiation, a grave illness, and ultimate redemption.

Another important theme in Moravia's novels is the condemnation of society's values. His works, such as *The Wheel of Fortune* (1935) and *Two Women* (1958), were censored and ultimately banned by the fascist government for their allegorical representation of capitalism and fascism as destroyers of innocence.

Moravia told an interviewer for *The Guardian,* "A writer has few themes if he is faithful to himself. He should not have much to say, but what he has to say he should give depth to and say in different ways." One recurring theme in Moravia's novels is the relationship between perception and reality, between one's internal thoughts and the outside world. Of his own reality, in terms of his writing, Moravia says, in *Life of Moravia,* "My books never satisfy me completely. I've always had the impression I could improve them, make them better."

Although Moravia may not have been satisfied with his writing, his list of prestigious honors confirms his talent. *Agostino* was awarded the Corriere Lombardo Prize in 1945. In 1952, he won the Chevalier de la Légion d'Honneur and the Strega Prize.

Another Work by Alberto Moravia

The Voyeur: A Novel. Translated by Tim Parks. New York: Farrar, Straus & Giroux, 1987.

A Work about Alberto Moravia

Peterson, Thomas E. *Alberto Moravia.* Boston: Twayne, 1996.

Mori Ōgai (Rintarō Mori) (1862–1922)

novelist, short-story writer, poet, essayist

Mori Ōgai was born in the remote town of Tsuwano to a physician during the last years of Japan's feudal system. A gifted student, he was studying the Chinese classics by the age of five, and at 19, he graduated from Tokyo Imperial University with a medical degree and joined the army. The government sent Mori in 1884 to study medical hygiene at German universities. While there, he also read widely in Western literature. Shortly after his return, he served as a medical officer during the Sino-Japanese War (1894–95) and the Russo-Japanese War (1904–05). In 1907, he became surgeon-general. Mori retired from the army in 1916 to become director of the Imperial Household Museum and head of the Imperial Art Academy.

On his return from Germany, Mori wrote several novellas, including *The Dancing Girl* (1890), a story about an affair between a Japanese student and a German woman in Berlin. Although his early stories were romantic, Mori became increasingly interested in history as a medium for storytelling. *The Wild Geese* (1911–13), a romantic story of un-

requited love, is relayed as an "old tale." Then, four days after the ritualistic suicide of Gen. Maresuke Nogi, who loyally followed Emperor Meiji into death in 1912, Mori wrote "The Last Testament of Okitsu Yagoemon," which examines the Confucian ideal of blind loyalty to one's master. This short story created a new Japanese literary genre called *rekishi shōsetsu* (historical fiction), which Mori used to explore ideals and character in the rapidly changing society of early 20th-century Japan.

Mori's renown stems from his medical accomplishments, complex prose style, and creation of a new genre, adopted by such writers as AKUTAGAWA Ryūnosuke and Yasushi Inoue. Mori also contributed to the modernization of Japanese theater by translating more than 50 European plays. For these accomplishments, he is regarded, along with NATSUME Sōseki, as one of the greatest influences on modern Japanese literature.

Other Works by Mori Ōgai

Dilworth, David, and J. Thomas Rimer, eds. *Saiki Kōi and Other Stories.* Honolulu: University of Hawaii Press, 1977.

Rimer, J. Thomas. *Youth and Other Stories.* Honolulu: University of Hawaii Press, 1994.

Works about Mori Ōgai

Marcus, Marvin. *Paragons of the Ordinary: The Biographical Literature of Mori Ōgai.* Honolulu: University of Hawaii Press, 1993.

Rimer, John Thomas. *Mori Ōgai.* Boston: Twayne, 1975.

Mrożek, Slawomir (1930–) *playwright, short-story writer*

Slawomir Mrożek was born in Borzecin, near Kraków, Poland. The son of a postal carrier, Mrożek first began his career as a journalist and cartoonist, writing satirical short articles that used wordplay and grotesque situations as a backdrop for their humor.

While writing for a Kraków newspaper, Mrożek began to write satirical short stories. The first collection of his works, *Slon* (1957; translated *The Elephant,* 1967) satirized various aspects of Polish communism in the 1960s. It was immediately successful both critically and publicly. The title story pokes fun at a small-town zoo which, when it is allocated government money to acquire an elephant, decides to save the government the money by inflating a large elephant-shaped balloon. They tell visitors that the elephant is very sluggish and that is why it hardly ever moves. Their scheme works until a gust of wind blows the elephant away. Other stories in the collection include a tale in which a lion refuses to take part in the eating of Christians because it knows that one day the Christians will rise to power and remember its actions. Another story focuses on an uncle who cannot tell his nephew what a giraffe looks like because he only reads books on marxism. When he looks through all of his Marxist books, he discovers they say nothing about giraffes, and the nephew, therefore, concludes that giraffes do not exist.

In the late 1950s, Mrożek left journalism to write plays. His first drama was *The Police* (1958). As a playwright, he is most noted for his subtle parody and his use of stylized language. His dramas present simple situations and human behaviors that are taken to the absurd. Mrożek's works belong to the style of theater known as the THEATRE OF THE ABSURD, which creates dramatic effect through distortion and parody.

In 1963, Mrożek emigrated to France and then to Mexico. His first full-length drama, *Tango* (1964; translated 1968), was first staged in 1964 and was eventually performed throughout Europe. The play presents a satirical psychological observation of totalitarianism.

In the 1990s, Mrożek focused his attention on war, the disintegration of morality, and a political system based on genocide. *Love in Crimea* (1994) focuses on the fall of the Russian empire; *The Beautiful Sight* examines the Balkan War from the point of view of two European tourists vacationing at the seaside in the former Yugoslavia who become annoyed by the interruption of the war; and *The Reverends* looks at religious hypocrisy.

Mrożek continues to write and to express his views about the tragedy still facing much of Eastern Europe in the 21st century. His works are influential both from their political standpoint and in their accurate representation of history in the making.

Another Work by Slawomir Mrożek
Striptease; Tango; Vatzlav: Three Plays by Slawomir Mrożek. New York: Grove, 1981.

A Work about Slawomir Mrożek
Stephan, Halina. *Translating the Absurd: Drama and Prose of Slawomir Mrożek.* Amsterdam: Rodopi, 1997.

Müller, Heiner (1929–1995) *dramatist*

Heiner Müller was born in Eppendorf, Saxony, into a working-class family. His father, a socialist, was beaten, arrested, and lost his job during the Nazi regime. Müller too became a socialist and was a civil servant in East Germany and later worked as a journalist and technical writer for the East German Writers' Union. He honed his skills as a dramatist working at the Maxim Gorki Theater in East Berlin in the late 1950s.

Müller wrote three plays with his wife, Inge Müller. The pair won the Heinrich MANN Prize in 1959. Their collaborative work *Der Lohndrücker* (*The Wage Shark,* 1957) was a critique of working conditions in East Germany. Because the Müllers refused to whitewash negative aspects of the socialist state, their own government disapproved of their plays, but their works were more successful in the West. After the government forced Müller to abandon contemporary subjects, he began to write adaptations of classical works in the 1960s; however, he added his own interpretations to the plays of Sophocles, Shakespeare, and the Soviet dramatist Mikhail SHOLOKHOV. These adaptations finally brought Müller fame in East Germany: He won the prestigious BÜCHNER Prize in 1985.

Müller's writing reflects a strong influence from Bertolt BRECHT. Although his dialectical dramas elicited official disapproval in East Germany, Müller's work with classic dramas earned him widespread acclaim. His biographer Jonathon Kalb notes in *The Theater of Heiner Müller* (1984) that Müller saw "that overvaluation of originality, the bourgeois-era cult of the absolutely new, was a factor in the devaluation of history (in the West and East), and responded with a string of texts that refused to treat originality with proper capitalistic seriousness." He is also known for combining lyrical prose with poetry to create language in his plays. Müller frequently depicted the individual's struggle with society, and his works address the causes of late 20th-century German angst.

Another Work by Heiner Müller

A Heiner Müller Reader: Plays, Poetry, Prose. Edited and translated by Carl Weber. Baltimore: Johns Hopkins University Press, 2001.

A Work about Heiner Müller

Kalb, Jonathon. *The Theater of Heiner Müller.* Munich: C. H. Beck, 1984.

Munonye, John (1929–) *novelist*

John Munonye was born in Akokwa, Imo State, Nigeria. He was the fourth of seven children. Munonye's father, a farmer, worked hard to send him to Christian schools. He first completed his undergraduate education at the University of Ibadan before leaving for London to obtain his masters in education at the University of London's Institute of Education. Munonye returned to Nigeria in 1954 and worked as a teacher for three years. He was promoted to the positions of administrator and school inspector in 1958, and he became principal of the Advanced Teachers College in 1970.

Munonye's writings reflect the cultural and psychological conflict he experienced balancing traditional Igbo values and Western ideology. His themes consist of the predicament of the common person's struggle in a rapidly modernizing world, colonial experience, cultural conflict, family fric-

tion, and love. In *The Oil Man of Obange* (1971), for example, Munonye tells the tragic tale of a palm-oil seller's sacrifice for his children in colonial Nigeria. Jeri, the main protagonist, literally works himself to death to give his children a Western education. In *The Only Son* (1966), Munonye begins a trilogy that examines issues of religious differences and the generation gap between old and young people in Nigerian society.

Munonye's literary achievements tend to be overshadowed by the popularity of fellow Nigerian Chinua ACHEBE, whom he used as a model for his writings. Unlike Achebe, however, Munonye incorporates humor into his reflections of the somber realities of life in colonial Nigeria. Munonye is a member of the first generation of Nigerian writers to write about their pasts in the initial stages of Nigeria's independence. His writing represents a voice among many, which bespeaks a clear optimism tainted by apprehension.

Works about John Munonye

Lindfors, Bernth. *Dem-Say: Interviews with Eight Nigerian Authors.* Austin, Tex: African and Afro-American Studies and Research Center, 1974.
Nnolim, Charles E. "Structure and Theme in Munonye's *The Oil Man of Obange.*" *African Literature Today* 12 (1982): 163–73.

Munro, Alice (1931–) *novelist, short-story writer*

Alice Munro was born Alice Laidlaw in Wingham, Ontario, to Robert Laidlaw and Ann Chamney. During the Depression, her father bred silver foxes. Munro began college at the University of Western Ontario but left in 1951 to marry James Munro. During the 1950s and 1960s, she privately wrote short stories. Her first collection, *Dance of the Happy Shades,* was published in 1968 and drew on her own experiences; for example, the story "Boys and Girls" begins, "My father was a fox farmer. That is, he raised silver foxes, in pens; and in the fall and early winter. . . ."

After the success of her first work, Munro continued publishing stories and novels. She writes "regional" fiction, realistic, domestic stories about ordinary people grounded in a particular region, Western Ontario; she was inspired by southern U.S. writers such as Eudora Welty. Her second work, *Lives of Girls and Women* (1971), is an episodic novel set in Jubilee, Ontario, and explores the emotional and imaginative development of the protagonist Del Jordan. Geoffrey Wolff of *Time* magazine noted the homespun realism of the work: "The book is a fiction for people who like to read brittle, yellow clips from newspapers published in towns where they never lived, who like to look through the snapshot albums of imperfect strangers."

Who Do You Think You Are? (1978), considered Munro's best work, is a collection of interrelated stories that follow the life of a character named Rose through childhood, college, marriage, and back to her childhood home. It explores the dark secrets underneath the surface of small-town life, such as incest and abuse: "He shakes her and hits her against the wall, he kicks her legs. She is incoherent, insane, shrieking. *Forgive me! Oh please, forgive me!*" One of Munro's hallmarks is the coherence of her short story collections, as critic Ildiko de Papp Carrington notes: "Although eight of the ten stories in *Who Do You Think You Are?* were originally published separately, the collection constitutes an organic whole." The collection was short listed for the BOOKER PRIZE. Munro's latest collection of short stories, *Hateship, Friendship, Courtship, Loveship, Marriage,* continues her exploration of life in rural Ontario. Critic Beverly Rasporich contends that "the fictional world that Munro creates is an expanding, visionary location but at the same time always recognizably hers."

Another work by Alice Munro
Selected Stories. New York: Knopf, 1996.

A Work about Alice Munro
Howells, Coral Ann. *Alice Munro.* New York: St. Martin's Press, 1998.

Murakami Haruki (1949–) *novelist, short-story writer*
Murakami Haruki was born in Kyoto, Japan, to Murakami Chiaki and Miyuki, both teachers, who often discussed classical poetry and medieval war tales at home. Thus instilled with a love of literature, Murakami entered the drama program at Waseda University with the intention of becoming a scriptwriter. After graduating, Murakami, with his wife, Yōko, opened a prosperous jazz club called Peter Cat in Tokyo. Then in 1986, Murakami moved to Europe, where he lived for most of a decade.

Reputedly inspired by a baseball game he attended in 1978, Murakami began to write novels, publishing his first a year later. *Hear the Wind Sing* (1979) is a retrospective story based on bar conversations between the unnamed protagonist, *boku* (I), and his friend "the Rat." The book won *Gunzō* magazine's New Novelist Prize.

His next novels further developed the character of *boku,* an everyman who represents the inner workings of the mind. In 1985, *Hard-Boiled Wonderland and the End of the World* split the world of *boku* in two: the real and the fantastic. Murakami then spent two years at Princeton University where he researched his next two books, *South of the Border, West of the Sun* (1998) and *The Wind-up Bird Chronicle* (1997). Since the 1995 sarin gas attack on a Tokyo subway, Murakami has published two volumes of interviews with both the victims and the members of the religious sect that took responsibility for the attack.

Murakami is regarded as one of the first Japanese authors at ease with the Westernization of Japan, largely due to his incorporation of foreign words into his prose and his open portrayal of postwar Japan. He has won the Tanizaki Jun'ichirō Prize and the Yomiuri Literary Award.

Other Works by Murakami Haruki
The Elephant Vanishes. Translated by Alfred Birnbaum and Jay Rubin. New York: Vintage International, 1993.

A Wild Sheep Chase. Translated by Alfred Birnbaum. Tokyo: Kodansha International, 1989.

Works about Murakami Haruki

Aoki Tamotsu. "Murakami Haruki and Contemporary Japan." Translated by Matthew Strecher. In John W. Treat, ed., *Contemporary Japan and Popular Culture*. Honolulu: University of Hawaii Press, 1996.

Rubin, Jay. "Murakami Haruki's Two Poor Aunts Tell Everything They Know About Sheep, Wells, Unicorns, Proust, and Elephants." In Stephen Snyder and Philip Gabriel, eds., *Ōe and Beyond: Fiction in Contemporary Japan*. Honolulu: University of Hawaii Press, 1999.

Musil, Robert von Edler (1880–1942)
novelist, playwright

Robert Musil was born in Klagenfurt, Austria, to Alfred Musil, a professor of engineering at the Technical University of Brunn and an arms manufacturer, and Hermine Musil. Robert Musil's childhood was difficult: His father was devoted to his career, and his mother was involved in an affair with Robert Musil's private tutor for many years. In elementary school, Musil had a nervous breakdown as a result of frequent family dramas at home. At the age of 12, he was sent away to a military academy by his father and, between 1898 and 1901, attended the Technical University of Brunn. Forced to study engineering by his domineering father, Musil finally revolted, left for Germany, and decided to study philosophy instead. In 1908, he received a doctorate in philosophy from the University of Berlin.

Musil began his writing career as a student at the University of Berlin. In 1906, he published his first novel, *Young Torless*, which was based on his experiences in the military academy. Although Musil's work was somewhat popular, he could not support himself by writing; from 1911 to 1914, he worked as a librarian in Vienna. He served in the Austrian army during World War I and, after being wounded, edited the army newspaper. After the war, Musil worked in various administrative capacities for the ministry of defense, but he lost his position and became a full-time writer and journalist in the 1920s.

After producing a number of short plays and satires, Musil concentrated on writing his major work, *The Man Without Qualities* (1930–43). This monumental novel describes the social, cultural, and political life during the last days of the Habsburg empire. In a style often compared to Marcel PROUST's, Musil focused on the emotional and intellectual development of the individual and concentrated on such themes as sexuality and survival. The attention that Musil devoted to this work led to the financial ruin of the family. Ulrich, the protagonist of the novel, a highly educated but psychologically immature man, desires to find his place in modern life. He undergoes a deep emotional transformation, marked by an almost psychologically incestuous relationship with his sister Agathe.

Married to a Jewish woman, Musil feared persecution by the Nazis and fled Austria for Switzerland in 1938. In Switzerland, he published a number of short essays; however, he remained an obscure writer. Robert Musil died in poverty and without due recognition. Most of his works have been rediscovered and published since his death. Today, Musil is considered one of the great writers of Austria. His works have been translated into more than 20 different languages.

Other Works by Robert Musil

Diaries, 1899–1941. Translated by Philip Payne. New York: Basic Books, 2000.

Five Women. Translated by Eithne Wilkins. New York: David R. Gordon, 1999.

Precision and Soul: Essays and Addresses. Chicago: University of Chicago Press, 1995.

A Work about Robert Musil

Jonsson, Stephen. *Subject Without a Nation: Robert Musil and the History of Modern Identity*. Durham, N.C.: Duke University Press, 2001.

Musset, Alfred de (1810–1857) *poet, play-wright*

Best known for his poetry, Alfred de Musset was inspired by Shakespeare and a love affair with George SAND. He can also be credited as having written the first modern French dramas. Born in Paris to a distinguished family, Musset graduated with honors from Collège Henri IV and briefly pursued a career in medicine before a dislike of blood prompted him to first try painting and then, ultimately, writing.

He published his first work, the ballad *A Dream*, in 1828, which was followed a year later with his first collection of poetry, *Contes d'Espagne et d'I-talie* (1830). The collection gained him the favor of Victor HUGO and earned his acceptance into the circle of ROMANTIC poets. In 1830, Musset was asked to write for the stage, but his first play, *La Nuit vénitienne* (*A Venetian Night*, 1830), was not successful.

In 1833, Musset met and began a passionate affair with poet George Sand. His autobiographical piece, *La Confession d'un enfant du siècle* (*Confession of a Child of the Century*, 1835), details their relationship. She abandoned him, however, after falling in love with another man during a trip to Venice. Returning to France alone and in despair, Musset used his feelings to produce some of his greatest theatrical works, including *Lorenzaccio* (1834) and *No Trifling With Love* (1834). He has been praised for his multidimensional female characters and his in-depth understanding of love. His works are commonly compared, in terms of popularity in France, to those of RACINE and MOLIÈRE.

Poor health began to haunt Musset in the 1840s in the form of a heart ailment that came to be referred to by scientists as Musset's symptom. Aggravated by excessive drinking and the depression caused by several failed affairs, his health caused a decline in his literary output. He spent the last two years of his life confined to his apartment and died on May 2.

Another Work by Alfred de Musset
Fantasio and Other Plays. Translated by Michael Feingold. New York: Theatre Communications Group, 1993.

A Work about Alfred de Musset
Bishop, Lloyd. *The Poetry of Alfred Musset: Styles and Genres.* New York: Lang, 1997.

N

Nabokov, Vladimir (1899–1977) *novelist, dramatist, literary critic, translator, poet*

Vladimir Vladimirovich Nabokov was born in St. Petersburg, Russia, into a wealthy, aristocratic family. His father, Vladimir Dmitrievich Nabokov, was a prominent liberal politician; his mother, Elena Ivanovna Nabokova, was a descendant of a wealthy, noble family. Nabokov learned French and English from various tutors and learned to read and write English before his native Russian. He described himself as "a perfectly normal trilingual child in a family with a large library." Nabokov's father served in the first Duma (the parliamentary body of Russia) and later held a post in the Provisional Government. After the Communists took control of the government, Nabokov's family left Russia in 1919 and temporarily settled in England. Nabokov's mother sold her jewels to finance his education at Trinity College, Cambridge, which he attended from 1919 to 1922. Nabokov graduated with honors from Cambridge, receiving a degree in Russian and French. The Nabokov family then moved to Berlin, Germany, when Nabokov's father accepted a position as the editor of the Russian newspaper. Nabokov's father was assassinated by right-wing monarchists in 1922.

Between 1922 and 1923, Nabokov published two collections of poetry and, in 1924, produced his first play, *The Tragedy of Mr. Morn.* In 1925, he married Vera Slonim. Although he worked in several genres of literature, Nabokov particularly excelled in fiction. In 1926, *Mary,* his first novel, was published in Berlin; two years later, he published his second novel *King, Queen, Knave.* Between 1929 and 1938, Nabokov published four novels and a collection of short stories.

The year 1938 was crucial for Nabokov's literary career. After moving to France, Nabokov decided he would try to write a novel in English; his first such work was *The Real Life of Sebastian Knight* (1914), a "biography" of a fictional writer, narrated by his brother.

In 1940, Nabokov emigrated to the United States, narrowly escaping the advancing Nazi troops. Between 1941 and 1959, Nabokov taught creative writing, literature, and Russian at Wellesley College, Stanford, Harvard, and Cornell. During the 1940s, he published short stories in *The New Yorker* and a scholarly work on Nikolai GOGOL. During these years, Nabokov's output of fiction was relatively small, partly because he was still adjusting to writing in English. In 1951, he published a memoir, *Conclusive Evidence.*

Nabokov's most famous novel, *Lolita,* was written during the early 1950s and published in France in 1955. The novel explores the psychological ramifications of a man's love affair with his 12-year-old stepdaughter. Although a number of critics immediately recognized the artistic virtues of the novel, it was banned in France in 1956 for its subject matter. When *Lolita* was finally published in the United States, it remained on *The New York Times* best-seller list for six months. The novel was adapted into film by Stanley Kubrick in 1962 and again by Adrian Lyne in 1997. *Lolita* remains one of the most powerful novels of 20th-century American literature. As critic Charles Rolo said in *The Atlantic Monthly* in 1958, *Lolita* is "an assertion of the power of the comic spirit to wrest delight and truth from the most outlandish materials."

In 1961, Nabokov moved to Montreux, Switzerland, where he remained until his death in 1977. During the 1960s and 1970s, he continued to write novels and translated his earlier works from Russian to English. One of the main criticisms of his work was its seeming lack of concern for social issues. Nabokov did not refute such criticism: "I have never been interested in what is called the literature of social comment." Indeed, his work comments on the experience of the individual, often exploring the character's psychological dimensions. "The true conflict is not between the characters in the novel, but between author and reader," he maintained. By the time of his death, Nabokov had established a worldwide reputation as a great writer and scholar.

Other Works by Vladimir Nabokov

Ada. New York: Vintage Press, 1990.
Despair. New York: Vintage Press, 1989.
Pale Fire. New York: Vintage Press, 1989.
Speak, Memory: An Autobiography Revisited. New York: Vintage Press, 1989.

A Work about Vladimir Nabokov

Cornwell, Neil. *Vladimir Nabokov.* Plymouth, U.K.: Northcote House Publishers, 1999.

Naidu, Sarojini (1879–1949) *poet*

Sarojini Naidu was born in Hyderabad, India, into an extremely Westernized family, which gave her the opportunity to pursue a lifestyle and education uncommon to most women of her time. Naidu wrote only in English and started writing poetry as a young girl. She went to England in 1895 to study at King's College, London, and returned to India in 1898.

Naidu's poetry was originally very well received in England because it portrayed an India with which Victorian England was familiar. Her poems were romantic portrayals of an aesthetically appealing, nonpolitical India that was friendly to its colonizers, the British, especially when Britain's rule was threatened.

As Naidu developed as a poet and became more involved in the political activities of the Indian National Congress Party, her poetry also changed. *The Golden Threshold* (1905), for example, presents a collage of poems about Indian life as seen through the native eye. The poems focus strongly on the social conditions of the nation under colonial rule. Because these poems were such a departure from Naidu's earlier works, which showed the influence of great Western poets such as Wordsworth and Keats, Naidu was called "the nightingale of India," an epithet given her by Mohandas GANDHI.

By her third and final collection of lyric verse, Naidu was already beginning to spend less time writing poetry and more time being actively involved in politics. She was a close friend of Gandhi and was often the only woman who would accompany him on his many political marches and rallies. Such involvement on her part also made her a powerful figure for women's causes. One of her contributions was working to abolish *purdah,* a social rule that forced women to seclude themselves inside homes and wear clothing that completely covered their bodies.

Naidu dedicated her last volume, *The Broken Wing* (1915–16), to India's patriotic freedom fighters. This work completed her transformation from a poetess of remarkable Western education and romantic sensitivity to one whose only concern was to encourage the patriotic zealousness of her time. She was the first Indian woman to become the president of the Indian National Congress in 1925, and in 1947, she was made governor of the state of Uttar Pradesh.

Other Works by Sarojini Naidu

The Bird of Time; Songs of Life, Death and the Spring. New York: J. Lane Company, 1916.

The Sceptred Flute: Songs of India. New York: Dodd, Mead & Co., 1923.

A Work about Sarojini Naidu

Naravane, Vishwanath S. *Sarojini Naidu: An Introduction to Her Life, Work, and Poetry.* New Delhi: Orient Longman Ltd., 1996.

Naipaul, V(idiadhar) S(urajprasad)

(1932–) *novelist, travel writer, essayist*

Born in Chaguanas, Trinidad, V. S. Naipaul is descended from Hindu Indians. His grandfather worked in a sugarcane plantation, and his father, Seepersad, was a journalist and short-story writer. As a child, Naipaul spent most of his time in the matriarchal Tiwari clan house in Chaguanas or in the streets of Port of Spain. He attended Queen's Royal College, Trinidad, and University College, Oxford, where he studied English literature.

After graduation, Naipaul stayed in England and worked for the BBC and the *New Statesman*, a literary journal. Inspired by his father, Naipaul began to write about his childhood experiences. Multiple publications followed, and selections of his published reviews and articles appear in *The Overcrowded Barracoon* (1972) and *The Return of Eva Peron with The Killings in Trinidad* (1980).

Western critics positively reviewed Naipaul's first novels, but others, especially those from the Caribbean and developing countries, vehemently criticized the treatment of colonial people in his writings. His first three novels—*The Mystic Masseur* (1957), *The Suffrage of Elvira* (1958), and *Miguel Street* (1957) which Naipaul wrote first but published last—ironically and satirically portray the absurdities of Trinidadian life while exploring the lives of East Indian community members.

Critical Analysis

A House for Mr. Biswas (1961), Naipaul's fourth work, earned substantially more recognition than his earlier novels. It focuses on Biswas, a sensitive man who is loosely modeled after Naipaul's father, who struggles with displacement, disorder, and alienation to establish his own identity. The hierarchical relations in Biswas's house symbolize and comment on colonial relationships. Many of Naipaul's subsequent novels also explore themes of alienation as his characters strive to integrate cultural tensions, especially those between native and Western-colonial traditions and influences.

The same year Naipaul published *A House for Mr. Biswas,* he received a grant from the Trinidad government to travel in the Caribbean. Extensive travel followed in the 1960s and early 1970s. His excursions to countries including Uganda, Argentina, Iran, Pakistan, Malaysia, and the United States informed his writing. *Mr. Stone and the Knight's Companion* (1963), which takes place in England, was Naipaul's first novel set outside the West Indian context.

More serious place-specific cultural studies replaced the more comedic aspects of Naipaul's earlier novels. The three short stories in *In a Free State* (1971), which won the Booker Prize in 1971, take place in different countries. Naipaul uses a novella as well as travel-diary excerpts in these three stories to explore individual and universal freedom. The novel *Guerrillas* (1975) follows an uprising in the Caribbean, and *A Bend in the River* (1979), which has been compared to Joseph Conrad's *Heart of Darkness,* examines the future of a newly independent state in Central Africa. The introspective *The Enigma of Arrival* (1979) juxtaposes autobiography and fiction to construct an almost anthropological exploration of the life of a writer of Caribbean origin living in rural England.

Although some praised Naipaul's complex and sometimes scathing cultural analyses of his journeys as honest and visionary, others criticized them as pessimistic portrayals of the developing world, as seen in two of his travel books on India: *An Area of Darkness* (1964) and *India: A Wounded Civilisation* (1977). Other nonfiction works include the more widely accepted *India: A Million Mutinies Now* (1990), *The Middle Passage: Impressions of Five Societies—British, French, and Dutch—in the West Indies* (1963), and *Among the Believers: An Islamic Journey* (1989), which critically assesses Muslim fundamentalists in non-Arab countries.

The Mimic Men, published in 1967, is considered by critics to be Naipaul's best novel. It traces the life of Ralph Singh, a politician in early retirement who explains his own position: "The career of the colonial politician is short and ends brutally. We lack order. Above all, we lack power, and we do not understand that we lack power." Set in the Caribbean island of Isabella and in England, the novel has generated many questions concerning authenticity, politics, and psychology.

After the publication of *The Loss of El Dorado* (1970), which describes Trinidad's colonial history, Naipaul returned to Trinidad. Dissatisfied, he went to England and began to blur fictional boundaries. As he wrote, "Fiction, which had once liberated me and enlightened me, now seemed to be pushing me toward being simpler than I really was." He explained this concept further in *Reading and Writing: a Personal Account* (2000): "So, as my world widened, beyond the immediate personal circumstances that bred fiction, and as my comprehension widened, the literary forms I practiced flowed together and supported one another; and I couldn't say that one form was higher than another." *A Way in the World* (1994), for instance, which contains nine thematically linked but segmented narratives, draws on the genres of fiction, history and memoirs, and documentary to address personal and sociopolitical issues.

Naipaul's distinctive incorporation of multiple genres in literary works has earned him the reputation of formal innovator. Themes of alienation, mistrust, and self-deception run through many of his works, but his latter works tend to embrace more than criticize.

In 1990, Naipaul, who has British citizenship, was knighted by Queen Elizabeth. After being a perennial nominee for the Nobel Prize in literature, Naipaul received the award in 2001. To quote Timothy F. Weiss, Naipaul,

> through an autobiographical art, has tapped experiences that have come to define aspects of people's lives in the colonial and postcolonial word. Spanning several decades, his works are about more than the problems of the developing world that are a deep concern running through every book; they are about a rapidly changing world order and a changing definition of home and belonging in that new order.

Other Works by V. S. Naipaul

Between Father and Son: Family Letters. New York: Vintage Books, 2001.

Half a Life. New York: Knopf, 2001.

"To a Young Writer." *New Yorker* (June 26–July 3 1995).

Works about V. S. Naipaul

Gupta, Suman. *V. S. Naipaul.* Plymouth, U.K.: Northcote House in Association with the British Council, 1999.

Khan, Md. Akhtar Jamal. *V. S. Naipaul: a Critical Study.* New Delhi: Creative Books, 1998.

King, Bruce. *V. S. Naipaul.* London: MacMillan, 1993.

Weiss, Timothy S. *On the Margins: the Art of Exile in V. S. Naipaul.* Amherst: University of Massachusetts Press, 1992.

Narayan, R(asipuram) K(rishnaswamy)
(1906–2001) *novelist, short-story writer*

R. K. Narayan was born in Madras, India. His father was a teacher who was repositioned in various South Indian states, which meant that Narayan frequently changed schools. Though he was not a model student, education was an important part of growing up in the Narayan household. Narayan was the third of eight children; to relieve some of the burden of bringing up so many children, his father sent Narayan to live with his maternal grandmother in Madras.

Narayan has often claimed that listening to his grandmother's stories inspired his own love for storytelling. Because writing was not considered a worthwhile profession at the time, his family received his decision to become a writer with shock and dismay. The creative spirit is not exclusive to R. K. Narayan in his family: His brother, R. K. Laxman, is one of India's most famous and highly published cartoonists and has illustrated several of Narayan's books. Like Laxman, Narayan depicts India through the eyes of a character from an "older" world, one that is detached from the modern world and is constantly bewildered by its machinations.

Narayan proved to be resourceful through his writing from the very beginning. While working on his first book *Swami and Friends* (1935), he was able to support himself by contributing short stories to magazines. This book first introduces Narayan's Malgudi village and its inhabitants. This fictional world appears to be completely estranged from the outside world, and its isolation clearly brings out more clearly the emotional ties that keep this village community together.

When Narayan began to write, he was one of numerous writers who created a turning point in Indian literature. For the first time, Indian writers were writing only in English, and many of them were writing for a national and international audience. At a time when writing in English was considered politically incorrect and when Indian politics were the most appropriate theme, Narayan placed himself outside of these constraints. He chose to use both English (the only language in which he wrote) and India's rural settings to create a version of an Indian life that was relatively free from colonial politics. One of his most popular works, *Malgudi Days* (1942), for instance, borrows the Malgudi of *Swami and Friends* to explore the effects of Western influence through human

relationships; it is also the name of a television series based on this collection of stories. The mythical village of Malgudi is set at the crossroads of an old India meeting a new one. These stories capture the image of the ordinary person amid simple surroundings to suggest an organic shift from a colonial India to an independent one. The central characters in *The English Teacher* (1945) and his story "Mithaiwalla" ("The Vendor of Sweets," 1967) are heroes set in this same transition.

The story "Mithaiwalla" focuses on the conflict that arises between a father and his son as they must learn how to understand their changing relationship without letting their differences create an emotional rift. In *The English Teacher,* a teacher's moral struggle against a decadent form of education is made more complicated by his growing responsibilities as a father. Also set in a small town, this novel explores the links between personal and social relationships. Being a good teacher, the protagonist learns, is contingent upon his maturity as a father and husband. The darker sides to Narayan's fiction are, however, always clothed in a humor that strives for frankness and compassion rather than judgment.

Narayan's novel *The Guide* (1958) won the Sahitya Akademi Award (India's highest literary award) and was made into a Hindi movie of the same name that has now become an Indian classic. It was the first Indian–English work to receive the award. In addition to writing fiction, Narayan interpreted and translated into English many of India's classic epics. His versions of *The Mahabharata* (1978) and *The Ramayana* (1972) made these texts available to new readers both in and outside India. Narayan is also known as the Grand Old Man of Indian English fiction.

Narayan won the Padma Bhushan (given in recognition of contributions to the nation) in 1964. In 1980, he was awarded the A. C. Benson Award by the Royal Society of Literature and made an Honorary Member of the American Academy Institute of Arts and Letters. In 1986, he joined Indian politics and became a member of Parliament; he was awarded this post for his contribution as an outstanding litterateur and held the position for six years.

Other Works by R. K. Narayan

The Financial Expert. Chicago: University of Chicago Press, 1995.
My Days: A Memoir. New York: HarperCollins, 1999.

A Work about R. K. Narayan

Kain, Geoffrey R., ed. *R. K. Narayan: Contemporary Critical Perspectives.* East Lansing: Michigan State University Press, 1993.

Natsume Kinosuke

See NATSUME SŌSEKI.

Natsume Sōseki (Natsume Kinosuke)
(1867–1916) *novelist, short story writer and essayist*

Natsume Sōseki was born Natsume Kinosuke in Tokyo, Japan. He was adopted shortly after his birth but was returned to his family home at age nine. While still very young, he studied Chinese literature and haiku, venturing into English literature at Tokyo Imperial University. After graduation, he began to teach in public schools. A turning point came in 1900 when the government sent him to England to continue his study of English literature. When he returned, he became a lecturer at Tokyo Imperial University. However, he soon resigned his teaching position to take up writing full time for the *Asahi Shimbun Newspaper* in 1907. He died nine years later from a stomach ulcer.

Shortly after returning from England, Natsume began his career with the comic novel *I Am a Cat* (1905). The story portrays the antics of a cat that lives with a teacher, indirectly revealing the relationship of the teacher and his wife. Within the next two years, he produced a number of short stories and novels, including a perennial favorite of Japanese students called *Botchan* (1906). In this novel, Natsume created a lovably bumbling protagonist who faces a series of awkward situations.

Toward the end of his life, Natsume wrote what has become one of the most recognized novels of Japanese literature, *Kokoro* (1914). This psychological novel took up the issue of individualism in a country in the throes of modernization.

Natsume is considered, along with Ogai MORI, to be the father of MODERNISM in Japanese literature, largely because of his effective portrayal of intellectuals at the turn of the century. Natsume's early writing was by and large satirical, but as be began to address issues such as alienation and morality, he adopted a more serious and often pessimistic tone.

Other Works by Natsume Sōseki

Botchan. Translated by Alan Turney. Tokyo: Kodansha International, 1992.
Grass on the Wayside. Translated by Edwin McClellan. Chicago: The University of Chicago Press, 1969.
The Miner. Translated by Jay Rubin. Stanford, Calif.: Stanford University Press, 1988.
The Wayfarer. Translated by Beongcheon Yu. Detroit: Wayne State University Press, 1967.

Works about Natsume Sōseki

Doi, Takeo. *The Psychological World of Natsume Sōseki.* Translated by William Jefferson Tyler. Cambridge, Mass.: Harvard University Press, 1976.
Iijima, Takehisa, and James M. Vardaman Jr., eds. *The World of Natsume Sōseki.* Tokyo: Kinseido Ltd., 1987.

naturalism (1860–1900)

Naturalism is perhaps best described as a literary movement in which writers attempted to be true to reality, accurate in their representation of life, and methodical and nonjudgmental in their observations of the various phenomena of life. The French writer Émile ZOLA first used the term *naturalism* to explain the application of elements of the scientific method to the examination of all aspects of life. In his essay *Le Roman expérimental* (1880), Zola wrote that the novelist should approach the craft of writing in the same manner as the scientist approaches the study of nature.

Proponents of naturalism believe that both hereditary and environmental influences combine to determine human behavior. For a writer to depict life as it really is, the ultimate goal of naturalist literature, he or she must present characters whose motivations can be clearly understood based on the surrounding causes. In other words, Zola and those who followed him replaced the classical idea of fate as the major factor behind human circumstances with the more scientific concept of determinism in which human beings are responsible for their own actions. Thus, some, if not all, human values can be seen to proceed in direct relationship to situational needs such as food, water, and shelter, placed in combination with environmental, sociological and psychological factors. The literature of the naturalist school, therefore, dealt more commonly with the observation of reality as it actually presents itself than with the construction of elaborate fantasies.

Naturalism in literature developed as a direct response to ROMANTICISM. Dissatisfaction with the representations of social conditions in literature led to a desire on the part of certain writers to create a body of work that stood in more direct correlation to actual life. Romanticism focused on high lyricism and was concerned with the beauty of language and self-expression, human emotions and personal values. Naturalism, on the other hand, was more concerned with cause-and effect relationships and logical outcomes to given circumstances. This trend was not entirely new; Realism had anticipated some of these concerns. However, naturalism was also a reaction to REALISM. The naturalists believed that realist literature, while it sought to portray life accurately, was not a true representation of the harsh realities faced by the lower social classes. Whereas the realists displayed a tendency within their work to aestheticize societal problems, making them more palatable to the bourgeois readership, naturalists developed more accurate portrayals of reality, making no attempt to pass judgment or to suggest a solution. They abandoned religion and philosophy, believing neither discipline capable of effecting change on society. Instead, they believed that literature had the power to create change simply by making the reader aware of the extent of the problem.

Common, therefore, among naturalist works is the emphasis on characters who are poor, undereducated, and trapped in lives filled with filth and corruption. These are the people whose lives are most controlled by social and cultural influences and whose decisions are most affected by the fulfillment of basic needs. As a result, much naturalist literature is a dreary representation of the harsh realities of life. Although similar to realism in many ways, naturalism goes beyond realism in its belief that social and biological factors take the place of free will entirely, as can be witnessed in the trappings of lower-class existence.

In addition to Zola, other noted French naturalists include the GONCOURT brothers, J. K. HUYSMANS, and Guy de MAUPASSANT. The Goncourts' works, such as *Soeur Philomène* (1861) and *Renée Mauperin* (1864; translated 1887) were based largely on notes from their travels and presented an accurate vision of life as they observed it. Prior to his absorption in DECADENCE, Huysmans's early works, such as *Marthe* (1876), can also be classified as naturalist pieces.

In the theater, the naturalist movement is most closely associated with the Théâtre Libre movement of the late 19th century. Again, the goal of drama, like that of literature, became the desire to represent life as accurately as possible. By placing a greater degree of emphasis on scenic design, which was realistically detailed, and costume design, which reflected the style and quality of the characters, as well as the development and encouragement of more natural acting methods, the movement was an attempt to break free from the conventions of artificial theatricality prevalent in the past.

The naturalist movement in France did not confine itself to one art form but existed in theatrical performances and the visual arts as well. Neither was the movement restricted to France. Similar movements occurred in the latter part of the 19th century throughout Europe and in America.

Works about Naturalism

Baguley, David. *Naturalist Fiction: The Entropic Vision*. New York: Cambridge University Press, 1990.

Bronson, Catharine Savage, ed. *Nineteenth Century French Fiction Writers: Naturalism and Beyond, 1860–1900*. Detroit: Bruccoli Clark Layman, 1992.

Nelson, Brian, ed. *Naturalism in the European Novel: New Critical Perspectives*. New York: St. Martin's Press, 1992.

Pagano, Tullio. *Experimental Fictions: From Émile Zola's Naturalism to Giovanni Verga's Verism*. Madison, Wisc.: Fairleigh Dickinson University Press, 1999.

Naubert, Benedikte (1756–1819) *novelist, writer of fairy tales*

Born into an academic family in Leipzig, Germany, Benedikte Naubert received an education unusual for a woman of her time. She was one of the most prolific and widely read authors of her age: Her publications—family novels, historical novels, and fairy tales—extend to 80 titles. Because of prejudice against women writers, she chose to publish anonymously. She influenced the historical novels of Sir Walter Scott and was appreciated by the romantics. The stories in Naubert's *Neue Volksmarchen der Deutschen* (1789–92), based on folktales, were original in combining the fantastic with the everyday and giving a voice to female narrators and protagonists. The brothers GRIMM were indebted to her, but their tales told a very different story about the ideal rise of women in the emerging bourgeois family. A few of her novels were translated into English during her lifetime, and one of her most interesting stories, *Der Kurze Mantel*, has more recently been translated as "The Cloak" in *Bitter Healing: German Women Writers: 1700–1830* (Blackwell and Zantop, eds., 1990).

Ndebele, Njabulo (1948–) *novelist*

Njabulo Ndebele was born in Western Native Township near Johannesburg, South Africa. His father, a Zulu, was a schoolteacher who later became an inspector of schools, and his mother, a Swazi, was a nurse. Ndebele's mixed parentage has an important influence on his perception of what it means to be African, which is revealed in his works. Ndebele moved with his family to a small mining town in Charterston Location in 1954 where he completed his primary-school education. Because Ndebele's parents did not think the apartheid South African government would allow Ndebele to exploit his intellect, they sent him to black-ruled Swaziland to attend high school. He went to Cambridge University for two years for his master's degree and taught briefly at the University of Lesotho before going on to the University of Denver for his Ph.D. In 1983, Ndebele returned to Africa where he filled several administrative and teaching positions before finally settling as vice chancellor of the University of Cape Town in September 2000.

Ndebele's most significant contribution to world literature is his desire to bring African literature out of its protest mood. In a series of articles, he questioned the conventional African approach to writing, which challenged white colonials' domination by appealing to their guilt. The most influential of these articles was "New South-African Literature or the Rediscovery of the Ordinary," published in *South African Literature and Culture: Rediscovery of the Ordinary* (1991). Ndebele believes that African writers should write for their fellow African readers, appealing to an African collective consciousness and heritage. African literature should not merely attack apartheid or oppression but should find a common ground where all Africans can express their values.

Ndebele's stories depict his various attempts to search for African values and to promote them as the essence of African identity that transcends all differences. In the short story, "Uncle" (1983), for example, the character Lovington teaches his nephew to recognize a new "map" of South Africa, drawn using traditional South African values, not colonial European laws. Within this framework, Ndebele also celebrates Africa's past by remembering heroic figures, such as King Moshoeshoe. In another short story, "The Music of the Violin" (1983), Ndebele presents music as a mock battleground where the indiscriminate adoption of Western culture is criticized by a child who sees the contradiction more clearly than his anglophile parents.

Ndebele's attempts to address the multidimensional aspects of colonialism on South Africa represent a refreshing approach to the different facets of colonialism that have been presented by past African writers as one dimensional. Perhaps the most remarkable contribution Ndebele makes to the literary world is his poignant and vivid description of the daily lives of ordinary Africans. By concentrating on daily struggles of ordinary people for survival rather than the sensational power struggles developing at the higher levels, Ndebele is able to show that little defeats and victories take place in spite of the larger nationalistic struggle. The true hero in Ndebele's mind is the ordinary person who, through diligence and resourcefulness, continues to survive.

Ndebele has won various writing awards including the Noma Award for Publishing in Africa, the SANLAM First Prize for outstanding fiction, and the Pringle and Mofolo–Plomer Awards. His only play, *UGubudele namazimuzimu* (*Gubudele and the Cannibals*, 1941), won the Esther May Bedford Prize in 1937, when it was first written.

Other Works by Njabulo Ndebele

Bonolo and the Peach Tree. New York: Manchester University Press, 1992.

Death of a Son. Johannesburg: Viva, 1996.

Fools and Other Stories. London: Reader's International, 1986.

Rediscovery of the Ordinary: Essays on South African Literature and Culture. Johannesburg: Congress of South African Writers, 1991.

Sarah, Rings and I. Johannesburg: Viva, 1993.

Works about Njabulo Ndebele

Shava, Piniel. *A People's Voice: Black South African Writing in the Twentieth Century.* London: Zed Books, 1989.

Trump, Martin. *Rendering Things Visible: Essays on South African Literary Culture.* Athens: Ohio University Press, 1990.

Necker, Anna Louise Germaine

See STAËL, GERMAINE DE.

négritude

In the early 1930s, French-speaking African and Caribbean writers living in Paris started the literary and ideological négritude movement with the leadership of poet Aimé CÉSAIRE from Martinique, poet Léon-Gontran Damas from French Guiana, and poet and later president of Senegal (1960–80) Léopold Sédar SENGHOR. Inspired by Harlem Renaissance writers in the United States, such as W. E. B. DuBois and Langston Hughes, and West Indian thinkers and poets, such as Jacques Roumain, René Maran, and Jean Price-Mars, black intellectuals began to examine critically Western values to reassess black cultural value and identity.

The publication of *Légitime Défense* (*Legitimate Defense*) in the early 1930s, a journal with a strong Marxist and anticolonial bent, prompted Senghor, Damas, and Césaire to print *L'Étudiant noir* (The black student) in 1934 "for all black students, regardless of origin, African, Antillean or American." According to Damas, the word *négritude* first appeared in an editorial by Césaire in *L'Étudiant noir.* For Césaire in his long poem, *Cahier d'un retour au pays natal* (*Return to My Native Land,* 1939), négritude originated in "Haiti, where Négritude first stood up and swore by its humanity." The term gained popularity after appearing in Césaire's poem, but some say the spirit of négritude was first expressed poetically by Damas in *Pigments* (1937).

After World War II, the group founded *Présence Africaine,* a publishing house and journal edited by Alioue Diop. One year later, Senghor's *Anthologie de la nouvelle poésie nègre et malgache de langue française* (Anthology of new Negro and Malagasy poetry in French, 1948) appeared. It included existentialist philospher Jean-Paul SARTRE's well-known essay, "Orphée noir" ("Black Orpheus"), which describes négritude from a Marxist perspective.

Initially, the négritude movement primarily influenced French-speaking colonial writers, but it gradually became more global. The core group expanded to include a number of African and West Indian poets, including Jacques Rabémananjara, a poet and playwright from Madagascar who met Senghor and Césaire in Paris in the 1950s, and Guy Tirolien, a West Indian poet who met Senghor in a German prison camp during the war. Many involved in the négritude movement critically examined assimilation, world wars, and the suffering of black people in their writing. They also promoted political and intellectual freedom, as well as the value of African life and traditions.

Senghor published his systematic statements on négritude in *Libertié I: Négritude et Humanisme* (1964), a collection of essays. On négritude, Senghor wrote, "To establish an effective revolution, *our* own revolution, we first had to cast off our borrowed clothes—the clothes of assimilation—and to assert our *négritude.*" Césaire took an even more revolutionary interpretation of négritude than Senghor, as can be seen in his *Discours sur le colonialisme* (*Discourse on Colonialism*), (1950) which displays his Marxist allegiances.

The spread of the négritude movement to black student writers in France, Africa, and the Caribbean during the 1930s, 1940s, and 1950s receded in the 1960s when fewer and fewer négritude themes appeared in writers' works. More recently, however, such writers as Abiole Irele, Biodun Jeyifu, and Omafume Onoge have been returning to the literary and ideological issues of négritude. Some have criticized the movement's reliance on NATIVISM and ahistoricism, as well as its representation of women and its failure to achieve revolutionary change. Many, however, still recognize négritude's significance as an empowering, historically grounded, and pertinent literary movement.

Works about Négritude

Ahluwalia, Pal. "'Negritude and Nativism': In Search of Identity." *Africa Quarterly* 39, no. 2 (1999).

Arnold, James A. "Négritude Then and Now." In James A. Arnold, ed., *A History of Literature in the Caribbean: Vol. I, Hispanic and Francophone Regions.* Philadelphia: Benjamins, 1994.

Asante-Darko, Kwaku. "The Co-Centrality of Racial Conciliation in Negritude Literature." *Research in African Literatures* 31, no. 2 (2000).

Claxton, Hadiya. "Colonialism, Negritude, and Experiences of Suffering." *JAISA: The Journal of the Association for the Interdisciplinary Study of the Arts* 5, no. 1 (Fall 1999).

Jack, Belinda E., and Sada Niang. "Literature and the Arts—Negritude and Literary Criticism: The History and Theory of 'Negro-African' Literature in French." *African Studies Review* 41, no. 2 (1998).

Jeyifo, Biodun. "Greatness and Cruelty: 'Wonders of the African World' and the Reconfiguration of Senghorian Negritude." *The Black Scholar* 30, no. 1 (Spring 2000).

Neruda, Pablo (Neftali Ricardo Reyes Basoalto) (1904–1973) *poet*

Pablo Neruda was born in Parral, Chile. His father, Jose del Carmen Reyes, was a railroad engineer. His mother, Rosa Basoalto, died of tuberculosis a few days after Neruda was born. In 1920, at age 16, Neruda moved to Santiago to study French literature at the Instituto Pedagogico; however, after three years of study he left school without graduating. It was at this time that Neruda adopted his pseudonym, taking the last name of Czech short-story writer Jan Neruda (1834–91).

In 1924, Neruda published *Twenty Love Poems and a Song of Despair,* which remains one of the most popular poetry collections in the Spanish-speaking world. Neruda's approach to love poetry is visceral and original; his emotions are vibrant and his sorrows poignant but without the least sentimentality. *Twenty Love Poems and A Song of Despair* combines rich and musical diction, striking images, and a strong sense of connection with the natural in human love.

As Neruda's literary reputation grew, he also began a political career. He was appointed as the Chilean consul in Rangoon, the capital of Burma, in 1927. He pursued his political career quite seriously throughout his life, serving as a senator and even running for president of Chile. He was a communist and worked to forward his ideals through both government service and poetry.

The collection *Residence on Earth* (1931, 1935, 1947) marked a significant change in style from his earlier books. It is written in the style for which Neruda is best known and that, during his life, was called Nerudaism—it is filled with irrational leaps of thought, eccentric uses of language, and powerful images presented without explanation. However, unlike the absurdist poetry of such French Surrealists as André BRETON, *Residence on Earth* is extremely emotional and expressive. Neruda's style of surrealism is not intended to shock or to make his reader laugh; rather, he uses the absurd to represent the complexity of the human mind and modern life.

Canto General (1950) represented another radical change in Neruda's poetry. Abandoning the obscurity of his earlier work, he attempted to create an epic poem about the grandeur of South America. *Canto General* is a free-verse poem written in a biblical cadence. It is a poetic catalogue of both the human and natural aspects of South American reality. In the poem, Neruda was trying to do for the Latin-American world what Walt Whitman had done for the United States in *Leaves of Grass:* to create an epic of democracy, not centered on a single elite hero but celebrating the majesty of every citizen.

In 1971, Neruda won the Nobel Prize in literature. Along with Jorge Luis BORGES, Neruda was one of the first Latin-American writers to become a major presence in international literary circles. Radically transforming his literary style again and again throughout his life, and working tirelessly for his political beliefs, his achievement is truly astounding. Neruda, who fought against oppression

his entire life, died in Santiago, 12 days after a coup d'état deposed the liberal government of President Allende and brought fascism to Chile.

Other Works by Pablo Neruda

Elementary Odes of Pablo Neruda. Translated by Carlos Lozano. New York: G. Massa, 1961.
Late and Posthumous Poems, 1968–1974. Edited and translated by Ben Belitt. New York: Grove Press, 1988.
Memoirs. Translated from the Spanish by Hardie St. Martin. New York: Farrar, Straus & Giroux, 1977.

Works about Pablo Neruda

De Costa, Rene. *The Poetry of Pablo Neruda.* Cambridge: Harvard University Press, 1982.
Nolan, James. *Poet-Chief: The Native American Poetics of Walt Whitman and Pablo Neruda.* Albuquerque: University of New Mexico Press, 1994.

Nerval, Gérard de (Gérard Labrunie)
(1808–1855) *poet*

Considered to be among the early French romantic poets, as well as an early Bohemian, Gérard de Nerval was born in Paris. The death of his mother when he was only two years old greatly affected the tone of his works, which are characterized by a fascination with dreams, visions, and fantasies, particularly those related to death, as well as the madness that these can produce. Throughout his life, he suffered from manic depression and an artistic vision that was destined to destroy him.

Nerval was greatly influenced by the German Romantic poets. He translated the works of GOETHE and also was interested in the occult and the poetry of the French Renaissance. The mystic world fascinated him, particularly esoteric, gnostic, and oriental philosophy.

Living in a heightened state of reverie, he began to suffer periods of madness. After an extreme manic episode in 1841, Nerval was hospitalized. During this time, he wrote *Christ on the Mount of Olives* (1841), which forms part of his final collection, and assumed the name *Nerval,* taken from an imaginary genealogy that he had created to replace his own family history. He fantasized that he was descended from Nerva, a Roman emperor, by way of Napoleon. It is this voice, a collected wisdom of the ages, through which he speaks in his poems.

His final poetic work, a collection of sonnets called, collectively, *The Chimeras* (1854), emphasizes themes of death and despair. The work is comprised of three parts. In the first section, six poems deal with the concept of a lost love who appears as bride, priestess, sorceress, queen, muse, and ultimately death. This latter vision ties directly to the death of Nerval's mother. The second section, "Christ on the Mount of Olives," details Christ's betrayal by both humankind and God. The final part, "The Golden Verses," reaffirms life after a deep depression.

Written while Nerval was undergoing a period of deep depression, *The Chimeras* was published only one year before the poet committed suicide.

His last great work, the short-story collection *Les filles du feu* (*The Daughters of Fire,* 1854), celebrates lost love and mythical aspects of women. The manuscript of *Aurélia,* an autobiographical and almost surrealistic story of breakdown and vision, was found in his pocket when he hanged himself at dawn on January 26.

Another Work by Gérard de Nerval

Selected Writings. Translated by Richard Sieburth. Hardmondsworth, U.K.: Penguin Books, 1999.

A Work about Gérard de Nerval

Lokke, Kari. *Gérard de Nerval: The Poet as Social Visionary.* Lexington: French Forum, 1987.

Neto, António Agostinho (1922–1979)
poet

António Agostinho Neto was born in Kaxikane, a Kimbundu village in the Icolo e Bengo region of Angola. His political awareness began at an early age: He became involved in cultural and political activities following his high-school graduation in

1944 when he was working in the Health Service in Luanda. In Lisbon, where Neto was attending university, he became very involved in the proindependence political activities of the overseas African students. He was arrested and imprisoned twice, in 1951 and 1955. By the time of his second imprisonment, he had become such a well-known figure that French intellectuals such as Jean-Paul SARTRE and Simone de BEAUVOIR pressured the Portuguese government to release him. After his release, Neto returned to Angola in 1959 and became the leader of the Popular Movement for the Liberation of Angola (MPLA). He spent most of his political career in and out of exile and prison until November 1975, when he declared Angola's independence. He was sworn in as Angola's first president, a position that he held until his death.

Neto's poetry clearly resonates with themes that most concern him, such as the nationalist struggle, his African roots, and assimilation. His writings also reveal his attempt to reconcile ideas of individual freedom and colonial domination. In "Nausea" (1974), for example, he examines the anguish of the colonized character João, whose anger intermixed with helplessness results in a physical state of unease. Neto's rejection of assimilation is best expressed in his poems "Marketwoman" (1974) and "Friend Mussunda" (1974), in which the characters, common people, celebrate the collective idea of "Africanness" and renounce colonial attempts to assimilate them.

Neto remains one of the most influential, founding poets of Angolan literature, and his poetry bespeaks the common African themes inherent in the relationship between the colonized and the colonizer.

Other Works by António Agostinho Neto

Ainda o Meu Sonho. Luanda: Uniao dos Escritores Angolanos, 1980.

Cikectabea de Poemas. Lisbon: Casa dos Estudantes do Imperio, 1961.

Sacred Hope. Dar es Salamm: Tanzania Publishing House, 1974.

Works about António Agostinho Neto

Burness, Donald. *Fire: Six Writers from Angola, Mozambique and Cape Verde.* Washington, D.C.: Three Continents, 1977.

Enekwe, Ossie O. "The Legacy of António Agostinho Neto." *Okike,* 18 (June 1981).

Martinho, Fernando. "The Poetry of Agostinho Neto." *World Literature Today,* 53 (Winter 1979).

New Novel

The New Novel, or Nouveau Roman, emerged in France in the 1950s. Representative authors include Claude SIMON, Nathalie SARRAUTE, Alain ROBBE-GRILLET, Marguerite DURAS, and Michel Butor. The term was introduced by critic Roland Barthes and theorized by Robbe-Grillet in his *For a New Novel* (1963). The main concept of the movement was to create fiction that opposed the constraints of conventional fiction and broke the rules that defined what a novel was.

To break realistic molds of storytelling, the new novelists abandoned the idea of continuity and standard chronological order, such as in Sarraute's 1951 work *Portrait of a Man Unknown.* They borrowed freely from poetry and the visual arts to produce works that were linguistic collages, as in Simon's *The Wind* (1959). The importance of memory and free association of ideas were often stressed as well.

The new novelists represented a vast and divergent array of stylistic and ideological perspectives. They had different aims and goals with regard to their works and, for the most part, were often opposed to being grouped together even in theoretical terms. The movement, in essence, suggested a move away from tradition and realized an attempt to experiment with new literary forms.

See also OBJECTIVISMO.

A Work about the New Novel

Babcock, Arthur E. *The New Novel in France: Theory and Practice of the Nouveau Roman.* Boston: Twayne, 1997.

Ngugi Wa Thiong'o (James Ngugi)
(1938–) *novelist, essayist, playwright*

Ngugi Wa Thiong'o was born in Kamiriithu in the Kiambu district of central Kenya, a district in which a large number of white people lived. Living where the two worlds of the black African and the white Christian met clearly had its impact on Ngugi's works. Although his parents were Gikuyu, the largest ethnic group in Kenya, they did not practice traditional religion, nor were they Christians. In 1948, Ngugi was exposed to the Gikuyu religion and values when he began school, which taught him about European subjects, traditional Gikuyu values, and Gikuyu history. Ngugi became especially interested in Gikuyu traditions after undergoing the Gikuyu rite of passage ceremony. He also developed a strong interest in reading European classics, especially adventure stories.

Ngugi's eloquent prose resonates with the emotions and conflicts of his personal life and the life of his country. It is not surprising, therefore, that his themes include alienation, love, loss, and struggle. His first novel, *Weep Not, Child* (1964), was the first English language novel to be published by an East African. The main protagonist, Njoroge, lost his opportunity to further his studies after having to face the dilemma of choosing between his idealistic dreams and opposing the harsh reality of colonial domination.

The colonial government's mission to destroy the independent guerrilla army of the Mau Mau peasant rebellions in the 1950s greatly affected Ngugi and his family. Ngugi's brother joined the Mau Mau, his stepbrother was shot, and his mother was arrested, interrogated, and tortured. Ngugi faced the dilemma of advancing his education (something very few black Africans had accomplished and which the colonial government made possible) and dealing with the government's persecution of his family. He depicts this conflict within himself and his community in, and uses the rebellions as a backdrop for, his novel *The River Between* (1965), which is about an unhappy love affair in a rural community whose Christian converts and non-Christian natives are at odds.

In 1977, Ngugi's active involvement in his village's communal theater led to his arrest and imprisonment. He was accused of promoting his strong political views via his play *I Will Marry When I Want* (1977). In addition, his novel *Petals of Blood* (1978), strongly depicts the exploitation and corruption of the colonial government in Kenya at that time. Ngugi was released from prison a few years later, and though he was a devout Christian, he rejected Christianity and changed his name to Wa Thiong'o in honor of his Gikuyu heritage. He also began to write his novels in Gikuyu, publishing the first modern novel written in that language, *Devil on the Cross* (1980). Ngugi argued that African literature written in a colonial language was not African literature.

Ngugi left Kenya in 1982 to live in self-imposed exile in London. He continues to write about Gikuyu culture. In his later and strongly influential work, *Matigari* (1987), for example, Ngugi narrates a satirical tale of a guerrilla fighter who seeks to find true liberation through the use of arms. The story is based on a famous Gikuyu folktale. Ngugi also encourages fellow African writers to continue to write in their native languages. He now teaches at New York University, where he has taught since 1992.

Other Works by Ngugi Wa Thiong'o

Decolonizing the Mind: The Politics of Language in African Literature. Westport, Conn.: Heinemann, 1986.
Petals of Blood. New York: E. P. Dutton, 1991.

A Work about Ngugi Wa Thiong'o

Cantalupo, Charles, ed. *Ngugi wa Thiong'o: Texts and Contexts.* Lawrence, N.J.: Africa World Press, 1995.

Nguyen Du (1765–1820) poet

Nguyen Du was born in Thing Long, Ha Tinh province, central Vietnam. The first 35 years of Nguyen Du's life were spent trying to survive the chaos of the Tay Son rebellion that began in 1771. Nguyen Du, a member of the northern scholar classes, was a loyal supporter of the then defunct Le dynasty and was extremely critical of the Tay Son rebellion, denouncing the rampant corruption and immoral behavior of the Tay Sons in his poetry. The Tay Son rebellion ended in 1802 with the ascension of the Nguyen emperor, Gia Long, to the Vietnamese throne in Hue. This southern-based dynasty (Ly), however, did not win Nguyen Du's support, despite his serving the dynasty for 20 years. Nguyen Du saw the Ly dynasty as an illegitimate successor to the Le dynasty, and his unwillingness to serve can be observed in his writings. He uses metaphors such as the bitterness of remarrying to illustrate his reluctance to serve a new master while he still felt loyal to the old. Nguyen Du served as an envoy in the 1813 mission to China, and he was to depart on another mission to China in 1820 when he died unexpectedly.

Nguyen Du's poetry deals with timeless issues that characterized Confucian Vietnamese society, such as personal morality and political obligations. His poems, such as the epic *Truyen Kieu* (*The Tale of Kieu*) bespeak his constant concern with morality and his respect for individual fortitude. The publication date of the poem is unknown. The poem relates the life of Kieu, whose determination in the face of misfortune and suffering earn her happiness in the end. Nguyen Du's poetry celebrates the high ideal of morality above love and selfish desire. Poems such as *The Tale of Kieu* and *The Guitar Player of Long Thanh* reflect his Buddhist ideology that places sacrifice, sorrow, and suffering as necessary obstacles to overcome before happiness can be obtained. Nguyen Du's poetry remains today a valuable repository of information and insight into late 18th- and early 19th-century perceptions of morality.

Other Works by Nguyen Du

"Calling the Wandering Souls." In Jacqui Chagnon and Don Luce, eds., *Quiet Courage: Poems from*

Viet Nam. Washington, D.C.: Indochina Mobil Education Project, 1974.

The Tale of Kieu: A Bilingual Edition. Translated by Huynh Sanh Thong. New Haven, Conn.: Yale University Press, 1987.

A Work about Nguyen Du

Woodside, Alexander. Introduction to *The Tale of Kieu: A Bilingual Edition.* Translated by Huynh Sanh Thong. New Haven, Conn.: Yale University Press, 1987.

Nichol, b[arrie] p[hilip] (1944–1988) *poet*

bpNichol, as he styles his name, was born in Vancouver, British Columbia, and grew up in three locations—Vancouver, British Columbia; Winnipeg, Manitoba; and Port Arthur, Ontario. While working toward a certificate from the University of British Columbia in elementary education (which he received in 1963), Nichol audited creative-writing courses. After teaching elementary school in British Columbia, he moved to Toronto in 1967.

Nichol's first published poem, "Translating Apollinaire," appeared in 1964. He soon gained notoriety for his concrete poetry. (Concrete poetry is written so that the words form a definite shape. George Herbert's "Easter Wings," in which the lines of poetry are arranged to form angel's wings, is a famous example. Another predecessor is Guillaume APOLLINAIRE with his *Calligrammes*). One of Nichol's concrete poems is "Blues," in which the word *love* is set six times, vertically, horizontally, and backwards, with a diagonal row of *e*'s across the center suggesting a cry of pain or perhaps astonishment. (The poem may be seen online at http://www.thing.net/~grist/l&d/bpnichol/ky-ebp01.htm.)

Nichol did not gain wide recognition, however, until the publication of *The Martyrology* (1972), a long narrative poem in five volumes that abandoned the concrete form of Nichol's previous work. (Subsequent books of *The Martyrology* were published in 1976, 1982, 1987, and 1992.) Nichol also published prose works, visual books, and miscellanies, usually through small presses. He liked to revisit themes and to work in series, as he did in the three volumes, *Love: A Book of Remembrances* (1972), *Zygal: A Book of Mysteries and Translations* (1985), and *Truth: A Book of Fictions* (1990). *Truth,* like the last volume of *The Martyrology,* was published posthumously; Nichol had just finished assembling the manuscript when he died.

In all of his work, Nichol explores the possibilities for meaning to be created by the structural and textual characteristics of words on the page—that is, their formal arrangement and layout. Concrete poetry marks an extreme form of this possibility, as can be seen in Nichol's poems.

In 1970, Nichol won the Governor General's Award for poetry. In addition to his many volumes of poetry, he also wrote 10 episodes of the children's program "Fraggle Rock." His concrete poetry is the subject of a 1969 documentary film by Michael ONDAATJE, *Sons of Captain Poetry.*

Other Works by bpNichol

An H in the Heart: A Reader. Edited by George Bowering and Michael Ondaatje. Toronto: McClelland & Stewart, 1994.

bpnicholcomics. Vancouver: Talonbooks, 2002.

A Work about bpNichol

Barbour, Douglas. *b.p. Nichol and His Work.* Toronto: ECW Press, 1992.

Nietzsche, Friedrich (1844–1900)
philosopher

Friedrich Nietzsche was born in Rocken, Germany, to Karl Ludwig Nietzsche, a Protestant pastor, and Franziska Nietzsche. Karl Ludwig died when his son was only five. The family moved to Naumburg, where Nietzsche attended *Domgymnasium,* a private preparatory school connected with a cathedral. At *Domgymnasium,* Nietzsche demonstrated great potential as a scholar and was consequently offered a scholarship to Schulpforta, the most famous high school in all of Germany. Nietzsche attended Schulpforta for six years; he was considered to be one of the best students in his class. Although he apparently failed a mathematics class in his final year of studies and jeopardized his graduation, in Robert Holub's 1995 biography, a teacher is quoted in defense of Nietzsche: "Do you wish perhaps that we allow the most gifted student that the school had since I have been here to fail?"

After graduating from Schulpforta in 1864, Nietzsche studied classical philology at the University of Bonn and the University of Leipzig. While studying at both universities, Nietzsche was influenced by the German philosopher Arthur Schopenhauer. The philosophical works that Nietzsche wrote later in his life were in many ways a response to Schopenhauer's philosophical ideas. In 1867, Nietzsche interrupted his studies for compulsory military service, but was declared unfit for duty in 1868 after falling off a horse. While recovering from the injury, he was befriended by the famous composer Richard Wagner and his wife, who became his mentors.

In 1869, at age 24, Nietzsche was appointed as a professor of classical philology at the University of Basel, Switzerland, where he remained for the next 10 years. The appointment was quite unusual because he never completed his dissertation. To accept this position, he had to renounce his Prussian citizenship and, because he never became a citizen of Switzerland, he remained a person without a country for the rest of his life. In 1870, at the outbreak of the Franco-Prussian War, he enlisted in the Germany army as a medical orderly, but he contracted diphtheria and had to resign the post.

Critical Analysis

During the 1870s, Nietzsche became progressively dissatisfied with his work as a philologist. Although he remained at the University of Basel until 1879, he contributed very little to classical philology. In 1872, he published *A Birth of Tragedy,* which Robert Holub calls "an odd mixture of classical philology, half-baked enthusiasm for Schopenhauer, and Wagner veneration." Using little philological evidence, Nietzsche attempted to connect the rise of tragedy with a coupling of Dionysian and Apollonian principles, to hinge the downfall of tragedy to rational thinking, and to present Richard Wagner as the renovator of German tragic art. His colleagues greeted *The Birth of Tragedy* with disparagement and perplexity, finding little relevance to philology in the work.

Nietzsche, suffering from numerous health problems and, utterly disappointed with his career as a philologist, retired from the university in 1879. With much more success, he turned his energy to cultural criticism, particularly focusing on the role of Christianity in the formation of Western ideas about psychology and social behavior. *Human, All Too Human* (1878–80) is the first published work in which he defends his famed perspectivism, the view that truths and all interpretations are formulated from particular perspectives. He claimed that, contrary to the claims of moralist theory, morality is not inherent in or determined by reality; it is, in fact, the invention of human beings. Moreover, Nietzsche sets morality against historical background, describing how the view of morality changed over time. The work explicitly contrasts Christian and Greek moral thought, typically claiming that Greek thought had been vastly superior.

Nietzsche further elaborates his critique of Christian morality in *Daybreak* (1881). In this work, he claims that Christianity somehow reshapes our notion of morality by implicating psychological guilt and constantly seeking spiritual reassurances—both acts that are destructive to the psychological and social health of society. In his famous work *The Gay Science* (1882), Nietzsche makes his perhaps most famous statement, proclaiming the death of God. Nietzsche once again renounces the Christian doctrine of afterlife and proposes an alternative system in which an individual should appreciate this life in its aesthetic terms. He suggests that ideal is the full experience of one's life, with all the turns of fate and flaws. Furthermore, he proposes the doctrine of eternal recurrence in this work: a concept that describes time as circular rather than linear, in which cyclical events recur over and over again.

Needless to say, Nietzsche's profound atheism was viewed as disturbing by his contemporaries. Yet, Nietzsche secured a small following, especially among the young members of the intelligentsia, with the publication of his major work *Thus Spake Zarathustra* (1883–94). The work, a combination of poetry, prose, and epigrams, describes the journey of Zarathustra who comes down from a mountain after years of meditation to offer his thoughts to the world. The work, structured as a parody of the Bible, praises all things denounced by Christian teachings, such as vanity, war, cruelty, and pure aestheticism. The work, often described as a culmination of Nietzsche's philosophical career but which breaks with conventional philosophical discourse, is his most widely read and appreciated work. Although *Thus Spake Zarathustra* was not widely appreciated during Nietzsche's lifetime, it influenced generations of philosophers and artists after his death.

Late in his life, Nietzsche remained a prolific writer. He lived in seclusion in Italy and Switzerland, maintaining very few contacts. In 1889, he suffered a complete nervous breakdown after witnessing a brutal beating of a horse on a street in Turin. He was transferred from clinic to clinic for the next 10 years, but, unable to work or recover his health, he finally died just as his popularity began to spread all over the world.

Today, Nietzsche is remembered as one of the most influential philosophers and writers of the 19th century. His works were translated into virtually every major language around the world. Nietzsche questioned the accepted notions of morality and values in the context of Christianity to emphasize the importance of the material, aesthetic world. It is not surprising that many artists found his message attractive and powerful. Many of his works are still read, discussed, and debated in universities all over the world.

Other Works by Friedrich Nietzsche
The Anti-Christ. Translated by H. L. Mencken. London: Sharp Press, 1999.
Twilight of the Idols or How to Philosophize with a Hammer. Translated by Duncan Large. Oxford: Oxford University Press, 1998.
The Will to Power. Translated by Walter Kaufmann. New York: Random House, 1987.

Works about Friedrich Nietzsche
Holub, Robert. *Friedrich Nietzsche.* Boston: Twayne, 1995.
Kauffman, Walter. *Basic Writings of Nietzsche.* New York: Random House, 1968.
Safransky, Rudiger. *Nietzsche: A Philosophical Biography.* New York: Norton, 2001.

Nkosi, Lewis (1936–) *novelist, literary critic*

Lewis Nkosi was born in Durban, South Africa. Before he turned eight, his parents died. He lived with his maternal grandmother, who worked as a washerwoman to support Nkosi's early education. During this time, Nkosi developed a love for literature, especially the works of 19th-century French novelists. Between 1952 and 1954, he was enrolled in a boarding school run by missionaries, and his Zulu language teacher gave him a thorough background in Zulu culture and history. After graduating, he worked briefly at a Zulu newspaper before being invited, in 1956, to join *The Drum,* an influential newspaper actively involved in the antiapartheid movement. Nkosi's acceptance of a Nieman Fellowship at Harvard University led to his exile from his homeland in 1961.

At Harvard, Nkosi wrote a play, *The Rhythm of Violence* (1964), as an entry for a drama competition. The play relates the violence and racism surrounding and following the first bombing in Johannesburg by African National Congress and Pan-Africanist Congress members. After Harvard, Nkosi worked as a literary editor of *The New African* in London from 1965 to 1968. Between 1970 and 1974, he took a four-year course in English literature at the University of London, spent several years in Europe and accepted a professorship in English at the University of Wyoming.

White supremacy and racial tension are recurring themes in Nkosi's writings. In his most acclaimed work, *Mating Birds* (1986), he satirizes the hypocrisy of the white court that condemned Sibiya, the main protagonist, to death mainly because he was black. In the novel, Sibiya narrates the series of events leading to his conviction of the rape of a white woman and his impending execution. By appropriating the plight of Sibiya, Nkosi contests the legitimacy of white justice and values in South Africa, which he portrays as being driven by self-interest. Another novel, *The Underground People,* about the personal and the political in the lives of antiapartheid activists, followed in 1993.

In 1965, Nkosi published a collection of essays, *Home and Exile,* which won a prize at the Dakar World Festival of Negro Arts in 1966. The essays in this collection deal with a variety of issues and themes, ranging from Nkosi's experience in exile to his views on African theater, black American poetry, and other African writers' works. He continues to publish criticism regularly.

Nkosi's main contributions lie in his ability to communicate the complexity and subtle aspects of racial politics and relationships in South Africa to a general reading public.

Other Works by Lewis Nkosi

The Black Psychiatrist. Lusaka: Lusaka Theatre Playhouse, 1983. Available online at http://weberstudies.weber.edu/archive/Vol.%2011.2/11.2Nkoski.htm.
Malcolm. London: ICA and Bush Theatres, 1972.
Tasks and Masks: Themes and Styles of African Literature. Harlow, U.K.: Longman, 1981.
The Transplanted Heart: Essays on South Africa. Benin City, Nigeria: Ethiope Publishing, 1975.

Works about Lewis Nkosi

Jacobs, Johan. "Lewis Nkosi: *Mating Birds.*" *Critical Arts,* 5:2 (1990).

Masuwa, Kristina Rungano. "South African Writing: Lewis Nkosi." *Wasafiri,* 19 (1994).
Watts, Jane. *Black Writers from South Africa: Towards a Discourse of Liberation.* New York: St. Martin's Press, 1989.

Nobre, António (1867–1900) *poet*

Born in Oporto, Portugal, to middle-class parents, Nobre suffered from ill health and died of tuberculosis at an early age. His illness changed his life and poetry. As a youngster, he spent many summers in northern Portugal. In 1898, he studied law in Coimbra, Portugal, but failed his courses and went on to Paris to attend the Sorbonne, where he received his degree in political science in 1895. Nobre traveled widely, always seeking better health. His finest poems were written while he was living in Paris's Latin Quarter.

Only one volume of poetry was published during Nobre's lifetime: *Só* (1892). It consists mainly of verse written in Portugal and Paris between 1884 and 1892. These poems express the loneliness and poverty the poet experiences on the death of his father. Two more volumes, containing a mixture of narcissism, folklore, realism, whimsy, and pessimism, appeared after the poet's death.

Another Work by António Nobre

Primeiros Versos e Cartas Inéditas. Lisboa: Editorial Notícias, 1983.

Noonuccal, Oodgeroo (Kath Walker)

(1920–1993) *poet, writer, political activist*
Oodgeroo Noonuccal was born in the land of Minjerribah on the coast of Brisbane, in Australia, to the Aboriginal couple Edward and Lucy Ruska. Kath Walker was her English name, but she returned later in her life to her traditional name Oodgeroo Noonuccal to identify with the Aboriginal people of Noonuccal, with whom she grew up. (Oodgeroo is the Aboriginal name for the paperbark tree.) Noonuccal attended the Dunwich State School on North Stradbroke Island. Her formal ed-

ucation ended when she turned 13, and she became a domestic servant as did most Aboriginal girls. In 1939, Noonuccal joined the Australian Women's Army Service (AWAS) and became a corporal.

The struggles of the Aboriginal people inspired Noonuccal to write when she was very young. Judith WRIGHT, an Australian poet, read Noonuccal's poems and introduced her to the Jacaranda Press in Brisbane. Noonuccal's first volume of poems, *We Are Going* (1964), was the first published work by an Aborigine. She writes of the oppression of the Aboriginal people and their sense of pride, using a free-verse style identified as "protest verse." In the poem "We Are Going," for example, the members of an Aboriginal tribe are given voice: "We are as strangers here now, We belong here." Noonuccal's second book, *The Dawn Is at Hand* (1966), is filled with rich imagery describing the tortures of the Aboriginal people.

Noonuccal's themes include the wrongs committed against the Aborigines, world peace, and a new life for her people. Noonuccal was one of Australia's best-known poets and was also known internationally as a political activist. She was a member of the realist writers' group (*see* REALISM) and wrote against social injustice. Noonuccal also wrote folk tales for children on the life and beliefs of the Aboriginal people. *Father Sky and Mother Earth* (1981) describes the bond of the Aboriginal people with nature. Fellow Australian poet Judith Wright wrote of Noonuccal's poems, "They were memorable, they were memorized and they will be remembered" (1994).

A Work about Oodgeroo Noonuccal

Collins, John, ed. *Noonuccal and Her People: Perspectives on Her Life's Work.* St. Lucia: University of Queensland Press, 1996.

Nortje, Arthur (1942–1970) *poet*

Arthur Nortje was born in the town of Oudtshoorn, Cape Province, South Africa. His mother was unmarried, and Nortje never knew who his father was. He attended school on scholarship and showed an early interest and propensity for writing poetry. In 1961, he moved to Cape Town, where he attended the University College of the Western Cape. The sharp class and racial distinctions that existed in the university led Nortje to resent the arbitrary nature of social segregation. He belonged to the "colored" group, the offspring of parents with mixed racial backgrounds, and his distaste for the opulent upper class is clear in his poetry, such as in "Thumbing a Lift" (1962), which won a Mbari Poetry Prize from Ibadan University.

Nortje briefly taught high school in Port Elizabeth before going to Oxford University in 1965, again on scholarship, one sponsored by the politically radical National Union of South African Students. After earning his B.A., he moved to British Columbia in Canada in 1967 to teach and then returned to London in 1970 to embark on his postgraduate study. He died on December 8.

Loneliness is perhaps the most acute emotion that surfaces in all Nortje's poems, which also speak of desolation and loss. His sense of estrangement from his homeland, following his self-imposed exile from South Africa, and his unfortunate encounter with love resonate through his characters and their experiences. Nortje's unfulfilled love for a young woman who separated from him to migrate to Canada, left him in despair. Discrimination intensified his anguish, loneliness, and alienation, which he depicts in political poems that condemn apartheid and its inherent hypocrisy. For example, in *Dead Roots* (1973), Nortje's first collection, a number of poems, such as "Continuation," relate his deterioration into depression and his dependency on drugs. In another poem, "The Long Silence," Nortje poignantly contrasts the forlorn resignation of the oppressed Africans with the "success" of the apartheid government. Though Nortje's literary career was brief, he successfully brought to the world a voice and a vision that, while pained and pessimistic, were very realistic.

Other Works by Arthur Nortje

The Collected Poems of Arthur Nortje. Edited by Dirk
    Klopper. Pretoria: University of South Africa
    Press, 2000.
Deep Roots. London: Heinemann, 1973.

Works about Arthur Nortje

Berthoud, Jacques. "Poetry and Exile: The Case of
    Arthur Nortje." *English in Africa,* 11:1 (1984).
Bunn, David. "'Some Alien Native Land': Arthur
    Nortje, Literary History, and the Body in Exile."
    World Literature Today, 70 (Winter 1996).
Dameron, Charles. "Arthur Nortje, Craftsman for his
    Muse." In Christopher Heywood, ed., *Aspects of
    South African Literature.* London: Heinemann,
    1976.
Leitch, Raymond. "Nortje: Poet At Work." *African Lit-
    erature Today,* 10 (1979).

Nwapa, Flora (1931–1993) *novelist*

Flora Nwapa was born in Oguta, East Central
State, Nigeria. Her parents were both teachers,
and Nwapa grew up in a popular and wealthy
family. She graduated from the University of
Ibadan in 1957 and received her postgraduate
diploma in education from the University of Edinburgh the following year. Nwapa returned to
Nigeria and worked as an education officer in
Calabar for a short time before assuming the position of geography and English teacher at
Queen's School in Enugu from 1959 to 1962.
She remained in Lagos until the Nigerian civil
war—the attempt by the Igbo people of Nigeria's
eastern area to establish a separate country called
Biafra—broke out in 1967. Like many members
of the Igbo elite, Nwapa and her family were
forced to return to the eastern region. Three years
after the war ended, she became the minister of
Health and Social Welfare of the east central state
from 1970 to 1971 and then the minister of
Lands, Survey and Urban Development from
1971 to 1974.

Nwapa was the first African woman writer to
publish her works in English. She is also the first
African woman to use the Igbo as the basis of her
stories. She established Tana Press in 1976, which
became the first indigenous publishing house to
be owned by a black African woman in West
Africa. The company published mainly adult fiction, but Nwapa soon set up another publishing
house, Flora Nwapa and Co., that specialized in
children's fiction. Nwapa took her role as an educator seriously: She continued to teach at colleges
and universities throughout her life and published works dealing with moral and ethical issues. She taught at various institutions in the
United States, including New York University,
Trinity College, and University of Michigan.
Nwapa died at age 62 in Enugu, Nigeria. At the
time of her death, she had just completed her
final manuscript of *The Lake Goddess* (1995)
about the goddess Mammy Water, who was a
source of inspiration for Nwapa's fiction.

Nwapa is best known for her recreation of Igbo
life and traditions from a woman's point of view.
In many ways, she could be considered one of
Nigeria's and Africa's first feminist writers. She
conveyed the positive optimism of her female protagonists and their strength and freedom to choose
their own paths. For instance, in *Idu* (1970), Idu's
quest for personal fulfillment leads her to take her
own life in defiance of her community's belief that
motherhood is the sole purpose of a woman's existence. Idu, however, prizes her qualitative life with
her husband above all else, including her child's
welfare. Her suicide is a commentary on a
woman's love.

Critical Analysis

Nwapa's debut novel, *Efuru* (1960), retells an Ibo
folktale about Efuru, a woman whose life mirrors
that of the lake goddess she worships. Efuru has
beauty and wealth but few children like the goddess. Efuru, however, has to struggle to find her
place in the society in which she lives. The novel is
indicative of Nwapa's portrayal of strong female
characters who are adventurous, independent, materially comfortable, and also have the freedom to
make their own decisions. These portrayals of

women in Ibo society, however, go against conventional views as presented in traditional Ibo texts, which tend to show Ibo women as weak, promiscuous, and fickle minded. Nwapa challenged these traditional views and set the foundation for later women writers to challenge and question the depiction of Ibo women in literature.

Nwapa also wrote short stories, poetry, and children's books. Her stories were not restricted to themes that dealt only with women's rights or a woman's place in society; she also drew on experiences from the Nigerian civil war, folktales, and other political conflicts that occurred during her lifetime. In *Never Again* (1975), which is set in the Nigerian civil war, her main character starts off as a fervent supporter of the Biafran cause but ends up trying to piece her life together and questioning her actions. In her children's stories, Nwapa drew on her rich reservoir of legends and folktales to emphasize the morals of the stories. Her major contribution to world literature rests in her characterization of the heroine as independent and strong and in her descriptions of the continual subjugation of women in Africa.

Other Works by Flora Nwapa

Efuru. London: Heinemann, 1966.

Never Again. Trenton, N.J.: Africa World Press, 1992.

One is Enough. Trenton, N.J.: Africa World Press, 1992.

This is Lagos and Other Stories. Trenton, N.J.: Africa World Press, 1992.

Wives at War and Other Stories. Trenton, N.J.: Africa World Press, 1992.

Women are Different. Trenton, N.J.: Africa World Press, 1992.

Works about Flora Nwapa

Brown, Lloyd W. *Women Writers in Black Africa.* Westport, Conn.: Greenwood Press, 1981.

Emenyonu, Ernest. "Portrait of Flora Nwapa as a Dramatist." In Marie Umeh, ed., *Emerging Perspectives on Flora Nwapa.* Trenton, N.J.: Africa World Press, 1998.

Ōba Minako (Shiina Minako) (1930–)
novelist, short-story writer, essayist, poet, playwright

Ōba Minako was born in Tokyo to Shiina Saburō and Mutsuko. From a very young age, Ōba nurtured an interest in reading. Her love of books was so intense that, even as she fled World War II air raids, she always grabbed a book to pass the time. Ōba witnessed the mushroom cloud of the atomic bomb dropped on Hiroshima and tended radiation sickness victims as they escaped the city. After the war, she studied American literature at Tsuda Women's College, where she met Ōba Toshio, whom she later married. The turning point in Ōba's life came when her husband was stationed in Alaska for 11 years. Removed from the restrictions placed on women in Japan, Ōba had the freedom to travel and to pursue a graduate-level education, although she never earned a degree.

Ōba completed her first short story, "A Picture with No Composition," in 1963 while she was attending a graduate art program at the University of Wisconsin. Four years later, she wrote "The Rainbow and the Floating Bridge" while attending a graduate art program at the University of Washington in Seattle and then "The Three Crabs" once she returned home to Alaska. In 1969, Ōba wrote "Fireweed," notable for its Alaskan setting and her depiction of an untraditionally ferocious nature. Her major works include *The Junk Museum* (1975), *Urashima Grass* (1977), *Without a Shape* (1982), and *Birds Singing* (1985), none of which have yet been translated into English.

Like the novelists ŌE Kenzaburō and Gabriel GARCÍA MÁRQUEZ, Ōba is noted for reusing characters and events from earlier stories. She frequently portrays strong female protagonists who challenge social mores, particularly with regard to women's roles. She has won numerous awards for her fiction, including the Gunzō New Writer's Prize, the Akutagawa Prize, and the Tanizaki Jun'ichirō Prize.

Other Works by Ōba Minako
"The Pale Fox." In Roberta Rubinstein and Charles R. Larson, eds., *Worlds of Fiction.* New York: Macmillan, 1993.
"The Smile of a Mountain Witch." In *Stories by Contemporary Japanese Women Writers.* Translated by Noriko Mizuta Lippit and Kyoko Irye Selden. Armonk, N.Y.: M. E. Sharpe, 1982.

A Work about Ōba Minako
Wilson, Michiko Niikuni. *Gender Is Fair Game: (Re)Thinking The (Fe)Male in the Works of Ōba Minako.* Armonk, N.Y.: M. E. Sharpe, 1999.

objectivismo

In the later half of the 20th century, *objectivismo* was a movement in Spain that was closely related to the French NEW NOVEL and particularly to the writings of Alain ROBBE-GRILLET and José Camilo CELA. *Objectivismo,* or objectivism, refers to the attempt to write novels that were completely free of subjective material and, therefore, closer to material reality. This involved the rejection of all conventional modes of narrative literature such as plot, chronological progression, and metaphorical description. The novels of *objectivismo* would, for example, feature extravagant, long descriptions of a piece of furniture or a geographic location and then repeat the same descriptions periodically throughout the book. Cela's *La Colmena* (*The Hive,* 1951) is a prime example.

Strongly influenced by existential philosophy of Heidegger, the main point of *objectivismo* is that reality, before human interpretation, is just there. Before any of the narrative meaning that human beings give to it, the most important feature of reality is its simple presence.

By refusing to concentrate on action or meaning, *objectivismo* texts have a sort of physical presence, in the philosophical sense of the word *physical*. More important, the texts imply that the author and human personality are essentially illusions. By an aesthetic act of will, the author may overcome these illusions and present a text free of his presence. The novels of Rafael Sánchez Ferlosio (1924–   ), such as *El Jarama* (1956; translated as *The One Day of the Week,* 1962), and the early work of Juan Marsé, are examples.

Literary critic Roland Barthes was a major influence on both the New Novel and *objectivismo*. He believed that too much importance had been given to the author's intentions in interpreting literature. He argued that, in fact, meaning, specifically the intentional meaning of the author, was an impermanent and changing thing based more on cultural context than anything else. *Objectivismo* is a literary style that supports and is supported by this idea.

The novels of *objectivismo* are texts that push the reader to supply interpretations. They are presented with compressed and repetitive events that are explained only in glimmers so that any meaning the reader gleans will not be definitive.

A Work about *Objectivismo*

Robbe-Grillet, Alain. *For a New Novel: Essays on Fiction.* Translated by Richard Howard. New York: Grove Press, 1966.

Ōe Kenzaburō (1935–   ) *novelist*

Ōe Kenzaburō was born in a small village in Ehime Prefecture on the island of Shikoku. By the time he entered school, Japan was at war, so he underwent strict moral training intended to instill unquestioning loyalty to the emperor. Before the end of the war, his father died, leaving him in the care of his mother. Under her guidance, Ōe developed an interest in literature, including Western novels. In 1954, he formalized that interest, entering the French literature department of Tokyo University.

While at Tokyo University, Ōe began to write plays for a student drama group. In 1957, he converted one of his plays into a short story, "A Peculiar Occupation," about a student who takes on a part-time job of exterminating dogs used for experiments. That story brought him to the attention of established writers, and he quickly found acceptance in the literary world. During the next two years, he published a number of stories, including *Nip the Buds, Shoot the Kids,* about a group of abandoned boys, which won the Akutagawa Prize, ensuring Ōe's place among the literati.

Ōe increasingly became politically active, notably opposing nuclear proliferation and the Japan–United States Mutual Security Treaty. His political concerns carried over into his writing and, in 1961, parodying a 17-year-old extremist who had assassinated a leader of a Socialist faction, he wrote the short story "Seventeen."

Ōe's literary career took a radical turn in 1963. Three years after his marriage to Itami Yukari, the sister of renowned film director Itami Jūzō, his son Hikari was born with a birth defect that damaged his brain. From this point, Ōe turned to more personal reflection in his writing.

Critical Analysis

In 1964, Ōe published one story and one novel that dealt specifically with the birth of his son. "Agwhee the Sky Monster" is the short story of a composer wrestling with a decision he made to let his son, diagnosed with a potentially fatal birth defect, die. The story is told from the perspective of a young college student who has been hired to watch over the composer. Ōe's novel *A Personal Matter* is widely regarded as his greatest work. In this novel, rather than killing the child, the protagonist, Bird, decides to save his son's life. The story trails the twists and turns of Bird's dilemma until he finally makes the decision to keep his child.

In his next major novel, *The Silent Cry* (1967), Ōe explores simultaneous story lines. The first involves a sibling rivalry in which one brother attempts to destroy a powerful supermarket chain and sleeps with both his brother's wife and his younger sister. The second story is set 100 years earlier. In it, their great-grandfather's younger brother foments an uprising against feudal authorities and has an affair with his brother's wife.

Although *The Silent Cry* received attention for its originality, critics regard his 1979 *A Game of Contemporaneity* as the pinnacle of this style of juxtaposing timeframes. The story is told in a series of letters from the narrator, Tsuyuki, to his sister, Tsuyumi. Tsuyuki is to develop a record of the history and myths of their village and, in doing so, relays a number of stories in fragmented form to his sister.

A Game of Contemporaneity also represented another significant development in Ōe's writing —myth making. Most of his recent works reflect this style, particularly *The Burning Green Tree* (1993–95), a trilogy that focuses on the story of a man named Gii. Having lived abroad in his youth, Gii moves to a village in Shikoku. Soon thereafter, a local medicine woman dies, and the villagers believe that Gii has inherited her healing powers.

In 1994, Ōe received the Nobel Prize in literature. During his Nobel speech, he called himself the last of the postwar writers—those who had witnessed the hardship of war but still retained hope for the future. He concluded his lecture, "As one with a peripheral, marginal and off-center existence in the world I would like to seek how—with what I

hope is a modest, decent and humanist contribution—I can be of some use in a cure and reconciliation of mankind."

Other Works by Ōe Kenzaburō

Teach Us to Outgrow Our Madness: Four Short Novels. Translated by John Nathan. New York: Grove Press, 1977.

The Catch and Other War Stories. Selected by Shoichi Saeki. New York: Kodansha International, 1981.

Works about Ōe Kenzaburō

Napier, Susan. *Escape from the Wasteland: Romanticism and Realism in the Fiction of Mishima Yukio and Ōe Kenzaburō.* Cambridge, Mass.: Harvard University Press, 1991.

Wilson, Machiko N. *The Marginal World of Ōe Kenzaburō: A Study in Themes and Techniques.* Armonk, N.Y.: M. E. Sharpe, 1986.

Ogot, Grace (1930–) *novelist*

Grace Ogot was born in Butere near Kisumu, district Central Nyanza, Kenya. She attended several girls' schools before training at the Nursing Training Hospital at Mengo, Uganda, from 1949 to 1953. From 1958 to 1959, she was a midwifery tutor and nursing sister at Makerere Hospital. She married Bethwell Ogot, history lecturer at Makerere University, in 1959. Two years later, Ogot became the principal of the Women's Training Center in Kisumu. In 1963, she returned to Makerere Hospital as nursing officer. She was also actively involved in activities that supported the women's movement. She was a member of the Maendeleo ya Wanawake Organization of Women and the Executive Committee of the Kenya Council of Women.

Ogot's writings reflect not only her feminist leanings but also her belief in the importance of perpetuating tradition and history in the face of technological progress and modernization. Her novel *The Promised Land* (1959) describes the Luo (an ethnic group in Kenya) migration from Uganda to the eastern shore of Lake Victoria during the colonial period. Migration, which is a dominant motif in this novel, highlights the sense of alienation and displacement experienced similarly by those who are victims of colonial exploitation and male domination. Ogot uses strong female characters, such as Nyapol, to comment on the hypocrisy of male domination by discrediting the male personalities in her novels and short stories. Nyapol's husband Ochola's mental deterioration in the new settlement is contrasted with Nyapol's strength and perseverance, and this challenges the misrepresentation of African females as meek and passive.

Ogot's volume of short stories, *Land Without Thunder* (1968), which was more successful and popular than *The Promised Land*, reinforces her attempts to undermine patriarchal authority by challenging ideas of male dominance. By developing the reversal of roles in her fiction, Ogot creates a platform for the female voice and discloses the male biases inherent in traditional African literature. In "The Old White Witch," for example, the white matron's shock at discovering that her female charges are more defiant and vociferous in their resistance to her domination than the men challenges the stereotypical view that men form the foundation of the African resistance movement.

Ogot's greatest contribution to African and world literature lies in her criticism of a male-dominated Africa and in her accurate and insightful depiction of many marginalized indigenous groups, such as the Luo, in Kenya.

Other Works by Grace Ogot

The Graduate. Nairobi: Uzima Press, 1980.
The Island of Tears. Nairobi: Uzima Press, 1980.
Miaha. Nairobi: Heinemann, 1983.
The Other Woman: Selected Short Stories. Nairobi: Transafrica Publishers, 1976.
The Strange Bride. Translated by Okoth Okombo. Nairobi: Heinemann, 1989.

Works about Grace Ogot

Conde, Maryse. "Three Female Writers in Modern Africa: Flora Nwapa, Ama Ata Aidoo and Grace Ogot." *Présence Africaine* 82 (1972).
Lindfors, Bernth. "Interview with Grace Ogot." *World Literature Written in English*, 18:1 (1979).

Okara, Gabriel (1921–) *novelist, poet*

Gabriel Okara was born at Bumoundi in the Ijo country of the Niger Delta in Nigeria. His parents were both members of the Ekpetinma clan. Okara received his early education at St. Peter's and Proctor's Memorial School and later attended the Government College of Umuahia. His education was temporarily interrupted by the outbreak of the World War II, but he resumed his studies during the war at Yaba Higher College. Under the guidance of renowned sculptor Ben Enwonwu, Okara became a painter; then later he turned to bookbinding, journalism, and creative writing. His first poems were published in the Ibadan-based journal *Black Orpheus* in the 1950s. He has been a part-time lecturer at the University of Nigeria, a government official, general manager of the Rivers State Broadcasting Corporation, and a founding member of the Association of Nigerian Authors.

Though Okara had no formal training in writing, his works effectively blend intense expression with masterful diction. Okara has written only one novel, *The Voice* (1964), which was critically acclaimed for its experimental and unorthodox style. This satire contains a strange narrative of events detailing a romantic hero's search for righteousness in a corrupted world. An eccentric writer, Okara amuses and inspires through his creative rendering of themes—colonialism, racism, and the fear of losing one's heritage—that consume most African writers of his time. He has also written two children's books: *Juju Island* and *Little Snake and Little Frog* (both 1982).

Folktales and myths are a strong source for Okara's poems, which attempt to revitalize the enchantment of Nigerian folklore through their representation of primordial acts of bravery and wisdom. Okara uses an unusual blend of ambiguous symbols and powerful imagery to relate these acts. The poem "You Laughed and Laughed and Laughed," for example (anthologized in Biddle), juxtaposes the cold laughter of the civilized world against the ancestral strength of Africa:

> Then I danced my magic dance
>   to the rhythm of talking drums
>   pleading, but you shut your
>   eyes and laughed and laughed and
>   laughed . . .

The poem relates how that cold laughter is ultimately thawed ("Now it is my turn to laugh"):

> . . . you whispered;
>   'Why so?'
>   And I answered:
>   'Because my fathers and I
>   are owned by the living
>   warmth of the earth
>   through our naked feet.'

His poems, which are written in a simple lyrical form, are also characterized by energy and vibrancy paralleled by a constant underlying protest against social injustice. "The Fisherman's Invocation," for instance, highlights Okara's concerns with the tribulations of nation building during the Nigerian civil war.

Okara received first prize in the British Council's 1952 short-story competition for his piece, "Iconoclast." In 1953, his poem, "The Call of the River Nun," won the best entry prize at the Nigerian Festival of Arts, and he won the Commonwealth Poetry Prize for "The Fisherman's Invocation" in 1979. Okara was also awarded an honorary doctorate by the University of Port Harcourt in Rivers State in 1982 in recognition for his efforts to involve Nigerians in their cultural and literary heritage.

Other Works by Gabriel Okara

Biddle, Arthur, ed. *Global Voices: Contemporary Literature from the Non-Western World.* Englewood Cliffs, N.J.: Prentice-Hall, 1995.

The Fisherman's Invocation. London: Heinemann Educational Books, 1978.

The Voice. New York: Holmes and Meier, 1987.

Works about Gabriel Okara

Anozie, S. O. "The Theme of Alienation and Commitment in Okara's *The Voice.*" *Bulletin of the Association for African Literature in English* 3 (1965).

Egudu, R. N. "A Study of Five of Gabriel Okara's Poems." *Okike* 13 (1979).

Shiarella, J. "Gabriel Okara's *The Voice:* A Study in the Poetic Novel." *Black Orpheus* 2:5–6 (1970).

Ondaatje, Michael (1943–) poet, novelist

Born in Colombo, Ceylon (now Sri Lanka), of Dutch, English, Sinhalese, and Tamil descent, Philip Michael Ondaatje is the youngest child of Mervyn Ondaatje, a tea-and-rubber-plantation superintendent, and Enid Doris, who ran a dance and theater school. In 1962, Ondaatje emigrated to Canada, where he studied English and history at Bishop's University in Quebec; he has baccalaureate and master's degrees.

Ondaatje is one of a few Canadian writers who also is published in the United States and Britain and is known internationally. His early poems appeared in *New Wave Canada: The New Explosion in Canadian Poetry* (1967). His poetry collection *Secular Love* (1984) explores the pain of the failure of his first marriage and celebrates his second.

In his first foray into fiction, *The Collected Works of Billy the Kid* (1970), Ondaatje retells the story of the outlaw William H. Bonney through a mixture of poetry, prose, photographs, and other illustrations. In *Coming through Slaughter* (1976), too, he interweaves biography, history, and fiction to relate the story of jazz cornetist Buddy Bolden, who went insane. *In the Skin of the Lion* retells the story of the building of Toronto's Prince Edward Viaduct. In 1978, after a 24-year absence, Ondaatje returned to his homeland, now Sri Lanka. In journals, he recorded family anecdotes and stories that developed into his "fictional memoir" *Running in the Family* (1982), which is composed of vivid, rhapsodic reminiscences.

In many of his novels, Ondaatje uses his central characters to explore a violent reality, mixing the ordinary and the fantastic to create a surreal montage, as can be seen in *The English Patient* (1993). Here a quartet of characters—Hana Lewis, a Canadian nurse; the "English patient," burned beyond recognition, who is in fact a Hungarian count; thief and double agent David Caravaggio; and sapper Kip Singh, who has been sent to clear the area of enemy mines—shelter in a dilapidated Italian villa during the last days of World War II. Douglas Barbour remarks, "As the complexly ordered fragments of the novel accumulate, their pasts, their presents, and their possible futures intertwine in an intricate collage," creating in the process, as Lorna Sage observes, "an improbable civilization of their own, a zone of fragile intimacy and understanding. . . ."

Fascinated by history, documentation, and biography, Ondaatje reinvents history through imagination. The dominant features of his style are a dynamic beauty and a scarcely contained violence. He has won many awards, including the Governor General's Award three times, the Booker Prize, and the Toronto Book Award.

A Work about Michael Ondaatje

Barbour, Douglas. *Michael Ondaatje.* Boston: Twayne, 1993.

Onetti, Juan Carlos (1909–1994) *novelist, short-story writer*

Juan Carlos Onetti, the son of Carlos Onetti and Honoria Borges, was born in Montevideo, Uruguay. Considering that he would go on to become a major novelist, the most remarkable thing about Onetti's childhood was that he never finished high school. He dropped out in his early teens and spent the next 20 years working at odd jobs and living the life of a bohemian. However, he continued to read constantly and educated himself in modern politics and literature.

Onetti was particularly fond of the novels of the Norwegian writer Knut HAMSUN. His first novel, *El Pozo* (*The Pit*, 1939), resembles Hamsun's novel *Hunger* (1890). Both works follow an alienated protagonist (similar to protagonists found in works by Jean-Paul SARTRE and Albert CAMUS) through an unfriendly city, concentrating on the main character's thoughts and his disconnection from everyone around him. Present in *Hunger* but far more pronounced in *El Pozo* is the introduction of elements of fantasy in what is mainly a realistic narrative. *El Pozo* was completely unsuccessful when it was first published; now, it is recognized as a precursor to the MAGIC REALISM movement and as perhaps the first truly modern Latin-American novel.

In *La Vida Breve* (*A Brief Life*, 1950), Onetti again focuses on a main character, Juan María Brausen, who is alienated from society and completely absorbed by his own thoughts. Brausen is himself a writer, and the reader watches him create narratives within the narrative. The novel takes place in the fictitious town of Santa Maria and combines REALISM with philosophical asides and elements of fantasy. Onetti would go on to write about Santa Maria again and again in his fiction. In this way, he resembles and is a precursor to GARCÍA MÁRQUEZ. Both authors worked at not only telling distinct stories but also creating an imaginary world. Unlike the mythic grandeur of García Márquez's Macondo, Onetti's imaginary world is restrained, tinged with the melancholy of philosophical dilemmas.

In 1974, Onetti was imprisoned by the Uruguayan government for selecting a controversial short story as the winner in a contest sponsored by the magazine *Marcha*. He was held for three months and finally released due to the outrage of the international community. He moved to Spain the next year and became a Spanish citizen.

Late in his life Onetti's pessimism increased. In *Dejemos hablar al viento* (*Let The Wind Speak*, 1979), he once again revisited Santa Maria, this time narrating its destruction by fire and a cleansing wind. This act of symbolically uncreating the imaginary world he had been building all his life resonates with both sorrow and purification. It is a final abandonment of nostalgia and a preparation for death.

In 1980, Onetti was awarded the Cervantes prize, the most prestigious award given in the Spanish-speaking world. He was the first Latin-American novelist to hit on the particular mixture of fantasy, reality, and formal experimentation, which such writers as Carlos FUENTES, García Márquez, and VARGAS LLOSA later developed into their own styles of magic realism. He is a writer of subtle humor and great philosophical insight.

Other Works by Juan Carlos Onetti

Goodbye and Stories. Translated by Daniel Balderston. Austin: University of Texas Press, 1990.

Past Caring? Translated by Peter Bush. London: Quartet Books, 1995.

The Shipyard. Translated by Nick Caistor. London: Serpent's Tail, 1992.

Works about Juan Carlos Onetti

Adams, Ian M. *Three Authors of Alienation: Bombal, Onetti, Carpentier.* Austin: University of Texas Press, 1975.

San Roman, Gustavo. *Onetti and Others: Comparative Essays on a Major Figure in Latin American Literature.* Albany: State University of New York Press, 1999.

Ortega y Gasset, José (1883–1955)
philosopher

José Ortega y Gasset was born in Madrid, Spain. Both his mother's and his father's families were powerful and successful publishers. Ortega y Gasset was trained to be a journalist, as well as to take over his family's publishing empire. However, when he graduated from the University of Madrid, despite an innate talent, he found the prospect of a career in journalism unsatisfying. Instead, he chose to study philosophy in Germany.

In 1914, at the outbreak of World War I, he published his first book *Meditations on Quixote.* The book is a collection of essays on topics ranging from the purely literary to features of life in modern-day Europe. All of the essays mix cultural commentary with the philosophical underpinnings that Ortega y Gasset had absorbed through his study of German philosophy, particularly that of Kant.

During the next 40 years, until his death, Ortega y Gasset was extremely prolific. His complete works, published in 1983, are 12 volumes of more than 500 pages each. He was also an important political figure in Spain, working tirelessly for moderate liberal reform until his impatience with extremism led him to retire in 1933.

Two of Ortega y Gasset's works stand out from the rest as having had a very large influence on later 20th-century thought. The first of these is *The Dehumanization of Art* (1925), in which he examines a unique modern phenomenon, the unheard-of unpopularity of modern art, and its rejection by the masses. Why, he asks, does the art that is generally acknowledged by critics and intellectuals as deserving of aesthetic merit receive such a negative reaction from common society? He finds that, unlike the highest forms of visual art from the past, modern art emphasizes the fictional aspect of the art medium and deemphasizes the "human concerns" of art's subject matter. Although this brings increased pleasure to knowing viewers who are educated to appreciate "pure" aesthetics, it alienates the uneducated viewers who want to find in art something to relate to their own lives.

In *The Revolt of The Masses* (1929), Ortega y Gasset examines another 20th-century phenomenon, the modern practice of sightseeing. Why, he asks, do countless people wish to go to sights, such as palaces or the Vatican, that formerly were accessible only to the privileged few? In former times, these places were used for specific functions. However, the masses go not to use the places as they were intended but simply to assert their own presence. Though somewhat elitist by today's standards, *The Revolt of The Masses* can be best understood as an indictment of the fascist tendencies of many European countries, including Spain, between the world wars. Ortega y Gasset feared, often correctly, that unfettered rule by the populace would end in brutality and fascism.

Ortega y Gasset is one of the most important Spanish philosophers of the 20th century. His efforts brought modern philosophical thought into Spanish culture. His influence has been worldwide, and his thought has influenced literature, philosophy, and art history.

Other Works by José Ortega y Gasset

History as a System, and Other Essays Toward a Philosophy of History. With an afterward by John William Miller. New York: Norton, 1961.

Man and Crisis. Translated by Mildred Adams. New York: Norton, 1962.

Meditations on Hunting. Translated by H. B. Westcott. New York: Scribner, 1986.

The Mission of the University. Translated by Howard Lee Nostrand. Piscataway, N.J.: Transaction Publishers, 2001.

The Origin of Philosophy. Translated by Toby Talbot. Champaign: University of Illinois Press, 2000.

Velasquez, Goya, and the Dehumanization of Art. New York: Norton, 1972.

A Work about José Ortega y Gasset

Díaz, Janet Winecoff. *The Major Themes of Existential-ism in the Work of José Ortega y Gasset.* Chapel Hill: University of North Carolina Press, 1970.

Osceola

See DINESEN, ISAK.

Ostrovsky, Nikolai (1904–1936) *novelist*

Nikolai Alexeevich Ostrovsky was born in the small village of Viliya, Russia. His father worked as a seasonal laborer, and the family was very poor. In 1914, his family resettled in the town of Sheptovka, where Ostrovsky briefly attended elementary school. As a young teenager, he worked at various laborer jobs and ran errands for the Bolshevik underground. He joined the Red Army in 1918 and fought for the Bolshevik cause. In 1920, he was seriously wounded in battle and subsequently contracted typhus.

Ostrovsky was officially declared an invalid in 1922. Bedridden by his physical breakdown, he dedicated his time to completing a correspondence course with Sverdlov University in Moscow, but a month after completing his course, he lost his vision and became partially paralyzed. He then began to write articles for newspapers and journals, to speak on the radio, and to begin his only full-length novel.

Ostrovsky completed *How the Steel was Tempered* in 1930. The novel, published in 1934, is firmly grounded in SOCIALIST REALISM and depicts the struggles of workers and soldiers in forging the Soviet Union, and its artistic aim of the novel is reflected in the simple, utilitarian language of the writer. Immediately hailed as a masterpiece of socialist art, the novel garnered him the Order of Lenin in 1935. His second novel *Born of the Storm,* about the civil war in the Ukraine, was incomplete when he died at the age of 32.

Ostrovsky achieved immense literary success with only one published novel. Although he was not prolific in his contribution to Russian literature, he did influence a new generation of fiction writers who attempted to glorify the building of a communist state.

Oz, Amos (Amos Klausner) (1939–   )
novelist, short-story writer, essayist

Amos Oz was born in a poor neighborhood of Jerusalem to conservative Zionist parents who both emigrated from Europe and met in Jerusalem. A sabra, or native Israeli, Oz grew up speaking and writing modern Hebrew. Oz's mother died when he was a teenager, and he left home at the age of 15 to join Kibbutz Hulda, one of Israel's oldest communes. There, striking out on his own, he changed his name from Klausner to Oz, a Hebrew word meaning "courage" or "strength."

At the commune, Oz was allowed to write just one day a week. Later, as his success grew, he was allowed to increase his writing time. He described life on a kibbutz in his first novel, *Elsewhere, Perhaps* (1973), and in *A Perfect Peace* (1982), set in a kibbutz in the 1960s. These and other of Oz's works explore the conflicts and tensions in modern Israeli society, examining human nature, its frailty, and its variety. Many of his stories take place either on a kibbutz or in Jerusalem, where he creates microcosms of Israeli society.

Oz is a full Professor at Ben-Gurion University of the Negev and was awarded the prestigious Israel Prize for Literature in 1998, the 50th anniversary year of Israel's independence.

Other Works by Amos Oz

Fima. Translated by Nicholas de Lang. New York: Harvest Books, 1994.
My Michael. Translated by Nicholas de Lang. New York: Vintage Books, 1992.
To Know a Woman. Translated by Nicholas de Lang. California: Harcourt Brace, 1992.

A Work about Amos Oz

Cohen, Joseph. *Voices of Israel: Essays on and Interviews With Yehuda Amichai, A. B. Yehoshua, T. Carmi, Aharon Appelfeld, and Amos Oz.* Albany: State University of New York Press, 1990.

Pa Chin

See BA JIN.

Pagis, Dan (1930–1986) *poet*

Dan Pagis was born in Bukovina, once a part of
Austria, Romania, and the Soviet Union. Today,
Bukovina is part of Ukraine and Romania. Pagis
spent his early years in the home of his grandparents. He had few friends but was a very enthusiastic reader from the age of six, spending much of his
time in his grandparents' apartment library. At the
age of 11, Pagis was deported to a Nazi camp,
where he spent three years. He emigrated to Palestine in 1946 and, after only four years in Israel,
began to write in his new language of Hebrew.

Said to be one of the most vibrant voices in
modern Israeli poetry, Pagis is also internationally
recognized as a major poet of his generation. He
has been called a poet of the unspeakable because
many of his poems are infused with the horror of
the Holocaust. Much of Pagis's subject matter is
grim, containing images of genocide, but Pagis also
explores other horizons, evoking biblical texts,
centuries-old mysticism, and the medieval Iberian
peninsula. Writers of his generation were known as
the emigré writers, consisting of those born in the
Diaspora (Jewish communities outside Palestine).

Along with other Israeli writers of his generation, Pagis helped to bring a more natural colloquial style to Hebrew poetry. His many volumes of
poetry have been described as "a poetry of allusion" in which he uses irony and plays on words to
mask sorrow. Yet, his poems also celebrate the
human spirit and contain compassion for his persecutors. His work remains popular and is celebrated not only in his home in Israel but also
around the world.

Other Works by Dan Pagis

Points of Departure. Translated by Stephen
    Mitchell. Philadelphia: Jewish Publication
    Society, 1981.
The Selected Poetry of Dan Pagis. Translated by
    Stephen Mitchell. Berkeley: University of
    California Press, 1996.
Variable Directions: Selected Poetry. Translated by
    Stephen Mitchell. San Francisco: North Point
    Press, 1989.

Works about Dan Pagis

Alter, Robert. "Dan Pagis and the Poetry of Displace-
    ment." In *Judaism: A Quarterly Journal of Jewish
    Life and Thought* 180, 45:4 (Fall 1996).
Jacobson, David C. "The Holocaust Survivor in
    Israeli Poetry: Dan Pagis." Paper delivered at

academic conference: Symposium on Trends in Contemporary Israeli Literature, University of Michigan, Ann Arbor, Michigan, 1977.

Pak Mogwol (Park Yong-jong)
(1916–1978) *poet, essayist, translator*

Park Yong-jong was born in Kyongju in Korea's Kyongsangnam province on January 6 and was educated through middle school. He is best known for his lyrical and nostalgic poems, which were popular with the Korean masses. His early pastoral poems of rural beauty, such as "Green Deer" and "The Mountain Peach Blossoms," were sentimental and evocative of his own childhood. Many were homages to his hometown and were infused with patriotic sentiments. He derived his rhythms from folk life and was deeply interested in folk culture.

Pak Mogwol moved from the countryside to the bustling metropolis of Seoul after Korea's liberation from Japanese colonialism in 1945. With his move, he made a similar shift in his poetry by moving toward REALISM, depicting city life, and pitting ordinary human beings against urban desolation. In "Sketch," for example, he tenderly describes a cast of haggard urban dwellers. In later years, Pak Mogwol's style and focus shifted once more—this time toward spiritualism and an acceptance of death—in poems such as "An Ordinary Day," in which the narrator marks his own grave.

In 1962, Pak Mogwol accepted a position teaching Korean literature at Hanyang University. He continued to write, producing essays, poems for children, translations, and the lyrical Korean poetry of which he is considered by many to be the modern master. He also edited the monthly journal, *The Image*. Pak Mogwol was honored with many awards, including the Free Literature Prize in 1955 and the Republic of Korea Literary Arts Prize in 1968. He died on March 24.

Another Work by Pak Mogwol
Selected Poems of Pak Mogwol. Translated by Kim Uchang. Fremont, Calif.: Asian Humanities Press, 1990.

Pamuk, Orhan (1952–   ) *novelist*

Orhan Pamuk was born in Istanbul, Turkey, and except for three years in New York, he spent his entire life there. Pamuk studied architecture at the Istanbul Technical University for three years but ultimately finished formal studies at the Institute of Journalism at Istanbul University. He began writing regularly in 1974 and published *Cevdet Bey and His Sons* in 1982, marking the beginning of his career. The novel was a family saga written in the REALIST style.

Pamuk's novels are very popular and at the same time highly controversial. His novel *Kara Kitap* (*The Black Book,* 1995), about a week in the life of the lawyer Galip whose wife Ruya has left him, became both a best-seller and an object of condemnation. Its postmodern style and ambiguous politics angered leftists and fundamentalists alike.

Pamuk's works have been translated into more than 20 languages. He is the recipient of major Turkish and international literary awards, including the 1984 Madarali Novel Prize for his second novel, *Sessiz Ev* (*The Silent House,* 1983); here, Pamuk shifted from the realist style of his first novel to a more in-depth psychosociological style. Pamuk won the 1991 Prix de la Découverte Européenne for the French translation of *Sessiz Ev*. His most notable subjects are Istanbul, Turkey's culture and politics, and human rights, and his novels, when taken as a whole, show a mixture of modern and traditional styles. In "Orhan Pamuk," Andrew Finkel states that "The point [of Pamuk's novels] seems to be that a person does not have to abandon the past in order to be part of the future."

Another Work by Orhan Pamuk
The White Castle. Translated by V. Holbrook. New York: George Braziller, 1991.

Pardo Bazán, Emilia de (1851–1921)
short-story writer, novelist

Pardo Bazán was born in La Coruña, Galicia. Her parents encouraged her studies, and her father's library supplied her with a great variety of reading material. She was fascinated by books about the French Revolution and loved *Don Quijote,* the Bible, and Homer's *Iliad.* She began to write poetry as a young child. Taught by private tutors, she refused to take music classes or to play the piano, as was traditional for young women; instead, she spent time reading and writing. Married at age 17, she moved to Madrid, where she became part of the social scene. Later, she went to France and traveled through Europe, learning French and German. She was influenced by French literature. In 1876, she gave birth to the first of three children and dedicated her only book of poems to this child. Her first novel, *Pascual López* (1879), was written on the birth of her second child. In 1880, she contracted hepatitis and went to Vichy to recuperate. There, she met the French poet and novelist Victor HUGO.

La Cuestión Palpitante (1883), a collection of articles explaining NATURALISM, (the theory that human behavior is controlled by instinct, emotion, and social and economic determinism), created a scandal, and her husband asked her to stop writing and to retract several statements. Two years later, in 1884, she left him and published *La Ama Joven* about matrimonial crises. *La Tribuna,* (1882), her third novel, is considered to be her first naturalist work. It is a study of the environment and workers in the cigar factories in La Coruña, similar to works by Benito PÉREZ GALDÓS (1843–1920). The two authors had a romantic relationship lasting some 20 years.

In 1890, she established the magazine *El nuevo teatro crítico.* At this time, denouncing educational differences between the sexes, she began a lifelong campaign for female emancipation. In 1906, she won a major battle in this area, becoming the first woman to preside over the literary section of the Ateneo of Madrid (a pioneer cultural institution) and the first female professor of literature at the Central University of Madrid. Only one student attended her class.

Pardo Bazán was given the title of *condesa* (countess) for her literary achievements.

Other Works by Emilia Pardo Bazán

The House of Ulloa. Translated by Lucia Graves. New York: Penguin USA, 1991.

The Tribune of the People. Translated by Walter Borenstein. Cranbury, N.J.: Bucknell University Press, 1999.

The White Horse and Other Stories. Translated by Robert M. Fedorchek. Cranbury, N.J.: Bucknell University Press, 1993.

Torn Lace and Other Stories. Translated by Maria Cristina Urruela. New York: Modern Language Association of America, 1997.

Works about Emilia Pardo Bazán

Gonzalez-Arias, Francisca. *Portrait of a Woman As Artist: Emilia Pardo Bazán and the Modern Novel in France and Spain.* New York: Garland, 1992.

Hemingway, Maurice. *Emilia Pardo Bazán: The Making of a Novelist.* Cambridge, U.K.: Cambridge University Press, 1983.

Tolliver, Joyce. *Cigar Smoke and Violet Water: Gendered Discourse in the Stories of Emilia Pardo Bazán.* Cranbury, N.J.: Bucknell University Press, 1999.

Park Yong-jong

See PAK MOGWOL.

Pasolini, Pier Paolo (1922–1975) *director, writer, poet, novelist, critic*

Pier Paolo Pasolini was born in Bologna, Italy, to Carlo Alberto Pasolini, an Italian army officer, and Susanna Colussi, a grade-school teacher. He attended the University of Bologna as an art history major before he switched to literature. He wrote his thesis on the poet Giovanni Pascoli. Pasolini was drafted into the Italian army in 1943 in the middle of his studies but served only a week. When his army unit was captured by the Germans, Pasolini escaped into the Italian countryside, after which he began to write poetry. During this time, he discovered he was homosexual.

Pasolini began to write novels in the 1950s. His early novels included *The Ragazzi* (1955), about poor young people in the slums of Rome, and *A Violent Life* (1959), which expresses his radical political beliefs. The former, a portrayal of the underside of Roman life, was considered so graphic and controversial that it led to charges of pornography.

In the 1960s, Pasolini turned to writing for film. He preferred the medium of film to paper, having once said, "Since Chaplin's *Modern Times,* movies have anticipated literature. . . . The movie has much more freedom." One of his key films is *The Gospel According to St. Matthew* (1964), which features his mother in the role of the older Virgin Mary. His final film was *One Hundred and Twenty Days of Sodom* (1975), which uses sex as a metaphor for the class struggle; this film stirred up controversy for its portrayal of Italian hedonistic society.

Pasolini was brutally murdered under ambiguous circumstances. Some believe a teenage prostitute bludgeoned Pasolini to death and then ran over him with Pasolini's car. Others believe he was assassinated, perhaps for his political beliefs. A provocative and controversial artist, writer, and filmmaker, Pasolini gained popularity after his death. Several of his works were released posthumously.

Other Works by Pier Paolo Pasolini

Petrolio. Translated by Ann Goldstein. New York: Pantheon, 1997.

Pier Paolo Pasolini: Poems. Translated by Norman MacAfee. New York: Noonday Press, 1996.

Roman Poems. Translated by Lawrence Ferlinghetti and Francesca Valente. San Francisco: City Lights Books, 1986.

Works about Pier Paolo Pasolini

Friedrich, Pia. *Pier Paolo Pasolini.* Boston: Twayne, 1982.

Rohdie, Sam. *The Passion of Pier Paolo Pasolini.* London: British Film Institute, 1996.

Pasternak, Boris (1890–1960) *novelist, poet, translator, short-story writer*

Boris Leonidovich Pasternak was born in Moscow to Leonid Pasternak, a celebrated painter, and Rosa Kaufman, a concert pianist. The family was established in the intellectual and cultural circles of Moscow. Indeed, Leo TOLSTOY was a family friend and played a role in the formation of Pasternak's literary style. An excellent student, Pasternak received the Russian equivalent of valedictorian rank and in 1908 began to study law at Moscow University. While there, he became very interested in philosophy and decided to pursue his studies at the University of Marburg in Germany in 1912.

Pasternak successfully completed his studies and in 1914 published his first volume of poetry, *The Twin in the Clouds.* Two subsequent collections, *Over the Barriers* (1916) and *My Sister, Life* (1917), established his reputation as a major Russian poet. His poetic works combined the elements of SYMBOLISM and FUTURISM, with verse that is lyrical and emotional, and contains some of the most profound images and metaphors found in Russian poetry.

At first, Pasternak supported the Bolshevik revolution, but he soon was disenchanted with the failed promises of the communist regime. During the 1920s, he began his prolific career as a fiction writer. In *The Childhood of Lovers* (1924), Pasternak explores the psychological makeup and emotions of a young girl. He published a short autobiographical work, *Safe Conduct* (1931), and a brilliant collection of poetry, *Second Birth* (1932). Because of his interest in exploring ethical themes and his political disillusionment, he came under repeated attacks from the government during the 1930s and was forbidden to publish. He supported himself by translating English and German poets into Russian. During these years, Pasternak gained the respect of Russian intellectual circles.

Pasternak received the Nobel Prize in literature in 1958 as a result of his most celebrated work, *Doctor Zhivago* (1957). The epic novel recounts the experiences of a young doctor, Yuri Zhivago, during the upheavals of the early 20th century. The novel's insights into the Communist regime quickly brought about government criticism and censure. It was first printed in Italy in 1957, followed by an English translation in 1958 and its publication in 1959 in the United States. Forced by the Soviet government to refuse the Nobel Prize, Pasternak was expelled from the Soviet Writers' Union and exiled to an artists' community outside Moscow. He died virtually abandoned by everyone except close friends. Critical acclaim for his work did not come in Russia until years after his death.

Pasternak is now recognized as one of the greatest writers of the 20th century. He left a legacy of courage and genius that is still admired today. He sacrificed his life for his work, to which his own countrymen were denied access until the 1970s.

A Work about Boris Pasternak

Barnes, Christopher. *Boris Pasternak: A Literary Biography.* Cambridge: Cambridge University Press, 1998.

Paton, Alan (1903–1988) *poet*

Alan Paton was born in Pietermaritzburg, Natal, South Africa. His father was James Paton, a Scot who had migrated to South Africa in 1895, and his mother was a descendant of English immigrants. His parents were not highly educated, but they were staunchly religious, and Paton grew up reading the Bible. His strict father often beat his sons when they were young, and the trauma of Paton's childhood deeply affected his views about authority and corporal punishment. His father's influence is not altogether negative, however; he encouraged Paton to love books and nature. Paton was an avid reader of literature, such as the works of Charles Dickens, Walter Scott, and Rupert Brooke. He attended high school at the Maritzburg College from 1914 to 1918 and completed his college education at Natal University College in 1924. Paton worked as a teacher at the Ixopo High School for White Students, where he met his first wife. In 1935, Paton was appointed principal of the Diepkloof Reformatory for young offenders. This experience formed the basis of his political consciousness. Paton resigned from his job

and, in 1953, formed the South African Liberal Party (disbanded in 1968).

Paton's most famous novel is *Cry, the Beloved Country,* which was published in 1948. By the time of Paton's death, the book had sold more than 15 million copies worldwide. It was also adapted into two films. Kumalo's journey in the book reflects Paton's concern with major themes that influenced his life, such as authority, racial discrimination, and religion. Paton's empathetic portrayal of Kumalo, a black Anglican priest, led many white South Africans to criticize his work for being too sentimental. At the peak of apartheid in South Africa, his disdain of racial discrimination and his idealized vision of eventual reconciliation of the two racial groups were deemed too revolutionary. Paton was a sort of liminal figure because he stood on the line that borders the two worlds of white and black South Africans. Most of the white Afrikaners rejected him for his sympathy for the black Africans, and some of the latter viewed his writing with suspicion, evidently shown in the mixed reactions to his portrayal of characters and interracial relationships in *Cry, the Beloved Country.* Paton's next international success, *Too Late the Phalarope* (1953), further explores the themes of racial and political inflexibility.

Paton's work against apartheid won him the annual Freedom Award in 1960. His other works include autobiographies and biographies of famous political figures such as Jan Hofmeyer, the cabinet minister. Paton's main contribution to African literature lies in his balanced perspective and optimism, untainted by the bitterness that often accompanies other African writings.

Other Works by Alan Paton

Journey Continued: An Autobiography. New York: Scribner, 1988.
Save the Beloved Country. New York: Scribner, 1989.
Towards the Mountains. New York: Scribner, 1980.

Works about Alan Paton

Alexander, Peter F. *Alan Paton: A Biography.* Oxford: Oxford University Press, 1994.

Chapman, Michael. *South African Literatures*. London: Longman, 1996.

Pavese, Cesare (1908–1950) *novelist, poet, translator*

Cesare Pavese was born in Santo Stefano Belbo, Italy, to Eugenio Pavese, a clerk at a law court in Turin, and Consolina Mesturini. His rural Italian roots are a big part of his identity, and his poetry and fiction are infused with images connected to his poor beginnings. As a young boy, he spent summers in the country and the rest of the year in Turin. When Pavese was six, however, his father died of a brain tumor. His mother, determined to give him a good education, enrolled him in the Liceo Massimo D'Azeglio school. Augusto Monti, his Italian and Latin teacher there, became an influential mentor in his life. Monti encouraged his bright pupil to read the works of Vittorio Alfieri, an 18th-century Italian dramatist whose works explored themes of political freedom and the dangers of tyranny. Monti introduced Pavese to politics, specifically the need for civic awareness, and helped instill in him a disdain for totalitarianism. In 1927, Pavese enrolled in the Faculty of Letters at the University of Turin. He wrote his thesis on U.S. poet Walt Whitman and graduated with a degree in literature in 1930. Other writers played a key role in Pavese's career as he translated many works of famous writers, beginning in 1931 with his translation of Sinclair Lewis's *Our Mr. Wrenn*. Other notable translations include Herman Melville's *Moby Dick* (1932), Daniel Defoe's *Moll Flanders* (1938), and Charles Dickens's *David Copperfield* (1939).

Pavese did not, however, limit himself to translating. *Hard Labor*, his collection of verse, was published in 1936. In her biography *Cesare Pavese*, Aine O'Healy says the collection is "one of Pavese's most challenging and ambitious works, and it contains the nucleus of all the thematic preoccupations of his subsequent writing," such as rural versus urban life, parenthood, and work.

Heavily influenced by Whitman and other poets, Pavese set out to create serious narrative poetry. His poem "South Seas," for example, is a recounting of a walk in the countryside with his cousin; yet, it takes on epic proportions.

Pavese's entry into novel writing took place toward the end of his life. His first novel, *The Beautiful Summer* (written in 1940), is a coming of age story about a working-class girl in Turin. *Among Single Women,* a novel that studied the "false tragic world of the upper class," followed in 1949. Pavese returns to the coming-of-age story in *The Devil in the Hills* (1948), but this time uses three young men as his characters and human freedom and limitation as his themes. These collective works earned Pavese the Strega Prize for fiction in 1950.

Pavese's contributions in the areas of poetry and fiction are noteworthy. His novels, translated into many languages, helped establish Italian neorealism, a movement in art, literature, and film characterized by its preoccupation with everyday, working-class life and leftist politics. In addition, his translations helped American classical literature reach a wider Italian audience. When he committed suicide in 1950, Pavese left this diary entry: "I have done my public share—as much as I could do. I have worked. I have given people poetry. I have shared the sufferings of many."

Another Work by Cesare Pavese
The Selected Works of Cesare Pavese. Translated by R. W. Flint. New York: Farrar, Straus & Giroux, 1968.

A Work about Cesare Pavese
Áine O'Healey. *Cesare Pavese*. Boston: Twayne, 1988.

Pavlova, Karolina Karlovna
(1807–1893) *poet, novelist*

Karolina Pavlova was born in Yaroslavl, Russia, but spent her childhood and most of her adulthood in Moscow with parents of German origin. Her father, Karl Yanish, was a professor of chemistry and physics, a physician, an amateur astronomer, and a scholar of literature and painting. Pavlova received a marvelous education as a child: She was an avid reader, was fluent in four languages by age 12, and often helped her father collect astronomical data.

Pavlova began her literary career in the late 1820s, translating Aleksandr PUSHKIN'S poetry into German and French. When she began to compose poetry, she also did so in French and German. Her translations were quite popular in the fashionable salons of Moscow, and Pavlova was inspired to compose poetry in Russian.

In 1836, she married N. F. Pavlov, a mediocre writer who was in constant trouble with authorities because of his political activities. Pavlova's poetry was at its most popular in the 1840s, and in 1848 Pavlova successfully published a novel, *A Double Life.* She soon found herself bankrupt, as her husband gambled away her inheritance. Indignant, Karl Yanish wrote a letter to government officials, fully describing the antigovernment activities of Nikolay Pavlov, who was subsequently imprisoned and sentenced to exile. Public indignation forced Pavlova to leave Moscow in 1853. She briefly settled in St. Petersburg until she finally left Russia in 1861 and settled in Drezden, Germany.

Her poems were collectively published only once during her lifetime, in 1863, but were overlooked. In 1915, however, Valery BRYUSOV edited a collection of her poems, and Pavlova's work became popular and appreciated, especially in literary circles. *A Double Life* is the only work of Pavlova translated into English. In the West, Pavlova's work is not well known, although some scholars have begun to reexamine her poetry, particularly in the context of feminism.

A Work about Karolina Pavlova

Fusso, Susanne, ed. *Essays on Karolina Pavlova.* Chicago: Northwestern University Press, 2001.

Paz, Octavio (1914–1998) *poet, essayist*

Octavio Paz was born in Mexico City, Mexico. His father, Octavio Paz, Sr., a lawyer, diplomat, and journalist, had represented the Mexican revolutionary Emiliano Zapata when he was tried in the United States. His mother, Josefina Lozano, was a first-generation Mexican born to Spanish parents. Paz was educated in his early years in a French school. In addition, his aunt tutored him in French and recommended French books for him to read. As a boy, his favorite authors were Victor HUGO and Jean-Jacques Rousseau. This affinity with French culture stayed with Paz throughout his life and influenced both his poetic style and his thought.

In his 20s, Paz's poetry was noticed by Pablo NERUDA, and he was invited to Spain to attend the Second Antifascist Writers Congress. He traveled in Europe and befriended André BRETON, French surrealist writer from whom Paz absorbed the ideas and psychological and philosophical concepts of surrealism. Paz approached these ideas with classical sensibility and measured logic.

In *Labyrinth of Solitude* (1950), a collection of essays, Paz speculates on the sociology of the Mexican national character. He finds that Mexico is a nation yet to arrive at a final national identity. It is a culture fragmented by the conflicts between the old world and the new. Because the culture is fragmented, its citizens are unable to connect with each other, and they find themselves trapped by solitude. Paz proposes a solution, which he takes directly from surrealism: The only way to escape solitude is through romantic love as an act of the imagination. Paz goes on to say that, for escape to be possible, Mexican women must be allowed more freedom to develop their own identities. *Labyrinth of Solitude,* thus, has an international appeal.

Though Paz's essays have come to be appreciated as much as his poems, his first success and literary impact was as a poet. His poem *Sun Stone* (1957) is perhaps the apex of his poetic vision and his powers of formal design. Its structure is cyclical and is metaphorically based on the famous Aztec calendar stone, a cosmological object that represents the Aztecs' religious and physical conception of the universe. It also has a practical purpose in that it can be used to help a person calculate the seasons. Paz, in essence, tried to create a poem that would represent analogously the universe of modern consciousness in all its grandeur and, at the same time, be accessible to an individual on a very personal level.

In both his poetry and his essays, one of Paz's primary concerns is how individuals connect to their society. He applied his formidable critical powers to the art of literature in his collection of essays *The Bow and the Lyre* (1953). His analysis explores poetic language, the role of the writer, and the social importance of literature. The book is filled with learned detail that Paz uses as he strives to synthesize poetry's historical and universal aspects.

In 1990, Octavio Paz won the Nobel Prize in literature. He was considered a mentor to many Mexican authors in the generation that came after him, most importantly to Carlos FUENTES. The two Mexican authors shared the qualities of a powerful imagination and a deep concern for history.

Another Work by Octavio Paz

A Draft of Shadows, and Other Poems. Edited and translated by Eliot Weinberger, with translations by Elizabeth Bishop and Mark Strand. New York: New Directions, 1979.

Works about Octavio Paz

Grenier, Yvon. *From Art to Politics: The Romantic Liberalism of Octavio Paz.* Lanham, Md.: Rowman & Littlefield, 2001.
Ivask, Ivar. *The Perpetual Present: The Poetry and Prose of Octavio Paz.* Norman: University of Oklahoma Press, 1973.
Quiroga, Jose. *Understanding Octavio Paz.* Columbia: University of South Carolina Press, 1999.

p'Bitek, Okot (1931–1982) *poet*

Okot p'Bitek was born in Gulu, northern Uganda. He attended Gulu High School and King's College in Budo before taking a two-year course at the Government Training College in Mbarara in 1952. He taught English and Religious Knowledge at Sir Samuel Baker's School near Gulu, where he was also the choirmaster. His interest in music began around this period and continued throughout his life. P'Bitek became increasingly interested in his African heritage and tradition. In 1962, he moved to Oxford University to pursue a degree in social anthropology and examine closely the richness of the African tradition. P'Bitek became active in politics, especially during the 1960s when a movement was established to gain independence for Uganda. He returned briefly to Uganda to change the agenda of the Ugandan Cultural Center in Kampala and then moved to Nairobi to teach at the university. He finally returned to Makerere University as a professor of creative writing in 1982 but died tragically five months later.

P'Bitek's poetry shows the rich influence of his interests in traditional African song, music, and oral tradition. He wrote his first poem, "The Lost Spear" (1952) while he was still a student in Mbarara. The poem retells the traditional Lwo folk story regarding the spear, the bead, and the bean.

P'Bitek's writings also express his concern with contemporary political issues and display his resourcefulness in blending these concerns with his musical talent. In *Song of Lawino* (1966), for example, p'Bitek employs strong imagery and lyrical rhythms to denounce Africans, especially politicians, who embrace Western ideology and discard their African heritage.

P'Bitek did not reject technological advancement and progress in Uganda, but he disagreed that these should come at the cost of losing Acoli cultural values. P'Bitek's contribution to world literature lies in his belief and efforts in bringing native language to the forefront of poetry writing in Africa, and his works express his concern that African nations be built on the basis of African beliefs, culture, and values, not on Western ones.

Other Works by Okot p'Bitek

African Religions in Western Scholarship. Kampala: East African Literature Bureau, 1970.
Hare and Hornbill. London: Heinemann, 1978.
The Horn of My Love. London: Heinemann, 1974.

Works about Okot p'Bitek

Heron, G. A. *The Poetry of Okot p'Bitek*. London: Heinemann, 1976.

Ofuani, Ogo. "The Poet as Self-Critic: The Stylistic Repercussions of Textual Revisions in Okot p'Bitek's *Song of Ocol*." *Research in African Literatures* 25, no. 4 (Winter 1994): 159–75.

Pederson, Knut

See HAMSUN, KNUT.

Perec, Georges (1936–1982) novelist

Georges Perec was born on March 7 in Paris, where he lived for most of his life. His father was killed in 1940 in World War II. Perec and other members of his family sought refuge in the country, but his mother disappeared from Paris in 1942, and it was later discovered that she died at Auschwitz. Perec was raised by his aunt and uncle, served in the army, married, and published his first works in magazines.

Perec's first novel, *The Things* (1965), was awarded the Prix Renaudot. He followed this achievement with 20 more books, no two of them having the same pattern. He joined a Paris-based writing group, OULIPO, the Workshop of Potential Literature, whose main goal was to expand literary possibilities by borrowing from the fields of mathematics and logic. Perec became intrigued by the palindrome, a sentence or word that reads the same both forward and backward. Perec wrote one palindrome consisting of more than 5,000 words.

Perec's literary output includes novels, short stories, and word games. He also composed a 466-word text using *a* as the only vowel. This experiment led to his fascination with the lipogram, a text in which one or more letters may not appear. *La Disparition* (1969) is a novel lipogram in E, meaning that the letter *e* is never used. This made translating difficult, as the literal English title, *The Disappearance*, would contain the forbidden letter. It was translated in 1994 by Gilbert Adair as *A Void*.

Largely secretive with regard to his private life, Perec did publish *W, or The Remembrance of Childhood* (1975), an odd assortment of memoirs interspersed with sections about a dystopian island called W, where life revolves around sports. His masterpiece, however, is *Life, A User's Manual* (1978), which tells stories about the residents of an apartment building. Perec built the work based on a complex system detailing the number and the length of the chapters, as well as the appearance of certain random elements within each of the stories. *Life, A User's Manual* was awarded the Prix Medici.

Another Work by Georges Perec

53 Days. Translated by David Bellos. London: Harvill, 1992.

A Work about Georges Perec

Bellos, David. *Georges Perec: A Life in Words*. London: Harvill, 1993.

Peretz, Isaac Lieb (1852–1915) poet, novelist, playwright

Isaac Lieb Peretz was born in Zamosc, Poland. Considered one of the founders of modern Yiddish literature, he was largely self-educated, gaining much of his knowledge through extensive reading. A career as a successful lawyer left little time for Peretz to write until a false accusation forced him to seek new employment. He was hired as a cemetery official for the Jewish cemeteries in Warsaw, Poland.

Peretz's career change left him with ample time to pursue his writing. He published fiction, plays, and poems and inspired younger writers to pursue their goals. He became active in socialist spheres and was often accused of radicalism. Attracting negative attention from the authorities, he was imprisoned once for his socialist activities.

A voice for the Jewish Enlightenment in Poland, a movement that stressed understanding and embracing Jewish heritage and culture, Peretz wrote his early work in Hebrew and his later work in Yiddish. Much of his work makes the point that, although Jews in Poland were materially poor, their lives were spiritually rich. He glorified the worker and showed compassion for the poor. For example, *Stories and Pictures* (1900; translated 1906), considered his finest work, is a series of Hasidic sketches in which Peretz offers a sympathetic look at Jewish life. With a tone that is sometimes loving, sometimes critical, he describes situations common not only to the Polish Jews of his time but also to all of humanity.

Peretz's heroes are the oppressed and the suffering who exemplify virtue, faith, and unselfishness that are often lacking in humanity as a whole. The hero of the short story "Bontsche the Silent" (in *Man's Search for Values* [translated by A. S. Rappoport, 1987]), for instance, is a virtuous man who spends his entire life suffering in silence. He receives his reward in the afterworld, where he is told that he can have whatever he desires; however, all the man can think of requesting is a hot roll and fresh butter for breakfast every morning. In this way, Peretz also exemplifies the simple pleasures of life that are most often taken for granted.

Another Work by Isaac Lieb Peretz

Selected Stories. Translated by Eli Katz. New York: Zhitlowsky Foundation for Jewish Culture, 1991.

A Work about Isaac Lieb Peretz

Wisse, Ruth R. *I. L. Peretz and the Making of Modern Jewish Culture.* Seattle: University of Washington Press, 1991.

Pérez Galdós, Benito (1843–1920)
novelist, playwright, historian

Benito Pérez Galdós was born on Grand Canary Island. He was the youngest of 10 children, and his mother was determined that he would be a lawyer, thereby bringing middle-class respectability to the family. Though an intelligent child and very talented in both the literary and visual arts, he did not apply himself at school and had no interest in being a lawyer. Nevertheless, when he was 18, his mother sent him to the University of Madrid to study law. Madrid was a true awakening for the young writer. Though Pérez Galdós had spent most of his youth in the Canary Islands, it was Madrid that became the focus of his novels, and he eventually became the quintessential writer of that city in the 19th century.

In 1865, he abandoned law school and became a journalist for the newspaper *The Nation.* His years reporting on the news of Madrid served as a literary apprenticeship in that the skills he acquired later helped him to develop his incredible REALISM. After Madrid, Pérez Galdós spent some time in Paris, where he began his first novel, *The Shadow* (1871), an odd phantasmagoric novel of psychological investigation. Its use of fantasy was uncharacteristic for Pérez Galdós and the realist style he would develop.

In 1873 Pérez Galdós wrote the first of a series of five works entitled *National Episodes,* in which he dramatizes events from 19th-century Spanish history as a way to explore issues of morality. In his concern for the moral character and national identity of Spain, he can be seen as a precursor and influence on the writers of the GENERATION OF 1898.

Pérez Galdós's historical interest became the major direction of his later works. Almost all of this series 46 novels depict the reality of his time or the recent past while commenting on how the forces of history affect individual lives. *The Disinherited Lady* (1881) is a perfect example. On the surface it is a realistic account of a woman's life in late 19th-century Spain; however, it is also a symbolic meditation on how the Spanish tendencies of self-deception and dreaming have led to certain political tragedies.

Later in his career, such novels as *Compassion* (translated 1962) would turn to examine more closely issues of the spirit and faith. Pérez Galdós continued to write in the realist mode, of which he was an exceptional master, but now, instead of layering his realism with political and historical ideas, his books began to focus on the metaphysical forces behind life.

Pérez Galdós wrote to illuminate the relationships between the individual and the forces of society. Those forces variously took the forms of history or metaphysical questions in his novels; however, they always represented the vast interconnected web of forces that make up reality. He could be compared to the French novelist BALZAC. The two authors were exacting realists who used realism in an attempt to communicate their visionary insights.

Other Works by Benito Pérez Galdós

The Golden Fountain Café. Translated by Walter Rubin. Pittsburgh, Pa.: Latin American Literary Review Press, 1989.

Our Friend Manso. Translated from the Spanish by Robert Russell. New York: Columbia University Press, 1987.

A Work about Benito Pérez Galdós

Ribbans, Geoffrey. *History and Fiction in Galdós's Narratives.* Oxford: Clarendon Press, 1997.

Perse, Saint-John (pseudonym of Marie-René-Auguste-Alexis Saint-Léger) (1887–1975) *poet, diplomat*

Saint-John Perse was born on the island of St. Léger des Feuilles near Point-à-Pitre, Guadeloupe. His father was a lawyer, and his mother's family owned plantations. In 1899, his family moved to France and settled in Pau. While studying law at Bordeaux, Perse befriended Paul CLAUDEL and other writers. He published his first collection of poems, *Éloges* (1911) shortly after graduating.

Perse wrote his epic poem *Anabase* (*Anabasis*, 1924) while he was working as a diplomat in China from 1916 to 1921. The title refers to the classical Greek writer Xenophon's account of an army's march through the ancient East. American-born English poet T. S. Eliot (1888–1965) thought so highly of this work that he translated it into English and wrote a preface in which he called it "a piece of writing of the same importance as the later work of James Joyce." Perse composed more poems

from 1921 to 1932 while he was secretary to French statesman Aristide Briand. In 1940, the Nazi secret police seized and destroyed manuscripts in his Paris apartment, and the collaborationist Vichy regime revoked Perse's citizenship and dismissed him from office.

Perse first fled to England and then settled in the United States, where he worked as a consultant on French poetry at the Library of Congress. He published many works after moving to the United States, including *Exil* (*Exile*, 1942), a collection of four poems. His collection *Amers* (*Seamarks*, 1957) has been called one of the greatest works to emerge from World War II, and its section titled "Etroits sont les vaisseaux" ("Narrow are the vessels") is considered one of the great erotic sequences in French literature.

The New York Times Book Review (July 27, 1958) wrote that "If one reads through all" Perse's poems, "one is immediately aware that each is, as it were, an instrument of one great oeuvre." As B. Lindblad, president of the Royal Academy of Sciences, said before Perse's acceptance speech for the 1960 Nobel Prize in literature, "with sublime intuition" Perse knows "how to describe in brilliant metaphors the reaction of the soul of humanity."

Other Works by Saint-John Perse

Anabasis. Translated and with a preface by T. S. Eliot. Fort Washington, Pa.: Harvest Books, 1970.

Collected Poems. With translations by W. H. Auden et al. Princeton, N.J.: Princeton University Press, 1983.

Exile, and Other Poems. Translated by Dennis Devlin. New York: Pantheon Books, 1953.

Selected Poems. Edited by Mary Ann Caws. New York: New Directions, 1982.

Works about Saint-John Perse

Krause, Joseph. "The Two Axes of Saint-John Perse's Imagery." *Studi Francesi* 36, no. 1 (January–April 1992): 81–95.

Sterling, Richard L. *The Prose Works of Saint-John Perse: Towards an Understanding of His Poetry.* New York: Peter Lang, 1994.

Pessoa, Fernando (Alberto Caeiro, Ricardo Reis, Álvaro de Campos)
(1888–1935) *poet*

Born in Lisbon, Portugal, to a cultured family, Pessoa was educated in South Africa and spoke English fluently. At age 15, he composed English sonnets in the style of Shakespeare.

In 1905, he returned to Portugal, attended the University of Lisbon, and became a commercial translator, an occupation that he held his entire life. He was one of the founders of *Orpheu* and *Presença,* two highly influential literary journals. At the time of his death, his work was not known outside of Portugal.

Pessoa began to write poetry in 1912. His poems express a longing for Portugal's glorious past, and they reflect the influence of the classical tradition and French SYMBOLISM. His earlier poems are nostalgic for a mythic past, whereas his later works deal more with consciousness and sensation.

His two main themes are the inherent limitations of one's power to apprehend reality and the elusive nature of personal identity. He invented literary alter egos to explore these themes. Pessoa wrote under 73 different names, and each persona reflects an individual outlook and Pessoa's belief that there is no one integrated personality. It is interesting to note that there is a recurrence of masks in his poems. His family name comes from the Latin *persona,* which refers to the masks worn by actors and, by extension, to the role the actors play. Also interesting is the fact that, in Portuguese, his family name means both "person" and "nobody."

Among his poetry collections are *Sonnets* (1918), *English Poems* (1922), and *Mensagem* (1934).

Another Work by Fernando Pessoa

Fernando Pessoa. Translated by Jonathan Griffin. Oxford: Carcanet, 1971.

A Work about Fernando Pessoa

Montero, George, ed. *The Man Who Never Was.* Providence, R.I.: Gavea Brown, 1982.

Pincherle, Alberto

See MORAVIA, ALBERTO.

Ping Hsin

See BING XIN.

Pirandello, Luigi (1867–1936) *playwright, novelist, short-story writer*

Luigi Pirandello was born in Caos, Italy, to Stefano Ricci-Gramitto, a sulfur dealer, and his wife, Caterina. His father expected him to join the family business, but Pirandello pursued academics instead. In 1887, he studied at the University of Palermo, then the University of Rome, before receiving a Ph.D. in Roman philology in 1891 from the University of Bonn in Germany. His dissertation explored the Sicilian dialect of his native region. After his university training, Pirandello returned to Rome and translated Goethe's *Roman Elegies.* He also published his first original work, *Joyful Ill*(1889), a collection of romantic and sentimental poetry.

In 1894, he entered an arranged marriage with Antoinetta Portulano, the daughter of his father's business associate. His wife suffered a severe nervous breakdown and violent outbursts. In 1919, once Pirandello became financially solvent in his work, she was sent to a sanitarium. The turbulent union produced three children and fueled the sense of tragedy and despair found in Pirandello's work.

In 1908, Pirandello became a professor of Italian literature at the Girls' Normal School in Rome. In 1921, he had dual theatrical successes with his plays *Six Characters in Search of an Author* and *Henry IV. Six Characters* experiments with theatrical conventions. The story revolves around actors and a director rehearsing Pirandello's own play

The Rules of the Game. During the rehearsal, a group of six people arrive, looking for someone to dramatize their story. As the tale unfolds, themes of morality, incest, and death intermingle. According to Susan Bassnett-McGuire in her book *Luigi Pirandello,* this work is a "two-fold process [that] takes place first in the author's mind and then on the stage when the actors and director take over."

When the play *Henry IV* (known in the United States as *The Living Mask*) came out, it was considered the Italian *Hamlet.* It is the most frequently performed of all of Pirandello's works in English. It centers on a costume party at which each guest is required to portray a famous historical character. One man chooses to be Henry IV. During the evening, he falls from a horse, hits his head, becomes deluded into believing he is actually the monarch, and is sequestered in a country villa set to resemble a medieval castle. His family, convinced that he is mad, plans to cure him of his insanity, but it is revealed that the man has been merely wearing the mask of insanity for a number of years and enjoying the ruse. In her introduction to *Three Plays,* Felicity Firth summarizes the theme in *Henry IV*: "[E]ach individual creates for himself a personal vision of the truth in order to make life bearable. . . ."

Luigi Pirandello is one of Italy's most respected playwrights. His ability to capture his own multitiered vision of truth has entertained audiences for many years. While he encountered initial resistance for his self-consciousness and experimentalism, he won the Nobel Prize in literature in 1934 and has become one of the most influential 20th-century dramatists. In 1935, Pirandello wrote of his critics, "The world of international literary criticism has been crowded for a long time with numerous Pirandellos—lame, deformed, all head and no heart, gruff, insane and obscure—in whom, no matter how hard I try, I cannot recognize myself, not even in the slightest degree."

Other Works by Luigi Pirandello

Firth, Felicity, ed. *Three Plays: "Enrico IV," "Sei Personaggi in Cerca d'Autore," "La Giara."* New York: St. Martin's Press, 1988.

Tales of Madness: A Selection from Luigi Pirandello's Short Stories for a Year. Translated by Giovanni R. Bussino. Brookline Village, Mass.: Dante University of America Press, 1984.
Three Major Plays. Translated by Carl R. Mueller. Hanover, N.H.: Smith & Kraus, 2000.

Works about Luigi Pirandello

Bassanese, Fiora A. *Understanding Luigi Pirandello.* Columbia: University of South Carolina Press, 1997.
DiGaetani, John Louis, ed. *A Companion to Pirandello Studies.* Westport, Conn.: Greenwood, 1991.

poetic realism

Poetic realism began in Germany, Scandinavia, and Central Europe, having its origins in the works of Poul Müller (1794–1838) and developing in the poetry and fiction of Theodor Storm (1817–88) and Theodor Fontane (1819–98), but its influence spread to Eastern European countries and to Russia as well. It developed as a result of dissatisfaction with the constraints and embellishments of ROMANTICISM, and in response to the often bleak social conditions of the late 19th century.

The major difference between poetic realism and other REALISM movements was the tendency for writers who associated with poetic realism to view the harsh realities of the world through a veil of artistic illusion, allowing some elements of the romantic movement to appear in their works. Higher poetic themes—such as love, aesthetics, death—were placed in the context of everyday life. Russian exponents of this principle notably include Aleksandr PUSHKIN.

As the age of realism progressed and war became more common among Central and Eastern European countries, as well as in America, poetic realism lost many of its ties to romanticism, moving away from a veil of illusion to a clear view of the human condition.

In the 1890s, poetic realism began to fade into the background and to be replaced throughout much of Central Europe by photographic realism, or NATURALISM. Reality was seen without the veil of illusion, and life was viewed impersonally, with no attempt to gloss over the unpleasant aspects of human existence. This change, however, arrived later in the Balkans and Russia, where poetic realism held sway until the middle of the 20th century. Even after the start of World War II, poetic realism explored the subjects of poverty and suffering and, at the same time, expressed hope within the bleakest of circumstances.

In the Balkans, poetic realism found an even greater expression in the visual arts, as represented by the works of Marko Celebonovic (1902–87), Nedjeljko Gvozdenovic (1902–88), Pedja Milosavljevic (1908–87), and Ivan Tabakovic (1898–1977). The tendency, however, in both the literature and art of this period was for artists to attempt to come to terms with reality, as opposed to escaping it.

Twentieth-century Russian poets who are considered poetic realists include Andrey Voznesensky (1933–), Yevgeny YEVTUSHENKO, and Joseph Brodsky (1940–96). In France, as well as in the Balkans, poetic realism continued to filter itself into the emerging field of film.

Works about Poetic Realism

Bernd, Clifford. *Poetic Realism in Scandinavia and Central Europe.* Columbia, S.C.: Camden House, 1995.

Pizer, John David. *Ego-Alter Ego: Double And/As Other in the Age of German Poetic Realism.* Durham: University of North Carolina Press, 1998.

Ponge, Francis (1899–1988) *poet, essayist*

French poet and essayist Francis Ponge was born in Montpellier, France, on March 27. He first studied law in Paris and then literature in Strasbourg. In the years between World War I and World War II, he worked as a journalist and newspaper editor. In 1937, Ponge became a member of the Communist Party. He was actively involved during World War II in the organization of a resistance movement among journalists. He left the party in 1947 and

lived for two years in Algeria prior to returning to Paris to teach. He retired in 1965 to give lectures in several countries.

Ponge's poetry first gained attention in the late 1940s when it was praised in an article by Jean Paul SARTRE. Ponge's poems were meticulous observations rather than emotional works. He described his ideas in rational terms that still remained lyrical. His collections include *The Voice of Things* (1942; translated 1972) and *La Rage de l'expression* (1952). He often looked at common objects as a means of expressing larger concerns such as in "L'Orange," from his collection *Le Parti pris des choses* (1942), in which an ordinary orange becomes a metaphor for ways of dealing with oppression.

Ponge died in Paris on August 6, leaving behind a legacy to world literature of the deeper understanding of the inherent simplicity of life.

Other Works by Francis Ponge

Selected Poems. Translated by C. K. Williams. Winston-Salem, N.C.: Lake Forest University Press, 1994.

The Delights of the Door: A Poem. Translated by Robert Bly. New York: Bedouin Press, 1980.

A Work about Francis Ponge

Sorrell, Martin. *Francis Ponge.* Boston: Twayne, 1981.

Poot, Linke

See DÖBLIN, ALFRED.

Popa, Vasko (1922–1991) *poet*

Vasko Popa was born in Grebenats, Banat, in Serbia. Although little is written of his life, he is one of the most widely translated modern Serbian poets. His works often describe the tragic experiences of the modern urban man in a time of war, and they express the fears and insecurities of humans trapped in a world that is becoming less and less human.

Popa's poetry is best known for its classical elements as it brings to life the myth of Kosovo as it appeared in the traditional epic songs, by translating them into the language of modern Yugoslav poetry. In *Earth Erect* (translated 1973), for example, Popa describes his country outside of war as "A field like no other / Heaven above it / Heaven below."

Classical images of Serbia's national culture dominate Popa's poetry, thus leading to its success not only in his own country but even more so abroad, where his works have been used as song lyrics for both children's classical folk-song anthologies and contemporary Serbian "rock" music. From surrealist fable to traditional folktale, combining autobiography with myth, Popa's poetry embodies the spirit of a country struggling to maintain its identity.

Other Works by Vasko Popa

Earth Erect. Translated by Anne Pennington. Iowa City: International Writing Program, University of Iowa, 1973.
Homage to the Lame Wolf: Selected Poems, 1956–1975. Tranlated with an introduction by Charles Simic. Oberlin, Ohio: Oberlin College, 1979.
The Golden Apple: A Round of Stories, Songs, Spells, Proverbs and Riddles. Translated by Andrew Harvey and Anne Pennington. London: Anvil Press Poetry, 1980.

Works about Vasko Popa

Alexander, Ronelle. *The Structure of Vasko Popa's Poetry (UCLA Slavic Studies, Vol. 14)*. Columbus, Ohio: Slavica Publishers, 1986.
Lekic, Anita. *The Quest for Roots: The Poetry of Vasko Popa (Balkan Studies, Volume 2)*. New York: Peter Lang, 1993.

postcolonialism

Postcolonialism is a complex phenomenon that has generated many interpretations. From a historical perspective, it refers to literature and cultures that have redefined themselves following the experience of Western colonization. It most commonly applies to the cultures of South Asia, Africa, and the Caribbean that have gained their independence since the Second World War (1939–45). Postcolonialism in Latin America has a longer history, going back to the 19th century. It also refers to a body of theory written primarily by diasporic academics—from the Caribbean, the Middle East, South Asia, and Africa—who now reside in Europe and the United States. Edward Said's seminal work *Orientalism* (1978) casts a postcolonial eye on the discourse of the "Orient" generated by colonialism. This work has inspired many revisions and reinterpretations of colonial discourse. Similarly groundbreaking are Hohmi Bahba's *Dislocations of Culture* (1994), which looks at the ways in which writers formed under colonialism turn the language of the colonizer into new forms of identity and resistance; and Gayatri Spivak's *In Other Worlds* (1987), which applies postmodern, poststructuralist, and feminist theories to the reading of postcolonial discourse and literature.

Although most colonized countries won their independence during the 20th century, Latin America has a unique postcolonial history. Colonized in the 16th century primarily by Spain and Portugal, it experienced postcolonial movements in the 19th century when many of its countries won their independence and sought to define their cultural specificity. This was achieved by, for example, incorporating elements that had been rejected or marginalized by the colonizers, such as indigenous and African cultures, or else by turning to northern Europe and North America, instead of Spain or Portugal, for cultural models and ideals. However, especially toward the end of the century, Latin America experienced forms of economic and cultural colonization that were imported from Great Britain, France, and the United States that posed new challenges to national definition and visions of independence. During the 20th century, many Latin-American liberation movements and many prominent writers and intellectuals were inspired by Communist responses, especially that of Cuba, to colonialism and its aftermath.

After the Second World War, the European empires that had dominated a large part of the world during the 19th century, exporting their cultures and their literary forms, began their retreat. Independence movements led not only to political and national redefinitions but to creative responses to Western influences and oppression. Since the independence of India in 1947, inspired by the writings of Mohandas K. GANDHI, South Asia has seen an extraordinary renaissance of writers from different religions and regions, exploring South Asian and diasporic identity. Many of these writers are internationally known. V. S. NAIPAUL, for example, was awarded the Nobel Prize for literature in 2002. Since independence, African literature has also found an international audience and includes Nobel Prize winners such as Nadine GORDIMER and Wole SOYINKA. Books by writers from many different parts of the world are being published at an ever-increasing speed; many different voices are being heard, including those of women and the politically disenfranchised.

The NÉGRITUDE movement in France of the 1940s and 1950s, led by Aimé CÉSAIRE and Léopold SENGHOR, valorized African identity and revitalized African and Caribbean poetry. When he became president of independent Senegal in 1960, Senghor used the concept of *négritude* as part of his political agenda, creating debate and controversy among other African and Caribbean writers about the meaning of being African.

In the 1950s and 1960s, the Civil Rights movement in the United States added impetus to the revival of African culture, long suppressed by slavery and its aftermath, and encouraged or inspired liberation movements throughout the world. In South Africa, often at the cost of imprisonment or death, black and white writers increasingly dared to oppose apartheid. Also, since the 1970s, liberation movements by indigenous peoples in Australasia and Latin American have transformed dying oral cultures, based on myth and ritual, and created new genres, such as the oral testimonial. *I Rigoberta Menchu: An Indian Woman in Guatemala* by Rigoberta MENCHÚ is one of many such testimonials that have brought to international attention the plight of indigenous cultures. Similarly, since the 1970s, the outcast Dalits of India have begun to reinvent their own culture and DALIT LITERATURE.

The question of language is crucial to postcolonial writers who were forced to learn the language of the colonizers, most often English, Spanish, or French. (In some cases, there are competing colonial languages, for example French and English in Canada, and Afrikaans and English in South Africa). After independence, for whom were these writers writing and in what language should they write? Some followed the example of the Martinican novelist Raphaël Confiant (1951–   ), who chose to write in his native Creole and then changed to French. For most writers, it was a question of finding a wider audience. Chinua ACHEBE, considered to be the first African novelist, chose to write in English to reach not only Western readers but also many African readers who speak hundreds of different languages but whose lingua franca is English. Addressing different constituencies, the Kenyan NGUGI WA THIONG'O writes in both English and Kikuyu.

Postcolonial writers have shown to what extent thay have been able to use their colonial languages in new and liberating ways. Their styles vary according to their specific cultural and historical circumstances. Drawing on oral and spiritual traditions alien to the modern, secular West, some writers, such as the Colombian Gabriel GARCÍA MÁRQUEZ and the Indian-born Salman RUSHDIE have combined myth and modernity, the sacred and the profane to create what has been called MAGIC REALISM, a popular postcolonial genre. Magic realism acknowledges the overlapping of cultures and the often absurd and ironic juxtapositions of competing beliefs, economic systems, and voices in the fragmented discourse of the postmodern and postcolonial world.

Postcolonialism has produced a strong immigrant and diasporic literature. For economic and political reasons, South Asians, Indonesians, Africans, Turks, and Caribbeans have established themselves in the West and have produced a new definition of what constitutes, for example, English or French or German or Dutch literature. Writers cannot easily be pinned down to a national identity. Dual nationality is common. Salman Rushdie wanders from Bombay to London to New York, always redefining the urban ground beneath his feet through the prism of his changing cultural experiences, including an India long left behind. The Trinidadian-born V. S. Naipaul reimagines the India, Africa, and Caribbean of his parents' diasporic past and chooses to live in England. Michael ONDAATJE moves from Sri Lanka to England to Canada. Other Indian, African, and Caribbean writers situate themselves within a tradition that includes, but is not reduced to, the colonial experience. Some of them emulate Arundhati ROY, a recipient of the Booker Prize, who has resisted the path of literary celebrity in the Indian diaspora and has remained in India, using her influence to support oppressed minorities—including tribal women—in their local cultural and political struggles.

Beginning with the collapse of the Berlin Wall in 1989, the disintegration of the empire of the Soviet Union, established since the Second World War, has produced its own, European form of postcolonial experience and literature. The fall of the Soviet Union has meant the reconfiguration of social and national identities in Eastern and Central Europe. Economic disorder and political unrest, especially due to the war in the former Yugoslavia and neighboring states, have also changed forms of literary expression and have increased the immigration of writers to Western Europe and the United States.

Electronic communications, the expansion of capitalism after the fall of the Soviet Union, and the economic liberalization of China have globalized the economy. For some peoples of the former colonial world, especially those opposed to Western forms of modernization, globalization, often interpreted as Americanization, is perceived as a threat to local cultures, religions, and forms of expression. For others, globalized forms of communication and dissemination of ideas are sources of new kinds of agency and self-determination. Because of their colonial histories, postcolonial writers remain especially alert to the dangers as well as the possibilities of globalization.

Works about Postcolonialism

Appiah, Kwame Anthony. *In My Father's House: Africa in the Philosophy of Culture.* New York: Oxford University Press, 1993.

Ashcroft, Bill, Gareth Williams, and Helen Tiffin. *The Empire Writes Back: Theory and Practice in Postcolonial Literatures.* New York: Routledge, 2002.

Fanon, Frantz. *Black Skin, White Masks.* Translated by Charles Markmann. New York: Grove Press, 1991.

———. *The Wretched of the Earth.* Translated by Constance Farrington. New York: Grove Press, 1996.

Glissant, Edouard. *Caribbean Discourse: Selected Essays.* Translated by J. Michael Dash. Charlottesville, Va.: Caraf Books (University of Virginia Press), 1992.

Gugelberger, Georg M., ed. *The Real Thing: Testimonial Discourse and Latin America.* Durham, N.C.: Duke University Press, 1997.

King, Anthony D., ed. *Culture, Globalization, and the World-System: Contemporary Conditions for the Representation of Identity.* Minneapolis: University of Minnesota Press, 1997.

Lazarus, Neil. *Resistance in Postcolonial African Fiction.* New Haven, Conn.: Yale University Press, 1990.

Ngugi Wa Thiong'o. *Decolonising the Mind: The Politics of Language in African Literature.* Portsmouth, N.H.: Heinemann, 1986.

Stratton, John. *Writing Sites: A Genealogy of the Postcolonial World.* Ann Arbor: University of Michigan Press, 1990.

Viswanathan, Gauri. *Masks of Conquest: Literary Study and British Rule in India.* New York: Oxford University Press, 1998.

postmodernism

Postmodernism emerged after World War II as a reaction against MODERNISM, which upheld the potentially restorative and integrating power of literature. Postmodernists do not attempt to correct or remedy the chaos and cacophony of language, but rather they imitate and often celebrate it. Many postmodernists, for example Samuel BECKETT and Peter HANDKE, emphasize the alienation of the individual in the modern social environment and seem highly aware of the domineering presence of technology—computers, telephones, faxes, weapons of mass destruction—in daily life. Although the intellectual beginnings of postmodernism are often identified with the French school of structuralist criticism, the aesthetic ideas of postmodern writers and artists can be found in contemporary works around the globe.

Postmodernist works often combine elements of diverse genres, such as television, cartoons, and music, that have a potential appeal to popular culture, and they often challenge the ideological assumptions of contemporary society. Opposing the notions of mimetic representation, postmodernists agree that language has its own singular reality.

The postmodern movement is identified with its own critical theories, namely deconstruction and cultural criticism. Cultural criticism questions the notions of "high" and "low" cultures and tends to treat all works of art, from comic books to statues, as equally legitimate cultural expressions. Deconstruction (often referred to as poststructuralism), the postmodern movement primarily based on the work of French philosopher Jacques Derrida (1930–   ), questions the notion of a single, unified meaning in a literary work. Through an act of close reading, the deconstructionists attempt to show that texts are self-contradictory and lack a single, unified center.

The postmodern movement is by no means limited to the arts. Our notions about the relationship between ideology and power underwent dramatic change based on the work of the French philosopher Michel Foucault (1926–84). Julia Kristeva (1941–   ), a psychoanalytic gender critic, changed our notions of femininity and its relationship to arts. Psychology also experienced dramatic changes, primarily in the field of psychoanalysis. Jacques Lacan (1901–81) refined Sigmund FREUD's ideas about the relationship of language, gender, and psyche.

In certain ways, postmodern thinkers demonstrate that the line between science and arts is not as self-demarcating as some would like it to be. Many postmodern scientists question the notion of a single, unified reality. The artificial intelligence expert Marvin Minsky (1927–   ) insists that computers can think. Chaos theory, developed by the chemist Ilya Prigogine (1917–   ), disrupts our concept of a unified universe. Currently, many postmodern thinkers are examining the role of computers and hypertext in our understanding of epistemology. These ideas closely relate to our changing understanding about the structure of language and discourse.

Postmodernism has influenced virtually every genre of literature, theater, and film. Even of greater significance, postmodernism has confronted our epistemological conceptions about language, image, and signs.

Works about Postmodernism

Appignanesi, Chris. *Introducing Postmodernism.* New York: Totem Books, 2001.

Docherty, Thomas, ed. *Postmodernism.* New York: Columbia University Press, 2002.

Eagleton, Terry. *The Illusions of Postmodernism.* Oxford: Blackwell, 1996.

Grenz, Stanley. *A Primer on Postmodernism.* Grand Rapids, Mich.: Wm.B. Eerdmans Publishing Co., 1996.

Heartney, Eleanor. *Postmodernism.* New York: Cambridge University Press, 2001.

Premchand, Munshi (Dhanpat Rai Srivastana) (1880–1936) *novelist, short-story writer*

Premchand was born outside the city of Benares, India. His family was very poor. The plight of the poor and the downtrodden is one of the prevalent themes in Premchand's literature. He is perhaps the most famous Hindi–Urdu novelist of Indian literature and is considered to be the father of the Urdu short story. One of the strongest influences in Premchand's earlier work was Gandhian politics. His later novels are a blend of his own faith in marxism and his growing disillusionment with GANDHI's brand of grassroots activism.

In 1899, Premchand became a schoolteacher and continued this profession for 20 years. Copies of his first collection of short stories *Passion for the Fatherland* (1908), written in his first penname Navab Rai, were burned by British officials because of their strong patriotic (anti-British) message. After this event, he wrote by the penname, Premchand. In 1915, Premchand stopped writing in Urdu completely and switched to writing in Hindi. This further increased his popularity because the Hindi language is spoken by a larger population in India.

By the time he wrote *Godān* (*Gift of the Cow*, 1936), published the year he died, Premchand had broken from his earlier optimistic portrayals of village life. Instead, he saw more clearly the dismal economic situation of India's rural poor. *God¯an* offers a stark look at the lack of social and economic reform in villages, while metropolitan India is busy with modernization. Hori, the main character, and the village setting are realistic portraits that reveal the growing chasm between urban and rural India.

Because Premchand had his own publishing house, he encountered little difficulty in publishing his more controversial works. These works, such as *Nirmala* (1928), address the social and psychological problems imposed on women by society's norms. In particular, Premchand challenges the standard treatment of widows and prostitutes; at the time, widows were forced into financially dependent relationships with their family members because they were not given employment and were not allowed to remarry.

While serving as editor of the literary magazine *Hans* in the 1930s, Premchand used his position to create a mutual ground for literature and progressive politics. In 1936, he briefly served as president of the All India Progressive Writers' Association (AIPWA). This group was one of India's first attempts to form a collective of leftist, socialist writers. Premchand's novels were also an international success. His novel *God¯an* has been translated into almost every Western language.

Other Works by Munshi Premchand

Gaban: The Stolen Jewels. Translated by Christopher R. King. Delhi: Oxford University Press, 2000.
Nirmala. Translated by Alok Rai. New York: Oxford University Press, 1999.

A Work about Munshi Premchand

Rai, Amrit. *Premchand: His Life and Times.* New York: Oxford University Press, 2002.

Proust, Marcel (1871–1922) *novelist*

Best known for his stream-of-consciousness autobiographical novel *À la recherche du temps perdu* (*In Search of Lost Time*, 1912; first published in English as *Remembrance of Things Past*), Marcel Proust was born in Auteuil, just outside of Paris, on July 10. The son of a wealthy doctor and his wife, a Jewish woman from a highly cultured background, Proust received an excellent education at the Lycée Condorcet. In spite of severe asthma, which plagued him throughout his life, he served one year in the military before attending the Sorbonne, where he received a degree in law.

Proust's literary skills became evident while he was still in his early teens. After graduation from the Sorbonne, he began to frequent the aristocratic salons in the wealthy sections of Paris. He also began to write for several of the Symbolist (*see* SYMBOLISM) magazines. His first books, *Portraits de peintres* (1896) and *Pleasures and Regrets* (1896), came out in rapid succession and established him as an emerging literary voice.

Between 1895 and 1899, Proust worked steadily on an autobiographical novel, which he never completed and which was never published. He returned to this genre with greater success later in life. Proust supported himself with family money and with money that he earned translating the works of English art critic John Ruskin. He also worked briefly as a lawyer, becoming active with Émile ZOLA in the Dreyfus affair. One of the prime examples of anti-Semitism in late 19th-century France, this case dealt with a false accusation of treason against Jewish army captain Alfred Dreyfus.

Proust's asthma increased in severity as he grew into adulthood, and he often spent large periods of time under the devoted care of his mother, to whom he became almost neurotically attached. The death of his father in 1903, followed by the death of his mother two years later, combined with the loss of his lover caused Proust to withdraw from his high-profile society life almost to the point of his becoming a total recluse. He took up residence in a soundproof flat and, until 1919, lived there, devoting himself entirely to his writing. He rarely left his dwelling except during the summer months, when he would retreat to coastal Cabourg. Financially secure, he was finally able to begin work in earnest on his masterpiece.

Inspired by the autobiographical works of GOETHE and CHATEAUBRIAND, Proust began work on *In Search of Lost Time*. He spent the majority of his time during this period locked in his bedroom writing late into the night and sleeping by day. He produced the first of seven volumes of the work in 1912.

Critical Analysis

In Search of Lost Time has no clearly constructed plot line. It is told entirely in a stream-of-consciousness style by a nameless narrator who, while he is not exactly Proust, resembles the author in many ways. He begins his journey in the novel completely ignorant, only beginning to rediscover his childhood memories after he is given a Madeleine cake soaked in linden tea, similar to those his aunt had given to him when he was a young boy. Memory becomes the central focus of the work, which traces the lives of the narrator's family as well as two other families, one aristo-cratic, the other Jewish. The smallest details within the work often prove to be the most important, and the characters are richly detailed.

Aside from his novels, Proust is also noted for his elaborate and lengthy letters. Collected volumes of his correspondence reveal his varied interests and his primary belief that a writer must be constantly seeking new information. He is considered by many critics to be one of the leading pioneers of the modern novel, and his influence can be seen in the works of Virginia WOOLF, Samuel BECKETT, Claude SIMON, and others. His skills as a literary critic remained undiscovered in his lifetime; it was not until the posthumous publication of *Contre Sainte-Beuve* (1954) that his nonfiction works received any serious attention.

The publication of the second volume of Proust's autobiographical masterpiece was delayed due to the start of World War I. It did not become available until 1919. This volume and the ones that followed, however, earned him international acclaim. It is a massive work, totaling more than 3,000 pages. Proust dedicated the final decade of his life to its perfection. On his deathbed, he was still making corrections, leaving the final volumes without what he considered to be their finishing touches. Proust died in Paris on November 18.

Other Works by Marcel Proust

The Captive. Translated by Charles Kenneth Scott-Moncrieff. New York: A. & C. Boni, 1929.
The Complete Short Stories of Marcel Proust. Translated by Joachim Neugroschel. New York: Cooper Square Press, 2001.
Selected Letters: 1880–1903. Translated by Ralph Manheim. New York: Doubleday, 1983.
Selected Letters Volume 2: 1904–1909. Translated by Philip Kolb. London: Collins, 1989.

Works about Marcel Proust

Carter, William C. *Marcel Proust: A Life.* New Haven, Conn.: Yale University Press, 2000.
Hindus, Milton. *A Reader's Guide to Marcel Proust.* New York: Syracuse University Press, 2001.

Shattuck, Roger. *Proust's Way: A Field Guide to In Search of Lost Time.* New York: W. W. Norton, 2000.

Pushkin, Aleksandr (1799–1837) *poet, novelist, short-story writer*

Aleksandr Sergeyevich Pushkin was born in Mihailovskoe, Russia, to aristocratic parents, Sergey Pushkin and Nadezhda Osipovna. On his mother's side, Pushkin descended from an African slave, given to Peter the Great as a state present from the Ottoman Empire. He had close relationships with his grandmother and his nurse, who brought him up on Russian folktales, and with the serfs on his family's estate. He was given a classical education from one of the best schools available in Russia, the Lyceum Tsarskoye Selo. It was there that he began to write poetry. He graduated with honors in 1817.

After graduation, Pushkin began to pursue a life of pleasure, freedom, and revolutionary thought in St. Petersburg. He published poetry that was considered scandalous at the time and brought the attention of the czar. In 1820, he published the long narrative poetic romance *Ruslan and Ludmilla*, which combined the traditional elements of a Russian fairy tale with the exquisite control of poetic language. The poem was immediately recognized as a masterpiece of Russian literature and brought fame to Pushkin.

That same year, Pushkin published *Ode to Liberty,* a poem that satirized famous figures of the czar's court and was viewed as politically and socially radical by the censors. Pushkin was exiled by the czar's police and forced to relocate in Ekaterinoslavl in southern Russia. This banishment provided an opportunity for Pushkin to travel to the exotic Caucasus and Crimea and gave him inspiration for his short stories, "The Prisoner of the Caucus" (1822) and "The Fountain of Bakhchisarai" (1824). Both stories center on the beautiful and inspiring mountainous landscape, and they reveal a strong influence of the poetry of the notorious Lord Byron. During his exile, Pushkin led a riotous lifestyle, and he was then ordered to return to his family's estate in Mikhailovskoe.

Far away from the court and stimulating society, in the solitude of Mikhailovskoe, Pushkin began to work without distractions. There he conceived his historical epic work, *Boris Godunov* (completed 1825; published 1831). The poem, broad in its scope, presents a tragic story of a downfall of a Russian czar. The poem was popularly received and was transformed into an opera by Modest Mussorgsky. Pushkin gave a public reading of the poem for which the government immediately reprimanded him. After the death of Alexander I in 1825, the new czar, Nicholas I, offered to be the personal censor of Pushkin; all future poems and stories were to be read directly by him before publication. Pushkin found this arrangement restrictive, however, and the czar ordered that he be put under constant government surveillance for the rest of his life.

Critical Analysis

Aleksandr Pushkin is considered the greatest poet of Russia. Often relying on historical foundations, his work established and shaped the country's poetic language. Influenced by the English romantic poets, such as Wordsworth and Lord Byron, however, Pushkin's attitude was ironic in the manner of Voltaire. His work was unprecedented in its scope, in imagery, and in its use of common Russian language.

In the long narrative poems *Poltava* (1829) and *The Bronze Horseman* (1837), Pushkin extols the achievements of Peter the Great. In both poems, the earthly figure of Russia's emperor is transformed through lyricism into a heroic deity who builds the Russian Empire.

Eugene Onegin (1833) is considered to be the definitive masterpiece of Russian literature. A novel in verse, *Eugene Onegin* dramatically describes the ill-fated relationship between lovers. The complex rhyme scheme and unprecedented, delicate treatment of poetic meter still amaze readers of Pushkin. Besides its poetic language, the work also contains a biting commentary on the social order of Russia during the 1820s. Some critics consider *Eugene Onegin* among the greatest works of all literature.

Although Pushkin is primarily known for his verse, his short stories also attained critical recognition. His stories and poems are based not only on historical facts but also on the deep cultural traditions of the Russian people. In "The Golden Cockerel" (1833), he introduces the traditional elements of a fairy tale into his prose, finding inspiration for his work in the bedtime stories that were told to him in childhood. He transformed several of these fairy tales into works of high poetic merit.

The Queen of Spades (1834) reveals deep psychological torments of a gambler who decides to risk his entire fortune in a game of cards. *Eugene Onegin* and *The Queen of Spades* were adapted into operas by Russian composer Tchaikovsky, while "The Golden Cockerel" became the basis for an opera by Rimsky-Korsakov. The adaptability of Pushkin's verse into music demonstrates the lyrical quality of the poet's work.

In 1837, Pushkin was wounded in a duel over an alleged affair between his wife and a young Frenchman; he died several days later, leaving a legacy for generations of Russian writers and for every major poetic movement. Pushkin clearly showed the poetic capacity of the Russian language, he also memorialized the rich cultural heritage of his motherland. Indeed, Pushkin is now considered to be an incomparable part of Russian language and culture.

A Work about Aleksandr Pushkin

Feinstein, Elaine. *Pushkin.* London: Weidenfield and Nicolson, 1998.

Qabbani

See KABBANI, NIZAR.

Quasimodo, Salvatore (1901–1968) *poet*

Salvatore Quasimodo, recipient of the 1959 Nobel Prize for literature, was born in the small town of Modica, Sicily. The son of a railroad worker, he began to develop a love of writing in his early childhood. His family, however, felt that it would be much more practical for him to pursue an education in a technical field; therefore, he moved to Rome in his late teens to study engineering. Financial difficulties forced him to abandon his education in 1923, but a series of odd jobs eventually led to a secure government position as a civil engineer in 1926. Stable in his employment, Quasimodo was then able to return to his thoughts of becoming a writer. His brother-in-law, the novelist Elio Vitorini, introduced Quasimodo into literary circles where he soon befriended fellow writers Eugenio MONTALE, and Guiseppe UNGARETTI.

Quasimodo published his first poetry in magazines. His first volume of collected works, *Water and Land* (1930), contained several poems that had been written when he was as young as 18 as well as numerous, more recent pieces. This collection falls into what has been defined as the early phase of Quasimodo's career. Divided by World War II, his works are distinctly marked as falling into two separate stylistic categories. Before the war, as in this collection, his writing style was complex and tended toward the metaphysical. Most of his poetry during this period was nostalgic, filled with images of Sicily as a backdrop for feelings of loneliness and melancholy. At the same time, he also concerned himself with themes of childhood memory and a love for the beauty and culture of Italy. He connects this culture to influences of various invaders, such as the Greeks and Romans, and the profound and lasting effect they had on his own literary heritage.

As Quasimodo's early poetic style developed, he began to come under the influence of the symbolist movement (*see* SYMBOLISM). *Sunken Oboe* (1932) and *Scent of Eucalyptus* (1933) both contain poems that exemplify the movement's adherence to suggestive imagery and mysticism. As a result, much of his work during this period is considered difficult to analyze because of the complex and metaphysical nature of his imagery content.

In 1938, becoming more involved in his writing, Quasdimodo left his government post to become an assistant to Cesare Zavattini, a well- known editor of several popular literary periodicals. He continued to work on his own poetry and to publish his works regularly in collections such as *Greek Lyrics* (1940), a compilation of ancient Greek lyrical poetry. In this work, he once again returned to the idea of past influences, making associations between modern style and ancient language. Quasimodo also became enamored of the academic lifestyle at this point. He devoted himself entirely to his writing, expanding his focus to include essays on poetry and other forms of literature as well as translations of classical poetry and drama, including the works of Shakespeare, Homer, Virgil, and Sophocles. In 1941, he gained employment as a professor of Italian literature at the Guiseppe Verdi Conservatory in Milan, allowing him to continue to spread his own poetic ideals to future generations.

The start of World War II marked a shift in Quasimodo's writing. He became a member of an anti-Fascist group and spent a brief period of time in prison. There, he began to develop a more humanistic approach to his work, becoming more concerned with social conditions, contemporary issues, and the atrocities of war and human suffering. His best-known work, *And Suddenly It's Evening* (1942), marks the beginning of this change in style.

Quasimodo briefly joined the Italian Communist Party at the end of the war, but he quickly resigned in protest of the party's insistence that he dedicate his talents to producing political poetry. In response, he published *Day after Day* (1947), a collection of poems in which he focuses on the hardships faced by Italian citizens during World War II and on his own disdain for his country and the role that it played in the war. Vivid in description, this work is often considered one of the strongest volumes of antiwar poetry to come out of any country during this period. It reflects strongly Quasimodo's own concerns for the fate of Italy, as well as his fear that the country will lose its culture and beauty. This falls in direct parallel to his early works and their tendency to exemplify those same values of cultural and natural beauty.

In the later years of his life, Quasimodo continued to focus on issues pertaining to the tragedy of human conditions and social injustices; however, he also began to return to some of his earlier nostalgia, this time not for places but for people whose lives impacted his own. Quasimodo had one child, a daughter Orietta, born in 1935 to Amelia Specialetti, a woman to whom he was never married. His first wife, Bice Donetti, had passed away in 1948. Although he remarried to the dancer Maria Cumani, they permanently separated in 1960, leaving him with three lost loves. His fond but often bittersweet memories of these women, as well as reminiscences over several friends who died before him, form much of the driving force behind his final volume of poetry, *To Give and To Have* (1966).

He continued to be active as a writer and a critic until his death. While in Amalfi where he was judging a poetry competition, Quasimodo suffered a cerebral hemorrhage. He was returned to Naples for treatment, where he died, leaving behind a legacy of poetry best known for its fight against the social injustice and tragedy of war.

Other Works by Salvatore Quasimodo

Complete Poems. Translated by Jack Bevan. New York: Schocken Books, 1984.

The Poet and the Politician, and Other Essays. Translated by Thomas G. Bergin and Sergio Pacifici. Carbondale: Southern Illinois University Press, 1964.

Queirós, José María de (Eça de Queirós) (1845–1900) *novelist*

Born in Portugal, Eça de Queirós was the illegitimate son of a magistrate and was raised by his grandparents. He was sent to boarding school at the age of five. This parental neglect may explain the satirical nature of his works.

After law school, he became a journalist and then entered the consular service in 1872. He resided mostly abroad, and his *Letters from England* (1870) provide us some amusing views on life in Victorian England.

Considered Portugal's greatest novelist, he was influenced by ROMANTICISM and NATURALISM. He uses very expressive, realistic language and is known for his character descriptions. His major novels are critical portrayals of upper-class Portuguese society. In *O crime do padre Amaro* (1876; *The Sin of Father Amaro*) and his masterpiece *Os Maias* (1888), Queiroz depicts the corruption he saw among the clergy and in high society. He is critical of the intellectual elite, which he believes suffers from moral deficiency. His works seem to say that Portugese society could not change unless there was a major catastrophe.

Other Works by José María de Eça de Queirós

The Illustrious House of Ramires. Translated by Anne Stevens. New York: New Directions, 1994.

The Relic. Translated by Margaret Jull Costa. New York: Hippocrene Books, 1995.

A Work about José María de Eça de Queirós

Coleman, Alexander. *Eça de Queirós and the European Realism.* New York: New York University Press, 1980.

Queiróz, Raquel de (1910–) *journalist, novelist*

Raquel de Queiróz was born November 17 in Fortaleza, a town in the state of Ceará in Brazil. Her great-grandmother was the cousin of another famous Brazilian writer, José de ALENCAR, also from the state of Ceará in northeastern Brazil. At age seven, she moved with her family to Rio de Janeiro, but they returned to Ceará just two years later, and she would remain there until she graduated from college in 1921.

Queiróz began to write early, and she had a long career as a journalist. She also wrote novels, the first of which, *The Fifteen,* was published in 1930. The novel was very well received, and it gave Queiróz a literary name in Brazil. She received the Graça Aranha Foundation prize for the novel in Rio de Janeiro in 1931. Just a few years later, she formed friendships with Graciliano Ramos and Jorge Lins do Rego, also from the northeast. Through the exceptional writing of Queiróz and others from this region, the northeastern novels of Brazil were born. In the 1930s, Queiróz married literary figure and poet José Auto da Cruz Oliveira. They had a daughter and later separated. She continued to write in various genres throughout her life, including journalistic chronicles, novels, short stories, theater, and even children's literature. One of her best-known novels, *The Three Marias* (1939), is often considered semiautobiographical because it recounts the story of a young woman through her developmental years, from the age of 12 until she turns 20.

Queiróz was also very politically active, and she represented Brazil at the session of the General Assembly of the United Nations in 1966, where she worked especially on the Human Rights Commission. On August 4, 1977, the Brazilian Academy of Letters elected her as its first female member, paving the way for future female authors in Brazil.

Other Works by Raquel de Queiróz

Castro-Klaren, Sara, Sylvia Molloy, and Beatriz Sarlo, eds. Selections in *Women's Writing in Latin America.* Boulder, Colo.: Westview, 1992.

A Work about Raquel de Queiróz

Ellison, Fred P. *Brazil's New Novel: Four Northeastern Masters.* Berkeley: University of California Press, 1954.

Queneau, Raymond (1903–1976) *poet, novelist*

Raymond Queneau was born in Le Havre, France. A man of many diverse intellectual interests, he was a mathematician, scholar, humorist, linguist, and poet. When he was 17, Queneau went to Paris, where he briefly associated with André BRETON's surrealism. He composed the manifesto *Permettez!* (1920) but soon broke with the group to write about the link he saw between surrealism and EXISTENTIALISM.

In his works, Queneau often uses colloquial speech patterns and phonetic spelling of words. Fascinated by languages, he felt that written French needed to free itself from archaic rules and restrictions. His first novel, *Le Chiendent* (*The Bark Tree*, 1933), was noted for its use of slang and casual language. Because of this, Queneau's works are difficult to translate, as the language itself is critical to the interpretation.

Queneau is best known internationally for his novel *Zazie dans le métro* (1959), the story of a young girl who comes to visit Paris and stays with her heterosexual uncle, who is employed as a dancer in a gay bar. Her one desire is to ride the metro, which she cannot do because the workers are on strike. Instead, she embarks on a journey toward adulthood. The novel was adapted to film in 1960, gaining both positive and negative critical attention for its bold use of language and its break from cultural norms.

After this first film endeavor, Queneau collaborated on several other occasions with "New Wave" film directors. His work in this genre marks his most notable contribution to world literature. In addition, one of his poems was made popular when it was set to music by Juliette Greco. Queneau was elected to the Goncourt Academy in 1952. He died on October 26, having left his mark in the destruction of traditional literary norms.

Another Work by Raymond Queneau

Stories and Remarks. Translated by Marc Lowental. Lincoln: University of Nebraska Press, 2000.

A Work about Raymond Queneau

Guicharnaud, Jacques. *Raymond Queneau.* Translated by June Guicharnaud. New York: Columbia University Press, 1965.

Quental, Antero Tarquínio de
(1842–1891) *poet*

Antero Tarquínio de Quental was born in Ponta Delgada, Portugal. He was from an aristocratic family of intellectuals, writers, and religious leaders. Nevertheless, all his life Quental was a rebel and had decidedly liberal leanings.

He was the key figure in the Generation of Coimbra, a group of students at the University of Coimbra who attempted to revitalize postromantic Portuguese literature. The Generation of Coimbra had a great deal in common with Latin-American MODERNISM, and Quental had many affinities with Rubén DARÍO, modernism's key figure.

Quental's *Modern Odes* (1865) abandons romantic decadence and returns to a vocabulary of classical images and symbols, presenting a heightened, purified view of reality with a pessimistic tone.

Though not an innovator, Quental was a master of the sonnet. He proved this in his *Complete Sonnets* (1886), a collection of 109 sonnets that serve as a spiritual autobiography.

Quental, though a minor figure, was an important voice of modernism and social reform in 19th-century Portugal.

Rao Srinivasa, Srirangam

See SRI SRI.

Rabéarivelo, Jean-Joseph (1903–1937)
poet

Jean-Joseph Rabéarivelo was born in Tananarive, Madagascar. His mother was a member of an aristocratic Madagascar family that had been impoverished by the French takeover of the island. Rabéarivelo was educated by his uncle in French schools but left school at 13. He worked in various occupations, including as a librarian, which gave him the opportunity to read widely. He began to write poetry, mostly in French but some in his native Malagasy, at first under pseudonyms. He also began to write for journals, and when his article on Madagascar poetry was accepted by the international journal *Anthropos* in 1923, Rabéarivelo decided to become a full-time writer. During the same year, he became a proofreader for a printing press, a job he kept until his death in 1937. He married in 1926 and had five children; his grief over the death of his youngest daughter in 1933, expressed in a short story entitled "Un conte de la nuit," may have contributed to his death. After struggling with addictions, Rabéarivelo committed suicide by poisoning himself.

A sensation of despair and foreboding overhang Rabéarivelo's poetry, which was influenced by the work of Charles BAUDELAIRE and the French symbolists (*see* SYMBOLISM) as well as by traditional Malagasy form. His melancholy resonates through his poems, as in "Valiha," which both celebrates and grieves for a transformation of nature into art, when bamboo shoots, rustling in the wind, are turned into a musical instrument, the traditional stringed valiha of Madagascar:

> There they will sound
> until an artist comes
> who will break their godlike youth
> and flay them in his village
> and stretch out their skins
> with shards of calabashes . . .

The isolation and sadness of the speakers of his poems derive from Rabéarivelo's personal life experiences. His sorrow was further accentuated by his perceived failure in life, giving his poems a poignant bitter-sweetness. His despair is tinged with a quiet resilience that was derived from his love of freedom and nature, echoing the chants of Madagascar's highlands. Gerald Moore and Ulli Beier remark, "In his poetry he has destroyed and dismembered reality. And out of the fragments he has built a new mythical world; it is a world of death and frustration, but also transcended by a sad beauty of its own."

Another Work by Jean-Joseph Rabéarivelo

Translations from the Night: Selected Poems of Jean-Joseph Rabéarivelo. Edited by John Reed and Clive Wake. London: Heinemann Educational, 1975.

Works about Jean-Joseph Rabéarivelo

Adejunmobi, Moradewun. *Jean-Joseph Rabéarivelo, Literature, and Lingua Franca in Colonial Madagascar.* New York: Peter Lang, 1996.

Moore, Gerald and Ulli Beier, eds. *Modern Poetry from Africa.* New York: Viking, 1963.

Rabinowitz, Sholem

See ALEICHEM, SHALOM.

Ravikovitch, Dahlia (1936–   ) *poet*

Dahlia Ravikovitch was born in Ramat Gan, a suburb of Tel Aviv (now in Israel), and spent her early years on a kibbutz (a communal farm or settlement in Israel) before attending high school in Haifa. She later studied at the Hebrew University of Jerusalem. Ravikovitch published her first collection of poems, *The Love of an Orange,* in 1959 when she was still in the army. She has worked as a journalist, teacher, and television reviewer and continues to write poetry.

Ravikovitch's early poems are often romantic, evoking distant places, love, and mythological figures. Her later work contains increased satire and sarcasm but still maintains intellectual understanding and sensitivity.

After the Israeli war in Lebanon in 1982, Ravikovitch became active in the Israeli peace movement, and her poetry often tackles the difficult subject of war. She has said, "Everyone wants peace but everyone thinks someone else should bring it." Yet, it remains difficult to categorize her work—she takes on womanhood, human rights, and war, alongside inner life and loneliness as some of her themes.

Ravikovitch is considered one of Israel's leading poets. She has also written some prose and several children's books, has translated poetry by William Butler Yeats, Edgar Allan Poe, and T. S. Eliot into Hebrew, and is the recipient of the Shlonsky, Brenner, Ussishkin, and Bialik Prizes.

Other Works by Dahlia Ravikovitch

A Dress of Fire. Translated by Chana Bloch. Camp Hill, Pa.: Horizon House Publishers, 1978.

The Window: New and Selected Poems. In collaboration with Ariel Bloch. New York: Sheep Meadow Press, 1989.

Works about Dahlia Ravikovitch

Cooperman, Alan. "Making Peace Where Politicians Fear to Tread." *U.S. News and World Report,* June 30, 1997. Available online at http://traubman.igc.org/makepeac.htm.

Lowin, Joseph. "Born to Dream: A Discussion into English of Dahlia Ravikovitch's 'The Reason for Falling.'" From the Literary Corner (17 April 2002) of The National Center for the Hebrew Language. Available online at www.ivrit.org/literary/born_to_dream.htm.

realism

Realism in literature is a worldwide movement that had its most profound effects in fiction and drama in the late 1800s. Born out of the ideas of the ROMANTIC novel but infused with concrete details and accurate descriptions of society, the characters of realist fiction are drawn from the events and contexts of modern life and face everyday obstacles. Realism, as it has spread throughout the world, has mutated into POETIC REALISM, NATURALISM, SOCIALIST REALISM, MAGIC REALISM, and (in Italy) VERISMO. Realism has molded the expectations of readers worldwide, and in spite of the antirealist trends in MODERNISM and POSTMODERNISM, it remains a force every writer must reckon with to this day.

French Realism

Realism is most commonly traced to the French novelist Honoré de BALZAC and his series of novels and stories which, grouped together, form *The Human Comedy* (1840). Balzac's intention was to portray, as accurately as possible, all aspects of French life and culture, from the lowest prostitute to the highest political leader. His attention to detail in setting and characterization provided the foundations for the movement, although the actual plots of his works, often absurd and almost unbelievable, were far from the goals to which realism ultimately aimed.

In 1857, Gustave FLAUBERT's *Madame Bovary* became the prototype for the realist novel. Like Balzac's work, Flaubert's novel was the result of systematic research; however, instead of fanciful plots, he focused instead on the issue of female adultery and the unhappy married life of a country woman, Emma Bovary. Considered mild according to modern standards, Flaubert's love scenes were so detailed that they resulted in the author facing charges of obscenity. He was called the anatomist of the heart.

Russian Realism

The shift from romantic idealism to realism in Russian literature was primarily initiated by the prose of Nikolay GOGOL, which addressed aspects of everyday life of the common people in Russia. In many respects, realism in Russia coincided with the development of a large class of government officials and merchants. The works of realism often depict the lives and conflicts of the Russian middle class and deal with themes such as marriage, money, and class relations. For the realists, literature needed to reflect the problems and issues pertinent to the economic, political, and social life of the nation.

In the 1850s, during the early phase of the realist movement, such writers as Aleksandr OSTROVSKY and Ivan GONCHAROV began to shift artistic focus toward the previously neglected merchant class, while poets such as Nikolay Nekrasov (1821–78) created long narrative poems that focused on the social ills suffered by the poor. The early works of realism often also depicted the moral degeneration of the Russian aristocrats.

Most of the realist masterpieces produced in Russia emerged during the movement's late phase, which is sometimes referred to as the golden age of Russian literature. The highly sophisticated prose of Ivan TURGENEV, for instance, focuses on the social dynamics of minor aristocrats and middle-class families. Turgenev also provided an unprecedented level of literary attention to the Russian peasantry. Fyodor DOSTOYEVSKY, however, concentrated on psychological realism. His novels carefully examine the emotional motivations and desires of his characters. Another giant of realism, Leo TOLSTOY, combined astute social commentary with observations about spirituality and religion. Most critics view Anton CHEKHOV as the last seminal figure of Russian realism. Like many other realists, Chekhov focused on the problems and moral dilemmas faced by middle-class families. Chekhov believed that the middle class was the backbone of Russian society and, therefore, centered his work on it.

Chinese Realism

In China, realism accompanied MODERNISM in literature into the 20th century. In a sense, many modernist writers, such as HU Shih, were realists in their use of objectivity to reflect the modern "condition."

Several literary groups and organizations formed during the May Fourth era, a period of unprecedented intellectual openness, innovation, and experimentation in China. Among them was a group of scholars who comprised the Literary Association. They also came to be known as the realist school. Mao Dun (1896–1981; also known as Mao Tun) was the leader of this group and its most prominent practitioner. He took over the journal *Short Story Monthly* and converted it to a journal of vernacular literature (*baihua* literature). The use of the vernacular was an important component of realism in that it best captured the language of the

Chinese people and contributed to an accurate representation.

Mao Dun and the realist school openly advocated "art for life's sake," which was a continuation of the idea that literature could effect social change. In contrast to the romantic tradition of "art for art's sake," the objective representation of reality had a sociopolitical purpose, and many realist writers had agendas for reform. BA Jin, an ardent anarchist and Communist, for example, was known for his realistic portrayals of Chinese society, as can be seen in *Family* (1931), his chronicle of the falling gentry. Mao Dun's 1933 work, *Midnight,* was another such work: Considered a major political novel of the era, it was noted for its objectivity, optimism for change, and revolutionary appeal.

Realism often manifested itself in short stories and novels about daily life and included criticism of government or society. BING Xin's short stories, such as "Loneliness" (1922), about young women confronting issues in love and life, were extremely popular, and because of her realistic portrayals, they often provided psychological insight readers could relate to.

The poetry school of realism also provided realistic depictions of Chinese life, adding innovative form and language. Realistic poetry focused on the preservation of natural rhythms as found in vernacular speech, as opposed to the poetic and formal diction of formalists or the experimental language of symbolist poetry. Realism's poets included Hu Shih, Li Jinfa (1900–76), and Dai Wangshu (1905–50), whose works were published in the journal *Poetry.*

By the onset of the communist revolution, realism had faded into the more direct objectives of socialist realism. Works took on a distinct socialist tenor, but components of realism, such as the close representation of reality to provide social critique, as well as writing in the vernacular, persisted. These powerful elements of realism render it a continuing popular force in Chinese literature today, although it frequently appears in new, slightly changed forms.

Works about Realism

Anderson, Marston. *Limits of Realism.* Berkeley: University of California Press, 1989.

Fanger, Donald, and Caryl Emerson. *Dostoevsky and Romantic Realism: A Study of Dostoevsky in Relation to Balzac, Dickens, and Gogol.* Evanston, Ill.: Northwestern University Press, 1998.

Lukacs, Georg. *The Theory of the Novel.* Translated by Anna Bostock. Cambridge, Mass.: MIT Press, 1974.

Mortimer, Armine Kotin. *Writing Realism: Representations in French Fiction.* Baltimore, Md.: Johns Hopkins University Press, 2000.

Reid, J. H. *Narration and Description in the French Realist Novel: The Temporality of Lying and Forgetting.* New York: Cambridge University Press, 1993.

Reis, Ricardo

See PESSOA, FERNANDO.

Remarque, Erich Maria (pseudonym of Erich Paul Kramer) (1898–1970) *novelist*

Erich Maria Remarque was born in Osnabruck, Germany, to Anna Marie and Peter Maria Kramer, a bookbinder. Despite the modest income of the family, Remarque was educated in the best private school in town, but his studies at the University of Munster were interrupted by the outbreak of World War I and his subsequent draft into the army at the age of 18. Remarque fought on the Western front and was wounded several times.

After discharge from the military, Remarque completed a pedagogy course offered by the government to veterans and soon began his writing career as a journalist for a sports magazine, *Sportsbild,* and then became its assistant editor.

Remarque's first novel, *All Quiet on the Western Front* (1929), is his most famous work. It realistically depicts the horrors faced by soldiers of both sides during World War I. The novel begins in 1917, after Paul Baumer, the protagonist, loses half of his friends in battle. Encouraged by their teacher to enlist in the German army, Baumer and his classmates find themselves in the trenches under constant attack by French machine guns and poisonous clouds of mustard gas. Baumer's romantic and nationalistic perspective of war, which the reader finds in the beginning of the novel, is replaced by sudden physicality, violence, and, ultimately, a sense of the futility of war. Today, *All Quiet on the Western Front* is considered one of the best depictions of war and a masterpiece of German literature. The work was internationally acclaimed and read worldwide. In Germany, however, the novel was politically controversial: Not only did it enrage members of the rising Nazi party, it was also labeled as defeatist and unpatriotic by many veterans whose sensibilities were injured by the frankness Remarque depicted.

In 1931, Remarque published *The Way Back.* A chilling sequel to *All Quiet on the Western Front,* the novel presents the collapse of the German government and army after the war and the return of the veterans into a world that has been shattered forever. In the 1930s, Remarque's position in Germany became precarious because of the rise of the Nazi regime. *All Quiet on the Western Front* was banned and was among the works that were publicly burned by the Nazis in 1933. The premier of the film adaptation was violently disrupted by Nazi gangs. In 1938, after accusations of pacifism, the Nazi government stripped Remarque of citizenship. Remarque fled to the United States and settled in Switzerland after World War II.

Remarque's later works did not receive the same critical acclaim as *All Quiet on the Western Front* but achieved a wide popularity among readers. He continued to describe a European society plagued by social and political upheavals. Remarque also addressed the oppression of the Nazi rule: *Arch of Triumph* (1946) portrays a German physician who flees from the Nazi rule. Remarque also closely collaborated with filmmakers in the United States, and several of his novels were adopted into screenplays.

Today, Erich Maria Remarque's work continues to remind readers of the horrors of war. His works are widely read and have been translated into more than 20 languages. A remarkable and heroic writer,

Remarque was not afraid to express his views, despite the constant threats and harassments by the Nazi regime. Remarque died in Locarno, Switzerland.

Other Works by Erich Maria Remarque

The Black Obelisk. Translated by David Lindley. New York: Fawcett Books, 1998.
Three Comrades. Translated by A. W. Wheen. New York: Fawcett Books, 1998.

A Work about Erich Maria Remarque

Barker, Christine. *Erich Maria Remarque.* New York: Barnes and Noble, 1980.

Reyes, Neftali Ricardo

See NERUDA, PABLO.

Rhys, Jean (Ella Gwendolyn Rees Williams) (1890–1979) *novelist, short-story writer*

Jean Rhys was born in Roseau, Dominica, West Indies, to William Rees Williams, a Welsh doctor, and Minna Williams (née Lockhart). She attended a Dominican convent school until immigrating to England at age 16, where she attended Cambridge's Perse School and London's Academy of Dramatic Art before joining a touring theater company. Three-and-a-half black notebooks, filled after a romantic break in 1913, were the basis for the novel *Voyage in the Dark* (1934).

During the 1920s, Rhys was loosely a part of the "Left Bank" writers, including such writers as James Joyce, Hemingway, and Ford Madox Ford, who represented the artistic and intellectual realm of politics. Ford helped Rhys publish her first work, *The Left Bank and Other Stories* (1927). Four more novels followed in the 1930s. Themes of denial, dissonance, rejection, discrimination, and alienation run through these and others of Rhys's works, which employ a controlled style, literal and figurative imagery, and first- and third-person points of view. Inquiries made by actress Selma Vaz Dias in 1949 to perform a dramatic adaptation of the modernist *Good Morning, Midnight* (1939) and in 1956 to broadcast the same novel as a radio play encouraged Rhys to complete her fifth novel, *Wide Sargasso Sea* (1966), the story of which is derived from Charlotte Brontë's *Jane Eyre* and tells the haunting tale of Rochester's first wife. In *The Letters of Jean Rhys* (1984), Rhys called the novel "a demon of a book" that "never leaves" her; the critics called the book a masterpiece.

During the years, British, American, and Caribbean critics have attempted to position Rhys's works as distinctively British, American, or Caribbean, respectively. In *Fifty Caribbean Writers* (1986), Jean D'Costa summarizes Rhys's importance to world literature when she says that "Rhys's works offer much to the analysts of society, of sexuality, of the psyche, of British imperial history, of Anglo-European letters, and of the Creole societies."

Other Works by Jean Rhys

After Leaving Mr. Mackenzie. New York: Harper & Row, 1982.

The Collected Short Stories. Introduction by Diana Athill. New York: Norton, 1987.

Smile, Please: An Unfinished Autobiography. Berkeley, Calif.: Donald S. Ellis/Creative Arts, 1983.

Works about Jean Rhys

Lykiard, Alexis. *Jean Rhys Revisited.* Exeter and Devon: Stride Publications, 2000.

Mellown, Elgin W. *Jean Rhys: A Descriptive and Annotated Bibliography of Works and Criticism.* New York: Garland Press, 1984.

Savory, Elaine. *Jean Rhys.* New York: Cambridge University Press, 1999.

Richardson, Elaine Potter

See KINCAID, JAMAICA.

Rilke, Rainer Maria (1875–1926) *poet, playwright, translator*

Rainer Maria Rilke was born in Prague, Czechoslovakia, to Josef Rilke, a minor railroad official, and Sophie Entz, a descendant of an aristocratic family. His mother dressed him in girls' clothes and called him Sophie until the age of eight to compensate for the loss of her infant daughter. Sophie Entz was a devout Catholic and often went on pilgrimages to shrines and other holy places; young Rilke accompanied her. This early experience with Catholicism left Rilke with a profound distrust and dislike of Christianity.

Rilke's parents separated when he was nine, and he was sent to a military academy by his father. Because of ill health, Rilke left the academy and traveled to Leinz, Austria, to study business. He was apprenticed to his uncle's law firm as a clerk. Rilke decided against a career in business and attended universities in Prague, Berlin, and Munich, where he studied art history, philosophy, and literature. He developed a talent for languages and became fluent in Russian, French, English, Danish, and Czech. Rilke developed a close relationship with several Russian intellectuals and accompanied them on a trip to Russia in 1899, where he met Leo TOLSTOY and studied Russian spiritual mysticism.

Critical Analysis

Today, Rilke is considered one of the greatest lyrical poets of the German-speaking world. He began his career as a poet in 1894 when he published a small, conventional volume of poems, *Leben und Leider*. While working as a correspondence secretary for Auguste Rodin in Paris, Rilke composed *The Book of the Hours: The Book of Monastic Life*. Saint Francis of Assisi is a major figure in the work. Rilke transforms this conventional image of Christian humility and piety into a kind of pagan nature spirit who permeates all things. Furthermore, Rilke praises traditional Christian values, such as poverty and spiritual purity, and often presents God as a humble, homeless man: "For blessed are those who never went away / And stood still in the rain without a roof."

Among Rilke's prose works, *The Tale of the Love and Death of Coronet Christoph Rilke* (1906), a long prose poem, became a great popular success. Set during the 1660s, the dynamic prose of the work tells of a young coronet who joins the European forces in their fight against the Ottoman Empire. The young coronet falls in love with a young lady, but he is killed during a sudden attack by the Turks the next day. Rilke, however, does not utterly glorify the military. The poem includes brutal scenes of violence and conveys the monotony of long military marches.

Rilke was a master of several genres. His famous novel *The Notebooks of Malte Laurids Brigge* (1910) takes the form of the diary of a Danish poet who arrives in Paris and describes his reactions to the cultural and intellectual life in the city. The novel uses flashbacks to describe the events of Laurids's childhood and the various European cities that he had visited. Lacking a traditional plot, the novel focuses on episodes in Laurids's life that create confrontation in his development as a writer. Eventually, Malte Laurids realizes that he has to transform himself metaphorically into an open vessel, receiving the outside events without preconceptions, to become a truly great poet.

Rilke's last seminal collections of poetry, *Duino Elegies* and *Sonnets to Orpheus*, were both published in 1923. Both works no longer dealt with ordinary images; instead, they concentrated on the larger themes of life and death, spirituality, philosophy, and materiality. Rilke presented material and spiritual worlds as entities and the individual as an observer entrapped between the both realms, only momentarily able to capture them. The alienated artist, however, can build a bridge between two worlds by creating a material translation of the spiritual realm. Indeed, the theme of alienation is one of the most dominant ones in the collection: "We are not at one / Are not in agreement like birds of passage / Overtaken and delayed, we force ourselves suddenly on the winds / and fall onto an indifferent pond."

Rainer Maria Rilke established himself as one of the most important figures of German literature. Although he is mainly remembered as a poet, he made a tremendous impact in virtually every genre. Rilke's influence on his generation of poets is simply enormous: he composed a significant corpus of poetic works in Russian and French, and he translated innumerable literary works from English, French, Russian, and Danish into German. Today, Rainer Maria Rilke is considered as the most important 20th-century poet of the German-speaking world: "Rilke was a large man, expansive in his concern for the fate of human beings in a difficult world," as Patricia Brodsky notes. Rilke's death was as strange as his life; he died from an infection that was contracted from a prick of a rose's thorn.

Other Works by Rainer Maria Rilke

Ahead of All Parting: Selected Poetry and Prose of Rainer Maria Rilke. Translated by Stephen Mitchell. New York: Modern Library, 1995.

The Book of Images. Translated by Edward Snow. Portland, Oreg.: North Point Press, 1994.

Rilke's Book of Hours: Love Poems to God. Translated by Joanna Macy. New York: Riverhead Books, 1997.

Works about Rainer Maria Rilke

Brodsky, Patricia. *Rainer Maria Rilke.* Boston: Twayne, 1988.

Freedman, Ralph. *Life of a Poet: Rainer Maria Rilke.* Chicago: Northwestern University Press, 1998.

Rimbaud, Arthur (1854–1891) *poet*

Arthur Rimbaud was born on October 20 in Charleville, a town in provincial France. He was the son of an army captain who deserted his family when Rimbaud was only six years old, forcing the family into poverty. This abandonment became a central theme in Rimbaud's poetry and was represented by the figure of a mythical father who was a man of action and an adventurer. Rimbaud's mother was afraid that her son would become hardened by his experience, especially when he became intrigued by the social conditions in which he was forced to live and began to sneak out to play with his peers. She eventually secured the means to move her family to the best part of town but still forbade Rimbaud to associate with boys his own age. She appears in his works as a controlling and domineering figure.

Deprived of the company of his peers, Rimbaud devoted himself to his studies until July 1870 when, with the outbreak of the Franco-Prussian War and the departure of his favorite teacher who left to serve with the army, he became despondent and fled his home to begin a life of rebellion.

Rimbaud spent a year of his life as a vagabond, denouncing women and the church, living on the streets in the most squalid conditions he could find. He studied the so-called immoral poets, such as BAUDELAIRE, and read everything from philosophy to the occult. He also began writing poetry, some of which he sent to Paul VERLAINE who, in 1871, invited the aspiring poet to visit him at his home in Paris.

Although the rest of the Parisian literary world rejected him, Rimbaud and Verlaine became lovers. In 1872, Verlaine left his wife and moved with Rimbaud to London. Their relationship was a difficult one, but it continued off and on for more than two years, giving Rimbaud a sense of spiritual and emotional disillusionment. After a drunken argument between the couple in Brussels, Verlaine shot Rimbaud in the wrist. Rimbaud, who had grown tired of the relationship, notified the police. Verlaine spent 18 months in prison. Rimbaud's guilt and disillusionment prompted him to write *A Season in Hell* (1873; translated 1932).

Rimbaud's affair with Verlaine eventually ended, and Rimbaud abandoned writing completely when he was not yet 20 years old. Returning to his earlier rebellious nature, he became a trader and gunrunner in Africa. He died 18 years later, on November 10, in Marseille, France, following the amputation of his right leg.

Rimbaud's literary legacy, however, lives on. He is known as the precocious boy-poet of SYMBOLISM and is credited with being one of the creators of free verse because of the rhythmic experimentation in his poem *Illuminations* (1886; translated 1932). Rimbaud's poetry is remarkable in its subtle suggestiveness. His work draws largely on subconscious sources, delving deeply into the human psyche. He helped to popularize synesthesia, a device commonly employed by symbolist poets in which one sensory experience is described in relation to another. In his "Sonnet of the Vowels" (1871; translated 1966), for example, each vowel is assigned a particular color and other sensory associations.

In addition, Rimbaud's influence can be seen in diverse works of modern literature, particularly that of the Beat poets. He has also been cited as the source of inspiration for modern musicians, such as Bob Dylan, Jim Morrison, and Patti Smith.

Another Work by Arthur Rimbaud
Rimbaud: Complete Works, Selected Letters. Translated by Wallace Fowlie. Chicago: University of Chicago Press, 1987.

Works about Arthur Rimbaud
Cohn, Robert Greer. *The Poetry of Arthur Rimbaud.* Columbia: University of South Carolina Press, 1999.
Robb, Graham. *Arthur Rimbaud.* New York: Norton, 2000.

Rinser, Luise (1911–) *novelist, short-story writer*
Luise Rinser was born in Pitzling, Bavaria. Her parents Josef and Luise Sailer Rinser were strict Catholics. After she finished grammar school in 1930, Rinser studied psychology and pedagogy at the University of Munich. She earned her teaching diploma in 1934 and spent four years teaching elementary school. After her first husband, conductor Horst-Günther Schnell, died fighting in World War II, Rinser married composer Carl Orff in 1954.

Rinser began to write in the 1930s and published her first story, "Die Lilie" ("The Lily") in 1938. Her first published volume *Die gläsernen Runge* (*Rings of Glass*, 1941) gained popular approval but was banned by the Nazis for promoting values different from those approved by the government. In 1944, Rinser was sent to a concentration camp for opposing the war effort. She described her prison experiences in *Gefängnis-Tagebuch* (*Prison Diary*, 1946). After World War II, Rinser wrote short stories and worked as a literary critic and columnist. Her novel *Mitte des Lebens* (*Nina*, 1956) became a major international success and was translated into 22 languages. In the 1970s and 1980s, she published six diary volumes and a best-selling autobiography. A political activist, she ran for president of West Germany in 1984 as the Green Party candidate.

Rinser's influences include the baroque Catholic tradition, Eastern philosophy, Carl Gustav Jung, and Ernest Hemingway. A major theme in her works is the plight of the disadvantaged and oppressed. Her specific topics include the fight for female equality in a patriarchal society and power politics in the Catholic Church. Critic Albert Scholz writes in "Luise Rinser's Gefängnistage-buch" that Rinser "is strongest and most effective in her positive attitude toward the fundamental questions of the present day, in her striving for truth, and in her portrayal of authentic human beings working and suffering."

Another Work by Luise Rinser

Abelard's Love. Translated by Jean M. Snook. Lincoln: University of Nebraska Press, 1998.

A Work about Luise Rinser

Falkenstein, Henning. *Luise Rinser.* Berlin: Colloquium Verlag, 1988.

Robbe-Grillet, Alain (1922–) *novelist*

Alain Robbe-Grillet was born in Brest, France, to a family of scientists and engineers. Before becoming a writer, he worked in a German tank factory during World War II and earned a degree from the National Institute for Agronomy. He worked as an agronomist, supervising several banana plantations in the West Indies, until 1955, when he took a job at Les Editions de Minuit, a well-known publishing house, as a literary consultant.

Robbe-Grillet had actually begun to write much earlier in his life, completing his first novel, *A Regicide,* in 1949, although it was not published until 1978. An illness in 1951 prompted his writing of *The Erasers* (1951), the work that established him as a novelist and gained him recognition and a leading position in the NEW NOVEL group. Robbe-Grillet followed this work with *The Voyeur* (1955) and *In the Labyrinth* (1959).

In response to the growing debate as to what constitutes the new novel, he wrote *For a New Novel* (1963). According to Robbe-Grillet, the perspective of the new novel is highly subjective and expresses the angle of vision of individual characters, not of the novelist or reader. He also condemned the use of metaphors, for which he received much criticism from his contemporaries Jean Paul SARTRE and Albert CAMUS who felt that his ideas were out of touch with reality.

Critical Analysis

Robbe-Grillet's works often lack the traditional or conventional elements of literature: a solid dramatic plot, character development, and coherent chronology. Instead, his works are often composed of recurring images and events from daily life.

Although Robbe-Grillet has worked in several literary genres, he is first and foremost a writer of mysteries, albeit nontraditional ones. His novel, *The Erasers,* which earned him the Feneon Prize for Literature in 1954, mixed a traditional mystery story with shifting perspectives and vividly detailed descriptions of common, natural objects, such as a tomato slice. In his most famous work to date, *Jealousy* (1957), which is considered to exemplify the new novel, the main character spies on his possibly adulterous wife. The plot is secondary, if not nonexistent, and Robbe-Grillet devotes the bulk of the work to studying the importance of the narrator to the creation of the text.

In addition, many of Robbe-Grillet's so-called mysteries, including *The Voyeur,* leave the reader without any concrete resolution. In this case, the novel (which was awarded the Critic's Prize in

1955, in spite of the fact that many members of the jury did not feel the work could be classified as a novel) is about a traveling watch salesman named Mathias who is never explicitly identified as the murderer.

Using the same fractured structure that he employed in his novels, Robbe-Grillet wrote and directed several works for the screen, including *Trans-Europ-Express* (1966), which incorporates ideas from Alfred Hitchcock films and the popular gangster genre, and *Topology of a Phantom City* (1976), which uses freeze-frame cinematography to focus on specific elements. The tale of a police investigation into the murder of a French prostitute, this film is often told from the first person perspective of David, the narrator, who is also the perpetrator of the crime.

Another of Robbe-Grillet's trademark devices was the use of bizarre descriptions of sexual violence. Many of these were based on images taken from the visual arts. *La Belle Captive* (1975) was inspired by the paintings of René Magritte, for example. In *Snapshots* (1976), he includes a story in honor of a work of painter Gustave Moreau, "The Secret Room," in which he vividly describes a chained and abused woman.

In his later novels, Robbe-Grillet turned his attention to the spy genre. *Djinn* (1981) recounts the fractured tale of a man who works for an American spy. In the process, he is forced to question his own existence when he is told that he is not real at all but merely the product of a dream.

In 1984, Robbe-Grillet published the first part of an autobiographical trilogy, *Ghosts in the Mirror*. In this work, he acknowledges Claude SIMON's idea that everything is autobiographical to some extent, indicating that much of his work is drawn, at least in part, from elements of his own life and memory.

Robbe-Grillet continues to write regularly. His most recent work, following his same themes, is *La Reprise* (2001), about a spy's sado-erotic experiences in postwar Berlin.

Another Work by Alain Robbe-Grillet

Project for a Revolution in New York: A Novel. Translated by Richard Howard. New York: Grove Press, 1972.

A Work about Alain Robbe-Grillet

Smith, Roch C. *Understanding Alain Robbe-Grillet.* Columbia: University of South Carolina Press, 2000.

Roberts, Charles (1860–1943) *poet, short-story writer*

Charles G. D. Roberts was born in Douglas, New Brunswick; the eastern Canadian landscape would have a profound impact on his work. He graduated from the University of New Brunswick and published his first book of poetry, *Orion and Other Poems,* in 1880. From 1879 to 1895, Roberts worked as a teacher in New Brunswick, as editor of the literary magazine *The Week,* and as a professor at King's College of Windsor, in Nova Scotia.

Regarded by many as the father of Canadian poetry, although he also wrote prose, Roberts, along with three contemporary writers, styled themselves the "Poets of the Confederation" and strove for a distinctly Canadian voice. During this period, he wrote one of his most celebrated collections, *In Divers Tones* (1887). Although in this and other works Roberts attempted to establish a Canadian national literature, he was profoundly influenced by British Victorian poets. The title of *In Divers Tones,* for example, is taken from Alfred, Lord Tennyson's long poem *In Memoriam.*

In 1897, Roberts moved to New York. He began, in part for financial reasons, to write prose; in particular, he pioneered the genre of the modern animal story. These stories are collected in the volumes *Earth's Enigmas* (1896) and *Eyes of the Wilderness* (1933). Roberts returned to Canada in 1925, settling in Toronto, and returned to writing poetry as well. Roberts was knighted in 1935.

Another Work by Charles Roberts

Keith, W. J., ed. *Selected Poetry and Critical Prose.* Toronto: University of Toronto Press, 1974.

romanticism

The term *romanticism* is applied to literary, intellectual, and artistic movements of the late 18th to mid-19th centuries that share a number of common characteristics, including strong emotion, imagination, freedom from classical correctness in art forms, and rebellion against social conventions. Many romantics advocated a return to nature and a belief that humanity, specifically the individual, was innately good or worthy, rather than inherently sinful, as the church had held for centuries. Romanticism was also, in part, a revolt against the age of reason and the ideals of rationalism.

Psychologically, romanticism was marked by a focus on emotions over intellect (the sense that the artist is an individual and thus the supreme creator of his or her own work) and on a deep feeling of national pride. Whereas the thinkers and writers of the Enlightenment paid homage to the classical writers by emphasizing reason, logic, order, and restraint, the romantics valued emotional experience. Romantic works emphasize subjective experience, individuality, and imagination. Romantics value emotional experience, individual style, and spontaneity in the individual expression of experience.

Imagination and emotions are linked to nature rather than to reason and logic. The romantics believed that human nature was generally good but was corrupted by society. Considering this philosophical viewpoint, it is not surprising that many romantics depicted and praised various aspects of nature because the natural environment outside the confines of civilization was supposedly a force that encouraged the possibility of authenticity and goodness. Nature, often seen as the antithesis of materialism and the social conflicts produced by civilization, became a prominent theme in the works of romantics. The romantics also revered childhood, which they saw as a natural state before the intervention of the corrupting forces of modern society.

Romantic writers, opposing the established order, also insisted on political and moral changes. Many took inspiration from the French Revolution of 1789, before the horrors of the Reign of Terror. Critics have sometimes attributed the romantic opposition to REALISM to the political affiliations of the movement. Many romantics became politically disenchanted after a series of failed European revolutions of the early 19th century. However, broadly speaking, the term *romanticism* applies to the arts, philosophy, and politics.

Romanticism in Germany

Romanticism originated in Germany and England during the 18th century as an opposition to the Enlightenment and neoclassicism. Eighteenth-century German philosopher Fredrich von SCHILLER was the first to apply the term to the literary movement.

In Germany, romanticism played an especially significant role in the development of national literature. Johann Wolfgang von GOETHE and Friedrich von Schiller are perhaps the most important figures associated with German romanticism. In his poetry and prose, Goethe created powerful emotional scenes often set against the background of wild, untamed nature. Likewise, Schiller created powerful emotional scenes, combining elements of folklore and traditional genres of literature. Many romantics also began to compose works celebrating the vernacular German and German culture. E. T. A. HOFFMANN and the GRIMM brothers wrote fairy tales that not only included fantastic and irrational elements but also celebrated the traditional culture of the German people. The humble heroes of their tales exemplified the courage, morality, and ingenuity of the common people. Achim von Arnim (1781–1831) and Clemens Brentano (1778–1842) collaborated on a collection of German tales that were orally transmitted to them by various common folk throughout Germany. Romanticism began during the process of unification of the German states, and thus greatly contributed to the establishment of a unified German national identity.

In certain ways, romantic literature in Germany was linked with the romantic tradition in music: Wilhelm Müller's (1784–1827) *Die Winterreise* was transformed into a series of musical pieces by Franz Schubert (1797–1828). Ludwig Uhland (1787–1862) wrote lyrical ballads that praised nature and human passions based on the traditional tales of German peasants.

German romanticism was perhaps one of the most influential movements in the history of European literature, affecting innumerable writers in England, France, Russia, and later America. The works of German romantics are still read and appreciated throughout the world. Romantics were visionary in their concern for emotions and psychology and their humanistic emphasis on the individual, particularly the individual who occupies a humble rank on the social ladder.

Romanticism in France

Romanticism arrived later in France than it did in Germany and England. The reasons for this are largely political. During the French Revolution and the Napoleonic Wars, France was too involved in its own internal struggles to be greatly affected by the outside world. In 1815, however, with the restoration of the monarchy, the return of the French nobility from exile brought about significant changes in literature and culture, as well as in politics. Many of those nobles who returned had lived for many years of exile in England. On arriving in France, they brought with them a variety of English cultural traditions, including the poetry of English romantic poet George Gordon, Lord Byron (1788–1824). Up until this point, French literature had for the most part held to the 17th-century literary ideal of neoclassicism. In a time when large-scale sociopolitical changes were occurring with great force, the works of Racine and Corneille and the expression of perfect harmony and clarity that had their roots in the Greek and Roman traditions were soon usurped by the rebellious beauty of romanticism.

Romanticism did not arrive in France without precedents, however. The works of the 18th-century writer Jean-Jacques Rousseau anticipated the trend by focusing on the social aspects of the human condition and questioning whether the concept of the soul could be dealt with rationally. In *Les Confessions* (1770), for example, Rousseau's subject, himself, becomes the most important figure in literature, granting the "I" form of identity a sense of supremacy that was lacking in literature to that point.

François-René CHATEAUBRIAND expresses the alienation of young aristocrats after the revolution, and with his *René* and *Atala* explores the themes of melancholy and exile. Germaine de STAEL's *De L'Allemange* introduced German mysticism and romanticism into France and contested universalist ideals in the name of a national literature. In French theater, Victor HUGO is credited with having set forth a definition of the movement in the *Préface* to his play *Cromwell* (1827). Hugo championed freedom of speech and freedom of the artist and individuality in all of his works, most notably in the novels *Les Misérables* (1862) and *Notre Dame de Paris* (1831).

In general, the romantic shared a few common goals. The focus on political freedom and the exploration of individual psyche, even to the point of the bizarre and the supernatural, became of utmost importance. The peculiar and the macabre were stressed as equally valid aspects of humanity. Gothic literature and the fantastic experienced a rise in popularity in the 1830s. Poetry, in particular, turned to nature as a source of primary inspiration. The romantic poet often felt the need to suffer to understand art as it related to the human condition. Political activism and the push for social change were also important aspects of the movement.

See also COSTUMBRISMO.

Works about Romanticism

Daniels, Barry V. *Revolution in the Theatre: French Romantic Theories of Drama.* Westport, Conn.: Greenwood Press, 1983.

Lacoue-Labarthe, Phillipe, ed. *The Literary Absolute: The Theory of Literature in German Romanticism.* Albany: State University of New York Press, 1988.

Moses, Claire Goldberg. *Feminism, Socialism and French Romanticism.* Bloomington: Indiana University Press, 1993.

Schulte-Sasse, Jochen, ed. *Theory as Practice: An Anthology of Early German Romantic Writings.* Minneapolis: University of Minnesota Press, 1997.

Rosas, Oscar (1864–1925) *poet*

Oscar Rosas was born in Florianópolis, Brazil. He was a minor member of the Brazilian symbolist movement whose leading figure was João CRUZ E SOUSA. Symbolism in Brazil was a manifestation of Latin American MODERNISM, a larger movement best exemplified by Rubén DARIO.

Later in life, Oscar Rosas became increasingly politically active, eventually serving in the Brazilian house of representatives. In 1925, he was attacked in a fight over politics and eventually died from the wound he sustained.

Rosenstock, Samuel

See TZARA, TRISTAN.

Roy, Arundhati (1961–) *novelist, nonfiction writer*

Arundhati Roy was born in Bengal, India, and grew up in Kerala. In 1986, her mother, Mary Roy, became famous for her court case that demanded equal rights for women in inheritance laws. Mary Roy also ran a liberal school, called Corpus Christi, where Arundhati Roy received her primary education. Born into a religious family, Roy was brought up in a traditional Syrian Christian household. When she was 16 years old, she left home and went to Delhi to study architecture.

Her first novel, *The God of Small Things* (1997), won the 1997 Booker Prize. She is the first nonexpatriate and the first Indian woman to win this award, and she has claimed that it will be the only novel she writes. Her novel, in fact, begins with the quote stating that this story will "be told as though it's the only one." *The God of Small Things* is a MAGIC REALISM depiction of Kerala's multireligious communities. Roy's brand of magic realism steers away from mere illusion, however, because of the text's lingering question on social identity. The secret love affair between two main characters foregrounds the still-existing burden of caste and religious (especially Syrian-Christian) divisions in Kerala. Roy poses time and place as protean categories in the narrator's memory as she tries to understand her roots within a family that is separated within itself by outside social forces.

Roy has also written many screenplays, including *In Which Annie Gives It Those Ones* (1988) and *Electric Moon* (1992), for which she became known for her straightforward and highly opinionated style. Since then and after her novel, she has dedicated herself to writing newspaper and journal articles about social issues in India. As a writer, she claims, this is the best form of activism of which she is capable. In 1999, her essay "The Greater Common Good," on the dispossession of tribal peoples during construction of the Narmada Dam, caused global concern. Her journalistic writing has given several underprivileged communities of India access to international media attention and has helped these kinds of social issues gain worldwide support.

Another Work by Arundhati Roy
Power Politics. Cambridge, Mass.: South End Press, 2001.

A Work about Arundhati Roy
Jones, Sonya L. "The Large Things of Arundhati Roy." In A. L. McLeod, ed., *The Literature of the Indian Diaspora: Essays in Criticism.* New Delhi: Sterling, 2000.

Rushdie, Salman (1947–) *novelist,*
essayist

Ahmed Salman Rushdie was born to wealthy, liberal, secularized Muslim parents, Anis Ahmed Rushdie and Negin Rushdie, in Bombay, India, but has lived much of his life in England. He is an agnostic Muslim and feels torn between different cultures. Referring to his short-story collection *East, West* (1994), Rushdie told the *Daily Telegraph,* "[t]he most important part of the title is the comma. Because it seems to me that I am that comma."

Rushdie's first three novels, *Grimus* (1975), *Midnight's Children* (1980), and *Shame* (1983), won critical approval. *Midnight's Children* was a multiple award winner: the Booker Prize, an award from the English Speaking Union, the James Tait Black Prize, and a special "Booker of Bookers" award as the best novel in the first 25 years of the Booker Prize.

Rushdie gained international fame even with nonreaders with his novel *The Satanic Verses* (1988), which rewrote the story of the Islamic prophet Muhammad, depicting him as a skeptic and a man driven by sexual desire. The prophet's scribe, "Salman," is initially faithful but says that when faced with religious hypocrisy, "I began to get a bad smell in my nose."

Satanic Verses enraged Islamic fundamentalists, leading Iran's spiritual leader at the time, the Ayatollah Ruhollah Khomeini, to issue a *fatwa,* or religious decree, pronouncing a death sentence against Rushdie for offending God. "Anyone who dies in the cause of ridding the world of Rushdie," said Khomeini, "will be a martyr and will go directly to heaven." After Khomeini's pronouncement, some bookstores that were believed to be carrying Rushdie's book were bombed, and riots occurred in places where he was believed to be staying. One translator of the book was stabbed to death. Many writers vocally announced their support for Rushdie, and politicians around the world condemned the death sentence. Critic Amir Mufti says, "The violence of the novel's reception . . . is an accurate indicator of the anger generated by its insistence on a sweeping rearrangement and rethinking of the terms of Muslim public culture." Pradyumna S. Chauan says, "*The Satanic Verses* was, and still remains, a major contribution to the contemporary novel."

Despite the death threat, which eventually was lifted, Rushdie continued to write. He even made unannounced public appearances, including one onstage during a well-attended, multimedia concert by the rock group U2.

After writing a nonfiction account of travels in Nicaragua, *The Jaguar Smile* (1987), Rushdie took a sympathetic interest in the United States, setting his novel *Fury* (2001) there. It is the story of Malik Solanka, professor and dollmaker, who tries to lose himself in New York City but discovers that one's deeds take on a life of their own as he watches his dolls become extremely popular. Solanka sees parallels between God's strange relationship to the humans he created, who have free will, and his own relationship to his dolls: "Nowadays, they started out as clay figurines. Clay, of which God, who didn't exist, made man, who did."

Solanka also struggles to control his own anger, often amplified by the chaos of the city: "He was never out of earshot of a siren, an alarm, a large vehicle's reverse-gear bleeps, the beat of some unbearable music." Rushdie argued in newspaper editorials in the years prior to *Fury* that America has generated hostility from both left-wing and right-wing groups around the globe precisely because it is an embodiment of freedom and change. In America's ability constantly to reinvent itself, Rushdie sees parallels to the dangerous power of fiction making and to his own status as a cultural nomad, a theme that arises repeatedly in his collection *Imaginary Homelands: Essays and Criticism 1981–1991* (1991).

Critical Analysis

Much of Rushdie's work is classifiable as MAGIC REALISM, combining realistic issues and events with elements of magic or mythology. *Grimus,* for instance, sends its Native American protagonist, Flapping Eagle, in search of his sister and involves him with magicians, intelligent stone frogs, extraterrestrials, and a host of other fantastic devices.

In *Midnight's Children,* political satire mixes with Hindu fantasy and psychic abilities as it is revealed that 1,001 children born at the stroke of midnight on August 15, 1947, the day of Indian independence from Britain, gained such superpowers as telepathy and telekinesis. Two of those children, one wealthy and one poor, are switched at birth, leading to political complications.

The Muslim Indian narrator, Saleem Sinai, says he is "handcuffed to history," the events of his life "indissolubly chained to those of my country." Sinai's psychic powers, says critic Dubravka Juraga, enable him "to empathize with members of all segments of India's complex, multilayered society," from a starving man to a rich man who bullies serfs and even to real-life political figures such as Prime Minister Nehru. Throughout the course of the novel, Saleem struggles to retain his own identity. Scholar Michael Reder remarks, "as Saleem's story demonstrates, individuals can fall victim to a discourse—such as a national myth—in which they themselves are denied a role." Individual identity is constrained by historical circumstances.

Shame, patterned after Gabriel GARCÍA MÁRQUEZ's *One Hundred Years of Solitude,* combines Pakistani civil war with the fairy–tale-like story of a little girl so wracked by shame that her blushes can set objects on fire. An accusatory narrative voice sometimes interrupts Rushdie's main narration, demanding to know whether Rushdie is close enough to Indian and Pakistani culture to tell this tale: "We know you, with your foreign language wrapped around you like a flag: speaking about us in your forked tongue, what can you tell but lies?" Critic Timothy Brennan calls this "Rushdie's most fully realized and densely crafted novel."

In *Haroun and the Sea of Stories* (1990) Rushdie artfully blends references to *The Thousand and One Nights* with Rushdie's philosophy that reality is open to many interpretations and his love of fiction as a playground of the mind where countless ideas, even heretical ones, can be displayed. It is the story of a boy who hopes to rescue his father by returning to him the gift of storytelling: "And because the stories were held here in liquid form, they retained the ability to change, to become new versions of themselves." Rushdie and his characters savor the ability to rework old tales and old beliefs.

Rushdie's blending of different cultural influences has been a chief interest of his critics, who have seen in him both a testament to the relevance of tradition and folklore and a reminder that the entire idea of nationhood is in some sense a fiction, maintained by common beliefs and touchstone stories. Further, as critic Timothy Brennan observes, by rewriting sacred stories with the imagination and freedom of a fiction writer rather than the ferocity of a heretic or adherent of a rival religion, Rushdie "unravels the religion from within." Scholar M. Keith Booker, in his introduction to a collection of essays on Rushdie, writes that "Rushdie has undoubtedly been one of the most important writers in world literature in the past quarter century . . . [and] a major commentator on Indian and other postcolonial cultures."

Other Works by Salman Rushdie

The Ground Beneath Her Feet. New York: Henry Holt, 1999.

The Moor's Last Sigh. Thorndike, Maine: Chivers Press, 1995.

Works about Salman Rushdie

Booker, M. Keith, ed. *Critical Essays on Salman Rushdie.* New York: G. K. Hall, 1999.

Cundy, Catherine. *Salman Rushdie.* Manchester, U.K.: Manchester University Press, 1996.

Harrison, James. *Salman Rushdie.* New York: Twayne, 1992.

Russian symbolism

See SYMBOLISM.

Saadawi, Nawal El
See SADAWI, NAWAL.

Sachs, Nelly Leonie (1891–1970) *poet*
Nelly Leonie Sachs was born in Berlin to Jewish parents, William and Margarethe (Karger) Sachs. Her father was a wealthy industrialist and inventor. Sachs attended Hoch Toechterschule but received most of her education privately. She developed an early interest in dancing and literature and began writing poetry and puppet plays as a teenager.

Sachs's first volume of poetry *Legenden und Erzählungen* (*Legend and Tales,* 1921) reflected her interest in the common roots of Judaism and Christianity. She was later influenced by German and Jewish mysticism, including the writings of Jakob Böhmne, and Hasidism. In the 1930s, Sachs published her poetry in newspapers and Jewish journals. With the help of friends, she escaped from Nazi Germany to Sweden in 1940. Sachs wrote her most significant poetry about the horrors of World War II and the Nazi death camps; these poems are included in volumes such as *In den Wohnungen des Todes* (*In the Habitations of Death,* 1946) and *Sternverdunkelung* (*Eclipse of the Stars,* 1949) and earned her worldwide acclaim.

While in Sweden, Sachs also translated the works of several Swedish poets, such as Erik Lindegren and Johannes Edfelt, into German.

The primary theme of Sachs's literary work is the Holocaust. Critics have noted that her poems elevated the Jews' suffering to a cosmic plane. Scholar Elisabeth Strenger writes in her essay "Nelly Sachs and the Dance of Language," that in Sachs's poems, "Jewish mystical voices cry out over the uninitiated language of the German oppressors." Sachs includes deep religious feeling, mourning, and elements of dance in her language. Her work provides an important poetic testimony to the Holocaust. She shared the Nobel Prize for literature in 1966 with Samuel Joseph AGNON.

Another Work by Nelly Sachs
The Seeker and Other Poems. Translated by Ruth Mead, Matthew Mead, and Michael Hamburger. New York: Farrar, Straus & Giroux, 1970.

A Work about Nelly Sachs
Bahti, Timothy, and Marilyn Sibley Fries. *Jewish Writers, German Literature: The Uneasy Examples of Nelly Sachs and Walter Benjamin.* Ann Arbor: The University of Michigan Press, 1995.

Sadawi, Nawal (al-Sa'dawi, El Saadawi)
(1931–) *essayist, memoirist, novelist*

Nawal Sadawi has authored some of Arab feminism's landmark texts. Her indictment of female genital mutilation in *The Hidden Face of Eve* is perhaps the aspect of Sadawi's work best known in the West; the English translation rearranges the Arabic text to begin with the author's searing memory of her clitorectomy at age six. Well known, too, are her attacks on Islamic fundamentalism and theory of ancient Egypt as originally matriarchal. Less well known in translation, perhaps because it is less palatable to her Western readership, is the fact that Sadawi denounces the patriarchy of all three Near Eastern religions—Islam, Christianity, and Judaism. Her protest against U.S. and global capitalism's exploitation of women in the developing world is another important theme in her work, which tends to be glossed over in English-language references in favor of emphasis on her critiques of Arab sexual mores. Sadawi's travelogue, *My Travels Around the World* (1992), which contains powerful condemnation of Western imperialism, is out of print.

In her fiction, Sadawi's protagonists are victimized women, beaten by overwhelming male domination in a world devoid of female friendship and male allies. In life, Sadawi earned her M.D. (1955) at Cairo University in a climate made possible by other Egyptian feminist men and women. Her parents, of rural Egypt, supported her career choice. In *Memoirs of a Woman Doctor* (1989) and other works, Sadawi drew on her clinical experiences for writing about women's sexual oppression. Abortion, honor killings, child molestation—Sadawi's indictment of patriarchy leaves no taboo unbroken. *Women and Sex* (1971) got her fired as Egypt's director of health education, and Sadat imprisoned her in 1981 for feminist activism, releasing her after international outcry. This is the basis of her *Memoirs from the Women's Prison* (translated by Miriam Cooke, 1986).

Sadawi's husband Sherif Hetata translates her novels to English. She has a daughter and a son from two earlier marriages; the family is active in the Arab Women's Solidarity Association, founded by Sadawi. Currently living in Cairo, she has seen her work translated into a dozen languages. *Woman at Point Zero* (translated by Hetata, 1983) is the most widely read of her novels. Some critics see its story of a friendless, poverty-stricken woman driven to murder by a life in which she has suffered every possible sexual abuse from child molestation to rape and forced prostitution as a stunning portrayal of patriarchy at its worst, while others find its popularity an example of the way in which Sadawi's complex, highly political feminist analysis is susceptible to being reduced to grist for sensationalist stereotypes of Arab women as sexual victims.

Other Works by Nawal Sadawi

Daughter of Isis. Translated by Sherif Hetata. London: Zed Books, 1999.

The Nawal El Saadawi Reader: Selected Essays 1970–1996. London: Zed Books, 1997.

Works about Nawal Sadawi

Malti-Douglas, Fedwa. *Men, Women, and God(s): Nawal El Saadawi and Arab Feminist Poetics*. Berkeley: University of California Press, 1995.

Tarabishi, George. *Woman Against Her Sex: A Critique of Nawal El-Saadawi, with a Reply by Nawal El-Saadawi*. London: Al Saqi Books, 1988.

Sa'id, Ali Ahmad

See ADONIS.

Saint-Exupéry, Antoine de (1900–1944)
novelist, nonfiction writer

Best known internationally for his children's fantasy *Le Petit Prince* (1943; translated as *The Little Prince*, 1943), Antoine de Saint-Exupéry was born in Lyons and educated in Switzerland at Jesuit schools. Obsessed with aviation, he joined the French air force in 1921 but left to become a commercial pilot in 1926. His novels and other works express his humanist beliefs regarding fairness and compassion to all humankind, as well as a deep respect for the art of flying.

As a commercial pilot, Saint-Exupéry's job involved flying air-mail routes over North Africa, the South Atlantic, and South America. He based his first novel, *Southern Mail* (1929; translated 1933), on these experiences. He married a young widow from Buenos Areis in 1931, publishing his second novel, *Vol de Nuit* (*Night Flight,* translated 1932), that same year.

During World War II, Saint-Exupéry returned to the military, joining the French air force once again; however, during combat, his plane was shot down. He escaped to the United States, where he joined the Free French Forces. *Flight to Arras* (1942; translated 1942) is an account of his wartime experiences.

Grounded from combat due to his age and multiple injuries, Saint-Exupéry began to serve as a flight instructor and reconnaissance pilot. During this time, he wrote his children's fantasy, *The Little Prince* (1943), for which he has gained lasting popularity.

Saint-Exupéry was last seen alive when he departed to fly a reconnaissance mission over southern France in 1944. His plane vanished without a trace. After his death, two notebooks that reflect on his life and ideas were published as *Wisdom of the Sands* (1948; translated 1950).

Another Work by Antoine de Saint-Exupéry

The Tale of the Rose: The Passion that Inspired The Little Prince. Translated By Esther Allen. New York: Random House, 2001.

A Work about Antoine de Saint-Exupéry

Schiff, Stacy. *Saint-Exupéry: A Biography.* New York: Alfred A. Knopf, 1995.

Saint–John Perse

See PERSE, SAINT-JOHN.

Saleh, Tayyib (Al-Tayyib Salih) (1929–   )

novelist, short-story writer, broadcast journalist
Tayyibb Saleh's name points his readers toward his connection to the Islamic African world. The word

tayeb, or *tayyeb,* in Arabic denotes purity, goodness, and piety. In addition, the prophet Saleh is an important prophet in The Qur'an. Saleh's contribution to world literature is his ability to fuse Western and Islamic-African realities in interesting and accessible ways.

Saleh was born into a farming community in the northern section of Sudan, a country that has had a troubled history of conflict with its larger, wealthier, northern neighbor, Egypt. The Sudan of which he writes is a country divided by racial, national, and religious schisms. The seeds of the geopolitical problems of the region stem from its European colonial heritage but are also tied to issues of religious and cultural differences that national boundaries too rarely reflect.

Saleh was raised in a traditional Islamic home, which meant that he studied the Qur'an regularly. He had originally intended to follow his father's lead and pursue a career in agriculture, but his path led him to a career in broadcasting. Notably, Saleh led the dramatic production division of BBC's Arabic Service. This experience undoubtedly helped him to put the struggle for "true" Sudanese independence into a larger geopolitical context.

His most well-known work is the novel *Season of Migration to the North*, which was first published in 1969. The novel operates as a sort of "response" to Joseph CONRAD's *Heart of Darkness* in that it traces the journey of an Islamic African named Mustafa as he visits the "horror" of London, the heart of the imperial center of the colonial world. The novel also echoes *Othello* and other literary encounters between dominant groups and "marginal" characters, stressing the deep chasms of cultural misunderstanding that appear when one encounters those who are different. As Mustafa puts it in the novel, "May God have mercy on someone who has turned a blind eye to error and has indulged in the outward aspect of things."

Like the Egyptian writer, Naguib MAHFOUZ, with whom Saleh shares many thematic interests, Saleh is not primarily a "protest" writer but one whose narratives speak to the richness of the culture out of which he has sprung and to the need to embrace the whole experience of a people.

Another Work by Tayyib Saleh
The Wedding of Zein and Other Stories. Washington, D.C.: Three Continents Press, 1985.

A Work about Tayyib Saleh
Boullata, Issa. *Critical Perspectives on Modern Arabic Literature.* Washington, D.C.: Three Continents Press, 1980.

Samman, Ghada (1942–) *novelist, short-story writer, essayist, journalist, poet*

Born in Damascus, Syria, Samman has written more than 30 books, including six short-story collections. The latest, *The Square Moon* (1994), uses supernatural elements. Her novel *Beirut '75* (1975) was considered prophetic for seeing the tensions under the surface of seemingly prosperous Lebanon; Samman wrote it just before the outbreak of the civil war that would rack the country for 15 years (1975–90). Her 1976 novel, *Beirut Nightmares,* placed her in a group of novelists who stayed in Lebanon during the civil-war years. Composed in more than 200 "nightmares," ranging in length from 10 lines to 10 pages each, *Beirut Nightmares* is a riveting experiment in form, as well as a stunning portrait of civil war from the apartment window of one woman trapped by crossfire. Samman's latest novel, *al-Riwaya al-mustahila* (1997), has not been translated into English. In addition to short stories and novels, she has written poetry, including *Love Across the Jugular Vein* (Arabic) in 1980, which treats love relationships in an ironic, wry tone that is, at the same time, infused with warmth and honesty.

Having lost her mother as a young girl, Samman was raised by her father, a law-school dean. She earned her B.A. in English literature at the University of Damascus and her master's at the American University of Beirut. She studied in Lon-

don for a time and lived in Europe from 1967 to 1969. Because of problems with Syria's strict regulations on Syrians abroad, Samman was unable to return to Syria. She settled in Lebanon where, in 1977, she established her own publishing company.

Samman cuts a striking figure as one of the best-known feminists of the Arab world. The heroines of her novels tend to be strong women breaking out of traditionally feminine roles. Her writing shows fierce awareness of the economic exploitation of the poor, in addition to an abiding concern with gender. Samman's tone is typically ironical, urbane, witty, and sometimes cynical, conveying profound commitment to social and political issues and attention to the craft of writing. Samman's work is translated into Russian, Romanian, Italian, Persian, German, Spanish, and English.

Another Work by Ghada Samman
The Square Moon. Translated by Issa J. Boullatta. Fayetteville: University of Arkansas Press, 1998.

Works about Ghada Samman
Cooke, Miriam. *War's Other Voices.* Cambridge: Cambridge University Press, 1988.
Zeidan, Joseph. *Arab Women Novelists.* Albany: State University of New York Press, 1995.

San Juan, Epifanio (1938–) *poet, novelist*

Epifanio San Juan was born in Manila, Philippines. He received his B.A. degree from the University of the Philippines in 1958, left for the United States in 1960, and received his M.A. and Ph.D. from Harvard University in 1962 and 1965, respectively. He has taught in various universities, and is currently the professor and chair of the Department of Comparative American Cultures at Washington State.

San Juan has written poetry, fiction, and literary criticism, in both Tagalog and English. His works address important issues, such as class conflict and political struggle in Filipino history, which had remained largely uninvestigated. He seeks to define the central role of race and racism in America, using his experience as an Asian intellectual living in the United States. San Juan believes that literature constitutes an important critical tool that should be used to examine and reflect social change.

San Juan has written more than 100 scholarly articles, published in journals in Europe, Japan, the Philippines, and the United States. Although he is an accomplished poet and novelist, he is better known for his work in comparative cultural studies. His 1972 work, *Carlos Buloson and the Imagination of the Class Struggle,* on Carlos Bulosan, a famous Filipino-American writer of the 1940s and 1950s, narrates the biography of a talented Filipino writer who published several important and influential works before his death in 1956. Bulosan did not manage to return to the Philippines or to become a U.S. citizen, but his works are celebrated for their depictions of the Filipino experience.

Another work, *From Exile to Diaspora: Versions of the Filipino Experience in the United States,* (1998) examines the diasporic experience of Filipinos, who constitute one of the major immigrant groups to the United States within the past century. In this work, San Juan argues that even in their overseas location, Filipinos continue to assess and reexamine their colonial past in view of their present. Their zeal for democracy and equality remains as vital to their existence in their new adopted home as in their homeland. This book as well as *The Rise of the Filipino Working Class and Other Essays* (1978), attribute a great degree of agency to the Filipino people.

San Juan was awarded the Fulbright lectureship from 1987 to 1988. His book, *Racial Formations/ Critical Transformations* (1992), won both the National Book Award and the Human Rights Award in 1993. He is the recent recipient of the 1994 Katherine Newman Award from the Society for the Study of Multi-ethnic Literatures in the United States.

Another Work by Epifanio San Juan

From the Masses, to the Masses: Third World Literature and Revolution. Minneapolis, Minn.: MEP Publications, 1994.

Sand, George (Amandine-Aurore-Lucile Dupin) (1804–1876) *novelist*

Noted for her skill as a writer as well as for her numerous love affairs with prominent men, such as Alfred de MUSSET and Frédéric Chopin, French romantic (*see* ROMANTICISM) novelist George Sand was born in Paris and raised and educated at her grandmother's country estate, which Sand inherited in 1821. In 1822, she married Baron Casimir Dudevant. Financially and socially secure, Sand bore two children with Dudevant, but she never found happiness with him nor reconciled her intellectual and artistic goals with those of wife and mother. She left her family in 1831 to return to Paris and embarked on a career as a writer.

Sand wrote and edited for several journals, including the prominent *Le Figaro, Révue de Deux Mondes,* and *La République.* Through her employment, she became acquainted with several well-known poets, artists, and philosophers. Her early works, in particular, show the influence these associations had on her. This was particularly true throughout the 1830s when, in response to rapidly expanding industrialization, Sand and her associates sought, through their works, to cure society of the evils of new technology. She was joined in this cause by Franz Liszt, with whom she became very good friends. Several other prominent figures with whom Sand was involved during this period and whose views distinctly reveal themselves in her writings include the revolutionary Michel de Bourges and Pierre Leroux.

One relationship in particular marked the start of Sand's career as a novelist: Her affair with fellow writer Jules Sandeau led them to coauthor and publish a novel, *Rose et Blanche* (1831), under the pseudonym Jules Sand. She assumed the name *George* for her second novel, *Indiana* (1832), which recounts the tale of a young woman who is both abused by her much older husband and deceived by her treacherous lover. The work was an instant success and was soon followed by the publication of popular novels in the 1830s, such as *Lélia* (1833), which exalted free love over conventional marriage.

In the 1840s, Sand began to break away from the molds provided for her by the men in her life and started to establish her unique writing voice. She became firmly committed to the ideals of socialism and, as a result, her works often provoked controversy. Alongside economic and social themes, Sand often questioned the preconceived notions of gendered identity. Her autobiography, *Histoire de ma vie* (1855), for example, raises questions about gender and sexuality that emerged from her complicated and unconventional life.

Sand's works were extremely popular during her lifetime. She wrote novels, memoirs, essays, short stories, and even children's fairy tales that often carried a deeper, more mature meaning. She died on June 8, having paved the way for female novelists, and left behind a lasting influence on fellow writers Fyodor DOSTOYEVSKY, Gustave FLAUBERT and Marcel PROUST.

Other Works by George Sand

The Castle of Pictures and Other Stories: A Grandmother's Tales. Translated by Holly Erskine Hirko. New York: Feminist Press at the City University of New York, 1994.

Horace. Translated by Zack Rogow. San Francisco: Mercury House, 1995.

Works about George Sand

Jack, Belinda Elizabeth. *George Sand: A Woman's Life Writ Large.* London: Chatto and Windus, 1999.

Massardier-Kenney, Françoise. *Gender in the Fiction of George Sand.* Atlanta, Ga.: Rodopi, 2000.

Saramago, José (1922–) *novelist*

José Saramago was born in Azinhaga, Portugal. His parents, José de Sousa and Maria da Piedade, were landless subsistence farmers. His last name, different from his father's, was written on his birth certificate as a joke by the public official who registered his birth. José de Sousa, the father, was called Saramago as a nickname because Saramago was a kind of wild green that was eaten in Azinhaga by the very poor.

Saramago was extremely close to his grandfather who, though illiterate, was an eloquent storyteller. The two of them, old man and young boy, would go on summer nights to sleep beneath a large fig tree by their house, and the grandfather would tell stories into the night. This formative experience instilled in Saramago a love of narrative and fantasy. Years later, he would begin to write in an attempt to preserve his memories of his grandfather and grandmother and his experiences of hearing stories under the fig tree.

Having moved to Lisbon, where Saramago's father worked as a policeman, Saramago went to elementary school and excelled. However, after a few years, his parents could no longer afford a liberal education for their son. He was sent to a technical school instead, where he trained to be a mechanic. Even at technical school, Saramago sought out the poems and stories contained in the literary anthologies that were used to teach grammar. He spent his evenings in the public library, reading whatever books he came across and practicing his French.

It was at this time that Saramago discovered the work of Fernando PESSOA, who was the inspiration for Saramago's novel *The Year of the Death of Ricardo Reis* (1984). Ricardo Reis was one of Pessoa's pseudonyms, and Saramago's novel explores the meaning of Pessoa's work in the face of the fascism that plagued Portugal in the 20th century.

Saramago worked for a few years as a mechanic and then managed to get a job as a civil servant. In 1950, he lost this job because of his affiliation with the Communist Party. He managed to find some work as a journalist and in the publishing industry, but as the political situation became more and more radically conservative, it became impossible for Saramago to find work anywhere. It was this situation that prompted him in 1976 at age 54 to dedicate himself to writing novels full time.

For the next 20 years, Saramago produced a steady stream of exceptional novels that blend allegorical symbolism, politics, and a unique narrative style. Finally, in 1998, Saramago was awarded the Nobel Prize in literature, the first Portuguese citizen to receive that award.

Critical Analysis

Saramago's novels share certain affinities with the MAGIC REALISM of some novels of Latin America, whose political contexts often center on colonialism. Though Portugal was a colonial power and not a colony, its separation from the rest of Europe, due to the fascist regimes that held power after World War II, create many similarities between Saramago's Portugal and Latin America.

He explores these political themes in his novel *The Stone Raft* (1986), in which the Iberian Peninsula breaks off from Europe and starts to float south on the ocean. *The Stone Raft* is a utopian novel in which the image of Portugal floating toward Africa represents Saramago's political vision of a world in which the oppressors in Europe come together with the oppressed peoples of developing nations.

In 1991, Saramago wrote *The Gospel According to Jesus Christ.* This book presents Christ in a very humanized form, emphasizing his family relationships and his love affair with Mary Magdalene. The novel was written as a critique of the strict Catholicism of Portugal and as an exploration of metaphysical doubt. The Portuguese government reacted strongly against it for its anti-Catholic views and vetoed its presentation for the European Literary Prize. In protest, Saramago moved to the Canary Islands.

In 1995, Saramago wrote *Blindness,* which is probably his most widely read book in the English-speaking world. It recounts an epidemic of a mysterious blindness that strikes people in an unnamed country seemingly at random. In his Nobel lecture, Saramago said of the book,

Blind. The apprentice thought, "we are blind," and he sat down and wrote *Blindness* to remind those who might read it that we pervert reason when we humiliate life, that human dignity is insulted every day by the powerful of our world, that the universal lie has replaced the plural truths, and that man stopped respecting himself when he lost respect for his fellow-creatures.

Largely unknown outside of Europe before winning the Nobel Prize, Saramago is quickly becoming the most popular Portuguese writer worldwide. His perceptiveness about human nature coupled with his strong moral and political concerns allow his novels to reveal to the reader a view of reality that was previously hidden. Saramago uses magic-realist techniques in a mode that both revitalizes his readers and stirs them to moral action.

Other Works by José Saramago

All the Names. Translated from the Portuguese by Margaret Jull Costa. New York: Harcourt, 1999.

Baltasar and Blimunda. Translated from the Portuguese by Giovanni Pontiero. San Diego: Harcourt Brace Jovanovich, 1987.

Journey to Portugal. Translated from the Portuguese and with notes by Amanda Hopkinson and Nick Caistor. London: Harvill Press, 2000.

Sargeson, Frank (1903–1982) *novelist*

Frank Sargeson was born to a middle-class family in Hamilton, New Zealand, completed his training as a solicitor in Auckland in 1926, and traveled in Britain and Europe for two years. He returned to New Zealand and took on various odd jobs before settling on his family land near Takapuna, remaining there for the rest of his life and making his living as a full-time writer. Between 1936 and 1954, Sargeson published 40 stories, most of which were completed before 1945. He continued writing in the postwar period, but he was unable to produce many works. Sargeson's writings reveal him as a writer who continued to develop and improve his art as he grew older. In his 60s, he experienced a new zest for writing, which culminated in the publication of his first complete collection of stories, *Collected Stories, 1935–1963* (1964). By the time Sargeson turned 70, he had begun to write a number of autobiographies and memoirs, veering away from the macabre and dark satirical style that characterize his writings of the previous decade. His trilogy of memoirs is, in comparison, anecdotal and lighthearted. These memoirs, which traces Sargeson's life as a writer from 1930 to 1970, are titled *Once Is Enough* (1973), *More Than Enough* (1975), and *Never Enough* (1977).

Sargeson's earlier works are remarkable for their stark depiction of human characters whose limited vision and lack of imagination represent the New Zealand working-class society. His central characters, usually the narrators of the stories, are often undistinguished and ordinary with puritanical upbringing that dictates actions and choices. Readers can appreciate these stories through Sargeson's mastery in conveying the poignant but realistic social circumstances of the working-class majority. In stories such as "The Making of a New Zealander" (1940) and "That Summer" (1946), the main characters are represented by unsettled laborers and unemployed men whose limited visions do not allow them to recognize and challenge the social forces that constitute the causes of their unhappy lives.

In the 1960s, Sargeson began to experiment with a different narrative technique. Using dark humor, he examines a new set of characters now taken from the middle classes whose better social positions ironically do not give them any advantage over the less-educated working classes of Sargeson's earlier short stories and novels. For instance, in the novel *The Hangover* (1967), Sargeson describes the dark world of a young university student caught between his duty to obey his puritanical but demented mother and his desire to indulge in the sensual pleasures of the city. The narratives of Sargeson's stories, unlike his earlier works, are elaborate and verbose.

In the 1970s, Sargeson began to write another form of narrative, reminiscent of his earlier writings but dealing with subjects closer to his heart. These were mainly autobiographies and critical writings. He managed to complete two novellas before his death in 1982: *Sunset Village* (1976), a comic crime mystery, and *En Route* (1979), a story relating a journey of self-discovery, which was published together with a novella by Edith Campion, another New Zealand author, in a joint volume entitled *Tandem*. Sargeson's achievements in fiction enable New Zealand writing to be appreciated and recognized all over the world.

Other Works by Frank Sargeson

Conversation in a Train, and Other Critical Writing. New York: Oxford University Press, 1990.

I Saw in My Dream. Auckland, N.Z.: Auckland University Press, 1974.

Joy of the Worm. London: MacGibbon and Kee, 1969.

Man of England Now; With, I for One . . ., And, a Game of Hide and Seek. London: Martin, Brian and O'-Keefe, 1972.

Memoirs of a Peon. London: MacGibbon and Kee, 1965; Auckland, N.Z.: Heinemann, 1974.

Never Enough: Places and People Mainly. Wellington, N.Z.: Reed. 1978.

Sunset Village. London: Martin, Brian, and O'Keefe, 1976.

Works about Frank Sargeson

King, Michael. *Frank Sargeson: A Life.* New York: Viking, 1995.

McEldowney, Dennis. *Frank Sargeson in His Time.* Dunedin, New Zealand: McIndoe, 1976.

Sarmiento, Félix Rubén García

See DARÍO, RUBÉN.

Sarraute, Nathalie (1900–1999) *novelist, essayist*

Pioneer and leading theorist of the French *nouveau roman* or NEW NOVEL, Nathalie Sarraute was born in Ivanova, Russia, on July 18 to intellectual parents: Her father worked in the field of sciences, and her mother published novels under the pseudonym of Vichrovski. They divorced, however, when Sarraute was two years old, and she went to live with her mother in Paris where, at a young age, French became her primary language. Her mother eventually remarried and the family returned to Russia when Sarraute was eight years old. She remained in close contact with her father, spending one month each year with him. When he began to encounter difficulties in Russia over his political views, he emigrated to France. Sarraute followed two years later to live with him in Paris and did not return again to her native Russia until 1936.

Sarraute received the bulk of her education at the Sorbonne, where she studied literature and law. In 1921, she spent a year at Oxford, prior to traveling to Berlin, where she continued to study legal science. She married Raymond Sarraute, a fellow law student, in 1925 and became a member of the French bar in 1926. She remained an active member until 1941 when she quit law to pursue a career as a writer.

Sarraute began writing while she was actively practicing law. Her first work, *Tropismes* (1932), was completed in 1932. It contains 24 short sketches based on nameless characters who are trapped by their interdependence on each other. Initially, the work was not well received or understood. It was rereleased in 1957 at the height of the popularity of the new-novel style and received greater success and critical acclaim.

During the 1950s and 1960s, Sarraute, alongside fellow writers such as Alain ROBBE-GRILLET, Claude SIMON, Marguerite DURAS, and Michel Butor, worked to pioneer the new-novel format. Exemplified by such works as Sarraute's *Portrait d'un homme inconnu* (*Portrait of an Unknown Man*, 1951), which Jean-Paul SARTRE dubbed an antinovel, the new novel discarded the conventional ideas of structure. In her works, Sarraute routinely abandoned chronological order and shifted point of view freely to focus instead on the conscious and subconscious minds of her characters.

Central to Sarraute's works is the idea of interpersonal relationships. *Portrait of an Unknown Man* explores a daughter's difficult relationship with her miserly father. *Martereau* (1953) recounts the internal tensions that arise in a family structure that is made up of individuals whose personalities are vastly different. In both of these works, the constantly shifting point of view calls into question the narrator's reliability. In *Le Planétarium* (1959), Sarraute does away with the narrator entirely in what is considered to be both an ironic comedy of manners and a parable of the creative process.

In the mid-1950s, Sarraute began to work on critical essays as she continued to write fiction. In *L'Ere de soupçon* (*The Age of Suspicion,* 1956), she attempts to analyze her own creative process and the goals she had for her works. In later years, she also devoted time to writing critical analyses on the works of other authors, including Paul VALÉRY and Gustave FLAUBERT. Sarraute expanded her writing further to include work on a number of radio and stage plays and on her partial autobiography, *Childhood* (1983), which was adapted for the stage. Sarraute died at the end of a lengthy and productive career in Paris on October 19.

Other Works by Nathalie Sarraute
Collected Plays. Translated by Maria Jolas and Barbara Wright. New York: George Braziller, 1981.
Here: A Novel. Translated by Barbara Wright. New York: George Braziller, 1997.

Works about Nathalie Sarraute
Barbour, Sarah. *Nathalie Sarraute and the Feminist Reader: Identities in Process.* Lewisburg, Pa.: Bucknell University Press, 1993.
Knapp, Bettina. *Nathalie Sarraute.* Atlanta, Ga.: Rodopi, 1994.

Sartre, Jean-Paul (1905–1980) *novelist, playwright, essayist*
Best known for his ties to EXISTENTIALISM, a philosophy that emphasizes the ultimate importance of human freedom, as well as for his long-term

relationship with fellow French philosopher and writer Simone de BEAUVOIR, Jean-Paul Sartre was born in Paris on June 21. The son of a naval officer who died when Sartre was very young, he spent his early years living with his mother and his grandfather. After his mother's remarriage in 1917, he moved to La Rochelle, where he attended school. He graduated from the École Normale Supérieure in 1929. He was a student at the time of his first meeting with de Beauvoir, and their relationship, along with Sartre's studies and exposure to other existential philosophers, proved to be important influences on both his life and his works.

After graduation, Sartre secured employment as a teacher. In 1945, he left teaching to devote his time exclusively to writing. He also traveled extensively in Egypt, Greece, Italy, and Berlin, where he studied the works of German philosophers Martin Heidegger and Edmund Husserl. At this time, Heidegger's most important work, *Being and Time* (1927), had been released. Uniting Søren Kierkegaard's and Friedrich NIETZSCHE's views on existentialism with Husserl's concept of phenomenology, Sartre began developing his own existential philosophy. During the late 1930s, Sartre began to gather around him a small group of intellectuals; together, they spent hours at cafés on the Left Bank, discussing philosophy and the importance of freedom.

In 1939, Sartre was drafted to serve in World War II. Less than a year later, he was captured and imprisoned in Germany, where he remained until 1941. Here, Sartre experienced firsthand the ramifications of the loss of what he valued most, his personal freedom. On returning to Paris, he joined the French Resistance Movement and put his growing talents as a writer to good use penning articles about the Resistance for magazines such as *Les Lettres Française* and *Combat*.

Sartre was deeply affected by his experience in the war and when it was over, decided to devote himself full-time to writing and political activism. He founded *Le Temps Modernes* (1946–   ), a monthly journal dedicated to literature and politics. Although he never became a member of the Communist Party, he worked closely with Communists in hopes of finding a solution to the problems of poverty and the poor social conditions of the working class. In his writing, he spent a great deal of time and effort trying to reconcile existentialism with marxism.

Aside from his work as a writer, Sartre exemplified his own beliefs by speaking out for freedom for oppressed peoples, such as the Hungarians in the mid- to late 1950s and the Czechoslovakians in the late 1960s. He became involved in numerous humanitarian causes and, as a result, twice had bombs set off in his place of residence. In 1967, he served as leader of the war-crimes tribunal, which investigated the actions of U.S. soldiers in Indochina, and, in 1968, he supported the student anti-Vietnam War protestors. He was also arrested in 1970 for selling an underground newspaper publication.

In 1975, Sartre's eyesight began to fail, and his health declined rapidly. No longer able to write, he nevertheless remained vocal and active; toward the end of his life, he was completely blind. He died on April 15 in Paris. His legacy remains as one of the strongest and most influential voices of the existentialist movement.

Critical Analysis

Sartre's first novel, *La Nausée* (1938), was greatly influenced by Husserl's concept of phenomenology, a movement devoted to describing experiences exactly as they present themselves with no reliance on theories, assumptions or deductions. Transferring this concept to human existence, Sartre's novel explores the idea that life has no essential purpose and that the main character is haunted by feelings of horror and nausea as he attempts to come to terms with the banality of life. During this period, Sartre also published a collection of short stories and a novella, *Le Mûr* (1938; published in English as *Intimacy*), which dealt with similar themes of identity and freedom.

Sartre's nonfiction work *L'Étre et le néant* (*Being and Nothingness,* 1943) begins to formulate the foundation of his own philosophy. He relates the idea of existence to his belief that it is composed of two distinct parts. In the first part are those things that exist simply because they are. They exist "en-soi" or *in* themselves. Human beings, however, belong to the second part, existing "pour-soi" or *for* themselves. According to Sartre, the demarcation between the two parts of existence is based on the fact that humans possess consciousness, in particular an awareness of mortality; thus, human beings exist in a constant state of dread. Sartre's premise, which he examines in later works, was this: To give meaning to those things that exist "en-soi," it is necessary for humans first to detach themselves from those things.

The importance of accepting responsibility for one's own actions is, therefore, also an essential part of Sartre's philosophy. His first dramatic work, *Les Mouches* (*The Flies*, 1943), examines this theme against the backdrop of ancient Greece, using the mythological characters of Electra and Orestes. Orestes, choosing to act by killing his murderous mother, rejects the guilt that has paralyzed his city since Agamemnon's death. His second play, *Huis-clos* (*No Exit,* 1944), presents three characters in a room with no way out, learning to face the truth that "Hell is other people."

Sartre also wrote works of literary criticism that explore the responsibility of artists in relation to their art, beginning with *Qu'est-ce la Littérature?* (*What Is Literature?*, 1947). He followed this in the same year with a study of BAUDELAIRE, and in 1952 he published a biography of Jean GENET, *Saint-Genet, Comédien et Martyr* (*Saint Genet, Actor and Martyr*). Sartre admired Genet for being free of the constraints of convention and making his own personal distinctions between right and wrong. Sartre was among a group of writers (including Albert CAMUS and Jean COCTEAU) who in 1948 successfully petitioned for Genet's release from a life sentence for burglary. From 1960 to 1971, he worked on a massive critical biography of Gustave FLAUBERT, *L'Idiot de la famille* (*The Family Idiot*). The work reached five volumes but remained unfinished, as in the last years of his life Sartre's failing eyesight prevented him from writing.

In 1963, Sartre published his memoir of childhood, *Les Mots* (*The Words*), in which he explored how language and literacy changed the consciousness of the growing child. In that year, the Nobel committee chose to honor Sartre with the Nobel Prize in literature, but Sartre refused to accept the award, feeling that it represented bourgeois values he rejected. Nonetheless, his reputation continued to grow, and his funeral drew thousands of mourners.

Other Works by Jean-Paul Sartre

Colonialism and Neo-Colonialism. Translated by Steve Brewer, Azzedine Haddour, and Terry McWilliams. London: Routledge, 2001.

Notebook for an Ethics. Translated by Davis Pellauer. Chicago: University of Chicago Press, 1992.

Truth and Existence. Translated by Adrian van den Hoven. Chicago: University of Chicago Press, 1992.

Works about Jean-Paul Sartre

Gordon, Haim. *Sartre's Philosophy and the Challenge of Education.* Lewiston, N.Y.: E. Mellen Press, 2001.

Howells, Christina, ed. *The Cambridge Companion to Sartre.* New York: Cambridge University Press, 1992.

Kamber, Richard. *On Sartre.* Belmont, Calif.: Wadsworth/Thomson Learning, 2000.

McBride, William L., ed. *Sartre's Life, Times and Vision-du-Monde.* New York: Garland Press, 1997.

Satyanarayana, Visvanatha (1895–1976)
poet, novelist, dramatist

Visvanatha Satyanarayana was born in Andhra Pradesh, India. He wrote in Telugu and is the author of more than 100 works. This alone places him among the most important figures in Telugu fiction. He has also rewritten ancient Hindu epics such as the *The Ramayana,* which dates from the fourth century B.C. When his version of the epic, *Ramayana—The Celestial Tree* appeared in 1953, it was seen as controversial because of his transformation of the original, formal Sanskrit into a more conventional style. This translation, however, made it accessible to a wider audience, and in 1971, it won him the Jnanpith Award (India's highest literary award).

Satyanarayana was widely read in European literature. One of his novels, *Veyipadagalu* (*A Thousand Hoods*, 1933–34), was inspired by the novels on industrialization by British writers Thomas Hardy (1840–1928) and D. H. Lawrence (1885–1930). Satyanarayana saw in their work his own belief that great literature is not only about issues but also form. Like them, Satyanarayana believed important themes such as social reform should not overshadow the mechanics of the literary genre and that the social message should not subsume the aesthetic element of the literary work.

Satyanarayana's literary legacy includes poetry, short stories, essays, plays, and novels. In 1970, he was made a Fellow of the Sahitya Akademi, which is reserved for the "immortals of Indian Literature."

A Work about Visvanatha Satyanarayana

S. P. Sen, ed. *History in Modern Indian Literature.* Calcutta, India: Institute of Historical Studies Press, 1975.

scapigliatura

A mid-19th-century Italian bohemian movement in art and literature, often associated with the French DECADENCE movement, *scapigliatura* takes its name from the title of a novel by one of the group's founding members, Cletto Arrighi, *The Scapigliatura and February 6th* (1862). In the book, the term refers to the restlessness and independent spirit of its characters, all ranging in age from 25 to 30 years old. Founded in Milan, the movement was greatly influenced by the works of BAUDELAIRE, and Edgar Allan Poe, as well as those of the French symbolist poets and German romantic writers (*see* SYMBOLISM and ROMANTICISM).

The main characteristics of the movement include an intense aversion to the sentimentalism and conformity of romanticism. In particular, artists of the *scapigliatura* movement held a common conviction that truth was the only valid form of poetry and art; anything less than brutal honesty was seen as substandard and unimportant. The works that came from this school featured bizarre and often pathological elements, as well as direct, realistic narration and vivid, often grotesque description, a theme held in common with French decadent writers. A second aim of *scapigliatura*, similar to many avant-garde and bohemian movements, was the rejection of bourgeois values and of the right to ownership of property.

The group was never large, consisting only of a select few artists, poets, and musicians. Its primary leader was Iginio Ugo Tachetti, who began his education in classical studies and was well acquainted with English literature. After a brief stint in the army, he began writing short stories and spending his free time in Milan, where he met with other members of the group, including the novelists and chief spokespeople for the movement, Giuseppe Rovani and Emilio Praga. Tachetti's works exemplified much of what the group sought to attain. He died young, at age 30, refusing to the end to accept hypocrisy, tradition, or conventions.

In the end, the group's most lasting influence on world literature came in its advancement of the avant-garde. The writers associated with the movement were largely considered isolated avant-garde writers who chose to live their lives and dedicate their art to revolt against middle-class conformity.

A Work about *Scapigliatura*

Del Principe, David. *Rebellion, Death, and Aesthetics in Italy: the Demons of Scapigliatura.* Madison, Wisc.: Fairleigh Dickinson University Press, 1996.

Schiller, Friedrich von (1759–1805) *playwright, essayist, poet*

Friedrich von Schiller was born in Marbach, Württenberg (present-day Germany), to Johannes Kaspar Schiller, an army officer and surgeon, and Elizabeth Schiller. Johannes Schiller was a pious

Lutheran and a harsh disciplinarian. He disapproved of his son's interests in literature and theater and many times forbade him to write poetry. At age 14, Schiller entered an academy to study law but subsequently decided to study medicine instead. His medical education was short-lived, however: He was expelled in 1780 for writing a controversial essay, *On Relation Between Man's Animal and Spiritual Nature,* which openly questioned the official theological dogma of the church.

On his return to Marbach, Schiller was forced to join his father's regiment of the army. Despite his father's strong efforts to suppress this "foolish" activity, Schiller continued to write. Schiller did not find the life of the soldier appealing and consciously avoided his duties as much as possible. Thoroughly resisting his father, Schiller continued to write and was almost arrested for neglecting his military duties.

Schiller's first play, *The Robbers* (1781), depicts a noble outlaw, Karl Moor, who violently and passionately rejects the conservative and reactionary notions of his father in his quest for justice. The play simultaneously reflected Schiller's own conflict with his father and the ideological struggle between the conservative and liberal political forces in Germany. The play was warmly greeted not only in Germany, especially among the university students, but also among the romantic writers in England. The play remains a groundbreaking work in the corpus of German romanticism. The major theme of liberty that appears in *The Robbers* permeates virtually all of Schiller's major works. The play *Don Carlos* (1787) similarly depicts a conflict between a father and son. *Don Carlos* is set during the reign of Philip II of Spain. It portrays the inner struggle of his eldest son, torn between passionate love and the vile political intrigues of his father's ministers in the court.

Between 1783 and 1784, Schiller worked as a playwright and stage manager for the theater in Mannheim. With the assistance of Johann Wolfgang GOETHE, Schiller was appointed professor of history at the University of Jena in 1789. For the next three years, Schiller worked almost exclusively on history, writing an account of the Thirty Years War. Schiller had to give up the professorship because of declining health. He worked as an assistant to Goethe, then the director of the theater at the Weimar Court.

Schiller also distinguished himself as a poet. "Ode to Joy" (1785), later set to music by Ludwig van Beethoven, is currently the anthem of the European Union. In *Wilhelm Tell* (1804), Schiller describes the close relationship with nature shared by the Swiss hero. The characteristics of Schiller's works—in their attention to nature, human emotions, and the ideals of liberty and political freedom—became the working definition of ROMANTICISM.

Schiller's interest in history resulted in several historical plays. *Mary Stuart* (1800) describes the turbulent relationship between Elizabeth I and Mary Queen of Scots in the final days before Mary's execution. The captive, wild environment of the castle of Fothernghay provides a dark, melancholy background that amplifies Mary as a tragic, romantic figure in the play. The dramatic trilogy *Wallenstein* (1796–1799) depicted Germany during the Thirty Years' War. Schiller captured the deep fragmentation of society along the lines of religion. The German national identity and the idea of nationhood is juxtaposed against the ruinous conflict created by the religious strife and political scheming of the rulers.

Schiller also wrote essays on topics ranging from religion and politics to art and humanity's relationship with nature. Many of Schiller's ideas were influenced by the works of the famous 18th-century German philosopher Immanuel Kant. In *On the Aesthetic Education of Man* (1795) Schiller deals with the bloody aftermath of the French Revolution and how it changed an understanding of notions of freedom. The key to freedom, the essay argues, is the fundamental aesthetic development of the individual and society. According to the essay, the experience of the sublime and the beautiful—two important philosophical categories in the works of Kant—is truly fundamental to one's education. A true sense of freedom and liberty is tightly connected to this experience.

In *On the Naïve and Sentimental in Literature* (1795), Schiller creates a series of dialectical dichotomies, such as feeling and thought, nature and culture, finitude and infinity, and finally sentimental and naïve modes of writing. Although describing himself as a sentimental or "reflective" writer, Schiller paid homage to his close friend Goethe, whom he described as the ultimate archetype of the naïve genius. Here, *naïve* is not used in the conventional sense of the word, but rather as a philosophical term that describes something that is utterly pure and good and closely connected with nature.

Critical Analysis

Friedrich von Schiller is considered today to be one of the foremost German writers. His drama and poetry are significant contributions to the literature of the romantic movement, although his reputation and legacy is recognized significantly more in Europe than it is in the United States. His magnificent control and elegant use of the German language inspired generations of readers, writers, and poets, and his works have had a long-lasting impact on the formation of the German national literature, as well as the German national identity.

Other Works by Friedrich von Schiller

Essays. New York: Continuum, 1993.
Schiller's Five Plays: The Robbers, Passion and Politics, Don Carlos, Mary Stuart, and Joan of Arc. Translated by Robert McDonald. New York: Consortium Books, 1998.

Works about Friedrich von Schiller

Carlyle, Thomas. *The Life of Friedrich Schiller: Comprehending and Examination of His Works.* Portland, Ore.: University Press of the Pacific, 2001.
Sharpe, Lesley. *Friedrich Schiller: Drama, Thought, and Politics.* Cambridge: Cambridge University Press, 1991.

Scherzer, Rosalie

See AUSLANDER, ROSE.

Schmitz, Ettore

See SVEVO, ITALO.

Schwarz-Bart, Simone (Simone Bruman) (1938–) *novelist*

Simone Schwarz-Bart was born Simone Bruman in Charente-Maritime, France, to a governess and a military man, according to a 1973 *Elle* interview; however, the novelist has since named the Guadeloupean capital Pointe-à-Pitre as her birthplace. Bruman was educated at Pointe-à-Pitre, Dakar, and Paris, where she met and married her husband, novelist André Schwarz-Bart, in the early 1960s.

Simone and André Schwarz-Bart coauthored *Un Plat de porc aux bananes vertes (A Dish of Pork with Green Bananas,* 1967), which employs nonlinear narratives, and *La mulâtresse Solitude (A Woman Named Solitude,* 1972), a fictional biography of a mulatto female struggling to exist in society. In 1972, Simone Schwarz-Bart also published *Pluie et vent sur Télumée Miracle (The Bridge of Beyond,* 1972), in which Télumée, the novel's female heroine, explores and consequently revises the painful history of her people.

One year after her return to Guadeloupe in 1978, Schwarz-Bart published *Ti Jean L'Horizon (Between Two Worlds,* 1979). In this novel, she uses MAGIC REALISM (elements of dreams, magic, fantasy, or fairy tales) and science fiction to tell the adventures of Ti Jean, a Guadeloupean folk hero, and to deconstruct traditional myths of Antillean identity.

All of Schwarz-Bart's novels have been internationally well received in multiple publications, including *The New York Times Book Review, Savacou,* and *Nouvelle Revue Française.* Her fictional retelling of personal Caribbean histories contributes to international contemporary expressions and examinations of the painful repercussions of patriarchal domination and exile.

Another Work by Simone Schwarz-Bart

Your Handsome Captain. Translated by Jessica Harris. In *Plays by Women: An International Anthology.* Edited by Francoise Kourilsky and Catherine Temerson. New York: Ubu Repertory Theatre Publications, 1989.

Works about Simone Schwarz-Bart

Karamcheti, Indira. "The Geographics of Marginality: Place and Textuality in Simone Schwarz-Bart and Anita Desai." In *Feminist Explorations of Literary Space.* Edited by Margaret R. Higonnet and Joan Templeton. Amherst: University of Massachusetts Press, 1994: 125–46.

McKinney, Kitzie. "Memory, Voice, and Metaphor in the Works of Simone Schwarz-Bart." In *Postcolonial Subjects: Francophone Women Writers.* Edited by Mary Jean Green et al. Minneapolis: University of Minnesota Press, 1996: 22–41.

Seferiadis, Giorgos

See SEFERIS, GEORGE.

Seferis, George (Giorgos Seferiadis)
(1900–1971) *poet*

George Seferis was born Giorgos Seferiadis in Smyrna, Turkey. As a child, he attended school in Smyrna and at the Gymnasium in Athens and, in 1918, moved with his family to Paris, where he attended the University of Paris to study law and where he also developed an interest in literature.

After graduating, Seferis returned to Athens in 1925. One year later, he was admitted to the Royal Greek Ministry of Foreign Affairs. In addition to his success as a writer, he had a long and successful diplomatic career. His final diplomatic post was as Royal Greek Ambassador to Great Britain from 1957 to 1962. Throughout his career, Seferis received numerous awards and recognitions. Included among these were honorary doctoral degrees from Cambridge University in 1960, Oxford University in 1964, the University of Salonika in 1964, and Princeton University in 1965.

His background in law and diplomacy, combined with his love of literature, allowed Seferis to make a profound impact on Greek poetry. His travels throughout the world gave him numerous ideas and provided the rich backgrounds for many of his works. What he experienced through war and through political negotiation influenced his decision to write poetry, almost exclusively with the themes of alienation, wandering, and death. Seferis's poetry is often surrealistic and always highly symbolic, sometimes to the point of being cryptic and difficult to interpret. He often invokes classical Greek themes as a means of exploring 20th-century Greek lifestyles and social consciousness.

Seferis's earliest poetry collections exist in two volumes. *Strophe* (*Turning Point,* 1931) consists of rhymed lyrical poems that were strongly influenced by the symbolist movement (*see* SYMBOLISM). His second collection, *E Sterma* (*The Cistern,* 1932), portrays through vivid imagery the idea that humankind must keep its true nature hidden from the everyday world that seeks to alienate and ignore humanity.

In his later poetry, Seferis shifts his focus to include a pervasive sense of awareness of the past, in particular Greek history. This awareness is not merely that of a historian but rather is indicative of the poet's desire to relate past events to those of the present and, ultimately, the future. This theme first becomes apparent in *Mythistorema* (1935; translated 1960), a collection consisting of 24 short poems that, when read as a group, translate the Odyssean myths into modern situations and circumstances. Seferis continued to develop these themes, using Homer's Odyssey as his symbolic basis, in several subsequent collections: *Book of Exercises* (1940), *Logbook I* (1940), *Logbook II* (1944), *Thrush* (1947), and *Logbook III* (1955). One notable exception to his use of Odysseus as a solitary source, however, occurs in "The King of Asine," one of the poems in *Logbook.* This poem is considered by many critics to be Seferis's greatest achievement because of its historical importance. This historical source consists of a single reference in Homer's *Iliad* to the King of Asine, who remains otherwise an all-but-forgotten character in Greek history.

Seferis did not limit himself to poetry and diplomatic relations, however. In addition to his collected poetic works, he published one book of essays, *Dokimes* (1944; translated *Essays on the Greek Style,* 1962). He also translated several works by T. S. Eliot and produced *Copies* (1965), a collection of translations from American, English, and French poets.

In the later years of his life, Seferis returned to writing in a style similar to that of his early poetry. His final collection of poems, *Three Secret Poems* (1966), contains, much like his first collection *Strophe,* 28 short lyrical poems that are highly surrealistic in nature. In 1963, Seferis was the first Greek writer to win the Nobel Prize in literature "for his eminent lyrical writing, inspired by a deep feeling for the Hellenic world of culture."

Other Works by George Seferis

Keeley, Edmund, ed. *Complete Poems of George Seferis.* Translated by Philip Sherrard. Greenwich, U.K.: Anvil Press Poetry, 1989.

Works about George Seferis

Hadas, Rachel. *Form, Cycle, Infinity: Landscape Imagery in the Poetry of Robert Frost and George Seferis.* Cranbury, N.J.: Bucknell University Press, 1985.

Kelley, Edmund, and Philip Sherrard, eds. *George Seferis.* Princeton, N.J.: Princeton University Press, 1995.

Tsatsos, Ioanna. *My Brother George Seferis.* Translated by Jean Demos. St. Paul, Minn.: North Central Publishing Company, 1982.

Seifert, Jaroslav (1901–1986) *poet*

Jaroslav Seifert was born in Prague, Czechoslovakia. He quit school at a young age to work for the Communist newspaper *Rudé Pravo,* where he acquired an extensive knowledge of Czechoslovakian history and culture, as exemplified in his first volume of poetry, *The City in Tears* (1920). The poems in this collection are characterized by simplicity and sensuality.

Seifert traveled throughout Europe, where he became familiar with literary trends. He initially regarded poetry as a tool for social change, and his early work expressed support for communism. Later, influenced by DADA and FUTURISM, his focus shifted toward poetry that was guided by sensual rather than intellectual motivations.

Because of his refusal to conform to orthodox political beliefs, Seifert's works were often censored by the Czechoslovakian government. He cofounded a society of avant-garde literary figures in Prague and, in 1929, was finally expelled from the Communist Party for refusing to oppose the elected Czechoslovakian government.

Seifert joined the Social Democrats, and his poetry began to change once again. *The Carrier Pigeon* (1929) focused on daily life, rejecting metaphor in favor of REALISM. During World War II, the publication of *Bozena Nemcová's Fan* (1939), with its passionate opposition to the Nazi occupation of Prague, put Seifert back in favor with the Communist Party, but by 1950 he was once again evicted from the party and charged with subjectivism.

Seifert then became a spokesperson for artistic freedom. In the 1970s, he headed the Union of Czech Writers and acted to oppose a ban on foreign publishing. *The Plague Column* (1977), which warned of the dangers of neo-Stalinism, was published in Cologne, West Germany, as a result of Czechoslovakian censorship. His final published work was his memoir, *All the Beauties of the World* (1981).

In 1984, Seifert became the first Czechoslovakian to receive the Nobel Prize in literature. Age and failing health prevented him from traveling to Stockholm to accept his award in person, and the Czechoslovakian government would not grant his son an exit visa to pick up the award for him. He died in Prague two years later.

Other Works by Jaroslav Seifert

Dressed in Light. Translated by Paul Jagasich and Tom O'Grady. New York: Dolphin-Moon Press, 1990.

The Early Poetry of Jaroslav Seifert. Translated by Dana Loewy. Evanston, Ill.: Hydra Books, 1997.

Sembène, Ousmane (1923–) *novelist, screenwriter*

Ousmane Sembène was born in Ziguinchor, in the Casamance region of southern Senegal. The son of a fisherman who was too poor to put his son through school, Ousmane left school before finishing to take various odd jobs, including those of bricklayer, fisherman, plumber, and apprentice mechanic. He was drafted into the French colonial army during World War II and served in both Italy and Germany. After the war, he returned to work as a manual laborer, first in Dakar, Senegal, and later in Marseilles, France. While in France, he was strongly influenced by French leftist thought and eventually became a trade-union leader. He joined the French Communist Party and became an active member until 1960 when Senegal gained its independence. After a year of instruction in cinema studies in Moscow, he devoted most of his attention and time to making films.

Sembène first made his mark as a novelist with *Le Docker noir* (*The Black Dockworker,* 1956) and moved into the film industry after 1962. In both his novels and his screenplays, he develops the themes of the nationalist struggle against colonialism, corruption, and racial discrimination. These are the issues that plagued most African writers who had firsthand experience of colonialism. What distinguishes Sembène is that he continues to write and explore these themes long after the colonial struggle ended. He completed three novels during the 1950s and 1960s. His most popular and, arguably, best novel is *Les Bouts de bois de Dieu* (*God's Bits of Wood,* 1960),

a story that vividly depicts the African workers' struggle against colonial oppression and exploitation. The book is set during the 1947 and 1948 Dakar-Niger Railway strike, an event that Sembène witnessed. He develops a sophisticated view of workers' rights and industrial relations, using a Marxist approach in this novel. *Xala* (1973) ironically bespeaks the anguish and disappointment following the postcolonial independence where Africans realized that their new leaders were incapable of making genuine progress or fulfilling promises that they pledged during the struggle.

Sembène's novels and screenplays are informed by his own personal experiences and encounters. He is most effective in depicting the complexities of the colonial and postcolonial struggle of many African nations, which, in many cases, did not end with the gaining of independence. Sembène has written all his works in French; approximately half have been translated into English.

Other Works by Ousmane Sembène

The Black Docker. London: Heinemann, 1987.

The Money-Order; with White Genesis. London: Heinemann, 1972.

Niiwam and Taww. Oxford: Heinemann, 1992.

Tribal Scars and Other Stories. London: Heinemann, 1974.

Films by Ousmane Sembène

Camp de Thiaroye. 1988. With Thiero Faty Sow.

L'Empire Sonhrai. 1963. In French.

Le Mandat (*The Money-Order*). 1968. In French and Wolof. English version, 1969.

Xala. 1974. In French and Wolof.

Works about Ousmane Sembène

Conde, Maryse. "Sembène Ousmane-Xala." *African Literature Today* no. 9 (1978).

Peters, Jonathan. "Sembène Ousmane as Griot: *The Money-Order with White Genesis.*" *African Literature Today* no. 12 (1982).

Pfaff, Françoise. *The Cinema of Ousmane Sembène, A Pioneer of African Film.* Westport, Conn.: Greenwood, 1984.

Senghor, Léopold Sédar (1906–2001)
poet

Léopold Sédar Senghor was born in the little coastal town of Joal, Senegal. As a boy, he moved around the circle of Serere farmers and fishermen and listened to the tales they told of precolonial Africa. These stories would greatly influence his poetry. He attended a Roman Catholic mission school in French West Africa when he was young and entered the Collège Libermann in Dakar in 1922 to study for the priesthood. He was, however, found participating in protests against racism and expelled from the school. Senghor finally completed his secondary education in a public school in 1928 and left Senegal after winning a scholarship to study in France.

Senghor studied contemporary French literature at the prestigious École Normale Supérieure in Paris. He was greatly influenced by the vibrant atmosphere of intellectual ferment in 1930s Paris. Black African writers were rediscovering their roots in exile away from their homeland, and this led them to establish the intellectual movement called NÉGRITUDE, which encouraged black students, artists, and writers to explore their common cultural roots and tradition. Senghor and his writer-friend Aimé CÉSAIRE were the cofounders of négritude and the newspaper, *L'Étudiant noir* (The black student).

Senghor established his literary and political career in the aftermath of World War II. In 1946, he and his mentor, Lamine Guèye, were both appointed as representatives of Senegal in the French Constituent Assembly in Paris. Senghor managed to be reelected and served in the assembly until 1958. When Senegal gained its independence in April 1960, Senghor became its first president. His rich cultural background and his keen intellect made him an effective leader, but his success did not last long. The persistence of Senegal's economic crisis and the futility of Senghor's programs led to his forced retirement in 1980. He resettled in Verson, France, where he spent the rest of his life.

Senghor's poems, written in French and translated into many languages, reflect his inner conflict between his Western predisposition and his determination to preserve the wealth of his African heritage. The poems in his first book, *Chants d'ombre* (Songs of shadow, 1945), are extremely effective in their dramatization of his search for identity. In these poems, he manages to extricate himself from the vicious cycle of self-doubt and find balance by retreating to his childhood and the past. This theme of the returning to his origins is best presented in the poem "Que m'accompagnent kôras et balaphong" ("To the Music of Kôras and Balaphon"), which also exhibits Senghor's aptitude for music. He believed that good musical rhythm was essential in poetry and often insisted that his poems should be read to the accompaniment of African music.

Senghor's personal experience as an exile living in France also influenced his writings. His sense of alienation derives from his dilemma as an educated African who felt torn between his black attributes and background and his Western intellectual inclinations. He felt distinctly the need to promote his black identity in the margins of Western society to establish his presence. Senghor's volume *Hosties noires* (Black victims, 1948) contains many poems written in the war years. A common thread runs through these poems: Senghor's growing disappointment and exasperation with losing his European "heritage." Senghor knew he could never be French, but his desire to retain his "Frenchness" was intermixed with a realization that his true roots lay in Africa. Senghor's ingenuity lies in his fluency in French, his extraordinary exploration of the range of human emotions, and his intellectual critique of French colonialism in Africa.

Other Works by Léopold Sédar Senghor

The Collected Poetry. Translated by Melvin Dixon. Charlottesville: University Press of Virginia, 1991.

Irele, F. A., ed. *Selected Poems of Léopold Sédar Senghor.* New York: Cambridge University Press, 1977.

Works about Léopold Sédar Senghor

Kluback, William. *Léopold Sédar Senghor: From Politics to Poetry.* New York: Peter Lang, 1997.

Spleth, Janet. *Léopold Sédar Senghor.* Boston: Twayne, 1985.

Vaillant, Janet G. *Black, French, and African: A Life of Léopold Sédar Senghor.* Cambridge, Mass.: Harvard University Press, 1990.

Serote, Mongane Wally (1944–) *poet, essayist, novelist*

Mongane Wally Serote was born in Sophiatown, South Africa. He received his early education in Alexandra Township and later attended the Morris Isaacson High School in Soweto. In 1974, after a succession of different jobs, he left South Africa on a Fulbright scholarship, which enabled him to study for a master's degree in fine arts at Columbia University in New York. Before leaving he had been awarded the Ingrid Jonker Prize for Poetry following the publication of his collection *Yakhal'inkomo* (1972).

Serote's most recent novel, *Gods of Our Time* (1999), documents the latter years of the liberation struggle in South Africa and conveys the bewilderment and uncertainty of those involved in the historic events of the time. In his text, Serote mimics the dislocated sensation of living in a time when people often disappeared without a trace by using a multitude of characters who enter the pages in an apparently random manner and then, inexplicably, disappear again. Much of Serote's work chronicles a disconnection with the past and attempts a realignment and reconfiguration with that past. His collection of poetry *The Night Keeps Winking* (1982) was banned in his home country. It contains vivid imagery of the cruelty of life under apartheid, but also lyrical notes:

> If life is so simple
> why can't it be lived
> if it is so brief
> why can't it be lived

After living in exile in Botswana and Britain, he returned to South Africa when the end of apartheid came. In 1991, he received an honorary doctorate from the University of Natal. He won the Noma Award for Publishing in Africa in 1993. Mongane Serote was elected to South Africa's Parliament in 1994 and became the chair of the Arts, Culture, Language, Science and Technology Parliamentary Portfolio committee. Serote continues to chronicle the history of the South Afican experience.

Another Work by Mongane Wally Serote

To Every Birth Its Blood. Westport, Conn.: Heinemann, 1983.

Works about Mongane Wally Serote

Brown, Duncan. "Interview with Mongane Wally Serote." *Theoria: A Journal of Studies in the Arts, Humanities and Social Sciences* 80 (October 1992): 143–49.

Horn, Peter. "A Volcano in the Night of Oppression: Reflections on the Poetry of Mongane Serote." Available online at http://homepages.compuserve.de/PeterRHorn/volcano.htm.

Seth, Vikram (1952–) *novelist, poet*

Vikram Seth was born in Calcutta, India, but grew up in Delhi. His father, Prem Seth, is an executive in a business company, and his mother, Lalitha Seth, is a judge. After completing his schooling in India, Seth went to England and America for further studies. At Stanford University in 1975, while studying for his doctorate in economics but frustrated by the tediousness of filling in data for a project, Seth decided to take a temporary leave from economics and thought to try writing a novel instead. He went to a bookstore and was so inspired by a PUSHKIN novel that he decided to write one himself.

What began as a break became Seth's lifetime profession—a cross-cultural exploration of the question of identity and human relationships. He has written about North America, Tibet, China, England, and India: In each instance, he does not create, as in the works of Salman RUSHDIE, postmodern cultural hybrids through his characters; rather, Seth's works can be said to be deliberately straightforward and direct without undermining the lyricism of his language. He does not complicate human nature but frankly and compassionately tries to communicate it. In *An Equal Music* (1998), which is set in England, the imminent separation of the lovers is an outcome destined by music and is not a result of a larger social or political cause. In this novel, the theme of love is contained within the context of the feelings the couple have for each other. The romantic intimacy between individuals in a drama devoid of politics places this work in a modernist framework.

Seth's difference from contemporary Indian writers of English can be found in a descriptive style that is as uncomplicated in form as it is in content. This, however, does not mean that he has not written on political issues: The poem "A Doctor's Journal Entry for August 6, 1945," from *All You Who Sleep Tonight* (1990), is a vivid exposition of a doctor's reaction to the atomic bomb at the moment of its fall into Hiroshima. Caught between saving himself and needing to do his duty to others as a doctor, the narrator realizes that silence and death are his only options.

Seth's first literary venture was not, as he intended, a novel. *Golden Gate* (1986) is written completely in rhyme and won him the Commonwealth Poetry Prize in 1986. *Golden Gate* follows the formal tradition of older poetry and is a satire of cosmopolitanism in sonnet form. It was inspired by the vibrancy of San Francisco and the lives of the youth who eke out a living there. Seth's second novel, *A Suitable Boy* (1993), is set in postindependent India in the 1950s. While a mother performs an exacting search for a perfect husband for her daughter, ethnic violence between Hindus and Muslims divides a nation. *A Suitable Boy* is the longest novel ever written in English. Because of its length and scope, covering the lives of four extended families, Seth was hailed as a "latter-day Tolstoy" by international critics when it was released.

Seth also studied classical Chinese poetry at Nanjing University (China) and has written about his travels in China and Tibet. Seth's travelogues uncover traces of India, found even in the remotest mountain in Tibet. After his studies in China, Seth published a collection of Chinese poems that he translated into English.

Seth has proven to be a truly versatile writer. Just as uncomplicated in form as he is in content, he has written in almost every literary genre. He has often said that rather than trying to combine different genres at one time, he prefers to pick a different form for a different theme. He has written six books of poetry, three novels, and a libretto, *Arion and the Dolphin* (1999), for an opera by British composer Alec Roth. His attention to form has twice placed him in the *Guinness Book of Records:* for *Golden Gate,* the first novel in English written entirely in sonnet form, and for *A Suitable Boy.*

Other Works by Vikram Seth
Arion and Dolphins. New York: Penguin Putnam, 1999.
From Heaven Lake. New York: Vintage Books, 1987.

Works about Vikram Seth
A. L. McLeod, ed. "The Gate and the Banyan: Vikram Seth's Two Identities," *The Literature of the Indian Diaspora.* Delhi, India: Sterling, 2000.
Atkins, Angela. *Vikram Seth's "A Suitable Boy": A Reader's Guide.* New York: Continuum International Inc., 2002.
Pandurang, Mala. *Vikram Seth: Multiple Locations, Multiple Affiliation.* New Delhi: Rawat, 2001.

Shalamov, Varlam (1907–1982) *poet, essayist*
The son of a priest, Varlam Tihonovich Shalamov was born in Vologda, Russia. As a young man, Shalamov joined the communist cause and actively participated in the Russian Revolution. Between 1926 and 1929, Shalamov studied law at the Moscow University. In 1929, he was arrested for

distribution of the so-called "Lenin's Will," a document that stated that Lenin opposed the appointment of Joseph Stalin to the leadership of the Communist Party and the Soviet Union. Shalamov was released in 1932 but was arrested once again in 1937 at the height of the period of Stalin's political repressions.

Shalamov spend the next 17 years in a labor camp in Kolyma, a remote location in Siberia. After he returned in 1952, he began to publish poems in various journals. In the meantime, he secretly worked on *Kolyma Tales*, which appeared in dissident circles around Moscow in 1966. *Kolyma Tales* describes Shalamov's experiences in Stalin's labor camps. The stories were officially published in London in 1977. After the London publication, the collection caused a scandal for the Soviet government, and Shalamov was forced to renounce his work publicly. He died alone in a nursing home five years before *Kolyma Tales* was officially published in the Soviet Union.

Varlam Shalamov's *Kolyma Tales* is considered by many to be a centerpiece of dissident fiction in Russia. His tales had a direct political impact in the Soviet Union, as they exposed the scandalous treatment of political prisoners in the Soviet Union and the injustices of the Soviet judicial system. Today, Shalamov is admired by many, and his work continues to bear relevance to the treatment of political prisoners by various totalitarian governments around the world.

Another Work by Varlam Shalamov

Graphite. Translated by John Glad. New York: Norton, 1981.

Shiga Naoya (1883–1971) *novelist, short-story writer, essayist*

Shiga Naoya was born in Ishimaki, Miyagi Prefecture, Japan, to Shiga Naoharu and Gin. When he was still very young, his grandparents took him to their residence in Tokyo. A member of an affluent and influential family, Shiga entered the elitist Gakushūin, a school established to educate the imperial family. He became interested in Christianity and joined a Christian study group while in middle school, and in 1906, he entered the English literature department of the Tokyo Imperial University. In 1914, Shiga married Sadako Kadenokōji. His father disapproved of the marriage, and Shiga responded by renouncing his inheritance, thus severing his ties with his family.

Shiga's formal literary career began with his publication of the short story "The Little Girl and the Rapeseed Flower" (1904) while he was still in high school. In 1910, Shiga and a group of friends from Gakushūin started a literary magazine as an outlet for their writing, and Shiga regularly contributed short stories. In 1912, he published *Ōtsu Junkichi*, his first long work. While critics called the novella uneven, its honesty of emotion ranks it highly among Japan's literary works. Five years later, while recovering from having been hit by a train, Shiga wrote his masterpiece "At Kinosaki," a reverie over the deaths of small animals. Shiga excelled in the arena of short stories, but he struggled with novel writing. Despite other attempts, he wrote only one full-length novel—*A Dark Night's Passing*—over a 16-year period, from 1921 to 1937. In the last 20 years of his life, Shiga entered into semiretirement, periodically writing personal essays based on his observations.

Shiga is regarded as the supreme stylist of his day. Using an economy of words, he depicted vivid vignettes based closely on his personal experiences. His literary power stems from his objectivity and honesty in portraying his characters' emotions. In 1949, he received the Order for Cultural Merit.

Other Works by Shiga Naoya

Morning Glories. Translated by Allen Say and David Meltzer. Berkeley, Calif.: Oyez, 1976.
The Paper Door and Other Stories. Translated by Lane Dunlop. San Francisco: North Point Press, 1987.

Works about Shiga Naoya

Mathy, Frances. *Shiga Naoya*. Boston: Twayne, 1974.
Starrs, Roy. *An Artless Art: The Zen Aesthetic of Shiga Naoya*. Richmond, Surrey: Japan Library, 1998.

Shiina Minako
See ŌBA MINAKO.

Sholokhov, Mikhail (1905–1984) *novelist, short-story writer*

Mikhail Aleksandrovich Sholokhov was born in a small village of Kruzhlinin, Russia. Sholokhov's father engaged in a number of farm-related trades; his mother was an illiterate Ukrainian peasant who learned to read and write late in her life to correspond with her son. Sholokhov was educated in several schools but left his educational pursuits to join the army in 1918. He fought on the Bolshevik side during the Russian civil war. He took part in the suppression of an anti-Bolshevik rebellion by the Don Cossacks (a semiautonomous group who was granted limited local independence by the czar, often in exchange for services in the military). Indeed, almost all of Sholokhov's prose is based on this experience during the war.

At the end of the war, Sholokhov relocated to Moscow where, between 1922 and 1924, he worked as a stonemason and an accountant. He occasionally participated in writers' seminars and published his first story, *The Birthmark,* in 1924. The same year, he decided to dedicate himself completely to writing; only a year later, he published his first collection of short stories, *Tales of the Don,* which depicted the bitter transformation of village life during the civil war.

Sholokhov's fame as a novelist came with the serialized publication of *And Quiet Flows the Don* (1928–40). Although the novel won the Stalin Prize in 1941, it was initially criticized for its objectivity in depicting the civil war. The work traces the tragic life of Cossack Grigory Melekhov and his ill-fated love. Along with the spiritual destruction of the protagonist, Sholokhov also depicts the downfall of traditional Cossack communities. His other major work, *Virgin Soil Uplifted* (1932–60), describes the agricultural collectivization in the Soviet Union. Although now recognized by many critics as mediocre at best, the novel received the Lenin Prize in 1960.

Sholokhov achieved high rank in the Communist Party. He accompanied the Soviet leader Nikita Khrushchev on a trip to Europe and the United States in 1959, and in 1961, he was elected as a member of the Central Committee. Many writers have criticized Sholokhov's work for its unscrupulousness in following official doctrines; still others questioned the authorship of *Tikhiy Don.* Despite these troubles, Sholokhov was the first officially sanctioned Soviet writer to receive the Nobel Prize in literature in 1965. By Sholokhov's death in 1984, more than 79 million copies of his work were published in 84 languages.

A Work about Mikhail Aleksandrovich Sholokhov
Ermolaev, Herman. *Mikhail Sholokhov and His Art.* Princeton, N.J.: Princeton University Press, 1982.

Shu Qingchun
See LAO SHE.

Sienkiewicz, Henryk (1846–1916) *novelist, short-story writer*

Henryk Sienkiewicz was born in Wola Okrzejska, part of the Russian area of Poland. His father's family were revolutionaries who fought for Polish independence, and his mother's family included scholars of history.

Sienkiewicz's talent for writing emerged at a young age. His earliest works were satirical sketches on social consciousness. In 1876, he visited America, publishing his travel accounts in Polish newspapers and gaining material for future works.

Returning to Poland, Sienkiewicz turned to historical studies, writing a trilogy about 17th-century Poland, which included *With Fire and Sword* (1884), *The Deluge* (1886), and *Pan Michael* (1888). A prolific writer, he followed these works in rapid succession with novels on a variety of contemporary subjects. *Without Dogma* (1891) was a psychological study of decadence, while

Children of the Soil (1894) focused on the lives of peasants.

In 1896 Sienkiewicz published *Quo Vadis*. This novel, for which he is most widely recognized internationally, told of the persecution of Christians at the time of Nero. He returned to historical subjects in *Krzyzacy* (1900), recounting the Poles' victory over the Teutonic knights in the Middle Ages, and *On the Field of Glory* (1906), a sequel to his previous trilogy. His final works, *Whirlpools* (1910) and *In Desert and Wilderness* (1912), again deal with contemporary issues.

In 1905, Sienkiewicz was awarded the Nobel Prize in literature for his "outstanding merits as an epic writer" (Nobel Lectures). Living in a time of cultural oppression, Sienkiewicz encouraged patriotism through his writing. Evidence of his success can be found in reports of Polish citizens pinning pages of his books to their clothing as a reminder of the fight for freedom. Sienkiewicz also wrote open letters to his people addressing political injustice, and in 1901, he helped to expose the persecution of Polish schoolchildren by the Prussians. He did not live to see the success of all he had fought to attain. He died two years before Poland's boundaries were restored.

Other Works by Henryk Sienkiewicz

Charcoal Sketches and Other Tales. Translated by Adam Zamoyski. Chester Springs, Pa.: Dufour Editions, 1990.

The Little Trilogy. Translated by Miroslaw Lipinski. New York: Hippocrene Books, 1995.

Works about Henryk Sienkiewicz

Giergielewicz, Mieczyslaw. *Henryk Sienkiewicz: A Biography.* New York: Hippocrene Books, 1991.

Kryanowski, Jerzy, ed. *The Trilogy Companion: A Reader's Guide to the Trilogy of Henryk Sienkiewicz.* New York: Hippocrene Books, 1992.

Simenon, Georges (1903–1989) *novelist*

Best known as a skilled writer of highly literate detective fiction, Georges Simenon was born in Liège, Belgium. The son of an accountant, he was forced to quit school because of his father's poor health. His mother died in 1921, and he worked for a time as a baker and a bookseller before launching his writing career with an apprenticeship at a local newspaper, *Gazette de Liège.*

Simenon began publishing when he was only 17 years old. He joined with a group of painters, writers, and artists who called themselves The Cask. This group spent the majority of their time drinking, experimenting with drugs, and having deep philosophical discussions. He recounts his experiences with this group in his novel *Le Pendu de Saint Pholier* (1931).

In 1922, Simenon moved to Paris, where he published numerous short stories and novels under a variety of pennames. Between 1922 and 1939, he produced more than 200 works of pulp fiction. The first work published under his real name was *The Strange Case of Peter Lett* (1931), in which Simenon introduces the character of Inspector Maigret, the Paris police detective about whom he would ultimately pen 84 mysteries, 18 of them written in the early 1930s. Simenon left the character behind for an eight-year hiatus at the start of World War II.

During the German invasion of France, Simenon moved to Fontenay, where he wrote successfully for the film business. After the war, under suspicion of having been a Nazi collaborator, he moved to the United States, where he wrote several mysteries with American settings, including *Belle* (1954) and *The Hitchhiker* (1955).

Simenon returned to Europe to live in Switzerland in 1955. Several of the Maigret novels enjoyed success as films. He announced his retirement in 1973, just after the publication of one last Maigret work, *Maigret et Monsieur Charles* (1972). He continued to write some nonfiction, including *Lettre a ma mère* (1974), which focuses on his relationship with his mother. Simenon died on September 4, leaving instructions that his body be cremated without ceremony. His legacy to literature lives on in the psychological depth he brought to the genre of detective fiction.

Other Works by Georges Simenon

Maigret Loses His Temper. Translated by Robert Eglesfield. San Diego, Calif.: Harcourt Brace Jovanovich, 1993.

The Rules of the Game. Translated by Howard Curtis. San Diego, Calif.: Harcourt Brace Jovanovich, 1988.

Works about Georges Simenon

Assouline, Pierre. *Simenon: A Biography.* Translated by Jon Rothschild. New York: Knopf, 1997.

Becker, Lucille. *Georges Simenon Revisited.* Boston: Twayne, 1999.

Simon, Claude (1913–   ) *novelist*

Closely associated with the emergence of the NEW NOVEL in the 1950s, Claude Simon was born in Tananarive, in the then French colony of Madagascar. His father was killed during World War II, leaving Simon to be raised by his mother and her family in Perpignan, a French city near the Spanish border.

Simon studied for a career in the navy but was ultimately dismissed and left to study art at both Oxford and Cambridge Universities. In the early 1930s, he visited the Soviet Union. Upon his return, he served with the French army. During World War II, he was captured by the Germans but managed to escape and join the Resistance.

It was not until after the end of World War II that Simon began his career as a writer. His first novel, *Le tricheur* (*The Cheat*, 1945), was followed by the autobiographical novel *La corde raide* (*The Tightrope*, 1947). These two works and Simon's two subsequent novels are traditional in structure, with easily identifiable plots and characters. Simon gained international recognition, however, with his "new novel"–styled *Le Vent* (*The Wind*, 1959). Here Simon began to develop a style in which the plot is really just one event viewed from several perspectives.

In *L'herbe* (1958) Simon began to emphasize visual perceptions. Nothing much happens in the novel, even though it is set in France in 1940, the tumultuous year of the German invasion. An old woman, Marie, is dying; her recollections, mainly of houses and gardens, form the substance of the book. A sequel, *La route des Flandres* (1960), is about Marie's nephew Georges, juxtaposing his wartime experiences with his present postwar reality. Much of Simon's work is largely biographical or historical in origin. Stylistically, he grew to favor a stream-of-consciousness style that was often devoid of regular punctuation and used parentheses excessively. For his works and contribution to the field of literature, Simon was awarded the Nobel Prize in literature in 1985.

Other Works by Claude Simon

The Georgics. Translated by Beryl and John Fletcher. New York: Riverrun Press, 1991.

The Invitation. Translated by Jim Cross. Normal, Ill.: Dalkey Archive Press, 1991.

The Jardin des Plantes. Translated by Jordan Stump. Evanston, Ill.: Illinois University Press, 2001.

The Trolley. Translated by Richard Howard. New York: New Press, 2002.

A Work about Claude Simon

Brewer, Maria Minich. *Claude Simon: Narratives Without Narrative.* Lincoln: University of Nebraska Press, 1995.

Singer, Isaac Bashevis (Icek–Hersz Zynger) (1904–1991) *novelist, short-story writer*

Isaac Bashevis Singer was born in Radzymin, Poland. Singer's father was a Hasidic rabbi, and his mother came from a family of rabbis. When he was four, he moved with his family to Warsaw where he received a traditionally Jewish education, combining academics with the study of Jewish law in Hebrew and Aramaic texts. An avid reader, he was also influenced by the works of Spinoza, GOGOL, DOSTOEVSKY, and TOLSTOY. Singer entered the Tachkemoni Rabbinical Seminary in 1920 but ultimately gave up this vocation to become a writer.

He began his writing career as a journalist in Warsaw, where he worked as a proofreader for

Literarische Bleter, a newspaper edited by his eldest brother Joshua Singer, who was more politically active than his brother and highly disillusioned with the Soviet political system. This disillusionment affected the younger Singer's awareness of the continuous sociopolitical and cultural upheaval in Poland.

Singer's chief subject was Jewish life, history, and tradition, centered primarily on the period before the Holocaust. He examines the importance of the Jewish faith through the lives of his characters.

Singer's earliest fictional works were short stories and novellas. His first novel, *Satan in Goray* (1932), was published in Poland. It addresses the theme of the power of the 17th-century false messiah Shabbatai Zvi. Written in a linguistic style similar to the medieval Yiddish book of chronicles, the novel is set in the 17th century during the time of the Cossaks and is based on the mass murder of Jews, peasants, and artisans. The characters are often at the mercy of circumstance but are also the victims of passion. The story examines the danger of messianic fever or overzealous prophet-worship. The destructive nature of passion and obsession are common themes in Singer's work.

Fearing Nazi persecution, Singer became a foreign correspondent and emigrated to the United States just after the publication of his first novel. He left behind his first wife, Rachel, and their son Israel. Settling in New York, he obtained employment with the Yiddish newspaper *Jewish Daily Forward.* In 1940 he married Alma Haimann, a German émigré, and was granted American citizenship in 1943.

His first collection of stories that was published in English was *Gimpel the Fool* (1957). He also published numerous stories in the *Jewish Daily Forward,* which were later collected in *In My Father's Court* (1966) and *More Stories from My Father's Court* (2000). The latter collection was published posthumously. In these stories, Singer depicts his own childhood in the overpopulated poor Jewish quarters of Warsaw before and during World War I. Singer's father is depicted as a pious man who studies the Talmud with great fervor; his mother is pictured as more practical, focusing on everyday problems.

The Family Moskat (1950) was Singer's first novel to be published in English. It forms the first volume of a trilogy along with *The Manor* (1967) and *The Estate* (1969). These novels describe how families are destroyed by the changing demands of society and a decline in religious faith.

Although Singer wrote all of his works in Yiddish, he collaborated with a number of well-known literary figures in the translation of his work, among them Saul Bellow and, most frequently, Cecil Hemley. He often published fiction under the penname Isaac Bashevis and journalism under Warshofsky.

In 1978, Singer was awarded the Nobel Prize in literature. In 1984, his short story "Yentil the Yeshiva Boy" was made into the popular film *Yentl.* The 1989 film *Enemies, a Love Story* was also based on one of his novels. Singer died in Surfside, Florida, on July 24, 1991.

Other Works by Isaac Bashevis Singer

Reaches of Heaven. New York: Farrar Strauss, 1980.
Scum. Translated by Rosaline Dukalsky Schwartz. New York: Farrar Straus, 1991.
The Penitent. New York: Farrar, Straus & Giroux, 1983.
The Slave. Translated by the author and Cecil Hemley. New York: Farrar, Straus & Giroux, 1962.

Works about Isaac Bashevis Singer

Friedman, Lawrence. *Understanding Isaac Bashevis Singer.* Columbia: University of South Carolina Press, 1988.
Hadda, Janet. *Isaac Bashevis Singer: A Life.* New York: Oxford University Press, 1997.

Škvorecký, Jozef (1924–) *novelist*

Jozef Škvorecký was born in 1924 in Náchod, Bohemia, Czeckoslovakia. He received his Ph.D. from Charles University in Prague. Škvorecký was fired from his job when his first novel, *The Cowards* (1958; translated 1970), was published; the novel was banned in Czechoslovakia soon after its publication for its ironic portrayal of the everyday lives of people living under communist rule. Undaunted, Škvorecký began freelancing, writing novels, film scripts, and nonfiction.

In response to the defeat of the Czech reform movement, Škvorecký left Czechoslovakia to settle in Canada in 1969. With his wife, he founded a Czechoslovakian publishing house in Toronto, where he began to build a solid reputation as a novelist. During a 20-year period, he developed a reputation as one of Canada's finest novelists, receiving the Governor General's Award for Fiction in 1984.

All of Škvorecký's novels have some basis in his experiences in Czechoslovakia and are often semi-autobiographical. Some of his works also focus on the problems of romantic love in a harsh sociopolitical climate. *The Engineer of Human Souls* (1984) is a comic novel that tells the tragic tale of novelist Danny Smiricky, a Czech immigrant living in Canada. *The Bride of Texas* (1995) is a historical novel about Czechoslovakian immigrants during the American Civil War who fought alongside the Union army.

Škvorecký taught at the University of Toronto from 1971 to 1991. Retired from teaching, he continues to write. His most recent novel, *Dead Man on Campus* (2000), is an autobiographical novel merged with a murder mystery.

Other Works by Jozef Škvorecký

Dvorák in Love: Alight-Hearted Dream. New York: Norton, 1988.

The Bass Saxophone: Two Novellas. New York: Ecco Press, 1994.

A Work about Jozef Škvorecký

Solecki, Sam. *Prague Blues: The Fiction of Josef Škvorecký.* New York: Ecco Press, 1990.

So Chōng-ju (Midang) (1915–2001) *poet*

So Chōng-ju was born in Sonuna village in Korea's North Cholla province. After receiving a high school education without graduating, he entered the monastery but soon left to pursue a career in writing.

So Chōng-ju, who was influenced by the Western writers Friedrich NIETZSCHE and Charles BAUDELAIRE, is considered one of Korea's first modern poets. He made a ripple in the Korean literary community by being the first writer to invoke sexual imagery, as in the poem "The Snake" (1938). Poems such as these marked his early sensual period.

So Chōng-ju also masterfully chronicled ordinary life. In the 1950s and 1960s, he drew on his Buddhist training and entered a Zen stage. Writing under his Buddhist name, Midang, he wrote of epiphany and Zen insight in "Legendary Karma Song" (1960) and "Beside a Chrysanthemum" (1955). He also focused on aesthetics and the natural world, both areas of Buddhist scholarship. Eventually, as So Chōng-ju aged, he returned to more personal poetry, reflecting upon his life and experiences and confronting the specter of his own mortality. "In Looking at Winter Orchids" (1976), for example, the narrator draws a parallel between his own mortality and flowers past bloom.

So Chōng-ju is one of the best-loved poets of modern Korea. He also achieved renown in the international community, which culminated in his nomination for the Nobel Prize in 1994, becoming the first Korean writer to receive this honor. A respected scholar, So Chōng-ju was a professor at Buddhist University and Dongguk University in Seoul. When he died on December 24, at the age of 85, the country mourned his death as a premier man of letters.

Another Work by So Chōng-ju

Poems of a Wanderer: Selected Poems of Midang So Chōng-ju. Translated by Kevin O'Rourke. Dublin: Dedalus Press, 1995.

socialist realism

Socialist realism was first recognized as an emerging literary movement in the Soviet Union in response to a May 1932 article in the *Literary*

Gazette. The article stated that, in response to modern times and a general trend toward embracing socialist doctrine, "The masses demand of an artist honesty, truthfulness, and a revolutionary, socialist realism in the representation of the proletarian revolution." This article was followed shortly thereafter by a 1933 article by Maxim GORKY, "On Socialist Realism," which emphasized the importance of artists taking "a new direction essential to us—socialist realism, which can be created only from the data of socialist experience." However, socialist realism was not officially defined as a literary and political term until 1934 when, at the First All-Union Congress of Soviet writers, it was officially adopted as the accepted standard for art and literature. In a speech at the congress, Gorky called on writers to "make labor the principal hero of our books."

Socialist realism was based on the principle that the arts should serve the purposes of communism and communist ideologies, both by glorifying worker heroes and by educating readers about the benefits of communist life. A first generation of socialist realists, including Maxim Gorky and Andrey Platonov (1899–1951), were not under state control and created works that portrayed the suffering of the poor and oppressed. However, socialist realism under Stalin persecuted writers who did not adhere to the party line. Writers, as well as visual and performing artists, were required to join the state-controlled Union of Soviet Artists and, as a condition of membership, were required to agree to abide by the union's restrictions. The movement began and spread quickly alongside the growth and expansion of communist ideology and government, becoming a dominant form of artistic expression in much of Eastern and Central Europe, but it also included writers from the United States, Latin America, Africa, and Asia.

Many writers and visual artists living under Communist governments found the demands of socialist realism stifling, so they emigrated to other countries. Others, such as the Polish writer Sławomir MROŻEK, without leaving, found ways to keep their creativity alive through the use of indirect satire. The first collection of Mrozek's works, *Slon* (1957; *The Elephant,* 1967), was an anthology of very short stories that satirized various aspects of Polish Communism in the 1950s. It was immediately successful with both critics and the general public but was not favored by strict socialists. Stalin's death in 1953 led to some relaxation of government control of the arts, but socialist realism continued as the official accepted literary and artistic practice into the 1980s.

Socialist realism is no longer a major movement, and very few works, if any at all, written today would fall under this category. It seems that socialist realism dissolved well before the collapse of the Soviet Union, and very few works of socialist realism, with the major exception of the first wave, are either read or appreciated today.

Socialist Realism in China

The growth of communism in the 1920s introduced socialist realism to China. A lack of mass awareness was discussed by writers, and quasi-socialist associations, such as the League of Left-Wing Writers (1930), were founded. But socialist realism did not materialize as an explicit literary and political directive in China until 1942, when Mao Zedong's talks at the Yenan Forum on Art and Literature gave the movement its foundation. By circumscribing the role of literature in a socialist society, Mao Zedong shaped communist literature for the remainder of the century. He drew heavily upon Soviet influence, and his primary tenet was the service of literature to revolutionary thought and politics.

Mao Zedong believed writers should not criticize the revolution but should emphasize the positive. Another main point at the Yenan talks was that literature must serve the masses. However, Mao Zedong also indicated that literature should not "lower" itself culturally to simple propaganda but should rise to a new artistic standard that concurrently served the revolutionary cause and urged the study of folk traditions.

Socialist realism was best served by writers indigenous to the movement. However, there were many writers who had been working for years who converted to communism, such as DING Ling and BA Jin. Adaptation to the newly stringent requirements of socialist realism was difficult. Some writers, including Ding Ling, Ba Jin, and the unfortunate scapegoat Wang Shiwei, were eventually purged by the party for a lack of mass awareness and other literary "crimes." The new writers were untrained students of revolution, such as Hao Ran, who wrote party-line fiction such as the three-volume novel *Bright Sunny Skies* (1965). Held up as a hallmark of literature for and by the masses, the novel follows three players—a landlord, a party secretary, and a fallen party member—in the difficult task of collectivizing their local economy.

Socialist realist works were to depict the revolutionary journey accurately. However, they also needed to portray revolutionary heroes or heroines, focus on the masses, and glorify the work of the revolution, such as industrialization, the militia of the People's Liberation Army, and agrarian reforms. The novels tended to be long and predictable, with idealistic young heroes, such as Yang Mo's romantic and revolutionary *Song of Youth* (1958). The military was the most popular topic, as in Chin Ching-mai's *The Song of Ou-Yang Hai* (1966), about a real-life People's Liberation Army soldier who acted selflessly. Ts'ao Ming's *The Motive Force* (1949) told the story of the rehabilitation of a destroyed hydroelectric plant and glorified industrial reconstruction in Manchuria.

The Communist Party had to launch periodic campaigns against forces that they deemed threatening to socialist realist literature. Two of the most infamous were the criticisms and purgings of Ding Ling and Hu Feng in 1955. Ding Ling, who was once lauded for her 1949 socialist-realist novel on land reform, *The Sun Shines Over Sanggan River,* was sent to labor reform for explicit and immoral writings and for her urgings for literary openness. Hu Feng was imprisoned for his criticisms of thought reform and the dogmatic views of party leaders regarding literature. Some writers, like Wang Shiwei, were even executed.

A brief respite against such persecution occurred from April 1956 to May 1957 in a period of tentative liberalization called the Hundred Flowers. In *Literature of the Hundred Flowers,* Mao Zedong said, "In the arts, let a hundred flowers bloom and in scholarship, let a hundred schools of thought contend." Here, Ding Ling and other writers who had been working under the demands of socialist realism for nearly a decade took the ills of the movement to task. Among the issues they raised were whether all literature had to be overtly political and whether poetry could be lyrical. The flowering was immediately followed by a purging anti-Rightist campaign.

The Cultural Revolution that began in 1966 and was led by Jiang Qing, Mao Zedong's wife, produced a high volume of works of propaganda that were of dubious artistic quality. Many cultural relics were destroyed; intellectuals, writers, and other artists were sent to labor reform camps; self-criticisms were forced; and mass persecutions were common.

After the Cultural Revolution, socialist realism had some mending to do. The first wave of writings from "rehabilitated" writers, such as Ding Ling and Ba Jin, were known as "scar literature" and revealed the wounds that resulted from the oppressive dictates of Chinese socialist-realist literature. Socialist realism persists in some form today, but with the changing face of Communist China it is hardly recognizable. Writers such as MO YAN document stories of ordinary life under communism with darkness and humor.

Works about Socialist Realism

Bisztray, George. *Marxist Models of Literary Realism.* New York: Columbia University Press, 1978.

Herdan, Innes. *The Pen and the Sword: Literature and Revolution in Modern China.* London: Zed Books Ltd., 1992.

Kemp-Welch, A. *Stalin and the Literary Intelligentsia, 1928–39.* New York: St. Martin's Press, 1991.

Lahusen, Thomas. *How Life Writes the Book: Real Socialism and Socialist Realism in Stalin's Russia.* New York: Cornell University Press, 1997.

Mao Zedong. *Selected Works of Mao Tse-Tung.* New York: Pergamon Press, 1977.

Robin, Régine. *Socialist Realism: An Impossible Aesthetic.* Translated by Catherine Porter; foreword by Léon Robel. Stanford, Calif.: Stanford University Press, 1991.

Yang Lan. *Chinese Fiction of the Cultural Revolution.* Hong Kong: Hong Kong University Press, 1998.

Södergran, Edith (1892–1923) poet

Edith Södergran was born in St. Petersburg, Russia, to Finnish–Swedish parents. Her father, Matts Södergran, was a mechanic and engineer who worked for Alfred Nobel for a time. Her mother, Helena Lovisa, was the daughter of a wealthy Swedish ironmaster. Södergran was educated at a German school in St. Petersburg and spent her summers at Raivola, Russia. As a teenager, she wrote poems in German, Swedish, French, and Russian. Södergran battled tuberculosis throughout her adolescence and spent several years in sanitariums in Switzerland and Finland.

An unhappy love affair with a Russian physician inspired Södergran's first collection of poetry *Dikter* (*Poems,* 1916). Her verse blended numerous influences, including Heinrich HEINE, Else LASKER-SCHÜLER, Walt Whitman, and Russian SYMBOLISM. Södergran's collection *Septemberlyran* (*September Lyric,* 1918), written after her wealth was erased by the Russian Revolution, was partially about the Finnish civil war. Her friendship with critic Hagar Olsson inspired the verse in *Rosenaltaret* (*The Rose Alter,* 1919). After Södergran adopted Rudolf Steiner's anthroposophy doctrines and Christianity, she ceased writing poetry until her final days. She died after long bouts with illness and malnutrition.

Södergran developed a cult following after her death. Young poets made pilgrimages to her Raivola home until it was destroyed in World War II. Södergran's works have been translated into French and German. Her poems combine childlike humor, frankness, and a passion for beauty, and she is credited with liberating Nordic verse from the restrictions of traditional rhyme, rhythm, and imagery. George Schoolfield's biography *Edith Södergran* (1984) contains a quote from Swedish poet Gunnar Ekelöf in a letter to W. H. Auden, describing Södergran as "a very great poet . . . brave and loving as your Emily Brontë."

Another Work by Edith Södergran

Love and Solitude: Selected Poems, 1916–1923. Translated by Stina Katchadourian. Seattle: Fjord Press, 1985.

A Work about Edith Södergran

Schoolfield, George C. *Edith Södergran: Modernist Poet in Finland.* Westport, Conn.: Greenwood Press, 1984.

Solovyov, Vladimir (1853–1900) philosopher, poet, translator

Vladimir Sergeyevich Solovyov was born in Moscow, Russia. His father, S. M. Solovyov, was a famous historian. Solovyov received an excellent education while growing up and attended the Moscow University, where he received a doctoral degree in philosophy. Afterward, he became a professor at the Moscow University until 1881, when he was forced to resign after publicly criticizing the death sentence passed on the assassins of Czar Aleksandr II.

Solovyov's poetry was closely connected with his philosophical and scholarly works, for which he is primarily remembered today. Deeply influenced by Plato, he adopted many of the Platonic ideals in the development of his own philosophy in conjunction with the beliefs of the Russian Orthodox Church. Although Solovyov was hardly a liberal in his political beliefs, he supported land reforms and other democratic reforms to ease the suffering of the Russian masses. His views became more and more reactionary as the Russian antigovernmental opposition became more and more violent.

Although initially sympathetic to the democratic cause and socialism, Solovyov's philosophy took a bitter turn toward the end of his life and became firmly grounded in Christian mysticism. He began to write about the end of history and the coming of the Antichrist.

A Work by Vladimir Solovyov

Politics, Law, and Morality: Essays by V. S. Solviev. London: Yale University Press, 2000.

A Work about Vladmir Solovyov

Kostalevsky, Marina. *Dostoevsky and Soloviev: The Art of Integral Vision.* London: Yale University Press, 1997.

Solzhenitsyn, Aleksandr (1918–)
novelist, historian

Aleksandr Isayevich Solzhenitsyn was born in Kislovodsk, Russia. His father died in a hunting accident six months before Solzhenitsyn's birth, and his mother supported the family by working as a typist. Solzhenitsyn studied mathematics and physics at the Rostov University, graduating with honors in 1941. While studying sciences, he also completed correspondence courses in literature at the Moscow State University. During World War II, he served as a captain of the artillery and was decorated for bravery. After writing a letter in which he criticized Stalin, he was sent to the political prison camps, where he remained from 1945 to 1953.

Most of Solzhenitsyn's work deals with his experiences during imprisonment. His first published novel, *One Day in the Life of Ivan Denisovich* (1958), appeared in the leading literary journal of the Soviet Union, *Novy Mir*. The novel dramatically portrays a day in the life of a political prisoner in one of the Stalin's labor camps. After the publication of the novel, Solzhenitsyn attracted negative attention from the government. His second novel, *Cancer Ward* (1968), was initially rejected. The novel describes the lives of patients suffering and dying from cancer as an allegory for Stalinist persecutions; it was

viewed as too radical by the authorities. *The First Circle* (1968), set during the late 1940s and the early 1950s, depicts a group of scientists who are forced to work on secret government projects in the labor camps.

By 1966, all of Solzhenitsyn's works were censored. In 1965, the KGB confiscated numerous manuscripts, and when Solzhenitsyn complained to the Soviet Writers' Union, he was expelled. Fortunately, Solzhenitsyn's works were smuggled abroad and were immediately recognized as dramatic testimony to Stalin's purges and persecutions. In Russia, Solzhenitsyn's work was secretly distributed in underground editions. Although he was awarded the Nobel Prize in literature in 1970, Solzhenitsyn was forced by the Soviet government to decline it. After *Gulag Archipelago* was published abroad in 1973, Solzhenitsyn was arrested and charged with treason. *Gulag Archipelago* contains personal testimony, interviews, and memories of the victims of Stalinist oppression. For the first time, the world could read about the unimaginable extent of Stalin's labor camps, where millions of political prisoners slaved for years. Solzhenytsin was stripped of Soviet citizenship and forcibly deported to Switzerland.

Solzhenytsin accepted his Nobel Prize in 1974, after his deportation from Russia. In 1990, his citizenship was reinstated, and all charges against him were dropped. He returned to Russia in 1994 and settled near Moscow.

Solzhenytsin's work is considered groundbreaking, particularly for its fearless exposure of the oppressive nature of the Soviet political system. Solzhenytsin remains the central figure of dissident literature, as well as one of the best-known Russian writers of the 20th century. His prose is distinct not only for its content but also for its well-developed narrative, highly descriptive diction, and realistic dialogue.

A Work about Aleksandr Solzhenitsyn

Scammell, Michael. *Solzhenitsyn: A Biography.* New York: Norton, 1984.

Souza, Eunice de (1940–) *poet, novelist, critic*

Eunice de Souza was born in Pune, India. She is of Goan Roman Catholic origin. Her father, an aspiring novelist, filled their house with books and inspired de Souza's love for literature and writing. In addition to writing four collections of poetry, she has put together anthologies of poems by other Indian poets. De Souza also writes folktales for children, is a regular contributor to newspapers and magazines, and is a respected literary critic. She is the head of the English department at St. Xavier's College, Mumbai, where she helped start an annual literary festival called Ithaka.

De Souza's anthology of Indian women poets of the 20th century is called *Nine Indian Women Poets* (1997). One of her inspirations for starting the project was her discovery of an obscure, ancient poem by a female monk. She began the anthology in the hopes that such moments of literary history would never again be neglected. *Nine Indian Women Poets* uncovers the contribution of women poets, such as Kamala Das and Sujata BHATT, and their role in advancing an old tradition of women writing in India. The anthology also reveals the different ways modern poetry has developed as a mode of expression for women in India.

De Souza's own poetry is in English, combined with its spoken version from Mumbai's streets, a sharp, witty and scathing language that reflects the author's own personality. Famous for her highly opinionated and critically discerning work, de Souza is often hailed as a feminist, she herself claims that poetry and propaganda do not belong together and that, if asked, she would have to admit she prefers writing about her pet parrots.

Other Works by Eunice de Souza

Conversations with Indian Poets. New York: Oxford University Press, 2001.
Dangerlok. New Delhi: Penguin Books, 2001.

Soyinka, Wole (Akinwande Oluwole Soyinka) (1934–) *playwright, poet, novelist, essayist*

Soyinka was born to Samuel Ayodele, a teacher, and Grace Eniola Soyinka, a shopkeeper, in western Nigeria. Both of his parents were Yoruba, a major tribal group in this West African country. He showed immense intellectual ability at an early age and was eventually able to go to England to study at the University of Leeds. Soyinka returned to Nigeria after graduating and worked to develop a Yoruba-based theater. He was influential in training many young people as the head of the Drama School of Ibadan University until he was arrested in 1967. Soyinka worked and wrote for the freedom of Biafra, a section of Nigeria, and his writings led to his imprisonment for almost two years. He details the experience in his text *The Man Died: The Prison Notes of Wole Soyinka* (1972), in the preface, of which, he says, "Books and all forms of writing have always been objects of terror to those who seek to suppress the truth."

Books were smuggled in to him while he was imprisoned. Soyinka read them ceaselessly and then wrote on these and other loose pieces of paper. In a sense, he inscribed his life in between the lines of other texts. Ultimately, the books were smuggled out, and the experience, as well as much poetry, was reconstituted. Some of the poetry can now be read in collections such as *A Shuttle in the Crypt* (1972). Soyinka's act of writing himself into existence within an unforgiving environment, using whatever materials were available, is an apt metaphor for how he has dealt with the legacy of colonialism in Nigeria. Like his countryman Chinua ACHEBE, Soyinka draws on his cultural inheritance to make sense of the postcolonial world he inhabits.

He has written several autobiographical books that also portray Nigeria from the 1940s to the 1960s. Soyinka depicts his coming of age in *Ake: The Years of Childhood* (1981) and his early adulthood in *Ibadan, The Penkelemes Years, A Memoir: 1946–1965* (1994).

Critical Analysis

In his play, *Death and the King's Horseman* (1975), Soyinka depicts a proud Yoruba leader who must make an impossible choice. His king has died, and he is expected to will himself to death and follow his king. A colonial administrator imprisons the king's "horseman" (a form of commander, and a very revered position), and the Yoruba takes this interference as a sign that his gods do not wish him to die. But the very people who had worshiped him now shun and insult the once-renowned warrior. In the most affecting portion of the play, the protagonist, Olori Elesin, sways and becomes one with the rhythmic pulse of the drums as they beat him on his way to the welcome embrace of eternity. Elesin's death is sad, yet honorable, even magnificent. His gesture is not futile—he does not act out of personal pride or desperation—rather, his embrace of this appropriate end fulfills the proper Yoruba tradition and leaves an honorable legacy.

Soyinka adapted the historical events of a 1946 incident to ground his play, but it is important to note that he refuses the label of a "clash of cultures" for his representations of such events. In much the same way that he inscribed himself into books while in prison, he takes the historical reality of colonialism and "writes" himself and his people into it. In this way, he examines the legacies left to his country while still insisting on the cultural vigor of his own people. Further, this form of writing his people into European versions of history allows Soyinka to avoid merely politicizing in favor of a joyous embrace of the power of theater itself.

Many of his plays deal with political themes. For example, *Madmen and Specialists* (1975) is set during the civil war in Nigeria in the 1960s and depicts the struggle between an interrogator and his prisoner.

Soyinka's poetry also deals with political subjects, but it is also often concerned with everyday Nigerian existence. For example, in the poem "Telephone Conversation," from the collection *Reflections* (1980), the speaker of the poem tries to entice a young woman into a date. The young woman wants to know just how dark, how "black" he is before she will agree. The young man simply wants her to see him for herself.

Soyinka's political thought is best viewed in his collection of essays, *The Open Sore of a Continent* (1996), which examines Nigeria's descent into turmoil in the 1990s. His outspoken criticism of the government led to a death sentence on the now-exiled writer.

It would be difficult to overstate the importance of Wole Soyinka to world literature. He was the first black African to win the Nobel Prize for literature (1986) and has a dazzling variety of texts that point to his prolific ability and his immense versatility.

Other Works by Wole Soyinka

Idanre and Other Poems. New York: Hill and Wang, 1967.

Madmen and Specialists. New York: Hill and Wang, 1971.

Myth, Literature, and the African World. Cambridge, U.K.: Cambridge University Press, 1976.

Works about Wole Soyinka

Katrak, Ketu. *Wole Soyinka and Modern Tragedy: A Study of Dramatic Theory and Practice.* Westport, Conn.: Greenwood Press, 1986.

Wright, Derek. *Wole Soyinka Revisited.* Boston: Twayne, 1993.

Sri Sri (Srirangam Rao Srinivasa)
(1910–1983) *poet, novelist*

Sri Sri was born in Vishakapatnam, Andhra Pradesh, India. After finishing his education in Madras, he became a subeditor for a daily newspaper and also worked for All India Radio. He wrote his first poem when he was seven and his first novel when he was nine.

Sri Sri is best noted for his radical attempts to use literature for social critique. His poetry is stylistically uncomplicated and composed of simple vocabulary, a trademark of "progressive poetry," a new school of Telugu poetry that Srinivasa started in the mid–1950s. The new movement attracted young writers because of its aim to change the style, content, and mythical and religious topics of traditional Telugu poetry. These poets were often called the militant young poets of Telugu literature. Their poetry characteristically resisted any romanticization and, instead, was concerned with reform and progress.

Sri Sri wrote creative, journalistic, and critical works that were collected into a six-volume anthology in Telugu titled *Sri Sri Sahityamu* (1972). The difference in genre, however, did not change the thematic kernel of his writing, which is to uncover the reasons for social inequalities. The poem "Hogwash" is a list of questions, posed to an imaginary "Sir." The speaker of the poem refuses to believe that the other man's economic privilege is a product of his own "illusion." Rejecting silence, he asks: the landlord's / Rolls Royce, / an illusion? / the prince's / fat wallet, / an illusion? / Sir / how can it be?

Sri Sri's contribution to Telugu literature was not only his original work. Profoundly influenced by dadaism (see DADA) and surrealism, he translated the works of Charles BAUDELAIRE (1821–61), André BRETON (1896–1966), and Salvador Dalí (1904–89) into Telugu. In 1966, Sri Sri was awarded the Lenin Peace Prize for his collection of poems called *Creation by the Sword*. In 1970, he became the first president of the Revolutionary Writers' Association of India.

Another Work by Sri Sri

Mahaprasthanam. Machilipatnam, India: Nalini Kumar Publishing House, 1950.

A Work about Sri Sri

Dharwadker, Vinay, and A. K. Ramanujan, eds. *The Oxford Anthology of Modern Indian Poetry.* London: Oxford University Press, 1994.

Srivastav, Dhanipat Rai

See PREMCHAND, MUNSHI.

Staël, Germaine de (Anna Louise Germaine Necker, Baronne de Staël-Holstein) (1766–1877) *novelist*

Anna Louise Germaine Necker was born in Paris to Swiss parents active in contemporary political and intellectual life. As a young child, she was tutored privately in her home and spent much time attending her mother's celebrated intellectual salon, where she had the opportunity to become acquainted with such leading intellectual figures as Edward Gibbon and Denis Diderot. As finance minister to Louis XVI, her father, Jacques Necker, directly experienced the turmoil of the revolution of 1789. He was a major influence on his daughter.

At age 20, Mademoiselle Necker married a Swedish diplomat, Baron Staël-Holstein. The baron was 17 years older than she and, though a titled nobleman, penniless. She supported the moderates during the revolution, but when her life was threatened, she fled to England and helped others escape the terror. Her major work on the revolution, *Considerations sur la Révolution Française* (*Thoughts on the French Revolution*), was not published until after her death. When she returned to Paris, her home became an intellectual and political salon of great power where writers, critics, and other artists gathered together to discuss not only politics and literature but also fashion trends and the development of social manners and customs. Although Staël and her husband separated in 1797, they remained on friendly terms.

Critical Analysis

Staël was a writer from a very young age. Influenced by Jean-Jacques Rousseau, she published the short stories "Mirza" and "Zulma" in 1795. Among the issues raised in these stories are the difficulties of being a writer when women were increasingly confined to a domestic role and the iniquities of the slave trade. In 1796, she published the major treatise *De l'influence des passions* (*On the Influence of the Passions*), following it in 1800 with *De la littérature* (*On Literature*). This work, which relates literature to social and political structures, transformed literary theory and founded comparative studies.

In 1794, Staël became romantically and intellectually involved with Benjamin CONSTANT, whose ideas were a great source of inspiration to her. Under his influence, she began to read the works of August Wilhelm SCHLEGEL (1767–1845) and his brother Friedrich (1772–1829) and dared to oppose Napoleon's policies.

Staël's first major novel, *Delphine* (1802), gained her attention both popularly and politically. Following the release of a nonfiction study of the effects of social conditions on literature, the novel is a politically challenging look at the destiny of women in a male-dominated, aristocratic society. Above all, the work questions the accepted norms of society as they pertain to the rights of women as intellectually independent people. Staël denied allegations that her work was intended to provoke a political response, claiming to be more intent on observations of fact than on causing open opposition to the norm. Napoleon, however, considered the work such a threat to the traditions of French society that he exiled Staël in 1803.

Staël retreated to Coppet on Lake Geneva, where she had an estate. There, she surrounded herself with a circle of highly influential and intelligent friends and associates. She traveled as much as possible, and a trip to Italy provided her with the inspiration for her second major novel, *Corinne* (1807). This work strips away all of the trappings of neoclassicism to express itself fully in the style of French ROMANTICISM. It is a tragic love story about an Italian woman, an intellectual, who falls for an English lord. The novel challenges, once again, the accepted norms for women in society—its main character, Corinne, is a celebrated poet, who ultimately loses her lover because he desires a less complex and more domestic partner. Other early feminist themes pervade the text as well, such as the rights of women to chose whom to love and to be intellectuals. These themes are developed alongside descriptions of Italy's artistic and architectural beauty and of evocations of the ideal of individual freedom not hampered by gender or class. The novel stands as one of Staël's most influential works, affecting not only the development of the French novel but also literary trends in England and the United States.

Staël's principal theoretical work, *De l'Allemagne* (*On Germany*, 1810) was also the result of her travels. It again brought her to Napoleon's attention. Although government censors did not see the book as a threat, Napoleon disliked it because he resented the comparisons Staël made between French and German cultures to the detriment of the French. In 1811, he ordered the destruction of the entire first edition, stating that it had no business being published in the first place because it was "un-French." Several copies of the book escaped destruction, however, and made their way to England, where they were published in a new edition and were well received. *De l'Allemagne* introduced German Romantic literature and idealist philosophy into France and was a major influence on the French Romantic movement.

In 1811, after a series of affairs with influential men, de Staël secretly married a young officer nearly half her age, Jean Rocca. Together they had one child, a boy, who was born mentally retarded. By this time, Staël had two other children, a boy fathered by a revolutionary whom she had helped escape to England in 1793 and a daughter, most probably fathered by Constant. Harassed repeatedly by the police, Staël exiled herself and her family, fleeing to Russia and then to England.

In 1815, Staël returned to Coppet and republished *De l'Allemagne*. Although her health was declining rapidly, she enthusiastically participated in the political life of France and, in spite of her long-standing history of problems with Napoleon, warned him of a threat that had been made on his life.

Staël suffered a stroke on July 14, and died in Paris. One of her best-known works, *Ten Years of Exile* (1821), which was largely autobiographical, was published posthumously.

Another Work by Germaine de Staël

An Extraordinary Woman: Selected Writings of Germaine de Staël. Translated by Vivian Folkenflik. New York: Columbia University Press, 1987.

Works about Germaine de Staël

Besser, Gretchen Rous. *Germaine de Staël Revisited.* Boston: Twayne, 1994.

Hogsett, Charlotte. *The Literary Existence of Germaine de Staël.* Carbondale: Southern Illinois University Press, 1987.

Stead, Christina (1902–1983) *novelist, short-story writer*

Christina Stead was the child of English parents who immigrated to Rockdale, New Sydney, Australia, where she was born. After the death of her mother, Ellen Butters Stead, when Christina was two years old, she was raised and influenced by her father, David George Stead, a naturalist who worked as an economist for the Australian fisheries. When her father remarried Ada Gibbons, Stead was expected to help care for the six children whom their marriage produced. She received her education in Sydney, graduating from Sydney University Teacher's College in 1922. After working for a short time at the university as a demonstrator in experimental psychology and then in Sydney Schools as a teacher of abnormal children, Stead became a secretary until she decided to leave Australia in 1928, working as a clerk first in London and then in Paris.

During her years in Europe, Stead began writing fiction, producing a collection of rather bizarre short stories, *Salzburg Tales* (1934), and a novel, *Seven Poor Men of Sydney* (1934). Soon after this, she met William Blake, an American financier, writer, economist, and socialist, whom she eventually married in 1952 and lived with until his death in 1968. Stead and Blake lived in Spain until the threat of civil war and then moved to the United States, living in New York and then Hollywood, where Stead worked as a screenwriter for MGM during World War II. They returned to Europe after the war, living in various countries until Blake's death. Stead finally returned to Australia in 1974, where she lived and wrote until her own death.

Although Christina Stead is the author of numerous novels and several collections of short stories, she is best known for her brilliant portrayal of a dysfunctional family in *The Man Who Loved Children* (1940). Loosely based on the lives and relationships of her father and her stepmother and their children, including herself, the novel depicts Sam and Hetty Pollit, each of whom seems unable to speak in a language that the other understands, so they employ their children as their means of communication, having them convey messages and carry notes back and forth between their parents. Also suffering from economic reversals after the death of Hetty's wealthy father, the family's struggles with angry creditors, Sam's passivity when it comes to fighting to keep his government job, Hetty's unwanted sixth pregnancy, the stepdaughter Louisa's defiance of her father, and an anonymous false accusation Sam receives that the baby is not really his, the family is unable to survive the passionate destructiveness and selfishness of the parents, whose battles become physical and life threatening. Louisa, who longs to save the children from their parents, wants to kill them both but manages to poison only Hetty, who actually realizes what is happening and thus chooses it as well. Sam, however, cannot believe that Louisa is indeed responsible for his wife's death, and Louisa is finally driven to escape from her father to survive. Stead's success in capturing the psychological truths of each character and the vividness with which she conveys their animosity has made *The Man Who Loved Children* a memorable book for which she has received the most acclaim, especially after its reissue in 1965 by an American publisher.

Another Work by Christina Stead

Letty Fox: Her Luck. New York: New York Review of Books, 2001.

Works about Christina Stead

Rowley, Hazel. *Christina Stead: A Biography.* New York: Henry Holt & Company, 1995.

Sheridan, Susan. *Christina Stead.* Bloomington: Indiana University Press, 1988.

Stendhal (Marie-Henri Beyle)

(1783–1842) *novelist, essayist*

Best known for his two masterpieces, *Le Rouge et le noir* (*The Red and the Black,* 1830) and *La Chartreuse de Parme* (*The Charterhouse of Parma,* 1839), Stendhal was born as Marie-Henri Beyle in Grenoble to a wealthy lawyer. His mother passed away in childbirth when Stendhal was very young. At age 16, he moved to Paris ostensibly to study, but he entered the military before ultimately settling on a career as a writer.

Stendhal enlisted in Napoleon's army in May 1800 and served for 18 months as a lieutenant, fighting in Russia, Germany, and Italy. His dreams, however, were not centered on achieving military accolades; he hoped to become one of the greatest comic poets of all time. When he resigned from active service, he took a post in civil and military administration, which he held until the fall of the French empire in 1814. At that point, he was given a 50 percent pay cut, making his income inadequate to his needs. He searched for other employment for several years but was unable to secure anything in France. Ultimately, he decided to move to Italy, where his first book, a travel piece entitled *Rome, Naples, and Florence in 1817* (1817), was published. This was also the first time he chose to use the penname of Stendhal.

Stendhal returned to Paris in 1821, taking advantage of his success as a writer and the steadily improving conditions in France. He frequented salons where he could discuss the latest ideas on art, literature, and politics. He continued to do well as a writer, publishing *On Love* (1822) and *Racine and Shakespeare* (1823) in quick succession. *On Love,* a psychology of love, is a collection of thoughts and ideas that show Stendhal as an early sympathizer, particularly with regard to his feelings on women's education. *Racine and Shakespeare* is an important romantic manifesto that insists that literature should reflect its historical moment. These works were well received, but his first novel, *Armance* (1827), a psychological study of impotence, was scorned by the critics.

Critical Analysis

The Red and the Black was a breakthrough for Stendhal. Inspired by a newspaper account of the trial of a young man for attempted murder of a married woman, it advanced the development of the novel in its complex and ironic interweaving of the psychological and the historical. It tells the story of Julien Sorel, a peasant, in the context of the post-Napoleonic period between 1815 and 1830. Sorel uses seduction and hypocrisy to rise in society, but believing that his mistress has betrayed him, he shoots the one woman he ever really loved. Finally, he rejects his lies and masks and, a condemned man, stands before the court to attack social inequality and oppression:

> Gentlemen, I have not the honour to belong to your social class. You see in me a peasant in revolt against the baseness of his fate. . . . I see men who would like in my person to punish and dishearten for ever that class of young people who, born in a lowly and poverty-stricken class, had the chance to educate themselves and the courage to associate with those circles which arrogance of the rich calls society. . . .

After the revolution of 1830 and the rise to power of King Louis-Philippe, Stendhal was appointed French consul in the small Italian port town of Civitavecchia. While there, he wrote *Memoirs of an Egoist,* (published 1892), in which he provides a vivid depiction of life in and among the salons, museums, and theatres of Paris. This work, along with two others, *Lucien Leuwen: The Green Huntsman,* which depicts the corruption under the reign of Louis-Philippe, and the largely autobiographical piece *The Life of Henry Brulard,* which was left unfinished, remained in manuscript at Stendhal's death, but were published in the 1890s.

Stendhal's political views were often motivated by his own success or failure under a prevailing regime. If he was doing poorly, he tended to mock and criticize the ruling body for his lack of success. However, as soon as he began to thrive, his views shifted and he became moderately conservative. He composed his second great work, *The Charterhouse of Parma* between 1836 and 1839, which is concerned with a search for identity. The protagonist, Fabrizio del Dongo, defines himself in areas as diverse as the battlefield at Waterloo and a Carthusian monastery. He experiences the frustrations of war, politics, love, and the loss of his child. He finally withdraws to the Charterhouse of Parma, where he dies. The work was published to great acclaim, rapidly gaining popularity, and critical success.

The Charterhouse of Parma was destined to be Stendhal's last major accomplishment. In 1841 he suffered a stroke, which forced him to take a leave of absence from his post and return to Paris. Late in the evening of March 22, Stendhal was taking a walk down a Paris street when he collapsed, unconscious, to the ground. He died a few hours later on March 23.

Another Work by Stendhal

Lamiel, or The Ways of the Heart. Translated by Jacques Le Clercq. New York: H. Fertig, 1978.

Works about Stendhal

Keates, Jonathan. *Stendhal.* London: Sinclair-Stevenson, 1994.

Pearson, Roger. *Stendhal's Violin: A Novelist and His Reader.* New York: Oxford University Press, 1992.

Talbot, Emile J. *Stendhal Revisited.* Boston: Twayne, 1993.

Storni, Alfonsina (Alfonsina Tao-Lao)
(1892–1938) *poet, dramatist, journalist*

Alfonsina Storni was born in Sala Capriasca, Switzerland, and moved with her cultured Italian-Swiss parents to Argentina at the age of four. When her father died in 1900, she was obligated to work in a cap factory, as an actress, and later as a schoolteacher. Her first poems were published in 1910, the year she moved to Buenos Aires. In 1911, she gave birth to an illegitimate child and later worked as a journalist and a teacher to support herself and her son.

Storni's first book of poems, *The Restlessness of the Rose Bush,* appeared in 1916, and her poetry between 1916 and 1921 reflects an intense romantic subjectivity. Her poetry was well received—in 1920, she won First Municipal Poetry Prize and Second National Poetry Prize.

By 1925, Storni's poetry was becoming more objective, as reflected in *Ochre* (1925), which focuses on the sea, and in *World of Seven Wells* (1934). Between 1926 and 1934, many of her plays were performed in theaters in Buenos Aires. During this period, she also authored, under the pseudonym Tao-Lao, various critical articles that appeared in the newspaper *La Nación.*

Her last books of poems, *Magnetized Circles* (1938) and *Mask and Trefoil* (1938), reflect her cynicism, her feminist rebelliousness, and her powerful language. By then, Storni had been dealing with breast cancer for three years, and when the cancer returned in 1938, she chose to commit suicide by filling her pockets with stones and drowning herself in the sea at Mar del Plata. She sent her final poem, "I Want to Sleep," now considered to be a suicide poem, to *La Nación* so that it would be received at the same time she entered the sea.

Another Work by Alfonsina Storni

Selected Poems of Alfonsina Storni. Translated by Mary Crow and Norman Ton. Fredonia, N.Y.: White Pine Press, Inc., 1996.

A Work about Alfonsina Storni

Phillips, Rachel. *Alfonsina Storni: From Poetess to Poet.* United Kingdom: Boydell & Brewer, Inc., 1975.

Strindberg, August (1849–1912)

playwright, short-story writer, novelist

August Strindberg was born in Stockholm, Sweden, to Carl Oscar Strindberg, a shipping agent, and Ulrika Eleanora Norling, a woman of working-class origins. Norling had been Carl Oscar's domestic servant but later became his mistress and mother to August. Strindberg's childhood was quite unhappy: He experienced the loss of his mother at age 13, endured poverty and family conflicts, and suffered abuse from his stepmother.

In 1867, Srindberg entered the University of Uppsala but failed to pass a preliminary examination in chemistry and had to leave. He worked at the Royal Dramatic Theater as an assistant manager and then returned to the University of Uppsala, where he finally received his degree in 1872. On graduation, Strindberg worked in Stockholm as a journalist and, from 1864 to 1882, served as an assistant librarian at the Royal Library.

Strindberg was married three times. His first, unsuccessful marriage was to the Baroness Siri von Essen, a member of the Swedish aristocracy in Finland, with whom he had three children. He married a second time in 1893 and a third time in 1901. These unions also ended in divorce, and he lost custody of his children.

Strindberg's first nationally successful novel, *The Red Room* (1879), focuses on the rise of industrialism in Sweden. The protagonist of the novel, Arvid Falk, is an aspiring youth who dreams of becoming a writer. Although he is talented, Falk rejects the uncertainties of a writer's life for a stable middle-class existence. Strindberg suggests that it is almost impossible to devote ones life to aesthetic pursuits in a world controlled by capitalistic values. The novel was popular throughout Sweden and established Strindberg as one of the foremost writers of Scandinavian literature.

During the years between 1883 and 1887, while living in France and Switzerland, Strindberg faced financial troubles and found himself on the verge of a nervous breakdown. This psychological imbalance culminated in clinical paranoia and a dependence on absinthe, a liquor made from wormwood. In 1884, Strindberg published *Getting Married*, a novel based on his experience during marriage. This frank portrayal of the institution of marriage outraged many in Sweden. Strindberg was put on trial charged with blasphemy, but he was eventually acquitted. He developed a deep distrust of women, whom he saw as persecutors, and believed that his wife was behind a plot to have him committed to a mental institution.

Critical Analysis

Strindberg's most famous play, *Miss Julie* (1888), was also one of his most controversial works. Julie, the daughter of a prosperous count, allows Jean, a male servant, to seduce her during a night of festivities. Jean understands that marriage between him and Julie is impossible. Fearing for his position, Jean psychologically corners Julie, and she commits suicide. *Miss Julie* combines the elements of NATURALISM and REALISM that made it a masterpiece. It depicts a Darwinian struggle between the sexes that is further amplified by the respective social roles and positions of the two main characters. Many critics have compared *Miss Julie* to Henrik IBSEN's *A Doll's House*. Both plays are classified as works of realism, but the representations of femininity found in the two plays are strikingly different. Julie is ultimately dominated by Jean, while Nora, even in defeat, is dominated by no one. Today, *Miss Julie* is Strindberg's most frequently performed play.

Between 1892 and 1897, Strindberg experienced one mental crisis after another. Constantly under attack by critics, and haunted by the guilt of loosing custody of his children, Strindberg was on a verge of a complete collapse. Still, he eventually recovered and entered the most productive period of his career. Between 1898 and 1909, Strindberg wrote 36 plays, most of which deal with life, death, and various aspects of marriage.

In a *A Dream Play* (1901), however, Strindberg breaks with the realism of the previous works. All actions are presented in the form of the thoughts, dreams, and psychological perceptions of Daughter of Indra, a mysterious, luminous figure who seemingly descends from heaven. The play seems to foreshadow the many theories of Austrian psychoanalyst Sigmund FREUD about the separation of the conscious from the unconscious and the active role of the former in the formation of the individual psyche. Most critics rejected the play as absurd, although some realized the genius of Strindberg's work.

Between 1907 and 1908, Strindberg experimented with various forms of theater. He introduced chamber music as part of his plays, and he exchanged the traditional single protagonist for a small group of equally important characters. These and other innovations had a long-lasting and dramatic influence on traditional conceptions of theater.

During his life, August Strindberg wrote more than 70 plays in addition to numerous novels, short stories, and essays. Today, he is considered to be among the most influential playwrights and theoreticians of the modern period. The controversial subjects of his plays challenged audiences to question what was suitable for theater and how plays should be performed. Strindberg's works have been the single most important source of inspiration for the German EXPRESSIONIST movement and for many contemporary playwrights as well.

Other Works by August Strindberg

Five Plays. Translated by Harry Carlson. Riverside: University of California Press, 1996.

Inferno and from Occult Diary. New York: Penguin, 1988.

Miss Julie and Other Plays. Oxford: Oxford University Press, 1999.

Works about August Strindberg

Lagercrantz, Olaf. *August Strindberg.* New York: Farrar, Straus, & Giroux, 1984.

Meyer, Michael. *Strindberg: A Biography.* Oxford: Oxford University Press, 1987.

Suleri, Sara (1953–) *novelist, critic*

Sara Suleri was born in Karachi, Pakistan. Her father, Ziauddin Ahmed, is Pakistani and an active political journalist. Her mother, Mair Jones, is Welsh and a professor of English literature. Suleri completed her master's degree at Punjab University and went on to Indiana University, where she received her doctorate degree in English in 1980. She became a professor at Yale University in 1981 and is the founder and editor of the *Yale Journal of Criticism.*

Her first novel, *Meatless Days* (1989), has several obvious similarities to her own life and is claimed by many critics to be an autobiographical memoir, though the author herself denies it. The narrator of the novel searches for her identity as it changes in time, memory, and space. Moving between Asia and America, the narrator depicts with longing what can be lost in transformations through cultural exchange and remembered relationships. Her search for her own identity, however, underlies the equally important search for Indian and Pakistani female identity in a history that has silenced them. *Meatless Days* is a personalized narrative on the search for women's presence and their voices.

Suleri is also the author of the critically distinguished work *The Rhetoric of English India* (1992). This book looks into the formation of colonial and postcolonial India and Pakistan through the English language by examining the works of authors such as Rudyard Kipling (1865–1936), E. M. Forster (1879–1970), V. S. NAIPAUL, and Salman RUSHDIE.

A Work about Sara Suleri

Smith, Sidonie, and Watson, Julia, eds. "Women Skin Deep: Feminism and the Postcolonial Condition." In *Women, Autobiography, Theory: A Reader.* Madison: University of Wisconsin Press, 1998.

Svevo, Italo (Ettore Schmitz) (1861–1928) *novelist, short-story writer*

Considered one of the pioneers of the Italian psychological novel, Italo Svevo was born Ettore Schmitz in the town of Trieste, then part of the

Austrian Empire. The son of a German Jewish glassmaker and his Italian wife, Svevo was sent to Germany at age 12 to attend boarding school. He later returned to Trieste to continue his education, which was abruptly terminated when he was in his late teens as a result of his father's failure in business. Svevo took a position as a clerk but continued to spend much of his free time reading and, ultimately, writing as well.

Svevo published his first novel, *Una Vita* (*A Life,* 1892), when he was 31 years old, using his pseudonym for the first time. The work gained attention immediately for its revolutionary introspective, analytic style. Svevo continued to publish works in this style, which were later classified as psychological novels; at the time, however, the newness of his tone made his works difficult to comprehend, resulting in their being ignored by critics once their curiosity wore off. Svevo's second novel, *As a Man Grows Older* (1898), received a similar lack of attention, at which point he officially gave up writing to pursue a career in his father-in-law's business. (He continued to write short stories throughout this period.)

Svevo's business career required him to travel, and many of his trips were to England. To improve his command of English, he employed as a tutor the young writer James Joyce, who was living in Trieste and teaching at the Berlitz school. In spite of their age difference, they rapidly forged an enduring friendship. Joyce allowed Svevo to read portions of his work in progress, *Dubliners,* and, in his turn, Svevo gave Joyce both of his novels to read. Joyce found the works to be enthralling and encouraged Svevo to resume his writing endeavors. As a result, his best-known work, *La Coscienza di Zeno* (*Confessions of Zeno,* 1923), was published. Written in the first person, it represents an attempt by the narrator to discover through analysis the source of his nicotine addiction. Again, the work was ignored, but two years after publication, Joyce arranged for publication of a French translation. Svevo became famous in France, and his popularity slowly grew in Italy, helped by the support of Eugenio MONTALE, as the psychological novel gained acceptance.

Svevo was in the process of working on a sequel to *Zeno* when he was killed in an automobile accident on September 13. His contribution to Italian literature, however, included a stream-of-consciousness style, which was present in both *Zeno* and several posthumously published short stories, as well as his advancement of the genre of the psychological novel in Italy.

Another Work by Italo Svevo
Emilio's Carnival (Senilità). Translated by Beth Archer Brombert. New Haven, Conn.: Yale University Press, 2001.

Works about Italo Svevo
Gatt-Rutter, John. *Italo Svevo: A Double Life.* Oxford: Clarendon Press, 1988.

Svevo, Livia Veneziani. *Memoir of Italo Svevo.* Translated by Isabel Quigly. London: Libris, 1989.

Weiss, Beno. *Italo Svevo.* Boston: Twayne, 1988.

symbolism
Predominant in France at the end of the 19th century, and evident in Belgium as well, the symbolist movement, strongly influenced by Charles BAUDELAIRE's essays on poetry and art, originated with the work of a group of French poets, including Paul VERLAINE, Stéphane MALLARMÉ, and Arthur RIMBAUD. It reached its peak around 1890, and the principles on which it was founded continued to influence MODERNIST movements of the early 20th century.

Symbolism began as a reaction against the prevailing literary trends of REALISM and NATURALISM. Because of the tendency of symbolist poets to focus on the artificial and grotesque as opposed to the natural, as well as their common thematic use of ruin and decay, the writers of this movement were also commonly associated with the subsequently emerging DECADENT movement.

Beginning in the 1830s, realism became the dominant form of literary expression in France. It was later followed by the similar but revised naturalist movement. Both schools of thought based their works entirely on factual observations of contemporary society and sought to portray life without glamorization or pretense. Toward the end of the century, particularly in Paris, symbolists began to challenge this style, believing that words and language as they currently existed were superficial. Therefore, they declared that to represent and transform the reality of modern life, the poet must recreate language. Through the use of symbols, poets could create patterns of meanings based on symbolic representation and allusion rather than direct statement. The symbolists affirmed the transcendent possibilities of the imagination.

There are a number of specific themes common to symbolist poetry, but the main focus is on the difficult role of the poet in modern urban life. The symbolist poets shared with the decadents a common FIN DE SIÈCLE sense of brooding melancholy and darkness.

Early symbolists experimented with form, resulting in the development of poetic free verse, poetry that, whether rhymed or unrhymed, disregards conventional rules regarding poetic meter. It often borrows patterns from natural speech in place of the more affected diction common to traditional poetry. This form is still the prevailing standard in modern poetry.

Another technique, which has existed since Homer but was exploited especially by French symbolists, is synesthesia, describing one sensation in terms of another (for example, describing sound with colors). Symbolist poets used synesthesia as a means of uncovering the correspondences between different sensory impressions, as in Baudelaire's famous "Correspondances" from *Les Fleurs du mal* (*The Flowers of Evil*, 1857).

While the symbolist movement had its origins in poetry, its influence eventually began to extend to fiction, drama, music, and the visual arts. The prominent members of the school, such as Rimbaud, Verlaine, and Mallarmé, can all trace their influence to the works of Charles Baudelaire, who was conversely influenced by Edgar Allan Poe, as their precursor; in turn, they influenced the writings of Paul CLAUDEL, Paul VALÉRY, Maurice MAETERLINCK, and others. Similar movements arose outside of France, and symbolism's effects reached as far as the United States in the works of writers such as Dylan Thomas and e.e. Cummings.

Russian Symbolism

Symbolism began in Russia a little later than in France and flourished until the Russian Revolution (1917). Deeply rooted themselves in mysticism, the Russian symbolists viewed themselves as a nexus between the Russian people and some higher spiritual realm. Like its French counterpart, Russian symbolism manifested itself in drama, poetry, prose, and graphic art; however, it achieved its full force almost exclusively in poetry. Like their French models, the Russian symbolists experimented with verse forms and especially with free verse.

The symbolists rejected realist notions about the social purposes of art. For the symbolists, the artist was a semidivine figure whose work would guide the Russian people to an ideal future. Symbolists often viewed the imagination as a different level of reality, and they used obscure images and strange metaphors to convey their feelings of detachment from the reality of everyday life.

Aleksandr Blok, Vladimir SOLOVYOV, and Andrey BELY were the leading figures of symbolism in Russia, but it is Solovyov who is considered the most important originator of the movement in Russia. Solovyov created a new form of mysticism based on the worship of the Eternal Feminine, dually identified as nature and as the muse that endowed poets with inspiration. Solovyov's work was the single most important foundation for the Russian symbolist movement.

The symbolist movement served an extremely important function in Russian literary history by bridging the gap between realism and ACMEISM. Although poets such as Anna AKHMATOVA later rejected symbolism, the movement was an extremely important early influence on her generation of poets and on later generations as well.

Works about Symbolism

Fowlie, Wallace. *Poem and Symbol: A Brief History of French Symbolism.* University Park: Pennsylvania State University Press, 1990.

Frantisek, Deak. *Symbolist Theater: The Formation of an Avant-garde.* Baltimore: Johns Hopkins University Press, 1993.

McGuinness, Patrick, ed. *Symbolism, Decadence and the Fin de Siècle: French and European Perspectives.* Exeter, U.K.: University of Exeter Press, 2000.

Pyman, Avril. *A History of Russian Symbolism.* New York: Cambridge University Press, 1994.

Szymborska, Wislawa (1923–) *poet*

Wislawa Szymborska was born in Bnin, now a part of Kornik, in western Poland. In 1931, she moved with her family to Krakow where, during the German occupation of Poland in World War II, she attended classes illegally. After the war, she studied Polish literature and sociology at the Jagiellonian University. She worked as a poetry editor and columnist for the Krakow literary magazine *Zycie Literacia* until 1981.

Szymborska's first published poem was "Szukam slowa" ("I Am Looking for a Word," 1945). She finished her first collection of poetry three years later, but the Communist Party's strict cultural policy deemed the work to be too complex, and it was not published. As a result, Szymborska concentrated on making her work more political, and her first collection, *Dlagtego Zyjemy,* appeared in 1952.

Szymborska's early works conformed to the style of SOCIALIST REALISM. Later, she became disillusioned with Communism and expressed her pessimism about humanity's future in her poems. Her 1996 poem "Tortures," with the line "Nothing has changed" that opens each stanza, connects the cruelties of the 20th century with the entire human experience over the ages: "Tortures are as they were, it's just the earth that's grown smaller."

In 1996, Szymborska won the Nobel Prize in literature "for poetry that with ironic precision allows the historical and biological context to come to light in fragments of human reality" (Nobel Lectures). She is one of the few female poets ever to have received this prize. Szymborska has published 16 collections of poetry. Her poems have been translated into numerous languages and have also been published in multiple anthologies of Polish poetry.

A private person by nature, Szymborska avoided public appearances but served as an inspiration for other female writers. In her acceptance speech for the Nobel Prize, she described her role not only as an artist but as a member of a larger humanity: ". . . inspiration is not the exclusive privilege of poets or artists generally. There is, has been, and will always be a certain group of people whom inspiration visits. It's made up of all those who've consciously chosen their calling and do their job with love and imagination. . . . Whatever inspiration is, it's born from a continuous 'I don't know.'" (Nobel Lecture, 1996)

Other Works by Wislawa Szymborska

Miracle Fair: Selected Poems of Wislawa Szymborska. Translated by Joanna Trzeciak. New York: Norton, 2001.

Poems New and Collected. Translated by Stanislaw Baranczak and Clare Cavanagh. Orlando, Fla.: Harcourt Brace, 1998.

Tagore, Rabindranath (Rabindranath Thakur) (1861–1941) *poet, novelist, dramatist, essayist*

Rabindranath Tagore was born in Calcutta, India, into an affluent family that was also very invested in Indian politics. His great-grandfather Dwarkanath Tagore was a businessman; Tagore's father, Debendranath Tagore, however, was more involved in religion than in politics and revived an old religious movement called the Brahmo Samaj. Rabindranath Tagore combined his grandfather's visions for the country with his father's religious asceticism, and his works, therefore, represent a unique synthesis of powerful national politics and spiritual poeticism. Tagore is the author and composer of India's national anthem, as well as the lyrical composer of a song by Bankim CHATTOPADHYAY called "Vande Materam" (Hail Motherland), which was adopted as India's unofficial national anthem during its problems before independence from British rule.

In his memoir *My Reminiscences* (1911), Tagore calls his memory a "picture-chamber . . . a series of pictures [which] correspond, but are not identical." A pioneer in integrating East–West poetic, political, and even scientific structures, Tagore is one of the key figures in the intellectual movement called the Bengal renaissance. The Bengal renaissance consisted of a group of writers who took advantage of colonial education and Western culture while at the same time contributing to Indian literature for an Indian audience.

This attitude reflected Tagore's own belief that education is interdisciplinary, bringing together science with humanism and politics with spirituality, and it was realized in the foundation of Shantiniketan (Abode of Peace), a school on the outskirts of Calcutta. This place, under the guidance of Tagore, who also taught there, grew into a meeting place for national and international scholars of music, painting, singing, and languages. Today, it thrives as one of West Bengal's prominent educational institutions.

In 1921, Tagore also founded Shriniketan (Abode of Plenty), a school that sought to bring Western scientific progress to India. At the same time, the preservation of nature was very important to Tagore, and this was enhanced by the foundation of Shriniketan, whose objective was to bring agricultural progress to the countryside. Tagore's works reflect his deep concern and respect for nature, and the need to bridge the gap between human and natural existence. In one of his letters he says that "I feel . . . I was one with the rest of the earth, that grass grew green upon me, that the autumn sun fell on me and its rays . . . wafted from every pore of my far-flung evergreen body." This is one of the most important themes in his poetry.

Tagore translated many of his own works into English. With the aid of W. B. Yeats and Thomas Sturge Moore, he brought out a translation of his religious and spiritual poetry called *Gitañjalī* (*Offering of Songs,* 1910). They were a huge success, and their publication caught the attention of renowned figures such as Albert Einstein, Ezra Pound, and André GIDE, with whom Tagore kept up regular correspondences. Their admiration of his work secured Tagore's position as an international poet. *Gitañjalī* borrows from India's ancient and traditional religious poetry. Written from a modern perspective, these poems take a new look at the conventional understanding of the relationships between nature, God, and spirituality. In these poems, the search for human spirituality goes beyond traditional religion.

Tagore's most famous novel, *The Home and the World* (1915–16), is about rural politics, though its tone is extremely nonpolitical. As the title suggests, the novel delves into how the domestic and political realms of power overlap. In this story, the woman protagonist defies social norm by coming out of the inner rooms of the house to join the men in their discussion of politics in the living room. She also allows herself to act on the gallant advances made to her by her husband's friend. The change in friendship between the two men is complicated through the female protagonist's fluctuating romantic attachment to both men. As the two male friends become increasingly estranged due to politics, it is the woman of the home who reveals the true meaning of faithfulness, loyalty, and commitment. Her honesty and open curiosity humanizes the novel's ruthless description of rural politics, and her story stresses the importance of domestic issues in the political struggles of the outside world.

By the time of his death, Tagore was idolized as one of India's leading political figures, a national poet, a painter, and an educational visionary. He experimented with almost all literary genres and

left behind a prodigious assortment of novels, short stories, songs, poetry, plays, essays, as well as correspondence with friends, family, and international contemporaries such as W. B. Yeats and Ezra Pound. In 1913, Tagore was awarded the Nobel Prize for literature for his translation of *Gitañjalī*. In 1919, he refused England's offer of knighthood in protest against human-rights violations under British rule.

Other Works by Rabindranath Tagore

Nationalism. London: Macmillan Publishers, 1917.
Selected Poems. Translated by William Radice. London: Penguin, 1985.
The Broken Nest. Columbia: University of Missouri Press, 1971.
The Hungry Stones and Other Stories. New York: Macmillan, 1916.

A Work about Rabindranath Tagore

Kipalani, Krishan. *Rabindranath Tagore: A Biography.* London: Oxford University Press, 1962.

Takamura Kotarō (1883–1956) *poet*

Takamura Kotarō was born in Tokyo to sculptor Takamura Kōun and his wife, Waka. His father, hoping that his son would follow in his footsteps, sent Takamura to Tokyo Fine Arts School in 1897. Even so, Takamura was already demonstrating an interest in literature and had begun to write and publish haiku and tanka. In 1906, he left to study in the United States, England, and France. When he returned to Japan, he fell in with dissolute artists and writers. In 1914, he married Naganuma Chieko. During the war, he acted as the head of the Japanese Literature Patriotic Association. Takamura took defeat hard and retreated to a country cabin in Iwate Prefecture for seven years, some believe to come to terms with the guilt he expressed over having encouraged young soldiers to battle and thus their deaths.

Takamura's first poems were written in traditional poetic forms. He began to write free verse, however, when he returned to Japan. His first poem of note, "The Lost Mona Lisa," published in 1911, was about the disappearance of a prostitute. His first collection of poetry, *The Road Ahead*, published in 1914, challenged conceptions of poetry by using subjects and diction that were not traditionally considered appropriate. *Chieko's Sky*, his second collection, was published in 1941 and consisted of love poems to his wife.

Takamura always considered himself first and foremost a sculptor, but he is more highly regarded as a poet who helped redefine the landscape of modern poetry. His most significant poetry is in free verse. In particular, his love poems to his wife garner the greatest praise for their moving emotional content and for their clear expression.

Other Works by Takamura Kotarō

A Brief History of Imbecility: Poetry and Prose of Takamura Kotarō. Translated by Hiroaki Sato. Honolulu: University Press of Hawaii, 1992.

Chieko and Other Poems of Takamura Kotarō. Translated by Hiroaki Sato. Honolulu: University Press of Hawaii, 1980.

Works about Takamura Kotarō

Keene, Donald. *Dawn to the West: Japanese Literature in the Modern Era: Poetry, Drama, Criticism.* New York: Holt, Rinehart and Winston, 1984.

Rabson, Steve. *Righteous Cause or Tragic Folly: Changing Views of War in Modern Japanese Poetry.* Ann Arbor, Mich.: Center for Japanese Studies, University of Michigan, 1998.

Tanikawa Shuntaro (1931–) *poet*

Tanikawa Shuntaro was born in Tokyo, Japan, to Tanikawa Tetsuzo, a philosopher, and Tanikawa Taki (Osada), a pianist. Tanikawa began writing poetry in his teens after a high-school friend asked him to contribute to a poetry magazine. When his father asked him what he intended to do instead of entering college, Tanikawa handed him notebooks that he had filled with poems. Recognizing talent, his father gave the poems to Miyoshi

Tatsuji, Japan's leading poet at the time, who helped get them published in the *Bungakkai (Literary World)* magazine when Tanikawa was still in his teens. Tanikawa's first book collection, *Twenty Billion Light Years of Loneliness* (1952), was published when he was 21.

Tanikawa says his early work was influenced by volumes of poetry from his father's library, but his work breaks with the major traditions of Japanese verse. He does not write haiku, although his strong, startling imagery is similar to the form's vivid word pictures. In a poem entitled "Colours," he ends with this surprising image: "Despair is a simple colour / Pure white." Many of his poems allude to icons of American popular culture, such as jazz musician Miles Davis and actor James Dean. His central theme is the isolation of the individual who stands alone facing an incomprehensible universe. In "The Isolation of Two Million Light Years," he comments, "The human race, on its little ball, / Sleeps, wakes, and works, / Wishing at times for companionship with Mars."

Tanikawa is Japan's most popular poet. He has published more than 60 volumes of poetry; has written scripts for television and film, children's books, song lyrics, and plays; and has translated Charles Schultz's comic strip "Peanuts" into Japanese. He has won many Japanese literary awards as well as an American Book Award for the English translation of *Floating the River in Melancholy* (1988). According to Geoffrey O'Brien of the *Village Voice*, Tanikawa "receives praise and the kind of lavish editions reserved in America for the long deceased."

Another Work by Tanikawa Shuntaro

Shuntaro Tanikawa: Selected Poems. Translated by William I. Elliott and Kazuo Kawamura. New York: Persea Books, 2001.

A Work about Tanikawa Shuntaro

Morton, Leith. "An Interview with Shuntaro Tanikawa," *Southerly* 58, no. 1 (Autumn 1998): 6–31.

Tanizaki Jun'ichirō (1886–1965) *novelist, short-story writer, playwright, essayist*

Tanizaki Jun'ichirō was born in Tokyo to Tanizaki Kuragorō and Seki. While he was a boy, his father lost the family fortune, so when Tanizaki, a gifted student, gained entrance to the prestigious Metropolitan Middle School and the First Higher School, his family could not afford tuition. To continue his education, Tanizaki worked as a houseboy for a wealthy family until he had an affair with a maid and was dismissed. In 1908, he entered the Japanese literature department of Tokyo Imperial University but was expelled for failing to pay his fees. In 1915, he married Ishikawa Chiyo, whom he divorced 15 years later. He quickly married reporter Furukawa Tomiko. However, this marriage lasted less than a year because he had begun to court another woman, Nezu Matsuko, whom he eventually married.

While attending university, Tanizaki published his first short story, "The Tatooer" (1910), which won the acclaim of critics. It was not until 1924 that Tanizaki produced his first novel, *Naomi,* which depicts a man who makes an ill-fated attempt to turn his lover into a Western woman. Five years later, Tanizaki's focus shifted to traditional Japan in his novel *Some Prefer Nettles* (1929). In 1933 he crafted a chilling masterpiece, "The Story of Shunkin," a short story about a servant who blinds himself to preserve in his mind the image of his mistress, who has become disfigured in an attack.

During the war years, Tanizaki worked on his most lyrical novel, *The Makioka Sisters* (1948). In the last year of his life, he published *Diary of a Mad Old Man,* the story of a scheming, aging man who suffers a stroke during a liaison with a woman.

Tanizaki insisted that fiction should be artifice. His stories, while reflecting the issues and trends of the time, were entirely created worlds rather than fictionalized accounts of personal experiences or historical events. His stories typically revolve around male protagonists and their relationships with women. In 1949, Tanizaki received the Imperial Order of Culture.

Other Works by Tanizaki Jun'ichirō

The Key. Translated by Howard Hibbett. New York: Knopf, 1961.
Seven Japanese Tales. Translated by Howard G. Hibbett. New York: Knopf, 1963.

Works about Tanizaki Jun'ichiro

Gessel, Van C. *Three Modern Novelists: Sōseki, Tanizaki, Kawabata.* Tokyo: Kodansha International, 1993.
Ito, Ken K. *Vision of Desire: Tanizaki's Fictional Worlds.* Stanford, Calif.: Stanford University Press, 1991.

Tao-Lao, Alfonsina

See STORNI, ALFONSINA.

Thakur, Rabindranath

See TAGORE, RABINDRANATH.

Thammachoat, Atsiri

See DHAMMACHOTI, USSIRI.

Theatre of the Absurd

Taking its name from the idea of the absurd as something not grounded in logic or reason, the Theatre of the Absurd is related to aspects of EXISTENTIALISM. The movement itself actually refers to a style of drama that began in Paris and flourished in the late 1940s and 1950s.

The roots of Theatre of the Absurd can be traced back as far as the morality plays of the Middle Ages, the Spanish religious allegories, the nonsensical writings of Lewis Caroll, and the macabre and grotesque drama of Alfred JARRY. It was anticipated by DADAISM and the surrealist movement of the 1920s and 1930s and gathers much of its theoretical accountability from Antonin ARTAUD's text *The Theatre and its Double* (1938; translated 1958). The term itself comes from the use of the word *absurd* by existentialist philosophers such as Albert CAMUS and Jean-Paul SARTRE in reference to the lack of a rational explanation for the human condition.

Although Alfred Jarry's *Ubu Roi* (1888) anticipates much of the foundation on which absurdist drama rests, the three playwrights most closely associated with the movement's popularity are Jean GENET, Eugène IONESCO, and Samuel BECKETT. Their works take on a nightmarish quality as they examine contemporary alienation and human anxiety over the absence of social coherence or transcendental meaning. Many playwrights, such as Beckett, wrote in French though it was not their native language, and communicated a sense of linguistic estrangement.

According to some sources, Beckett was the most influential writer of the period. His *Happy Days* expresses humanity's fear of death through the character of a woman who, in the first act, is buried up to her waist in a mound of dirt. By the second act, the mound has grown so that only her head remains visible, a metaphoric vision of the ultimate journey from life to death and burial.

Other playwrights of this school wrote of similar anxieties. Ionesco emphasizes the fear of mediocrity and the inability to communicate in *The Bald Soprano* (1950). Genet's works, on the other hand, fuse illusion with reality in an often violently erotic manner to exemplify the absurd roles that people play in daily existence.

The influence of Theatre of the Absurd, created by a group of international writers living in Paris, extends beyond France to the works of Czechoslovakian playwright Václav HAVEL, British writers Harold Pinter and Tom Stoppard, and U.S. dramatists Edward Albee and Sam Shepard.

A Work about Theater of the Absurd

Esslin, Matin. *Theatre of the Absurd.* New York: Overlook Press, 1969.

Theodorescu, Ion N.

See ARGHEZI, TUDOR.

Tian Jian (Tien Chien; Tong Tianjian)
(1916–1985) *poet*

Tong Tianjian was born on May 14 in Anhui province's rural Wuwei County, in China. He moved to Shanghai in 1933 and studied foreign languages at Guanghua University, where he edited the journals *New Poetry* and *Literary Mosaic*. He published poems written during his college years in *Before Dawn* in 1935.

Tian Jian's poetry was known as declamatory poetry because of its political nature and revolutionary ideas. Much of his work was influenced by the Japanese occupation of Nanking and the Sino-Japanese War and had a very nationalistic slant.

Before the Sino-Japanese War, Tian Jian focused on the lives of Chinese peasants, for whom he wrote two volumes of poetry, *Pastoral Songs* (1936) and *Stories of the Chinese Countryside* (1936). The latter is a long poem comprised of three parts: "Hunger," "On the Yangtze River," and "Go Ahead." Tian Jian used the river as a metaphor for China and depicted the hardships of peasant life and resistance against the old regime.

In the spring of 1937, Tian Jian traveled to Japan and returned to China after the Sino-Japanese War began later that year. He served as a war correspondent with the Service Corps on the Northwestern Battlefield. He wrote poems influential for their military fervor and rhythms during the war in two volumes, *Odes to Soldiers on Patrol in a Sandstorm* (1938) and *Poems Dedicated to Fighters* (1943).

Tian Jian joined the Chinese Communist Party in 1943. He held high-level information posts and participated in land reform. He also continued his literary pursuits. He began a drive for "street verse," edited a new party literary magazine called *New Masses,* and joined the Chinese Writers Association after its 1949 formation. He then taught at the Central Institute of Literature in Beijing.

During the Korean War, Tian Jian served again as a war correspondent and visited Eastern Europe and Africa in 1954. He produced many volumes of poetry and essays, including *A Hero's Battle Song*

(1959), *Travels in Africa* (1964), and *A Sketch on a Trip to Europe* (1956), before the onset of the Cultural Revolution, when he was suppressed.

After the revolution ended, Tian Jian began to write poetry again in 1976. His work celebrated the new life of "liberated" peasants, such as *China in her Prime* (1986). Tian Jian died August 30 in Beijing.

Toer, Pramoedya Ananta (1925–)
novelist

Pramoedya Ananta Toer was born in Blora, a small town on the north coast of Java, Indonesia. His father was a former teacher and an activist of the Blora branch of the PNI (Indonesian National Party). His mother was the daughter of a mosque official and a former student of his father. Toer was the eldest of nine children. He graduated from the Radiovakschool in Surabaya in 1941. To avoid conscription into the Dutch army, Toer fled back to Blora. During the first four months of the Japanese occupation, he looked after his ill mother and his younger siblings. When his mother died, the family moved to Jakarta.

Toer wandered over much of Java after he had been passed over for promotion. He returned to Jakarta after he learned about the declaration of independence by Sukarno, Indonesia's former president, in August. Following the reorganization of the Indonesian army in late 1946, he became the editor of the journal *Sadar,* the Indonesian edition of *The Voice of Free Indonesia.*

Toer was imprisoned for two years for possessing anti-Dutch political documents and was one of the last men to be released in 1949. He was immediately given a position by the government literary bureau, Balai Pustaka, an appointment he temporarily postponed because of his father's death. Between 1950 and 1951, Toer was an editor for the modern-literature department of Balai Pustaka and for the magazines, *Indonesia* and *Kunang-Kunang (Firefly).* He became a member of the Lekra (Institute for People's Culture), an affiliated organization of the Indonesian Communist Party, and

lectured in the Res Publica University in Jakarta. He also edited "Lentera," the literary column in the daily paper *Bintang Timur.*

His sympathy for the despised Chinese in Indonesia landed him in trouble with Sukarno's "Guided Democracy" government. He was arrested in 1969 and sent to Buru Island, where he spent 10 years in exile. He was released in 1979 but was placed under house arrest by the new-order government a few years later. Toer's works had been banned in Indonesia since 1965, but they were extremely popular outside Indonesia, were printed in at least 28 languages, and won him international fame as a defender of truth and human rights. Finally in 1997, with the toppling of the Suharto regime, Toer was released from house arrest, and the ban on his works was lifted. Toer now travels around the world and gives talks at various universities.

Critical Analysis

Toer's works are extremely valuable to the study of Indonesian history. In *The Girl from the Coast,* Toer tells the story of his grandmother, derived from his interactions with her, others' perceptions of her, and his own imagination. Interwoven into the tale is a complex exploration of class conflict and gender relations at the village level. As in many of Toer's works, he intersperses his story with references to historical events, such as Kartini's death, enabling the reader to place episodes within a temporal context. Kartini was a princess of the Javanese royal family who was extremely influential in providing education for all. This story, which was first published in Indonesian in 1987, is the first in an untitled semiautobiography. Unfortunately, the second and third parts have been lost.

Toer's voice clearly emerges in his works. He writes with an intensity that emanates emotions ranging from anguish and melancholy to soft compassion and harsh indignation. His writings appeal through their sheer reflection of lived experiences that are both real and sadly universal. Toer is able to draw his readers into his world by enabling them to live vicariously through his own experience and tragedy. In *The Fugitive* (1962), a novel of betrayal and bravery during the Japanese occupation of Indonesia during World War II, the plight of Raden Hardo, the hero of the tale, bears similarity to Toer's own experience during the war. His attachment to Javanese attitudes and cultural beliefs is also revealed. The characters in the story, such as Hardo and Dipo, clearly resemble heroic characters that can be found in the Javanese traditional art form, the *wayang*, a shadow-puppet theatrical medium of performance.

Toer's storytelling skill is best exemplified in his 1999 work, *Tales from Djakarta: Caricatures of Circumstances and Their Human Beings*. In this collection of short essays, he is able to paint with great accuracy and biting wit the scenes of daily life in 1950s Jakarta, the capital of Indonesia. Through his writing, the bustling city with its ironic contrast of the luxurious quarters of the rich and the simmering squatters of the poor comes to life. He narrates with sarcastic wit the plight of the common people, some of whom rise above their station and others who miserably fail. Toer's stories do not always end in tragedy; for instance, in "Maman and His World" (1999), Maman, a poor *kampung* boy is able to build and own his own factory through hard work and perseverance. Maman's kindness and generosity also enable him to enlarge his wealth. Toer's heroes are taken from a variety of backgrounds, but his most poignant ones are those who remain untouched by avarice and other vices.

Toer was first propelled to fame when he completed the novel *Kranji-Bekasi Jatuh* in 1947. During his imprisonment in the Bukit Duri jail from 1948 to 1949, he wrote the short-story collections *Percikan Revolusi* and *Perburuan*. The latter won him first prize from Balai Pustaka. His greatest works are *Bumi Manusia, Anak Semua Bangsa*, and *Jejak Langkah*.

Toer's popularity in the literary world bespeaks his power to write convincingly and realistically about the plight of the common person not only in Indonesia but all over the world. His characters are universal, and his use of historical contexts and periods enables readers to better understand Indonesia's past.

Other Works by Pramoedya Ananta Toer

Child of All Nations (Buru Quartet, Volume 2). Translated by Max Lane. New York: Penguin USA, 1996.

Footsteps (Buru Quartet, Volume 3). Translated by Max Lane. New York: Penguin USA, 1996.

House of Glass (Buru Quartet, Volume 4). Translated by Max Lane. New York: Penguin USA, 1997.

The Mute's Soliloquy: A Memoir. Translated by Willem Samuels. New York: Hyperion, 1999.

This Earth of Mankind (Buru Quartet, Volume 1). Translated by Max Lane. New York: Penguin USA, 1996.

Works about Pramoedya Ananta Toer

Hering, Bob, ed. *Pramoedya Ananta Toer 70 Tahun: Essays to Honour Pramoedya Ananta Toer's 70th Year*. Indonesia: Yayasan Kabar Seberang, 1995.

Koh, Young Hoon. *Pemikiran Pramoedya Ananta Toer dalam Novel-novel Mutakhirnya*. Kuala Lumpur: Dewan Bahasa dan Pustaka, 1996.

Tolstoy, Leo (Count Lev Nikolayevich Tolstoy) (1828–1910) *novelist, short story writer, dramatist*

Leo Tolstoy was born in the town of Yasnaya Polyana, Russia, in a landowning family. His mother, Princess Volkonskaya, died when he was two years old, and his father when he was nine. He and his siblings were raised by relatives and educated by private tutors. At 16, Tolstoy entered the University of Kazan, but after dabbling in oriental languages and law, he returned to the family estate in 1847. A restless and high-spirited youth, he soon tired of the country and spent the next several years in St. Petersburg and Moscow, living a profligate life and keeping a diary in which he recorded even the most outrageous of his adventures. In 1852, seeking adventure, he joined his brother in the army. He was cited for bravery in the defense of Sebastopol. He left the army in 1856 and returned to the family estate with the idea, radical for the time, of educating and emancipating his serfs.

Tolstoy's early education included grounding in several European languages and literatures, and he continued to enlarge this knowledge over the next several years with extensive travels. He read widely and was particularly taken with the ideas of the 18th-century French writer Jean Jacques Rousseau. He was also well acquainted with the English novelists Laurence Sterne and Charles Dickens, who helped form his approach to the novel, while Rousseau and the New Testament influenced his later religious and philosophical works.

Tolstoy had begun his literary career with the publication, while he was still in the army, of an autobiographical work, *Childhood* (1852), and this was followed by *Boyhood* in 1854 and *Youth* in 1857. Material for these works came from his prodigious memory, substantially abetted by reference to the detailed diary he had begun in 1847. Though the facts of Tolstoy's early life form the basis of these books, their rearrangement and modification show us the budding writer of fiction learning his craft. Other short stories, based on his army experiences, followed in 1855 and 1856. In 1862, Tolstoy married Sofiya Bers, with whom he would have 13 children. His obsessive honesty led him to give her his diaries to read, and the young bride was, at the least, startled. She later got even by giving Tolstoy *her* diary to read. But marriage had a settling influence, and in the next 15 years following that, Tolstoy produced his greatest works, *War and Peace* (1865–69) and *Anna Karenina* (1875–77).

Tolstoy's approach to his work of this period was to observe carefully even the most minute details of his characters' lives and to record them faithfully, building the story in the same way that real life reveals itself. The great English critic and essayist Matthew Arnold said that if life could write its own story, it would write like Tolstoy. The two novels are not led by preconceived literary ideas of how structure, plot, and narrative are to be delineated; they happen, as life happens.

Critical Analysis

War and Peace is the story of five aristocratic Russian families, their associates, and the effects of Napoleon's wars from 1805 to 1820. The novel also contains essays that reflect Tolstoy's philosophy of history. The central love story involves Natasha Rostova and Pierre Bezukhov. Natasha finds fulfillment in marriage and motherhood, serving as an example of the value of life's simple processes. Meanwhile, Pierre searches for the philosophical system that will explain to him the meaning of life, but he comes, for a while at least, to believe that no such system exists outside of the common routines of existence.

In the essays on history and in the novel's chaotic plots, Tolstoy repudiates the theory that great men make history and that events are shaped by human intention. He views Napoleon and the Russian emperor Aleksandr as pompous men whose bumblings cause great misery. The pretenses of noble society are shown to be hollow as well. The character Prince Andrey Bolkonsky eschews the false values and artificialities of social life, substituting for a while the values of heroism and bravery in battle. He is severely wounded at Austerlitz and, while attempting to recuperate, realizes that these values as well are worthless. Tolstoy's own values are exemplified by the less sophisticated characters. Critics often have noted that Tolstoy describes his characters' thinking and behavior in minute detail, like a painter adding small brushstrokes, until, through sheer accretion, a full portrait appears. As the novel proceeds through its many years, the characters age; Natasha, for instance, grows from a giddy and self-centered girl to a portly and concerned mother.

Anna Karenina, though set in the same aristocratic milieu as *War and Peace*, is not as panoramic in scope. Based on the true story of a young woman's suicide in Tolstoy's province, it tells of the aristocratic Anna, who conducts an adulterous love affair with the dashing army officer Aleksey Vronsky. For him, she leaves both her husband and her beloved little boy. In contrast to her self-defeating romantic attachment is the true love of

Kitty and Konstantin Levin. Kitty is the sister of the unhappy Dolly Oblonsky, whose careless husband Stiva has been unfaithful to her.

Anna is Stiva's sister and in some ways is as careless as he; she wants romance and persuades herself that it is owed her. Society does not accept Anna's self-assertion in the face of convention, and she is ostracized. When she comes eventually to see the flaws in her lover, she has lost the love of her good but dull husband and sees no way out of her guilt-ridden life except suicide. Levin and Kitty meanwhile have bonded with a true love that accepts the daily limitations of being human.

Underlying both these works and the great changes that took place in Tolstoy's life soon after the publication of *Anna Karenina* are the philosophical musings of Jean Jacques Rousseau, apostle of what has come to be known as ROMANTICISM. Central to this doctrine is the idea of the *noble savage,* which holds that only those not infected with civilization's postures and deceptions are truly good. Civilization includes high society, secular and sacred institutions, commerce and money, legalisms and rank. Though Tolstoy used his reading of Rousseau to profound effect in his two great novels, when he tried to put these theories into practice, he ran into serious trouble, both artistic and personal. Among other things he was excommunicated from the Russian Orthodox Church, and he seriously alienated most of his family, particularly his wife, by repudiating the great novels and attempting to give away all his worldly goods. His writing suffered from his preoccupations, although his two later novellas, *The Death of Ivan Ilyich* (1886) and *The Kreutzer Sonata* (1891), are still widely read. A third long novel, *Resurrection,* was published in 1899, and at about this time he wrote a play, *The Living Corpse.*

Tolstoy proceeded into an ascetic and anarchistic old age. Although his philosophical meditations do not have the standing today they once had, his influence was profound, especially on the young Mohandas GANDHI: Passive resistance toward evil was a principle advocated by Tolstoy that Gandhi used with great effect to liberate India from foreign rule. Tolstoy's later convictions and behavior so contradicted his earlier ones that he sought literally to run away from them. Hounded by the demons of his own philosophy, he died while attempting to escape media attention in a provincial railroad station.

Works about Leo Tolstoy

Berlin, Isaiah. *The Hedgehog and the Fox: An Essay on Tolstoy's View of History.* New York: Simon & Schuster, 1986.

Bloom, Harold, ed. *Leo Tolstoy: Comprehensive Research and Study Guide.* Broomall, Pa.: Chelsea House, 2001.

Gifford, Henry. *Tolstoy.* New York: Oxford University Press, 1982.

Orwin, Donna Tussing, ed. *The Cambridge Companion to Tolstoy.* New York: Cambridge University Press, 2002.

Shirer, William. *Love and Hatred: The Stormy Marriage of Sonia and Leo Tolstoy.* Upland, Pa.: DIANE Publishing Co., 1994.

Troyat, Henri. *Tolstoy.* Translated by Nancy Amphoux. New York: Grove Press, 2001.

Tong Tianjian

See TIAN JIAN.

Tornimparti, Alessandra

See GINZBURG, NATALIA.

Torres Bodet, Jaime (1902–1974) *novelist, poet*

Jaime Torres Bodet was born in Mexico City. He was the son of Alejandro Torres Girbent, a theatrical producer, and Emilia Bodet. Torres Bodet believed it was important for a writer to work a "regular" job and to be involved in the world. He was an educator and would eventually be appointed minister of education for Mexico.

He and his literary group, the Contemporaneos, were seminal in bringing modern European literature to the attention of Mexican intellectuals in the first half of the 20th century. His novel *Movie Star* (1933) contrasts the world of psychology and imagination with the reality of everyday life in a modern style that brought intellectual vitality to the Mexican novel.

Later in his life, when he was involved in his political career, he dedicated himself almost exclusively to the writing of poetry. In 1965, he published a volume titled *Poems by Jaime Torres Bodet,* which included his own selection of his 50 most important poems. His poetry demonstrates his ideas about the importance of everyday life as a subject for literature. In it, he writes passionately about simple experiences.

Torres Bodet is remembered for his great expressive force in writing. He received the National Literature Award in 1966, and the Mexican government issued a commemorative stamp in his honor in 1975. Torres Bodet's poetry is considered thoughtful, sensitive, and humanistic.

Another Work by Jaime Torres Bodet

Selected Poems. A bilingual edition with translations by Sonja Karsen. Bloomington: Indiana University Press, 1964.

A Work about Jaime Torres Bodet

Karsen, Sonja. *Jaime Torres Bodet: A Poet in a Changing World.* Saratoga Springs, N.Y.: Skidmore College, 1963.

Trakl, Georg (1887–1914) *poet*

Georg Trakl was born in Salzburg, Austria, into a middle-class Protestant family. Although his early childhood was quite happy, Trakl began to show signs of trouble in his adolescence. In his youth, he was close to his sister Grete, so close that many have speculated about an incestuous relationship. In high school, Trakl frequented brothels, drank, and used opium heavily. After failing his courses in high school, he was forced to repeat a year and eventually dropped out.

He apprenticed to a local pharmacist, many believe, to have an easier access to drugs. By his early adulthood, he showed clear signs of mental illness and emotional disturbance.

Trakl moved to Austria, where he studied to be a pharmacist. In Vienna, he began to write his first serious poems, publishing them in several literary journals. He also met prominent artists of the expressionist movement (*see* EXPRESSIONISM), including Oskar KOKOSCHKA. Shortly before completing his degree, Trakl lost all financial support as a result of his father's death.

Trakl published only one collection of poetry during his lifetime, *Poems* (1913). The poems, permeated by dark themes of sorrow and decay, reveal his deep disgust with imperialist society. Two posthumous collections, *The Autumn of the Lonely* (1920) and *Song of the Departed* (1933), reveal similar themes, often distorting reality to amplify the disturbed emotional state of the poet. The bleak verses are pierced by nightmarish images of twilight, death, and somber religious symbolism.

At the outbreak of World War I, Trakl was recruited into the Austrian army in the capacity of a pharmacist. He was hospitalized on several occasions for depression, attempted suicide, and was released seemingly without any improvement. Three days after having witnessed several locals hanged from a tree by the Austrian army, Trakl intentionally overdosed on cocaine.

Although Trakl was by no means a prolific poet, he left a significant contribution for the expressionist movement. His poetry is widely read and appreciated in Germany, the United States, and Europe as a whole. Trakl's work has been translated into nine languages.

Other Works by Georg Trakl

Autumn Sonata: Selected Poems of Georg Trakl. Translated by Daniel Simko. London: Asphodel Press, 1998.

Poems and Prose. Translated by Alexander Stillmark. New York: Libris, 2001.

A Work about Georg Trakl

Williams, Eric, ed. *The Dark Flutes of Fall: Critical Essays on Georg Trakl.* Rochester, N.Y.: Camden House, 1991.

Tsushima Yūko (Tsushima Satoko)

(1947–   ) *short-story writer, novelist*

Tsushima Yūko was born in Tokyo to novelist Dazai Osamu and his wife, Michiko. Soon after her birth, her father committed suicide with his lover. Her mother raised her, her older sister, and an older brother, who was mentally handicapped, on her own. When Tsushima was very young, she attended a music school for children. In 1965, she began to study English literature at Shirayuri Women's College in Tokyo, graduated in 1969, and went on for one year of postgraduate study at Meiji University. She married in 1972 but later separated from her husband after having two children.

Tsushima's writing career began while she was still an undergraduate when she won a university prize for her story, "Requiem for a Dog and an Adult" (1969). Her first novel, *The House Where Living Things are Gathering,* followed in 1973. She continued to write at a rapid rate, producing short-story collections that appeared almost annually, including *A Bed of Grass* in 1977. Her second novel, *Child of Fortune* (1978), is about a 36-year-old music teacher raising a child on her own. The novel *Driven by the Light of Night* (1986), about the efforts of a woman to retain the memories of her dead son, marked a new direction in Tsushima's writing. She picked up the theme of bereavement and memory again in *To the Daylight* (1988).

Tsushima's protagonists are generally single mothers who experience an awakening, and her novels typically explore the internal world of female protagonists. Tsushima herself has claimed that her writing stems from a desire to articulate herself, which was repressed during childhood because of her nonverbal relationship with her handicapped brother. She has won many literary prizes, including the Kawabata Yasunari Prize in 1982 and the Yomiuri Newspaper Prize in 1987.

Other Works by Yūko Tsushima

The Shooting Gallery and Other Stories. Translated by Geraldine Harcourt. New York: Pantheon Books, 1988.

Woman Running in the Mountains. Translated by Geraldine Harcourt. New York: Pantheon Books, 1991.

"Water's Edge." In *Reexamination of Modern Subjectivity in Japanese Fiction.* Saitama-ken Sakado-shi, Japan: Center for Inter-cultural Studies and Education, Josai University, 1994.

Tsvetaeva, Marina (1892–1941) *poet*

Born in Moscow, Marina Ivanovna Tsvetaeva grew up in an affluent family. Her father was an art-history professor at the University of Moscow, and her mother a talented pianist. Tsvetaeva's family frequently traveled abroad, and she attended schools in Italy, Switzerland, Germany, and France. In school, Tsvetaeva excelled in literature, history, and languages. She published her first collection of poems, "Evening Album" (1910), at the age of 18. The collection explored the themes of childhood and subsequent transition to adulthood. It was noticed and praised by Valery BRYUSOV.

In 1912, Tsvetaeva married Sergei Efron; two daughters were born, in 1912 and 1917. Tsvetaeva opposed the Bolshevik revolution of 1917, and Efron volunteered to serve in the oppositional forces of the White Army. Tsvetaeva remained in Moscow, where she suffered from poverty and hunger. Her daughter Irina died of starvation in 1920. In spite of all, Tsvetaeva wrote intensely, producing six verse dramas and several narrative poems including *The Demesne of the Swans,* an epic about the Russian civil war, and many lyrics. Eventually, Tsvetaeva and her family emigrated from Russia, spending time in Berlin and Prague and settling in Paris in 1925, the year her son Gyorgy was born.

During these years Tsvetaeva published five collections of poetry, the last—and the last published in her lifetime—being *After Russia* (1928), a collection that dealt with the themes of national identity and displacement. Tsvetaeva was the only source of income for her family in Paris, and she eventually turned to writing prose because it paid more than poetry. She wrote critical essays, memoirs, and short stories. Tsvetaeva's prose, however, never achieved the level of skill and literary genius found in her verse. Furthermore, Tsvetaeva did not identify herself with the Russian émigré community. After writing a friendly and admiring letter to the Soviet poet MAYAKOVSKY, Tsvetaeva was ostracized from the émigré community and found it virtually impossible to have her work published. Efron had become more sympathetic to the Soviets, as had their daughter Alya, and in 1937 Alya and Efron returned to Russia.

Tsvetaeva was never able spiritually and emotionally to separate from Russia, as her nostalgic and expressive poems "Homesick for Motherland" (1935) and "Motherland" (1936) indicate. Tsvetaeva's last collection of verse, *Poems to the Czechs* (1938–39), explored the anguish of the Nazi occupation of Czechoslovakia. Tsvetaeva returned to Russia in 1939, with Gyorgy, and soon found herself in the same predicament as she had been during the 1920s. Besides the occasional translation work that was provided to Tsvetaeva by Boris PASTERNAK, she was unable to find employment. Efron and Alya were arrested for espionage during the height of the Stalinist purges. Alone, impoverished, and in deep despair, Tsvetaeva committed suicide in 1941.

Tsvetaeva's use of traditional poetic diction and classical images went against the cultural politics of SOCIALIST REALISM. For Tsvetaeva, poetry was a personal rather than a social experience. Her contribution to Russian literature was not recognized until years after her death. Now, however, she generally ranked with Anna AKHMATOVA, Osip MANDELSTAM, and Boris PASTERNAK as one of the four greatest Russian poets of the 20th century.

Other Works by Marina Tsvetaeva

Earthly Signs. Translated by Jamey Gambrell. New Haven, Conn.: Yale University Press, 2002.

Milestones. Translated by Robin Kemball. Evanston, Ill.: Northwestern University Press, 2002.
Poem of the End: Selected Narrative and Lyrical Poetry, with Facing Russian Text. Translated by Nina Kossman. Ann Arbor, Mich.: Ardis, 2000.
The Ratcatcher: A Lyrical Satire. Translated by Angela Livingstone. Evanston, Ill.: Northwestern University Press, 2000.
Selected Poems. Translated by Elaine Feinstein. New York: Penguin Books, 1994.

Works about Marina Tsvetaeva

Dinega, Alyssa E. *A Russian Psyche: The Poetic Mind of Marina Tsvetaeva.* Madison: University of Wisconsin Press, 2002.
Feiler, Lily B. *Marina Tsvetaeva: The Double Beat of Heaven and Hell.* Durham, N.C.: Duke University Press, 1994.
Schweitzer, Viktoria. *Tsvetaeva.* Translated by Peter Norman. New York: Farrar, Straus & Giroux, 1993.

Turgenev, Ivan Sergeyevich (1818–1883)
novelist, dramatist, short-story writer

Ivan Turgenev was born in Orel, Russia, to Sergey and Varvara Turgenev, rich aristocratic landowners. Turgenev's childhood was defined by the domineering personality of his mother. In 1827, the family relocated to Moscow, and Turgenev, who up to that point had been educated by his mother, was now tutored by prominent intellectuals and writers of the period. A brilliant student, he was admitted to Moscow University at the age of 15. The family moved to St. Petersburg in 1834, where Turgenev continued his studies.

While studying in St. Petersburg, Turgenev met a number of important literary figures, among them Aleksandr PUSHKIN and Nikolay GOGOL. In 1838, he moved to Berlin to continue his studies of philosophy and literature. While in Germany, Turgenev developed a warm friendship with Mikhail Bakunin, a famous anarchist and social theoretician. Turgenev returned to Russia in 1841 and began work on short stories about the lives of peasants. He published his first story, "Khor and

Kalinich," in 1847. Many of these stories, depicting daily lives and suffering of common people, appeared together as *A Hunter's Sketches* in 1852. The collection revealed Turgenev's love of nature as well as his concern for the social conditions of common Russians. In *A Hunter's Sketches,* he criticized the institution of serfdom, in which the social status of peasants was equivalent to that of slaves. It was widely rumored that reading this story was what inspired Aleksandr II to emancipate the serfs.

In 1856, Turgenev traveled extensively throughout Europe. He had a following in French literary circles and developed friendships with such influential writers as FLAUBERT and ZOLA. After a hostile response to his novel *Fathers and Sons* (1862), Turgenev left Russia and settled in Paris. By 1870s, Turgenev was recognized as one of the world's leading writers.

The decade 1850–1860 was the most productive in Turgenev's career as a writer. Turgenev always concentrated on social and political issues in his work, as his novels *Rudin* (1856), *A Nest of Gentlefolk* (1859), and *On the Eve* (1860) readily attest. Turgenev often juxtaposes the daily struggles of the peasants with disruption in the social structure of country aristocrats. The parallel placement of spiritual and physical struggles in the narrative often plays an important role in his work. His most famous novel, *Fathers and Sons,* deals with nihilism and the role of the individual within a family and the social dynamics of the state. The work was widely criticized for its "social irresponsibility" and supposed "misrepresentation" of Russia's youth. Despite this criticism, Turgenev continued to examine social issues in his work. His novels *Smoke* (1867) and *Virgin Soil* (1877) deal with the transformation of Russian society and its subsequent effects on the peasantry and country gentry.

Turgenev also wrote a number of plays. *A Month in the Country* (1855) contained a number of dramatic innovations in style and subject matter. This play became a catalyst for the dramatic works of Anton CHEKHOV. In the comical play *A Provincial Lady* (1851), Turgenev satirically treats the moral and ethical beliefs of country aristocrats. Both plays demonstrate Turgenev's ability to illuminate a certain social issue without demonizing a certain class or social group. Turgenev's criticism is often intricately interwoven into the fabric of the segment of society represented on stage.

When Turgenev died in 1883, his contribution to world literature was already recognized, and his literary influence extended far beyond the borders of Russia. Henry James, for instance, considered Ivan Turgenev one of the greatest writers of the 19th century. Turgenev's work also inspired social changes in Russia and contributed to the development of liberal political thought.

Another Work by Ivan Turgenev
Three Novellas About Love. Translated by Tatiana Litvinov. Moscow: Raduga, 1990.

A Work about Ivan Turgenev
Knowles, Anthony Vere. *Ivan Turgenev.* Boston: Twayne Publishers, 1988.

Tuwim, Julian (1894–1953) *poet*
Julian Tuwim was born in Lodz, Poland. His father's family was strongly Jewish and included several Zionists. His mother was an assimilationist who insisted that Tuwim be educated in a strictly Polish manner. He never attempted to conceal his Jewish identity and upbringing; as a result, during the years preceding World War II, he was subjected to numerous brutal attacks by extreme Polish nationalists.

Tuwim lived in exile in France, South America, and the United States throughout the Nazi era. He was an active antifascist, and part of one of his poems became the anthem of the Polish resistance movement.

Tuwim was also one of the leaders of the Skamander group, a group of experimental poets. He became a major figure in Polish literature largely as a result of his collection *Slowa we Krwi* (*Words Bathed in Blood,* 1926). The poetry in this volume fervently expresses the sense of emptiness that accompanies the violence of urban life. Although Tuwim clearly sympathized with the poor and underprivileged, he did not become as actively involved in the proletariat revolutionary movement as he had in speaking out against fascism. Instead, his poems voiced the protest of an isolated intellectual. He used his works to illustrate the dangerous effects of capitalism.

In addition to *Slowa we Krwi,* Tuwim also wrote a collection of poems for children called *Locomotive* (1938; translated 1940) and published translations of PUSHKIN, for which he won the Pen Club Award in 1935, and of other Russian poets. Many of Tuwim's poems were also set to music and became extremely popular.

Another Work by Julian Tuwim

The Dancing Socrates, and Other Poems. Translated by Adam Gillon. Boston: Twayne Publishers, 1968.

Tzara, Tristan (Samuel Rosenstock)

(1896–1963) *poet, essayist*

Known primarily as one of the founders of DADA, Tristan Tzara was born in Moinesti, Romania, on April 16. While living in Zurich during World War I, he wrote *La Première Aventure céleste de Monsieur Antipyrine* (*The First Heavenly Adventure of Mr. Antipyrine,* 1916) and *Twenty-Five Poems* (1918). These two works are commonly considered to be the first dadaist texts. He also wrote the movement's manifesto, *Seven Dada Manifestos* (1924).

Tzara eventually moved to Paris, where he became involved with fellow writers André BRETON, Louis ARAGON, and Philippe Soupault. Together this group shocked readers and critics alike with their nihilistic works, which sought to subvert the conventional structures of language and society.

In the early 1930s, Tzara began to tire of nihilism and turned, instead, to the newly emerging surrealism as a more constructive form of artistic expression. In 1936, he joined the Communist Party and became actively involved in seeking ways to integrate surrealism with Marxist doctrine.

During World War II, Tzara joined the French resistance movement. His political activities brought him into close contact with the realities of oppression and made him brutally aware of human suffering. His later works, such as *The Approximate Man* (1931), *Speaking Alone* (1950), and *The Inner Face* (1953), reflect this new understanding of the human condition.

Tzara continued to be active as both a poet and an essayist until his death in Paris on December 24.

Another Work by Tristan Tzara

Approximate Man and Other Writings. Translated by Mary Ann Caws. Detroit: Wayne State University Press, 1973.

Works about Tristan Tzara

Lindsay, Jack. *Meetings with Poets: Memories of Dylan Thomas, Edith Sitwell, Louis Aragon, Paul Eluard, Tristan Tzara.* New York: Ungar, 1969.

Peterson, Elmer. *Tristan Tzara: Dada and Surrational Theorist.* New Brunswick, N.J.: Rutgers University Press, 1971.

U

Ueda Fumi

See ENCHI FUMIKO.

Unamuno y Jugo, Miguel de

(1864–1936) *novelist, playwright, poet, essayist*

Miguel de Unamuno y Jugo was born in Bilbao, Spain. He grew up and was educated there until he was 16, absorbing the Basque culture and independent spirit of that city. At 16, he went to Madrid to study literature and philosophy at the university.

Unamuno went on to become a professor of Greek and Spanish literature at the University of Salamanca. Because he spoke out publicly against the dictatorship of Primo de Rivera in the 1920s, he was banished and fled to France. He lived just over the Spanish border in the town of Hendaye so that he could continue to express his views against the regime to his fellow Spaniards.

In 1930, he was able to return to Spain. During the Spanish civil war, he sided with Franco, although he eventually spoke out against the dictator. Unamuno was one of the most famous members of the group of Spanish writers known as the GENERATION OF 1898. Like other members of the movement, he sought to present a revital-ized model of Spanish nationalist identity be expunging certain decadent cultural habits that had infiltrated Spanish culture. To this end, he was against bullfights and the veneration of the Hapsburg and Bourbon royalty that had ruled Spain for the past few centuries. He called for a return to the Spanish traditions of the Middle Ages before the Spanish Inquisition had homogenized Spanish culture.

He was the most versatile of the Generation of 98, writing novels, poetry, and philosophy with equal skill. In line with his political views, Unamuno's most important essays examine Spanish history and the potential roles the Spanish nation might play in the modern world.

His novels and poetry focus more on the plight of the modern individual. In *Mist* (1914), a typical novel and one of his most successful, Unamuno traces the life of Augusto Perez, a man who lacks a strong personality and any self-knowledge. Gradually, Unamuno depicts how Perez arrives at self-knowledge through the pain of unsuccessful romances. The mist of the title becomes a metaphor both for Perez's personality and the forces that obscure it.

Unamuno's most famous poem is "Atheist's Prayer," which portrays the irony of praying to a god whom one cannot truly believe exists. It is representative of Unamuno's typical blend of intensely spiritual feeling and skepticism.

Along with José ORTEGA Y GASSET, Unamuno is the member of the Generation of 1898 who has the largest international reputation. He is certainly the most internationally known novelist of his generation. His influence on later Spanish authors who followed his particularly open style of narrative structure and ideas was immense. He demonstrated a mode of philosophical literature that was particularly suited to the themes of existential philosophy and, along with Pío BAROJA Y NESSI, pioneered the modern Spanish novel.

Other Works by Miguel de Unamuno y Jugo

The Agony of Christianity; and, Essays on Faith. Translated by Anthony Kerrigan. Princeton, N.J: Princeton University Press, 1974.

Our Lord Don Quixote: The Life of Don Quixote and Sancho, with Related Essays. Translated by Anthony Kerrigan. Princeton, N.J.: Princeton University Press, 1976.

A Work about Miguel de Unamuno y Jugo

Ilie, Paul. *Unamuno; An Existential View of Self and Society.* Madison: University of Wisconsin Press, 1967.

Undset, Sigrid (1882–1949) *novelist, short-story writer, essayist*

Born in Kalundborg, Denmark, Sigrid Undset grew up in Christiana (present-day Oslo), Norway. Her father Ingvald Undset was an archaeologist and a historian who encouraged her interest in history and literature. Her mother Anne Charlotte, the daughter of a Danish attorney, had to support the family after Ingvald died in 1893. To help her mother, Undset took a job as a secretary at age 16. She cultivated her literary talent during the 10 years she worked in offices. In 1909, she started to write full-time.

Undset's first novels and short stories drew from her work experience and portrayed women trying to decide between career and family. In the 1920s, she turned to historical novels and published her masterpiece, the *Kristin Lavransdatter* (1920–22) trilogy. Undset's next set of works on medieval Norwegian history, translated into English as *The Master of Hestviken* (1928–30), earned her the Nobel Prize in literature. In the 1930s, Undset returned to writing about modern concerns and became one of the first Norwegians to oppose fascism. During World War II, she fled to the United States to escape Nazi occupation.

Undset was a keen observer of contemporary events. Her works about women caught between public and private spheres deal with careers, love, marriage, and infidelity. Undset's historical novels display an impressively detailed knowledge of medieval Norway. Her search for ethics and religion led to her conversion to Catholicism in 1925. Although Undset's religious views offended some, her biographer Mitzi Brunsdale pointed out in *Sigrid Undset* (1988) that even Undset's critics praised her sincerity: "She assailed not only Norwegian social conditions but the dangerous materialism and sentimental humanitarianism that she felt threatened all Western civilization."

Other Works by Sigrid Undset

Gunnar's Daughter. Translated by Arthur B. Chater. New York: Penguin USA, 1998.

Kristin Lavransdatter: The Cross. Translated by Tina Nunnally. New York: Penguin USA, 2000.

Kristin Lavransdatter: The Wreath. Translated by Tina Nunnally. New York: Penguin USA, 1997.

Kristin Lavransdatter II: The Wife. Translated by Tina Nunnally. New York: Penguin USA, 1999.

A Work about Sigrid Undset

Brunsdale, Mitzi. *Sigrid Undset: Chronicler of Norway.* New York: Berg Publishers, Ltd., 1988.

Ungaretti, Giuseppe (1888–1970) *poet*

Giuseppe Ungaretti was born in Alexandria, Egypt. He spent his childhood in North Africa, however, where the nomadic culture influenced many of his future life choices as well as his writing. Educated in Paris, he lived a free-spirited life along with many other members of the emerging literary and artistic avant-garde. Their ideas, particularly those of the French symbolists, would eventually impact the direction of his poetry.

During World War I, Ungaretti served in the Italian infantry. He fought with the 3rd Army on the lower Isanzo front from 1915 to 1918. In the spring of 1918, he was transferred to the Western front where the Italian army fought with much distinction. It was this experience that gave the aspiring poet the background for his mature works, particularly his war poetry, such as *Vigil* (1915) and *Brothers* (1916).

Writing in the style of the symbolists, in which the works are reduced to their simplest and most essential elements, Ungaretti's major themes are love and the precarious and temporary nature of the human existence. This is particularly evident in *I Am a Creature* (1916). He chose each word carefully, stressing the musicality of language and avoiding elaborate structure within his poems. His style was so unique that it prompted an entire poetic movement that became known as hermeticism.

Ungaretti's poetry is collected in English translation in a series titled *The Life of Man* (1969). As well as writing poetry, he also translated the works of Shakespeare and Racine and held teaching posts in Brazil and Rome.

Another Work by Giuseppe Ungaretti

Selected Poems: Bilingual Edition. Translated by Andrew Frisardi. New York: Farrar, Straus & Giroux, 2002.

Valéry, Paul (1871–1945) *poet, essayist*

A writer who devoted his life and work to worshiping what he referred to as the "idol of intellect," Paul Valéry was born in the small Mediterranean seaside town of Sète on October 30. The son of a customs clerk, he spent his childhood by the sea. He grew to be fascinated by the rhythmical quality of waves and the intrinsic natural beauty of water. This early childhood aesthetic delight translated itself into a later interest in both architecture and poetry.

As an adult, Valéry left the seacoast to travel to Paris, where he made the acquaintance of a small group of friends who shared his interests and encouraged his artistic endeavors, among whom was fellow writer André GIDE. The two became lifelong friends and influenced each other greatly. Valéry was also influenced by Stéphane MALLARMÉ and the symbolist poets. His earliest works were published in symbolist journals, where they were well received, but Valéry chose initially to place his artistic endeavors secondary to his study of mathematics and the sciences. He did, however, publish a collection of vignettes, such as *Mr. Head* (1895), depicting human intellect as distinct and segregated from the world as a whole. This theme would manifest itself in much of Valéry's later work.

A failed romance prompted Valéry to withdraw completely from the arts, maintaining some of his artistic friendships but taking a job in the civil-service branch of the French war office and focusing solely on scientific pursuits. He wrote no poetry during this period. He wrote only his observations on the scientific aspects of language and consciousness and one substantial work on Leonardo da Vinci. He praised Leonardo as being a perfect example of man because of his ability to remain emotionally detached in his mastery of both science and the arts.

In 1912, 20 years after his retreat from poetry, Valéry was encouraged by André Gide to go back and revise some of his earlier works. Five years later, the poems were collected and published to widespread acclaim. Of particular interest both popularly and critically was the publication of his long poem *The Youngest Fate* (1917). The work details the awakening of human consciousness and intellect symbolically through the youngest fate, which represents the earliest stage of human development. This work solidly emphasizes Valéry's *idol of intellect,* which he eventually defined as a state of pure reason existing separately from the emotional demands of society. He also stressed the conflict between the human desire to think and the human will to act.

The works produced in 1917 gained Valéry widespread fame as a poet. He continued to publish poetry throughout the rest of his life, but the majority of his work remained focused on the sciences, as well as cultural and political concerns. His interest in the sciences brought him into direct contact with many influential thinkers, including Einstein and Faraday. He became a prominent personality in Parisian high society where his wit and intelligence provided much entertainment at otherwise dry social functions. The degree to which he knew and understood politics also made him an extremely popular speaker on current events.

In 1925, Valéry was elected to the Académie Française, and the position of professor of poetry at the Collège de France was created specifically for him. He died soon after the liberation of France at the end of World War II. He was given a state funeral, in keeping with his honored place in French society.

Another Work by Paul Valéry

Sea Shells. Translated by Ralph Manheim. Boston: Beacon Press, 1998.

Works about Paul Valéry

Kluback, William. *Paul Valéry: A Philosopher for Philosophers: The Sage.* New York: Peter Lang, 2000.

Putnam, Walter. *Paul Valéry Revisited.* Boston: Twayne, 1995.

Vallejo, César (1892–1938) *poet, novelist*

César Abraham Vallejo was the youngest of 11 children born to a family in Santiago de Chuco, a small Andean town north of Peru. His parents, Francisco de Paula Vallejo and María de los Santos Mendoza, were both children of Chimu Indian mothers and Spanish Catholic priests. Vallejo's family was very poor, and financial problems haunted the poet throughout his life.

In 1910, he enrolled in the University of Trujillo, but his studies were repeatedly interrupted due to financial hardship. Vallejo took different jobs, such as teaching and a clerical position in a sugar estate's accounting department, to survive. His job at the sugar estate showed him the poverty and poor working conditions of the workers, an experience that helped refine Vallejo's sense of solidarity with and empathy for those who suffer.

It was in Trujillo that Vallejo first came into contact with writers, and there he wrote his first poems, including the draft of his first book of poetry, *The Black Heralds* (1918). The poetry in this collection shows both MODERNIST and ROMANTIC tendencies and was well received. He received his master's degree in 1915 in Spanish literature and, in 1917, moved to Lima, where he became acquainted with many important Peruvian writers and intellectuals of the day, including the anarchist Manual Gonzalez Prada.

After the crushing loss of his mother in 1920, and having lost a teaching position, he returned home to visit. Disturbances broke out while he was there—an official was assassinated and a store was burned down—and he was accused of being an instigator. Even though there was an overwhelming supportive response in the form of letters by important intellectuals and newspaper editors, Vallejo still served 105 days in jail. This experience, as well as the changes occurring in European literature, affected his next collection of poetry, *Trilce* (1922), which marked a fundamental change in Hispanic-American literature. By separating himself from the more traditional models he had followed in the past, and by pursuing unexplored experiences of the human condition, Vallejo helped renovate poetic language and form.

Having lost yet another job and fearing being put back in jail, Vallejo moved to Paris in 1923. Although he met such important vanguard figures as Vicente Huidobro, Juan Gris, Pablo Picasso, Jean COCTEAU, and Antonin ARTAUD, Vallejo eventually abandoned his own experimental writings due to his readings in marxism. By 1927, he was engaged in the communist cause and became an intellectual and political activist. In 1930, he was arrested at a train station for producing communist propaganda and was ordered to leave France.

Vallejo went to Madrid where, in 1931, he joined the Spanish Communist Party and wrote his novel *Tungsten* (1931). He returned to Paris in 1933 via a resident permit that banned him from becoming involved in any type of political activities.

In 1934, he married Georgette Phillipart, with whom he had been living since 1929. In 1936, the fascist uprising in Spain sparked in Vallejo a period of unparalleled creativity. In 1937 he was voted Peruvian representative at the Second International Congress of Writers for the Defense of Culture, which took place in Spain. There he had a chance to see firsthand the horror of the civil war, and out of this experience in the next few months came a tragedy, *La piedra cansada* (*The exhausted rock*), and more than 80 poems, including the 15 poems that form *Spain, Take This Cup from Me*.

In his poem "Black Stone on Top of a White Stone" Vallejo wrote: "I shall die in Paris, in a rainstorm." These words were prophetic. His last words expressed his desire to go to Spain and fight against the fascist forces that were tearing through the country. At the time of his death, much of his work was still unpublished. In 1939, his *Spain, Take This Cup from Me* and *Human Poems* were published posthumously. His poetry is characterized by experimentation with language, which often makes it difficult to read; real historical elements; and intense images of human pain and connection. His poem "To My Brother Miguel In Memoriam," for example, poignantly draws a parallel between the brothers' childhood games of hide-and-seek and Miguel's death: "Miguel, you went into hiding . . . but, instead of chuckling, you were sad." Vallejo is remembered as being Peru's greatest poet, as well as one of the seminal voices of 20th-century Hispanic-American poetry, and one of the most original Spanish voices of all time.

Other Works by César Vallejo

Bly, Robert, ed. *Neruda and Vallejo: Selected Poems.* Translated by John Knoepfle and James Wright. Boston: Beacon Press, 1993.

César Vallejo: The Complete Posthumous Poetry. Translated by Clayton Eshleman and Jose Rubin García. Berkeley: University of California Press, 1992.

The Black Heralds (Discoveries). Translated by Richard Schaaf and Katherine Ross. Pittsburgh, Pa.: Latin American Literary Review Press, 1990.

Trilce. Translated by Rebecca Seiferle. New York: Sheep Meadow Press, 1992.

Tungsten. Translated by Robert Mezey. Syracuse, N.Y.: Syracuse University Press, 1989.

Works about César Vallejo

Niebylski, Dianna C. *The Poem on the Edge of the Word: The Limits of Language and the Uses of Silence in the Poetry of Mallarmé, Rilke and Vallejo.* New York: Peter Lang, 1993.

Sharman, Adam, ed. *The Poetry and Poetics of César Vallejo: The Fourth Angle of the Circle.* Lewiston, N.Y.: Edwin Mellen Press, 1997.

Vargas Llosa, Mario (1936–) *novelist*

Mario Vargas Llosa was born in Arequipa, Peru. Shortly after his birth, his father and mother separated, and his mother took him to live in Bolivia. His grandfather was the Peruvian consul there, and Vargas Llosa spent the next eight years in a privileged and happy atmosphere. He read adventure stories and, because he could not stand it when the books came to an end, he invented additional chapters.

When Vargas Llosa was 10 years old, his parents reconciled, and he returned to Peru. As a teenager, he began to write poems. His father, wishing to discourage his son from being a writer, sent him to the Leoncio Prado Military School. This traumatic experience had the opposite effect on Vargas Llosa: Forced to keep his literary interests secret, he became more committed to his writing and developed a strong need to rebel against conventional society.

When Vargas Llosa's first novel *The Time of the Hero* (1962) was published, it won several literary prizes and was highly praised. It also caused a great controversy at the Leoncio Prado Military School because of his harsh criticism of the military. A thousand copies were burned publicly on orders of the school administration.

The Time of the Hero focuses on sections of society and taboos frequently avoided by Peruvian writers. In the book, Vargas Llosa pays a great deal of attention to his character's fantasies, which become an active part of the plot. One of Vargas Llosa's main interests is how real life and fantasy combine to form a reality which would not exist without both of them.

In 1967 Vargas Llosa met Gabriel GARCÍA MÁRQUEZ in Caracas. The two men, both central figures in the MAGIC REALISM movement, held a series of public discussions on the art of fiction writing. At this time, Vargas Llosa was arriving at his mature conception of the purpose of the novel in society. He saw the novel as a mode for the writer to struggle with and attempt to change human reality. He viewed the novel both as a means to preserve moments of time from one's personal past and to exorcise personal demons.

Vargas Llosa became increasingly concerned with politics during the 1970s and, in 1981, wrote *The War of the End of the World*, which examines and harshly criticizes the tendency toward political fanaticism so prevalent in Latin-American history. Set in 19th-century Brazil, it blends an actual historical event with fantasy and the psychological exploration of its characters. The overall effect is to make visceral the atrocity of an event that otherwise might have been become a history remembered without emotion. Vargas Llosa's techniques emphasize that history is itself a kind of fiction and our view of it can change the future.

In 1990, Vargas Llosa took his political interests from the world of literary discourse and decided to put them into action. He ran for president of Peru against Alberto Fujimori. Unfortunately, he lost, and Fujimori went on to impose an authoritarian and corrupt government on the people of Peru.

Vargas Llosa continues to write. His most recent novel, *The Feast of the Goat* (2002), examines the reign of Dominican dictator Gen. Rafael Trujillo with Vargas Llosa's characteristic blend of history, fantasy, and political insight.

Other Works by Mario Vargas Llosa

Aunt Julia and the Scriptwriter. Translated by Helen R. Lane. New York: Farrar, Straus & Giroux, 1982.

A Fish in the Water: A Memoir. Translated by Helen Lane. New York: Farrar, Straus & Giroux, 1994.

Verga, Giovanni (1840–1922) *novelist, dramatist*

Giovanni Verga was born in Catania, Sicily. He intended initially to pursue a career in law; he abandoned his studies to concentrate on writing novels. His early works were romantic in tone, but his later and, subsequently, better-received novels beginning with *The Malavogolia Family* (1881) were written in the emerging Italian realist style known as VERISMO.

Modeled after ÉMILE ZOLA's *Rougon-Macquart* series, *The Malavogolia Family* was initially intended to be part of a larger sequence of novels collectively titled *The Vanquished*, dealing with the life of Sicilian fishermen. Although only one other novel was completed in the saga, *Maestro Don Gesualdo* (1884), the works firmly established Verga as a leading writer in the verismo school. His attention to detail in his faithful depictions of late 19th-century life in both Sicily and southern Italy gained him much praise.

Although Verga began his career writing novels, he is best known for his dramatic works. His first play was an adaptation of his short story *Rustic Chivalry* (1884). A tale of lust, love, and murder, the play, set in his native Sicily, gained popularity when it was further adapted as an opera by the composer Mascagni. *Cavalleria Rusticana* continues to be performed throughout the world.

Verga's second dramatic work, *In Porter's Lodge* (1885), again treats the themes of love and violence. This time, he moves the setting to the city of Milan, thus exemplifying the universality of his themes. In fact, the major criticism against Verga's dramas has been that he indulges in the violent nature of reality, focusing on murder, lust, adultery, suicide, and other crimes of passion at the expense of the poetry and humor of Sicily. This is equally true in several of his later plays including *The She-Wolf* (1896) and *The Wolf Hunt* (1902). However, it is his unsentimental depiction of reality that make his plays successful. Verga's one attempt at social drama, *The Fox Hunt* (1902), received little attention critically and was a failure in production.

Verga wrote his last play, an adaptation of his novel *Dal tuo al Mio,* in 1905. The remainder of his life, during which many translations of his works were produced internationally, passed quietly. He died in 1922, well remembered for his contributions to Italian realistic literature.

Other Works by Giovanni Verga

Appelbaum, Stanley, ed. *Sicilian Stories/Novelle Siciliane: A Dual-Language Book.* New York: Dover, 2002.

Little Novels of Sicily: Stories. Translated by D. H. Lawrence. South Royalton, Vt.: Steerforth Press, 2000.

The House by the Medlar Tree. Translated by Raymond Rosenthal. Berkeley: University of California Press, 1984.

verismo

Similar in form to other REALIST movements of the late 19th and early 20th centuries, the Italian *verismo* movement developed as a means of objectively presenting life in simple language, with vivid details and natural dialogue. In particular, writers of the movement focused on the social conditions and hardships of the lower classes, bringing to focus much of the tragedy of the dominant human condition.

Two primary novelists of the *verismo* movement were Luigi Capuana (1839–1915) and Giovanni VERGA. They were influenced by the French realist movement, especially the writings of Honoré de BALZAC, and, closer to home, the short-lived Milanese Bohemian movement SCAPIGLIATURA.

Capuana is actually credited with having begun the movement with his collection of short stories *Studies of Women* (1877), a work which was extremely psychologically motivated as well as objective in its depictions to the point of almost excluding all traces of human emotion. Verga's works, while also objective in nature, tended to be softer than Capuana's, lending a trace of emotional warmth to an otherwise dismal portrait of 19th-century Sicily and its social conditions.

As the movement grew, other writers also began to adopt some of its traits, generally focusing their works on the places they knew the best, such as their hometowns, and the prevailing social conditions faced by the lower-class residents. Minor writers of the movement who are worthy of note included Matilde Serao (1865–1927) and Grazia Deledda (1871–1936), who was awarded the Nobel Prize for literature in 1926.

Verismo also found expression in opera. In the last decade of the 19th century, violence and melodrama found their way to the stage in the form of operatic works taken directly from everyday life. Here, the influence of the movement is felt most strongly. In particular, Puccini's *Tosca* (1900) shows strongly the impact of *verismo*.

A Work about *Verismo*

Sergio, Pacifici, ed. *From Verismo to Experimentalism: Essays on the Modern Italian Novel.* Bloomington: Indiana University Press, 1970.

Verlaine, Paul (1851–1896) *poet*

A leading poet of the French symbolist movement (*see* SYMBOLISM), Paul Verlaine was born in Metz. In 1881, he moved to Paris, where he attended school and read Charles BAUDELAIRE's *Flowers of Evil,* which influenced his decision to become a writer.

Verlaine studied law for two years but abandoned his studies to pursue writing. He befriended several young poets with whom he spent long hours in philosophical discussions. Excessive consumption of absinthe, the favored drink among writers and artists, eventually led to the demise of many of his relationships and to his own ultimate hospitalization.

Verlaine's father refused to support his son's bohemian way of life, but Verlaine managed to forge an existence based primarily on drinking and writing. His first published works, *Poèmes saturniens* (1866) and *Fêtes Galantes* (1869), echoed the emerging symbolist style.

In 1870, although he had already begun to display homosexual tendencies, Verlaine married Mathilde Maute de Fleurville. For her, he wrote *La Bonne Chanson* (1870), in which he expressed his darkest fears and hopes for happiness. The marriage ended when Verlaine began an affair with the younger French poet Arthur RIMBAUD. Verlaine left his wife to return to a bohemian existence with Rimbaud until, after a drunken argument, he shot Rimbaud in the wrist. Verlaine was sentenced to 18 months in prison, during which time he wrote what is arguably his finest collection, *Songs Without Words* (1874).

In 1873, Verlaine converted to Catholicism. He moved to England to teach French and began work on the collection *Wisdom* (1881). These poems reflect his new faith in God. He left his teaching post in 1889 and adopted his favorite student.

In 1883, Verlaine's student died of typhus. His mother's death followed in 1886. Again Verlaine sought refuge in alcohol. He continued to write but spent his royalties on prostitutes and constantly reflected on his loss of Rimbaud, whom he claimed to dream about every night.

Verlaine achieved great fame as a poet and was elected France's Prince of Poets in 1894. His way of life ultimately got the better of him, and he died two years later on January 8, in complete poverty.

Another Work by Paul Verlaine

Women and Men: Erotica. Translated by Philip Shirley. New York: Stonehill, 1980.

A Work about Paul Verlaine

Chadwick, Charles. *Verlaine.* London: Athlone Press, 1973.

Vigny, Alfred de (1797–1863) *playwright, poet, novelist*

Best known for his *Chatterton* (1835), one of the most influential plays of the French romantic period (*see* ROMANTICISM), Alfred de Vigny was born in Loches, Indre-et-Loire, to Leon Pierre de Vigny, a former officer of the king's army. As a student, he wrote several neoclassical tragedies based on the lives of such figures as Anthony and Cleopatra, but he destroyed these works and, at age 16, followed in his father's footsteps by entering the military. He soon became disillusioned with military life, however, finding it less glamorous than it is portrayed in fiction. He spent most of his time in the barracks reading classical texts and writing poetry.

Vigny met Victor HUGO in 1820 and became enamored of the new trend toward romanticism. He published a collection of poetry, *Poèmes antiques et modernes* (1826), and a historical novel, *Cinq-Mars* (1826), inspired by the works of Sir Walter Scott.

In 1827, Vigny resigned from military service and went to Paris to write. He wrote of his disappointment with the military experience in *Servitude et grandeur militaires* (*The Military Necessity,* 1835). In this work, he condemns the savage nature of war but praises the friendships that develop between soldiers.

Vigny planned to marry Delphine Gay who, 20 years later, became the inspiration for many of his poems, but his mother opposed the idea, and he married instead Lydia Bunbury. In 1827, after an English Shakespearean theater group came through France, he became interested in theater, writing adaptations of Shakespeare's plays. He wrote his first original play, *La Maréchale D'Ancre* (1831), based on Louis XIII.

His best-known work, *Chatterton* (1835), was written for his mistress, actress Marie Dorval. It describes the death of a young poet who was incapable of surviving in a brutal, materialistic world. Its success gained Vigny recognition as a literary rival to Hugo, with whom his friendship had declined. Although he remained successful in his literary career, the end of his life was difficult. His marriage and his affair both turned sour, and he was rejected by the French Academy five times before being accepted in 1845. He published only a few poems in later years, dying in Paris on September 17.

Other Works by Alfred de Vigny

Alfred de Vigny's "Chatterton". Translated by Philip A. Fulvi. New York: Griffon House, 1990.
Stello: A Session with Doctor Noir. Translated by Irving Massey. Montreal: McGill University Press, 1963.

Works about Alfred de Vigny

Dolittle, James. *Alfred de Vigny.* Boston: Twayne, 1967.
Shwimer, Elaine K. *The Novels of Alfred de Vigny: A Study of Their Form and Composition.* New York: Garland Press, 1991.

Villiers de L'Isle-Adam, Auguste
(Mathias de Villiers) (1838–1889)
novelist, playwright

A believer in God as well as in the mysteries of the occult, Villiers was a visionary who anticipated SYMBOLISM, promoted idealism, lived his beliefs in spite of the harsh reality of the world around him, and remained proud of his heritage. Born in Brittany on November 28, he came from a family whose ancestors had defended and rebuilt France, fought in the Crusades, and exemplified what Villers believed to be the true ideals of virtue. The temporary nature of physical existence, the importance and reality of the spirit world and its forbidden mysteries, as well as the beauty and nobility of intellect all find their way into his writing.

Villiers's works, influenced by the gothic elements of ROMANTICISM, are also commonly associated with the then-emerging symbolist movement. Although extremely prolific, he is most noted for the play *Axel* (1890), the short-story collection *Sardonic Tales* (1883; translated 1927), and the novel *L'Eve Future* (1886). In these works, Villiers turns to magic and the supernatural in a search for idealism that is lacking in the material world.

Loved and admired by fellow writers Paul VERLAINE and Maurice MAETERLINCK, Villiers was unknown to most of the world and scorned by many who did know him and believed him to be a madman. His early works, of which there were many, such as the spiritual romance *Isis* (1862) and the macabre *Claire Lenoir* (1867), went unnoticed by the public and the critics. *L'Eve Future* (1886), his parody of science and technology, finally gained him some measure of recognition in 1886.

Villiers died on August 19 while working on the final revisions to the posthumously published *Axel.* The recognition that had been denied him in life, as is often true for those individuals whose work is visionary, found him in death, and he paved the way for much of the emerging symbolist work that followed.

A Work about August Villiers de L'Isle-Adam

Conroy, William Thomas. *Villiers de l'Isle-Adam.* Boston: Twayne, 1978.

Voinovich, Vladimir (1932–) *novelist*

Vladimir Vladimirovich Voinovich was born in the city of Dushanbe, the capital of Tajikistan, in the Soviet Union. His father was a journalist, and his mother a mathematics teacher. Although his father wrote poetry and prose, virtually none of it was published. From an early age, Voinovich loved books and he later remarked about his childhood, "Our principal wealth was our books. . . ." Voinovich grew up during World War II and began to work at age 11. As he admits, he had little formal schooling and was principally educated by his father. He worked at various jobs, such as carpenter and metal worker, before starting to write.

Working with various composers, Voinovich began his writing career in 1960 by writing about 50 songs; he also wrote poetry and was published nearly at once. In 1961, his first short story, "We Live Here," was published in *Novy Mir,* a prestigious literary journal. Early in his career, the poignant realism of Voinovich's prose alarmed the Soviet government, which resulted in Voinovich being openly badgered in newspapers throughout the country. Voinovich emigrated from Russia in 1980. He was stripped of his Soviet citizenship in 1981 by decree of Leonid Brezhnev, the leader of the Soviet Union.

No longer restricted by censors, Voinovich was prolific and productive while he lived in Germany and the United States. His best-known novel, *The Life and Extraordinary Adventures of Private Ivan Chonkin,* was published in Paris in 1975. Combining political criticism and humor, the novel satirizes the absurdity of the Soviet regime. Voinovich experimented with various genres of fiction, ranging from striking realism to dystopian science-fiction visions of a communist future. *Moscoe 2042* (1986) exaggerated and reflected the reality of the crumbling Soviet regime. In this novel, the narrator time-travels into 21st-century Moscow and discovers a culturally and socially degenerate society that supposedly achieved the theoretical goals of communism.

After the fall of the communist regime, the government returned Russian citizenship to Voinovich. He currently lives in Moscow and in Munich, Germany. Voinovich is a member of the prestigious Bavarian Academy of Arts and the Mark Twain society. His prose has been translated into 10 languages.

Another Work by Vladimir Voinovich

Fur Hat. Translated by Susan Brownberger. New York: Harvest Books, 1991.

W

Walcott, Derek (Alton) (1930–   ) *poet, playwright, producer, teacher, journalist, painter*

Derek Alton Walcott was born in Castries, St. Lucia, an ex-British colony. His grandmothers were slave descendants, and his grandfathers were English and Dutch. Both Walcott's father, Warwick, a Bohemian poet and artist, and his mother, Alix, who ran Castries' Methodist school and recited Shakespeare in the house, influenced the pursuits of Derek and his twin brother, Roderick, who later became a distinguished playwright. Walcott's mentor Harold (Harry) Simmons, a painter, folklorist, and family friend, gave the young man painting and drawing lessons, as well as access to his library of poetry and art books and his collection of classical records. By the age of eight, Walcott decided he wanted to become a poet.

Educated at St. Mary's College, a high school for boys in Castries, Walcott published his first poem at age 14 in *The Voice of St. Lucia.* As an 18 year old, he published his first volume of poetry, *25 Poems* (1948), followed by his long poem *Epitaph for the Young* (1949). *25 Poems* attracted the attention and encouragement of Frank COLLYMORE. Looking back at his earlier verse writing in "What the Twilight Says," a 1970 autobiographical essay, Walcott wrote

that he strove to "legitimately [prolong] the mighty line of Marlowe and Milton."

In 1950, the British awarded Walcott a Colonial Development and Welfare Scholarship to the University College of the West Indies in Jamaica. While there, Walcott published a small collection of poetry, entitled *Poems.* He stayed at the University College of the West Indies to do graduate work in education after earning a B.A. in English, French, and Latin. Before leaving, Walcott designed and directed the student drama society's presentation of *Henri Christophe* (1950), Walcott's first and best-known play, previously produced in 1950 by the St. Lucia Arts Guild, which Walcott founded.

From 1953 to 1957, Walcott worked as a teacher at the Grenada Boys' School, St. Mary's College, and Jamaica College, and in 1956, he started working in journalism as a feature writer for *Public Opinion,* a Jamaican weekly in Kingston. Later, he became a feature writer and drama critic for the Trinidad *Guardian.* Sponsored by a Rockefeller Foundation theater fellowship, he went to New York in 1958 and studied directing and set design. Dissatisfied, he settled in Trinidad one year later. In 1960, he founded the Little Carib Theatre Workshop (which later became the Trinidad Theatre Workshop). There he trained actors and produced a number of his earlier plays, many on the myths and rituals of West Indian folk life.

Walcott's plays examine Caribbean identity and life by employing verse and prose, elements of pantomime, realism, fable, and fantasy. In "What the Twilight Says," Walcott wrote that he wanted to use "a language that went beyond mimicry," "which begins to create an oral culture, of chants, jokes, folk-songs, and fables." Of his many plays, Walcott's *Dream on Monkey Mountain* (1967) is among his most impressive. It won an Obie Award as the best foreign play of 1971 after being staged in New York. Three other plays—*The Last Carnival*, which looks at the recent decades of Trinidad's history; *A Branch of the Blue Nile*, about a conflict in the central character's mind between drama and the church, with characters partly based on the actors Walcott worked with at the Trinidad Theatre Workshop); and *Beef, No Chicken*, a comedy about the absurdities of postcolonial politics in the Caribbean—appear in *Three Plays* (1986).

In addition to playwriting, Walcott has worked with Galt MacDermott, known for the musical *Hair*, and has written musicals: *The Joker of Seville* (first performed in 1974; an adaptation of Tirso de Molina's *El Burlador de Sevilla* from Roy Campbell's English translation); and *O Babylon!* (first performed in 1976; a portrayal of Rastafarians in Jamaica that examines capitalism).

Drawing on various literary and dramatic traditions—classical and contemporary, African, Asiatic, and European—Walcott writes in standard English and West Indian dialect. His work uses imagery and traditional literary techniques to explore themes of exile, injustice, oppression, and identity formation while reconstructing history. *In a Green Night* (1962), his first widely distributed and commercially published volume of poetry, fuses traditional verse with examinations of Caribbean experiences. In a review cited in the Academy of American Poets Poetry Archive, Robert Graves asserted, "Derek Walcott handles English with a closer understanding of its inner

magic than most (if not any) of his English-born contemporaries."

Since the 1970s, Walcott has periodically lived and worked in the United States, serving as a visiting lecturer at several universities, including Columbia, Rutgers, Yale, Princeton, Harvard, and Boston University.

Meanwhile, Walcott has continued to write prolifically. Between 1970 and 1974, he published essays on literary culture, including "What the Twilight Says: An Overture" (1970), "Meanings" (1970), and "The Muse of History" (1974). His publications consistently garner critical acclaim. They include *Sea Grapes* (1976) and *The Star Apple Kingdom* (1979), collections in which he turned from the lush celebrations of the Caribbean landscape that characterized his earlier poems to examine the cultural tensions of island life, and *Midsummer* (1984), which focuses on the poet's own situation, living in America and isolated from his Caribbean homeland. In his most ambitious work, the epic poem *Omeros* (1990), Walcott uses terza rima, a rhyme scheme of interlocking tercets most famously used by Dante in *The Divine Comedy*, and Creole idioms to retell the Homeric legends in a modern Caribbean setting.

In 1992, two years after *Omeros*'s publication, Walcott received the Nobel Prize in literature. Rex Nettleford, a former classmate of Walcott's at the University of West Indies, vice-chancellor of the University of West Indies, and artistic director of Jamaica National Dance Theatre Company, said, in "1992, he's the West Indian writer most deserving of recognition. His work signifies the cultural integrity emerging from tremendous cross-fertilization in Caribbean life and history. It reminds us that we have no common mint of origin, only a common mint of relations." D. S. Izevbaye comments that his "skill in creating new meanings out of old, that is, the creation of a new language based on his commitment to standard English and a mythohistoric interpretation of West Indian identity, is a central part of Walcott's achievement."

Other Works by Derek Walcott

The Bounty. New York: Farrar, Straus, & Giroux, 1997.

Tiepolo's Hound. New York: Farrar, Straus & Giroux, 2000.

What the Twilight Says: Essays. New York: Farrar, Straus, & Giroux, 1999.

Works about Derek Walcott

Breslin, Paul. *Nobody's Nation: Reading Derek Walcott.* Chicago: University of Chicago Press, 2001.

Burnett, Paula. *Derek Walcott: Politics and Poetics.* Gainesville: University Press of Florida, 2000.

Izevbaye, D. S. "The Exile and The Prodigal: Derek Walcott as West Indian Poet." *Caribbean Quarterly* 26 (March–June 1980).

King, Bruce. *Derek Walcott, a Caribbean Life.* New York: Oxford University Press, 2000.

Walker, Kath

See NOONUCCAL, OODGEROO.

White, Patrick (1912–1980) *poet, novelist*

Patrick Victor Martindale White was born in Knightsbridge, London, to Victor Martindale and Ruth Withycombe. He came to Australia as an infant and grew up in Kings Cross, Sydney. In 1925, he went to England to attend Cheltenham College and returned to Australia in 1929. White's interest in writing came early as a child, and he also wanted to be an actor. His mother encouraged him to write while in primary school, and when he was nine, he was published in the children's page of a newspaper.

White's collection of poems, *The Ploughman* (1935), gained prominence, and other of his poems were published in the *London Mercury.* He rewrote his novel *The Immigrants,* which was published as *Happy Valley* in 1939, for which he won the Australian Literature Society's gold medal. In 1939, he came to the United States and published *The Living and the Dead* (1941).

White's main themes are alienation, the Australian landscape, the cultures of Europe and Australia, and the Aborigines. His central theme is the search for meaning and value in life. He was influenced by the French poet Charles BAUDELAIRE and came to be known as a symbolist (*see* SYMBOLISM) writer. He uses symbolism to convey a sense of the splendor of Australia, which to many people seemed dull. White's narrative techniques include autobiographical elements, dramatization, symbolism, merging of his self with his characters, and flashbacks. For White, plot was not as important as character development.

White was also known to be a transcendentalist because of his portrayal of an Australia above the ordinary. He wrote the novel *The Tree of Man* (1955) with the goal of finding a secret core or purpose of Australia. In the novel, Stan and Amy long for a new beginning for their country, beyond ordinary politics. In *The Aunt's Story* (1948), White writes about the national homelessness of Theodora, who is placed between the two cultures of Britain and Australia. He also expresses his doubts about Europe because of nuclear armament and the Holocaust. Ellen in *A Fringe of Leaves* (1976) feels ill at ease in Europe. The Australian landscape is a major presence in this novel. As he writes of his own reaction to Europe in his autobiography, *Flaws in the Glass* (1981), "It was landscape that made me long to return to Australia."

In *Voss* (1957), we see a primitive picture of the Aborigines. Voss, the main character, communicates with the Aborigines in a language of nature, as if they were not human. In *A Fringe of Leaves,* we also read of Eliza Fraser, who is stranded on an island and is living with the Aborigines. She becomes one with them, and her cannibalism is a metaphor for European destruction of Aboriginal culture.

Patrick White won the Nobel Prize in literature in 1973, the only Australian to have this honor. In 1965, he won the Australian Literature Society's gold medal for *Riders in the Chariot* (1961). He received the Australia Day Councils' Australian of the Year Award for 1974. He is considered to be one of the most intellectual, original, and preeminent Australian novelists. White died in Sydney after a long illness.

Other Works by Patrick White

Selected Writings. Edited by Alan Lawson. St. Lucia: University of Queensland Press, 1994.

The Twyborn Affair. New York: Penguin, 1980.

Works about Patrick White

Marr, David. *Patrick White: A Life.* New York: Knopf, 1991.

Wolfe, Peter, ed. *Critical Essays on Patrick White.* Boston: G. K. Hall, 1990.

Wicomb, Zoë (1948–) *short-story writer, novelist*

Born near Cape Town, Wicomb was educated at universities in South Africa and in Great Britain. Although everyone in the rural town in which she was raised spoke Afrikaans, the dialect spoken by the Afrikaner descendants of South Africa's Dutch settlers, she taught herself to speak English by "copying the radio." She wanted to be a writer of English stories and, encouraged especially by her father, Robert, she wrote "horrible little poems." The dismantling of apartheid and the first truly free elections in South Africa's history (in 1992) have meant that the country's writers must look beyond apartheid for subjects. Wicomb is one of a wave of "new" South African authors whose work does not revolve around colonialism, in general, or apartheid issues, in particular. She writes feelingly and lyrically about personal identity and the connectedness, or lack of it, between and among people of color.

Wicomb has written two books. The first, *You Can't Get Lost in Cape Town* (1987), is a series of related short stories set in and around the strikingly beautiful Cape Province. The central character of this "novel in parts" is an educated, young, mixed-race ("coloured") woman. In the closing story in the collection, "A Trip to the Gifberg," Wicomb's first-person narrator details the occasionally difficult interaction with her Griqua (tribal African) mother as they journey to a mountain that her mother had always meant to visit. The older woman, uneducated and accustomed only to the old ways, had often looked up at the "unat-

tainable blue of the mountain" from a seat on her porch. The personal relationship, especially when her mother is "genuinely surprised that our wishes do not coincide," speaks to the political and public lack of any real connection between even those whose "color" had previously defined them as a coherent group.

In both this work and in her second novel, *David's Story* (2001), Wicomb explores the various landscapes, physical and emotional, of her characters' existence as neither black nor white in the "new," postapartheid Africa. Like many other writers of contemporary South Africa, the overthrow of the racially based segregation policies of the apartheid-era government has compelled and allowed Wicomb to deal with increasingly difficult issues of personal identity. For example, the protagonist of *David's Story* has to come to grips with his self-identification as a political activist when his opponent, apartheid, has been defeated. David confronts the power of an unpleasant past in a present where all is supposed to be "better."

As of July 2002, Wicomb was a finalist for a new and prestigious fiction award sponsored by the *South Africa Times.* She is one of a group of South African writers who speaks to issues beyond the sociological and the political, and her growing status among critics and writers outside of South Africa attests to her power and reach.

Another Work by Zoë Wicomb

"Shame and Identity: The Case of the Coloured in South Africa" (pp. 91–107). *Writing South Africa: Literature, Apartheid, and Democracy, 1970–1995.* Edited by Derek Attridge and Rosemary Jolly. Cambridge, England: Cambridge University Press, 1998.

Wiesel, Elie (1928–) *novelist, nonfiction writer*

Elie Wiesel was born in Sighet, Transylvania. When he was 15, his family was sent to Auschwitz, a Nazi death camp. His mother and younger sister died there, but his two older sisters survived, and Wiesel and his father were transferred to Buchenwald, where his father perished shortly before the liberation of the camps in 1945.

When World War II was over, Wiesel lived in a French orphanage until 1948 when he began to study journalism at the Sorbonne in Paris. The French writer and Nobel laureate François Mauriac persuaded Wiesel to break his silence and write about his time in the concentration camps. The resulting memoir, *Night* (1958), established Wiesel as a writer. A passage from the book recalls his shattered childhood: "Never shall I forget the little faces of the children, whose bodies I saw turned into wreaths of smoke beneath a silent blue sky. Never shall I forget those flames which consumed my faith forever."

Wiesel has written more than 40 works on the Holocaust and humanity's responsibility to fight racism and genocide. These works include several novels and two additional volumes of memoirs.

Wiesel became an American citizen in 1963 and, in 1978, was appointed chairman of the President's Commission on the Holocaust. He has since founded the U.S. Holocaust Memorial Council, received more than 100 honorary degrees, and defended causes ranging from those of the Soviet Jews to Cambodian refugees, famine and apartheid victims in Africa, and victims of war in Yugoslavia. He has received numerous awards for his literary and human-rights activities, including the Nobel Peace Prize in 1986.

Other Works by Elie Wiesel

And the Sea Is Never Full: Memoirs. Translated by Marion Wiesel. New York: Knopf, 1999.
The Fifth Son. Translated by Marion Wiesel. New York: Schocken Books, 1998.
The Testament. Translated by Marion Wiesel. New York: Schocken Books, 1981.

A Work about Elie Wiesel

Kolbert, Jack. *The Worlds of Elie Wiesel: An Overview of his Career and Major Themes.* Selinsgrove, Pa.: Susquehanna University Press, 2001.

Williams, Ella Gwendolyn Rees

See RHYS, JEAN.

Wittig, Monique (1935–) *poet, novelist, essayist*

A prominent name in feminist and lesbian literature, Monique Wittig was born in France. She earned a degree in languages from the University of Paris and published her first novel, *L'opopomax* (1964) shortly thereafter. In the late 1960s, she became increasingly outspoken about women's rights, helping to organize the separatist group Féministes Révolutionaires, for which she became the spokeswoman in 1970. She also took part in numerous organized protests and published a second novel, *Les Guérillères* (1970).

In 1973, Wittig became increasingly unable to reconcile her own goals as a writer with the idea of separatism. Although she understood its importance for some women, she also felt that oppression, whether based on gender differences or sexual orientation, exists primarily as a result of the preconceived concept that heterosexuality is inherently at the foundation of society. The way to negate discrimination, therefore, is to negate this belief, an idea that became major theme in Wittig's writing.

In 1976, Wittig moved to the United States and began working on the journal *Questions Féministes* with Simone de BEAUVOIR. She received her Ph.D. in 1986 and took a position on the faculty at the University of Arizona at Tucson in 1990.

Wittig's works, including the well-known pieces *One Is Not a Woman Born* (1981) and *The Lesbian Body* (1973), speak of gender equality and rights for women. She continues to express her views in her works as a means of abolishing gender distinctions in society.

Other Works by Monique Wittig

Lesbian People: Material for a Dictionary. New York: Avon Books, 1979.
The Straight Mind and Other Essays. Boston: Beacon Press, 1992.

A Work about Monique Wittig

Gray, Nancy. *Language Unbound: On Experimental Writing by Women.* Urbana: University of Illinois Press, 1992.

Wolf, Christa (Christa Ihenfeld)

(1929–   ) *novelist, short-story writer, essayist*
Christa Wolf was born in Landsberg an der Warthe, Germany (today Gorzów Wielkopolski, Poland). During World War II, her father Otto Ihelenfeld, a salesman, was forced to move the family to Mecklenburg. After completing grammar school in 1949, Wolf studied literature at the Universities of Leipzig and Jena. She joined East Germany's Socialist Unity Party (SED) and worked as a journal editor and reader for publishing houses. In 1951, she married essayist Gerhard Wolf.

In the 1950s, Wolf began to write essays and coedited two anthologies on East German literature with her husband. Her first major literary success *Der Geteilte Himmel* (*The Divided Heaven,* 1963) dealt with the issue of divided Germany and made her the best-known writer in East Germany. Wolf followed the SED's call for writers to work in factories and incorporate working themes into their books. However, she later wrote novels that were critical of East Germany. In 1976, Wolf lost her membership in the East German Writers' Union for protesting the revocation of singer Wolf Biermann's citizenship. Wolf continued writing and, in 1980, won the prestigious Büchner Prize. She frequently addressed political topics in her numerous essays and, in 1989, joined writer Volker BRAUN in opposing German reunification.

Wolf's important influences include Anna Seghers and Ingeborg BACHMANN. She writes with frankness and believes that literature should help the reader grow personally. Wolf combines elements of pessimism with resourceful approaches to feminism and individualism. She addresses contemporary concerns but does not allow East Germans to escape dealing with their Nazi past. In 1997, scholar Marit Resch wrote in *Understanding Christa Wolf* (1997) that "one of Wolf's most important messages to all German citizens today is that it is imperative to discuss and honestly examine the totality of GDR [East German] history, not just politically expedient excerpts of it."

Other Works by Christa Wolf

Accident: A Day's News. Translated by Heike Schwarzbauer and Rick Takvorian. London: Virago, 1989.
Cassandra: A Novel and Four Essays. Translated by Jan van der Heurck. New York: Farrar, Straus & Giroux, 1984.

A Work about Christa Wolf

Resch, Margit. *Understanding Christa Wolf: Returning Home to a Foreign Land.* Columbia: University of South Carolina Press, 1997.

Wolff, Kurt

See BENN, GOTTFRIED.

Woruk, Kona

See HARRIS, WILSON.

Wright, Judith (1915–2000) *poet*

Judith Wright was born to Philip Arundel Wright and Ethel Wright in Thalgarrah Station in Australia. Wright's mother died in 1927, and a governess educated Wright. From 1929 to 1933, she attended the New England Girls' School in Armidale. She started writing poems when she was very young, and her first poems appeared in 1933. In 1934, she attended the University of Sydney.

Many of Wright's poems appeared in leading journals including the *Sydney Morning Herald, Bulletin,* and *Meanjin Papers.* Significant themes of her poetry include relationships with nature, Australian culture, Aboriginal culture, human rights, and reverence for life. *The Moving Image* (1946), her first collection of poems written during World War II, considers death and evil.

Wright writes in lyric form, as in *Woman to Man* (1949), which compares poetic imagination to the love between a man and woman: "Then all worlds I made in me: / all the world you hear and see." *The Two Fires* contains poems on the threat to humanity by humanity itself by means of nuclear weapons. There is also an emphasis on the exploration of language and the importance of myth. Her poetry is influenced by T. S. Eliot, Wallace Stevens, and W. B. Yeats, as can be seen in the wasteland images and prosaic language of *Phantom Dwelling* (1985).

Wright is renowned as poet, short-story writer, environmentalist, and children's writer. *Going-on Talking: Tales of a Great Aunt* (1998), her last book, was for children. She has received several honors: In 1949 she won the Grace Leven Prize for Poetry; she was elected to the Australian Literature Council; she won the Robert Frost Memorial award in 1976; she won the World Prize for Poetry in 1984; and, her greatest honor, she received the Queen's gold medal for poetry. Wright has published more than 56 volumes of poetry and short stories. She is acclaimed as one of Australia's greatest writers.

Another Work by Judith Wright

Collected Poems, 1942–1985. Sydney: Angus & Robertson, 1994.

Works about Judith Wright

Strauss, J. *Judith Wright.* Melbourne: Oxford University Press, 1995.

Walker, S. P. *Flame and Shadow: A Study of Judith Wright's Poetry.* St. Lucia, B.W.I.: University of Queensland Press, 1991.

Xie Wanying

See BING XIN.

Y

Yacine, Kateb (1929–1989) *novelist, poet, playwright*

Kateb Yacine was born in Condé-Smendou, near Constantine, Algeria. *Kateb* means "writer" in Arabic, which designates Yacine's family as highly literate. Yacine was raised on both tales of Arab achievements and Algerian legends. These childhood memories had an important influence on his writings. Yacine's father sent him to a French high school rather than a Qur'anic school when he was a young boy. In 1945, he participated in a nationalist demonstration in Sétif, which led to his expulsion from the Collège de Sétif. He was sent to prison without trial for a few months. During this time, he discovered his love for poetry and revolution. In 1950, he moved to France after paying several short visits to the country. His involvement in the Algerian revolution forced him to leave France in 1955, shortly after he had been offered a job at a publishing company. Yacine lived in many countries including Germany, the Soviet Union, Tunisia, and Vietnam, before returning finally to Algeria in 1970. He formed a theatrical company after his return and began to write plays. Yacine died in Grenoble, France.

At age 17, Kateb published his first book, *Soliloques* (1946), a collection of poems, and in 1948, he published the long poem "Nedjma ou le poeme ou le couteau," in which the character of Nedjma (the name means "star"), a mysterious woman, first appears. Kateb used the figure of Nedjma in many later poems and plays.

Revolution constitutes an important theme in Yacine's works. His visits to different countries greatly enhanced his determination to spearhead the Algerian nationalist struggle for independence. In the love story, *Nedjma* (1956), which recounts a tale of intraclan struggle set against the background of French colonial Algeria, the main protagonist Nedjma is loved by four revolutionaries. Nedjma, the name of the cousin with whom Yacine fell in love, is a mysterious character, obviously influenced by early childhood fantasies that were resurrected from his memories of Algerian legends.

Yacine's writings explore other important themes as well, such as change and the resilience of Algerian traditional values. Yacine's heroes are often Marxist revolutionaries, including historical characters in other cultures and societies, such as Ho Chi Minh and Mao Zedong. Ho Chi Minh is featured in Yacine's play, *L' Homme aux sandales de caoutchouc* (*The Man in the Rubber Sandals*) (1970).

Until his death, Yacine believed it was the responsibility of the writer to educate the public that the constant struggle between the proletariat (the working class) and the bourgeoisie (the upper and middle classes) was unceasing. Yacine wrote all his works in French.

A Work about Kateb Yacine

Salhi, Gamal. *The Politics and Aesthetics of Kateb Yacine: From Francophone Literature to Popular Theatre in Algeria and Outside.* Lewiston, N.Y.: Edwin Mellen Press, 1999.

Yamada Eimi (Yamada Futaba)
(1959–   ) *novelist, short-story writer, cartoonist*

Yamada Eimi was born in Tokyo. As a high school student, she became a devoted reader and chose Japanese literature as her area of study when she attended Meiji University in 1978. However, she never graduated, having already begun writing in her junior year *manga* (narrative comics) for high-school girls. Yamada soon tired of producing *manga* and decided to take up fiction writing. She adopted a sensational lifestyle as a bar hostess, a nude model, and a "queen" of a sado-masochists' club. She began to write seriously when her relationship soured with an African-American soldier based in Japan.

Her first work, the autobiographical novella *Bedtime Eyes,* published in 1985, was about a relationship between a Japanese woman and an African-American soldier based in Japan. A year later, Yamada produced eight stories, including "Jessie's Spine," about a Japanese woman's difficult relationship with her African-American lover's son. Increasing her rate of production even more, she published another eight short stories and three novels in 1987. One of the novels, *A Foot-bound Butterfly,* is a story about the experiences of a young girl as she navigates adolescent pressures.

Yamada is a prolific writer whose stories revel in the exotic. Her characters are generally young women living on the edge and often involved in relationships with African Americans. She incorporates an unusually large amount of slang English into her stories to evoke vivid imagery. As such,

Yamada's stories represent a new voice in Japanese literature. She has won the Bungei Award and the Naoki Prize and been nominated for the Akutagawa Prize.

Other Works by Yamada Eimi

"Kneel Down and Lick My Feet." Translated by Terry Gallaher. In Alfred Birnbaum and Elmer Luke, eds., *Monkey Brain Sushi: New Tastes in Japanese Fiction.* New York: Kodansha International, 1993.
Trash. Translated by Sonya L. Johnson. New York: Kodansha International, 1995.

A Work about Yamada Eimi

Cornyetz, Nina. "Power and Gender in the Narratives of Yamada Eimi." In Paul Gordon Schalow and Janet A. Walker, eds., *The Woman's Hand: Gender and Theory in Japanese Women's Writing.* Stanford, Calif.: Stanford University Press, 1996.

Yáñez, Mirta (1947–   ) *poet, screenwriter, critic*

Mirta Yáñez was born in Havana, Cuba, and attended the University of Havana, where she later taught. Considered to be one of Cuba's best contemporary poets who has written for Cuban film and television, she is also one of Cuba's foremost literary critics and has written extensively about feminism in Cuban literature.

In 1996, she assembled a collection of writing by Cuban women, and in 1998, it was released in the United States with the title *Cubana.* This collection of 16 stories and an introductory essay by Yáñez gives the reader a moving glimpse into the difficult social situation of Cuban woman today.

Yáñez lives in Havana where she writes and lectures.

Yathay Pin (1944–   ) *novelist*

Yathay Pin was born in Oudong, a village about 25 miles north of Phnom Penh, Cambodia. Yathay's father, Chhor, was a small trader, and his family, though not impoverished, was poor.

Yathay was the eldest of five children. His father had high expectations of him: Knowing that Yathay was an excellent student, Chhor sent him to a good high school in Phnom Penh. Yathay received a government scholarship after completing high school, and he went to Canada to further his studies. In 1965, Yathay graduated from the Polytechnic Institute in Montreal with a diploma in civil engineering. He went back to Cambodia and joined the Ministry of Public Works. He married his first wife soon after, and they had one son. His first wife and second baby died in childbirth in 1969. Afterward, Yathay married his wife's sister, Any, and they had two sons. In 1975, the Khmer Rouge overthrew the Lon Nol government in Phnom Penh and began a regime of terror. The communist Khmer Rouge persecuted educated professionals and intellectuals and accused them of being bourgeois capitalists. Yathay and his family, consisting of eight members, were sent to work as unpaid agricultural workers in the countryside. By 1977, most of his family members had perished from malnutrition, overwork, or sickness. Yathay, who had managed to disguise his educated background for a few years, was finally betrayed by an acquaintance. Fearing execution, he made a run for freedom by walking over the mountains that separated Cambodia from Thailand. Yathay safely reached Thailand two months later; he had, however, lost his wife in a forest fire. From his Cambodian past, Yathay has one surviving son whom he fears is already dead. Yathay now works as a project engineer in the French Development Agency in Paris. He has also remarried and now has three sons.

Yathay's best and only known work is *Stay Alive, My Son* (1987), which is an acrid account of his hellish experience in Cambodia under the terror of the Khmer Rouge regime. His harrowing tale of anguish and distress is one among many voices that have since emerged from the writings of Cambodian refugees who have lived to tell about the horrors. *Stay Alive, My Son* is a remarkable book not merely because it is a moving tale but also because it is a true story. Only the late Haing Ngor's memoir, *A Cambodian Odyssey* (1987), can rival its poignant reality.

Yesenin, Sergey (Esenin, Sergei)
(1895–1925) *poet*

Born in Konstantinovo, Russia, in a peasant family, Sergey Aleksandrovich Yesenin was raised by his maternal grandparents. He vigorously engaged in all the physical activities afforded by the countryside, such as swimming, hunting, and riding horses. He began to compose verse when he was only nine. After finishing grammar school in 1909, he was sent to a seminary to be trained as a teacher. While in seminary, he became serious about writing poetry and, upon the advice of a teacher, left for Moscow to pursue writing as a career.

After an unsuccessful marriage that lasted only a year, Yesenin moved to St. Petersburg in 1914. His first poetry collection, *Radunitsa* (*Mourning for the Dead*) was published in 1916. The poems were composed in the traditional lyrical style, emphasizing rhyme, meter, and metaphor. Yesenin focused on his personal experience with nature, family relationships, and love. To the disapproval of the exponents of SOCIALIST REALISM, Yesenin's poetry continued to stress image rather than message. His fame spread quickly, and he even read his poetry for the empress and her daughters. Nonetheless, he welcomed the October Revolution of 1917, seeing it as a vindication of the peasant values he celebrated in his collection *Inoyiya* (*Otherland*, 1918). But before long he was disillusioned with Bolsheviks, criticizing them in poems such as "The Stern October Has Deceived Me." Yesenin's application to join the Communist Party was rejected in 1919, supposedly due to his lack of political discipline.

In 1922, Yesenin published *Pugachev*, a tragic epic poem about an 18th-century peasant rebellion. The same year, he married American dancer Isadora Duncan, who had opened a ballet school in Moscow. Duncan and Yesenin traveled together in Europe and the United States and had spectacular public quarrels. After their 1923 separation,

Yesenin returned to Moscow where he gave poetry recitals in cafes and drank heavily, sober only when he was actually composing verse.

The collections published in 1924 and 1925 demonstrate a major shift in Yesenin's poetry. *Moscow of the Taverns* (1924) and *Soviet Rus* (1925) comment on social and cultural changes in Communist Russia. Although Yesenin's diction remains lyrical and imaginative, he has moved away from the solipsistic study of the individual.

Subdued by alcoholism, Yesenin developed major psychological problems during the last year of his life. His marriage to Sofia Tolstoy, granddaughter of Leo TOLSTOY, was essentially unsuccessful. Yesenin committed suicide by hanging himself. His suicide note was a poem written in his own blood. His works, popular though they were, were banned under Stalin but were republished in Russia in 1966.

Other Works by Sergey Yesenin

Confessions of a Hooligan: Fifty Poems. Translated by Geoffrey Thurley. Manchester, U.K.: Carcanet Press, 1973.
The Collected Poems of Yesenin. Translated by Gregory Brengauz. Tallahassee: Floridian Publisher, 2000.

Works about Sergey Yesenin

McVay, Gordon. *Isadora and Esenin: The Story of Isadora Duncan and Sergei Esenin.* Ann Arbor, Mich.: Ardis, 1978.
Visson, Lynn. *Sergei Esenin, Poet of the Crossroads.* Wurzburg: Jal-Verlag, 1980.

Yevtushenko, Yevgeny (1933–) *poet, dramatist*

Yevgeny Yevtushenko was born in Irkutsk, Russia. When he was 11, his family moved to Moscow. From an early age, he loved literature and decided to pursue a career in a literary field. He studied at the Gorky Institute of Literature from 1951 to 1954. He was closely attached to his father and sometimes accompanied him on geological expe-

ditions. In 1948, they traveled to distant regions of Kazakhstan and Altai. The experiences of this trip appear in Yevtushenko's first published collection of verse, *Zima Junction* (1956).

Yevtushenko became internationally renowned with the publication of *Babi Yar,* a long narrative poem that denounces Nazi anti-Semitism and memorializes victims of the Holocaust. The poem also criticizes actions of the Russian people toward the Jews. For this reason, the poem did not appear in Russia until 1984. Yevtushenko proceeded to publish verse of a more political nature. In *Heirs of Stalin* (1961), he warns readers about the dangers that Stalinism poses even after Stalin's death. In 1963, Yevtushenko published *A Precocious Autobiography* in English. The work was criticized by the government for its open criticism of Soviet policies, and he was not allowed to leave the country for two years.

In 1972, Yevtushenko shifted his artistic interests from poetry and produced a hugely successful play, *Under the Skin of the Statue of Liberty.* Yevtushenko is a prolific artist and expanded his artistic scope to directing, acting, and photography. He also edited poetry for *Ogonek,* a journal that published many previously repressed writers and poets.

Yevgeny Yevtushenko has achieved enormous success during his lifetime. He was appointed as an honorary member of American Academy of Arts and Sciences in 1987. In 1989, he was elected as a member of the Congress of People's Deputies, and he has served as vice president of an organization of Russian writers (PEN). After the collapse of the Soviet Union, Yevtushenko played a central role in the erection near the former KGB headquarters of a monument to the victims of Stalinism.

Other Works by Yevgeny Yevtushenko

Don't Die Before You're Dead. Translated by Antonina W. Bouis. New York: Random House, 1995.
The Collected Poems, 1952–1990. Translated by James Ragan. New York: Henry Holt, 1991.
Yevgeny Yevtushenko: Early Poems. Translated by George Reavey. New York: Marion Boyars, 1989.

Yosano Akiko (Shō Hō) (1878–1942)

poet, essayist, critic, children's story writer

Yosano Akiko was born in the city of Sakai near Osaka, Japan, to a merchant family. When she was young, she helped out with the family business, reading Japanese classical literature from her father's library in her spare time. After she completed a junior-high-school education, she began to write poetry. During this time, she wrote a letter to Tokyo poet Tekkan Yosano (1873–1935), to establish a professional relationship. She later married him. In an effort to further education for women, Yosano helped establish a high school for women in 1921. Seven years later, she started a poetry magazine called *Tōhaku* (Cameria-Camelia). She died of a cerebral hemorrhage.

Yosano's first poem was published in an anthology of Osaka-area poets in 1896. She continued to work with these local poets until she met Tekkan, who published a literary magazine *Myōjō* (*Morning Star*). In 1901, she left Osaka for Tokyo and began to publish poems, novels, and essays at a rapid rate. During this period, she published her most famous collection of poetry, *Midaregami* (*Tangled Hair,* translated 1987). She also wrote essays on social and political issues, translated *The Tale of Genji* into modern Japanese, and created a collection of children's stories.

Yosano primarily wrote tanka and free verse that expressed honest emotions. To develop honesty in her writing, she based her poems on her personal experiences and feelings, notably her love for Tekkan. Her style challenged traditional poetry themes and methods of expression, thereby establishing her own modern poetic style. By the time of her death, Yosano had written approximately 50,000 tanka.

Other Works by Yosano Akiko

River of Stars: Selected Poems of Yosano Akiko. Translated by Keiko Matsui Gibson. Boston: Shambhala Publications, 1997.

Tangled Hair: Love Poems of Yosano Akiko. Translated by Dennis Maloney. Fredonia, N.Y.: White Pine Press, 1991.

Travels in Mongolia and Manchuria. Translated by Joshua A. Fogel. New York: Columbia University Press, 2001.

Works about Yosano Akiko

Rodd, Lauren Rasplica. "Yosano Akiko and the Taisho Debate over the 'New Woman.'" In Gail Lee Bernstein, ed., *Recreating Japanese Women, 1600–1945.* Berkeley: University of California Press, 1991.

Ueda, Makoto. *Modern Japanese Poets and the Nature of Literature.* Stanford, Calif.: Stanford University Press, 1983.

Yourcenar, Marguerite (Marguerite de Crayencour) (1903–1987) *novelist, poet, essayist*

Born to an aristocratic family in Brussels, Belgium, Yourcenar spent much of her childhood traveling with her father. After his death, she became independently wealthy and was able to pursue writing, a passion that had begun to manifest itself when she was a teenager. Her historical novels, which deal with modern themes such as the psychological manifestations of homosexuality and deviant behavior, gained her international fame and recognition.

Chinese legend fascinated Yourcenar in her early works, as did the role and life of the artist. In her early short story collection, *Oriental Tales* (1938), she draws from Chinese and Sanskrit legend to write about art and the artist's frustration. In one particular piece, "How Wang-Fo was Saved," she recounts the tale of an aging painter who is imprisoned by a ruler who fears the power of art.

Memoirs of Hadrian (1951) is among the best known of Yourcenar's works. Detailing the reflections of a dying man and set on the eve of Hadrian's death, the emperor recounts his memories in a letter addressed to the person who will take his place. The novel took 15 years to complete and was published shortly after Yourcenar moved to the United States at the start of World War II.

Yourcenar took a position in New York at Sarah Lawrence College as professor of French literature and began to live with her translator Grace Frick. The two remained partners for the duration of Yourcenar's life. She continued to write, publishing *Le Coup de grâce* (1939), the story of a Prussian officer who, because he secretly loves her brother, decides to kill the woman who has fallen in love with him. She also published *The Abyss* (1976), in which she creates a fictional Renaissance man who is essentially a combination of the historical figures Da Vinci, Paracelsus, Copernicus, and Giordano Bruno. Like many of the male characters she presents, he is depicted as a homosexual.

Yourcenar wrote only one work with a contemporary setting. The novel, *Denier du rêve* (*A Coin in Nine Hands,* 1934), revolves around the attempted assassination of Mussolini. The novel is also unique in that it revolves around several female characters and examines the female psyche. The majority of Yourcenar's characters in her works are men who are trapped between the demands of society and the desire for passion.

Yourcenar also wrote two volumes of family memoirs, *Souvenirs Pieux* (*Dear Departed,* 1974) and *Archives du Nord* (*Northern Archives,* 1977), as well as a number of essays, poems, and plays. As a translator, she worked to translate English and American novels as well as Negro spirituals into her native French. In 1980, Yourcenar became the first woman ever to be elected to the Académie Française. She died seven years later on December 17 in Maine.

Other Works by Marguerite Yourcenar

Dreams and Destinies. Translated by Donald Flanell Friedman. New York: St. Martin's Press, 1999.
How Many Years. Translated by Maria Louise Ascher. New York: Farrar, Straus & Giroux, 1995.
Mishima: A Vision of the Void. Translated by Alberto Manguel. Chicago: University of Chicago Press, 2001.

Works about Marguerite Yourcenar

Horn, Pierre L. *Marguerite Yourcenar.* Boston: Twayne, 1985.

Saint, Nigel. *Marguerite Yourcenar: Reading the Visual.* Oxford: Legenda, 2000.

Yu Guangzhong (Yü Kwang-chung)
(1928–) *poet, essayist*

Yu Guangzhong was born in Nanjing, China, the capital of Fukien Province. He studied foreign languages at Ginling and Xiamen Universities in China before moving to Hong Kong with his family in 1948.

In 1950, Yu Guangzhong fled to Taiwan as a student refugee. He attended Taiwan's most prestigious institution, the National Taiwan University, where he began to write poetry. He graduated in 1952 and that same year published his first collection of poems, *Blues of a Sailor.* Highly sentimental and nostalgic, it was very popular.

Yu Guangzhong worked as an army interpreter until 1956 when he turned to teaching. Eventually, he decided to pursue a graduate degree in the United States. He earned a Masters of Fine Arts from the University of Iowa in 1959. He returned to Taiwan in 1959 and taught at Taiwan Teachers University and the Political University of Taiwan. Later, he taught at the Chinese University in Hong Kong.

Yu Guangzhong remained committed to literature, however, and formed the Blue Star Poetry Society with a friend, Qin Zihao. In the 1960s, he moved away from the sentimental style of his past writing and studied both traditional Chinese and modern forms of poetry. He published an article, "Good-bye, Mr. Nothingness!" on this subject, advocating change but discouraging the complete Westernization of Chinese literature.

Yu Guangzhong continued to teach English literature at National Taiwan Normal University until 1972 when he became the chair of the Department of Western Languages and Literature at National Chengchi University. Since then, he has lived in the United States twice as a Fulbright scholar and is the author of many volumes of poetry, including *Stalactite* (1960), *Associations of the*

Lotus (1964), and *A Bitter Gourd Carved in White Jade* (1974). He is also a prolific translator of poetry and a prominent literary critic and essayist. Today, he is considered one of Taiwan's premier men of letters.

Yun Tongju (Yun Hae-hwan) (1917–1945)
poet

Yun Hae-hwan was born on December 30 in Myongdong, North Kando province of Korea. He regularly published children's poems while studying literature at Yonhui College and wrote poems for a volume he hoped to publish later. After graduating in 1941, he chose to continue his studies in English literature.

Like many students in Japanese-occupied Korea, Yun Tongju traveled to Japan, first enrolling at Rikkyo University in 1942 and then transferring to Doshisha University in Kyoto. At the time, resistance to Japanese colonial rule was high, and restrictions on Koreans in Korea and Japan were increasingly stringent. Yun Tongju was forced to take a Japanese name and read, write, and speak in Japanese. He wrote secretly in his native language.

Yun Tongju actively participated in the Korean independence movement. As a result, in July 1943, he was arrested for subversive activity by the Japanese government. It is thought he was mistreated and abused in Japan's Fukuoka prison, where he died under unknown circumstances at the age of 28.

His one volume of poetry, *Sky, Wind, Stars and Poetry,* was published posthumously in 1948. The poems closely reflected Yun Tongju's feelings as a subject of Japanese colonialism. Particularly because he studied in Japan, he had to deal with a marked isolation from his native country and culture. His poems capture his displacement and resentment. "Counting the Stars" is replete with melancholic remembrances of the past, while "Awful Hour" examines the depths of the narrator's sense of alienation, perhaps in a period of intense solitude.

Yun Tongju's writing is the poetry of an exile. He searched for spiritual integrity and a Korean identity under an oppressive foreign regime. As he was battling outward influences of oppression, his inner struggle manifested itself in tortured, anguished, highly personal poems that seem to document both his individual struggle between self-love and self-hate and Korea's national crisis to articulate its independence. Because his writing is a testament to Korea's struggle against colonialism and provides a moving portrait of a young person's inner struggles, they were extremely popular, especially among younger readers.

Yun Tongju did not live to see Korea's liberation in 1945. In 1968, his alma mater, Yonhui College, erected a monument in his honor.

Z

Zamyatin, Yevgeny (1884–1937) *novelist*

Yevgeny Ivanovich Zamyatin was born in the small provincial town of Lebedyan, Russia. His father was a priest, and his mother an extremely well-educated woman who loved music. As a young child, Zamyatin read Dostoevsky and Turgenev. Zamyatin graduated Voronezh Gymnasium in 1902 with the Gold Medal (the highest academic honor in Russia, equivalent to a valedictorian), which he pawned for 25 rubles some months later. He moved to St. Petersburg and worked in the shipyards. Zamyatin joined the Bolsheviks, and his political beliefs got him into trouble. He was beaten by the police, placed in solitary confinement for several months, and was finally banished from St. Petersburg by the czar's police force.

Zamyatin's literary debut in 1908 was a subversive short story "Alone," for which he was briefly exiled to Lakhta. In 1914, he was tried for political subversion and expression of antimilitarist sentiments on the basis of his short story "At the End of the World." He was eventually acquitted. In 1917, Maxim GORKY offered Zamyatin a position with *Vsemirnaya Literatura,* a journal specializing in world literature. Zamyatin was in charge of the English and American sections in the journal. Throughout this period, he continued to publish short stories.

Zamyatin described his literary works as neorealism, a style according to Zamyatin that concentrates on the grotesque and brutal aspects of life. Zamyatin's most famous work, *We* (1924), is one of the earliest dystopias of science fiction. The setting of the novel is a future One State, governed by perfect laws of mathematics. All citizens have numbers instead of names, and their consumption (including sex) is completely regulated by the state. *We* comments on the structure of Soviet society, as well as the role of an individual within this social matrix. After the publication of *We*, Zamyatin could no longer publish his work in the Soviet Union. He moved to Paris in 1931. Zamyatin was readmitted to the Writers' Union but died in 1937 before returning to Russia.

Zamyatin never received proper recognition for his work during his lifetime. His style was an enormous influence on many writers, including George Orwell and Ursula Le Guin. Zamyatin's work has been translated into more than a dozen languages.

Another Work by Yevgeny Zamyatin

The Dragon: Fifteen Stories. Translated by Mirra Ginsburg. New York: Random House, 1967.

Zhao Zhenkai
See BEI DAO.

Zhou Shuren
See LU XUN.

Zola, Émile (1840–1902) *novelist, essayist*

Noted both as the founder of the naturalist movement (*see* NATURALISM) and for his active participation in the Dreyfus affair, Émile Zola was born in Paris, France. His father died when he was seven years old, leaving the family with severe financial problems. He spent his childhood in the south of France, in Aix-en-Provence, returning with his mother to Paris at age 18. He befriended French painter Paul Cézanne and, influenced by ROMANTICISM, began to write. His mother had great hopes that he would pursue a career in law and ease the family's financial burdens, but he failed his exams. Popular legend holds that there were times in which Zola's family was so poor that he would capture birds on his windowsill to provide meat for the supper table.

Unable to pursue law, Zola secured employment first as a clerk for a shipping firm, then at the Louis-Christophe-François-Hachette publishing house, all the while working toward his goal of becoming a published author. His journalistic writings included art criticism and literary reviews as well as political articles in which he openly expressed his animosity toward Napoleon III.

Zola's earliest published works of fiction include *Contes à Ninon* (*Stories for Ninon,* 1864) as well as several essays, plays and short stories. He attracted little attention for his work until the publication of his scandalous and sordid autobiographical work *La Confession de Claude* (*Claude's Confession,* 1865). This attention, however, came not so much from the public as it did from the authorities. As a result, Zola was fired from his job at the publishing firm, but he gained recognition as an emerging author.

Thérèse Raquin (1867), Zola's first novel to be considered a major work, was published two years later and was a moderate success. He followed it immediately with the first of a series of works collectively referred to as the *Rougon-Macquart* cycle (1871–93), which revolves around the life of a family living under Napoleon III and the Second Empire. Zola initially presented this idea to his publisher in 1868. The family is split into two branches: the working-class Rougons, and the Macquarts, who are alcoholics and smugglers. In the course of time, some would rise to the highest levels of society, and others would fall victim to the evils of society and the malformations of their own character. The series reached 20 volumes, each one slightly different in theme but all of them sharing a common element of detailed research. Zola conducted interviews and attempted to experience as much as he could firsthand to understand and present his characters fully. He was particularly interested in the effects of heredity and social determinism. This marked the beginning of the new naturalist period of French literature.

The novel that brought him fame was *L'Assommoir* (*The Drunkard,* 1877). After its publication, he bought property and continued to compile detailed notes about all aspects of life. *Germinal* (1885) was written based on notes compiled on labor conditions for coal miners. Having centered his novel on a worker's strike, Zola again attracted the attention of the authorities, who viewed his work as advocating and encouraging revolution.

On January 13, 1898, Zola became even more openly involved in controversy. He published an open letter entitled *J'accuse* in which he defended Albert Dreyfus, a Jewish officer who had been sent to prison for allegedly giving military secrets to Germany. This letter was ultimately instrumental in gaining Dreyfus a new trial and his eventual release, but not until Zola was forced to flee to England to escape imprisonment for writing it. He returned in 1899, after Dreyfus was released.

On September 28, 1902, Zola was found dead in his home of carbon monoxide poisoning. Strong evidence points to the possibility that this was not an accident but a murder, carried out by those who disagreed with his views.

Other Works by Émile Zola

The Masterpiece. Translated by Thomas Walron. New York: Oxford University Press, 1993.

Pot Luck. Translated by Brian Nelson. New York: Oxford University Press, 1999.

A Work about Émile Zola

Brown, Frederick. *Zola: A Life.* New York: Farrar, Straus & Giroux, 1995.

Zynger, Icek–Hersz

See SINGER, ISAAC BASHEVIS.

SELECTED BIBLIOGRAPHY

Abrahams, Cecil. *Alex La Guma.* Boston: Twayne, 1985.

Abrahams, C., ed. *The Tragic Life: Bessie Head and Literature in Southern Africa.* Lawrenceville, N.J.: Africa World Press, 1990.

Abramson, Glenda. *The Writing of Yehuda Amichai: A Thematic Approach.* Albany: State University of New York Press, 1989.

Adams, Ian M. *Three Authors of Alienation: Bombal, Onetti, Carpentier.* Austin: University of Texas Press, 1975.

Adereth, Max. *Elsa Triolet and Louis Aragon: An Introduction to Their Interwoven Lives and Works.* Lewiston, N.Y.: Edwin Mellen Press, 1994.

Adler, Jeremy. *Franz Kafka.* New York: Overlook Press, 2002.

Adler, Laure. *Marguerite Duras: A Life.* Translated by Anne-Marie Glasheen. Chicago: University of Chicago Press, 2000.

Aichinger, Isle. *The Bound Man and Other Stories.* Translated by Eric Mosbacher. New York: Noonday Press, 1956.

Akutagawa Ryunosuke. *Tales Grotesque and Curious.* Translated by Glen W. Shaw. Tokyo: Hokuseido, 1948.

Alberti, Rafael. *The Owl's Insomnia: Poems Selected and Translated by Mark Strand.* New York: Atheneum, 1973.

Alcalay, Ammiel. *Keys to the Garden, New Israeli Writing.* New York: City Light Books, 1996.

Alexander, Peter F. *Alan Paton: A Biography.* Oxford: Oxford University Press, 1994.

Alldridge, James C. *Ilse Aichinger.* Chester Springs, Pa.: Dufour Editions, 1969.

Alpers, Antony. *The Life of Katherine Mansfield.* New York: Viking Press, 1980.

Amoia, Alba della Fazia. *Feodor Dostoevsky.* New York: Continuum Press, 1993.

Anand, Mulk R. *Anthology of Dalit Literature.* Columbia, Mo.: South Asia Books, 1992.

Anastasia, Olga, ed. *Isak Dinesen: Critical Views.* Athens: Ohio University Press, 1993.

Anderson, Marston. *Limits of Realism.* Berkeley: University of California Press, 1989.

Angulo, Maria-Elena. *Magic Realism: Social Context and Discourse.* New York: Garland, 1995.

Anyidoho, Kofi, Abena Busia, and Anne V. Adams, eds. *Beyond Survival: African Literature and the Search for New Life.* Lawrenceville, N.J.: Africa World Press, 1998.

Arenas, Reinaldo. *The Ill-Fated Peregrinations of Fray Servando.* Translated by Andrew Hurley. New York: Avon, 1987

Arghezi, Tudor. *Poems: Tudor Arghezi.* Translated by Andrei Bantas. Bucharest: Minerva Publishing House, 1983.

———. *Selected Poems of Tudor Arghezi*. Translated by Michael Impey and Brian Swann. Princeton, N.J.: Princeton University Press, 1976.

Arico, Santo L. *Oriana Fallaci: The Woman and the Myth*. Carbondale: Southern Illinois University Press, 1998.

Arnold, James A., ed. *A History of Literature in the Caribbean*. Philadelphia: Benjamins, 1994.

Assouline, Pierre. *Simenon: A Biography*. Translated by Jon Rothschild. New York: Knopf, 1997.

Atkins, Angela. *Vikram Seth's "A Suitable Boy": A Reader's Guide*. New York: Continuum International Inc., 2002.

Attridge, Derek, and Rosemary Jolly, eds. *Writing South Africa: Literature, Apartheid, and Democracy, 1970–1995*. Cambridge: Cambridge University Press, 1998.

Atwell, David. *J. M. Coetzee: South Africa and the Politics of Writings*. Berkeley: University of California Press, 1993.

Auslander, Rose. *Selected Poems of Rose Auslander*. Translated by Ewald Osers. London: London Magazine Editors, 1977.

Babcock, Arthur E. *The New Novel in France: Theory and Practice of the Nouveau Roman*. Boston: Twayne, 1997.

Bachelard, Gaston. *Lautreamont*. Translated by Robert S. Dupree. Dallas, Tex.: Dallas Institute of Humanities and Culture, 1986.

Bahti, Timothy, and Marilyn Sibley Fries. *Jewish Writers, German Literature: The Uneasy Examples of Nelly Sachs and Walter Benjamin*. Ann Arbor: The University of Michigan Press, 1995.

Bair, Dierdre. *Samuel Beckett: A Biography*. New York: Harcourt Brace Jovanovich, 1978.

Baker, Gary. *Understanding Uwe Johnson*. Columbia: University of South Carolina Press, 1999.

Barbour, Douglas. *b. p. Nichol and His Work*. Toronto: ECW Press, 1992.

———. *Michael Ondaatje*. Boston: Twayne, 1993.

Barbour, Sarah. *Nathalie Sarraute and the Feminist Reader: Identities in Process*. Lewisburg, Pa.: Bucknell University Press, 1993.

Barker, Christine. *Erich Maria Remarque*. New York: Barnes and Noble, 1980.

Barlow, Tani E., and Gary J. Bjoge, eds. *I Myself Am a Woman: Selected Writings of Ding Ling*. Boston: Beacon Press, 1990.

Barnes, Christopher. *Boris Pasternak: A Literary Biography*. Cambridge: Cambridge University Press, 1998.

Barnett, Ursula. *A Vision of Order: A Study of Black South African Literature in English (1914–1980)*. Amherst: University of Massachusetts Press, 1983.

Barnstone, Aliki, and Willis Barnstone, eds. *A Book of Women Poets from Antiquity to Now*. New York: Schocken Books, 1980.

Barnstone, Willis, ed. *Borges at Eighty: Conversations*. Bloomington: Indiana University Press, 1982.

Barnstone, Willis, and Tony Barnstone, eds. *Literature of Asia, Africa, and Latin America*. Upper Saddle River, N.J.: Prentice Hall, 1999.

Barron, Stephanie, and Wolf-Dieter Dube, eds. *German Expressionism: Art and Society*. New York: Rizzoli, 1997.

Bassanese, Fiora A. *Understanding Luigi Pirandello*. Columbia: University of South Carolina Press, 1997.

Baudelaire, Charles. *Baudelaire: Poems*. Translated by Laurence Lerner. London: J. M. Dent, 1999.

Bauer, Nancy. *Simone de Beauvoir, Philosophy and Feminism*. New York: Columbia University Press, 2001.

Bauermeister, Erica, Jesse Larsen, and Holly Smith, eds. *500 Great Books by Women*. New York: Penguin, 1994.

Beasley, W. G., ed. *Modern Japan: Aspects of History, Literature and Society*. Berkeley: University of California Press, 1975.

Becker, Lucille F. *Louis Aragon*. Boston: Twayne, 1971.

Beichman, Janine. *Masaoka Shiki*. New York: Kodansha International, 1986.

Bell-Villada, Gene H. *Borges and His Fiction*. Arlington: University of Texas Press, 1999.

Bellos, David. *Georges Perec: A Life in Words*. London: Harvill, 1993.

Benn, Gottfried. *Prose, Essays, Poems*. New York: Continuum, 1987.

Berlin, Isaiah. *The Hedgehog and the Fox: An Essay on Tolstoy's View of History.* New York: Simon & Schuster, 1986.

Bermel, Albert. *Artaud's Theatre of Cruelty.* New York: Taplinger, 1977.

Bernstein, Gail L., ed. *Recreating Japanese Women, 1600–1945.* Berkeley: University of California Press, 1991.

Bertram, James. *Charles Brasch.* Wellington: Oxford University Press, 1976.

Besser, Gretchen Rous. *Germain de Stael Revisited.* Boston: Twayne, 1994.

Birbalsingh, Frank, ed. *Frontiers of Caribbean Literatures in English.* New York: St. Martin's Press, 1996.

———. *Indo-Caribbean Resistance.* Toronto: TSAR, 1993.

Birch, Cyril, ed. *Chinese Communist Literature.* New York: Frederick A. Praeger, 1963.

Birnbaum, M. D., and R. Trager-Verchovsky, eds. *History, Another Text.* Ann Arbor: University of Michigan Press, 1988.

Bishop, Lloyd. *The Poetry of Alfred Musset: Styles and Genres.* New York: Peter Lang, 1997.

Bisztray, George. *Marxist Models of Literary Realism.* New York: Columbia University Press, 1978.

Blackwell, Jeannine, and Susanne Zantop, eds. *Bitter Healing: German Women Writers: 1700–1830.* Lincoln: University of Nebraska Press, 1990.

Bloom, Harold, ed. *Isaac Babel: Modern Critical Views.* Broomall, Pa.: Chelsea House, 1987.

Boeschentein, Hermann. *A History of Modern German Literature.* New York: Peter Lang, 1990.

Bohn, William. *Apollinaire and the International Avante-Garde.* Albany: State University of New York Press, 1997.

Bondanella, Peter. *Umberto Eco and the Open Text: Semiotics, Fiction, Popular Culture.* Cambridge: Cambridge University Press, 1997.

Bonifaz, Oscar C. *Remembering Rosario: A Personal Glimpse into the Life and Works of Rosario Castellanos.* Translated by Myralyn F. Allgood. Madrid: Scripta Humanistica, 1990.

Bouchard, Norma, and Veronica Pravadelli, eds. *Umberto Eco's Alternative.* New York: Peter Lang, 1998.

Boullata, Issa. *Critical Perspectives on Modern Arabic Literature.* Washington, D.C.: Three Continents Press, 1980.

Bower, Kathrin M. *Ethics and Rememberance in the Poetry of Nelly Sachs and Rose Auslander.* Rochester, N.Y.: Camden House, 2000.

Brasch, Charles. *Indirections: A Memoir 1909–1947.* Edited by James Bertram. Wellington, N.Z.; New York: Oxford University Press, 1980.

Breslin, Paul. *Nobody's Nation: Reading Derek Walcott.* Chicago: University of Chicago Press, 2001.

Brewer, Maria M. *Claude Simon: Narratives Without Narrative.* Lincoln: University of Nebraska Press, 1995.

Brock, Peggy, ed. *Women, Rites and Sites: Aboriginal Women's Cultural Knowledge.* Boston: Allen and Unwin, 1900.

Brod, Max. *Franz Kafka: A Biography.* New York: Da Capo Press, 1995.

Brodsky, Patricia. *Rainer Maria Rilke.* Boston: Twayne, 1988.

Bronner, Stephen E. *Camus: Portrait of a Moralist.* Minneapolis: University of Minnesota Press, 1999.

Brotherson, Gordon. *Manuel Machado: A Revaluation.* Cambridge: Cambridge University Press, 1968.

Brown, Frederick. *Zola: A Life.* New York: Farrar, Strauss & Giroux, 1995.

Brown, Lloyd W. *Women Writers in Black Africa.* Westport, Conn.: Greenwood Press, 1981.

Brown, Stewart, ed. *The Art of Kamau Brathwaite.* Bridgend, Mid Glamorgan, Wales: Seren, 1995.

Brown, Stewart, et al. *Voiceprint: An Anthology of Oral and Related Poetry from the Caribbean.* Essex, England: Longman Group UK Limited, 1989.

Brunsdale, Mitzi. *Sigrid Undset: Chronicler of Norway.* New York: Berg Publishers, Ltd., 1988.

Burness, Donald. *Fire: Six Writers from Angola, Mozambique and Cape Verde.* Washington, D.C.: Three Continents Press, 1977.

Burnett, Paula. *Derek Walcott: Politics and Poetics.* Gainesville: University Press of Florida, 2000.

Buruma, Ian, ed. *India: A Mosaic.* New York: New York Review of Books, 2000.

Buxton, John. *The Grecian Taste: Literature in the Age of New-Classicism 1740–1820.* New York: Barnes and Noble, 1978.

Bynum, Brant B. *The Romantic Imagination in the Works of Gustavo Adolfo Bécquer.* Chapel Hill: University of North Carolina, Department of Romance Languages, 1993.

Cady, Andrea. *Measuring the Visible: The Verse and Prose of Philippe Jaccottet.* Atlanta, Ga.: Rodopi, 1992.

Calvocaressi, Richard, and Katharina Schultz. *Oskar Kokoschka, 1886–1980.* New York: Solomon R. Guggenheim Foundation, 1986.

Camber, Richard. *On Camus.* Belmont, Calif.: Wadsworth/Thompson Learning, 2002.

Caranfa, Angelo. *Claudel: Beauty and Grace.* Lewisburg, Pa.: Bucknell University Press, 1989.

Carlyle, Thomas. *The Life of Friedrich Schiller: Comprehending and Examination of His Works.* Portland, Oreg.: University Press of the Pacific, 2001.

Cate, Curtis. *André Malraux: A Biography.* London, England: Hutchinson, 1995.

Cavafy, Konstantin. *Before Time Could Change Them: The Complete Poems of Constantine P. Cavafy.* Translated by Theoharis Constantine Theoharis. Orlando, Fla.: Harcourt Brace, 2001.

Caws, Mary Ann. *René Char.* Boston: Twayne, 1977.

Celan, Paul. *Selected Poetry and Prose of Paul Celan.* Translated by John Felsteiner. New York: Norton, 2000.

Chadwick, Charles. *Verlaine.* London, England: Athlone Press, 1973.

Chagnon, Jacqui, and Don Luce, eds. *Quiet Courage: Poems from Viet Nam.* Washington, D.C.: Indochina Mobil Education Project, 1974.

Chambers, Helen. *The Changing Image of Theodor Fontane.* Columbia, S.C.: Camden House Inc., 1997.

Champagne, Roland A. *Georges Bataille.* Boston: Twayne, 1998.

Chapman, Michael. *South African Literatures.* London, England: Longman, 1996.

Chartier, Armand B. *Barbey d'Aurevilly.* Boston: Twayne, 1977.

Cheung, Dominic. *Feng Chih.* Boston: Twayne, 1979.

Chevalier, Tracy, ed. *Contemporary World Writers.* Detroit: St. James Press, 1993.

Chung, Chong-wha, ed. *Modern Korean Literature, An Anthology, 1908–1965.* New York: Kegan Paul International, 1995.

Cixous, Helene. *Reading with Clarice Lispector.* Minneapolis: University of Minnesota Press, 1990.

Cliff, Michelle. *The Land of Look Behind: Prose and Poetry.* Ithaca, N.Y.: Firebrand Books, 1985.

Clurman, Harold. *Ibsen.* New York: Da Capo Press, 1989.

Cobb, Carl. *Antonio Machado.* Boston: Twayne, 1971.

Coghlan, Brian. *Hofmannsthal's Festival Dramas.* Cambridge: Cambridge University Press, 1964.

Cohen, Georg. *Henrik Ibsen, A Critical Study. With a 42-Page Essay on Bjørnstjerne Bjørnson.* New York: Classic Books, 1964.

Cohen, Joseph. *Voices of Israel: Essays on and Interview with Yehuda Amichai, A. B. Yehoshua, T. Carmi, Aharon Applefeld, and Amos Oz.* Albany: State University of New York Press, 1990.

Cohn, Robert G. *The Poetry of Arthur Rimbaud.* Columbia: University of South Carolina Press, 1999.

Collins, John, ed. *Noonuccal and Her People: Perspectives on Her Life's Work.* St. Lucia, B.W.I.: University Queensland Press, 1996.

Collymore, Frank. *The Man Who Loved Attending Funerals and Other Stories.* Edited by Harold Barratt and Reinhard Sander. Portsmouth, N.H.: Heinemann, 1993.

Conde, Maryse. *Tales from the Heart: True Stories from My Childhood.* Translated by Richard Philcox. New York: Soho, 2001.

Conroy, William T. *Villiers de L'Isle-Adam.* Boston: Twayne, 1978.

Cooke, Miriam. *War's Other Voices.* Cambridge: Cambridge University Press, 1988.

Cooke, Nathalie. *Margaret Atwood: A Biography.* Toronto: ECW Press, 1998.

Copeland, Rebecca L. *Lost Leaves: Women Writers of Meiji Japan.* Honolulu: University of Hawaii Press, 2000.

Cornwell, Neil. *Vladimir Nabokov.* Plymouth, Mass.: Northcote House Publishers, 1999.

Cook, David, and Michael Okenimkpe. *Ngugi wa Thiong'o: An Exploration of His Writings.* London, England: Heinemann, 1983.

Couste, A. *Julio Cortázar.* South America: Oceano Group, 2002.

Coutinho, Edilberto. *Gilberto Freyre.* Rio de Janeiro, Brazil: Agir, 1994.

Cox, Brian, ed. *African Writers.* New York: Charles Scribner's Sons, 1997.

Crane, Ralph J. *Ruth Prawer Jhabvala.* Boston: Twayne, 1992.

Crichfield, Grant. *Three Novels of Madame de Duras.* The Hague: Mouton, 1975.

Crockett, Roger A. *Understanding Friedrich Dürrenmatt.* Columbia: University of South Carolina Press, 1998.

Cronin, Anthony. *Samuel Beckett: The Last Modernist.* London, England: HarperCollins, 1996.

Csaire, Aime. *Lyric and Dramatic Poetry, 1946–82.* Translated by Clayton Eshleman and Annette Smith. Charlottesville: University Press of Virginia, 1990.

———. *Aimé Césaire: The Collected Poetry.* Translated by Clayton Eshleman and Annette Smith. Berkeley: University of California Press, 1983.

Cuomo, Glenn R. *Career at the Cost of Compromise: Gunter Eich's Life and Work in the Years 1933–1945.* Atlanta, Ga.: Rodopi, 1989.

Currie, William. *Metaphors of Alienation: The Fiction of Abe, Beckett and Kafka.* Ann Arbor, Mich.: University Microfilms, 1973.

Curtis, J. A. E. *Mikhail Bulgakov: A Life in Letters and Diaries.* New York: Overlook Press, 1992.

Czeslaw, Milosz. *Who Is Gombrowicz?* New York: Penguin, 1986.

Daglarca, Fazil H. *Secme Siirler. Selected Poems.* Translated by Talat Sait Halman. Pittsburgh: University of Pittsburgh Press, 1969.

Dana, Doris, ed. *Selected Poems of Gabriela Mistral.* Translated by Doris Dana. Baltimore: Johns Hopkins University Press, 1971.

Dance, Daryl C., ed. *Fifty Caribbean Writers: A Bio-Bibliographical Critical Sourcebook.* Westport, Conn.: Greenwood Press, 1986.

Daniels, Barry V. *Revolution in the Theatre: French Romantic Theories of Drama.* Westport, Conn.: Greenwood Press, 1983.

Danly, Robert L. *In the Shade of Spring Leaves: The Life and Writings of Higuchi Ichiyo, a Woman of Letters in Meiji Japan.* New Haven, Conn.: Yale University Press, 1981.

Davies, Carole B., and Anne Adams Graves, eds. *Nagambika: Studies of Women in African Literature.* Lawrenceville, N.J.: Africa World Press, 1986.

Davies, Carole B., and Elaine Savory Fido, eds. *Out of the Kumbla: Caribbean Women and Literature.* Lawrenceville, N.J.: Africa World Press, 1990.

Davis, Gregson. *Aimé Césaire.* Cambridge: Cambridge University Press, 1997.

Dawes, Kwame, ed. *Talk Yuh Talk: Interviews with Anglophone Caribbean Poets.* Charlottesville: University Press of Virginia, 2001.

Day, A. Grove, and Edgar C. Knowlton, Jr. *Vicente Blasco Ibáñez.* Boston: Twayne, 1972.

Del Principe, David. *Rebellion, Death, and Aesthetics in Italy: The Demons of Scapigliatura.* Madison, Wis.: Fairleigh Dickinson University Press, 1996.

Demetz, Peter. *After the Fires: Recent Writing in the Germanies, Austria, and Switzerland.* New York: Harcourt Brace Jovanovich, 1986.

———. *Postwar German Literature: A Critical Introduction.* New York: Pegasus, 1970.

Dever, Aileen. *Radical Insufficiency of Human Life: The Poetry of R. de Castro and J. A. Silva.* Jefferson, N.C.: McFarland, 2000.

Dharwakder, Vinay, and A. K. Ramanujan, eds. *The Oxford Anthology of Modern Indian Poetry.* London, England: Oxford University Press, 1994.

Dhqwan, R. K. *The Novels of Amitav Ghosh.* New York: Prestige Books, 1999.

DiGaetani, John L., ed. *A Companion to Pirandello Studies.* Westport, Conn.: Greenwood Press, 1991.

Dodiya, Jaydipsinh, ed. *The Fiction of Rohinton Mistry: Critical Studies.* London, England: Sangam, 1998.

Dodiya, Jaydipsinh. *The Plays of Girish Karnad: Critical Perspectives.* New Delhi: Prestige Books, 1999.

Doherty, Justin. *The Acmeist Movement in Russian Poetry: Culture and the Word.* Oxford: Oxford University Press, 1995.

Doi, Takeo. *The Psychological World of Natsume Soseki.* Translated by William Jeffeson Tyler. Cambridge: Harvard University Press, 1976.

Dolezelova-Velingerova, M., ed. *The Chinese Novel at the Turn of the Century.* Toronto: University of Toronto Press, 1980.

Dolittle, James. *Alfred de Vigny.* Boston: Twayne, 1967.

Dollenmayer, David. *The Berlin Novels of Alfred Doblin.* Berkeley: University of California Press, 1988.

Donahue, Thomas J. *The Theater of Fernando Arrabal: A Garden of Earthly Delights.* New York: New York University Press, 1980.

Dooling, Amy D., and Kristina M. Torgeson. *Writing Women in Modern China: An Anthology of Women's Literature from the Early Twentieth Century.* New York: Columbia University Press, 1998.

Edstrom, Vivi Bloom. *Selma Legerlof.* Boston: Twayne, 1982.

Ehre, Milton. *Isaak Babel.* Boston: Twayne, 1986.

Eich, Gunter. *Pigeons and Moles: Selected Writings of Günter Eich.* Translated by Michael Hamburger. Columbia, S.C.: Camden House, 1990.

Eilersen, Gillian. *Bessie Head: Thunder Behind Her Ears: Her Life and Writing.* Cape Town, Claremont: David Philip, 1995.

El-Enany, Rasheed. *Naguib Mahfouz: The Pursuit of Meaning.* New York: Routledge, 1993.

Ellis, Keith. *Critical Approaches to Rubén Dario.* Toronto: University of Toronto Press, 1974.

Ellison, David R. *Ethics and Aesthetics in Modernist Literature: From the Sublime to the Uncanny.* New York: Cambridge University Press, 2001.

Ellison, Fred P. *Brazil's New Novel: Four Northeastern Masters.* Berkeley: University of California Press, 1954.

Elytis, Odysseus. *The Collected Poems of Odysseus Elytis.* Translated by Jeffrey Carson and Nikos Sarris. Baltimore: Johns Hopkins University Press, 1997.

Erickson, John D. *Dada: Performance, Poetry and Art.* Boston: Twayne, 1984.

Ermolaev, Herman. *Mikhail Sholokhov and His Art.* Princeton, N.J.: Princeton University Press, 1982.

Erwin, Edward. *The Freud Encyclopedia: Theory, Therapy, and Culture.* New York: Garland, 2002.

Espinet, Ramabai, ed. *Creation Fire: A CAFRA Anthology of Caribbean Women's Poetry.* Toronto: Sister Vision, 1990.

Esslin, Martin. *Brecht, a Choice of Evils: A Critical Study of the Man, His Works, and His Opinions.* New York: Methuen Drama, 1984.

———. *Theatre of the Absurd.* New York: Overlook Press, 1969.

Ezenwa-Ohaeto. *Chinua Achebe: A Biography.* Bloomington: Indiana University Press, 1997.

Falb, Lewis W. *Jean Anouilh.* New York: Frederick Unger, 1977.

Falk, Thomas. *Elias Canetti.* Boston: Twayne, 1993.

Faurot, Jeannette L., ed. *Chinese Fiction from Taiwan: Critical Perspectives.* Bloomington: Indiana University Press, 1980.

Fekkema, Douwe, and Elrud Ibsch. *Modernist Conjectures: A Mainstream in European Literature 1910–1940.* New York: St. Martin's Press, 1988.

Felsteiner, John. *Paul Celan: Poet, Survivor, Jew.* New Haven, Conn.: Yale University Press, 2001.

Ferguson, Robert. *Enigma: The Life of Knut Hamsun.* New York: Noonday Press, 1988.

Ferre, Rosario. *Sweet Diamond Dust and Other Stories.* New York: Plume, 1996.

Feuerwerker, Yi-tsi Mei. *Ding Ling's Fiction: Ideology and Narrative in Modern Chinese Literature.* Cambridge, Mass.: Harvard University Press, 1982.

Fioretos, Aris. *The Solid Letter: Reading of Friedrich Holderlin.* Stanford, Calif.: Stanford University Press, 2000.

Firda, Richard. *Peter Handke.* Boston: Twayne, 1993.

Fishburn, Katherine. *Reading Buchi Emecheta: Cross-Cultural Conversations.* Westport, Conn.: Greenwood Press, 1995.

Flores, Angel. *Spanish American Authors.* New York: H. W. Wilson Company, 1992.

Flores, Angel, and Kate Flores, eds. *The Defiant Muse: Hispanic Feminist Poems from the Middle Ages to the Present.* New York: The Feminist Press, 1986.

Fong, Gilbert C. F. *The Other Shore: Plays by Gao Xingjian.* Hong Kong: The Chinese University Press, 1999.

Fortescue, William. *Alphonse de Lamartine: A Political Biography* New York: St. Martin's Press, 1983.

Fowlie, Wallace. *Poem and Symbol: A Brief History of French Symbolism.* University Park: Pennsylvania State University Press, 1990.

Franco, Jean. *An Introduction to Spanish-American Literature.* Cambridge: Cambridge University Press, 1994.

Frank, Joseph. *Dostoevsky: The Seeds of Revolt, 1821–1849.* Princeton, N.J.: Princeton University Press, 1976.

———. *Dostoevsky: The Years of Ordeal, 1850–1859.* Princeton, N.J.: Princeton University Press, 1984.

———. *Dostoevsky: The Years of Liberation, 1860–1865.* Princeton, N.J.: Princeton University Press, 1986.

———. *Dostoevsky: The Miraculous Years, 1865–1871.* Princeton, N.J.: Princeton University Press, 1996.

———. *Dostoevsky: The Mantle of the Prophet, 1871–1881.* Princeton, N.J.: Princeton University Press, 2002.

Frantisek, Deak. *Symbolist Theater: The Formation of an Avant-Garde.* Baltimore: Johns Hopkins University Press, 1993.

Freedman, Ralph. *Life of a Poet: Rainer Maria Rilke.* Chicago: Northwestern University Press, 1998.

Frey, John A. *A Victor Hugo Encyclopedia.* Westport, Conn.: Greenwood Press, 1999.

Friedman, Lawrence. *Understanding Isaac Bashevis Singer.* Columbia: University of South Carolina Press, 1988.

Friedrich, Pia. *Pier Paolo Pasolini.* Boston: Twayne, 1982.

Fusso, Susanne, ed. *Essays on Karolina Pavlova.* Chicago: Northwestern University Press, 2001.

Garrard, John. *Mikhail Lermontov.* Boston: Twayne, 1982.

Gatt-Rutter, John. *Italo Svevo: A Double Life.* Oxford: Oxford University Press, 1988.

———. *Oriana Fallaci: The Rhetoric of Freedom.* Washington, D.C.: Berg, 1996.

George, Stefan. *The Works of Stefan George.* Translated by Olga Marx and Ernst Morwitz. Chapel Hill: University of North Carolina Press, 1974.

Gessel, Van C., and Tomone Matsumoto, eds. *The Showa Anthology: Modern Japanese Short Stories.* Tokyo: Kodansha International, 1985.

Giergielewicz, Mieczyslaw. *Henryk Sienkiewicz: A Biography.* New York: Hippocrene, 1991.

Gifford, Henry. *Tolstoy.* New York: Oxford University Press, 1982.

Gifford, Paul, and Johnnie Gratton, eds. *Subject Matters: Subject and Self in French Literature from Descartes to the Present.* The Netherlands: Rodopi, 2000.

Gikandi, Simon. *Writing in Limbo: Modernism and Caribbean Literature.* Ithaca, N.Y.: Cornell University Press, 1992.

Giles, James, ed. *French Existentialism: Consciousness, Ethics and Relations with Others.* Atlanta: Rodopi, 1999.

Goldberg, Anatol. *Ilya Ehrenburg, Revolutionary, Novelist, Poet, War Correspondent, Propagandist: The Extraordinary Epic of a Russian Survivor.* New York: Viking Press, 1984.

Goldblatt, Howard, ed. *Worlds Apart: Recent Chinese Writing and Its Audiences.* Armonk, N.Y.: M. E. Sharpe, 1990.

Goldman, Merle. *Modern Chinese Literature in the May Fourth Era.* Cambridge, Mass.: Harvard University Press, 1977.

Gonzalez, Roberto E. *Alejo Carpentier, The Pilgrim at Home.* Ithaca, N.Y.: Cornell University Press, 1977.

Goodwin, K. L. *Understanding Poetry: A Study of Ten Poets.* London, England: Heinemann, 1982.

Gordon, Haim, ed. *The Dictionary of Existentialism.* Westport, Conn.: Greenwood Press, 1999.

Gordon, Haim. *Naguib Mahfouz's Egypt: Existential Themes in his Writings.* Westport, Conn.: Greenwood Press, 1990.

———. *Sartre's Philosophy and the Challenge of Education.* Lewiston, N.Y.: Edwin Mellen Press, 2001.

Gordon, Lois. *The World of Samuel Beckett.* New Haven, Conn.: Yale University Press, 1996.

Gotlieb, Vera, and Paul Allain, eds. *The Cambridge Companion to Chekhov.* Cambridge: Cambridge University Press, 2000.

Graham, Robb. *Balzac: A Biography.* New York: Norton, 1994.

Grant, Judith S. *Robertson Davies: Man of Myth.* New York: Viking, 1994.

Gray, Nancy. *Language Unbound: On Experimental Writing by Women.* Urbana: University of Illinois Press, 1992.

Green, Mary Jean, ed. *Postcolonial Subjects: Francophone Women Writers.* Minneapolis: University of Minnesota Press, 1996.

Greider, Jerome B. *Hu Shih and the Chinese Renaissance: Liberalism in the Chinese Revolution, 1917–1937.* Cambridge, Mass.: Harvard University Press, 1970.

Gross, John, ed. *The Modern Movement.* London: Harvill, 1992.

Grossman, Joan. *Valery Bryusov and the Riddle of Russian Decadence.* Berkeley: University of California Press, 1985.

Guibert, Rita. *Seven Voices: Seven Latin American Writers Talk of Rita Guibert.* Translated by Frances Partridge. New York: Knopf, 1972.

Guicharnaud, Jacques. *Raymond Queneau.* Translated by June Guicharnaud. New York: Columbia University Press, 1965.

Guignon, Charles and Derk Pereboom, eds. *Existentialism: Basic Writings.* Indianapolis, Ind.: Hackett, 2001.

Guillen, Jorge. *Guillen on Guillen: The Poetry and the Poet.* Translated by Reginald Gibbons. Princeton, N.J.: Princeton University Press, 1979.

Gupla, Suman. *V. S. Naipaul.* Plymouth, New Zealand: Northcote House in Association with the British Council, 1999.

Haberly, David. *Three Sad Races: Racial Identity and National Consciousness in Brazilian Literature.* New York: Cambridge University Press, 1983.

Hadda, Janet. *Issaac Bashevis Singer: A Life.* New York: Oxford University Press, 1997.

Hale, Thomas, ed. *Critical Perspectives on Aimé Césaire.* Washington, D.C.: Three Continents Press, 1992.

Hanrahan, Gene Z. *Heavensent.* London: J. M. Dent and Sons, 1951.

Harris, Jane G. *Osip Mandelstam.* Boston: Twayne, 1988.

Harris, Wilson. *Selected Essays of Wilson Harris: The Unfinished Genesis of the Imagination.* New York: Routledge, 1999.

Harss, Luis, and Barbara Dohmann. *Into the Mainstream: Conversations with Latin-American Writers.* New York: Harper & Row, 1969.

Hasek, Jaroslav. *The Bachura Scandal and Other Stories and Sketches.* Translated by Alan Menhennet. London, England: Angel, 1991.

Hasluck, Nicholas. *Anchor and Other Poems.* Fremantle, Australia: Fremantle Arts Center Press, 1976.

Hassall, Anthony J. *Dancing on Hot MacAdam: Peter Carey's Fiction.* St. Lucia, B.W.I.: University of Queensland Press, 1998.

Hawley, John C., ed. *Writing the Nation: Self and Country in the Postcolonial Imagination.* The Netherlands: Rodopi, 1996.

Havel, Václav. *The Garden Party and Other Plays.* New York: Grove Press, 1993.

Hayman, Ronald. *Eugène Ionesco.* New York: Frederick Ungar, 1976.

Head, Bessie. *A Woman Alone: Autobiographical Writings.* Oxford: Heinemann, 1990.

Heilbut, Anthony. *Thomas Mann: Eros and Literature.* Riverside: University of California Press, 1997.

Hemingway, Maurice. *Emilia Pardo Bazan: The Making of a Novelist.* Cambridge: Cambridge University Press, 1983.

Herdan, Innes. *The Pen and the Sword: Literature and Revolution in Modern China.* London: Zed Books Ltd., 1992.

Hermond, Joest. *Heinrich Heine's Contested Identities: Politics, Religion, and Nationalism in Nineteenth Century Germany.* New York: Peter Lang, 1999.

Heron, G. A. *The Poetry of Okot p'Bitek.* London: Heinemann, 1976.

Hettinga, Donald. *The Brothers Grimm: Two Lives, One Legacy.* London: Clarion Books, 2001.

Hewitt, Nicholas. *The Life of Celine: A Critical Biography.* Malden, U.K.: Blackwell, 1999.

Heywood, Christopher, ed. *Aspects of South African Literature.* New York: Africana, 1976.

Higgonnet, Margaret R., and Joan Templeton, eds. *Feminist Explorations of Literary Space.* Amherst: University of Massachusetts Press, 1994.

Hintz, Suzanne S. *Rosario Ferre, A Search for Identity.* New York: Peter Lang, 1995.

Hsia, C. T. *A History of Modern Chinese Literature.* New Haven, Conn.: Yale University Press, 1961.

Hofmannsthal, Hugo von. *The Lyrical Poems of Hugo von Hofmannsthal.* Translated by Charles Wharton Stark. New Haven, Conn.: Yale University Press, 1918.

———. *Selected Plays and Libretti.* Edited by Michael Hamburger. New York: Oxford University Press, 2000.

Hogsett, Charlotte. *The Literary Existence of Germain de Stael.* Carbondale: Southern Illinois University Press, 1987.

Holman, Martin. *The Book of Masks.* London: Readers International, 1976.

Holub, Robert. *Friedrich Nietzche.* Boston: Twayne, 1995.

Hopwood, Mererid, and David Basker, eds. *Sarah Kirsch.* Cardiff: University of Wales Press, 1997.

Horn, Pierre L. *Marguerite Yourcenar.* Boston: Twayne, 1985.

Howells, Christina, ed. *The Cambridge Companion to Sartre.* New York: Cambridge University Press, 1992.

Howells, Coral A. *Alice Munro.* New York: St. Martin's Press, 1998.

Huggan, Graham. *Peter Carey.* Oxford, England: Oxford University Press, 1997.

Hulme, Peter, and William H. Sherman. *The Tempest and Its Travels.* Philadelphia: University of Pennsylvania Press, 2000.

Hyslop, Lois B. *Charles Baudelaire Revisited.* Boston: Twayne, 1992.

Idema, Wilt L., and Lloyd L. Haft. *A Guide to Chinese Literature.* Ann Arbor, Mich.: Center for Chinese Studies, 1997.

Ilie, Paul. *Unamuno; An Existential View of Self and Society.* Madison: University of Wisconsin Press, 1967.

Indyk, Ivor. *David Malouf.* New York. Oxford University Press, 1993.

Innes, C. L. *Chinua Achebe.* New York: Cambridge University Press, 1992.

Ito, Ken K. *Vision of Desire: Tanizaki's Fictional Worlds.* Stanford: Stanford University Press, 1991.

Ivask, Ivar. *The Perpetual Present: The Poetry and Prose of Octavio Paz.* Norman: University of Oklahoma Press, 1973.

Jack, Belinda E. *George Sand: A Woman's Life Writ Large.* London: Chatto and Windus, 1999.

Janecek, Gerald. *Andrey Bely: A Critical Review.* Lexington: Kentucky University Press, 1978.

Jeannet, Angela M., and Giuliana Sanguinetti Katz, eds. *Natalia Ginzburg: A Voice of the Twentieth Century.* Toronto: University of Toronto Press, 2000.

Ji-Moon, Suh, and Julie Pickering. *The Descendants of Cain.* Armonk, N.Y.: M. E. Sharpe, Inc., 1997.

Jolly, Rosemary. *Colonization, Violence, and Narration in White South African Writing: André Brink, Breyten Breytenbach, and J. M. Coetzee.* Athens: Ohio University Press, 1996.

Jonsson, Stephen. *Subject Without a Nation: Robert Musil and the History of Modern Identity.* Durham, N.C.: Duke University Press, 2001.

Jrade, Cathy. *Rubén Dario and the Romantic Search for Unity: The Modernist Recourse to Esoteric Tradition.* Austin: University of Texas Press, 1983.

Kain, Geoffrey R., ed. *R. K. Narayan: Contemporary Critical Perspectives.* East Lansing: Michigan State University Press, 1993.

Kalb, Jonathon. *The Theater of Heiner Muller.* Munich, Germany: C. H. Beck, 1984.

Kamber, Richard. *On Sartre.* Belmont, Calif.: Wadsworth, 1999.

Kanes, Martin. *Père Goriot: Anatomy of a Troubled World.* Boston: Twayne, 1993.

Kanes, Martin, ed. *Critical Essays on Honoré de Balzac.* Boston: G. K. Hall, 1990.

Kanik, Orhan V. *I, Orhan Veli: Poems by Orhan Veli.* Translated by Murat Nemet-Nejat. Brooklyn, N.Y.: Hanging Loose Press, 1989.

Karsen, Sonja. *Jaime Torres Bodet; A Poet in a Changing World.* Saratoga Springs, N.Y.: Skidmore College, 1963.

Kaschnitz, Marie L. *Selected Later Poems of Marie Luise Kashnitz.* Translated by Lisel Mueller. Princeton, N.J.: Princeton University Press, 1980.

———. *Circe's Mountain: Stories by Marie Luise Kaschnitz.* Translated by Lisel Mueller. Minneapolis: Milkweed Editions, 1990.

Katrak, Ketu. *Wole Soyinka and Modern Tragedy: A Study of Dramatic Theory and Practice.* Westport, Conn.: Greenwood Press, 1986.

Keats, Jonathan. *Stendhal.* London: Sinclair-Stevenson, 1994.

Keeley, Edmund. *Cavafy's Alexandria.* Princeton, N.J.: Princeton University Press, 1995.

Keene, Donald. *Dawn to the West: Japanese Literature of the Modern Era: Fiction.* New York: Columbia University Press, 1998.

Keene, Donald, ed. *Modern Japanese Literature.* New York: Grove Press, 1956.

Kemp-Welch, A. *Stalin and the Literary Intelligentsia, 1928–1939.* New York: St. Martin's Press, 1991.

Ketchian, Sonia I. *The Poetic Craft of Bella Akhmadulina.* University Park: Pennsylvania State University Press, 1993.

Keys, Roger. *The Reluctant Modernist: Andrei Belyi and the Development of Russian Fiction.* Oxford: Clarendon Press, 1996.

Khan, Md. Akhtar Jamal. *V. S. Naipaul: A Critical Study.* New Delhi: Creative Books, 1998.

Killam, G. D. *An Introduction to the Writings of Ngugi.* London: Heinemann, 1980.

King, Bruce. *Derek Walcott, a Caribbean Life.* New York: Oxford University Press, 2000.

———. *V. S. Naipaul.* London: Macmillan, 1993.

King, Michael. *Wrestling with the Angel: A Life of Janet Frame.* Washington, D.C.: Counterpoint Press, 2000.

Kipalani, Krishan. *Rabindranath Tagore: A Biography.* London: Oxford University Press, 1962.

Kirsner, Robert. *The Novels and Travels of Camilo Jose Cela.* Chapel Hill: University of North Carolina Press, 1964.

Klein, Leonard S. *Latin American Literature in the 20th Century.* New York: Frederick Ungar, 1986.

Kluback, William. *Paul Valery: A Philosopher for Philosophers: The Sage.* New York: Peter Lang, 2000.

Knapp, Bettina L. *Jean Cocteau.* Boston: Twayne, 1989.

———. *Maurice Maeterlinck.* Boston: Twayne, 1975.

———. *Nathalie Sarraute.* Atlanta, Ga.: Rodopi, 1994.

———. *Paul Claudel.* New York: Frederick Ungar, 1982.

Knight, Kelton W. *Anne Hebert: In Search of the First Garden.* New York: Peter Lang, 1998.

Knowles, Anthony V. *Ivan Turgenev.* Boston: Twayne, 1988.

Knowlson, James. *Damned to Fame: The Life of Samuel Beckett.* New York: Simon & Schuster, 1996.

Knox, Bernard. *Backing into the Future: The Classical Tradition and Its Renewal.* New York: Norton, 1994.

Kobler, J. F. *Katherine Mansfield: A Study of the Short Fiction.* Boston: Twayne, 1990.

Koepke, Wulf. *Understanding Max Frisch.* Columbia: University of South Carolina Press, 1991.

Kolbert, Jack. *The Worlds of Elie Wiesel: An Overview of His Career and Major Themes.* Selinsgrove, Pa.: Susquehanna University Press, 2001.

Kolinsky, Eva, and Wilfried van der Will, eds. *The Cambridge Companion to Modern German Culture.* New York: Cambridge University Press, 1998.

Kossoff, Philip. *Valiant Heart: A Biography of Heinrich Heine.* London: Cornwall Books, 1983.

Kostalevsky, Marina. *Dostoevsky and Soloviev: The Art of Integral Vision.* New Haven, Conn.: Yale University Press, 1997.

Kourilsky, Francoise, and Catherine Temerson. *Plays by Women: An International Anthology.* New York: Ubu Repertory Theatre Publications, 1989.

Kremer, Roberta S., ed. *Memory and Mastery: Primo Levi as Writer and Witness.* Albany: State University of New York Press, 2001.

Kriseova, Eda. *Václav Havel: The Authorized Biography.* New York: St. Martin's Press, 1993.

Krispyn, Egbert. *Gunter Eich.* Boston: Twayne, 1971.

Kunene, Mazisi. *The Ancestors and the Sacred Mountain.* London: Heinemann, 1982.

Kuo, Helena. *The Quest for Love of Lao Lee.* New York: Reynal and Hitchcock, 1948.

Kurahashi Yumiko. *The Woman with the Flying Head and Other Stories of Kurahashi Yumiko.* Translated by Atsuko Sakaki. Armonk, N.Y.: M. E. Sharpe, 1998.

Kurpershoek, P. M. *The Short Stories of Yusuf Idris: A Modern Egyptian Author.* Leiden, The Netherlands: Brill, 1981.

Lacoue-Labarthe, Philippe, ed. *The Literary Absolute: The Theory of Literature in German Romanticism.* Albany: State University of New York Press, 1988.

Lagercrantz, Olaf. *August Strindberg.* New York: Farrar, Straus & Giroux, 1984.

Lahusen, Thomas. *How Life Writes the Book: Real Socialism and Socialist Realism in Stalin's Russia.* Ithaca, N.Y.: Cornell University Press, 1997.

Larson, Wendy. *Women and Writing in Modern China.* Stanford, Calif.: Stanford University Press, 1998.

Last, Rex W. *German Dadaist Literature: Kurt Schitters, Hugo Ball, Hans Arp.* Boston: Twayne, 1973.

Lau, Joseph S. M., and Howard Goldblatt, eds. *The Columbia Anthology of Modern Chinese Literature.* New York: Columbia University Press, 1995.

Lawrie, Steven W. *Erich Fried: A Writer Without a Country.* New York: Peter Lang, 1996.

Leatherborrow, William J. *Feodor Dostoevsky: A Reference Guide.* Boston: G. K. Hall, 1990.

Lederer, Wolfgang. *The Kiss of the Snow Queen: Hans Christian Andersen and Man's Redemption by Woman.* Berkeley: University of California Press, 1990.

Lednicki, Waclaw. *Adam Mickiewicz in World Literature.* Berkeley: University of California Press, 1956.

Lee, Leo Ou-fan. *Voices from the Iron House: A Study of Lu Xun.* Bloomington: Indiana University Press, 1987.

Lee, Mabel. *Soul Mountain.* New York: HarperCollins, 1999.

Lee, Peter H., ed. *The Silence of Love: Twentieth-Century Korean Poetry.* Honolulu: University of Hawaii Press, 1980.

Le Gassick, Trevor, ed. *Critical Perspectives on Naguib Mahfouz.* Washington, D.C.: Three Continents Press, 1991.

Lennon, Nigey. *Alfred Jarry: The Man with the Axe.* Los Angeles: Panjandrm Books, 1984.

Lerner, Michael G. *Maupassant.* New York: G. Braziller, 1975.

Lindfors, Bernth. *Dem-Say: Interviews with Eight Nigerian Authors.* Austin, Tex.: African and Afro-American Studies and Research Center, 1974.

———. *Conversations with Chinua Achebe.* Jackson: University Press of Mississippi, 1997.

Linn, Rolf N. *Heinrich Mann.* Boston: Twayne, 1967.

Lippit, Noriko, and Kyoko Selden, eds. *Stories by Contemporary Japanese Women Writers.* New York: M. E. Sharpe, 1982.

Lloyd, Rosemary. *Mallarmé: The Poet and His Circle.* Ithaca, N.Y.: Cornell University Press, 1999.

Lokke, Kari. *Gerard de Nerval: The Poet as Social Visionary.* Lexington, Ky.: French Forum, 1987.

Lombard, Charles M. *Lamartine.* Boston: Twayne, 1973.

Long, J. J. *The Novels of Thomas Bernhard: Form and Its Function.* Rochester, N.Y.: Camden House, 2001.

Loose, Gerhard. *Ernst Junger.* Boston: Twayne, 1974.

Luce, Jacqui, and Don Luce. *Quiet Courage: Poems from Viet Nam.* Washington, D.C.: Indochina Mobile Education Project, 1974.

Lukacs, Georg. *The Theory of the Novel.* Translated by Anna Bostock. Cambridge, Mass.: MIT Press, 1974.

Lutzeler, Paul M. *Hermann Broch: A Biography.* Translated by Janice Fureness. London: Quarter, 1987.

Lyell, William A. *Cat Country: A Satirical Novel of China in the 1930s.* Columbus: Ohio State University Press, 1970.

———. *Lu Hsun's Vision of Reality.* Berkeley: University of California Press, 1976.

Lykiard, Alexis. *Jean Rhys Revisited.* Exeter, U.K.: Stride Publications, 2000.

MacDonald, Paul S., ed. *The Existentialist Reader: An Anthology of Key Texts.* New York: Routledge, 2001.

Magidoff, Robert, ed. *Russian Science Fiction: An Anthology.* Translated by Doris Johnson. New York: New York University Press, 1964.

Magill, Frank N. *Masterpieces of Latino Literature.* New York: HarperCollins, 1994.

Magnarelli, Sharon. *Understanding Jose Donoso.* Columbia: University of South Carolina, 1993.

Makward, Edris, et al. *The Growth of African Literature.* Lawrenceville, N.J.: Africa World Press, 1998.

Malik, Hafeez, ed. *Iqbal, Poet-Philosopher of Pakistan.* New York: Columbia University Press, 1971.

Malti-Douglas, Fedwa. *Men, Women, and God: Nawal El Saadawi and Arab Feminist Poetics.* Berkeley: University of California Press, 1995.

Mandel, Siegfried. *Group 47: The Reflected Intellect.* Edwardsville: Southern Illinois University Press, 1973.

Mann, Heinrich. *Henry, King of France.* Translated by Eric Sutton. New York: Knopf, 1939.

Mao, Chen. *Between Tradition and Change: The Hermeneutics of May Fourth Literature.* Lanham, Md.: University Press of America, 1997.

Marable, Manning, ed. *Dispatches from the Ebony Tower.* New York: Columbia University Press, 2000.

Marcus, Marvin. *Paragons of the Ordinary: The Biographical Literature of Mori Ogai.* Honolulu: University of Hawaii Press, 1993.

Marinetti, F. T. *The Futurist Cookbook.* Translated by Suzanne Brill, edited and introduction by Lesley Chamberlain. San Fransico: Bedford Arts, 1989.

Maron, Monika. *Silent Close No. 6.* Translated by David Newton Marinelli. Columbia, La.: Reader's International, 1993.

Marr, David. *Patrick White: A Life.* New York: Knopf, 1991.

Martin, Helmut, and Jeffrey Kinkley, eds. *Modern Chinese Writers: Self-Portrayals.* Armonk, N.Y.: M. E. Sharpe, 1992.

Masaoka Shiki. *Masaoka Shiki: Selected Poems.* Translated by Burton Watson. New York: Columbia University Press, 1997.

Massardier-Kenney, Françoise. *Gender in the Fiction of George Sand.* Atlanta: Rodopi, 2000.

Mathy, Frances. *Shiga Naoya.* Boston: Twayne, 1974.

Matthews, J. H. *Theatre in Dada and Surrealism.* Syracuse, N.Y.: Syracuse University Press, 1974.

McBride, William. *Sartre's Life, Times and Vision-du-Monde.* New York: Garland, 1997.

McDougall, Bonnie S., and Kam Louie. *The Literature of China in the Twentieth Century.* New York: Columbia University Press, 1997.

McGlathery, James. *E. T. A. Hoffmann.* Boston: Twayne, 1997.

McGuinness, Patrick, ed. *Symbolism, Decadence and the Fin de Siècle: French and European Perspectives.* Exeter, U.K.: University of Exeter Press, 2000.

McLaughlin, Martin. *Italo Calvino.* Edinburgh: Edinburgh University Press, 1998.

McRae, Robert. *Resistance and Revolution.* Ottawa: Carleton University Press, 1997.

Meeks, Brian. *Voiceprint: An Anthology of Oral and Related Poetry from the Caribbean.* Essex, England: Longman Group UK Limited, 1989.

Mellown, Elgin W. *Jean Rhys: A Descriptive and Annotated Bibliography of Works and Criticism.* New York: Garland, 1984.

Merini, Rafika. *Two Major Francophone Women Writers: Assia Djebar and Leila Sebbar: A Thematic Study of Their Works.* New York: Peter Lang, 1999.

Metzger, Michael M., and Erika A Metzger. *Stefan George.* Boston: Twayne, 1972.

Meyer, Michael. *Strindberg: A Biography.* Oxford: Oxford University Press, 1987.

Mileck, Joseph. *Hermann Hesse: Life and Art.* Riverside: University of California Press, 1981.

Miller, Yvette E., and Charles Rossman. *Gabriel García Márquez.* Pittsburgh, Pa.: University of Pittsburgh, 1985.

Milosz, Czeslaw. *The History of Polish Literature.* Berkeley: University of California Press, 1983.

Mistral, Gabriela. *Selected Poems.* Translated Doris Dana. Baltimore: Johns Hopkins University Press, 1971.

Misurella, Fred. *Understanding Milan Kundera: Public Events, Private Affairs.* Columbia: University of South Carolina Press, 1993.

Mitchell, Stephen. *Freud and Beyond: A History of Modern Psychoanalytical Thought.* New York: Basic Books, 1996.

Mitler, Louis. *Contemporary Turkish Writers: A Critical Bio-Bibliography.* Bloomington: Indiana University Press, 1988.

Moon, Vasant. *Growing up Untouchable in India: A Dalit Autobiography.* Translated by Gail Omvedt. New Delhi: Vistaar Publishing, 2002.

Moore, Gerald. *Twelve African Writers.* London: Hutchinson University Library for Africa, 1980.

Moosa, Matti. *The Early Novels of Naguib Mahfouz: Images of Modern Egypt.* Gainesville: University Press of Florida, 1994.

Moran, Dominic. *Questions of the Liminal in the Fiction of Julio Cortázar.* Oxford: Oxford University Press, 2001.

Mortimer, Armine K. *Writing Realism: Representations in French Fiction.* Baltimore: Johns Hopkins University Press, 2000.

Mortimer, Mildred P. *Journeys Through the French African Novel.* Westport, Conn.: Heinemann, 1990.

Mortimer, Mildred P., ed. *Maghrebian Mosaic: A Literature in Transition.* Boulder, Colo.: Lynne Rienner Publishers, 2001.

Moses, Claire G. *Feminism, Socialism and French Romanticism.* Bloomington: Indiana University Press, 1993.

Mueller, Heiner. *A Heiner Muller Reader: Plays, Poetry, Prose.* Translated by Carl Weber. Baltimore: Johns Hopkins University Press, 2001.

Mulhern, Chieko I., ed. *Japanese Women Writers: A Bio-critical Sourcebook.* Westport, Conn.: Greenwood Press, 1994.

Munsterer, Hanns Otto. *The Young Brecht.* Concord, Mass.: Paul and Company Publishers Consortium, 1992.

Naess, Harald. *Knut Hamsun.* Boston: Twayne, 1984.

Naipaul, V. S. *Between Father and Son: Family Letters.* New York: Vintage Books, 2001.

———. *Half a Life.* New York: Knopf, 2001.

Nantell, Judith. *Rafael Alberti's Poetry of the Thirties: The Poet's Public Voice.* Athens: University of Georgia Press, 1986.

Napier, Susan. *Escape from the Wasteland: Romanticism and Realism in the Fiction of Mishima Yukio and Ōe Kenzaburō.* Cambridge, Mass.: Harvard University Press, 1991.

Naughton, John. *The Poetics of Yves Bonnefoy.* Chicago: University of Chicago Press, 1984.

Naravane, Vishwanath S. *Sarojini Naidu: An Introduction to Her Life, Work, and Poetry.* New Delhi: Orient Longman Ltd., 1996.

Nasta, Sheila, ed. *Motherlands: Black Women's Writing from Africa.* New Brunswick, N.J.: Rutgers University Press, 1992.

Nathan, John. *Mishima: A Biography.* New York: Da Capo Press, 2000.

Nathan, Leonard, and Arthur Quinn. *The Poet's Work: An Introduction to Czeslaw Milosz.* Cambridge, Mass.: Harvard University Press, 1991.

Nathan, Robert L. *The Dreamtime.* Woodstock, N.Y.: Overlook Press, 1975.

Nelson, Emmanuel S., ed. *Contemporary African American Novelists: A Bio-Bibliographical Critical Sourcebook.* Westport, Conn.: Greenwood Press, 1999.

Nevin, Thomas. *Ernst Junger and Germany: Into the Abyss, 1914–1945.* Durham, N.C.: Duke University Press, 1997.

Niebylski, Dianna C. *The Poem on the Edge of the Word: The Limits of Language and the Uses of Silence in the Poetry of Mallarmé, Rilke and Vallejo.* New York: Peter Lang, 1993.

Nieh, Hauling. *Literature of the Hundred Flowers.* New York: Columbia University Press, 1981.

Nugent, Robert. *Paul Éluard*. Boston: Twayne, 1974.

Oba Minako. *Stories by Contemporary Japanese Women Writers*. Translated by Noriko Mizuta Lippit and Kyoko Irye Selden. Armonk, N.Y.: M. E. Sharpe, 1982.

O'Ceallachain, Eanna. *Eugenio Montale: The Poetry of Later Years*. Oxford: Legenda, 2001.

O'Healey, Aine. *Cesare Pavese*. Boston: Twayne, 1988.

O'Neil, Patrick. *Günter Grass Revisited*. Boston: Twayne, 1999.

Osbourne, John. *Gerhart Hauptmann and the Naturalist Drama*. London: Routledge, 1999.

Painter, George D. *Chateaubriand: A Biography*. New York: Knopf, 1978.

Pandurang, Mala. *Vikram Seth: Multiple Locations, Multiple Affiliation*. New Delhi: Rawat, 2001.

Panny, Judith D. *I Have What I Gave: The Fiction of Janet Frame*. New York: George Braziller, 1993.

Paperno, Irina. *Chernyshevsky and the Age of Realism*. Stanford, Calif.: Stanford University Press, 1988.

Paravisini-Gerbert, Lizabeth. *Jamaica Kincaid: A Critical Companion*. Westport, Conn.: Greenwood Press, 1999.

Parrot, Cecil. *The Bad Bohemian: The Life of Jaroslav Hašek, Creator of the Good Soldier Svejk*. London, England: Bodley Head, 1978.

Partridge, Monica. *Alexander Herzen*. Paris: Unesco, 1984.

Patt, Beatrice P. *Pío Baroja y Nessi*. Boston: Twayne, 1971.

Paul, Georgina, and Helmut Schmitz, eds. *Entgegenkommen: Dialogues with Barbara Kohler*. Atlanta, Ga.: Rodopi, 2000.

Peixoto, Marta. *Passionate Fictions: Gender, Narrative, and Violence in Clarice Lispector*. Minneapolis: University of Minnesota Press, 1994.

Peled, Mattityahu. *Religion My Own: The Literary Works of Najib Mahfuz*. New Brunswick, N.J.: Transaction Books, 1983.

Pelensky, Olga A. *Isak Dinesen: Critical Views*. Athens: Ohio University Press, 1993.

Penrod, Lynn. *Hélène Cixous*. Boston: Twayne, 1996.

Peretz, Isaac L. *Selected Stories*. Translated by Eli Katz. New York: Zhitlowsky Foundation for Jewish Culture, 1991.

Peterman, Michael. *Robertson Davies*. Boston: Twayne, 1986.

Peterson, Thomas E. *Alberto Moravia*. Boston: Twayne, 1996.

Petro, Peter, ed. *Critical Essays on Milan Kundera*. New York: G. K. Hall, 1999.

Pfaff, Francoise. *The Cinema of Ousmane Sembene, a Pioneer of African Film*. Westport, Conn.: Greenwood Press, 1984.

Pilarde, Jo-Ann. *Simone de Beauvoir Writing the Self: Philosophy Becomes Autobiography*. Westport, Conn.: Praeger, 1999.

Piore, Nance K. *Lightning: The Poetry of René Char*. Boston: Northeastern University Press, 1981.

Plunka, Gene A., ed. *Antonin Artaud and the Modern Theatre*. Madison, N.J.: Fairleigh Dickinson University Press, 1994.

Polcari, Stephanie. *Abstract Expressionism and the Modern Experience*. Cambridge: Cambridge University Press, 1993.

Popkin, Michael, ed. *Modern Black Writers*. New York: Frederick Ungar, 1978.

Porter, Laurence M. *Victor Hugo*. Boston: Twayne, 1999.

Preston, Paul. *Salvador de Madariaga and the Quest for Liberty in Spain*. Oxford: Clarendon Press, 1987.

Proffer, Ellendea. *A Pictorial Biography of Mikhail Bulgakov*. Ann Arbor, Mich.: Ardis, 1984.

Prokushev, Yuri. *Sergei Yesenin: The Man, the Verse, the Age*. Moscow: Progress Publishers, 1979.

Pulver, Elsbeth. *Marie Luise Kaschnitz*. Munich, Germany: C. H. Beck, 1984.

Putnam, Walter. *Paul Valéry Revisited*. Boston: Twayne, 1995.

Rabson, Steve. *Righteous Cause or Tragic Folly: Changing Views of War in Modern Japanese Poetry*. Ann Arbor: University of Michigan, Center for Japanese Studies, 1998.

Rai, Amrit. *Premchand: His Life and Times*. New York: Oxford University Press, 2002.

Rayfield, Donal. *Anton Chekhov: A Life*. Chicago: Northwestern University Press, 2000.

Reddick, John. *Georg Büchner: The Shattered Whole*. Oxford: Clarendon Press, 1994.

Redwitz, Eckenbert. *The Image of the Woman in the Works of Ingeborg Bachmann.* New York: Peter Lang, 1993.

Reeder, Roberta. *Anna Akhmatova: Poet and Prophet.* New York: Picador, 1995.

Reid, J. H. *Narration and Description in the French Realist Novel: The Temporality of Lying and Forgetting.* Cambridge: Cambridge University Press, 1993.

Reiss, Timothy J. *For the Geography of a Soul: Emerging Perspectives on Kamau Brathwaite.* Lawrenceville, N.J.: Africa World Press, 2001.

Resch, Margit. *Understanding Christa Wolf: Retuning Home to a Foreign Land.* Columbia: University of South Carolina Press, 1997.

Rhys, Jean. *The Collected Short Stories.* New York: Norton, 1978.

Ribbans, Geoffrey. *History and Fiction in Galdós's Narratives.* London, England: Oxford University Press, 1993.

Rice, Martin P. *Valery Bruisov and the Rise of Russian Symbolism.* Ann Arbor, Mich: Ardis, 1975.

Richardson, Angelique, and Chris Willis, eds. *The New Woman in Fiction and in Fact: Fin de Siècle Feminisms.* New York: Palgrave, 2001.

Richardson, Joanna. *Baudelaire.* New York: St. Martin's Press, 1994.

Ridge, George R. *Joris-Karl Huysmans.* Boston: Twayne, 1968.

Rimer, John T. *Mori Ōgai.* Boston: Twayne, 1975.

Ritchie, J. M. *Gottfried Benn: The Unreconstructed Expressionist.* London: Oswald Wolff, 1972.

Robb, Graham. *Arthur Rimbaud.* New York: Norton, 2000.

Robbe-Grillet, Alain. *For a New Novel: Essays on Fiction.* Translated by Richard Howard. New York: Grove Press, 1966.

Robin, Regine. *Socialist Realism: An Impossible Aesthetic.* Translated by Catherine Porter. Stanford, Calif.: Stanford University Press, 1991.

Robinson, Roger, and Nelson Wattie, eds. *The Oxford Companion to New Zealand Literature.* Oxford: Oxford University Press, 1998.

Robson, Clifford. *Ngugi wa Thiong'o.* London: Macmillan, 1979.

Rojas, Sonia R., and Edna Aguirre Rehbeim, eds. *Critical Approaches to Isabel Allende's Novels.* New York: Peter Lang, 1991.

Rose, Henry. *Henrik Ibsen: Poet, Mystic, and Moralist.* New York: Haskell, 1972.

Roumani, Judith. *Albert Memmi.* Philadelphia: Celfan, 1987.

Rowley, Hazel. *Christina Stead: A Biography.* New York: Henry Holt & Company, 1995.

Rubin, Jay, ed. *Modern Japanese Writers.* New York: Charles Scribner's Sons, 2001.

Russell, Ralph. *Ghālib.* Cambridge, Mass.: Harvard University Press, 1969.

Sachs, Nelly. *The Seeker, and Other Poems.* Translated by Ruth Mead, Matthew Mead, and Michael Hamburger. New York: Farrar, Straus & Giroux, 1970.

Safransky, Rudiger. *Nietzche: A Philosophical Biography.* New York: Norton, 2001.

Saint, Nigel. *Marguerite Yourcenar: Reading the Visual.* Oxford: Legenda, 2000.

Salma, Jayyusi. *Trends and Movements in Modern Arabic Poetry.* Leiden, The Netherlands: Brill, 1977.

Samson, Earl. *Nikolai Gumilev.* Boston: Twayne, 1979.

Samuel, Maurice. *The World of Sholom Aleichem.* New York: Dramatists Play Series, 1948.

San Juan, E. *Aimé Césaire: Surrealism and Revolution.* Bowling Green, Ohio: Bowling Green State University Press, 2000.

————. *From the Masses, to the Masses: Third World Literature and Revolution.* Minneapolis: MEP Publications, 1994.

Savory, Elaine. *Jean Rhys.* New York: Cambridge University Press, 1999.

Scammell, Michael. *Solzhenitsyn: A Biography.* New York: Norton, 1984.

Schalow, Paul G., and Janet A. Walker, eds. *The Woman's Hand: Gender and Theory in Japanese Women's Writing.* Stanford, Calif.: Stanford University Press, 1996.

Schierbeck, Sachiko. *Japanese Women Novelists in the Twentieth Century: 104 Biographies 1900–1993.* Copenhagen: Museum Tusculanum Press, 1994.

Schiff, Stacy. *Saint-Exupéry: A Biography.* New York: Knopf, 1995.

Schoolfield, George C. *Edith Sodergran: Modernist Poet in Finland.* Westport, Conn.: Greenwood Press, 1984.

Scholtz, Sally. *On de Beauvoir.* Belmont, Calif.: Wadsworth/Thomson Learning, 2000.

Schulte-Sasse, Jochen, ed. *Theory as Practice: An Anthology of Early German Romantic Writings.* Indianapolis: University of Minnesota Press, 1997.

Schulze, Julia. *Rigoberta Menchu Tum: Champion of Human Rights.* New York: Burke, John Gordon Publisher, Inc., 1997.

Schwarz, Roberto. *Misplaced Ideas: Essays on Brazilian Culture.* New York: Verso, 1992.

Schwartz, Ronald. *Spain's New Wave Novelists, 1950–1974.* Lanham, Md.: Scarecrow Press, 1976.

Schwartz-Bart, Simone. *Between Two Worlds.* Translated by Barbara Bray. New York: Harper & Row, 1981.

———. *The Bridge and Beyond.* Translated by Barbara Bray. New York: Atheneum, 1974.

Schweitzer, Victoria. *Tsvetaeva.* New York: Farrar, Straus & Giroux, 1993.

Schwertfeger, Ruth. *Else Lasker-Schuler: Inside This Deathly Solitude.* Oxford: Berg Publishers, Ltd., 1991.

Scott-Stokes, Henry. *The Life and Death of Yukio Mishima.* New York: Farrar, Straus & Giroux, 1974.

Seifert, Jaroslav. *The Early Poetry of Jaroslav Seifert.* Translated by Dana Loewy. Evanston, Ill.: Hydra Books, 1997.

Sergio, Pacifici, ed. *From Verismo to Experimentalism: Essays on the Modern Italian Novel.* Bloomington: Indiana University Press, 1970.

Shaked, Gershon. *Shmuel Yosef Agnon: A Revolutionary Traditionalist.* Translated by Jeffery M. Green. New York: New York University Press, 1989.

Sharman, Adam, ed. *The Poetry and Poetics of César Vallejo: The Fourth Angle of the Circle.* Lewiston, N.Y.: Edwin Mellen Press, 1997.

Sharpe, Lesley. *Friedrich Schiller: Drama, Thought, and Politics.* Cambridge: Cambridge University Press, 1991.

Shava, Piniel. *A People's Voice: Black South African Writing in the Twentieth Century.* London: Zed Books, 1989.

Sheridan, Susan. *Christina Stead.* Bloomington: Indiana University Press, 1988.

Silva, A. J. Simoes da. *The Luxury of Nationalist Despair: George Lamming's Fiction as Decolonizing Project.* Atlanta, Ga.: Rodopi, 2000.

Simms, Norman. *Silence and Invisibility: A Study of the New Literature from the Pacific.* Washington, D.C.: Three Continents Press, 1986.

Simons, Margaret. A. *Beauvoir and the Second Sex: Feminism, Race and the Origins of Existentialism.* Boston: Lanham, Rowman and Littlefield, 1999.

Simpson, Michael, and John Untfrecker. *Dreams of the Rainbow: Poems by Kauraka Kauraka.* Honolulu: University of Hawaii at Manoa, East-West Center, 1986.

Singh, Amritjit, Joseph T. Skerrett, Jr., and Robert E. Hogan, eds. *Memory and Cultural Politics: New Approaches to American Ethnic Literatures.* Ann Arbor, Mich.: Edwards Brothers, 1996.

Singh, G. *Leopardi and the Theory of Poetry.* Lexington: University of Kentucky Press, 1964.

Smart, Ian I. *Nicolas Guillen, Popular Poet of the Caribbean.* Columbia: University of Missouri Press, 1990.

Smethurst, Colin. *Chateaubriand, Atala and René.* London: Grant and Cutler, 1995.

Smith, Roch C. *Understanding Alain Robbe-Grillet.* Columbia: University of South Carolina Press, 2000.

Snyder, Stephen, and Philip Gabriel, eds. *Ōe and Beyond: Fiction in Contemporary Japan.* Honolulu: University of Hawaii Press, 1999.

Sodergran, Edith. *Love and Solitude: Selected Poems, 1916–1923.* Translated by Stina Katchadourian. Seattle: Fjord Press, 1985.

Sole, Carlos A. *Latin American Writers.* New York: Charles Scribner's Sons, 1989.

Solecki, Sam. *Prague Blues: The Fiction of Josef Skvorecky.* New York: Ecco Press, 1990.

Soto, Francisco. *Reinaldo Arenas.* Boston: Twayne, 1998.

Spector, Robert D. *Pär Lagerkvist.* Boston: Twayne, 1973.

Spivak, Gayatri. *In Other Worlds: Essays in Cultural Politics.* New York: Routledge, 1987.

Stafford, Helene. *Mallarmé and the Poetics of Everyday Life: A Study of the Concept of the Ordinary in His Verse and Prose.* Atlanta, Ga.: Rodopi, 2000.

Standish, Peter. *Understanding Julio Cortázar.* Columbia: University of South Carolina Press, 2001.

Stavans, Ilan. *Julio Cortázar: A Study of the Short Fiction.* Boston: Twayne, 1996.

Stead, C. K. *In the Glass Case: Essays on New Zealand Literature.* Auckland, N.Z.: Auckland University Press, 1981.

———. *Kin of Place: Essays on New Zealand Writers.* Auckland, N.Z.: Auckland University Press, 2002.

Stephan, Halina. *Translating the Absurd: Drama and Prose of Slawomir Mrozek.* The Netherlands: Rodopi, 1997.

Sterling, Richard L. *The Prose Works of Saint-John Perse: Towards an Understanding of His Poetry.* New York: Peter Lang, 1994.

Stevens, Shelley. *Rosalia de Castro and the Galician Revival.* London: Tamesis Books Ltd., 1986.

Stilman, Leon. *Gogol.* New York: Columbia University Press, 1990.

Stratton, Florence. *Contemporary African Literature and the Politics of Gender.* New York: Routledge, 1994.

Strauss, J. *Judith Wright.* Melbourne: Oxford University Press, 1995.

Strong-Boag, Veronica J., and Carole Gerson. *Paddling Her Own Canoe: The Times and Texts of E. Pauline Johnson.* Toronto: University of Toronto Press, 2000.

Sucher, Laurie. *The Fiction of Ruth Prawer Jhabvala: The Politics of Passion.* New York: St. Martin's Press, 1989.

Suk, Jeannie. *Postcolonial Paradoxes in French Caribbean Writing: Césaire, Glissant, Condé.* Oxford: Clarendon Press, 2001.

Szymborska, Wislawa. *Miracle Fair: Selected Poems of Wislawa Szymborska.* Translated by Joanna Trzeciak. New York: Norton, 2001.

Talbot, Emile J. *Stendhal Revisited.* Boston: Twayne, 1993.

Tam Kwok-kan. *Soul of Chaos: Critical Perspectives on Gao Xingjian.* Hong Kong: The Chinese University Press, 2001.

Tanaka, Yukiko, ed. *To Love and to Write: Selections by Japanese Women Writers 1913–1938.* Seattle: Seal Press, 1987.

Tapia, John R. *The Indian in the Spanish-American Novel.* Durango, Colo.: University Press of America, 1981.

Tarabishi, George. *Woman Against Her Sex: A Critique of Nawal El-Saadawi, with a Reply by Nawal El-Saadawi.* London: Al-Saqi Books, 1988.

Terras, Victor. *Vladimir Mayakovsky.* Boston: Twayne, 1983.

Thomas, H. *Elias Canetti.* Boston: Twayne, 1993.

Thurman, Judith. *Isak Dinesen: The Life of a Storyteller.* New York: St. Martin's Press, 1982.

———. *Secrets of the Flesh: A Life of Colette.* New York: Knopf, 1999.

Tisdall, Caroline, and Angela Bozolla. *Futurism.* Oxford, England: Oxford University Press, 1978.

Tollerson, Marie. *Mythology and Cosmology in the Narratives of Bernard Dadie and Birago Diop.* Washington, D.C.: Three Continents Press, 1984.

Tomalin, Claire. *Katherine Mansfield: A Secret Life.* New York: Knopf, 1988.

Tong-gyu Hwang. *Strong Winds at Mishi Pass.* Groveport, Ohio: White Pines Press, 2001.

———. *Wind Burial: Selected Poems of Hwang Tong-gyu.* Laurenberg, N.C.: St. Andrew's Press, 1990.

Treat, John W., ed. *Contemporary Japan and Popular Culture.* Honolulu: University of Hawaii Press, 1996.

Treece, David. *Exiles, Allies, Rebels: Brazil's Indianist Movement, Indigenist Politics, and the Imperial Nation-State.* Westport, Conn.: Greenwood Press, 2000.

Trump, Martin. *Rendering Things Visible: Essays on South African Literary Culture.* Athens: Ohio University Press, 1990.

Tsatsos, Ioanna. *My Brother George Seferis.* Translated by Jean Demos. St. Paul, Minn.: North Central, 1982.

Tuwim, Julian. *The Dancing Socrates, and Other Poems.* Translated by Adam Gillon. Boston: Twayne, 1968.

Ueda Makoto. *Modern Japanese Writers.* Stanford, Calif.: Stanford University Press, 1976.

Umeh, Marie, ed. *Emerging Perspectives on Flora Nwapa.* Lawrenceville, N.J.: Africa World Press, 1998.

Unger, Richard. *Friedrich Holderlin.* Boston: Twayne, 1984.

Uraizee, Joya F. *This Is No Place for a Woman: Nadine Gordimer, Nayantara Sahgal, Buchi Emecheta, and the Politics of Gender.* Lawrenceville, N.J.: Africa World Press, 2000.

Vernon, Victoria V. *Daughters of the Moon: Wish, Will and Social Constraint in Fiction by Modern Japanese Women.* Berkeley: University of California Press, Institute of East Asian Studies, 1988.

Viain, Robert. *The Poetry of Hugo von Hofmannsthal and French Symbolism.* New York: Oxford University Press, 2000.

Vohra, Ranbir. *Lao She and the Chinese Revolution.* Cambridge, Mass.: Harvard University Press, East Asian Research Center, 1974.

Vucinich, Wayne, ed. *Ivo Andric Revisited: The Bridge Still Stands.* Berkeley: University of California Regents, 1996.

Wade, Michael. *Peter Abrahams.* London: Evans Bros., 1972.

Wagner, Irmagard. *Goethe.* Boston: Twayne, 1999.

Wagner, Rudolf G. *Inside a Service Trade: Studies in Contemporary Chinese Prose.* Cambridge, Mass.: Council on East Asian Studies, Harvard University, 1992.

Wall, Cheryl, ed. *Changing Our Own Words: Essays on Criticism, Theory, and Writing by Black Women.* Piscataway, N.J.: Rutgers University Press, 1989.

Watts, Jane. *Black Writers from South Africa: Towards a Discourse of Liberation.* New York: St. Martin's Press, 1989.

Weimar, Karl S., ed. *German Language and Literature: Seven Essays.* Englewood Cliffs, N.J.: Prentice Hall, 1974.

Weiss, Beno. *Italo Svevo.* Boston: Twayne, 1987.

———. *Understanding Italo Calvino.* Columbia: University of South Carolina Press, 1995.

Weiss, Timothy F. *On the Margins: The Art of Exile in V. S. Naipaul.* Boston: University of Massachusetts Press, 1992.

Wellington, Beth. *Reflections on Lorca's Private Mythology: Once Five Years Pass and the Rural Plays.* New York: Peter Lang, 1993.

Welsh, David J. *Adam Mickiewicz.* Boston: Twayne, 1966.

White, Clement A. *Decoding the Word: Nicolas Guillen as Maker and Debunker of Myth.* Miami, Fla.: Universal, 1993.

Whitford, Frank. *Oskar Kokoschka: A Life.* New York: Atheneum, 1986.

Whitmore, Katherine P. R. *The Generation of 1898 in Spain as Seen Through Its Fictional Hero.* Northampton, Mass.: Smith College, 1936.

Willbanks, Ray. *Australian Voices: Writers and Their Work.* Austin: University of Texas Press, 1991.

Williams, Eric, ed. *The Dark Flutes of Fall: Critical Essays on Georg Trakl.* Rochester, N.Y.: Camden House, 1991.

Williams, John. *Goethe: A Critical Biography.* Oxford, England: Blackwell Publishers, 2001.

Williams, Raymond L. *The Writings of Carlos Fuentes.* Austin: University of Texas Press, 1996.

Wilson, Machiko N. *The Marginal World of Ōe Kenzaburō: A Study in Themes and Techniques.* Armonk, N.Y.: M. E. Sharpe, 1986.

Wisse, Ruth R. *I. L. Peretz and the Making of Modern Jewish Culture.* Seattle: University of Washington Press, 1991.

Wolf, Christa. *Cassandra: A Novel and Four Essays.* Translated by Jan van Heurck. New York: Farrar, Straus & Giroux, 1984.

Wolfe, Peter, ed. *Critical Essays on Patrick White.* Boston: G. K. Hall, 1990.

Wolpert, Stanley. *Gandhi's Passion: The Life and Legacy of Gandhi.* New York: Oxford University Press, 2001.

Wright, Derek. *Wole Soyinka Revisited.* Boston: Twayne, 1993.

Wright, Edgar, ed. *The Critical Evaluation of African Literature.* London: Heinemann, 1973.

Wullschlager, Jackie. *Hans Christian Andersen: The Life of a Storyteller.* New York: Knopf, 2001.

Yamada Eimi. *Monkey Brain Sushi: New Tastes in Japanese Fiction.* Translated by Terry Gallagher. New York: Kodansha International, 1991.

Yang, Winston L. Y., and Nathan K. Mao, eds. *Modern Chinese Fiction: A Guide to Its Study and Appreciation; Essays and Bibliographies.* Boston: G. K. Hall, 1981.

Yip Wai-Lim, ed. *Modern Chinese Poetry: Twenty Poets from the Republic of China, 1955–1965.* Iowa City: University of Iowa Press, 1970.

Yourcenar, Marguerite. *Mishima: A Vision of the Void.* Translated by Alberto Manguel. New York: Farrar, Straus & Giroux, 1986.

Yu Beongsheon. *Akutagawa: An Introduction.* Detroit: Wayne State University Press, 1972.

———. *Han Yong-un and Yi Kwang-su: Two Pioneers of Modern Korean Literature.* Detroit: Wayne State University Press, 1992.

Zeidan, Joseph. *Arab Women Novelists.* Binghamton: State University of New York Press, 1995.

Zhao, Henry Y. H. *Towards a Modern Zen Theatre: Gao Xingian and Chinese Theatre Experimentalism.* London, England: School of Oriental and African Studies, 2000.

Ziolkowski, Theodore. *Herman Broch.* New York: Columbia University Press, 1964.

INDEX

✦⧼⧽✦